BLACKSTONE'S

EMPLOYMENT LAW PRACTICE

BLACKSTONE'S

EMPLOYMENT LAW PRACTICE

2010

EDITORS

GAVIN MANSFIELD
Barrister, Littleton Chambers

JOHN BOWERS QC
Barrister, Littleton Chambers, Recorder

DAMIAN BROWN
Barrister, Littleton Chambers

SIMON FORSHAW
Barrister, 11KBW

ANTHONY KORN
Barrister, No. 5 Chambers

JULIA PALCA
Partner, Olswang, Part-time Employment Tribunal Chair

CONTRIBUTORS

JONATHAN SCHWARZ
Barrister, Temple Tax Chambers

BRIAN NAPIER (QC Scot.)
Barrister, Cloisters

PRINCIPAL CONSULTANT EDITOR

JOHN MACMILLAN
Regional Chairman, Employment Tribunals

OXFORD
UNIVERSITY PRESS

OXFORD
UNIVERSITY PRESS

Great Clarendon Street, Oxford OX2 6DP

Oxford University Press is a department of the University of Oxford.
It furthers the University's objective of excellence in research, scholarship,
and education by publishing worldwide in

Oxford New York

Auckland Cape Town Dar es Salaam Hong Kong Karachi
Kuala Lumpur Madrid Melbourne Mexico City Nairobi
New Delhi Shanghai Taipei Toronto

With offices in

Argentina Austria Brazil Chile Czech Republic France Greece
Guatemala Hungary Italy Japan Poland Portugal Singapore
South Korea Switzerland Thailand Turkey Ukraine Vietnam

Oxford is a registered trade mark of Oxford University Press
in the UK and in certain other countries

Published in the United States
by Oxford University Press Inc., New York

First published 2010

British Library Cataloguing in Publication Data
Data available

Library of Congress Cataloging in Publication Data
Data available

Typeset by Glyph International, Bangalore, India
Printed in Great Britain
on acid-free paper by
CPI Antony Rowe, Chippenham and Eastbourne

ISBN 978–0–19–958041–5

1 3 5 7 9 10 8 6 4 2

Foreword to the first edition

This is a very welcome addition to the employment law library, produced by a very distinguished and hard-working team of editors and contributors. The whole of the employment law field is, by dint of a great deal of thoughtful and sensible selection and summarization, squeezed into one volume. It will be of immense value for academics and practitioners, trade unions, employers, and employees alike. It does not shrink from making clear and well-researched assertions on the law and the procedure, not too cluttered by footnotes, and yet the source for such assertions can easily be identified. The authors do not restrict themselves to narrative, but include a good deal of well-informed comment. I have no doubt they will ensure that this book continues to keep up to date in this ever-changing legal environment: but, as of date of publication, it succeeds in giving an excellent view, both panoramic and detailed, of all that needs to be known to bring or defend an employment issue before the courts or tribunals. I dare say that we judges will feel the more comfortable as we see the tome on the desk in front of the advocate or litigant in person appearing before us.

Sir Michael Burton
President of the Employment Appeal Tribunal
Chairman of the Central Arbitration Committee
High Court Judge

Preface

The idea behind this book is very simple. It should contain everything you need to know about a case at the employment tribunal, Employment Appeal Tribunal, and Central Arbitration Committee, as well as in the High Court and Court of Appeal, without needing to cart around many looseleaf volumes. It is slanted towards an analysis of the practice and procedure adopted by the tribunal. It also contains a summary of the substantive law in the areas most likely to arise day to day in tribunals. This is in the form of an introduction and checklists; it does not attempt to cover every case but examines the key points which may arise at tribunal. The extracts of statutes and statutory instruments are selective, but comprise those which the practitioners who wrote the volume believe are most used. The book is published annually to ensure that it provides an up-to-date reference source.

This year there have been two important changes to the team of authors.

First, John Bowers QC steps down from the role of general editor, which is now taken up by Gavin Mansfield. This book is very much John's work. It was he who first wrote the book's predecessor *Employment Tribunal Practice and Procedure*. It was his vision which led to the creation of the book in its current form. We are all grateful to him for the great knowledge, insight and energy that he has brought to the role of editor. He will remain a valued part of the writing team.

Secondly, Catherine Taylor steps down from the team of authors. She has made a valuable contribution to each of the previous editions, and the work has benefitted greatly from her legal and practical insights into employment law. The remaining authors wish her well.

This book incorporates the earlier work *Employment Tribunal Practice and Procedure*, and we recognize the contribution of Geoffrey Mead to earlier editions. In addition to the named authors a large number of people have contributed to the work and have read chapters. We would particularly like to thank our colleagues at Littleton Chambers, many of whom have provided great assistance. We also thank Sally Cowen, Corinna Ferguson (Old Square Chambers), Janet Simpson, Katherine Tucker, and Professor Roy Lewis.

We also wish to thank Mr John Macmillan, Regional Chair, Nottingham, for his comprehensive comments on various chapters, and we are grateful for the Foreword by Sir Michael Burton.

This year we have incorporated changes brought about by the Employment Act 2008, which came into effect on 6 April 2009. However, we have thus included the existing law (with its complex case law), which will continue to have relevance for some years to come.

We have attempted to cover the law up to 5 January 2010.

Acknowledgements

Pages 11–12 from *Guidelines for the Assessment of General Damages in Personal Injury Cases* edited by Judicial Studies Board (9th edn, 2008) are reproduced by permission of Oxford University Press © Judicial Studies Board 2008.

The AA Motoring Costs tables 2007–2009 are reproduced by permission of the Automobile Association © the Automobile Association Limited 2007, 2008, and 2009.

Equality and Human Rights Commission: Code of Practice on Equal Pay (2003), Code of Practice on Sex Discrimination: Equal Opportunity Policies, Procedures and Practices in Employment (1985, as amended), and Commission for Racial Equality: Code of Practice on Racial Equality in Employment (2005) are reproduced with permission of the Equality and Human Rights Commission. The copyright and all other intellectual property rights in the material to be reproduced are owned by, or licensed to, the Commission for Equality and Human Rights, known as the Equality and Human Rights Commission (the EHRC). Further information can be found on the EHRC website <http://www.equalityhumanrights.com>.

Crown copyright material is reproduced with the permission of the Controller of Her Majesty's Stationery Office.

Contents—Summary

Contents

Table of Cases

Table of UK Legislation

Paragraph references in **bold** indicate that the text is reproduced in full

A Statutes

B STATUTORY INSTRUMENTS

(ETR 2001 and 2004 see Sch 1 to Employment Tribunals (Constitution and Rules of Procedure) Regulations 2001 and 2004; 2004 EV Rules see Sch 6)

Table of European and International Legislation

Paragraph references in **bold** indicate that the text is reproduced in full

EC PRIMARY LEGISLATION

EC SECONDARY LEGISLATION

Regulations

Directives

INTERNATIONAL LEGISLATION

Codes of Practice and Practice Directions

Paragraph references in **bold** indicate that the text is reproduced in full

List of Abbreviations

1990 Order	Employment Tribunals (Interest) Order 1990, SI 1990/479, as amended
1991 Order	High Court and County Courts Jurisdiction Order 1991, SI 1991/724, as amended
2001 Regulations	Employment Tribunals (Constitution and Rules of Procedure) Regulations 2001, SI 2001/1171, as amended
2004 Regulations	Employment Tribunals (Constitution and Rules of Procedure) Regulations 2004, SI 2004/1861, as amended
ACAS	Advisory and Conciliation Service
ACAS Code	ACAS Code of Practice 1: Disciplinary and Grievance Procedures, April 2009
ACAS Guidance	Discipline and Grievances at Work: The ACAS Guide, April 2009
ADR	Alternative dispute resolution
BIS	Department for Business Innovation and Skills
CAB	Citizens Advice Bureau
CAC	Central Arbitration Committee
CCA 1984	County Courts Act 1984
CEDR	Centre for Dispute Resolution
CEHR	Commission for Equality and Human Rights
CMC	Case management conference
CMD	Case management discussion
COET	Central Office of Employment Tribunals
CPR	Civil Procedure Rules 1998
CRE	Commission for Racial Equality
DDA 1995	Disability Discrimination Act 1995
DRC	Disability Rights Commission
EA 2002	Employment Act 2002
EA(DR)R 2004	Employment Act 2002 (Dispute Resolution) Regulations 2004
EAT	Employment Appeal Tribunal
EAT Rules	Employment Appeal Tribunal Rules 1993, SI 1993/2854, as amended
EC Treaty	Treaty establishing the European Community
ECHR	European Convention on Human Rights
ECJ	European Court of Justice
ECtHR	European Court of Human Rights
EDT	Effective date of termination
EEAR 2006	Employment Equality (Age) Regulations 2006, SI 2006/1031
EHRC	Equality and Human Rights Commission
EOC	Equal Opportunities Commission
EP(C)A 1978	Employment Protection (Consolidation) Act 1978
EqPA 1970	Equal Pay Act 1970
ERA 1996	Employment Rights Act 1996
ER(DR)A 1998	Employment Rights (Dispute Resolution) Act 1998
ERelA 1999	Employment Relations Act 1999
ER(NI)O	Employment Rights (Northern Ireland) Order
ET	Employment tribunal
ETA 1996	Employment Tribunals Act 1996
ETO reason	Economic, technical, or organizational reason
ETR 2001	Employment Tribunal Rules of Procedure 2001
ETR 2004	Employment Tribunal Rules of Procedure 2004

ETS	Employment Tribunals Service
EV Rules	Employment Tribunals (Equal Value) Rules of Procedure
EWC	European Works Council
FH	Full hearing
FTER 2002	Fixed Term Employees (Prevention of Less Favourable Treatment) Regulations 2002, SI 2002/2034
FWR	Flexible Working Regulations
GAD	Government Actuary's Department
GLO	Group Litigation Order
GMF	Genuine material factor
GP	General Practitioner
HMRC	HM Revenue & Customs
HRA 1998	Human Rights Act 1998
ICER	Information and Consultation of Employees Regulations 2004, SI 2004/3426
IE	Independent expert
IRA 1971	Industrial Relations Act 1971
ITB	Industrial Training Board
ITEPA 2003	Income Tax (Employment and Pensions) Act 2003
JES	Job evaluation study
MPLR 1999	Maternity and Parental Leave etc Regulations 1999, SI 1999/3312
NIC	National insurance contributions
NIRC	National Industrial Relations Court
NMWA 1998	National Minimum Wage Act 1998
ONS	Office for National Statistics
PAYE	Pay as you earn
PD	Practice direction
PH	Preliminary hearing
PHR	Pre-hearing review
PILON	Payments in lieu of notice
PTO	Preparation time order
PTWR 2000	Part-time Workers (Prevention of Less Favourable Treatment) Regulations 2000, SI 2000/1551
RBR 2003	Employment Equality (Religion or Belief) Regulations 2003, SI 2003/1660
RDO	Register deletion order
ROET	Regional Office of Employment Tribunals
RPI	Retail Prices Index
RRA 1976	Race Relations Act 1976
RRO	Restricted reporting order
RSC	Rules of the Supreme Court
SCA 1981	Supreme Court Act 1981
SDA 1975	Sex Discrimination Act 1975
SNB	Special Negotiating Body
SOR 2003	Employment Equality (Sexual Orientation) Regulations 2003, SI 2003/1661
SRCR 1977	Safety Representatives and Safety Committees Regulations 1977, SI 1977/500
SSP	Statutory Sick Pay
SSPA	Social Security Pensions Act 1975
TICER 1999	Transnational Information and Consultation of Employees Regulations 1999, SI 1999/3323

TULR(C)A 1992	Trade Union and Labour Relations (Consolidation) Act 1992
TUPE 1981	Transfer of Undertakings (Protection of Employment) Regulations 1981, SI 1981/1794
TUPE 2006	Transfer of Undertakings (Protection of Employment) Regulations 2006, SI 2006/246
WTR 1998	Working Time Regulations 1998, SI 1998/1833

Part A

Tribunal Procedure

1

Jurisdiction and Constitution

SUMMARY

(1) Employment tribunals are established and governed by statute to hear a wide range of employment law disputes.

(2) A tribunal must be chaired by a qualified lawyer, and normally also includes two lay members from panels drawn up by the Lord Chancellor (previously the Secretary of State for Business, Enterprise and Regulatory Reform performed this role). Tribunal decisions are usually unanimous, but a decision can be made by a majority.

(3) A judge may sit alone for case management discussions, pre-hearing reviews, and for hearings of defined classes of cases. In each of the latter two situations the judge may be required at least to consider sitting with two lay members.

(4) Regulation 19(1) of the Employment Tribunals (Constitution and Rules of Procedure) Regulations 2004 imposes territorial limits on the tribunals' jurisdiction.

(5) The tribunals are headed by the President of Employment Tribunals, and each region has a Regional Chairman. Employment Tribunal Offices are found in most major cities in England and Wales and are administered by the Tribunals Service.

(6) There are no restrictions on rights of audience in the tribunals.

A. INTRODUCTION

Employment tribunals were first established under the Industrial Training Act 1964 to hear appeals from assessments of industrial training levies. The matters in respect of which the tribunals have jurisdiction have grown beyond all recognition since 1964. In 1965 they became responsible for deciding redundancy payment disputes; from 1972 they heard claims for unfair dismissal, which had been introduced by the Industrial Relations Act 1971. In 1975 and 1976 with the introduction of the key sex and race discrimination legislation (Equal Pay Act 1970, Sex Discrimination Act 1975, Race Relations Act 1976) the tribunals became responsible for 1.01

determining complaints of discrimination under those statutes in the employment field. The classes of discrimination claim in respect of which the tribunal has jurisdiction have grown rapidly since the mid 1990s, covering notably disability, religion, sexual orientation, and age. The tribunals were given limited jurisdiction in relation to certain contractual disputes in 1994. From 1998 onwards there has been an increasing amount of statutory regulation of the workplace, often European led, and the tribunals have been given further jurisdiction in relation to the new legislation. A full list of complaints in respect of which the employment tribunals have jurisdiction is set out in Table 1 on p xx *et seq*.

1.02 Employment tribunals are created by and derive their powers from statute. The Employment Tribunals Act 1996 and the Employment Tribunals (Constitution and Rules of Procedure) Regulations 2004, SI 2004/1861, which came into effect on 1 October 2004, govern the constitution and regulation of the tribunals. The tribunals' rules of procedure are contained in Sch 1 to the 2004 Regulations, the Employment Tribunal Rules of Procedure 2004 (ETR 2004). The 2004 Regulations contain five further Schedules which add to or amend the ETR 2004. In practice, apart from Sch 6 dealing with equal pay claims, claims under these specialist jurisdictions are rare. Chapter 16 deals with the tribunals' specialist jurisdictions. The ETR 2004 were amended by the Employment Tribunals (Constitution and Rules of Procedure) (Amendment) Regulations 2008, SI 2008/3240 with effect from 6 April 2009.

1.03 The employment tribunals are not courts of record. However, for the purposes of the Contempt of Court Act 1981 they are inferior courts, so that contempt of court in tribunal proceedings is punishable by the Divisional Court of the High Court (*Peach Grey & Co v Sommers* [1995] ICR 549, [1995] IRLR 363, DC).

1.04 The 2004 Regulations for the first time create a unified body of rules for both England and Wales, and Scotland. Under the previous regime, England and Wales was governed by the Employment Tribunals (Constitution and Rules of Procedure) Regulations 2001, SI 2001/1171, and Scotland by the Employment Tribunals (Constitution and Rules of Procedure) (Scotland) Regulations 2001, SI 2001/1170, although the rules were very similar. Although the administration of tribunals is provided centrally for England, Wales, and Scotland, the detail of practice in Scotland remains slightly different and it is a distinct jurisdiction.

1.05 The original vision for the employment tribunals was that they should be 'easily accessible, informal, speedy and inexpensive' (Donovan Commission on Trade Unions and Employers' Associations 1965–8). As much as possible tribunals try to maintain this approach. The tribunal shall, so far as it appears to be appropriate, seek to avoid formality in its proceedings, and shall conduct hearings in such manner as it considers appropriate for the clarification of the issues before it, and generally to the just handling of the proceedings (ETR 2004, r 14(2)–(3)). The laws of evidence do not apply (ETR 2004, r 14(2)). However, although the tribunals continue to strive for these objectives, over the years the claims upon which the tribunals have been required to adjudicate have become more and more complex, and the rules of procedure for dealing with those cases have become more extensive. Hearings in the tribunal are conducted in a format very similar to that applied in the civil courts. In recent years there has been a trend towards a case management approach more in line with the approach in the civil courts under the Civil Procedure Rules 1998, SI 1998/3132 (CPR).

1.06 The 2001 Regulations introduced for the first time an overriding objective, to which a tribunal shall seek to give effect whenever it exercises a power under the rules, or interprets such a rule. By reg 3 of the 2004 Regulations the overriding objective of the rules is to enable tribunals to deal with cases justly. Dealing with a case justly includes so far as practicable:

(a) ensuring that the parties are on an equal footing;
(b) saving expense;
(c) dealing with the case in ways which are proportionate to the complexity of the issues;
(d) ensuring that it is dealt with expeditiously and fairly.

Further, by s 2 of the Human Rights Act 1998 (HRA 1998), the tribunal must take into account any judgment or decision of the European Court of Human Rights (ECtHR) when considering any matter in respect of which a human rights issue has arisen. **1.07**

The employment tribunal is a public authority, and as such may not itself act in a manner incompatible with rights under the European Convention on Human Rights (ECHR). In its procedures a tribunal must respect the right of all parties before it to a fair trial under ECHR, Article 6(1). **1.08**

The tribunal must, so far as possible, read and give effect to legislation in a way which is compatible with Convention rights (HRA 1998, s 3). This may affect the substantive decision-making of the tribunal. In *X v Y* [2004] EWCA Civ 662, [2004] IRLR 625 the Court of Appeal held that when considering the fairness of a dismissal under s 98(4) of the Employment Rights Act 1996 (ERA 1996) a tribunal was required to give effect to Convention rights under s 3 of HRA 1998. See also *Copsey v WWB Devon Clays Ltd* [2005] EWCA Civ 932, [2005] IRLR 811. **1.09**

A tribunal may not make a declaration that primary legislation is incompatible with the ECHR (HRA 1998, s 4). That power is limited to the High Court, Court of Appeal, and House of Lords. The Employment Appeal Tribunal (EAT) has held that neither the employment tribunal nor the EAT has jurisdiction to hear a submission as to the incompatibility of legislation with the ECHR (*Whittaker v P & D Watson (t/a P & M Watson Haulage)* [2002] ICR 1244, EAT). Nor may a tribunal hear a freestanding claim for interference with Convention rights under s 6 of HRA 1998. **1.10**

B. COMPOSITION OF EMPLOYMENT TRIBUNALS

A tribunal must be constituted in accordance with s 4 of the Employment Tribunals Act 1996 (ETA 1996) and the 2004 Regulations. A tribunal must be chaired by an appropriately qualified lawyer. Normally a tribunal consists of a panel of three, with the judge joined by two lay members. Under s 4(1) all cases should be heard by a panel of three unless s 4 or ETR 2004 provide for the case to be heard either by a judge alone or a judge with one member. **1.11**

Although the judge is the sole legally qualified member, and will be responsible for the management of proceedings before the tribunal, all three members of the tribunal participate equally in the decision-making of the tribunal. **1.12**

Members

Judges

The Tribunals, Courts and Enforcement Act 2007 inserted a new s 3A into the ETA 1996, pursuant to which chairmen are to be known as 'Employment Judges' with effect from 1 December 2007. The judge must have satisfied the judicial appointment eligibility condition within the meaning of the Tribunals, Courts and Enforcement Act 2007 for a period of five years. In Scotland or Northern Ireland the judge must be a barrister, advocate, or solicitor of five years' standing (2004 Regulations, reg 8(3)). Part-time judges will normally be practising solicitors or barristers. They may not appear as representatives before a tribunal in the region in which they have been appointed as a part-time judge. **1.13**

Lay members

The two lay members who sit on each tribunal are selected one from a panel of 'employer representatives' and one from a panel of 'employee representatives'. The panels are drawn up by the Lord Chancellor after consultation with such organizations or associations of organizations representing respectively employers and employees as the Lord Chancellor sees fit (2004 Regulations, reg 8(3) as amended). In fact, the practice in modern times is that lay members are recruited by public advertisement and interview. This appears to have resulted in a broadening of the range of lay members, in particular an increase in the number of younger members, **1.14** although with some loss of 'hands-on' industrial experience, particularly from the employee panel.

1.15 The lay members are not intended to be delegates of their respective organizations; rather they should be independent and open-minded. They should, and do, judge each case on its merits without preconception, fear, or favour: see the remarks of Burton J in *Rabahallah v BT Group plc* [2005] ICR 440, [2005] IRLR 184, EAT, paras 13–14; see also *de Haney v Brent MIND* [2003] EWCA Civ 1637, [2004] ICR 348. The Lord Chancellor looks for candidates who have practical experience of industrial relations and who are capable of acting impartially in reaching decisions on facts presented to them. The lay members can be perceived as the safety valve of the employment adjudication system, deflecting much of the criticism of the unions that the system is biased against them. They reflect the tripartism which has been a feature of British employment relations as reflected in bodies such as the Advisory, Conciliation and Arbitration Service (ACAS).

1.16 Since 1999 lay members have been appointed for a renewable period of three years. During his period of appointment a lay member in England and Wales may be removed upon a written notice from the Lord Chancellor upon five grounds (misbehaviour, incapacity, failure as to training, failure to satisfy the sitting requirements, and sustained failure to observe the standards reasonably to be expected of a holder of the office). The Lord Chancellor cannot remove a lay member unless, having first consulted with the President of the Employment Tribunals, he then notifies the Lord Chief Justice of his concern and requests him (in consultation with the President) to nominate a judge to investigate all circumstances. Only if the report of the investigating judge is that grounds for removal are made out and if the Lord Chief Justice concurs in the removal can the Lord Chancellor then remove the member. A lay member will automatically be offered reappointment at the end of his term, unless specified grounds for non-renewal are made out. The Lord Chancellor's power of non-renewal is subject to judicial control similar to that in cases of removal. For an explanation of the changes to the system of appointment of lay members, see the EAT's decision in *Scanfuture UK Ltd v Secretary of State for Trade and Industry* [2001] IRLR 416.

1.17 Under the pre-1999 system periods of office were shorter, and the power of removal was not restricted. In *Scanfuture* the EAT held that prior to the 1999 changes the employment tribunal was not an independent and impartial tribunal for the purposes of ECHR, Article 6 in cases where the Secretary of State was a party. The EAT held that there was no ground to doubt the independence and impartiality of the tribunal after the 1999 changes.

1.18 There are no requirements in the rules for the composition of tribunals to suit particular types of employment or particular types of claim. It was held in *Halford v Sharples* [1992] ICR 146 that, apart from cases of sex and race discrimination, appointment to tribunals should be by random selection and not based on type of employment. The practice in England and Wales in race and sex discrimination cases is different. During the passage of the Bill which became the Race Relations Act 1976 the Government (House of Lords, Lord Jacques, 15 October 1976) said that steps would be taken to appoint to the panel of lay members persons who, in addition to their general knowledge or experience of employment, also had special knowledge or experience of relations between persons of different racial groups in the employment field and that, wherever possible, one such member would sit in cases where racial discrimination is alleged by the claimant. This has always been the normal practice. However, failure to appoint such a person does not affect the legal validity of a tribunal's composition: *Habib v Elkington & Co Ltd* [1981] ICR 435, [1981] IRLR 344, EAT. Further, a certificate given by the President of the Employment Tribunals for England and Wales that one lay member 'was selected as having special knowledge or experience of relations between persons of different racial groups in the employment field' could not be challenged in the absence of any convincing evidence that what is certified is either wholly inaccurate or is false. In sex discrimination cases, steps are normally taken to ensure the tribunal includes at least one female member.

Independence and impartiality

All members of a tribunal must be independent and impartial—bias, or the appearance of bias, must be avoided. Bias is dealt with in detail in Chapter 10. **1.19**

Majority decision

Where the tribunal members are unable to agree, the decision may be by a majority (ETR 2004, r 28(4)). Each of the three members has an equal vote, so it is possible for the lay members to outvote the judge. In rare circumstances where a judge sits with only one lay member, the judge has a casting vote in the event of disagreement (ETR 2004, r 28(4)). In practice the vast majority of decisions are unanimous. See further paras 11.27–11.33 in relation to majority decisions. **1.20**

All members of the tribunal who sit must take part in every aspect of the questions which they have to decide. This was made clear by the National Industrial Relations Court in *Morris v Gestetner Ltd* [1973] ICR 587, where one member failed to agree with the majority view that, since the tribunal could take no account of pressure exercised by employees in a strike threat, the employee had been unfairly dismissed. Having taken this view on the main issue against the claimant, the dissentient took no part in the further decision of whether to make a recommendation for the employee's re-engagement. Sir John Donaldson, then President, however, rebuked the tribunal on the grounds that all must participate in the decisions accorded them by statute. **1.21**

Cases where a judge may sit alone

ETR 2004 classifies hearings into five types: case management discussions, pre-hearing reviews, interim relief hearings, hearings, and reviews (ETR 2004, r 14). The requirements for the composition of the tribunal panel vary from one type of hearing to another. **1.22**

Case management discussion

Case management discussions are interim hearings which deal with matters of procedure and the management of hearings. ETR 2004, r 17(1) provides that case management discussions shall be conducted by a judge sitting alone. **1.23**

Pre-hearing review

Pre-hearing reviews are interim hearings which may make more substantial decisions concerning a case. For example, there are powers to strike out a claim or a response at a pre-hearing review. ETR 2004, r 18 sets out the powers that may be exercised at a pre-hearing review. **1.24**

Rule 18(1) provides that a pre-hearing review shall be conducted by a judge unless (r 18(3)): **1.25**

(a) a party has made a request in writing not less than 10 days before the date on which the pre-hearing review is due to take place that the pre-hearing review be conducted by a tribunal instead of a judge; and
(b) a judge considers that one or more substantive issues of fact are likely to be determined at the pre-hearing review, that it would be desirable for the pre-hearing review to be conducted by a tribunal and he has issued an order that the pre-hearing review be conducted by a tribunal.

Rule 18(3)(b) broadly reflects the position established by the authorities prior to ETR 2004. Under the 1993 and 2001 versions of the Rules judges had jurisdiction to sit alone to determine jurisdictional points, and to hear all other matters in connection with an originating application, and in hearing such applications they could hear evidence and determine disputed factual issues (*Tsangacos v Amalgamated Chemicals Ltd* [1997] IRLR 4). However, in *Edusei v (1) Ledwith, (2) Nynex Cablecoms Ltd*, 27 February 1997, EAT/1326/95, the EAT emphasized that in cases which raised difficult disputes of fact, or mixed fact and law, the judge should consider carefully the wisdom of sitting alone, since in those types of case the experience of the lay members may be especially valuable. In *Sutcliffe v Big C's Marine* [1998] ICR 913 a judge sitting alone **1.26** had heard an issue as to which of three companies was actually the employer of the claimants. The EAT said that although on the facts of the case it was a legitimate route to take, tribunals should think carefully before dispensing with lay members and must bear in mind the interests of justice, and not simply the saving of expense, when making such decisions. It is suggested that this guidance remains relevant to the exercise of the judge's discretion under r 18(3).

Review

1.27 A review should be heard by the judge or tribunal which made the decision under review (ETR 2004, r 36(1)). If the decision subject to a review was made by a full tribunal, the review should be by that tribunal. If the review is of a decision of a judge sitting alone, then the review should be conducted by that judge sitting alone.

Hearings under the Employment Tribunals Act 1996, s 4(3)

Proceedings to which s 4(3) applies

1.28 By ETA 1996, s 4, the following proceedings shall be heard by a judge alone, unless having regard to particular matters (set out below), it is appropriate for the case to be heard by a full tribunal:

(a) proceedings under ss 68A or 87 of the Trade Union and Labour Relations (Consolidation) Act 1992 (TULR(C)A 1992) (right not to suffer deductions of unauthorized or excessive trade union subscriptions);
(b) proceedings under s 192 of TULR(C)A 1992 (claim to receive compensation for failure to inform and consult over collective redundancies);
(c) proceedings under ss 161, 165, or 166 of TULR(C)A 1992 (claims for interim relief in cases of dismissal for trade union membership or activities);
(d) proceedings under s 126 of the Pension Schemes Act 1993 (complaints that the Secretary of State has failed to make required payments of unpaid contributions to pension schemes);
(e) proceedings under s 11 of ERA 1996 (right to a written statement of terms and conditions of employment);
(f) proceedings under s 23 of ERA 1996 (unauthorized deductions from wages);
(g) proceedings under s 34 of ERA 1996 (right to guarantee payments);
(h) proceedings under ss 64 and 70(1) of ERA 1996 (right to remuneration during suspension on medical grounds);
(i) proceedings under s 163 of ERA 1996 (right to a redundancy payment);
(j) proceedings under s 170 of ERA 1996 (right to a redundancy payment from the Secretary of State in the event of the employer's insolvency or refusal/failure to make the payment);
(k) proceedings under s 188 of ERA 1996 (right to payment from Secretary of State in the event of insolvency);
(l) proceedings under ss 128, 131, or 132 of ERA 1996 (interim relief in certain unfair dismissal cases);
(m) proceedings under ETA 1996, s 3 and the Employment Tribunals Extension of Jurisdiction (England and Wales) Order 1994, SI 1994/1623 and the Employment Tribunals Extension of Jurisdiction (Scotland) Order 1994, SI 1994/1624 (claims for breach of contract or money owing under a contract);
(n) appointment by a tribunal under s 206(4) of ERA 1996 of a person to act on behalf of a deceased person before a tribunal;
(o) proceedings under reg 15(10) of the Transfer of Undertakings (Protection of Employment) Regulations 2006, SI 2006/246 (to recover money ordered by a tribunal to be paid for failure to inform and consult over a transfer of an undertaking);
(p) proceedings on a complaint under s 11 of the National Minimum Wage Act 1998;
(q) proceedings on an appeal under ss 19 or 22 of the National Minimum Wage Act 1998;
(r) proceedings in which the parties have given their written consent to the case being heard by a judge alone;
(s) proceedings in which the respondent has not contested, or is not contesting, the proceedings;

(t) proceedings under reg 30 of the Working Time Regulations 1998 relating to an amount due under regulation 14(2) or 16(1) of those Regulations (claims for holiday pay);
(u) proceedings under reg 18 of the Merchant Shipping (Working Time: Inland Waterways) Regulations 2003 relating to an amount due under reg 11 (claims for holiday pay);
(v) proceedings under reg 18 of the Civil Aviation (Working Time) Regulations 2004 relating to an amount due under reg 4 (claims for holiday pay); and
(w) proceedings under reg 19 of the Fishing Vessels (Working Time: Sea-fishermen) Regulations 2004 relating to an amount due under reg 11 (claims for holiday pay).

Prior to the introduction of the final four categories listed above, it was not possible for a claim under the Working Time Regulations 1998 to be heard by a judge alone. Nor was it permissible to use a reference for a determination of terms and conditions of employment (which did fall within s 4(3)) to determine issues of the scope of an employee's rights under the WTR 1998, see *British Bakeries Ltd v Herminio Costa Nascimento* UKEAT/0888/04, [2005] All ER (D) 20 (Sep). The Government's consultation paper 'Dispute Resolution: Secondary legislation consultation' (Department for Business, Enterprise and Regulatory Reform, July 2008) proposed that holiday pay cases should be added to the list of jurisdictions within r 4(3) and the Employment Tribunals Act 1996 (Tribunal Composition) Order 2009 SI 2009/789 introduced new subss (ce) to (ch) to give effect to the proposal from 6 April 2009.

Consideration of hearing by a full tribunal

Section 4(5) of ETA 1996 provides that the proceedings listed in s 4 shall be heard by a full tribunal if the judge decides at any stage of the proceedings to do so, having regard to: **1.29**

(a) whether there is a likelihood of a dispute arising on the facts which makes it desirable for the proceedings to be heard by a full tribunal;
(b) whether there is a likelihood of an issue of law arising which would make it desirable for the proceedings to be heard by a judge alone;
(c) any views of any of the parties as to whether or not the proceedings ought to be heard by a judge alone or by a full tribunal; and
(d) whether there are other proceedings which might be heard concurrently but which are not proceedings specified in s 4(3).

In a case where the views and experience of the lay members are likely to be of assistance to the decision-making process, a judge should generally decide pursuant to s 4(5) that the case be heard by a full tribunal (Post Office v Howell [2000] ICR 913, EAT). **1.30**

A judge must exercise the discretion under s 4(5) if the issue is raised by one of the parties. It is desirable for a judge to consider s 4(5) even if the issue is not raised by the parties, although it is not an error of law to fail to do so: *Morgan v Brith Gof Cyf* [2001] ICR 978, Lindsay J, departing from a number of earlier decisions (*Sogbetun v Hackney LBC* [1998] ICR 1264; *Post Office v Howell* [2000] ICR 913; *Professional Selection & Development Ltd v Wahab* EAT/64/00). In *Gladwell v Secretary of State for Trade and Industry* [2007] ICR 264, the EAT under Elias P followed the approach taken in *Morgan*, but added a second situation in which a judge is obliged actively to exercise his discretion: where one of the parties is a litigant in person, or at least a litigant in person who may not be aware of the possibility, or relative merits, of a differently constituted panel. Elias P also agreed with the EAT in *Clarke v Arriva Kent (Thameside) Ltd* [2001] All ER (D) 485 (Jul) that the discretion should be kept under review, as the circumstances may change from those existing at the time the decision was made. *Gladwell* has since been followed by a differently constituted EAT in *Sterling Developments (London) Ltd v Pagano* [2007] IRLR 471, HHJ Clark presiding. **1.31**

Judge sitting with one lay member

A tribunal has power to sit with the judge and one lay member provided either that all of the parties consent, or else all of those who are present or represented at the beginning of the hearing **1.32** consent (ETA 1996, s 4(1), as amended by the Employment Rights (Dispute Resolution) Act 1998). This occurs in the event of illness or travel difficulties of a tribunal member. If one party does not give its consent to the hearing going ahead on this basis, it must be adjourned.

1.33 Where the tribunal proposes sitting with only one lay member, the tribunal must inform the parties from which panel the absent member was taken (employer's panel or employee's panel): *Rabahallah v BT Group plc* [2005] ICR 440, [2005] IRLR 184 following *de Haney v Brent MIND* [2003] EWCA Civ 1637, [2004] ICR 348, where the Court of Appeal dealt with the identical situation in relation to the composition of the EAT. Absence of this information vitiates the consent of the parties. In *Rabahallah*, Burton J (para 35) suggested that it would be sensible for a form to be signed by the parties, giving consent to a case commencing or continuing before a panel of two rather than three. It should contain an express reference to the identity of the judge and one member who will try or continue to try the case, with a statement of the panel from which that member is drawn.

1.34 Where a tribunal consists of a judge and one lay member, the judge has a casting vote (ETR 2004, r 28(4)).

Determination of claims without a hearing

1.35 The Employment Act 2008 introduced an amendment to the ETA 1996 in the form of a new subs 3AA to s 7. The provisions allow regulations to be introduced to authorize a 'fast track' system for adjudicating certain disputes without a hearing if all the parties consent or the respondent has either presented no response or does not contest the claim. At the time of writing no such regulations have been made. The categories of cases for which the Government believes this system would be suitable are claims for unlawful deduction from wages, breach of contract, redundancy pay, holiday pay, and national minimum wage.

C. JURISDICTION

1.36 The tribunal has only the jurisdiction given to it by statute. There are now over 70 statutory jurisdictions in respect of which the tribunal may hear claims. Most of these are to determine rights which are defined in some detail by statute. Others, however, amount to a statutory jurisdiction to determine a common law cause of action: ETA 1996, s 3, for example, gives the employment tribunal jurisdiction to hear certain claims of breach of contract (see Chapter 8). The tribunal has no power to determine any matter or give any remedy falling outside its specific statutory jurisdictions. A list of the tribunal's jurisdictions is set out in Table 1 (page 14 *et seq.*).

1.37 Whether a tribunal has jurisdiction in respect of any particular claim is largely a matter of substantive law depending on the jurisdictional requirements of the particular statute upon which the claim is based. The tribunal's common law contractual jurisdiction is considered in Chapter 8. The interplay of the tribunal's jurisdiction and the jurisdiction of the civil courts is considered in Chapter 20.

Territorial jurisdiction

1.38 A number of statutory rights are subject to territorial limitations: see, for example, Sex Discrimination Act 1975, ss 6 and 10; Race Relations Act 1976, s 8; Disability Discrimination Act 1995, s 68; TULR(C)A 1992, s 285(1). The ERA 1996 confers rights in relation to claimants employed in Great Britain at the time of their dismissal, and in certain exceptional cases, for example where employees based in Great Britain are posted overseas for the purposes of a business based in Great Britain: *Lawson v Serco* [2006] UKHL 3, [2006] IRLR 289. A different approach may be required where the claims of employees are based on rights conferred by European Union laws, rather than domestic laws: see *Bleuse v MBT Transport* [2008] IRLR 264, where the EAT held that those claims of the employee that were founded on EU legislation fell within the tribunal's jurisdiction, while those based on legislation with no origin in EU law did not. Detailed consideration of the territorial limitations on statutory employment rights is outside the scope of this work.

In addition to the requirements of the particular statute upon which any claim is based, under reg 19(1) of the 2004 Regulations an employment tribunal in England and Wales shall only have jurisdiction to deal with proceedings where: **1.39**

(a) the respondent or one of the respondents resides or carries on business in England or Wales;
(b) had the remedy been by way of action in the county court, the cause of action would have arisen wholly or partly in England and Wales;
(c) the proceedings are to determine a question which has been referred to the tribunal by a court in England and Wales; or
(d) in the case of proceedings to which Schedule 3, 4, or 5 applies, the proceedings relate to matters arising in England and Wales.

Regulation 18(2) contains an equivalent provision in respect of Scotland.

The Employment Protection (Offshore Employment) Order 1976, SI 1976/766 provides that the main employment legislation applies to any activities in British territorial waters (other than activities connected with a ship in the course of a navigational survey or a ship engaged in dredging or fishing), activities connected with the exploration of the sea bed, sub-soil, or the exploitation of their natural resources, and any activities connected with the exploration or exploitation of the Frigg gas field. The provisions confer jurisdiction on employment tribunals whether or not individual claimants or respondents are British subjects, and whether or not any respondent company is incorporated under the laws of the United Kingdom. **1.40**

Questions on the geographical scope of tribunals have arisen in several cases. A company may carry on business in England and Wales for the purposes of reg 19(1)(a) even though its registered office is abroad: see *Knulty v Eloc Electro-Opteik and Communicatie BV* [1979] ICR 827. **1.41**

In the civil courts the phrase 'carried on business' has been held to refer to something of a permanent character. A temporary carrying on of a business in a district by a person whose permanent place of business is elsewhere does not make it his place of business for the purpose of being sued (see *Shiels v Great Northern Railway Co* (1861) 30 LJ QB 331; *Gorslett v Harris* (1857) 29 LT OS 75). **1.42**

Cases can be transferred between England and Scotland by order of the President or Regional Employment Judge if it appears to him that the case can be more conveniently tried on transfer, and if the 'transferee' President has consented to the transfer (ETR 2004, r 57; see r 60 on service of notices). **1.43**

D. ADMINISTRATION

President

The overall head of employment tribunals in England and Wales is the President of the Employment Tribunals, who must be a barrister or solicitor of at least seven years' standing appointed to the position by the Lord Chancellor. He holds his position for a term or terms of five years, with a compulsory retirement age of 70. There is a separate President for Scotland who is appointed by the Lord President of the Court of Session. In Scotland there is also a Vice-President, a position which is equivalent to a Regional Chairman in England and Wales. The President's duties include nominal responsibility for selection of judges and lay members for the hearing of particular cases, giving directions for their sittings, and determining the number of tribunals to be established. He also receives complaints about the conduct of employment judges and members. He may also sit as a judge of a tribunal himself, and is responsible for Regional Chairmen. Since the Tribunals, Courts and Enforcement Act 2007, the apex of the tribunal **1.44** judiciary is the Senior President of Tribunals (currently Carnwath LJ), who has responsibility not just for the employment tribunals and EAT, but for numerous other statutory tribunals falling within the remit of the Tribunals Service.

Employment tribunal offices

1.45 The employment tribunals operate through a number of offices in cities around England and Wales, and Scotland. Most tribunals sit between 10 am and 4 or 4.30 pm, although practice varies in different parts of the country. Tribunal offices are open between 9 am and 5 pm on weekdays.

1.46 Prior to the 2004 Regulations, there was a Central Office of Employment Tribunals (COET), and there were also Regional Offices of Employment Tribunals. Both have now been abolished, leaving only employment tribunal offices, as referred to in the previous paragraph. The position of Regional Chairman has been retained, and employment judges remain grouped in regions comprising of a number of tribunal offices and hearing centres.

1.47 Administrative matters for the tribunals are the responsibility of the Secretary of Employment Tribunals. There is one Secretary for England and Wales and one for Scotland. Each employment tribunal office will have a person who exercises the powers of the Secretary for that office (see ETR 2004, r 60(3)).

1.48 Administrative support for employment tribunals and the EAT is provided by the Tribunals Service, an executive agency under the control of the Ministry of Justice.

Regional Employment Judges

1.49 Regional Employment Judges are drawn from the panel of full-time judges, and are appointed by the Lord Chancellor (2004 Regulations, reg 6).

Clerk

1.50 Each tribunal has a clerk who does not act as a court clerk but merely performs administrative functions, such as recording the times of sittings and administering oaths. The clerk deals with administrative matters with the parties before the start of any hearing, such as recording the names of those attending, ascertaining what form of oath the witnesses wish to take, and ensuring that the tribunal has copies of the bundle and witness statements.

Tribunals, Courts and Enforcement Act 2007

1.51 The employment tribunals and the EAT emerged largely unscathed by the Legatt review of tribunals, which led to the Tribunals, Courts and Enforcement Act 2007. This Act introduced an integrated system for the majority of statutory tribunals, but left the constitution and procedure of the employment tribunals largely untouched. The Act made a number of changes principally at administrative level. The key changes are as follows:

(a) The Lord Chancellor has a statutory duty to ensure that there is an efficient and effective system to support the carrying on of the business of the employment tribunals and the EAT, and to ensure that appropriate services are provided for the tribunals (s 40).
(b) In common with other statutory tribunals, the employment tribunals and the EAT come under the auspices of the Senior President of Tribunals.
(c) The employment tribunals and EAT are subject to the oversight of the Administrative Justice and Tribunals Council, which replaces the abolished Council on Tribunals.
(d) A new s 7B of the ETA 1996 provides that regulations may provide for practice directions establishing judicial mediation of claims before the employment tribunals.
(e) There is a new mechanism for enforcement of ACAS conciliated settlements through the county court (s 142).

E. REPRESENTATION

1.52 Employment tribunals are intended to be less daunting and cheaper for those appearing than are the ordinary courts. Ideally, the parties should be able to dispense with legal representation. About two-thirds of claimants do appear unrepresented by lawyers. They may, however, receive help with their case from a trade union, law centre, Citizens Advice Bureau, or a friend more articulate than themselves. There are limited restrictions on the range of representation, and indeed claimants are fully entitled to represent themselves, as frequently happens. Many employers are also tempted to represent themselves, and some personnel managers have acquired considerable expertise in doing so.

1.53 In recent years, tribunals have seen an increase in representation of employers by employment consultants, often as part of employer insurance schemes. Most are not covered by a code of professional conduct. In response to concerns over the highly variable quality of advice and representation being provided, a regulatory framework was introduced by the Compensation (Regulated Claims Management Services) Order 2006, SI 2006/3319, which came into force on 23 April 2007. Those who provide 'claims management services' must obtain authorization from the Regulator; a failure to do so is a criminal offence. There are a number of exemptions to the requirement for regulation: barristers; solicitors; charities; not-for-profit organizations; and independent trade unions provided that they comply with the code of practice for the provision of regulated claims management services by trade unions issued by the Secretary of State on 28 November 2006. Further detail about authorization can be found at <http://www.claimsregulation.gov.uk>.

1.54 For an interesting study on the effect of legal representation in tribunal proceedings, see 'Making a Difference? Legal Representation in Employment Tribunal Cases: Evidence from a Survey of Representatives' PL Latreille, JA Latreille, and KG Knight (2005) 34 ILJ 308.

1.55 Most employment judges actively assist an unrepresented party, for example, in cross-examining the witnesses of the other side. Kilner Brown J said in *Mortimer v Reading Windings Ltd* [1977] ICR 511: 'The little man, or the little woman, trying to put a case of grievance, should be given every assistance so that his or her case will have been put and properly considered.'

1.56 The EAT has deprecated representation by a member of management who has been involved in an internal appeal by the claimant employee. Phillips J stated in *Singh v London Country Bus Services Ltd* [1976] IRLR 176, 291:

> It can obviously give rise to misunderstanding if a man who has appeared as a member of an Appeal Board subsequently appears at a tribunal as an advocate, as it were, officially representing the respondent employer. To do so can give rise to misunderstanding, however ill-founded in the mind of the employee. We think that as far as possible such a course should be avoided.

1.57 Ultimately, however, the choice of representative is a matter for the party (subject only to authorization where that representative is a provider of claims management services). A party to proceedings indeed has a statutory right under s 6 of ETA 1996 to be represented by the representative of his or her choice. In *Bache v Essex County Council* [2000] IRLR 251 the employment judge purported to 'sack' the claimant's representative on the grounds that he was not conducting the case competently. The Court of Appeal held that the tribunal had no power to do so; the tribunal's power to control the way in which a party conducts its case does not extend to the power to control the choice of representative. Further in *Douglas v Dispatch Management Services (UK) Ltd* [2002] IRLR 389, the claimant was represented by solicitors who had previously acted for the respondent, and the tribunal held, following *Bache*, that it has no power to dismiss the solicitors from acting as a representative in the proceedings.

1.58 There is no legal aid available for representation in employment tribunals. Formerly the Commission for Racial Equality (CRE), the Equal Opportunities Commission, and the Disability Rights Commission could assist with representing individual complainants in cases of racial, disability, or gender discrimination or equal pay, where a question of principle arose or where it was unreasonable, having regard to the complexity of the case, to expect the individual to deal with the case unaided. The Equality Act 2006 merged these Commissions into a single Equality and Human Rights Commission (EHRC), which was established in October 2007 and took over the functions of the CRE in April 2009. Section 28 gives the EHRC the power to give legal assistance to individuals in proceedings relating to the equality enactments.

Table 1 Employment tribunal jurisdiction list

The following list produced by the Tribunals Service, can be found at <http://www.employmenttribunals.gov.uk/FormsGuidance/jurisdictionList.htm>. A key to the legislation abbreviations used appears at the end of the table.

Jurisdiction	Originating legislation
Suffer a detriment and/or dismissal resulting from a failure to allow an employee to be accompanied, or to accompany a fellow employee at a disciplinary/grievance hearing	ERelA 1999 ss 11–12
Application for a declaration that the inclusion of discriminatory terms/rules within certain agreements or rules causes the aforesaid to be invalid	SDA 1986 s 6(4A)
Application by an employee, their representative or trade union for a protective award as a result of an employer's failure to consult over a redundancy situation	TULR(C)A 1992 s 189
Breach of Contract	ETA 1996 s 3
Failure of the employer to consult with an employee representative or trade union about a proposed contracting out of a pension scheme	SSPA 1975
Application or complaint by the EOC, CRE or DRC in respect of discriminatory advertisements or instructions or pressure to discriminate (including preliminary action before a claim to the county court)	SDA 1975 ss 72–73, 76; RRA 1976 ss 63–64, 68; DDA 1995 s 17B and Sch 3, para 3
Discrimination or victimisation on grounds of age	EE (Age) Regs 2006
Suffered a detriment, discrimination and/or dismissal on grounds of disability or failure of employer to make reasonable adjustments	DDA 1995 ss 17A and 25(8) and Sch 3, para 3
Suffered a detriment and/or dismissal resulting from requiring time off for other (non-work but not Health and Safety) duties, study, training or seeking work	ERA 1996 ss 46, 47, 48, 102–103, 105, 108–109 and 111
Discrimination or victimisation on grounds of religion or belief	EE (Religion or Belief) Regs 2003 regs 28 and 34
Discrimination or victimisation on grounds of sexual orientation	EE (Sexual Orientation) Regs 2003 regs 28 and 34
Application by the Secretary of State for Trade & Industry to prohibit a person from running an Employment Agency	Employment Agencies Act 1973 ss 3A and 3C
Failure to provide equal pay for equal value work	EPA 1970 ss 2 and 7A
Failure of the employer to consult with an employee rep. or trade union about a proposed transfer	TUPE 1981 reg 11(1)–(4) and (8)
Suffer a detriment and/or dismissal for claiming under the flexible working regulations or be subject to a breach of procedure	ERA 1996 ss 47E, 80F–80I and 104C FW (Procedural Requirements) Regs 2002 FW (Eligibility, Complaints and Remedies) Regs 2002

Application by an employee that an employer has failed to pay a protected award as ordered by a tribunal	TULR(C)A 1992 s 192
Failure to pay remuneration whilst suspended from work for health and safety reasons whilst pregnant or on mat. leave	ERA 1996 ss 67–68 and 70(1) and (4)
Failure to provide a written statement of terms and conditions and any subsequent changes to those terms	ERA 1996 s 11(1)
Suffered less favourable treatment and/or dismissal as a fixed term employee, than a full time employee or, on becoming permanent, failed to receive a written statement of confirmation from employer	FTE 2002 regs 7 and 9 ERA 1996 s 105
Failure to allow time off for trade union activities or duties, for ante-natal care or for public duties	TULR(C)A 1992 ss 168–170; ERA 1996 ss 51 and 57
Failure to provide a guarantee payment	ERA 1996 s 34
Failure to pay remuneration whilst suspended for medical reasons	ERA 1996 ss 64 and 70(1)
Failure to allow time off to seek work during a redundancy situation	ERA 1996 s 54
Failure of an employer to comply with an award by a tribunal following a finding that the employer had previously failed to consult about a proposed transfer of an undertaking	TUPE 1981 s 11(5–8)
Failure to allow or to pay for time off for care of dependants, union learning representatives duties, pension scheme trustee duties, employee representatives duties, young person studying/training and European Works Council duties	ERA 1996 ss 57B, 60, 63 and 63C; TICER 1999 reg 27
Failure to provide a written pay statement or an adequate pay statement	ERA 1996 s 11(2)
Failure to provide a written statement of reasons for dismissal or the contents of the statement are disputed	ERA 1996 s 93
Appeal against an enforcement, improvement or prohibition notice imposed by the HSE or Environmental Health Inspector, or by the Environment Agency	NESE 1994 reg 6 or HSWA 1974 s 24(2) or COMAH 1999 s 18
Failure to pay for or allow time off to carry out Safety Rep duties or undertake training	Health & Safety at Work etc Act 1974s 80 Safety Representatives & Safety Committees Regs 1977 reg 11 Health & Safety (Consultation with Employees) Regs 1996 Sch 2 EPA 1970 s 2(1)
Suffer a detriment, dismissal or redundancy for health and safety reasons	ERA 1996 ss 44, 48, 100, 105, 108–109 and 111
Application for interim relief	ERA 1996 s 128 or TULR (C) A 1992 ss 161–167
Failure by the SOS to make an insolvency payment in lieu of wages and/or redundancy	ERA 1996 s 188
Appeal against the levy assessment of an Industrial Training Board	Relevant Industrial Training Levy Order—either Construction or Engineering Construction Board
Loss of office as a result of the reorganisation of a statutory body	Miscellaneous statutes

Suffer a detriment and/or dismissal on grounds of pregnancy, child birth or maternity	ERA 1996 ss 47C, 48, 99, 108–109 and 111 MPL 2002 regs 19–20 PAL Regs 2002 regs 28–29
Appeal against an enforcement or penalty notice issued by the Inland Revenue	NMWA 1998 ss 19 and 22
Suffer a detriment and/or dismissal related to failure to pay the minimum wage or allow access to records	ERA 1996 ss 104A, 105, 108–109 and 111 NMWA 1998 s 11
Appeal against a non-discrimination notice issued by either the CRE, DRC or EOC	DRC 1999 Sch 3, para 10 or RRA 1976 ss 59 and 68 or SDA 1975 ss 68 and 76
Failure of the employer to comply with a certificate of exemption or to deduct funds from employees pay in order to contribute to a trade union political fund	TULR 1992 s 68A
Failure of the employer to prevent unauthorised or excessive deductions in the form of union subscriptions	TURER 1993 s 15(68)
Failure of the Secretary of State to pay unpaid contributions to a pensions scheme following an application for payment to be made	Pensions Schemes Act 1993 s 126
Suffered a detriment and/or dismissal due to exercising rights under the Public Interest Disclosure Act	ERA 1996 ss 47B, 48, 103A, 105, 108–109 and 111
Suffer a detriment and/or dismissal due to requesting or taking paternity or adoption leave or time off to assist a dependant	ERA 1996 ss 47C, 48, 57A and 80 MPL 1999 reg 19 PAL 2002 s 28
Suffer less favourable treatment and/or dismissal as a result of being a part time employee by comparison to a full time employee	PTW 2000 reg 8 ERA 1996 s 105
Failure to pay a redundancy payment	ERA 1996 ss 163 and 177
Failure of the SOS to pay a redundancy payment following an application to the NI fund	ERA 1996 s 170
Discrimination or victimisation on grounds of race or ethnic origin	RRA 1976 ss 54 and 68
Suffer a detriment and/or dismissal for refusing to work on a Sunday	ERA 1996 ss 44, 48, 101, 105, 108–109 and 111
Discrimination or victimisation on grounds of sex, marriage or transgender	SDA 1975 ss 63 and 76 SDA 1986 s 4c
Suffered less favourable treatment and/or dismissal as a temp. employee than a full time employee	FTE Regs 2002
Suffer discrimination in obtaining employment due to membership or non-membership of a trade union	TULR(C)A 1992 ss 137 and 139
Suffer a detriment and/or dismissal relating to being, not being or proposing to become a trade union member	TULR(C)A 1992 ss 145A–145C, 146–147 and 152–160 ERA 1996 Part X
(a) Failure of the employer to consult or report about training in relation to a bargaining unit (b) Suffered a detriment on grounds related to recognition of a trade union for collective bargaining	TULR(C)A 1992 ss 70c, Sch A1 paras 156–157
Suffer discrimination in obtaining the services of an employment agency due to membership or non-membership of a trade union	TULR(C)A 1992 ss 138 and 139

Suffered a detriment and/or dismissal due to exercising rights under the Tax Credits Act	ERA 1996 ss 47D, 48, 104B, 105, 108–109 and 111
Unfair dismissal after exercising or claiming a statutory right	ERA 1996 ss 104, 105, 108–109 and 111
Unfair dismissal on grounds of capability, conduct or some other general reason including the result of a transfer of an undertaking	ERA 1996 s 111
Unfair dismissal in connection to a lock out, strike or other industrial action	TULR(C)A 1992 ss 237–239 ERA 1996 s 105
Failure of employer to pay or unauthorised deductions have been made	ERA 1996 s 23
Appeal by a person who has been served with an improvement or prohibition notice under the Working Time Regulations 1998	WTR 1998 Sch 3, para 6
Failure to limit weekly or night working time, or to ensure rest breaks	WTR 1998 regs 4, 6, 10, 12–17 ERA 1996 ss 45A, 48, 101A, 105, 108–109 and 111 WTR 1998 reg 30 Merchant Shipping (Working Time: Inland Waterways) Regs 2004 reg 18
Complaint by a worker that employer has failed to allow them to take or to pay them for statutory annual leave entitlement	WTR 1998c regs 13, 14(2) or 16(1)

Originating Legislation—Abbreviation and Full Title

CEC 1975	Colleges of Education (Compensation) Regulations 1975
COMAH 1999	Control of Major Accident Hazards Regulations 1999
DCOA 1994	Deregulation and Contracting Out Act 1994
DDA 1995	Disability Discrimination Act 1995
DRC 1999	Disability Rights Commission Act 1999
EE (Age) Regs 2006	Employment Equality (Age) Regulations 2006
EE (Religion or Belief) Regs 2003	Employment Equality (Religion or Belief) Regulations 2003
EE (Sexual Orientation) Regs 2003	Employment Equality (Sexual Orientation) Regulations 2003
EPA 1970	Equal Pay Act 1970
ERA 1996	Employment Rights Act 1996
ERelA 1999	Employment Relations Act 1999
ETA 1996	Employment (Industrial) Tribunals Act 1996
FTE 2002	Fixed Term Employees (Prevention of Less Favourable Treatment) Regulations 2002
FWR 2002	Flexible Working (Procedural Requirements) Regulations 2002 and Flexible Working (Eligibility, Complaints and Remedies) Regulations 2002
HSCE 1996	Health and Safety Consultation with Employee Regulations 1996
HSWA 1974	Health and Safety at Work Act 1974
MPL 1999	Maternity and Parental Leave Regulations 1999
MPL 2002	Maternity and Parental Leave (Amendment) Regulations 2002

NESE 1994	Notific: ;ion of Existing Substances (Enforcement) Regulations 1994
NMWA 1998	National Minimum Wage Act 1998
PAL 2002*f*	Paternity and Adoption Leave Regulations 2002
PIDA 1998	Public Interest Disclosure Act 1998
PTW 2000	Part Time Worker (Prevention of Less Favourable Treatment) Regulations 2000
RRA 1976	Race Relations Act 1976
SDA 1975	Sex Discrimination Act 1975
SRSC 1977	Safety Representatives and Safety Committees Regulations 1977
SSPA 1975	Social Security Pensions Act 1975
STA 1994	Sunday Trading Act 1994
TCA 2002	Tax Credits Act 2002
TICER 1999	The Transnational Information and Consultation of Employees Regulations 1999
TULR(C)A 1992	Trade Union and Labour Relations (Consolidation) Act 1992
TUPE 1981	Transfer of Undertakings (Protection of Employment) Regulations 1981
TURER 1993	Trade Union Reform and Employment Rights Act 1993
WTR 1998	Working Time Regulations 1998

art = (Article) **par** = (Part) **reg** = (Regulation) **Sch** = (Schedule) **s** = (Section)

2

Claim Form

SUMMARY

(1) Claims before employment tribunals have become more formal as a result of ETR 2004 (and associated legislation).

(2) In addition there are now pre-acceptance procedures where a claim form is vetted to ensure that a claimant has complied with any relevant workplace dispute resolution procedures before the tribunal can accept the claim.

(3) What has emerged from the EAT demonstrates that despite the restrictive wording of ETR 2004 some flexibility will be permitted and that access to justice remains a major principle outweighing technical or minor defaults.

A. INTRODUCTION

Prior to 1 October 2005 a claim to a tribunal could be presented in a relatively informal manner with minimum mandatory requirements. While there were some authorities suggesting that the old IT1 was not a formal pleading and did not need the detail that would be expected in the civil courts, there was also authority to the effect that claimants would be restricted to matters set out in their claim especially in discrimination cases (see *Chapman v Simon* [1994] IRLR 124 approved by the House of Lords in *Nagarajan v London Regional Transport* [1998] IRLR 73). The effect of the Employment Tribunals (Constitution and Rules of Procedure) (Amendment) Regulations 2005, SI 2005/435 is that there is now a prescribed claim form that must be used in all cases. **2.01**

The claim form can be obtained online (<http://www.employmenttribunals.gov.uk>) or from any local office of the Employment Tribunals Service. There is also guidance as to how to fill it in. **2.02**

B. REQUIRED INFORMATION

2.03 The required information is set out in ETR 2004, r 1(4) as:

(a) the claimant's full name;
(b) the claimant's address;
(c) the name of each person against whom the claim is made ('the respondent');
(d) their address;
(e) details of the claim;
(f) whether or not the claimant was the employee of the person against whom the claim is made (see *Richardson* below);
(g) whether or not the claim includes a complaint that the claimant was dismissed or the respondent has contemplated doing so;
(h) whether or not the claimant has raised the subject matter of the claim with the respondent in writing at least 28 days before presenting the claim; and
(i) if not, why not.

2.04 There are certain circumstances in which the information does not need to be provided (ETR 2004, r 1(5)):

(a) if the claimant is or was not an employee of the respondent the information in (g) to (i) above need not be supplied;
(b) if the claimant was an employee of the respondent and was dismissed there is no need to provide the information in (h) and (i) above—that information concerns grievances and non-dismissal claims;
(c) if the claimant was an employee of the respondent but not dismissed and has raised the subject matter of the complaint with the respondent in writing in accordance with (h) above, then (i) above will not need to be provided.

From 6 April 2009 the Claim Form does not need to contain the matters in (f) to (i) above (Employment Tribunals (Constitution and Rules of Procedure) (Amendment) Regulations 2008). Similarly r, SI 2008/3240 1(5) is repealed.

2.05 Rule 3(2)(a) states that if the above information is not provided the claim will not be accepted by the Secretary to the tribunal but will instead be referred to a judge who must consider whether to accept it. If he decides not to accept it, he must inform the claimant of his decision and the reasons for it as soon as is reasonably practicable. The judge must also provide details as to how to appeal or review the decision. If the reason for not accepting the claim form is that there has been a failure to comply with the provisions of the statutory grievance procedures (see paras 2.10 *et seq.* below), the Secretary must inform the claimant of the relevant time limit and of the consequences of not complying with s 32 of the Employment Act 2002. In *Richardson v U Mole Ltd* [2005] IRLR 668 the EAT rejected a claim for non-compliance with r 1(4)(f)—the claimant had not used the new form and had failed to indicate that he was an employee (there was no issue between the parties that he was in fact an employee). Burton J held that the averments in the form were sufficient for compliance with r 1(4)(f)—the claimant had filled in the section entitled 'Please give the dates of your employment'. In any event had there not been compliance the claim should have been accepted on review as this was an immaterial error and/or it was explained and/or justice and equity required it (see *Moroak* (*t/a Blake Envelopes*) *v Cromie* [2005] IRLR 353 (see para 4.03 below) for the parallel approach to the response).

C. PRESENTATION OF THE CLAIM FORM

2.06 The claim can be presented by hand, post, fax, or online (see *Tyne and Wear Autistic Society v Smith* [2005] ICR 663) and email (ETR 2004, r 63(1)). A claim is presented online when it is successfully submitted online to the Employment Tribunals Service website—that is, it is submitted and accepted there even if it is not then forwarded by the website host to the tribunal office. In *McFadyen and ors v PB Recovery Ltd and ors* UKEATS/0072/08/BI, the Scottish Employment Appeal Tribunal (EAT) held that presenting a claim online is effective only for the tribunal to which the claim is directed and does not amount to effective presentation to all UK tribunals generally. The host server receiving online claims acts as an agent for the tribunal nearest to the address of the respondent provided on the form and it is this tribunal to which the form is submitted. A solicitor's error meant that the claim form was directed to the Bristol tribunal, where it was rejected, rather than the Glasgow tribunal. The EAT held that it was correct to use the date the form was resubmitted to Glasgow when considering if the claims were in time, rather than the date the claim was first presented online.

If a claim form is sent by post the EAT has stressed that there is a duty on claimants, and those **2.07** representing them, to ensure that it has been received. In *Capital Foods Retail Ltd v Corrigan* [1993] IRLR 430, the application was posted well within time, but for some unexplained reason the tribunal did not receive it; the EAT was critical of the failure by the applicant's solicitor to pursue the tribunal to confirm receipt after a lengthy silence, and held that the application had not been presented and it was not right to extend the time. In *Camden and Islington Community Health Services NHS Trust v Kennedy* [1996] IRLR 351, the EAT stressed that the test laid down in *Corrigan* above is a stringent one. For a solicitor to act reasonably and without fault, there must be a system in place which enables the solicitor to find out, contemporaneously, whether the conduct of business is taking a normal course and to check, at or near the time, that replies which should have been received at a given date have in fact been received. A competent solicitor practising in this field must be taken to appreciate the vital importance of complying with time limits strictly and having in place a system designed to ensure that such limits are complied with at the time when they are supposed to be being complied with. In *Camden* the employment judge had erred in finding that a system which involved only a check several weeks after the solicitor expected an acknowledgement from the tribunal that the application had been received could be regarded as satisfying the requirement that solicitors should take all reasonable steps to see that an application was timeously presented.

In the case of postal claims, see paras 3.49–3.53 below. **2.08**

D. ACTIONS ON RECEIPT

On receipt the claim form is date stamped and retained along with the envelope and this is **2.09** generally treated as the date of presentation. This can be rebutted, for example by showing that the claim form was posted physically through the tribunal letter box (see *Post Office v Moore* [1981] ICR 623).

E. ACCEPTANCE PROCEDURES

The claim will not be accepted or registered where the required information is not provided (see **2.10** para 2.05 above). However, in *Grimmer v KLM Cityhopper Ltd* [2005] IRLR 596, Judge Prophet ruled that the 2004 Regulations must not be interpreted so as to deny a claimant access to the employment tribunal system. The case concerned a woman who sought to complain that her request for flexible working for childcare reasons had been refused. She put 'flexible working' on her claim form and gave as details of her claim that: 'The company's business argument for refusing my application is based upon their assumption that, if they concede to my request, others would be requesting similar/same working arrangements.' The employment tribunal refused to admit the claim on grounds that she did not provide 'details of the claim' as required by the new r 1(4)(e). Allowing the appeal Judge Prophet stated (at 599) that:

> the Rules of Procedure cannot cut down on an employment tribunal's jurisdiction to entertain a complaint which the primary legislation providing an employment right empowers it to determine. If there is a conflict, the Rules must give way.

2.11 He further went on to state that the threshold for access should, in the interests of justice, be kept low. When determining whether a claim form contains the required details of the claim, the test for the tribunal is 'whether it can be discerned from the claim as presented that the claimant is complaining of an alleged breach of an employment right which falls within the jurisdiction of the employment tribunal'. If the judge thinks that further particulars are necessary, they can be ordered.

2.12 Where the tribunal does not have the power to consider the claim, or part of it, the claim, or the relevant parts, will not be accepted. This may occur where the claim concerns a grievance and it has been presented to the tribunal without complying with the provisions of s 32(2) of the Employment Act 2002 (see Appendix 1). The Employment Act 2008 repeals the statutory dispute resolution procedures (including s 32) from 6 April 2009 (see SI 2008/3232). The cases and procedure set out in para 2.13 below are not applicable for claims commenced after 6 April 2009, but remain relevant to cases prior to that date. Where the statutory grievance procedures continue to apply, the following are the key points to be taken from the authorities and regulations:

(a) A grievance is a complaint by an employee about action which the employer has taken or is contemplating taking in relation to him (ETR 2004, reg 2).
(b) A resignation letter may be sufficient (*Galaxy Showers v Wilson* [2006] IRLR 83 at para 10).
(c) A letter before action or other document from a third party including a solicitor (*Mark Warner v Aspland* [2006] IRLR 87) will qualify: it is not fatal if it is without prejudice (*Arnold Clark Automobiles v Stewart*, UKEAT/0052/05/RN) nor if it is a request for flexible working (*Commotion Ltd v Rutty* [2006] IRLR 17 at para 17) and it is irrelevant that it also refers to other matters outside the grievance (see reg 2(2) and *Canary Wharf Management v Edebi* [2006] IRLR 416 at para 19).
(d) It need only set out the grievance and not the basis (*Thorpe and Soleil Investments v Poat and Lake* [2006] All ER (D) 30).
(e) The grievance must be current but there are no hard and fast rules (*Galaxy* at para 17).
(f) There is no need for it to state that it is a grievance in terms (*Shergold v Fielding Medical Centre* [2006] IRLR 76 at para 33, and in that case the claimant expressly declined to pursue a grievance under the employer's own procedure but was nonetheless held to have lodged one for statutory purposes—see also *Galaxy Showers* at para 10).
(g) If fresh matters arise in the course of an internal hearing it is not always necessary to set out a new grievance if they are simply shifts in focus as opposed to other distinct acts (*Silman v ICTS (UK) Ltd* UKEAT/0630/05/LA); there may also be a subsequent grievance about the way in which an initial grievance has been conducted (*Mudchute Association v Petheridge* UKEAT/0569/05).
(h) Whether or not a letter comprises a grievance depends on whether the employer on a 'fair reading of the statement and having regard to the particular context in which it is made, can be expected to appreciate that the relevant complaint is being raised' (*Canary Wharf* at para 25 and *Muhammad v Royal Mail* [2007] All ER (D) 342 (Dec) in which a grievance simply about bullying and harassment was not capable of being read as relating to race and religion, and in *Highland Council v TGWU* UKEATS/0048/07, the EAT held that letters written by the claimants' trade unions to their employer, complaining of ongoing equal pay issues and failure to implement the Single Status Agreement, were not collective grievances under regulation 9 of the Employment Act 2002 (Dispute Resolution) Regulations 2004, as they did not name any of the claimants. Neither were they grievance letters under the Standard Grievance Procedure, since they were not about any action directed at the particular claimants and had not been sent by the claimants); the issue must not be approached in a technical way (para 10).
(i) That said, the subject matter of the grievance and any subsequent proceedings must be 'materially similar' rather than identical (*Shergold* at paras 35 and 36 and *Canary Wharf* where complaints about health and safety did not equate to a subsequent DDA claim).

(j) An equal value questionnaire (or any other statutory questionnaire) does not amount to a grievance as they are expressly excluded by reg 14 (*Holc-Gale v Makers UK Ltd* [2006] IRLR 178).
(k) In the case of a protected disclosure it will only amount to a grievance if information is disclosed to an employer in circumstances where the information relates to a matter which could be raised as a grievance and the employee intends it to be raised as a grievance (EA 2002, Sch 2, para 15).

The claim will not be accepted or registered where the required information is not provided (see para 2.05 above, but note the different regime after 6 April 2009). In addition, where the tribunal does not have the power to consider the claim or part of it, the claim or the relevant parts will not be accepted. **2.13**

If a claim is accepted by the Secretary he or she will: **2.14**

(a) send a copy of the claim to each respondent and record in writing the date on which it was sent;
(b) inform the parties in writing of the case number of the claim (which must from then on be referred to in all correspondence relating to the claim) and the address to which notices and other communications to the Employment Tribunal Office must be sent;
(c) inform the respondent in writing about how to present a response to the claim, the time limit for doing so, what may happen if a response is not entered within the time limit, and that the respondent has a right to receive a copy of any judgment disposing of the claim;
(d) when any enactment relevant to the claim provides for conciliation, notify the parties that the services of a conciliation officer may be available to them; and
(e) if only part of the claim has been accepted, inform the claimant and any respondent which parts of the claim have not been accepted and that the tribunal shall not proceed to deal with those parts unless they are accepted at a later date.

F. FILLING IN THE CLAIM FORM

The prescribed form reminds claimants to read the guidance notes and that items marked with a * are mandatory and information concerning those marked with a • should be provided where relevant. The claim form states that it may be used by multiple claimants and, if so, their names and addresses should be provided on a separate sheet of paper. The sections of the form are described below. **2.15**

Box 1 'Your details'

The claimant must provide his first name and surname and his address. These are mandatory details. In addition, claimants must give their sex and date of birth, their telephone number, and their preference for communications—post is usually used but email is an option. If an address other than the claimant's home address is to be used for communications, then this should be provided. This can be changed by giving notice to the tribunal and the other parties (ETR 2004, r 61(5)). **2.16**

Box 2 'Respondent's details'

The name and address of the employer, or person against whom relief is sought, is mandatory here. Their telephone number should also be included and if the claimant worked at a different address from that given for the employer this should be provided along with the postcode. There is a separate section to provide details of additional respondents against whom relief is sought. Particular problems may arise where the respondent is an unincorporated association. Although a trade union is an unincorporated association it may sue or be sued in its own name by virtue of statute (see TULR(C)A 1992, s 10(1)(b)). The correct respondent for all other such bodies is the individual officers who have effective control of the organization—usually either **2.17** the management committee or the Chairman and/or secretary (see *Affleck v Newcastle Mind* [1999] IRLR 405).

2.18 Where the respondent is a company in administration, tribunal proceedings may only be commenced with the permission of the High Court or the administrator (see *Carr v International Helicopters Ltd* [1994] ICR 18 and Insolvency Act 1986, s 11(3)). If permission is not given, the proceedings will be stayed until it is obtained. The administrator may also be joined as an interested party but in some circumstances he or she may be personally liable because he or she has adopted the employee's contract of employment.

2.19 If the respondent is bankrupt their trustee in bankruptcy will have a clear interest in the outcome of the proceedings and would be entitled to apply to be joined as a party. The Secretary of State will also be an interested party (since many payments will be met from the National Insurance Fund: see ERA 1996, s 186). Usually the tribunal notifies the Department for Business, Enterprise and Regulatory Reform of the claim and asks whether the Secretary of State wishes to be joined.

Box 3 'Action before making a claim'

2.20 The information requested here seeks to identify whether the claimant has used the disciplinary or grievance procedures under the Employment Act 2002 (see paras 3.97 *et seq*. below and 2.04 above: when the EA 2002 is repealed this information will not be required). Completion of this box is mandatory and if, in answering the questions, it is clear that a claimant has not waited 28 days from submitting a grievance for a response, the claim will be rejected by the tribunal.

Box 4 'Employment details'

2.21 This box deals with the details concerning the claimant's employment with the respondent—dates, pay, hours, etc. The information is not mandatory. It also asks about the type of work done by the claimant and whether there was a notice period and if so whether it was worked or paid.

Box 5 'Unfair dismissal or constructive dismissal'

2.22 In this box the claimant will set out the substance of the complaint. Questions are also asked about membership of the employer's pension scheme and as to what remedy the claimant is seeking if the case is successful. The options are reinstatement, re-engagement, and/or compensation. It is not mandatory to give this information and even if the claimant gives an indication, the matter can be revisited at a later stage.

Box 6 'Discrimination'

2.23 The claimant is asked to provide details as to what sort of discrimination is being alleged and is also asked to provide dates of incidents and the people involved. The case of *Ali v Office for National Statistics* [2005] IRLR 201 shows the importance of completing claim forms thoroughly, and setting out all potential claims. Mr Ali had made a complaint of race discrimination, when his application for employment was rejected by the Office for National Statistics (ONS). He initially succeeded in the tribunal in showing direct discrimination, although he failed in a victimization claim. The ONS appealed to the EAT, and the direct discrimination finding was overturned and the matter remitted to the tribunal. At this stage, Mr Ali sought leave to amend his claim form, to add a complaint of indirect race discrimination, in view of evidence that had come to light during disclosure and cross-examination in the first hearing. The tribunal said this could be permitted as it was merely adding a different label. The EAT and Court of Appeal disagreed: it was a new claim, direct and indirect discrimination being distinct causes of action. The matter was remitted to the tribunal for consideration of whether it was just and equitable to allow the claim to be presented out of time. The earlier statement in *Quarcoopome v Sock Shop Holdings Ltd* [1995] IRLR 353 that an originating application that makes a claim for race discrimination incorporates any claim for race discrimination, whether direct or indirect, was disapproved.

Box 7 'Redundancy payments'

The claimant is asked why he believes he is entitled to a redundancy payment and what steps have been taken to obtain it. **2.24**

Box 8 'Other payments you are owed'

This section should contain details of whether the complaint is for holiday pay, notice pay, or other unpaid amounts as well as the precise amount being claimed, and whether this is gross or net. The reasons as to why the sums are claimed should also be given. **2.25**

Box 9 'Other complaints'

The claimant is asked to fill in this section if he or she has a complaint that is not covered by the other sections. **2.26**

Box 10 'Other information'

This section instructs the claimant not to send a covering letter but to add any further information. It may be used, for example, to seek disclosure of documents or to explain why the claim is out of time. **2.27**

Box 11 'Your representative'

If the claimant has a representative, his or her name and address should be provided. **2.28**

G. CLAIMS BROUGHT ON BEHALF OF DECEASED PERSONS

On the death of an employee s 206 of ERA 1996 provides that, in cases concerning unfair dismissal, redundancy, and other individual employment rights, proceedings can be instituted or continued by a personal representative of the deceased employee, or where there is no personal representative, by a person appointed by the tribunal. **2.29**

Any award made in favour of a deceased employee may be enforced on behalf of his estate by his personal representative or any such person appointed by the tribunal (Employment Tribunals Awards (Enforcement in Case of Death) Regulations 1976, SI 1976/663, regs 5 and 6). **2.30**

Although there is no equivalent to ERA 1996, s 206 in the discrimination legislation, claims under the SDA 1975, RRA 1976, and DDA 1995 can nevertheless be instituted or continued after the death of the complainant by virtue of s 1(1) of the Law Reform (Miscellaneous Provisions) Act 1934 (see *Harris (Personal Representatives of Andrews (deceased)) v Lewisham and Guys Mental Health NHS Trust* [2000] IRLR 320). A claim of discrimination, being in the nature of a statutory tort (see *Sheriff v Klyne Tugs (Lowestoft) Ltd* [1999] IRLR 481, [1999] ICR 1170), is a cause of action within the meaning of s 1(1) of the 1934 Act which will survive for the benefit of the complainant's estate after death. The court held that there is nothing in the RRA 1976 (nor in the SDA 1975 or DDA 1995) which disapplies that section and precludes existing causes of action from vesting in the deceased's estate. **2.31**

H. CLAIMS BY AND AGAINST BANKRUPT AND INSOLVENT PARTIES

A bankrupt is limited in the claims (and appeals) he can pursue, all claims 'for property' vesting in the trustee in bankruptcy. In the case of *Grady v HM Prison Service* [2003] IRLR 474 the Court of Appeal held that unfair dismissal claims are personal in nature and can be pursued by **2.32** a bankrupt—a finding influenced by the fact that, when addressing the question of remedy, a tribunal must consider reinstatement and re-engagement (essentially personal remedies). In *Khan v Trident Safeguards Ltd* [2004] EWCA Civ 624, [2004] ICR 1591, the Court of Appeal held that if a bankrupt pursuing a discrimination claim limits his claim for relief to a declaration and compensation for injury to feelings, he is permitted to proceed. This is because the cause of action can be categorized as personal rather than a property claim.

3

Time Limits

SUMMARY

(1) Time limits are generally a matter of jurisdiction, and a failure to comply may result in a tribunal refusing to entertain a claim.

(2) The first question to consider is the date from when time starts to run; this will depend upon the wording of the specific statute under consideration.

(3) The date of presentation of the complaint is the second matter to consider; care should also be taken not to present a premature application.

(4) If an application is presented late there is normally a discretion to extend the time limit and again this depends upon the provisions of the relevant statute.

(5) The dispute resolution regime may mean that complaints are rejected for non-compliance or may lead to an extension of time.

A. JURISDICTION

Time limits are generally expressed in mandatory terms in the various statutes; s 111 of ERA 1996, for example, states that a tribunal 'shall not consider' a complaint unless it is presented within the time limit. The Court of Appeal confirmed in *Dedman v British Building & Engineering Appliances Ltd* [1973] IRLR 379 that time limits are a matter of jurisdiction in unfair dismissal (see also *Secretary of State for Employment v Atkins Auto Laundries Ltd* [1972] ICR 76). One consequence of this is that the tribunal may raise the question of its own volition regardless of the parties' views. Secondly, questions of jurisdiction may be raised at any stage even at the remedies hearing (see *Rogers v Bodfari (Transport) Ltd* [1973] IRLR 172) or for the first time on appeal. **3.01**

B. WHEN TIME STARTS TO RUN—GENERALLY

3.02 The most important time limits are three months in the case of unfair dismissal and six months for redundancy payments. The table setting out time limits and qualifying periods is at Appendix 6. The Gibbons Review ('A review of employment dispute resolution in Great Britain' DTI March 2007) suggested that time limits and their extension periods should be standardized. However, no steps have yet been taken to do so.

3.03 When time starts to run from a particular date, the general rule is that this means the whole period of 24 hours from midnight to midnight, so that in general no account is taken of fractions of a day (*Trow v Ind Coope (West Midlands) Ltd* [1967] 2 QB 899). Thus, where the effective date of termination is 1 January, time runs from the start of that day and the claim form must be presented not later than midnight on 31 March (that is three months from the effective date of termination in a case of unfair dismissal; a month is defined in Sch 1, para 5 of the Interpretation Act 1978 as a calendar month). Where time runs from 31 January, the month ends on 28 February (or 29 February in a leap year).

3.04 Where the statute specifies that a claim must be brought 'beginning with' a date, that date is included in the calculation of time (see *Hammond v Haigh Castle and Co Ltd* [1973] ICR 148); when a claim must be presented 'from', 'after', or 'of' a particular date that date is excluded from the calculation (see *Trow*). There is an exception where time runs from a day where there is no corresponding day in the later month, for example, time running from 31 January ends on 30 March (see *Pruden v Cunard Ellerman Ltd* [1993] IRLR 317 and *University of Cambridge v Murray* [1993] ICR 460). Further assistance may be obtained from CPR r 2.8 which shows how to calculate any period of time for doing any act specified within the CPR and includes specific examples. Regulation 15 of the 2004 Regulations provides the method for calculating time under Schs 1–5 (ETR 2004) and also sets out examples:

(a) Where any act must or may be done within a certain number of days of or from an event, the date of that event shall not be included in the calculation. For example, a respondent is sent a copy of a claim on 1 October. He must present a response to the Employment Tribunal Office within 28 days of the date on which he was sent the copy. The last day for presentation of the response is 29 October (reg 15(2)).
(b) Where any act must or may be done not less than a certain number of days before or after an event, the date of that event shall not be included in the calculation. For example, if a party wishes to submit representations in writing for consideration by a tribunal at a hearing, he must submit them not less than seven days before the hearing. If the hearing is fixed for 8 October, the representations must be submitted no later than 1 October (reg 15(3)).
(c) Where the tribunal or a judge gives any decision, order, or judgment which imposes a time limit for doing any act, the last date for compliance shall, wherever practicable, be expressed as a calendar date (reg 15(4)).
(d) ETR 2004, r 14(4) (requirement to send the notice of hearing to the parties not less than 14 days before the date fixed for the hearing) should not be construed as a requirement for service of the notice to have been effected not less than 14 days before the hearing date, but as a requirement for the notice to have been placed in the post not less than 14 days before that date. The example given is a hearing fixed for 15 October. The last day on which the notice may be placed in the post is 1 October.

3.05 Finally, where any act must or may have been done within a certain number of days of a document being sent to a person by the Secretary, the date when the document was sent will be regarded, unless the contrary is shown, as the date on the letter from the Secretary which accompanied the document. For example, a respondent must present his response to a claim to the Employment Tribunal Office within 28 days of the date on which he was sent a copy of the claim. If the letter from the Secretary sending him a copy of the claim is dated 1 October, the last day for presentation of the response is 29 October.

Where the last day of a month has no corresponding day in a following month—for example, a dismissal on 30 November—then the previous day is to be taken—28 February. Care should be taken with a dismissal on 28 February—the corresponding date is 27 May. 3.06

C. SPECIFIC CASES

Unfair dismissal

The ERA 1996 defines the normal time limit of three months in such cases as running from the effective date of termination (EDT) (see s 97(1)). For example, in *Gisda CYF v Lauren Barratt* [2009] EWCA Civ 648 the Employment Appeal Tribunal (EAT) had been entitled to uphold a decision that a letter of dismissal, which had arrived by post at the recipient's address whilst she was away from home, did not become effective until the recipient read the letter. An exception is permitted in a case where a claimant can present a claim after notice has been given but before the EDT occurred (see ERA 1996, s 113(3)). Further, the time can be extended if it was not reasonably practicable to present in time and the presentation was within a reasonable period thereafter (see also paras 3.57–3.85). 3.07

See paras 3.65 and 3.93 below for the impact of the 2004 statutory dispute resolution procedures which allow for an extension of the time limit in certain circumstances. The three months less one day rule above is the same under reg 15(1) EA(DR)R 2004 (see *Joshi v Manchester City Council* [2008] All ER (D) 246). 3.08

In a constructive dismissal case the claimant may also give notice and present a claim before the EDT (see ERA 1996, s 95(1)(c) and *Presley v Llanelli Borough Council* [1979] ICR 419). 3.09

In the case of a fixed term contract its expiry on its due date is not a termination by notice and therefore an unfair dismissal complaint may only be presented after expiry of the term. 3.10

Written particulars and itemized pay

Claims arising from a failure by the employer to provide statements of employment particulars and itemized pay statements must be brought during employment or within three months of termination (ERA 1996, s 11). The time may be extended if it was not reasonably practicable to present in time and the presentation was within a reasonable period thereafter (see also paras 3.57–3.85). 3.11

Discrimination cases

The standard time limit for discrimination claims is three months from the act complained of. In most discrimination cases, time runs from the date the act complained of was done. This applies to race, sex, disability claims, religion and beliefs, sexual orientation, and age discrimination. Extensions are permitted on a 'just and equitable' basis. See Appendix 6 for the particular time limits and extensions permitted. Commonly, however, claimants rely upon the fact that there was an act extending over a period, in which case time will run from the date of the last act complained of. In the case of service personnel the time limit is six months from the act complained of and they must invoke the applicable Service Redress Procedure before presenting a claim (see Appendix 6). 3.12

Three matters are important when considering discrimination time limits: 3.13

(a) An inclusion of a term in a contract that renders the making of the contract an unlawful act extends throughout the duration of the contract.
(b) Acts extending over a period are treated as having been done at the end of the period.
(c) A deliberate omission is treated as made when the person in question decided upon it.

3.14 The leading case on (b) above is *Barclays Bank plc v Kapur* [1991] IRLR 136, HL, which concerned a term in a pension scheme introduced in 1970 that discriminated against employees whose previous service was in Africa rather than in Europe. The employees were able to bring claims in 1987 because the act extended over the period in question. Similarly, where the employer fails to remedy acts of racial harassment, time runs from the end of the period in which the employer failed to act (see *Littlewoods Organisation plc v Traynor* [1993] IRLR 154).

3.15 Confusion has arisen over the distinction between an act *extending over a period* and the *consequences* of such an act. This distinction was illustrated in a sex discrimination case where a man was promoted to a position over a woman and it was held that, in the absence of a policy of discrimination, the promotion was a single act of discrimination (*Amies v Inner London Education Authority* [1977] 2 All ER 100; see also *Sougrin v Haringey Health Authority* [1992] IRLR 416 and *Owusu v London Fire and Civil Defence Authority* [1995] IRLR 574 where the EAT cautioned against deciding on whether there is a continuing act or a series of single acts as often a succession of specific acts can indicate the existence of a practice: the same point was made by the Court of Appeal in *Hendricks v Commissioner of Police of the Metropolis* [2003] IRLR 96). In *Lyfar v Brighton and Hove University Hospitals Trust* [2006] EWCA Civ 1548, the Court of Appeal approved the practice of dealing with the question of whether acts extend over a period at a pre-hearing review (PHR) in general (although it declined to give guidance on the particular circumstances when it would be appropriate and when not). In addition in *Owusu* the EAT ruled that the statutory words 'an act extending over a period' required a 'policy, practice or regime'.

3.16 In *Hendricks* the Court of Appeal took a different view. In the words of Mummery LJ the reference to a 'practice, policy or regime' was merely an example and was not intended to be exhaustive. He said that 'the burden is on (the applicant) to prove, either by direct evidence or by inference from primary facts, that the numerous alleged incidents of discrimination are linked to one another and that they are evidence of a discriminatory state of affairs'. The Court of Appeal in *Lyfar* ruled that the *Hendricks* test was the correct one.

3.17 In *Arthur v London Eastern Railway Ltd* [2007] ICR 193, IRLR 58, the Court of Appeal held that a tribunal had erred in deciding whether acts were part of a series and therefore whether a claim of being subjected to a detriment for making a protected disclosure was brought in time without hearing any evidence, although stressing that the burden was on the claimant who must show a prima facie case.

3.18 The mere repetition of a request cannot convert a single managerial decision into a policy. See in particular *Cast v Croydon College* [1997] IRLR 14 in which the Court of Appeal judgment draws an important distinction between a decision which is a fresh consideration and one which is merely a reference back to an earlier determination, the latter falling outside of what constitutes a continuing act.

3.19 In *Swithland Motors plc v Clarke* [1994] ICR 231, the EAT considered the time limits for an omission to act. Section 76(6)(c) of SDA 1975, states that 'a deliberate omission shall be treated as done when the person in question decided upon it'. The applicants were not offered new employment when their employer was bought from receivership because, they claimed, the purchaser had a policy of women-only sales staff. They were interviewed by the purchaser and some time later the purchase took place. The EAT held that time ran from the date the purchase took place, not the interviews, because that was the date when the purchasers were in a position to decide whether or not to re-employ the applicants.

3.20 In a discriminatory dismissal case time runs from the date of expiry of the notice—not, as one might think, from the decision to dismiss. In *Lupetti v Wrens Old House Ltd* [1984] ICR 348, the applicant was given oral notice on 3 February 1983 that his employment would terminate on 28 February 1983. He did not present his claim for race discrimination until 19 May 1983. At the hearing, both parties accepted that the dismissal had taken place on 3 February, and that the complaint was out of time. They relied upon authorities concerning the different statutory provisions for the effective date of termination for unfair dismissal. The EAT accepted the employee's argument that the proper date to consider was when the applicant found himself without a job, 28 February, and the application was in time.

There are special rules applying in a case of an appeal against dismissal and the date from which time runs. If the contract provides that the employment or the contract continues pending the appeal, then the date on which the unsuccessful appellant is notified of the result is the date from which time runs (*Adekeye v The Post Office (No 2)* [1997] ICR 110). If the contract does not subsist pending the appeal then time runs from the date of dismissal. Where the claim is based on a failure to promote an applicant, the tribunal looks to when the cause of action crystallized, not when the applicant felt that he was discriminated against (see *Clarke v Hampshire Electro-Plating Co Ltd* [1991] IRLR 490, where the EAT held that when an action crystallizes is a question of fact for the tribunal to find). **3.21**

The statutory grievance procedure applies to discrimination claims and consequently the extension of time under reg 15(3) also applies (see paras 3.97–3.103 and EA 2002 Sch 3 in Appendix 1). **3.22**

Interim relief

There is a short time limit in these cases because of the nature of the relief involved. The claim may be made involving trade union activity or membership cases, health and safety, protected disclosures, and the protected activities of employee representatives. Claims must be brought at any time up to seven days *after* the EDT (for example, dismissal on Monday requires presentation the following Monday: ERA 1996, s 128). **3.23**

There is no discretion to extend time for the interim relief application in such claims. **3.24**

Equal pay

In a standard case, claims for breach of an equality clause under the Equal Pay Act 1970, s 2 should be brought during the existence of the contract or within six months of the employee leaving employment (see ss 2(4) and 2ZA). The relevant consideration is neither the end of the job nor the employee leaving the employer but the end of the contract in respect of which the equality clause has been breached. *National Power v Young* [2001] IRLR 32 is authority for the proposition that time does not run from the end of a particular job, the tribunal having found (or proceeded on the assumption) that the claimant was employed under the same contract throughout each job change. **3.25**

In addition to a standard case, there are three categories in which the normal six-month time limit is modified (s 2ZA). They are: **3.26**

(a) a case in which there is 'concealment';
(b) a disability case; and
(c) a 'stable employment case'.

In order for the employee to rely upon the 'concealment' provisions, the employer must have deliberately concealed any fact which is relevant to the breach of the Act to which the proceedings relate. There is thus a causative link that must be established as the woman must also show that without knowledge of that fact the proceedings could not have been commenced and the fact was not discovered until after the last day on which she was employed or the day on which her 'stable employment relationship' ended (see further, below). **3.27**

If there has been concealment the claim must be presented within six months of the date on which the fact was discovered or could have been discovered using reasonable diligence. **3.28**

A 'disability case' is one where the woman is not disabled under DDA 1995 but where she was a minor or of unsound mind at any time during the six months after the date on which she ceased to be employed, her stable employment relationship ended, she discovered the concealed fact, **3.29** or could have discovered it with reasonable diligence if that date was later than the last day of employment.

3.30 The time limit is then six months from that day after the day she ceased to be under a disability.

3.31 A 'standard case' is a case which is not one of the other types and proceedings must be brought within six months of the last date of employment.

3.32 Special rules apply where a woman is engaged on a series of fixed term contracts in a stable relationship. When a stable relationship arises depends in part upon the intention of the parties, but the features that characterize a 'stable employment relationship' are that there is a succession of short-term contracts, meaning three or more contracts for an academic year or shorter; concluded at regular intervals, in that they are clearly predictable and can be calculated precisely, or where the employee is called upon frequently whenever a need arises; relating to the same employment; and to which the same pension scheme applies. In such circumstances the termination of each of the contracts does not trigger the obligation to lodge a claim—only termination of the final contract does so (see *Preston v Wolverhampton NHS Trust (No 3)* [2004] IRLR 96). The point was specifically considered in *Slack v Cumbria CC* [2009] IRLR 463 where the Court of Appeal was concerned with equal pay claims where women had worked under a series of contracts with the same local authority employer. Over the years the contents of their contracts had varied, and conditions had changed. The Council argued that the original contracts had terminated and been replaced by new contracts, and any arrears payable under the equal pay claim were limited to the period covered by the final contract. The Court of Appeal accepted that there was a 'stable employment relationship' where the same work continued to be done under a series of successive contracts, and where the only difference between contracts was a reduction in working hours. Where there were other changes of a more substantial nature, affecting the nature of the work done and other conditions of employment (such as the acquiring of a new right to sick pay), the question whether there was such a relationship was a matter of fact, to be decided by the tribunal.

Redundancy

3.33 Under s 164(1) of ERA 1996, in a redundancy case the employee must show that within six months from the date of termination:

(a) the redundancy payment has been agreed and paid;
(b) a claim for the payment has been made in writing to the employer;
(c) a question as to the right to the payment or the amount of it has been referred to an employment tribunal; or
(d) a complaint of unfair dismissal has been made to an employment tribunal.

3.34 This means that, where the employer accepts the employee's right to a redundancy payment but disputes its amount, the employee is protected provided he has submitted a written claim for the payment within six months. The employee may then actually submit an application to a tribunal to settle any argument about the actual amount at any time (see *Bentley Engineering Co Ltd v Crown and Miller* [1976] ICR 225). This is satisfied by a letter provided it is clear that what is sought is a redundancy payment (see *Price v Smithfield and Zwanenburg Group Ltd* [1978] ICR 93).

3.35 Section 164 goes on to provide that if the employee fails to take any of the steps within the initial six months, provided the employee refers a redundancy claim or makes a complaint of unfair dismissal to the tribunal within the *next* six months, the tribunal has a discretion to award a redundancy payment if it is just and equitable having regard to the reason shown by the employee for his failure to take one of the prescribed steps and all the other relevant circumstances. There is no discretion to extend time for taking the necessary steps beyond the second six months period, so any application even a day late will be out of time (*Secretary of State for Employment v Banks* [1983] ICR 48).

Deduction of wages claims ERA 1996, s 23

In claims under s 23 of the ERA 1996 for deductions of wages, the time limit of three months commences from the date of payment of wages from which the deduction was made or the date on which the payment was received by the employee. Where there has been a series of deductions, time runs from the date the last deduction could have been made in accordance with the contract, and the entire series is recoverable (see *Group 4 Nightspeed v Gilbert* [1997] IRLR 398). **3.36**

The statutory grievance procedure applies, and there is an automatic extension of time under the DRR, reg 15(3). **3.37**

Further, the time can be extended if it was not reasonably practicable to present in time and the presentation was within a reasonable period thereafter (see also paras 3.57–3.85). **3.38**

Other claims

Time runs from the date the act complained of was done in trade union and health and safety discrimination cases (TULR(C)A 1992, ss 66(2), 68A(1), 139(1), 147, and 175 and ERA 1996, ss 48–49). The time period is three months with the usual extension if it was not reasonably practicable to present in time and the presentation was within a reasonable period thereafter. **3.39**

European claims

Time limits under European claims are dealt with in paras 22.16–22.18. **3.40**

D. PRESENTATION OF COMPLAINT: SPECIFIC PROBLEMS

Expiry of time outside office hours

The expiry date for an application may be a day on which the tribunal offices are closed, because it falls at the weekend or on a statutory holiday. In *Anglo Continental School of English (Bournemouth) Ltd v Gardiner* [1973] ICR 261, the National Industrial Relations Court (NIRC) held that when, on the final day, the office was closed the time was automatically extended until the next day. **3.41**

The decisions of *Post Office v Moore* [1981] ICR 623 and *Hetton Victory Club v Swainston* [1983] ICR 139, however, took a different approach. In *Swainston*, the Regional Office of Employment Tribunals (ROET) in Manchester was closed on a Sunday, which was the last day on which the applicant was entitled to present his claim for unfair dismissal and he therefore presented his complaint on the Monday. The EAT considered that an application was 'presented' when placed in the letter box or dealt with in some other way which was held out by the ROET as a means whereby it will receive communications. **3.42**

The EAT held that the application was presented in time but the Court of Appeal disagreed, deciding that the three-month time limit expired at midnight on the last day of the period even where that was not a working day. For the purposes of the rules, 'presentation' was complete when the application was put through the letter box, which the applicant could easily have done. The case of *Pritam Kaur v Russell & Sons* [1973] 1 QB 336 was distinguished on the grounds that although in the High Court a writ that does not arrive on a working day, which is required as it must be issued by the court staff, receives an automatic extension to the next working day, 'presentation' does not require any action on the part of the body to whom the presentation is made. A submission that there would be injustice if the ROET did not have a letter box was dealt with by Waller J who suggested that the applicant in such a case 'might be able to show that it was not reasonably practicable for him to present the complaint within the relevant period' (see further paras 3.57–3.83 below). The Court of Appeal's judgment leaves a question mark over when an applicant can rely on the automatic extension and when he must argue that it was **3.43** not reasonably practicable to present a complaint in time. The Court of Appeal was silent as to which rule would apply where there was no post box at the tribunal. This is perhaps resolved in *Ford v Stakis Hotels and Inns Ltd* [1988] IRLR 46, where the originating application was pushed under the door of the Cardiff ROET, which had no letter box, on a bank holiday which was the last day for presenting the complaint. The EAT decided that in this case time was automatically extended to the next day.

3.44 In *Lang v Devon General Ltd* [1987] ICR 4, there was evidence of a special arrangement between the ROET and the Post Office whereby post received for delivery on a Saturday would be kept until the Monday. The EAT held that the Post Office was thus made a bailee of the mail, and a letter which was actually received at the ROET on Monday could be treated as if received on the Saturday (see *Anglo Continental*, above, for the difficulties of establishing bailment). These cases were decided before COET had fax machines which are now available at all times at employment tribunal offices.

3.45 Claims can also now be made online at any time at <http://www.employmenttribunals.gov.uk>. The 'ordinary course of email', without any contrary indication that an email message has not been sent, is to expect delivery within a reasonable time thereafter, perhaps half an hour up to an hour (see *Initial Electronic Security Systems Ltd v Avdic* [2005] IRLR 671).

Premature applications

3.46 In respect of unfair dismissal, s 111(3) of ERA 1996 provides that an application may be considered even though sent in before the effective date of termination. Where the employee terminates with notice in a constructive dismissal case it was suggested, in *Presley v Llanelli Borough Council* [1979] IRLR 381, that the premature application may be considered by the tribunal. However, the wording in s 111(3) seems to indicate that this is incorrect and that the focus is on the notice given by the employer, so the position is far from clear. It should be noted that the Act requires 'termination' and so an application anticipating non-renewal of a fixed term contract will be premature (see *Throsby v Imperial College of Science and Technology* [1977] IRLR 337). Where the application is made after notice of termination has been given, the fact that the employer subsequently summarily dismisses does not deprive the tribunal of jurisdiction (see *Patel v Nagesan* [1995] IRLR 370).

3.47 There is no equivalent for redundancy payment claims which must be made after the notice expires (*Watts v Rubery Owen Conveyancer Ltd* [1977] IRLR 112). In *Banking Insurance and Finance Union v Barclays Bank plc* [1987] IRLR 495 the EAT held that it was not premature to bring a claim for failure to consult under reg 10 of the TUPE 1981, before the transfer had taken place.

Delays in the post

3.48 In *St Basil's Centre v McCrossan* [1992] ICR 140 it was suggested that the High Court procedure as set out in CPR r 6.7 (which provides that a first class letter takes two working days to arrive after posting—Saturdays, Sundays, bank holidays, Christmas Day, and Good Friday are excluded from this computation) should be applied in the Tribunal. In *Metcalfe v Cygnet Healthcare* [2002] 3 All ER 801 the claimant's solicitors posted a letter on a Thursday in circumstances where the time limit was due to expire on Saturday at midnight and received by the Tribunal on a Monday. EAT held that applying the postal rule the letter was deemed delivered on the Saturday as that was a posting day. The approach in *St Basil's* was approved by the Court of Appeal in the case of *Consignia plc v Sealy* [2002] EWCA Civ 878, [2002] ICR 1193, where Brooke LJ set out (at para 31) the following guidance:

(1) Section 111(2) of the Employment Rights Act 1996 speaks of 'presenting' a complaint to a tribunal. It is now well established that a complaint is 'presented' when it arrives at the Central Office of Employment Tribunals or an Office of the tribunals ('the Office').

(2) If a complainant or his/her agent proves that it was impossible to present a complaint in this way before the end of the time prescribed by section 111(2)(a)—for example because the Office was

found to be locked at a weekend and it did not have a letter-box—then it will be possible to argue that it was not reasonably practicable for the complaint to be presented within the prescribed period.

(3) If a complainant chooses to present a complaint by sending it by post, presentation will be assumed to have been effected, unless the contrary is proved, at the time when the letter would be delivered in the ordinary course of post (see, by analogy, section 7 of the Interpretation Act 1978).

(4) If the letter is sent by first class post, it is now legitimate to adapt the approach contained in CPR 6.7 and conclude that in the ordinary course of post it will be delivered on the second day after it was posted (excluding Sundays, bank holidays, Christmas Day, and Good Friday, being days when post is not normally delivered).

(5) If the letter does not arrive at the time when it would be expected to arrive in the ordinary course of post, but is unexpectedly delayed, a tribunal may conclude that it was not reasonably practicable for the complaint to be presented within the prescribed period.

(6) If a form is date-stamped on a Monday by a Tribunal Office so as to be outside a three-month period which ends on the Saturday or Sunday, it will be open to a tribunal to find as a fact that it was posted by first class post not later than the Thursday and arrived on the Saturday, alternatively to extend time as a matter of discretion if satisfied that the letter was posted by first class post not later than the Thursday.

(7) This regime does not allow for any unusual subjective expectation, whether based on inside knowledge of the postal system or on lay experience of what happens in practice, to the effect that a letter posted by first class post may arrive earlier than the second day (excluding Sundays etc: see (4) above) after it is posted. The 'normal and expected' result of posting a letter must be objectively, not subjectively, assessed and it is that the letter will arrive at its destination in the *ordinary* course of post. As the present case shows, a complainant knows that he/she is taking a risk if the complaint is posted by first class post on the day before the guillotine falls, and it would be absurd to hold that it was not reasonably practicable for it to be presented in time if it arrives in the ordinary course of post on the second day after it was posted. Nothing unexpected will have occurred. The post will have taken its usual course.

In *Initial Electronic Security Systems Ltd v Avdic* [2005] IRLR 671 and *Metcalfe* (above), the EAT reiterated that *Consignia* should be relied upon as establishing the test of objective reasonable expectation of a claimant sending his claim form to the ET: it does not impose an obligation to prove an 'unforeseen circumstance'. Only if the '*Consignia* escape route' is established, however, is a claimant free from justifying his or her delay during the three-month period. **3.49**

Guidance on whether it is reasonable to rely on next day posting was given in *Beanstalk Shelving Ltd v Horn* [1980] ICR 273, where evidence that a letter posted first class from Liverpool could be expected to arrive in London the next day was heard, but it was also stated that 'it is an extremely dangerous practice for applicants to industrial tribunals to leave the posting of their application until the penultimate day' (see also *Sturges v A E Farr Ltd* [1975] ICR 356 where it was stressed that the tribunal will want to know the exact date and time when the application was posted). **3.50**

A different issue arose in *Capital Foods Retail Ltd v Corrigan* [1993] IRLR 430, where the application was posted well within time but for some unexplained reason the tribunal did not receive it. The EAT was critical of the failure by the applicant's solicitors to pursue the tribunal to confirm receipt after a lengthy silence and held that the application had not been presented and it was not right to extend the time (see also *Camden and Islington Community Health Services NHS Trust v Kennedy* [1996] IRLR 351). **3.51**

For claims 'served' via the Employment Tribunals Service website, see *Tyne and Wear Autistic Society v Smith* [2005] ICR 663 at para 2.06 above. **3.52**

E. EXTENSIONS

Not reasonably practicable

Many time limits allow the applicant an extension for a further period which the tribunal considers 'reasonable in a case where it is satisfied that it was not reasonably practicable for a complaint to be presented before the end of the period' (ERA 1996, s 111(2)(b)). This applies **3.53** to unfair dismissal and most other employment protection rights. The different provisions of SDA 1975, RRA 1976, and DDA 1995 are considered separately below.

3.54 The statutory test can be reduced to two distinct questions:

(a) was it reasonably practicable to present the complaint in time, or
(b) if it was not, did the applicant bring the complaint within a further reasonable period?

3.55 It is for the claimant to prove that it was not reasonably practicable to bring the claim in time and it is a question of fact for the tribunal to decide. The EAT and the Court of Appeal are reluctant to interfere with such a decision (see *Wall's Meat Co Ltd v Khan* [1979] ICR 52; *Riley v Tesco Stores Ltd* [1980] IRLR 103; and *Palmer and Saunders v Southend-on-Sea Borough Council* [1984] IRLR 119). In approaching this question, the Court of Appeal, in *Dedman v British Building and Engineering Appliances Ltd* [1974] ICR 53, stated that a liberal interpretation in favour of the employee should be adopted by the tribunal.

3.56 The question of practicability has been described as being whether something can be done (see *Singh v Post Office* [1973] ICR 437). Lord Denning MR in *Dedman* (at 61) considered practicability and stated that:

> if in the circumstances the man knew or was put on enquiry as to his rights, and as to the time limit then it was practicable for him to have presented his complaint within the four weeks and he ought to have done so. But if he did not know and there was nothing to put him on enquiry, then it was not practicable and he should be excused. . .If a man engages skilled advisers to act for him and they mistake the limit and present it too late—he is out. His remedy is against them.

3.57 More general consideration was given in *Palmer and Saunders v Southend-on-Sea Borough Council* (above), where May LJ stated (at 125):

> to construe the words 'reasonably practicable' as the equivalent of reasonable is to take a view too favourable to the employee. On the other hand 'reasonably practicable' means more than what is reasonably capable physically of being done. . .in the context in which the words are used in the 1978 Consolidation Act, however inaptly as we think, they mean something between the two. Perhaps to read the word 'practicable' as the equivalent of 'feasible'. . .and to ask colloquially and untrammelled by too much legal logic—was it reasonably feasible to present the complaint to the industrial tribunal within the relevant 3 months?—is the best approach to the correct application of the relevant subsection.

3.58 A number of factors were set out, although May LJ emphasized that they could not be exhaustive, but should form a useful starting point, and the tribunal should consider, amongst other things:

(a) the manner in which, and the reason for which, the employee was dismissed, including any internal 'conciliatory appeals procedure';
(b) the substantial cause of the employee's failure to comply with the statutory time limit;
(c) whether he knew he had the right to complain that he had been unfairly dismissed;
(d) whether there had been any 'misrepresentation' about any relevant matter by the employer to the employee;
(e) whether the employee was advised at any material time and, if so, by whom; the extent of the adviser's knowledge of the facts of the case and the advice given to the employee.

3.59 Other factors to be considered were suggested in *Wall's Meat* (para 3.55 above) by Brandon LJ where (at 60) he gave the following guidance:

> the performance of an act, in this case the presentation of a complaint, is not reasonably practicable if there is some impediment which reasonably prevents, or interferes with, or inhibits such performance. The impediment may be physical, for instance the illness of the complainant or a postal strike; or the impediment may be mental, namely, the state of mind of the complainant in the form of ignorance of, or mistaken belief with regard to essential matters. Such states of mind can, however, only be regarded as impediments making it not reasonably practicable to present a complaint within the period of three months, if the ignorance on the one hand, or the mistaken belief on the other, is itself reasonable. Either state of mind will, further, not be reasonable if it arises from the fault of his

> solicitors or other professional advisers in not giving him such information as they should reasonably in all the circumstances have given him. ([1979] ICR 52, 60–1)

The EAT will rarely interfere with a tribunal's decision on reasonable practicability; however, it will do so where the tribunal has reached a decision that can be categorized as perverse (see *Birmingham Optical Group plc v Johnson* [1995] ICR 459, where the EAT reversed a tribunal decision that it was not reasonably practicable to submit an application because of ongoing commercial relations between the parties). We now consider in turn the factors set out by May LJ (see para 3.58 above). **3.60**

The manner in which, and the reason for which, the employee was dismissed, including any internal 'conciliatory appeals procedure'

One frequently encountered explanation for delay is that internal disciplinary proceedings arising out of the dismissal were pending at the same time, and these often take several weeks or months to resolve. Tribunals have rejected the argument that the pursuit of such remedies generally postpones the effective date of termination until their conclusion (*Savage v J Sainsbury plc* [1980] IRLR 109). In the absence of a delayed starting point, applicants have sought to use the extension of time discretion in those circumstances. In *Crown Agents for Overseas Governments and Administration v Lawal* [1979] ICR 103, Kilner Brown J said (at 109): **3.61**

> Merely as a statement of general principle, it would seem to us that in cases where a person is going through a conciliation process or is taking up a domestic appeals procedure whether it be for discipline or whether it be for medical purposes that common sense would indicate that while he is going through something which involves him and his employer directly he should be able to say it was not reasonably practicable for me to lodge any application within three months.

This view has not, however, commanded universal acceptance. In *Bodha (Vishnudut) v Hampshire Area Health Authority* [1982] ICR 200, Browne-Wilkinson J reminded tribunals that the statutes set out the tests and they require the tribunal to have regard to what could be done, albeit approaching what is practicable in a common-sense way. The statutory tests are not satisfied just because it was reasonable not to do what could be done. The phrase 'reasonably practicable' means reasonably capable of being done: **3.62**

> there may be cases where the special facts (additional to the bare fact that there is an internal appeal pending) may persuade an industrial tribunal, as a question of fact, that it was not reasonably practicable to complain to the industrial tribunal within the time limit. But we do not think that the mere fact of the pending appeal by itself, is sufficient to justify a finding of fact that it was not 'reasonably practicable' to present a complaint to the industrial tribunal. ([1982] ICR 200, 205)

In that case it was held that it was reasonably practicable to present a complaint within the time limit, notwithstanding the internal appeals procedure. In *Palmer and Saunders* (para 3.55 above) the applicants were charged in 1980 with theft of fuel from Southend Airport where they worked. They were immediately suspended on half-pay, and the letter stated that 'in the event that you are adjudged to be not blameworthy, your suspension will be lifted and you will be entitled to reimbursement of lost pay. On the other hand, a conviction by a court will establish gross misconduct which could lead to instant dismissal.' The two applicants were convicted of theft in April 1981 and their employment was summarily terminated. On 22 April 1981 their internal appeals were rejected but they were told that if their criminal appeal succeeded, the employers would reconsider their positions. In December 1981, the Court of Appeal quashed the convictions but the employers refused to reinstate them. On 28 April, a year after the dismissal but only days after the successful appeal, the applicants presented their complaints to a tribunal. The tribunal, which was upheld by the EAT and Court of Appeal, decided that it was reasonably practicable to have presented the complaints in time. The applicants' argument that they acted reasonably in waiting for the internal procedures to be exhausted was rejected by the tribunal, since they could have presented the complaints in time and postponed the tribunal hearing until the resolution of the criminal proceedings (it should be noted that the continuation of civil proceedings is also not usually relevant for similar reasons). The case must be distinguished from the situation in which the employer specifically requests the employee to refrain from **3.63** making a tribunal application because there are ongoing negotiations (see *Owen v Crown House Engineering Ltd* [1973] ICR 511; contrast with *Times Newspapers Ltd v O'Regan* [1977] IRLR 101; and *Ruff v Smith* [1976] ICR 118 where the tribunal will nearly always grant extra time).

3.64 Problems have arisen in relation to the terms of disciplinary procedures. The fact that a procedure provides that a successful appellant will be reinstated with back-pay does not assist the unsuccessful appellant and the effective date of termination (EDT) remains the original date when termination becomes effective. In *Savage v J Sainsbury plc* the procedure stated that the employee was suspended pending appeal and would be reinstated with full back-pay if successful. Where the applicant was summarily dismissed, this did not keep the employment relationship alive until the date on which the appeal was refused because it was only if the appeal was successful that the employee was reinstated with back-pay. While several cases have held that in the absence of a suspensory provision in the procedure an agreement in advance can remedy the problem (see, for example, *Booth v USA* [1999] IRLR 16) in *London Probation Board v Kirkpatrick* [2005] IRLR 443 the EAT held that it is not necessary as a term can be implied and also that it is possible to have a retrospective agreement.

3.65 An appeal is part of the statutory dismissal and disciplinary procedures and reg 15 of the EA(DR) R 2004, provides that if the claimant had reasonable grounds to believe that an appeal was continuing at a point when the normal time limit expired an extension of three months will be granted in certain circumstances (see para 3.94 below).

The substantial cause of the employee's failure to comply with the statutory time limit

3.66 This means that the tribunal must examine the reasons proffered by the employee and must decide whether the delay was outside the applicant's control. Postal delays are commented upon below. Physical impediment, such as serious illness or absence abroad, will be relevant, as will the fact that the applicant was serving a prison sentence during some or all of the three-month period. In *Schultz v Esso Petroleum Ltd* [1999] IRLR 488 the Court of Appeal had to consider a case in which the claimant had been ill with depression towards the end of the time limit. The Court of Appeal held that while there was a seven-week period at the start when the claimant could have presented his claim, it was not fair to give this the same weight as the later period and accordingly it had not been reasonably practicable to lodge the claim in time. In *Imperial Tobacco v Wright* [2005] All ER (D) 325 (Jul) an employee was incapable of lodging his claim in time due to a relapse into drug abuse following his dismissal. The EAT accepted that a tribunal had correctly equated this with *Esso* (the employer on appeal wished to argue that, given that it is a criminal offence to be in possession of a controlled drug, and it is a general principle of common law that a party may not rely on his own wrong to secure a benefit, it would be wrong to allow the employee to rely on his drug use to excuse his late claim, but whilst it was arguable this had not been raised). On the other hand, in *Agrico v Ireland* EAT 0024/05 where a solicitor had left issuing an unfair dismissal claim to the last few days of the limitation period, his secretary's unexpected illness was not sufficient reason for the claim to be accepted a day late. An employment judge decided to accept the claim on the basis that it had not been reasonably practicable for the complaint to be presented in time. Given that there would have been nothing wrong with the application being presented on the last day the judge focused on the last few days of the three-month period. He concluded that, in those days the solicitor had done everything he could by leaving the matter with his experienced secretary. The failure to present the claim in time arose from the secretary's unforeseen illness. On the employer's appeal the EAT concluded that the judge had been wrong to focus entirely on the last three days of the three-month period. He had failed to take account of the fact that, although there is nothing wrong with a claim being presented on the last day of that period, a firm runs serious risks if it deliberately files claims so late. A competent solicitor must be taken to have appreciated the vital importance of complying with time limits strictly. To show that he or she acted reasonably, a solicitor must have a rather better system for ensuring that claims were issued in time when he or she was away from the office than simply relying on a secretary.

As there had been no evidence as to why the secretary had failed to contact the office to instruct someone else to issue the claim form there was no real evidence as to whether the solicitor's firm, as opposed to the individual solicitor, had done everything it could in the circumstances. **3.67**

In *Churchill v A Yeates & Son Ltd* [1983] ICR 380, the applicant presented his claim for unfair dismissal after hearing that his previous job had apparently been filled, thus nullifying the employer's claim that he was redundant. The EAT held that it might not be reasonably practicable to bring a complaint of unfair dismissal until he had knowledge of a fundamental fact which rendered the dismissal unfair. It is irrelevant that the employee could have brought a claim on another ground of unfairness. The case was remitted to a tribunal to decide whether the applicant could 'demonstrate . . . that until he was aware of the possibility of challenging the reason for dismissal given by the employers he reasonably took the view that he had no reasonable grounds to complain of unfair dismissal' (contrast this with *Borland v Independent Vegetable Processors Ltd* (CA, 9 December 1982), where on similar facts it was held that the employee did not make inquiries as to the situation at the company and ignorance of the true facts in those circumstances was not reasonable). See also *Cambridge & Peterborough NHS Trust v Crouchman* EAT 8/5/09 where the EAT held that it had not been reasonably practicable for a claimant to present an unfair dismissal claim within the time limit prescribed by the Employment Rights Act 1996, s 111(2) where written reasons for the dismissal of his internal appeal, delivered after the expiry of the time limit, differed from oral reasons delivered before the expiry of the time limit, such that they disclosed crucial facts making him reasonably and genuinely believe that he had grounds to pursue a claim. **3.68**

Whether he knew that he had the right to complain that he had been unfairly dismissed

The mistaken belief or ignorance of an applicant as to his rights must be reasonable in order to support the claim that it was not reasonably practicable to present the application in time. The employee may be ignorant as to the existence of the right, the way to exercise it, or the time limit. In each case that ignorance must be reasonable. A good illustration is the fact that an employee who knows of the right but not of the time limit will not be reasonable since he should be put on notice about claiming those rights (*W Press & Son Ltd v Hall* [1974] ICR 21; *Avon County Council v Haywood-Hicks* [1978] ICR 646; *House of Clydesdale Ltd v Foy* [1976] IRLR 391; and also *Trevelyans Ltd v Norton* [1991] ICR 488). **3.69**

In *Dedman* (para 3.55 above), the Court of Appeal set out some of the relevant questions that tribunals might ask when considering a claim that the employee was ignorant as to his rights: **3.70**

(a) what opportunities did the applicant have for finding out about his rights;
(b) did he take them; or
(c) was he misled or deceived (clearly this overlaps, to a degree, with item (d) of the *Palmer* guidance, considered at para 3.58 above).

In *Porter v Bandridge* [1978] ICR 943, the Court of Appeal stressed that pure and simple ignorance is not enough. The real issue is that the applicant ought to have known and tribunals will, in general, be reluctant to accept a claim that intelligent and well-educated individuals are unaware of their rights or that such ignorance is reasonable (as in the *Avon* case above). In some cases, the fact that an applicant had poor English is relevant but not decisive to this question (*Bhatt v Pioneer Plastic Containers Ltd* EAT/108/90). **3.71**

It is important to distinguish between ignorance of the law and ignorance of material facts (as in the *Churchill* case, see para 3.68 above). In *Machine Tool Industry Research Association v Simpson* [1988] ICR 558, Simpson discovered that someone else was doing her former job shortly before the expiry of the unfair dismissal time limit, at which point she thought she might not have been dismissed for redundancy. The Court of Appeal upheld her claim that it had not been **3.72** reasonably practicable to bring the claim in time and that the employee's subjective belief was the focus of the inquiry. Applicants in those sorts of cases must demonstrate three things:

(1) It was not reasonable to expect the applicant to have been aware of the factual basis upon which a claim or complaint could have been brought during the time limit.
(2) The applicant gained the knowledge thereafter reasonably and it was crucial, fundamental, or important to the change in the applicant's belief that he now did have grounds for applying to a tribunal.
(3) The belief that there are grounds for an application must be reasonable and genuinely held.

3.73 This has been followed in *James W Cook & Co (Wivenhoe) Ltd v Tipper* [1990] IRLR 386 and by Mummery J in *Marley (UK) Ltd v Anderson* [1994] IRLR 152 (affirmed [1996] IRLR 163). After his redundancy, Anderson discovered that his former post still existed and that he had been dismissed for his work performance. The EAT accepted that these facts were capable of providing independent grounds justifying the late presentation of the application and that the applicant does not have to demonstrate the *truth* of the facts that cause him to change his mind. The analysis where an applicant is unaware of the right to make a claim is slightly different. The applicant in *Biggs v Somerset County Council* [1996] IRLR 203 was a part-time teacher who was dismissed in 1976. In 1994 the House of Lords declared that the restriction on part-time employees claiming unfair dismissal was contrary to EC law. Mrs Biggs brought her claim within three months of the House of Lords judgment. However, her claim was dismissed on the basis that she could and should have sought to challenge the law in 1976 and it was not possible to claim that the law was only recently clarified as this would seriously undermine the principle of legal certainty. *Biggs* was a case involving the 'reasonably practicable' test and a slightly different approach was adopted in *British Coal Corporation v Keeble* [1997] IRLR 336 which dealt with the just and equitable extension. The EAT in that case held that the discretion applying the 'just and equitable' test is wide and comparable to that under s 33 of the Limitation Act 1980 and the court can consider prejudice to the parties, the length of any delay and the excuse advanced for it, and the fact that as a result of a change in the law the applicant has a 'new' right. Each of these factors must be considered in turn by the tribunal.

Whether there had been any 'misrepresentation' about any relevant matter by the employer to the employee

3.74 The facts of *Marley* are a good example of such misrepresentations. Other examples include the *Churchill* case at para 3.68 above.

Whether the employee was advised at any material time, and if so, by whom; the extent of the adviser's knowledge of the facts of the case and the advice given to the employee

3.75 The starting point must be the famous passage in *Dedman* (paras 3.55 and 3.56 above) where Lord Denning MR said:

> If a man engages skilled advisers to act for him and they mistake the limit and present it too late—he is out. His remedy is against them.

3.76 Skilled advisers include trade union representatives and voluntary advisers such as CAB workers and the Free Representation Unit (see *Croydon Health Authority v Jaufurally* [1986] ICR 4). In *Riley v Tesco Stores Ltd and Greater London Citizens Advice Bureaux Service Ltd* [1980] IRLR 103 the Court of Appeal disapproved of the construction of 'skilled adviser' as if it were part of the statute and stated that the issue was one of fact. In *Wall's Meat Co Ltd v Khan* [1979] ICR 52, 57 Shaw LJ stated:

> the test is empirical and involves no legal concept. Practical common sense is the keynote and legalistic footnotes may have no better results than to introduce a lawyer's complication into what should be a layman's pristine province. These considerations prompt me to express the emphatic view that the forum to decide such questions is the industrial tribunal and that their decision should prevail unless it is plainly perverse or oppressive.

The *Dedman* principle has been doubted by the Court of Appeal in *London International College Ltd v Sen* [1993] IRLR 333, where the Master of the Rolls questioned the basis of any rule of law to the effect that consulting an adviser makes it reasonably practicable to present a complaint in time. In *Marks and Spencer v Williams Ryan* [2005] IRLR 562 the Court of Appeal upheld a tribunal's decision that it had not been reasonably practicable for an employee to bring an unfair dismissal claim in accordance with the applicable three-month time limit where, having received advice from a CAB, the employee had believed it necessary to exhaust the employer's internal appeal procedure before bringing her claim. The reasoning is far from compelling however. (See para 3.94 below for statutory disciplinary and grievance procedure rules.) **3.77**

The Court of Appeal concluded that whilst the decision of the tribunal was generous to the claimant it was not outside the ambit of conclusions available to it. It was not for the Court of Appeal to review findings of fact unless there was no basis for those findings or they were perverse. It noted that no authorities were referred to where the Court of Appeal had reversed a decision on the facts and the present case should not be a first. Further it was held that s 111(2) of ERA 1996 should be interpreted liberally in favour of employees and the tribunal was entitled to reach the conclusion it had. **3.78**

Where an applicant has missed the time limit because of erroneous or misleading advice from tribunal staff, tribunals are more sympathetic (see *Jean Sorelle Ltd v Rybak* [1991] IRLR 153 and *London International College Ltd v Sen* [1993] IRLR 333). In the *Sen* case, the applicant's solicitor told him the date for presenting the originating application and he confirmed it with a member of the tribunal staff. The date was one day out of time and he failed to present his claim within the time limit. The Court of Appeal stated that it was clear that the 'effective cause of the failure was the advice, on all the facts, of the industrial tribunal'. **3.79**

Further period

If the applicant fails to establish that he did bring the claim in time, he should apply for an extension to bring it within 'such further period as the tribunal considers reasonable'. The tribunal's decision is, of course, a question of fact and successful challenges on appeal will be rare. Two cases offering guidance are *James W Cook and Co (Wivenhoe) v Tipper* [1990] IRLR 386, CA, and *Marley (UK) Ltd v Anderson* [1994] IRLR 152. In the former case the applicants were dismissed, but there were attempts to keep the shipyard open. After the expiry of the time limit the shipyard closed and two weeks later the applicants presented claims to the tribunal. This was held to be a reasonable further period. In the latter case, the tribunal had held that the applicant had delayed too long in bringing his complaint without focusing on the reasons for the delay, which must be relevant. **3.80**

The principles upon which the discretion hinges will be similar to those in the 'reasonably practicable' cases. It will be rare for a tribunal to allow an extension where the applicant is represented by his trade union or has not pursued a claim through his own neglect. **3.81**

Extension of time on a just and equitable basis

The test that applies in, for the main, the discrimination legislation potentially affords a tribunal a far wider discretion than in the case of the reasonably practicable extension as emphasized in *Hutchison v Westward Television* [1977] IRLR 69. For the impact of that test see *British Coal Corporation v Keeble* [1997] IRLR 336, in which the EAT held that the discretion applying the 'just and equitable' test is wide and comparable to that under s 33 of the Limitation Act 1980, and the court can consider prejudice to the parties, the length of any delay and the excuse advanced for it, and the fact that as a result of a change in the law the applicant has a 'new' right. Each of these factors must be considered in turn by the tribunal. The discretion to extend time should be exercised in exceptional circumstances (see *Robertson v Bexley Community Centre* [2003] IRLR 434 as endorsed by the Court of Appeal in *Department of Constitutional Affairs v Jones* [2008] IRLR 128 and followed by the EAT in *Chief Constable of Lincolnshire Police v Caston* UKEAT/0530/08). **3.82**

3.83 In *Chohan v Derby Law Centre* [2004] IRLR 685 Judge McMullen QC summarized the principles from the authorities as follows (paras 12–16):

> A tribunal demonstrably taking the wrong approach or not taking account of a fact which it should have done errs in law—see *Hutchison v Westward Television* [1977] IRLR 69 EAT.
>
> The availability of legal advice is a relevant question—see *British Coal Corporation v Keeble* [1997] IRLR 336 EAT at paragraph 8 per Smith J.
>
> The use of a check list under the Limitation Act is often useful: *British Coal Corporation v Keeble* EAT/413/94 unreported 6 July 1995 EAT Holland J at paragraph 10, upon which Mrs Justice Smith based her judgment above.
>
> Although it is not a requirement that a tribunal go through the check list, failure to consider a significant factor will amount to an error of law: *London Borough of Southwark v Afolabi* [2003] IRLR 220 CA paragraph 33 per Peter Gibson LJ.
>
> The failure by a legal adviser to enter proceedings in time should not be visited upon the claimant for otherwise the defendant would be in receipt of windfall: *Steeds v Peverel Management Services Ltd* [2001] EWCA Civ 419 pp 38–40.

3.84 The Limitation Act checklist requires the court to consider the prejudice which each party would suffer as the result of the decision to be made and also to have regard to all the circumstances of the case and in particular to:

(a) the length of and reasons for the delay;
(b) the extent to which the cogency of the evidence is likely to be affected by the delay;
(c) the extent to which the party sued had cooperated with any requests for information;
(d) the promptness with which the claimant acted once he or she knew of the facts giving rise to the cause of action; and
(e) the steps taken by the claimant to obtain appropriate professional advice once he or she knew of the possibility of taking action.

3.85 Whilst the Court of Appeal has held that it is not mandatory to go through the checklist (see *London Borough of Southwark v Afolabi* [2003] EWCA Civ 15, [2003] IRLR 220) it is recommended that any witness evidence and/or skeleton arguments use the checklist as a template. In particular for respondents the issue of specific prejudice—for example, that evidence has been destroyed—will most often be determinative (although there is no rule of law to this effect—see *Apelogun-Gabriels v London Borough of Lambeth* [2001] EWCA Civ 1853, [2002] IRLR 116).

3.86 *Chohan* was a case in which the EAT overruled the tribunal's decision that incorrect advice by the claimant's solicitor did not amount to a just and equitable excuse. The tribunal had not been persuaded by the case of *Hawkins v Ball* [1996] IRLR 258 which only held that it was not a mistake in law to take the adviser's error in calculating time into account, but the EAT went further in following the *Steeds* case above. It is still the case, however, that the claimant's own delay in instructing lawyers or in issuing proceedings will be a relevant factor, as will the adviser's fault in simply failing to send the claim in time or any inexcusable delay. The EAT in *Virdi v Commissioner of Police of the Metropolis* [2007] IRLR 24 has confirmed that the fault of a solicitor will be a 'highly material' factor in deciding whether to extend time on a just and equitable basis to allow a complaint of discrimination to proceed out of time. Finally, there is no rule of law that a CAB adviser should be regarded as a 'skilled adviser', comparable to a solicitor, so as to fix the claimant with the adviser's fault (*Royal Bank of Scotland v Theobald* UKEAT/0444/06).

Specific examples

3.87 In *Berry v Ravensbourne National Health Service Trust* [1993] ICR 871, the applicant's claim of race discrimination was additional to, and overlapped with, an existing unfair dismissal complaint which was made in time but had not yet been heard. The applicant was given notice of redundancy by her employers on 4 January 1992 and made a complaint of unfair dismissal, alleging that she had been unfairly selected for redundancy. Her employment terminated on

31 March 1992. At the end of August 1992 the applicant learnt that on 14 April 1992 the employers had advertised a vacancy for a pharmacist which they had not brought to her attention, though under their redundancy procedure an employee who was made redundant was, where practicable, given preferential consideration for suitable vacant posts up to four weeks after the termination of employment. On 2 November 1992 she sought to amend her complaint to add a claim of racial discrimination.

An extension of time was granted to allow the race claim to be heard as there was the overlap, and she had not discovered the facts in relation to the discrimination claim immediately. **3.88**

In *Robinson v Post Office* [2000] IRLR 804, a delay caused by a claimant invoking an internal grievance or disciplinary appeal procedure prior to commencing proceedings was held to justify the grant of an extension of time. However, this is merely one factor that must be weighed in the balance along with others that may be present (the case was approved by the Court of Appeal in *Apelogun-Gabriels v London Borough of Lambeth* above). On the facts of *Robinson*, the employee delayed making a disability discrimination claim whilst he pursued an internal disciplinary appeal. He was ultimately refused an extension of time as he knew of the time limit for bringing a discrimination claim and refused to take his union's advice to lodge the application in time. In *Apelogun-Gabriels*, the Court of Appeal rejected the earlier decision of Morison J in *Aniagwu v London Borough of Hackney* [1999] IRLR 303 that there is a general principle that an extension should always be granted where a delay is caused by a claimant invoking an internal grievance or appeal procedure, unless the employers could show some particular prejudice. **3.89**

An extension of time was granted to a claimant who did not discover the evidence which led to his race discrimination claim (concerning the failure to appoint him to a particular grade) until nine years after the expiry of the time limit: *Southwark London Borough v Afolabi* above. Factors taken into account were that he had no reason to discover the evidence earlier; that he presented his complaint within three months of discovering it; and that the nine-year delay would be equally prejudicial to both parties. **3.90**

Employment Act 2002

The Employment Act 2008 (Commencement No 1, Transitional Provisions and Savings) Order 2008 SI 2008/3232 confirmed 6 April 2009 as the date on which the Employment Act 2008 would repeal the dispute resolution procedures. The Order also contains transitional provisions governing when the statutory disciplinary, dismissal, and grievance procedures will continue to apply after 6 April. As there are still many cases brought at a time when the EA 2002 procedures applied we will continue to deal with that regime. **3.91**

Schedule 2 to the Employment Act 2002 sets out a three-stage internal procedure that must be followed if an employee lodges a written grievance with his or her employer. Section 32 of EA 2002 prevents an employee from presenting a complaint to an employment tribunal unless he or she has complied with Step 1 of the grievance procedure and has given the employer 28 days to respond. A claim form will therefore be rejected as inadmissible if it is presented before s 32 has been complied with. Extensions are permitted in the following circumstances: **3.92**

(a) Where the employee has submitted a claim within the normal time limit but that claim is inadmissible because the employee has not sent the Step 1 grievance letter. The employee must then submit the letter within one month after the expiry of the normal time limit (EA 2002, s 32(4)(b)). The claim must then be submitted within three months of the expiry of the normal time limit.
(b) Where the employee has sent the Step 1 grievance letter within the normal time limit but has not waited 28 days. The employee must wait the full 28 days and resubmit the claim within three months of the expiry of the normal time limit.
(c) Where the employee sends the Step 1 grievance letter within the normal time limit and then submits a claim within three months of the expiry of that time limit (reg 15(3)).

3.93 Where the statutory disciplinary procedure applies (see EA 2002, Sch 3, Appendix 1 for a list of claims to which it applies), reg 15(1)(a) and (2) of the EA(DR)R 2004 extend the normal time limit by three months where the employee had reasonable grounds for believing, when the normal time limit expired, that a dismissal or disciplinary procedure, whether statutory or otherwise was being followed in respect of matters that consisted of or included the substance of the complaint. The purpose of reg 15 is effectively to impose a moratorium of three months before the normal time limit commences in order to allow for the statutory procedures to run their course. Apart from that, its effect on the operation of the primary time limit contained should be neutral. However, in both situations it can only apply if the relevant statutory procedure was engaged at the time when the original time limit expired. If the procedure is completed very late but still within the limit this benefit of the regulation cannot be claimed (although it may be a basis for claiming relief under the 'not reasonably practicable' extension: see *Royal Bank of Scotland v Bevan* [2007] UKEAT/440/07, where the employer suddenly and without warning concluded the procedure on the day before the time limit, and *Ashcroft v Haberdashers Aske's Boys School* [2007] UKEAT/151/07).

3.94 Where the time limit has been extended in accordance with reg 15, the tribunal retains its usual discretion to extend it further (see below). In *Martins v Bisset* [2006] EAT 0022/06, the EAT held that where a claim is brought by an employee against both his or her employer and a fellow employee, the submission of a written grievance to the employer does not operate to extend the time limit for lodging a claim against the fellow employee (although in *London Borough of Lambeth v Corlett* [2007] ICR 88 another division of the EAT cast doubt on this). In *Codemasters v Wong* UKEAT/0639/06/DA (in what was a fact sensitive case), the EAT upheld a tribunal decision that an employee who lodged an appeal against dismissal had a reasonable belief that a procedure was being followed even where the employer had written informing him that the appeal he had submitted was out of time. In *Towergate London Market Limited v Harris* [2008] EWCA Civ 433 [2008] IRLR 536, an employee failed to appeal her dismissal for redundancy under the company procedures but, after her employment ended, she sent her employer a 'grievance' challenging the dismissal. The employer subsequently provided her with further information about the process and had a meeting. She made a claim to a tribunal for unfair dismissal, which was out of time. The EAT and, subsequently, the Court of Appeal, held that she had, in fact, presented her employer with an appeal against dismissal which fell within reg 15; because of the employer's follow-up, she had 'reasonable grounds for believing . . . that a dismissal . . . procedure, whether statutory or otherwise, was being followed'. Therefore, under reg 15(2), the time for bringing a claim was extended. In *Eagles v Rugged Systems* UKEAT/0018/09 the EAT held that an employee who was in the process of negotiating a compromise of her claim could claim the extension as negotiations to compromise are capable of being a procedure to resolve matters in dispute. It is not the label that one attaches to the procedure but the employee's reasonable belief that is important.

3.95 The reg 15(2) automatic extension does not apply in cases of constructive unfair dismissal because the employer is not contemplating dismissal (see *Lothian Buses plc v Nelson* UKEATS/0059/05) but it is a cause of action in relation to which the statutory grievance procedure applies and therefore the extension under reg 15(3) may apply. In *Pisticelli v Zilli Fish Ltd* UKEAT/0638/05/DZM, the claimant was summarily dismissed and whilst there were negotiations on settlement they were not concluded. The claimant lodged his claim 10 days out of time and sought to rely on the argument that an earlier letter before action, in which his solicitors had alleged that his dismissal was unfair, could be read as an appeal, and further that the employers had no appeal procedure. The EAT rejected his contention that the letter could be read in this way and stated that where the employer rejects an appeal, or has no procedure, the employee cannot have reasonable grounds for believing that an appeal is being followed, and so must follow the usual time limit (although the employer may be penalized in compensation).

3.96 There is also a trap for the unwary in presenting a claim before the 28-day period for a grievance response has elapsed. In *Basingstoke Press Ltd v Clarke* UKEAT/0375/06 a grievance was lodged on Friday 7 October 2005, and the claim form was received by the Employment Tribunal on the Internet at 19:01 on Thursday 3 November. Drawing on the CPR (where what is required is the elapsing of a period of time before an event can occur) the 28 days must come and go before the action can be taken—so a grievance put in on Sunday 1 October could not be the subject of a claim presented to a tribunal until Monday 30 October, leaving 28 clear days between 1 and 30 October (28 days plus a day). The claim here was put in two days early and could not be accepted.

In *Spillett v Tesco* and *BUPA Homes v Cann* [2006] IRLR 248 the EAT clarified the issue as to whether the claimant can rely upon any other discretionary extension of time (in that case the just and equitable extension under the DDA 1995, Sch 3, Part 3). HHJ Clark sitting alone had to address the question whether the expression 'original time limit' (in s 32(4) of the EA 2002 it is undefined) refers to the primary three-month limitation period or to the primary period as extended by the tribunal where either it was not reasonably practicable to present a complaint of unfair dismissal in time or it is just and equitable to extend time. He concluded (at para 37): **3.97**

> In my judgment the 'original time limit for making the complaint' is the time limit provided for in the relevant legislation, here the DDA. That includes giving a tribunal the power to consider a complaint made outside the primary limitation period where it is just and equitable to do so.

For the purpose of the extension of the time afforded by reg 15 of the EA(DR)R 2004, an employee's grievance is to be treated as lodged 'within the normal time limit' even if it is lodged before the effective date of termination or other date from which time starts to run (*Barua v HM Prison Service* [2007] ICR 671).

The position appears to be different in relation to amending the claim form. It is still not clear whether an amendment which seeks to raise a matter to which the statutory procedure applies would be allowed if the employee has not submitted a Step 1 grievance letter in relation to that matter and allowed 28 days for a response. To disallow the amendment would seem to be contrary to the overriding objective to deal with cases in a just and cost-effective manner, but to allow the amendment would enable the employee to circumvent the statutory procedure, and would potentially be open to challenge on the ground that the tribunal has no jurisdiction under s 32 of EA 2002. Perhaps some guidance can be obtained from the case of *Smith v Network Rail Infrastructure Ltd* [2007] All ER (D) 253 (May) in which the EAT held that an employee could not raise a grievance about a specific incident of discrimination and then in the claim form seek to rely on other specific incidents. Similarly, a grievance could not be raised about sex discrimination, and then a claim brought in respect of race unless there had been a further grievance letter. The position is different when what is complained of in the grievance letter is a continuing complaint and the claimant seeks to amend the claim form to add further acts of discrimination of the same nature. **3.98**

4

The Response

SUMMARY

(1) In the case of the response the time limit for entering it is 28 days after the claim form has been sent to the respondent.

(2) Extensions of time are possible but, if the respondent fails to lodge a response within the specified or extended time, he is not entitled to take part in the proceedings except to a very limited degree.

A. TIME LIMITS

The respondent has 28 days after the claim form has been sent to submit his response. A claim against a foreign state is governed by the State Immunity Act 1978, s 12(2) which provides that the time limit is two months and provides special rules for service which are incompatible with, and therefore supersede, the provisions of ETR 2004. The 28-day period will be strictly construed as running from the date when the document was actually sent by the tribunal, and there is no scope for construing it as running from the date when it was received (see *Bone v Fabcon Projects Ltd* [2006] ICR 1421). **4.01**

If no response is entered or it is out of time a judge may issue a default judgment (ETR 2004, r 8). Even if a default judgment is not entered under para 8, the Secretary may refuse to accept the response under r 6(2) with the effect that the respondent can play no further part in the proceedings pursuant to r 9 (see para 4.23 below). **4.02**

Regulation 4(7) of the 2008 Regulations amends rule 8 of Schedule 1 to remove an employment judge's discretion not to issue a default judgment in certain circumstances. The new procedure is as follows: **4.03**

> In any proceedings where a relevant time limit for presenting a response has passed an employment judge shall issue a default judgment to determine the claim without a hearing (subject to the two expectations set out below). If the employment judge is not satisfied that he has sufficient information to issue a default judgment, he should make an order requiring such additional information as he considers appropriate to enable him to issue a default judgment.

Where such an order is made and the information not received within any specified time limit, a default judgment should be issued.

The two exceptions are first that no default judgment need be issued where the employment judge is not satisfied that the tribunal has jurisdiction to consider the claim, or part of it, or has sufficient evidence to conclude that the claim form has not been received by the respondent, and second a default judgment should not be issued where the parties have settled the proceedings (either by means of a compromise agreement or through ACAS). If a default judgment is issued in these circumstances it shall have no effect.

B. LATE RESPONSE

4.04 In *Moroak (t/a Blake Envelopes) v Cromie* [2005] IRLR 353, Burton P had to consider a response lodged at the tribunal 44 minutes late. The tribunal ordered that the respondent could play no further part in proceedings and refused a review on the basis that there was no provision for it in ETR 2004. While he accepted that there was no power under r 4 to consider an application for an extension of time once the 28-day period had expired and that the tribunal could set aside a judgment in default, in this case no judgment had been entered. He held that r 34 allows a review on the grounds of it being just and equitable and therefore the response could be accepted.

4.05 Rule 11 allows, in the ordinary course of events, for an application for an extension of time. This must however be applied for before the 28-day period has elapsed (see r 4(4)).

4.06 If an application to extend time is made (and r 11 applies to such applications), the party's legal representative must provide all other parties with the following information at the same time as the application is sent to the tribunal:

(a) Details of the application and why it is sought; this must include an explanation as to how the direction or order would assist the tribunal or judge in dealing with the proceedings efficiently or fairly.
(b) That any objection to the application must be sent to the tribunal within seven days of being informed of the application.
(c) That any objection to the application must be copied to both the tribunal and all other parties.

4.07 The requirement to provide the information at (a) and (b) is only imposed on the applying party if they are legally represented. If there is no legal representative the Secretary to the tribunal takes the responsibility to copy the application to the opposing party.

4.08 The respondent can apply for a review of any default judgment made against him for failing to present a response in time, in which case he will not only have the right but will be under an obligation to apply for an extension of time in the course of making that application (see further para 13.53).

4.09 Rule 4(4) states that the tribunal should allow the extension if a judge considers that it is just and equitable to do so. In *Kwik Save Stores Ltd v Swain* [1997] ICR 49, the EAT stated that a judge considering whether to extend time must take account of all of the relevant factors and reach a conclusion which is justified on the grounds of reason and justice.

4.10 When a legally represented respondent applies to extend the 28-day period allowed for responding to a claim, all other parties must be notified of the details of the application and of the manner in which objections may be made.

C. CONTENTS OF THE RESPONSE

The Form

4.11 Since 1 October 2005 it has been mandatory to use form ET3. ETR 2004, r 6 states that a response will not be accepted if it does not contain all the required information. It may be that the respondent is unable to complete various parts of the response because of insufficient information on the claim form. In such circumstances the response should be completed to the best of the respondent's ability and an order for further information should be applied for. In *Butlins Skyline Ltd v Beynon* [2007] ICR 121, EAT, the response was rejected by the tribunal Secretary as it was not in the prescribed form (this appears debatable as it was properly filled in but could not be scanned into the ETS system) and the respondent was debarred from taking any further part in proceedings. There is an express power to review a 'decision' by a judge but none where the decision is that of the Secretary. The EAT held that this decision was still susceptible to review as the power in r 34 must have envisaged this situation. This is really the corollary of *Hamling v Coxlease School Ltd* [2007] IRLR 8, [2007] ICR 108, which allows for latitude in determining whether the claim form has been properly completed.

The respondent can set out his defence to a number of different claims in the same document, if the remedy claimed arises out of the same set of facts, provided that the respondent intends to resist all the claims and the grounds for doing so are the same in relation to each claim or the respondent does not intend to resist any of the claims (see ETR 2004, r 4(5)). **4.12**

Two practice points need mentioning at this stage. The first concerns pleading in the alternative. The respondent may wish to put forward more than one argument. The most obvious example is that of a constructive dismissal. A respondent frequently pleads that the applicant was not dismissed but resigned and, in the alternative, if he was dismissed it was for a permissible reason and was fair in all the circumstances. In some cases, a respondent who fails to plead the alternative ground has been unable to present evidence or argument on the fairness of the dismissal (for example, *Derby City Council v Marshall* [1979] ICR 731) but in many cases a tribunal will nevertheless allow such amendment. **4.13**

The second matter is incorrect labelling of the reason for dismissal. Employers should not be penalized by using the wrong label to describe the reason for dismissal. In *W Devis & Sons v Atkins* [1977] IRLR 314, for example, the employer gave a different reason from the real one out of kindness to the employee. The wrong label does not disqualify the employer from relying on the real one (see *Abernethy v Mott, Hay & Anderson* [1974] ICR 323) but a change of reason will not reflect well on an employer's credibility, nor on the question of reasonableness. **4.14**

In particular, the change of label may mean that a dismissal is unfair because the employee has not had a chance to answer the new allegation. In *Hotson v Wisbech Conservative Club* [1984] ICR 859, the EAT held that a dismissal was unfair on this basis where the employers sought to change the reason from one of capability to dishonesty (see also *Hannan v TNT-IPEC (UK) Ltd* [1986] IRLR 165, where there was no injustice to the employee in allowing a change of label). **4.15**

Box 2 'Action before a claim'

The contents of this box are not mandatory and ask: **4.16**

(a) whether the claimant was an employee;
(b) if the complaint is about dismissal, whether the respondent agrees that the claimant was dismissed;
(c) if the complaint is about something else, whether it relates to action taken on the ground of the claimant's conduct or capability;
(d) whether the substance of the complaint has been raised in writing under a grievance procedure.

The respondent is then asked what stage of any internal procedures has been reached and to set out details of all meetings. It may be that the question of dismissal is in dispute. The tribunal will often hear this as a preliminary issue at a pre-hearing review or simply identify it as an issue to be determined at the substantive hearing.

Box 3 'Employment details'

4.17 Confirmation of the claimant's employment dates is required here and if there is disagreement, reasons should be given. This is clearly in order to flush out any disputes concerning continuity and/or basic award at an early stage. The respondent is also asked whether the claimant's job title is correct and if not, why not. Similarly there are questions concerning notice pay and hours of work, basic pay, and other benefits.

Box 4 'Unfair dismissal or constructive dismissal'

4.18 This asks about whether pension details are correct.

Box 5 'Response'

4.19 It is mandatory to indicate whether the claim is resisted or not. The respondent may wish to resist only part of the claim, for example, remedy and not liability, and this can be shown on the form. It is often useful to indicate here whether and, if so, why there is a need for PHR or CMD. For example, is disability in issue or not and, if so, why? While Box 6 is the place to indicate whether there is a need for a CMD or PHR, this is the place to plead the circumstances.

4.20 Responses tend to be quite full now and there is provision for continuation on a separate sheet. Particular care should be taken in filling out the response in all cases but more so in discrimination cases as inferences may be drawn (see *Dattani v Chief Constable of West Mercia Police* [2005] IRLR 327).

4.21 All the discrimination statutes provide for the Secretary of State by order to prescribe 'forms by which the person aggrieved may question the respondent on its reasons for doing any relevant act'. They then provide that 'where the person aggrieved questions the respondent (whether in accordance with an order . . . or not)', any reply is admissible and if the tribunal considers that the reply, is 'evasive or equivocal', it 'may draw any inference from that fact that it considers it just and equitable to draw, including an inference that he committed an unlawful act' of discrimination. In *Dattani* one of the issues was whether an inference of discrimination could be drawn from incorrect information as to the reason for the transfer provided by the employers in their response, further and better particulars, and a written explanation given to the claimant. The EAT held that the use of the words in accordance with an order 'or not' means that the question and answer provisions cover replies given in a form other than that prescribed in the statutory discrimination questionnaires. This broadens the scope of the question and answer procedure by making it clear that tribunals have a responsibility to consider drawing an inference from an evasive or equivocal reply to any question in writing from the claimant, regardless of whether the statutory form has been used.

Box 6 'Other information'

4.22 The respondent is informed that no covering letter should be sent with form ET3 and that therefore any additional information should be included in this box. For example, the respondent may be seeking early orders for further information or for a pre-hearing review. It may be that the respondent considers that he has been incorrectly named in the proceedings or that another party should be joined (note that under the old rules only persons against whom relief was sought could be joined, but under ETR 2004 anyone with an interest in the proceedings may be joined).

Box 7 'Your representative'

4.23 The details of any representative including his or her preferred method of communication should be included in this box.

D. CONSEQUENCES OF FAILING TO ENTER A RESPONSE

A respondent who fails to enter a response or whose response is not accepted is governed by ETR 2004, rr 8 and 9 which state that he is no longer entitled to take a part in 'proceedings' except either to defend on quantum or to: **4.24**

(a) make an application for a review of a default judgment (r 33);
(b) make an application for a review under r 34 (see *Moroak* below);
(c) make an application for a preliminary consideration of an application for a review (r 34(3)(a));
(d) be called as a witness for another person;
(e) be sent a copy of a document or corrected entry (rr 8(4), 29(2), or 37).

The tribunal may, in its discretion, issue a default judgment. A default judgment may determine liability only or liability and remedy (ETR 2001 rule 8(3)). **4.25**

Such a respondent, however, can appeal a decision of the tribunal to the EAT whether that decision is the default judgment or a decision on compensation. This was the decision of the EAT in *Atos Origin IT Services UK Ltd v Haddock* [2005] IRLR 20. The facts of the case were that the employers had failed to enter a response to a claim under DDA 1995 and following a hearing the tribunal awarded compensation to the claimant. The case then took some unusual procedural detours and was remitted to the tribunal to determine the claimant's entitlement to a discrete aspect of compensation. The tribunal found in the claimant's favour and the employers appealed to the EAT against that decision. The EAT held that notwithstanding the employers' failure to lodge a notice of appearance (now 'response') and the restriction on their participation in the tribunal proceedings defined by ETR 2001, those 'proceedings' were not the same as the appeal to the EAT, which was governed by different rules and a Practice Direction, and therefore the employers could take part at the appellate level. **4.26**

In *NSM Music v Leefe* [2006] ICR 450, the employer was late entering its response. The employer applied for a review, which was rejected without consideration of the merits. The employer then failed to lodge an appeal against the refusal of the review, which Burton P stated should be 'the sensible course for a Respondent'. The employer was therefore not entitled to defend the compensation which was assessed at £48,000. The employer wrote to the tribunal asking for written reasons for the judgment but the tribunal refused on the grounds that r 9, prohibiting the employer from taking any further part in the proceedings, included a prohibition on requesting written reasons. **4.27**

On appeal Burton P held: **4.28**

- rather than a point blank refusal to provide written reasons, it would be good practice for an employment tribunal to first ask the employer why it wants them;
- that the rules—properly interpreted—allow an employer to request written reasons for the purpose of a *review*, even when it has been debarred from taking further part in the proceedings;
- but the rules do not allow the employer to seek written reasons for the purpose of an *appeal.* However, this problem can be bypassed if the employer presents an appeal, and then the EAT requests written reasons under r 30(3)(b);
- the EAT has no power to order that the employer pay the judgment debt as a condition of being permitted to continue with the appeal—but it is open to a claimant to go to the county court and ask that the judgment debt be paid into court pending the outcome of any appeal.

A respondent can also have costs, or preparation time, orders made for or against him in relation to the conduct of any part which he has taken in the proceedings (ETR 2004, rr 38(4) and 42(4), and see *British School of Motoring v Fowler* UKEAT/509/06, where the EAT ordered the costs of an appeal caused by an employer who had not entered a response: similarly, in the tribunal, reviews in similar circumstances might attract such orders). The EAT clarified the extent of such **4.29** an order in *Sutton v The Ranch Ltd* [2006] ICR 1170, where it held that a tribunal's jurisdiction to award costs, when an employer fails to enter a response, is limited to costs caused or incurred in dealing with one of the express matters set out in r 9, (essentially making an application for review of a default judgment). The EAT's reasoning was based on the lack of any obligation on an employer to enter a response and so there is no breach of any rule if it fails to do so.

Review of Default Judgments

4.30 On the face of ETR 2004, responses that are out of time will not be accepted. A refusal to accept a response must be given in writing with reasons (see further para 4.03 'Late Response' above). In *British School of Motoring v Fowler* [2006] UKEAT 0059/06 the employer failed to lodge a notice of appearance and applied for a review claiming that it had no notification of the claim at all. The tribunal considered the application and the employee's comments on paper and refused a review as it rejected this explanation. The EAT held that at the very least when rejecting an explanation the employee's comments should have been sent to the employer for comment and there should have been a hearing.

4.31 In *Pendragon v Copus* [2005] ICR 1671 the employer was out of time filing a response to the claim and the tribunal issued a default judgment. The employer applied to revoke the judgment and for an extension of time for it to submit its response, but the judge was not satisfied by the explanation for not filing the response on time and refused to set aside the judgment.

4.32 On appeal Burton P, sitting alone, stated that such cases involve a balance and that an employment judge should always consider the following:

(a) the employer's explanation as to why an extension of time is required: the more serious the delay, the more important it is that the employer provides a satisfactory and honest explanation, but the time limits for a respondent do not go to jurisdiction;
(b) the balance of prejudice: would the employer, if his request for an extension of time were refused, suffer a greater prejudice than that which the complainant would suffer if the extension of time were granted?
(c) the merits of the defence: if the employer's defence is shown to have some merit, justice will often favour the granting of an extension of time—otherwise the employer might be held liable for a wrong which he had not committed.

4.33 He also noted that although r 33 does not refer to the need for employment judges to exercise their discretion justly and equitably, they are obliged to deal with cases justly under the overriding objective set out in reg 3 of the 2004 Regulations, and that the principles in *Kwik Save v Swain* apply to the present rules as well as to the previous rules. In *Pestle and Mortar v Turner* UKEAT/0652/05 the employer had no good reason for not entering a response (it was posted late) but the EAT accepted that was only one factor, and the other factors—the prejudice suffered by the respondent, that there was an attempt to fax the response form within time, and that the actual delay was only two days—were more important.

E. COUNTERCLAIMS

4.34 If the claimant makes a complaint of breach of contract, the respondent may want to include a counterclaim and, if so, he must provide adequate details (pursuant to ETR 2004, r 7(1)). The judge may or may not then require a reply from the claimant depending upon the complexity of the issues. For the circumstances in which a counterclaim may be brought see paras 8.23 to 8.27.

5

Conciliation and Settlement

SUMMARY

(1) ACAS has a duty to endeavour to promote settlement of disputes. In respect of many claims ACAS's duty will extend only over a fixed period at the early stages of a claim.

(2) There are restrictions on contracting out of most statutory employment rights. A settlement of a dispute concerning a statutory employment right will not be effective unless it conforms with the requirements of an ACAS conciliated settlement agreement, or the requirements for a compromise agreement, or unless a consent order is made by the tribunal.

(3) If a settlement agreement does not meet the requirements of an ACAS conciliated agreement or a compromise agreement it will not prevent a claimant from pursuing a claim in the tribunal.

(4) If a party fails to perform a valid compromise agreement, the agreement can be enforced in the civil courts in an action for breach of contract. In limited circumstances a claim for breach of the settlement or compromise agreement can be brought in the tribunal.

(5) A settlement or compromise agreement may be set aside on grounds of mistake, misrepresentation, illegality, duress, or undue influence.

A. INTRODUCTION

5.01 Most civil disputes are resolved by compromise. This is as true, if not more so, of disputes in the employment tribunal as it is of disputes conducted in the civil courts. The court and tribunal systems in recent years have increasingly encouraged compromise and alternative dispute resolution as a means of easing the burden of litigation on the public purse. Parties to a dispute may view a compromise as an attractive solution for a number of reasons:

(a) it avoids the uncertainty of the trial process;
(b) there is a saving of cost, particularly relevant in the tribunal where costs are unlikely to be recovered even by the winning party;
(c) a compromise will often lead to a quicker solution than a trial, and therefore may avoid litigation becoming a distraction;
(d) a compromise may avoid publicity;
(e) parties may agree between themselves terms which are outside the tribunal's power to order by way of remedy (for example, terms as to an agreed reference or a protocol as to future behaviour).

5.02 It is open to the parties to reach a settlement at any stage from the moment when the dispute arises, before proceedings commence, until the moment before judgment is entered by the tribunal. Even after that point, the parties may settle a case between the decision and the hearing of any pending appeal. Many disputes are settled without the need for tribunal proceedings to be issued at all. Even where a claim is issued, the majority of cases settle without the need for a determination at a hearing. Throughout each stage of a claim in the tribunal the parties are likely to be involved in a process of assessment of the benefit of settlement, in the context of an analysis of the merits of each party's case and the time and cost of pursuing the claim to a hearing.

5.03 Where settlement is considered as an option, the following questions arise:

(a) By what process is settlement best achieved? There are a number of methods of alternative dispute resolution ('ADR'): private negotiation between the parties and their representatives; ACAS conciliation; ACAS arbitration; other forms of commercially provided mediation.
(b) What terms of agreement can be negotiated?
(c) Once an agreement is reached, how should the parties best give effect to the agreement?
(d) Once agreement is reached, how should the proceedings be disposed of consistent with the terms of the agreement?

5.04 There are a number of special features which impact upon settlement of disputes in the employment tribunal:

(a) A system is provided for the intervention of ACAS to assist in conciliation of most tribunal claims.
(b) As a matter of common law, an agreement to settle a claim is a contract like any other, and is subject to the normal rules of formation and interpretation of contracts. However, statute imposes stringent restrictions on contracting out of many statutory employment rights, and the capacity of parties to compromise many statutory rights is limited by important procedural restrictions.

5.05 We will outline the principles applicable to three methods of ADR (ACAS conciliation, ACAS arbitration, and mediation) before turning to consider in detail the statutory restrictions on settlements of statutory claims. A specimen compromise agreement, and drafting notes for compromise agreements, are contained at Section O of this chapter.

B. THE ROLE OF ACAS

Section 18 of ETA 1996 provides that where a claim under one of the relevant statutory jurisdictions has been presented before an employment tribunal, and a copy has been sent to a conciliation officer (which is required under s 19), then he must endeavour to promote a settlement if either (1) he receives a request from both parties to do so, or (2) he considers that he could act with a reasonable prospect of success of achieving such an outcome. The jurisdictions to which this provision applies are listed in s 18(1), and include all the principal jurisdictions of the employment tribunal. **5.06**

Once a tribunal claim has been presented the parties (or, as appropriate, their representatives) will receive a letter from ACAS informing them of the identity of the officer who has been 'assigned' to the case, and inviting the parties to contact that officer with a view to discussing whether a settlement can be reached. The role of the conciliation officer is to inform parties of their legal rights, examine the strengths and weaknesses of their case, and explore the options open to them. The conciliation officer may facilitate some bargaining to take place and if settlement is reached it is the parties and not the conciliation officer who determine the settlement. **5.07**

The process normally does not involve any face-to-face meetings between the parties. Rather, conciliation officers relay the perspectives of one party to the other. Officers will not reveal information that one party wishes to keep from the other, and information given to a conciliation officer in connection with conciliation is not admissible in evidence before a tribunal without the consent of the person who gave it. If conciliation does not resolve the dispute before the date fixed for the tribunal hearing, the matter will be decided by the employment tribunal. **5.08**

A conciliation officer may become involved even before any tribunal proceedings have been commenced. Section 18(3) of ETA 1996 provides that where a person claims that he has grounds for bringing a tribunal claim and, before any such application is made, either he or the potential respondent requests the conciliation officer to make his services available, then the conciliation officer shall endeavour to promote a settlement of any such proceedings which might be commenced. In order to justify the intervention of an officer, it is not necessary that the potential claimant has reached the stage of presenting a claim before the tribunal. To satisfy s 18(3), it is sufficient that a claim that a party has grounds to bring a tribunal claim may be implied from the acts and attitudes of the employee: *Moore v Duport Furniture Products Ltd* [1982] ICR 84, [1982] IRLR 31, HL. **5.09**

In June 2007 ACAS announced that it would extend its conciliation services to selected cases referred to it by the EAT. The type of cases expected to be referred by the EAT include: **5.10**

- cases where the parties' employment relationship is ongoing;
- cases which could be referred back to the employment tribunal; and
- appeals relating to monetary awards.

'Endeavour to promote a settlement'

What does the ACAS Conciliation Officer actually have to do to endeavour to promote settlement and thus meet his statutory obligations? The officer's role is to try and help the parties reach a settlement; but not to act as an arbitrator on the merits. Further, the conciliation officer: **5.11**

(a) has no duty, when promoting a financial settlement, to ensure that it is fair to both sides (see *Moore v Duport Furniture Products Ltd* [1982] ICR 84, [1982] IRLR 31, HL and *Clarke v Redcar & Cleveland Borough Council* [2006] ICR 897);
(b) does not have to explain to the parties the legislative framework in which the claim or potential claim is made; and

(c) does not have to advise the employee on his rights and remedies, and in fact advising a party as to the worth of his/her claim could actually undermine the function of the conciliation officer (see *Clarke v Redcar & Cleveland Borough Council* [2006] ICR 897).

Provided that the conciliation officer has not acted in bad faith or adopted unfair methods, a conciliated settlement cannot be set aside because he has failed in his duty (see *Slack v Greenham (Plant Hire) Ltd* [1983] ICR 617 and *Clarke* (above)).

5.12 Where the claim which has been presented, or which might be presented, is for unfair dismissal, the conciliation officer is required to seek to promote reinstatement or re-engagement (ETA 1996, s 18(4)). However, where reinstatement or re-engagement is either not desired by the complainant, or is not practicable (and it will usually be within one of these categories), the conciliation officer shall seek to promote an agreement for the payment of a cash sum. In many cases it will be plain that reinstatement or re-engagement is not practicable, and in such cases, an officer is not 'compelled, with no possibility of his doing any good at all, to go through the motions of acting in a way which was wholly inappropriate to the circumstances of the particular case with which he is concerned' (*Moore*, above).

5.13 A vital question is whether a conciliation officer is acting legitimately if he merely 'rubber stamps' an agreement which has already been reached before he came on the scene. In *Moore* the House of Lords gave a wide construction of the words now found in s 18 of ETA 1996 which require the officer to 'endeavour to promote a settlement'. Their Lordships said that the words were 'capable of covering whatever action by way of such promotion is applicable in the circumstances of the particular case'. In that case, the officer did not play any part in formulating the terms of the settlement. He suggested that the parties should meet and try to reach an agreement but was not present at the meeting. The House of Lords held that it was sufficient that once an agreement had been reached he recorded the terms on a COT3 form, and ensured that the parties understood those terms and the implications of signing them. The circumstances faced by the conciliation officer were that there was no prospect of reinstatement of the employee, and an amount of compensation had already been agreed. Therefore action under s 18(4) to promote reinstatement or to promote agreement as to the amount of compensation was futile and not applicable in the circumstances of the case. In the circumstances, the acts taken by the conciliation officer did amount to a sufficient degree to endeavouring to promote a settlement within the meaning of s 18(2).

Confidentiality

5.14 Anything communicated to the conciliation officer in connection with his endeavours to promote settlement is not admissible in evidence in any proceedings before an employment tribunal, except with the consent of the party making the communication: ETA 1996, s 18(7). Whether this is an absolute prohibition in respect of any and all communications, or whether the words in the subsection 'in connection with the performance of his functions under this section' imply a limitation on the scope of the prohibition analogous to the scope of protection afforded to 'without prejudice' communications, has not been the subject of any appellate decision.

5.15 Further in *Freer v Glover* [2006] IRLR 521 it was held that communications with a conciliation officer will be protected from defamation proceedings under the common law of absolute privilege and could not therefore be made use of in any proceedings. This case was determined under the common law relating to absolute privilege rather than on a construction of ETA 1996, s 18(7). In that case solicitors acting for the respondent to employment tribunal proceedings had written to the claimant indicating that the respondent would not be prepared to settle on any terms and that they would 'not be blackmailed by you and your friends'. The conciliation officer had been copied into the correspondence and the claimant subsequently issued defamation proceedings in the High Court against the respondent's solicitors. It was argued by the claimant that the relevant communication was not protected by absolute privilege because it was not a communication which was 'incidental to the dispute' since the respondent was indicating why it was not prepared to negotiate with the claimant on any terms. It was held, however, that the relevant communication was covered by absolute privilege since the conciliation officer was under a duty to promote settlement and in order to do so, it was necessary for her to understand why one or other of the parties was not willing to enter into negotiations. Therefore, the communication was incidental to the employment tribunal proceedings and absolute privilege was 'practically necessary for the administration of justice' and the situation fell within the scope of the rules of privilege as set out in *Lincoln v Daniels* [1962] 1 QB 237.

C. THE ACAS ARBITRATION SCHEME

ACAS has responsibility for an arbitration scheme under the Employment Rights (Dispute Resolution) Act 1998 as a means to resolve claims of unfair dismissal and flexible working claims. The arbitrator hears from both sides and then makes a binding decision. The decision is therefore the arbitrator's and the parties lose their power over the settlement. The arbitrator's award is final and the case cannot then proceed to a tribunal. Parties therefore make a choice between arbitration and going to court. **5.16**

The ACAS arbitration scheme was set up to offer a distinct alternative to tribunals, and one of its key features is that it is designed to be free of legalism. Hearings are private and confidential, and inquisitorial rather than adversarial. No cross-examination is permitted and clarification or questioning is conducted only through the arbitrator and with the arbitrator's permission. The parties are given the opportunity to state their own cases and comment on the case of the other side. The arbitrator rules on procedural and evidential matters rather than directly on points of law. The arbitrator can only make awards of compensation, reinstatement, and re-engagement, so the settlements reached are limited to those provided by law. **5.17**

In the arbitration scheme there is no appeal in respect to the arbitrator's award, except on grounds of serious irregularities. The scheme is voluntary so both parties will have to opt for it. **5.18**

D. MEDIATION

In mediation the mediator, an independent, neutral, third party, assists disputing parties to reach a settlement. The mediator is not a judge or arbitrator of the dispute before him and will not seek to impose a solution. Mediation does not attempt to determine the rights and wrongs of the case but to identify and focus on the real issues, and seek to create 'win–win' options for resolution that satisfy the needs of both parties. It is the parties, not the mediator, who decide the terms of the agreement, keeping the outcome of the dispute firmly in their hands. Like all ADR processes, mediation is voluntary, private, and informal. The process usually involves bringing the parties together for at least one face-to-face meeting, but the degree to which parties continue to meet in joint session will vary depending on the practice of the mediator and the willingness of the parties to have joint meetings. Mediators may give an opinion or make suggestions for settlement. They test the reality of the positions of the parties to a greater or lesser extent depending on the particular mediation. Giving an opinion on the merits is usually out of bounds. A pilot mediation scheme run by the employment tribunal itself was tested in the Birmingham, London, and Newcastle Regions, and since January 2009 the scheme has been rolled out to all Employment Tribunals for a specific subset of claims including many discrimination claims. The mediations may last for up to two days and will be conducted by employment judges as mediators. **5.19**

Mediation may be used for a range of non-statutory workplace disputes, such as disputes between employees or between employer and employee, and as a stage within an organization's grievance or complaints procedure. It may work especially well in harassment and discrimination cases which are the most intractable of the statutory rights and where the parties may have to continue to work together. Indeed, the Cambridge Study on Reform of Discrimination Law **5.20** recommended that there should be a pilot project to examine the use of mediation for sexual harassment cases. Courts may order a stay of proceedings pending mediation, in which case participation may be seen to lose some of its voluntary flavour.

5.21 Mediation is thus flexible in terms of both process and outcomes and may be ideally suited for problems concerned with relationships or behaviour. Mediated agreements can include protocols about future behaviour, a written apology, an explanation of what took place, and decisions about what might happen in the future. None of these is within the direct power of an employment tribunal or the court.

5.22 The majority of mediations last one day. Mediation may be particularly beneficial where the employee is still with the employer and all parties want to continue the relationship. The early resolution of problems coupled with the non-adversarial nature of mediation is more likely to restore and safeguard relationships.

5.23 A further key advantage of ADR for many parties is that it is private. While the public forum of an employment tribunal may be important in some cases, parties may prefer the more supportive and private forum that ADR processes provide. Although the Employment Tribunal Rules provide that there may be no reporting of sexual harassment cases (which are especially sensitive) during their hearings, the press may report such cases *after* the hearings are concluded, and there is no such restraint in other areas where embarrassing details may emerge.

5.24 In most cases, nothing said during mediation can be used against a party at a later time; the entire process is strictly 'without prejudice' to legal rights. If a satisfactory outcome is not reached through mediation, parties can still pursue a grievance or bring a claim to an employment tribunal (subject to time limits).

When to begin mediation

5.25 The general principle is the earlier the better, not least in order that the issue does not become more bitter as time goes on, but also because the cost and time savings are the greatest. However, it is inappropriate to hold a mediation if further documents or information have to be provided by one party to enable the other party to fully understand the first party's allegations. Also, part of mediation's flexibility is that it can be used at any stage in a dispute and can run in parallel to a formal grievance or tribunal process. Sometimes, conversely, time is a healer and the best time to mediate will be some time after a claim has been lodged.

5.26 If mediation is part of an organization's internal grievance or complaints process, then raising the mediation option with the other side is relatively easy. If a judge or tribunal recommends that mediation be attempted, the task of persuading the other side is considerably easier since it has been raised in a neutral way.

5.27 If mediation is neither part of an internal grievance process nor court-referred, the only way forward is to persuade the other side to try mediation. One party can approach the other party directly or indirectly. The direct approach is contact between the parties themselves or through their respective lawyers or representatives. The indirect approach to the other side is likely to be through a mediation provider, which has the advantage of giving the other party the opportunity to discuss any concerns and be informed about the process in more detail. Which approach to use will depend on the particular circumstances and personalities of each case. One way to facilitate the path to the mediation table is to offer to meet in order to discuss mediation and this can include a representative from a mediation provider.

The mediation agreement

5.28 The terms on which the mediation is to take place are usually outlined in a short document that should be agreed by the parties and the mediator. The mediation agreement sets out the practical details of the mediation such as the date, time, venue, selected mediator, etc. The agreement also establishes the legal features of the mediation such as its 'without prejudice' nature, confidentiality, mediator immunity, and authority to settle. The document should be simple and straightforward so that all parties will be willing to sign it. The mediation should be attended by those parties with first-hand knowledge of the issues and full authority to settle the dispute. If lawyers or other representatives do attend the mediation with their clients it is important that they understand that their role is not to represent their client in the traditional sense, but rather to support them in seeking a solution going forward.

It is common for parties to submit to the mediator a brief summary of the dispute (preferably agreed between them) highlighting the key issues from each of their perspectives. This can help parties to focus on the real issues in dispute that they wish to address. In many disputes there will also be some relevant documentation which it is appropriate for the mediator to see in advance. The case summaries and relevant documents are then exchanged between the parties and copied to the mediator at an agreed date before the mediation. Parties may bring additional documents to the mediation for only the mediator to see or send such documents to the mediator before the mediation. **5.29**

Length of the mediation

Most mediations (not including the pre-mediation meetings) take no longer than one day (ie about eight hours), but, occasionally, mediations last two or three days for particularly complex cases. The parties will decide in advance how long they want the mediation to last. Even if the mediation is agreed at eight hours, parties are usually keen for it to continue on the same day if there has been no settlement at the end of the eight hours and one is in sight. If so, the mediation will continue by consent either until the dispute is resolved or it is agreed that there will be no resolution. Occasionally, mediations are adjourned after they have started if, during the course of the mediation, it is agreed that the parties require further information and that the mediation cannot be resolved without that information. **5.30**

Often the parties use all the available time and do not make their best offer (or even close to their best) until the final stage of these proceedings. The length of a mediation depends on what parties feel comfortable with in terms of time and cost. Sometimes the mediator(s) will meet both parties separately prior to the mediation. This provides an opportunity for the mediator to become more familiar with the case, to establish rapport with both parties, and to address any concerns that they may have. Pre-mediation meetings have the advantage of freeing up more time on the day of the mediation since some of the exploratory stage will have taken place. **5.31**

Role of private meetings or caucuses

Private sessions between the mediator and the individual parties are a useful opportunity for open and confidential discussion of the issues and settlement options. They can be used for a variety of reasons, such as to examine privately the strengths and weaknesses of a particular proposal, to build more trust with each party, or to challenge positions and judgements. Private meetings (sometimes called caucuses) are usually crucial to progress in a mediation, and the degree to which a mediator will use them will depend on the mediator's preference and on the circumstances as they arise. A key aspect of the private meeting is its confidential nature and mediators should always check what can and cannot be conveyed to another party. The danger of using caucus meetings is that the mediator will become a shuttle negotiator, moving back and forth between the two parties until agreement is reached. Joint meetings are important for building relations and necessary trust between the parties and encouraging parties to see the process as one of working together to find a mutually acceptable agreement. As a result, many mediators encourage the parties to continue to have joint meetings throughout the day. **5.32**

The settlement agreement

At the conclusion of the mediation, the mediator may assist the parties to prepare a list of the points they have agreed upon. Once the agreement has been written it can be signed and **5.33** formally typed up later. No agreement will be considered to be legally binding until it is written down and signed by the parties or their authorized representatives in the form of a compromise agreement. It is important to ensure that the settlement which comes out of an employment mediation meets the criteria of compromise agreements within the Employment Rights Act 1996 because otherwise they will not restrain the employee from taking the issue to an employment tribunal (see para 5.37). The most important requirement is that the employee states that he or she has been independently advised by a relevant adviser.

Post-settlement issues

5.34 An important feature of mediation is that it may provide for a review process, which is not possible in the once and for all circumstance of the tribunal. This may be important in cases of, for example, alleged sexual harassment where the result may be that the 'harasser' is moved away from contact with the 'victim' or a protocol is agreed for future behaviour. In such cases it is important to build in a review mechanism after say six months with, possibly, provision for a further mediation session to be held then.

When is it suitable?

5.35 Any employment dispute, in theory, can be mediated; but mediation is not always the best option for resolving a dispute. The suitability of a case for mediation is determined less by the type of case and more by the circumstances of the individual case at the particular timeframe when the mediation takes place.

5.36 When there is a relationship to preserve, mediation is a better option since it is a non-adversarial process that unlike litigation or arbitration does not produce a winner and a loser but an acceptable settlement for both sides. Mediation is suitable especially when the parties want to save the time, money, and stress of a protracted dispute.

E. STATUTORY RESTRICTIONS ON SETTLEMENT OF CLAIMS

5.37 There are statutory restrictions on contracting out of or waiving most statutory employment rights. The policy behind these restrictions is to ensure that employees, who may be in a vulnerable position vis-à-vis their employers, are not subjected to improper pressure to give up their rights. These restrictions apply until all questions of liability and remedy have been determined by a tribunal (*Courage Take Home Trade Ltd v Keys* [1986] ICR 874, [1986] IRLR 427, EAT). There are exceptions to these restrictions which permit contracting out in narrowly defined circumstances where it is considered that employees are adequately protected. In the context of compromise of claims, the relevant exceptions are (1) ACAS conciliated settlements and (2) compromise agreements (referred to as compromise contracts in some statutes) meeting strict criteria.

5.38 Section 203 of ERA 1996 renders any provision in an agreement (whether a contract of employment or not) void insofar as it purports to exclude or limit the operation of any provision of ERA 1996, or to preclude a person from bringing any proceedings under ERA 1996 before an employment tribunal.

5.39 'Purports to exclude or limit' does not require a purpose or intention to exclude or limit the operation of a provision of s 203, but encompasses any term which has the effect of excluding such a provision, see *Joseph v Joseph* [1967] Ch 78, *per* Denning MR at 87F–G and Diplock LJ 89F–90D (in the context of similar language in s 38, Landlord and Tenant Act 1964), cited in *M & P Steelcraft Ltd v Ellis* [2008] IRLR 355, EAT.

5.40 In some cases, a difficult distinction may arise between a clause which purports to exclude a right, and a clause which forms part of the defining characteristics of a type of contract under which the rights never arise in the first place. On the one hand if, for example, a contract is not a contract of employment then a right not to be unfairly dismissed does not arise, and there are no rights which s 203 could protect. On the other hand, the courts look with caution on attempts to avoid s 203 by 'dressing up' an exclusion of rights which would otherwise arise as a contract under which the rights never arise in the first place, for example by a clause stating that an agreement (which would otherwise be a contract of employment) is not a contract of employment, or that it has no legal effect at all.

In *M & P Steelcraft* Elias J said that it would seriously weaken the policy objective which s 203 was designed to achieve if employers could, by the simple expedient of including a clause denying an agreement legal effect, thereby avoid the extensive statutory rights conferred upon employees. Elias J identified two questions, both of which must be satisfied if a clause is to fall foul of s 203. Firstly, but for the clause, would rights under the ERA 1996 be enforceable? Secondly, is the only purpose of the clause to alter, or seek to alter, what would, absent the clause, be the legal effect of the contractual arrangements? **5.41**

Similar provisions to s 203 in relation to compromises of statutory claims are found in TULR(C) A 1992, s 288; the Working Time Regulations 1998, SI 1998/1833, reg 35; the National Minimum Wage Act 1998, s 49; and the Transnational Information and Consultation of Employees Regulations 1999, SI 1999/3323, reg 41. See also the Part-time Workers (Prevention of Less Favourable Treatment) Regulations 2000, SI 2000/1551, reg 9 and the Fixed Term Employees (Prevention of Less Favourable Treatment) Regulations 2002, SI 2002/2034, reg 10, which apply ERA 1996, s 203 to those regulations. This chapter focuses on s 203 of ERA 1996, the most commonly encountered of these provisions. The analysis of that section applies equally to these equivalent provisions. **5.42**

The approach in relation to claims under TUPE 2006 is complex. TUPE, reg 18 provides that s 203 of ERA 1996 shall apply in relation to TUPE 2006 as if they were contained in the ERA 1996, save that that section shall not apply in so far as TUPE 2006 provides for an agreement (whether in a contract of employment or not) to exclude or limit the operation of the Regulations. A claim based upon TUPE 2006 may arise in two ways: **5.43**

(1) where a claim based on breach of TUPE 2006 takes the form of a complaint under an existing jurisdiction of ERA 1996 (such as unfair dismissal or unlawful deduction from wages), ERA 1996, s 203 applies in the usual way, as described above; or
(2) where the claim is a freestanding claim under TUPE 2006, such as a failure to notify employee liability information (reg 12), or failure to inform or consult (reg 15), ETA 1996, s 18 is deemed to apply to such a claim (reg 12(7) and reg 16(1)), and the claim may thus be settled by an ACAS conciliated settlement under ERA 1996, s 203(e). However, it appears that such a claim cannot be compromised by a compromise agreement under ERA 1996, s 203(2)(f). Section 203(2)(f) applies only to claims under certain specified paragraphs of ETA 1996, s 18 (as listed in s 203(2)(f) itself), and claims under reg 12 and reg 15 TUPE 2006 are not included in the list. A similar problem existed under TUPE 1981: see *Solectron Scotland Ltd v Roper* [2004] IRLR 4, EAT.

The formulation in respect of discrimination claims is slightly different; rather than rendering the relevant provision in an agreement void, s 77(3) of SDA 1975 provides that a term in a contract which purports to exclude or limit any provision of the Act is 'unenforceable by any person in whose favour the term would operate apart from this subsection'. See also in the same terms: RRA 1976, s 72(2); DDA 1995, Sch 3A, para 1(3); the Employment Equality (Sexual Orientation) Regulations 2003, SI 2003/497, Sch 4, para 1(3); the Employment Equality (Religion or Belief) Regulations 2003, SI 2003/1660, Sch 4, para 1(3); and the Employment Equality (Age) Regulations 2006, SI 2006/1031, Sch 5, para 1(3). There are also exceptions relating to conciliated settlements and compromise agreements similar to those under ERA 1996, s 203. **5.44**

Where these statutory restrictions apply, a dispute may be compromised in the following ways: **5.45**

(a) By an agreement reached as a result of an ACAS conciliation (ERA 1996, s 203(2)(e); SDA 1975, s 77(4)(a)).

(b) By an agreement complying with the requirements for a compromise agreement (ERA 1996, s 203(2)(f)) or a compromise contract (SDA 1975, s 77(4)(aa)).

5.46 Further, any claim can be compromised by the parties causing or permitting the tribunal to make a judgment or order disposing of the proceedings by consent. Each of these methods of settlement will be considered in detail below.

5.47 There are no statutory restrictions on compromise of common law claims (ie breach of contract claims) brought in the employment tribunals. Such claims may be settled by agreement in the same manner as any other civil proceedings. An agreement to compromise a contract claim may be valid even if it is contained in an agreement which also contains a void compromise of statutory claims (*Sutherland v Network Appliances Ltd* [2001] IRLR 12; *Lunt v Merseyside TEC* [1999] IRLR 458, EAT).

5.48 It would appear also that the statutory restrictions do not preclude an agreement to refrain from appealing a decision to the EAT. The EAT in *Hoeffler v Kwik Save Stores* EAT/803/97 held that s 77 of SDA 1975 did not restrict the rights of parties to compromise a right of appeal to the EAT. The EAT also held that the agreement was in any event void as it also compromised the claimant's right to have a determination of remedy for a complaint of unfair dismissal, an agreement which undoubtedly was covered by s 203 of ERA 1996. On the terms of the particular agreement before it, the EAT was unable to separate out the parts of the agreement dealing with sex discrimination and those concerning unfair dismissal.

5.49 The reasoning in *Hoeffler* on the latter point is open to doubt. As Lindsay J pointed out in *Sutherland*, the effect of s 203(1) is not that any agreement which includes a requirement in contravention of its terms is totally void. It is not even that the whole of any separately identifiable provision which includes a requirement in contravention of s 203 is void. What is rendered void is only that provision 'in so far as it purports' to exclude or preclude a right to claim in contravention of s 203. Where a provision in an agreement offends s 203 so far as it relates to statutory claims, we would suggest that there is no reason to sweep aside the whole contract.

5.50 Whether a settlement is contained in a conciliated agreement or in a compromise agreement or contract, the determination whether the agreement applies to prohibit any particular claim by a claimant depends on two questions:

(a) As a matter of construction of the contract, does the agreement cover the claim?
(b) If, as a matter of contract, the agreement would settle the claim, is the agreement rendered ineffective by the statutory restrictions on contracting out?

We now consider both issues in turn.

F. CONSTRUCTION OF THE CONTRACT

5.51 Whether the settlement is contained in a compromise agreement or in a COT3 it will always be a question of construction of the agreement as to precisely what claims were intended by the parties to be settled by the agreement. As a matter of common law, a COT3 or compromise agreement will be interpreted in accordance with the normal principles of contractual interpretation. The general contractual principles summarized in *Investors Compensation Scheme Ltd v West Bromwich Building Society* [1998] 1 WLR 896, HL, 912–13 (*per* Lord Hoffman) apply to the construction of such agreements: *BCCI v Ali* [2001] UKHL 8, [2001] IRLR 292, para 8, *per* Lord Bingham.

5.52 The more clearly the claims are set out in the agreement, the less room there will be for uncertainty. In *BCCI v Ali* above, for example, the employee had signed a COT3 in the widest terms: in return for a sum of money the agreement was stated to be 'in full and final settlement of all or any claims . . . of whatever nature that exist or may exist'. At the time of the COT3 the employee had no reason to believe that he had any basis for claiming stigma damages arising out of the corrupt manner in which it transpired that BCCI had conducted its business over many years. Later, in the wake of the decision in *Malik v BCCI* [1998] AC 20, HL to the effect that stigma damages might be claimed in such circumstances, he wished to bring such a claim. As the compromise concerned a contractual rather than a statutory claim, there was no *statutory* restriction on the employees contracting out of their rights. The issue was thus whether the employee had, as a matter of *contract*, compromised rights of which he was not and could not have been aware at the time of making the agreement. The House of Lords held that there was no reason in principle to prevent a party from compromising, in an agreement supported by valuable consideration, rights of which he was not and could not be aware. However, the courts will be slow to infer that he had done so in the absence of clear language to such effect. Despite the apparently wide language of the agreement, the House of Lords held that on its true construction neither party had intended to compromise claims which they could never have had in contemplation.

In *Royal National Orthopaedic Trust v Howard* [2002] IRLR 849, EAT, the claimant entered into a COT3 agreement under which she accepted a payment on the following terms (at para 2): **5.53**

> In full and final settlement of these proceedings and of all claims which the claimant has or may have against the respondent (save for claims for personal injury and in respect of occupational pension rights) whether arising under her contract of employment or out of the termination thereof on 29 November 1998, or arising under the Employment Rights Act 1996, the Sex Discrimination Act 1975 or under European Community law.

She subsequently brought a claim of victimization under the SDA 1975, and alleged that the act of victimization occurred after the date of the COT3. The question was whether she had effectively compromised any claims in respect of future acts by the COT3. The EAT rejected an argument that as a matter of public policy parties could not agree to settle claims of which they were unaware, or claims which had not yet come into existence. The question was thus a matter of interpretation of the agreement as to whether the parties had intended to compromise such claims. The EAT followed the approach in *Ali*: **5.54**

> If the parties seek to achieve such an extravagant result that they release claims of which they have and can have no knowledge, whether those claims have already come into existence or not, they must do so in language which is absolutely clear and leaves no room for doubt as to what it is they are contracting for.

The EAT found that the agreement did not have the effect of compromising future claims, and that 'have or may have' did not suggest that the agreement included future claims. However, the EAT's comments that there is in principle no restriction on the ability to contract out of future claims were in the context of an analysis of the position at common law. Having decided that, as a matter of construction, the contract did *not* cover future claims, the EAT did not need to decide whether there was any statutory restriction on contracting out of future claims, and it declined to do so. The most that it was prepared to say was that it had 'some doubts' as to whether the tribunal had been right that a COT3 agreement made under s 18 of ETA 1996 is not capable of compromising a future cause of action. The difficult issue of exclusion of future claims was also considered in *Hilton UK Hotels Ltd v McNaughton* UKEAT/0059/04, where a list of statutory claims covered by the agreement was prefaced by the words 'all claims that you believe you have against the company for. . .' The reference to the employee's belief indicated that the agreement could not cover future claims, of the existence of which the employee was unaware at the time of the agreement.

Difficult issues also arose in *University of East London v Hinton* [2005] EWCA Civ 532, [2005] IRLR 552. The relevant clause of a compromise agreement said that the agreement was: **5.55**

> in full and final satisfaction of all claims in all jurisdictions (whether arising under statute, common law or otherwise) which the employee has or may have against the University officers [*sic*] or employees arising out of or in connection with his employment with the University, the termination of his employment or otherwise including in particular the following claims which have been raised by or on behalf of the Employee as being claims which he may have for. . .

There then followed a long list of claims, which did not include the claim eventually brought by the claimant in the tribunal (a claim under s 47B of ERA 1996 of detriment by reason of whistle-blowing).

5.56 The main interest in the decision in *Hinton* is the Court of Appeal's analysis of the requirement under s 203 of ERA 1996 that a compromise agreement must '*relate to* the particular proceedings'. This point is dealt with in para 5.67 below. However, the Court of Appeal also dealt with the contractual construction of the clause. Purely as a matter of contractual construction, the agreement covered the s 47B claim in general terms, even though the claim was not specifically referred to. It should be noted that in contrast to the situations in *Ali* and *Royal National Orthopaedic Trust* above, the s 47B claim did arise on facts which occurred prior to the date of the agreement. The omission of express reference to it appears to have been a drafting error. However, the language of the clause was in very broad terms, and the list was illustrative, not exhaustive. Another example is *Palihakkara v British Telecommunications plc* UKEAT/0185/06, where a compromise of claims 'arising out of the termination of employment' did not compromise claims existing prior to the date of termination.

G. STATUTORY REQUIREMENTS FOR COMPROMISE AGREEMENTS

5.57 It is possible for the parties to reach a binding settlement of statutory claims without the intervention of a conciliation officer but only by entering into a compromise agreement (or compromise contract) which has its own criteria which must be met. In order for a compromise agreement in relation to a claim under ERA 1996 to be valid, it must fulfil the following conditions (ERA 1996, s 203(3)):

(a) the agreement must be in writing;
(b) the agreement must relate to the particular proceedings;
(c) the employee or worker must have received advice from a relevant independent adviser as to the terms and effect of the proposed agreement and in particular its effect on his ability to pursue his rights before a tribunal;
(d) the adviser must be covered by a contract of insurance or an indemnity provided for members of a profession or professional body in respect of any claim which may be brought by the employee in respect of loss caused by the advice;
(e) the agreement must identify the adviser;
(f) the agreement must state that the conditions regulating compromise agreements under the Act are satisfied.

5.58 The provisions in relation to discrimination claims are identical, save that, as noted above, the expression 'compromise contract' is used instead of compromise agreement for reasons which are obscure. (In this chapter the expression 'compromise agreement' is used to refer also to 'compromise contracts' unless otherwise stated in the text.) The contract must also relate to 'the particular complaint': see, for example, SDA 1975, s 77(4A)(b). See Section O of this chapter for a specimen compromise agreement, and drafting notes.

Claims which may be covered by a compromise agreement

Agreement reached prior to the issue of proceedings

5.59 Although s 203(3)(b) refers to particular 'proceedings' a compromise agreement may be used to settle a cause of action where proceedings have not yet been issued: *University of East London v Hinton* [2005] EWCA Civ 532, [2005] IRLR 552, para 17(6). Section 203(2) refers to an agreement 'to refrain from instituting or continuing any proceedings'. If a compromise agreement could not be used before proceedings were issued the reference to refraining from 'instituting' proceedings could not be given effect; see also *Bennett v De Vere Hotels Ltd* EAT/1113/95, IDS Employment Law Brief 568, applying the same reasoning. The Court of Appeal in *Hinton* observed that no sensible or useful purpose would be served by requiring an employee to issue proceedings for the sole purpose of enabling a valid compromise agreement to be made.

The legislative wording in SDA 1975, RRA 1976, and DDA 1995 is somewhat different from s 203: for example, s 77(4)(aa) of SDA 1975 refers to 'a contract settling a complaint to which section 63(1) applies' (s 63(1) provides for a complaint that a person has committed an unlawful act of discrimination to be presented to the employment tribunal). The better view is that a compromise agreement can settle a complaint even if tribunal proceedings have not been instituted: the section refers to complaints which 'may be presented to an employment tribunal' rather than that they 'have been presented'. Moreover, as a matter of policy, there is every reason why the various statutory provisions should be interpreted consistently. The Court of Appeal's reasoning in *Hinton* that it would be pointless to have to issue proceedings purely to be able to enter into a valid compromise agreement applies equally to cases of discrimination. **5.60**

More than one complaint/proceedings

A single compromise agreement may be used to settle more than one cause of action or set of proceedings: *Lunt v Merseyside TEC Ltd* [1999] IRLR 458; *Hinton* above, para 17(7). **5.61**

Relating to the particular proceedings

Section 203(3)(b) requires the agreement to relate to 'the particular proceedings' (the formulation in the discrimination statutes is 'the particular complaint': for example, SDA 1975, s 77(4A)(b)). The legislative policy is to protect employees from signing away rights except where a number of closely defined conditions have all been satisfied. As the Court of Appeal commented in *Hinton*, the code of protection set out in ERA 1996 would be worthless if it could be removed, at the stroke of a pen, by a general release or waiver. A compromise agreement cannot therefore be used to achieve a 'clean break' settlement of all conceivable claims, whether presently contemplated by the parties or not. **5.62**

A compromise agreement thus cannot be made in respect of claims which have not been raised by the employee, although until the decision of the Court of Appeal in *Hinton* a degree of latitude was allowed as to the complaints which would be regarded as having been raised and capable of settlement. **5.63**

It thus may be sufficient that a complaint has been made in correspondence. In *Lunt v Merseyside TEC Ltd* [1999] IRLR 458 the claimant had raised a number of different complaints in correspondence. She later signed a compromise agreement expressed to be 'in full and final settlement of all claims that [she] may have, whether arising out of her employment or its termination'. The EAT held that the compromise agreement was effective in respect of those matters about which she had complained in correspondence, and expressly adopted a passage from *Harvey on Industrial Relations and Employment Law*: **5.64**

> A compromise agreement cannot seek to exclude potential complaints that have not yet arisen on the off-chance that they might be raised. However, where a number of different claims have been raised by the employee, whether in an originating application or in correspondence prior to the issue of the proceedings, there does not seem to be any good reason why these should not all be disposed of in the one compromise agreement.

However, in *Hinton* the Court of Appeal held that *Lunt* could not be regarded as authority for the proposition that the words 'relate to' in s 203(3)(b) simply refer to proceedings or claims which have been raised, as opposed to the necessity of setting them out in the body of the compromise agreement. The Court of Appeal said that *Lunt* was not directed to the 'particular proceedings' point arising under s 203(3)(b) and is not authority on it. **5.65**

In *Byrnell v British Telecommunications plc* UKEAT/0383/04 the compromise agreement purported to be in full and final settlement of all claims 'both contemplated and not contemplated at the date hereof'. The EAT held that the subsequent claim for unfair dismissal and sex discrimination had been validly compromised, on the basis that prior to the agreement (1) the claimant had raised with his employers a potential claim for unfair dismissal, and the facts **5.66** of the discrimination claim were closely linked to the unfair dismissal claim; and (2) he had received advice from his solicitor in relation to both unfair dismissal and sex discrimination, a fact recorded in the compromise agreement itself. The EAT declined to comment on whether the agreement to compromise claims 'not contemplated' could be valid, but it is difficult to see how such a provision could satisfy the statutory requirement that the agreement relate to a particular complaint.

5.67 The requirement that the agreement relate to 'particular proceedings' was given a restrictive interpretation by the Court of Appeal in *Hinton*. In that case, the Court decided that purely as a matter of contractual construction the compromise was wide enough to cover the whistle-blowing claim brought by the claimant even though the claim was not specifically referred to (see para 5.56 above). However, the agreement fell foul of s 203(3)(b). The Court of Appeal held that the agreement did not cover the whistle-blowing claim, because there was no reference to either the factual or statutory basis for such a claim. The effect of the decision of the Court of Appeal is that the proceedings will need to be clearly identified in the agreement itself in order to be sure that they have been compromised. A general waiver such as 'all statutory rights' or 'all claims' is not sufficient for this purpose. The agreement must instead identify the particular claims to be covered. Smith LJ, going further than Mummery LJ, stated that it would not be enough to refer to *all* rights provided for under a particular statute (at least where the particular statute includes a number of rights). Either the particular claim must be identified by description (for example, 'unfair dismissal') or by the section number of the statute under which it arises.

5.68 The Court of Appeal indeed went so far as to suggest that as a matter of good practice the agreement should contain a brief factual and legal description of the nature of the allegations and the statute under which they are made or the common law basis for the claims, irrespective of whether the claim being compromised is the subject of proceedings, or whether or not proceedings have yet been issued.

Independent adviser

5.69 A 'relevant independent adviser' is defined as one of the following (ERA 1996, s 203(3A)):

(a) a qualified lawyer (ie a solicitor or barrister, or in Scotland an advocate);
(b) a trade union officer, employee, or member who has been certified by the union as competent to give such advice and is authorized to do so on behalf of the union;
(c) a worker or volunteer at an advice centre who has been certified by the centre as competent to give advice, and is authorized to do so on behalf of the centre; or
(d) a person of a description specified in an Order made by the Secretary of State (no Order yet having been made).

5.70 However, an adviser is not independent:

(a) if he is employed by or acting in the matter for the employer; or
(b) in the case of a union or advice centre, if the union or the advice centre is the employer; or
(c) in respect of advice from a worker at an advice centre, if the employee makes a payment for the advice received from that worker.

5.71 The Government consulted on a proposal to extend the scope of relevant independent advisers to include members of the Chartered Institute of Personnel and Development (see 'Dispute Resolution: Secondary legislation consultation', Department for Business, Enterprise and Regulatory Reform, July 2008). However, the response to the consultation was mixed and in December 2008 the Government indicated that they would not extend the scope of relevant independent advisers at this time.

The advice

5.72 The relevant independent adviser must give advice as to the terms and effect of the proposed agreement and in particular its effect on the claimant's ability to pursue his rights before a tribunal: ERA 1996, s 203(3)(b). With regard to the advice as to the 'terms and effect of the agreement', the adviser must give a view on whether the terms being offered are in the interests of the employee, or whether he should seek an improvement on them. However, the agreement is still valid even if, against the advice of the adviser, the employee signs it. Thus, the adviser does not have to *approve* the deal; he merely has to *advise* on it. Provided that advice is given by an appropriate adviser, the tribunal will not inquire into the nature or quality of the advice. The only issue is whether advice has been given. If the employee clearly acknowledges in the compromise agreement that such advice has been given, the agreement itself will be sufficient evidence that the requirements of the statute have been met: *Hilton UK Hotels Ltd v McNaughton* UKEAT/0059/04, para 22.

Further, there is no legal requirement that the adviser actually sign the agreement to confirm that he has given the advice. Section 203(3)(e) requires only that the agreement *identifies* the adviser. It is, however, considered good practice for the adviser to sign a declaration (usually as a schedule to the agreement) that he is a relevant legal adviser, is covered by appropriate insurance, and that he has given advice for the purposes of s 203(3). 5.73

As regards paying the adviser, there is no legal requirement on the employer to meet any costs incurred by the employee in obtaining the requisite advice, although many employers are prepared to do so. 5.74

H. ACAS CONCILIATED SETTLEMENTS

The role played by ACAS in facilitating settlement has been considered at para 5.06 above. This section considers the requirements which must be satisfied for an agreement facilitated by ACAS to comply with s 203 of ERA 1996 and its equivalents. 5.75

Effect of ACAS facilitated settlement

Section 203(2)(e) of ERA 1996 and its equivalents provide that the rule rendering void an agreement by an employee not to pursue his statutory rights 'does not apply to any agreement to refrain from instituting or continuing proceedings where a conciliation officer has taken action under section 18 of the Employment Tribunals Act 1996'. 5.76

Section 77(4)(a) of SDA 1975 and its equivalents provide that where such an agreement is made '"with assistance of" a conciliation offer, then it is likewise binding'. 5.77

FORM OF SETTLEMENT

There are no special formal requirements for an agreement reached through an ACAS conciliation, in contrast to the requirements for a valid compromise agreement set out at para 5.57 above. Indeed a settlement is binding once terms have been agreed orally with the conciliation officer, even if the COT3 is not subsequently signed by a party (*Gilbert v Kembridge Fibres Ltd* [1984] IRLR 52). Hence parties should be careful when discussing settlement terms with a conciliation officer, and if they have any doubts as to whether they wish to accept the terms that are being proposed, they ought to tell the officer that they wish to consider them further and then revert to him. In practice, the settlement agreement is almost invariably reduced to writing. Form COT3 is provided by ACAS for this purpose. Where an ACAS settlement has been reached, ETR 2004, r 25A provides the mechanism for dismissal of the proceedings. 5.78

Scope of settlement

In contrast to a compromise agreement, an ACAS conciliated settlement need not relate to 'particular proceedings', or to a 'particular complaint'. An ACAS conciliated settlement may indeed be used to achieve a full and final settlement of all claims arising out of the claimant's employment or its termination. However, care must be taken to properly identify 5.79

the claims covered by the agreement, and the claims in respect of which the ACAS officer is taking steps.

5.80 An ACAS officer will not be presumed to be taking steps to conciliate all possible claims which could arise between the parties, and unless the parties tell the officer they wish to achieve a final clean break, and provide for this in their agreement, then there is a risk that the agreement will be taken as settling only the immediate proceedings which were before the tribunal. In *Livingstone v Hepworth Refractories plc* [1992] IRLR 63, the EAT held that the ACAS officer is to be taken to be dealing with complaints within the presumed contemplation of the parties at the time of the agreement. It held that a COT3 agreement drawn up pursuant to s 203 of ERA 1996 does not cover a claim under SDA 1975 or EqPA 1970 unless expressly stated to do so. The COT3 agreement in *Livingstone* stated that it was 'in full and final settlement of all claims which the claimant may have against the respondent arising from his employment with the respondent or out of its termination' save for personal injury and pension exclusions. On the face of it, it is difficult to see why such wide language would not cover a claim under the SDA. It should be noted, however, that the particular claim which was held not to be covered by the agreement only became open to the claimant following a decision of the ECJ which post-dated the COT3: *Barber v Guardian Royal Exchange Assurance Group* [1990] IRLR 240. The decision is perhaps best explained on the basis that the parties should not be taken as having in their contemplation a future claim which is not open to the claimant at the time of the agreement being reached. In the light of *Livingstone*, whilst it is possible to achieve a 'clean break' in a COT3 form it would seem prudent to make as clear as possible the precise claims to which the settlement relates, preferably by reference to statutory provisions. We deal further with the construction of the meaning of settlements as a matter of common law at paras 5.51–5.56 above.

I. EFFECT OF AN AGREEMENT WHERE THE STATUTORY REQUIREMENTS HAVE NOT BEEN MET

5.81 Where a settlement agreement does not meet the strict requirements of statute, the employee is not precluded from bringing an action in the employment tribunal. This is well illustrated by the EAT's decision in *Riverside Health Authority v Chetty* EAT/1168/95. In that case, the claimants had entered into an agreement in which they accepted payments 'in full and final settlement' of their unfair dismissal claims. However, the settlement agreement did not satisfy the conditions of being a compromise agreement. Both the tribunal and the EAT refused to strike out the claims.

5.82 If a settlement agreement fails in any respect to satisfy the requirements for a compromise agreement, the employee is entitled to pursue proceedings, even if the failure is what might be regarded as a minor technicality. In *Lunt v Merseyside TEC Ltd* [1999] IRLR 458, an agreement dealing with a number of claims, including unfair dismissal and sex discrimination, failed to state that the conditions regulating compromise under SDA 1975 had been satisfied, although it did state that the equivalent conditions under ERA 1996 had been satisfied. The agreement was thus a valid compromise of the unfair dismissal complaint, but was void in relation to the sex discrimination complaint. See *Palihakkara v British Telecommunications plc* UKEAT/0185/06 to similar effect.

5.83 In *CPS v Bamieh* EAT/309/99, the parties had apparently concluded a compromise agreement (but not signed it) one working day before the tribunal hearing was due to commence. When the case was about to begin, however, the claimant indicated that she was not prepared to continue with the agreement. The tribunal found that it was in the interests of justice for the case to proceed, and the EAT rejected an appeal on the basis that, if it was necessary to conduct a 'trial within a trial' to determine whether the agreement was reached, the power to strike out should not be exercised. It was also held not to be necessary for the tribunal to recuse themselves because they had been made aware of the agreement.

In the cases mentioned above, the claimant changed his or her mind about the compromise *before* the proceedings were disposed of. Where the claimant agrees to a compromise, and on the basis of that compromise withdraws his claim or otherwise permits it to be dismissed by the tribunal, then the claimant will be bound by that dismissal, even though he would not have been bound by the agreement which led to it: see *Mayo-Deman v University of Greenwich* [2005] IRLR 845, EAT. There is nothing to prevent a party from voluntarily abandoning proceedings, but what cannot be done is to compel him to do so because of an agreement he made, if he changes his mind before he does so abandon them. Once proceedings are abandoned they cannot be resuscitated, see *Times Newspapers Ltd v Fitt* [1981] ICR 637; *Council of Engineering Institutions v Maddison* [1977] ICR 30. In relation to proceedings which are withdrawn but not dismissed see para 5.93 below. **5.84**

In *Carter v Reiner Moritz Ltd* [1997] ICR 881, EAT, the tribunal dealing with a remedy hearing found that there had been an agreement to compromise claims for a certain sum, but that the agreement fell foul of the predecessor to s 203 (EP(C)A 1978, s 140). The tribunal nonetheless awarded compensation in the sum upon which the parties had agreed even though the claimant's solicitors had indicated almost immediately after the purported agreement that a mistake had been made in calculating the figure. The EAT held that s 140 did not preclude the parties from reaching an agreement, albeit that such an agreement has to be considered by the tribunal and would not become enforceable unless the tribunal exercised its discretion to make an order in the terms of the agreement. It must be doubted whether the tribunal would have a discretion to make an order in the terms of the agreement in such circumstances. If the agreement falls foul of s 203, then a party cannot be precluded from changing his mind and abandoning the agreement. If the agreement is not binding, and one party no longer consents to its terms, then the tribunal cannot, we consider, make an order by consent. If a tribunal has a discretion to give effect to an agreement which the claimant has rejected, then the claimant is deprived of the protection of s 203. It is difficult to see on what principles the tribunal could exercise such a discretion. **5.85**

That is not to say that a tribunal will disregard the fact that a void agreement has been reached, if sums have been paid under that agreement. Sums paid will be taken into account in the assessment of any compensation due if the claim succeeds. In *Courage Take Home Trade Ltd v Keys* [1986] ICR 874, for example, the claimant agreed a sum in settlement of his claim, received the agreed monies, and then continued with his claim. As the agreement was not a valid compromise agreement he could not be prevented from pursuing the claim, but the EAT held that in assessing compensation, and taking into account the sums which he had already received, it would not be just and equitable to make any award of compensation. A claimant who proceeded in such circumstances but did not recover more than the sum originally agreed would be at risk of an order for costs. **5.86**

J. ENFORCEMENT OF A SETTLEMENT AGREEMENT

Where a party fails to comply with the terms of the compromise agreement, the aggrieved party may sue in the civil courts in the normal way in an action for breach of contract. The aggrieved party may claim damages for breach of contract, and may be able to claim specific performance of the agreement. In a clear case of breach of a binding compromise agreement, the aggrieved party may be able to obtain summary judgment from the court, but in any event, a claim in the courts is likely to be expensive and time consuming. Since 1 April 2009 an ACAS approved settlement is generally enforceable as if it were a county court order. s 19A ETA 1996 (introduced by the Tribunals Courts and Enforcement Act 2007 s 142). **5.87**

In some circumstances it may be possible to sue on the agreement in the tribunal, but only if the claim can be said to be a contract claim within the meaning of the Employment Tribunals Extension of Jurisdiction Orders 1994, SI 1994/1623 and SI 1994/1624. For the tribunal to have jurisdiction over a claim for breach of contract under the Order, the claim must be **5.88** for breach of an employment contract, or a contract connected with employment. In *Rock-It Cargo v Green* [1997] IRLR 581, the EAT held that where an employer failed to pay to a former employee the sums due under a compromise agreement, the compromise agreement could be sued on in the tribunal as an agreement connected with employment.

5.89 It should be noted, however, that under art 3(c) of the 1994 Orders a further jurisdictional requirement is that the claim arises or is outstanding on termination of employment. In *Rock-It Cargo* the compromise agreement was made and was breached *prior* to termination of employment, and it was thus conceded that the claim was outstanding on termination of employment. Where a compromise agreement is made *after* termination, the claim cannot be said to arise or be outstanding on the termination of employment. This was indeed the conclusion reached (albeit reluctantly) by the EAT in *Miller Bros & F P Butler Ltd v Johnston* [2002] IRLR 386. Further, given that the claim in the contract case arises from the breach of contract and not the formation of the contract, it would seem that where a compromise agreement is made prior to termination, but the breach does not occur until after termination, the conditions of art 3(c) would not be satisfied.

K. CONSENT ORDERS

5.90 Very often, parties reach settlement at the tribunal just before the hearing; it is indeed often because the parties realize the weakness of their case and start worrying about cross-examination by the other side. Settlement may hold added attractions for the claimant/employee who has received, before the hearing, substantial state benefit payments since, if an award is made by a tribunal, such benefits received must be paid back, but this is not required to be done in an out-of-court settlement (including where agreement as to the compensation to be paid to the claimant is reached after a finding by the tribunal on liability). Settlement in these circumstances may also have attraction for the respondent employer who may be able to reduce his liability for the same reason (see Chapter 26 for detailed consideration of the recoupment provisions).

5.91 In such cases, it may not be practicable to involve a conciliation officer, nor to enter into a compromise agreement (for example because one of the parties does not have access to independent legal advice). The normal practice when a late settlement is reached in this manner is to ask the tribunal to make a consent order. If both or all the parties agree in writing upon the terms of a decision to be made by the tribunal, the tribunal may decide accordingly (ETR 2004, r 28(2)).

5.92 However, the parties may be reluctant to incorporate the party's agreement into a decision entered by consent, to avoid the risk of an order for the payment of money being subject to the recoupment provisions referred to above. Arguably the recoupment provisions would not apply where a tribunal makes an order in the terms of an agreed sum, particularly if the sum is a single lump sum which does not separately identify the basic award, past loss of earnings, and future loss of earnings to be paid. In practice many practitioners, to avoid any risk of recoupment, ask the tribunal to dismiss the claim on withdrawal on the basis of terms agreed between the parties and contained in a schedule to the dismissal order (see further under the heading of 'Tomlin Orders' below). If confidentiality is required, terms of settlement may be merely endorsed on counsel's brief, or by a separate agreement by representatives.

5.93 A claimant may withdraw all or part of his claim at any time by notifying the tribunal office (ETR 2004, r 25). The withdrawal takes effect on the date the tribunal receives notification and the proceedings are brought to an end on that date (save in relation to costs, wasted costs, or preparation time). Where a claim is withdrawn a respondent may apply to have the claim against him dismissed (r 25(4)). If the proceedings are dismissed, the claimant may not commence a further claim against the respondent for the same or substantially the same cause of action. Where proceedings are withdrawn but not dismissed, the proceedings cannot be continued, but there is no cause of action estoppel barring a second set of proceedings on the same cause of action (*Khan v Heywood & Middleton Primary Care Trust* [2006] EWCA Civ 1087, [2006]

IRLR 793). For cause of action estoppel see further para 11.98 *et seq.*; for further commentary on r 25(4) see para 11.105 *et seq.* ETR 2004, r 25A provides a mechanism for dismissal where a claim, or part of it, is withdrawn following an ACAS brokered settlement.

Once an order has been made dismissing the claim there is no scope to argue that the agreement which led to the dismissal fell foul of s 203 of ERA 1996 (or its equivalents in other legislation). A tribunal is not required to ensure that an agreement for proceedings to be dismissed complies with s 203 (or its equivalents) before it permits a claim to be dismissed: *Mayo-Deman v University of Greenwich* [2005] IRLR 845, EAT. Section 203 is designed to protect employees from entering into misguided bargains before their claim is heard by the tribunal; once the claim has come before the tribunal and has been disposed of, the purpose of the section is exhausted in the absence of fraud or misrepresentation (*Times Newspapers v Fitt* [1981] ICR 637, EAT). **5.94**

L. 'TOMLIN' ORDERS

Dismissing the claim on terms agreed between the parties presents difficulties if the settlement goes wrong for some reason: once the proceedings have been dismissed, they cannot be reopened, and the only remedy for the aggrieved party will be to attempt to sue on the settlement agreement, assuming that the agreement can be shown to be valid. **5.95**

To avoid the risk of difficulties if the settlement goes wrong, tribunals often order that all further proceedings on the claim be stayed, except for the purpose of carrying the terms agreed between the parties into effect, with liberty to apply for that purpose. This means that if things go wrong the parties may go back to the tribunal. The terms of settlement may be scheduled to the order. This practice is based on the terms of the 'Tomlin Order' much used in the civil courts. The tribunal will invariably include a further order (provided the parties consent) that if no application is made under the liberty to apply within a fixed period (usually a short period after the date on which money is to be paid under the agreement) the proceedings will be dismissed on withdrawal. The purpose of such an order by the tribunal is to achieve a balance between, on the one hand, allowing the parties to apply if something goes wrong with the agreement and, on the other hand, achieving an efficient final disposal of the claim so that parties are not left in a state of uncertainty. The option of staying the proceedings, so that the parties may return to the tribunal if something goes wrong, was regarded as preferable to a simple dismissal of the claim by the EAT in *Hoeffler v Kwik Save Stores* EAT/803/97. **5.96**

In the civil courts, the effect of a Tomlin Order is to replace the party's original cause of action with rights arising under the settlement agreement scheduled to the Tomlin Order (assuming the statutory provisions rendering an agreement void do not apply). In the civil courts once the compromise has been reached the court has no further power to deal with the original cause of action and the same applies in the tribunal. In *Green v Rozen* [1955] 1 WLR 741, the leading case in the civil courts, Slade J said (at 746): **5.97**

> the Court has no further jurisdiction in respect of the original cause of action, because it has been superseded by the new agreement between the parties to the action, and if the terms of the new agreement are not complied with the injured party must seek his remedy upon the new agreement.

If a party defaults on the agreement (for example, the defendant fails to pay monies agreed) the innocent party's remedy is not to reopen the proceedings, but to sue on the agreement comprised in the schedule to the Tomlin Order. In the civil courts, there is no jurisdictional difficulty in a party doing so under the liberty to apply which is regularly contained in the Tomlin Order. **5.98**

The analogous position in the tribunal is dictated by two factors: **5.99**

(1) The restrictions on the settlement of most statutory claims will impinge on the validity of an agreement made at the door of the tribunal.
(2) The tribunal's jurisdiction in relation to claims for breach of contract is limited by statute.

5.100 If the 'agreement' is a void com romise of statutory claims (because it fails to comply with the requirements of s 203 of ERA 1996 or its equivalents), it would not prevent the claimant from pursuing a hearing of his claim, and the claimant may apply under the liberty to apply for such a hearing. In *Milestone School of English v Leakey* [1982] IRLR 3 the tribunal made an order adjourning the proceedings generally on terms agreed between the parties; when the respondent failed to pay, the claimant was permitted to have his claim heard as the agreement fell foul of the predecessor to s 203. Indeed, if the agreement fails to satisfy the relevant statutory requirements it is open to the claimant to change his mind even if the other party is still prepared to abide by the agreement or has already abided by it: the agreement cannot be effective to exclude the claimant's right to a determination of the statutory claims. Therefore whenever possible it is prudent for parties to enter into a compromise agreement, even where the agreement is entered at the door of the tribunal, to avoid the risk of a change of mind, or to ask the tribunal to make a consent order in the agreed amount.

5.101 On the other hand, if the agreement is valid but one party fails or refuses to comply with it:

(a) The aggrieved party cannot apply to have the case reopened. The position is the same as that in the civil courts: the underlying cause of action has been replaced by a right to sue on the contract which comprises the settlement agreement.
(b) The aggrieved party can sue on the contract in the courts, but the aggrieved party would be unlikely to be able to sue on the agreement in the tribunal: whilst the contract claim may be connected with the contract of employment it does not arise on the termination of employment so that any enforcement would be in the county court (see above, paras 5.87–5.89, and see in particular *Miller Bros & F P Butler Ltd v Johnston* [2002] IRLR 386, EAT).

M. AUTHORITY OF REPRESENTATIVES TO COMPROMISE

5.102 Parties to tribunal proceedings will often have appointed advisers (often, but not always, solicitors) to act for them, including dealing with a conciliation officer to seek to settle the case. Where someone, such as a solicitor, is named as a representative and holds himself out as such, the other party is entitled to assume that he does indeed have authority so to act, unless he receives notice indicating to the contrary. This general principle applies to non-qualified representatives, as it does to legally qualified representatives. See *Freeman v Sovereign Chicken Ltd* [1991] ICR 853, [1991] IRLR 408, EAT, where the EAT held that the respondents were entitled to rely on an agreement signed by a Citizens Advice Bureau worker on behalf of the claimant. However, the representative must act with the actual or ostensible authority of the party. Ostensible authority arises from the party himself holding out that a person is authorized to act on his behalf, not from a holding out by the representative (see *Gloystarne & Co Ltd v Martin* [2001] IRLR 15, EAT). If there is such ostensible authority but the representative did not in fact have authority to do what he did, then the party whom he was 'representing' may have an action against him, but the resulting agreement still stands. In practical terms, those advising parties should ensure that the party has seen and approved settlement terms before the representative formally agrees to them.

N. OVERTURNING AGREEMENTS

5.103 A settlement, whether reached through an ACAS officer or by compromise agreement, may be set aside on the same grounds as any other contract: incapacity of the parties, mistake, misrepresentation, illegality, duress, and undue influence.

5.104 In *Hennessy v Craigmyl & Co Ltd and ACAS* [1986] IRLR 300, the Court of Appeal decided that s 203 did not provide an exhaustive code of situations in which an agreement is valid or void and that the agreement could be set aside on the normal grounds of invalidity. The EAT in *Spikas & Son v Porter* EAT/927/96 considered what amounts to unlawful duress in the context of the settlement of employment claims. The employee argued that the settlement of his wages claim was signed only after the employer had applied improper pressure on him, namely refusing to make the payment until he agreed to accept a lesser amount than his full entitlement. The EAT rejected the employee's submission, noting that when negotiating to settle a dispute, it is quite common for each party to seek to exploit the weaknesses of the other. The EAT also noted that the individual had a 'cheap and quick procedure' for enforcing his claims, namely recourse to the tribunal. This case demonstrates just how difficult it will be for an employee to overturn a settlement agreement on the grounds of alleged economic duress.

In practice, particular difficulties may exist in seeking to set aside an agreement reached through a conciliation officer. The EAT has said that if the conciliation officer acted in bad faith or adopted unfair methods when promoting a settlement, 'the agreement might be set aside and might not operate as a bar of the proceedings' (*Slack v Greenham (Plant Hire) Ltd* [1983] IRLR 271, 275, affirmed in *Clarke v Redcar & Cleveland Borough Council* [2006] ICR 897). There is, however, no reported case of a successful application on this basis. **5.105**

There are inconsistent authorities as to whether a common law or equitable challenge to the validity of a compromise agreement can be raised in the tribunal, rather than in the civil courts. We suggest that the better view is that such challenges can be raised in the tribunal. This is the more recent view of the EAT, although there are a number of earlier authorities which state that the tribunal does not have jurisdiction to determine such issues: *Hirsch v Ward & Goldstone plc* [1984] 280 IDS Employment Law Brief 9, COIT 1535/15 (misrepresentation); *Larkfield of Chepstow Ltd v Milne* [1988] ICR 1, EAT (mistake of fact); *Byrnell v British Telecommunications plc* EAT/0383/04 (total failure of consideration). In each case a claim within the tribunal's jurisdiction (eg unfair dismissal) was defeated on grounds that the claim was precluded by a compromise agreement, and the EAT declined jurisdiction to consider whether there were common law or equitable grounds to avoid the agreement. The reasoning of the EAT is open to doubt. In *Byrnell*, for example, the EAT held that the tribunal had jurisdiction only to determine whether the statutory requirements for a compromise agreement in ERA 1996, s 203(2)(f) were satisfied. Any common law challenge to the validity of the agreement was a matter for the civil courts. However, s 203(2)(f) provides that the restriction on contracting out of claims does not apply to 'any *agreement* to refrain from instituting or continuing . . . any proceedings' (emphasis added) of a kind to which the subsection applies 'if the conditions regulating compromise agreements under this Act are satisfied'. It would seem open to the tribunal to determine whether there is an agreement at common law, and not just whether the statutory requirements for such an agreement are met. Such a conclusion was reached in the EAT in *Hennessy v Craigmyle* [1985] ICR 879: a tribunal can investigate the circumstances in which it is alleged that an agreement, within the meaning of what is now ERA 1996, s 203 is liable to be avoided at common law or in equity. This principle was not disputed (though not expressly affirmed) in the Court of Appeal (cited above). *Greenfield v Robinson* EAT/811/95 reached the same conclusion, as, more recently, did the EAT in *Industrious Ltd v Horizon Ltd and Vincent* [2009] UKEAT/0478. **5.106**

Statements of fact by one or other of the parties may form pre-contractual representations, or may be included within the settlement agreement as warranties. As a matter of practice, compromise agreements often include warranties on the part of the employee as a condition of payment under the agreement. Thus, in a compromise agreement in which a claim relating to termination of employment is compromised for a payment of money, the employee may warrant that there are no circumstances which would have entitled the employer to dismiss summarily without payment. The employer may be able to withhold payment under the agreement if it later discovers that the facts were not as warranted: see, for example, *Collidge v Freeport plc* [2008] EWCA Civ 485, [2008] IRLR 697. See further the specimen compromise agreement and drafting notes at Section O of this chapter. **5.107**

The EAT has no power to entertain an appeal by a party from a settlement, according to the EAT in *Eden v Humphries and Glasgow Ltd* [1981] ICR 183, where the employee sought to appeal against the amount of compensation awarded on his unfair dismissal. On the day when **5.108** the appeal was due to be heard he announced that he withdrew it on the understanding that the employers would pay an additional sum and offer him a testimonial. Later, the employee changed his mind about the settlement and sought to appeal against it, but the EAT determined that it had no power to set aside such a compromise and that it was a matter for the courts.

5.109 In some circumstances, an otherwise valid compromise agreement may be attacked on grounds that it contains a penalty clause. Often employers may wish to attempt to enforce confidentiality obligations (or indeed other obligations such as post-termination restrictions on competition) written into a compromise agreement by means of a 'claw-back' provision. By this provision, the employer is entitled to recover a proportion of the contractual consideration paid in respect of the compromise where obligations of confidentiality are not met. Such clauses are unlikely to be enforceable and are likely to be considered as penalty clauses by the courts. This requires a consideration of whether the claw-back is a genuine pre-estimate of loss or a penalty designed to prevent breach. The position was considered in the Court of Appeal in *CMC Group plc v Zhang* [2006] EWCA Civ 408, where it was held that a 'claw-back' provision was unenforceable as amounting to a penalty clause since it was repayable on a breach of contract irrespective of the loss occasioned. The Court of Appeal gave helpful guidance on identifying penalty clauses in *Murray v Leisureplay* [2005] IRLR 946. It is first necessary to identify the amount payable under the contract on breach by a party. Further, it is necessary to identify the loss occasioned by the other party on breach. To the extent that there is a difference between the two, the court must then consider why there is a difference. Where there is no reasonable explanation, it is likely that the clause in question is not a genuine pre-estimate of loss and is a penalty clause.

O. SAMPLE COMPROMISE AGREEMENT

SETTLEMENT AND WITHDRAWAL OF CLAIMS

Sample Compromise Agreement
[On employer's headed notepaper]

STRICTLY PRIVATE AND CONFIDENTIAL

[*Name*]
[*Address*]
[*Date*]

WITHOUT PREJUDICE AND SUBJECT TO CONTRACT

Dear [ ]

Termination of your employment with [ ]

This letter sets out the terms that have recently been discussed in relation to the termination of your employment with [ ]('Company').

You [allege that you] have potential claims arising from your employment and its termination [*insert brief details of the relevant circumstances of termination*] which include: [all claims in the Proceedings (as defined in clause 3.8 below),] unfair dismissal, wrongful dismissal, [sex][race][disability][discrimination] [equal pay] [*insert brief description of the other relevant potential claims*] ('Employment Claims').[1]

This Agreement settles the Employment Claims. In addition, it reflects the intention of both you and the Company [and all Group Companies] that this Agreement should also settle any other claim(s) that you may have against the Company [or any Group Company], subject to and in accordance with the terms set out in this letter.

---

1 Use extreme care when completing this paragraph as you risk alerting the employee to claims they may not know they have.

1. Termination

1.1 Your employment with the Company [will terminate] [terminated] on [*date*] ('Termination Date') [by reason of [ ]. Your P45 [will be] [has been] issued [shortly after the Termination Date].

1.2 The payments provided for by this Agreement are made without admission of liability but are in full and final settlement of any claims made or to be made by you as more fully set out in clause [3].

2. Payments

2.1 You [will] [have] receive[d] your salary up to and including the Termination Date (less applicable tax and employee's National Insurance contributions [and less a repayment to the Company of £[ ] in respect of holiday taken by you in excess of your accrued entitlement [and you confirm your consent to this deduction]]).

2.2 The Company will pay, without admission of liability, within 14 days of the later of: the Termination Date, the issue of your P45[,] [and] receiving a copy of this Agreement, signed by all the parties and your Adviser (as defined below), the following:

2.2.1 a payment of £[ ] (less applicable income tax and employee's National Insurance contributions) in lieu of your [ ] notice;

2.2.2 a payment of £[ ] (less applicable income tax and employee's National Insurance contributions) in lieu of [ ] [day's] [days'] holiday accrued but untaken as at the Termination Date;

2.2.3 [a payment of £[ ] (less applicable income tax and employee's National Insurance contributions) as compensation for loss of your contractual benefits during your notice period];

2.2.4 [a redundancy payment of £[ ] [which includes a statutory redundancy payment of £[ ]] ('Statutory Redundancy Payment')]. [The Statutory Redundancy Payment has been calculated as set out in Schedule [2]]; [and]

2.2.5 [a payment of £[ ] (less applicable tax and employee's National Insurance contributions) in consideration of your obligations set out in [any clauses containing post-termination restrictions]; and]

2.2.6 a payment of £[ ] as compensation for the termination of your employment ('Compensation Payment').

2.3 For the avoidance of doubt your entitlement to all salary and benefits [including [*specify PHI, private medical cover, life insurance, pension, etc*]] [will end] [ended] on the Termination Date.

3. Claims against the Company and warranties

3.1 Subject to clause 3.2, you accept the terms of this Agreement in full and final settlement of all and any claims, costs, expenses, or rights of action of any kind, whether contractual, statutory, or otherwise arising out of circumstances of which the parties were aware before, on or after the date of this Agreement, and whether having already occurred or arising in the future [in the United Kingdom or in any other country in the world,] which you have or may have against the Company [or any Group Company] (or its [or their] shareholders, directors, officers, consultants, workers, or employees) from time to time, which arise out of or in connection with your employment by the Company [or any Group Company] or its termination including (but not limited to) any claim: [*Consider deleting obviously irrelevant claims from the list below.*]

3.1.1 which is an Employment Claim;

3.1.2 in relation to notice or pay in lieu of notice;

3.1.3 for unauthorized deductions from wages, for detriment in employment (on any ground), for detriment or dismissal or selection for redundancy on grounds related to having made a protected disclosure, for paid time off for ante-natal care, for the right to time off for dependants, for the right to a written statement of reasons for dismissal, for unfair dismissal, for automatically unfair dismissal (on any ground), for a redundancy payment, for automatically unfair selection for redundancy on any ground, and any other claim under the Employment Rights Act 1996;

3.1.4 under the Employment Act 2002;

3.1.5 for equal treatment under the Equal Pay Act 1970;

3.1.6 for direct and/or indirect sex discrimination, discrimination on the grounds of gender reassignment, direct and/or indirect discrimination against married persons, discrimination by way of victimization, and any other claim under the Sex Discrimination Act 1975;

3.1.7 for direct and/or indirect discrimination, discrimination by way of victimization, harassment, and any other claim under the Race Relations Act 1976;

3.1.8 for discrimination, harassment, failure to make adjustments, and any other claim under the Disability Discrimination Act 1995;

3.1.9 for refusal of employment, action short of dismissal, dismissal and/or other detriment on grounds related to trade union membership, for failure to comply with collective consultation obligations and/or to pay a protective award and/or any other claim under the Trade Union and Labour Relations (Consolidation) Act 1992;

3.1.10 for the national minimum wage and/or additional remuneration, failure to allow access to records and detriment in employment on grounds related to the national minimum wage under the National Minimum Wage Act 1998;

3.1.11 for the right to be accompanied and for detriment and/or dismissal on the grounds relating to the right to be accompanied under the Employment Relations Act 1999;

3.1.12 for dismissal for reasons related to a relevant transfer, for failure to inform and/or consult, and/or any other claim under the Transfer of Undertakings (Protection of Employment) Regulations 2006;

3.1.13 for compensation for entitlement to annual leave, payment in respect of annual leave, refusal to give paid annual leave, daily and/or weekly and/or compensatory rest and/or rest breaks, and any other claim under the Working Time Regulations 1998;

3.1.14 relating to any rights to and/or during any period of maternity leave and/or parental leave, relating to the right to return after maternity and/or parental leave, detriment relating to maternity and/or paternity rights, automatic unfair dismissal on maternity or parental grounds, contractual rights to and/or during maternity and/or parental leave under the Maternity and Parental Leave etc Regulations 1999;

3.1.15 under the Transnational Information and Consultation of Employees Regulations 1999;

3.1.16 for less favourable treatment, for the right to receive a written statement of reasons for less favourable treatment, automatic unfair dismissal and/or detriment in employment under the Part-time Workers (Prevention of Less Favourable Treatment) Regulations 2000;

3.1.17 for less favourable treatment, for the right to receive a written statement of reasons for less favourable treatment, automatic unfair dismissal and/or detriment in employment under the Fixed Term Employees (Prevention of Less Favourable Treatment) Regulations 2002; or

3.1.18 for any rights to and/or during paternity and/or adoption leave, the right to return after paternity and/or adoption leave, for detriment relating to paternity and/or adoption leave, automatic unfair dismissal and/or contractual rights to and/or during paternity and/or adoption leave under the Paternity and Adoption Leave Regulations 2002 and/or the Statutory Paternity Pay and Adoption Pay (General) Regulations 2002;

3.1.19 for detriment and/or dismissal or failure to allow the right to be accompanied under the Flexible Working (Procedural Requirements) Regulations 2002;

3.1.20 for discrimination, victimization, and/or harassment on grounds of religion and/or belief under the Employment Equality (Religion or Belief) Regulations 2003;

3.1.21 for discrimination, victimization, and/or harassment on grounds of sexual orientation under the Employment Equality (Sexual Orientation) Regulations 2003;

3.1.22 for discrimination, victimization, and/or harassment on grounds of age under the Employment Equality (Age) Regulations 2006;

3.1.23 in relation to any breach of your contract of employment including (but not limited to) unpaid wages, unpaid holiday pay and/or unpaid sick pay, permanent health insurance, private medical insurance, bonus or commission, or any other contractual or discretionary benefit, and any other contractual and/or tortious claim;

3.1.24 in relation to any office or directorship(s) of the Company [or any Group Company] you may hold;

3.1.25 in relation to any share option scheme, bonus scheme, or other profit-sharing scheme or arrangement between you and the Company [or any Group Company] [including (but not limited to) [*specify scheme name*];

3.1.26 in relation to the conduct of the Company [or any Group Company] in relation to any retirement benefits scheme (as defined in section 611 of the Income and Corporation Taxes Act 1988) of which you are or claim to be a member including, without limitation, the payment of contributions to, the accrual of benefits under, or the exercise of any powers or discretion in relation to such a scheme;

3.1.27 under the Protection from Harassment Act 1997;

3.1.28 in respect of which a Conciliation Officer is authorized to act;

3.1.29 under European Union law; [or]

3.1.30 [in the Proceedings (as defined in clause [3.8]);] [or]

3.1.31 any other statutory claim or claim for breach of statutory duty.

3.2 For the purposes of clause [3.1], 'claim' excludes [any claim for personal injury [that has been notified to the Company in writing before the Termination Date]] that may be brought in a county court or the High Court and] [pension rights accrued up to the Termination Date under any occupational pension scheme (as defined in Pension Schemes Act 1993) operated by the Company [or any Group Company] and of which you are a member ('Pension Rights')]. [You undertake and warrant that, to the best of your knowledge, information and belief, after due and careful inquiry, you have [no claim for personal injury and][no claim against the Company [or any Group Company] in respect of Pension Rights] as at the date of this Agreement.]

3.3 For the purposes of clause [3.1], 'claim' includes (without limitation):

3.3.1 any claim of which, at the date of this Agreement, neither the Company nor you is aware; and

3.3.2 any claim of which, at the date of this Agreement, you are aware but neither the Company [nor any Group Company] nor any of its [or their] consultants, directors, employees, officers, shareholders, or workers is aware.

3.4 You represent, warrant, and undertake that:

3.4.1 you have received advice from [ ] of [ ] ('Adviser') who is a relevant independent adviser (within the meaning of section 203 of the Employment Rights Act 1996 as amended) as to the terms and effect of this Agreement and in particular its effect on your ability to pursue your rights before an employment tribunal;

3.4.2 you were advised by the Adviser that there was in force, at the time you received the advice referred to above, a contract of insurance, or an indemnity provided for members of a professional body, covering the risk of a claim by you in respect of loss arising in consequence of that advice;

3.4.3 you [have not presented or brought and] will not present or bring any [other] complaint, proceedings, action, or claim before any court, employment tribunal or other judicial body in England or any other jurisdiction in connection with, relating to, or arising out of your employment and/or its termination and nor has nor will anyone acting on your behalf;

3.4.4 [the Adviser has advised you as to whether you have any claim of any kind arising out of or in connection with your employment by the Company [or any Group Company] or the termination of any such employment and, to the extent that you have or may have any such claims, these have been asserted or intimated to the Company by you or the Adviser on your behalf prior to the date of this Agreement and this Agreement and the waiver and release in clause [3.1] above expressly relate to each and every one of those claims;] [OR] [any claims of any kind that you may have arising out of or in connection with your employment by the Company [or any Group Company] or the termination of such employment have been asserted or intimated to the Company by you or the Adviser on your behalf prior to the date of this Agreement and this Agreement and the waiver and release in clause [3.1] above expressly relate to each and every one of those claims;]

3.4.5 except for those claims asserted as indicated in paragraph [3.4.4] above, you have no other complaints or claims of any nature against the Company [or any Group Company] or any of its [or their] directors, officers, consultants, employees, agents, workers, or shareholders;

3.5 You accept that the Company [(on behalf of itself, and its Group Companies)] is entering into this Agreement in reliance upon the representations, warranties and undertakings provided by you in this clause [3].

3.6 You agree that the conditions regulating compromise agreements contained in the Sex Discrimination Act 1975, the Race Relations Act 1976, the Disability Discrimination Act 1995, the Employment Rights Act 1996, the National Minimum Wage Act 1998, the Working Time Regulations 1998, the Transnational Information and Consultation of Employees Regulations 1999, the Part-time Workers (Prevention of Less Favourable Treatment) Regulations 2000, the Fixed Term Employees

(Prevention of Less Favourable Treatment) Regulations 2002, the Employment Equality (Religion or Belief) Regulations 2003, the Employment Equality (Sexual Orientation) Regulations 2003, and the Employment Equality (Age) Regulations 2006 are intended to be and have been satisfied.

3.7 [The Company agrees to pay, directly to the Adviser's firm, the Adviser's firm's reasonable legal fees incurred by you exclusively for advice given to you in relation to the termination of your employment and the terms of this agreement up to a maximum of £[ ] (inclusive of VAT) after receipt by the Company of an appropriate invoice from the Adviser's firm addressed to you and marked payable by the Company.]

3.8 [It is a condition of this Agreement that within three working days of the date of this Agreement you notify the [ ] Employment Tribunal (in writing, copied to the Company, in the form set out in Schedule [3]) that the whole claim against the Company [and all other respondents] lodged under case number [ ] ('Proceedings') has been settled, and is immediately withdrawn by you.][2]

4. The validity, construction, and performance of the terms set out in this Agreement shall be governed by and construed in accordance with English law. Each of the parties irrevocably submits to the exclusive jurisdiction of the courts of England.

5. This Agreement, although marked 'without prejudice/subject to contract', will upon signature by us both and upon the Adviser signing the acknowledgement in Schedule [1] be treated as an open document evidencing an agreement binding on us both.

Please confirm your agreement to the terms set out in this Agreement by signing, dating, and returning to me both of the enclosed copies. Please note that it is a condition of this Agreement that your Adviser signs the acknowledgement at Schedule [1].

I look forward to hearing from you.

Yours sincerely

[ ]

Duly authorized for and on behalf of the Company

I have read and understood and agree to the terms of this Agreement.

....

....

[*Name of Employee*] [*Dated*]

SCHEDULE 1

ADVISER'S ACKNOWLEDGEMENT

I [ ], confirm that I have given independent legal advice to [ ] of [ ] ('Employee') as to the terms and effect of this Agreement and in particular its effect on the Employee's ability to pursue the Employee's rights before an employment tribunal.

I confirm that I am a qualified lawyer within the meaning of section 203(4) of the Employment Rights Act 1996 (as amended) holding a current practising certificate and that I am neither employed by nor acting for [*name of employer*][, nor acting in this matter for any Group Company]. I confirm that there is, and was at the time I gave the advice referred to above, in force a contract of insurance or indemnity provided for members of a professional body covering for the risk of a claim by the Employee in respect of any loss arising in consequence of the advice referred to above.

Signed... Dated...

SCHEDULE 2

STATEMENT OF CALCULATION OF STATUTORY REDUNDANCY PAYMENT

Name:

Date of birth:

Date on which continuous employment commenced: / /

Effective date of termination of employment: / /

Number of completed years' service

(subject to statutory maximum of 20 years) Years

Week's pay (subject to statutory maximum of £350): £

Calculated as follows:

- For every year during the whole of which you were 41 or over 1.5 × week's pay
- For every earlier year during the whole of which you were 22 or over 1.0 × week's pay
- For every earlier year (years under the age of 18 do not count) 0.5 × week's pay

So:

[ ] × 1.5 × [350] =
[ ] × 1.0 × [350] =
[ ] × 0.5 × [350] =
Total =

[*Set out any reduction here.*]

Schedule 3
Letter to Employment Tribunal

The Chairman

[ ] Employment Tribunal

[Address]

[Date]

Dear Sir

[Case Number] [Name of Case]

We write to confirm that settlement terms have been agreed in this matter and a compromise agreement has been signed.

The Claimant therefore wishes to withdraw [all] [his/her] claim[s] against [all] [the] Respondent[s].

We look forward to receiving a notice of withdrawal accordingly.

Yours faithfully

[Adviser]

cc: [The Company]

[The Company's solicitors]

P. DRAFTING NOTES FOR A COMPROMISE AGREEMENT

This section proceeds on the basis that you are advising the employer in the drafting of a compromise agreement. It should be read together with the checklist of issues below, which covers many of the practical issues you should consider when drafting a compromise agreement. See also the form of compromise agreement above. This contains the main substantive provisions which should be included in a compromise agreement to ensure it is binding on the employee. 5.110

General considerations

As a starting point, consider the contractual documents (contract of employment, handbook, benefit documents, share benefit documents). See the checklist section below for the type of issues that may arise from this consideration. 5.111

Be particularly careful to ensure you identify the correct employer, especially if an employee is employed by one group company but working for another one. Also, if an individual employee 5.112

has been named as a respondent in discrimination proceedings, should he or she be a party to the compromise agreement too? Are share options or other benefits granted by a different company within the group? If so the relevant company will also need to be joined as a party. Is there a TUPE transfer in the background which means that the transferor or transferee should also be a party to the agreement?

5.113 Consider also the background to the dispute. Are there any specific points which need to be considered in the full and final settlement clause as a result? Should the compromise agreement also cover the withdrawal of any grievances, statutory questionnaires, or requests under the Data Protection Act 1998?

5.114 Generally the agreement should be marked 'without prejudice and subject to contract' until it is actually executed.

Taxation considerations—general

Termination date and reason

5.115 Preferably, the compromise agreement should be signed *after* the termination date. If the agreement is signed before the termination date, HM Revenue & Customs can argue that the agreement in fact represents a variation of the employee's contract of employment (or is a new fixed term contract of employment) and that £30,000 exemption from tax (under s 401, ITEPA 2003) that usually applies to termination payments will not apply. In practical terms, this is less likely if the agreement is signed only days in advance of termination. In addition, signing the compromise prior to termination arguably affects the validity of the compromise: a valid agreement must 'relate to the particular proceedings' (ERA 1996, s 203(3)(b)), usually (but not always) on termination of employment. There may therefore be no valid 'proceedings' if termination has not occurred.

5.116 Reference to termination by mutual consent should be avoided wherever possible. A termination by mutual consent constitutes a discharge of a contract, not a breach. A breach is now required by HM Revenue & Customs before any termination payment is treated as damages (see *Tax Bulletin*, Issue 63 on Payments in Lieu of Notice (PILON) treatments). HM Revenue & Customs will most likely consider a mutual consent termination to be a variation of contract, so that the £30,000 exemption will not apply. Attempt therefore to agree an acceptable reason for dismissal, but the employer should beware of any attempt to collude with the employee, for example in a fraudulent claim for income support following 'redundancy' etc.

Redundancy payments

5.117 Statutory redundancy payments are exempt from liability to tax as earnings pursuant to s 309 of ITEPA 2003. However, the exemption does not extend to s 401 of ITEPA 2003 and consequently such payments fall within s 401 of ITEPA 2003 as specific employment income. Consequently, statutory redundancy payments in effect go towards 'using up' the £30,000 exemption. If the payment includes a statutory redundancy payment, the employee must be given a written statement showing how the amount is calculated. Failure to do so without reasonable excuse is a criminal offence.

PAYE deductions

5.118 PAYE will apply to termination payments which are taxable, whether under ss 6, 401, or 225 of ITEPA 2003. However, provided the employment has terminated and the employer has issued the employee with his P45 (so that the payment is not referred to in the P45) the employer is only obliged under the PAYE regulations to deduct tax at the basic rate (currently 20 per cent for the tax year 2008/09) rather than in accordance with the employee's coding (see reg 37(1), (2) of the Income Tax (Pay As You Earn) Regulations 2003, SI 2003/2682). The employee still has to account for any applicable higher rate tax (generally in the January following the end of the tax year when payment is made) but has a cash-flow advantage as he will do this under self-assessment.

Payments in lieu of notice

HM Revenue & Customs in May 2003 updated their rules of interpretation on the tax treatment of PILONs in *Tax Bulletin*, Issue 63. Briefly: 5.119

(1) Under the rules, the absence of a PILON no longer determines whether notice pay can be given tax free to an employee.
(2) HM Revenue & Customs will consider the following questions of fact:
   (a) whether a payment has been reduced to take into account mitigation of the employee's loss. If it has not, it is more likely to be taxable as earnings;
   (b) whether the payment has been adjusted to reflect the difference in tax and NIC consequences (ie paid to the employee gross or net). The purpose of damages is to put an employee in the position he would have been had the contract been performed, so any loss of earnings awarded by a court/tribunal for the notice period would usually be net losses. (There is no strict legal obligation on the employer to offer gross notice pay but many do so as a gesture of goodwill. It must therefore be questionable for HM Revenue & Customs to consider that such 'adjustments' determine the tax status);
   (c) whether a payment for loss of benefits for the notice period has been included in the notice pay. Many express PILON clauses *exclude* any entitlement to benefits. Any damages award would *include* them; and
   (d) whether the employer's decision not to exercise a PILON has been evidenced in writing.

Non-contractual PILONS may still be caught where they are 'an integral part of the employer–employee relationship'. This would arise where a PILON is paid as 'an automatic response to a termination'. Unless an employer has evidence that it has breached the employee's contract by not giving notice and has paid damages instead, an automatic payment in substitution of the employee's notice period will be caught as 'earnings' regardless of whether there is any express PILON clause.

In light of the above, it is usual for PILON payments to be made under the PAYE system, and therefore subject to tax and employer's and employee's NIC in full. Departures from this general practice should only be undertaken where the employer has considered the risks involved. 5.120

Tax indemnity

Consider including a tax indemnity whereby, if the employer is ordered to pay additional tax to HM Revenue & Customs because s 403 of ITEPA 2003 does not apply and the £30,000 exemption from tax or some other tax exemption is not available, the employee will indemnify the employer for that tax and any fines or penalties imposed on the employer as a result of late payment. The primary liability for basic rate tax in the situation where the £30,000 exemption from tax does not apply will be that of the employer, and usually HM Revenue & Customs will treat the amount paid as the net amount and gross it up for basic rate tax. A tax indemnity may, therefore, give the employer some comfort, although the indemnity will only be as good as the employee's ability to pay. 5.121

Taxation issues—specific

Retirement

Take particular care if the termination is occurring on the employee's retirement. *Ex gratia* payments made on retirement do not benefit from the £30,000 exemption in s 401 of ITEPA 2003 (see ITEPA 2003, s 393 and HM Revenue & Customs' Statement of Practice 13/91); rather they fall within the pension scheme tax rules and are chargeable to income tax. The payment may fall within s 401 of ITEPA 2003, however, as long as the reason for the payment is as damages for breach of contract or for severance of employment due to redundancy or loss of office. The distinction will not always be clear. Take specialist tax advice and consider applying for advance clearance from HM Revenue & Customs. Avoid all references to 'retirement' in the agreement, relevant board minutes, correspondence, etc. 5.122

Legal expenses tax concession

5.123 No tax charge is imposed on payments made by the former employer direct to the former employee's solicitor, in full or partial discharge of the solicitor's bill of costs incurred by the employee *only* in connection with the termination of his/her employment *and* under a specification in the settlement agreement providing for that payment (HM Revenue & Customs Concession A81). Where the solicitor's bill relates to other matters as well as termination costs, the amount relating to the termination must be clearly identifiable in the bill. The fees of accountants and other professionals *do not* in themselves fall within HM Revenue & Customs' Concession A81. However, HM Revenue & Customs accept that 'where, exceptionally, the employee's solicitor found it necessary to consult other professionals for the specific claim, the cost to the solicitor would represent a disbursement and would therefore, as legal costs, be within the concession'. So if tax issues are particularly complex, accountant's fees may fall within the concession if they are charged as a disbursement on the solicitor's bill.

5.124 Note that the above concession applies only when the termination payment (or part of it) falls to be taxed as specific employment income under s 401 of ITEPA 2003; it does *not* apply where the payment is fully taxable under s 6 of ITEPA 2003 as general earnings or as specific employment income other than under s 401 (for example, payments under a contractual non-discretionary PILON clause).

5.125 Note that where a party (ie the employer) is paying another's legal costs, the question is one of indemnity (ie the terms of the clause in the compromise agreement) not of VAT. The following principles apply:

(1) the solicitor whose costs are being paid must deliver a VAT invoice to his own client (the employee). The invoice should be addressed to the employee but the bill marked as payable by the relevant company;
(2) if the solicitor's client is not VAT registered and cannot therefore obtain input tax credit (which will almost without exception be the case for an employee) the indemnifying party is liable to pay the full VAT inclusive costs, but cannot recover the VAT as the legal services were not supplied to the company. The company may attempt an argument that it is not 'allowed' to pay VAT if it cannot recover it. That appears to be incorrect—it is not 'paying' VAT—it is indemnifying the employee for his expenses in full (ie the VAT inclusive amount). If it does not reimburse the VAT element, the employee will be out of pocket;
(3) under no circumstances should a VAT invoice be issued by the solicitor to the employer, as the services have not been rendered to the employer. If such an invoice were to be issued, it would be a fraud on HM Revenue & Customs.

It is therefore essential to ensure that the term in the compromise agreement always specifies whether indemnity includes VAT, as the terms of that indemnity will be definitive.

Taxation of payments in relation to restrictions

5.126 Section 225 of ITEPA 2003 provides (in summary) that payments (or other valuable consideration) to individuals for the giving of restrictive undertakings (such as post-termination restrictive covenants, confidentiality undertakings, intellectual property provisions, etc) or the total or partial fulfilment of an undertaking, in either case where such undertaking is given in connection with his current, future, or past employment, are to be treated as earnings chargeable to tax (under s 6 of ITEPA 2003) in the tax year in which payment is made. Consequently, PAYE tax is payable on such payments/consideration (at basic rate if payment made after termination and issue of P45). Statement of Practice SP3/96 provides that HM Revenue & Customs 'will not attribute part of a termination payment made in settlement of employment claims to restrictive covenants which formed part of the terms of employment and which are re-affirmed in the settlement'. This does not, however, affect the application of s 225 of ITEPA 2003 to sums that are referable to other restrictive undertakings which individuals give in relation to an employment, whether those undertakings are contained in a job termination settlement or otherwise. Depending on the importance of the restrictions the employer should consider:

(a) merely referring to (any) existing restrictions contained in a contract/service agreement if the employer is satisfied these are adequate. These should not fall within s 225 of ITEPA 2003;
(b) if the restrictions are of critical importance, repeating existing/new restrictions in the compromise agreement and specifically allocating consideration to them (which will be taxable within s 225). The consideration should be adequate or it risks raising the suspicion of HM Revenue & Customs on an investigation.

Note that, as payments under s 225 are earnings, they will also be subject to employer's and employee's NIC and appropriate deductions should be made before payment to the employee. **5.127**

Tax treatment of the repayment provision

Compromise agreements sometimes include a provision whereby the employee will have to repay any amounts of compensation if he breaches the terms of the compromise agreement, brings a claim against the employer, or otherwise claims the compromise agreement is invalid (see para 5.143 below for further information on this type of provision). There are tax implications if such clauses are included. Certain tax inspectors were concluding that the inclusion of clauses such as this rendered the compensation payment (and possibly other payments under the agreement) fully taxable. HM Revenue & Customs have now, helpfully, confirmed that the inclusion of a repayment clause will not ordinarily, of itself, mean that the whole or part of the settlement payment should be attributed to the undertaking. **5.128**

Ill-health dismissal

If the employee is being dismissed for ill-health there may be total exemption from tax (ITEPA 2003, s 406). In the case of an ill-health dismissal, it must be on account of injury to, or disability of, an employee. In these circumstances, 'disability' requires a specific illness or disability, mental, or physical, whether chronic or not, making the employee unfit for his/her job. Medical evidence will be required. **5.129**

Foreign service exemption

Sections 413 and 414 of ITEPA 2003 provide that certain (full or partial) exemptions to tax on termination payments may apply where an employee has spent part of their employment overseas. **5.130**

Practical arrangements, payment, and benefits

There are many general practical considerations and issues relating to benefits. See the checklist below in relation to this. However, note that the employee is also likely to be entitled to the continued provision of other benefits during the notice period or compensation for their loss if termination is immediate. Consider: bonus entitlement (or other deferred payments), car allowance, other allowances, payments to personal pension schemes, holiday pay (and pay in lieu of untaken entitlement accrued to the termination date), private health insurance, PHI schemes, life assurance, use of company mobile, Blackberry, laptop, etc, and share options. **5.131**

Post-termination restrictions

Most compromise agreements will include a confidentiality clause. This will restrict the employee from discussing the terms of settlement and, in some cases, it will go further and also restrict discussion of the reasons for the termination of employment or events during the employment. In the latter case, both employer and employee will need to consider whether there needs to be **5.132** a separate agreement or exclusions about announcements and responses to third party queries or discussions with legal advisers or family members.

5.133 Many compromise agreements include a provision that the departing employee will not make or publish any disparaging or derogatory or defamatory statements concerning the company or any of its officers or employees. This has obvious advantages for an employer in terms of controlling an employee's statements. However, it usually results in the employee's lawyers requiring a parallel undertaking from the company. Such a parallel undertaking must be carefully drafted to avoid depriving the company of defences which would be available under the law of defamation and imposing on the employer a higher burden than any which would otherwise apply. It is particularly important to bear in mind the necessity for executives of the employer to be able to speak freely in their internal discussions without laying themselves open to a claim if the departing employee finds out about their discussions. The departing employee need not concern himself about the intricacies of the law of defamation but would simply sue for breach of contract under the compromise agreement. If such a restriction is being demanded of the employer, you should always advise the employer that this is more onerous than the standard position under the law.

5.134 The employee may also request a reference. If he does, the employer needs to consider whether it is prepared to give one at all and, if so, whether it will be a 'dates only' reference or something which is in fuller form. If it is the latter, the employee should seek to annex the form of reference to the agreement. The employer should include in the agreement details of a specified person, who will be responsible for issuing the reference and may wish to retain the right to alter the terms of the reference if new facts about the employee's performance come to light. The employer should also include a standard disclaimer in the reference, to protect it from claims from future employers in relation to the contents of the reference.

5.135 Consider whether it is desirable to include any other post-termination restrictions controlling competition, dealings with clients, dealings with employees, and representations about the employee's involvement with the business. If so, the easiest way to address this may be to refer back to such restrictions in the original agreement, if they are likely to be enforceable. If not, bear in mind that these provisions will be subject to all the usual rules of restraint of trade which apply to post-termination restrictions in the employment context. See paras 5.126–5.127 above on the taxation of payments in relation to restrictions.

Full and final settlement

Settlement of 'all or any claims'—general release

5.136 See paras 5.52–5.80 for the current legal position in relation to full and final settlement. Consider the following:

(1) Bear in mind for the purposes of compliance with ERA 1996, s 203, the general guidance that using a rolled-up expression such as 'all statutory rights' is not sufficient, identifying the proceedings only by reference to the statute under which they may arise, for example 'under the ERA', is not sufficient, and that the particular claims or potential claims to be covered must be identified, either by a generic description such as 'unfair dismissal' or by the section of the statute giving rise to the claim (see clause 3.1 of the compromise agreement above).

(2) Consider including a brief description of the complaints alleged in the body of the agreement (see the second paragraph of the sample compromise agreement, above). The employer may not wish to do this, particularly where it fears it may be alerting the employee to claims of which he or she was not aware, but it is preferable to do so. In any case, the employer can always do this without any admission of liability.

(3) Ensure the full and final settlement clause in the compromise agreement is specifically tailored to the situation; do not merely include a shopping list of each and every claim an employee could bring.

Warranties

Note also that although the case of *Lunt v Merseyside TEC Ltd* [1999] ICR 17, [1999] IRLR 458, EAT was doubted by the Court of Appeal in *Hinton v University of East London* [2005] EWCA Civ 532, [2005] ICR 126 on other issues, it is likely to continue to influence the drafting of compromise agreements in relation to warranties. *Lunt* stated that only those claims 'indicated' by the employee could be validly compromised in a compromise agreement. The EAT approved the statement as an accurate statement of the law: 'A compromise agreement cannot, therefore, seek to exclude potential complaints that have not arisen on the off chance that they may be raised'. Many employers will therefore continue to include a specific warranty to deal with this (see clause 3.4.4 of the compromise agreement) notwithstanding *Hinton*. **5.137**

Consider using full form warranties about future claims if this is of crucial importance (see clause 3.3 of the compromise agreement). Note that the employee may as a result become aware of further claims which may lead to demands for increased compensation. In practice, the likelihood of a compromise agreement being set aside is small. **5.138**

Note that any attempt to contract out of liability under an occupational pension scheme is void and unenforceable by virtue of the Pensions Act 1995 and so a carve-out from the settlement for such claims will be one it is proper to request (see clause 3.2 of the compromise agreement). If the employer has no occupational pension scheme, however, this carve-out will not be relevant and should not be included. **5.139**

It is usual for the employee's adviser to require a carve-out of personal injury claims. This is not usually unreasonable, but consider requiring a warranty that the employee is not aware of claims at the termination date to give the employer some comfort (see clause 3.2 of the compromise agreement). **5.140**

As the employer, you may also wish to include a warranty from the employee that he has not obtained and is not about to obtain another job. This will then give the employer some comfort at least that the employee's negotiating position in relation to mitigation is accurate, although such a provision may be very strongly resisted by the employee concerned. **5.141**

The employer could also include a warranty by the employee in relation to breaches of his employment and/or fiduciary duties. Such a warranty may, however, trigger a request from the employee for a waiver of all claims the employer may have against him. An employer should think carefully about granting such a waiver where the employee is senior, and any such waiver should be accompanied by the warranty described above. Where the employee is a statutory director, the employer also needs to consider the limitations imposed by company law. **5.142**

The employer could include a provision which allows it to require the employee to repay some or all of the compensation paid on the occurrence of certain events, for example, breach of a material provision of the compromise agreement, the assertion of a claim against the employer which has supposedly been waived under the terms of the agreement, or other assertion that the compromise agreement is void. Such clauses may be enforceable, but the drafting must be done carefully or the provision may be void as a penalty clause (*CMC Group plc v Zhang* [2006] EWCA Civ 408, see para 5.109 above). **5.143**

If employment tribunal proceedings are ongoing it is necessary to ensure that they are properly withdrawn and dismissed, and provisions should be included in the agreement dealing with this (see clause 3.8 of the compromise agreement). Note the impact of the Employment Tribunal Rules of Procedure 2004 in this regard. Although the claimant employee may apply for his or her claim to be withdrawn, such a withdrawal does not affect any proceedings for costs, preparation time, or wasted costs. To ensure that the proceedings cannot be revived for such claims, employers should avail themselves of the procedure in r 25 and apply, within 28 days of the notice of withdrawal being sent to it, for the proceedings to be dismissed. If the application is **5.144** granted and the proceedings are dismissed, those proceedings cannot be continued by the claimant employee (unless the decision to dismiss is successfully reviewed or appealed).

5.145 It is traditional but not obligatory to pay the legal fees of the employee's adviser. In relation to this, see the tax requirements above and clause 3.7 of the compromise agreement. The adviser should sign an acknowledgement in the form of Schedule 1 to the compromise agreement above.

Company law considerations

5.146 Remember that a statutory director whose employment has ended remains entitled to notice of and to attend board meetings until he or she resigns or is removed as a director. If the statutory director is not given due notice, the business of the meeting is invalid. Consider the articles of association carefully.

5.147 Sections 215–222, Companies Act 2006 require that a compensatory payment to a director for 'loss of office' or upon retirement from office must be disclosed to and approved by the shareholders, unless the payment is made in good faith in discharge of a legal obligation, in payment of damages for breach of the director's employment contract, in compromise of a claim relating to termination of employment or loss of office, or by way of a contribution to pension to reflect past services.

5.148 Remember that a resolution from a holding company to terminate a directorship or approve a compensation payment will only operate as against that company, and separate resolutions must be proved in relation to directorships of subsidiary companies.

5.149 Consider also the Stock Exchange Rules: a relevant company must notify the Company Announcements Office of the UK Listing Authority upon the resignation or removal of a director. Placing a director on garden leave is arguably such a notifiable event if it is likely that, should the decision become public information, it would be price sensitive. Consider the City Code on Takeovers and Mergers: variations in contracts or 'poison pills' in contracts with companies 'in play' may require further consideration. Seek specialist corporate law advice if necessary.

5.150 Consideration should also be given to best practice in terms of corporate governance concerning termination packages. Is consultation with a remuneration committee or an investor protection committee appropriate? Public opinion may also be an issue.

5.151 Take note of the fiduciary duties of the departing director and those remaining. Breach of that duty is a risk if the directors approve a particularly generous or complex severance package. Any actual or potential conflict of interest must also be avoided (Companies Act 2006, ss 175 and 182).

CHECKLIST OF ISSUES

General considerations

Review copy of current contract of employment, any relevant handbook provisions, and relevant benefit documents. Check:

- Who is the correct employer? Consider also the definition of Group Company.
- The salary and benefits—have these been changed since the contract was drafted? Are there further non-contractual benefits you wish to include/exclude?
- Is there a pay in lieu of notice clause? If so, this will affect the tax treatment of any payment.
- Are there post-termination restrictions? Do you wish to rely on them—in which case are they enforceable?

- Does any other company and/or individual need to be a party to the agreement? For example, the entity granting any share benefits, any individual listed as a respondent in the employment tribunal, those involved in TUPE situations.

Consider the reason for termination of employment and relevant background. What reason will be stated in the agreement? Is the employer prepared to state a 'neutral' reason. (See also full and final settlement below.) Is the agreement marked 'without prejudice/subject to contract'? It should be.

Tax considerations

Does the employee wish to sign the agreement before the termination date? Beware as this may have adverse tax consequences and may bring the validity of the compromise agreement into question.

Does the employee wish to specify that the termination is by mutual consent? Beware of this as it may have adverse tax consequences.

Is the employee being made redundant? If so, the statutory redundancy payment will take up some of the £30,000 exemption and should be properly documented in the compromise agreement (see Schedule 2 to the compromise agreement above).

Is there a PILON in the contract of employment? If so, the employer should probably deduct tax and NICs.

Has the P45 been issued or will it be issued shortly? If so, it may be possible to pay the employee the termination amounts less tax at basic rate only.

Do you wish to include an indemnity obligation on the employee for any tax which becomes payable by the employer? If so, bear in mind that the indemnity will only be as effective as the employee's ability to pay.

Is the employee at or near retirement age? If so, consider the particular tax consequences which may arise.

Is there to be a contribution towards the employee's legal fees? If so, it may be possible for them to be paid without tax liability for the employee under an HM Revenue & Customs concession. However, to qualify, there are very specific rules which must be adhered to.

Are there post-termination restrictions in the compromise agreement? If so, and they are not simply a restatement of those which appeared in the contract of employment, beware as this may mean that the £30,000 exemption to tax may not apply.

Is this an ill-health dismissal? A specific tax exemption may apply.

Has the employee any service abroad with the employer? A tax exemption may apply to compensation relevant to that service.

Practical considerations

Is the employee currently on garden leave or otherwise excluded from the company's premises? Does the company wish to include a provision that the employee will not contact or attempt to contact employees, customers, etc?

Will the employee be expected to attend the office as required to effect a handover? If so, include a provision dealing with this in the agreement.

Does the employee have any company property which must be returned, for example documents containing confidential information, mobile, laptop, company car, etc? If so, include a provision to deal with this in the agreement.

What are the arrangements for payment of salary up to and including the termination date?

Benefits

Are there any outstanding loans, loans for relocation expenses, season ticket loans? Will the final salary payment be sufficient to meet repayment of these or will alternative arrangements be necessary?

Are there any outstanding expenses? What are the arrangements for the payment/approval of these?

Does the employee have any accrued but untaken holiday? The company will need to pay in lieu of annual leave in accordance with the Working Time Regulations 1998 and may have to pay in lieu of all of it under the relevant contractual provisions.

Equally, has the employee taken more than their accrued holiday entitlement? In this case the employer may be able to claw back payment in respect of the excess holiday if there is an appropriate contractual provision to this effect.

Does the employee have a company car? What are the arrangements for its retention or return? Consider issues such as insurance and running costs.

Is the employee going to buy the car? If so and even if the car is going to be transferred to the employee at no cost, for tax reasons the fair market value of the car will needed to be ascertained.

If the car is leased, consider arrangements for obtaining consent of the leasing company etc. Note that it may be a breach of the leasing agreement for an employee to keep the car after employment has terminated.

What are the current pension arrangements and what is proposed in relation to these? Consider contributions to a personal pension scheme, rights under any occupational pension scheme, additional pension contributions by the company, the use of funded unapproved retirement benefit schemes, etc.

Does the employee hold any vested but unexercised share options? It is necessary to see the relevant share option scheme to determine what can be done in relation to them. Are there any arrangements in place to finance the exercise of the options? Is it proposed that the employer procure that the scheme's committee use its discretion to permit exercise?

What is proposed in relation to other benefits? Note that in many cases the company will have already paid the relevant annual premium to the service provider and, subject to the rules of the scheme(s), may be able to extend cover beyond the termination date at no additional cost which is likely to be an attractive incentive to the employee. Consider:

- private health care;
- directors' and officers' liability insurance;
- life insurance;
- permanent health insurance.

Note that other contractual benefits may cease automatically under their terms on the termination date, for example life insurance, death in service benefit. You will need to check these issues and clarify the position in the agreement.

Termination benefits

Will the company pay for outplacement counselling and assistance for the employee? Up to what limit? (Note this can be relatively expensive but is advantageous tax wise.)

Is the company prepared to contribute to legal expenses? Up to what limit?

Ongoing arrangements

Is the company likely to wish to call on the employee at a later date, for example in relation to an ongoing project, litigation, etc? If so, consider the inclusion of a clause providing for this future assistance to the company.

Does the employer require the terms of the events leading up to the termination of employment and/or the compromise agreement to be kept confidential? Is it prepared to keep them confidential? If so, include a confidentiality provision but be ready for the employee to ask for a parallel undertaking from the employer.

Does the employer wish to prevent the employee:

- making derogatory statements about it and its employees, directors, etc;
- making representations on behalf of the company?

If so, include the relevant provision but be ready for the employee to ask for a parallel undertaking from the employer.

What (if anything) is proposed by the company in relation to a reference? Will it provide a 'dates only reference' or something more detailed?

Are the employee's existing restrictions in his service agreement concerning confidentiality, intellectual property, and post-termination restrictions adequate and enforceable? If not, consider the inclusion of new ones in the compromise agreement but note the possible tax implications.

Is there to be an agreed announcement regarding the employee's departure?

Full and final settlement

If known, who will be advising the employee? Is he or she an independent solicitor or a trade union adviser?

Is the employer prepared to insert brief details of the complaints alleged by the employee? If so, do so as it will make the full and final settlement clause more likely to be enforceable.

Has the list of statutory clauses been properly edited to ensure it refers to each of the possible claims properly and to prevent allegations of a 'shopping list' settlement clause?

Has a warranty been included that these are all the claims the employee is asserting to prevent allegations that *Lunt v Merseyside TEC Ltd* [1999] ICR 17, [1999] IRLR 458, EAT applies?

Is this an exceptional case where the company is prepared to waive claims it may have against the employee? (Note: it is very rare to include this in first draft.)

Has the employee already presented a complaint to the employment tribunal? If so, the existing complaint will need to be withdrawn on settlement and an application for its dismissal made.

Does the employer require a warranty that the employee has not obtained employment elsewhere? This can be useful to ensure that what the employee is saying about mitigation is correct.

Does the employer want a provision requiring the employee to repay the payments made under the agreement should the employee breach any material term under the agreement and/or bring a claim in relation to the issues purportedly waived under the terms of the agreement? If so, bear in mind that such a provision must be carefully drafted to ensure it is enforceable.

Does the employer require the employee to withdraw a grievance, grievance appeal, statutory questionnaire, or a request under the Data Protection Act 1998? If so, you should include drafting to cover this off.

Company law considerations

Is the employee a director/company secretary of the company or any group company? If so the employee will need to sign the relevant resignation forms etc.

Does the employee hold any nominee/founder shares in the company? If so, it is necessary to include provision for their transfer back to the company.

Does the compensation package require Board or other approval?

Consider Stock Exchange and corporate governance requirements.

6

Case Management

SUMMARY

(1) Tribunals have the power to make interim orders and directions on a wide variety of matters.

(2) Applications for case management orders may be dealt with by written submissions without a hearing.

(3) If a hearing is needed, applications are generally dealt with by a judge alone at a case management discussion.

A. CASE MANAGEMENT DISCUSSIONS

Before ETR 2004 came into force employment tribunals increasingly held interim hearings, particularly in the more complex cases, at which the issues were defined and any outstanding matters were dealt with before the main hearing. The rules now formalize this practice and there is a new power for the President of Employment Tribunals to make Practice Directions about the procedure of tribunals including Directions concerning the exercise by tribunals or judges of powers in relation to, for example, granting or refusing orders. In all case management decisions the tribunal should have at the forefront the overriding objective that it is to deal with cases justly (2004 Regulations, reg 3(1)) and this includes, so far as is practicable: (a) ensuring that the parties are on an equal footing; (b) dealing with cases in ways which are proportionate to the complexity of the issues; (c) ensuring that the case is dealt with expeditiously and fairly; and (d) saving expense (2004 Regulations, reg 3(2)). This is largely a replication of the CPR overriding objective (rr 1.1–1.3), and a tribunal or judge must seek to give effect to the overriding objective either when exercising any power given to it or him by the regulations or the rules in the schedules, or when interpreting any of the regulations or rules (2004 Regulations, reg 3(3)). There is also an obligation on the parties to assist the tribunal to further the overriding objective which ought not to be overlooked (2004 Regulations, reg 3(4)). **6.01**

A case management discussion (CMD) is an interim hearing held by a judge alone and shall be held in private (ETR 2004, r 17(1) as amended by SI 2005/1865, reg 2). There is a restriction on **6.02** what it can achieve since a CMD may not determine a person's 'civil rights or obligations' which is why it may be held in private. This language is borrowed from Article 6 of the ECHR and the aim is to ensure that Article 6 (see Chapter 16) does not apply to the conduct of the CMD. As a consequence, matters such as striking out a claim or part of it may not be determined at a CMD but must be dealt with at a pre-hearing review (PHR) which is a public hearing. Rule 10(2) of ETR 2004 sets out a list of examples of orders that may be dealt with at a CMD. They include orders:

(a) as to the manner in which the proceedings are to be conducted, including any time limit to be observed; this will include a term estimate and possibly the timetabling of witnesses;
(b) that a party provide additional information; for example because their claim or response is not clear or that schedules of loss should be provided;
(c) requiring the attendance of any person in Great Britain either to give evidence or to produce documents or information;
(d) requiring any person in Great Britain to disclose documents or information to a party to allow a party to inspect such material as might be ordered by a county court (or in Scotland, by a sheriff);
(e) extending any time limit, whether or not expired (subject to rr 4(4) extension of time limit for response, 11(2) application for an order to be not less than 10 days before the date of the hearing, 25(5) time limit for withdrawal of proceedings, 30(5) time limit for requesting written reasons, 33(1) time limit for a review of default judgment, 35(1) time limit for a review, 38(7) time limit for costs application, and 42(5) time limit for preparation time order, and to r 3(4) of Sch 2 time limit in national security cases);
(f) requiring the provision of written answers to questions put by the tribunal or judge;
(g) that, subject to r 22(8), a short conciliation period be extended into a standard conciliation period (this will be repealed after 6 April 2009);
(h) staying (in Scotland, sisting) the whole or part of any proceedings;
(i) that part of the proceedings be dealt with separately; this may cover a split liability and remedy hearing;
(j) that different claims be considered together;
(k) that any person who the judge or tribunal considers may be liable for the remedy claimed should be made a respondent in the proceedings;
(l) dismissing the claim against a respondent who is no longer directly interested in the claim;
(m) postponing or adjourning any hearing;
(n) varying or revoking other orders;
(o) giving notice to the parties of a pre-hearing review or the hearing;
(p) giving notice under r 19;
(q) giving leave to amend a claim or response;
(r) that any person whom the judge or tribunal considers has an interest in the outcome of the proceedings may be joined as a party to the proceedings;
(s) that a witness statement be prepared or exchanged; or
(t) as to the use of experts or interpreters in the proceedings.

6.03 A CMD may take place on either the application of a party or at the judge's own motion. The importance of holding CMDs has been stressed by the appellate courts in the following areas:

(1) *Race discrimination cases* In *Martins v Marks & Spencer plc* [1998] IRLR 326, Mummery LJ suggested before the rule changes that, in most cases, it would be good practice to hold a meeting for directions in order to identify the issues before the hearing of the case began. The judge could then consider making directions on such matters as the issues falling for determination and, if appropriate, the exchange of witness statements in advance of the substantive hearing. It would be important to obtain from the parties a reliable time estimate of the length of the hearing, which the parties should be asked to justify by reference to the number of documents which the tribunal was likely to be asked to examine and to the number of witnesses who were likely to be called to give evidence on the relevant issues.

It should then be possible for the regional office 'to allot a realistic slot in the list to ensure an uninterrupted hearing of the whole case, without damaging disruptions which had occurred in the present and other cases'. In *Hendricks v Metropolitan Police Commissioner* [2003] IRLR 96, para 54, Mummery LJ gave the following guidance for dealing with discrimination cases which involve numerous incidents by many people over a long period (in that case over 11 years):

> Before the applications proceed to a substantive hearing, the parties should attempt to agree a list of issues and to formulate proposals about ways and means of reducing the area of dispute, the number of witnesses and the volume of documents. Attempts must be made by all concerned to keep the discrimination proceedings within reasonable bounds by concentrating on the most serious and the more recent allegations. The parties' representatives should consult one another about their proposals before requesting another directions hearing before the chairman. It will be for him to decide how the matter should proceed, if it is impossible to reach a sensible agreement.

(2) *Disability discrimination* The importance of this approach in disability discrimination cases was emphasized by the EAT in *Goodwin v Patent Office* [1999] IRLR 4, [1999] ICR 302. In cases where the parties have not identified the real questions at issue in the claim and response, the tribunal should either give standard directions or arrange for a directions hearing in order to clarify the issues, as 'generally, it will be unsatisfactory for the disability issue to remain unclear and unspecific until the hearing itself'. Moreover, if expert evidence is to be called, directions should be given at an early stage, as 'it would be quite undesirable for any such evidence to be given without proper advance notice to the other party and the early provision of a copy of any expert report to be referred to'. If the degree of impairment required for disability is an issue, tribunals are encouraged to use the directions procedure to remind the parties, particularly where they are unrepresented, of the need in most cases for qualified and informed medical evidence to be obtained (see *McNicol v Balfour Beatty Rail Maintenance Ltd* [2002] IRLR 711, [2002] ICR 1498, para 26 and *De Keyser Ltd v Wilson* [2001] IRLR 324). It is appropriate to have an examination for the purposes of discovering the causes of an alleged disability but it may be legitimate to investigate whether a claimed impairment is genuine (see *Hospice of St Mary of Furness v Howard* [2007] IRLR 944). In *De Keyser* Lindsay P (at para 36) set out the following guidance when considering the instruction of expert witnesses:

(a) Careful thought needs to be given before any party embarks upon instructions for expert evidence. It by no means follows that because a party wishes such evidence to be admitted that it will be. A prudent party will first explore with the employment tribunal at a directions hearing or in correspondence whether, in principle, expert evidence is likely to be acceptable.
(b) Save where one side or the other has already committed itself to the use of its own expert (which is to be avoided in the absence of special circumstances), the joint instruction of a single expert is the preferred course.
(c) If a joint expert is to be instructed, the terms which the parties need to agree include the incidence of that expert's fees and expenses. Nothing precludes the parties *agreeing* that they will abide by such a view as the tribunal shall later indicate as to that incidence (though the tribunal will not be obliged to give any such indication), but the tribunal has no *power* as to costs beyond the general provisions of ETR 2004, r 12.
(d) If the means available to one side or another are such that in its view it cannot agree to share or to risk any exposure to the expert's fees or expenses, or if, irrespective of its means, a party refuses to pay or share such costs, the other party or parties can reasonably be expected to prefer to require their own expert, but even in such a case, the weight to be attached to that expert's evidence (a matter entirely for the tribunal to judge) may be found to have been increased if the terms of his instruction shall have been submitted to the other side, if not for agreement then for comment, ahead of their being finalized for sending to the expert.

(e) If a joint expert is to be used, tribunals, lest parties dally, may fix a period within which the parties are to seek to agree the identity of the expert and the terms of a joint letter of instruction and the tribunal may fix a date by which the joint expert's report is to be made available.
(f) Any letter of instruction should specify, in as much detail as can be given, any particular questions the expert is to be invited to answer and all more general subjects which he is to be asked to address.
(g) Such instructions are as far as possible to avoid partisanship. Tendentiousness, too, is to be avoided. Insofar as the expert is asked to make assumptions of fact, they are to be spelled out. It will, of course, be important not to beg the very questions to be raised. It will be wise if the letter emphasizes that in preparing his evidence the expert's principal and overriding duty is to the tribunal rather than to any party.
(h) Where a joint expert is to be used, the tribunal may specify, if his identity or instructions have not been agreed between the parties by a specified date, that the matter is to be restored to the tribunal, which may then assist the parties to settle that identity and those instructions.
(i) In relation to the issues to which an expert is or is not to address himself (whether or not he is a joint expert) the tribunal may give formal directions as it does generally in relation to the issues to be dealt with at the main hearing.
(j) Where there is no joint expert the tribunal should, in the absence of appropriate agreement between the parties, specify a timetable for disclosure or exchange of experts' reports and, where there are two or more experts, for meetings (see below).
(k) Any timetable may provide for the raising of supplementary questions with the expert or experts (whether there is a joint expert or not) and for the disclosure or exchange of the answers in good time before the hearing.
(l) In the event of separate experts being instructed, the tribunal should encourage arrangements for them to meet on a without prejudice basis with a view to their seeking to resolve any conflict between them and, where possible, to their producing and disclosing a schedule of agreed issues and of points of dispute between them.
(m) If a party fails, without good reason, to follow these guidelines and if in consequence another party or parties suffer delay or are put to expense which a due performance of the guidelines would have been likely to avoid, then the tribunal may wish to consider whether, on that party's part, there has been unreasonable conduct as to costs.

There is also considerable guidance in CPR Part 35 (Experts and Assessors), and the associated Practice Direction (PD), which ought to be carefully considered by all those seeking to rely upon expert evidence. This includes reminding parties in the High Court that the late production of expert evidence or the unavailability of a chosen expert will not usually be grounds to vary directions and/or a trial date. For example, in *Rollinson v Kimberley Clark Ltd* [2000] CP Rep 85, the Court of Appeal held that it was not acceptable for a solicitor to instruct an expert shortly before trial without checking on his availability.

Generally the use of expert evidence should be limited to that which is reasonably required to resolve the proceedings (CPR r 35.1) and it is the duty of the expert to assist the court rather than the parties (CPR r 35.3). This latter point may need to be emphasized when the expert is someone who treats, or has care for, a party. The expert's report, whether a joint or party's own, should comply with the practice direction which includes setting out the basis of instructions and expressly acknowledging the duty to the court.

(3) *Protected disclosure cases* In protected disclosure (whistle-blowing) cases it has also been suggested that a hearing is needed 'in order to identify the issues and ascertain what evidence the parties intend to call on those issues' (*ALM Medical Services Ltd v Bladon* [2002] IRLR 807, [2002] ICR 1444). The reason for this is that the protected disclosure provisions of ERA 1996, ss 43A–43L require a number of different elements to be established on the evidence before a claimant can succeed in his claim; for example, whether he has made a qualifying protected disclosure, whether he acted with the necessary reasonable belief

under s 43B, or with the required good faith under s 43C, or whether he acted reasonably in making an external disclosure under s 43G.

(4) *Equal Pay cases* The special procedure to follow in equal pay cases is set out in Chapter 15 and, as is pointed out, the aim is to reduce the delays that occur in such claims and various timetables are set out.

B. ORDERS AND DIRECTIONS AT CASE MANAGEMENT DISCUSSIONS

How to apply for an order

An application for an order must be made in writing not less than 10 days before the hearing at which it is to be considered unless it is not reasonably practicable to do so or the judge or tribunal considers it in the interests of justice that shorter notice should be allowed. It should state the case number and the reasons for the request. However the rule is not operated inflexibly: while 10 days should be allowed in order for objections this is invariably circumvented and many applications, because of their urgency, are not in writing but are by fax or phone (for example postponements). **6.04**

If the application is for a CMD to be held it should identify the precise orders to be sought (r 11(3)) although some flexibility is allowed by most judges. It should also set out an explanation as to why the orders are sought and how the order will assist the judge in dealing with the proceedings efficiently and fairly. **6.05**

When a party is legally represented in relation to an application (except for a witness order) the party or representative must provide all other parties with the following information in writing: **6.06**

(a) details of the application and why it was sought;
(b) notification that any objection to the application must be sent to the tribunal within seven days of receiving the application or before the date of the hearing (whichever date is the earlier);
(c) notification that any objection to the application must be copied to both the tribunal and all other parties (r 11(4)).

The power to make orders is extensive and can include an application to a tribunal hearing a case that it recuse itself and that there be a rehearing in front of a differently constituted tribunal on the grounds of bias (see *Charman v Palmers Scaffolding Ltd* [1979] ICR 335 and *Peter Simper & Co Ltd v Cooke (No 1)* [1984] ICR 6). **6.07**

Varying or setting aside

A party may apply for an order to be issued, varied, or revoked at any stage in the proceedings (r 10(2)(n)). As an order made at a CMD is an interim order rather than a final judgment the limited grounds on which a final judgment can be reviewed (r 34(3)) do not apply to applications under r 10(2)(n); see however para 6.04 for other limitations on an employment judge's power to vary such an order. **6.08**

The grounds on which an application may be made under r 10(2)(n) are not prescribed, and therefore not limited, and may include where an order made by a judge on his own initiative where the parties have not been given an opportunity to make representations, or where one party has had the opportunity to do so. In such circumstances the matter may be reconsidered by the tribunal upon application by the absent party. **6.09**

An application must be made before the time for complying with the order has expired and must include the reasons for the application (ETR 2004, r 11(4)(a)). The right to make an objection within seven days must be communicated to all parties by the legal representative or by the Secretary to the tribunal and this is usually done by a template box at the end of the letter. **6.10**

An order made or refused by one judge cannot simply be revisited by another. If there is a subsequent application tribunals should follow the same principles applicable under the CPR and **6.11** only set aside or vary such an order where there has been a change in the circumstances since it was made (see CPR 29PD, para 6.4). In *Goldman Sachs Services Ltd v Montali* [2002] ICR 1251 a tribunal reversed an interim order (made by a different tribunal) providing for a limitation issue to be heard at a directions hearing, and instead ordered it to be dealt with at the substantive hearing. It was held on appeal that, in the absence of any change of circumstances, this was both 'a wrong exercise of discretion and wrong in principle'.

Sanctions for non-compliance

6.12 If a party does not comply with an order made by the tribunal, a judge or tribunal may exercise powers under r 13 and:

(1) make an order in respect of costs or preparation time (see Chapter 12);
(2) at a pre-hearing review or hearing (subject to notice being given under r 19) strike out the whole or part of the claim or response, or order that a respondent be debarred from responding to the claim altogether;
(3) issue an order that, unless an order is complied with, the claim or response shall be struck out on the date of non-compliance without further consideration of the proceedings or the need to give notice under r 19 or hold a pre-hearing review or hearing.

6.13 A strike out under r 13 may be reviewed as it is a 'judgment' even where it is for default of an unless order (see *Neary v Governing Body of St Alban's Girls School* UKEAT 0281/08). In so doing the tribunal is exercising a similar power to that of the High Court in exercising relief from sanctions, and an employment judge must consciously consider all nine factors in the CPR r 3.9(1) when determining an application for review of such an automatic strike out. Such an application must, in the High Court, be supported by evidence and it is useful to record the factors here:

(a) the interests of the administration of justice;
(b) whether the application for relief has been made promptly;
(c) whether the failure to comply was intentional;
(d) whether there is a good explanation for the failure;
(e) the extent to which the party in default has complied with other rules, practice directions, court orders and any relevant pre-action protocol;
(f) whether the failure to comply was caused by the party or his legal representative;
(g) whether the trial date or the likely trial date can still be met if relief is granted;
(h) the effect which the failure to comply had on each party; and
(i) the effect which the granting of relief would have on each party.

6.14 Contrast the position with the striking out of a response which does not give rise to a final determination of proceedings, and therefore does not fall within the definition of a 'judgment' in Sch 1 para 34(1)(b) and Sch 1 para 28(1)(a); see *North Tyneside Primary Care Trust v Aynsley & Others* [2009] All ER (D) 125. An employer whose response is struck out is liable to have a default judgment issued just as if he had failed to present a response in the first place. As such there was no need to examine the factors in CPR 3.9(1). A respondent may, however, apply for the order to be reconsidered under r 10(2)(m) (see para 13.09 below).

Particular orders that may be applied for

6.15 As set out at para 6.02 above, particular examples of orders which may be made are listed in r 10(2) and each is considered below.

Additional information: general

6.16 (a) A tribunal may order a party to provide further details of the allegations in a claim or response.
(b) The tribunal can so order at the request of a party or at the tribunal's own motion either before or at a hearing.

(c) Parties should try to avoid long and complicated requests, and the earlier that such requests are made the more likely they are to be granted.
(d) The purpose of a request for further information is to inform the other side of the case that they have to meet, to prevent parties from being taken by surprise by enabling them to prepare rebutting evidence, and to define the issues in dispute.
(e) A party who fails to comply with an order to provide further information may find his claim or response, or relevant parts, dismissed or struck out although tribunals are naturally reluctant to take this draconian step (see paras 6.27 and 6.28).

Rules 1 and 4 of ETR 2004 require the claimant to set out the details of a claim and the respondent to state the grounds for resisting a claim. If either party's allegations are vague or ambiguous, further details may be sought. A common example is where a party refers to a conversation that has allegedly taken place. The opposing party will seek details as to when it was and who was involved so that rebutting evidence can be obtained. The employer may request further information before the response has been entered in cases where the claim is very obscure. **6.17**

Tribunals are, in general, anxious that cases do not become a complex battle of pleadings reminiscent of a case in the High Court in times past. **6.18**

Important guidance on the proper scope of orders for further information under the old rules was given in *White v University of Manchester* [1976] ICR 419, 423, by Phillips J, who said: **6.19**

> it is a matter of straightforward sense. In one way or another the parties need to know the sort of thing which is going to be the subject of the hearing. Industrial tribunals know this very well and, for the most part, seek to ensure that it comes about. Of course, in the end, if there is surprise they will ordinarily grant an adjournment to enable it to be dealt with, but by and large it is much better if matters of this kind can be dealt with in advance so as to prevent adjournment taking place.

The EAT thus required particulars of the generalized allegation made by the employers that the employee, a typist, was 'unable to cope with her job duties'. This guidance was echoed by Wood J in *Byrne v Financial Times* [1991] IRLR 417. **6.20**

An employer was also held to be entitled to particulars of an allegation that the employer condoned fraudulent claims for expenses so that it should know precisely the case which was going to be put against it, and to enable it to prepare its evidence (*International Computers Ltd v Whitley* [1978] IRLR 318). **6.21**

In *Honeyrose Products Ltd v Joslin* [1981] IRLR 80, Waterhouse J pointed out the essential principles. Claims should be sufficiently simple to enable employers to identify with reasonable clarity the case that they have to meet and the range of argument that is likely to occur before the tribunal. On the other hand, it would be 'most unfortunate if it became the general practice for employers to make requests when the nature of the case is stated with reasonable clarity'. An interesting issue arose in the case of *P & O European Ferries (Dover) Ltd v Byrne* [1989] IRLR 254 as to when particulars should be revealed of the identity of a 'relevant employee' who had taken part in industrial action but had not been dismissed. This was essential in the case because the tribunal had at the time no jurisdiction to hear a case if all the employees taking part in the industrial action had been dismissed (TULR(C)A 1992, s 238(2)). The employers argued that the identity of the individual should be revealed as it was an oversight that he had not been dismissed if he had taken part in the industrial action and they would remedy it once they knew the employee's name. The Court of Appeal held that the employers were entitled to particulars to enable them to know the case they had to meet, even though this would result in the identification of a witness, since this was outweighed by the ability of the employers to take the jurisdictional point. **6.22**

An order for further information will, however, be refused where it is unnecessary, overly burdensome, or oppressive. Part of the overriding objective relates to proportionality in any event. Thus a request for details of incidents that occurred many years ago may be refused as both unnecessary and burdensome since the witnesses are unlikely to recall the matters. Requests that **6.23** are very detailed and relate to statistical or other matters may also fail on the grounds that they are too burdensome.

6.24 Where actual or constructive knowledge of a particular fact is alleged, for example, 'the applicant knew he would be dismissed for fighting', further information would normally be ordered to discover how the applicant knew this; was he told, was it a rule derived from custom and practice, etc.

Form of application

6.25 An application for an order for further information must be made in accordance with r 11 (see paras 6.04–6.07 above). It is good practice for an informal request for further information to be made before an order from the tribunal is sought. The application to the tribunal should be brief and should enclose the previous request and reply (if any) and should state clearly why the order is sought. The request for further information should be set out clearly and preferably in a separate document. The employment judge, who may often be the duty judge in the particular tribunal office and not normally the person ultimately hearing the case, may then simply tick off such requests as are granted and strike out those that he thinks impermissible. Where unrepresented parties are involved on the other side, it is useful to send two copies of the request (one for them to keep) and to set out the request with space beneath for the reply, thus ensuring that each of the requests are answered.

6.26 If the request is in relation to a pleading, it should identify the specific part of the other side's pleading that is being questioned, usually by setting out the phrase that is under consideration, and setting out the details required.

6.27 The tribunal will state the time within which the further information should be provided. This time can be extended and a party can apply to vary or set aside the order for further information.

6.28 The representative of a party subject to a request for further information should send a copy of it to his client, preferably retyped with space for the client's response to the requests. This has the advantage of avoiding the client attending on the representative and the replies coming across in the client's own words, not those of the representative. They may then be edited.

Further requests for further information

6.29 If the replies that come back from the other party are still vague or raise even more issues, the party in receipt is entitled to make a further request for further information (although whether an order will be made for its production is a matter for the discretion of the tribunal). Before making such an application, however, a party should bear in mind the general guidance set out above and the risk of a party who asks for more being criticized for unnecessarily complicating the process.

Sanctions for non-compliance

6.30 The sanctions for non-compliance with any order of a tribunal are set out at para 6.12 above. The circumstances in which it is appropriate to strike out a claim or response for non-compliance with an order for further information have been considered by the EAT under the old rules (although it is unlikely that any difference in principle would apply under the new rules). In *Dean v Islamic Foundation* [1981] IRLR 491, the applicant's employment tribunal application claiming unfair dismissal and race discrimination was so unclear that the respondents made an extensive request for further and better particulars. The applicant's reply was still not satisfactory after he had been given two opportunities to reply. The employers applied for the application to be struck out on the grounds that he had not complied with the order. The tribunal granted the application but the EAT reversed the decision. Bristow J thought that although 'it would be difficult to imagine an originating application filled in worse' this was 'an occupational hazard for industrial tribunals'. It was apparent to the tribunal that this was a claim for unfair dismissal compensation and from the notice of appearance 'there was no misunderstanding by the employers about what Mr Dean was on about in his claim'. It was not appropriate, however, to strike out the whole claim since this would result in preventing Mr Dean from 'presenting that part of his claim which is intelligible and which may or may not be well founded'. The applicant argued that there was no provision expressly in the rules to strike out part of his originating application, and even though this was technically correct at the time (under ETR 1980) the EAT held that it could order 'by its inherent jurisdiction to get the proceedings into the proper shape in which they can be dealt with' that the unfair dismissal part only should go ahead and not the allegations of discrimination. The Court of Appeal upheld the decision.

It is instructive to compare *Dean* with the approach of the tribunal in *Medallion Holidays Ltd v* **6.31** *Birch* [1985] IRLR 406. The employers justified the dismissal of the employee on the grounds of his 'failure to perform his duties in a manner consistent with the good of the company resulting in substantial losses and losses of contracts'. The employee's solicitors obtained orders for further particulars and discovery but the employers failed to comply with them even though they were given extensions of time. The employment judge ordered that the whole of the notice of appearance be struck out, and the EAT would not interfere with this use of the judge's discretion. Such an order was required in order 'to demonstrate that the interlocutory directions of a tribunal are not made lightly and that parties who treat them casually are liable to do so at risk of losing their case altogether'. However, in *James v Blockbuster Entertainment* [2006] IRLR 360, the claimant failed to provide adequate further particulars of his claims, refused to allow his employer to photocopy his disclosure documents, and attended the tribunal on day one of a six-day hearing with previously unseen documents (including an undisclosed tape recording of an important conversation). In addition to the above breaches of tribunal orders he also refused to sign his witness statement, and attended on the morning of the hearing having made changes without notice to the employer. The tribunal struck his claim out. On appeal the Court of Appeal held that despite this set of breaches the power to strike out should be exercised sparingly. Sedley LJ gave the following guidance: that the first object of any system of justice is to get triable cases tried and it does not necessarily matter if the litigant is difficult and uncooperative. He further observed that it is undesirable for a strike-out application to be made (or granted) on the first day of a six-day hearing. If non-compliance is serious enough to warrant a strike-out application, this ought to be clear before the trial begins—although it is not clear what the employer ought to have done here. This liberal decision in favour of claimants is likely to reduce the number of strike outs.

Special rules in race, sex, and disability discrimination claims

In the case of race, sex, equal pay, disability, religion, sexual orientation, and age discrimination, **6.32** claimants are assisted by the fact that they may issue a questionnaire to the employer (RRA 1976, s 65(1); SDA 1975, s 74(1); EqPA 1970, s 7B(1); DDA 1995, s 56(2); RBR, reg 33(1); SOR, reg 33(1); and AR, reg 41(1)). This is considered in Chapter 31. The questions and replies are admissible as evidence in the tribunal, and if the employer deliberately omits to reply within the statutory period of eight weeks (for all except sex discrimination cases; it was formerly within a reasonable period) or is misleading, evasive, or equivocal in the replies, the tribunal may infer, if it considers it just and equitable to do so, that this failure or refusal is evidence that the employer has committed the unlawful act in question (see *King v Great Britain-China Centre* [1991] IRLR 513; *Virdee v ECC Quarries Ltd* [1978] IRLR 295; *Chapman v Simon* [1994] IRLR 124; *Igen Ltd v Wong* [2005] ICR 931, [2005] IRLR 258; and *Madarasy v Nomura* [2007] IRLR 246). The EAT in *Dattani v Chief Constable of West Mercia Police* [2005] IRLR 327 extended the drawing of inferences to form ET3 and other documents. Similar provisions are found in regs 28 and 33 of the Employment Equality (Religion and Belief) Regulations 2003 and the Employment Equality (Sexual Orientation) Regulations 2003.

Reply

In general, a formal reply to the matters in a response is not required and should be used only **6.33** in complex cases where a specific legal point is raised or to make it clear that the respondent's account of the facts is strongly disputed. This may assist in clarifying the issues in advance of the hearing.

Written answers

6.34 (1) The tribunal can, of its own motion or on application, require a party to provide a written answer to a question.
(2) The power will be exercised where it appears to the tribunal that such an answer would clarify matters and it would assist the progress of the proceedings for that answer to be available before the hearing.
(3) The written answer is not evidence but is treated in the same way as written submissions.

6.35 This power was first introduced in 1993 and allows the tribunal to require a party to provide a written answer to a question provided it clarifies an issue that arises for determination in the proceedings and will assist the progress of the proceedings if it is available before the hearing. The advantage of the written answer over requests for further information is that the former are not tied to the 'pleadings' and the material facts contained in them. So, for example, when a party claims that he was pressurized into resigning (in a witness statement or other than in the Claim Form), a written answer can be sought asking what pressure was allegedly brought to bear and by whom. The power may also be used in order to clarify the authorship of a document that has emerged in disclosure or whether a particular document was received by a party.

6.36 Any written answers that are provided have the same status as written representations in r 14(5). They are not direct evidence but may nonetheless form the basis of cross-examination if inconsistent answers are given.

Amendments

6.37 (1) Both the claimant and respondent can amend their pleadings and in deciding whether to grant any such amendment the tribunal should attempt to do justice between the parties.
(2) This amendment can include addition of new claims, in limited circumstances, where the time limit for the new claim has expired.
(3) Similarly, respondents can add new grounds of resistance with relative ease where there is simply a change of legal label put on the facts alleged.
(4) Where amendment leads to an adjournment of the hearing, the party at fault will frequently have to pay the costs incurred.

General

6.38 In *Chapman v Goonvean & Rostowrack China Clay Co Ltd* [1973] ICR 50, the NIRC stated that the general discretion to amend was an exercise of seeking to do justice between the parties. This follows the normal practice in civil litigation. If an amendment leads to an adjournment, the amending party will generally have to pay the costs occasioned by that adjournment.

Amending the claim

6.39 The claimant may amend his claim only with the leave of the tribunal once the primary time limit for presenting the claim has expired. This is so even where the claimant seeks to add a new claim, for example, for a redundancy payment in addition to a claim for unfair dismissal, even though the time limit for the presentation of the new claim has expired (*Home Office v Bose* [1979] ICR 481, on the basis that the facts were the same or very similar).

6.40 In exercising its discretion whether to allow an amendment, however, the tribunal should consider in particular 'any injustice or hardship which may be caused to any of the parties if the proposed amendment were allowed or, as the case may be, refused' (*Cocking v Sandhurst* (*Stationers*) *Ltd*

[1974] ICR 650). That case sets out (at 656–7) a useful checklist for tribunals to follow when considering amendments to the originating application (and was followed in *British Newspaper Printing Corporation (North) Ltd v Kelly* [1989] IRLR 222):

(a) Does the unamended claim form comply with the rules for presentation of a claim form?
(b) If it does not, a new claim form should probably be presented.
(c) If it does comply, was the claim presented within the time for the proposed amendment? This is not determinative of the issue, however, but is simply a factor to put in the scales (*British Newspaper Printing Corporation (North) Ltd v Kelly*, above).
(d) If it was in time, does the tribunal have the discretion to allow an amendment?
(e) If the amendment involves adding or substituting a new respondent or other party, this should only be allowed if the tribunal is satisfied that the non-inclusion was a genuine mistake and was not misleading or such as to cause reasonable doubt as to the identity of a party; a tribunal may at any time of its own volition or at the application of any person add a respondent (this is considered further below).
(f) The tribunal should have regard to the injustice or hardship which may be caused to any of the parties if the proposed amendment were allowed or, as the case may be, refused as stated above.
(g) The tribunal may make costs a condition of the amendment being granted.

In *Harvey v Port of Tilbury London Ltd* [2000] ICR 1030, Lindsay J appeared to doubt elements of the *Kelly* principles, particularly any suggestions that time limits do not apply to amendments. This may be overstating the matter and in any event the orthodoxy is contained in *Selkent Bus Co Ltd v Moore* [1996] ICR 836, where Mummery J stated that the general guiding principle is that the discretion should be exercised in a way that is consistent with the requirements of 'relevance, reason, justice and fairness inherent in all judicial discretions'. In *Selkent* Mummery J suggests that there are a number of different types of amendment, some attracting the time limits, others not. The following were the matters that were suggested for consideration: **6.41**

The nature of the amendment

Applications to amend are of many different kinds: on the one hand, the correction of clerical and typing errors, the addition of factual details to existing allegations, and the addition or substitution of other labels for facts already pleaded; and, on the other hand, the making of entirely new factual allegations which change the basis of the existing claim. The tribunal has to decide whether the amendment which is sought is one of the minor matters or is a substantial alteration pleading a new cause of action. An amendment of a broad claim of discrimination to include indirect discrimination was considered to be a minor amendment in *Quarcoopome v Sock Shop Holdings Ltd* [1995] IRLR 353. However, the tide of authority is moving away from this to a more rigorous approach. In *Smith v Zeneca (Agrochemicals) Ltd* [2000] ICR 800 Charles J concluded that a claim of direct discrimination is different and separate from both a claim of indirect discrimination and of victimization, and so cannot be deemed to include either of those claims. The point at issue in *Smith v Zeneca* was not whether an amendment should have been allowed, for no application was made to amend, but whether the pleaded case that the employers were vicariously liable for acts of sexual harassment by a fellow employee was wide enough to cover an additional claim raised at the hearing that the employers' handling of the complaint itself amounted to direct sexual discrimination by them. The tribunal held that it had no jurisdiction to consider this additional point as there had been no application to amend. The EAT held that the new point was a separate claim and could not be regarded as simply putting a different label on facts already asserted. If an application had been made to amend, the time limit would have had to be considered as the new claim was a separate 'act complained of' for the purpose of SDA 1975, s 76(1). Contrary to the decision in *Quarcoopome*, the fact that it was a further allegation of sex discrimination could not prevent time running. *Smith v Zeneca* was followed in *Ali v Office for National Statistics* [2005] IRLR 201. Mr Ali had sought leave to amend his claim form after a successful appeal by the Office for National Statistics in order to add a complaint of indirect race discrimination in light of evidence that had come to light during disclosure and cross-examination in the first hearing. The Court of Appeal overturned **6.42** the decision of the tribunal that the claimant was merely applying a new label to the same claim, holding that direct and indirect discrimination are distinct causes of action and the amendment therefore amounted to a new claim. The matter was remitted to the tribunal for consideration of whether it was just and equitable to allow the claim to be presented out of time. The facts of *Selkent* itself provide another good illustration—a late application to amend an unfair dismissal claim to allege that the reason for dismissal was trade union activities was refused as this was an application to add a fresh cause of action rather than a change of label.

6.43 In *BMA v Chaudhary* [2003] EWCA Civ 645 the Court of Appeal held that it was permissible for a claimant to amend a claim to raise allegations post-dating the original complaint (at paras 79–82) although the basis is far from clear from the judgment which largely related to issue estoppel. In *Prakash v Wolverhampton City Council* UKEAT/0140/06 the EAT held that it is permissible to amend a claim form, so as to include a claim which did not exist at the time the claim form was originally presented. This can be done by the employment tribunal exercising its discretion to allow a claim to be amended so as to permit a second claim to be included that could not have been included when the claim form was originally presented, because the second claim had accrued at a later date.

The applicability of time limits

6.44 If a new substantive complaint or cause of action is proposed to be added by way of amendment, it is essential for the tribunal to consider whether that complaint is out of time and, if so, whether the time limit should be extended under the applicable statutory provisions. An amendment of a claim form to add a new head of complaint which in itself would be out of time was only allowed if the grounds already given in the claim form clearly reveal the requisite causal connection between the original complaint and the claim form. The claimant in *Housing Corporation v Bryant* [1999] ICR 123 brought a claim for unfair dismissal (in time) and sex discrimination (out of time). The tribunal refused to allow the amendment to plead victimization because there was no suggestion of it in the unfair dismissal action and it was not just and equitable to extend time, and this approach was upheld by the Court of Appeal (see also *Ashworth Hospital Authority v Liebling* EAT/1436/96). For the relevance of the new statutory grievance and dispute resolution procedures, see Chapter 2 above.

6.45 However, in *Lehman Brothers v Smith* EAT/0486/05 the EAT contrasted the tightly drawn provision of the CPR dealing with amendment with those in r 10(2)(q) and held, at para 43, that:

> Whilst the question as to whether an amendment application seeking to add a new claim (as opposed to a minor amendment) is itself made out of time, is an important factor, it is not determinative of the question. The balance of hardship and justice as between the parties must always be considered in carrying out the exercise of discretion to grant or refuse the amendment.

The EAT reasoned that had Parliament wished to restrict tribunals' powers to amend where the new claim was out of time it would have so legislated. Despite this *Selkent* remains good law.

The timing and manner of the application

6.46 An application should not be refused solely because there has been a delay in making it unless the delay has caused prejudice. There are no time limits laid down in ETR 2004 for the making of amendments. The amendments may be made at any time—before, at, and even after the hearing of the case. Delay in making the application is, however, a discretionary factor. It is relevant to consider why the application was not made earlier and why it is now being made: for example, the discovery of new facts or new information appearing from documents disclosed. In taking any factors into account, the paramount considerations are the relative injustice and hardship involved in refusing or granting an amendment. Questions of delay, as a result of adjournments, and additional costs, particularly if they are unlikely to be recovered by the successful party, are relevant in reaching a decision. In *Berry v Ravensbourne National Health Service Trust* [1993] ICR 871 a claimant was allowed to amend the claim alleging race discrimination even though more than three months had passed since the last act complained of, because she was unaware of the act until the time limit had expired. Further, she had acted promptly on discovering this and the facts of the complaint were similar to her existing unfair dismissal claim and it was therefore just and equitable to extend time.

Although there is no obligation to hold an oral hearing to deal with every application for leave to amend, if the refusal of an application would lead to a claimant's case failing a hearing should be held (see *Smith v Gwent District Health Authority* [1996] ICR 1044, although in *Selkent* above, which is now the most frequently cited decision on the point, Mummery J suggested that a failure to hold a hearing will not necessarily amount to an error of law). **6.47**

An amendment to change the nature of the relief sought is often a simple matter, particularly where the claimant seeks to add a claim for reinstatement or re-engagement, since ERA 1996 allows the claimant to choose remedies once liability has been determined, but it is clearly best practice to choose the appropriate remedy as soon as possible, as the employer might fill vacancies without notice of the claimant's claim. **6.48**

Adding/dismissing respondents

A tribunal or judge may add a respondent at the application of any person, or on its own initiative, at any time. Rule 10(2) specifically envisages that the following orders may be made: **6.49**

(a) an order that a person whom the judge or tribunal considers may be liable for the remedy claimed be made a respondent in the proceedings;
(b) an order dismissing a claim against a respondent who is no longer directly interested in the claim;
(c) an order that a person whom the judge or tribunal considers has an interest in the outcome of the proceedings be joined as a party to the proceedings.

In *Watts v Seven Kings Motor Co Ltd* [1983] ICR 135, an application to amend by the respondent was allowed even after the tribunal had reached its decision, on the proviso that the employer had appropriate safeguards, such as an opportunity to enter a response or apply for a review (see also *Linbourne v Constable* [1993] ICR 698). The effect of delay was again stressed to be merely a factor in the absence of time limits for amendments in *Gillick v BP Chemicals Ltd* [1993] IRLR 437 and *Linbourne v Constable* above, both of which concerned amendments to add new respondents against whom new claims would be time-barred. The fact that two respondent companies are related is again only a factor and not the grounds upon which the discretion is exercised (see *Gillick*). **6.50**

The EAT in the *Linbourne* case stressed that where it is evident during the tribunal hearing that the wrong respondent is present, the tribunal should make this clear to the applicant and invite an application to amend. However, potential new respondents should be given the chance to address the tribunal on the issue of whether joinder should be permitted (*Gillick v BP Chemicals* [1993] IRLR 437). **6.51**

It may not be appropriate for a party to be, or continue to be, a respondent in the proceedings where no remedy could be sought against it (*Sandhu v Department of Education and Science* [1978] IRLR 208). **6.52**

Amending the response

A response can also be amended at any time with the leave of the tribunal, although the later that an amendment is left the less likely it is to be granted and the less likely any factual claim made in the amendment is to have credibility. An example of a late application that was refused is *Kapur v Shields* [1976] ICR 26, where the respondents sought to amend at the hearing from a defence that the claimant had asked for dismissal to assist in an application for a council flat, to a defence of capability and conduct. The application was refused on the grounds of lateness and fairness (see also *Ready Case Ltd v Jackson* [1981] IRLR 312, where the application was refused as the application was late, the respondents had professional advice, and they had not complied with a request for further information). If there is no prejudice to the claimant and no new evidence is needed, the application is far more likely to be granted. **6.53**

Witness orders

6.54 (1) Witnesses may be compelled to attend the tribunal and to produce documents, either on application by the parties or by the tribunal of its own motion.
(2) For a witness order to be made the witness must be relevant to the proceedings and must be unwilling to attend unless compelled.

6.55 Either party may apply to an employment tribunal for a witness order against a person in any part of Great Britain to attend the employment tribunal and for that person to produce any documents in his or her possession. The power generally corresponds to the witness summons power in the ordinary civil courts. The tribunal may now order the attendance of a witness of its own motion and in such circumstances the witness should be called by the tribunal, with both parties having an opportunity to cross-examine. In *Dada v Metal Box Co Ltd* [1974] IRLR 251 it was stated that, before issuing a witness order, tribunals should satisfy themselves that:

(a) the witness prima facie can give evidence which is relevant to the issues in dispute; and
(b) it is necessary to issue a witness order to compel attendance (that is because the witness has refused to come voluntarily, for example, because his employer objects).

6.56 It is an error of law to refuse a witness order where the witness has relevant documents in his possession (see *Wilcox v Humphreys & Glasgow Ltd* [1975] IRLR 211). However, the Court of Appeal emphasized in *Noorani v Merseyside TEC Ltd* [1999] IRLR 184 that tribunals have a wide discretion in deciding whether to issue a witness order.

6.57 A problem can arise for a party where the witness attends under a witness order and gives evidence that is unfavourable to the party who has called him. The general rule applicable in both criminal and civil cases is that a party cannot challenge the credibility of his own witness. There are, however, two situations that must be distinguished and they involve the unfavourable witness and the hostile witness. An unfavourable witness is one who, although he does not display any hostility to the party calling him, fails to come up to proof (that is, does not give the evidence expected of him) or gives evidence unfavourable to the party who has called him. The only avenue left open to the party is to call other evidence in rebuttal but he cannot challenge the witness directly (see *Ewer v Ambrose* (1825) 3 B & C 746).

6.58 A hostile witness is one who has no desire to tell the truth and displays hostility to the party calling him. The tribunal must be invited to find that the witness is hostile and the party who has called him may be permitted to cross-examine him. The tribunal can take into account the attitude and demeanour displayed by the witness, his willingness to cooperate, and inconsistent prior statements. If cross-examination is allowed, the party who called the witness may ask leading questions but cannot present evidence to show that the witness cannot be believed on oath.

6.59 The attendance of the witness should be requested by letter before an order is sought. The witness may claim travelling expenses to and from the tribunal from the Employment Tribunals Service. Failure without reasonable excuse to comply with a witness order may result in a fine not exceeding level 3 on the standard scale (ETA 1996, ss 4(6) and 7(4)).

Disclosure orders

6.60 (1) Disclosure may be ordered to facilitate the fair disposal of the case and to save costs.
(2) Unless there is an order for disclosure or inspection, no party is under any obligation in relation to disclosure, but any party who chooses to make voluntary disclosure of any documents in his possession or power must not be unfairly selective in his disclosure.
(3) To succeed in an application for an order for disclosure the documents must be relevant to the issues and therefore it is usually important to establish what the issues are at as early a stage as possible.

Each party may need documents which are currently in the possession of the other party in order to prove its case. For instance, it may be necessary to have access to a report made by the employer on a particular alleged incident of misconduct. A tribunal may, on the application of a party or of its own motion, order a party to grant disclosure or inspection of a document to another party. Such orders are not limited to documents; photographs and video evidence can also be obtained. **6.61**

In contrast with the position in the civil courts under CPR Part 31, there is no general duty on the parties to give disclosure in tribunal proceedings. Tribunals are nevertheless directed by r 10(2)(d) to adopt the same principles as the county court. The principles of standard disclosure under the CPR require a party to disclose those documents on which he relies, any documents which support or adversely affect his or another party's case, and any other documents which a party is required to disclose pursuant to a relevant practice direction. CPR 31PD, para 5.4 states that in deciding whether to make an order for specific disclosure the court will take into account all of the circumstances of the case and, in particular, the overriding objective (to deal with cases justly and in a cost-effective manner). **6.62**

The general rule is that a document is relevant 'which it is reasonable to suppose contains information which may, not which must, either directly enable the party either to advance his own case or to damage the case of his adversary (including) a document which may fairly lead him to a train of inquiry which may have either of these two consequences' (*Compagnie Financière v Peruvian Guano Co* (1882) 11 QBD 55; see also *Ballantine* (*George & Sons*) *v FER Dixon* [1974] 2 All ER 503). The documents sought must be relevant and be necessary to be disclosed for the fair disposal of the proceedings (*Dolling Baker v Merrett* [1990] 1 WLR 1205) and the fact that they are available and would be disclosed normally is not the correct approach—the relevance and necessity is the key. In *Okuda v (1) Photostatic Copies (Southern) Ltd, (2) Japan Office Equipment Ltd* COIT 2663/183, the tribunal stressed that documents must be relevant and material, and the respondents failed to convince the employment tribunal to order disclosure of the applicant's bank statements on either ground. **6.63**

In *Copson v Eversure Accessories Ltd* [1974] ICR 636, Sir John Donaldson said: **6.64**

> cases are intended to be heard with all the cards facing upwards on the table. It was said that the tribunal's power of ordering further and better particulars, discovery or issuing witness orders will be of little value in the pursuit of justice if the parties do not know they exist. Tribunals should therefore be vigilant to ensure that their existence is known in appropriate cases.

In *Birds Eye Walls Ltd v Harrison* [1985] IRLR 47, 52, Waite J stated the general principle that: **6.65**

> No party is under any obligation, in the absence of an order upon the Industrial Tribunal, to give discovery in the Tribunal proceedings. That is subject, however, to the important qualification that any party who chooses to make voluntary discovery of any documents in his possession or power must not be unfairly selective in his disclosure. Once, that is to say, a party has disclosed certain documents (whether they appear to him to support his case or for any other reason) it becomes his duty not to withhold from discovery any further documents in his possession or power (regardless of whether they support his case or not) if there is any risk that the effect of withholding them might be to convey to his opponent or to the tribunal a false or misleading impression as to the true nature, purport or effect of any disclosed document.

There are two principles to be borne in mind so that no party should suffer injustice by reason of the rule being applied. The first is that the duty of every party not to withhold from disclosure any document whose suppression would render the disclosed document misleading is a high duty which the tribunals should interpret broadly and enforce strictly. The second is that the tribunal should use its wide and flexible powers as the master of its own procedure to ensure that if any party can be shown at any stage of the proceedings to have been at risk of having his claim or defence unfairly restricted by the denial of an opportunity to become aware of a document in the possession or power of the other side, which is material to the just prosecution of his case, he does not suffer any avoidable disadvantage as a result. In certain circumstances, an application **6.66** for an order for disclosure will be refused if to grant it may lead to such significant expenditure of time and cost to the respondent as to be oppressive (see *Wilcox v HGS* [1975] ICR 306 and *Perera v Civil Service Commission* [1980] ICR 699).

6.67 The general approach has been set out by Wilkie J in *South Tyneside Metropolitan Borough Council v Anderson* EAT/0002/05 (the facts of which are considered below). When faced with an application for disclosure the tribunal should order disclosure of such documents as appear relevant at that stage and then later, if necessary, consider applications for specific disclosure—as opposed to order mass disclosure and leaving it to the parties to determine relevance later. If specific disclosure is then sought it would be sensible if the party applying produced either evidence or a skeleton argument as to why the disclosure already ordered was insufficient for the purpose of disposing of the issues at the hearing (see para 6.73 below).

6.68 CPR 31PD, para 2A requires parties to search for and disclose documents held in electronic form as well as on paper. The definition of such a 'document' includes not only file stores on servers and back-up systems but also those that have been deleted. It also covers additional information stored and associated with electronic documents called 'metadata'—the data that describe the structure and workings of an organization's use of information, and which describe the systems it uses to manage that information. The new List of Documents form in civil cases (N265) requires parties to give details of the steps they have taken to search for electronic documents (eg the devices—PCs, databases, back-ups, mobile phones, PDAs) and where they have not searched for types of documents to say so (eg spreadsheets, calendars, mail files).

6.69 Just as in a search for a paper document the extent of a search is not without limit and will depend upon:

(a) the number of documents involved;
(b) the nature and complexity of the proceedings;
(c) the ease and expense of retrieval of any particular document: this includes accessibility and location of documents and data including emails, servers, back-up systems, and other devices or media (eg phones, flash cards, portable USBs, PDAs), the likelihood of retrieving the data, the cost of it, and the significance of any document located in the search.

6.70 When any such document is sought the PD stresses the importance of the parties discussing any electronic search prior to the first Case Management Conference (so the CMD in the tribunal). This may involve the parties providing information about:

(a) the categories of documents under their control;
(b) the computer systems, electronic devices, and media on which they may be held;
(c) the storage systems maintained and their document retention policies—this is particularly useful as it will give an indication of the shelf life of documents and when it is reasonable to destroy them.

6.71 In cases involving a large amount of documentation it may be necessary to use keyword searches and this costly procedure places a particular onus on the parties to narrow the area of dispute and to discuss:

(a) the types and format of documents to be searched and disclosed (eg metadata, deleted data, back-up data);
(b) the likely volume of documentation to be reviewed and/or disclosed;
(c) the categories of documentation to be aggregated before the keyword search;
(d) the terms of the keyword search;
(e) the method of exchanging the documents (printed or electronic);
(f) the basis of charging for the process.

6.72 Not all of this will be relevant or immediately applicable in tribunals, and certainly not in the straightforward claims, but where it is the PD should be followed as closely as possible.

Equal pay cases

In *Clwyd CC v Leverton* [1985] IRLR 197, the employee, a female nursery nurse, was held to be entitled to discovery of the job descriptions of male clerical workers employed by the appellants in certain grades of the local government clerical scale, even though she had not yet named her male comparator on the grounds that all she needed to show was a prima facie case. However, in *South Tyneside Metropolitan Borough Council v Anderson* above, the EAT had to consider an application for disclosure by 218 claimants in an equal pay claim where it was contended that the employer's job evaluation scheme was not valid and they sought disclosure of the scoring, rankings, and bandings, as well as what had been agreed and what remained to be agreed in respect of the job evaluation study. The employment judge who dealt with the application at a CMD considered r 10(4) of ETR 2001 and ordered disclosure of a large amount of documents commenting that the parties could, once they had seen them, then determine what was relevant between them. On appeal, the EAT (Wilkie J) held that any order for disclosure should only be as much as 'but no more than necessary for' the effective disposal of the litigation and that step-by-step disclosure is often to be preferred. The essential issue in this case was whether the study was agreed and this could be determined, initially at least, by looking at the relevant minutes and/or correspondence. Accordingly Wilkie J ordered only disclosure of the second category of documentation and criticized the judge's approach which had the effect of disclosing all documents and then leaving it to the parties to determine relevance. The correct approach is to order disclosure of such documents as appear relevant at that stage and then later to consider applications for specific disclosure. **6.73**

Discrimination cases

The tribunal will only order that confidential personnel reports be revealed in cases where it is reasonably necessary to do so. In *Science Research Council v Nassé* [1979] IRLR 465, the employees sought details of employment records of all other persons interviewed for jobs they had sought but to which they had not been appointed, including service records, personal history forms, personal assessment records, and details of commendations, together with their application forms for the particular posts advertised. This presented a clear conflict between the principles of facilitating proof of discrimination and preserving the confidentiality of staff reports. All members of the House of Lords agreed that there was no general proposition of law that documents are protected from discovery by reason of confidentiality alone; their relevance, although a necessary condition, was not by itself sufficient. The true test was whether discovery 'is necessary for fairly disposing of the proceedings'. Lord Wilberforce stated this principle (at 468): **6.74**

> The process is to consider fairly the strength and value of the interest in preserving confidentiality and the damage which may be caused by breaking it, then to consider whether the objective to dispose fairly of the case can be achieved without doing so and only in the last resort to order discovery.

Where the court or tribunal is impressed with the need to preserve confidentiality in a particular case, it should consider carefully whether the necessary information has been or can be obtained by other means not involving a breach of confidence. In especially sensitive cases, the court or tribunal may cover up parts of the relevant documents (known as redaction), insert anonymous references, or proceed in private (see *British Railways Board v Natarajan* [1979] 2 All ER 794). **6.75**

In *Perera v Civil Service Commission* [1980] ICR 699, the EAT gave the *Nassé* principle further consideration. In order to prove that he had been turned down several times for jobs with the Civil Service on the grounds of his race the applicant sought discovery of all documents relating to those applications. Notwithstanding that the assembly of all the relevant information would be difficult and expensive since there were 1,600 applicants, Slynn J called for sufficient material to be disclosed so that the applicant could pursue his relevant inquiry where other candidates had as high qualifications as he possessed. In particular, he called for the application forms of 78 candidates interviewed in 1977 to be revealed, together with details of their nationality **6.76** and fathers' nationalities and their final reports and assessment, with identifying material covered over.

6.77 In *Selvarajan v Inner London Education Authority* [1980] IRLR 313, the claimant sought to refer, in support of his discrimination claim, to a series of incidents between 1961 and 1976 concerning abortive applications for jobs with the respondents. The EAT held that these could be logically probative and disagreed with the tribunal's cut-off point of 1973. Since the request was limited to the application forms of the appointed candidates, minutes of appointment, and Selvarajan's own file, no unfairness or oppression would result to the respondents.

6.78 A particularly contentious question has been the power to order a summary of the persons of various ethnic groups who were appointed by a respondent during a particular period. In *Jalota v Imperial Metal Industries (Kynoch) Ltd* [1979] IRLR 313, the EAT thought that such material need not be disclosed. The position was reviewed in *West Midlands Passenger Transport Executive v Singh* [1987] IRLR 351, where Popplewell J rejected the contention that the fact of previous discrimination could have no probative value as to present discrimination, especially since the code of practice on race relations recommends that employers monitor the ethnic background of their employees. On appeal the Court of Appeal [1988] IRLR 186 set out the following principles for guidance when considering discovery applications in race or sex discrimination cases:

(a) There is normally no overt evidence of discrimination, and the claimant has an uphill struggle.
(b) The evidence adduced in a discrimination case does not need to prove decisively that the respondent acted on racial grounds.
(c) Direct discrimination involves unfavourable treatment because the claimant is a member of a group. Statistical evidence may establish a pattern in the treatment of that group, for example under-representation at the workplace, and this is why ethnic monitoring is recommended.
(d) Where a practice is being operated against a group, in the absence of a satisfactory explanation it is reasonable to infer that there has been discrimination. Evidence of discriminatory behaviour towards a group may be more persuasive than discrimination against the claimant as the latter may be motivated by personal dislike.
(e) Employers often adduce evidence that they employ both black and white employees to demonstrate that they do not discriminate and there is no reason why evidence that the employer is generally discriminatory or the ethnic breakdown of the workforce is imbalanced should not have the same probative effect.
(f) The suitability of candidates can be measured objectively. Subjective judgments are often made and if there is a high failure rate for members of an ethnic group this may indicate a conscious or unconscious racial attitude involving stereotyped assumptions.

6.79 When ordering the release of application forms of other candidates the tribunal should limit disclosure to relevant details on the claim before it and should try and ensure that comparators are not identified (see, for example, *Oxford v Department of Health and Social Security* [1977] IRLR 225). In *Williams v Dyfed County Council* [1986] ICR 449, Wood J pointed to the balance that must be maintained between the essential maintenance of trust and confidence between employer and employee and the necessary information to be supplied to the claimant so as to ensure that he has a fair hearing. The matters which would be relevant to a discrimination claim relating to failure to gain the appointment on the grounds of sex would be the sex of other applicants, their age, qualifications, and work experience. The matter should be dealt with by the regional chairman and any matters which go to identify the other applicants should be kept to a minimum.

Redundancy selection

6.80 To what extent is an individual selected for redundancy who claims that selection is unfair entitled to disclosure of the documents of the retained employees? This is a question grappled with by a number of courts over recent years. The first point to emphasize is that there must be an issue on the pleaded case that makes disclosure of such documents relevant (see *Green v British Aerospace* [1995] IRLR 433). So the claimant must allege that either the whole or a particular part of the selection process was unfair in the claim form or risk a tribunal refusing disclosure. *Green* suggested that such general disclosure of other employee's documents would be exceptional. However, in *FDR Ltd v Holloway* [1995] IRLR 400 (concerning the need to make one employee redundant out of a workforce of eight) the EAT granted disclosure of documents relating to the assessments of all eight employees as being necessary in order to dispose of the issue whether the selection criteria had been fairly applied.

However, there have been reminders not to enter into an exercise of re-marking each candidate's assessment, in particular where the initial process was subjective and depended on value judgements (see also *Eaton v King* [1995] IRLR 75). **6.81**

Medical reports

In *Department of Health and Social Security v Sloan* [1981] ICR 313, the employee wanted discovery of medical reports about herself. The employers, in response to the applicant's claim for unfair dismissal, stated that she had been retired on medical grounds because she was incapable of doing her work. The tribunal granted discovery of certain medical reports prepared by doctors on behalf of the employers, but, with the consent of the employee's legal advisers, restricted the circulation of the documents to the employee's solicitor and general practitioner. Her solicitors then applied for a variation of the order, since they wished to refer to the reports at the hearing. A different judge considered the employers' submission that disclosure to the applicant would be harmful to her health, and held that, since a litigant was entitled to see all the relevant documents unless there was a principle of law preventing it, they should be made available to the employee. **6.82**

On appeal, the EAT held that, where it was agreed that certain evidence might be harmful to an applicant if revealed, the proper course for the party's legal adviser was to cooperate to ensure that the applicant was protected, but that since it was not clear whether or not there was a fact in issue as to her medical state in this case, the decision as to whether the medical reports were relevant and ought to be disclosed would be postponed for consideration by the party's legal advisers when the employee's own medical report had been obtained. **6.83**

In *Ford Motor Co v Nawaz* [1987] IRLR 163, the EAT agreed with a tribunal that had ordered the respondent to reveal medical reports on the applicant notwithstanding that it was the employer's policy never to disclose medical reports to lay people. The fact that in ill-health cases the management are entitled to act on the say-so of their medical advisers does not absolve the management from carrying out, through their medical advisers, the proper investigation which is required in any dismissal case. In deciding whether the medical expert had sufficient material before him on which to advise, the tribunal had to see the medical material itself. Thus, the employers had to disclose the consultant's report on the applicant, instructions given to him prior to the examination, and the notes made by the in-house doctor. **6.84**

The EAT has decided that there will be no breach of a person's right to respect for private and family life under Article 8 of the ECHR where he or she is obliged to attend a medical examination or disclose medical records for the purpose of a claim for personal injury (*De Keyser v Wilson* [2001] IRLR 324). **6.85**

The Access to Medical Records Act 1988 gives employees a statutory right of access to medical reports prepared for employment purposes by a medical practitioner who has been responsible for the employee. This does not include one-off reports or those of independent consultants. **6.86**

If an employer wants access to a report prepared by the employee's doctor, he must notify the employee and obtain his consent. The employee is allowed access to the report and may refuse to forward it to the employer. He can also amend the report and attach his own views to it. **6.87**

The principle of non-disclosure where it would have harmful effects on the employee's physical or mental health is embodied in s 7(1) of the 1988 Act. Similarly, where disclosure would be likely to reveal information about another person without his consent or would reveal the identity of a source of information (other than a health professional) disclosure will not be allowed (s 7(2)).

Disclosure by non-parties

6.88 A tribunal may make an order, either on application or of its own motion, requiring a person who is not a party to attend (see witness orders, at para 6.54 above) and to produce any document relating to the matter to be determined. This will be particularly useful in (a) insolvency cases as it means the liquidator can be required to attend and to bring important documents that the former employer and employee are unlikely to have; and (b) transfer of undertaking cases where an alleged transferee may require documents from the possession of the transferor. A similar power exists in the civil courts which is much used.

6.89 Rule 10(5) of ETR 2004 states that such an order may be made only when the disclosure sought is necessary in order to dispose fairly of the claim or to save expense.

Form of application

6.90 The party requiring the information should initially approach the other side by letter with a copy to the tribunal. If the other side refuses a reasonable request an order for disclosure should be sought from the tribunal (in accordance with r 11). The letter should set out the documents sought and the request may be facilitated by a schedule or draft order identifying the documents sought, and the judge considering the application can simply tick off the documents to be disclosed.

Failure to comply

6.91 A refusal, without reasonable excuse, to comply with an order for discovery may lead to a fine (ETA 1996, s 7(4)) although this rarely happens or the party's claim or response may be struck out. The party at risk of having his pleading struck out must be given notice under r 19.

Restrictions on disclosure

Confidentiality

6.92 In *Nassé* (para 6.74 above), it was held that where a party claims that it is not appropriate to disclose a document, the tribunal may inspect the document and decide whether the claim is valid. As we have seen, confidentiality in *Nassé* was a consideration, but not a determinative factor, and the test should be whether discovery would fairly dispose of the proceedings. There is no rule whereby confidential documents are excluded from discovery merely because they are confidential. This was emphasized in *Alfred Compton Amusement Machines Ltd v Customs and Excise Commissioners (No 2)* [1974] AC 405, where it was stated that, in the absence of some additional factor, such as the fact that the claimant is exercising a statutory function which would be impeded by disclosure, confidentiality would not justify the non-disclosure of a document.

6.93 When considering an informant's information the principles of confidentiality may be relevant. In *British Steel Corporation v Granada Television Ltd* [1981] AC 1096, the House of Lords stated that the courts have a discretion to disclose the name of an informer but this must be balanced against other interests in the case.

Public interest immunity

6.94 Another possible ground for withholding a document is that it would damage the public interest (see CPR r 31.19). Public interest immunity arises in a number of ways and is usually claimed on the basis that withholding documents is necessary for the proper functioning of the public service. This must, however, be balanced in each case against the public interest in the fair administration of justice (*D v NSPCC* [1977] 1 All ER 589 and *Evans v Chief Constable of Surrey* [1989] 2 All ER 594). The requirement of a fair trial under Article 6 of the ECHR is relevant to this balancing exercise. The public interest is not static and the categories 'are not closed and must alter from time to time whether by restriction or extension as social conditions and social legislation develop' (*D v NSPCC*).

In *Conway v Rimmer* [1968] AC 910 the courts reasserted their right, over that of the executive, to decide whether in any case disclosure is in the public interest. The principles in *Conway* were applied in *Halford v Sharples* [1992] ICR 146, EAT (affirmed [1992] ICR 583, CA), where it was stated that tribunals should use the power to inspect documents with extreme care and it was stressed that the onus to justify exclusion is a heavy one. The person claiming that a document attracts public interest immunity is acting under a duty and the immunity can extend to the contents of particular documents or to a class of documents (see *Campbell v Tameside Metropolitan Borough Council* [1982] QB 1065). **6.95**

Evidence is sometimes excluded in employment tribunals on the grounds of national security, the defence of the realm, or good diplomatic relations. In *Balfour v Foreign and Commonwealth Office* [1994] ICR 277, for example, the Court of Appeal held that disclosure of certain diplomatic information was precluded by certificates signed by the Foreign Secretary and the Home Secretary claiming public interest immunity. The courts were not qualified to evaluate a minister's claim that national security would be damaged by disclosure and discovery was refused. **6.96**

In cases where a Minister of the Crown is of the opinion that the disclosure of information would be injurious to national security the information must not be disclosed (ERA 1996, s 202). The cases to which the provisions apply are those involving the giving of employment particulars, health and safety cases, ante-natal and maternity cases, written statements of reasons for dismissal, and unfair dismissal cases under Part I, ss 44 and 47, 48 and 49, 55–57, 61–63, 66–68, 69 and 70; Part VIII, ss 92 and 93; ss 99(1)–(3), 100 or 103 of ERA 1996. **6.97**

Diplomatic immunity

Where diplomatic immunity is claimed, embassy documents are protected by absolute privilege from disclosure. Even where a respondent has waived that privilege the immunity can be claimed by the embassy concerned (*Fayed v Al-Tajir* [1987] 2 All ER 396). **6.98**

Legal professional privilege

Communications between a party and his solicitor are privileged from disclosure provided that they are confidential and made for the purpose of obtaining and giving legal advice (*Balabel v Air India* [1988] 2 All ER 246). Communications between a party and his lawyer and third parties (such as expert witnesses) are also privileged, provided the dominant purpose is the preparation for contemplated or pending litigation (*Waugh v British Railways Board* [1979] 2 All ER 1169). **6.99**

The communication must have been confidential and if not actually made during the legal relationship it must have been made with a view to establishing one (see *Minter v Priest* [1930] AC 558). **6.100**

There is no rule of law which prevents the disclosure of the fact that there has been correspondence between the lawyer and client and/or that there have been meetings, only the advice given at those meetings. **6.101**

Initially, it was thought that privilege could be claimed by non-lawyers appearing before tribunals (see *M & W Grazebrook v Wallens* [1973] IRLR 139) but in *New Victoria Hospital v Ryan* [1993] IRLR 202, the EAT refused to extend privilege beyond legally qualified members of professional bodies to a firm of industrial relations consultants. **6.102**

6.103 The scope of legal professional privilege was somewhat extended in *Three Rivers Council and BCCI v Bank of England* [2004] UKHL 48, [2005] 1 AC 610 in which the House of Lords held that legal privilege covered legal advice privilege and litigation privilege, and that only litigation privilege was restricted to proceedings or anticipated proceedings in a court of law. Legal advice privilege covered advice and assistance in relation to public law rights, liabilities, and obligations as well as private law rights, and for policy reasons should not be confined to telling the client the law, and had to include advice as to what should prudently and sensibly be done in the relevant legal context.

6.104 It is possible to waive privilege by disclosing any part of the document in question in compliance with a general order for disclosure (*Pozzi v Eli Lilley & Co* The Times, 3 December 1986) and if part of a privileged document is read to the tribunal without further qualification that amounts to a waiver of privilege even if the party has not expressly authorized it (*Great Atlantic Insurance Co v Home Insurance Co* [1981] 2 All ER 485), although the document may still be excluded on the grounds of relevance (see *GE Capital Corporate Finance Group v Bankers Trust Co* [1995] 1 WLR 172). If the client raises in evidence something that he said to his solicitor on one occasion he may be questioned about what was said about the same matter on other occasions (*George Doland Ltd v Blackburn, Robson, Coates & Co* [1972] 1 WLR 1338). However, a mere reference to a privileged document does not amount to waiver (*Tate & Lyle International Ltd v Government Trading Corporation* The Times, 24 October 1984).

Absolute privilege

6.105 According to the Court of Appeal in *Lincoln v Daniels* [1962] 1 QB 237 the absolute privilege which covers proceedings in or before a court of justice can be divided into three categories. The first category covers all matters that are done before a court and extends to everything that is said in the course of proceedings by judges, parties, counsel, and witnesses, and includes the contents of documents put in as evidence. The second covers everything that is done from the inception of the proceedings onwards and extends to all pleadings and other documents brought into existence for the purpose of the proceedings, starting with the writ or other document which institutes the proceedings. The third category extends to the proof taken by a solicitor of evidence which a witness will give in court. It is immaterial whether the proof is or is not taken in the course of proceedings. The privilege also attaches to what was said in the course of an interview by a solicitor with the person who might or might not be in a position to be a witness on behalf of his client in contemplated proceedings. In *South London and Maudsley NHS Trust v Dathi* [2008] IRLR 350 Mrs Dathi tried to claim that letters written by the respondents to herself and the tribunal in response to her application for costs amounted to victimization. The letters were akin to pleadings and accordingly attracted immunity.

Self-incrimination

6.106 Section 14 of the Civil Evidence Act 1968 provides that a party does not have to give disclosure if it would tend to incriminate him or his spouse or expose them to proceedings which might lead to a penalty.

'Without prejudice' communications

6.107 Communications between the parties made with a view to seeking a settlement are not generally admissible documents (see *Rush and Tompkins v GLC* [1989] AC 1280). In *Independent Research Services v Catterall Ltd* [1993] ICR 1 Knox J, in the EAT, stated that the guiding principle on admissibility of 'without prejudice' communications is whether the negotiations are genuine and, if they are not, the documents should be admitted. There, an employee claimed a breakdown of trust and confidence and subsequently wrote a letter seeking further employment on different terms. The employers understandably wished to adduce the letter as evidence that trust and confidence had not broken down, but the EAT held it did not come within the exceptions to the 'without prejudice' rule, as it could not be said to be dishonest. There was nothing, however, to prevent the employers referring to the correspondence or the fact of the negotiations: it was only the contents of the documents so produced that were excluded.

The label 'without prejudice' is not itself determinative one way or the other of whether a document is really written without prejudice. The tribunal has to decide whether the communications were bona fide attempts at settlement before exercising the discretion to exclude them. In *BNP Paribas v Mezzotero* [2004] IRLR 508 the EAT upheld the decision of a tribunal that a meeting which the employer expressed to be without prejudice at which sexually discriminatory comments were allegedly made could be referred to in the proceedings, referring to the unequal relationship of the parties, the vulnerable position of the applicant, and the fact that the suggestion was made by the employer only once the meeting had begun, and also *Vaseghi v Brunel University* [2006] EWCA Civ 1681, in which highly material without prejudice evidence was allowed, as in discrimination claims the necessity of revealing the truth of what had occurred, and the public interest in the eradication of discrimination, tipped the scales as against the necessity of protecting the without prejudice privilege. **6.108**

Communications with ACAS

Communications with an ACAS conciliation officer, whether written or oral, are not subject to discovery unless the privilege is expressly waived by the party who communicated with the officer (ETA 1996, s 18(7)). **6.109**

Disclosure by mistake

If a privileged document is mistakenly sent to the opposing party it does not necessarily become properly disclosed and its return should be sought once the mistake is realized. However, the question as to whether a disclosure has been made by mistake is decided by primarily looking at the context in which the disclosure took place—for example it is easier to conclude that it was a mistake where there is one privileged document disclosed amongst many that cannot be so described. The test to determine whether privilege is lost is if it would not be obvious to a reasonable solicitor that a mistake had been made, the onus being on the party mistakenly disclosing to show this (see *Al Fayed v Commissioner of Police of the Metropolis* [2002] EWCA Civ 780 and *ISTIL Group Inc v Zahoor* [2003] EWHC 165). If so, the documents should be returned (see *Breeze v John Stacey & Sons Limited* [2000] CP Rep 77). This is to be contrasted with a waiver of privilege which can occur where the contents of the document are referred to during the proceedings. The principles underlying mistaken disclosure were summarized in *ISTIL* at para 74 as follows: **6.110**

> First, it is clear that the jurisdiction to restrain the use of privileged documents is based on the equitable jurisdiction to restrain breach of confidence . . . Second, after a privileged document has been seen by the opposing party, the court may intervene by way of injunction in exercise of the equitable jurisdiction if the circumstances warrant such intervention on equitable grounds. Third, if the party into whose hands the document has come (or his solicitor) either (a) has procured inspection of the document by fraud or (b) on inspection, realises that he has been permitted to see the document only by reason of an obvious mistake, the court has the power to intervene by the grant of an injunction in exercise of the equitable jurisdiction. Fourth, in such cases the court should ordinarily intervene, unless the case is one where the injunction can properly be refused on the general principles affecting the grant of a discretionary remedy, e.g. on the ground of delay.

If a party wishes to recover documents mistakenly disclosed an application to the tribunal should be made promptly and/or an application may be made for an injunction to restrain improper use. **6.111**

In *Pizzey v Ford Motor Company Limited* [1994] PIQR P15 a similar situation arose where the claimant's solicitors mistakenly sent a privileged document to the defendants. The same test is to be applied—whether it is evident to a reasonable person with the qualities of the recipient that there had been a mistake even though the mistake is not in fact evident to the recipient. **6.112**

7

Interim Applications: Pre-hearing Review and Other Preliminary Issues

SUMMARY

(1) A determination of a preliminary issue can take place at a hearing (where the tribunal considers part of the proceedings should be dealt with separately) or at a pre-hearing review.

(2) A pre-hearing review is designed to deal with preliminary matters that cannot be dealt with at a case management discussion.

(3) A claim or response or part of one may be struck out at a pre-hearing review.

(4) When determining an application to strike out, the tribunal should adopt the same approach to assessment of a party's conduct as in an application for costs.

(5) Pre-hearing reviews are usually held by a judge, but can also be held by a full tribunal.

A. PRE-HEARING REVIEW

Rule 17 of ETR 2004 provides that any determination of a person's civil rights or obligations shall not be dealt with in a case management discussion (see para 6.02 above). Such restriction does not, however, apply to pre-hearing reviews where orders amounting to a final determination of the case can be made. 7.01

Rule 18 of ETR 2004 states that, at a pre-hearing review 'the judge may carry out a preliminary consideration of the proceedings' and may: 7.02

(a) determine any interim or preliminary matter relating to the proceedings;
(b) issue any order in accordance with rule 10 or do anything else which may be done at a case management discussion;
(c) order that a deposit be paid in accordance with rule 20 without hearing evidence;
(d) consider any oral or written representations or evidence;
(e) deal with an application for interim relief made under section 161 of TULR(C)A or section 128 of the Employment Rights Act.

Pre-hearing reviews are conducted by a judge sitting alone unless a party makes a written request not less than 10 days before the hearing that it be conducted by a tribunal, and the judge 7.03

considers that one or more substantive issues of fact are likely to be determined and it would be desirable for the pre-hearing review to be conducted by a tribunal (r 18(3)).

B. DETERMINATION OF PRELIMINARY ISSUES

7.04 Tribunals can hold hearings on a wide range of preliminary issues including matters of jurisdiction and questions of law. Such hearings may be in the form of a pre-hearing review, under r 18, or a full hearing under r 26 where the tribunal has determined that part of the proceedings be dealt with separately.

7.05 The specific issue to be determined must be capable of resolution separate to the substantive case (*Post Office Counters v Malik* [1991] ICR 355). In a case of constructive dismissal, for example, it will not normally be appropriate to determine whether or not there has been a dismissal because the question of who caused the dismissal is the central issue in the case.

7.06 There are a number of EAT judgments warning of the dangers inherent in determining issues at a preliminary stage (see, for example, *Secretary of State for Education v Birchall* [1994] IRLR 630). While it may be superficially a cheaper and faster course of action to isolate an issue, it is often better to find all the facts first and then to decide matters of law. As a result there may be only one appeal to the EAT rather than a whole series of appeals which may throw out the timescale and be more costly for the parties. In *Smith v Gardner Merchant Ltd* [1998] IRLR 510, Ward LJ said (at para 5):

> I would discourage industrial tribunals from trying to identify preliminary points of law in cases in which the facts are in dispute and when it is far from clear what facts will ultimately be found by the tribunal and what facts should be assumed to be necessary to form the basis of the proposed point of law.

7.07 Issues of jurisdiction are, however, commonly determined as preliminary issues. An example may be to determine who is the transferor or transferee in transfer of undertakings cases and whether there has been a transfer of an undertaking and if so which (see *Allan v Stirling District Council* [1994] IRLR 208). Without these matters being clearly determined the remainder of the structure of the hearings cannot be determined. The distinction between jurisdictional and substantive issues may nevertheless be difficult to draw. In *Warren v Wylie and Wylie* [1994] IRLR 316 the judge, sitting alone, held a preliminary hearing on whether the claimant had qualifying service to bring a claim for unfair dismissal. The facts in the case were not in dispute and the matter was a pure question of law. Similarly there are many appellate authorities warning against attempting to determine matters such as continuing acts of discrimination or the existence of a practice or policy of discrimination at such hearings. *Hendricks v Metropolitan Police Commissioner* [2003] IRLR 96 stresses that determining whether matters are out of time in a case of continuing discrimination is not suitable for preliminary determination as there are disputes of fact involved.

C. PAYMENT OF A DEPOSIT

7.08 Rule 20 of ETR 2004 provides that a judge may make an order in a pre-hearing review that a party pay a deposit of an amount up to £500 as a condition of being permitted to continue and take part in the proceedings, where he considers that the contentions put forward by that party have little reasonable prospect of success. The judge must take reasonable steps to ascertain the ability of the party to comply with the order before making it, and take that into account when determining the amount.

7.09 The deposit must be paid within 21 days of the order for payment being sent to the party. An extension of a further 14 days may be allowed if the party against whom the order is made applies within the 21 days. Failure to pay will result in the part of the claim or response to which the order relates being struck out. This is mandatory under r 20(4). The order to pay the deposit is not reviewable as r 20 is an order and not a judgment (see *Sodexho v Gibbons* [2005] ICR 1647). In fact relatively few of these orders have been made.

See Chapter 12 in relation to orders for costs or preparation time orders where a deposit has been paid. **7.10**

D. STRIKING OUT

A claim or response or any part of one can be struck out for some or all of the following reasons: **7.11**

(a) all or part of the claim or response is scandalous or vexatious or has no reasonable prospect of success (r 18(7)(b));
(b) the manner in which the proceedings have been conducted by or on behalf of the claimant or the respondent has been scandalous, unreasonable, or vexatious (r 18(7)(c));
(c) the claim has not been actively pursued (r 18(7)(d));
(d) the claimant or respondent has not complied with an order or practice direction (r 18(7)(e);
(e) it is no longer possible to have a fair hearing of the proceedings (r 18(7)(f)).

This list is exhaustive, and tribunals' general case management powers do not extend to striking out for any other reason (*Care First Partnership Ltd v Roffey* [2001] IRLR 85). Rule 18(7)(a) permits a tribunal to dismiss a claim where the claimant is not entitled to bring proceedings. The distinction between a strike out and a dismissal for want of jurisdiction is that the former requires an exercise of judicial discretion (to some extent) and the latter is a jurisdictional barrier imposed by law. Rule 19 provides that the party at risk of being struck out must be given an opportunity to give reasons why the order should not be made, either orally or in writing (see also *James v Blockbuster Entertainment* [2006] EWCA Civ 684, where the Court of Appeal stressed the necessity to consider other sanctions before striking out and its extreme nature). **7.12**

An application for an order striking out a claim or response should be made in accordance with r 11 (see paras 6.27–6.28 above). An order striking out a claim or part of claim is reviewable as it is a final determination of the proceedings, or part of them, and therefore a judgment (r 28(1)(a)). In *Sodexho v Gibbons* [2005] ICR 1647 the EAT contrasted the ETR 2004 with the 2001 Rules, the latter drawing a distinction between strike out orders which could be reviewed and those which could not and the former making no such distinction **7.13**

Scandalous or vexatious claim or response

A scandalous claim or response is one which is both irrelevant and abusive to the other side. A vexatious claim or defence is one which is not pursued with the expectation that it will be successful but with the intention of harassing the other side out of some improper motive. **7.14**

In *Ashmore v British Coal Corp* [1990] ICR 485 the Court of Appeal in an employment case expressed the view that: **7.15**

> A litigant has the right to have his claim litigated, provided it is not frivolous, vexatious or an abuse of process. What may constitute such conduct must depend on all the circumstances of the case; the categories are not closed and considerations of public policy and the interests of justice may be very material.

A persistently vexatious litigant can be declared as such using the power contained in s 33 of ETA 1996. The Attorney-General, or the Lord Advocate in Scotland, can apply to the EAT for an order for the restriction of vexatious proceedings. The effect of the order means that before the vexatious litigant can institute or continue proceedings in a tribunal or the EAT, the specific leave of the EAT is required to do so. Similarly, the EAT's leave is required before the vexatious litigant can make an application in any proceedings. **7.16**

7.17 The EAT must, before an order is made, be satisfied that a person has habitu. lly and persistently, without any reasonable ground, instituted vexatious proceedings in the employment tribunal or the EAT, whether against the same person or not, or made vexatious applications in any proceedings in the employment tribunal or the EAT.

7.18 The order may be made for a specified period or indefinitely (s 33(3)). The EAT will not give leave to the vexatious litigant unless it is satisfied that the proceedings or application are not an abuse of the process of the tribunal in question, and that there are reasonable grounds for the proceedings or application (s 33(4)). There can be no appeal against the EAT's decision to refuse leave for the institution of proceedings or continuance of existing ones or for the making of claims (s 37(3)).

7.19 An order may cover the whole of Great Britain whether made in England, Wales, or Scotland and a copy of it must be published in the *London Gazette* and *Edinburgh Gazette* (s 33(5)).

7.20 Section 42 of the Supreme Court Act 1981 is the equivalent High Court power and when considering whether to declare a person a vexatious litigant the court, under that provision, looks not only at the cause of action in the instant case but at the whole manner in which the litigation has been conducted (see *Re Vernazza* [1959] 1 WLR 622).

No reasonable prospect of success

7.21 The test for striking out on the basis of the merits of the claim or response has altered to become easier from 'frivolous' to 'misconceived' (ETR 2001, but defined as 'having no reasonable prospect of success' in those Rules) to 'no reasonable prospect of success' (ETR 2004). This brings the striking-out procedure broadly into line with the civil courts' powers to strike out statements of case (CPR r 3.4). 'No reasonable prospect of success' means, in effect, that a case is hopeless. For example dismissal was plainly and unarguably within the range of reasonable responses (a response may be struck out as well).

7.22 A second claim on the same grounds as one which has been withdrawn will not automatically be struck out. In *Mulvaney v London Transport Executive* [1981] ICR 351, the applicant's claim of unfair dismissal because of ill-health was withdrawn. He made a second application, which the respondents sought to strike out. Slynn J repeated the accepted meaning of 'frivolous' but stated that a claim of absence due to ill-health, by its nature, required careful consideration and so it should not be struck out. The EAT said (at 354):

> It seems to us that it is right to ask the question: 'Why was the first application withdrawn: is there a good reason for making a second application?' If there is, and if on the face of it the claim is not manifestly misconceived and can have no prospect of success, then a tribunal has a discretion not to strike out the application even though it is a second case.

7.23 The opposite conclusion was, however, reached in *Acrow (Engineers) Ltd v Hathaway* [1981] 2 All ER 161, where the employee withdrew his first claim the day before the hearing was due to take place, as he claimed to be unwell and no representative was available. He then made a second claim within the three-month time limit but the EAT considered this vexatious, as he should have applied to the tribunal to review the case and to take into account any detriment to the employers if the decision were set aside. There is no doubt, however, that the burden of proving the abuse is on the party making the allegation (see *Department of Education and Science v Taylor* [1992] IRLR 308) and the mere fact that previous proceedings have been brought is not a determining factor—special circumstances are needed. In *Ashmore* there were special circumstances justifying the decision to strike out, as there had been sample cases chosen as most representative and they had been dismissed. No fresh evidence in the claimant's case could change that decision.

7.24 In *AKO v Rothschild Asset Management Ltd* [2002] IRLR 348, the Court of Appeal suggested that it would be advisable for tribunals, on being notified of the withdrawal of an originating application, to ask the applicant for a statement of the circumstances of the decision to withdraw before deciding whether to make an order dismissing the proceedings.

There is nothing to stop a claimant seeking a declaration that he has been unfairly dismissed even if his employers have offered to pay him the full amount of compensation that could be awarded (*Telephone Information Services Ltd v Wilkinson* [1991] IRLR 148) or where he has received an amount of compensation in excess of the statutory limit (see *NRG Victory Reinsurance Ltd v Alexander* [1993] ICR 675, where the tribunal refused to strike out such a claim). **7.25**

Scandalous, unreasonable, or vexatious conduct

Tribunals have no contempt power and the power to strike out on this ground may be seen as a means of regulating the behaviour of unruly litigants in person following the difficulties highlighted in *O'Keefe v Southampton City Council* [1988] ICR 419, although the Court of Appeal sounded a note of caution in *James v Blockbuster* (above at para 7.12). **7.26**

The EAT set out in *Bolch v Chipman* [2004] IRLR 140 the stages that must be undertaken by a tribunal in considering any application to strike out on grounds of conduct of the proceedings: **7.27**

(a) There must be a conclusion by the tribunal not simply that a party has behaved unreasonably but that the proceedings have been conducted by or on his behalf unreasonably. The EAT commented that this proposition is supported by the decision of the Court of Appeal in *Bennett v Southwark London Borough Council* [2002] IRLR 407, where the conclusion was that conduct in the tribunal by an advocate, by way of aberrant and offensive behaviour (saying to the tribunal 'If I were an Oxford educated white barrister with a plummy voice I would not be put in this position') was not, in those circumstances, relevant conduct within the rule. In *Harmony Healthcare plc v Drewery* Independent, 20 November 2000, the EAT upheld a decision to strike out a response where the respondent's representative assaulted the claimant's representative in the tribunal waiting room.
(b) Assuming there is a finding that the proceedings have been conducted scandalously, unreasonably, or vexatiously, that is not the final question so far as leading on to an order that the response must be struck out. What is required before there can be a strike-out of a response or indeed a claim is a conclusion as to whether a fair trial is or is not still possible.
(c) Once there has been a conclusion, if there has been, that the proceedings have been conducted unreasonably etc, and that a fair trial is not possible, there still remains the question as to what remedy the tribunal considers appropriate, which is proportionate to its conclusion.

It is possible that the specific guidance on the availability of a fair hearing is less applicable now that such considerations are dealt with separately under r 18(7)(f). **7.28**

Fair hearing not possible

Tribunals generally follow the same guidelines as apply under CPR r 3.4, which gives the civil courts an unqualified discretion to strike out a claim where a party has failed to comply with a fixed time limit or order or Practice Direction. However, the prospect of a fair trial no longer being possible is a high threshold to attain. The Court of Appeal has stressed, in any event, that usually other alternatives to strike out may be more appropriate such as costs (see *Biguzzi v Rank Leisure plc* [1999] 1 WLR 1926). **7.29**

In *Evans' Executors v Metropolitan Police Authority* [1992] IRLR 570, however, the Court of Appeal accepted that when applying the old High Court principles to tribunals the courts would be less tolerant of delay than in other civil proceedings because there is a shorter limitation period and tribunals ought to decide cases quickly. The Court of Appeal stressed that **7.30** prejudice must be shown and this is often obvious since memories get worse over time. This will not be so obvious when the case turns on pure law (as it did in *Evans' Executors*, which concerned equality in pensions).

Failure to comply with an order

7.31 See Chapter 6, and for review see Chapter 13.

8

Contractual Claims

SUMMARY

(1) A narrowly defined range of claims for breach of contract can be brought in the employment tribunal.

(2) The tribunal may award damages for breach of contract up to a maximum of £25,000.

(3) The time limit for a claim is three months, and may be the subject of extension on grounds that it was not reasonably practicable to claim in time.

(4) An employer may counterclaim for breach of contract only if the employee has brought a claim for breach of contract. The restrictions on the type of claim an employer may bring mirror those applying to employee claims.

(5) The relationship between contractual claims in the tribunal and in the civil courts requires careful tactical consideration.

A. INTRODUCTION

The Employment Tribunal's Extension of Jurisdiction (England and Wales) Order 1994, SI 1994/1623 ('the 1994 Order') permits tribunals to hear certain specified claims for breach of contract. **8.01**

Matters originally excluded from their jurisdiction included claims for wrongful dismissal, and claims for contractual notice payments relating to the period after termination of employment. Sums owing under these heads were generally for fairly small amounts, with the consequence that dismissed employees would not find it worthwhile to pursue their remedies in the ordinary courts. **8.02**

Hence, a dismissed employee might succeed in an unfair dismissal claim before a tribunal, yet have no realistic opportunity of recovering sums owing in respect of these contractual claims. As Lord Browne-Wilkinson said in *Delaney v Staples* [1992] 1 AC 687, 'to be forced to bring **8.03** two sets of proceedings for small sums of money in relation to one dismissal is wasteful of time and money . . . it is not calculated to ensure that employees recover their full legal entitlement when wrongfully dismissed'. Under the 1994 Order, it is possible for a tribunal to hear all of the relevant claims together and make awards accordingly.

B. CONDITIONS FOR A CONTRACT CLAIM

8.04 The effect of s 3(2) of ETA 1996 and the 1994 Order is to give an employment tribunal a jurisdiction to hear a narrowly defined class of claims for breach of contract and a number of types of contract claim which may commonly arise in the employment context are excluded from the tribunal's jurisdiction. Once it is determined that a claim falls within the terms of the 1994 Order, the tribunal's jurisdiction is concurrent with the civil courts' common law jurisdiction to hear claims of breach of contract (see ETA 1996, s 3(4)), and the claims fall to be determined applying normal common law principles of contract law. The overlap between the jurisdictions of the tribunal and the courts is considered at para 8.32 and in Chapter 20.

8.05 If an employee brings a contract claim a tribunal may also consider a contract claim brought by an employer (1994 Order, art 4); in effect a counterclaim. An employer has no independent right to sue in the tribunal for breach of contract. Employers' claims are dealt with at para 8.23 below.

8.06 The conditions for an employee's contract claim are as follows (1994 Order, art 3):

(1) The claim must be of one of the following types (ETA 1996, s 3(2)):
   (a) a claim for damages for breach of a contract of employment or other contract connected with employment;
   (b) a claim for a sum due under such a contract;
   (c) a claim for recovery of a sum in pursuance of any enactment relating to the terms of performance of such a contract.
(2) The claim must be one which a court in England, Wales, or Scotland would have jurisdiction to hear and determine (ETA 1996, s 3(2)).
(3) The claim must arise or be outstanding on the termination of the employee's employment (1994 Order, art 3(b)).
(4) The claim must not be in respect of personal injuries or fall within the categories of claim excluded by art 5 of the 1994 Order.

Contract claim

8.07 The tribunal's jurisdiction covers claims for damages for breach of contract and claims for sums due under the contract (or under an enactment relating to the terms or performance of such a contract) (ETA 1996, s 3(2)). The jurisdiction is therefore limited to money claims, whether in debt or damages. The employment tribunal is not given jurisdiction to grant injunctions, order delivery up of property, or make declarations, even if the civil courts could do so on the same facts. A maximum of £25,000 can be awarded in respect of each such claim; this is discussed in more detail at paras 8.32–8.35 below.

8.08 The tribunal does not have jurisdiction to determine common law or equitable claims which are not founded on contract. There is therefore no jurisdiction to determine tortious claims (for example negligence or economic torts) or equitable claims (for example breach of fiduciary duty, or claims relating to trusts over an employer's property).

8.09 In *Pilley v British Steel Engineering Steels UK Ltd* EAT/182/99 the claimants complained that they had entered into a redundancy agreement on the basis of misrepresentations made by their employer. The EAT held that whatever the precise juridical basis of the claim for damages for misrepresentation it was not a claim for damages for breach of contract, and was therefore outside the tribunal's statutory jurisdiction. It should be noted, however, that the EAT remitted the case to the tribunal on the claimants' amended claim that the representations amounted to a collateral contract. There was a possibility that such a collateral contract would be a contract connected with employment for the purposes of s 3(2) of ETA 1996.

Contract connected with employment

claim must be for breach of an employment contract, or a contract connected with employment (ETA 1996, s 3(2)(a)). **8.10**

A compromise agreement entered into between an employer and an employee in respect of the employee's employment is a contract connected with employment. Thus a party to the agreement may sue in the tribunal for damages for breach of such an agreement: see *Rock-It Cargo v Green* [1997] IRLR 581, EAT. However, in relation to compromise agreements careful consideration should be given to whether the claim arises or is outstanding on termination of employment (see para 8.18 below). In the light of *Pilley* (above) a contract collateral to a collective redundancy agreement may also be a contract connected with employment. **8.11**

Jurisdiction of the courts of England and Wales

The tribunal's territorial jurisdiction in respect of contract claims is the same as the jurisdiction of the courts (ETA 1996, s 3(2)). See further Chapter 1 for the territorial jurisdiction of employment tribunals. **8.12**

Arising or outstanding on the termination of employment

Article 3(c) of the 1994 Order provides that the claim must 'arise or is outstanding on the termination of the employee's employment'. The word 'on' is used in a temporal sense: that is, the claim must be outstanding on the date of termination, or arise on that date (*Miller Bros & F P Butler Ltd v Johnston* [2002] IRLR 386, EAT). **8.13**

A claim cannot be brought while the employee is still employed. The tribunal has no jurisdiction to hear a contract claim which is lodged before the date of termination of employment, even if the employment has terminated by the date of the hearing (*Capek v Lincolnshire County Council* [2000] ICR 878, CA). **8.14**

Conversely, provided the claim arises or is outstanding on termination, a claim may be brought even if the termination occurred before the employee started work under the contract: *Sarker v South Tees Acute Hospitals NHS Trust* [1997] IRLR 328, EAT. There is no minimum qualifying period for bringing a claim under the 1994 Order: *Masiak v City Restaurants Ltd* [1999] IRLR 780, EAT. **8.15**

Where dealing with a claim for bonuses or commission, particular care must be taken to analyse whether the claimant's entitlement arises or is outstanding on termination. If the sum claimed fell due on a date after termination of employment, then the tribunal will not have jurisdiction in respect of the claim. For example, in *Peninsula Business Services Ltd v Sweeney* [2004] IRLR 49, EAT, under the terms of a commission scheme, commission due on work carried out during the claimant's employment did not fall due for payment until a date after termination of his employment. The EAT held that as at the date of termination he had no more than a prospective right to payment, which had not yet matured, and so his claim neither arose on termination, nor was it outstanding on termination. The EAT held that a claim will only be 'outstanding' on the date of termination if it is in the nature of a claim which, as at that date, was immediately enforceable but remained unsatisfied. **8.16**

As the Court of Appeal pointed out in *Capek*, where there is no jurisdiction to hear a contract claim because employment has not been terminated, it may be possible for the claimant to formulate his claim as one for an unlawful deduction from wages under Part I of ERA 1996. **8.17**

As noted at para 8.11 above a compromise agreement will be regarded as a contract connected with employment. However, the timing of when a compromise is made may exclude the **8.18** tribunal's jurisdiction. In *Rock-It Cargo* the compromise agreement was made *prior* to termination of employment, and the breach of contract also occurred prior to termination of employment; it was thus conceded that the claim was outstanding on the termination of employment. Where a compromise agreement is made *after* the termination of employment, whilst the contract may, on the authority of *Rock-It,* be connected with the employment, the claim in respect of it cannot be said to arise or be outstanding on the termination of employment (1994 Order, art 3(c)). The EAT in *Miller Bros & F P Butler Ltd v Johnston* (above) decided that there was no jurisdiction to hear a claim in relation to a contract where negotiations had begun prior to the termination of employment, but had not been concluded until after termination. However, the EAT clearly had some reservations about the undesirable practical consequences of this decision, given that there is little reason in principle to distinguish between compromises concluded before and after the termination of employment. One further point has not yet been canvassed by the authorities: given that the cause of action in the contract claim arises from the breach of contract, it is arguable that where a compromise agreement is made prior to termination, but breach does not occur until after termination, the conditions of art 3(c) would not be satisfied.

Claims in respect of personal injuries

8.19 A claim cannot be brought in the tribunal for damages, or a sum due, in respect of personal injuries (ETA 1996, s 3(3), 1994 Order, art 3). 'Personal injuries' includes any disease and any impairment of a person's physical or mental condition.

8.20 The exclusion is of potentially wide application. Obvious examples include claims in respect of injuries sustained at work as a result of the employer's culpable act or omission, the traditional territory of personal injury litigation. However, there is no requirement in s 3(3) that the claim need be one where the claimant is alleging that the personal injuries are the fault of the defendant. Where an employee's entitlement to a contractual benefit depends upon the employee demonstrating that he has suffered personal injury, then the claim is likely to fall within the exclusion, irrespective of whose fault the injury was, or indeed, by whom it was caused. In *Flatman v London Borough of Southwark* [2003] EWCA Civ 1610 the employer operated a personal injury allowance scheme in respect of injuries sustained during the course of work. The claimant's complaint was not that his employers had caused his injury, but that they had refused to pay him an allowance to which he was entitled, having satisfied the conditions for payment. He claimed for an award under the scheme, or for the loss of a chance of being awarded a sum. The Court of Appeal held that this was a claim for damages in respect of personal injuries, and was excluded from the tribunal's jurisdiction under s 3(3). Similar reasoning is likely to apply in respect of benefits under long-term disability and permanent health insurance schemes, although given their typically high value, such claims are unlikely to be suitable for the tribunal in any event.

8.21 The rationale for the exclusion would appear to be that claims in respect of personal injury invariably involve consideration of expert medical evidence, and as such raise matters which are thought unsuitable to determination in the tribunal (see for example *Flatman* above, *per* Schiemann LJ, at para 38). There is less force in this rationale now than there would have been at the time that the predecessor of s 3 of ETA 1996 was enacted. Tribunals now regularly have to deal with medical evidence in claims under DDA 1995, and also in assessing damages for personal injury as a head of loss under RRA 1976 and SDA 1975.

Claims excluded by art 5

8.22 Article 5 of the 1994 Order also excludes claims for breach of a contractual term of any of the following descriptions:

(1) a term requiring the employer to provide provision or occupation of living accommodation, or a term imposing obligations on the employer or employee in respect of living accommodation;

(2) a term relating to intellectual property;
(3) a term imposing an obligation of confidence;
(4) a term which is a covenant in restraint of trade.

C. EMPLOYER COUNTERCLAIM

An employer may bring a claim for breach of contract against the employee (1994 Order, art 4). The conditions setting out the nature of the claim are the same as those applicable to an employee's claim, ie the claim must fall within s 3(2) of ETA 1996; the claim must not fall within the excluded categories set out above; and the claim must arise or be outstanding on the termination of the employment of the employee against whom it is made. **8.23**

There are, however, important further restrictions in relation to employers' claims. The tribunal will only entertain a complaint which arises out of a contract with the employee (art 8(b)), and only if the employee has brought a contract claim (art 4(d)). An employer can only present a claim at a time when there is before the tribunal a complaint in respect of a contract claim of the employee which has not been settled or withdrawn (art 8(a)). In other words, an employer's claim can only be brought by way of counterclaim. **8.24**

When, however, a valid employer's claim has been presented, the tribunal will have jurisdiction to determine it, even if the employee's claim is subsequently withdrawn or settled. This was held to be the case from the wording of art 8 in *Patel v RCMS Ltd* [1999] IRLR 161, EAT. In *Patel* the EAT went so far as to hold that there was jurisdiction to entertain an employer's claim even though the employee's claim was not presented in time, and therefore could not proceed in the tribunal. This was because the presentation of a form IT1 (now ET1) in respect of an out-of-time claim was not a nullity, and therefore, in the language of art 4(d), proceedings in respect of a claim of the employee had been *brought before an employment tribunal.* **8.25**

The employee is in a vulnerable position, since at the time of making the initial claim he may not know that the employer may seek to counter it. As a consequence, the employee may actually refrain from making the initial contract claim, especially if the claim is for a relatively small amount. If the employer can substantiate a counterclaim in respect of serious breaches by the employee, or breaches going back over a long period, the counterclaim may indeed significantly exceed the original claim. If the employee claims only unfair dismissal, the employer will not be able to counterclaim for breach of contract. If the employee adds in a claim for wrongful dismissal, no matter how short the notice period, he exposes himself to a risk of a counterclaim for damages of up to £25,000. **8.26**

On the other hand, the circumstances in which the employer can bring a contract claim in the tribunal are all dependent on the claims the employee chooses to pursue. Even if the employee brings a contract claim, the employer may need to act swiftly in submitting a counterclaim, to avoid the risk of the employee withdrawing his claim before the counterclaim is presented. **8.27**

D. COMMENCEMENT AND TIME LIMITS

Article 7 of the 1994 Order provides that the complaint shall be presented to a tribunal within three months of the effective date of termination or, if there is no such date, the last day of the relevant employment. In cases where it is not reasonably practicable to present it within that time, it must be presented within such further period as the tribunal considers reasonable. For the purposes of art 7, no definition of effective date of termination is given, but tribunals normally adopt the definition contained in s 97(1) of ERA 1996. This view is reinforced by the fact that art 2 defines the effective date of termination in terms of s 97(1). **8.28**

Any counterclaim by the employer must be presented within six weeks of the date when the employer receives from the employment tribunal a copy of the claim in respect of the employee's **8.29** contract claim, or in cases where that is not reasonably practicable, such further period as is reasonable.

E. STATUTORY GRIEVANCE PROCEDURES

8.30 Many contract claims will be subject to the provisions concerning grievance procedures in the Employment Act 2002 and the Employment Act 2002 (Dispute Resolution) Regulations 2004, SI 2004/752 (where those procedures still apply). Claims which are not concerned with dismissal (for example bonus claims) will be likely to be subject to the requirement to follow a standard or modified procedure under reg 6 of the 2004 Dispute Resolution Regulations. Regulation 6 will apply to a claim which is outstanding after termination of employment unless it is not reasonably practicable for the employee to raise a grievance in writing (reg 6(4)), an exception which is likely to be of limited scope in practice. If a statutory grievance procedure applies, a claimant must take care to follow the procedure in order to avoid having his claim rejected by the tribunal. Chapter 2 deals with the application of the statutory procedures and the tribunal's power to reject claims for non-compliance. Subject to transitional provisions the statutory grievance procedure was abolished with effect from 6 April 2009.

F. HEARING OF A CONTRACT CLAIM

8.31 An employment judge sitting alone may hear any contractual claim (ETA 1996, s 4(3)(d)). In deciding whether to hear a case alone or with lay members, the judge must take into account whether there are other proceedings which might be heard concurrently. If there are other such proceedings, such as a claim for unfair dismissal, this may weigh against having a judge sitting alone. See further paras 1.28–1.31 above.

G. COMPENSATION LIMITS AND RELATIONSHIP WITH THE CIVIL COURTS

8.32 As has been stated, all of the claims falling within the contractual jurisdiction may also be brought in the ordinary courts; a claimant thus faces a choice whether to bring a claim in the tribunal or in the High Court or the county court. A number of factors are likely to be relevant in choosing where to proceed:

(a) The value of the claim: will the claim exceed the £25,000 cap imposed in the tribunal?
(b) Remedy: does the claimant seek a remedy other than a monetary award (for example an injunction, an order for delivery up or an account)? If so, the court is the appropriate forum.
(c) Other claims: does the claim stand alone, or is it to be brought alongside other claims? If there are other claims, are they to be brought in the tribunal (for example unfair dismissal or discrimination) or in the courts (for example personal injury or restrictive covenant claims)? There may well be an advantage in having the contract claim determined along with the other claims, if this is possible.
(d) Speed: the tribunal is likely to provide a quicker remedy than the courts.
(e) Cost: court proceedings are more procedurally complex and are normally likely to cost more. The tribunal claim is likely to be determined on the basis that each side will bear its own costs—in the courts the claimant is likely to recover his costs if he wins, but risks paying the other side's costs if he loses.
(f) Limitation: the tribunal claim must be brought within three months (subject to extension), whereas a claim can be brought in the courts within the normal six-year limitation period for a claim for breach of contract.

8.33 One aspect is the level of award that may be made in the employment tribunal for a contract claim. Article 10 of the 1994 Order provides that the tribunal: 'shall not in proceedings in respect of a contract claim, or in respect of a number of contract claims relating to the same contract, order the payment of an amount exceeding £25,000'. This compensation limit has not been changed since 1994. In *Fraser v HLMAD Ltd* [2006] EWCA Civ 738, [2006] IRLR 687 Mummery LJ remarked that the time might have arrived for the Secretary of State to reconsider the limit, particularly in the light of the tribunal's experience of dealing with high value compensation claims in discrimination cases (see paras 5–6 and 33). A law society survey of members between 19 March and 2 April 2009 showed that 70 per cent of members responding felt that the cap should be removed or increased, <http://www.lawsociety.org.uk/documents/downloads/employ-tribunal-survey-results-may09.pdf>.

The tribunal is entitled as a matter of fact to determine that the amount of loss or debt is a sum in excess of £25,000, but can only award a capped sum of £25,000 (as in the analagous position of the statutory cap for unfair dismissal). Where a contract claim exceeds £25,000, it is not permissible to sue for the first £25,000 in the tribunal, and then claim the excess in the civil courts. The reason for this is the civil law doctrine of merger. If the tribunal adjudicates on the contract claim, the cause of action becomes merged into the judgment. Once judgment is given, there is no remaining cause of action upon which the claimant can sue. *Fraser v HLMAD* (above) was an application of the doctrine of merger in this context; see also *Republic of India v India Steamship Co Ltd* [1993] AC 410 and *Clarke v Yorke* (1882) 52 LJ Ch 32. It is important to note that the operation of the doctrine of merger is strict: unlike abuse of process there is no scope for discretionary factors to be taken into account. Thus in *Fraser* the claimant brought claims in the tribunal for unfair dismissal and breach of contract. He obtained judgment on both claims. His ET1 recognized that his contract claim exceeded £25,000, and expressly put the respondent on notice that he intended to claim in the High Court for the excess. Indeed, his court proceedings were commenced (but not concluded) before the tribunal judgment. The tribunal assessed his breach of contract damages at £80,000, but applied the statutory cap. His claim in the courts to recover the shortfall was struck out. The Court of Appeal expressed sympathy for his position: if the claimant had withdrawn his contract claim from the tribunal, not only would he have been entitled to pursue it in the High Court, but the tribunal's findings would have operated as an issue estoppel in his favour. There was no prejudice to the respondent. However, the application of the doctrine of merger was strict, and there was no scope to take into account matters such as prejudice (or absence of it) (see paras 29–30 *per* Mummery LJ). **8.34**

In practice a problem often arises where proceedings have been started in the tribunal but it subsequently transpires that the sum of £25,000 will prevent full recovery of the value of the claim in the tribunal. This may be because the claimant commenced proceedings in person and was unaware of the cap; or it may be that the claim is difficult to evaluate, and it is only after disclosure of documents that it emerges that the claim is worth more than £25,000. In these circumstances, the claimant may wish to abandon the tribunal proceedings and pursue his claim in the civil courts. The approach of the courts to the appropriate procedure for bringing the tribunal proceedings to an end has been complicated. The position is considered in detail at para 11.94 *et seq*. below. See also paras 20.10–20.22 in relation to the overlap of claims between the employment tribunal and the civil courts. **8.35**

9

The Hearing

SUMMARY

(1) There are four types of hearing: case management discussions, pre-hearing reviews, full hearings, and review hearings.

(2) Parties are entitled to 14 days' notice of a hearing (other than for case management discussions). Parties are expected to do their utmost to adhere to listing timetables, but the tribunal has the power to postpone or adjourn any hearing.

(3) The tribunal has a broad discretion to conduct hearings in a manner most appropriate for the just handling of the proceedings. Tribunals should avoid formality as far as appropriate and are not bound by the rules of evidence.

(4) A hearing must normally be held in public. A hearing may only be held in private if the evidence contains information which cannot be communicated without breach of an enactment, confidential information, or information which, if disclosed, would cause substantial injury to the employer's undertaking.

(5) A restricted reporting order may be made in certain cases involving allegations of sexual misconduct, and in certain cases of disability discrimination. The effect of such an order is to prohibit the media from publishing matter which is likely to identify specified persons involved in the proceedings.

A. INTRODUCTION

9.01 The ETR 2004 draw a distinction between five different types of hearing (ETR 2004, r 14(1), as amended):

(a) A case management discussion under r 17;
(b) A pre-hearing review under r 18;
(bb) A hearing dealing with interim relief under r 18A;
(c) A hearing under r 26;
(d) A review hearing under r 33 or 36.

9.02 A hearing under r 26 is defined as follows (r 26(1)):

> A Hearing (written with a capital for this purpose) is held for the purpose of determining outstanding procedural or substantive issues or disposing of the proceedings. In any proceedings there may be more than one Hearing and there may be different categories of Hearing, such as a Hearing on liability, remedies, costs (in Scotland, expenses) or preparation time.

9.03 This chapter deals primarily with preparation and conduct of the main hearing. However, many of the principles, particularly in relation to natural justice and practical steps to prepare evidence, may apply to hearings more generally where evidence is to be heard and where issues in the case are to be determined.

9.04 For the composition of tribunals, see Chapter 1.

B. LISTING AND NOTICE OF HEARING

9.05 The Secretary to the tribunal should send to the parties notice of any hearing (other than a case management discussion) not less than 14 days before the date fixed (ETR 2004, r 14(4)). The notice shall inform the parties that they have the opportunity to submit written representations and to advance oral argument. In relation to case management discussions, by contrast, r 14(4) requires only that the Secretary gives reasonable notice. Rule 26(4) provides that the tribunal should send with the notice of a hearing information and guidance as to the procedure at the hearing.

9.06 The requirement is that the notice is placed in the post not less than 14 days before the date fixed for the hearing; in practice the parties may receive the notice less than 14 days before the hearing (Employment Tribunals (Constitution and Rules of Procedure) Regulations 2004, reg 15(5)).

9.07 In most cases the parties will have the opportunity to have input into the time estimate for the hearing. If there is a CMD, the judge will fix a hearing based on a time estimate which has been discussed with the parties. In a case with no CMD, a judge will normally make an estimate on the basis of the papers available to him, but may give the parties a short period of time to make representations to the tribunal if the time estimate is inadequate.

9.08 Parties should attempt to assess the likely length of hearing as realistically as possible, in order to avoid hearings overrunning their allotted time and having to be adjourned 'part-heard' for long periods before the same panel can sit together again (see comments of Court of Appeal in *Martins v Marks and Spencer plc* [1998] IRLR 326, paras 60 and 61). This means that tribunal members may forget the evidence heard on the first hearing date. Problems arise in particular where hearings are spread out, with the result that it may be difficult for the tribunal to remember the demeanour of a witness over a long period. The problem is exacerbated in cases where the judge is a part-time judge and thus only sits irregularly. In *Barnes v BPC (Business Forms) Ltd* [1976] 1 All ER 237 the High Court stated that 'as many steps as possible ought to be taken so that consecutive hearings may be obtained . . . the real answer is that it cannot be helped particularly in the case of tribunals such as this which include part-time members'. In *Shashi Kumar v University of Strathclyde* EATS/0003/02, The Times, 19 July 2002, the EAT considered that it was unsatisfactory for a final hearing before an employment tribunal to be listed deliberately with gaps between every day of the hearing and such scheduling should be avoided unless absolutely necessary.

C. PREPARATION FOR THE HEARING

In many cases all important case management decisions for preparation of a case will have been taken prior to the commencement of the hearing. Either a CMD will have taken place, or the tribunal may have issued directions of its own motion. The directions should set out the timetable for disclosure of documents, preparation of bundles, exchange of witness statements, and expert reports. An estimate for the length of the hearing will have been made (either with or without the views of the parties), and the case will be listed accordingly. Case management is dealt with in more detail in Chapter 6. If there has been a CMD, the issues to be determined at a hearing should have been defined. The need for interim applications should have been identified, and by the time of the final hearing these interim applications should have been dealt with. Interim applications are dealt with in Chapter 7. **9.09**

The following paragraphs outline the main steps to be considered in preparation for a hearing (subject of course to any specific directions given by the tribunal or agreed between the parties). **9.10**

Bundles

A bundle of documents should be agreed between the parties and exchanged ahead of time. **9.11**

The guidance on preparation of bundles in civil proceedings is pertinent in the tribunal: see CPR 39PD, para 3. The following provisions are worthy of note: **9.12**

> 3.3 The originals of the documents contained in the trial bundle, together with copies of any other court orders should be available at the trial.
>
> 3.5 The trial bundle should be paginated (continuously) throughout, and indexed with a description of each document and the page number. Where the total number of pages is more than 100, numbered dividers should be placed at intervals between groups of documents.
>
> 3.6 The bundle should normally be contained in a ring binder or lever arch file. Where more than one bundle is supplied, they should be clearly distinguishable, for example, by different colours or letters. If there are numerous bundles, a core bundle should be prepared containing the core documents essential to the proceedings, with references to the supplementary documents in the other bundles.
>
> 3.7 For convenience, experts' reports may be contained in a separate bundle and cross-referenced in the main bundle.
>
> 3.8 If a document to be included in the trial bundle is illegible, a typed copy should be included in the bundle next to it, suitably cross-referenced.
>
> 3.9 The contents of the trial bundle should be agreed where possible.
>
> 3.10 The party filing the trial bundle should supply identical bundles to all the parties to the proceedings and for the use of the witnesses.

The *Chancery Guide*, Appendix 2 also provides detailed and practical guidance on preparation of bundles. A badly organized bundle can waste a great deal of tribunal time, and be confusing both for tribunal members and witnesses. Following the spirit of CPR PD39, para 3.1, a sensible order for the bundle in most cases is as follows: **9.13**

(a) claim form and response;
(b) any responses to requests for further information;
(c) questionnaires;
(d) orders and directions by the tribunal;
(e) documents. Whilst there are various ways of organizing the documents depending on the issues in the case, in most cases a single chronological sequence of documents is most helpful; however, variations from this structure may be appropriate; for example, it may be

convenient to put contract documents and employer's handbooks and policies in a separate section if they are voluminous;
(f) witness statements and expert evidence.

9.14 All documents on which each party will rely should be included in the bundle but unnecessary documents should be excluded. The fact that a bundle is agreed between the parties does not mean that the parties admit the contents of the documents, but merely that it is agreed that those documents may go before the tribunal. The truth of any material contained in the document may need to be proved by oral evidence but documents generally do not have to be formally proved.

9.15 If a question arises as to whether a particular document should be excluded from a party's bundle of documents (or an agreed bundle), the judge should decide whether the document should be excluded or not, either at a separate CMD or at the outset of the hearing. There is no requirement that such matters should be dealt with in advance of the hearing. If the admissibility of the document is determined at the hearing and there is a fear of potential prejudice arising from the lay members seeing the disputed document in advance, the judge may direct that they shall not be given the bundle until the issue has been decided (*X v Z Ltd* [1998] ICR 43, CA).

9.16 Six copies of the bundle should be brought to the tribunal on the day of the hearing. Note that one bundle may be made available to the press although they are not allowed to take it away from the tribunal room or to copy it.

Witnesses and witness statements

9.17 Witness statements should be exchanged in advance. Six copies should be brought to the tribunal plus one copy marked 'Not to be removed from the tribunal' to be made available to the public. The statements should have been signed by the maker prior to exchange, although it is not uncommon for witnesses to sign their statements on the morning of the hearing. Some judges are more particular about this than others.

9.18 Once the notice of hearing has been received, witnesses should be warned of the dates when they are likely to be needed and advised to keep themselves available for those dates. If witnesses are unwilling to attend, witness orders may be obtained from the tribunal.

9.19 Representatives should ensure that each witness reads his witness statement shortly prior to the hearing and is happy with its content. Witnesses should also be given the opportunity to familiarize themselves with the bundle of documents. It may be helpful, if time and cost permit, for each witness to be given a brief explanation of the procedure that will be followed in the tribunal. Some witnesses may choose to attend a public hearing in another case to familiarize themselves with the tribunal environment and procedure; if possible, this is helpful.

9.20 It is, of course, inappropriate for a representative to 'coach' a witness in preparation for the hearing, and inappropriate to practise cross-examination on the evidence in the case. English practice here differs from that common in the United States. There has been a recent trend in large value cases to make use of 'witness familiarization' programmes, where professional trainers carry out a mock tribunal and give training on the giving of evidence. This is permissible within prescribed limits, designed to prevent contamination of the evidence. The familiarization must take place in a context unrelated to the proceedings. Any case study should not be based on the facts of the case, nor similar facts. The representatives in the case should never be involved in the training. For detailed guidance in the context of the criminal courts, see *R v Momodou* [2005] EWCA Crim 177, [2005] 1 WLR 3442. For an application of that guidance in civil proceedings see *Ultraframe (UK) Ltd v Fielding*; *Northstar Systems Ltd v Fielding* [2005] EWHC 1638, *per* Lewison J at paras 21–31. There is Bar Standards Board Guidance at <http://www.barstandardsboard.org.uk/standardsandguidance/codeguidance/witnesspreparation-momodouandlimani/>.

Special arrangements

Representatives should consider whether special arrangements will be necessary for the hearing. For example: 9.21

(a) If audio or video recordings or links are to be used in evidence, arrangements should be made to ensure that there are facilities for the recordings to be played. It may be necessary for the representatives to provide equipment. The Hearing may be conducted by use of electronic communications provided that the Tribunal considers it just and equitable to do so (r 15 (1) as substituted by SI 2008/340). However, it must be remembered that where hearings are required to be held in public they must be held in a place to which the public has access and using equipment that allows them to see and hear all parties to the communication when witness evidence is heard (r 15 (2)). If the hearing is to be held in private the Tribunal must likewise be able to see and hear all parties to the communication when witness evidence is heard (r 15 (3)).
(b) If a professional interpreter is needed, the tribunal office dealing with the case should be notified, who will then make arrangements for an interpreter to be engaged.
(c) If any party or witness suffers from a disability, representatives should check access to the tribunal, and should take steps to ensure that he or she is able to participate and follow the proceedings. Will a deaf witness need a signer? Will a witness with a condition causing poor concentration or energy levels need extra breaks?

All of these arrangements are likely to have an effect on the time estimate, and the listing should take these factors into account. Where a case has been listed, parties should inform the tribunal as soon as they are aware of any special features which may affect the time estimate. 9.22

Chronology, skeleton, and authorities

A chronology of main events is helpful for the tribunal in all but the most simple case. This should be agreed between the parties if possible and provided to the tribunal prior to the commencement of the hearing. 9.23

In a complex case, the tribunal may be assisted by an opening skeleton argument or at least a list of issues (if these have not already been defined at a CMD). 9.24

Legal authorities should be exchanged between the parties on the morning of the hearing. In a complex case where exchange of skeleton arguments has been directed, representatives should exchange lists of authorities along with the skeleton arguments. 9.25

Review of time estimate

The parties should review the time estimate for the case in the light of each stage of its progress, in particular following disclosure and exchange of witness statements. The tribunal should be notified as soon as possible if it appears that the time estimate is inadequate. The tribunal is more likely to be able to find extra days for the hearing the earlier it is aware of the problem. Similarly, if it appears that the original listing is excessively long, the tribunal should be informed so that they can list other matters on the days which will not be needed. 9.26

Settlement

The parties should inform the tribunal as soon as possible if a settlement is reached. 9.27

D. ADJOURNMENT AND POSTPONEMENT

General considerations

The tribunal has a wide discretion whether or not to postpone or adjourn a hearing: this power falls within its general powers to regulate its own procedure. The tribunal also has a specific power 9.28

to adjourn where conciliation procedures are available for the purpose of giving an opportunity for the complaint to be settled.

9.29 The tribunal has a complete discretion, but it is to be exercised judicially (ie not arbitrarily or capriciously and after taking into account the representations of the parties), and may grant an adjournment if there is a good, reasonable ground to do so (*Jacobs v Norsalta Ltd* [1977] ICR 189). The tribunal should assess what is required in the best interests of justice in each case (*Carter v Credit Change Ltd* [1979] ICR 908, [1979] IRLR 361, CA).

9.30 In exercising their discretion to postpone hearings, tribunals should seek to weigh in the balance the need for speedy determinations, especially in the interests of claimants, against the requirement that, for example, witnesses be available at the hearing to enable justice to be done to all parties.

9.31 The policy of tribunals differs throughout the country, with some regions taking a stronger line than others on resisting adjournments. In recent years, however, most tribunals have been tougher in resisting adjournments because of the major backlog in cases.

9.32 The tribunal has the power to make costs orders in respect of costs incurred as a result of a postponement or adjournment. Rule 40(1) ETR 2004, is not subject to the more stringent conditions of r 40(2), so it is not necessary to show that a party has behaved vexatiously, abusively, disruptively, or otherwise unreasonably; the tribunal has a broad discretion to make any such order for costs as befits the justice of the case. In practice, however, tribunals are unlikely to make an order for costs on an adjournment unless there has been some unreasonable behaviour on the part of the party applying for the adjournment.

9.33 The tribunal has no power to attach conditions to an adjournment, and so should not make an adjournment dependent on the payment of costs which the party seeking the adjournment has been ordered to pay (*Cooper v Weatherwise (Roofing and Walling) Ltd* [1993] ICR 81, EAT).

Proceedings pending in another forum

9.34 Applications for a postponement or a stay often arise where proceedings relating to the same employment are pending in the High Court, county court, or Crown Court (*Jacobs v Norsalta Ltd* [1977] ICR 189). These would most commonly concern claims for breach of confidence, damages for wrongful dismissal, a criminal charge, or an action for unfair prejudice as a shareholder of a company pursuant to s 994 of the Companies Act 2006. An adjournment may be granted in respect of proceedings pending in a foreign jurisdiction (*JMCC Holdings Ltd v Conroy* [1990] ICR 179).

9.35 The question to be considered is essentially in which court the action is most conveniently and appropriately to be tried, bearing in mind all the surrounding circumstances. There is no legal presumption in favour of or against adjournments when other proceedings are afoot (*Carter v Credit Change Ltd* [1980] 1 All ER 252). It is not an error of law to refuse an adjournment of a tribunal pending High Court proceedings, bearing in mind the need for speed in tribunals (*Automatic Switching Ltd v Brunet* [1986] ICR 542).

9.36 The following factors were identified in *First Castle Electronics Ltd v West* [1989] ICR 72, 78 (*per* Wood J) as relevant to the exercise of the discretion to adjourn:

(a) The degree of overlap of the issues in the court proceedings and the tribunal proceedings.
(b) The complexity of the issues and the evidence.
(c) The amounts at stake in the respective proceedings.
(d) The risk of findings by the tribunal which will bind the High Court: 'findings of fact by the tribunal on issues coming before both proceedings in the High Court could prove embarrassing to the trial judge in the High Court . . . clear findings of fact in a judgment from a High Court judge could well prove helpful to a tribunal at a later hearings'.

(e) The procedural complexity of the case: High Court procedure is better suited to dealing with procedural and evidential complexities, for example expert evidence, large-scale disclosure, or disputes about privilege.
(f) The rules of evidence: 'in a complicated matter such as the present it is probably best that the strict rules of evidence as applied in the High Court are more suitable—excessive informality can lead to injustice to one side or the other'.
(g) Delay: the claimant may be prejudiced by the delay in that receipt of compensation is delayed and may make reinstatement or re-engagement impracticable. Either party may potentially be prejudiced by delay in resolving issues which put the parties' reputations and integrity at stake.

See also *Bowater plc v Charlwood* [1991] ICR 798; *Warnock v Scarborough Football Club* [1989] ICR 489; *Cahm v Ward and Goldstone Ltd* [1979] ICR 574.

In *Chorion plc v Lane* The Times, 7 April 1999, the High Court ordered an employee involved in High Court and tribunal proceedings to apply for a stay of the tribunal proceedings or to consent to the employer's application for a stay. There was a significant overlap between the proceedings with both involving alleged breaches of fiduciary duty and breach of contract. Since allegations of dishonesty were made it was preferable for the matters to be heard in the High Court. In *GFI Holdings Ltd v Camm* [2008] All ER (D) 74 (Sep) the EAT held that a tribunal had erred when refusing to grant a stay on the grounds that there was no overlap of issues with High Court proceedings. A finding of dismissal was an important first stage in both sets of proceedings, and there was also a real risk that the Tribunal would make findings going to the implied term contended for in the High Court. A stay should therefore be ordered. **9.37**

Although it will usually be in the interests of the employer and not in the employee's interest to postpone tribunal proceedings, delay may also (but less frequently) suit a claimant employee if, for example, he expects to be acquitted of a criminal charge, and thus wishes the magistrate or the Crown Court to adjudicate before the unfair dismissal case is heard. He will in particular not wish to be cross-examined in the employment tribunal in advance of a criminal trial. **9.38**

Postponements ought normally to be granted where the claimant has indicated that he only instituted tribunal proceedings as a protective measure to avoid being debarred by reason of the time limit. If proceedings are brought on this basis, claimants should make this clear in their originating applications and they can then easily be dealt with accordingly (see *First Castle* and *Warnock*). **9.39**

Tribunals have stressed that complainants were entitled to an early hearing of their applications in the interests of justice and tribunals should go ahead where there are straightforward issues of fact which they were competent to determine. They are generally reluctant to grant postponements without good reason; see, for example, *Bastick v James Lane (Turf Accountants) Ltd* [1979] ICR 778, where an adjournment was refused because the issues in the tribunal were not sufficiently closely linked to those in parallel criminal proceedings. Where, however, it was essential that a witness's credibility be challenged in a criminal case, the tribunal granted a postponement even though the claimant was not himself the subject of the prosecution (*Smith-Evans v Wyre Forest District Council* COIT 1590/129). **9.40**

The tribunal will examine carefully the degree of overlap between the sets of proceedings in each case. In *BUPA Care Homes (CFC Homes) Ltd v Muscolino* [2006] ICR 1329, the claimant was dismissed for gross misconduct having been found asleep while on duty. The employers applied to adjourn the unfair dismissal claim pending the claimant's appeal to the Care Standards Tribunal against a determination made by the Secretary of State that she was unsuitable to work with vulnerable adults. The EAT upheld the employment tribunal's rejection of that application. The EAT did not consider that the overlap between the different issues which the two statutory tribunals were to decide was sufficiently great. It should also be noted that the tribunal's findings of fact would not be binding on the Care Standard's Tribunal, by reason of the particular statutory provisions governing that tribunal. **9.41**

Inability of party, witness, or representative to attend

General

9.42 In exercising their discretion to postpone hearings, tribunals seek to weigh in the balance the need for speedy determinations against the requirements of a fair hearing. Delay caused by adjournment potentially causes prejudice to both sides. The adjournment usually causes additional expense. There is prejudice from an unresolved dispute hanging over the parties, particularly in cases of discrimination. In unfair dismissal cases where reinstatement is sought the longer the proceedings take, the less likely reinstatement will be a practical solution. Adjournments also entail a waste of the tribunal's limited resources.

9.43 However, the tribunal must not sacrifice the right of the parties to a fair trial in the interests of speed and efficiency. An adjournment should normally be granted where a refusal would deny a fair trial. This most frequently arises if a party or important witness is unable to attend the hearing. In *Teinaz v London Borough of Wandsworth* [2002] EWCA Civ 1040, [2002] IRLR 721, paras 20–1, Peter Gibson LJ said:

> Although an adjournment is a discretionary matter, some adjournments must be granted if not to do so amounts to a denial of justice. Where the consequences of the refusal of an adjournment are severe, such as where it will lead to the dismissal of the proceedings, the tribunal or court must be particularly careful not to cause an injustice to the litigant seeking an adjournment.
>
> A litigant whose presence is needed for the fair trial of a case, but who is unable to be present through no fault of his own, will usually have to be granted an adjournment, however inconvenient it may be to the tribunal or court and to the other parties. That litigant's right to a fair trial under Article 6 of the ECHR demands nothing less. But the tribunal or court is entitled to be satisfied that the inability of the litigant to be present is genuine, and the onus is on the claimant for an adjournment to prove the need for such an adjournment.

Absence of a witness

9.44 In most cases, the tribunal will send out a listing letter well in advance of a potential hearing date, asking the parties to indicate what dates are inconvenient for witnesses and representatives, and if a party has accepted a date as convenient, the tribunal is unlikely to accept an adjournment because it has at a later stage become inconvenient.

9.45 Parties are well advised to apply for an adjournment as soon as they become aware that a witness will not be able to attend the hearing, and to give reasons for the absence, and reasons why the adjournment application could not have been made sooner. Factors relevant to the tribunal's decision will include the importance of the evidence of the witness who cannot attend, the reasons for the witness's absence, the prejudice likely to be caused by delay, and whether the party seeking the adjournment had acted promptly in seeking the adjournment. In *Tillingbourne Bus Co Ltd v Norsworthy* EAT/947/99, the EAT said that the tribunal should have regard to the conduct of the parties such as whether they have complied with time limits and how much warning has been given of the application to adjourn. The tribunal should look at the reason for the application and how pressing it is. If an important witness cannot be present, it is necessary to consider whether the evidence might be presented in some other manner.

9.46 In *Priddle v Fisher & Son* (1968) 3 ITR 358, the High Court stated that: 'a tribunal is acting wrongly in law if, knowing that a claimant has all along intended to give evidence. . . and being satisfied as they must have been, that he was for one reason or another unable to attend they refused to adjourn merely because he had not asked expressly for an adjournment'. (See also *Giblett v MSC* EAT/249/81.)

Ill-health

9.47 Requests for adjournments are often made on grounds that a party, or a witness, is unable to attend the hearing due to ill-health. If a party is genuinely unfit to attend the hearing, then, in line with general guidance in *Teinaz v London Borough of Wandsworth* [2002] EWCA Civ 1040, [2002] IRLR 721, paras 20–1, an adjournment ought to be granted.

This should generally be the case however late the application is made, as ill-health is not only unavoidable, but frequently unforeseen. Where there are grounds to criticize the ill party for not applying sufficiently quickly once it is known that he or she will not be able to attend, however, the appropriate remedy is in costs, and it would not be appropriate to proceed in the absence of the ill party. **9.48**

The practical problem for the tribunal is in assessing the medical reason upon which the application for an adjournment is based. From time to time, for their own reasons, parties are reluctant to attend hearings, and from time to time the unscrupulous may advance a false or exaggerated medical ground for non-attendance. **9.49**

Save for cases of extreme emergency (for example if a party is taken ill or involved in an accident immediately before the hearing), a tribunal will not normally allow an adjournment without cogent medical evidence of the fact that the party is unable to attend. What is to be expected of the evidence will depend very much on the circumstances, and upon the time available between the onset of the incapacity and the hearing. **9.50**

Assessing the genuineness of the evidence presents a difficult practical problem for the tribunal. Where the tribunal has doubts about the genuineness or sufficiency of the medical evidence, it may give directions to assist in resolving its doubts. In *Teinaz* above, Peter Gibson LJ (at para 22) suggested some possible approaches which may be suitable depending on the circumstances of the case. One possibility is to direct for further medical evidence to be provided promptly. Another is to invite the party seeking the adjournment to authorize the other side's representatives to have access to the doctor who provided the evidence. A short adjournment may be appropriate for further inquiries to be made (*Teinaz*, Arden LJ, at para 39). **9.51**

The results of these further inquiries may assist the tribunal in the exercise of the discretion. Further medical evidence may reinforce the initial advice that the party was unfit to attend; or the absence of further evidence may justify the tribunal in reaching the conclusion that the ill-health is not genuine or not sufficient to warrant an adjournment. In *Andreou v Lord Chancellor's Department* [2002] EWCA Civ 1192, [2002] IRLR 728, the tribunal took the view that the medical evidence originally submitted was inadequate. The tribunal gave directions for further evidence to be provided, and spelt out the matters which it wished to see medical evidence about. The further medical evidence was wholly inadequate compliance with the direction. The Court of Appeal (consisting of two of the same judges who sat in *Teinaz*) said that the tribunal was entitled to have regard to the fact that the party seeking the adjournment had had time to produce sufficient evidence and had failed to do so as justifying its inference that the ill-health was not so serious as to warrant an adjournment. **9.52**

Andreou is also a useful reminder that the key question for the tribunal is whether the party is fit to attend the hearing. This is not the same as whether the party is fit to attend work. An illness may frequently render a party both unfit to work and unfit to attend a hearing, but this is not automatically so, and whether it is the case is a matter of evidence. **9.53**

Parties applying for an adjournment on grounds of ill-health should therefore ensure that their medical evidence: **9.54**

(a) gives a full account of the nature of the illness and its symptoms;
(b) specifically addresses the question of whether the person is fit to attend a hearing;
(c) sets out the period over which the person has suffered from the illness—if an application is made at the last minute on the basis of a condition that had been known of for some time, the party applying will have to explain the delay;
(d) if possible, sets out the prognosis for recovery, which will assist the parties and the tribunal in re-listing the case. In an urgent case this may not be possible.

If a party chooses not to attend, this is material to the exercise of the discretion to adjourn. However, if a doctor has advised his patient not to attend on medical grounds, it is unfair to **9.55** describe the party as choosing not to attend. The party cannot be expected to attend the hearing to demonstrate the fact that he is not fit (*Teinaz*).

9.56 These principles should apply to ill-health of a witness as well as to ill-health of a party. However, there are some further considerations in relation to witnesses: how important to the case is the evidence of the witness? Have reasonable steps been taken by the party to produce evidence from an alternative witness? The more peripheral the evidence of the witness, and in particular if another witness can give evidence as to the same matter, the less likely an adjournment will be granted. If however the evidence is important to the case, and there is no other witness who can cover the evidence, then an adjournment should be granted so as not to deprive the party of a fair chance to advance his case (see, for example, *Rotherham Metropolitan Borough Council v Jones* UKEAT/0726/04).

9.57 Where a party advances a false reason in support of an application to adjourn, he risks the tribunal striking out his claim, regardless of whether a fair trial would still be possible: see, for example, *Carter v Highway Express* UKEAT/0813/01, where the claimant had falsely claimed that he could not attend the hearing on grounds of ill-health. It should be noted that in *Carter* the tribunal had found that the claimant had intentionally misled the tribunal and the EAT appears to have treated the case as equivalent to 'contumelious default'. This conclusion was reached by the EAT in *Rolls Royce Plc v Riddle* [2008] IRLR 873, where a misrepresentation about the claimant's health had been made to the Tribunal which he knew to be false and took no steps to correct subsequently. Short of contumelious default, a strike-out will not normally be appropriate on grounds of unreasonable conduct if a fair trial is still possible (see *Bolch v Chipman* [2004] IRLR 140, EAT; *De Keyser Ltd v Wilson* [2001] IRLR 324, EAT and *Abegaze v Shrewsbury College of Arts and Technology* [2009] All ER (D) 209 (Feb)).

Lack of representation

9.58 In *Masters of Beckenham Ltd v Green* [1977] ICR 535, the EAT decided that the tribunal should have granted an adjournment when told that the company secretary who had represented the company at the prior hearing had recently left their employ, and no one else at that stage knew the details of the case. A similar decision was reached in *Smith v Alsecure Guards Ltd* EAT/264/82, where the employee wanted to be represented by his local welfare rights office. The EAT has, however, decided that there is no general rule of law that tribunals should permit a request for postponement made merely because a party's legal representative will not be available on the listed date. It went on to commend the practice adopted in the (then) London Central and Scotland regions that both parties be consulted in advance of a date being fixed, by means of a form on which convenient dates would be ringed (*Hewson v Travellers Club* EAT/338/85). In most tribunal regions now, the listing offices and employment judges, if an application is made to them, will not accept the inconvenience of a date for the party's representatives as a reason for adjourning a case.

Cases where interim relief is available

9.59 Where interim relief is available under s 128 of ERA 1996 (dismissals for trade union and employee representative activities and whistle-blowing), s 128(2) provides that the tribunal shall not postpone the hearing unless it is satisfied that special circumstances exist which justify it in doing so. Speed in such cases is of the essence.

Appeals against adjournment decisions

9.60 The EAT is reluctant to interfere with the employment tribunal's discretion in the matter of adjournment. In *Bastick v James Lane (Turf Accountants) Ltd* [1979] ICR 778, it was held that before the EAT could overturn a tribunal's decision it was necessary to show either that it had improperly taken into account some matter in exercising its discretion to adjourn, or that its decision was perverse in all the circumstances.

E. NON-ATTENDANCE BY A PARTY

From time to time, a party fails to attend the hearing. This may of course be for a variety of reasons. There may have been a last-minute difficulty preventing him from attending (for example ill-health, childcare problems, transport problems); it may transpire that he had not received notice of the hearing, or made a mistake as to the date for the hearing. Occasionally litigants, particularly unrepresented litigants, simply decide to abandon their claim without telling the tribunal or the other side. Some litigants see non-attendance as a tactic for achieving an adjournment in situations where their case is not ready. **9.61**

The tribunal faces a choice. It may adjourn the hearing to give the absent party the opportunity to attend. Or it may dismiss or dispose of the proceedings in the absence of the party (ETR 2004, r 27(5)). **9.62**

It goes without saying that the reason for absence is unlikely to be known to the tribunal, or the other party, at the time the tribunal must make its decision as to how to deal with the case. The tribunal and the other party face a dilemma as to the most efficient and cost-effective way of dealing with the case. On the one hand, an adjournment may do an injustice to the party who has prepared and attended and will face another day's costs on the adjourned hearing. If the absent party has indeed abandoned his case, then that second day too will be wasted. Whilst the party not at fault can in theory be compensated in costs, costs orders cannot be enforced against an impecunious claimant. On the other hand, if the tribunal proceeds with the hearing, it risks injustice to the absent party if there is a good reason for absence. Further, there is a risk of further time and cost for the other party in dealing with any review or appeal subsequently brought by the absent party. **9.63**

Before making a decision whether to adjourn or proceed the tribunal should consider trying to telephone the party or his representative to ascertain the reason for absence. In *Cooke v Glenrose Fish Company* [2004] IRLR 866, EAT, Burton J said that although the tribunal does not have to telephone the absent litigant in every case where there is an absent party, such a call should always be considered. Where solicitors were on record as representing the absent party, there would have to be a very good reason why a telephone call was not made (see also *London Borough of Southwark v Bartholomew* [2004] ICR 358, EAT). **9.64**

In *Cooke* Burton J went on to say that where a tribunal takes a stringent attitude to a party's absence, it is a necessary concomitant that there be a less stringent attitude on a review if that party comes forward with a genuine and full explanation and shows that the original hearing was not one from which he deliberately absented himself. **9.65**

If the tribunal chooses not to adjourn, it may dismiss or dispose of the proceedings under r 27(5). Rule 27(6) provides that if the tribunal wishes to dismiss or dispose of the proceedings under r 27(5) it shall first consider any information in its possession which has been made available to it by the parties. **9.66**

Rule 27(5) gives the tribunal a wide discretion about how to deal with cases to which it applies. The tribunal's consideration of the case must take account of the material referred to in r 27(6), but the tribunal is not obliged to conduct a full hearing in the absence of the party. In *Roberts v Skelmersdale College* [2003] EWCA Civ 954, [2004] IRLR 69, Mummery LJ said (at paras 15–16) that the rule does not impose on the tribunal a duty to investigate the case, nor to be satisfied that, on the merits, the respondent to a case has established a good defence to the claim of the absent claimant. In the exercise of its discretion, the tribunal would be entitled to require the respondent to produce evidence, but the rule does not impose any duty on the tribunal to follow that course. At para 15 he gave the following example: **9.67**

> For example, in an unfair dismissal case where, as here, it is common ground that there has been dismissal, the burden of establishing the reason for the dismissal is on the respondent/employer.

But rule 9(3) does not require the employment tribunal to hear evidence from the respondent in order to determine for itself substantively the reason for the dismissal, or to satisfy itself as to whether, if the dismissal was for a potentially fair reason, it was fair and reasonable to dismiss the claimant/employee for that reason.

9.68 The scope of application of r 27(5)–(6) is unclear. It appears in a rule headed 'What happens at the Hearing', and its language is specific in referring to a 'Hearing':

> (5) If a party fails to attend or to be represented (for the purpose of conducting the party's case at the Hearing) at the time and place fixed for the Hearing, the tribunal may dismiss or dispose of the proceedings in the absence of that party or may adjourn the Hearing to a later date.

9.69 There would seem to be no reason in principle why the same approach should not apply to other types of hearing particularly where that hearing may result in disposal of the proceedings (for example a review under rr 33 or 36, or a r 18 pre-hearing review to consider striking out the claim). However, there is no equivalent to r 27(5) in the rules dealing with those types of hearing, nor in r 14 which contains general guidance concerning hearings. The predecessors to the rule (ETR 2001, r 11(3); ETR 1993, r 9(3)) appeared in rules which dealt with 'the hearing of an originating application', although neither set of rules contained a rule categorizing hearings like ETR 2004, r 14. Arguably, the tribunal has sufficient powers under r 10 and r 60(1) to dismiss or dispose of proceedings even where r 27(5) does not apply, but there is no reported authority dealing with the situation.

F. WRITTEN REPRESENTATIONS

9.70 The parties may, if they wish, submit written representations to the tribunal if they are given in not less than seven days before the hearing (ETR 2004, r 14(5)). A clear distinction must be drawn between written representations which must comply with the requirements of r 14(5) to be admissible and written evidence (for example witness statements) and aids to an oral submission (for example a skeleton argument), which need not. In practice tribunals will accept written aids to oral submissions, such as skeleton arguments, lists of issues, and chronologies on the day of the hearing, and will not regard them as written representations falling within r 14(5).

9.71 The tribunal will naturally pay rather less attention to written representations than oral evidence, since the latter (unlike the former) can be challenged by cross-examination. Where both parties submit written representations and there is an acute conflict of fact, the tribunal is in an impossible position, and should call the parties for oral evidence (*Tesco Stores Ltd v Patel* The Times, 15 March 1986). Where there is no substantial conflict of fact, written representations on the law may be more appropriate.

G. CONDUCT OF THE HEARING

General considerations

9.72 The judge has a wide degree of discretion as to how the hearing should be conducted. The rules provide for a great degree of informality in tribunal procedure. However, tribunals must observe the overriding objective of dealing with cases justly, and must ensure that all parties are afforded a fair trial.

Informality

9.73 Rule 14(2)–(3) of ETR 2004 provides:

> (2) So far as it appears appropriate to do so, the judge or tribunal shall seek to avoid formality in his or its proceedings and shall not be bound by any enactment or rule of law relating to the admissibility of evidence in proceedings before the courts.

(3) The judge or tribunal (as the case may be) shall make such enquiries of persons appearing before him or it and of witnesses as he or it considers appropriate and shall otherwise conduct the hearing in such manner as he or it considers most appropriate for the clarification of the issues and generally for the just handling of the proceedings.

Rule 60(2) of ETR 2004 provides that, subject to the provisions of the rules and any Practice Directions, the tribunal or judge may regulate its or his own procedure. **9.74**

The detail of practice varies. Some judges are strict about the rules of evidence and run the tribunal as if it were a court. Others adopt a more informal approach. Others still take a more inquisitorial approach. **9.75**

The judge's discretion as to the conduct of the hearing is not unfettered; the judge must conduct the proceedings in accordance with: **9.76**

(a) the overriding objective;
(b) the parties' right to a fair trial, both under Article 6 of the ECHR, and at common law.

The tension between informality on the one hand and ensuring a fair hearing on the other hand is constantly present in employment tribunals. **9.77**

In *Aberdeen Steak Houses Group plc v Ibrahim* [1988] ICR 550, the EAT indicated that too much informality may be counter-productive and may lead to actual or perceived unfairness to a party, and it was important that parties should know in advance what rules are to apply. **9.78**

Whilst the vast majority of cases are conducted along the lines of adversarial court proceedings, a more inquisitorial approach may from time to time be appropriate. In *Ridley v GEC Machines Ltd* (1978) 13 ITR 195, 196, the EAT said: **9.79**

> The cases which are heard by industrial tribunals are very different from ordinary cases heard by regular courts, and the litigation of necessity takes—or certainly at all events ought to take—something of the form of an enquiry; so that ordinary customary legal proceedings need to be applied with that requirement in mind. It is really essential that at the end of the day the parties should feel that the whole of the facts had been investigated.

On the other hand, employment judges have to be careful not to go too far the other way and to appear to be 'entering the ring'. The tribunal must be even-handed and ensure that the parties are afforded a fair trial. **9.80**

The overriding objective

The overriding objective (reg 3 of the 2004 Regulations) is to deal with cases justly. This includes as far as practicable: **9.81**

(a) ensuring that the parties are on an equal footing;
(b) dealing with cases in ways which are proportionate to the complexity or importance of the issues;
(c) ensuring that cases are dealt with expeditiously and fairly;
(d) saving expense.

Whenever a tribunal exercises a power or interprets a provision of ETR 2004 it should seek to give effect to the overriding objective. The parties are under a duty to assist the tribunal to further the overriding objective. The overriding objective underpins the exercise of the tribunal's discretion in the matters covered in this chapter. **9.82**

The right to a fair trial

An employment tribunal is a public authority for the purposes of the Human Rights Act 1998. Therefore: **9.83**

(a) the tribunal must, so far as possible, read and give effect to legislation in a way which is compatible with Convention rights (s 3);

(b) the tribunal must not itself act in a way which is incompatible with Convention rights (s 6).

9.84 Article 6(1) of ECHR provides:

> In the determination of his civil rights and obligations . . . everyone is entitled to a fair and public hearing within a reasonable time by an independent and impartial tribunal established by law.

9.85 The tribunal should ensure equality of arms between the parties.

9.86 Quite apart from Article 6, the right to a fair trial is a fundamental principle of the common law. The Court of Appeal has said that Article 6 reflects the pre-existing approach of the common law: *R v Lord Chancellor, ex p Witham* [1998] QB 575; *Ebert v Venvil* [2000] Ch 484, 497. The common law has long recognized the right to a hearing by an independent and impartial tribunal, and the right to be heard (often referred to as the principles of natural justice).

The order of the hearing

Normal sequence of events

9.87 In the vast majority of cases the order of events and the calling of evidence follows the format of the civil courts, save that opening speeches are rare in the tribunal. Normally, the sequence of events will be as follows:

(a) Discussion of opening and preliminary matters between the parties' representatives and the judge.
(b) Calling of witnesses: each witness will in turn give evidence in chief, and then answer questions in cross-examination from the other party/parties, and from the tribunal. The party's representative may then re-examine. Local practice varies as to whether re-examination takes place before or after the tribunal's questions.
(c) Closing submissions.

The right to go first

9.88 The normal rule in the civil courts is that the party bearing the burden of proof on the main issue in the case has the right to open (ie to go first)—this principle is followed in the tribunal (*Gill v Harold Andrews Sheepbridge Ltd* [1974] IRLR 109, [1974] ICR 294, NIRC).

9.89 In an unfair dismissal case where dismissal is admitted, the respondent will normally go first, as the employer must prove the reason for dismissal. Where dismissal is denied (for example in a constructive dismissal case) then the claimant must prove the dismissal, and accordingly the claimant will normally go first. The claimant will normally go first in discrimination cases. See *Hawker Siddeley Power Engineering Ltd v Rump* [1979] IRLR 425.

9.90 The normal rule is that the right to go first carries with it the right to the last word in closing submissions. So, for example, in an ordinary unfair dismissal case, the respondent will call its witnesses first, then the claimant and his witnesses will be called. When it comes to submissions, the claimant will go first, and then the respondent.

Opening and preliminary matters

9.91 Most tribunals read the claim form and the response before the beginning of the hearing, but representatives should never assume that this has happened. It is rare that a tribunal has had the opportunity to read the bundles of documents or witness statements before the beginning of the hearing unless some reading time has been allocated. It is important for representatives to ensure at this early stage that the tribunal has before it all the necessary material, and that nothing is missing.

9.92 It is not the practice in most tribunals to allow the parties opening speeches. The party going first may get the opportunity to make a short opening address outlining the nature of the case, particularly in a complex case. Many tribunals are impatient with long introductions, and are usually eager to start the evidence. However, this eagerness should be balanced by the need to manage the hearing efficiently, and in modern practice it is common for the tribunal to spend some time before hearing evidence going through preliminary and housekeeping matters and identifying the issues to be determined.

The judge will usually identify what materials the tribunal has been provided with. The representatives should ensure that all members of the tribunal and the witness table are provided with all relevant documents (bundles, witness statements, skeletons, chronologies, etc). **9.93**

The judge will usually outline his understanding of the main issues in the case, and ask the parties' representatives what they see the issues as being. In complex cases in particular it is helpful to prepare a list of issues for the beginning of the case, or to include such a list of issues in a skeleton argument. Some judges have been known to adjourn for a short period on the first morning whilst the parties' representatives draw up an agreed list of issues. **9.94**

If it is not obvious from the judge's opening comments, the representatives should seek to ascertain what documents the tribunal has had the chance to read before the hearing. **9.95**

Correct identification of the issues at the outset of the hearing is important, as it is the duty of the parties, and not the tribunal to ensure that all relevant issues are raised, and that all relevant evidence is put before the tribunal. This is so even when one of the parties is not legally represented (*Kumchyk v Derby County Council* [1978] ICR 1116, EAT). This was confirmed in *Mensah v East Hertfordshire NHS Trust* [1998] IRLR 531, CA, where the Court of Appeal held that the tribunal had no duty to consider a part of the claim not raised by the claimant. However, the EAT has held that there are some matters which are so well established that they should be considered by a tribunal even if a party does not raise them, for example the principal criteria for an unfair redundancy (see *Langston v Cranfield University* [1998] IRLR 172, EAT). However, although judges should provide all possible help to litigants in person or those represented by unqualified friends, such assistance has to be balanced against the need to ensure fairness to the opposing party. In *Birmingham City Council v Laws* UKEAT/0360/06/MAA the EAT held that in formulating an additional issue at the closing submissions stage, the tribunal had overstepped the boundary of providing proper assistance so that an injustice was suffered by the council. **9.96**

The judge may seek to impose a timetable for the hearing, including time taken for hearing evidence from each witness and reading documents referred to in the evidence; time for cross-examination of each witness, and time for closing submissions. Representatives should be prepared to give such time estimates on the first morning. Some judges use a timetable as a guide; others are stricter and will impose a 'guillotine' if a representative goes materially beyond his estimate. **9.97**

In addition to identifying the issues and timetabling the case, there may be contested preliminary matters which may need to be resolved at the outset of the hearing. By the time the date of the 'main' hearing comes around, the result of the case management decisions should be that the issues are clearly defined, the evidence and documents are in order, and the parties and the tribunal are ready to get on with hearing the case. In practice, this is often not the case, and case management decisions will need to be taken at the beginning of the hearing. The following issues commonly need to be dealt with at the beginning of the hearing: **9.98**

(a) Definition or redefinition of the issues.
(b) Applications to admit or exclude witness evidence produced after the date for exchange of witness statements or late disclosed documents.
(c) Applications for late amendments of the parties' cases.
(d) Issues arising from the non-attendance of witnesses or parties.

Each of these issues is at the very least likely to give rise to timetabling questions, and may give rise to applications for adjournment. Often issues such as these may arise after the hearing has **9.99** commenced, for instance prompted by the evidence given by a witness, or by questions from the tribunal. The tribunal will have to decide how to deal with such issues as and when they arise. The principles that apply to such applications are dealt with in more detail in Chapters 6–7 dealing with case management and interim applications.

Split hearings; defining the issues

9.100 In a number of contexts tribunals may split a case so that different issues are dealt with at different stages. Even in a straightforward case, tribunals generally deal separately with questions of liability and the appropriate remedies (*Copson v Eversure Accessories Ltd* [1974] ICR 636). It is common for a case to be listed so that the tribunal may deal with liability, give its decision, and then immediately proceed to deal with remedy. It is not uncommon for there to be insufficient time once a liability decision is reached for remedy to be dealt with. In this situation directions will be given for remedy to be dealt with at a later hearing. In a complex case, particularly if there are multiple causes of action, there may be reasons why the tribunal will deal with some issues at one hearing, leaving other issues to a later hearing.

9.101 The tribunal should ensure that all parties are fully aware of what aspects are to be argued at what stage and that the parties have a proper opportunity to address all relevant points (*Slaughter v C Brewer & Sons Ltd* [1990] ICR 730; *Ferguson v Gateway Training Centre Ltd* [1991] ICR 658). Care should be taken to ensure that it is clear at the beginning of the hearing what issues are to be dealt with at the liability stage, and what is being left over to the remedy stage, so that the parties know what evidence needs to be called at which stage. Tribunals may refuse to allow evidence to be revisited at the remedies stage (see *Iggesund Converters Ltd v Lewis* [1984] IRLR 431; *King v Eaton (No 2)* [1998] IRLR 686, Court of Session).

The evidence

Exclusion of evidence

9.102 The tribunal has the power under rr 14 and 60(2) of ETR 2004 to control the way a party or his representative conducts his case before the tribunal. The tribunal is not bound by the rules of evidence which apply in civil and criminal courts. The tribunal can exclude irrelevant evidence and argument and stop lines of questioning and submissions which do not assist the tribunal: *Bache v Essex County Council* [2000] IRLR 251, CA.

9.103 Where a dispute arises as to the admissibility of evidence the primary question is whether the evidence is relevant to the issues in the case. Evidence which is irrelevant to the issues is inadmissible as a matter of the law of evidence, and ought not to be admitted in tribunal proceedings; see *XXX v YYY* [2004] EWCA Civ 231, [2004] IRLR 471, where the Court of Appeal upheld the tribunal's decision to refuse to admit certain video evidence on the ground that it had no probative value.

9.104 Whilst a party is entitled to adduce evidence which is relevant to the issues in the case, it is, of course, a matter for the tribunal as to whether evidence is relevant or not. In *ALM Medical Services Ltd v Bladon* [2002] EWCA Civ 1085, [2002] IRLR 807 the Court of Appeal decided that the tribunal had wrongly held that the evidence which the respondent wished to call (and in respect of which witness statements had been submitted) was irrelevant. Mummery LJ said (at para 15):

> A party is entitled to adduce evidence relevant to the issues in the case and to put questions on relevant matters to the other party and to his witnesses. It is for the tribunal, with the assistance of the parties and their representatives, to identify the relevant issues for decision and to exercise its discretionary case management powers to decide whether the evidence adduced or the questions put to the witnesses in cross-examination are relevant. The exercise of the discretion will rarely be disturbed on appeal: it can only be successfully challenged if it can be shown that the tribunal has exercised it contrary to legal principle or otherwise in a manner which is plainly wrong.

9.105 However, there is some debate in the authorities as to whether the tribunal has the power, on grounds of efficient case management, to exclude evidence which is relevant to the issues.

The point was not directly in issue in *ALM*, where the Court of Appeal held that the excluded evidence was relevant, and the tribunal had been wrong to regard it as irrelevant. The EAT in *Digby v East Cambridgeshire District Council* [2007] IRLR 585, held that a tribunal does have a discretion, in accordance with the overriding objective, to exclude relevant evidence which is, for example, unnecessarily repetitive or of only marginal relevance in the interests of proper, modern day case management. However, that discretion must be exercised judicially. It may properly be challenged on appeal on *Wednesbury* principles. The guiding principle is to ensure justice between the parties. Earlier authorities were in conflict on this issue: see *Rosedale Mouldings Ltd v Sibley* [1980] IRLR 387, approved in *Aberdeen Steak Houses Group plc v Ibrahim* [1988] IRLR 420, [1988] ICR 550, and contrast *Snowball v Gardner Merchant Ltd* [1987] ICR 719. For the time being at least, *Digby* has resolved the issue, and has reached a result that would seem correct in principle.

Hearsay evidence

Although there is no strict rule against hearsay evidence, the EAT in *Aberdeen Steak Houses Group plc* sounded a note of caution in relation to hearsay, in saying that whilst a tribunal can and should on occasion admit hearsay, it must be remembered that rules of procedure and evidence have been built up over many years in order to guide courts and tribunals in the fairest and simplest way of dealing with and deciding issues. **9.106**

Where a witness upon whose evidence a party wishes to rely cannot attend the hearing, a statement should be submitted on behalf of the witness, together with an explanation as to why the witness is not available to give live evidence. The tribunal will assess the weight to be attached to the evidence. Inevitably, evidence untested by cross-examination will carry less weight than the evidence of witnesses whom the tribunal has seen questioned at the hearing. In assessing the weight to be attached to such hearsay evidence, it is suggested that the factors to be considered in the civil courts set out in s 4 of the Civil Evidence Act 1995 are relevant: **9.107**

(1) In estimating the weight (if any) to be given to hearsay evidence in civil proceedings the court shall have regard to any circumstances from which any inference can reasonably be drawn as to the reliability or otherwise of the evidence.
(2) Regard may be had, in particular, to the following—
   (a) whether it would have been reasonable and practicable for the party by whom the evidence was adduced to have produced the maker of the original statement as a witness;
   (b) whether the original statement was made contemporaneously with the occurrence or existence of the matters stated;
   (c) whether the evidence involves multiple hearsay;
   (d) whether any person involved had any motive to conceal or misrepresent matters;
   (e) whether the original statement was an edited account, or was made in collaboration with another or for a particular purpose;
   (f) whether the circumstances in which the evidence is adduced as hearsay are such as to suggest an attempt to prevent proper evaluation of its weight.

Without prejudice communications

Without prejudice communications between the parties and their representatives are privileged and may not be put in evidence: *Rush and Tompkins v GLC* [1989] AC 1280. The principle extends to all negotiations genuinely aimed at settling the matters in dispute between the parties, and applies to both oral and written communications. The key question is whether the communication forms part of a genuine negotiation of a settlement: *Independent Research Services v Caterall* [1993] ICR 1. **9.108**

Questions of putting without prejudice communications in evidence will normally be resolved at the stage of disclosure, or in preparation of the bundle for the hearing. References to without prejudice communications in witness statements should be excised before the hearing. Not infrequently, however, a witness may start to refer to without prejudice communications in the course of evidence. Most judges are astute to issues of privilege, and will stop the witness as soon **9.109** as it is apparent that he is about to give evidence of privileged matters. The same can be said of matters which are subject to legal privilege.

9.110 Whether a communication is without prejudice or not depends upon the substance of the communication: ie whether it forms part of a genuine attempt to settle. Therefore, whilst it is common practice to label documents produced for the purpose of negotiation 'Without Prejudice', such a label is neither necessary nor sufficient: the label will not attach privilege to a document which is not without prejudice in nature, and the absence of the label will not deprive a true without prejudice communication of privilege.

9.111 In an employment dispute, it can often be difficult to ascertain the point at which without prejudice begins to apply. An employer may seek to start without prejudice discussions at an early stage: for example, where the employer is contemplating a dismissal, he may seek to have a without prejudice discussion to explore a consensual departure without the need to dismiss. If such a meeting is protected by without prejudice privilege, then the tribunal may see an incomplete picture of the events leading to dismissal, and of the reason for dismissal. Further still, it is possible, in a discrimination claim, for the events in the without prejudice meeting themselves to be acts of discrimination. This was the case in *BNP Paribas v Mezzotero* [2004] IRLR 508, EAT. The employee had raised a grievance whilst on maternity leave, and was called to a meeting with her employers. At the start of the meeting, the employers said that they wanted the discussions to be 'without prejudice' and suggested that it would be best for the business and for her if she terminated her employment. The EAT held that the tribunal was right to admit evidence of what occurred at the meeting. At the point that the meeting occurred, there was no dispute between the parties, and therefore the meeting could not have been in furtherance of settlement of a dispute. No privilege therefore attached to the contents of the meeting. In *Framlington Group Ltd v Barnetson* [2007] EWCA Civ 502 the Court of Appeal addressed the question of when, in exchanges between employer and employee, a 'dispute' can be said to have arisen such as to engage the 'without prejudice' rule. The Court stated that what was important was the subject matter of the exchanges, rather than how long before the threat, or start, of litigation they were aired. The crucial consideration was whether in the course of negotiations the parties contemplated or might reasonably have contemplated litigation if the dispute could not be resolved.

9.112 The privilege may be waived, but it must be waived by both parties, as the privilege is that of both parties. In *Chaudhary v Secretary of State for Health* [2006] EWCA Civ 1648, the Court of Appeal decided that the fact that a 'without prejudice' communication had been openly referred to in a tribunal case did not automatically mean that it could be referred to in a subsequent appeal. The question was whether the person claiming the privilege had waived it (which on the facts the Department of Health had not done) rather than whether the material had already been referred to in other proceedings. In *Brunel University v Webster* [2007] EWCA Civ 482, [2007] IRLR 592, both parties had given evidence of the allegedly privileged communications in an internal grievance meeting which had been conducted by an independent panel and amounted, in effect, to a mini-trial. The Court of Appeal held that privilege had been waived, although it stressed that the waiver arose in the context of the particular nature of the internal hearing. The Court of Appeal also held that privilege had been waived when each party referred to the without prejudice communications in the ET1 and the ET3.

9.113 Privilege will be lost if there is 'unambiguous impropriety' and an abuse of the without prejudice occasion: *Unilever plc v Proctor & Gamble* [2000] 1 WLR 2436 and *Savings and Investment Bank Ltd v Fincken* [2004] 1 WLR 667. There has been some suggestion by the EAT that privilege may more easily be lost in a discrimination case if it is necessary for the tribunal to hear evidence of without prejudice communications in order to fully investigate the allegations: that was the view of the EAT in *Brunel University v Webster* UKEAT/0307/06, purporting to follow *Mezzotero* (see above). However, the Court of Appeal in *Brunel*, whilst declining to decide the point, did not endorse the EAT's approach. In *Brodie v Nichola Ward t/a First Steps Nursery* EAT

0526/07 the EAT declined an invitation to widen the 'unambiguous impropriety' exception to allow a claimant to rely on a solicitor's letter offering a compromise agreement as the 'last straw' in her constructive dismissal claim: the letter had been a proper attempt to settle a dispute and as such was privileged.

Admissibility of evidence and human rights

In deciding whether to admit or exclude evidence, the court may on occasion have to weigh in the balance the right of the party seeking to rely on the evidence to a fair trial under Article 6 of ECHR, with a competing Convention right of the other party. Most commonly, this will be the right to private life under Article 8. See, for example, *XXX v YYY* [2004] EWCA Civ 231, [2004] IRLR 471—although the Court of Appeal decided the case on grounds of relevance, it accepted that had the evidence been relevant there would have needed to be a weighing up of the competing human rights, on the one hand the right to a fair trial, and on the other the right to privacy. **9.114**

Convention rights are not absolute, and most provide for legitimate restrictions. Article 8(2) permits interference with the right to private life in pursuit of a number of defined legitimate interests. Notable in the current context is the protection of rights and freedoms of others, which would include the right of another person to a fair trial under Article 6. Both the Court of Appeal and the EAT have been willing to allow in evidence material which is otherwise admissible and probative, even though the material was obtained by a party in a manner which interfered with the privacy of the other party. Thus in *Jones v University of Warwick* [2003] EWCA Civ 151, [2003] 1 WLR 954, a personal injury claim, evidence obtained by covert video surveillance was admitted. Evidence of a recorded telephone conversation was admitted in *Avocet Hardware plc v Morrison* EAT/0417/02; given that the telephone call was the evidence relied on by the employer in deciding to dismiss the employee, the employer could not have had a fair trial without being able to put the evidence before the tribunal. In *Amwell View School Governors v Dogherty* [2007] IRLR 198, the claimant covertly recorded disciplinary proceedings against her: both the open hearings and the panel's private deliberations. The EAT allowed the recordings of the open hearing in evidence, holding that no right to privacy was engaged. The recordings of the private deliberations were held to be inadmissible on the grounds of the public interest in maintaining the integrity of the private deliberations of adjudicating bodies. However, in balancing this interest against the claimant's right to a fair trial, the EAT expressly relied on the fact that the agreed procedure was that the panel would deliberate in private and then give full reasons for the decision. Further, the EAT indicated that the decision may have been different in a discrimination claim where the recording showed the only, and incontrovertible evidence of discrimination. The court must weigh the competing interests of fair trial and privacy in the particular circumstances of each case (see the approach of the ECtHR in *Jersild v Denmark* (1995) 19 EHRR 1). Where an employee has been dismissed in circumstances alleged to amount to a breach of Article 8, a distinction must be drawn between the tribunal's procedural decision whether to admit evidence obtained in breach of privacy (as in *Avocet*) and the tribunal's substantive decision as to whether the dismissal was unfair. For consideration of the substantive question of the impact of Article 8 on the fairness of a dismissal, see *McGowan v Scottish Water* [2005] IRLR 167 EAT, *X v Y* [2004] EWCA Civ 662, [2004] IRLR 625; and *Copsey v WWB Devon Clays Ltd* [2005] EWCA Civ 932, [2005] IRLR 811. **9.115**

Witness evidence

Provisions of the rules

Rule 27(2) of ETR 2004 provides that at the hearing a party shall be entitled to give evidence, to call witnesses, to question witnesses, and to address the tribunal. **9.116**

Evidence is given on oath or affirmation (ETR 2004, 27(3)). If a witness needs an interpreter, there is a special interpreters' oath that is used. As evidence is given on oath, the law in relation to perjury applies to evidence given to the tribunal. **9.117**

9.118 Rule 27(4) of ETR 2004 provides that the tribunal may exclude from the hearing any person who is to appear as a witness in the proceedings until such time as they have given their evidence if it considers it is in the interests of justice to do so. In practice this power is rarely exercised in tribunals in England and Wales.

Witness statements

9.119 It is standard practice for a witness's evidence in chief to be given by witness statement. Tribunals often give such directions for evidence in chief to be by way of witness statement, and for witness statements to be exchanged ahead of the hearing. Even where there is no such direction, parties would be well advised to prepare statements for their witnesses to be used at the hearing. Parties without representatives will be given more latitude in this respect. Where witness statements have been prepared, the tribunal may require the witness to read the statement out, or may take the statements as read (as is the practice in the civil courts). Practice varies from tribunal to tribunal, and depends upon the time available, the length of the statement, and the complexity of the matters in issue. When witness statements are taken as read, copies should be made available to the press.

9.120 A tribunal will normally allow a witness to give some oral evidence to amplify his witness statement or to give evidence as to additional matters, for example to comment on matters arising from the other side's evidence in chief. In the civil courts a witness giving oral evidence at trial may, with the permission of the court, amplify his witness statement and give evidence in relation to new matters which have arisen since the witness statement was served on the other parties. The court will only give such permission if it considers that there is good reason not to confine the evidence of the witness to the contents of his witness statement (CPR r 32.5). An employment tribunal is not bound by this approach, and in practice a certain latitude is allowed especially for unrepresented parties. However, there are dicta to the effect that tribunals should be parsimonious in giving the parties leave to amplify their statements (*Shahronki v NATFHE* EAT/486/99). Sometimes however it may be helpful to amplify matters, and it may be necessary to deal with matters arising since exchange of statements.

9.121 In public hearings (ie in the vast majority of hearings) at least one copy of each witness statement should be made available to be left at the back of the tribunal room marked 'Not to be removed from the tribunal'. These copies are available for inspection by the public. Directions at a CMD may sometimes provide for this, but even if there is no direction, copies should be provided in any event. It is an aspect of a public hearing that the public should be entitled to know what evidence is given by a witness, regardless of whether it was given orally or in a witness statement (see the High Court case of *Cox v Jones* [2004] All ER (D) 385, *per* Mann J).

Examination in chief

9.122 During any additional examination in chief a representative of the party calling the witness should not ask leading questions which presuppose a particular answer. The witness evidence should be confined to matters of fact, and the witness should not be asked to give opinion evidence, or to speculate about matters outside his knowledge. Where the witness's evidence is hearsay, it will be admissible in the tribunal, as the rules of evidence do not apply, but the source of the hearsay should be identified so that the tribunal may assess the weight of the evidence.

9.123 Witnesses are not normally permitted in court proceedings to read notes when giving evidence. A clean copy of the witness statement will be available on the witness table, and the witness will not normally be allowed to use his own marked-up copy of his statement. However, the EAT held in *Watson-Smith v Tagol Ltd (t/a Alangate Personnel)* EAT/611/81, that where parties represent themselves at hearings before employment tribunals they should be allowed to refer to notes. This takes account of the fact that a solicitor or barrister or other skilled representative will normally have a statement from a witness to assist in his cross-examination.

Cross-examination

After examination in chief, the other party or parties may cross-examine the witness. The aims of cross-examination are to challenge the material parts of the evidence in chief; to elicit new evidence that may be helpful to the cross-examining party; and to undermine the credit of the witness. As a rule of practice the party cross-examining must put his case to the witness, insofar as the matter is within the witness's knowledge. That is to say that the material facts which form part of the cross-examining party's case, and which are in issue, must be put to the witness so that he can respond to them. It is particularly important in discrimination cases and whistle-blowing cases, where it is often necessary for the tribunal to draw inferences as to the reason why individuals acted in a particular manner, that these matters are put to the witness under cross-examination in order that they are given the opportunity to comment on them. Thus where it is alleged by a respondent in a whistle-blowing case that the claimant's disclosure was not made in good faith, the allegations of bad faith must be made clear to the claimant and the claimant must be given an opportunity to comment on them (see *Lucas v Chichester Diocesan Housing Association Limited* UKEAT/0713/04). Similarly, in *Doherty v British Midland Airways Limited* [2006] IRLR 90 EAT, the tribunal found that the claimant was malicious without that allegation having been put to the claimant under cross-examination. An appeal was allowed and the matter was remitted to a fresh employment tribunal for determination. **9.124**

The tribunal may impose restrictions on the cross-examination of witnesses under its general case management powers, and in furtherance of the overriding objective. By analogy with the High Court, limits may be imposed on cross-examination in two ways. A limit may be imposed on the issues explored in cross-examination (see *Watson v Chief Constable of Cleveland* [2001] EWCA Civ 1547); or a time limit on cross-examination may be imposed (see *Hayes v Transco plc* [2003] EWCA Civ 1261), leaving the advocate to decide how best to use his time. **9.125**

A party does not have an absolute right to cross-examine come what may. The tribunal is not obliged to allow lengthy and detailed cross-examination on matters that do not appear to the tribunal to be of assistance, and has a duty to keep the inquiry before it within proper bounds (*Gulson v Zurich Insurance Co* [1998] IRLR 118, EAT, Kirkwood J, approved by the Court of Appeal in *Bache v Essex County Council* [2000] IRLR 251). A refusal to allow cross-examination may be compatible with Article 6(1) of ECHR if the cross-examination would not assist the court: *X v Austria* (1972) 42 CD 145, E CommHR. **9.126**

However, the employment judge must tread a delicate line between efficient case management, entailing the avoidance of wasted time and cost, and the need to ensure that the hearing is fair and can be seen to be fair. In *McBride v British Railways Board* (1972) 7 ITR 84, the employee was not given a chance to cross-examine witnesses, as the tribunal felt that this would be a waste of time. On appeal, the NIRC felt it doubtful that any different decision would have been reached had the cross-examination actually taken place, but it thought in all the circumstances justice had not been seen to be done, and remitted the case for further consideration. Whilst it would be rare in modern times to find a case where a party was denied all right to cross-examine, excessive limitation of, or interference with, cross-examination may amount to a denial of a fair trial, and render the tribunal's decision liable to be set aside. See, for example, *Moir v Heart of England Housing & Care Ltd* UKEAT/0918/04. **9.127**

Tribunal questions and re-examination

After cross-examination the employment tribunal may then ask questions of its own. Either before or after the tribunal's questions (depending on local tribunal practice) the representative calling the witness may re-examine. **9.128**

The role of re-examination of one's own witness (which can be a very powerful weapon if used wisely) is to clear up misleading answers to questions or responses when the witness did not fully understand the nature and extent of the question. The limits of re-examination are often not well understood by laymen appearing in the tribunal. First, re-examination should be limited **9.129** to matters arising out of cross-examination; it is not an opportunity for a 'second bite of the cherry' in evidence in chief. Secondly, as with examination in chief, the representative should not lead the witness.

Recalling witnesses

9.130 Witnesses are normally released so they can leave the tribunal after they have given evidence and are then free to leave the tribunal, although in exceptional circumstances they may be ordered to be recalled but only because some evidence is given which could not have been anticipated when the decision to release was made. These matters are within the general discretion of the employment tribunal to regulate its own procedures (see, for example, *Aberdeen Steak Houses Group plc v Ibrahim* [1988] ICR 550). Parties should always ask the tribunal whether a particular witness can be released; they will usually be told that they can.

Party's decision as to what witnesses to call and the order in which they are called

9.131 It should normally be a matter for the parties, and not the tribunal, to determine how they call their evidence. In *Barnes v BPC (Business Forms) Ltd* [1976] IRLR 397, the employer's solicitor was instructed by the judge to call witnesses in a certain order to prevent their long absence from work. Phillips J reprimanded the judge and said that: 'representatives are entitled to conduct the proceedings as they see fit within the rules and in particular to call witnesses in the order they wish . . . it was an unwise decision for the chairman to have made and should not be repeated'.

9.132 The EAT reached a contrary view in *Snowball v Gardner Merchant Ltd* [1987] IRLR 397, 399, [1987] ICR 719, 723. *Barnes* was, however, subsequently approved by the EAT (Wood J) in *Aberdeen Steak Houses Group plc*.

9.133 It is the parties' responsibility to ensure that all relevant issues are raised, and that all relevant evidence is put before the tribunal (*Kumchyk v Derby County Council* [1978] ICR 1116, EAT). This was confirmed in *Mensah v East Hertfordshire NHS Trust* [1998] IRLR 531, CA.

Tribunal calling witness of own motion

9.134 Under r 14(3) of ETR 2004 the tribunal has a power to call witnesses of its own motion, including parties to the proceedings. Where it does so, each party has a right to cross-examine the witness. In *Clapson v British Airways plc* [2001] IRLR 184, the EAT, however, warned that tribunals should be 'very cautious' before deciding to call a witness whom neither of the parties wishes to call, and should be particularly wary where the witness is one of the parties to the case. In ordinary circumstances, where there was a dispute of fact, the tribunal would deal with the situation by drawing an adverse inference against the party who had not given evidence.

Documents

9.135 For the preparation and composition of bundles, see para 9.11 above.

9.136 The tribunal will not normally have read the documents in the bundle (other than the claim form and the response) prior to the commencement of the hearing, and any documents on which a party wishes to rely must be read by the tribunal during the course of the hearing. Practice varies from judge to judge, and will depend on the circumstances of the particular case. Normally documents are introduced during the course of the evidence of witnesses who deal with them. One common approach is for the witness to give evidence, and when a document is mentioned, for the representative to refer to the document, which the tribunal members then read, whilst the witness remains at the witness table. If lengthy documents need to be read, the tribunal may take time to adjourn and read the documents. This may be fitted into a timetable agreed at a CMD so that the tribunal has a reading day before the parties need attend. An alternative, and increasingly common approach, is for the tribunal at the beginning of the hearing to adjourn after the preliminary discussion to read the witness statements and essential documents referred to in them. A variation on this is for the tribunal to adjourn for a short period before each witness to read that witness's statement and the documents to which it refers.

Whichever course is adopted, the representatives must ensure that they and their clients understand the procedure that is being followed, and that all documents upon which the party relies are drawn to the tribunal's attention. Representatives must be prepared to assist the tribunal at the beginning of the hearing by agreeing a key reading list with the other side. Representatives should note what documents are read by the tribunal during the course of the hearing, so that, after his client's last witness has given evidence, any documents not already referred to can be drawn to the tribunal's attention. **9.137**

Submission of no case to answer

An application of no case to answer is made at 'half-time' in the case: ie after the evidence of the party bearing the burden of proof is complete, but before hearing evidence from the other party. It is an opportunity for the party going second to argue that the other party cannot succeed even on his own evidence, so that the second party should not be put to the expense of continuing with the hearing. The procedure is established in the civil courts and, more particularly, in the criminal courts (where of course the standard of proof is higher). **9.138**

It is possible to make a submission of no case to answer in the employment tribunal, but such submissions have never been encouraged, see for example *Ridley v GEC Machines Ltd* (1978) 13 ITR 195; *Coral Squash Clubs Ltd v Matthews and Matthews* [1979] IRLR 390; and *George A Palmer Ltd v Beeby* [1978] ICR 196. **9.139**

In *Logan v Commissioners of Customs & Excise* [2003] EWCA Civ 1068, 18–19, Ward LJ said that it should be rare for a submission of no case to answer to be made and rare for it to succeed. He summarized the law as follows (by reference to *Clarke v Watford Borough Council* 4 May 2000, EAT, *per* Judge Peter Clark): **9.140**

(a) There is no inflexible rule of law and practice that a tribunal must always hear both sides, although that should normally be done (*Ridley v GEC Machines Ltd* (1978) 13 ITR 195).
(b) The power to stop a case at 'half-time' must be exercised with caution (*Coral Squash Clubs Ltd v Matthews and Matthews* [1979] IRLR 390).
(c) It may, however, be a complete waste of time to call upon the other party to give evidence in a hopeless case (*Ridley v GEC Machines Ltd*).
(d) Even where the onus of proof lies on the claimant, as in discrimination cases, it will only be in exceptional or frivolous cases that it would be right to take such a course (*Oxford, Owen and Briggs v James* [1981] IRLR 133; *British Gas plc v Sharma* [1991] IRLR 101, 106). (This proposition applies to whistle-blowing cases, which to some extent are treated as a form of discrimination cases (see *Boulding v Land Securities Trillium (Media Services) Ltd* UKEAT/0023/06, applying, *Logan*. This proposition applies also to constructive dismissal cases.)
(e) Where there is no burden of proof, as under s 98(4) of ERA 1996, it will be difficult to envisage arguable cases where it is appropriate to terminate the proceedings at the end of the first party's case.
(f) Where a party makes an unsuccessful submission of no case to answer, he will not be regarded as having elected to call no evidence (*Walker v Josiah Wedgwood & Sons Ltd* [1978] ICR 744, 753). However, he will be bound by a specific statement that he will not call evidence (*Stokes v Hampstead Wine Co Ltd* [1979] IRLR 298). In civil and criminal proceedings, the party wishing to make a submission of no case to answer is generally put to his election whether he will call evidence or not (see *Alexander v Rayson* [1936] 1 KB 169, CA; *Miller v Cawley* [2002] EWCA Civ 1100).

Closing submissions

After all of the evidence has been concluded, each party's representatives makes a closing speech. **9.141**
The party bearing the burden of proof has the last word. Many employment judges discourage

long closing speeches. Some impose time limits for oral submissions. The ECtHR has recognized that it is generally for national courts to regulate their own procedure, including the time allowed for oral submissions: *Brown v UK* (1999) 28 EHRR CD 233.

Skeleton arguments

9.142 A written skeleton argument, or outline of submissions, is often helpful to the tribunal, particularly in a complex case, or in a case where there will be little time for oral submissions. Sometimes the tribunal may have ordered skeleton arguments to be filed at a CMD, or may have invited the submission of skeletons during the course of the hearing. A skeleton argument (as opposed to full written submissions) is not intended as a substitute for oral argument, and should be as brief as the nature of the issues permits. A skeleton argument should identify concisely:

(a) the nature of the case generally, and the background facts insofar as they are relevant;
(b) the propositions of law relied upon with references to the relevant authorities;
(c) the submissions of fact to be made with reference to the evidence.

9.143 It is important for representatives to make a skeleton as easy to use for a tribunal as possible. Paragraphs should be numbered, and appropriate use made of section headings and sub-headings. Cross-references to the evidence are helpful, as they mean the judge does not have to make a note of references during the oral submissions. Abbreviations and appropriate defined terms are to be encouraged. (These principles are adapted from the *Chancery Guide*, Appendix 3, paras 1–3.)

Use of authorities

9.144 A representative can assume that the tribunal will be familiar with the leading cases, such as *Devis v Atkins* [1977] AC 931; *British Home Stores v Burchell* [1978] IRLR 379; and *Polkey v Dayton* [1988] 1 AC 344. Any authorities upon which the party wishes to rely should be copied for the tribunal members and for the other side. Authorities should be handed up to the tribunal at the beginning of the hearing, having been exchanged between the parties' representatives beforehand by agreement between the representatives.

Written submissions

9.145 Not infrequently the tribunal will adjourn at the end of the evidence for written submissions. This can arise because the evidence has used up all the listed time and there is no time left to do justice to oral submissions. The parties may prefer to prepare written submissions for use by the tribunal when deliberating, rather than to return for a further day of hearing. Alternatively, written submissions may be thought appropriate because the case is a long or complex one and the tribunal would prefer the assistance of written submissions before reaching its judgment. Where the parties are to provide written submissions, this may either be in substitution for any oral submissions, or to supplement oral submissions to be made at a hearing after the submissions have been produced.

9.146 In *London Borough of Barking and Dagenham v Oguoko* [2000] IRLR 179, the EAT gave guidance to employment tribunals on the correct procedure to be adopted for written closing submissions, if the parties are not to return to the tribunal to make oral submissions:

(a) The procedure for written submissions should be implemented only with the consent of all parties.
(b) It is the judge's responsibility to ensure that the procedure adopted complies with natural justice.
(c) Upon receipt of both sets of submissions, the tribunal should serve each party with the written submission of the other.
(d) Each party should be informed that if they have any appropriate comment to make on the submission of their opponent, they should send those comments to the tribunal within a further fixed period. They should be warned that if, within that time, no comment is received back by the tribunal, it will be assumed they have no comment to make and the tribunal will proceed to make its decision on the basis of the submissions already tendered.

In *Sinclair Roche & Temperley v Heard* [2004] IRLR 763, EAT, Burton J considered the position where written submissions were filed prior to a further day of hearing for closing submissions. Burton J remarked that an 'American system of briefs' was valuable but not intended to be a substitute for oral argument. His *obiter* remarks must be seen in the context of the type of long, complex case with which he was dealing. It is doubtful that he intended to suggest that there were not cases where it was appropriate to take written submissions without additional oral submissions: indeed, as noted above, in many cases (particularly simpler ones) the parties may feel that such an approach is the most efficient and cost-effective way of dealing with the submissions in the case. **9.147**

Burton J's real concern was with the timescale in which the tribunal had required submissions to be produced in such a complex case. After 12 days of evidence the tribunal heard oral closing submissions effectively on the next working day (with only the Easter weekend in between). He thought that the value of written submissions is lost if neither the parties nor the tribunal has time to read and assimilate the submissions before the commencement of oral submissions. Burton J said that in a long case where written submissions were ordered the following procedure should be followed: **9.148**

(a) The timescale for preparation of the submissions must be a sensible one to allow the representatives time to prepare their submissions without unfair pressure.
(b) It is essential that the timescale should provide for the submissions to be provided to the other party in sufficient time before the oral submissions for the other party to be able to read them so that that party can, in his oral submissions, comment upon, address, and seek to answer them.
(c) It is equally, if not more, essential that the tribunal has had the opportunity to read the submissions before the oral submissions.

H. CONTEMPT OF COURT

An employment tribunal is an inferior court for the purposes of RSC Ord 52, r 1, and thus a person may be found guilty of contempt of court in connection with tribunal proceedings: *Peach Grey & Co v Sommers* [1995] IRLR 363. The contempt is punishable on committal by the Divisional Court. (See also dicta in *Attorney-General v British Broadcasting Corporation* [1978] 1 WLR 477.) **9.149**

A wide variety of different acts and omissions may be in contempt of court; the following may be particularly relevant in the tribunal: **9.150**

(a) Contempt in the face of the court: this covers a wide variety of forms of disrespectful and disruptive behaviour in the tribunal.
(b) Words (written or spoken) scandalizing the court.
(c) Publication of matter which creates a substantial risk that the course of justice in proceedings which are active will be impeded or prejudiced.
(d) Publication of matter which the court has decided should be kept confidential in the interests of justice.
(e) Acts calculated to prejudice the course of justice, for example interference with witnesses.
(f) Further consideration is outside the scope of this work, interested parties and representatives should consult specialist works on civil procedure or contempt of court (for example *Supreme Court Practice 2005*, § 52.1.8, *Arlidge, Eady & Smith on Contempt*, 3rd edn, 2005).

In cases of disruptive behaviour by a party or his representative during the course of the hearing, contempt proceedings before the Divisional Court are unlikely to be a practical solution. The tribunal has powers within its own rules to deal with such situations: the tribunal may strike out a claim or response on the grounds that the proceedings have been conducted by a party or his representative in a manner which is scandalous, vexatious, or unreasonable (ETR 2004, r 18(7)(c)) (see Chapter 7); the EAT has held that threats made in the tribunal car park to a claimant by **9.151** an employee of the respondent who was playing a 'key role' in handling its case were also grounds for the exercise of this power (*Force One Utilities Ltd v Hatfield* [2009] IRLR 45). The tribunal may make an order for costs against a party or his representative, if behaviour at the hearing has led to costs being wasted. A tribunal may not, however, refuse to allow a party his choice of representative (*Bennett v London Borough of Southwark* [2002] EWCA Civ 223, [2002] IRLR 407, following *Bache v Essex County Council* [2000] IRLR 251). Nor does the Tribunal have the power to ask the Official Solicitor to investigate the mental capacity of a litigant, however apparently delusional, or to appoint a litigation friend: *Johnson v Edwardian International Hotels Ltd* UKEAT 0588/07. Faced with disruptive behaviour the judge should first try to defuse the situation, by pointing out the potential consequences if the behaviour continues, and perhaps by allowing the parties a short break to reflect on their positions.

I. PRIVATE HEARINGS AND RESTRICTED REPORTING ORDERS

Public hearings

9.152 Rule 26(3) of ETR 2004 provides that any hearing of a claim shall be held in public, unless specific powers to hold the hearing in private apply.

9.153 Rule 26(3) applies to 'Hearings' which, pursuant to r 14, are one of five types of hearing which a tribunal may hold (see para 9.01 above). The position would therefore appear to be that the requirement of a public hearing does not apply to a CMD, a pre-hearing review, an interim relief hearing, or a review. This would appear to be the case even though a pre-hearing review may involve witness evidence and may be determinative of the proceedings (for example, if the tribunal determines as a preliminary issue that a claim is out of time). Where a hearing (or part of it) is conducted by electronic means, r 15 provides for public access to the hearing.

9.154 The position under ETR 2004 reflects the pre-existing practice whereby tribunals did not sit in public to make interlocutory directions in cases. In *Jones v Enham Industries* [1983] ICR 580, the EAT endorsed this practice, on the basis that an interlocutory order dealing with directions was not 'a decision' within reg 2 of ETR 2001, so that a sitting to enable a tribunal to make such an order was not a hearing, and did not have to be in public.

9.155 Where r 26(3) does apply, the requirement to hold a public hearing is a stringent one. The importance of a public hearing was, however, stressed in the somewhat surprising decision in *Storer v British Gas plc* [2000] IRLR 495. In that case there was a coded door lock restricting entry to the part of the tribunal building where the hearing took place. The hearing was held not to have been in public, as the public did not have access to the hearing, even though there was no evidence that any person who wished to attend had been prevented from attending. Henry LJ stated that 'the obligation to sit in public was fundamental to the function of an employment tribunal'. He went on to observe that Parliament had not provided in respect of tribunals for any 'chambers-type procedure'. Strictly speaking, *Storer* concerned a decision on a jurisdiction point, clearly requiring a public hearing; a statement of wider principle applying to interim applications was *obiter*. However, since the Human Rights Act 1998 came into effect, imposing on tribunals an obligation to comply with Article 6 of ECHR (right to a fair trial) there has been a greater emphasis on the need for justice to be carried out openly in public.

Restrictions on publicity

9.156 A tribunal has a number of powers to restrict the principle that hearings should be heard and reported on publicly:

(a) A tribunal may conduct a hearing, or part of it, in private in circumstances defined by ETR 2004, r 16.
(b) A tribunal may impose restricted reporting orders in cases involving allegations of sexual misconduct, or disability cases involving sensitive personal information (ETR 2004, r 50).

(c) Special procedures for private hearings apply to cases involving national security (ETR 2004, r 54).

Private hearings

9.157 Under ETR 2004, r 16, a hearing or part of one may be conducted in private for the purpose of hearing from any person, evidence or representations which in the opinion of the tribunal or the judge is likely to consist of information:

(a) which he could not disclose without contravening a prohibition imposed by or by virtue of any enactment;
(b) which has been communicated to him in confidence, or which he has otherwise obtained in consequence of the confidence placed in him by another person; or
(c) the disclosure of which would, for reasons other than its effect on negotiations with respect to any of the matters mentioned in s 178(2) of TULR(C)A 1992, cause substantial injury to any undertaking of his or any undertaking in which he works.

9.158 The tribunal's power to sit in private is limited to the specific situations mentioned above. The tribunal may not sit in private as part of its powers to conduct the proceedings as it considers most appropriate (ETR 2004, r 14(2)–(3)): *R v Southampton Industrial Tribunal, ex p INS News Group Ltd and Express Newspapers plc* [1995] IRLR 247.

9.159 Where a decision is taken to hold a hearing, or part of a hearing, in private, the tribunal or judge (as the case may be) must give reasons for the decision (ETR 2004, r 16(2)).

9.160 Tribunals are naturally reluctant to exclude the public and rarely do so but it is appropriate for private hearings, for example, where details about a burglar alarm installation would have to be given (see *Neal v Christie Intruder Alarms Ltd* COIT 546/157) and where evidence about police reports was necessary to establish the parties' respective cases (see *Wilson v Crown Office* COIT 61/4; *Boyer (UK) Ltd v Kirkham* IT/23287/85).

9.161 *XXX v YYY* [2004] EWCA Civ 231, [2004] IRLR 471 concerned a dispute as to the admissibility of a video recording showing the claimant (a nanny), her employer, and the child of her employer. An argument arose as to the protection of the right to privacy of the child. The EAT held that the evidence was potentially relevant and that to refuse to admit it may infringe X's right to a fair trial, but to play it in public would infringe the child's right to privacy. The EAT reconciled the competing rights by directing that the tribunal receive the evidence in a private hearing. The Court of Appeal overturned this decision holding that the evidence was not relevant and therefore not admissible. However, the Court of Appeal noted that there was no challenge to the EAT's power to direct that the tribunal view the video in private. The EAT held that the jurisdiction to hear the evidence in private was in what is now r 16(1)(a): playing the video in public would infringe the child's Article 8 rights, and the tribunal has an obligation to act in accordance with those rights under s 6 of the Human Rights Act 1998. The evidence would be likely to consist of information which could not be disclosed without contravening a prohibition imposed by or by virtue of an enactment.

Determining whether to hear the case in private

9.162 A party has no right to insist on a preliminary hearing to decide whether the hearing itself should be held in private. In *Milne and Lyall v Waldren* [1980] ICR 138, the respondent firm of solicitors sought a private preliminary hearing on the ground that confidential matters would be raised in the claimant's complaint of unfair dismissal. They also wanted the application for the private hearing considered at a date prior to the hearing, so that they could appeal from that decision if they so wished. The judge refused to hold a preliminary hearing to consider the point and the employers appealed from this refusal. The EAT thought that, even if this was a 'direction' within the rules from which the appellants were entitled to appeal at all, the tribunal was empowered to regulate its own procedure in such a matter within its absolute discretion, so that the appeal was dismissed.

Meaning of hearing in private

9.163 When a case is heard in private, the husband of the claimant was entitled to attend. The extent of the persons so entitled to attend was a matter of fact and degree (*Fry v Foreign and Commonwealth Office* [1997] ICR 512).

National security

9.164 Special rules apply to cases concerning Crown employment. Under r 54(1) of ETR 2004 in such cases a Minister of the Crown may, if he considers it expedient in the interests of national security, direct a tribunal to:

(a) sit in private;
(b) exclude the claimant or his representatives from all or part of the proceedings;
(c) take steps to conceal the identity of a witness in the proceedings.

9.165 The tribunal may take any of these steps of its own motion if it considers it expedient in the interests of national security to do so (r 54(2)). A tribunal may also in such a case make directions limiting the persons to whom documents may be disclosed (r 54(2)). A tribunal is under a duty to ensure that information is not disclosed contrary to the interests of national security.

9.166 The Employment Tribunals (National Security) Rules of Procedure 2004, r 16(2) (see 2004 Regulations, Sch 2) modify ETR 2004 in cases where a power is exercised under r 54 of ETR 2004. Of particular note is the procedure for the Attorney-General to appoint a special advocate to represent the interests of a claimant if either he or his representative is excluded from the proceedings (Sch 2, r 8).

Restricted reporting orders

Introduction

9.167 A restricted reporting order (RRO) may be made in certain cases involving allegations of sexual misconduct and in certain cases of disability discrimination. The effect of such an order is to prohibit the media from publishing information which is likely to identify specified persons involved in the proceedings.

Cases in which a restricted reporting order may be made

9.168 The powers to make a restricted reporting order are contained in ss 11–12 of ETA 1996. The rules governing RROs are set out in ETR 2004, r 50. These provisions permit an RRO to be made in:

(a) cases involving sexual misconduct;
(b) certain disability cases.

9.169 The power to make an RRO in either circumstance is permissive: ss 11–12 and r 50 identify situations where an RRO may be made. Whether an RRO should be made in a particular case is a question of discretion for the tribunal.

9.170 See paras 9.225–9.228 below for a discussion as to whether the tribunal has wider powers to make restrictions on publicity outside of these provisions.

Sexual misconduct cases

9.171 A tribunal may make a restricted reporting order in any case involving allegations of sexual misconduct (ETA 1996, s 11(1)(b) and ETR 2004, r 50(1)(a)).

Sexual misconduct

9.172 Sexual misconduct means (ETA 1996, s 11(5)):

> the commission of a sexual offence, sexual harassment, or other adverse conduct (of whatever nature) related to sex, and conduct is related to sex whether the relationship with sex lies in the character

of the conduct or in its having reference to the sex or sexual orientation of the person at whom the conduct is directed.

Disability cases

A tribunal may make an RRO on a complaint under ss 17A or 25(8) of DDA 1995 in which evidence of a personal nature is likely to be heard (ETA 1996, s 12(1) and ETR 2004, r 50(1)(b)). **9.173**

Evidence of a personal nature means (ETA 1996, s 12(7)): **9.174**

> any evidence of a medical, or other intimate, nature which might reasonably be assumed to be likely to cause significant embarrassment to the complainant if reported.

The effect of a restricted reporting order

In either type of case, an RRO is an order which prohibits the publication in Great Britain of 'identifying matter' in a written publication available to the public or its inclusion in a relevant programme for reception in Great Britain. **9.175**

'Identifying matter' in relation to a person is defined as follows: **9.176**

(a) Sexual misconduct cases: 'any matter likely to lead members of the public to identify him as a person affected by, or as the person making, the allegation' (ETA 1996, s 11(6));
(b) Disability cases: 'any matter likely to lead members of the public to identify the complainant or such other persons (if any) as may be named in the order' (ETA 1996, s 12(7)).

Where a tribunal makes an RRO it must specify the persons who may not be identified (ETR 2004, r 50(8)(a)). **9.177**

The effect of a restricted reporting order is not to prevent a case from being reported, or to suppress allegations; rather it prevents publication of material likely to identify the persons who are the subject of the order. **9.178**

In *R v Southampton Industrial Tribunal, ex p INS News Group Ltd and Express Newspapers plc* [1995] IRLR 247, Brooke J said (at para 22) that tribunals should make such orders as clear as they can so that the press is left in no doubt about what they may and may not do. **9.179**

Scope

Involving allegations of sexual misconduct

The power to make an RRO arises in cases involving allegations of sexual misconduct. Such allegations will typically arise in cases brought under the SDA 1975; however, s 12 of ETA 1996 is not limited to claims under the SDA 1975. For example, a claim of constructive unfair dismissal may be brought on the basis of allegations of sexual harassment, or a claimant in an unfair dismissal claim may have been dismissed for the reason that his employer believed him to have sexually harassed a co-worker. In each of these examples, the case involves an allegation of sexual misconduct, regardless of the cause of action relied on. **9.180**

Conversely, there may be claims brought under the SDA 1975 which involve no allegation of sexual misconduct, and where, therefore, s 12 does not apply. In *Chief Constable of West Yorkshire Police v A* [2000] IRLR 465, the EAT held that 'sexual misconduct' did not extend so far as to cover the case of a claimant who alleged that she was rejected for a job on the grounds of her status as a transsexual. If all that was required for 'sexual misconduct' was that it was conduct which was 'adverse' and was 'related to sex' by way of having reference to the sex or sexual orientation of the person to whom it was directed, every case of sex discrimination would be a case of 'sexual misconduct'. **9.181**

A case may involve allegations of sexual misconduct even if those allegations do not form the basis of the cause of action in the claim, and even if the allegations may not be central to the tribunal's decision-making. A legalistic analysis of the pleadings is not necessary, nor is proof of the allegations. Thus, for example, in *X v Stevens* [2003] IRLR 411 the claim was that the claimant **9.182** had been denied a vacancy because of her status as a post-operative transsexual. The respondent denied that this was the reason that the claimant was denied the vacancy, and alleged a number of reasons for the decision, including an unproven suspicion that the claimant had in the past been involved in a sexual assault. The EAT (Burton J) held that the tribunal would need to hear some evidence which touched on the suspected assault, and that the claim therefore involved an allegation of sexual misconduct.

Persons making or affected by an allegation of sexual misconduct

9.183 In sexual misconduct cases, the legislation is aimed at preventing identification of a person affected by or a person making the allegation.

9.184 There are certain categories of person who may naturally be thought to fall within the scope of an RRO: principally victims, alleged perpetrators, and witnesses. However, the statute does not define the concept of 'affected by' and the courts have declined to place a gloss on its meaning. In *R v London (North) Industrial Tribunal, ex p Associated Newspapers Ltd* [1998] ICR 1212, [1998] IRLR 569, QBD, Keene J said that each case must be viewed on its particular facts to ascertain whether the person in respect of whom an RRO is being sought is a person affected by the allegations.

9.185 An RRO should, however, be no wider in scope than is necessary to achieve the purposes of the legislation. The judge must consider the extent of the RRO on the basis of each individual of whom it is sought to prevent reporting. A blanket approach to such a prohibition is improper (see *ex p Associated Newspapers* above). In *Scottish Daily Record and Sunday Mail Ltd v McAvoy* EATS/1271/01, the EAT held that the tribunal had erred in making a blanket order in respect of all the witnesses in the case, when some of those witnesses were not persons 'affected by' the allegation of sexual harassment at all.

9.186 It is necessary to appreciate two different ways in which the reporting of the identity of, or evidence of, a person may be covered by an RRO:

(1) Who is a person making or affected by the allegation of sexual misconduct? Such a person is the permissible subject of an RRO.
(2) What constitutes identifying matter: that is, matter which is likely to lead to identification of a person affected by, or making an allegation.

9.187 It is quite possible that the publication of the identity of, or evidence of, a witness who is not himself an affected person would be likely to cause identification of an affected person. In this situation, the witness is not a person affected, but the press may not report his evidence in a way which would lead to identification of someone who is a subject. Such a person may be included in the RRO: *Tradition Securities & Futures SA v Times Newspapers Ltd* [2009] IRLR 354.

9.188 For example:

(a) X brings a claim under the SDA 1975 against the company employing her (Y), alleging sexual harassment by her line manager (A); she alleges the managing director (B) failed properly to deal with her complaint about the harassment. She intends to call as a witness a co-worker (C) who witnessed some instances of harassment.
(b) X may be a person identified in an RRO as the person making an allegation of sexual misconduct.
(c) So too may A: he is the alleged perpetrator, and therefore a person affected by the allegation.
(d) B (the investigating manager), however, is not the maker of the allegation, nor is he affected by it. He is not entitled to have his identity protected. The press must be cautious, however, in reporting B's evidence to ensure that matter is not reported which would be likely to lead to the identification of X or A.

(e) C, as a witness to the harassment, may be affected by the allegation (see, for example, *ex p Associated Newspapers* above).
(f) The position of Y, as a body corporate, requires further consideration: see the following section.

In *ex p Associated Newspapers*, Keene J stated (at para 12) that it is unnecessary for an RRO itself to ban the identification of one person simply on the basis that it is likely to lead to the identification of the person whose identity it is truly sought to protect or conceal: it is for the press to exercise its judgment as to what is likely to lead to such identification, and powerful sanctions exist if they transgress: see also Staughton LJ in *X v Z Ltd* [1998] ICR 43, 46. **9.189**

Bodies corporate

There have been conflicting decisions as to whether the persons to whom an order may apply may include corporate bodies. In *M v Vincent* [1998] ICR 73, EAT, it was held that a 'person', the word used in the rules, could include a corporate body, so that an order was made in respect of a company. In *ex p Associated Newspapers* above, Keene J doubted that a local authority could be a person within the meaning of s 11. Keene J pointed out, however, that reporting of the identity of a corporate body may in effect be restricted (if, for example, reporting the name of the body is likely to lead to the identification of an individual himself covered by an RRO). In *Leicester University v A* [1999] ICR 701, EAT, the EAT, preferring the approach of Keene J in *ex p Associated Newspapers*, held that the words 'person affected by. . . the allegation' in s 11(6) of ETA 1996 could only apply to an individual and not to a corporate body. The EAT said it was not the intention of Parliament to provide anonymity for corporate respondents who may be vicariously liable for acts of sexual misconduct in order to protect their commercial reputation. **9.190**

Disability cases

In a disability case, an RRO may prohibit publication of matter likely to lead to identification of the complainant 'or such other persons (if any) as may be named in the order' (ETA 1996, s 12(7)). **9.191**

There is no express qualification of the power to name other persons in the order. The proper scope of the provision is unclear. Clearly the main intention of the provision is to protect publication of the identity of the complainant about whom evidence of a personal nature is likely to be heard. It is suggested that other persons may be named only to the extent necessary to protect the identity of the complainant. Given the importance of freedom of the press and open justice, and given the degree of dispute as to the scope of the (older) provisions under s 11, it seems unlikely that Parliament intended the tribunal to have an unfettered power to protect the identity of persons other than the complainant. **9.192**

Multiple proceedings

Where an RRO has been made in respect of a complaint, and that complaint is being dealt with together with any other proceedings, the tribunal or judge may order that the RRO applies in relation to those other proceedings or part of them (ETR 2004, r 50(9)). **9.193**

This is a new provision in ETR 2004. The provision applies to both sexual misconduct cases and disability cases. The provision is underpinned by express statutory provision in relation to disability claims (ETA 1996, s 12(2)(b)), but it is interesting to note that there is no such equivalent provision in s 11 of ETA 1996. **9.194**

The power is apparently wide ranging. However, it should be borne in mind that the statutory power under ss 11–12 remains unaltered. So, to take the example of sexual misconduct cases, the power under s 11 is limited to prohibiting information which is likely to reveal the identity of a person making an allegation of sexual misconduct or affected by the allegation. Where two sets of proceedings are being heard together, one raising an allegation of sexual misconduct **9.195** (the first proceedings), the other not (the second proceedings), it is suggested the position is as follows:

(a) Rule 50(9) permits the tribunal to make an order in respect of both proceedings. It is not a ground of objection to making an order in the second proceedings that no allegation of sexual misconduct is involved in those proceedings.
(b) However, the tribunal should satisfy itself that publication of matter from the second proceedings would be likely to lead to the identification of a person who is properly protected by an RRO in the first proceedings.
(c) Mindful of the interests of public justice and freedom of the press, the tribunal will need to examine carefully whether, and to what extent, it is necessary to restrict publication of matter relating to the second proceedings in order to protect the identity of the complainant in the first proceedings.

Exercise of the discretion

9.196 In exercising its discretion whether to make an RRO a tribunal must balance a number of competing human rights interests: the right to a fair trial (including the need for a public judgment); the right to respect for private life; and the right to freedom of expression.

9.197 In relation to allegations of sexual misconduct there is a delicate balance between:

(1) the importance of stamping out sexual harassment and thus encouraging those with a proper grievance to bring claims to the attention of the employment tribunal; and
(2) the principles of open justice in a democratic society.

9.198 In *ex p Associated Newspapers* above, Keene J stated that an RRO was an infringement of freedom of the press; any interference with such a basic constitutional right should be narrowly construed. Therefore an RRO should extend so far as, and no further than, is necessary to achieve the purpose of the legislation (at para 45). The purpose of the legislation (based on consideration of *Hansard*) was to enable complaints of sexual harassment in the workplace to be brought and witnesses to give evidence without being deterred by fear of intimate sexual details about them being published (at para 36).

9.199 Women who have potential claims for sexual harassment were often shy of making them for fear of damaging publicity. Potential claimants were being discouraged from bringing complaints through fear that they would suffer identification, adverse publicity, the trauma of giving evidence, and meeting the perpetrator of the harassment in the stressful situation of the employment tribunal room. Such discouragements are not, of course, confined to sexual harassment claims, but they are particularly acute in such circumstances.

9.200 The dangers in terms of publicity are also not, of course, confined to the *victim* of sexual harassment. Some employers are pushed into making large settlements because of the fear of lurid publicity, and are in effect open to 'blackmail' claims because of the likelihood of publicity at the hearing. Some claimants do alert the press in advance of a hearing, in order to embarrass the employer, and to force a better settlement.

9.201 Publicity for sexual harassment cases, on the other hand, may be seen to have some advantages as a matter of public interest to some degree for the following reasons:

(a) It may cause the issue to obtain a greater degree of public awareness. Such harassment is often seen as just a fact of working life which women have to suffer, and not a legal wrong which can cause a great deal of harm. If women see that other women are complaining about it to tribunals by those facts being reported widely, and that those complaints are being taken seriously (with large awards against the perpetrators), they too may be made aware of their legal rights and seek to enforce them. In essence, the press, in responsibly reporting such cases, can be put to good use in getting this matter dealt with, not only in the workplace, but also in a wider arena.

(b) It is important that the public become aware of which employers are guilty of harassing staff.

The tribunal will have to weigh each of these matters on the facts of the particular case: **9.202**

(a) The wishes of each party for privacy or publicity.
(b) The fact that each of the parties had previously put aspects of the allegations in the public domain may be a relevant factor weighing against making an RRO: *Scottish Daily Record and Sunday Mail Ltd v McAvoy* EATS/1271/01, citing *Cinderella Bowyer v Armajit Singh Sandhu* ET/S/102262/99.

Duration of restricted reporting order

A tribunal may make either a temporary RRO or a full RRO. The temporary RRO is a new concept, introduced for the first time in ETR 2004 (r 50(3)). **9.203**

Temporary RRO

A judge or tribunal may make a temporary RRO without a hearing, and without sending a copy of the application to the other parties (r 50(3)). As soon as possible after making a temporary RRO the Secretary shall inform all parties of the fact that the order has been made. Any party may apply within 14 days of the date the temporary order was made to have the temporary order discharged, or converted into a full RRO (r 50(4)(b)). **9.204**

The duration of the temporary RRO depends upon the response of the parties: **9.205**

(a) If no party makes an application, then the temporary RRO will lapse on the fifteenth day after it was made (r 50(5)).
(b) If a party makes an application under r 50(4)(b) then the temporary order will continue to have effect until the hearing at which the application is considered.

Full RRO

A full RRO will remain in force until both liability and remedy have been determined, unless revoked earlier (r 50(8)(b)). A judge or tribunal may revoke an RRO at any time (r 50(10)). **9.206**

Liability and remedy are determined on the date recorded as being the date on which the judgment disposing of the claim was sent to the parties (r 50(11)). **9.207**

Application for restricted reporting order

An order may be made on the application of either party in cases involving allegations of sexual misconduct. In disability cases, only the complainant may apply for an order. In either case, an order may be made by the tribunal of its own motion (r 50(2)). **9.208**

The application may be made in writing or orally at a hearing. **9.209**

A tribunal should not make a full RRO unless it has given each party the opportunity to advance oral argument at a hearing (either a pre-hearing review or a hearing) (r 50(6)). **9.210**

In some cases tribunals have imposed orders by reason of the agreement of the parties, even where the case did not fall within the scope of ss 11–12 of ETA 1996. The validity of such an order must be open to doubt: first, the order is made outside the tribunal's statutory powers; secondly, the public interest in open justice suggests that restrictions on reporting should not be left to the agreement of the parties. In cases where both parties consent to an RRO, the tribunal ought still to satisfy itself that the conditions for making an order are satisfied, and that it is appropriate to exercise the discretion to make an order. **9.211**

Challenge to a restricted reporting order by a non-party

The groups most interested in challenging the making of restricted reporting orders are naturally the press and media organizations, who have an interest in reporting cases, and who may wish to object to an RRO on grounds of freedom of the press and freedom of speech. **9.212**

9.213 Rule 50(7) of ETR 2004 provides that any person may make an application to the judge or tribunal to have a right to make representations before a full RRO is made. The judge or tribunal shall allow such representations to be made where he considers that the claimant has a legitimate interest in whether or not the order is made.

9.214 Rule 50(7) is a provision introduced for the first time in ETR 2004. It provides a mechanism for the press to make representations objecting to the making of an RRO. It would also permit a non-party (for example a witness) to make representations in support of, or in opposition to, a party's application for an RRO. Such a person (referred to in r 50(7) as the 'applicant') will be heard by the tribunal without becoming a party to the proceedings.

9.215 The new rule is to be welcomed given the previously uncertain state of the law in relation to handling objections by the press to the making of an RRO. It is expected that the procedure in r 50(7) will now ensure that the difficulties described below will no longer arise:

(a) One route followed in a number of cases was to apply for judicial review of a tribunal decision to make a restricted reporting order (see *ex p Associated Newspapers* above). However, such a route could be expensive, and the limitations upon the court's willingness to interfere with decisions by way of judicial review made this procedure a poor substitute for being heard by the tribunal prior to making a decision.
(b) There was some doubt whether the press had formal *locus standi* in the employment tribunal to challenge the making of the order, although many employment judges have in practice permitted the press to appear for the purpose of making representations to oppose an order being made. In *A v B, ex p News Group Newspapers Ltd* sub nom *Chessington World of Adventures Ltd v Reed, ex p News Group Newspapers Ltd* [1998] ICR 55, [1998] IRLR 56, EAT, Morison J held that the press had standing to be joined as a party to the proceedings in the EAT for the purposes of making representations on an RRO made by the EAT (note that judicial review does not lie against a decision of the EAT). In *McAvoy* above, the Scottish EAT doubted that joining a press organization as a party to the proceedings was the appropriate approach, but held that the tribunal could hear representations from a non-party as part of its power to regulate its own procedure.

9.216 After an RRO has been made, however, the position is unclear. One view is that, at that point in time, the only persons who can apply for the revocation of a full RRO are those who are parties to the case: ETR 2004 do not provide for an interested non-party to apply to revoke a full RRO: see r 11(1), r 50(10) ETR 2004, and *Dallas McMillan v Davidson* UKEATS/0006/07/MT (para 49). However, joinder of media organizations to seek a variation of a full RRO was permitted in *Tradition Securities & Futures SA v Times Newspapers Ltd* [2009] IRLR 354, the EAT purporting to follow *ex p Associated Newspapers*.

Procedure at the hearing

9.217 The fact that an order has been made will be displayed on the noticeboard of the tribunal, and on the door of the room in which the hearing takes place (r 50(8)(c)) to ensure that the press is fully aware of the risks it runs if it breaches the order. As a matter of practice, the judge will normally remind all present of the existence of the RRO at the commencement of the hearing.

Penalties for breach of a restricted reporting order

9.218 Contravention of an RRO is a criminal offence, punishable in the criminal courts on summary conviction by a fine (ETA 1996, ss 11(2) and 12(3)). Sections 11(2) and 12(3) set out in detail the persons (both individual and corporate) who may commit an offence in respect of a publication in breach of an RRO (for example the editor, publisher, or proprietor of a newspaper). There is a defence for any such person if he 'proves that at the time of the alleged offence he was not aware, and neither suspected nor had reason to suspect, that the publication or programme in question was of, or included, identifying matter' (ETA 1996, ss 11(3) and 12(4)).

Decisions in cases concerning sexual offences

In any proceedings appearing to involve allegations of the commission of a sexual offence the tribunal, judge, or Secretary shall omit from the register, or delete from the register or any judgment document or record of the proceedings which is available to the public, any identifying matter which is likely to lead members of the public to identify any person affected by or making such an allegation (ETR 2004, r 49; ETA 1996, s 11(1)(a)). **9.219**

An order under the predecessor to this rule has been described as a 'Register Deletion Order' (RDO) by Burton J in *X v Stevens* [2003] IRLR 411. **9.220**

Rule 49 relates only to the content of the judgment or record of the proceedings, it does not affect the conduct of the hearing, nor the reporting of the hearing. It is quite common for an order under r 49 to be made in tandem with an order under r 50. **9.221**

The language of r 49 differs from that of r 50(1)(a) in two respects, the first material, the second probably immaterial. **9.222**

An RDO may be made only in cases of 'sexual offences' as opposed to sexual misconduct. Sexual offences are defined in s 11(6) of ETA 1996, which provides a list of relevant criminal offences. The concept is much narrower than the concept of sexual misconduct which is all that is necessary for an RRO. **9.223**

Rule 49 relates to proceedings '*appearing* to involve allegations' whereas r 50 relates to any case 'which involves allegations'. It is suggested that there is no material difference between these formulations: in *X v Stevens* above, Burton J doubted (at para 26) that there was much if any difference between the two tests. Furthermore, rr 49 and 50 both derive from s 11(1) of ETA 1996 where paras (a) and (b) of subs (1) both use the language 'cases involving allegations'. **9.224**

Restrictions on publicity outside the provisions of ETA 1996 and ETR 2004

We have seen (paras 9.180–9.182) that in many sex discrimination cases there may be no power to make an RRO, because sex discrimination does not necessarily involve sexual misconduct. **9.225**

There is some authority for the proposition that an RRO may be made outside the scope of ETR 2004 and ETA 1996, if such an order is necessary to promote a claimant's right to equal treatment under the Equal Treatment Directive (Council Directive 76/207/EEC [1976] OJ L39/40). In *X v Commissioner of Police of the Metropolis* [2003] ICR 1031, the EAT rejected an argument that an employment tribunal had the power to make an RRO under its power to regulate its own procedure. However, the EAT went on to hold that there was jurisdiction deriving from the Equal Treatment Directive where the respondent was an emanation of the State, and the claimant would be denied effective protection of rights under Article 6 of the Equal Treatment Directive, if, in the absence of an RRO she would be deterred from bringing a claim. The EAT's reasoning was that: **9.226**

(a) The employment tribunal and the EAT have a power and are under a duty to apply the provisions of the Equal Treatment Directive. In particular Article 6 of the Directive requires Member States to ensure that judicial and administrative procedures are put in place to ensure the enforcement of obligations under the Directive and to ensure that all those people who consider themselves wronged by a failure to apply the principle of equal treatment are able to make use of such procedures.
(b) Both the employment tribunals and the EAT have the power to regulate their own procedure. That must include, where a claimant would otherwise be deterred from bringing a claim, the making of an RRO in order to ensure the confidentiality in respect of the identity of the claimant.
(c) As such, the EAT concluded at para 56 of its decision:

> In those circumstances, we conclude that both in the employment tribunal and in the appeal tribunal there is a power for those bodies to regulate their own procedure, so as to include, in a

proper case, a restricted reporting order or a register deletion order or other order analogous to them or to make some provision in respect of confidentiality of the identity of the applicant, or, no doubt in an appropriate case, a respondent, not limited by the precise terms of the existing Rules.

9.227 The decision in *X v Commissioner of Police of the Metropolis* has simplified the law. Prior to that authority the EAT's decision in *Chief Constable of West Yorkshire Police v A* [2001] ICR 128 indicated that the EAT's jurisdiction to make an RRO in a case on similar facts to *X v Commissioner of Police of the Metropolis* was based on a combination of the EU law principle of effectiveness and the EAT's inherent jurisdiction to make such an order. That authority indicated therefore that the EAT's power to make RROs may go beyond the powers of the employment tribunal who had no such inherent jurisdiction (see *A v B, ex p News Group Newspapers*). Such a position would plainly be undesirable and *X* sets out the position for both the EAT and the employment tribunals.

9.228 An example of an order 'analogous to a restricted reporting order' being made occurred in the EAT in *Q v National Union of Teachers UKEAT/0354–0355/06*. In that case it was argued that in the absence of an RRO the claimant, a transsexual, would be deprived of an effective remedy due to her fear of publicity and prejudice and that, therefore, Article 6 of the Equal Treatment Directive required that an order be made. The EAT agreed, relying on *Stevens* and *X v Commissioner of Police of the Metropolis*, and made the order sought even though the order did not fall within rr 49 or 50 of the 2004 Rules.

10

Bias and Improper Conduct of the Hearing

SUMMARY

(1) All parties are entitled to a fair trial, and the tribunal must ensure the parties have a fair opportunity to put their case and to answer the case against them. The tribunal must avoid bias or the appearance of bias.

A. INTRODUCTION

Tribunals must conform to the general principles of natural justice, act fairly, and refrain from bias. Article 6(1) of ECHR provides that: **10.01**

> In the determination of his civil rights and obligations . . . everyone is entitled to a fair and public hearing within a reasonable time by an independent and impartial tribunal established by law.

Article 6 is given effect in English law by virtue of s 6 of the Human Rights Act 1998. An employment tribunal is a public body for the purposes of s 6, and thus must not act in a manner which breaches a litigant's rights under Article 6(1). The rights to a fair hearing, to a public hearing, and to a hearing within a reasonable time are separate and distinct rights from the right to a hearing before an independent and impartial tribunal established by law. This means that a complaint that one of these rights was breached cannot be answered by showing that the other rights were not breached. **10.02**

B. BIAS

10.03 Parties are entitled to a hearing by an independent and impartial tribunal. In *Findlay v UK* (1997) 24 EHRR 221, 244–5 (para 73) the ECtHR said:

> The Court recalls that in order to establish whether a tribunal can be considered as 'independent', regard must be had *inter alia* to the manner of appointment of its members and their term of office, the existence of guarantees against outside pressures and the question whether the body presents an appearance of independence. As to the question of 'impartiality', there are two aspects to this requirement. First, the tribunal must be subjectively free from personal prejudice or bias. Secondly, it must also be impartial from an objective viewpoint, that is, it must offer sufficient guarantees to exclude any legitimate doubt in this respect. The concepts of independence and objective impartiality are closely linked.

10.04 The existence or appearance of bias on the part of any person sitting in a judicial capacity will ordinarily lead to the disqualification of that person from sitting, or, if the proceedings have been concluded, to the hearing being declared a nullity and the decision set aside. In considering whether to recuse himself, the judge has no discretion to weigh different factors in the balance. Either there is the appearance of bias, in which case the judge must recuse himself; or there is not, in which case there is no valid objection to the judge hearing the case (see *AWG Group Limited v Morrison* [2006] 1 WLR 1163).

10.05 The general principles as to bias set out below relate to hearings before employment tribunals as they do to courts. The EAT has on occasions thus remitted a case to another employment tribunal because of material irregularity in the procedure of the first hearing. Very few allegations of bias have been proved, which can itself be seen as a testimony to the success of tribunals in dealing with hard-fought industrial issues, notwithstanding that a majority of their members come from the two sides of employment.

10.06 Bias can be divided for legal purposes into two categories: actual bias and the appearance of bias. Apparent bias can itself be divided into two 'sub-categories': presumed bias, and other cases of apparent bias (see *Locabail (UK) Ltd v Bayfield Properties Ltd* [2000] IRLR 96, CA).

10.07 Cases of actual bias on the part of a judge are rare, not least because its existence is difficult to prove.

10.08 The fundamental principle in relation to the appearance of bias is that 'justice should not only be done, but should manifestly and undoubtedly be seen to be done' (*R v Sussex Justices, ex p McCarthy* [1924] 1 KB 256, 259). The cases on the appearance of bias identify two categories. In *R v Bow Street Metropolitan Stipendiary Magistrate, ex p Pinochet Ugarte (No 2)* [2000] 1 AC 119, 132–3, Lord Browne-Wilkinson said:

> (1) Where a judge has a direct personal interest, other than *de minimis*, in the outcome of a case, bias is presumed and disqualification is automatic. The leading case is *R v Bow Street Metropolitan Stipendiary Magistrate, ex p Pinochet Ugarte (No. 2)* [2000] 1 AC 119.
> (2) The conduct or behaviour of a judge may give rise to a suspicion that he is not impartial. Here the test for apparent bias in *Porter v Magill* [2001] UKHL 67, [2002] 2 AC 357 should be applied.

10.09 In *Lawal v Northern Spirit Ltd* [2003] UKHL 35, [2003] ICR 856, the House of Lords stated (at para 22) that the indispensable requirement of public confidence in the administration of justice requires higher standards today than was the case even a decade or two decades ago. What the public was content to accept many years ago is not necessarily accepted in the world of today.

Presumed bias

10.10 Where a judge has a direct personal interest, other than *de minimis*, in the outcome of a case, bias is presumed and disqualification is automatic. The fundamental principle is that a man may not be judge in his own cause.

Such an interest will arise where the judge is a party to the action, or has a financial or proprietary interest in the outcome of the action. However, the principle is not limited to cases of pecuniary interest. The principle applies where the judge's decision would lead to promotion of a cause in which the judge was actively involved together with one of the parties (see *R v Bow Street Metropolitan Stipendiary Magistrate, ex p Pinochet Ugarte* (*No 2*) [2000] 1 AC 119, where the judge was a director of Amnesty International, which took part in the proceedings). However, *Pinochet* was clearly an exceptional case, and Lord Browne-Wilkinson was at pains not to overstate the scope of relevant non-financial interests. Rejecting the suggestion that judges would be unable to sit in cases involving charities with whose work they were involved, he said that a judge should only be concerned to recuse himself, or disclose his position, where he took an active role as trustee or director of a charity closely allied to and acting with a party to the proceedings (at 134). **10.11**

In *Meerabux v The Attorney-General of Belize* [2005] UKPC 9, [2005] 2 AC 513, Lord Hope, giving the opinion of the Privy Council, said that the decision in *Pinochet* 'appears, in retrospect, to have been a highly technical one' (at para 21). *Meerabux* concerned the judge of a tribunal which had been convened to investigate complaints by the Bar Association of Belize against a judge. It was alleged that a presumption of bias arose as the judge was a member of the Bar Association which brought the complaints. The Privy Council rejected the bias argument. Mere membership of an organization by which proceedings were brought would not automatically disqualify a member from sitting in the proceedings, but active involvement in the institution of the particular proceedings would. **10.12**

The test is whether the outcome could realistically affect the judge's interest, allowing for a *de minimis* exception (*Locabail* (*UK*) *Ltd v Bayfield Properties Ltd* [2000] IRLR 96, paras 8–10). For example, if a judge has a small number of shares in a large company, and the sums at stake in the litigation are not so large that the litigation could affect the value of the shares or the dividend payable (*Locabail*, at para 8), the interest would be *de minimis* and would have no effect. **10.13**

The relevant interest must be a direct interest of the judge's: see *Jones v DAS Legal Expenses Insurance Co Ltd* [2004] EWCA Civ 1071, [2004] IRLR 218, where no presumption of bias arose where the employment judge's husband was a barrister who received instructions from time to time from one of the parties. The judge's interest was only indirect, and in any event, even her husband's interest was in his own well-being, not in the fortunes of DAS. **10.14**

Where a judge is a party to the action, or has a relevant interest in the proceedings, the judge is disqualified from hearing the case without any investigation of whether there was likelihood or suspicion of bias. **10.15**

Apparent bias

The test for apparent bias is set out by the House of Lords in *Porter v Magill* [2001] UKHL 67, [2002] 2 AC 357, para 102, *per* Lord Hope, a case concerning alleged misconduct by councillors and an inference of apparent bias by the council auditor which approved the approach of the Court of Appeal in *Re Medicaments* (*No 2*) [2001] 1 WLR 700. The test requires that: **10.16**

(a) the court must first ascertain all the circumstances which have a bearing on the suggestion that the judge was biased;
(b) it must then ask whether those circumstances would lead a fair-minded and informed observer to conclude that there was a real possibility that the tribunal was biased.

The appearance of bias may arise from the nature of any connection between the tribunal members and anyone involved in the case; or the appearance of bias may arise from the way in which the tribunal members conduct themselves during the course of the hearing. **10.17**

Material circumstances

What forms part of the material circumstances will of course depend on the facts of the particular case. **10.18**

10.19 In *Locabail (UK) Ltd v Bayfield Properties Ltd* [2000] IRLR 96, the Court of Appeal held that in cases in the second category of apparent bias (as opposed to presumed bias) the reviewing court might properly inquire whether the judge knew of the matter alleged to undermine his impartiality, as ignorance would preclude a danger of bias.

10.20 Any explanation given by the judge may form part of the material circumstances. In *Re Medicaments (No 2)* [2001] 1 WLR 700, para 86, the Court of Appeal said:

> The material circumstances will include any explanation given by the judge under review as to his knowledge or appreciation of those circumstances. Where that explanation is accepted by the claimant for review it can be treated as accurate. Where it is not accepted, it becomes one further matter to be considered from the viewpoint of a fair-minded observer. The court does not have to rule whether the explanation should be accepted or rejected. Rather it has to decide whether or not the fair-minded observer would consider that there was a real danger of bias notwithstanding the explanation advanced.

Fair-minded and informed observer

10.21 The fair-minded and informed observer is taken as being a person both with knowledge of the litigation process, and with knowledge of the particular case. Other factors in ascertaining who is an informed observer are:

(a) The informed observer is 'not one who made his judgment after a brief visit to the court but was familiar with the detailed history of the proceedings and with the way cases of the present kind were tried' (*Arab Monetary Fund v Hashim (No 8)* The Times, 4 May 1993, (1994) 6 Admin LR 348). See also *Sengupta v Holmes* [2002] EWCA Civ 1104.

(b) The informed observer will be taken as being aware of the legal tradition and culture of the jurisdiction (*Taylor v Lawrence* [2003] QB 528, para 61). This entails awareness of the oath of office taken by judges to administer justice without fear or favour, and their ability to carry out that oath by reason of their training and experience (*Locabail (UK) Ltd v Bayfield Properties Ltd* [2000] IRLR 96, para 21).

(c) However, the informed observer is not to be taken to be wholly uncritical of the legal culture and system, and should be taken to be 'neither complacent nor unduly sensitive or suspicious' (*Lawal v Northern Spirit Ltd* [2003] UKHL 35, [2003] IRLR 538, paras 14 and 22).

10.22 In the specific context of the employment tribunal, it is irrelevant that any individual accused of bias forms part of a panel of three members (despite some earlier views to the contrary). The following points should be noted:

(1) In *Jones v DAS Legal Expenses Insurance Co Ltd* [2004] EWCA Civ 1071, [2004] IRLR 218, para 28, the Court of Appeal held that it was a relevant circumstance that the tribunal was a panel of three. The charge of impartiality has to lie against the tribunal and this tribunal consisted not only of its judge but also of two independent wing-members who were equal judges of the facts as the judge was. The Court of Appeal noted that their impartiality was not in question and their decision was unanimous. This may be taken to suggest that it will be harder to establish bias where one member of three is subject to the allegation of bias, than it would be to establish bias against a single judge.

(2) However, in the House of Lords in *Lawal* above it was said that the reasonable observer is likely to approach the matter on the basis that lay members look to the judge (in the EAT context) for guidance on the law, and can be expected to develop a fairly close relationship of trust and confidence with the judge (at para 21).

(3) In *Lodwick v Southwark LBC* [2004] EWCA Civ 306, [2004] IRLR 554 the fact that the judge was only one of three members all with an equal vote was said not to be a good reason for the judge to refuse to recuse himself. As the legally qualified and presiding member of the tribunal, the judge's position was an important one, and any apparent bias was not nullified by the presence of two lay members (at para 20).

(4) It would appear therefore that despite the comments in *Jones v DAS*, an appearance of bias will not be dispelled by the fact that only one member of the tribunal is alleged to have shown bias, at least where that member is the judge.

Apparent bias: particular examples

In the employment tribunal questions of bias may arise more commonly than in the courts due to the composition of an employment tribunal. It is part of the very nature of the system that lay members will have business or professional interests outside their role as a tribunal member. Further, it is common for tribunals to be chaired by part-time judges who carry on practice as solicitors or barristers. These interests increase the chances of a case being listed in front of a member with some connection with one of the parties. **10.23**

In *Locabail (UK) Ltd v Bayfield Properties Ltd* [2000] IRLR 96, the Court of Appeal, whilst acknowledging that each case must turn on an examination of all the material circumstances, gave some examples of the types of relationships which may or may not be likely to give rise to an appearance of bias: **10.24**

(1) It was 'inconceivable' that an objection could be soundly based on the religion, ethnic or national origin, gender, age, class, means, or sexual orientation of the judge.
(2) Nor, ordinarily and without more, would an appearance of bias arise from the judge's:
  (a) social or educational or service or employment background or history, nor that of any member of the judge's family;
  (b) previous political associations, membership of social or sporting or charitable bodies, or Masonic associations;
  (c) previous judicial decisions or extra-curricular utterances (whether in textbooks, lectures, speeches, articles, interviews, reports, or responses to consultation papers);
  (d) previous receipt of instructions to act for or against any party, solicitor, or advocate engaged in a case before him;
  (e) membership of the same Inn, circuit, local Law Society, or chambers;
  (f) the fact that a judge, earlier in the same case or in a previous case, had commented adversely on a party or a witness, or found the evidence of a party or witness to be unreliable would not without more give rise to the appearance of bias.
(3) On the other hand, an appearance of bias may arise from the following circumstances (at para 25):

> By contrast, a real danger of bias might well be thought to arise if there were personal friendship or animosity between the judge and any member of the public involved in the case; or if the judge were closely acquainted with any member of the public involved in the case, particularly if the credibility of that individual could be significant in the decision of the case; or if, in a case where the credibility of any individual were an issue to be decided by the judge, he had in a previous case rejected the evidence of that person in such outspoken terms as to throw doubt on his ability to approach such person's evidence with an open mind on any later occasion; or if on any question at issue in the proceedings before him the judge had expressed views, particularly in the course of the hearing, in such extreme and unbalanced terms as to throw doubt on his ability to try the issue with an objective judicial mind. . .; or if, for any other reason, there were real ground for doubting the ability of the judge to ignore extraneous considerations, prejudices and predilections and bring an objective judgment to bear on the issues before him.

In *Howell v Lees Millais* [2007] EWCA Civ 720, one of the parties was a partner in a firm of solicitors. The judge had recently had unsuccessful negotiations to join the firm. The judge refused to recuse himself, but the Court of Appeal overturned his decision. An appearance of bias arose from the combination of the judge's apparent irritation at the failure of the negotiations, and from the judge's intemperate conduct towards the firm during the recusal application. **10.25**

In *Hamilton v GMB (Northern Region)* [2007] IRLR 391, the EAT held that a tribunal member should have stood down from the hearing of a claim involving the legality of the GMB's equal **10.26** pay strategy. The fact that she had previously held a senior position in a union with an identical policy was sufficient to justify a finding of apparent bias. The court found that a reasonable person might conclude that she would have had a natural desire to uphold the legality of that policy. In *City and County of Swansea v Honey* EAT/0030/08/RN the EAT allowed a bias appeal where a wing member was a union member who had been involved in a campaign against the employer and had a negative view of the employer council as a whole.

Part-time judges

10.27 The *Terms and Conditions of Service and Terms of Appointment of Part-time Chairmen of Employment Tribunals* (October 2000) provides that no part-time judge may appear as an advocate before any employment tribunal in the whole of the region to which they are assigned to sit as a judge.

10.28 In *Lawal v Northern Spirit Ltd* above, apparent bias arose out of the fact that counsel appearing for one of the parties before the EAT sat as a part-time judge of the EAT, and had sat with one or more of the lay members in the past. Both the EAT and the Court of Appeal (by a majority) held that there was no apparent bias; the House of Lords held that there was an appearance of bias. The lay members are likely to look to the judge for guidance on the law, and to develop a relationship of trust and confidence with the judge. The informed observer would also be likely to consider the fact that a part-time judge of the employment tribunal cannot appear at all in the region in which he sits. The House of Lords directed that EAT practice should be assimilated to that in the employment tribunal by introducing a restriction on part-time judges appearing as counsel before a panel of the EAT consisting of one or two lay members with whom they had previously sat.

Professional connections of judge

10.29 Traditionally it has been not uncommon for judges to have appearing before them members of the Bar and solicitors who are known to them (and with whom they may have been in chambers), without any concern as to bias.

10.30 Barristers in private practice are independent self-employed practitioners and do not have responsibility for, or (usually) detailed knowledge of, the affairs of other members of the same chambers (*Locabail* above, at para 20). The fact that a party is represented by a barrister from the same chambers as the judge or employment judge does not, of itself, give rise to an appearance of bias. See *Birmingham City Council v Yardley* [2004] EWCA Civ 1756 applying *Locabail* in the context of a Recorder with counsel from his chambers appearing before him. Further in *Smith v Kvaerner Cementation Foundations Ltd* [2006] EWCA Civ 242, [2007] 1WLR 370, the Court of Appeal cited *Yardley* in finding that ordinarily, the fact that a judicial officer was a barrister and was a member of the same chambers as one or both of the advocates did not prevent that judicial officer from hearing the case. However, it was pointed out, *obiter dicta*, by the Court of Appeal that the position may be different where one or more of the advocates is acting under a conditional fee agreement since in those circumstances, the success or failure of that party may have an effect on the financial standing of the set of chambers as a whole.

10.31 In *Jones v DAS Legal Expenses Insurance Co Ltd* [2004] EWCA Civ 1071, [2004] IRLR 218, the employment judge's husband was a barrister who received instructions from time to time from the respondent. The Court of Appeal rejected the presumption of bias on grounds that the judge did not herself have an interest in the outcome of the proceedings. The Court of Appeal also held that in the circumstances there was no apparent bias. The fair-minded and informed observer, proceeding on the basis that the judge knew in general how the employers' system of appointing barristers operated and that her husband was to some extent a beneficiary of it, would not conclude that the judge herself, still less the tribunal as the decision-making body, was biased.

10.32 The position of a solicitor as judge (or employment judge) is more difficult since, in contrast to barristers in chambers, a solicitor in a partnership has a common financial interest with his partners. As a partner, the solicitor will owe duties to clients of whom he may personally know nothing (*Locabail* above, at para 20). The judge should consider whether there is any conflict of interest which would have prevented him from acting against any party to the proceedings. However, the Court of Appeal rejected an inflexible rule that if there is such a conflict the judge must recuse himself. All the circumstances must be considered: *Locabail* above, at para 58.

An appearance of bias arose in *Cleveland Transit v Walton* EAT/578/91 from the fact that the employers had sought tenders from firms of solicitors to act as their legal advisers and one of those submitting an unsuccessful tender was the firm of which the employment judge was a senior partner. **10.33**

The effect of a judge's former role as a partner in a firm of solicitors was further considered in *BCCI v Ali* (Ch D, 3 December 2001). Lawrence Collins J was assigned to determine costs sharing between employees involved in litigation against BCCI. An allegation of bias was made on the ground that the judge had been a partner in a firm of solicitors which had acted for BCCI's auditors in claims brought against the auditors by some of the employees in the instant proceedings. The judge refused to recuse himself. There was no presumption of bias: although the auditors might have an interest in the former employees being ordered to pay costs, that could not give a partner in the solicitors' firm representing them a financial interest in their success. In any event, as a *former* partner in that firm, it was clear that the judge could have no financial or other interest in the success or failure of the proceedings against the auditors. The judge also rejected the allegation of apparent bias: the auditors were not parties to the instant proceedings; the judge had not represented the auditors in the previous action by the employees and was no longer a partner in the firm that had represented them. **10.34**

Tribunal member having previously adjudicated on a case involving a party or representative

The mere fact that a judge, earlier in the same case or in a previous case, had commented adversely on a party or a witness, or found the evidence of a party or witness to be unreliable, would not without more found a sustainable claim of apparent bias (*Locabail* above, at para 25). This is the case even in circumstances where there are outstanding complaints against a tribunal member resulting from the conduct of previous litigation in which one or more of the parties were involved. Thus, in *Ansar v Lloyds TSB Bank plc* [2006] EWCA 1462, [2007] IRLR 211, the Court of Appeal approved the decision of an employment judge not to recuse himself from hearing a pre-hearing review in circumstances where he had previously heard litigation between the parties which had resulted in an appeal to the EAT and the making of complaints against the judge by one of the parties. See also *Henry v London Metropolitan University* EAT/0252/06, where the EAT refused the recusal of a lay member on the grounds that he had expressed a view on the live issue in the case during an earlier appeal in the same case. There must be something more which is of substance and which would lead the fair-minded and informed observer to conclude that there is a real possibility that the decision-maker who is impugned will not be able to bring an open mind and objective judgment to bear. **10.35**

This principle also applies with at least as much force to previous adverse comments upon a party's representative (*Lodwick v Southwark London Borough Council* [2004] EWCA Civ 306, [2004] ICR 884). See also paras 10.77–10.83 below. **10.36**

Judge's previous legislative role

In *Davidson v Scottish Ministers* [2004] UKHL 34, (2004) HRLR 34, however, the House of Lords held that where a judge was required to rule on the meaning of legislation which he had previously been involved in drafting or promoting, there was a real risk of apparent bias. The informed observer would conclude that there was a real possibility that the judge would subconsciously strive to avoid a conclusion that undermined advice the judge had given to Parliament during the promotion of the legislation. **10.37**

Connection between lay members and parties

10.38 Where a lay member has business connections with, or has been employed by one of the parties, there may be a risk of the appearance of bias, and such connections should be disclosed to the parties at the outset of the proceedings. Further, pending or proposed applications by lay members for employment with a party may well give rise to the appearance of bias.

10.39 The *Medicaments* case (para 10.16 above) concerned the Restrictive Practices Court, which in common with the employment tribunal has lay membership. One of the lay members applied for a job with the firm of economic consultants who were giving expert evidence for one of the parties in the case. The member disclosed the application to the President of the Restrictive Practices Court who notified the parties; the firm of economic consultants indicated that there were no vacancies available; and the member undertook initially not to pursue an application until after the trial, and then not to do so until two years after trial. The Court of Appeal held that the fair-minded observer may nevertheless be concerned that the member may still harbour hopes of working for the consultants, and that this may affect her ability to make an impartial appraisal of the expert evidence. In *London Underground v Ayanbadejo* EAT/1160/97, a lay member of the tribunal had worked for, and for a time been in dispute with, a predecessor of the employers, but did not disclose the connection. The EAT made clear that the fact should have been disclosed but was not prepared to overturn the decision ultimately reached.

10.40 In *Gillies v Secretary of State for Work and Pensions* [2006] UKHL 2, [2006] ICR 267 the House of Lords considered the membership of the Disability Appeal Tribunal which like the employment tribunals and EAT has a legally qualified judge and two wing members. One of the members of the Disability Appeal Tribunal is a 'medical member' who has medical expertise. The claimant alleged that there was the appearance of bias on the part of the medical member of the panel given that that member was a doctor and had spent many years providing reports as an examining practitioner for the Benefits Agency. The House of Lords held that there was no appearance of bias and that the reasonable and right minded observer would conclude that the medical member would approach the evidence objectively and, in the light of her own knowledge and expertise, would not prefer the evidence of the examining medical practitioner to the other available evidence simply because of that member's relationship with the Benefits Agency.

10.41 The appearance of bias may arise from a wide variety of contacts between tribunal members and the parties. In *University College Swansea v Cornelius* [1988] ICR 735, EAT, for example, the claimant named a professor of the university as respondent in a sex discrimination complaint. It was only after the employment tribunal upheld her complaint that it was disclosed that one of the lay members of the tribunal was the mother-in-law of that professor. Wood J said that the importance of disclosing any connection with persons or bodies involved in proceedings before them should be impressed upon lay members, and it might be that, before the start of the hearing, it would be wise for a judge to pose a specific question and to impress upon the members how important it was that if, during the hearing, any relevant matter should arise, he should be informed at once. The EAT cited a passage from Lush J in *Sergeant v Dale* [1887] 2 QBD 558, 567: 'at all events it is to clear away everything which might engender suspicion and distrust of the tribunal, and so to promote the feeling of confidence in the administration of justice which is so essential to social order and security'.

10.42 In *Source Publications v Ellison* EAT/872/83, apparent bias arose from the fact that a member of the tribunal had recently been in dispute with the employers about a bill. In *Peninsula Business Services Ltd & others v Ress & others* EAT/0333/08/RN, the EAT held that the test for apparent bias was met where a part-time employment judge was a partner in a small firm of solicitors which had placed an advertisement expressing derogatory views about non-solicitor employment consultants, and one of the parties in the case before the part-time judge was a company of non-solicitor employment consultants. However, in an appeal on the same grounds in a later case the test was not met as the passage of time since the advertisement and the fact that the part-time judge was no longer a partner in the firm of solicitors meant that there was no appearance of bias.

The EAT held there to be an appearance of bias in *Halford v Sharples* [1992] ICR 146, where a lay member had been chosen for the case which involved the Assistant Chief Constable of Merseyside Police because of his relevant experience, in that he was employed by another police force as an equal opportunities officer. He had interviews with members of that force who were involved in the instant proceedings, and had knowledge of a number of officers involved in the case. **10.43**

On the other hand, in *ASI v Glass Processing Ltd* 27 April 1999, CA, the employment tribunal refused to review a decision on the ground that having lost, the employer found that one of the lay members knew the respondent. The point could have been taken before but was not so taken; no satisfactory explanation was given for the review application being long out of time; the objection was misconceived because the connection was tenuous and did not give rise to a real danger of bias. **10.44**

In *Colback v Ena Ferguson* [2001] EWCA Civ 1027, although it was said that it had been unwise for two lay members of a tribunal to accept a lift in a taxi with one of the parties, it had not created a real risk or danger of bias. **10.45**

C. IMPROPER CONDUCT AND PROCEDURAL IRREGULARITIES

Both Article 6 of ECHR and the common law concept of natural justice require a tribunal to afford parties a fair hearing. The requirements of a fair hearing are not fixed, but will depend on the circumstances of each case. Essential elements are the right to be heard on the issues in the case, and the right to be placed on an equal footing with the other parties. **10.46**

The tribunal's overriding objective and procedural rules are designed to achieve a fair trial for all parties. Interim decisions of the tribunal and the conduct of the tribunal at the hearing may give rise to a concern that a party has been denied a fair trial. A wide range of case management decisions both prior to and at the hearing may lead to an allegation that a party has been deprived of a fair trial: for example a refusal to allow an amendment, or the late admission, or refusal to admit evidence (see, for example, *Yellow Pages Ltd v Garton* EAT/0375/02). Many of these situations have been dealt with already in this chapter. This section considers specifically cases where the conduct of the tribunal at the hearing may be said to be improper or procedurally irregular so as deny a party a fair hearing, and the related issue of cases where the conduct of the tribunal at the hearing may give rise to the appearance of bias. **10.47**

Interventions by the tribunal

The tribunal must take care to ensure in its conduct of the proceedings, and in its comments during the hearing, that all parties feel that they have the opportunity to bring forward their case, and the tribunal must refrain from any expression which may appear partial. The tribunal must avoid conducting the hearing in a manner which indicates a closed mind. **10.48**

Avoidance of immoderate language and personal comment

In *Tchoula v Netto Foodstores Ltd* EAT/1378/98, the EAT stressed that the tribunal should avoid making and expressing judgments on the claimant in person. The tribunal should in particular avoid any appearance of being patronizing towards a litigant in person when issues of law were being considered. In *Diem v Crystal Services plc* UKEAT/0398/05, the employment judge, in the course of enquiring whether the claimant was seeking to depart from her case, questioned the claimant about her skin colour and made comparisons between his own skin colour and hers. The EAT found that the judge's enquiry would lead a fair-minded observer to conclude that there was a real possibility of unconscious bias on the part of the judge. **10.49**

The importance of courtesy being shown by a tribunal was stressed by the EAT in *Laher v London Borough of Hammersmith and Fulham* EAT/215/91. Immoderate or intemperate language should be avoided by tribunals, according to the EAT in *Kennedy v Metropolitan Police* **10.50**

Commissioner The Times, 8 November 1990. Wood J commented that 'what could be tolerated by the Bar could give the wrong impression [of bias] to a layman'.

10.51 The tribunal must maintain a particularly difficult balance where one party is unrepresented. On the one hand, it is proper for the judge to assist an unrepresented party to ensure that he brings out his case; on the other hand, the judge must not act in such a way as to allow the appearance of bias, or to restrict the other party in the conduct of its case. This point was stressed in *Riverside Restaurants Ltd (t/a Harry Ramsden) v Tremayne* EAT/1168/95.

Statements indicating predisposition against a party

10.52 Comments made by the employment judge may give rise to an appearance of bias. In *Harada Ltd (t/a Chequepoint UK Ltd) v Turner (No 1)* [2001] EWCA Civ 599, the Court of Appeal held that there was a real danger that the judge would not approach the case with an open mind in the light of comments made by him at the beginning of the hearing that the respondent did not come to the hearing with a clean slate, and criticisms of the respondent's conduct of other proceedings which had been before the same tribunal. In *Breeze Benton Solicitors v Weddell* UKEAT/0873/03 the judge listed to hear a nine-day case against the respondent firm had, a year previously, heard a case involving the same respondent where he was alleged to have made disparaging remarks about the partner who represented the respondent—the respondent had subsequently written to complain to the regional chairman and to the Lord Chancellor's Department, although the complaints had not been pursued. Even though the disparaging remarks were disputed, the EAT held that there was a real possibility of bias, and the chairman should have recused himself. Accordingly the case was remitted for rehearing by a different tribunal. However, the significance in *Breeze Benton* attached to the mere fact of the former complaint has been disapproved in *Ansar v Lloyds TSB Bank plc* [2006] EWCA 1462, [2007] IRLR 211, see paras 10.77–10.83 below.

Statements indicating prejudgment of the issues

10.53 In many cases, the tribunal, through the judge, may make comments indicating the difficulties which a party may face on one or more of the issues. It is inevitable that a tribunal will react to what is put before it, and the judge is entitled to try to obtain answers from the party to points which trouble the judge as being matters of great relevance: *BLP UK Ltd v Marsh* [2003] EWCA Civ 132. Whilst the judge cannot be expected to sit in silence through the hearing (and in most cases parties would not be assisted by the judge keeping his concerns to himself), care must be taken to avoid the appearance of prejudgment.

10.54 Allegations of prejudgment often arise where the tribunal has sought to encourage the parties to settle. Such encouragement is quite common in practice, and in giving such encouragement the tribunal may indicate its preliminary views of the case based on the evidence heard thus far. There are benefits to such an approach in terms of achieving amicable resolution for the parties, a saving of costs, and a saving of tribunal time. However, such comments can leave the lingering suspicion with one or more of the parties that tribunal members have already made up their minds on the issue.

10.55 There is no impropriety in a tribunal encouraging the parties to settle; nor is there anything wrong in principle with the tribunal expressing a provisional view on the case for the purposes of assisting the parties: *Jiminez v London Borough of Southwark* [2003] IRLR 477; *Harada Ltd (t/a Chequepoint UK Ltd) v Turner (No 1)* [2001] EWCA Civ 599.

10.56 In *Harada*, Pill LJ stated that judges may make remarks at the beginning or in the course of hearings which indicate the difficulties a party faces upon one or more of the points at issue. Provided a closed mind is not shown, such comments are permissible. Such comments from the Bench are at the very heart of the adversarial procedure by way of oral hearing. It enables the party to focus on the point and to make such submissions as he properly can. In principle there is nothing wrong with a judge, having explored the difficulties on the facts or legal issues of the case with counsel, giving an opportunity for settlement discussions. Pill LJ's comments were cited and followed in *Jiminez*.

Where comments are made as to the merits of the case while the case is ongoing, the key distinction, emphasized by *Harada* and *Jiminez*, is between the expression of a provisional view, and the expression of a concluded view or closed mind. Whether any particular statement by the tribunal falls on one side of the line will depend on the circumstances of the case, the manner in which the statement is made, and the stage of the hearing at which the statement is made. **10.57**

If a judge expresses a view too forcefully, or too early, or without making clear that the view is provisional, there is a risk that the appellate court may decide that the tribunal's mind was closed. So, for example: **10.58**

(a) In *Peter Simper & Co Ltd v Cooke* [1986] IRLR 19, unqualified remarks hostile to the employer's case were made by the judge during the course of cross-examination of the employee on the opening day, before the employer had led any evidence. The EAT held that this was not the appropriate time for such strongly expressed views.
(b) Similarly, in *Graham v Ivan Boardley* EAT/444/84, when, at the end of the examination in chief of the second witness, the tribunal announced that it was completely satisfied that a redundancy situation existed. The EAT thought that it could not have formed a concluded view of fairness at this stage, and remitted the case to another tribunal for rehearing.
(c) A rehearing was also ordered in *Mortimer v Reading Windings Ltd* [1977] ICR 511, where the judge, in introducing the case, said: 'Why are we here today, because you have obviously resigned'. He also continually pushed the claimant to finish his case.
(d) In *Chris Project v Hutt* UKEATS/0065/06, before any evidence was called the employment judge made a comment that the appellant employer faced an uphill struggle with its case. As a result of the comment the employer's lay representative conceded that the employee had been unfairly dismissed. The EAT held that the tribunal had appeared to be biased by giving the impression that the case had been prejudged; further the comment was such that an observer would have considered that it put undue pressure on the employer's representative to refrain from advancing the defence.
(e) In *Ezsias v North Glamorgan NHS Trust* [2007] EWCA Civ 330, (2007) 104(12) LSG 34, the Court of Appeal held that the fact that the employment judge had expressed a view of the claimant's prospects in concluded terms at an earlier hearing led to an appearance of bias. In the circumstances it was reasonable for a fair-minded and informed observer to take the view that the judge, at the second hearing, had a closed mind as to the claimant's prospects of success.
(f) In contrast in *Jiminez* the judge's views were expressly said to be provisional, and at a stage when the bulk of the evidence had been heard.
(g) In *Advance Security UK Limited v Musa* UKEAT/0611/07 the tribunal had stated, immediately after hearing closing submissions, that they expected to reach their decision within 20 minutes. The EAT rejected an argument that this was unfair. In the circumstances, where the tribunal had heard only one day of evidence, an indication that a decision would or might be made in 20 minutes would not show to an impartial observer that the tribunal may have been treating unfairly one party or the other.

Remarks made after the conclusion of the hearing may be seen in a different light. In *Greenway Harrison Ltd v Wiles* [1994] IRLR 380, the judge was alleged to have said 'that will teach them not to settle when I tell them'. The EAT held that, even if this had been said, it was after the conclusion of the proceedings and would not amount to bias since it was a casual remark made at the conclusion of the hearing and not during the tribunal's deliberations. **10.59**

The EAT will look at the evidence as to the handling of the proceedings by the judge in the context of the proceedings as a whole, and of the issues raised by the parties; see, for example, *Anthony v Governors of Hillcrest School* EAT/1193/00, where comments from the judge which **10.60** on their own suggested that he had prejudged the claimant's case did not give rise to the appearance of bias when seen in the context of the four-day hearing as a whole.

Reliance on matters not canvassed at the hearing

10.61 The tribunal should exercise caution if it wishes to consider matters not raised before it by the parties, in the pleadings, witness statements, and submissions. There are two relevant principles:

(1) The tribunal has jurisdiction to determine issues raised in the claim form (and any amendment allowed to the claim form). It does not have jurisdiction to determine a complaint which is not included in the claim form: *Chapman v Simon* [1994] IRLR 124, CA.
(2) Even if a particular claim falls within the tribunal's jurisdiction, the right to a fair hearing requires notice to be given to the parties of all material matters of fact and law upon which the tribunal intends to rely.

10.62 In *Hereford & Worcester County Council v Neale* [1986] IRLR 168, 175, Ralph Gibson LJ said that an employment tribunal should not rely on matters which occur to it *after* the hearing and which have not been mentioned or treated as relevant without the party against whom the point is raised having an opportunity to deal with it, unless the tribunal could be entirely sure that the point is so clear that the party could not make any useful comment or explanation. (See to similar effect *Laurie v Holloway* [1994] ICR 32; *British Gas v McCaull* [2001] IRLR 60, EAT; *Bradford Hospital NHS Trust v Al-Shabib* [2003] IRLR 4, EAT). If, after the hearing and before reaching its judgment, the tribunal becomes concerned by a new point, it should recall the parties and give them the opportunity for further submissions on the point: *Vauxhall Motors Ltd v Ghafoor* [1993] ICR 376.

10.63 The steps that the tribunal must take to give the parties the opportunity to be heard on the new point will depend on the nature of the point, and its significance to the case as a whole. In some cases it may be sufficient for the tribunal to give the parties the opportunity to submit further written submissions on the point, for example if the tribunal wants submissions on a new legal authority. However, where the tribunal's point is more fundamental, and may affect the evidence which the parties would want to put before the tribunal, the tribunal should reconvene a hearing. In *Easter v Governing Body of Notre Dame High School* UKEAT/0615/04, the tribunal during its deliberations rejected gross misconduct as the reason for dismissal (which had been the reason advanced by the employer throughout) but decided instead that the reason was some other substantial reason. It was held by the EAT that it was insufficient simply to invite written submissions on this new reason: the hearing should have been reconvened and the parties given the opportunity to submit more evidence.

10.64 For further cases concerning the denial of opportunity to make representations, see *Murphy v Epsom College* [1984] IRLR 271; *Ellis v Ministry of Defence* [1985] ICR 257; and *Hotson v Wisbech Conservative Club* [1984] IRLR 422. For more recent examples, see also *Tarbuck v Sainsbury's Supermarkets Ltd* [2006] IRLR 184, para 62 and *Lewis v HSBC Bank plc* [2006] UKEAT 0364/06. However, it may be unlikely that the EAT would remit a case for a full rehearing where the loss of opportunity to make submissions is the only point on appeal, and there is no error of law disclosed by the decision itself.

New evidence raised late in the hearing

10.65 A party may be denied a fair hearing if a matter is raised at the hearing in a way that does not give the party proper opportunity to deal with it. In *Panama v London Borough of Hackney* [2003] EWCA Civ 273, [2003] IRLR 278 evidence concerning fraud on the part of the claimant, which the tribunal later found relevant to the question of compensation, was not raised for the first time until cross-examination of the claimant. The Court of Appeal approved a statement by the EAT in *Hotson* that once dishonesty is introduced into a case, the relevant allegation has to be put with sufficient formality and at an early enough stage to provide a full opportunity for answer. It is suggested that the same principle should apply whenever new evidence which is highly relevant to the tribunal's decision comes to light late in the hearing. The tribunal should ensure that the parties are given adequate opportunity to deal with the new evidence.

Reliance by the tribunal on authorities not canvassed with the parties

In *Albion Hotel (Freshwater) Ltd v Maia e Silva* [2002] IRLR 200, EAT, the employment tribunal had erred in relying on authorities which had not been cited by the parties' advocates. Where an employment tribunal considers that an authority is relevant, significant, and material to its decision but it has not been referred to by the parties, the tribunal should refer that authority to the parties and invite their submissions before concluding its decision. Failure to do so may amount to a breach of natural justice and of the right to a fair hearing. **10.66**

The limits of this principle must be recognized. The mere fact that a tribunal relies in its decision on authorities which have not been cited at the hearing does not give an automatic right of appeal. The Court of Appeal in *Stanley Cole Wainfleet Ltd v Sheridan* [2003] EWCA Civ 1046, [2003] IRLR 885 identified two elements before a decision can be said to be unfair by reason of failure to draw authority to the parties' attention: **10.67**

(1) The authority must be central to the tribunal's decision, in the sense of 'relevant, significant and material'. Ward LJ said (at para 32):

> the authority must alter or affect the way the issues have been addressed to a significant extent so that it truly can be said by a fair-minded observer that the case was decided in a way which could not have been anticipated by a party fixed with such knowledge of the law and procedure as it would be reasonable to attribute to him in all the circumstances.

(2) It must be shown that a material injustice has resulted. The hearing will not have been unfair if it causes no substantial prejudice to the party complaining.

Use by members of industrial experience

The requirements of natural justice may also come into conflict with the desirability of the use by the lay members of their industrial experience. In *Hammington v Berker Sportcraft Ltd* [1980] ICR 248, a claimant complained that a lay member had used his personal knowledge in reaching a conclusion on compensation, and had thus not confined himself to the evidence placed before the employment tribunal. The EAT stated that if the lay member was minded to do this, it was not only necessary to indicate to the parties that the tribunal member was a specialist in the field, but also to bring facts known by him to the attention of the parties, so they could deal with them by calling other evidence if necessary. **10.68**

This approach was reiterated in *Halford v Sharples* [1992] ICR 146, where it was held that it was improper for lay members to make investigations of their own into a case, since it was impossible for either party to know the circumstances on which their decision was based. It was important that the findings of fact were based on the evidence heard by the tribunal, and not on investigations carried out by the members themselves. Here, a lay member had been chosen for the case, which involved the Assistant Chief Constable of Merseyside Police, because of his relevant experience, in that he was employed by another police force as an equal opportunities officer and he had interviews with members of that force who were involved in the instant proceedings. **10.69**

Tribunal member asleep

The parties may be denied a fair hearing where a member of the tribunal falls asleep, or otherwise fails to pay attention to the hearing. See, for example, *Whitehart v Raymond Thompson Ltd* EAT/910/83; *Red Bank Manufacturing Co Ltd v Meadows* [1992] ICR 204, EAT; and *Kudrath v Ministry of Defence* EAT/422/97 (where the EAT criticized the employment judge's practice of closing his eyes to indicate that an advocate was not being persuasive). A hearing by a tribunal which includes a member who has been drinking alcohol to the extent that he appeared to fall asleep and not to be concentrating on the case does not give the appearance of the fair hearing to **10.70** which every party is entitled. Public confidence in the administration of justice would be damaged if the court took the view that such behaviour by a member of an employment tribunal did not matter: *Stansbury v Datapulse plc* [2003] EWCA Civ 1951, [2004] IRLR 466. In *Fordyce v Hammersmith & Fulham Conservative Association* [2006] UKEAT 0390/05, the parties raised the issue with the tribunal that one of the wing members appeared to be asleep but agreed to continue with the hearing. The wing member appeared to resume sleeping but the issue was not raised again by either of the parties. The losing party appealed and a rehearing was ordered. It was emphasized by the EAT that the decision of the tribunal was a decision of all three members and where one of the members was asleep, that member could not play a full part in the decision-making process.

D. RAISING AN ALLEGATION OF BIAS OR PROCEDURAL IMPROPRIETY

10.71 Issues of bias or unfairness in the conduct of the hearing may arise during the course of the hearing itself, or they may arise after the tribunal has given its decision. If they are raised before the tribunal decision, the tribunal has the power to recuse itself and to direct that the proceedings are reheard before a differently constituted tribunal. If raised after the decision, the allegations may form the basis of an application for review, or a ground of appeal. There is conflicting case law as to the extent to which such allegations should be raised during the hearing (see paras 10.84–10.90).

The tribunal's power to recuse itself

10.72 It is clear that the tribunal has power to recuse itself and to order a rehearing by a differently constituted tribunal: see *Charman v Palmers Scaffolding Ltd* [1979] ICR 335, where the EAT held that although there was no specific reference to rehearings in ETR 1993, the power fell within the tribunal's general power to give directions on any matter arising in connection with the proceedings and to regulate its own procedure. However, where a tribunal finds that the principle of judicial impartiality has been breached it must recuse itself. In this regard the power is exercised in a different manner to other case management decisions. The tribunal cannot decide to continue with the hearing weighing all the considerations in the balance (see *AWG Group Limited v Morrison* [2006] EWCA Civ 6, [2006] 1 WLR 1163).

Disclosure by the tribunal and waiver by the parties

10.73 Judges, chairmen, and tribunal members are under a duty to raise matters which may disqualify them from hearing a particular case. The Court of Appeal in *Locabail (UK) Ltd v Bayfield Properties Ltd* [2000] IRLR 96 stated that in cases of personal embarrassment or automatic disqualification, the judge should recuse himself at the earliest possible stage; in any other case, where a judge became aware of a matter which could give rise to a real danger of bias he should disclose this to the parties as soon as possible.

10.74 The party affected then has the opportunity to ask for the judge to recuse himself. A party could waive a right to call for a judge to be disqualified provided the waiver was clear and unequivocal and is given in full knowledge of the relevant facts (*Pinochet* [2000] 1 AC 119, 137, *per* Lord Browne-Wilkinson). Where, following appropriate disclosure by the judge, no objection was taken to his hearing the case, no subsequent complaint of bias could be made in respect of the matter disclosed (see *Locabail* above, at paras 15 and 20). A party may waive any right to complain of presumed bias or apparent bias (*Jones v DAS* [2004] EWCA Civ 1071, [2004] IRLR 218, para 30). However, in circumstances where a party has not been made aware of all the relevant information, an apparent waiver of the right to object will not amount to a proper waiver (see *Smith v Kvaerner Cementation Foundations Ltd* [2006] EWCA Civ 242, [2007] IWLR 370). In the *Kvaerner* case, the party had not been made aware of how long it would take for a new trial date to be obtained and counsel acting for the party had sought to influence the decision of the party by making reference to the costs which would be thrown away.

Guidance on disclosure

In *Jones v DAS* the Court of Appeal gave the following guidance (at para 35): **10.75**

(i) If there is any real as opposed to fanciful chance of objection being taken by that fair-minded spectator, the first step is to ascertain whether or not another judge is available to hear the matter. It is obviously better to transfer the matter than risk a complaint of bias. The judge should make every effort in the time available to clarify what his interest is which gives rise to this conflict so that the full facts can be placed before the parties.

(ii) Some time should be taken to prepare whatever explanation is to be given to the parties and, if one is really troubled, perhaps even to make a note of what one will say.

(iii) Because thoughts that the court may have been biased can become festering sores for the disappointed litigants, it is vital that the judge's explanation be mechanically recorded or carefully noted where that facility is not available. That will avoid the kind of controversy about what was or was not said which has bedevilled this case.

(iv) A full explanation must be given to the parties. That explanation should detail exactly what matters are within the judge's knowledge which give rise to a possible conflict of interest. The judge must be punctilious in setting out all material matters known to him. Secondly, an explanation should be given as to why the problem had only arisen so late in the day. The parties deserve also to be told whether it would be possible to move the case to another judge that day.

(v) The options open to the parties should be explained in detail. Those options are, of course, to consent to the judge hearing the matter, the consequence being that the parties will thereafter be likely to be held to have lost their right to object. The other option is to apply to the judge to recuse himself. The parties should be told it is their right to object, that the court will not take it amiss if the right is exercised and that the judge will decide having heard the submissions. They should be told what will happen next. If the court decides the case can proceed, it will proceed. If on the other hand the judge decides he will have to stand down, the parties should be told in advance of the likely dates on which the matter may be re-listed.

(vi) The parties should always be told that time will be afforded to reflect before electing. That should be made clear even where both parties are represented. If there is a litigant in person the better practice may be to rise for five minutes. The litigant in person can be directed to the Citizens Advice Bureau if that service is available and if he wishes to avail of it. If the litigant feels he needs more help, he can be directed to the chief clerk and/or the listing officer. Since this is a problem created by the court, the court has to do its best to assist in resolving it.

In giving this guidance the Court of Appeal emphasized that it was guidance, and not a definitive checklist, and may not be applicable in every case. **10.76**

Dangers of inappropriate recusal

Whilst the recent trend may have been towards fuller disclosure in order to avoid the risk of allegations of bias, there is potential injustice in a tribunal acceding too readily to a request for a rehearing before a differently constituted tribunal. A rehearing will cause the parties additional costs and the further delay may affect the reliability of the evidence when the case is reheard. Particularly where the application for recusal arises out of conduct at the hearing, there is a risk that a party may manipulate the procedure in order to achieve a change to what he perceives may be a more favourable tribunal. There is a danger in complaints of bias or impropriety becoming 'self-fulfilling'. The Court of Appeal in *Dobbs v Triodos Bank NV* [2005] EWCA Civ 468 warned against judges too readily recusing themselves in the face of criticism (*per* Chadwick LJ at para 7): **10.77**

> If judges were to recuse themselves whenever a litigant—whether it be a represented litigant or a litigant in person—criticised them (which sometimes happens not infrequently) we would soon

re. ch the position in which litigants were able to select judges to hear their cases, simply by criticising all the judges they did not want to hear their cases. It would be easy for a litigant to produce a situation in which a judge felt obliged to recuse himself simply because he had been criticised—whether that criticism was justified or not.

10.78 In *Locabail* the court said that if an objection was made, it would be the duty of the judge to consider the objection and exercise his judgment upon it, but 'he would be as wrong to yield to a tenuous or frivolous objection as he would to ignore an objection of substance'. In *BCCI v Ali* 3 December 2001, Ch D, following *Locabail,* Lawrence Collins J said that it is important that judges discharge their duty to sit and do not, by acceding too readily to complaints of bias, encourage parties to believe that they may have their case tried by someone thought to be more sympathetic.

10.79 In *Taylor v Lawrence* [2003] QB 528, the Court of Appeal said that judges should be circumspect about disclosing relationships where no possibility of bias could arise in the mind of the fair-minded and impartial observer. If a relationship existed which might give rise to such a possibility, and in a borderline case, the relationship should be disclosed to the parties. The judge had been under no obligation to disclose the fact that a party's solicitor had acted for the judge in a personal matter: it was unthinkable that such a relationship would give rise to a possibility of bias in the mind of the fair-minded and impartial observer. In *Automobile Proprietary Ltd v Healy* [1979] ICR 809, the tribunal, whilst rejecting the allegation of bias, decided that it could not properly proceed with the case if the employee had no confidence in it, and thus ordered a rehearing before a different tribunal. The EAT criticized it for this action, on the ground that the lack of confidence was insufficient to form a ground for a rehearing.

10.80 The appropriateness of a tribunal's decision to recuse itself was raised before the Court of Appeal in *Bennett v London Borough of Southwark* [2002] EWCA Civ 223, [2002] IRLR 407, where the tribunal had recused itself after the claimant's representative had suggested racial bias on the part of the tribunal; the tribunal concluded that they could not hear a race discrimination case in which it had been accused of racism. When faced with allegations of this nature from a representative, the tribunal should first invite the representative to withdraw the comments. If he does so, the case can continue. If he does not withdraw, the tribunal must consider the justification for the comments. If no proper justification is offered, the tribunal will need to consider whether, given the potential injustice to the other side and the public expense which recusing itself will bring, it cannot continue with the hearing with an unclouded mind.

10.81 However, the EAT's decision in *Breeze Benton Solicitors v Weddell* UKEAT/0873/03 suggested an approach more favourable to recusal. Cox J stated the following principles (at paras 44 and 53):

(a) The tribunal is required to recuse itself if there is a real possibility of bias (*per* the test in *Porter* and *Lawal*). If such a risk is found, the tribunal is not entitled to balance against that risk considerations of prejudice to the other party resulting from delay.
(b) If in any case there is a real ground for doubt, that doubt should be resolved in favour of recusal.
(c) It is no answer to a recusal application to say that the judge was only one of three members (following *Lodwick*).
(d) The claim of the person asked to recuse himself that he will not be or is not partial is of no weight because of 'the insidious nature' of bias.
(e) If the application for recusal is well founded, the fact that it could have been made at an earlier interlocutory stage is relevant only to the question of costs and not to the question of recusal.

10.82 In *Breeze Benton* one factor alleged to give rise to the appearance of bias was that the judge was aware of a complaint made against him by the respondent (see para 47). There must be some caution in relation to this factor; as noted above, it is undesirable for applications for recusal to become self-fulfilling. *Bennett* (at para 19) and *Dobbs* cited above clearly show that tribunals should avoid manipulation, whether intentional or otherwise. *Bromley Appointments.com Ltd v Mackinnon* UKEAT/0640/04 (Bean J) concerned a complaint of bias on the part of the judge arising out of an interim decision made between the liabilities hearing and the remedies hearing. The employer complained about the judge to the Regional Chairman (even threatening proceedings against the ETS) and applied for the judge to recuse himself from the remedies hearing. The EAT found that no appearance of bias arose from the interim decision. The fact of the complaint did not give grounds for recusal: it would be a recipe for chaos if a party dissatisfied with an interlocutory decision of a tribunal could achieve a recusal by threat to sue the ETS, where a recusal was not otherwise appropriate (at para 29). The Court of Appeal in *Ansar v Lloyds TSB Bank plc* [2006] EWCA Civ 1462, [2007] IRLR 211 followed the robust approach in *Dobbs*, holding that the mere fact of complaint could not give rise to a decision to recuse.

In *AWG v Morrison* [2006] EWCA Civ 6, [2006] 1 WLR 1163, the Court of Appeal observes that in many of the cases the allegation of bias arose during the course of the trial or hearing. Where the issue arises prior to the commencement of the trial, there is room for 'the sensible application of the precautionary principle' on the basis that it is better to be safe than sorry (para 9). The Court's comments must, however, have been pragmatic: the test for the appearance of bias is clear and there can be no difference in the test applied depending upon the stage in the proceedings when the bias allegation is made. However, if the court can avoid an argument as to recusal, and the risk of disturbing the efficient case management of the case, there is sense in trying to do so. The Court of Appeal in *El Farargy v El Farargy* [2007] EWCA Civ 1149 took a similar approach, at para 32, *per* Ward LJ: **10.83**

> It is invidious for a judge to sit in judgment on his own conduct in a case like this but in many cases there will be no option but that the trial judge deal with it himself or herself. If circumstances permit it, I would urge that first an informal approach be made to the judge, for example by letter, making the complaint and inviting recusal. Whilst judges must heed the exhortation in *Locabail* not to yield to a tenuous or frivolous objections, one can with honour totally deny the complaint but still pass the case to a colleague. If a judge does not feel able to do so, then it may be preferable, if it is possible to arrange it, to have another judge take the decision, hard though it is to sit in judgment of one's colleague, for where the appearance of justice is at stake, it is better that justice be done independently by another rather than require the judge to sit in judgment of his own behaviour.

Application for recusal

Where an application for a recusal and rehearing is made by one of the parties during the course of the hearing itself on the grounds of bias, it should be considered by all members of the tribunal and not by the judge alone. An opportunity must also be given to the other parties in the case to consider the grounds of the application, and to be heard on it, since a rehearing may result in injustice and would certainly increase the costs of that other party (see *Peter Simper & Co Ltd v Cooke* [1986] IRLR 19, EAT). **10.84**

Where the tribunal discloses material which may give rise to the appearance of bias, the party affected has a clear choice of whether or not to object to the hearing proceeding. Where an allegation of bias or denial of a fair hearing arises from the conduct of the tribunal during the course of the hearing the party affected has a more difficult decision whether to raise the matter in the course of the hearing, or to wait until the decision and use the bias allegation as a ground of appeal. **10.85**

There is no hard and fast rule as to whether an objection must be taken at the hearing (so that failure to do so means that the objection cannot be raised as a ground of appeal), or whether the objection may be raised for the first time in an appeal. In *Stansbury v Datapulse plc* [2003] EWCA Civ 1951, [2004] IRLR 466, the Court of Appeal allowed a complaint concerning a sleeping tribunal member to be raised on appeal for the first time. A failure to raise an objection before the employment tribunal should be considered against the test of reasonableness in all the circumstances of the case. Whilst it is always desirable that a point on the behaviour of the employment tribunal should be raised at the tribunal in the course of the hearing, it is unreal- **10.86** istic not to recognize the difficulty, even for legal representatives, in raising with the tribunal a complaint about the behaviour of one of its members who, if the complaint is not upheld, may yet be part of the tribunal deciding the case.

10.87 Similarly, in *Peter Simper & Co Ltd v Cooke* above, Peter Gibson J stated (at para 21) that such complaints should not be raised during the hearing:

> Save in extraordinary circumstances, it cannot be right for a litigant, unhappy with what he believes to be the indications from the Tribunal as to how the case is progressing, to apply, in the middle of the case, for a re-hearing before another Tribunal. It is undesirable that the Tribunal accused of giving the opinion [*sic*] of bias should be asked itself to adjudicate on that matter. The dissatisfied litigant should ordinarily await the decision and then, if he thinks it appropriate, he would make his dissatisfaction with the conduct of the Tribunal a ground of appeal.

10.88 However, some caution must be exercised in treating this as a statement of general principle. As was made clear in *Stansbury*, much depends upon the circumstances of the particular case, and the particular matter about which complaint is made. In *Harada Ltd (t/a Chequepoint UK Ltd) v Turner (No 1)* [2001] EWCA Civ 599, after the judge's preliminary comments, the respondent invited the tribunal to recuse itself, and when the tribunal refused to do so, it withdrew from any further part in the hearing. Pill LJ, whilst acknowledging the force of the approach in *Peter Simper*, stated that the appropriate procedure depends upon all the circumstances, including the subject matter of the case, the statement which is complained of, and the circumstances in which it is made. There may be cases where the alleged conduct of the tribunal is such, or where there is to be a long hearing and the point arises at a very early stage, that it would not be appropriate simply to carry on with the case and then take the point on appeal.

10.89 Where the complaint is of a matter which might be remedied at the hearing, both principle and common sense dictate that the party should raise it at the hearing; it will not be right for parties to await the outcome of the decision and only at that stage raise such transient matters (*Red Bank Manufacturing Co Ltd v Meadows* [1992] ICR 204, EAT). However, the EAT in *Kudrath v Ministry of Defence* EAT/422/97, noted that whilst it was preferable to raise the matter during the course of the hearing, it is unrealistic to expect this always to be sensible or practicable.

10.90 *Anthony v Governors of Hillcrest School* EAT/1193/00 is another decision which indicates that a party may lose the right to complain of bias if it fails to raise the issue at the time of the conduct complained of, but instead waits to see whether it has won or lost. In *Anthony* the allegation of bias arose from the comments of the judge during the course of the hearing, and interference with cross-examination by the claimant's representative. The EAT held, in a case which it described as borderline, that the judge's comments did not give rise to the appearance of bias. The EAT also held that the claimant had effectively waived the right to complain: the comments had been made early in a four-day hearing, yet neither the claimant nor his representative complained during the hearing, nor during submissions, nor at any time until after the reserved decision had been given. It is perhaps doubtful that the same result would now be reached in the light of *Stansbury*, but clearly under the principles set out in *Stansbury* much will depend on the circumstances of the particular case.

Approach of the EAT

10.91 Where on appeal it is found that there was actual or apparent bias, the normal course will be to remit the matter for rehearing. It is not clear whether the decision *must* be set aside, or whether in some circumstances the court may allow the decision to stand if it can be said to be plainly right. In *Re Medicaments* (*No 2*) [2001] 1 WLR 700, the effect of the decisions of the ECtHR was said to be that the decision of the judge must be set aside. In *Turner v Harada* above, Pill LJ considered it to follow from that proposition that once the legitimate fear that the judge might not have been impartial is established, the decision of the judge must be set aside; if it ever can be otherwise, it would be an exceptional case. He did not give any guidance as to what might amount to an exceptional case. Mantell LJ, whilst agreeing with Pill LJ, said that irrespective of the correctness or otherwise of the decision which was eventually reached, what is at stake in cases of bias is public confidence in the administration of justice.

The EAT in *Anthony*, purporting to follow Pill LJ in *Turner v Harada*, said that the test was that once a real danger of bias is shown, except in exceptional cases, the decision must be set aside. It is not sufficient to establish exceptional circumstances to show that the decision would inevitably have been the same. The case must be one where it can be said with certainty that to permit the decision to stand would not affect confidence in the administration of justice. The EAT found that the facts of *Anthony* would give rise to such an exceptional case; however, as the EAT also found that there was no appearance of bias, its decision on this point is *obiter*. **10.92**

Where any complaint is to be made on appeal to the EAT alleging bias or misconduct on the part of the employment tribunal, full particulars of such matters must be set out in the grounds of appeal. The EAT Practice Direction 2004, para 11, establishes a special procedure following the EAT's guidelines in *Facey v Midas Retail Security* [2000] IRLR 812 (see paras 19.41–19.51). **10.93**

11

Judgments, Decisions, and Orders

SUMMARY

(1) A tribunal's decision finally determining issues between the parties is given in a judgment. A tribunal's decision on interim matters is given in an order. Judgments and orders are recorded in writing and entered into the register.

(2) A tribunal must give reasons for any judgment, and must give reasons for orders if a request is made by a party or by the EAT.

(3) A tribunal may give its judgment or order, or the reasons for it, orally at a hearing, or may reserve its decision to a later date. Reasons will be given in writing if so requested by a party at the hearing, or within 14 days of being sent the judgment.

(4) A decision may be unanimous, or by a majority. Where a tribunal comprises a judge and only one lay member, the judge has a casting vote.

(5) Reasons should be in sufficient detail to explain to the parties why they have won or lost. Reasons should contain an outline of the story which has given rise to the complaint and a summary of the tribunal's basic factual conclusions and a statement of the reasons which have led them to reach the conclusion which they do on those basic facts.

(6) There are limited grounds to challenge a decision before registration.

(7) A judgment is binding on the parties and may give rise to *res judicata* or issue estoppel in subsequent proceedings. Raising a claim in proceedings which could or should have been raised in earlier proceedings between the parties may be an abuse of process.

A. CLASSIFICATION OF JUDGMENTS AND ORDERS

11.01 The tribunal may make the following types of decision (ETR 2004, r 28(1)):

(a) A 'judgment', which is defined (r 28(1)(a)) as a final determination of the proceedings or of a particular issue in those proceedings. It may include an award of compensation, a declaration, or recommendation and it may include orders for costs, preparation time, or wasted costs.
(b) An 'order', which, according to r 28(1)(b) may be issued in relation to interim matters and will require a person to do or not do something.

11.02 It would seem on the face of it that r 28(1) was meant to be exhaustive of the types of decision that a judge or tribunal is able to make. Rules 28–32 deal generally with the requirements for judgments, orders, and reasons.

11.03 However, on a daily basis tribunals make many orders which do not fit within r 28(1)(b), because they are directions which do not require a person to do or not to do something. In *Onwuka v Spherion Technology UK Ltd* [2005] ICR 567, the EAT observed that a refusal of permission to amend an ET1 did not fall within r 28(1). Whilst noting that the correct characterization of such a ruling under the rules was 'a bit of a mystery', the EAT held that such a ruling was 'an order' for the purpose of r 10 (which sets out the tribunal's general powers to make orders), even if it is not an 'order' for the purpose of r 28.

11.04 There is no reason why order is so narrowly defined in r 28, and why the formal requirements in relation to orders, and the reasons for orders set out in rr 30–1 should apply to some types of order and not others. The distinction would appear arbitrary. For example, as pointed out by *Onwuka*, a decision refusing an application to amend would not fall within r 28(1)(b). Nor, for that matter, would a decision allowing an amendment. Yet each of these decisions may have an important impact on the conduct of the proceedings. On the other hand, a decision which required the amending party to file and serve the amendment would fall within r 28(1)(b), as the order would require someone to do something. Even a mundane direction, such as a direction requiring the parties to prepare an agreed bundle, would fall within r 28(1)(b).

11.05 An unless order which provides for proceedings to be struck out if certain steps are not taken by a specified time is a conditional judgment which becomes a final determination of the proceedings if the parties fail to comply with the underlying order. Such an order is amenable to review, at least once the strike-out has taken effect: see *Uyamnwa-Odu v Schools Offices Services Ltd* Independent, 1 December 2005, EAT.

11.06 The distinction between judgments and orders is an important one as most orders are not amenable to review under r 34. They may be varied or revoked under r 10(2)(q). See further paras 13.08–13.10 below.

B. PROCEDURAL REQUIREMENTS FOR JUDGMENTS AND ORDERS

Form and content of judgment

11.07 All judgments, whether issued orally or in writing, must be recorded in writing and signed by the judge (r 29(1)) (subject to r 31, see para 11.26 below).

11.08 The Secretary of the tribunal must provide a copy of the judgment to each party (r 29(1)) and give guidance to the parties on how the judgment may be reviewed or appealed (r 29(2)).

11.09 Where the judgment includes an award of compensation or a determination that one party is required to pay a sum to another (excluding an order for costs, expenses, allowances, preparation time, or wasted costs), the judgment must contain a statement of the amount of compensation awarded, or the sum to be paid (r 28(3)).

The duty to give reasons

A distinction must be drawn between a judgment and an order, and the reasons for such a judgment or order. A judgment or order will express quite shortly the tribunal's determination on each of the issues that are live before the tribunal. A judgment, for example, may simply say that the tribunal finds that the claimant was unfairly dismissed and that the respondent is ordered to pay a certain sum; or that the claimant's claim is dismissed. An order will typically set out the timetable for directions decided upon by the tribunal. The tribunal's reasons will set out the reasons why the tribunal reached its judgment or order. **11.10**

A tribunal or judge must give reasons (either orally or in writing) for any judgment (r 30(1)(a)). **11.11**

A tribunal or judge need only give reasons for an order: **11.12**

(a) if a request for reasons is made before or at the hearing at which the order is made (r 30(1)(b));
(b) if requested by the EAT at any time (r 30(3)(b)).

This represents a change from the position under the previous rules. The duty to give reasons for decisions under r 12 of ETR 2001 was held to apply equally to interlocutory decisions: *Independent Research Services v Catterall Ltd* [1993] ICR 1, followed by the Court of Session in Scotland in *South Ayrshire Council v Morton* [2002] IRLR 256. **11.13**

The content of the duty to give reasons is considered in detail at para 11.34 below. **11.14**

Reserved judgments, orders, and reasons

Rule 28(3) of ETR 2004 gives a judge or tribunal the power either to issue a judgment or order orally at the end of a hearing, or to reserve the judgment or order to be given in writing at a later date. If judgment is reserved, a written judgment shall be sent to the parties as soon as practicable (r 29(1)). All judgments, whether issued orally or in writing, shall be recorded in writing and signed by the judge. **11.15**

There is no similar provision to r 29(1) applying to orders, but there would seem to be no sensible ground for the distinction. It is just as important for the parties and the tribunal to have a written record of an order as it is to have a written judgment; it is equally important to have such a record as soon as practicable. In practice, any order made by the tribunal at a hearing or CMD will be set out in writing and sent to the parties. **11.16**

Just as a judge or tribunal may reserve its judgment, so too it may reserve its reasons. Rule 30(2) provides that a tribunal or judge may give reasons orally at the time of issuing a judgment or order, or the reasons may be reserved to be given in writing at a later date. **11.17**

Whether a decision is given orally at the end of the hearing or reserved to be given in writing is a matter of discretion for the judge or tribunal. The approach taken will depend on the complexity of the issues in the case, and the time of the day at which the hearing ends. If the tribunal, after retiring for discussion, is not agreed and faces the prospect of a majority decision, it should reserve its decision: *Anglian Home Improvements Ltd v Kelly* [2004] EWCA Civ 901, [2004] IRLR 793, and see para 11.27 *et seq.* below. **11.18**

Written or oral reasons

A tribunal's judgment must be recorded in writing, whether given orally at the hearing or reserved (r 29(1)). The obligation to provide reasons in writing is more limited. Written reasons shall only be provided (r 30(3)): **11.19**

(a) In relation to judgments, if requested by a party, either orally at the hearing where the judgment is issued, or in writing within 14 days of the date when the judgment was sent to the parties. This time limit may be extended if a judge considers it just and equitable to do so (r 30(5)).

(b) In relation to any judgment or order, if requested by the EAT at any time.

11.20 Written reasons must be signed by the judge and sent to the parties (r 30(2) and (4)). The reasons must record the date on which the reasons are sent: this is the date from which time for an appeal to the EAT runs.

Delay in giving judgment or reasons

11.21 Under Article 6 of the European Convention on Human Rights a litigant has the right to the determination of a tribunal within a reasonable time: *Porter v Magill* [2001] UKHL 67, [2002] 2 AC 357, para 108, *per* Lord Hope.

11.22 Delay can arise at any stage of a case. One potential cause of delay for the tribunal is in promulgating a reserved decision after a hearing. For a number of reasons a judgment may be reserved after the end of a hearing: for example because insufficient time is available on the day for the tribunal to reach a decision, or because the tribunal wishes to have written submissions before considering its decision. To reach a decision the tribunal panel will need to meet for a day in chambers (deliberating in private), and the judge will then need to draw up the reasons, and to circulate a draft to the lay members for comment. A final version then needs to be typed up and sent to the parties. All of this creates the potential for delay. The aim of sending a written decision within four weeks of the hearing in 85 per cent of cases is contained in the charter statement published by the Employment Tribunals Service.

11.23 The consequences of unreasonable delay in promulgating a decision after a hearing was considered by the Court of Appeal in *Bangs v Connex South Eastern Ltd* [2005] EWCA Civ 14, [2005] IRLR 389. In *Bangs* the EAT had considered a number of joined appeals dealing with delay in promulgating decisions (under the name *Kwamin v Abbey National plc* [2004] IRLR 516). The EAT followed the approach taken to delay by the civil courts: delay can in itself be an independent ground of appeal if the delay creates a probability or possibility that the decision is wrong or unsafe on grounds of delay (see *Cobham v Frett* [2001] 1 WLR 1775, 1783, PC and *Goose v Wilson Sandford & Co* CA Transcript No 196 of 1998). A similar approach had been adopted by the EAT in *Barker v The Home Office* EAT/804/01, EAT/835/01 and *Chinyanga v Buffer Bear Ltd* EAT/0300/02. Burton P also gave guidance on steps to be taken by the tribunals to avoid delay.

11.24 The Court of Appeal overturned the decision of the EAT in *Bangs*, holding that the test adopted in the civil courts could not be applied in the employment tribunals, given that, unlike the civil courts, appeal lies from a decision of an employment tribunal only on a question of law (Employment Tribunals Act 1996, s 21). Mummery LJ stated the following principles as applicable to appeals from the tribunal on grounds of unreasonable delay (at para 43):

(a) An appeal from the tribunal is confined to questions of law.

(b) No question of law arises from the decision itself just because it was not promulgated within a reasonable time. Unreasonable delay is a matter of fact, not a question of law. It does not in itself constitute an independent ground of appeal. Unreasonable delay may result in a breach of Article 6 and possibly give rise to State liability to pay compensation to the victim of the delay, but it does not in itself give rise to a question of law. (Note that in the subsequent decision of *Carpenter v City of Edinburgh Council* UKEATS/0038/07/MT a delay of over three years was held to have given rise to a real risk that the claimant had been denied his Article 6 right to a fair trial.)

(c) No question of law arises and no independent ground of appeal exists simply because, by virtue of material factual errors and omissions resulting from delay, the decision is 'unsafe'.

(d) In order to succeed in a challenge to the facts found by the tribunal it is necessary to establish that the decision is, as a result of the unreasonable delay, a perverse one.

(e) It is not incompatible with Article 6 of ECHR for domestic legislation to limit the right of appeal from an employment tribunal to questions of law.
(f) Even if it were incompatible with Article 6 to limit appeals to questions of law, it is not possible by use of s 3(1) of the Human Rights Act 1998 or otherwise to interpret s 21(1) of ETA 1996 as expanding a right of appeal expressly limited to questions of law to cover questions of fact.
(g) There may, however, be exceptional cases in which unreasonable delay by the tribunal in promulgating its decision can properly be treated as a serious procedural error or material irregularity giving rise to a question of law in the 'proceedings before the tribunal'. That would fall within s 21(1) of ETA 1996, which is not confined to questions of law to be found in the substantive decision itself. Such a case could occur if the appellant established that the failure to promulgate the decision within a reasonable time gave rise to a real risk that, due to the delayed decision, the party complaining was deprived of the substance of his right to a fair trial under Article 6(1), and it would be unfair or unjust to allow the decision to stand. A point on whether or not a person has had a fair trial in the employment tribunal is capable of giving rise to a question of law.

Mummery LJ agreed (at para 20) with the general guidance given by Burton P in the EAT on the steps to be taken by tribunals to avoid unreasonable delay: see paras 6–10 and 16 of the EAT's judgment. The effect of that guidance, in summary, is as follows: **11.25**

(1) Delay after the commencement of the proceedings ought to be capable of being minimized by way of active case management and the imposition of sanctions.
(2) To avoid delay after the hearing of the case begins, if there need to be adjournments and restarts of hearings:
    (a) the parties, and the tribunal, should cooperate in arriving at the best possible estimate of time, and revisit that estimate from time to time: the tribunal may need itself to look at the estimate again in the light of the papers lodged, shortly prior to the hearing;
    (b) the fixing of any such adjourned hearing should be immediate (if at all possible before the parties (or their representatives) leave the building) and for a date with as little intervening delay as can be achieved.
(3) The employment tribunals should observe a three-and-a-half months' deadline for promulgating a decision, beyond which there is thus culpable delay in the absence of proper explanation. The period runs, where closing speeches are delivered orally, from the end of the hearing itself; in a case where subsequent written submissions are provided for (either instead, or by way of supplementation, of any oral submissions), then in almost every case the three and a half months will be considered to run from the delivery of those submissions.
(4) Time must be allowed for consideration of cases and for judgment in writing. The tribunal, in relation to a case which is estimated to last more than a few days, should automatically (and without reference to the parties) add one or two days to the end of the hearing for that purpose, both to reserve the members and to prevent the judges from having to move straight on to another decision.
(5) A system should be introduced in every regional office by which judges are notified of, and reminded about, the passage of time in relation to uncompleted reserved judgments on a regular basis, and explanations sought and assistance given, as necessary, by giving the relevant judges extra judgment-writing time, by rearranging his or her sittings, and facilitating communication with the lay members.

Judge unable to sign judgment, order, or reasons

Where it is not possible for a judge to sign a judgment, order, or reasons, due to death, incapacity, or absence, either a lay member may sign, or, if the judge dealt with the case sitting alone, the Regional Chairman, Vice-President, or President may sign when it is practicable for him to do so. Whoever signs must certify that the judge was unable to sign (r 31). **11.26**

Majority decisions

11.27 A tribunal panel will normally consist of a judge and two lay members (see paras 1.22–1.34 above for situations in which a judge may sit alone or with one lay member only).

11.28 Where a tribunal is composed of three persons, any order or judgment may be made or issued by a majority (r 28(4)).

11.29 Where a tribunal is composed of two persons only, the judge has a second or casting vote (r 28(4)).

11.30 In practice, the vast majority of judgments and orders are unanimous. The Court of Appeal has indeed said that it is undesirable for tribunals to reach split decisions, and all efforts should be made to achieve unanimity: *Anglian Home Improvements Ltd v Kelly* [2004] EWCA Civ 901, [2004] IRLR 793.

11.31 Where the tribunal is split, it is preferable for the tribunal to reserve the decision, rather than to give an oral decision at the hearing (*Anglian Home Improvements*, approving the approach in *Holden v Bradville Ltd* [1985] IRLR 483, EAT). This allows the judge to write a draft decision, recording both majority and minority views, and to circulate it to the lay members, ensuring that the lay members' views are properly expressed, and also allowing for reflection on the areas of disagreement.

11.32 Where the judge is in the minority, he must not sign the judgment until the majority have seen and approved the text: *Maure v Macmillan Distribution Ltd* [1977] IRLR 215, EAT. The majority and minority views should be set out clearly in separate paragraphs (*Parkers Bakeries Ltd v Palmer* [1977] IRLR 215, EAT, approved in *Anglian Home Improvements*).

11.33 The fact that a majority and a minority of a tribunal came to differing views on the evidence before them does not, however, of itself amount to a ground of appeal; indeed, it may serve to emphasize the care with which the tribunal has considered the matter (*Chief Constable of Thames Valley Police v Kellaway* [2000] IRLR 170).

C. THE TRIBUNAL'S REASONS

11.34 It has always been the duty of the tribunal to give reasons for its decision. However, the EAT and Court of Appeal have had to grapple repeatedly with the question of what is entailed by this duty: how detailed must the tribunal's reasons be? What are the consequences of a failure to give adequate reasons? The first of these questions is considered in the following paragraphs, the second at paras 11.69–11.78 below.

General principles

11.35 For the first time in the tribunal's rules of procedure, ETR 2004 makes express general provision for the *content* of reasons. Previous versions of the rules were either silent as to the content of reasons (as opposed to the obligation to provide such reasons), or dealt with the matter in a piecemeal and incomplete way.

11.36 Rule 30(6) of ETR 2004 provides:

> Written reasons for a judgment shall include the following information—
>
> (a) the issues which the tribunal or judge has identified as being relevant to the claim;
> (b) if some identified issues were not determined, what those issues were and why they were not determined;
> (c) findings of fact relevant to the issues which have been determined;
> (d) a concise statement of the applicable law;
> (e) how the relevant findings of fact and applicable law have been applied in order to determine the issues; and

(f) where the judgment includes an award of compensation or a determination that one party make a payment to the other, a table showing how the amount or sum has been calculated or a description of the manner in which it has been calculated.

It is not mandatory for a tribunal expressly to set out each of these matters provided that the important matters relevant to the judgment are set out. However, a tribunal which does not follow the framework provided by the rules runs the risk that it will fail in its duty towards the parties (see *Spaulding v BMI Health Care Limited* EAT/0551/06). **11.37**

Rule 30(6) must be seen in the context of the existing body of case law concerning the scope and content of the duty to give reasons. The requirement for reasons arises not just in the employment tribunals, but across the whole range of judicial decision-making. The duty to provide reasons arises under the common law, as an aspect of natural justice and the right to a fair trial, and is also required by Article 6 of ECHR (given effect in England and Wales by the Human Rights Act 1998). Article 6(1) requires that adequate and intelligible reasons must be given for judicial decisions (see *Ruiz Torija v Spain* (1994) 19 EHRR 553; *Garcia Ruiz v Spain* (2001) 31 EHRR 22). **11.38**

The leading authority on the content of judicial reasons is *English v Emery Reimbold & Strick* [2002] EWCA Civ 605, [2003] IRLR 711. The case concerned the adequacy of reasons given by judges in High Court trials, but the Court of Appeal's guidance was plainly meant to be of general application. The Court of Appeal gave the following guidance (at paras 18–22, *per* Lord Philips MR): **11.39**

(a) It is the duty of a judge to produce a judgment that gives a clear explanation for his or her order.
(b) The judgment should make it apparent to the parties why they have won or lost, and should enable the appellate court to understand why the judge reached his decision.
(c) There is no duty on a judge to deal with every argument presented to him, and a judgment need not be lengthy. While a judgment may often need to refer to evidence or submissions, it may be unnecessary to detail or even summarize the evidence or submission.
(d) However, issues which are vital to the judge's conclusion should be identified and the manner in which they are resolved should be explained. The judgment should identify and record the matters which are critical to the decision.
(e) If the critical issue is one of fact, it may be enough to say that one witness was preferred to another because he manifestly had a clearer recollection, or the other gave answers which demonstrated that his recollection could not be relied upon.
(f) Where there is a conflict of expert evidence, the judge should provide an explanation as to why he accepted the evidence of one expert and rejected that of another.

The Court of Appeal also dealt with the approach to amplification of a judge's reasons. This topic is dealt with at paras 11.69–11.78 below. **11.40**

Obviously, whether a particular judgment gives adequate reasons depends on the facts and circumstances of the particular case (*English* above, at para 17; see also *Flannery v Halifax Estate Agencies Ltd* [2000] 1 WLR 377, 381–2, *per* Henry LJ, approved in *English*). The *English* guidance (and for that matter r 30 of ETR 2004) leaves room for argument as to whether a particular judgment complies with the guidance or not (see also Chapter 19). **11.41**

The leading authority on reasons relating specifically to the employment tribunals has for many years been *Meek v City of Birmingham District Council* [1987] IRLR 250, CA. In *Meek*, Bingham LJ said (at 251) that reasons should: **11.42**

> contain an outline of the story which has given rise to the complaint and a summary of the tribunal's basic factual conclusions and a statement of the reasons which have led them to reach the conclusion which they do on those basic facts. The parties are entitled to be told why they have won or lost. There should be sufficient account of the facts and of the reasoning to enable the EAT or, on further appeal, this court to see whether any question of law arises; and it is highly desirable that the

decision of an [employment] tribunal should give guidance both to employers and trade unions as to practices which should or should not be adopted.

11.43 Bingham LJ in his judgment in *Meek* approved and applied two earlier passages from decisions of the Court of Appeal. First, *Union of Construction, Allied Trades and Technicians v Brain* [1981] ICR 542, Donaldson LJ (as he then was) said (at 551):

> Industrial tribunals' reasons are not intended to include a comprehensive and detailed analysis of the case, either in terms of fact or in law. Their purpose remains what it has always been, which is to tell the parties in broad terms why they lose, or as the case may be, win. I think it would be a thousand pities if these reasons began to be subjected to a detailed analysis and appeals were to be brought based upon such analysis. This, to my mind, is to misuse the purpose for which reasons are given.

11.44 Secondly, *Martin v MBS Fastenings (Glynwed) Distribution Ltd* [1983] IRLR 198, 202, *per* Sir John Donaldson MR:

> The duty of an Industrial Tribunal is to give reasons for its decision. This involves making findings of fact and answering a question or questions of law. So far as the findings of fact are concerned, it is helpful to the parties to give some explanation of them, but it is not obligatory. So far as the questions of law are concerned, the reasons should show expressly or by implication what were the questions to which the Industrial Tribunal addressed its mind and why it reached the conclusions which it did, but the way in which it does so is entirely a matter for the Industrial Tribunal.

11.45 In *Martin* the Court of Appeal rejected the contention that it was the tribunal's duty to state the law, its primary findings of fact, secondary findings of fact, and conclusions. See also to similar effect *Kearney & Trecker Marwin v Varndell* [1983] IRLR 335, CA, *per* Eveleigh LJ. This passage from *Martin* should not now be interpreted too broadly. The modern trend in the cases has been to require fuller reasons to be given by the tribunal, and r 30(6) now expressly requires reasons to contain a statement of the findings of fact, the applicable law, and conclusions drawn.

11.46 The guidance in *English* has swiftly been adopted by the EAT and the Court of Appeal as applying to appeals against decisions of the employment tribunals: see *Logan v Commissioners of Customs & Excise* [2003] EWCA Civ 1068, [2004] IRLR 63, para 25, where Ward LJ regarded the principles in *English* as an authoritative statement of a test already embodied in *Meek*; see also *Burns v Consignia (No 2)* [2004] IRLR 425, EAT, where Burton P described *English* as 'a seminal decision' plainly intended to be of universal application.

11.47 The guidance in *Meek* has been followed repeatedly in subsequent cases as the touchstone for the content of reasons: see, for example, *High Table v Horst* [1997] IRLR 513, CA; *Miriki v General Council of the Bar* [2002] ICR 505; *Tran v Greenwich Vietnam Community* [2002] IRLR 735, CA; and *Anya v University of Oxford* [2001] EWCA Civ 405, [2001] IRLR 377. Indeed the EAT and Court of Appeal have come to describe the question of adequacy of a tribunal's reasons as whether those reasons are '*Meek* compliant' (see *Tran*, at para 17, *per* Sedley LJ).

11.48 Whether the tribunal's reasons are adequate to satisfy the tests in *Meek* and *English* will depend upon the particular issues and circumstances of each case and no hard and fast guidelines can be given.

11.49 The appellate courts have repeatedly discouraged overlong and elaborate decisions. They will generally give a generous interpretation to the tribunal's reasoning, and will not apply the standards to be expected of a judgment from a High Court judge. Lord Nicholls in *Shamoon v Chief Constable of the Royal Ulster Constabulary* [2003] ICR 337, 59, said:

> It has also been recognized that a generous interpretation ought to be given to a tribunal's reasoning. It is to be expected, of course, that the decision will set out the facts. That is the raw material on which any view of its decision must be based. But the quality which is to be expected of its reasoning is not that to be expected of a High Court Judge. Its reasoning ought to be explained, but the circumstances in which a tribunal works should be respected. The reasoning ought not to be subjected to an unduly critical analysis.

Particular aspects of the duty to give reasons

Dealing with the issues

The reasons should set out the issues which the tribunal is to determine. The modern practice is for those issues to have been defined before the evidence is heard: either at a case management discussion, or at the beginning of the hearing. Often the parties' representatives are asked to agree those issues. **11.50**

Whilst a tribunal must consider all that is relevant, it need only deal with the points which are seen to be in controversy relating to those issues, and then only with the principal important controversial points: *High Table Ltd v Horst* [1997] IRLR 513, 518, CA, *per* Peter Gibson LJ. Peter Gibson LJ repeated this proposition in *Comfort v Lord Chancellor's Department* [2004] EWCA Civ 349, [2004] All ER (D) 313 (Mar), in finding that a tribunal's reasons were defective because they failed to make findings on an important factual dispute. A tribunal must make findings upon the factual issues essential to its conclusions; it does not, however, have to explore the circumstances of every event in the evidence placed before it: *Wheeler and Newton v Durham County Council* [2001] EWCA Civ 844, paras 50, 54, and 55; *Anya v University of Oxford* [2001] ICR 847, 862; *Madarassy v Nomura International plc* [2007] EWCA Civ 33, [2007] IRLR 246. Similarly in *Deman v Association of University Teachers* [2003] EWCA Civ 329, para 37, Potter LJ said that each case must be decided in the light of its own particular circumstances. It cannot be right that in every case the tribunal must make findings on every piece of circumstantial evidence, however peripheral, merely because the claimant chooses to make it the subject of complaint. **11.51**

In *Miriki v General Council of the Bar* [2002] EWCA Civ 1973, [2002] ICR 505, it was argued that *Anya* set a higher standard for reasons, in that even on peripheral matters of complaint it is for the tribunal to state its findings and its reasons for rejecting the complaint. Peter Gibson LJ (at para 46) rejected this argument. What is required of the reasons depended on the circumstances of each particular case. He reiterated the approach that he had first set out in *High Table v Horst* [1997] IRLR 513. **11.52**

Dealing with findings of fact

Although tribunals are not required to set out their reasons in great detail, they should set out their main findings of fact. This is now required by r 30(6)(b). The tribunal should state its primary findings of fact. **11.53**

There is no need to recite all of the evidence in the case. The tribunal should state its findings of fact in a sensible order (often chronological) indicating in relation to any significant finding the nature of the conflicting evidence and the reason why one version has been preferred to another (*Tchoula v Netto Foodstores Ltd* EAT/1378/98). **11.54**

Where a tribunal is faced with a conflict of evidence on a significant issue of fact, its view of the evidence must be made plain and discernible from the reasons (*Levy v Marrable & Co Ltd* [1984] ICR 583, EAT). The tribunal should state which evidence it believes or prefers (*British Gas plc v Sharma* [1991] IRLR 101; *Wadman v Carpenter Farrer Partnership* [1993] IRLR 374). The tribunal should avoid bald statements that it prefers the evidence of one party rather than another: reasons should be given for such a conclusion (*Tchoula v Netto Foodstores Ltd* above, approved in *Anya v University of Oxford* and *Deman v Association of University Teachers*, para 11.51 above). **11.55**

An uncritical belief in the witnesses' credibility without proper examination of the relevant evidential issues through to a reasoned conclusion will not be sufficient: *Anya v University of Oxford* above, at para 25. **11.56**

The degree of detail required will depend on the nature of the case. Discrimination claims can raise particularly complicated issues, in that they will frequently turn on the inferences to be drawn from primary facts. A tribunal should take care to set out its findings of primary fact, and **11.57** then to explain the inferences which it draws, and why it draws them. In *Deman v Association of University Teachers*, the Court of Appeal (at para 44) contrasted an unfair dismissal case on the one hand with a racial discrimination and victimization case on the other hand. In the first case, once the primary facts are found, the case turns upon applying objective and accepted standards of fairness; in the latter, the case will often depend on assessing nuances and drawing inferences as to the true reason underlying particular actions. The latter type of case will usually involve the necessity for a more careful and elaborate statement of reasons than the former in order for the parties to understand why they have won or lost, and in order for the EAT to know that there has been no error of law (see also *Chapman v Simon* [1994] IRLR 124, CA).

11.58 As to the importance of the tribunal making findings of fact before drawing inferences, see *Anya v University of Oxford* [2001] EWCA Civ 405, [2001] IRLR 377; *Bahl v The Law Society* [2004] EWCA Civ 1070, [2004] IRLR 799. As to the drawing of inferences in discrimination cases generally, see *King v The Great Britain-China Centre* [1991] IRLR 513, CA and *Glasgow City Council v Zafar* [1997] 1 WLR 1659, [1998] IRLR 36, HL, and in relation to the statutory reversal of the burden of proof in discrimination cases, see *Igen Ltd v Wong* [2005] EWCA Civ 142, [2005] IRLR 258; *Barton v Investec Henderson Crosthwaite Securities Ltd* [2003] ICR 1205, EAT; and *EB v BA* [2006] EWCA Civ 132, [2006] IRLR 471.

11.59 The tribunal should not simply set out the relevant evidential issues, but should follow them through to a reasoned conclusion. If the tribunal feels it unnecessary to state a conclusion on an issue, it should explain why (*Anya*). It is insufficient merely to recite the background and then state a conclusion. The reasons should show how the tribunal got from its findings of fact to its conclusion (*Tran*, at para 17 (see para 11.47 above)).

Dealing with disputed expert evidence

11.60 Where an issue turns on expert evidence, the tribunal is under a duty to summarize and take into account the expert evidence, and if it rejects the evidence, to explain why: *Edwards v Mid Suffolk DC* [2001] IRLR 190, EAT.

Dealing with the law

11.61 Rule 30(6)(e) requires a concise statement of the applicable law. It is of course difficult for an appellate court to determine whether the tribunal has made any error of law if the tribunal does not state the legal principles it has applied. In *Conlin v United Distillers* [1994] IRLR 169, the EAT had stressed the importance of setting out the applicable statutory provisions and the correct statutory test in an unfair dismissal case.

11.62 Some of the earlier cases discouraged detailed treatment of legal authorities in tribunals' reasons. In *Anandarajah v Lord Chancellor's Department* [1984] IRLR 131, Waite J stated that industrial tribunals are not required to and should not be invited to subject the authorities to the same analysis as a court of law searching in a plethora of precedent for binding or persuasive authority. However, this does not reflect the reality of the exercise facing many tribunals in modern times. The tribunal's jurisdiction has expanded significantly since the 1980s, both in relation to the legal questions the tribunal must address, and the potential sums that it may be invited to award by way of compensation. In many cases the tribunal has no choice but to grapple with complex legal issues, often where authorities conflict or are unclear. A tribunal would not discharge its duty to explain how it reaches its decision if it does not state the principles of law it applies, and in some cases this may require detailed consideration of the authorities.

Dealing with guidance and codes of practice

11.63 In a number of areas, the tribunal is obliged to have regard to statutory guidance and codes of practice. In *Goodwin v Patent Office* [1999] ICR 302, [1999] IRLR 4 (a disability discrimination case), Morison J emphasized the importance of express reference to guidance and to codes.

11.64 However, Burton P in *Steel v Chief Constable of Thames Valley Police* UKEAT/0793/03, pointed out that Morison J gave that guidance at a stage when the DDA 1995 was in its early period of operation; as employment tribunals become more familiar and comfortable with the operation of these procedures, express reference to particular provisions becomes less significant. Burton P said (at para 40):

> We do not conclude that there is any need in every case for spelling out, by reference to every paragraph of a relevant code, a conclusion as to whether there has been breach, and whether there is an inference to be drawn one way or the other from that breach, where a tribunal does not conclude that such breach or such inference is central, or essential, or significant to its conclusion, or at any rate where an appeal court, on looking at the matter, does not so conclude.

Similarly in *McDonald v London Borough of Ealing* EAT/406/99, Charles J stated (at para 33) that it was not necessary, where there was an allegation of breach of a code of practice, for the provisions of the code of practice to be expressly referred to in the tribunal's reasons, if none of them pointed to a different conclusion or approach from that reached and taken by the tribunal. **11.65**

Reasons for interim orders

In *English v Emery Reimbold & Strick* [2002] EWCA Civ 605, [2003] IRLR 710, paras 13–14, Lord Philips MR observed that Strasbourg jurisprudence in relation to Article 6 of ECHR acknowledged that there were some decisions where fairness does not demand that the parties should be informed of the reasoning underlying the decision. He gave interim decisions in the course of case management as 'an obvious example'. **11.66**

Reasons for costs orders

In *English* (above), Lord Philips MR (at paras 14 and 27–30) noted that costs orders in the civil courts were often given in summary form without reasons. Whilst it remains in the interests of justice that a judge should be able to dispose of costs applications in a speedy and uncomplicated way, a costs order without reasons would only comply with Article 6 of ECHR if the reason for the order was implicit from the circumstances of the case. In the normal case in the civil courts costs follow the event (ie the winner gets his costs paid by the loser) and the reasoning will be plain. If the reasons for the costs order are not obvious, in particular if the costs order departs from the norm, a brief explanation should be given. The Court of Appeal will only give permission to appeal on grounds of inadequate reasons if no explanation is given, and there is no obvious explanation. **11.67**

The same approach, in principle, should apply to the making of orders for costs in the tribunal. Indeed, there is likely to be a greater need for reasons in the tribunal. The tribunal's jurisdiction to make an order for costs is narrower than that of the civil courts, and the tribunal will at least need to explain briefly why the jurisdictional requirements of the rules are met, and why it is exercising its discretion, both in principle and as to amount. **11.68**

Amplification of the reasons

Jurisdiction

For now, it appears settled that the EAT may remit a case to the tribunal to amplify its reasons: such a practice is provided for in the EAT Practice Direction 2004. The practice was recognized and approved in *Burns v Consignia plc (No 2)* [2004] IRLR 425, and *Burns* itself was approved by the Court of Appeal in *Barke v SEETEC Business Technology Centre Ltd* [2005] EWCA Civ 578, [2005] IRLR 633 and *Bone v London Borough of Newham* [2008] EWCA Civ 435, [2008] IRLR 546. **11.69**

In *Burns*, Burton P had held that s 35 of ETA 1996 gave the EAT jurisdiction to remit a case to the tribunal to amplify its reasons. In *Barke*, the Court of Appeal rejected this interpretation, holding that the words 'disposing of' meant 'dealing conclusively with'. The Court of Appeal found jurisdiction for the *Burns* procedure by other routes. First, r 30 of ETR 2004 obliges a tribunal to give reasons for a judgment. The tribunal is not *functus officio* for all purposes once **11.70** a judgment is registered, and in particular the tribunal cannot be said to be *functus officio* if the tribunal has failed to comply with its duty to give reasons by giving inadequate reasons (at paras 27–8). Secondly, the Court of Appeal found jurisdiction for the *Burns* procedure as part of the EAT's power to regulate its own procedure (ETA 1996, s 30(3)).

11.71 The practice approved in *Barke* was controversial. It ran counter to earlier decisions of the Court of Appeal to the effect that remission in such circumstances was not possible: *Leverton v Clwyd County Council* [1988] IRLR 239, CA and the majority view in *Tran v Greenwich Vietnam Community* [2002] IRLR 735. However, the *Barke* decision seems now to be well established.

Scope of the power

11.72 Burton P said in *Burns* above that the EAT was entirely satisfied that in most cases the practice ordinarily appropriate in the civil courts enshrined in *English* is also appropriate, proper, and necessary for employment tribunals.

11.73 The *English* guidance (at paras 25–6, *per* Lord Philips MR) is as follows:

(a) If an application for permission to appeal on grounds of lack of reasons is made to the trial judge, the trial judge should consider whether his reasons are defective for lack of reasons, and should adjourn for that purpose if necessary.
(b) If the judge concludes that the reasons are lacking, he should provide additional reasons, and refuse permission to appeal on grounds that he has made good the lack of reasons.
(c) If he considers that he has given adequate reasons, he should refuse permission to appeal.
(d) If an application for permission to appeal on grounds of lack of reasons is made to the appellate court and the application appears well founded, the appellate court should consider adjourning the application and remitting the case to the trial judge with an invitation to provide additional reasons (either for the judgment as a whole, or in relation to specific findings).
(e) Where permission to appeal is granted on grounds that the judgment does not contain adequate reasons, the appellate court should review the judgment, in the context of the material evidence and submissions at trial, to determine whether it is apparent why the judge reached the decision he did. If the reason is apparent, and is a valid basis for the judgment, the appeal will be dismissed. If the reason for the decision is not apparent, the appellate court will have to decide whether to proceed itself with a rehearing, or to direct a new trial.

11.74 The detail of the guidance must be seen in the context of two features of civil procedure which differ from procedure in the tribunals:

(1) most types of appeal in the civil courts require permission to appeal; and
(2) the option for the appeal court to conduct a rehearing is only available in the civil courts as the jurisdiction of the appellate courts in civil proceedings is wider than that of the EAT (and the higher courts on appeal from the EAT), which is limited to corrections of errors of law.

11.75 In *Burns*, Burton P referred to a 'carefully controlled' remission, and clearly did not intend to give the tribunal a second bite at the cherry in order to change its mind, or change the basis for its decision. He said (at 427):

> Of course there are dangers in remitting to the original tribunal a case where the ground of appeal is inadequacy of reasoning, and there will be some cases in which the reasoning is so inadequate that it would be unsafe to remit to the same tribunal. Equally, there will be the potential danger of giving the opportunity to a court below to reconsider its decision on an entirely different basis. However, remission, carefully controlled, makes, as we see it, entire sense. The remission in this case was expressly on the basis that the tribunal should not call any further oral evidence; it would, of course, have its notes of evidence, and it would be able to express its reasons, which would be based upon the original findings of fact.

However, he went on to note that in an appropriate case a tribunal could decide to review its own decision under r 34 of ETR 2004. **11.76**

In *Barke*, the Court of Appeal rejected the suggestion that the *Burns* procedure should be applied with caution and only in tightly defined circumstances. The overriding objective would be frustrated if an unduly restrictive approach was taken. The Court of Appeal refrained from giving guidelines, leaving that to Burton P should he consider it appropriate. The Court of Appeal has subsequently stated that when using the *Burns/Barke* procedure the EAT must take care to identify the point upon which the tribunal's reason might be inadequate; the tribunal should answer the questions asked of it by the EAT, and should not attempt to justify its reasoning: *Woodhouse School v Webster* [2009] IRLR 568. **11.77**

Request for clarification by the parties

Rather than appeal a decision and seek a remission for further reasons, the parties may request clarification of a decision from the tribunal. If there has been a material omission in the tribunal's findings of fact or in its consideration of the issues of fact and law before it, parties should ask the tribunal to amplify its reasons, either when oral reasons are given or as soon as possible after receiving written reasons: *Bansi v Alpha Flight Services (Note)* [2007] ICR 308 approved in *Royle v Greater Manchester Police Authority* [2007] ICR 281. **11.78**

D. DECISIONS IN CASES CONCERNING SEXUAL OFFENCES

In cases involving allegations of the commission of a sexual offence the tribunal must omit or delete from the register and from any decision or record of the proceedings available to the public, identifying matter which is likely to lead members of the public to identify any person affected by or making such allegations (ETR 2004, r 49). Relevant sexual offences are specified in the Sexual Offences (Amendment) Acts 1976 and 1992, and for Scotland in the Criminal Procedure Scotland Act 1995, s 274(2) (ETA 1996, s 11(6)). **11.79**

E. CHANGING THE DECISION

After registration

There are two situations in which a tribunal may change its decision after registration (other than as a result of a successful appeal): **11.80**

(1) The tribunal may review its own decision under rr 33–6 of ETR 2004.
(2) The tribunal may alter its decision or reasons under the 'slip rule' (ETR 2004, r 37) which provides that clerical mistakes and errors arising from an accidental slip or omission may at any time be corrected by the judge by certificate.

Reviews and corrections under the slip rule are dealt with more fully in Chapter 13. **11.81**

Before registration

There are a number of apparently conflicting authorities on the question of the tribunal's powers to recall and alter a decision after an oral decision has been given, but before the decision has been registered. Many of the decisions pre-date the introduction of the tribunal's power to review its own decision, first introduced in ETR 1993. Given that the tribunal may review its decision under rr 34–6 of ETR 2004, the power to recall is now of limited relevance save where the formalities for seeking a review have not been complied with. **11.82**

In the civil courts there is a power in exceptional circumstances to recall a decision before it has been perfected. The court is not *functus officio* until the decision has been perfected (see, for example, *Re Barrell Enterprises* [1973] 1 WLR 19, CA; *Robinson v Bird* [2003] EWCA Civ 1019). In employment tribunal proceedings it is important to identify the point at which the **11.83** decision is finally binding and the tribunal is *functus officio*. Whilst a decision may be given orally at the hearing, decisions are not perfected until registered.

11.84 A number of cases establish a limited power of recall prior to such registration. In *Hanks v Ace High Productions Ltd* [1979] IRLR 32, EAT, Phillips J said (at 33):

> It is that class of case, where the error or omission is obvious and comes to light soon after the hearing and before the order is drawn up, which is suitable to be dealt with in this way, rather than by way of review. Putting the matter negatively, it would obviously be wrong to make use of the power, in effect to re-hear the case, or merely to hear further argument on matters of fact with the possibility of changing the mind of the tribunal on the facts, when already a clear decision has been reached upon them. It is intended for the simple error which can be put right and matters of that sort.

11.85 In *Lamont v Fry's Metals Ltd* [1985] IRLR 470, the tribunal gave an oral decision, and then changed its mind before the written reasons were completed or registered. The EAT held ([1983] IRLR 434) that the tribunal had the power to recall its decision before the decision was registered, and to invite further argument upon it. In the Court of Appeal Lawton LJ assumed, without deciding, that a tribunal could recall its judgments before they have been perfected, and that a decision of a tribunal is not perfected until it is registered in accordance with the regulations. The actual decision in the case turned on the finding that there was a miscarriage of justice, in that the claimant had not in fact had the opportunity to address the tribunal on the matters which led to the tribunal reversing its oral decision; and the Court of Appeal decided that the proper course was to allow the oral decision to stand.

11.86 There are some authorities, such as *Jowett v Earl of Bradford* [1977] ICR 342, EAT, to the effect that an orally announced decision was *ipso facto* binding, and cannot be reopened other than under the slip rule. This decision was doubted in *Hanks* and is inconsistent with the position as it was assumed to be in *Lamont*.

11.87 Although subsequent decisions have recognized the power to recall, they have on the whole followed the narrow approach of *Hanks* as to the circumstances in which the power may be exercised. It is doubtful whether the power would extend to allow the tribunal to reopen the case as it tried to do in *Lamont*. The EAT followed *Hanks* in *Arthur Guinness Son & Co (GB) Ltd v Green* [1989] IRLR 288, [1989] ICR 241, where the tribunal announced its decision on compensation orally at the end of the hearing, but in its subsequent written reasons changed its decision as to the cut-off point for compensation. It was held that an oral decision must stand other than in the very limited circumstances identified in *Hanks* where the tribunal could exercise the power of recall. Further, even where it was appropriate to recall the decision the tribunal should notify the parties of its intention to do so and invite their comments.

11.88 It is important to preserve the principle that the tribunal should never contemplate departing from its previous oral decision without giving the parties the opportunity to make representations. In *Spring Grove Services Group v Hickinbottom* [1990] ICR 111, the EAT held that the power to recall did not, however, allow the tribunal to invite argument on a new authority reported after the oral decision was handed down.

11.89 The above discussion concerns the recall of final orders: the position differs in respect of interim orders. An interim order is effective as soon as it is announced, and it would appear that there can never be a recall of it: *Casella London Ltd v Banai* [1990] ICR 215. However, an interim decision can subsequently be varied or revoked (see para 13.10 below), so the power of recall is, for practical purposes, unnecessary.

F. RES JUDICATA, ISSUE ESTOPPEL, AND ABUSE OF PROCESS

Introduction

11.90 The question of the effect of previous decisions of courts or tribunals involving the same or similar parties arises from time to time in all civil litigation (see also Chapter 19). In the most straightforward case, a party seeks to bring proceedings which relitigate a matter which the court or tribunal has already decided on. Employment litigation creates particular difficulties with respect to the effect of earlier decisions because of the overlapping jurisdiction of the tribunal and the civil courts. There are a number of situations in which issues raised in tribunal proceedings may overlap with issues which may be raised in the civil courts (Chapter 19). For example, issues raised in an unfair dismissal complaint may also be raised in High Court breach of contract proceedings. Further, the tribunals and the courts have concurrent jurisdiction in relation to certain claims for breach of contract. Damages may be claimed in the tribunals in respect of personal injuries caused by unlawful discrimination. There may be an overlap between such a claim and a claim for damages for personal injury arising out of the employer's negligence, which may be pursued in the courts. As a result of these overlaps it will often be necessary for a court or tribunal to determine the effect of an earlier decision on related issues.

There are three relevant doctrines which arise from the general law: **11.91**

(1) Res judicata, or *cause of action estoppel* A final adjudication against a party on a particular cause of action will be conclusive in later proceedings involving the same parties and the same cause of action as to all points decided in the previous judgment.
(2) *Issue estoppel* A judgment which includes a decision on a particular issue forming a *necessary* ingredient in the cause of action will be binding as to that particular issue if it arises in subsequent proceedings between the same parties or related parties where that issue is relevant, subject to narrow exceptions.
(3) *Abuse of process* It may be an abuse of process to make a claim which could and should have been brought forward as part of earlier proceedings.

Application of principles of estoppel to tribunal decisions

A decision of the employment tribunal may give rise to an issue estoppel, or to *res judicata* in High Court proceedings, so that no evidence may be led in High Court proceedings to contradict the decision of the tribunal (*Green v Hampshire County Council* [1979] ICR 861, Ch D; *Munir v Jang Publications Ltd* [1989] IRLR 224, [1989] ICR 1, CA; *Soteriou v Ultrachem Ltd* [2004] IRLR 870, EWHC, approved in *Fraser v HLMAD* [2006] EWCA Civ 738, [2006] IRLR 687 at para 28). **11.92**

Cause of action and issue estoppel

Conditions for cause of action and issue estoppel

The following conditions apply to both forms of estoppel: **11.93**

(a) There must be a *final* adjudication on the merits (see paras 11.94–11.109 below).
(b) The parties must be the same, or privies to the original parties (see para 11.110 below).
(c) The subject matter must be the same (see paras 11.111–11.117 below).

Final decision on the merits

A potential trap frequently arises when a party has started proceedings in the employment tribunal, but later decides to abandon those proceedings in favour of a claim in the High Court. A decision may be a decision on the merits even if there has been no argument upon it. In the employment tribunals, a dismissal on withdrawal by a claimant has been treated as a decision on the merits, giving rise to a cause of action estoppel. This has presented problems in the tribunals for a number of years, as there has been no procedure in the tribunal for discontinuance or a dismissal which did not give rise to a cause of action estoppel. Unwary litigants and their representatives have therefore on numerous occasions found themselves debarred from having their case determined on the merits through failing to appreciate the consequences of a dismissal on withdrawal. Although ETR 2004 introduced a new rule (r 25) dealing with withdrawal of claims, the opaque language of the rule (described by both the EAT and the Court of Appeal as 'lamentable' in *Khan v Heywood & Middleton Primary Care Trust* [2006] EWCA Civ **11.94**

1087, [2006] IRLR 793) has created its own problems of interpretation, and the rule has been amended with effect from 6 April 2009 (see para 11.105 below).

11.95 In *Barber v Staffordshire CC* [1996] IRLR 209, the Court of Appeal held that the principles of cause of action or issue estoppel apply to the dismissal of an application by a tribunal following its withdrawal by the claimant. The court stated that there is nothing which stipulates that the doctrine of estoppel can only apply in cases where a tribunal has given a reasoned decision on the issues of fact and law. An order dismissing a complaint upon withdrawal is a judicial decision rather than a mere administrative act.

11.96 In *Lennon v Birmingham City Council* [2001] IRLR 826, CA the Court of Appeal, applying *Barber*, again held that adjudication necessary to give rise to an issue estoppel is not limited to a trial on the merits. What matters is that there has been an actual decision of a competent court dismissing the process. The doctrine of issue estoppel does not turn on the reason why the court's decision to dismiss the claim was consented to by the party making the claim, nor on the reason why a court made the order, but on the simple fact that the order was made (*per* Buxton LJ at para 30).

11.97 Three subsequent decisions of the Court of Appeal, however, suggested a less strict approach, and allowed the consequences of a dismissal on withdrawal to depend upon the reasons for the withdrawal: *Sajid v Sussex Muslim Society* [2001] EWCA Civ 1684, [2002] IRLR 113; *Ako v Rothschild Asset Management Ltd* [2002] EWCA Civ 236, [2002] IRLR 348; and *Enfield LBC v Sivanandan* [2005] EWCA Civ 10.

11.98 The approach adopted in those cases is illustrated by *Ako v Rothschild Asset Management Ltd* [2002] EWCA Civ 236, [2002] IRLR 348:

(a) The claimant presented a complaint of unfair dismissal and race discrimination. She subsequently wrote to the tribunal asking to withdraw the application; the tribunal dismissed the application on withdrawal. Less than a week later, the claimant presented a fresh complaint repeating the original allegations and adding some further allegations, and also adding a second respondent. It was subsequently found that the claimant's intention had at all times been to replace the original application with the second application, and that she did not intend or understand that she would not be permitted to pursue the claim after the dismissal on withdrawal (ie there was no intention to abandon the claim, the withdrawal being purely for procedural reasons).

(b) As in *Sajid*, the Court of Appeal's approach was to look at the *purpose* for which the claimant withdrew her application. Mummery LJ stated (at para 27) that although the decision in *Lennon* was binding on the court, and was correctly decided, that decision did not preclude the application of the general principle that a court may have regard to the factual circumstances surrounding a consensual act in order to understand its meaning and effect.

(c) The problem in the employment tribunal was that there was no distinction in the applicable procedural rules between dismissal and discontinuance. The Court of Appeal held that neither the case of *Barber* nor *Lennon* require that cause of action estoppel should apply to employment tribunal cases where it is clear, on examination of the surrounding circumstances, that the withdrawal of the application is in substance a discontinuance of the proceedings (at para 30).

(d) Mummery LJ suggested that before dismissing an application on withdrawal the claimant should be asked for a statement of the circumstances of the decision to withdraw (at para 30).

11.99 It is difficult to reconcile the approach in *Sajid* and *Ako* with the apparently unqualified statement of Buxton LJ in *Lennon* that the doctrine of estoppel arises from the fact of the order made. The cases concerned what on the face of it is a simple order dismissing an application. The effect of such an order appeared to be clear after *Barber* with no need to construe the order against the factual circumstances in which it was made. The decisions in *Ako* and *Sajid* appeared to achieve justice on their particular facts, and avoided the procedural difficulties which arise from the absence of a power to discontinue or transfer tribunal proceedings. However, they led to uncertainty as to the effect of any such order in a particular case, and as to where the necessary boundaries are to be drawn. If the effect of a dismissal on withdrawal depends upon the circumstances in which the claimant asked for the withdrawal, it is difficult for parties to know what is the precise effect of the order, unless there is an investigation of the facts and an adjudication upon them by another tribunal. *Ako* illustrates this: neither the respondent nor the tribunal would have been aware of the circumstances of the withdrawal until the estoppel defence was raised in the second proceedings.

In *Enfield LBC v Sivanandan* [2005] EWCA Civ 10, the Court of Appeal expressly approved *Sajid* ('an entirely appropriate exception to the *res judicata* rule', para 124, *per* Peter Gibson LJ), and Peter Gibson LJ (at para 122) gave some guidance (consistent with *Sajid*) on the manner in which a claim should be withdrawn if it is to be pursued in another forum: **11.100**

> I am in no doubt that on a matter as important as the withdrawal of a claim, or part of a claim, a clear procedural discipline is required. Thus, in my judgment, if a claim is to be withdrawn from the Employment Tribunal on the basis that it is to be pursued elsewhere, as in *Sajid*, the position must be made clear, and it would be desirable for the Employment Tribunal to adjudicate by making an order dismissing the claim on withdrawal. That would mean that either on the face of the order itself, or in the record kept by the Employment Tribunal, there would be unambiguous evidence of the circumstances in which, and the reasons for which, the application was withdrawn. In my judgment, expressions of intent are insufficient. It is of the utmost importance that the issues on which an Employment Tribunal is being asked to adjudicate are clearly defined, and good practice requires that if a claim is to be withdrawn, both the fact that it is being withdrawn and the reasons for its withdrawal should be clear.

The suggestion that there be a dismissal on withdrawal is of course directly contrary to the position in *Barber* and *Lennon*. Buxton LJ, who gave the lead judgment in *Lennon*, sat in *Sivanandan*, yet the status of *Barber* and *Lennon* were not commented on (and indeed *Lennon* was not cited to the court). **11.101**

ETR 2004 contain an express rule in relation to withdrawal of proceedings. Rule 25(1) provides that a claimant may withdraw all or any part of his claim at any time. Rule 25(3) provides that the effect of a withdrawal is that 'proceedings are brought to an end'. Rule 25(4) provides that when a claimant withdraws a claim a respondent may make an application to have the proceedings against him dismissed. In its amended form (see Employment Tribunals (Constitution and Rules of Procedure) (Amendment) Regulations 2008) r 25(4) provides that if the proceedings are dismissed the claimant cannot bring a further claim against the respondent for the same or substantially the same cause of action. **11.102**

The language of the rule, even as amended, leaves a number of issues unclear. The rule leaves open the possibility for proceedings to be withdrawn under r 25(1) but not dismissed under r 25(4). The status of the proceedings in such a situation is entirely unclear. Further, the rule says nothing at all about the effect of either a withdrawal under r 25(3) or a dismissal under r 25(4) on any subsequent proceedings. The rule has, in its original form, caused the EAT and the Court of Appeal considerable difficulty in construction. The original rule was interpreted by the Court of Appeal (*Khan v Heywood & Middleton Primary Care Trust* [2006] EWCA Civ 1087) as follows: **11.103**

(1) The purpose of the distinction between a withdrawal under r 25(3) and a dismissal under r 25(4) is to cover the lacuna, identified in *Sajid* and *Ako*, that there is no procedure in the tribunal for a discontinuance.
(2) Where proceedings are withdrawn under r 25(3) and subsequently dismissed under r 25(4) the principle in *Barber* applies, and a cause of action estoppel arises out of the dismissal.
(3) Where the proceedings are withdrawn, but are not dismissed, no cause of action estoppel arises, as proceedings are brought to an end automatically by operation of r 25(3), not by judicial decision. The claimant would therefore be free to pursue subsequent proceedings based on the same facts.

(4) However, once the proceedings are withdrawn under r 25(3) it is not possible for the tribunal to revoke or set aside the withdrawal. Rule 25(3) states that the proceedings are brought to an end (save for certain specified purposes). Had the draftsman intended there to be a power to set aside the withdrawal, the Rules would have needed to make provision for such a procedure.

11.104 Although he was able to reach this construction of the rule, Wall LJ agreed that the drafting of r 25 was lamentable and ambiguous, and suggested that it should be reconsidered when the ETR are next revised (see paras 78–9). The amendment to r 25(4) only partially solves these problems.

11.105 It has been held by the EAT in *British Association for Shooting and Conservation v Cokayne* [2008] ICR 185, that the route taken in the *Ako* line of cases is no longer available to tribunals since the introduction of r 25. According to HHJ Richardson (para 35), the underlying principle illustrated by *Ako* is that there may be exceptions to the application of cause of action estoppel where it is necessary to do justice. The approach taken in *Ako* was only necessary when the tribunal rules had no mechanism for withdrawing proceedings without dismissing them. Given that a tribunal may permit withdrawal without dismissal under r 25, if the tribunal goes the extra step and dismisses the claim, then the claim must be taken as dismissed for all purposes, and it is not open to a claimant to avoid the application of cause of action estoppel by reliance on *Ako*.

11.106 However, the EAT in *Cokayne* went on to note that a trap still remains for an unrepresented litigant who does not appreciate the significance of the distinction between dismissal and withdrawal under r 25. The EAT recommended that the tribunal, when faced with an application under r 25 in a case with an unrepresented claimant, should itself consider whether there is material on file which would suggest that it is unjust to dismiss the claim (para 37). Further, if the claim is dismissed in cases where the claimant intends to commence fresh proceedings, the claimant's remedy is to seek an application for review of the dismissal. On the review the tribunal can consider whether it would be an abuse of process to set aside the dismissal, opening the way for the claimant to commence fresh proceedings (para 36).

11.107 Rule 25 creates a further difficulty, in that on its face it offers no guidance as to how the power to dismiss under r 25(4) should be operated. The power would appear to be discretionary, but there is no indication as to the principles upon which the discretion is to be exercised. This problem was considered by the EAT in *Verdin v Harrods Ltd* [2006] IRLR 339. The EAT confirmed that the power under r 25(4) was discretionary, and gave some guidance as to when it should be exercised. Once again, the key to the rule lay in the application of the principles of estoppel and abuse of process to decisions of the tribunal. A respondent will generally be entitled to have the proceedings dismissed. There may, however, be circumstances in which it would be just to refuse to dismiss the proceedings if the dismissal is for the purpose of pursuing other proceedings. The questions for the tribunal to determine are those identified in *Ako*. Is the withdrawing party intending to abandon the claim? If the withdrawing party is intending to resurrect the claim in fresh proceedings, would it be an abuse of process to allow that to occur? If the answer to either of these questions is yes, then it will be just to dismiss the proceedings. If the answer to both questions is no, it will be unjust to dismiss the proceedings. The reasoning in *Verdin* as to the legislative intent of the rule was approved by the Court of Appeal in *Khan*.

11.108 *Verdin* also addressed one further technical gap in the drafting of r 25. Whilst it is clear from r 25(1) and r 25(2) that a party may withdraw part of a claim, r 25(3) refers only to the consequence of withdrawal if the whole of the claim is brought to an end. The EAT held that where part of a claim is withdrawn the proper construction of r 25(3) is that only the withdrawn part of the claim is brought to an end.

11.109 The decisions which do not give rise to a cause of action estoppel are set out below:

(a) A decision on the grounds of lack of jurisdiction (although in reaching its decision a court may decide issues which give rise to an issue estoppel on those issues (see, for example, *The Sennar No 2* [1985] 1 WLR 490, HL)).

(b) A refusal to allow an amendment to permit a claim to be brought (*Air Canada v Basra* [2000] IRLR 683, EAT, para 39).
(c) A 'decision' of the tribunal recording the terms of a settlement between the parties, but which does not order a sum to be paid or dismiss the claim is not a decision at all and therefore cannot give rise to a *res judicata* (*Dattani v Trio Supermarkets Ltd* [1998] IRLR 240, CA).

Same parties or their privies

Privies may be privy to the parties by blood, title, or identity of interest (*Carl Zeiss Stiftung v Rayner and Keeler Ltd* [1967] 1 AC 853, 910, *per* Lord Reid). So, for example, a judgment against a person will be binding on his heirs and executors. Further examples include office holders and their successors and members of a representative class in representative proceedings. Privity of interest arises where a party has sufficient involvement in proceedings to which he is not a party that it is just for the decision in those proceedings to be binding upon him. The circumstances giving rise to privity of interest are not well defined. The mere fact that a company's commercial success depended on the outcome of proceedings is not sufficient, nor is the fact that a person has provided a witness statement in the proceedings. Some element of control of the proceedings or the matters in issue in the proceedings is likely to be required. See in addition to the *Carl Zeiss* case, *Gleeson v Wippell & Co* [1977] 1 WLR 510, ChD and *Kirin-Amgen Inc v Boehringer Mannheim GmbH* [1997] FSR 289, CA. **11.110**

Same subject matter

Where cause of action estoppel is relied on, the cause of action in the subsequent case must be the *same* as the cause of action determined in the first case. **11.111**

Where issue estoppel is relied on, the issue in the second proceedings must be the same as the issue in the first proceedings. Further, the issue must have been an issue which was necessarily determined in the first case. A party will not be bound by a finding of fact which it was not necessary for the tribunal in the first case to have decided in reaching its decision. **11.112**

It is necessary to take some care in determining whether the cause of action or issue is indeed identical in the two sets of proceedings. **11.113**

In *Jones v Mid-Glamorgan County Council* [1997] IRLR 685, [1997] ICR 815, CA: **11.114**

(a) County court proceedings were brought for breach of contract in relation to pension benefits. The key issue was whether, in accepting voluntary retirement terms, an employee had been acting under duress. The court held that he had not been subjected to duress, but that he had in fact retired voluntarily on the agreed terms.
(b) In a subsequent unfair dismissal complaint, the issue for the employment tribunal was whether the employee had been dismissed. The tribunal, having heard evidence, concluded that he had not been dismissed (thus in effect reaching the same conclusion as the county court), but in its reasons it referred to the county court's findings on the question of voluntary retirement as being 'binding' on it.
(c) The EAT and the Court of Appeal held that no issue estoppel arose. The issue in the county court was whether, under the law of contract, duress had vitiated the employee's acceptance of the early retirement offer, whereas, in the tribunal, the relevant question was whether the threat of dismissal was the operative factor in the employee accepting early retirement. As the two issues were quite different, requiring different analyses, the question of issue estoppel did not arise.
(d) The Court of Appeal, however, overturned the EAT's decision and upheld the tribunal's decision, finding that on a true construction of the reasons the tribunal had decided the issues itself, and had not applied an issue estoppel (but cf Browne-Wilkinson J in *O'Laiore v Jackel International Ltd* [1991] ICR 718).

11.115 In *Friend v Civil Aviation Authority* [2001] IRLR 819, CA:

(a) The claimant was dismissed after complaining about certain safety procedures. In employment tribunal proceedings his dismissal was found to have been procedurally unfair, but his conduct was held to have contributed 100 per cent to his dismissal and he received no compensation.
(b) He later issued High Court proceedings claiming wrongful dismissal and various employment-related torts.
(c) The Court of Appeal held that no issue estoppel arose from the finding of contributory conduct. A decision under s 123(6) of ERA 1996 that the claimant's conduct contributed to his dismissal, and that it would be just and equitable to reduce the amount of the compensatory award by 100 per cent, cannot be regarded as a decision that any loss resulting from the dismissal was not caused by any tort or breach of contract of the employers but by the claimant's own behaviour.

11.116 In *British Airways v Boyce* [2001] IRLR 157, Court of Session:

(a) The claimant brought a race discrimination complaint, alleging that he had been discriminated against on grounds of his English *ethnic* origins. The complaint was dismissed, because the English were not an ethnic group.
(b) The claimant brought a second race discrimination complaint on identical facts, the only difference being that he claimed discrimination on grounds of his English *national* origins.
(c) The Court of Session regarded the complaint as *res judicata*. The type of complaint, and the facts alleged were the same. The change reflected no more than a different legal approach in support of the same underlying proposition. The proper approach was to ask what was litigated and what was decided. Lord Marnoch said (at 159):

> The *media concludendi* should in general be taken as covering everything in the legislation, both in its legal and factual aspects, which is pertinent to the act or acts of the employer made subject of the complaint—here the act of the employer in refusing the respondent's job application on allegedly racial grounds.

11.117 In *Bainbridge v Redcar and Cleveland Borough Council* [2008] EWCA Civ 885, [2008] IRLR 776:

(a) The claimants brought equal pay claims relating to a period of time in respect of which earlier equal pay claims had already been determined, albeit in relation to different comparators. The respondents argued that a cause of action estoppel arose.
(b) The respondent categorized the cause of action as being the alleged breach of the equality clause in respect of the claimants for the particular period of time.
(c) The EAT, by a majority, had rejected this argument and instead found in favour of the claimants. The reasoning of the majority in the EAT was that a promise to pay A the same as B is not the same as a promise to pay A the same as C: a single contractual term may contain a number of contractual obligations.
(d) The Court of Appeal, dismissing an appeal from the EAT's decision, held that although the equal pay claim was for contravention of a term of a contract, the content of the term was determined by the terms of the statute and not by agreement of the parties. The cause of action was asserted pursuant to statute. Within and by virtue of the statute there was more than one cause of action. Accordingly, there was nothing in the doctrine of *res judicata* which restricted the claimants to confine themselves to one way of putting their case.

Issue estoppel—special circumstances

11.118 A cause of action estoppel is an absolute bar to further proceedings based on the same cause of action. The principle of issue estoppel, however, is more flexible. There is an exception to the rule of issue estoppel in the special circumstances where further material has become available to a party which was relevant to the correct determination of the point involved in the earlier proceedings but which could not by reasonable diligence have been adduced in those proceedings: *Arnold v National Westminster Bank plc* [1991] 2 AC 93. In *Watt (formerly Carter) v Ahsan*

[2007] UKHL 51, [2008] 2 WLR 17, [2008] ICR 82 the House of Lords held that it would be unjust to allow a party to one action (A) to rely on this exception where it had in unrelated proceedings appealed on the point of law decided against it in action A but made no attempt to stay action A pending the hearing of the appeal in the unrelated proceedings. Thus even though the unrelated appeal later succeeded, the tribunal and the parties in action A remained bound by the earlier tribunal decision, however incorrect in law that had now proven to be.

The principle in *Henderson v Henderson*

General principle

In general, a litigant must raise all relevant points at the trial of the complaint he has brought. The courts have long adhered to the principle that when a litigant brings a case he must bring forward his whole case and will not, except in special circumstances, be permitted to bring fresh proceedings in respect of a matter which could and should have been litigated in earlier proceedings. The starting point for this principle is the decision of the Court of Appeal in *Henderson v Henderson* (1843) 3 Hare 100. Sir James Wigram VC said (at 115): **11.119**

> Where a given matter becomes the subject of litigation in, and of adjudication by, a court of competent jurisdiction, the court requires the parties to that litigation to bring forward their whole case, and will not (except under special circumstances) permit the same parties to open the same subject of litigation in respect of matter which might have been brought forward as part of the subject in contest, but which was not brought forward, only because they have, from negligence, inadvertence, or even accident, omitted part of their case. The plea of res judicata applies, except in special cases, not only to points upon which the court was actually required by the parties to form an opinion and pronounce a judgment, but to every point which properly belonged to the subject of litigation, and which the parties, exercising reasonable diligence, might have brought forward at the time.

Application in the employment sphere

The principle in *Henderson v Henderson* above presents a particular trap in employment litigation because of the potential for claims which could be brought either in the employment tribunal, or in the courts. **11.120**

In *Sheriff v Klyne Tugs (Lowestoft) Ltd* [1998] IRLR 481, CA: **11.121**

(a) The claimant claimed to have been subjected to racial harassment as a result of which he suffered a nervous breakdown.
(b) He brought a claim of race discrimination in the employment tribunal which was dismissed on withdrawal after terms of settlement were reached between the parties.
(c) The claimant subsequently brought proceedings in the county court claiming that his psychiatric injury had been caused by abusive and detrimental treatment by his employer. The particulars relied on were substantially the same matters alleged in the tribunal claim.
(d) The Court of Appeal held that damages for personal injury arising out of unlawful race discrimination could have been recovered in the tribunal proceedings.
(e) Relying on the rule in *Henderson v Henderson* the Court of Appeal struck out the county court claim on the basis that the claimant could and should have brought forward his whole claim in the tribunal proceedings.
(f) The Court of Appeal rejected the argument that procedural differences between the tribunal and the court (limitation periods, costs regimes, power to award interim payments, and provisional damages) amounted to special circumstances. The fact that the medical condition was undiscovered at the time of the tribunal hearing may amount to a special circumstance.
(g) The Court of Appeal also held that the terms of the compromise reached in the tribunal proceedings had compromised any claim in relation to personal injuries. The relevant provision of the settlement provided:

> The Applicant accepts the terms of this agreement in full and final settlement of all claims which he has or may have against the respondent arising out of this employment or the termination thereof being claims in respect of which an industrial tribunal has jurisdiction.

11.122 A strict application of the principle can lead to harsh results. It was not clear as a matter of law that the tribunal could award damages for personal injury in a discrimination claim until *Sheriff* itself, yet the claimant was precluded from bringing a court action because he should have raised such a claim in the tribunal. See also *Barber v Staffordshire County Council* [1996] ICR 379.

11.123 The principle may apply even though a party may have little time to decide whether to pursue a claim in the earlier set of proceedings: *Divine-Borty v London Borough of Brent* [1998] IRLR 525, CA. In *Divine-Borty*, during the hearing of a claim for unfair dismissal, evidence from one of the employer's witnesses suggested that the claimant's race may have been a factor in the dismissal. No application was made to bring a claim under the Race Relations Act 1976. The tribunal dismissed the unfair dismissal application, making no express finding as to the racial issue.

11.124 The claimant issued a second tribunal application alleging race discrimination. The Court of Appeal held, on the basis of *Henderson v Henderson*, that the second complaint should not be allowed to proceed. The fact that the evidence upon which the race claim was based emerged during the hearing of the unfair dismissal was not a special circumstance. The race discrimination complaint should have been raised at the hearing, or if necessary an adjournment sought.

11.125 *Sheriff* was followed by the Court of Appeal in *Enfield LBC v Sivanandan* [2005] EWCA Civ 10. In striking out a High Court claim for breach of contract, the primary reasoning of the Court of Appeal in *Sivanandan* was that the same claim had been raised in the tribunal and had been struck out on the grounds of vexatious conduct. However, the Court of Appeal considered, and accepted, an alternative argument: even if the contract claim had been withdrawn from the tribunal proceedings prior to the strike-out, it was an abuse of process to 'reinvent' in the guise of a breach of contract a claim that was really the same as the race discrimination claim that had been struck out in the employment tribunal.

11.126 In so deciding, the Court of Appeal was influenced by the following:

(a) The facts giving rise to the breach of contract claim were encompassed by the race discrimination claim.
(b) The loss claimed in the contract claim could have been recovered in the race discrimination claim.

11.127 The Court of Appeal therefore closely followed *Sheriff* in holding that the second claim arose out of the same facts, and claimed the same losses as were claimed in the first claim, therefore the second claim was an abuse. Note, however, it was clear that the Court of Appeal regarded Sivanandan's conduct of the proceedings as unreasonable (see in particular Buxton LJ's judgment), and it was a relevant factor that in order to bring the contract claim she had significantly changed her position as to if and when her employment was terminated ([2005] EWCA Civ 10, para 138, *per* Peter Gibson LJ).

Relaxation of the strictness of the rule

11.128 The civil courts have in recent years taken a more liberal approach to the principle of *Henderson v Henderson*.

11.129 In *Johnson v Gore Wood Ltd* [2002] 2 AC 1, the House of Lords made clear that although closely connected with cause of action estoppel and issue estoppel, the principle in *Henderson v Henderson* is a form of abuse of process. Two important points arise, which alleviate the strict application of the principle: (1) a broad merits based approach, taking into account all the circumstances, should be taken; (2) the onus is on the defendant to show abuse, rather than on the claimant to show special circumstances why the claim should be allowed to proceed. Lord Bingham of Cornhill said (at 90):

> The bringing of a claim or the raising of a defence in later proceedings may, without more, amount to abuse if the court is satisfied (*the onus being on the party alleging abuse*) that the claim or defence should have been raised in the earlier proceedings if it was to be raised at all. I would not accept that it

is necessary, before abuse may be found, to identify any additional element such as a collateral attack on a previous decision or some dishonesty, but where those elements are present the later proceedings will be much more obviously abusive, and there will rarely be a finding of abuse unless the later proceeding involves what the court regards as unjust harassment of a party. It is, however, wrong to hold that because a matter could have been raised in early proceedings it should have been, so as to render the raising of it in later proceedings necessarily abusive. That is to adopt too dogmatic an approach to what should in my opinion be *a broad, merits based judgment which takes account of the public and private interests involved and also takes account of all the facts of the case, focusing attention on the crucial question whether, in all the circumstances, a party is misusing or abusing the process of the court by seeking to raise before it the issue which could have been raised before.* (emphasis added)

The courts have resisted attempts to define or categorize what may be an abuse of process. However, a number of elements which would be likely to render relitigation an abuse were identified by Auld LJ in *Bradford & Bingley Society v Seddon* [1999] 1 WLR 1482, CA, as: **11.130**

(a) a collateral attack on an earlier judicial decision;
(b) dishonesty;
(c) successive actions amounting to harassment of the defendant;
(d) pursuit of a claim after having pursued a mutually exclusive alternative claim;
(e) pursuit of a claim which had previously been abandoned.

In *Stuart v Goldberg Linde (a firm)* [2008] EWCA 2 the Court of Appeal provided further guidance on the question of abuse of process: **11.131**

(a) the broad merits based approach to which *Johnson* referred related to the merits of the argument that it was an abuse of process to bring a second claim, not to the substantive merits of the claim itself. It would only be in an extreme case that the merits of the case would be relevant (for example, where the merits were such that summary judgment was appropriate, in which case the necessary application can be made for that purpose: *Walbrook Trustees (Jersey) Ltd v Fattal* [2009] EWCA Civ 297, para 6);
(b) delay of itself is not relevant (absent questions of limitation); and
(c) there is no general duty on the claimant to exercise reasonable diligence in finding out facts going to whether or not he has a new claim, and, as a general rule, a claimant's failure to exercise such diligence is not relevant to the question of abuse of process.

The more liberal approach, following *Johnson v Gore Wood Ltd* above, can be seen in the employment context in *Friend v Civil Aviation Authority* [2001] IRLR 819, CA, and *Chaudhary v Royal College of Surgeons* [2003] ICR 1510, paras 70–83; see also *Bradford & Bingley Building Society v Seddon* [1999] 1 WLR 1482, CA. It should be noted that *Seddon* was not cited in *Sheriff* and neither *Seddon* nor *Johnson v Gore Wood* were referred to in *Sivanandan*. **11.132**

In Scotland, the doctrine of *res judicata* differs from that in England and Wales and does not go so far as does the rule in *Henderson* in England and Wales. However, in *British Airways v Boyce* [2001] IRLR 157, the Court of Session held that the general principle of *res judicata* should apply to tribunal proceedings in Scotland, and a broad approach taken to what was litigated and what was decided so that in practice the practical outcome of cases should be similar in both jurisdictions. **11.133**

Other instances of abuse of process

Res judicata and issue estoppel will only arise where a dispute is relitigated between the same parties. Similarly, in *Johnson v Gore Wood Ltd*, Lord Millet said that the principle in *Henderson v Henderson* only applies where a claim is brought between parties who had been parties to the previous proceedings. **11.134**

However, there may be circumstances in which proceedings are held to be an abuse of process because of their close connection with an earlier dispute, even if the party claiming abuse was not a party to the previous proceedings. Quite apart from the interests of a defendant in not being sued twice over the same matter, there is a general public interest in the same issue not **11.135** being litigated over again. There is a policy interest in finality, and also in avoiding inconsistent decisions. This policy can be used to justify the extension of the rules of issue estoppel to cases in which the parties are not the same but the circumstances are such as to bring the case within the spirit of the rules (see *Arthur J Hall & Co v Simons* [2000] 3 WLR 543, HL).

11.136 In *Ashmore v British Coal Corp* [1990] 2 QB 338, A was one of 1,500 women employees of the respondent who made equal pay complaints to the tribunal. The tribunal decided to hear 14 sample cases, six selected by the employees and eight by the employers, to lay down general principles according to which the others could be decided. The tribunal decided all the cases adversely to the applicants on grounds which were equally applicable to A's application. She then asked for a separate hearing of her case. The Court of Appeal decided that it should be struck out as an abuse of the process of the court. A had not been a party to the sample proceedings but the sensible procedure there adopted would be undermined if all other members of the group were entitled to demand a separate hearing.

11.137 Similarly, in *Acland v Devon CC* EAT/1220/98, in 1997, 145 home care workers employed by three councils had brought claims for breach of contract claiming that they were not bound by the terms of a collective agreement. They also brought equal pay claims. These claims were settled but the underlying dispute continued. In 1998, 130 home care assistants, all members of the same unit for whom two unions were bargaining agents, claimed equal pay. There was no *res judicata* as the parties were not the same. The 1997 proceedings had been brought by named individuals on behalf of the bargaining unit. The tribunal dismissed the applications as an abuse of process because substantially the same workforce was reopening the same issue.

11.138 In *Dexter Ltd v Vlieland-Boddy* [2003] EWCA Civ 14, the Court of Appeal recognized that successive actions based on similar facts, but brought against different defendants who were not privies, could be an abuse of process. However, on the facts, applying the 'broad merits based approach' advocated in *Johnson v Gore Wood Ltd*, the circumstances did not amount to an abuse.

11.139 It may be an abuse of process to bring proceedings for the purpose of mounting a collateral attack on a final decision made against a party by another court of competent jurisdiction in previous proceedings, in which the party had a full opportunity to contest the decision in the court by which it was made (see *Hunter v Chief Constable of West Midlands Police* [1982] AC 529, HL, 541, *per* Lord Diplock).

Part A Tribunal Procedure

12

Costs

SUMMARY

(1) Costs are not usually awarded in tribunals.

(2) Tribunals have the power to order costs not only against a party but also their representative ('wasted costs') and also in favour of in-house representatives and litigants in person ('preparation time orders').

(3) A tribunal can award either a fixed sum that is either agreed or up to a maximum of £10,000 or the costs can be determined, or assessed, in the county court.

A. INTRODUCTION

An important distinction between proceedings in the courts and those in the tribunal is that the tribunal's powers to award costs to a successful party are very limited. In a civil claim the losing party will invariably have to pay the winner's costs; in the tribunal this will usually not be the case, and each side will bear its own costs. It is important therefore to assess the likely costs of pursuing or defending any claim at an early stage with this in mind. **12.01**

The jurisdiction to award costs under ETR 1993 was not frequently exercised. In the year 2000/01 there were 247 awards of costs out of 129,725 cases disposed of. The average amount of costs awarded was £295 (ETS Annual Report 2000/01). By the time of the 2003 Annual Report 126,793 cases were disposed of and there were 976 costs orders. The average costs awarded had risen to £1,859 (Annual Report 2003/04). By the time of the 2005/06 Annual Report there were 432 costs orders made and the average award made was £2,256 (although in the 2007/08 Report the average award had fallen to £2,095. **12.02**

Statistically costs have tended to be awarded more frequently as the tribunal rules have changed and the amounts of orders made have also increased over the years. **12.03**

12.04 Tribunals may sometimes indicate to a party during the hearing that they are at risk of costs. In *Gee v Shell* [2003] IRLR 82, the Court of Appeal held that a tribunal should only give a costs warning where there is a real risk that an order for costs will be made against an unsuccessful claimant at the end of the hearing. The court recognized that there is a line to be drawn between 'robust, effective and fair case management', on the one hand, and inappropriate pressure, on the other. In deciding which of the two to choose, a number of factors must be considered, such as the circumstances in which the warning was given, the strength of the case against the party, the nature and extent of the warning (for example, whether it referred to the possibility of a summary or a detailed assessment being made), and the manner in which it was given.

B. OVERVIEW

12.05 Costs can be made in the following circumstances:

(a) an adjournment occasioned by a failure to adduce evidence to deal with a request for reinstatement or re-engagement (ETR 2004, r 39(1));
(b) vexatious, unreasonable, etc conduct (see para 12.15 below) (ETR 2004, r 40(3));
(c) failing to comply with an order or Practice Direction (ETR 2004, r 40(4));
(d) where a party has been ordered to pay a deposit as a condition of being permitted to continue to participate in the proceedings and the tribunal or judge has found against that party (ETR 2004, r 47(1));
(e) where a claim form or response has not been accepted by the tribunal, a party may still be awarded costs in respect of his participation in the proceedings (ETR 2004, r 38(4)). This rule applies both to the situation where a respondent has put in a response but has not had it accepted by the tribunal and to the situation where a respondent has not presented any response at all. In each situation a tribunal only has power to make an order for costs against or in favour of such a respondent in relation to the conduct of a part of the proceedings in which he is entitled to take part (ie under any of the exceptions in r 9 (for example, applying for a review) and in which he has actually taken part (*Sutton v The Ranch Ltd* [2006] ICR 1170, EAT)).

12.06 Preparation time orders (PTOs) can be made in similar circumstances where the party has not been legally represented at, for example, the hearing (see further para 12.38 below). Wasted costs orders may be made against a party's legal representatives in certain circumstances (see further para 12.44 below).

12.07 A tribunal cannot make a costs order and a PTO in favour of the same party in the same proceedings (r 46(1)). If a tribunal makes a costs order or a PTO before the proceedings are determined it can decide to make the award for costs or preparation time after the proceedings have been determined—effectively reserving the final determination on costs (r 46(2)).

C. KEY TERMS

12.08 'Paying party' means the party against whom an order for costs is made. 'Receiving party' means the party in favour of whom costs are made. A 'costs order' is known in Scotland as an 'expenses order'. It can be made only when the receiving party is legally represented (r 38(2), (5)). Where the party is unrepresented, a PTO may be made.

D. TIMING OF ORDERS

12.09 An order can be made at any stage in the proceedings. An application which is made at the end of a hearing can either be oral or in writing. In each case it must be made within 28 days of an oral judgment or the date on which any reserved judgment was sent to the parties (r 38(7)) (if later than 28 days the application can only be considered if it is in the interests of justice to do so). The Secretary to the tribunal must send notice to the party against whom an order is sought allowing them the opportunity to give reasons as to why the order should not be made. There is no requirement to send a notice where the party has had the opportunity to respond orally.

Where a tribunal makes a costs order or PTO it should provide written reasons for doing so if a request for written reasons is received within 14 days of the date of the order. **12.10**

E. WHEN ORDERS MUST BE MADE

An order for costs (as opposed to a PTO) must be made against a respondent in an unfair dismissal case where the claimant has expressed a wish to be reinstated or re-engaged which has been communicated to the respondent not less than seven days before the hearing and the respondent has obtained an adjournment based on its inability to adduce reasonable evidence as to the availability of the job from which the claimant was dismissed or comparable or suitable employment. The respondent can avoid such an order if the request was made less than seven days before the hearing and it can show a 'special reason' as to why it could not adduce the evidence. In many cases claimants will tick the box on the claim form indicating that they are seeking reinstatement/re-engagement. It is difficult to envisage circumstances in which a respondent will not have had at least seven days' notice as the schedule of loss and/or witness statements may also contain such an indication. **12.11**

A party who has paid a deposit as a condition of being permitted to continue proceedings (under r 20) will have to pay costs if the tribunal finds against him and the tribunal considers that he has: (1) conducted the proceedings unreasonably in persisting in having the matter determined, and (2) the grounds on which he has failed are substantially the same as those recorded in the order for considering that the party's contentions had little reasonable prospect of success. Rule 47(1) provides, however, that this order can only be made provided no other order for costs has been made in the proceedings. The deposit will be forfeited as part of this costs order: if there is an excess it will be refunded. **12.12**

F. DISCRETIONARY ORDERS

The tribunal has a discretion whether to order costs where there has been an adjournment of a hearing or pre-hearing review. The order will be against the party who has caused the adjournment. **12.13**

There is also the discretion to order costs against a party who has in bringing the proceedings acted vexatiously, abusively, disruptively, or otherwise unreasonably. Costs may be ordered against the paying party where the bringing or conducting of the proceedings has been misconceived. Costs may be ordered against the party or his representative where they have behaved vexatiously, abusively, disruptively, or otherwise unreasonably. In *Health Development Agency v Parish* [2004] IRLR 550, the EAT held that the conduct of a party prior to proceedings, or unrelated to proceedings, cannot form the basis of an order for costs (see also *Davidson v John Calder (Publishers) Ltd and Calder Educational Trust Ltd* [1985] IRLR 97—prior conduct can be relevant to an assessment of whether it was reasonable to bring or defend the claim, but it cannot be treated as the act of vexatiousness or unreasonableness upon which an award of costs can be founded). However, in *McPherson v BNP Paribas* [2004] IRLR 558, the Court of Appeal held that there is no requirement for the causal link between the party's unreasonable behaviour and the costs incurred by the receiving party. The tribunal should have regard to the nature, gravity, and effect of the unreasonable conduct as factors relevant to the exercise of its discretion but there is no need to link the conduct to any specific loss (this was followed in *Salinas v Bear Stearns Holdings Inc* [2005] ICR 1117). **12.14**

Vexatious

12.15 The formulation used to describe conduct attracting an award of costs in the rules before 1993 was 'frivolous and vexatious' and the classic description of this was given by Sir Hugh Griffiths in *Marler (ET) Ltd v Robertson* [1974] ICR 72, 76:

> If the employee knows that there is no substance in his claim and that it is bound to fail, or if the claim is on the face of it so manifestly misconceived that it can have no prospect of success, it may be deemed frivolous and an abuse of the procedure of the tribunal to pursue it. If an employee brings a hopeless claim not with any expectation of recovering compensation but out of spite to harass his employers or for some other improper motive or acts vexatiously and likewise abuses the procedure [his action is vexatious].

Misconceived

12.16 A claim or response that is misconceived 'includes having no reasonable prospect of success' (2004 Regulations, reg 2). The definition is not exhaustive and clearly leaves the tribunal with a wide discretion.

12.17 The categorization extends not only to a party who knows that there is no merit in the case but also to one who ought to have known that the case had no merit. In *Cartiers Superfoods Ltd v Laws* [1978] IRLR 315, the EAT held that a tribunal should inquire as to what a party knew or ought to have known had he gone about the matters sensibly. The question of whether a party knew or ought to have known that a claim was without merit should be considered throughout the hearing and not just at the time of commencement. So, while it might be reasonable to commence proceedings, it may later become clear that they are misconceived. In *Beynon v Scadden* [1999] IRLR 700, the EAT suggested that it may be unreasonable conduct to fail to seek further information, written answers, or disclosure in order to assess the merits of the case (at para 28). In that case the EAT also said (at para 20):

> one does not necessarily judge a party who has had the benefit of advice as one would a lay person left only to his own perhaps inadequate devices.

12.18 The fact that a party has sought legal advice is a relevant factor but not determinative of itself. The tribunal ought, however, to be wary of the dangers of hindsight. The fact that a party loses before the tribunal does not mean that the case was misconceived or vexatious. What becomes clear to the parties, for example after cross-examination, at the end of the proceedings may not have been clear at the start.

12.19 A judge may also order costs against a party who has not complied with an order or a Practice Direction (r 40(4)) (see Chapter 6).

Collateral or improper purposes

12.20 In *Beynon* above, the employees pursued a TUPE claim which the union knew or ought to have known had no prospect of success. One reason for awarding costs was that the claims were proceeded with for the collateral purpose of forcing the employer to recognize the union. Similarly, in *Kovacs v Queen Mary and Westfield College* [2002] IRLR 414, the tribunal awarded costs on the basis, amongst other things, that there was no real claim against the respondent and they had been dragged in as part of a vendetta against the principal witness.

Otherwise unreasonably

12.21 Even if a party's case is meritorious, the way in which it is handled by the party or his advisers may be unreasonable. Late disclosure of documents or late withdrawals often form the basis of an application for costs under this heading. The rule also covers conduct during the hearing or outside it including intimidating witnesses.

12.22 When considering whether an award of costs should be made against a claimant who withdraws his claim, the crucial question is whether he has acted unreasonably in the conduct of the proceedings, not whether the withdrawal of the claim is itself unreasonable (*McPherson v BNP Paribas* [2004] IRLR 558). Mummery LJ at para 28 gave this guidance:

> [it would be] legally erroneous if, acting on a misconceived analogy with the CPR, tribunals took the line that it was unreasonable conduct for employment tribunal claimants to withdraw claims and that they should accordingly be made liable to pay all the costs of the proceedings.

In the next paragraph, however, he recognized the equal weight to be given to the principle of discouraging speculative claims with a hope of a settlement. **12.23**

Withdrawal is not in itself to be equated with unreasonableness and in each case it must be shown that the claimant's conduct of the proceedings has been unreasonable. This is determined by looking at the conduct overall. If it is adjudged to have been unreasonable, then costs can be awarded but only in respect of the period after the conduct became unreasonable. However, the receiving party does not have to show that any particular item of expense after that was actually caused by the unreasonable conduct (*McPherson*, above). In *Daleside Nursing Home Limited v Mathew* 2009 UKEAT 0519 the Tribunal found that the claim was based on a lie but declined to make an order for costs. The EAT held that having made such a finding the tribunal should have gone on to conclude that the claimant had acted unreasonably and order costs. **12.24**

G. *CALDERBANK* LETTERS

In proceedings in the civil courts a winning party who fails to do better than an offer made to him by the losing party will usually expect to pay the losing party's costs from the date of the offer (see generally CPR Part 36). The use of '*Calderbank* letters' is common—an offer to settle without prejudice, save as to costs. The letter is not revealed to the court until the end of the trial. Initially the practice of *Calderbank* letters was not looked upon favourably in tribunals (see Lindsay J in *Monaghan v Close Thornton Solicitors* EAT/3/01). In *Kopel v Safeway Stores plc* [2003] IRLR 753, however, it was held that a failure by a party to beat a *Calderbank* offer will not, by itself, result in an award of costs against him. What must be shown is 'that the conduct of an appellant in rejecting the offer was unreasonable before the rejection becomes a relevant factor in the exercise of its discretion under [r 38]' (at para 18). On the facts of that case, the EAT upheld a tribunal's award of £5,000 costs against the claimant where she had failed in her unfair dismissal and sex discrimination claims, and had not only turned down a 'generous' offer to settle the case but had persisted in alleging breaches of the provisions of the ECHR prohibiting torture and slavery, which the tribunal categorized as 'frankly ludicrous' and 'seriously misconceived'. In the circumstances, the EAT held that the tribunal was entitled to find that the rejection of the offer was unreasonable conduct of the proceedings justifying the award of costs that was made. **12.25**

In *Power v Panasonic* EAT/439/04, the EAT again stressed that the rule in *Calderbank v Calderbank* [1976] Fam 93 has no place in the employment tribunal jurisdiction and cited with approval *Kopel v Safeway Stores plc* [2003] IRLR 753, paras 17–18. However, where a party has obstinately pressed for some unreasonably high award despite its excess being pointed out and despite a warning that costs might be asked for against that party if it were persisted in, the tribunal could in appropriate circumstances take the view that that party had conducted the proceedings unreasonably. **12.26**

H. COSTS AGAINST RESPONDENTS

In *Cartiers Superfoods Ltd v Laws* [1978] IRLR 315, the EAT stated that great care should be exercised by tribunals before awarding costs against respondents as they must be entitled to defend proceedings. However, the proceedings must still be defended reasonably. **12.27**

I. AMOUNT

12.28 Where it has been decided to make a costs order against a party, a tribunal or judge may make one of the following orders (see r 41(1)):

(a) an order for a specified sum not exceeding £10,000;
(b) an order for a specified sum agreed by the parties; or
(c) an order that the whole or a specified part of the costs to be determined by way of a detailed assessment in a county court in accordance with the CPR or, in Scotland, as taxed according to such part of the table of fees prescribed for proceedings in the sheriff court as shall be directed by the order. A detailed assessment is where the court will assess whether the amounts claimed as costs are reasonable in relation to the length of time spent on any work and the hourly rate, for example, claimed by a party's representative. See para 12.34 below.

12.29 The latter two types of order may exceed £10,000. When considering either whether to make an order, or the amount of the order, the tribunal may have regard to the paying party's ability to pay (r 41(2)). This reverses the position under the previous rules where there was no such power, and it had been held that there was no discretion to take means into account (*Kovacs v Queen Mary and Westfield College* [2002] IRLR 414). It is not mandatory to take means into account and it may be that the tribunal cannot, in some circumstances, ascertain what those means are. In *Jilley v Birmingham & Solihull Mental Health NHS Trust* [2008] All ER (D) 35 (Feb) the EAT held that rules 41(1) and (2) taken together were wide enough to allow a tribunal to take account of ability to pay by placing a cap on an award of costs even where it ordered a detailed assessment. If a tribunal was satisfied that a paying party had not been frank as to his means, it might be positively desirable to do so as it might render it unnecessary to go through the expense of a detailed assessment, or assist parties to reach terms of payment. If a tribunal decided not to take ability to pay into account, it had to say why. If it decided to take into account ability to pay, it should set out its findings about ability to pay, state what impact that had had on its decision whether to award costs or on the amount of costs, and explain why.

12.30 Even if means are taken into account, the Court of Appeal in *Kovacs* quoted with approval the principle set out by the tribunal (at 417):

> It does not appear, on the face of the relevant Regulations, that it was intended that poor litigants may misbehave with impunity and without fearing that any significant costs order will be made against them, whereas wealthy ones must behave themselves because otherwise an order will be made.

12.31 In *Walker v Heathrow Refuelling Services Co Ltd* EAT/0366/04 the EAT had to consider its own power to award costs under r 34B(2) of the EAT (Amendment) Rules 2004 which provides that the Appeal Tribunal may have regard to the paying parties' ability to pay when considering the amount of the costs order. The EAT in that case took into account the fact that the claimant was backed by his union when having regard to his ability to pay.

12.32 A costs order includes the legal costs and the allowances paid by the Secretary of State for witnesses' allowances (r 38(1)) and those fees, charges, disbursements, or expenses incurred by or on behalf of a party in the proceedings. Solicitors', counsels', and experts' fees, letter-writing, conferences, and written advice, travelling time, and hearing time are all within this description. In *Verma v Harrogate NHS Trust* 2009 UKEAT 0155 a costs order was made pursuant to dismissal of a 'hopeless' strike out application made by the respondent. The EAT held that in such circumstances it is perverse to allow recovery of Counsel's fees for attending the pre-hearing review (PHR) and drafting a skeleton argument, whilst excluding recovery of the solicitor's costs of preparation for the PHR and attendance on Counsel at the hearing.

12.33 In an equal value claim, an order for costs may include the costs or expenses incurred by a party in connection with any investigation carried out by an expert preparing his report (r 38(3)).

J. ASSESSMENT

An assessment is the process by which the court or tribunal decides the amount of any costs orders made. An assessment can either be summary or detailed, the former usually an assessment of the costs performed by the tribunal and the latter by a costs officer in the county court or High Court (although wasted costs orders are assessed by the judge making the order). In either case it is advisable for a party to prepare a schedule of costs and, wherever possible, serve it on the paying party so that he can make representations on it. **12.34**

K. COSTS SCHEDULES

There is guidance on the format for a schedule of costs in CPR 43PD, section 4 (and *Health Development Agency v Parish* [2004] IRLR 550 states that regard should be had to CPR principles). Of particular note is para 4.6 which sets out the various headings that can be claimed which include: **12.35**

(a) attendances on the court;
(b) attendances on and communications with the receiving party;
(c) attendances on and communications with witnesses;
(d) communications with the court and counsel;
(e) work done on documents;
(f) work done in connection with negotiations.

The summary should show the total profit costs and disbursements claimed separately from the VAT claimed. **12.36**

L. WITNESS ALLOWANCES

If an order is made for the payment of witness allowances they will usually cover the loss of wages, travel costs, and other expenses incurred by the individual concerned. Section 5(3) of ERA 1996 sets out the fixed scales that are applicable for each head. **12.37**

M. PREPARATION TIME ORDERS

In *Kingston Upon Hull City Council v Dunnachie* (No 3) [2003] IRLR 843, the EAT held that under the 2001 Rules there was no jurisdiction to award costs in favour of a litigant in person The circumstances in which a PTO must now be made and those in which it is discretionary are the same as those relating to orders for costs. In both sets of circumstances the PTO may only be made in favour of a receiving party who has not been legally represented at a hearing or in proceedings determined without a hearing where the party has not been represented when the proceedings are determined. **12.38**

It would appear that employment consultants do not count as legal representatives because of the definition in r 38(5) which covers only those with qualifications within: (a) the meaning of the Courts and Legal Services Act 1990, s 71; (b) advocates and solicitors in Scotland; and (c) solicitors and barristers in Northern Ireland. **12.39**

Preparation time

Preparation time is the time spent: (1) by the receiving party or his employees carrying out preparatory work directly relating to the proceedings, and (2) by the receiving party's legal and other representatives (for example, accountants, human resources consultants) relating to the conduct of the proceedings. In both cases preparation time covers that spent up to the hearing, but not the hearing itself. The time spent by advisers must relate to the conduct of the proceedings so it would not cover any advice given at a stage before proceedings were commenced. **12.40**

12.41 In accordance with r 42(4) PTOs may be made against respondents who have not had their response accepted.

The amount of a preparation time order

12.42 Once it has decided to make a PTO the tribunal has to assess the number of hours spent on preparation. It is directed to do so using information provided by the receiving party and its own assessment of what is a reasonable and proportionate amount of time bearing in mind the complexity of the proceedings, the number of witnesses, and the documentation required. This figure is then applied to an hourly rate (currently £25 and increasing by £1 each year after 6 April 2006) with a maximum of £10,000.

12.43 The tribunal may have regard to the paying party's ability to pay when considering whether to make the order and how much it should be.

N. WASTED COSTS

12.44 Tribunals can now make a wasted costs order against a party's representative. Representatives include legal or other representatives (r 48(2)), but only where an application was presented after 1 October 2004. Wasted costs means any costs incurred by a party as a result of any improper, unreasonable, or negligent act or omission, or any costs incurred by such conduct which the tribunal considers it unreasonable for a party to pay.

12.45 It seems clear that a party may apply for the wasted costs order against his own, or the other side's, representative (see r 48(5)), but it is not so clear as to whether the tribunal may do so of its own motion (compare with the High Court position in *Brown v Bennett* [2002] 2 All ER 73, where the court may proceed of its own motion).

12.46 The tribunal must ask itself three questions:

(1) Has the legal representative acted improperly, unreasonably, or negligently?
(2) Did such conduct cause the party to incur unnecessary costs?
(3) If so, is it unreasonable that the other party should pay those costs?

12.47 The tribunals will draw on the principles in the civil cases of *Ridehalgh v Horsefield* [1994] Ch 205 and *Medcalf v Weatherill* [2002] UKHL 27 (see *Ratcliffe Duce & Gammer v* (1) *L Binns* (*t/a Parc Ferme*) (2) *N McDonald* [2008] UKEAT/0100/08 in which the EAT confirmed this).

12.48 Improper conduct includes that which is very serious under the representative's professional code of conduct (*Medcalf*). Negligent is to be defined in the normal sense of failing to act with reasonable competence but also something akin to abuse of process (see *Persaud (Luke) v Persaud (Mohan)* [2003] EWCA Civ 394 and *Charles v Gillian Radcliffe & Co* 5 November 2003, ChD). Problems of privilege have arisen, for example, where a hopeless case has been pursued. A representative against whom the application is made does not have to waive privilege on advice given (and indeed the client may not allow him to do so). The Court of Appeal has held that it cannot be inferred from those circumstances that the representative has advised the course of action taken. The task for the court is to ask whether or not a reasonably competent legal adviser would have evaluated the chances of success such as to continue with it, but the judge may only come to a conclusion adverse to the party's advisers if he has seen their advice (*Dempsey v Johnstone* [2003] EWCA Civ 1134).

12.49 The order may be one, or a combination, of the following:

(a) the representative pays costs to another party;
(b) the representative pays costs to his own client;
(c) the representative pays any witness allowances of any person who has attended the tribunal by reason of the representative's conduct of the proceedings.

'Representatives' means a party's legal or other representatives and any employee of such representatives (r 48(4)). Excluded from wasted costs orders are representatives who do not act in pursuit of profit—principally law centres and Citizens Advice representatives—although those acting under conditional fee arrangements are deemed to be acting in pursuit of profit. Wasted costs orders against representatives who are the employees of a party may not be made. They can be made in favour of a party regardless of whether he or she is legally represented. **12.50**

When can wasted costs orders be made?

An order does not have to be made at the end of the case but the party's representative should be given the notice in writing of the wasted costs proceedings and any order made. The representative should be given a reasonable opportunity to make oral or written representations as to why the order should not be made. The tribunal may have regard to the representative's ability to pay when considering whether to make an order or the amount. **12.51**

Amount

There is no limit to the amount of a wasted costs order and the order should specify the amount to be paid or disallowed which is decided by the tribunal (as opposed to the county court). The tribunal should give written reasons for any order provided a request for them has been made within 14 days of the date of the order. It is expressly provided that no extension may be made to this time limit under r 10. **12.52**

13

Review

SUMMARY

(1) A tribunal may review its own decision if the decision was made through administrative error, if a party did not receive notice of the hearing or did not attend, if new evidence becomes available which could not reasonably have been put before the tribunal, or if the interests of justice so require.

(2) A party may apply for a review, or the tribunal may review a decision of its own motion.

(3) A tribunal may review a default judgment. The tribunal will consider the reason for default, and whether the respondent has a reasonable prospect of success.

(4) A tribunal may correct administrative errors in a judgment or order under the 'slip rule'.

A. INTRODUCTION

There are a number of ways in which a decision of an employment tribunal may be challenged: **13.01**

(a) an appeal to the Employment Appeal Tribunal (see Chapter 19);
(b) a review of the decision by the employment tribunal under ETR 2004, rr 33–6;
(c) an application under the 'slip rule' (ETR 2004, r 37) for correction of a clerical mistake in any order, judgment, decision, or reasons, or of an error arising in such documents from an accidental slip or omission;
(d) there may be cases in which a tribunal may, in very limited circumstances, recall a decision between promulgating the decision orally and the entry of the decision in the register—see

Hanks v Ace High Productions Ltd [1979] IRLR 32, [1979] ICR 1155, EAT and *Lamont v Fry's Metals Ltd* [1985] IRLR 470, CA. This power is dealt with more fully at para 11.85 *et seq*.;

(e) an interim order may be varied or revoked during the course of proceedings (see ETR 2004, r 10(2)(n) and r 11). In particular an order made without giving the parties opportunity to make representations may be varied or revoked under ETR 2004, r 12(2)(b).

13.02 This chapter is concerned with reviews under rr 33–6 and slip rule corrections under r 37.

13.03 In contrast to an appeal to the EAT, an application for review is heard by the employment tribunal (either by the same or by a different tribunal panel, depending on the circumstances (see para 13.48 below)). A review is likely to be a quicker and cheaper way of changing a decision than an appeal. However, the types of decision which may be reviewed, and the grounds upon which a review may be granted, are limited.

B. DECISIONS WHICH MAY BE REVIEWED

Default judgments

13.04 A judgment in default granted against a party may be reviewed under r 33. Rule 33 sets out a separate scheme for review, both in terms of procedure and grounds to that applicable to other decisions. Rule 33 is considered further at para 13.53 below.

Judgments

13.05 Under r 34, certain types of judgment or order may be reviewed. Rule 34 applies to the following categories of judgment or order:

(a) a decision not to accept a claim, response, or counterclaim;
(b) a judgment (other than a default judgment but including an order for costs, expenses, preparation time, or wasted costs); and
(c) a decision made under r 6(3) of Sch 4 to the 2004 Regulations (Health and Safety Prohibition Notices).

13.06 Rule 34 expressly provides that any decision or order which does not fall within these three categories cannot be reviewed under rr 34–7.

13.07 Rule 28 defines a 'judgment' as:

> a final determination of the proceedings or of a particular issue in those proceedings; it may include an award of compensation, a declaration or recommendation and it may also include orders for costs, preparation time or wasted costs.

Interim orders

13.08 In contrast, the other type of decision provided for by r 28 is an 'order' which may be issued in relation to interim matters and it will require a person to do or not to do something. It follows therefore that an order cannot be reviewed under rr 34–7. Therefore case management decisions, for example orders in relation to further information, disclosure, or witness statements, cannot be reviewed under rr 34–7. That 'orders' or other rulings of the employment tribunal are not reviewable has been confirmed by the EAT in *Hart v English Heritage* [2006] ICR 655. This position is in line with ETR 2001 and previous rules before that (but see the following paragraph for one particular change). Under ETR 2001 only a 'decision' could be reviewed and the definition of 'decision' in reg 2(2) of the 2001 Regulations excluded most interim orders. Under r 2(2) orders striking out an originating application or notice of appearance for failure to comply with orders for particulars, discovery, or written answers, and orders striking out on grounds of frivolous or vexatious conduct or pleadings were all included in the definition of decision, but other interim orders were not. Accordingly the previous case law identifying which decisions and orders were not capable of review under the old rules may remain relevant: see *Peter Simper & Co Ltd v Cooke (No 1)* [1984] ICR 6, EAT and *Casella London Ltd v Banai* [1990] ICR 215, EAT.

The distinction between judgments and orders may create some apparently anomalous situations in relation to reviews. For example, a decision to order a deposit to be paid is not a judgment capable of review, but a decision to strike out a claim on grounds that a deposit has not been paid is a judgment and may be reviewed: see *Sodexho Ltd v Gibbons* [2005] IRLR 836, EAT. Another example of an anomalous situation created by the distinction is demonstrated by *North Tyneside Primary Care Trust v Aynsley & Others* [2009] All ER (D) 125 where the EAT held that an automatic strike-out of a response is not a judgment, and a respondent wishing to challenge the strike out has to rely on r 10(2)(m), whereas a claimant in the same position can rely on r 34; however, see *EPI Coaches Ltd v Lafferty* UKEAT/0065/09/RN decided one month earlier and not referred to in *Aynsley*, where the EAT treated an order striking out a response as amenable to review under r 34. **13.09**

An interim order which is not amenable to review under rr 33–6 may be challenged by an application to vary or revoke on grounds of change of circumstance: see *Goldman Sachs Services Ltd v Mantali* [2002] ICR 1251, EAT, in relation to the position under ETR 2001. In *Onwuka v Spherion Technology UK Ltd* [2005] ICR 567, EAT the EAT considered an application to review a decision of a judge not to permit an amendment to an originating application. It is clear that such a decision cannot be reviewed under r 34, as it is not one of the categories of decision in r 34(1). However, the EAT held that rr 33–7 are not a complete code of cases where a tribunal can review its own decisions. Although r 34(1) says 'Other decisions or orders may not be reviewed under these rules', the EAT interpreted 'under these rules' to mean under rr 34–7, not as meaning under ETR 2004 as a whole. There are wider powers to vary or revoke orders outside the scope of rr 34–7: a judge has the general power to vary or revoke an order under r 10(2)(n), and r 11(1) and r 12(2)(b) each provide for a party to apply to vary or revoke orders. The EAT held that a judge has the power to vary or revoke an earlier case management decision (such as a refusal to grant an amendment). However, the EAT held that it would not ordinarily expect such a power to be exercised in the absence of a material change of circumstances. See also *Kuttapan v London Borough of Croydon* [1999] IRLR 349, EAT and *Nikitas v Metropolitan Borough of Solihull* [1986] ICR 291. **13.10**

C. GROUNDS FOR REVIEW

Summary of grounds

An application for review under rr 34–6 may be brought on the following grounds (r 34(3)): **13.11**

(a) the decision was wrongly made as a result of an administrative error;
(b) a party did not receive notice of the proceedings leading to the decision;
(c) the decision was made in the absence of a party;
(d) new evidence has become available since the conclusion of the hearing to which the decision relates, provided that its existence could not have been reasonably known of or foreseen at that time; or
(e) the interests of justice require such a review.

A decision by the tribunal to reject a claim can only be reviewed on grounds (a) and (e) (r 34(4)). **13.12**

Administrative error

Review on this basis will be unusual as errors on the part of the tribunal's administrative staff would usually be capable of correction under the slip rule (r 37, see para 13.67 below). **13.13**

13.14 An administrative error on the part of a party may constitute grounds for review under r 34(3)(a): for example, an error in giving the address on the claim form, as a result of which the party does not receive an order and therefore fails to comply with the order (see *Sodexho Ltd v Gibbons* [2005] IRLR 836, EAT, paras 34–40).

13.15 The party seeking to obtain a review must show that the decision was wrongly obtained as a result of the error. Minor errors and factual inaccuracies not affecting the outcome of the proceedings would not therefore give rise to a review on this ground.

13.16 In *Butlins Skyline Ltd v Beynon* [2007] ICR 121, EAT, Burke J held that an administrative error, namely an erroneous rejection of a response, amounted to a decision within r 34(1) (a) and was therefore reviewable. He found that 'Although the decision was not one reached by a chairman, it was a decision which had the effect of bringing the part which could be played by the respondents in the proceedings to an end'.

Notice not received

13.17 A party may apply to have a decision reviewed where he did not receive notice of the proceedings. This should be taken to include both a situation where there has been no notice of the claim as a whole (for example where the respondent was never served with the claim form, or any subsequent papers), and a situation where a party does not have notice of a particular hearing.

13.18 In practice this may be a difficult ground to establish where the reason for the failure of notice is that the document has been lost in the post. The notice of hearing may have gone astray but s 7 of the Interpretation Act 1978 deems service by ordinary post to have been effective unless the contrary is proven: *Migwain Ltd v TGWU* [1979] ICR 597; *T & D Transport (Portsmouth) Ltd v Limburn* [1987] ICR 696; *Zietsman (t/a Berkshire Orthodontics) v Stubbington* [2002] ICR 249, EAT; *Gdynia American Shipping Lines (London) Ltd v Chelminski* [2004] EWCA Civ 871, [2004] IRLR 725. ETR 2004 now contain an express provision in similar terms: by r 61(2), any document or notice which may be served by post under the rules is to be deemed to be received by the party to whom it is addressed in the ordinary course of the post, unless the contrary is proved. The party applying for review therefore has the burden of proving that he did not receive the notice. This deeming provision would not of course apply if the reason for lack of notice is that the tribunal failed to send out a notice of hearing, or sent it to the wrong address (though note that service at a company's last known place of business may suffice for the purposes of r 61: see *Zietsman*).

Absence of party

13.19 An absent party must establish a good reason for absence in order to succeed: see, for example, *Morris v Griffiths* [1977] ICR 153.

13.20 Reviews on this ground will only arise where the tribunal has decided, in the face of the absence of a party, to go on to hear and determine the case. The current practice encouraged by the EAT where a party does not attend the hearing is for the tribunal to consider telephoning the party or its advisers to investigate the party's whereabouts, and the reason for absence: *Cooke v Glenrose Fish Company* [2004] IRLR 866, EAT; *London Borough of Southwark v Bartholomew* [2004] ICR 358, EAT. Such steps should reduce the risk of a decision being made which is open to attack on review: if investigations show that a party is absent for good reason, for example ill-health, or failure of service of a notice of a hearing, then the tribunal may postpone the hearing instead of proceeding to determine the case (see also para 9.61 *et seq.*).

13.21 If the tribunal, taking a more stringent approach, decides not to make inquiries of the absent party on the day of the hearing, then if that party later comes forward with a good explanation for absence, a less stringent approach should be taken on an application to review (see *Cooke v Glenrose*, para 21).

There may be situations in which there is doubt about the genuineness of the absent party's explanation. This may be the case either where that explanation is given over the telephone on the morning of the hearing, or if the explanation is first given at a later date. Where, on an application for review, there is a dispute as to the genuineness of the reason for absence, the issue is best resolved by hearing oral evidence from the absent party at the review hearing (*Morris v Griffiths* [1977] ICR 153). **13.22**

New evidence

In the interests of finality of proceedings tribunals are understandably cautious about allowing decisions to be reopened on grounds of new evidence (see also restrictions in the EAT, paras 19.176–19.183 below). The power to review on this ground is therefore constrained by a number of conditions. **13.23**

First, the new evidence must be such that it was not reasonably available or foreseen at the conclusion of the original hearing, see r 34(3)(d). **13.24**

In addition, tribunals follow the approach taken by the Court of Appeal in determining whether to permit fresh evidence on appeal: *Ladd v Marshall* [1954] 1 WLR 1489. Therefore, to be admissible on review or appeal such evidence must satisfy three conditions (see *Wileman v Minilec Engineering Ltd* [1988] IRLR 144; note that the case concerned admission of new evidence on appeal, but the EAT indicated that the same approach should be adopted on appeal and on review (at para 14), cf *Borden (UK) Ltd v Potter* [1986] ICR 647): **13.25**

(1) the evidence could not have been obtained with reasonable diligence for use at the trial (as provided in r 34(3)(d)); and
(2) the evidence must be such that if given it would probably have an important influence on the result of his case, though it need not be decisive; and
(3) the evidence must be apparently credible.

Thus, new evidence which demonstrates that a witness on whose evidence much turned was telling lies is likely to lead to a review, but only if it would make a material difference to the outcome. For examples of decisions on this ground see *Moncrieff (DG) (Farmers) v MacDonald* [1978] IRLR 112; *Ladup v Barnes* [1982] IRLR 7; *Qureshi v Burnley Borough Council* EAT/916/92; and *Burnley Borough Council v Qureshi* EAT/917/92. **13.26**

A party seeking to introduce fresh evidence on a review ought to lodge a statement of the evidence on which he seeks to rely: *Vauxhall Motors Ltd v Henry* (1978) 13 ITR 432; *Drakard (PJ) & Sons Ltd v Wilton* [1977] ICR 642. The party will also need to give an explanation as to why the evidence was not relied on prior to the decision under review. **13.27**

Interests of justice

In *Flint v Eastern Electricity Board* [1975] IRLR 277, the EAT held that the ground of interests of justice is a residual category, intended to confer a wide discretion on the employment tribunals. See also *Caines v Kuang (t/a Red Dragon Garage)* EAT/254/83 and *Redding v EMI Leisure Ltd* EAT/262/81. **13.28**

In *Trimble v Supertravel Ltd* [1982] IRLR 451, the EAT stated that the review procedure should only be available in exceptional circumstances. This approach was adopted over many years; see, for example, *Moncrieff (DG) (Farmers) v MacDonald* [1978] IRLR 112, EAT. In *Williams v Ferrosan* [2004] IRLR 607, however, the EAT doubted the requirement of 'exceptional circumstances' because, first, there is no such requirement in the rule, the language of which ('in the interests of justice') is in broad terms. Secondly, since 2001 the Employment Tribunals Regulations and Rules have contained an overriding objective of dealing with cases justly (2004 Regulations, r 3). This includes dealing with cases expeditiously, fairly, and in ways that save expenses. The need to observe the overriding objective suggests that an 'exceptional circumstances' requirement is inappropriate. **13.29**

13.30 In an appropriate case it may be in the interests of the overriding objective to review a case rather than pursue the slower and more expensive route of an appeal. The more flexible approach in *Williams v Ferrosan* was followed and endorsed by the EAT in *Sodexho Ltd v Gibbons* [2005] IRLR 836, EAT. Indeed, in *D&H Travel Ltd v Foster* [2006] 2 ICR 1537, EAT, the EAT held it would have been proportionate and in accordance with the overriding objective to have granted a review and allowed the respondents to participate in a Remedies Hearing. The EAT found that a judge had wrongly assumed that unless he set aside a default judgment which had been specifically limited to liability, the respondents could play no part at the Remedies Hearing. The EAT found that the respondent should have been treated as making an application to permit the late submission of a response, saying 'After all, the essence of a review of a default judgment is that the Tribunal is being asked to accept a response out of time'. Thus, the judge's refusal at the Remedies Hearing to allow the respondent to submit a response was a decision made at a hearing and open to review. Further, the EAT found that the fact that the senior manager of the respondent attended the Remedies Hearing and sought to put his case was an oral application for a review of that decision under r 35(2) on the grounds of interests of justice.

13.31 A review on grounds of the interests of justice may also be an appropriate way of a party seeking relief from the consequences of his failure to comply with a rule or order. It may be appropriate to review on this ground where a claim form has been rejected due to an immaterial or otherwise explicable error by the party in completing the claim form: *Richardson v U Mole Ltd* [2005] IRLR 668, EAT. Similarly, a review on the grounds of interests of justice may be appropriate where a claim has been struck out for non-compliance with an order of the tribunal. In dealing with such an application for review, the judge may have regard to the factors listed in CPR 3.9, however, he is not under a positive duty to do so (*The Governing Body of St Albans Girls' School v Neary* [2009] EWCA Civ 1190). These factors are as follows: (a) the interests of the administration of justice; (b) whether the application for relief has been made promptly; (c) whether the failure to comply was intentional; (d) whether there is a good explanation for the failure; (e) the extent to which the party in default has complied with other rules, practice directions, court orders, and any other relevant pre-action protocol; (f) whether the failure to comply was caused by the party or his legal representative; (g) whether the trial date or the likely date can still be met if relief is granted; (h) the effect which the failure to comply had on each party; and (i) the effect which the granting of relief would have on each party.

Error of law

13.32 Applications for a review in the interests of justice may involve complaints of errors of law, which raises an issue as to when it is appropriate to review, and when it is appropriate to appeal.

13.33 Whilst in the normal case an error of law on the face of the tribunal's decision should be challenged by way of appeal, it is not appropriate for a tribunal to refuse to review a decision simply because the review involved consideration of an error of law: *Trimble v Supertravel Ltd* [1982] IRLR 451. In *British Midland Airways Ltd v Lewis* [1978] ICR 782, the EAT said that review is appropriate when the tribunal makes a mistake and soon realizes the error. That is the case even if the mistake results in an error of law. In *Trimble*, the true distinction perceived by the EAT between appeal and review was not between minor and major errors of law, but whether or not a decision alleged to be erroneous in law has been reached after there has been a procedural mishap ([1982] IRLR 451, 453):

> If the matter has been ventilated and properly argued, then errors of law of that kind fall to be corrected by this appeal tribunal. If, on the other hand, due to an oversight or to some procedural occurrence one or other party can with substance say that he had not had a fair opportunity to present his argument on a point of substance, then that is a procedural shortcoming in the proceedings before the tribunal which in our view can be correctly dealt with by a review . . . however difficult the point of law or fact may be. In essence, the review procedure enables errors occurring in the course of the proceedings to be corrected but would not normally be appropriate when the

proceedings had given both parties a fair opportunity to present their case and the decision had been reached in the light of all relevant argument.

This distinction, whilst still helpful, should not be seen as a hard and fast rule: *Williams v Ferrosan* [2004] IRLR 607, EAT, makes clear that the power under r 34(3)(e) is a broad one to be exercised in the interests of justice and in accordance with the overriding objective. **13.34**

Procedural mishaps

Applications for review on this ground have been successful where a procedural mishap occurred which deprived a party of a fair opportunity to present his case. For example, in *Trimble v Supertravel Ltd* [1982] IRLR 451, the party applying for a review was denied the opportunity to address the tribunal on the question of mitigation of loss. In *Harber v North London Polytechnic* [1990] IRLR 190, a claimant's representative withdrew a claim on the basis of a mistaken belief that the claimant did not meet the jurisdictional requirements for the claim. Whilst that was a mistake on the part of the representative, it was brought about in part by the respondent's failures during disclosure, and in part by a misapplication of the law by the employment judge. The Court of Appeal held that a review was in the interests of justice. **13.35**

Where there is simply failure on the part of a party's representative, an application for a review will be unlikely to succeed. In *Ironside Ray & Vials v Lindsay* [1994] IRLR 318, Mummery J said that to permit a review on grounds of the inadequacy of a representative's presentation of a case was 'a dangerous path to follow'. He stated that it involved the risk of encouraging a disappointed claimant to seek to reargue his case by blaming his representative for the failure of his claim. That may involve the tribunal in inappropriate investigations into the competence of the representative. Similarly, in *Dhedhi v United Lincolnshire Hospitals NHS Trust* [2003] All ER (D) 366, the EAT observed that in the absence of a procedural shortcoming, a decision should not be reviewed simply because a party's representative had made inadequate submissions. **13.36**

In *Williams v Ferrosan* [2004] IRLR 607, EAT, the parties had not been denied an opportunity to present their case. An error arose in the decision because both the parties and the tribunal proceeded on a mistaken belief as to the incidence of taxation on an award of compensation for loss of future earnings in a discrimination claim. The EAT held that a review should have been allowed: although it did not fall within the procedural mishap category, there was an error in the decision which had resulted from the mistake of the parties and the judge. Whilst the decision could have been challenged by way of an appeal, it was in accordance with the overriding objective to follow the quicker and cheaper route of a review. **13.37**

New evidence

A number of the cases on this ground concern attempts to rely on new evidence which would not fall within r 34(3)(d), usually because the new evidence was, or should have been, available at the hearing. In such cases, r 34(3)(e) ought not to be used to 'outflank' the requirements of r 34(3)(d). A review could not be granted simply because of the importance of the case. A review in the interests of justice could in these circumstances only arise by reason of some circumstance or mitigating factor relating to the failure to bring the evidence sought now to be adduced: *General Council of British Shipping v Deria* [1985] ICR 198. Failure on the part of the party's representative to identify or rely on relevant evidence is unlikely to amount to such a circumstance: see, for example, *Stanley Cole (Wainfleet) Ltd v Sheridan* [2003] IRLR 885, [2003] EWCA Civ 1046. **13.38**

Subsequent events

Subsequent events can include a change in the law (*Griffin v City & Islington College* UKEAT/0459/06). A review was also held not to be appropriate on the basis that the tribunal had underestimated the amount of time a claimant would be out of work for the compensatory award (see *Brennan and Ging v Elward (Lancs) Ltd* [1976] IRLR 378). However, where the employee gets another job after the hearing at a much higher rate of pay, a review may be appropriate (see *Yorkshire Engineering v Burnham* [1973] IRLR 316 and *Help the Aged v Vidler* [1977] IRLR 104). **13.39**

D. PROCEDURE FOR REVIEW

The application

13.40 A party may apply for a review, or the tribunal may review a decision on its own initiative (r 34(5)). A party who has been debarred from taking part in the tribunal's proceedings under r 9 is entitled to apply for a review but on limited grounds (see r 9(b)). Where the decision or judgment of a tribunal is reviewable but could also be appealed to the EAT, it is highly desirable that the review option is taken. A review is 'speedier, less cumbersome and in all probability less expensive than an appeal' (see *Butlins Skyline, Smith v Beynon* [2007] ICR 121, EAT).

Application by a party

13.41 The application for a review must be made within 14 days of the date the decision was sent to the parties (r 35(1)). The application may be made at the hearing where the decision is pronounced (r 35(2)). A judge may extend the time limit if it is just and equitable to do so (r 35(1)). Where a party who has been debarred from taking part in the proceedings under r 9 applies for a review, that party is entitled to seek reasons from an employment tribunal pursuant to r 30 for the purpose of making that application (*NSM Music Ltd v JH Leefe* [2006] ICR 450).

13.42 The application should be in writing (unless the decision was made at a hearing, and the application is made at that hearing). The application must identify the ground(s) that r 34(3) relied on. Whilst the rule may strictly be complied with by identifying the relevant paragraph number of r 34(3), the application should set out the detailed grounds for contending that the decision challenged was wrong, along with the reasons for the request for a review: *Drakard (PJ) & Sons Ltd v Wilton* [1977] ICR 642. On the other hand, an application will not be defective if it does not refer to the relevant paragraph of r 34(3), provided that the application sets out material from which it can be discerned what grounds are relied on: *Sodexho Ltd v Gibbons* [2005] IRLR 836, EAT, paras 32–3. It is of course open to the other party to seek further particulars of the grounds of review (*Sodexho*, para 33).

13.43 More than one application for review may be made in the exceptional circumstances that the interests of justice so require, although it is unclear whether the grounds can be the same or must be different for each application (see *Raybright TV Services Ltd v Smith* [1973] ICR 640 and *Stevensons (Dyers) Ltd v Brennan* [1974] ICR 194).

Review by the tribunal on its own initiative

13.44 Where no application has been made by a party, but the decision is being reviewed on the initiative of the tribunal:

(a) The tribunal must send each party a notice explaining in summary the grounds upon which it is proposed to review the judgment and giving an opportunity to give reasons why there should be no review. The notice must be sent before the expiry of 14 days from the date on which the original judgment was sent to the parties (r 36(2)).
(b) The review will not be subjected to the preliminary consideration procedure under r 35(3). There is a distinction in the drafting of the rules between an application by a party for review, and a review at the initiative of the tribunal. It would, of course, make no practical sense for a tribunal to decide to review a claim of its own initiative if the tribunal considered there were no grounds for review or the review has no reasonable prospect of success.

Preliminary consideration

13.45 The first stage of the process of review is that the application will be considered by a judge, without the need for a hearing (r 35(3)). The application for a review will be refused if the judge considers that:

(a) there are no grounds to review under r 34(3); or
(b) there is no reasonable prospect of the decision being varied or revoked.

The preliminary consideration will be carried out by a judge alone, even if the decision was made by a full tribunal. The preliminary consideration should be by the judge who made the decision, unless it is not practicable to do so, in which case the preliminary consideration may be by the Regional Chairman, Vice-President, or President or by another judge nominated by the Regional Chairman or Vice-President. 13.46

If the review is refused at this stage, the judge must give written reasons for the decision to the party applying for the review. 13.47

The hearing

The review itself should be heard by the original judge or tribunal which made the decision. There is a distinction between reviews on an application by a party, and reviews of the tribunal's initiative: 13.48

(a) Where a party has applied for a review, if it is not practicable for the original tribunal to carry out the review, a different judge or tribunal may be appointed by the Regional Chairman or Vice-President.
(b) Where the tribunal conducts a review of its own motion, the original judge or tribunal *must* carry out the review.

A review should not be heard in the absence of a party (*Ali v Nilgar Fashions Ltd* (1978) 13 ITR 443). A tribunal cannot make the granting of a review conditional upon costs being paid by a party (*Lawton v British Railways Board* EAT/29/80). 13.49

A tribunal or judge who reviews a decision may confirm, vary, or revoke the decision. If the decision is revoked, the tribunal or judge must order the decision to be taken again. When an order is made that the original decision be taken again, if the original decision was taken by a judge without a hearing, the new decision may be taken without hearing the parties and if the original decision was taken at a hearing, a new hearing must be held. 13.50

Reviews and pending appeals to the Employment Appeal Tribunal

It may be that an appeal is pending at the time of the review application, but this is no bar to the review proceedings, unless the employment judge considers it undesirable, in which case he should contact the registrar of the EAT on the appropriate course to adopt (see *Blackpole Furniture v Sullivan* [1978] ICR 558). 13.51

The EAT Practice Direction 2004 now requires an appellant to include with his notice of appeal a copy of any application for a review, together with either the decision on the review or a statement that it is still pending. The EAT will itself therefore be aware, before any case management of an appeal, if a review is pending before the tribunal. 13.52

E. REVIEW OF DEFAULT JUDGMENTS

ETR 2004, r 33 contains a separate procedure for review of default judgments. Under r 8 of ETR 2004 a default judgment may be entered by a judge without a hearing where a respondent fails to present an ET3 in time, or the response is not accepted under r 6, or if a respondent has indicated that he does not intend to resist the claim. Where a default judgment has been entered against a party, he may apply for a review under r 33. 13.53

Time limit

The time limit for an application under r 33 is 14 days from the date on which the default judgment was sent to the parties. The time limit may be extended by a judge if he feels it just and equitable to do so (r 33(1)). 13.54

The application

13.55 The application must be made in writing and must state the reasons why the default judgment should be varied or revoked. In absence of a written application, the employment tribunal will be unable to hear an application for review. The tribunal has no power to dispense with the requirement of a written application (*Direct Timber Ltd v Hayward* UKEAT/0646/05). A respondent applying to vary or review must include a draft response to the ET1, an application for extension of time to present the ET3, and an explanation why the ET3 was not presented in time. An employment judge may refuse the application without a hearing if these requirements are not met (r 33(2A), as amended).

Hearing

13.56 The application for review is to be conducted by a judge at a hearing in public unless all the parties consent to a review without a hearing. All other parties must be served with notice of the hearing and with a copy of the application (r 33(3)).

The judge's powers on review

13.57 The judge may refuse the application for review, vary the judgment, revoke the judgment, or confirm the judgment (r 33(4)). If the default judgment is revoked then the respondent's response (which should have been attached to the application for review) is accepted and the case will then proceed in the normal way (r 33(7)).

Grounds for review

13.58 There are two mandatory grounds to set aside a default judgment (r 33(5)):

(1) If the whole of the claim was satisfied before the judgment was issued.
(2) If the claim is settled (either by a compromise agreement or through ACAS) before the default judgment is entered. In these circumstances the default judgment has no effect, and if a party applies for review the judge must revoke the judgment (see also r 8(6)–(7)).

13.59 Apart from these mandatory grounds, the power to revoke a default judgment is discretionary. There are two factors expressly referred to in the rule itself:

(a) The judge may vary or revoke all or part of the judgment if the respondent has a reasonable prospect of success (r 33(5)).
(b) In considering the application for review the judge must have regard to whether there was a good reason for the response not having been presented within the applicable time limit (r 33(6)).

13.60 Where the judge has a discretion whether to revoke a judgment, two points of ambiguity in the rules have now been answered in a series of judgments delivered in the EAT. Those points were:

(1) whether, the existence of a reasonable prospect of success is a necessary condition, or whether the judge has wider discretion, to revoke the judgment;
(2) whether the mandatory consideration (reason for failure) is the only relevant consideration, or whether the judge, in exercising his discretion, may consider a wider range of matters.

13.61 As to the first of these points, the EAT held in *The Pestle & Mortar v Turner* UKEAT/ 0652/05 that a judge only has a discretion to review a default judgment in circumstances where a respondent has a reasonable prospect of successfully defending the claim. Having a reasonable prospect of success is the 'gateway to the discretion'. As such, it would appear that there is no jurisdiction for an employment tribunal to review a default judgment in circumstances where there is some other reason why the respondent ought to be permitted to defend proceedings. In this respect, r 33 differs from the equivalent provision in CPR 13 which gives a broader discretion to a judge to set aside judgment in default of defence in the civil courts.

As to the factors relevant to the judge's discretion, it is suggested that while r 33(6) is mandatory it is not exhaustive. The judge has a discretion as to whether to set aside, and provided the judge has regard to the mandatory factor (reason for failure: r 33(6)), and otherwise exercises the discretion judicially, it is open to the judge to consider a range of other factors in deciding whether to set aside the default judgment. **13.62**

This is the approach that has been adopted by the EAT: Burton P in *Moroak (t/a Blake Envelopes) v Cromie* [2005] IRLR 353 and in *Pendragon plc (t/a CD Bramall Bradford) v Copus* [2005] ICR 1671, EAT said that the basis for the discretion to review a judgment in default should be the same as an application for an extension of time for filing a response under r 4(4) (whether the extension is just and equitable), save that r 33 contains the additional express requirement for reasonable merits to be shown. The discretionary factors set out in *Kwik Save Stores Ltd v Swain* [1997] ICR 49, EAT, *per* Mummery P should apply, that is to say the tribunal should take account of all relevant factors including: **13.63**

(a) the explanation for the non-compliance;
(b) the merits of the defence;
(c) the balance of possible prejudice to each party.

That the 'explanation for the non-compliance' is a factor specifically mentioned in r 33(6) does not mean that that consideration should be given more weight than the other considerations. Indeed, it is necessary to weigh the balance of prejudice to each of the parties in every case (*The Pestle and Mortar v Turner* UKEAT/0652/05). **13.64**

It may be useful to look at the grounds for setting aside judgment in default of defence under the CPR in determining other factors which might be relevant to the exercise of a judge's discretion to set aside judgment in default. In considering whether to set aside or vary a judgment entered under CPR Part 12, the matters to which the court must have regard include whether the person seeking to set aside the judgment made an application to do so promptly (CPR r 13.3(2)). **13.65**

Cases where a default judgment has not been entered

Where a respondent fails to present a response to a claim form within the relevant time limit, the tribunal may enter judgment in default (under r 8) or it may refuse to accept a late response under r 6 without making a default judgment. The judge has a discretion whether to enter a default judgment. A decision refusing to accept a response cannot be reviewed under r 33, which applies only to default judgments. Further, the respondent cannot make an application to extend time for the response after the time limit has expired (r 4(4)). However, the respondent can apply for a r 34 review of the refusal to accept the response, on the grounds that the interests of justice require such a review: *Moroak (t/a Blake Envelopes) v Cromie* [2005] IRLR 353, EAT. Burton P saw no reason why a review of a refusal to accept a response should be limited to the content of the response, as opposed to the timing. On such a review, the tribunal has a just and equitable discretion to extend time for the response, to be exercised on the same grounds as a review under r 33 (see also *Pendragon plc (t/a CD Bramall Bradford) v Copus* [2005] ICR 1671, EAT). **13.66**

F. CORRECTIONS UNDER THE SLIP RULE

Clerical mistakes in any order, judgment decision, or reasons, or errors arising from an accidental slip or omission may be corrected by the judge (or by the Regional Chairman, Vice-President, or President) (r 37(1)). **13.67**

The Civil Procedure Rules 1998 contain a similar power to correct an accidental slip or omission: see CPR r 40.12. ETR 2004, r 37 should be interpreted consistently with the equivalent CPR provision. The rule should only be used to correct genuine slips or omissions, and should not be used to alter the substance of the court or tribunal's decision, *Markos v Goodfellow* [2002] EWCA Civ 1542. If the need for correction is such that the tribunal in fact issues what amounts **13.68** to a fresh judgment, this may amount to a review by the tribunal on its own initiative under r 34(5) (see *Aziz-Mir v Sainsbury's Supermarket plc* UKEATPA/0537/06/JOJ). The slip rule should not be used to allow the tribunal to have second thoughts, or for the parties to seek to persuade the tribunal to do so. Whilst the tribunal may not change the substance of a decision under the slip rule, the slip rule may be used to alter a judgment or order to give clear meaning and effect to the tribunal's intention: *Bristol-Myers Squibb v Baker Norton Pharmaceuticals Inc* [2001] EWCA Civ 414; *Foenander v Foenander* [2004] EWCA Civ 1675. The slip rule should not be used by a tribunal to add a fresh finding on an important matter of substance to their decision: *Bone v London Borough of Newham* [2008] IRLR 546. The unusual circumstances of that case were that the tribunal made a finding of unfair dismissal, but omitted to record a decision that the dismissal had also been an act of sex discrimination and victimization. The tribunal had intended so to find, and purported to correct its decision under the slip rule. The Court of Appeal held that this was an inappropriate use of the slip rule, and allowed an appeal against the tribunal's order under r 37. However, in order for the tribunal to be able to reach the decision it had apparently intended to reach, the case was remitted to the tribunal under the *Burns/Barke* procedure (see *Barke v Seetec Business Technology Centre Ltd* [2005] IRLR 633, CA) with a direction that the tribunal should formally announce and give in writing its reasons for concluding that the constructive dismissal was an act of direct sex discrimination and victimization. Whilst the decision in *Bone* achieves justice on the unusual facts of the case, it is open to question whether the use of the *Burns/Barke* procedure was appropriate: the tribunal was not being asked to supplement its reasons for a judgment already made, but to make a fresh finding which had not formed part of its original judgment.

13.69 The correction is made by a certificate (r 37(1)), which will be sent to the parties, and any entry on the register will be altered so as to conform with the certificate (r 37(2)). A certificate of correction should not purport to delete the entirety of the reasons and substitute corrected reasons as this may amount to a fresh judgment. Further, the tribunal should make it clear that the original promulgation date of the judgment still stands (see *Aziz-Mir v Sainsbury's Supermarket plc* UKEATPA/0537/06/JOJ).

13.70 Where a party applies under r 37, and the interests of another party to the proceedings might be affected, the tribunal must give the other party the opportunity to make representations concerning the application: *Times Newspapers Ltd v Fitt* [1981] ICR 637, EAT.

14

Enforcement of Tribunal Awards

SUMMARY

(1) Tribunals cannot enforce their own awards.

(2) Awards for money can be enforced against the respondent in the county court.

(3) The Tribunals, Courts and Enforcement Act 2007, which will deal with the enforcement of tribunal awards in the future, received Royal Assent on 19 July 2007. Aspects of the new Act are already in force but much remains to be brought into force as at the date of the preparation of this edition.

A. INTRODUCTION

It is a curious feature of the system that the tribunals do not have their own power of enforcement. Instead, the machinery of the county court is used (ETA 1996, s 15(1), (2)) in respect of any sum payable in pursuance of a decision of an employment tribunal in England and Wales which has been registered in accordance with the regulations. Two important things must be noticed about this formulation: **14.01**

(a) The county court has no power to enforce orders or agreements other than for the payment of money, for example reinstatement orders or agreements to provide a reference to the county court, even in respect of the monetary aspects of a reinstatement order (*O'Laiore v Jackel International Ltd* [1990] ICR 97, [1990] IRLR 70, CA).
(b) The order cannot be enforced against anyone other than the respondent mentioned in the order of the employment tribunal (*Stow v John Bell* 29 July 1985, Aldershot County Court).

An applicant can apply to the county court even though the respondent has appealed (*Zabaxe v Nicklin* The Times, 30 October 1990) although usually enforcement will be stayed pending the outcome of the appeal. **14.02**

From 1 April, 2009, any legal person who has an employment tribunal judgment registered against them by the County Court will have their name entered in the Register of Judgments, Orders and Fines (see the Register of Judgments, Orders and Fines Regulations 2005, SI 2005/3595). The register is available for inspection by members of the public as well as institutions wishing to consider the creditworthiness of such persons for the purpose of extending credit to them. **14.03**

B. METHODS OF ENFORCEMENT

14.04 Enforcement may take effect by:

(a) a warrant of execution (or warrant of control as this will become when s 69 of the Tribunals, Courts and Enforcement Act 2007 is brought into force);
(b) a third party debt order;
(c) a charging order, stop order, or stop notice;
(d) in the county court, an attachment of earnings order;
(e) by the appointment of a receiver.

Rule 70.5 of CPR applies to any enforcement procedures. The CPR procedures apply to monetary awards, including costs, but not to ACAS arbitration awards.

C. FORM OF APPLICATION

14.05 The successful party seeking to enforce the judgment may present an application to the county court, together with a copy of the award. This should be done in the district in which the defaulting party resides or carries on business.

14.06 The application may be heard and determined by any 'proper officer' and the order on the application must be in form N322A of the county court forms. Fixed costs apply (CPR r 45.6). If interest is being claimed, details of the interest must also be included (CPR r 70.5 and CPR PD70).

14.07 Where an employee has been awarded compensation by an employment tribunal and that money has been paid into the county court on the taking of enforcement proceedings, the money should remain in court if a High Court action is pending in respect of an employer's claim for a larger amount (*Schofield v Church Army* [1986] 2 All ER 715, CA).

D. ENFORCEMENT IN THE CASE OF DEATH

14.08 On the death of an employee in cases concerning unfair dismissal, redundancy, and other individual employment rights, under ERA 1996 proceedings may be instituted or continued by a personal representative of the deceased employee, or, where there is no personal representative, by a person appointed by the tribunal (ERA 1996, s 206). Further, rights accruing under ERA 1996 after the death of the employee devolve to the deceased's estate as if they had accrued before death. In such cases an award made in favour of a deceased employee may be enforced on behalf of his estate by his personal representatives or any such person appointed by the tribunal (Employment Tribunals Awards (Enforcement in Cases of Death) Regulations 1976, SI 1976/663, regs 5 and 6). Although there are no provisions equivalent to s 206 in the discrimination legislation, a claim under RRA 1976 can be instituted or continued after the death of the complainant by the personal representatives of his estate pursuant to s 1(1) of the Law Reform (Miscellaneous Provisions) Act 1934 (*Harris* (*Personal Representatives of Andrews* (*deceased*)) *v Lewisham and Guys Mental Health NHS Trust* [2000] ICR 1170, [2000] IRLR 320; *Executors of the Estate of Gary Soutar, Deceased v* (1) *James Murray and Co* (*Cupar*) *Ltd*, (2) *Scottish Provident Institution* [2000] IRLR 22). The reasoning applies similarly to other discrimination claims.

E. INSOLVENT EMPLOYER

14.09 Certain sums may be recovered from the National Insurance Fund. The applicant must submit a written application to the Department for Business, Innovation and Skills who must be satisfied that:

(a) the employer is insolvent within the statutory definition in s 183 of ERA 1996;
(b) the employment of the employee has been terminated;

(c) the debt is capable of being claimed under s 184;
(d) the debt was due on the appropriate date as defined in s 185.

Debts in respect of which claims can be made are as follows (ERA 1996, s 184): **14.10**

(a) arrears of pay in respect of one or more but not more than eight weeks;
(b) any amount which the employer is liable to pay for statutory minimum notice, or for failure to give such notice;
(c) holiday pay in respect of holiday not exceeding six weeks to which the employee became entitled during the months ending with the appropriate date;
(d) basic award for unfair dismissal;
(e) any reasonable sum by way of reimbursement of the whole or part of any fee or premium paid by an apprentice or articled clerk.

The amount payable is capped to a maximum amount in respect of any one week, currently £350 (in line with the maximum week's pay for redundancy pay and basic award calculations). If the Department for Business, Innovation and Skills does not pay the debt, or pays less than that claimed, an applicant can present a complaint to an employment tribunal (ERA 1996, s 188) within three months of the Department for Business, Innovation and Skills' decision (the tribunal has a discretion to extend the time if it was not reasonably practicable to comply). **14.11**

15

Equal Pay Procedure

SUMMARY

Tribunals have a number of special jurisdictions with slightly different procedures. One such jurisdiction has regard to claims for equal pay.

A. EQUAL PAY CLAIMS

The Equal Pay Act 1970 (EqPA 1970) enables women or men to bring claims in the tribunal where they are paid less or their contract is detrimental in any other way when compared with an employee of the opposite sex doing work of equal value. If the claim is upheld the tribunal will make a declaration that the claimant's contract contains an equality clause, so that the term or terms of the contract which are less favourable are modified so as not to be less favourable, or the contract is treated as including the beneficial term or terms which the comparator's contract contains. Claimants may also in certain circumstances rely directly on Article 141 (formerly 119) of the EC Treaty and/or the Equal Pay Directive (Council Directive 75/117/EEC [1975] OJ L45/19)—see Chapter 32. **15.01**

The claimant is free to choose his or her comparator, but it must be someone employed by his or her employer or any associated employer at the same establishment or at establishments in Great Britain which include that one and at which common terms and conditions of employment are observed (EqPA 1970, s 1(6)). Where the claimant relies on Article 141, the terms and conditions of his or her contract and that of the comparator must derive from a single source (*Lawrence v Regent Office Care Limited* [2003] ICR 1092; *Allonby v Accrington and Rossendale College* [2004] IRLR 224; *Robertson v Department for Environment, Food and Rural Affairs* [2005] EWCA Civ 138) or be in the same service. The concept of comparator has been given a wider meaning than the EqPA 1970 under Article 141 EU Treaty. The comparator does not need to have been employed at the same time in the sense that a complainant can rely on a predecessor as a comparator: see *McCarthys Ltd v Smith* [1980] ICR 672. However, it appears in the light of the decision of the EAT in *Walton Centre for Neurology v Bewley* [2008] IRLR 588 that a complainant may not rely on a successor as a comparator either as a matter of domestic law or as a matter of European law. **15.02**

When comparing the claimant's work to that of the comparator, there are three 'gateways' to a claim under the EqPA 1970: **15.03**

(1) The claimant claims to be employed on *like work* with the comparator—'like work' is defined in s 1(4) of EqPA 1970 as work 'of a same or broadly similar nature', where the differences (if any) between the things the claimant does and the things the comparator does

'are not of practical importance in relation to terms and conditions of employment' (see *Eaton Limited v Nuttall* [1977] IRLR 71 and *Thomas v National Coal Board* [1987] ICR 757).

(2) The claimant claims to be employed on *work rated as equivalent* or work rated as being of a higher value (see *Redcar & Cleveland Borough Council v Bainbridge* [2007] IRLR 984) to that of the comparator. The work will only be regarded as rated as equivalent if the two jobs have been given an equal value in terms of the demands made on a worker under various headings (for instance effort, skill, decision) on a job evaluation study, or would have been given an equal value but for the evaluation giving different values for men and women on the same demand under any heading (EqPA 1970, s 1(5) and see *Springboard Sunderland Trust v Robson* [1992] ICR 554 and *Redcar & Cleveland Borough Council v Bainbridge (No 2)* [2007] IRLR 984).

(3) The claimant claims to be employed on work which is in terms of the demands made on him or her of *equal value* or a higher value (see *Murphy v An Bord Telecom Eireann* [1988] ECR 673) to that of the comparator. This type of claim can only be brought if the claimant's case does not fall within the first two categories.

Procedure

Starting a claim

15.04 Equal pay claims are started in the normal manner by submitting an ET1 claim form. Two or more claimants may present their claims on the same form if they arise out of the same or similar facts and very frequently there are hundreds of claims combined together. This can be particularly useful in equal pay cases, where there are likely to be numerous claimants in the same position (ETR 2004, r 1(7)) and multiple claim forms can be submitted online for up to 50 claimants. Where there are multiple claimants the parties may agree that lead claimants be identified. These should be as representative as possible of all the issues to be determined by the tribunal in the particular series of cases.

15.05 The time limit for bringing a claim is usually six months from the last date of employment. The relevant consideration is neither the end of the job nor the employee leaving the employer but the end of the contract in respect of which the equality clause has been breached. *National Power v Young* [2001] IRLR 32 is authority for the proposition that time does not run from the end of a particular job, the tribunal having found (or proceeded on the assumption) that the claimant was employed under the same contract throughout each job change. Where a TUPE transfer takes place, it appears that time may run on a claim for equal pay from the date of the TUPE transfer since although TUPE preserves rights and continuity of service, for the purposes of the EqPA 1970, the relevant employment has ended. The scope of the principle is, however, unclear: see *Powerhouse Retail v Burroughs* [2006] IRLR 381; *Unison v Allen* [2007] IRLR 975; and *Sodexo Ltd v Gutridge* [2009] IRLR 721. The tribunal has no discretion to extend the time limit, but s 2ZA of the EqPA 1970 provides for some modifications to the time limit in specified circumstances:

(1) A concealment case, in which the employer deliberately concealed from the claimant any fact which is relevant to the proceedings and without which he or she could not reasonably have been expected to institute proceedings: the time limit is six months from the day on which the claimant discovered the fact (or could with reasonable diligence have discovered it).

(2) A disability case, in which the claimant is 'under a disability' (ie a minor or of unsound mind) at any time during the six months after the last date of employment: the time limit is six months from the day on which the claimant ceased to be under a disability.

(3) A stable employment case, in which the proceedings related to a period during which a stable employment relationship subsisted between the claimant and the employer, notwithstanding that the period includes any time after the ending of a contract of employment when no further contract of employment is in force: the time limit is six months from the date on which the stable employment relationship ended (see *Preston v Wolverhampton*

Healthcare NHS Trust [2004] IRLR 96 and *Slack v Cumbria County Council* [2009] IRLR 463).

(4) A standard case, which is a case not falling within any of the other categories: the time limit is six months from the last date of employment.

Claims brought between 1 October 2004 and 5 April 2009 required an employee to raise a statutory grievance before commencing the claim: see EA 2002, s 32 and *Suffolk Mental Health Partnership NHS Trust v Hurst* [2009] IRLR 12. However, from 6 April 2009 EA 2002, s 32 has been repealed. Transitional provisions state that where the facts giving rise to a claim began before 6 April 2009 and continued after that date and a grievance or a claim is brought on or before 4 October 2009, then EA 2002, s 32 will continue to apply. Otherwise, the requirement to raise a grievance will no longer apply. **15.06**

Questionnaires

Section 7B of EqPA 1970 entitles claimants or potential claimants to request information from their employer by serving a statutory questionnaire pursuant to the Equal Pay (Questions and Replies) Order 2003, SI 2003/722. The questionnaire may be served at any time before the claim form is presented or within 21 days of the claim form being presented. The tribunal may on application allow a longer period for service of a questionnaire. Article 5 of the 2003 Order provides that the employer must reply to the questionnaire within eight weeks, but the tribunal has no power to order a party to serve a reply. If the tribunal decides that a respondent has deliberately and without reasonable excuse omitted to reply to questions from a claimant within eight weeks, or that replies given are evasive or equivocal, the tribunal may draw any inference that it considers just and equitable to draw, including the inference that the respondent has contravened a term modified or included by an equality clause. See also para 32.09. **15.07**

Equal value claims

While like work and work rated as equivalent claims are dealt with under the ordinary tribunal rules, equal value claims are subject to a special procedure because of the particular evidential difficulties in comparing the value of two jobs which may be entirely different. An equal value claim is commenced in the ordinary manner, but the determination of the question of equal value is subject to the Equal Value Rules (see below), which facilitate the commissioning of a report from an independent expert (IE), if the tribunal considers it to be necessary in the particular case(s). ACAS maintains a list of IEs for this purpose and designates an IE to a case when the tribunal directs that one is to be appointed. **15.08**

The Employment Tribunals (Equal Value) Rules of Procedure (EV Rules) are contained in Sch 6 to the 2004 Regulations. They modify and supplement the general tribunal rules in certain respects, and are designed to be operated only by judges who specialize in equal pay cases (see 2004 Regulations, reg 8(5)). The EV Rules take effect subject to the Tribunal's general case management powers and that, therefore, a Tribunal may decide to conduct an equal value case in a manner other than as suggested by the EV Rules: *JD Baldwin v Haberdashers Monmouth School for Girls* (unreported EAT, 15 November 2007). **15.09**

The overall aim of the EV Rules is to reduce the excessive delays which have become customary in equal value cases. The Annex to the EV Rules sets out an 'indicative timetable' of 25 weeks for cases not involving an IE and 37 weeks for those involving an IE. This timetable, however, applies only to the period from presentation of the claim form to determination of the question of equal value, and therefore resolution of a whole claim may take significantly longer if the claim is brought on alternative bases and/or the respondent seeks to rely on a genuine material factor defence. It is noteworthy that the timetable is only indicative. The very large series of cases involving local authorities and the NHS largely located in the North East in the mid 2000s has suggested that it is difficult to fulfil the timetable in practice where very large claims are brought raising a wide variety of issues. **15.10**

Stage 1 equal value hearing

15.11 If there is a dispute as to whether the work is of equal value, the tribunal must convene a stage 1 equal value hearing. From 6 April 2009, an employment judge sitting alone may hear a stage 1 hearing. The following steps must be taken at the stage 1 hearing (EV Rules, r 4(3)):

(1) If the work of the claimant and that of the comparator have been given different values on a job evaluation study (JES), the tribunal must strike out the equal value claim at the stage 1 hearing unless it has reasonable grounds for suspecting that the evaluation was made on a system which discriminated on grounds of sex or is 'otherwise unsuitable to be relied upon' (EqPA 1970, s 2A(2A); see also *Bromley v H & J Quick Ltd* [1988] IRLR 249). The claimant must be sent a notice giving him or her the opportunity to make representations to the tribunal before the claim is struck out.

(2) The tribunal must decide whether it will determine the question of equal value, or whether a member of the panel of IEs shall prepare a report with respect to equal value. When deciding whether to require an IE to prepare a report, the tribunal may consider whether there are any reasonable grounds for determining that the claimant's work and that of the comparator are of equal value. However, in *Wood v William Ball* [1999] IRLR 773, the EAT held that the tribunal had erred in dismissing nine equal value complaints because there were no reasonable grounds for determining that the work was of equal value to that of the comparators, and thus no basis for commissioning an IE's report, without giving the parties an opportunity to adduce their own expert evidence.

(3) The tribunal must make standard orders as follows, unless it considers it inappropriate to do so (EV Rules, r 5):
   (a) Within 14 days of the stage 1 hearing: the claimant shall disclose in writing to the respondent the name of any comparator or such information as enables the comparator to be identified by the respondent, and the period of comparison.
   (b) Within 28 days of the stage 1 hearing: the parties shall provide each other with written job descriptions for the claimant and comparator, and identify to each other in writing the facts which they consider to be relevant to the question of equal value.
   (c) The respondent shall grant access to the claimant and his or her representative to its premises for them to interview any comparator.
   (d) Within 56 days of the stage 1 hearing: the parties shall present to the tribunal a joint agreed statement in writing of (i) job descriptions, (ii) relevant facts, and (iii) facts on which the parties disagree and a summary of their reasons for disagreeing.
   (e) At least 56 days prior to the hearing: the parties shall disclose to each other, to any experts, and to the tribunal written statement of any facts on which they intend to rely in evidence at the hearing.
   (f) At least 28 days prior to the hearing: the parties shall present to the tribunal a statement of facts and issues on which the parties agree and on which they disagree and a summary of the reasons for disagreeing.

(4) If the tribunal has decided to require an IE to prepare a report, it will require the parties to copy all disclosures to the IE, and fix a date for the stage 2 equal value hearing.

(5) If the tribunal has decided not to require an IE to prepare a report, it will fix a date for the substantive hearing.

(6) The tribunal must also consider whether any further orders are appropriate.

15.12 The duties and powers of the IE are set out in r 10 of the EV Rules, and include:

(a) a duty to assist the tribunal in furthering the overriding objective;
(b) a duty to comply with the requirements of the EV Rules and any orders;
(c) a duty to keep the tribunal informed of any delay in complying with any order;
(d) a duty to comply with the timetable set by the tribunal insofar as it is reasonably practicable;
(e) a duty to inform the tribunal on request of progress in the preparation of the report;
(f) a duty to make him or herself available to attend hearings.

The IE may also make an application for any order or for a hearing as if he or she were a party to the proceedings. **15.13**

The tribunal may, on the application of a party, hear evidence and submissions on the issue of the genuine material factor (GMF) defence under s 1(3) of the EqPA 1970 before determining whether to require an IE to prepare a report (EV Rules, r 4(5)). **15.14**

Stage 2 equal value hearing

A stage 2 hearing is only held where the tribunal has decided to require an IE to prepare a report. Its purpose is for the tribunal to make a determination of facts on which the parties cannot agree. The facts determined by the tribunal and any agreed facts are provided to the IE for the purposes of preparing the report. **15.15**

The tribunal must also make the following orders, unless it considers it inappropriate to do so: **15.16**

(a) The IE shall prepare a report and send copies to the tribunal and to the parties by a specified date.
(b) The IE shall prepare the report on the basis of the facts provided to him or her by the tribunal and on no other facts.

The tribunal will also fix a date for the equal value hearing. **15.17**

Other steps

The tribunal may require the respondent to grant to the IE access to its premises in order to interview any person whom he or she considers to be relevant to the preparation of the report. It may also, at any stage of the proceedings, order the expert to assist in establishing the facts on which the report is based (EV Rules, r 6(2)). **15.18**

Section 2A(1A) of the EqPA 1970 provides that a tribunal may withdraw an instruction given to an IE and determine the question of equal value itself, although in practice tribunals will be reluctant to do so. **15.19**

The parties are still able to call their own experts on the question of equal value provided that they have the permission of the tribunal (EV Rules, r 11) and such permission will probably be given when there are many claimants and complicated issues of methodology. Expert evidence is restricted to that which the tribunal considers reasonably required to resolve the proceedings. Any report which a party proposes to rely on must be disclosed to the other parties at least 28 days before the hearing. The tribunal also has the power to order a joint expert to be instructed (EV Rules, r 11(6)). The idea behind the process is that the tribunal is wholly responsible for fact finding and not the independent expert, which marks a change from the previous Rules. **15.20**

The parties are entitled to put written questions to the IE or any other expert within 28 days of receipt of the report, but, unless the Employment Judge agrees otherwise, only for the purpose of clarifying the factual basis of the report (EV Rules, r 12). They must copy any such questions to the other parties. The expert's answers, which must be given within 28 days of receiving the questions, form part of his or her report. **15.21**

Rule 13(2) specifically provides that the EV Rules do not preclude the tribunal from holding other hearings as permitted by the general tribunal rules. Pre-hearing reviews are likely to be common in equal pay claims because of the numerous stages involved in proving any equal pay case. **15.22**

The hearing

At the substantive hearing the tribunal will determine whether the work of the claimant and that of the comparator are of equal value. Where an IE's report has been prepared, the report must be admitted in evidence unless the tribunal determines that the report is not based on 'the facts relating to the question' (ie the facts determined at the stage 2 hearing). If the report **15.23** is not admitted the tribunal may determine the question itself or require another IE to prepare a report.

15.24 The EV Rules remove the ability formerly in the rules for a party to challenge the admissibility of the IE's report on the basis that it is not 'satisfactory'. The IE's time and public funds will thus be less often wasted by the report being declared inadmissible, although the tribunal may still hear submissions on whether it should adopt the conclusions of the report and may hear expert evidence on this.

16

Special Jurisdictions

SUMMARY

Tribunals have a number of special jurisdictions with slightly different procedures. There are different procedures in relation to national security, appeals against levy assessments, appeals against health and safety improvement notices, and appeals against unlawful act notices.

A. NATIONAL SECURITY

16.01 Schedule 2 to the Employment Tribunals (Constitution and Rules of Procedure) Regulations 2004 applies to national security proceedings or proceedings where a Minister of the Crown has exercised his right to address the tribunal (pursuant to ETR 2004, r 54) in order to direct it to:

(a) conduct proceedings in private for all or part of particular Crown employment proceedings;
(b) exclude the claimant from all or part of particular Crown employment proceedings;
(c) exclude the claimant's representative from all or part of particular Crown employment proceedings;
(d) take steps to conceal the identity of a particular witness in particular Crown employment proceedings.

16.02 The procedure in relation to the claim form will follow that used in relation to ETR 2004. In any proceedings an Employment Judge may exercise similar powers if it is expedient in the interests of national security. Applications must be made at London Central, and invariably the hearing will be there as well.

Responding to a claim

16.03 If before the expiry of the period for entering the response:

(a) a direction of a Minister of the Crown excluding the claimant (ETR 2004, r 54(1)(b)) (exclusion of claimant) applicable to this stage of the proceedings is given; or
(b) a Minister of the Crown has informed the Secretary that he wishes to address the tribunal or judge with a view to the tribunal or judge making an order under r 54(2) to exclude the claimant;

r 4(3)(d) of ETR 2004 (grounds for the response) shall not apply.

16.04 There are two possible courses to follow: one where the exclusion has been ordered/directed, the other where it has not.

16.05 If the tribunal or judge decides not to make an order to exclude the claimant the respondent must within 28 days of the decision present to the Employment Tribunal Office the written grounds on which he resists the claim. On receiving the written grounds the Secretary shall send a copy of them to all other parties and they shall be treated as part of the response (2004 Regulations, Sch 2, r 3).

16.06 Where the tribunal or judge makes the order or the minister so directs the respondent must within 44 days of the direction or order being made, present to the Employment Tribunal Office the written grounds on which he resists the claim and they shall be treated as part of the response. If a special advocate has been appointed he or she should also be sent a copy.

16.07 These time limits may be extended if it is just and equitable to do so and if an application is presented to the Employment Tribunal Office before the expiry of the relevant time limit. The application must explain why the respondent cannot comply with the time limit.

Serving of documents by the Secretary

16.08 Once an exclusion order is made the Secretary should not send a copy of the response or grounds for the response to the person excluded.

16.09 Where a Minister of the Crown has informed the Secretary in accordance with ETR 2004, r 54(3) that he wishes to address the tribunal or judge with a view to an order being made under r 54(2)(a) to exclude the claimant's representative from all or part of the proceedings, the Secretary shall not at any time before the tribunal or judge has considered the minister's representations, send a copy of the response or the grounds for the response to any person who may be excluded from all or part of the proceedings by such an order if it were made.

Default judgment

16.10 The rules on default judgments (ETR 2004, r 8(1)) apply in relation to the time limit for presenting a response. If a response is not submitted then a default judgment will follow. However, if the minister has made a direction or a tribunal has excluded a claimant, representative, etc (see above) the limits do not apply to the 28- and 44-day periods for entering written grounds.

Witness orders and disclosure of documents

16.11 In cases where a minister has issued a direction or the tribunal or a judge has made an order to exclude a claimant or his representative from all or part of the proceedings and a judge or the tribunal is considering whether to make, or has made, an order described in ETR 2004, r 10(2)(c) or (d) (requiring a person to attend and give evidence or to produce documents) the minister (whether or not a party to the proceedings) may make an application to the tribunal or judge objecting to the imposition of a requirement described in ETR 2004, r 10(2)(c) or (d) or under Sch 3 or 4 to the 2004 Regulations.

If such an order has been made the minister may make an application to vary or set aside the order. The claim should be heard and determined in private and the minister is entitled to address the tribunal or judge. The application should be made by notice to the Secretary and the Secretary should give notice of the application to all parties. **16.12**

Case management discussions and pre-hearing reviews

In proceedings in which a special advocate has been appointed in respect of the claimant, if the claimant has been excluded from a case management discussion or a pre-hearing review, at such a hearing the claimant shall not have the right to advance oral argument, but oral argument may be advanced on the claimant's behalf by the special advocate. **16.13**

Special advocate

In any proceedings in which there is an excluded person the tribunal or judge shall inform the Attorney-General (or in Scotland, the Advocate General) of the proceedings with a view to the Attorney-General (or the Advocate General, in Scotland), if he thinks it fit to do so, appointing a special advocate to represent the interests of the claimant in respect of those parts of the proceedings from which— **16.14**

(a) any representative of his is excluded;
(b) both he and his representative are excluded; or
(c) he is excluded, where he does not have a representative.

A special advocate shall have a general qualification for the purposes of s 71 of the Courts and Legal Services Act 1990 or shall be an advocate or a solicitor admitted in Scotland. **16.15**

Where the excluded person is the claimant, he shall be permitted to make a statement to the tribunal or judge before the commencement of the proceedings, or the part of the proceedings, from which he is excluded. **16.16**

The special advocate is restricted in relation to communications, whether direct or indirect, with the excluded claimant: **16.17**

(a) (except in the case of the tribunal, judge, and the respondent) on any matter contained in the grounds for the response referred to in r 3(3) of Sch 2;
(b) (except in the case of a person who was present) on any matter discussed or referred to during any part of the proceedings in which the tribunal or judge sat in private in accordance with a direction or an order given or made under ETR 2004, r 54.

More generally the special advocate may apply for orders from the tribunal or judge authorizing him to seek instructions from, or otherwise to communicate with, an excluded person— **16.18**

(a) on any matter contained in the grounds for the response; or
(b) on any matter discussed or referred to during any part of the proceedings in which the tribunal or judge sat in private in accordance with a direction or an order given or made under ETR 2004, r 54.

Any such application should be made in writing to the Employment Tribunal Office and should include the title of the proceedings and the grounds for the application. Once received the Secretary should notify the minister of it and the minister is then entitled to address the tribunal or judge on the application. **16.19**

Hearings

16.20 Unless there is a direction or order as discussed above, any hearing of or in connection with a claim shall take place in public (subject to ETR 2004, r 16 as to which see paras 9.157–9.167).

16.21 In a private hearing a member of the Council on Tribunals is not entitled to attend.

16.22 If there has been a direction or order there may be limits on the entitlement of a party to give evidence, call witnesses, question any witnesses, and to address the tribunal at a hearing.

Reasons in national security proceedings

16.23 The tribunal's reasons may be subject to restrictions also. Before the Secretary sends a copy of the full written reasons to any party, or enters them in the register, he must send a copy of the full written reasons to the minister. If the minister considers it in the interests of national security and he has given a direction or the tribunal or a judge has made an order excluding persons etc the minister may—

(a) direct the tribunal or judge that the full written reasons shall not be disclosed to persons specified in the direction, and to prepare a further document ('the edited reasons') setting out the reasons for the judgment or order, but with the omission of such of the information as is specified in the direction;
(b) direct the tribunal or judge that the full written reasons shall not be disclosed to persons specified in the direction, but that no further document setting out the tribunal or judge's reasons should be prepared.

16.24 Where the minister has directed the tribunal or judge in accordance with (a) above, the edited reasons should be signed by the judge and initialled in each place where an omission has been made.

16.25 Where a direction has been made that edited reasons should be supplied the Secretary should—

(a) send a copy of the edited reasons referred to, to any person specified in the direction and to the respondent, the claimant, or the claimant's representative if they were not otherwise excluded, if applicable, the special advocate, where the proceedings were referred to the tribunal by a court, to that court; and where there are proceedings before a superior court (or in Scotland, an appellate court) relating to the decision in question, to that court;
(b) enter the edited reasons in the register, but omit from the register the full written reasons; and
(c) send a copy of the full written reasons to the persons set out in (a) above.

16.26 Where a direction has been made that no further document should be prepared the Secretary shall send a copy of the full written reasons to the persons listed in (a) above, but he shall not enter the full written reasons in the register.

Correction of written reasons

16.27 Where written reasons (whether 'full' or 'edited' as above) have been omitted from the register in accordance with r 10 of Sch 2 and they are corrected by certificate under ETR 2004, r 37, the Secretary shall send a copy of the corrected reasons to the same persons who had been sent the reasons in (a) at para 16.25 above.

Review of judgments or decisions

16.28 In ETR 2004, r 34(3) (review of other judgments and decisions), the reference to decisions being made in the absence of a party does not include reference to decisions being made in the absence of a party where this is done in accordance with a direction given or an order made in national security proceedings for obvious reasons.

B. EMPLOYMENT TRIBUNAL LEVY ASSESSMENT APPEALS

The Industrial Training Act 1982 provides for assessments of a levy to be made by the various Industrial Training Boards (ITBs). Schedule 3 to the 2004 Regulations sets out the rules of procedure for appeals against such assessments. **16.29**

The 'usual' tribunal rules in ETR 2004 apply to levy appeals. The rules in Sch 3 modify the rules in ETR 2004 and if there is a conflict the rules in Sch 3 prevail. **16.30**

The 'respondent' in all cases is the ITB. All references in ETR 2004 to a claim or claimant are to be read for these purposes as references to a levy appeal or to an appellant in a levy appeal respectively. **16.31**

Exclusions

The following rules in ETR 2004 do not apply in relation to levy appeals: **16.32**

r 1	Starting a claim
r 2	What the tribunal does after receiving the claim
r 3	When the claim will not be accepted by the Secretary
r 4	Responding to the claim
r 5	What the tribunal does after receiving the response
r 6	When the response will not be accepted by the Secretary
r 7	Counterclaims
r 8	Default judgments
r 9	Taking no further part in proceedings
r 16(1)(c)	Hearings which may be held in private: ability to hold hearing in private where disclosure of information may harm an undertaking
r 18(2)(c) and (e)	Conduct of pre-hearing reviews: ordering deposits and interim relief
r 20	Requirement to pay a deposit in order to continue with proceedings
rr 21–4	Conciliation
r 25	Right to withdraw proceedings
r 33	Review of default judgments
r 34(1)(a), (2) and (4)	Review of other judgments and decisions: review of decision not to accept a claim, response, or counterclaim
r 38(4)	General power to make costs and expenses orders: ability to make costs order to respondent who has not had a response accepted
r 39	When a costs or expenses order must be made
r 42(4)	General power to make preparation time orders: ability to make order to respondent who has not had a response accepted
r 43	When a preparation time order must be made
r 47	Costs, expenses, or preparation time orders when a deposit has been taken
rr 49–50	Restricted reporting orders
r 51	Proceedings involving the National Insurance Fund
r 52	Collective agreements
r 53	Employment Agencies Act 1973
r 55	Dismissals in connection with industrial action
r 61(4)(a), (7) and (8)	Notices etc: notices to be served on the Insolvency Service in appropriate cases.

16.33 Rule 61 of ETR 2004 is amended so that in the case of a notice of an appeal brought under the Industrial Training Act 1982 the address for sending documents is the ITB's address for service specified in the assessment notice. In the case of any other document directed to the ITB it is the ITB's address for service.

Starting an appeal

16.34 A person wishing to appeal an assessment to a levy should send to the ITB two copies of a notice of appeal which must be substantially in accordance with form 1 in the Annex to Sch 3, and they must include the grounds of their appeal.

Action on receipt of appeal

16.35 Unless there is a request for information the ITB must, within 21 days of receiving the notice of appeal, send the following documents to the Employment Tribunal Office (Sch 3, r 4):

(a) one copy of the notice of appeal;
(b) a copy of the assessment notice and of any notice by the Board allowing further time for appealing;
(c) a notice giving the Board's address for service under these rules where that address is different from the address specified in the assessment notice as the address for service of a notice of appeal; and
(d) any representations in writing relating to the appeal that the Board wishes to submit to the tribunal.

16.36 However, a failure to comply with any provision of this rule or r 5 of Sch 3 (requests for further information) shall not make the appeal invalid.

Requests for further information

16.37 On receipt of the appeal, the ITB may consider that it requires further information on the appellant's grounds for the appeal and of any facts relevant to those grounds. If it does so consider it should send a notice to the appellant specifying the further information required within 21 days of receiving the notice of appeal (Sch 3, r 5).

16.38 The appellant must send the ITB two copies of the further information within 21 days of receiving the notice requesting the information, or within such further period as the ITB may allow.

16.39 Once the ITB has received the information it has 21 days in which to send the following documents to the Employment Tribunal Office (Sch 3, r 5(4)):

(a) the documents listed in r 4(1);
(b) a copy of the notice requesting further information;
(c) any further information which has been provided to the Board; and
(d) any representations in writing regarding such information which the Board wishes to submit to the tribunal.

16.40 If the further information is not received by the ITB within the time limit, the appeal and assessment notice should be sent to the Employment Tribunal Office (Sch 3, r 5(5)):

(a) within 50 days of the receipt of the notice of appeal by the Board; or
(b) if the Board has allowed a further period of time for delivery of further particulars . . . within seven days of the end of that period.

16.41 It is then open to the ITB to apply for an order (Sch 3, r 8). A judge or tribunal may order the appellant to supply the further information and the appellant will be directed to send two copies of it to the Employment Tribunal Office within such time as the judge or tribunal may direct. Once received the Secretary should send a copy to the ITB.

Any such order made will be treated as an order for the purposes of ETR 2004, r 13 (sanctions for compliance with orders and Practice Directions). 16.42

Withdrawal of appeal or assessment

The appellant may withdraw the notice of appeal by notice given to the ITB at any time and in that event no further action shall be taken in relation to the appeal. 16.43

When an assessment is withdrawn by the ITB, there is an obligation upon it to notify the Employment Tribunal Office and no further action shall be taken in relation to the appeal. 16.44

Entry of appeal

The Secretary shall, as soon as reasonably practicable after receiving from the ITB the relevant documents, give notice to the appellant and to the ITB of the case number of the appeal (which must from then on be referred to in all correspondence relating to the appeal) and of the address to which notices and other communications to the Employment Tribunal Office shall be sent (Sch 3, r 6). 16.45

The Secretary must also (Sch 3, r 7(1)(b), (c)): 16.46

(b) give notice to the appellant of the Board's address for service; and
(c) send to the appellant a copy of any representations in writing that the Board has submitted to the tribunal.

C. APPEALS AGAINST HEALTH AND SAFETY IMPROVEMENT NOTICES

The ETR 2004 apply to appeals against a health and safety improvement or prohibition notice with some modifications. If there is conflict between the rules, those in Sch 4 to the 2004 Regulations shall prevail. 16.47

All references in ETR 2004 to a claim shall be read as references to a notice of appeal or to an appeal against an improvement notice or a prohibition notice, as the context may require, and all references to the claimant shall be read as references to the appellant in such an appeal. 16.48

The following rules in ETR 2004 shall not apply in relation to appeals against improvement and prohibition notices: 16.49

r 1	Starting a claim
r 2	What the tribunal does after receiving the claim
r 3	When the claim will not be accepted by the Secretary
r 4	Responding to the claim
r 5	What the tribunal does after receiving the response
r 6	When the response will not be accepted by the Secretary
r 7	Counterclaims
r 8	Default judgments
r 9	Taking no further part in proceedings
r 10(1)	General power to manage proceedings
(2)(g)	Extension of conciliation period
(i)	Part of proceedings may be dealt with separately
(k)	Adding respondents
(l)	Dismissing a claim against a respondent who is no longer interested in proceedings
(r)	Joinder of party (as opposed to respondent) with an interest in the proceedings
r 12	Judge acting on his own initiative

r 13	Compliance with orders and Practice Directions
r 16(1)(c)	Hearings which may be held in private: ability to hold hearing in private where disclosure of information may harm an undertaking
r 18(2)(c) and (e)	Conduct of pre-hearing reviews: ordering deposits and interim relief
(8)	Strike-out of claim
r 20	Requirement to pay a deposit in order to continue with proceedings
rr 21–4	Conciliation
r 25	Right to withdraw proceedings
r 29(3)	Form and content of judgments: judgment to specify amount of compensation or costs
r 33	Review of default judgments
r 34(1)(a), (2) and (4)	Review of other judgments and decisions: review of decision not to accept a claim, response or counterclaim
r 38(4)	General power to make costs and expenses orders: ability to order costs order to respondent who has not had a response accepted
r 39	When a costs or expenses order must be made
r 42(4)	General power to make preparation time orders: ability to make order to respondent who has not had a response accepted
r 43	When a preparation time order must be made
r 47	Costs, expenses, or preparation time orders when a deposit has been taken
rr 49–50	Restricted reporting orders
r 51	Proceedings involving the National Insurance Fund
r 52	Collective agreements
r 53	Employment Agencies Act 1973
r 55	Dismissals in connection with industrial action
r 61(4)(a), (7) and (8)	Notices etc: notices to be sent to Secretary of State in certain proceedings

Notice of appeal

16.50 A person wishing to appeal an improvement notice or a prohibition notice issued pursuant to the Health and Safety at Work etc Act 1974 should send to the Employment Tribunal Office a notice of appeal which must include the following (Sch 4, r 3):

(a) the name and address of the appellant and, if different, an address to which he requires notices and documents relating to the appeal to be sent;
(b) the date of the improvement notice or prohibition notice appealed against and the address of the premises or the place concerned;
(c) the name and address of the respondent;
(d) details of the requirements or directions which are being appealed; and
(e) the grounds for the appeal.

Time limit for bringing appeal

16.51 The notice of appeal must be sent to the Employment Tribunal Office within 21 days from the date of the service on the appellant of the notice appealed against. A tribunal may extend the time mentioned above where it is satisfied, on an application made in writing to the Secretary, either before or after the expiration of that time, that it is or was not reasonably practicable for an appeal to be brought within that time (Sch 4, r 4). Given that the formulation is the same as the discretion to extend in unfair dismissal cases the case law set out at para 3.59 above will apply.

Once the Secretary has received the notice of appeal a copy is sent to the respondent and the Secretary will inform the parties in writing of the case number of the appeal and of the address to which notices and other communications to the Employment Tribunal Office shall be sent. **16.52**

Application for a direction suspending the operation of a prohibition notice

When an appeal is brought an application may be made by the appellant under s 24(3)(b) of the Health and Safety at Work etc Act 1974 for a direction suspending the operation of the prohibition notice until the appeal is determined or withdrawn. **16.53**

The application must be presented to the Employment Tribunal Office in writing and must include (Sch 3, r 6(1)): **16.54**

(a) the case number of the appeal, or if there is no case number sufficient details to identify the appeal; and
(b) the grounds on which the application is made.

The Secretary should then send a copy of the application to the respondent as soon as practicable after it has been received and inform the respondent that he has the opportunity to submit representations in writing if he so wishes, within a specified time but not less than seven days. **16.55**

A judge should consider the application and any representations submitted by the respondent, and may (Sch 4, r 6(3)): **16.56**

(a) order that the application should not be determined separately from the full hearing of the appeal;
(b) order that the operation of the prohibition notice be suspended until the appeal is determined or withdrawn;
(c) dismiss the appellant's application; or
(d) order that the application be determined at a hearing (held in accordance with r 26 of Sch 1).

The judge must give reasons for any decision made which may be reviewed (adopting the same principles as in r 34 of ETR 2004, see Chapter 13). **16.57**

General power to manage proceedings

The judge may at any time on the application of a party make an order in relation to any matter which appears to him to be appropriate—either those listed in ETR 2004, r 10(2) (subject to r 11 below) or such other orders as he thinks fit (see Chapter 6). **16.58**

Orders may be issued as a result of a judge considering the papers before him in the absence of the parties, or at a hearing (see reg 2 of the 2004 Regulations for the definition of 'hearing'). If the parties agree in writing upon the terms of any decision to be made by the tribunal or judge, the judge may, if he thinks fit, decide accordingly (Sch 4, r 7(2)). **16.59**

Appointment of an assessor

The President, Vice-President, or a Regional Employment Judge may, if he thinks fit, appoint in accordance with s 24(4) of the Health and Safety at Work etc Act 1974 a person having special knowledge or experience in relation to the subject matter of the appeal to sit with the tribunal or judge as an assessor. **16.60**

Right to withdraw proceedings

An appellant may withdraw all or part of the appeal at any time. This may be done either orally at a hearing or in writing. To withdraw an appeal or part of one in writing the appellant must **16.61** inform the Employment Tribunal Office in writing of the appeal or the parts of it which are to be withdrawn. The Secretary must then inform all other parties of the withdrawal. Withdrawal takes effect on the date on which the Employment Tribunal Office (in the case of written notifications) or the tribunal or judge receives notice of it and, where the whole appeal is withdrawn, proceedings are brought to an end against the respondent on that date and the tribunal or judge shall dismiss the appeal (Sch 4, r 9).

Costs and expenses

16.62 A tribunal or judge may make an order that a party make a payment in respect of the costs incurred by another party.

16.63 'Costs' means fees, charges, disbursements, expenses, or remuneration incurred by or on behalf of a party in relation to the proceedings. In Scotland all references in this Schedule to costs or costs orders shall be read as references to expenses or orders for expenses.

16.64 Under r 10(3) of Sch 4, the amount of a costs order against the paying party can be determined as follows:

(a) the tribunal may specify the sum which the party must pay to the receiving party, provided that sum does not exceed £10,000;
(b) the parties may agree on a sum to be paid by the paying party to the receiving party and if they do so the costs order shall be for the sum so agreed;
(c) the tribunal may order the paying party to pay the receiving party the whole or a specified part of the costs of the second party with the amount to be paid being determined by way of detailed assessment in a county court in accordance with the Civil Procedure Rules or, in Scotland, as taxed according to such part of the table of fees prescribed for proceedings in the sheriff court as shall be directed by the order.

16.65 The amounts which may be agreed or ordered under (b) and (c) above may exceed £10,000. The tribunal or judge should have regard to the paying party's ability to pay when considering whether it or he shall make a costs order or how much that order should be (Sch 4, r 10).

D. APPEALS AGAINST UNLAWFUL ACT NOTICES

Application of ETR 2004

16.66 The ETR 2004 will apply to appeals against an unlawful act notice (issued under s 21 of the Equality Act 2006) except as where excluded or modified in Sch 5 to the 2004 Regulations. If there is conflict between ETR 2004 and Sch 5, the rules in Sch 5 prevail.

16.67 The ETR 2004 are modified to the extent that all references to a claim shall be read as references to a notice of appeal or to an appeal against an unlawful act notice and all references to the claimant shall be read as references to the appellant in such an appeal.

16.68 In any such appeals references to the 'respondent' mean the Commission for Equality and Human Rights established under s 1 of the Equality Act 2006.

Exclusions

16.69 The following rules in ETR 2004 do not apply:

r 1	Starting a claim
r 2	What the tribunal does after receiving the claim
r 3	When the claim will not be accepted by the Secretary
r 4	Responding to the claim

r 5	What the tribunal does after receiving the response
r 6	When the response will not be accepted by the Secretary
r 7	Counterclaims
r 8	Default judgments
r 9	Taking no further part in proceedings
r 10(1)	General power to manage proceedings
(2)(g)	Extension of conciliation period
(i)	Part of proceedings may be dealt with separately
(k)	Adding respondents
(l)	Dismissing a claim against a respondent who is no longer interested in proceedings
(r)	Joinder of party (as opposed to respondent) with an interest in the proceedings
r 12	Judge acting on his own initiative
r 13	Compliance with orders and Practice Directions
r 16(1)(c)	Hearings which may be held in private: ability to hold hearing in private where disclosure of information may harm an undertaking
r 18(2)(c) and (e)	Conduct of pre-hearing reviews: ordering deposits and interim relief
r 20	Requirement to pay a deposit in order to continue with proceedings
rr 21–4	Conciliation
r 33	Review of default judgments
r 34(1)(a), (2) and (4)	Review of other judgments and decisions: review of decision not to accept a claim, response, or counterclaim
r 38(4)	General power to make costs and expenses order: ability to order costs order to respondent who has not had a response accepted
r 39	When a costs or expenses order must be made
r 42(4)	General power to make preparation time orders: ability to make order to respondent who has not had a response accepted
r 43	When a preparation time order must be made
r 47	Costs, expenses, or preparation time orders when a deposit has been taken
rr 49–50	Restricted reporting orders
r 51	Proceedings involving the National Insurance Fund
r 52	Collective agreements
r 53	Employment Agencies Act 1973
r 55	Dismissals in connection with industrial action
r 61(4)(a), (7) and (8)	Notices etc: notices to be sent to Secretary of State in certain proceedings

Notice of appeal

A person wishing to appeal an unlawful act notice must send a notice of appeal to the Employment Tribunal Office (Sch 5, r 3). The notice should be in writing and must include: **16.70**

(a) the name and address of the appellant and, if different, an address to which he requires notices and documents relating to the appeal to be sent;
(b) the date of the non-discrimination notice appealed against;
(c) the name and address of the respondent;
(d) details of the requirements which are being appealed; and
(e) the grounds for the appeal.3

Action on receipt of appeal

16.71 On receipt of the appeal the Secretary must send a copy of the notice of appeal to the respondent and inform the parties in writing of the case number of the appeal (which must from then on be referred to in all correspondence relating to the appeal) and of the address to which notices and other communications to the Employment Tribunal Office shall be sent (Sch 5, para 4).

17

Human Rights Claims

SUMMARY

(1) The main practical effect of the Human Rights Act 1998 was that those seeking to rely upon it could proceed in domestic courts rather than in the European Court of Human Rights in Strasbourg.

(2) Tribunals, however, do not have jurisdiction to hear free-standing complaints under the Human Rights Act 1998.

(3) Human rights jurisprudence has been important in developing employment case law:

(a) in relation to procedural fairness Article 6 ECHR;

(b) in cases involving a claimant's private and/or family life under Article 8 ECHR;

(c) in cases involving religious discrimination under the Employment Equality (Religion or Belief) Regulations 2003 and Article 9 ECHR;

(d) in cases involving trade union freedom and freedom of association under Article 11 ECHR.

A. CLAIMS UNDER THE HUMAN RIGHTS ACT 1998

The Employment Tribunal does not have jurisdiction to hear freestanding claims under ss 7–10 **17.01** of the Human Rights Act 1998 (HRA) or otherwise. It does not have the power to make a declaration of incompatibility under s 4 of the HRA. However, it does have a duty under s 3 of the HRA to interpret legislation and subordinate legislation so far as it is possible to do so in such a way as is compatible with the Convention rights. Further it has a duty under s 2 of the HRA in determining a question which has arisen in connection with a Convention right to take account of judgments of the European Court of Human Rights, the Commission, and the Committee of Ministers.

In X v Y [2004] IRLR 625, Mummery LJ held that HRA (and Convention rights) could only be **17.02** raised in the tribunals by way of interpretation of UK statutes and statutory instruments.

17.03 Mummery LJ set out the following framework for tribunals:

(a) Do the circumstances of the dismissal fall within the ambit of one or more of the Articles of the Convention? If they do not, the Convention right is not engaged and need not be considered.
(b) If they do, does the State have a positive obligation to secure enjoyment of the relevant Convention right between private persons? If it does not, the Convention right is unlikely to affect the outcome of an unfair dismissal claim against a private employer.
(c) If it does, is the interference with the employee's Convention right by dismissal justified? If it is, proceed to (e) below.
(d) If it is not, was there a permissible reason for the dismissal under ERA 1996, which does not involve unjustified interference with a Convention right? If there was not, the dismissal will be unfair for the absence of a permissible reason to justify it.
(e) If there was, is the dismissal fair, tested by the provisions of s 98 of ERA 1996, reading and giving effect to them under s 3 of HRA 1998 so as to be compatible with the Convention right?

17.04 It is therefore still open to rely upon Convention rights in order to aid interpretation or in order to ensure that the tribunal's own conduct and procedure conform to, for example, human rights obligations, in particular Article 6. The following are the more likely Articles of ECHR to be engaged in tribunals:

Article 4	prohibiting forced labour.
Article 6	right to a fair trial.
Article 8	right to respect for private and family life.
Article 9	freedom of thought, conscience, and religion.
Article 10	freedom of expression.
Article 11	freedom of assembly and association.
Article 14	prohibition of discrimination.

Article 6: fair trial

17.05 Since the enactment of the HRA, Article 6 has been argued in employment cases both in relation to the employment tribunal's own procedure and more broadly in relation to procedural fairness. As an ordinary dismissal from employment is not a determination of civil rights and obligations Article 6 and its case law has had a most limited effect on the law of unfair dismissal (see eg *C v UK* Application 1182/85 7 October 1987).

Article 6 and the employer's procedure

17.06 *In R(on the application of Malik) v Waltham Forest Primary Care Trust* [2006] IRLR 526, QBD the Divisional Court held that the jurisprudence of the European Court of Human Rights (ECtHR) and the Commission establishes that in general interim measures (such as suspension) do not engage Article 6 since they are not determinative of civil rights and are administrative. However, dismissal may have a determinative effect on an individual's ability to practice a profession because of a system of provisional listing (*R (on the application of Wright) v Secretary of State for Health* [2009] UKHL 3, [2009] All ER 129) or the sending of alert letters to all NHS trusts in the context of a doctor's dismissal (*Kulkarni v Milton Keynes NHS Trust* [2009] EWCA Civ 789).

17.07 The High Court in *R(on the application of G) v X School and Y Council* [2009] EWHC 504 (Admin) (currently under appeal) held that the potential for an individual to be included on the list of those unsuitable to work with children as a result of his dismissal meant that Article 6 (1) required that the claimant must have the right to legal representation.

Article 6 in the ET

As with the CPR the ET rules contain an obligation to comply with the overriding objective which includes the principle of proportionality. 17.08

One of the early cases in which Article 6 was argued in relation to the procedural fairness of the employment tribunal's rules was *Teinaz v Wandsworth London Borough Council* [2004] EWCA Civ 104 [2002] ICR 1471, [2002] IRLR 721. The Court of Appeal held that a litigant whose presence is needed for the fair trial of a case but who is unable to be present through no fault of his own will usually have to be granted an adjournment, however inconvenient it may be to the tribunal or court and to the other parties. However, the tribunal or court is entitled to be satisfied that the inability of the litigant to be present is genuine, and the onus is on the applicant for an adjournment to prove the need for such adjournment (para 21). Specific medical evidence is required, not just of unfitness to work. The evidence must deal specifically with the witnesses' unfitness to attend and give evidence to the tribunal: *Andreou v Lord Chancellors Department* [2002] EWCA Civ 1192, [2002] IRLR 728). 17.09

The question of whether the right to a fair trial (Article 6) had been infringed by a delay of a year between the tribunal hearing a case and the decision being promulgated was considered by the Court of Appeal in *Bangs v Connex South Eastern Ltd* [2005] EWCA Civ 14, [2005] IRLR 389. The court considered that unreasonable delay is generally a matter of fact, not law, and it does not in itself constitute an independent ground of appeal. In order to succeed in such a challenge, it would be necessary to satisfy the notoriously difficult perversity test. There may, however, be exceptional cases in which unreasonable delay can properly be treated as a serious procedural error, giving rise to a question of law, where a party is deprived of the substance of his or her right to a fair trial. On the facts of this case, won by the appellant employee, the employer had not been deprived of a fair hearing. 17.10

Article 6 has had a bearing in a number of cases concerning the composition and procedure of the Employment Tribunal: 17.11

- *AG v Wheen* [2001] IRLR 91: vexatious litigant order did not conflict with Article 6.
- *Scafuture v Secretary of State for Trade and Industry* [2001] IRLR 416: the Employment Tribunal now constituted is an independent and impartial tribunal within the meaning of Article 6(1) for the purposes of claims to which the Secretary of State is a party.
- *Lawal v Northern Spirit* [2003] IRLR 538, in which the House of Lords held that there is no difference between the common law test for bias and the requirements of Article 6: accordingly counsel appearing before the EAT ought not to have previously sat there in a judicial capacity as there was a real risk of bias. See also Chapter 10.
- *Stansbury v Datapulse plc* [2004] IRLR 466, in which the Court of Appeal held that an allegation that a member of a tribunal did not appear to be alert during the hearing may cause that hearing to be held to be unfair, both under English law and under Article 6(1).
- *Williams v Cowell* [2000] ICR 85, where it was held that a challenge to the exercise of the discretion under ETA 1996, s 20(2) to refuse to conduct a hearing in Wales was not invalidated by any of the provisions of the Welsh Language Act 1993 or of Articles 6 and 14 (linguistic equality was argued for).

Article 8: private and family life

Article 8 was considered in *McGowan v Scottish Water* [2005] IRLR 167, where Mr McGowan had been the subject of covert surveillance. His employers suspected, and the surveillance confirmed, that he was falsifying his timesheets. Given that the movements of all the inhabitants of his home were being tracked, an issue for determination was whether there had been a breach of his right to a private and family life (Article 8). While the EAT considered that there was a 'strong presumption' of infringement, it upheld the tribunal's decision to reject Mr McGowan's complaint. Lord Johnston, sitting in Edinburgh, considered the employer's actions to have been 17.12

justified and proportionate under Article 8(2) in circumstances where it was protecting its assets and investigating what in effect was a criminal activity.

17.13 In *Pay v UK* [2009] IRLR 139 the ECtHR considered Article 8 in the context of the dismissal of a probation officer discovered to have in his spare time pursued a business selling sadomasochistic and bondage products. In the context of his work as a probation officer working with sexual offenders the dismissal was held to be a proportionate infringement. The claimant's conduct affected the employer's reputation and the confidence of the general public.

17.14 In *De Keyser v Wilson* [2001] IRLR 324, it was argued that references to the claimant's private life in a letter of instruction to an expert witness amounted to a breach of her right to respect for her private and family life under Article 8. This was rejected as the material was not confidential and because the claimant's right would also conflict with the employer's right to a fair trial under Article 6.

17.15 In *Chairman and Governors of Amwell School v Dogherty* [2007] IRLR 198 concerned the use of covert surveillance by employees. The claimant had covertly recorded her disciplinary hearing and the deliberations of the panels on her mobile phone without asking for the panel's consent. She wished to rely on the recording in the ET. The employer sought to argue that the panel members' Article 8 rights were infringed. The EAT held that there was no infringement of Article 8.

Article 9: religious freedom

17.16 The Employment Equality (Religion or Belief) Regulations 2003 implement the Framework Directive on Equality 2000/73. The Framework Directive expressly refers in the recitals to the ECHR. Tribunals regularly refer to jurisprudence of the ECHR when interpreting the Regulations.

Article 11: freedom of association

17.17 The rights of trade unions and their members are both protected by Article 11 ECHR (*Aslef v UK* [2007] IRLR 361). Article 11 protections include the right to form and join a trade union, the prohibition of closed-shop agreements, and the right for a trade union to seek to persuade the employer to hear what it has to say on behalf of its members (see *Demir v Turkey* [2009] IRLR 766 para 145 Grand Chamber).

17.18 The 'right to strike' has been recognized by the ECJ as a fundamental principle of European Community law (*International Transport Workers' Federation v Viking Line* Case C-438/05 [2008] IRLR 143, para 44).

17.19 However, there has been a reluctance of the English courts to find that the restrictions and conditions applied to trade unions' right to strike under TULR(C)A 1992 to be disproportionate (*Metrobus v Unite the Union* [2009] EWCA Civ 829).

18

Group Litigation

SUMMARY

(1) In the civil courts group litigation orders may be applied for in the case of mass claims.

(2) In the employment tribunal there is no specific order under the rules but similar results may be achieved by the use of the general power for employment judges to 'make any order in relation to any matter which appears to him to be appropriate' to manage proceedings.

A. INTRODUCTION

Where claims are brought by more than one claimant or (which is less likely in the employment field) against several respondents, which give rise to common issues of fact or law, all the claims should be dealt with on a group basis whether in the civil court or employment tribunal. Such an approach could include managing all the claims from one court centre or in one tribunal region, staying some claims whilst appropriately selected test cases are tried, and trying common issues as preliminary issues. **18.01**

The civil courts have specific provision in the CPR to make group litigation orders to manage such litigation. No such rules for that specific purpose exist in the employment tribunal, but many of their characteristics and efficiency savings can be obtained by use of the tribunal's ordinary case management powers which can be adapted to reflect the needs of mass litigation. **18.02**

B. GROUP LITIGATION ORDERS IN THE CIVIL COURTS

In 2000 new procedures were adopted for the management of multi-party claims in the civil courts (but not the employment tribunals). The new rules promote the following objectives recommended by Lord Woolf's *Final Access to Justice Report* (July 1996, Chapter 7, para 2) to: **18.03**

(a) provide access to justice where large numbers of people have been affected by another's conduct, but individual loss is so small that it makes an individual action economically unviable;

(b) provide expeditious, effective and proportionate methods of resolving cases, where individual losses are large enough to justify individual action but where the number of claimants and the nature of the issues involved mean that the cases cannot be managed satisfactorily in accordance with normal procedure;
(c) achieve a balance between the normal rights of claimants and defendants, to pursue and defend claims individually, and the interests of a group of parties to litigate the action as a whole in an effective manner.

18.04 The rules establish such a procedural framework to provide the flexibility for the court to deal with the particular characteristics of these sorts of cases. They provide a mechanism to manage group litigation, for identifying generic issues applicable to the entire group, and for resolving cases at a cost that is proportionate to the value of an individual claim. They are located at CPR rr 19.10–19.15, and in CPR 19BPD.

18.05 A group litigation order (GLO) is defined in CPR r 19.10 as 'an order made under rule 19.11 to provide for the case management of claims which give rise to common or related issues of fact or law ('the GLO issues')'. The court may make such a GLO where there are, or are likely to be, a number of claims giving rise to GLO issues (CPR r 19.11).

18.06 The special procedural rules that then apply to GLO cases essentially provide for the following:

(a) either before or after the commencement of litigation, a party may apply for a GLO;
(b) the GLO will identify the issues to be managed as part of the group litigation ('the GLO issues') and any individual claim must raise these issues to fall under the terms of the order ('a GLO claim');
(c) a register of GLO claims will be maintained and a specified court will be given responsibility for managing them;
(d) the managing court has wide case management powers to ensure the effective coordination and resolution of the GLO claims;
(e) a judgment on any GLO issue will bind all other GLO claims.

18.07 In the general field of employment, situations that might merit the use of such a procedure dedicated to the handling of civil claims involving multiple parties include personal injury claims arising from industrial disease or accident; financial loss arising from mishandling of pension schemes, where disputes exist as to terms and conditions of employment after business transfers, where similar contractual debts are claimed; or there is a claim for enhanced redundancy payments due under contract.

Preliminary matters

18.08 Before applying for a GLO, the solicitor acting for the proposed applicant should consult the Law Society's Multi Party Action Information Service in order to obtain information about any other cases giving rise to the proposed GLO issues (CPR 19BPD, para 2.1).

18.09 The Practice Direction also recommends that the claimant's solicitors form a group, appoint one of their number to be the lead solicitor, and carefully define in writing the lead solicitor's role and relationship with other members of the group (CPR 19BPD, para 2.2).

Application for a GLO

18.10 Any application for a GLO must be made in accordance with CPR Part 23 (CPR 19BPD, para 3.1). The following information should be included in the application notice or in written evidence filed in support (CPR 19BPD, para 3.2):

(1) a summary of the nature of the litigation;
(2) the number and nature of claims already issued;
(3) the number of parties likely to be involved;

(4) the common issues of fact or law that are likely to arise in the litigation; and
(5) whether there are any matters that distinguish smaller groups of claims within the wider group.

The application for the GLO should be made to the Senior Master in the Queen's Bench Division or the Chief Chancery Master in the Chancery Division. For claims that are proceeding or are likely to proceed in a specialist list (such as the Commercial Court), the application should be made to the senior judge of that list (CPR 19BPD, para 3.5). Outside London, the application should be made to a Presiding Judge or a Chancery Supervising Judge of the Circuit in which the District Registry which has issued the application notice is situated. County court applications should be made to the Designated Civil Judge for the area in which the county court which has issued the application notice is situated (CPR 19BPD, para 3.6). **18.11**

The court may also make a GLO of its own initiative (CPR 19BPD, para 4) although this is rarely done. **18.12**

A GLO may only be made with the consent of the following individuals: in the Queen's Bench Division, the Lord Chief Justice; in the Chancery Division, the Vice Chancellor; and in the county court, the Head of Civil Justice. The court will seek the necessary permission as part of its own administration of the application. **18.13**

Characteristics of a group litigation order

The GLO must: **18.14**

(a) contain directions about the establishment of a 'group register' on which the claims managed under the GLO will be entered;
(b) specify the GLO issues which will identify the claims to be managed under the GLO; and
(c) specify the court which will manage the claims on the group register (CPR r 19.11).

In addition, the GLO may: **18.15**

(a) in relation to claims which raise one or more of the GLO issues direct their transfer to the management court (that is the court where the claims will be heard), order their stay until further order, and direct their entry onto the group register;
(b) direct that from a specified date claims which raise one or more of the GLO issues should be started in the management court and entered on the group register; and
(c) give directions for publicizing the GLO (CPR r 19.11).

The group register

Once a group register has been established, any party to a particular case may apply for the case to be entered on to it, but such an order will only be granted if the case gives rise to at least one of the GLO issues (CPR 19BPD, para 6). Rule 19.14 provides that a party entered on the group register may apply to the management court for the claim to be removed from the register, and if it does make such an order the court is given the power to give directions about the future management of that claim. **18.16**

Allocation

Every claim entered onto the group register will be automatically allocated, or reallocated, to the multi-track, and any case management directions that have been given by a court other than the management court will be set aside (CPR 19BPD, para 7). **18.17**

Case management

Practice Direction 19B envisages one judge having responsibility for case management throughout the life of the group litigation case. A Master or district judge may be appointed to deal with **18.18** procedural matters, which he will do in accordance with any directions given by the managing judge (CPR 19BPD, para 8).

18.19 The management court will also normally require all new claims to be commenced in it, although failure to comply will not invalidate such a claim; instead it should be transferred to the management court to be entered on the group register as soon as possible (CPR 19BPD, para 9).

18.20 In addition to the general management powers of the court contained in CPR Part 3, r 19.13 sets out the following directions that may be given by the management court:

(a) varying GLO issues;
(b) providing for one or more claims on the group register to proceed as test claims (which is the great advantage of the GLO);
(c) appointing the solicitor of one or more parties to be the lead solicitor for the claimants or defendants;
(d) specifying the details to be included in a statement of case in order to show that the criteria for entry of the claim on the group register have been met;
(e) specifying a date after which no claim may be added to the group register unless the court gives permission; and
(f) the entry of any particular claim which meets one or more of the GLO issues on the group register.

18.21 The management court may direct that the GLO claimants serve 'Group Particulars of Claim' which set out the various claims of all the claimants on the group register at the time of filing the particulars. Such particulars of claim will usually contain general allegations relating to all claims and a schedule containing entries relating to each individual claim specifying which of the general allegations are relied on and any specific facts relevant to the claimant (CPR 19BPD, para 14).

18.22 Test claims, which are not defined by the CPR, are specifically addressed by CPR r 19.15. Where a direction has been given for a claim on the group register to proceed as a test claim and that claim is settled, the management court may order that another claim on the register be substituted as the test claim. Where such an order is made, any order made in the test case before the date of substitution is binding on the substituted claim unless the court orders otherwise.

18.23 There are other methods of managing group litigation than using test cases as such, and these include division of the group into sub-groups, identification of common issues, trial of preliminary issues, and some investigation of a sample or all individual claims.

Judgments and orders

18.24 Under CPR r 19.12, where a judgment or order is given or made in a claim on the group register in relation to one or more GLO issues:

(a) that judgment or order will be binding on the parties to all other claims on the group register at the time it is made, unless the court orders otherwise; and
(b) the court may give directions as to the extent to which that judgment or order is binding on the parties to any claim which is subsequently entered on the group register.

18.25 Any party who is adversely affected by a judgment or order binding on him may seek permission to appeal the order, unless a party to a claim which was entered onto the group register after that judgment or order was given, in which case that party may not appeal it or apply for it to be set aside, varied, or stayed, but may apply to the court for an order that the judgment or order is not binding on him (CPR r 19.12(2) and (3)).

18.26 CPR r 19.12(4) provides that unless the court orders otherwise, disclosure of any document relating to the GLO issues by a party to a claim on the group register is disclosure of that document to all parties to the claims who are at the time on the group register and those who are subsequently entered onto it.

Trial

The management court may give directions about the trial of common issues and of individual issues. Common issues or test cases will normally be tried at the management court although it may be convenient for the parties to have other issues tried at courts located elsewhere (CPR 19BPD, para 15). **18.27**

Costs

Costs will be apportioned between the parties taking account of those costs relating to common issues and those that relate to issues in particular cases. CPR r 48.6A provides a basic framework for costs where the court has made a GLO. The following principles have been established by authorities on some of the issues of assessment that may arise: **18.28**

(1) Costs payable by those parties who discontinue their litigation before its conclusion should not be determined until after the outcome of the common issues part of the proceedings has been completed: *Afrika v Cape plc* [2001] EWCA Civ 2017, CA.
(2) No costs-sharing order had been made regarding five test cases (out of 369), but all parties were ordered to share the claimant's costs equally: *BCCI SA v Ali* (*Assessment of Costs*) [2000] 2 Costs LR 243.
(3) The importance of the courts' exercise of case management powers to limit costs was stressed in *Griffiths v Solutia UK Ltd* [2001] EWCA Civ 736.
(4) There may be joint and several liability of unsuccessful claimants in actions involving closely related claims tried together but where no GLO had been made: *Bairstow v Queens Moat Hotels plc* (*Assessment of Costs*) [2001] CP Rep 59.

C. MANAGEMENT OF GROUP LITIGATION IN EMPLOYMENT TRIBUNALS

Group litigation in the employment tribunal is most likely to involve similar claims for equal pay (for example, *Newcastle City Council v Allan* [2005] ICR 1170) arising out of TUPE 2006, for deductions from wages or where many employees are dismissed on a business reorganization or during a strike. It is believed that the largest ever single group actions are by those dismissed during the Wapping News International dispute in 1984–5 and 12,000 brought by retained fire-fighters under the Part Time Workers Regulations. Recently equal pay claims against NHS Trusts from all over the UK have been centralized in the Newcastle Region at least for the purposes of case management directions. This has the advantage of some common approach being taken to such issues. **18.29**

Rule 10(1) of ETR 2004 provides a general power for employment judges to 'make any order in relation to any matter which appears to him to be appropriate' to manage proceedings. Amongst those examples given in ETR 2004, r 10(2) of orders which may be made, the following may assist those seeking to set up a form of group litigation (using the letters as they appear in the subrule): **18.30**

(h) staying (in Scotland, sisting) the whole or part of any proceedings;
(i) that part of the proceedings be dealt with separately;
(j) that different claims be considered together;
(q) giving leave to amend a claim or response.

Rule 10(1) further enables a judge to make any other order which he thinks fit in the particular circumstances of the case.

18.31 Further procedural aspects of when and how directions may be given are contained in Chapter 6. Employment judges are encouraged to manage cases actively and this is required more for mass claims than elsewhere. The issues which frequently arise in such cases are:

(a) The centralization of cases—sometimes claims in relation to the same issue are lodged in many different regions because they are brought against a single employer which has many different places of business. The appropriate course is to write to the President of Employment Tribunals to ask him to make an order that all cases are heard in one region. Thus, in the thousands of cases arising out of part-time pensions litigation, the hearings were centralized in London Central region.

(b) It is important that, as far as possible, multiple appeals at different stages are avoided since this has the effect of postponing the conclusion of the litigation. The cases should therefore be managed in such a way that one case is taken to appeal and the others await the outcome of that appeal.

(c) It is often appropriate that an end date be stated after which new cases will not be treated as part of the multiple. This is done in order to avoid a situation where the cases are being prepared for trial and then new cases are added, which extends the preparation time for them and may lead to adjournments. However, in most cases the claims which are outside the multiple will fall in line with the decision in principle reached in the multiple in accordance with cases such as *Ashmore v British Coal* [1990] ICR 485.

(d) Schedules should be prepared of all of the claimants and these should ideally be agreed with the respondents to ensure that there is no ambiguity as to who will be covered by the decisions which are made in the multiple.

(e) A clear register should be drawn up of those involved in the group litigation so that it is clear whose cases are covered by orders and decisions made in the litigation without further ado.

18.32 Case management is often needed very early on in these cases and regular discussion should be encouraged between representatives and ET judges (with active involvement by the administration) and most appropriately often by telephone (although the large number of representatives involved in some such cases may render this logistically difficult). This can save endless time and cost later on. Early identification of sample/test case issues is helpful where possible. Once they are settled it is easier to move to further directions about further information, disclosure, and witness statements.

18.33 Where more than one claim is being pursued within a mass claim, eg unfair dismissal, discrimination, and/or breach of contract, and the generic claim is not applicable to all, claimant representatives should clearly identify at the outset which of the claims each claimant is pursuing and what structure of hearings is desired.

18.34 The same employment judge should deal throughout if possible with the mass claims in order to achieve continuity. A senior clerk should also be appointed to deal with all claims and ensure continuity of treatment.

18.35 Frequently, there are similar issues arising in different mass claims going on around the country but there is no clear information system (save informal discussion) which allows these matters to be tracked, still less to be reviewed to check whether such issues could be centralized. It would be sensible for all other cases to be stayed and for bulletins to then be issued to practitioners as to the progress on those test cases with appropriate directions made on a national basis. This would be similar to the approach taken in the part-time pensions cases but not apparently in other cases.

19

Employment Appeal Tribunal

SUMMARY

(1) A party may appeal to the EAT on the grounds that an employment tribunal has wrongly applied a principle of law, misunderstood a statute, reached a decision that no reasonable tribunal could have reached (perversity), or come to a conclusion that was perverse since there was no evidence whatever to support it.

(2) The EAT is reluctant to overturn tribunal decisions on fairness unless an error of law can clearly be identified.

(3) The EAT will not hear academic appeals which do not affect the decision in the case, nor will it allow, save in exceptional circumstances, new points of law to be raised which were not taken in the tribunal from which the appeal is brought.

(4) The EAT will only in exceptional circumstances overturn awards of compensation and it has no jurisdiction to set aside an agreement to compromise an appeal.

(5) New evidence which was not before the tribunal will be allowed only in exceptional circumstances.

(6) Interim matters may be heard before the main hearing usually in preliminary hearings, and the EAT has the power to award costs and to review its own decisions in ways which are similar to that exercised by the employment tribunal.

(7) A party which is unsuccessful in the EAT may appeal to the Court of Appeal, but only with permission of the EAT or the Court of Appeal, and an application for permission should be made before the EAT as soon as possible after the hearing from which the appeal is brought and within four weeks of the date when the decision, judgment, or order was entered, perfected, or signed.

A. INTRODUCTION

19.01 Those litigants who are not satisfied with either the outcome of their case in the employment tribunal or alternatively, the way in which their case was dealt with by the tribunal have the right to appeal to the Employment Appeal Tribunal (EAT) but only on a point of law. The EAT's jurisdiction is now provided for by the Employment Tribunals Act 1996 (ETA 1996) and is limited, on the whole, to jurisdiction over individual labour disputes.

19.02 The EAT has a division which sits in Scotland but it remains part of the national EAT. The EAT has occasionally sat in Wales since 2001. This was as a result of the decision of the Court of Appeal in *Williams v Cowell (t/a The Stables)* [2000] ICR 85. In that case the Court of Appeal held that there was no requirement that the EAT permit the use of Welsh since an appeal heard by the EAT in England did not amount to 'legal proceedings in Wales' within s 22(1) of the Welsh Language Act 1993 even though an appeal might be from an employment tribunal which sat in Wales. In Northern Ireland, appeals from the decisions of the employment tribunals are brought by way of case stated to the Northern Ireland Court of Appeal and there is no equivalent to the EAT.

19.03 Cases are usually heard within three months of the notice of appeal being presented.

B. CONSTITUTION AND PROCEDURAL RULES

19.04 Although titled a tribunal, the EAT is in fact a superior court of record consisting of a High Court or county court judge and a union and management lay member with industrial relations knowledge and experience (ETA 1996, s 22). Thus the EAT usually sits as a three-member court but where cases of particular difficulty are dealt with four lay members may sit (see, eg, *Government Communications Staff Federation v Certification Officer* [1993] ICR 163).

19.05 Several High Court judges are assigned to the tribunal, although typically only two sit on any one day. Circuit judges have also sat in the jurisdiction since 1991. Phillips J was the first President of the EAT and he was succeeded by Slynn J, Browne-Wilkinson J, Waite J, Popplewell J, Wood J, Mummery J, Morison J, Lindsay J, Burton J, and Elias J. The present President of the EAT is Underhill J. In Scotland, Lord Macdonald, a judge of the Court of Session, presided between 1974 and 1986. His successors have been in turn Lords Mayfield, Coulsfield, and Johnson, and now Lady Smith. Applications for lay members are sought as and when they are required, from trade unions and employer organizations.

The EAT's decision may be given on a majority basis and as such, since the EAT member has just one vote, the judge may be outvoted by the lay members. This is a unique position within the appellate courts and rarely happens but did, for example, in the cases of *Inner London Education Authority v Nash* The Times, 18 November 1978 and *Smith v Safeway plc* [1995] ICR 472. The judgment is always given by the judge even if he is in the minority, although he will express the minority view in the judgment as well as the dominant majority view. **19.06**

The administration of the EAT is headed by the registrar, presently Ms P Dunleavy, with a small staff. **19.07**

On a typical day, four or five divisions of the EAT sit in London and one in Scotland. The address of the EAT for England and Wales is Audit House, 58 Victoria Embankment, London EC4Y 0DS and in Scotland 11 Melville Crescent, Edinburgh EH3 7LU. **19.08**

The procedural rules

The EAT has been governed since 16 December 1993 by the Employment Appeal Tribunal Rules 1993, SI 1993/2854. These rules have been amended by the Employment Appeal Tribunal (Amendment) Rules 2001, SI 2001/1128 and the Employment Appeal Tribunal (Amendment) Rules 2004, SI 2004/2526. However, the EAT retains a general power to regulate its own procedure under s 30(3) of ETA 1996. As such, the EAT has issued a number of important Practice Directions. The most recent of these is the Practice Direction which came into force on 22 May 2008 (the 2008 Practice Direction) replacing but not much amending that which was effective from 9 December 2004. By para 1.1 of the 2008 Practice Direction it supersedes all other Practice Directions. **19.09**

Paragraph 1.4 of the 2008 Practice Direction requires and enables the EAT to apply the overriding objective which is also contained in the EAT Rules. That objective is to deal with cases justly. Dealing with cases justly includes, so far as is practicable: **19.10**

(a) ensuring that the parties are on an equal footing;
(b) dealing with cases in ways which are proportionate to the importance and complexity of the issues;
(c) ensuring that a case is dealt with expeditiously and fairly;
(d) saving expense.

The parties are required to help the EAT to further the overriding objective by virtue of para 1.5 of the 2008 Practice Direction so that a representative may be penalized in costs if she or he does not do so and instead is obstructive toward the EAT. **19.11**

C. JURISDICTION

The EAT's jurisdiction is set out exhaustively in s 21 of ETA 1996 which states that an appeal lies to the EAT in respect of 'any question of law arising from any decision of, or arising in any proceedings before an employment tribunal'. Further, s 21 requires that the appeal be in respect of a question of law arising under or by virtue of one of the following statutes or statutory instruments: **19.12**

(a) Equal Pay Act 1970;
(b) Sex Discrimination Act 1975;
(c) Race Relations Act 1976;
(d) Trade Union and Labour Relations (Consolidation) Act 1992;
(e) Disability Discrimination Act 1995;
(f) Employment Rights Act 1996;
(g) Employment Tribunals Act 1996;
(h) National Minimum Wage Act 1998;
(i) Employment Relations Act 1999;

(j) Working Time Regulations 1998, SI 1998/1833;
(k) Transnational Information and Consultation of Employees Regulations 1999, SI 1999/3323;
(l) Part-time Workers (Prevention of Less Favourable Treatment) Regulations 2000, SI 2000/1551;
(m) Fixed Term Employees (Prevention of Less Favourable Treatment) Regulations 2002, SI 2002/2034;
(n) Employment Equality (Sexual Orientation) Regulations 2003, SI 2003/1661;
(o) Employment Equality (Religion or Belief) Regulations 2003, SI 2003/1660;
(p) Merchant Shipping (Working Time: Inland Waterways) Regulations 2003, SI 2003/3049;
(q) European Public Limited-Liability Company Regulations 2004, SI 2004/2326;
(r) Fishing Vessels (Working Time: Sea-fishermen) Regulations 2004, SI 2004/1713;
(s) Information and Consultation of Employees Regulations 2004, SI 2004/3426;
(t) Employment Equality (Age) Regulations 2006, SI 2006/1031.

19.13 In addition to the general jurisdiction conferred by s 21 of ETA 1996, appeals lie to the EAT on questions of law arising from the Transfer of Undertakings (Protection of Employment) Regulations 2006.

19.14 The EAT also has jurisdiction to hear appeals from the decision of the certification officer under the Trade Union and Labour Relations (Consolidation) Act 1992 (see para 22.41). Section 9 of TULR(C)A 1992 provides jurisdiction for the EAT to hear appeals relating to the refusal of a certification officer to enter an organization's name in the list of trade unions or a refusal to issue a certificate of independence. Similarly, s 126 of TULR(C)A 1992 allows the EAT to hear appeals from the decision of a certification officer in respect of the entry of an organization's name on the list of employers' associations. Section 45D provides jurisdiction in respect of ss 25, 31, and 45C which deal with the administration of trade unions. Appeals from the decision of the certification officer as to Part IV of TULR(C)A 1992, which deals with trade union elections, lie to the EAT by virtue of s 56A. Similarly, appeals from the certification officer under Chapter VI (application of funds for political purposes), Chapter VIIA (breach of rules), and s 103 (resolutions approving union amalgamations or transfers). These decisions of the certification officer can be appealed to the EAT by virtue of ss 95, 108C, and 104 respectively.

19.15 The EAT has no jurisdiction to hear appeals from the Central Arbitration Committee (CAC) in respect of its main function of resolving statutory trade union recognition disputes under ERA 1996, or indeed any of its functions; save that the EAT has a limited appellate jurisdiction over the CAC in respect of its decisions with regard to European Works Councils, under the Transnational Information and Consultation of Employees Regulations 1999. Any challenge to the CAC's decisions, save in that limited respect, lies by way of judicial review to the Administrative Court.

19.16 Where the EAT has no jurisdiction to hear an appeal from a decision of the employment tribunal such as improvement or prohibition notices (see para 16.47), appeals on questions of law still lie with the High Court by virtue of s 11 of the Tribunals and Inquiries Act 1992. However, there are very few appeals from the employment tribunals which are heard by the High Court. In those cases the appeal is governed by CPR r 52 and RSC Ord 94, r 8. The appellant's notice of appeal must be served on the employment tribunal and the respondent within 42 days of the decision of the employment tribunal.

Original jurisdiction of the Employment Appeal Tribunal

19.17 In addition to its appellate jurisdiction, the EAT has original jurisdiction in certain circumstances:

(a) to hear complaints under regs 20(1) and 21(1) of the Transnational Information and Consultation Regulations 1999 which relate to failures to establish European Works Councils or information or consultation procedures, and disputes relating to the operation of the above. The EAT has the power to issue a written penalty notice to the relevant central management which requires it to pay a penalty to the Secretary of State in respect of the failure unless it is satisfied that the failure resulted from a reason beyond its control, or that it has some other reasonable excuse. In addition the EAT may decide that the central management has not complied with the terms of an agreement setting up a European Works Council or consultation procedure. In that instance the EAT may order a defaulter to take steps that are necessary to comply.

(b) to hear applications under reg 33 of the European Public Limited-Liability Company Regulations 2004 for a penalty notice to be issued following the CAC's declaration that there has been a failure to comply with an employee involvement agreement of the standard rules on employee involvement. An employer who is issued with a penalty notice will have to pay a penalty to the Secretary of State unless he is able to show that the failure resulted from circumstances beyond the employer's control or that he has some other reasonable excuse for his failure.

(c) to hear applications under reg 22 of the Information and Consultation of Employees Regulations 2004 for a penalty notice to be issued following the CAC's declaration that there has been a failure to comply with a negotiated agreement or the standard information and consultation provisions. If issued with a penalty notice the employer will have to pay a penalty to the Secretary of State unless he is able to show that the failure resulted from circumstances beyond the employer's control or that he has some other reasonable excuse for his failure.

D. GROUNDS OF APPEAL

Appeal on a point of law

Appeals lie to the EAT (pursuant to ETA 1996, s 21) generally on any question of law arising out of those specified statutes and statutory instruments which the EAT has jurisdiction to hear appeals from. To succeed in an appeal on a point of law, an appellant must be able to establish that: **19.18**

> the employment tribunal has wrongly applied a principle of law; misunderstood a statute; reached a decision that no reasonable tribunal could have reached; or come to a conclusion that was perverse since there was no evidence whatever to support it (*Watling v William Bird & Son Contractors* (1976) 11 ITR 70).

If a tribunal has properly directed itself as to the law and has reached a permissible conclusion on the facts, its use of language in its decision which may appear to be inconsistent with the direction of its reasoning will not necessarily amount to an error of law (*Jones v Mid Glamorgan CC* [1997] ICR 815, 826). As Lord Denning MR stated in *Hollister v National Farmers' Union* [1979] ICR 542, 552:

> Parliament has expressly left the determination of all questions of fact to the industrial tribunals themselves. An appeal to the appeal tribunal lies only to a point of law; and from the tribunal to this Court only on a point of law. It is not right that points of fact should be dressed up as points of law so as to encourage appeals.

There are certain categories of cases in which the EAT and the Court of Appeal have stated that in general no points of law are likely to be raised since the matters in question are essentially matters of fact. This includes but is not limited to the following: **19.19**

(a) whether or not there has been a direct dismissal (*Western Excavating (ECC) Ltd v Sharp* [1978] IRLR 27, EAT);
(b) whether there has been a constructive dismissal (*Woods v WM Car Services (Peterborough) Ltd* [1982] IRLR 413; *Pederson v Camden London Borough Council* [1981] ICR 674);
(c) the assessment of fairness in unfair dismissal cases (*Earl v Slater & Wheeler (Airlyne) Ltd* [1973] 1 All ER 145);
(d) whether a person is employed or an independent contractor (*O'Kelly v Trust House Forte plc* [1983] IRLR 413; *Pederson v Camden London Borough Council* [1981] ICR 674);

(e) the assessment of contributory fault (*Hollier v Plysu Ltd* [1983] IRLR 260; *Warrilow v Robert Walker Ltd* [1984] IRLR 304);
(f) whether a person has taken part in industrial action (*Naylor v Orton & Smith Ltd* [1987] IRLR 233; *Faust v Power Packing Casemakers Ltd* [1983] IRLR 117);
(g) whether an employee has resigned (*Makin v Greens Motors (Bridport) Ltd* The Times, 18 April 1986);
(h) whether and when there has been a transfer of an undertaking for the purposes of the TUPE provisions (*Apex Leisure Hire v Barratt* [1984] IRLR 224).

19.20 The EAT has not tended, historically, to interfere with the amounts of compensation which are awarded to successful claimants before the employment tribunals since there is a recognition on the part of the EAT that damages are calculated making use of a broad brush approach (*Fougere v Phoenix Motor Co Ltd* [1977] 1 All ER 237). However, there has of late been a recognition, particularly with regard to discrimination cases, that awards should reflect compensation that would be made for injury to feelings in personal injury cases (*Vento v Chief Constable of West Yorkshire Police* [2002] IRLR 177, EAT). As such, the award of compensation has become a more exact science and therefore appeal points are more likely to be taken and are more likely to be successful. If they are to be successful appellants will still have to demonstrate that the assessment of compensation amounts to an error of law on the part of an employment tribunal rather than merely being a reasonable exercise of the employment tribunal's discretion.

Perversity

19.21 The EAT will only interfere with a finding of fact made by the employment tribunal where that finding is perverse since a perverse finding of fact amounts to an error of law. Perversity is a difficult ground of appeal to establish since the test is a very high hurdle to overcome. In *Chiu v British Aerospace plc* [1982] IRLR 56 the EAT pointed out that a finding of an employment tribunal could only be described as perverse where no tribunal, properly directed in law, could have reached the decision which the particular tribunal had reached. It would not be enough that the finding was 'contrary to the weight of the evidence' or that 'the tribunal heard evidence it is hard to believe'.

19.22 The classic statement of perversity as a ground of appeal can be found in *Neale v County Council of Hereford and Worcester* [1986] IRLR 168. The EAT had overturned the employment tribunal's decision relating to the fairness of the dismissal. However, the EAT decision was overturned by the Court of Appeal and it was rebuked for substituting its own view as to the fairness of the dismissal for that of the 'industrial jury'. May LJ stated at para 45 of his judgment:

> An [employment] tribunal has been described as an 'industrial jury', and so in many ways it is. It knows its area; it comprises a lawyer, a representative of employees and a representative of employers within that district; each has substantial experience of industrial problems and they are hearing this type of case regularly. Their job is to find the facts, to apply the relevant law and to reach the conclusion to which their findings and their experience lead them. It will not, in my opinion, be often that when an industrial tribunal has done just that, and with the care, clarity and thoroughness which the Industrial Tribunal in the present case displayed, that one can legitimately say that their conclusion 'offends reason', or that their conclusion was one to which no reasonable industrial tribunal could have come. Deciding these cases is the job of industrial tribunals and when they have not erred in law neither the EAT nor this Court should disturb their decision unless one can say in effect: 'My goodness, that was certainly wrong'.

19.23 However, the *Neale* formulation of perversity, despite frequently being cited by appellate courts, is not universally accepted. In *Piggott Brothers v Jackson* [1992] ICR 85, Lord Donaldson MR was of the view that the *Neale* formulation was liable to confuse appellate courts since the EAT, for example, could fall into error by deciding that it would have come to a different conclusion to that reached by the employment tribunal. It might then decide that the decision of an employment tribunal was certainly wrong. A decision of the employment tribunal is not perverse merely because an appellate court would have come to a different view. Lord Donaldson MR therefore proposed that the test be stricter. Appellate courts should look to see if the finding of fact could be supported by *any* evidence at all or alternatively whether there was a clear misdirection in law by the tribunal. If the tribunal's decision was not open to criticism on either of these grounds, then the appellate court might wish to reconsider whether the decision of the employment tribunal was perverse.

In *Stewart v Cleveland Guest (Engineering) Ltd* [1994] IRLR 443, Mummery P reviewed the authorities relating to perversity and stated: **19.24**

> [The EAT] should only interfere with the decision of the Industrial Tribunal where the conclusion of that Tribunal on the evidence before it is 'irrational', 'offends reason', 'is certainly wrong' or 'is very clearly wrong' or 'must be wrong' or 'is plainly wrong' or 'is not a permissible option' or 'is fundamentally wrong' or 'is outrageous' or 'makes absolutely no sense' or 'flies in the face of properly informed logic'. This variety of phraseology is taken from a number of well-known cases which describe the circumstances in which this Tribunal (and higher courts) have characterised perversity. The result is that it is rare or exceptional for an appeal to succeed on the grounds of perversity.

This was reiterated by the Court of Appeal in *Yeboah v Crofton* [2002] EWCA Civ 794, [2002] IRLR 634. The court explained that 'even where the appeal tribunal had grave doubts about the decision it had to proceed with great care' where allegations of perversity were made. Mummery LJ said (at para 93): **19.25**

> Such an appeal [perversity appeal] ought only to succeed where an overwhelming case is made out that the Employment Tribunal reached a decision which no reasonable tribunal, on a proper appreciation of the evidence and the law, would have reached. Even in cases where the Appeal Tribunal has 'grave doubts' about the decision of the Employment Tribunal it must proceed with 'great care'. (See also *James v LB of Greenwich* [2008] IRLR 302 para 7; *McGregor v Intercity East Coast* 1998 SC 440.)

For an example of a case where it was found that an employment tribunal had come to a perverse finding, see the decision of the EAT (sitting in Scotland) in *United Distillers v Conlin* [1992] IRLR 502. In that case the claimant was dismissed from his job for having engaged in fraud against his employer while under a final written warning for the same offence. It was accepted that the procedure adopted by the employer was fair but the employment tribunal found the dismissal to be unfair in substance given the low value of the fraud and inconsistency in the approach by the employer. The EAT overturned the decision of the employment tribunal as being a perverse decision in the sense that the decision was not a permissible option in all the circumstances (see also *Anglian Home Improvements Ltd v Kelly* [2005] ICR 242 at para 32). **19.26**

Paragraph 2.6 of the Practice Direction 2008 states with regard to the drafting of a notice of appeal in cases of perversity appeals that: **19.27**

> an appellant may not state as a ground of appeal simply words to the effect that 'the judgment or order was contrary to the evidence', or that 'there was no evidence to support the judgment or order', or that 'the judgment or order was one which no reasonable Tribunal could have reached and was perverse' unless the Notice of Appeal also sets out full particulars of the matters relied on in support of those general grounds.

It is thus important to set out very clearly precisely what findings it is said are perverse and why with reference to the evidence if necessary.

Examples of perversity: finding of fact unsupported by any evidence

The EAT will allow an appeal where the employment tribunal makes a finding of fact which is not supported by any evidence. This form of appeal is really a subset of perversity since if a tribunal makes a finding of fact which is unsupported by any evidence, that is, in effect, the same as saying that the tribunal has made a finding of fact which no tribunal, properly directed in law could have made. It will not be enough for an appellant to show that the weight of evidence was against a particular finding of fact since the weight that a tribunal attached to evidence is a **19.28** matter for itself (see *Eclipse Blinds Ltd v Wright* [1992] ICR 723, 733). The appellant must show that there was no evidence at all which could enable the tribunal to make a finding of fact that it has made, which usually means producing notes of evidence.

19.29 Therefore, in *British Telecommunications plc v Sheridan* [1990] IRLR 27, the Court of Appeal explained that it was not enough, in order to constitute a ground of appeal, that the employment tribunal had misunderstood or misapplied the facts. The error of the tribunal had to be more serious and it must have come to a conclusion for which there was absolutely no evidence in order to convert a finding of fact into an error of law.

Inadequate reasoning

19.30 The EAT is also entitled to interfere with the decision of an employment tribunal in circumstances where it is of the view that the tribunal's reasons are inadequate. The extent of the reasons required will depend on the circumstances of the case. In *Meek v City of Birmingham DC* [1987] IRLR 250, para 8, the Court of Appeal classically explained what was required of an employment tribunal:

> It has on a number of occasions been made plain that the decision of an Industrial Tribunal is not required to be an elaborate formalistic product of refined legal draftsmanship, but it must contain an outline of the story which has given rise to the complaint and a summary of the Tribunal's basic factual conclusions and a statement of the reasons which have led them to reach the conclusion which they do on those basic facts. The parties are entitled to be told why they have won or lost. There should be sufficient account of the facts and of the reasoning to enable the EAT or, on further appeal, this court to see whether any question of law arises; and it is highly desirable that the decision of an Industrial Tribunal should give guidance both to employers and trade unions as to practices which should or should not be adopted.

19.31 Subsequently, in *English v Emery Reimbold & Strick Ltd* [2002] EWCA Civ 605, [2003] IRLR 710, the Court of Appeal stated that as a matter of law arising both from (a) Article 6 of the European Convention on Human Rights, and (b) the common law duty to provide reasons, that a judgment must contain sufficient reasoning so that the parties know why one won and the other lost. Further, any appellate court or tribunal in asking whether it is apparent to the parties why they have won or lost should not merely refer to the judgment as it appears on its face. Rather it must look at the judgment of the tribunal in the context of the material evidence and submissions which were placed before that tribunal. Similarly if on the broad brush approach the judgment is plainly inadequate then detailed legal arguments should not be employed to repair it. Thus in *Anya v University of Oxford* [2001] IRLR 377 Sedley LJ stated that it was not appropriate:

> to comb through a patently deficient decision for signs of the missing elements and to try and amplify these by argument into an adequate set of reasons.

19.32 In the final analysis, the extent to which detailed reasoning will be required may depend on the nature of the case in hand. Thus the Court of Appeal stated in *Deman v Association of University Teachers* [2003] EWCA Civ 329 that more would be expected from an employment tribunal in a detailed race or sex discrimination case which required the tribunal to draw inferences in order to determine a person's true motivation for behaving in a particular manner than would be required if the tribunal were simply applying an objective norm to a set of facts as the tribunal does when it decides whether a dismissal is fair in all the circumstances.

19.33 Where an appeal is allowed by the EAT on the grounds that the employment tribunal has not given sufficient reasons for its decision, the matter will normally be remitted to the same tribunal in order that it can complete its statutory duty or alternatively to a different tribunal for rehearing (on the principles to be applied see paras 11.35–11.50). It will not simply be overturned by the EAT unless it is convinced that whatever the further reasoning it will reveal another error by the employment tribunal (see, for example, *Burns v Consignia Ltd No. 2* [2004] IRLR 425 and *Barke v SEETEC* [2005] EWCA Civ 578, [2005] IRLR 633 discussed at paras 19.199–19.202 below).

Delay

The EAT may in certain limited cases intervene in situations where there has been excessive delay by an employment tribunal in promulgating its decision. The jurisprudential basis for such intervention has been the subject of some debate in the case law and the Court of Appeal diverged from the approach taken by the EAT itself. **19.34**

In *Kwamin v Birmingham City Council* [2004] IRLR 516, the EAT held that an independent ground of appeal would arise in the case of delay where the decision of a tribunal was unsafe. A decision would become unsafe when the delay in promulgating the decision had led to a tribunal falling into error even if such error would not have resulted in the tribunal's decision being perverse and therefore amounting to an error of law. **19.35**

The *Kwamin* appeal was made up of a number of conjoined appeals. One of those was subsequently appealed to the Court of Appeal and the appeal became known as *Bangs v Connex South Eastern Ltd* [2005] EWCA Civ 14, [2005] 2 All ER 316. The leading judgment of Mummery LJ did not accept the EAT's reasoning in *Kwamin*. Mummery LJ held that the following principles govern appeals to the EAT where the ground of appeal is that the employment tribunal has delayed unreasonably in promulgating its decision: **19.36**

(a) Appeals could only be brought before the EAT on questions of law by virtue of s 21 of ETA 1996. No appeals could be brought in respect of findings of fact which were made by the employment tribunal.
(b) Unreasonable delay was ordinarily a matter of fact and not a question of law. No independent ground of appeal existed simply because a decision was unsafe as a result of factual errors or omissions which had been caused by the delay.
(c) If an appellant was to succeed in arguing that an appeal ought to succeed as a result of an employment tribunal unreasonably delaying the promulgation of its decision, it would need to be shown that the tribunal had come to a perverse decision in respect of its overall conclusion or in respect of specific matters of fact or credibility.
(d) There may be situations in which an appellant could argue that unreasonable delay can be treated as a procedural error or material irregularity giving rise to a question of law in the proceedings of the tribunal. Such a situation would occur if the appellant could show that the failure to promulgate the decision within a reasonable time gave rise to a real risk that the appellant had been deprived of his right to a fair trial under Article 6 of ECHR.

In the light of *Bangs v Connex* it is unlikely that there will be many successful appeals on the sole basis that litigants have experienced delays in the promulgation of a decision by the employment tribunal. Most delays are unlikely to be severe enough to deprive litigants of their Article 6 right to a fair trial—indeed, that was the conclusion of the Court of Appeal on the facts in *Bangs v Connex* itself. Moreover, if the delay leads to a perverse decision, an appellant will be able to rely on perversity as a ground of appeal without making reference to the delay. **19.37**

Allegations of bias or procedural impropriety

Allegations of bias or procedural impropriety levelled against a tribunal (see Chapter 10) can raise a question of law provided that they are not obviously so lacking in substance that there is, in reality, no challenge to the tribunal's decision. This point was investigated in *Lodwick v Southwark London Borough Council* [2004] EWCA Civ 306, [2004] IRLR 544, where the EAT had declined jurisdiction over a bias appeal on the basis that it raised no question of law and therefore the EAT had no jurisdiction. Pill LJ stated, however, at para 15 of his judgment that all but the most unfounded allegations of bias would raise a question of law and therefore the EAT would have jurisdiction to entertain such appeals: **19.38**

> While there may be cases in which, upon findings of fact by the tribunal, the allegation of bias disappears, the appeal against the ruling of the employment tribunal was in my judgment an appeal on a question of law arising from a decision of the tribunal. The Employment Appeal Tribunal had

jurisdiction unless the allegation of bias was on its face so lacking in substance that it could not be said to amount to a real challenge to the decision.

19.39 Moreover, the effect of Article 6 of ECHR (restated in the overriding objective as the duty to act fairly) is to place a tribunal under a duty to conduct a proper hearing without any form of prejudice (see *Kraska v Switzerland* (1993) 18 EHRR 188, 200, para 30). A breach of Article 6 would amount to an error of law on the part of the tribunal and therefore invoke the jurisdiction of the EAT.

19.40 The EAT has developed rules of practice for dealing with appeals where allegations of bias or procedural impropriety are made in the 2008 Practice Direction.

19.41 The appellant must include in the notice of appeal full particulars of each complaint made (2008 Practice Direction, para 11.1). It is particularly important that a party making an allegation of bias or procedural impropriety sets out clearly the allegations made about the conduct of the employment tribunal. Thus, if the allegations are not set out adequately the registrar or a judge may direct that the appellant or his representative provide an affidavit setting out full particulars of all allegations of bias or misconduct relied upon (2008 Practice Direction, para 11.2). It is unusual now to require an affidavit but its use here stresses the degree of certainty that there should be before such a criticism is made.

19.42 If the appeal is allocated to the preliminary hearing track or the full hearing track, then the EAT may take the following steps:

(a) require the appellant or a representative to provide, if not already provided, an affidavit (it is thought that a witness statement is insufficient because of the gravity of the allegations);
(b) require any party to give an affidavit or to obtain a witness statement from any person who has represented any of the parties at the tribunal hearing, and any other person present at the tribunal hearing or a relevant part of it, giving their account of the events set out in the affidavit of the appellant or the appellant's representative;
(c) seek comments, upon all affidavits or witness statements received, from the judge of the employment tribunal from which the appeal is brought, and may seek such comments from the lay members of the tribunal;
(d) The EAT will on receipt supply to the parties copies of all affidavits, statements, and comments received.

19.43 Paragraph 11.6 of the 2008 Practice Direction provides that:

(a) the EAT will not permit complaints of bias or procedural impropriety to be raised or developed at the hearing of the appeal unless this procedure has been followed (and this is in practice strictly adhered to);
(b) the EAT recognizes that pursuant to the Employment Tribunal (Constitution and Rules of Procedure) Regulations 2004 judges and employment tribunals are themselves obliged to observe the overriding objective and are given wide powers and duties of case management, so appeals in respect of their conduct of employment tribunals, which is pursuant to these provisions, are less likely to succeed;
(c) unsuccessful pursuit of an allegation of bias or improper conduct, particularly in respect of case management decisions, may put the party raising it at risk of an order for costs.

19.44 The EAT issued a Conciliation Protocol on 9 December 2004 which may apply to any appeal which is amenable to conciliation, but it is expressed to be likely to apply to complaints of bias or procedural irregularity on the part of the employment tribunal. The Protocol states at para 10 that the EAT can stay an appeal for a period of '(say) 28 days' in order that the parties might make use of the conciliation services of ACAS. If ACAS is successful in negotiating a settlement, the appeal may be dismissed on withdrawal by the appellant or alternatively the appeal may be allowed by consent. If the appeal is to be allowed by consent then the judge will give directions under para 15 of the 2008 Practice Direction. Further, in June 2007 ACAS announced that it would extend its conciliation services to selected cases referred to it by the EAT. The cases which are expected to be referred by the EAT include in particular:

(a) cases where the parties' employment relationship is ongoing;
(b) cases which could be referred back to the employment tribunal;
(c) appeals relating to monetary awards.

It is too early to determine how significant an impact this channel of avoiding the hearing of appeals will be.

An appeal on grounds of bias or procedural impropriety may appear to draw the EAT into a position where it has to adjudicate upon factual disputes as to precisely what has occurred before the tribunal from which the appeal is brought, but naturally the EAT has tried to avoid being drawn into such a role. As such, in *Kennedy v Metropolitan Police Commissioner* The Times, 8 November 1990, the EAT was of the view that if there is a dispute as to what happened at a hearing before the employment tribunal, the practice of the EAT should be to 'accept the word and the evidence and comments of the learned chairman unless there is clearly a mistake'. **19.45**

The decision of the EAT in *Facey v Midas Retail Security* [2000] IRLR 812, however, indicates that the EAT may have to determine factual disputes since the resolution of such disputes may well resolve the question of whether the judge or tribunal was biased or prejudiced. In *Facey* the appellant sought to bring the tribunal members to the EAT to give evidence as to what had occurred before the tribunal. The EAT decided that the procedure it ought to adopt in determining such matters of primary fact was that while the judge and lay members may be requested to provide sworn written evidence as to matters of primary fact and adverse inferences can be drawn in a suitable case from their failure to do so, they can neither voluntarily submit themselves for cross-examination, nor can they be compelled to answer questions under cross-examination. **19.46**

Moreover, in *Stansbury v Datapulse plc* [2003] EWCA Civ 1951, [2004] IRLR 466, the Court of Appeal accepted the EAT's view as expressed in *Facey*, that in situations where there was a factual dispute, the EAT may well have to assume the role of being judges of fact. An acute case of this was seen in *Stansbury*; the allegation was that one of the wing members had fallen asleep and had appeared drunk during the hearing. Needless to say, there was a substantial dispute as to what had, in fact, occurred. The EAT had found that it was not necessary for it to resolve the issues of fact since even if the wing member had fallen asleep during the tribunal hearing, that would not render the hearing unfair since the tribunal had reserved its decision, which in the event, had been unanimous. The Court of Appeal disagreed. Peter Gibson LJ stated (at para 26): **19.47**

> If the hearing was unfair because of the misbehaviour of a member of the ET the decision is not saved from being unfair by the fact that the decision was unanimous and reserved.

Thus the Court of Appeal found that it was not only appropriate, but indeed necessary, for the EAT to resolve the issues of fact which would enable it to determine whether or not the hearing was fair.

Guidance as to whether or not an appeal on grounds of bias is likely to succeed was given to tribunals by the Court of Appeal in *Locabail (UK) Ltd v Bayfield Properties Ltd* [2000] IRLR 96. Paragraph 25 of the judgment sets out a number of factors which might lead to a successful appeal on grounds of bias and sets out other grounds which would ordinarily not lead to a successful appeal: **19.48**

> It would be dangerous and futile to attempt to define or list the factors which may or may not give rise to a real danger of bias. Everything will depend on the facts, which may include the nature of the issue to be decided. We cannot, however, conceive of circumstances in which an objection could be soundly based on the religion, ethnic or national origin, gender, age, class, means or sexual orientation of the judge. Nor, at any rate ordinarily, could an objection be soundly based on the judge's social or educational or service or employment background or history, nor that of any member of the judge's family; or previous political associations; or membership of social or sporting or charitable bodies;

> or Masonic associations; or previous judicial decisions; or extra-curricular utterances (whether in textbooks, lectures, speeches, articles, interviews, reports or responses to consultation papers); or previous receipt of instructions to act for or against any party, solicitor or advocate engaged in a case before him; or membership of the same Inn, circuit, local Law Society or chambers. By contrast, a real danger of bias might well be thought to arise if there were personal friendship or animosity between the judge and any member of the public involved in the case; or if the judge were closely acquainted with any member of the public involved in the case, particularly if the credibility of that individual could be significant in the decision of the case; or if, in a case where the credibility of any individual were an issue to be decided by the judge, he had in a previous case rejected the evidence of that person in such outspoken terms as to throw doubt on his ability to approach such person's evidence with an open mind on any later occasion; or if on any question at issue in the proceedings before him the judge had expressed views, particularly in the course of the hearing, in such extreme and unbalanced terms as to throw doubt on his ability to try the issue with an objective judicial mind; or if, for any other reason, there were real ground for doubting the ability of the judge to ignore extraneous considerations, prejudices and predilections and bring an objective judgment to bear on the issues before him.

19.49 Successful challenges to tribunal decisions on grounds of bias have been in fact few (see also para 19.38 *et seq.*).

19.50 In *Ansar v Lloyds TSB Bank plc* [2007] IRLR 211, the Court of Appeal, upholding the judgment of Burton J, decided that the EAT should test the employment tribunal's decision as to recusal by considering the proceedings which had taken place before the tribunal as a whole and should decide whether a perception of bias had arisen from the conduct of those proceedings. The mere fact that a judge or employment judge or member earlier in the same case or in a previous case had commented adversely on the conduct of a party or a witness or had found the evidence of a party or witness to be unreliable would not, without something more, found a sustainable objection. Here the claimant had sought to rely on the fact that he had already made a complaint about the particular judge, and thus sought his recusal from the case, but the Court of Appeal held that a mere complaint could not give rise to an automatic decision to recuse.

E. RESTRICTIONS ON THE SCOPE OF APPEAL

19.51 There are certain types of appeal which the EAT has indicated are unlikely to be successful even though the decision of the employment tribunal contains an error of law. These are:

(a) academic points of appeal;
(b) points of law which were not argued in the employment tribunal;
(c) appeals in relation to compromise agreements.

Academic points

19.52 The EAT takes the same approach to academic appeals as does the Court of Appeal. This is that in order for the appeal to be considered, it must affect the actual decision in the case. Thus, if an appeal relates to an aspect of the reasoning of an employment tribunal which, even if overturned, would not affect the result of the case, then the EAT will not hear the appeal. The classic statement of the principle is to be found in the House of Lords decision of *Ainsbury v Millington* [1987] 1 WLR 379, where Lord Bridge stated (at 381):

> It has always been a fundamental feature of our judicial system that the courts decide disputes between the parties before them; they do not pronounce on abstract questions of law when there is no dispute to be resolved.

19.53 The principle was applied by the Court of Appeal to an employment case in *Riniker v University College London* [2001] EWCA Civ 597 in which Miss Riniker had succeeded in establishing sufficient continuity of service to bring her claim, but was concerned about the date of termination of certain contracts of employment as determined by the EAT and in particular the problems that this might cause her for future proceedings. Since Miss Riniker had established sufficient continuity of service and therefore an appeal would make no difference to the result of Miss Riniker's case, the Court of Appeal refused her permission to appeal.

19.54 In *Riniker's* case, the Court of Appeal expressly approved the EAT's treatment of the principle relating to academic appeals in *Harrod v Ministry of Defence* [1981] ICR 8. In that case, the appellant sought to challenge a finding of fact made by the employment tribunal that there was no mobility clause in the appellant's contract of employment. Before the appeal the appellant's solicitor wrote to the EAT and explained that the appellant did not wish to challenge the employment tribunal's overall decision that he had not been constructively dismissed. The EAT declined jurisdiction to hear the appeal. May J stated (at 11):

> it is inherent in any appeal that the Appellant must be seeking to set aside the decision, judgment or order, whatever it may have been of the tribunal below and. . . it would need very clear words to entitle a party to any proceedings to appeal to an appellate tribunal on the basis that, although the decision below was right, nevertheless the reasons for it were wrong.

19.55 Similarly, in *Carter v Tower Hamlets LBC* EAT/1073/99 an employee who had been a swimming instructor was found work as a classroom helper but was paid at a higher rate of pay of a swimming instructor. A complaint of unfair dismissal was upheld by the employment tribunal and an order was made as to re-engagement. The tribunal then ordered at a further hearing that it would not be reasonably practicable for the employment tribunal to comply with the order for re-engagement and that she was not entitled to compensation since she had failed to take reasonable steps to mitigate her loss. The employee sought to appeal in respect of the order for re-engagement but the EAT was satisfied that there could be no benefit to the employee in pursuing an appeal and that, therefore, it would be inappropriate for the EAT to hear it.

19.56 It should be noted that since the decision of the House of Lords in *Ainsbury v Millington* (see para 19.52) both the Court of Appeal and House of Lords have sometimes taken the view that they should hear certain academic appeals where they raise points of general public importance. Thus in *Don Pasquale v HM Customs and Excise* [1990] 1 WLR 1108 the Court of Appeal was prepared to hear an appeal in relation to the assessment of value added tax despite the fact that no live issue remained between the parties. In addition, in *R v Secretary of State for the Home Department, ex p Salem* [1999] 2 All ER 42 the House of Lords accepted that its decision in *Ainsbury v Millington* only applied to questions of private rights and therefore the House of Lords was free to hear an appeal on a point of public law even though there was no issue between the parties.

19.57 The EAT has so far declined to hear academic appeals. However, in the light of the retreat of the Court of Appeal and House of Lords from the strictness of the principle set out in *Ainsbury v Millington* the EAT might choose to do so in the future. There is nothing in the EAT's rules that would prevent it doing so since the jurisdiction provided for in s 21 of EAT 1996 is invoked whenever the employment tribunal falls into an error of law.

Points of law which were not argued in the employment tribunal

19.58 It is very unusual that a party will be able to argue a point on appeal which was not argued in the employment tribunal. The general principle was set out by the EAT in *Kumchyk v Derby County Council* [1978] ICR 1116. In that case a car park attendant was dismissed after he refused to work in a different place from his usual place of work. His claim for unfair dismissal failed before the tribunal on the basis that there was an express mobility clause in this contract of employment. He sought to argue on appeal that there was an implied term in his contract of employment which restricted the express mobility clause. The point had not, however, been argued below. The EAT found that there was nothing in the statute which prevented the EAT from taking new points on appeal. However, in most cases it would be unjust to do so. It may be just to allow a new point where there had been some deception on the part of the respondent to the appeal which entitled the appellant to say:

> This really is a case in which we were headed off from running the point which we are now seeking to run before the appellate court by conduct which cannot possibly be condoned in justice by the appellate court.

However, the EAT (Arnold J presiding) went on to state that (at 1123):

> It certainly is not enough, in our judgment, that the point was not taken owing to a wrong, or what turns out in the light of events to have been a wrong, tactical decision by the appellant or his advocate. It would certainly not be enough that the omission was due to the lack of skill or experience on the part of the advocate. It would certainly not, we think, be enough that the omission could have been made good had the industrial tribunal chosen to suggest the point for consideration to the appellant or his advocate.

19.59 The basis for the rule set out in *Kumchyk* is that there is a public interest in the finality of litigation and this is especially acute in employment cases with their short time limits and lack of a costs jurisdiction. This rationale was set out by Robert Walker LJ in *Jones v Governing Body of Burdett Coutts School* [1998] IRLR 521, para 29, where he stated:

> the search for justice requires some difficult reconciliations of conflicting principles, and there is a strong public interest in finality in litigation. The rule or practice embodied in [*Kumchyk*] is not regarded as a matter of technicality, but of justice to a respondent who may be plunged into yet more litigation.

19.60 The rule set out in *Kumchyk* is of wide-ranging application and it will be generally difficult for appellants to introduce points of law before the EAT which were not argued before the employment tribunal. The rule is more strictly applied in the EAT than in the Court of Appeal. However, the rule is subject to certain exceptions:

(a) The rule will not be applied where the appellant was prevented from arguing a point before the employment tribunal by a deception on the part of the respondent to the appeal (see *Kumchyk*).

(b) It was held by the EAT in *House v Emerson Electrical Industrial Controls* [1980] ICR 785 that where a point related to the employment tribunal's jurisdiction to hear the issue, the *Kumchyk* principle should not be applied.

19.61 The extent to which the exception to the *Kumchyk* principle set out in *House* ought to be applied has been considered by the EAT and Court of Appeal on a number of occasions since. In *Glennie v Independent Magazines (UK) Ltd* [1999] ICR 38, EAT argument had taken place before the tribunal on a preliminary issue as to whether the claim was brought in time or not. The effective date of termination was agreed between the parties at the employment tribunal hearing. Ms Glennie, having lost before the employment tribunal, sought to argue before the EAT that the effective date of termination was a different date on the basis that her contract of employment had a provision requiring notice. The EAT allowed her to present that argument but its decision was overturned by the Court of Appeal ([1999] IRLR 719) which reasoned that:

(a) There was a conflict between the decision of the EAT in *House* which suggested that any jurisdictional issue could be taken as a new point on appeal and the subsequent authorities of *Russell v Elmdon Freight Terminal Ltd* [1989] ICR 629 and *Barber v Thames Television plc* [1991] IRLR 236. Those authorities held that not all jurisdictional points which were not raised before the tribunal of first instance could be taken on appeal before the EAT and that in each case the EAT had to decide whether justice required that the new point be taken. The EAT would be particularly reluctant to allow a point to be argued where new evidence was required for it to be properly considered. As was stated by Knox J in *Barber* (at 268):

> It does not however follow from this that all jurisdictional points must be allowed at any stage even if they involve a further hearing to establish further facts. In our view in each case the

appeal tribunal has to decide on balance whether justice requires that the new point should be allowed to be taken. If it appears on existing evidence that the decision appealed from is a nullity that will be a consideration of overwhelming strength. Where what is relied upon is a chance of establishing a lack of jurisdiction by calling fresh evidence which was always available the case is far less straightforward.

(b) In the *Barber* case, Knox J had been wise to leave open the possibility that, in the case of an unrepresented party, justice might demand that the EAT put right what appeared to be a glaring injustice, even though, strictly, the evidence on which the unrepresented party sought to rely would have been available before the tribunal. However, Knox J had not envisaged the possibility that, when a represented party has fought and lost a jurisdictional issue on agreed facts before the tribunal, it should then be allowed to resile from its agreement and seek a new tribunal hearing in order to adduce evidence which would then be challenged, and invite the tribunal to decide the question of jurisdiction all over again on new facts.

(c) The Court of Appeal appeared to be impressed by the fact that the appellant in the *Glennie* case would not be deprived of relying on an 'obvious knock-out point' by its refusal to allow the point to be run.

In the light of the *Glennie* decision, it will be difficult for appellants who were represented before the employment tribunal to run jurisdictional points before the EAT which were not run below. They will have to show some exceptional reason why they should be permitted to run the argument. The EAT will be more likely to allow such points where they would not require a fresh analysis of evidence by the employment tribunal or where there was an 'obvious knock-out point' which had not been taken. Litigants who were unrepresented below will have an easier task of convincing the EAT to allow them to run fresh jurisdictional points, particularly in circumstances where there has been a 'glaring injustice' as a result of the failure of the litigant in person to take a point (see also *Vakante v Governing Body of Addey* and *Stanhope School (No 2)* [2005] ICR 231; *Atkins v Coyle Personnel plc* [2008] IRLR 420). **19.62**

An exceptional case where the EAT did allow new arguments to be made was *O'Connell v Thames Water Utilities plc*, EAT/903/98. That case turned on a complicated issue where the employment tribunal wrongly held that the matter was covered by the Water Reorganization (Pensions) Regulations 1989, SI 1989/1161. **19.63**

Where the EAT allows a new point to be taken on appeal, it must give reasons for doing so and in *Jones v Governing Body of Burdett Coutts School* [1998] IRLR 521 the Court of Appeal overturned the decision of the EAT to do so because it had not given reasons, and unusually the decision fell outside the range within which the appeal tribunal could reasonably exercise its discretion. **19.64**

The Court of Appeal in *Hellyer Bros Ltd v McLeod* [1987] ICR 526 suggested that while it was for the EAT to regulate its own procedure, it was surprising that the EAT adopted a more stringent rule than that which was applied by the Court of Appeal, although this hint that a more relaxed view should be taken has not in fact been taken up. The Court of Appeal practice was set out in *Wilson v Liverpool Corporation* [1971] 1 WLR 302, where it was stated that a new point may be taken (at 307): **19.65**

> if the [Court of Appeal] is in possession of all the material necessary to enable it to dispose of the matter finally, without injustice to the other party and without recourse to a further hearing below.

In *Secretary of State for Health v Rance* [2007] IRLR 665 Judge McMullen collected the authorities together as follows at para 14: **19.66**

> I regard those two passages as key statements of the law, together with the interpretation by Brooke LJ of previous judgments of the EAT dealing with concessions. From the authorities reviewed in those cases, I draw the following principles of law:
>
> (1) There is a discretion to allow a new point of law to be argued in the EAT. It is tightly regulated by authorities; *Jones* paragraph 20.

(2) The discretion covers new points and the re-opening of conceded points; ibid.
(3) The discretion is exercised only in exceptional circumstances; ibid.
(4) It would be even more exceptional to exercise the discretion where fresh issues of fact would have to be investigated; ibid.
(5) Where the new point relates to jurisdiction, this is not a trump card requiring the point to be taken; *Barber v Thames Television plc* [1991] IRLR 236, EAT Knox J and members at paragraph 38; approved in *Jones*. It remains discretionary.
(6) The discretion may be exercised in any of the following circumstances which are given as examples:

(a) It would be unjust to allow the other party to get away with some deception or unfair conduct which meant that the point was not taken below; *Kumchyk v Derby City Council* [1978] ICR 1116, EAT Arnold J and members at 1123.
(b) The point can be taken if the EAT is in possession of all the material necessary to dispose of the matter fairly without recourse to a further hearing; *Wilson v Liverpool Corporation* [1971] 1 WLR 302, 307, per Widgery LJ.
(c) The new point enables the EAT plainly to say from existing material that the Employment Tribunal judgment was a nullity, for that is a consideration of overwhelming strength; *House v Emerson Electric Industrial Controls* [1980] ICR 795 at 800, EAT Talbot J and members, followed and applied in *Barber* at paragraph 38. In such a case it is the EAT's duty to put right the law on the facts available to the EAT; *Glennie* paragraph 12 citing *House*.
(d) The EAT can see a glaring injustice in refusing to allow an unrepresented party to rely on evidence which could have been adduced at the Employment Tribunal; *Glennie* paragraph 15.
(e) The EAT can see an obvious knock-out point; *Glennie*, paragraph 16.
(f) The issue is a discrete one of pure law requiring no further factual enquiry; *Glennie* para 17 per Laws LJ.
(g) It is of particular public importance for a legal point to be decided provided no further factual investigation and no further evaluation by the specialist Tribunal is required; Laws LJ in *Leicestershire* para 21.

(7) The discretion is not to be exercised where by way of example:

(a) What is relied upon is a chance of establishing lack of jurisdiction by calling fresh evidence; *Barber* para 20 as interpreted in *Glennie* para 15.
(b) The issue arises as a result of lack of skill by a represented party, for that is not a sufficient reason; *Jones* para 20.
(c) The point was not taken below as a result of a tactical decision by a representative or a party; *Kumchyk* at page 1123, approved in *Glennie* at para 15.
(d) All the material is before the EAT but what is required is an evaluation and an assessment of this material and application of the law to it by the specialist first instance Tribunal; *Leicestershire* para 21.
(e) A represented party has fought and lost a jurisdictional issue and now seeks a new hearing; *Glennie* para 15. That applies whether the jurisdictional issue is the same as that originally canvassed (normal retiring age as in *Barber*) or is a different way of establishing jurisdiction from that originally canvassed (associated employers and transfer of undertakings as in *Russell v Elmdom Freight Terminal Ltd* [1989] ICR 629, EAT Knox J and members). See the analysis in *Glennie* at paras 13 and 14 of these two cases.
(f) What is relied upon is the high value of the case; *Leicestershire* para 21.

19.67 On the facts of the particular case the EAT held that:

a. it is relevant to ask what the period of time has been since the date of the judgment or possibly from the date of the 'concession'. A short period of time, or a short period of time in the context of very protracted litigation, would point in favour of the Respondents.
b. It is relevant to ask what the reason was for the change of position. An administrative mistake, or an oversight by a lawyer doing a routine audit of a very substantial number of files, is more venial than a tactical decision made by a representative in the proceedings. A mistake which arises in the course of handling 11,000 cases according to protocols directed by the Employment Tribunal from the centre should not readily be held against the Respondents, even if the number is upwards of 120 out of the 11,000.

c. genuine attempts were made to raise the matter on review before the Tribunals which were unsuccessful is also a relevant factor, as is the reason for the Tribunal's refusal. It would generally be unjust to allow the re-opening of a concession if the Claimant had made an agreement to forego any part of her claim in exchange for the conceded point, unless the matter could be put right entirely on a financial settlement.

In *Lipscombe v Forestry Commission* [2007] EWCA Civ 428 the EAT allowed a new point to be argued where the employee was a litigant in person and the new point arose from an EAT decision which was issued after the decision of the tribunal and no further evidence was required. **19.68**

The Practice Direction lays down a process for dealing with such challenges. Where a respondent intends to contend at the full hearing of an appeal that the appellant has raised a point which was not argued below, the respondent should inform the EAT within 14 days of receiving the notice of appeal in a case where a preliminary hearing has been ordered and in a case which is set down for a full hearing without need for a preliminary hearing, in the respondent's answer (2008 Practice Direction, para 8.5). In the event of a dispute between the parties as to whether a point was argued before the employment tribunal, the employment judge will be asked for his comments. This in fact rarely happens as it should be obvious from the decision of the employment tribunal, especially now that tribunals are encouraged to set out what are the issues they decided. **19.69**

In a surprising result the EAT accepted (Mitting J presiding) in *Atos Origin IT Services UK Ltd v Haddock* [2005] IRLR 20 that a respondent who failed to enter a response before the employment tribunal and was therefore not allowed to take any part in the tribunal proceedings might still appeal the decision of the tribunal. The EAT held that r 3(3) of ETR 2001 which stated that 'a respondent who has not entered an appearance shall not be entitled to take part in any proceedings' applied only to proceedings before the tribunal and not proceedings before the EAT. The EAT held that it governed its own procedure and that there was nothing in ETA 1996 or in the EAT Rules which would restrict the right of a respondent who had not entered a notice of appearance from participating in an appeal. Moreover, para 16 of the 2008 Practice Direction provides a procedure for a situation where an appellant has not presented an ET3 to the tribunal. However, this appears to leave a respondent who does not enter a response at all in a better position as regards an appeal to the EAT, as compared to a respondent who enters a response and takes part in the tribunal hearing but fails at the hearing to argue a particular point of law. Such a position does not appear to be grounded in principle. **19.70**

Compromise agreements

The EAT has no jurisdiction to set aside an agreement by which the appellant has compromised his appeal before the EAT since the jurisdiction of the EAT is purely statutory and is confined to hearing appeals (see *Eden v Humphries and Glasgow Ltd* [1981] ICR 183; cf *Hirsch v Ward & Goldstone plc* COIT 1535/15). Any action brought on the compromise agreement must be brought as a contractual claim in the civil courts. However, where the parties settle the remedy or quantum part of an unfair dismissal claim that does not prevent an appeal as to the fairness of the dismissal since this will usually be entered into without prejudice to the issue of fairness (*Associated Tyre Specialists (Southern) Ltd v Lewis* 233 Industrial Relations Information Bulletin 13). **19.71**

F. PRECEDENT

It might be expected that the doctrine of precedent applied to the EAT with the same rigour as in other civil appellate bodies (as to precedent in the Court of Appeal see *Davis v Johnson* [1979] AC 264). However, the EAT approaches the doctrine in a somewhat flexible manner. For example, in recent years there has been a willingness to depart from previous decisions where it is considered that those decisions are wrongly decided although this will only be done **19.72** 'in exceptional circumstances or where there are previous inconsistent decisions' (*Secretary of State for Trade and Industry v Cook* [1997] IRLR 150).

19.73 The EAT indicated in *Digital Equipment Co Ltd v Clements (No 2)* [1997] IRLR 140 that its approach in the face of inconsistent decisions would be to try and reconcile such decisions in order to preserve consistency but if this could not be done then to direct tribunals which of the inconsistent authorities ought to be followed. An example of this practice in action is in the decision of the EAT in *Woodward v Abbey National plc (No 2)* [2005] ICR 1702 in which the EAT directed employment tribunals to no longer follow the decision of the EAT in *Midland Packaging v Clark* [2005] 2 All ER 266.

19.74 In *Clarke v Frank Staddon* [2004] EWCA Civ 422, a decision on rolled-up holiday pay and the Working Time Regulations 1998, the Court of Appeal dealt with the question of whether decisions of the Scottish Court of Session were binding on the EAT. In that case there was authority in the form of a decision of the EAT sitting in Scotland in *MPB Structures Ltd v Munro* [2003] IRLR 350 which was inconsistent with the decision of the EAT sitting in London in *Marshalls Clay Products v Caulfield* [2004] ICR 436. The Court of Appeal held that there was no rule of law binding on any court in England or Wales to follow a decision of a court whose jurisdiction runs in Scotland only. Thus, although as a matter of pragmatic good sense, the EAT ought to follow decisions of the Scottish Court of Session (the equivalent of the Court of Appeal) where the point of law before them is indistinguishable from the point of law dealt with in the Scottish case, the EAT and Court of Appeal are not obliged to (*Airbus UK Ltd v Webb* [2008] IRLR 309). In the event, the Court of Appeal preferred the approach set out in *Marshalls Clay Products* to that in *Munro*.

G. APPEALS AGAINST INTERIM ORDERS

19.75 The EAT's approach to dealing with appeals against interim orders by employment tribunals is the same as the EAT takes in dealing with final orders and judgments. As such, there must be found to be an error of law in order to invoke the jurisdiction of s 21 of ETA 1996 and therefore allow the EAT to intervene. This approach was set out by the EAT in *Adams v West Sussex CC* [1990] ICR 546. Wood J stated (at 551–2):

> It seems to us desirable, and indeed we would have expected, that the same principle would apply to interlocutory appeals as for final appeals even though the former will in the main be the result of the exercise of a discretion. Thus, in examining an interlocutory order of an industrial tribunal or of a chairman sitting alone we would define three issues: (a) Is the order made one within the powers given to the tribunal? (b) Has the discretion been exercised within guiding legal principles? (e.g. as to confidential documents in discovery issues); (c) Can the exercise of the discretion be attacked on the principles in *Associated Provincial Picture Houses Ltd v Wednesbury Corporation* [1948] 1 KB 223?

The same principles apply to an appeal against the refusal on the part of a tribunal to review its decision.

19.76 The approach adopted by the EAT in *Adams v West Sussex CC* amounted to a change in approach. Previously *British Library v Palyza* [1984] ICR 504 indicated that the EAT would be prepared to take a more interventionist approach to supervising the exercise of discretion on the part of the employment tribunals in interim matters. The same principles apply to an appeal against the refusal on the part of a tribunal to review its decision. (See also *Amey Services Ltd v Cardigan* [2008] IRLR 279). In *X v Z Ltd* [1998] ICR 43 Waite LJ at para 54 said in regard to case management decisions:

> the tribunals themselves are the best judges of the case management decisions which crop up every day as they perform the function . . . of trying to do justice with the maximum of flexibility and the minimum of formality.

H. COMMENCING AN APPEAL

The notice of appeal

The appellant must present a notice of appeal to the EAT in a specified form depending upon which tribunal the appeal is in respect of. Appeals as to decisions of the employment tribunal should be completed in the form of 'Form 1' which is attached to the 2008 Practice Direction. This requires copies of the ET1 and ET3 to be filed with the notice of appeal or alternatively an explanation as to why such documents are not included. Appeals from decisions of the CAC should be completed in the form of 'Form 1A' and appeals from a decision of a certification officer should be completed in the form of 'Form 2'. Forms 1A and 2 are attached to the EAT Rules. **19.77**

The formal printed notice of appeal need not always be used and both the EAT Rules and the 2008 Practice Direction allow for a notice of appeal which is presented substantially in the prescribed form. However, appellants should exercise caution in making use of a document other than the prescribed forms. Such a document would have to include sufficiently defined grounds of appeal (2008 Practice Direction, para 2.4) and in *Martin v British Railways Board* [1989] ICR 27, the EAT held that a letter merely indicating a wish to appeal was not sufficient to commence proceedings. **19.78**

Paragraph 2.4 of the 2008 Practice Direction requires that the notice of appeal sets out the order which the appellant will ask the EAT to make. This might be overturning the decision of the tribunal or a remission of the case to the same tribunal or a differently constituted tribunal for reconsideration. These orders may be sought in the alternative. **19.79**

By para 2.1 of the 2008 Practice Direction the notice of appeal must have the following attached to it: **19.80**

(a) a copy of the judgment, decision, or order appealed against and of the tribunal's written reasons; and
(b) a copy of the ET1 and ET3; or
(c) if any documents are not attached then a written explanation as to why they are not attached must be provided.

If the notice of appeal is presented without these documents then 2.1 of the 2008 Practice Direction states that it will not be validly lodged. The EAT has, however, in the past, been prepared to take a flexible approach where full reasons had not been sought but where the summary reasons were 'in essence quite full' (*Wolesley Centres Ltd v Simmons* [1994] ICR 503; cf *Griffiths v NE Derbyshire DC* EAT/612/99). In cases where a written explanation is provided as to why the notice of appeal does not have a copy of the judgment, decision, or order appealed against attached, at the time of lodging the notice of appeal the appellant must apply in writing to the EAT to exercise its discretion to hear the appeal without written reasons or to request that the EAT exercises its power to request written reasons for the judgment from the tribunal.

In the light of the decision of Burton P in *Kanapathiar v Harrow LBC* [2003] IRLR 571, however, it is likely that the registrar of the EAT will adopt a strict approach and refuse to accept notices of appeal which do not have the required documents attached. In that case the appellant had posted a notice of appeal with the relevant documentation attached to the EAT the day before the time limit for presentation expired. In addition, on the day that the deadline expired the appellant attended the EAT in person, despite there being concerns about his health, and lodged a copy of the notice of appeal but without any attached documentation. Burton P held that the registrar had not erred in granting the appellant a one-day extension of time to lodge the relevant documents in the circumstances of Mr Kanapathiar's **19.81** case. However, Burton P wished to make it clear that the somewhat lax approach of permitting notices of appeal would no longer be adopted. He stated (at para 14):

> it is equally clear that, in the discretion of the Registrar, this was an appropriate case, not only because of the particular compassionate circumstances, but also because this would be the case used as an affirmative signal of the end of the previous lax practice, for the grant of what is, after all, only a one-day extension.

19.82 Indeed, on 3 February 2005 a Practice Statement was handed down by the President of the EAT ([2005] ICR 660) making it clear that notices of appeal would not be accepted without the required documents.

19.83 It is not uncommon for an appellant to seek both an appeal before the EAT and a review of an employment tribunal's decision. If this course is adopted, the application to the employment tribunal for review should be attached to the notice of appeal. If the employment tribunal has dealt with the application for review, the judgment and written reasons should also be attached. In other cases a statement should be provided stating that judgment is awaited (2008 Practice Direction, para 2.2).

19.84 Paragraph 2.5 of the 2008 Practice Direction restates the position as set out in r 3(7)–(10) of the EAT Rules that the registrar may decide that no further action should be taken in respect of a notice of appeal which discloses either no reasonable grounds for the bringing of the appeal, or that the appeal is an abuse of the EAT's process or is otherwise likely to obstruct the just disposal of proceedings. In these circumstances, the registrar will notify the appellant setting out written reasons for his decision. The appellant may then take one of two alternative courses of action. First, the appellant can appeal the decision of the registrar by way of oral hearing before a judge. In order to do this, the appellant must 'express dissatisfaction' with the reasons which have been given and request a hearing before a judge. The appellant has 28 days from the date that written reasons were sent by the EAT to do this (EAT Rules, r 3(10)). In addition, pursuant to r 3(8) of the EAT Rules an appellant can resubmit a notice of appeal within 28 days from the date on which notification was sent to him. By r 3(9) of the EAT Rules, the new notice of appeal will be considered to be a fresh notice of appeal and therefore the appellant ought to be able to take completely fresh points of appeal. In practice this procedure is not often made use of by the EAT and such matters tend to be dealt with at preliminary hearings and appropriate orders made. In *Haritaki v South East England Development Agency* [2008] IRLR 945, the EAT commented that when an appellant seeks to submit a fresh notice of appeal that is generally put back in front of the same judge who decided and gave an opinion under r 3(7).

Time limits for commencing an appeal

19.85 Rule 3(3) of the EAT Rules and paras 3.2–3.3 of the 2008 Practice Direction require a notice of appeal to be filed within the following time limits:

(a) In a case where the appeal is against an order or decision of the tribunal then the appeal must be commenced within 42 days of the order or decision.
(b) If the appeal is against a judgment of an employment tribunal the appeal must be instituted within 42 days of the date on which the written record of the judgment was sent to the parties unless written reasons were requested orally at the hearing, in writing within 14 days of the written record of the judgment being sent to the parties or if the tribunal reserved its reasons and gave them subsequently in writing. In these cases the time limit will be 42 days from the date when written reasons were sent to the parties.

19.86 The date on which the extended reasons were sent to the appellant is the date on which the document was transmitted to the party concerned and not when it was received by him. The position has been placed beyond doubt by the decision of the Court of Appeal in *Gdynia American Shipping Lines (London) Ltd v Chelminski* [2004] EWCA Civ 871, [2004] IRLR 725, where the Court of Appeal affirmed the EAT's decisions in *Sian v Abbey National* [2004]

IRLR 185 and *Hammersmith & Fulham London Borough Council v Ladejobi* [1999] ICR 673 and found that the EAT's decisions in *Immigration Advisory Service v Oomen* [1997] ICR 683 and *Scotford v Smith Kline Beecham* [2002] ICR 264 to the contrary were wrongly decided. That was because the parties could not in this case, where the rules were clear on their face, rely on s 7 of the Interpretation Act 1978, that is the presumption that a document sent by first class post would arrive the following day. The Court of Appeal found that the deeming rules which were set out in the Interpretation Act 1978 had no bearing on the application of the EAT Rules which simply referred to the date on which the reasons were sent. The Court of Appeal, while viewing the question of law principally as a matter of statutory construction, also accepted Burton P's conclusion in *Sian v Abbey National* that it was more administratively convenient for the date from which the 42 days ran to be the date on which the decision was transmitted to the parties by the employment tribunal. Burton P considered that the opposite result would cause great uncertainty, in particular, to the respondent, since it would never be clear from which date time ran.

Sian v Abbey National is an instructive example of the strictness with which the rules relating to time limits can be applied by the registrar. The appellant did not receive the written reasons at all until after the expiry of the 42-day period in which the appellant was required to appeal. The appellant's solicitor wrote to the employment tribunal asking for an extension of time in which to appeal and was told that the tribunal had no jurisdiction to grant such a request. The appellant then made an application to the EAT seeking an extension of time in which to appeal and arguing that the appeal had been brought within time. The registrar not only found that the notice of appeal had not been lodged within time but refused to grant an extension of time to the appellant. **19.87**

Rule 37(1A) of the EAT Rules states that a notice of appeal must be lodged by 4 pm on the relevant day. This has raised problems as to what happens when a notice of appeal is partially presented, for example by fax, before 4 pm and partially after 4 pm. The EAT considered that question in *Midland Packaging v Clark* [2005] 2 All ER 266. Burton P found that: **19.88**

(a) in circumstances where a notice of appeal was received by the EAT's fax machine prior to 4 pm on the relevant day, that such a notice of appeal would have been lodged in time even if the EAT's fax machine did not print it off until after the 4 pm time limit.
(b) a notice of appeal which had started to be delivered to the EAT's fax machine by the 4 pm deadline would be validly lodged within time. Burton P concluded (at para 23):

I say nothing as to what would happen if, for example, there were to be communication by e-mail, and someone was still typing an e-mail, halfway through it, at 4.00 pm, and as to whether that would count, but it seems to follow by analogy that such would not be sufficient, in that it is the communication which is crucial, though not the printing out—a printer could be jammed or overloaded. Where the document has in fact been completed, it is in either electronic or readable form, and is in the process of dispatch, and the dispatch has, on the balance of probabilities, started at the time of the expiry of the deadline, in my judgment that should count as good service or lodgment of the document.

However, in *Woodward v Abbey National plc (No 2)* [2005] ICR 1702, the EAT (Burton P presiding) found that *Midland Packaging v Clark* was wrongly decided and that all of the notice of appeal and accompanying documentation must be lodged at the EAT by 4 pm on the relevant day in order that the notice of appeal is lodged in time. In cases where the notice of appeal is faxed, the time at which it is lodged will be determined with reference to the EAT's fax log and the fax containing the notice of appeal and its accompanying documents must be complete. In making this decision Burton P was influenced both by the wording of the EAT's own 2008 Practice Direction and CPR 5PD (Court Documents). Neither of these had been before the EAT in *Midland Packaging v Clark*. (On time limits for response see *Echendu v Wm Morrison Supermarkets plc* UKEATPA/1675/07.) **19.89**

Application for an extension of time to lodge the notice of appeal

19.90 Under r 37(1) of the EAT Rules, the EAT has a discretion to extend time for a notice of appeal to be presented although in practice this is rarely granted. Therefore, if a notice of appeal is presented out of time, it must be accompanied by an application for an extension of time, setting out in detail the reason for the delay. It is not possible for a party to seek to extend time prior to the presentation of a notice of appeal since para 3.5 of the 2008 Practice Direction states that an application for an extension of time can only be considered once the notice of appeal has been received by the EAT.

19.91 Paragraph 3.6 of the 2008 Practice Direction sets out the procedure which will be adopted by the EAT on receipt of an application to extend time. The application must be made as an interim application to the registrar who will determine whether to grant an extension of time having considered written representations from each side. The registrar will seek to decide this type of question in an expeditious manner and the parties will typically be given a relatively short amount of time to prepare written representations. Having received representations from the parties, the registrar will determine whether or not time ought to be extended.

19.92 An appeal from such a decision of the registrar lies to a judge and as with other interim appeals before the EAT, the EAT must be notified of the appeal within five days of the date that the registrar's decision was sent to the parties. Appeals in relation to applications to extend time are often heard at preliminary hearings (see para 19.115 below) although a potential respondent has the right to be heard, unlike the practice at a normal preliminary hearing.

19.93 Paragraphs 3.7 and 3.8 of the 2008 Practice Direction set out the principles by which the registrar will exercise the discretion granted to him by r 37(1) of the EAT Rules and therefore by which an application to extend time will be determined. These principles have been developed by the NIRC, EAT, and Court of Appeal. The paragraphs state:

> 3.7 In determining whether to extend the time for appealing, particular attention will be paid to whether any good excuse for the delay has been shown and to the guidance contained in the decisions of the EAT and the Court of Appeal, as summarised in *United Arab Emirates v Abdelghafar* [1995] ICR 65; *Aziz v Bethnal Green City Challenge Co Ltd* [2000] IRLR 111; and *Jurkovska v HLMAD* [2008] EWCA Civ 231, [2008] ICR 842.
>
> 3.8 It is not usually a good reason for late lodgment of a Notice of Appeal that an application for litigation support from public funds has been made, but not yet determined; or that support is being sought from, but has not yet been provided by, some other body, such as a trade union, employers' association or the Equality and Human Rights Commission.

19.94 *Marshall v Harland & Wolff* [1972] ICR 97 decided that the fact that a party is seeking support to fund an appeal is not, of itself, a good reason for the EAT to exercise its discretion to extend time. The 2008 Practice Direction advises appellants, at para 3.9, to lodge a notice of appeal in time in 'any case of doubt or difficulty' and then to make an application to the registrar for directions.

19.95 Since para 3.7 of the 2008 Practice Direction refers specifically to the summaries of case law provided by the EAT and Court of Appeal in *Abdelghafar* and *Aziz*, some analysis of these leading decisions is required.

19.96 In *Abdelghafar* Mummery P set out a summary of the authorities which deal with extensions of time generally and concluded that they showed that:

(a) It is necessary to weigh up or balance all the relevant factors when making a decision to extend a time limit. In particular it was necessary to weigh on the one hand the public interest in promoting the expeditious dispatch of litigation and on the other hand the principle that litigants should not be denied an adjudication on the merits of their claim as a result of a procedural default.

(b) Where a party seeks an extension of time to present an appeal, that party will already have enjoyed a judicial determination of his or her claim and therefore the public interest and interest of the parties in having finality in the proceedings may make the court stricter about

the application of time limits. Therefore, an extension of time may be refused even though the failure to observe the time limit had not caused prejudice to any party to the proceedings.
(c) No party is entitled to an extension and therefore it is incumbent upon any party seeking an extension of time that he or she provides the court with a 'full, honest and acceptable' explanation of the reasons for the delay.

Applying those general principles to the specific context of the EAT and to applications for an extension of the time limits for the presentation of a notice of appeal, Mummery P adumbrated the following guidelines: **19.97**

(1) Although sympathy may be extended to an unrepresented litigant who may be in ignorance of the time limit or may not appreciate the importance of complying with it, the time limit will only be relaxed in rare cases where the EAT is satisfied that there is a reason which justifies departure from the limits.
(2) The EAT will not exercise its discretion unless it is provided with a full and honest explanation of the reason for the non-compliance with the time limit. The following explanations have been rejected by the EAT in the past and therefore are unlikely to excuse a failure to comply with the time limit:
    (a) ignorance of the time limit;
    (b) oversight of the passing of the limit as a result of, for example, pressure of work;
    (c) prior notification to the EAT, the employment tribunal, or to the other party of intent to appeal;
    (d) the existence of pending applications for review of the decision or for remedies (see the 2008 Practice Direction, para 3.4); and
    (e) delay in the processing of an application for legal aid or of an application for advice or support from elsewhere.
(3) If an explanation for the delay is offered, then any number of factors may be considered by the EAT. The EAT will be particularly astute about any evidence of procedural abuse or wilful non-compliance. In addition, while the length of the delay, the merits of the appeal and any prejudice which has been occasioned to the other party may be considered, they are unlikely to be very important in determining whether or not the EAT ought to exercise its discretion.

Mummery P concluded, therefore, that the questions which the EAT must ask itself are: **19.98** '(a) what is the explanation for the default? (b) does it provide a good excuse for the default? (c) are there circumstances which justify the tribunal taking the exceptional step of granting an extension out of time?'

In *Abdelghafar*, the EAT was prepared to extend time for the presentation of an appeal despite **19.99** the fact that no acceptable excuse had been put forward because the case unusually raised particular issues relating to the State Immunity Act 1978 and that Act bound all courts and tribunals to give effect to the immunity conferred by it. *Abdelghafar* itself demonstrates therefore that it is difficult to set out exhaustive guidelines explaining how the EAT will exercise a general discretion as to which of any number of factors could be relevant.

In *Aziz v Bethnal Green City Challenge Company* [2000] IRLR 111, the Court of Appeal affirmed **19.100** the guidance given by the EAT in *Abdelghafar* even though the result was that the approach in EAT was stricter than that adopted in the Court of Appeal. The Court of Appeal accepted that there were differences in the manner in which the EAT and Court of Appeal approached appeals since the two courts had different jurisdictions on appeal. In any case, the Court of Appeal recognized that there was a trend in favour of applying time limits in a stricter manner in the civil courts and therefore the Court of Appeal itself may have to adopt a stricter approach in the future.

Woods v Lambeth Service Team Ltd EATPA/251/99 saw the EAT extend time for a notice of **19.101** appeal which was received one day out of time on the basis that the function of the EAT was wider than that arising in the specific case. Morison P decided that the EAT's supervisory jurisdiction over employment tribunals required it to ensure that procedural mishaps did not occur which would render the proceedings defective. While this case demonstrates the breadth of factors which might be taken into account by the EAT in deciding whether to extend time and the fact that those will inevitably differ from case to case, it must, respectfully, be doubted as a general proposition. The strictness of the rules has been emphasized in a series of decisions of the EAT including that in *Sian v Abbey National plc* [2004] IRLR 185, where Burton P stated that the EAT's 'discretion is to be used sparingly'. The EAT will look at the whole period of delay to decide why the notice of appeal was not lodged in time but this may require a different analysis to be applied to different parts of the time (*Muschett v London Borough of Hounslow* EATPA/0/281/07; see also *Waller v Bromsgrove DC* EATPA/00/19/07). An excuse might not be sufficient to explain delay if it failed to explain why a notice was not lodged throughout the entirety of the period though it was not fatal that an appellant was able to comply during part of the time (*Muschett v Hounslow LBC* [2009] ICR 424).

19.102 It is well established that a change in the law by an appellate court will not usually tempt the EAT to exercise its discretion to extend time limits in order to consider an appeal. In *Setiya v East Yorkshire HA* [1995] IRLR 348 a notice of appeal was served two years after the employment tribunal's decision was reached. The notice of appeal was filed in response to the landmark decision of the House of Lords in *R v Secretary of State for Employment, ex p EOC* [1994] ICR 317. The EAT was not prepared to extend time in order to consider Dr Setiya's appeal merely as a result of a change in the law since it was of the view that Dr Setiya could have taken the arguments which ultimately succeeded in the *EOC* case. Mummery P concluded (at 352) that:

> Life, including law, is subject to the chance of change. Dr Setiya's claim against the authority was subject to the 'hazards of time' inherent in change.

19.103 In *Jurkovska v HLMAD* [2008] EWCA Civ 231, [2008] ICR 842 the Court of Appeal upheld a decision of the EAT Judge to extend time by 33 minutes when the Notice of Appeal had been presented in time but not the written reasons for decision. They rejected an argument that the introduction of the overriding objective into the EAT required a more relaxed approach to EAT time limits generally. Rimer LJ expressed the view that any explanation for delay should be provided in a witness statement by someone who could speak to the relevant facts (para 32).

I. RESPONDENT'S ANSWER AND CROSS-APPEALS

19.104 If an appeal is set down for a full hearing, the EAT will send a copy of the notice of appeal to all named respondents to the appeal along with any submissions or skeleton arguments lodged by the appellant. Within 14 days of the seal date of the EAT order the respondent must lodge at the EAT and serve on all other parties a respondent's answer (2008 Practice Direction, para 10.1). In cases where an appeal is set down for preliminary hearing the respondent(s) will be given the opportunity to produce written submissions prior to the preliminary hearing but will only be required to lodge and serve a respondent's answer if the appeal is set down for a full hearing. This is often not understood by litigants who lodge the respondent's answer if, for example, they are sent a notice of appeal by the appellant merely as a matter of courtesy. This is not necessary until the case has proceeded through the sift.

19.105 Rule 6(2) of the EAT Rules requires that the respondent must answer the notice of appeal in accordance, or substantially in accordance with the specified form which is to be found in 'Form 3' appended to the EAT Rules. If a respondent fails to deliver an answer (or indeed a response where the EAT exercises its original jurisdiction) the EAT may order that the respondent is debarred from taking any further part in the proceedings by virtue of r 26 of the EAT Rules. The respondent's answer may only be a short document if the reasons given by the employment tribunal are relied on as will often be the case. A respondent may not wish to give succour to the appellant by itself criticizing the employment tribunal's reasoning albeit from a different direction.

A cross-appeal is an appeal by the respondent against part or the whole of the tribunal's decision; it is not where the respondent wishes to uphold the conclusion on other grounds. If the respondent wishes to cross-appeal, it may do so, but it is not bound to do so. If it does, it includes a statement of grounds within the respondent's answer. For example, where an appeal is set down for a preliminary hearing at the sift, respondents should include a cross-appeal within the written submissions which a respondent must lodge and serve within 14 days of service of the notice of appeal (2008 Practice Direction, para 9.8). Strangely other than where a case is set down for a preliminary hearing, there is no time limit for the service of a cross-appeal although, in practice, litigants tend to include a cross-appeal together with the respondent's answer and should do so speedily given the fast turnaround time of the EAT and the risk that a cross-appeal which a party seeks to launch just before the hearing will be disallowed. Should a respondent not wish to contest the appeal then pursuant to r 6(5) of the EAT Rules, the parties can agree a draft order to be placed before the EAT for approval although it is a matter for the EAT whether it will approve such an arrangement (see para 19.207 below). **19.106**

Where the respondent's answer contains a cross-appeal, the appellant must within 14 days of service lodge at the EAT and serve on the other parties a reply (2008 Practice Direction, para 10.1). In addition, where the respondent's answer contains a cross-appeal and therefore the appellant's appeal has been set down for a full hearing without the need for a preliminary hearing, the respondent must apply to the EAT immediately so that the EAT can determine whether the cross-appeal should be set down for a preliminary hearing. The respondent must give notice of such application to the appellant (2008 Practice Direction, para 9.12). **19.107**

J. AMENDMENTS TO THE NOTICE OF APPEAL OR RESPONDENT'S ANSWER

Paragraph 2.7 of the 2008 Practice Direction deals with amendments to the notice of appeal or respondent's answer: **19.108**

> A party cannot reserve the right to amend, alter or add, to a Notice of Appeal or a Respondent's Answer. Any application for leave to amend must be made as soon as practicable and must be accompanied by a draft of the amended Notice of Appeal or amended Answer which makes clear the precise amendments for which permission is sought.

Paragraph 9.4 of the 2008 Practice Direction states as to the form in which applications to amend the notice of appeal or the respondent's answer are made: **19.109**

> An application to amend a Notice of Appeal or Respondent's Answer must include the text of the original document with any changes clearly marked and identifiable, for example with deletions struck through in red and the text of the amendment either written or underlined in red. Any subsequent amendments will have to be in a different identifiable colour.

In practice amendments are made quite readily although the trend may be towards a more rigorous approach as foreshadowed in *Khudados v Leggate* [2005] IRLR 540. The EAT held that the usual principles that applied to amendments to statements of case (which had been set out by the Court of Appeal in *Cobbold v London Borough of Greenwich* [1999] EWCA Civ 2074—that they should generally be permitted provided that the prejudice to the other party can be compensated for in costs and the public interest in the efficient administration of justice is not significantly harmed) ought not to be applied when dealing with applications to amend notices of appeal for a number of reasons: **19.110**

(a) The approach of the EAT in ensuring that parties deal with proposed appeals expeditiously is stricter than the approach taken by the Court of Appeal. This was noted by the Court of Appeal in the *Aziz* case.
(b) The EAT takes a strict view of anything which might delay a hearing. That approach is consistent with a desire to ensure that proceedings must be brought before an employment

tribunal quickly and the usual three-month period in which claimants must present a claim is significantly less than the limitation periods in most civil claims.

(c) The EAT's regime is, for the most part, a cost-free regime and costs can only be awarded in very limited circumstances.

19.111 The EAT also drew attention to the fact that, under the 2002 Practice Direction, amendments had to be made 'as soon as the need for amendment is known' and that there was no equivalent provision in the CPR. However, the requirement for amendments to be made as soon as the need is known by the relevant party has been removed from the 2004 and 2008 Practice Directions. Amendments must be made, pursuant to the 2008 Practice Direction, as soon as it is practicable to do so.

19.112 The EAT concluded at para 86 of *Khudados* that the following matters would be relevant in determining whether an appellant should be given permission to amend their notice of appeal:

(a) Whether or not the appellant is in breach of the EAT Rules or a relevant Practice Direction. In this vein the EAT referred again to the requirement in the 2002 Practice Direction that the amendment be made as soon as the need for amendment is known and explained that 'the requirement is not simply aspirational or an expression of hope'. Presumably, the requirement that amendments be made as soon as practicable imports a little more flexibility into the criterion.
(b) Any extension of time is an indulgence and the EAT is entitled to a full, honest, and acceptable explanation for any delay of failure to comply with the EAT, the Rules, or Practice Direction.
(c) The extent to which, if the amendment was allowed, it would cause a delay. The EAT explained that crisp new points of law closely related to existing grounds are more likely to be allowed than new perversity points which will require an analysis of complex factual material.
(d) The extent to which allowing an amendment will cause prejudice to the opposite party and the extent to which refusing an amendment will do prejudice to the appellant by depriving him of fairly arguable points of law.
(e) It may be necessary to consider the merits of a proposed amendment. They must raise a point of law which gives the appeal a reasonable prospect of success.
(f) Regard must be had to the public interest in ensuring that business in the EAT is conducted expeditiously and that resources are used efficiently.

19.113 The 2008 Practice Direction suggests that the same principles should be applied to amendments in respect of the respondent's answer as well as the notice of appeal. However, it is noteworthy that many of the concerns expressed above apply with less force to amendments to the respondent's answer than they would to notices of appeal.

K. INTERIM MATTERS

19.114 There are various interim matters which may come before the EAT in the course of an appeal. The most important of these are dealt with below.

The sift and the setting of directions by the Employment Appeal Tribunal

19.115 The present process for case management in the EAT was introduced by the 2002 Practice Direction and was maintained with minimal amendments in the 2004 and 2008 Practice Directions. The approach, pursuant to para 9.5 of the 2008 Practice Direction, involves sorting cases and placing them on one of four tracks. Those tracks are:

(a) r 3(7) (of the EAT Rules) cases;
(b) preliminary hearing cases;
(c) full hearing cases;
(d) fast-track full hearing cases.

An appeal will be sorted or sifted onto one of these tracks by a judge or by the registrar in order to determine the most effective way in which to manage the case. The track on which the case is placed will usually determine the nature of the directions which are issued with regard to the appeal. However, there is no set manner in which directions should be given under the 2008 Practice Direction and the EAT has scope to give such directions as are appropriate in any case. As such, pursuant to para 9.2 of the 2008 Practice Direction a party can seek directions for case management at any time before or after the registration of a notice of appeal. Alternatively, by para 10.2 of the 2008 Practice Direction, after lodgement and service of the respondent's answer and of any reply to a cross-appeal, the registrar may, where necessary, invite applications from the parties in writing, on notice to all other parties, for directions, and may give any appropriate directions on the papers or may fix a day when the parties should attend an appointment for directions. The setting of directions is provided for by para 9.1 of the 2008 Practice Direction: **19.116**

> Consistent with the overriding objective, the EAT will seek to give directions for case management so that the case can be dealt with quickly, or better considered, and in the most effective and just way.

In r 3(7) cases the judge or registrar may consider on the papers that the notice of appeal does not contain any grounds of appeal which have a reasonable prospect of success. Alternatively it may be decided (although this will be highly unusual) that the notice of appeal amounts to an abuse of process or will otherwise obstruct the just disposal of proceedings. If a judge or the registrar forms the view that the case is thus a r 3(7) case, summary reasons will be sent to the appellant for this view. No further action will be taken unless the appellant serves a fresh notice of appeal or requests an oral hearing before a judge pursuant to r 3(10). **19.117**

Paragraph 9.7 of the 2008 Practice Direction sets out the purpose of a preliminary hearing before the EAT: **19.118**

> 9.7 the purpose of a PH is to determine whether:
> 9.7.1 the grounds in the Notice of Appeal raise a point of law which gives the appeal a reasonable prospect of success at a FH; or
> 9.7.2 for some other compelling reason the appeal should be heard eg that the appellant seeks a declaration of incompatibility under the Human Rights Act 1998; or to argue that a decision binding on the EAT should be considered by a higher court.

Prior to any preliminary hearing automatic directions will be given pursuant to para 9.8 of the 2008 Practice Direction. By para 9.8 of the 2008 Practice Direction, such directions may require, but in any event will enable, the respondent(s) to serve written submissions within 14 days of the seal date of the order for a preliminary hearing. These written submissions are themselves not a respondent's answer which will only be produced if the case is set down for a full hearing. Rather they are submissions directed to demonstrating that there is no point of law raised in the appeal. If the respondent is to cross-appeal then the grounds for such cross-appeal must be included in those written submissions setting out whether the respondent wishes to advance the cross-appeal irrespective of whether the appellant succeeds at the preliminary hearing (an unconditional cross-appeal) or whether the respondent only wishes to pursue the cross-appeal if the appellant succeeds at the preliminary hearing (a conditional cross-appeal which is the more usual) (2008 Practice Direction, para 9.9). **19.119**

In the normal case, only the appellant and/or a representative should attend to make submissions to the EAT on the issue of whether the notice of appeal raises a point of law with a reasonable prospect of success (2008 Practice Direction, para 9.10). The hearing should last for no longer than one hour (2008 Practice Direction, para 9.11). The procedure may be applied to cross-appeals where appropriate. **19.120**

If satisfied that the appeal (and/or the cross-appeal) should be heard at a full hearing on all or some of the grounds of appeal, the EAT will give directions relating to, for example, a time estimate, any application for fresh evidence, a procedure in respect of matters of evidence before the employment tribunal not sufficiently appearing from the judgment or written reasons, the **19.121** exchange and lodging of skeleton arguments, and an appellant's chronology as well as bundles of documents and authorities (2008 Practice Direction, para 9.13). A list of issues may be required.

19.122 At the preliminary hearing, the EAT will either:

(a) dismiss the appeal wholly or in part and give a judgment setting out the reasons for doing so; or
(b) permit the appeal to go to a final hearing on all grounds in which case a reasoned judgment need not be given.

19.123 In relation to transcripts of unreserved judgments at a preliminary hearing EAT Practice Direction 2002, para 17 states that:

1. where an appeal, or any ground of appeal, is dismissed in the presence of the appellant, no transcript of the judgment is produced unless, within 14 days of oral delivery of the judgment, either party applies to the EAT for a transcript;
2. where an appeal is dismissed in the absence of the appellant, a transcript will be supplied to the appellant;
3. where an appeal is allowed to proceed to a full hearing, a judgment will not normally be delivered, but, if it is, the judge may order it to be transcribed, in which case a transcript is provided to the parties.

19.124 In relation to transcripts of unreserved judgments at a full hearing where judgment is delivered at the hearing, no transcript will be produced and provided to the parties unless:

(1) either party applies for it to the EAT within 14 days; or
(2) the EAT of its own motion directs that the judgment be transcribed, eg where it is considered that a point of general importance arises or that the matter is to be remitted to, or otherwise continued before, the employment tribunal.

19.125 Where the EAT is only allowing an appellant's appeal to proceed to a full hearing on some of the grounds of appeal it should make clear which grounds are permitted to proceed and which are not (*IPC Magazines Ltd v Clements* EAT/456/99). However, in an exceptional case the EAT might exercise its general case management powers at the hearing to allow an appellant to depart from those points. In *Miriki v General Council of the Bar* [2002] ICR 505, the Court of Appeal stated that this might be permitted where:

(a) the point was raised before the employment tribunal;
(b) the appellant explained why he did not appeal against the limiting of the grounds of appeal at the preliminary stage; and
(c) the EAT gave full opportunity to the respondent to argue against the departure and explained its reasons for allowing the departure.

19.126 In *Vincent v MJ Gallagher Construction Ltd* [2003] EWCA 640, the appellant put forward six grounds but the EAT allowed an appeal to proceed only in respect of two of them. The Court of Appeal considered that the other grounds were arguable. Pill LJ urged the EAT (at para 15) to act with great care when allowing appeals to proceed on one ground but not others when 'the entire compass of the case is a narrow one'. Further, if the matter was raised before the EAT at the preliminary hearing and the EAT which sat on that occasion refused to give directions to enable the appeal to proceed, the EAT hearing the full appeal would have to be satisfied that there was some material change of circumstances or other good reason to allow the additional ground of appeal to proceed.

19.127 In a few cases the Court of Appeal has allowed an appeal from the conclusion of the EAT that there was no point of law which raised a reasonable prospect of success at a full hearing. The Court of Appeal in *Lambe v 186K Ltd* [2005] ICR 307, where this occurred, had to consider whether in this case the appeal should be remitted to the EAT or be heard by the Court of Appeal and decided that the latter was the appropriate course.

Where an appeal is permitted to continue to a full hearing it will be assigned a listing category. This will either be P where the appeal is recommended to be heard in the President's list, A where the appeal is complex and raises points of law which are of public importance, and B in any other case. The President reserves the discretion to alter any relevant category as circumstances require (2008 Practice Direction, para 9.18). There was before 2008 a category C which has been abolished. 19.128

In the full hearing track where the judge or the registrar considers that a preliminary hearing is not appropriate, directions will be given relating, for example, to amendment, further information, any application for fresh evidence, a procedure in respect of matters of evidence at the employment tribunal not sufficiently appearing from the judgment or extended reasons, allegations of bias, apparent bias or improper conduct, provisions for skeletons, appellant's chronology and bundles of documents, and of authorities, time estimates, and listing categories (2008 Practice Direction, para 9.19). 19.129

Pursuant to para 9.20 of the 2008 Practice Direction, a judge of the EAT or the registrar will allocate cases to the fast-track full hearing track where such cases involve: 19.130

(a) appeals where the parties have made a reasoned case on the merits for an expedited hearing;
(b) appeals against interim orders or decisions of the employment tribunal, particularly those which involve the taking of a step in proceedings within a specified period, for example adjournments, particulars, amendments, disclosure, witness orders, refusal to give extended reasons, to extend time, to grant a review;
(c) appeals on the outcome of which other applications to the employment tribunal or the EAT or the civil courts depend;
(d) appeals in which a reference to the European Court of Justice, or a declaration of incompatibility under the Human Rights Act 1998, is sought;
(e) appeals involving reinstatement, re-engagement, interim relief, or a recommendation for action (in discrimination cases).

In addition, the EAT has a power to allocate category B cases which are estimated to take two hours or less to the fast track (2008 Practice Direction, para 9.21). 19.131

Interim applications

Paragraph 4 of the 2008 Practice Direction states: 19.132

> Interim applications should be made in writing (no particular form is required) and will be initially referred to the Registrar who after considering the papers may deal with the case or refer it to a judge. The judge may dispose of it himself or refer it to a full EAT hearing. Parties are encouraged to make any such applications at a Preliminary Hearing or an Appointment for Directions if one is ordered.

There are a wide variety of interim applications which could be made to the EAT. The EAT Rules specifically provide for some powers which might be exercised on an interim application. Thus, the EAT can (a) debar a party from proceeding in relation to the appeal because of a failure to comply with its orders by r 26, (b) order the production of documents or the attendance of a witness by r 27, (c) join parties by r 18, (d) extend or abridge time by r 37, and (e) waive procedural requirements in the interests of justice by r 39. 19.133

An appeal lies from the decision of the registrar on an interim application to a judge. Such an appeal must be notified to the EAT within five days of the date on which the registrar's decision was sent to the parties by virtue of para 4.3 of the 2008 Practice Direction. 19.134

Conciliation

Since the insertion of r 36 in the EAT Rules by the Employment Appeal Tribunal (Amendment) Rules 2004 and the issuing of the Conciliation Protocol on 9 December 2004, the EAT has the power to stay appeals for a period of '(say) 28 days' while the parties make use of the services of 19.135

ACAS. This procedure is likely to be made use of in cases which involve allegations of bias and procedural impropriety (see para 2 of the Conciliation Protocol), but pursuant to para 8 of the Conciliation Protocol:

> Other appeals may also be amenable to conciliation, particularly those relating to monetary awards only, or where the overwhelmingly likely result of a successful appeal would be a remission to the ET.

Where conciliation is successful, the appeal may be dismissed on withdrawal or alternatively allowed by consent. Where the appeal is allowed by consent, a judge will give directions in accordance with the 2008 Practice Direction, para 15. This is to render the EAT procedure analogous to that before the ET under its new rules.

L. VEXATIOUS LITIGANTS

19.136 Section 33(1) of the ETA 1996 states:

> If, on an application made by the Attorney General or the Lord Advocate under this section, the Appeal Tribunal is satisfied that a person has habitually and persistently and without any reasonable ground—
>
> (a) instituted vexatious proceedings, whether before the Certification Officer, in any employment tribunal or before the Appeal Tribunal, and whether against the same person or against different persons, or
>
> (b) made vexatious applications in any proceedings, whether before the Certification Officer, in any employment tribunal or before the Appeal Tribunal,
>
> the Appeal Tribunal may, after hearing the person or giving him an opportunity of being heard, make a restriction of proceedings order.

19.137 This is based on a long-established practice in the civil courts but it was only introduced in the employment tribunal and the EAT in 1998 as a result of the passage into law of the Employment Rights (Dispute Resolution) Act 1998. In *Attorney-General v Wheen* [2000] IRLR 461, the EAT considered the operation of s 33 of ETA 1996. Mr Wheen had instituted 15 sets of proceedings against various respondents alleging discrimination on the grounds of race, sex, disability, and marital status. The cases all followed the same pattern which is that Mr Wheen had applied for a job with the respondent, had been turned down, and had then instituted proceedings in the employment tribunal. The majority of the claims had been struck out by the tribunal as being frivolous, vexatious, or an abuse of process. Drawing on a passage of Lord Bingham CJ in *Attorney-General v Barker* [2000] 1 FLR 759, the EAT clarified that the meaning of vexatious proceedings is that it has little or no basis in law (or at least no discernible basis), that whatever the intention of the proceedings may be, its effect is to subject the respondent to inconvenience, harassment, and expense out of all proportion to any gain likely to accrue to the claimant, and that it involves an abuse of process of the court, that is the use of the court process for a purpose or in a way that is significantly different from the ordinary and proper use of that process.

19.138 Mr Wheen appealed to the Court of Appeal. The Court of Appeal ([2001] IRLR 91) held that:

(a) The fact that 18 months had elapsed between Mr Wheen's most recent submission of an originating application and the Attorney-General's application under s 33 of ETA 1996 did not prevent the EAT from properly concluding that an order should be made against Mr Wheen.

(b) The s 33 order did not breach Article 6 of the ECHR on fair trial since access to the courts was not prohibited but rather was provided for on certain terms. The Court of Appeal indeed described it as 'wholly unarguable' that s 33 conflicted with the ECHR.

19.139 Where an order is made under s 33 of ETA 1996, the vexatious litigant is required to gain leave of the EAT before commencing further proceedings (s 33(2)). Orders may be made indefinitely or for a specified period (s 33(3)). The Attorney-General and Lord Advocate have not applied for many of these orders.

M. LISTING THE CASE

The listing arrangements are now set out in para 12 of the 2008 Practice Direction. As a result of these arrangements, the waiting time at the EAT has been reduced to approximately three months from lodging the notice of appeal. **19.140**

Generally, a date will be fixed for a hearing as soon as practicable after the sift has taken place. In cases which are allocated to the preliminary hearing track, the preliminary hearing will be fixed for a hearing as soon as practicable after the sift and then will be listed for a full hearing, if necessary, after the preliminary hearing (2008 Practice Direction, para 12.3). The listing officer will generally consult the parties on dates and will try to accommodate reasonable requests but is not bound to do so. Once a date is fixed the appeal will be set down in the list (2008 Practice Direction, para 12.4). **19.141**

If a party wishes to change the date fixed for an appeal, they should inform the EAT listing officer and may apply for it to be changed but must give the reasons why they wish this to be done. This will only be done if the date listed causes serious difficulties and a party must notify all other parties of such an application and the reasons for it (2008 Practice Direction, para 12.4). **19.142**

In addition to the usual process for the listing of appeals, the EAT maintains a 'warned list'. This list will ordinarily be made up of short cases or cases which require expedition. Once a case is placed in the warned list, the parties are, in effect, on notice that the case will be listed at short notice. As much notice as possible will then be given to the parties of the intention to list the case for hearing but the 2008 Practice Direction suggests that this might well be fewer than seven days. The parties can object to the listing of their case at first instance to the listing officer and then on appeal to the registrar or a judge. The parties may also apply for a fixed date for the hearing. Other cases may be placed in the warned list such as cases which are settled, withdrawn, or cases which will appear to take less time than was originally anticipated. (See paras 12.6 and 12.7 of the 2008 Practice Direction as to the operation of the warned list.) **19.143**

The bundle of papers for use at the hearing

The 2002 Practice Direction introduced a major change in the way in which bundles for use in hearings before the EAT were prepared since it placed the responsibility on the parties to prepare a core bundle of papers for use at the hearing. Previously the EAT prepared the bundle on the basis of documents supplied by the employment tribunal and the parties. This change has been maintained in para 6 of the 2008 Practice Direction. Ultimate responsibility for the bundle lies with the appellant and pursuant to para 6.1 of the 2008 Practice Direction the bundle must include only those documents which are relevant to the points of law raised in the appeal and which are likely to be referred to at the hearing. It is the responsibility of parties to retain copies of all documents including hearing bundles sent to the EAT. **19.144**

Paragraph 6.2 of the 2008 Practice Direction states: **19.145**

> 6.2 The documents in the core bundle should be numbered by item, then paginated continuously and indexed, in the following order:
> 6.2.1 Judgment, decision or order appealed from and written reasons
> 6.2.2 Sealed Notice of Appeal
> 6.2.3 Respondent's Answer if a Full Hearing . . ., Respondent's Submissions if a PH
> 6.2.4 ET1 Claim (and any Additional Information or Written Answers)
> 6.2.5 ET3 Response (and any Additional Information or Written Answers)
> 6.2.6 Questionnaire and Replies (discrimination and equal pay cases)
> 6.2.7 Relevant orders, judgments and written reasons of the Employment Tribunal
> 6.2.8 Relevant orders and judgments of the EAT
> 6.2.9 Affidavits and Employment Tribunal comments (where ordered)
> 6.2.10 Any documents agreed or ordered . . .

19.146 The total number of pages in the core bundle must not exceed 100 unless permission of the registrar is granted. If permitted or ordered, further pages may follow with consecutive pagination in additional bundles (2008 Practice Direction, para 6.3). In complex cases the registrar will usually give that permission but parties should be prepared to explain why it is necessary to do so. It is sometimes helpful to divide the papers into a core and non core bundle.

19.147 The rules relating to the preparation of the bundles depend on the track to which the case is allocated (see 2008 Practice Direction, paras 6.5–6.7):

(a) In preliminary hearings, appeals from an order of the registrar, r 3(10) hearings, and appointments for directions, the appellant should prepare and lodge four copies of the bundle as soon as possible after the service of the notice of appeal and no later than 21 days from the seal date of a relevant order unless otherwise directed.
(b) In final hearings the parties must cooperate in agreeing a bundle of papers for the hearing. By no later than 35 days from the seal date of a relevant order, unless otherwise directed, the appellant is responsible for ensuring that four copies of a bundle agreed by the parties is lodged at the EAT. This must be complied with even in a case where a preliminary hearing took place since the EAT will not retain papers from a preliminary hearing.
(c) In the warned list or fast-track final hearing cases the bundles should be lodged as soon as possible with the EAT and in any event within seven days of being notified that the case has been expedited or placed on the warned list (unless the hearing date is within seven days).

19.148 Where there is a disagreement between the parties as to the preparation of the bundles, the registrar may give directions on an application by the parties or on the registrar's own initiative (2008 Practice Direction, para 6.8). All documents should be legible and unmarked (2008 Practice Direction, para 6.8). The question of what documents should go into the bundle often becomes heated between the parties but is rarely of influence on the final outcome of the appeal. Brevity is welcomed by the EAT and it is clear that only those documents relevant to the point of law to be argued should be before the EAT.

N. SKELETON ARGUMENTS

19.149 Skeleton arguments must be provided in all hearings before the EAT unless the EAT is notified by a party or representative that the notice of appeal or respondent's answer contains the full argument which a party wishes to advance on paper (2008 Practice Direction, para 13.1). This will be a rare case in fact.

19.150 Pursuant to para 13.9 of the 2008 Practice Direction, skeleton arguments must be lodged at the EAT and exchanged in a case where both parties have been ordered to be present:

(a) in the case of a preliminary hearing, appeal against an order of the registrar, a r 3(10) hearing, or appointment for directions, not less than 10 days before the hearing, or, if the hearing is fixed at less than seven days' notice, as soon as possible after the hearing date has been notified;
(b) not less than 21 days before a full hearing (although this is often reduced to 14 days by order);
(c) in the case of warned list and fast-track final hearing cases, as soon as is possible and in any event (unless the hearing date is less than seven days later) within seven days of the parties having been notified that the case is expedited or in the warned list.

19.151 Paragraph 13.8 of the 2008 Practice Direction provides that parties may submit skeleton arguments with the notice of appeal or respondent's answer (as occurs in the Court of Appeal).

19.152 Where a party does not comply with the procedure with regard to skeleton arguments, it may lead to an adjournment of the appeal or alternatively (and unusually) a dismissal for non-compliance with the Practice Direction and to an award of costs. The party in default may also have to attend the EAT to explain their failure (2008 Practice Direction, para 13.10) which is likely to prove embarrassing. Often the parties will attach a bundle of authorities to the skeleton argument but this may also be done separately. In *Sage UK Ltd v Bacco* EAT/597/06 the EAT laid down a practice direction that bundles of authorities should contain IRLR or ICR reports when the case is reported so as to avoid wasteful pre-reading (paras 15 to 17). They should not be taken from the Internet.

A party in default should immediately despatch any delayed skeleton argument to the EAT by hand, fax, or email (londoneat@ets.gsi.gov.uk or edinburgheat@ets.gsi.gov.uk) and unless notified by the EAT to the contrary, bring to the hearing a minimum of six copies of the skeleton argument and any authorities referred to. Paragraph 13.10 of the 2008 Practice Direction makes clear that the EAT staff will not be responsible for copying or supplying authorities or skeletons on the morning of the hearing. **19.153**

A skeleton argument should: **19.154**

(a) be concise (2008 Practice Direction, para 13.2);
(b) identify and summarize the points of law relied on (2008 Practice Direction, para 13.2);
(c) identify and summarize the steps in the legal argument and the statutory provisions and authorities to be relied on, identifying them by name, page, and paragraph and stating the legal proposition sought to be derived from them (2008 Practice Direction, para 13.2);
(d) state the form of the order which the party will ask the EAT to make at the hearing (2008 Practice Direction, para 13.3); this is very important given the wide range of disposals of the case which may be available in a particular case (the question whether a case if remitted should be remitted to the same or a different tribunal should be addressed);
(e) in the case of the appellant's argument, be accompanied by a chronology of events, to be agreed if possible (2008 Practice Direction, para 13.4);
(f) be prepared, unless impracticable, using the pagination in the index to the appeal bundle (2008 Practice Direction, para 13.5).

At para 13.6 of the 2008 Practice Direction, represented parties are informed that they must 'give the instructions necessary for their representatives to comply with this procedure within the time limits'. Further, it is no excuse for the failure of a party to produce a skeleton argument that conciliation or settlement negotiations were being conducted (2008 Practice Direction, para 13.7). **19.155**

Skeleton arguments are merely an opportunity to set out the steps of their legal argument on paper and should not be used as an opportunity to argue the case in detail (2008 Practice Direction, para 13.2). Parties should not cite an unnecessary number of authorities in skeleton arguments (2008 Practice Direction, para 14.3). It is, however, the first document which the EAT is likely to read in a case so it is vital to set out the party's contentions clearly. **19.156**

O. HEARING LENGTH

Paragraph 12.1 of the 2008 Practice Direction requires parties to give accurate time estimates since lay members of the EAT are part-time and it may well be difficult to re-list an appeal should the initial time estimate which has been given prove to be insufficient for the hearing. Moreover, the EAT reserves the right at para 12.2 of the 2008 Practice Direction to avoid any adjournment of an appeal by placing the parties under appropriate time limits in order to complete the presentation of submissions within the available time. Therefore, parties are best advised to inform the listing officer of any change in the estimate or disagreement with an estimate made by the EAT as soon as possible. The hearing length should include the time likely to be needed by the EAT to reach its decision as it prefers to give judgment at once rather than reserve its decision. **19.157**

P. RESTRICTED REPORTING ORDERS

The EAT has the power to make restricted reporting orders under the EAT Rules where the case involves an appeal as to the grant of such an order or the refusal of an employment tribunal to grant an order (see ETA 1996, ss 31(2) and 32(1)). In addition, the EAT can make a restricted **19.158** reporting order in any appeal from an interim decision of the employment tribunal where the employment tribunal has made a restricted reporting order which has not been revoked. It is to be noted that a decision of the tribunal on liability is not considered to be an interim decision even where quantum is yet to be determined. Rule 23 of the EAT Rules deals with cases where allegations of sexual misconduct have been made or where the commission of a sexual offence is relevant. Rule 23A deals with disability discrimination cases. The employment tribunal is able to make a restricted reporting order in respect of disability discrimination cases where evidence of a personal nature is likely to be heard (see ETR 2004, r 50(8)(b)).

19.159 In addition, if an appeal appears to raise allegations of a sexual offence having been committed, the registrar must omit from the register or delete from any order, judgment, or other document which is available to the public any material which is likely to lead members of the public to identify any person affected by or making the allegation (EAT Rules, r 23(2)).

19.160 In *X v Commissioner of Police of the Metropolis* [2003] ICR 1031, the EAT (Burton P presiding) considered the phrase 'appeared to involve allegations of the commission of a sexual offence' in the EAT Rules—the same phrase appears in ETR 2004. The EAT considered that in determining whether or not the case appeared to involve such allegations it was not limited to a consideration of the pleadings. The EAT or employment tribunal had to make a determination on the basis of everything that it had read as to whether or not the case would involve such allegations.

19.161 The EAT will not usually make a restricted reporting order unless it has given the parties opportunity to advance oral argument at a hearing (EAT Rules, r 23(5)). However, the EAT need not comply with that requirement in the case of a temporary order and may make one pursuant to r 23(5A) even without the need for a hearing. Where a temporary order has been made the registrar will inform the parties of it as soon as possible. The parties may then apply within 14 days to have the temporary order revoked or converted into a full order (EAT Rules, r 23(5B)). If no such application is made, then the temporary order will cease to have effect on the fifteenth day after it was made. If an application is made, it will continue in effect until the hearing takes place at which the application is considered (EAT Rules, r 23(5C)).

19.162 Interested parties of the media may be joined as parties to a case in order that they are able to make representations as to whether or not a restricted reporting order should be made. The power to join parties to proceedings before the EAT is contained within r 18 of the EAT Rules. However, the press will have to show good cause to be joined as such joinder will not occur automatically (*A v B, ex p News Group Newspapers Ltd* [1998] ICR 55, 66).

19.163 The discretion of the EAT to make a restricted reporting order will be exercised by reference to whether or not the making of the order is in the public interest. In *X v Z Ltd* [1998] ICR 43, 46–7, Staughton LJ explained:

> It is important that those who have to exercise that power should realise that it is not to be exercised automatically at the request of one party, or even at the request of both parties. The industrial tribunal still has to consider whether it is in the public interest that the press should be deprived of the right to communicate information to the public if it becomes available. It is not a matter which is to be dealt with on the nod so to speak. *Scott v Scott* [1913] A.C. 417, 438 establishes that, when both sides consent to an order prohibiting publication, that is exactly the moment when a court ought to examine with particular care whether, as a matter of discretion, such an order should be made.

19.164 The EAT has been invited to find, on a number of occasions, that its powers to make a restricted reporting order are wider than the extent which is set out in the ETA 1996 and the EAT Rules. In *A v B, ex p News Group Newspapers* the EAT was asked to find that it had an inherent jurisdiction to make a restricted reporting order. The EAT (Morison P presiding) saw the force of the argument that the EAT had an inherent jurisdiction to make a restricted reporting order but was not prepared, on the facts of that case, to cut through the statutory regime provided for by the ETA 1996 and the EAT Rules by issuing a restricted reporting order.

The EAT considered the issue again in *X v Commissioner of Police of the Metropolis* [2003] ICR 1031. In that case the appellant, who had undergone gender reassignment surgery, brought a claim for sex discrimination as a result of the rejection of her application to join the police force. The police alleged that the appellant was suspected of criminal offences and that was part of the reason that her application was rejected. The appellant's application before the tribunal for a restricted reporting order had been declined as not being a case which fell within the rules by which the employment tribunal could make a restricted reporting order. The appellant appealed to the EAT. The EAT (Burton P presiding) declined to offer conclusive guidance as to whether or not the EAT has an inherent jurisdiction to make a restricted reporting order. In that case, it was unnecessary for the EAT to do so since the EAT found that it could make a restricted reporting order by a different route even though the case was not covered by the statutory provisions. The EAT's reasoning was that: **19.165**

(a) The employment tribunal and the EAT have a power and are under a duty to apply the provisions of the Equal Treatment Directive (Council Directive 76/207/EEC [1976] OJ L39/40). In particular Article 6 of the Directive requires Member States to ensure that judicial and administrative procedures are put in place to ensure the enforcement of obligations under the Directive and to ensure that all those people who consider themselves wronged by a failure to apply the principle of equal treatment are able to make use of such procedures.
(b) Both the employment tribunals and the EAT have the power to regulate their own procedure. That must include, where a claimant would otherwise be deterred from bringing a claim, the making of a restricted reporting order in order to ensure the confidentiality in respect of the identity of the claimant.
(c) As such, the EAT concluded at para 56 of its decision:

> In those circumstances, we conclude that both in the employment tribunal and in the appeal tribunal there is a power for those bodies to regulate their own procedure, so as to include, in a proper case, a restricted reporting order or a register deletion order or other order analogous to them or to make some provision in respect of confidentiality of the identity of the applicant, or, no doubt in an appropriate case, a respondent, not limited by the precise terms of the existing Rules.

The decision in *X v Commissioner of Police of the Metropolis* has simplified the law. Prior to that authority, the EAT's decision in *Chief Constable of West Yorkshire Police v A* [2001] ICR 128 indicated that the EAT's jurisdiction to make a restricted reporting order in a case on similar facts to *X v Commissioner of Police of the Metropolis* was based on a combination of the EU law principle of effectiveness and the EAT's inherent jurisdiction to make such an order. The authority of *A* indicated, therefore, that the EAT's power to make restricted reporting orders may go beyond the powers of the employment tribunal who had no such inherent jurisdiction (see *A v B, ex p News Group Newspapers*). This would plainly be undesirable and *X* sets out the position for both the EAT and the employment tribunals. **19.166**

Where material is published in contravention of a restricted reporting order, the punishment on summary conviction is a fine not exceeding level 5 on the standard scale (see ETA 1996, s 31(3)). **19.167**

Q. NATIONAL SECURITY APPEALS

Rules 30A and 31A of the EAT Rules provide that where a Minister of the Crown considers it to be expedient in the interest of national security, he may in Crown employment proceedings direct the EAT to sit in private for all or part of a hearing, exclude the party who was the claimant before the employment tribunal and his representative, and take steps to conceal the identity of particular witnesses. **19.168**

Further, the EAT may choose to exercise its own authority and make any of the orders referred to above of its own volition (r 30A(2)). In addition, the EAT may prevent disclosure **19.169** of documents (including any decision) to any excluded person such as the claimant or his representative or alternatively to any person who has been excluded from a private hearing. The EAT may also take steps to keep secret all or any part of the reasons for any order which it makes. In the case of a claimant or his representative being excluded from the proceedings, the EAT must pursuant to r 30A(4) and (5) inform the Attorney-General who may appoint a special advocate to represent the interests of the claimant. The special advocate must not communicate directly or indirectly with anyone including the excluded applicant about any of the grounds of appeal or the basis on which the appeal is resisted. Neither may the special advocate communicate any matter referred to during the private sitting pursuant to r 30A(7).

19.170 A minister may also, where he considers it expedient in the interests of national security, direct that a document is prepared containing the reasons for a decision of the EAT but with material omitted from it for the benefit of a person who was excluded from the proceedings. Alternatively, a minister may simply state that no separate document should be prepared but that no reasons are disclosed to a party who was excluded from the proceedings. These powers are contained in r 31A(2)–(5) of the EAT Rules.

R. EVIDENCE

Notes of evidence

19.171 The vast majority of the work undertaken by the EAT involves the EAT exercising its appellate jurisdiction and usually, in order for it to exercise such jurisdiction, there is no need for it to consider the evidence heard by the employment tribunal. However, where an appellant seeks seriously to argue that a finding of fact of the employment tribunal cannot be supported with reference to any of the evidence heard by the employment tribunal, it might be necessary for the EAT to consider the precise evidence which the employment tribunal heard. The only way in which evidence before the employment tribunal is formally recorded is in the form of a note taken by the judge. The parties may keep their own record of proceedings but there is no requirement on them to do so and those representing themselves will find this difficult to do. The judge's note need not, however, contain an account of all proceedings—there is no need for the note to contain the detail of an advocate's submissions, for example. However, the note should be a verbatim or near verbatim account of the witness evidence.

19.172 An application for the use of the judge's note should only be made by a party in appropriate circumstances. In particular it should not be used merely to seek further grounds of appeal which are not apparent on the face of the tribunal's decision. In *Webb v Anglian Water Authority* [1981] IRLR 494 (decided under the old practice but still authoritative on this point) the EAT stated that notes should not be provided to a party unless the notice of appeal raised a ground of attack relating to the findings of fact made by the employment tribunal. Such grounds will be likely to be perversity appeals and in particular those perversity appeals where it is suggested that there was no evidence at all on which the employment tribunal could have properly reached a finding of fact. This principle is now succinctly enshrined in para 7.7 of the 2008 Practice Direction.

> A note of evidence is not to be produced and supplied to the parties to enable the parties to embark on a 'fishing expedition' to establish grounds or additional grounds of appeal or because they have not kept their own notes of evidence. If an application for such a note is found by the EAT to have been unreasonably made . . . the party behaving unreasonably is at risk of being ordered to pay costs.

19.173 The EAT is naturally reluctant to allow access to the notes of evidence on the basis that it adds cost to appeals and inevitably delays them, and an appellant which seeks access to the notes will usually find that the point must be argued orally before the EAT save in a very clear case.

An appellant who considers that a point raised in the notice of appeal cannot be argued without reference to the evidence heard by the employment tribunal should submit an application with the notice of appeal (2008 Practice Direction, para 7.1). Where the application is not made at the same time as the notice of appeal it should be made: **19.174**

(a) in the skeleton or written submissions lodged prior to the preliminary hearing in cases where there is a preliminary hearing;
(b) if no preliminary hearing is ordered and the case is sent straight to a final hearing then an application should be made within 14 days of the seal date of the order which provides for such hearing.

The complexity of this subparagraph was criticized by the Court of Appeal in *Wheeler v Quality Deep Ltd* [2005] ICR 265 at paras 65–8 on the basis that litigants in person would not be able to understand it. Hooper LJ invited the EAT President to consider whether the judge who conducts the sift and orders a full hearing should consider in each case whether judge's notes should be required.

An application for the evidence heard by the employment tribunal to be used at the appeal hearing should include the following by virtue of para 7.2 of the 2008 Practice Direction: **19.175**

(a) the issue in the notice of appeal or respondent's answer to which the matter is relevant;
(b) the names of the witnesses whose evidence is considered relevant, alternatively the nature of the evidence the absence of which is considered relevant;
(c) (if applicable) the part of the hearing when evidence was given;
(d) the gist of the evidence (or absence of evidence) alleged to be relevant; and
(e) (if the party has a record), saying so and by whom it was made, or producing an extract from a witness statement given in writing at the hearing.

The more detail that can be given in the application the better and the party must give as much background to the case to enable the registrar to master the issues arising on the application.

By para 7.3 of the 2008 Practice Direction the application may be considered on the papers or alternatively by the registrar or a judge at a preliminary hearing. Usually it will be ordered that the party seeking to place employment tribunal evidence before the EAT give notice to the other parties to the appeal, although orders determining the application or alternatively giving directions for written representations may be made. Where such notice is ordered, it will require the parties to cooperate and use best endeavours to agree a note of the relevant evidence or alternatively a statement that there was no such evidence within 21 days. Paragraph 7.7 of the 2008 Practice Direction threatens uncooperative parties with the payment of costs. Paragraph 7.4 of the 2008 Practice Direction further provides that where it proves impossible to agree the evidence within 21 days any party can apply to the EAT for directions within seven days. The directions might include: **19.176**

> the resolution of the disagreement on the papers or at a hearing; the administration by one party to the others of, or a request to the Chairman to respond to, a questionnaire; or, if the EAT is satisfied that such notes are necessary, a request that the Chairman produce his/her notes of evidence in whole or in part.

A few employment tribunals are tape recorded as part of a pilot scheme. Paragraph 7.6 of the 2008 Practice Direction states that the principles set out above will apply to a transcript of the recording of proceedings. **19.177**

Where a party disputes the contents of the judge's note of evidence the procedure set out in *Dexine Rubber Co Ltd v Alker* [1977] ICR 434 will be made use of. Any party who seeks to criticize the note should submit his criticism to the advocate for the other party in order to determine whether or not both sides agree that the note is inaccurate and then send his criticisms to the employment judge. If the judge replies, stating that after consideration **19.178** of the matter he is satisfied that his note is correct, then the judge's conclusion must be accepted.

19.179 An unusual situation arose in *Houston v Lightwater Farms Ltd* [1990] ICR 502, where the employment judge refused to provide his note of evidence to the EAT on its request stating that it was an aide-memoire for his use and need only be supplied to the EAT out of courtesy. The EAT was of the view that since a judge sat in a judicial capacity and had a judicial duty to make notes the judge had to comply with the EAT's request.

Introducing new evidence

19.180 The EAT has a discretion (rarely exercised in fact) to admit fresh evidence which was not placed before the employment tribunal. Paragraph 8.2 of the 2008 Practice Direction states:

> 8.2 In exercising its discretion to admit any fresh evidence or new document, the EAT will apply the principles set out in *Ladd v Marshall* [1954] 1 WLR 1489, having regard to the overriding objective, ie:
> 8.2.1 the evidence could not have been obtained with reasonable diligence for use at the Employment Tribunal hearing;
> 8.2.2 it is relevant and would probably have had an important influence on the hearing;
> 8.2.3 it is apparently credible.

Accordingly the evidence and representations in support of the application must clearly address these principles.

19.181 Thus, the EAT has borrowed the strict principles as regards the admissibility of fresh evidence which are used in the Court of Appeal. This is consistent with the EAT as a body which deals only with points of law and not fact. In *Ladd v Marshall* itself, the Court of Appeal refused to allow fresh evidence to be called where a witness admitted that she had lied at the original trial. The judges accepted that such evidence was relevant and would have an important influence on the hearing but declined to accept that such evidence was credible:

> A confessed liar cannot usually be accepted as credible. To justify the reception of the fresh evidence, some good reason must be shown why a lie was told in the first instance, and good ground given for thinking the witness will tell the truth on the second occasion. If it were proved that the witness had been bribed or coerced into telling a lie at the trial, and was now anxious to tell the truth, that would, I think, be a ground for a new trial, and it would not be necessary to resort to an action to set aside the judgment on the ground of fraud.

19.182 The EAT has discouraged the introduction of fresh evidence from its earliest days (*Bagga v Heavy Electricals (India) Ltd* [1972] ICR 118, 120) and it is clear that where a party chooses not to raise a category of evidence at trial, he cannot seek to reopen that issue by calling the evidence on appeal (*Bingham v Hobourn Engineering Ltd* [1992] IRLR 298).

19.183 In spite of the strict approach taken by the EAT, in *Borden (UK) Ltd v Potter* [1986] ICR 647, Popplewell J explained that the EAT would look more favourably on the failure of a litigant in person to adduce evidence at trial than on the part of professional representatives. In that case the employer dismissed the claimant in circumstances where it was alleged that he had assaulted a fellow employee. A tribunal found that the dismissal was unfair and the employer sought to appeal that finding by introducing medical evidence to discredit the claimant. The EAT declined to admit the fresh evidence since no reasonable explanation was given as to why it had not been obtained and placed before the tribunal.

19.184 Similarly, in *Wileman v Minilec Engineering Ltd* [1988] ICR 318, the EAT declined to admit fresh evidence. In that case the employer lost a claim for sexual harassment and sought to introduce before the EAT a photograph which had been published in a newspaper of the claimant posing in a 'flimsy costume' after the employment tribunal hearing. The employer argued that the photograph demonstrated that the claimant did not suffer a detriment as a result of the harassment. Although the evidence could not have been available at the hearing, the EAT was not convinced that it was relevant or probative.

However, fresh evidence is sometimes accepted by the EAT. One such case is *Photostatic Copiers (Southern) Ltd v Okuda and Japan Office Equipment Ltd (In Liquidation)* [1995] IRLR 11. In that case the claimant admitted before the EAT that he had been in receipt of a payment from the employer's business rival. The evidence had become available since the tribunal hearing and its existence could not have been known or foreseen by the employer. Moreover, the existence of the evidence was likely to have an impact on the result of the case albeit only on remedies. **19.185**

As with the EAT's exercise of discretion in other areas (see *United Arab Emirates v Abdelghafar* [1995] ICR 65) special considerations may arise in certain circumstances. For example, under the State Immunity Act 1978 there is an overriding duty on the EAT under the Act which overrides the usual rules (*Egypt v Gamal-Eldin* [1996] ICR 13). **19.186**

The procedure for admitting new evidence is that it should be filed with the EAT at the same time as the notice of appeal or respondent's answer along with an application to admit such new evidence (2008 Practice Direction, para 8.1). A party who wishes to resist an application to admit new evidence should submit written representations to the EAT and other parties within 14 days of the application being sent to them (2008 Practice Direction, para 8.3). The application will then be considered by the registrar or a judge of the EAT (2008 Practice Direction, para 8.4). **19.187**

S. ORDERS OF THE EMPLOYMENT APPEAL TRIBUNAL

Where the EAT allows an appeal, it may, pursuant to s 35 of ETA 1996: **19.188**

(a) exercise any of the powers of the body or officer from whom the appeal was brought, or
(b) remit the case to the body or officer from whom the appeal was brought.

In the case of the employment tribunals, therefore, the usual orders made by the EAT are to substitute its own decision for that of the tribunal, remit the case to the same tribunal for reconsideration or further reasoning, or, alternatively, remit the case to a differently constituted tribunal for rehearing on some or all points. In addition, the EAT has the power to accept an agreed order, to grant permission to appeal to the Court of Appeal, to review its own decision, or to make a reference to the European Court of Justice (see Chapter 22). **19.189**

The EAT has no power to make a declaration of incompatibility under the Human Rights Act 1998 (HRA 1998) since it is not a court as defined in s 4(5) of HRA 1998. This question was considered in *Whittaker v P & D Watson* [2002] ICR 1244, where the EAT, presided over by Lindsay P, commented (at 1249): **19.190**

> It is to be noted that definition of 'court' does not include the employment tribunal or the Employment Appeal Tribunal. The effect is a little odd so far as concerns the Employment Appeal Tribunal because were I to be sitting alone, 500 yards away, in my erstwhile role in the Chancery Division, and were a corresponding question to come in front of me, I would be able to make a declaration of incompatibility in an appropriate case. But here, where I am assisted by a carefully balanced panel to represent both sides of industry, I cannot so decide.

It might be that the correct approach is for the EAT to dismiss the appeal in hand but then to grant permission to appeal. The Court of Appeal then has the power to make a declaration of incompatibility (see also Chapter 16).

Substitution

The EAT is entitled to substitute its own view for that of the tribunal where the decision reached by the tribunal is plainly and unarguably wrong on the facts as a result of a misdirection of law. In order to determine whether the decision is plainly and unarguably wrong on the facts those facts must not require any amplification or further investigation. That was the view of the Court of Appeal in *McLeod v Hellyer Brothers Ltd* [1987] IRLR 234, where the Court of **19.191**

Appeal refused to interfere with a decision of the EAT to substitute its own view for that of the tribunal. In *Dobie v Burns International Security Services (UK) Ltd* [1984] IRLR 329, Sir John Donaldson MR set out the test (at para 18) as follows:

> Once you detect that there has been a misdirection, and particularly that there has been an express misdirection of law, the next question to be asked is not whether the conclusion of the Tribunal is plainly wrong, but whether it is plainly and unarguably right, notwithstanding that misdirection, that the decision can stand. If the conclusion was wrong or might have been wrong, then it is for the appellate tribunal to remit the case to the only tribunal which is charged with making findings of fact.

19.192 The EAT's willingness to substitute its own decision for that of the employment tribunal, in cases where it is able to do so without further factual investigation, perhaps stems from a reluctance to allow a litigant a 'second bite at the cherry' particularly given the delay and additional expense that is caused by remitting cases to the employment tribunals.

Remission

19.193 Where the EAT exercises its power to remit a case to the employment tribunal, the tribunal is only entitled to reconsider the case to the limited extent that is ordered by the EAT. Sometimes the EAT is not crystal clear about the scope of remission; parties should be prepared to argue before the EAT as to precisely what subjects should be dealt with on such a remitted hearing and whether fresh evidence may be given or simply submissions to be made. In *Aparau v Iceland Frozen Foods* [2000] IRLR 196, the Court of Appeal allowed an employee's appeal against the decision of an employment tribunal which had allowed a respondent employer to amend a response so as to add alternative potentially fair reasons for a dismissal once the matter had been remitted on a much narrower question. The Court of Appeal explained that the tribunal has no jurisdiction to hear or determine other matters and no power to allow a party to amend its case to raise new matters.

19.194 The EAT is entitled to remit to the same employment tribunal or to a differently constituted tribunal. The EAT has given important guidance as to how it should determine whether to remit to the same tribunal (*Sinclair, Roche & Temperley v Heard* [2004] IRLR 763). The following factors will be relevant:

(a) Proportionality must be considered and in particular the amount of money at stake must be weighed against the cost and distress to the parties of ordering a complete rehearing.
(b) It is necessary to consider whether or not the same tribunal will remember the case. If the tribunal will have forgotten the case, then it should not be sent back to it. Whether or not the tribunal will remember the case is likely to depend on how much time has passed since the hearing as against the length of the hearing when it occurred.
(c) It would not be appropriate to send cases back to the same tribunal where the EAT had found that the tribunal was biased or there was a risk of pre-judgment or partiality.
(d) The EAT must have confidence that the tribunal, with appropriate guidance, can get the matter right on a reconsideration of the case. Therefore where the first hearing was totally flawed or where there was complete mishandling of the case, the EAT should send the matter to a differently constituted tribunal.
(e) There must be careful consideration not to provide the tribunal with what has been described as a 'second bite at the cherry'. The EAT must not send a case back to the same tribunal where it does not have confidence that the tribunal will be able to consider the matter again and look at such further matters as are required and, if necessary, come to a different conclusion.
(f) On balance, in the ordinary case it is likely that the EAT will consider that the tribunal below is capable of taking a professional approach to dealing with the matter on remission (see also *HM Prison Service v Johnson* [2007] IRLR 951, para 126).

There are some cases where the EAT finds that the tribunal's approach to the case has been so poor that the party which lost cannot have confidence that justice will be done on remission. This is a matter of 'feel' for the EAT.

Pursuant to para 9.4 of the 2008 Practice Direction, the EAT can adjourn an appeal for up to 21 days and in effect remit an appeal to the employment tribunal: **19.195**

> pending the making or the conclusion of an application by the appellant to the Employment Tribunal (if necessary out of time) for a review or pending the response by the Employment Tribunal to an invitation from the judge or Registrar to clarify, supplement or give its written reasons.

Therefore, that the EAT can remit an appeal to the employment tribunal in order that the tribunal clarifies or supplements its reasoning is now beyond doubt as a result of the 2008 Practice Direction and the cases of *Burns v Consignia plc (No 2)* [2004] IRLR 425 and *Barke v SEETEC Business Technology Centre Ltd* [2005] EWCA Civ 578, [2005] IRLR 633. However, the courts have adopted contradictory and confusing positions with regard to this power in the past.

For example, in *Yusuf v Aberplace Co Ltd* [1984] ICR 850 the EAT (presided over by Nolan J) was of the view that the employment tribunal was not *functus officio* until it had told the parties why they had won or lost and that therefore it was possible for the EAT to remit a case to the tribunal in order that the tribunal elaborated on its reasoning. However, in *Reuben v LB Brent* [2000] IRLR 176 a differently constituted EAT (presided over by Morison P) held that once the tribunal's decision had been promulgated in the register, the tribunal was *functus officio* and therefore had no further function to perform in the case. Thus, if the decision was defective because of a lack of reasoning, an appeal should be granted rather than the matter sent back to the same tribunal. **19.196**

The area was reviewed by the Court of Appeal in *Tran v Greenwich Vietnam Community* [2002] IRLR 735. The issue arose since one of the matters considered by the court was whether the EAT could have remitted the case back to the tribunal at a preliminary stage of the appeal and prior to hearing the substance of the appeal. In the event, the appeal was not determined on this point since the Court of Appeal decided that adequacy of reasons had not been argued below and that, therefore, the court had no jurisdiction to entertain the point on appeal. However, the Court of Appeal was prepared to offer its advice on the matter. The majority of the Court of Appeal (Brooke and Arden LJJ) noted that the power to remit a case back to the employment tribunal only arose under s 35 of ETA 1996 in order to dispose of an appeal. The majority argued that remitting a case back to the tribunal in order that it could provide further reasons would not be disposing of the appeal at all, but would, in fact, amount to retaining the appeal or, at best, an interim order to remit the case to the tribunal prior to a further hearing of the appeal. Sedley LJ found himself in the minority arguing (at para 21) that: **19.197**

> For my part I would have held that the section 35 power is not confined to orders made at the conclusion of an appeal: it exists 'for the purpose of disposing of an appeal' and can therefore in my judgment be exercised at any appropriate stage.

However, seven days after the decision in *Tran* was handed down, the then Master of the Rolls, Lord Phillips, gave judgment in *English v Emery Reimbold & Strick Ltd* [2003] IRLR 710 and stated at para 25: **19.198**

> if an application for permission to appeal on the ground of lack of reasons is made to the appellate court and it appears to the appellate court that the application is well founded, it should consider adjourning the application and remitting the case to the trial judge with an invitation to provide additional reasons for his decision or where appropriate his reasons for a specific finding or findings.

In *Burns v Consignia plc (No 2)* [2004] IRLR 425, the EAT (Burton J presiding) had to follow either the approach of the majority of the Court of Appeal in *Tran* or, alternatively, to follow the minority approach of Sedley LJ in *Tran* and the similar approach as set out by Lord Phillips MR in *English*. In *Burns* the claimant had issued an application alleging sex and race discrimination **19.199** which had subsequently been withdrawn. After the withdrawal she issued a second application making the same allegations of sex and race discrimination but in addition alleging constructive unfair dismissal. The employment tribunal struck out her application as an abuse of process. The EAT would have been prepared to allow her appeal in respect of the constructive unfair dismissal claim but noted that the tribunal had failed to consider whether, given Mrs Burns' behaviour, a fair trial was still possible. The EAT therefore adjourned the appeal and remitted the matter back to the employment tribunal. On the adjourned hearing of the appeal, counsel for Mrs Burns took the point that he should be able to challenge the order for remission. He relied on the majority's decision in *Tran*. The EAT declined to follow the decision of the majority of the Court of Appeal in *Tran* on two bases:

(a) The views of the majority of the Court of Appeal in *Tran* were 'plainly obiter' and therefore were not binding on the EAT.
(b) Even if the views of the majority formed part of the *ratio decidendi* of the case it was necessary for the EAT to take account of the important case of *English* to which no reference could have been made in *Tran*. Although *English* did not deal with s 35 of the ETA 1996, any hostility to the idea of a 'second bite at the cherry' which must have formed the basis of the decision in *Tran* would be overtaken and ousted by the contrary decision of Lord Phillips MR in *English*.

19.200 The EAT did, however, issue this warning ([2004] IRLR 425, para 13, *per* Burton P):

> Of course there are dangers in remitting to the original tribunal a case where the ground of appeal is inadequacy of reasoning, and there will be some cases in which the reasoning is so inadequate that it would be unsafe to remit to the same tribunal. Equally, there will be the potential danger of giving the opportunity to a court below to reconsider its decision on an entirely different basis.

19.201 This matter has been dealt with by the Court of Appeal in *Barke v SEETEC Business Technology Centre Ltd* [2005] EWCA Civ 578, [2005] IRLR 633. In that case, the argument first set out by Morison J in *Reuben v LB of Brent* [2000] IRLR 176, that the employment tribunal was *functus officio* once it had given its reasons and its decision had been recorded on the register, was relied on by counsel. Dyson LJ pointed out, however, that there were still several functions which an employment tribunal could perform after it had recorded its judgment, such as correcting clerical errors, providing the judge's notes to the EAT, and review. Therefore it was incorrect to say that the employment tribunal was *functus officio* for all purposes once its written reasons have been entered on the register. The Court of Appeal found that even if there was no power for the employment tribunal to clarify or supplement its reasons under its own rules, the EAT had the power to regulate its own procedure under s 30(3) of ETA 1996. Therefore the Court of Appeal went on to uphold the *Burns* procedure—which is now codified in para 9.5 of the 2008 Practice Direction—of remitting cases to the employment tribunals in order for them to elaborate on their reasoning. However, the Court of Appeal agreed with Burton P that there would be some occasions when the procedure would not be appropriate, for example, when there was an allegation of bias against a member of the employment tribunal or:

> where the inadequacy of reasoning is on its face so fundamental that there is a real risk that supplementary reasons will be reconstructions of proper reasons rather than unexpressed actual reasons for the decision... The Employment Appeal Tribunal should always be alive to the danger that an employment tribunal might tailor its response to a request for explanations or further reasons (usually subconsciously rather than deliberately) so as to put the decision in the best possible light. (*Barke v SEETEC* para 46, *per* Dyson LJ)

19.202 Dyson LJ also stated that the Court of Appeal would be slow to interfere with the EAT's exercise of the power to remit to the employment tribunal for clarification or supplementation since the power was a discretionary case management power which should be left to the employment appeal tribunal to apply (*Barke v SEETEC* above, at para 49). There are some dangers with the process. Thus in *Woodhouse School v Webster* [2009] IRLR 568, Mummery LJ emphasized that the purpose of the *Burns/Barke* procedure was to give the tribunal the opportunity of fulfilling its duty to provide adequate reasons, but the tribunal should do no more than answer the specific request. It should not advance arguments in defence of the decision against the grounds of appeal.

T. PERMISSION TO APPEAL

Appeals from the EAT lie to the Court of Appeal in England and Wales. Permission to appeal is required and may be granted by order of the EAT. Pursuant to para 21.1 of the 2008 Practice Direction permission must be sought at the end of the hearing or when a reserved judgment is handed down. If permission is refused then it may be sought from the Court of Appeal within 14 days of the sealed order. Pursuant to para 21.2 of the 2008 Practice Direction where a party seeks permission to appeal it must first state the point of law to be advanced and the grounds of appeal. **19.203**

In Scotland an appeal lies from the EAT to the Court of Session. Permission must be sought from the EAT to appeal to the Court of Session within 42 days of the date of the hearing where judgment is delivered (2008 Practice Direction, para 21.3). **19.204**

There are no rules which govern the EAT's discretion to give permission to appeal. However, permission to appeal is likely to be granted by the EAT only if the appeal raises an important point of principle or practice or if there is some other compelling reason for the appeal court to hear the appeal. **19.205**

The EAT has no power to grant a party permission to appeal straight to the House of Lords. This was noted by the EAT (presided over by Bean J) in *Botham v Ministry of Defence* UKEAT/0503/04 (one of the appeals subsequently joined with *Lawson v Serco* [2006] UKHL 3, [2006] IRLR 289). In that case the EAT stated (at para 23): **19.206**

> We note that if the hearing before us had been in the High Court an application could have been made (with the consent of all parties) for a certificate under section 12 of the Administration of Justice Act 1969 permitting a petition to be presented to their Lordships for leave to bring a 'leap-frog' appeal direct to the House. . . the power applies only in proceedings before a single judge of the High Court or a Divisional Court. We venture to suggest that consideration be given to whether the Employment Appeal Tribunal, which did not exist in 1969, might be brought within the scope of the section.

U. AGREED ORDER

An agreed order may be agreed between the parties in an attempt to achieve one of two results. The parties might agree that the appeal will be withdrawn by way of settlement. Alternatively the parties might agree that an appeal is allowed by way of settlement. **19.207**

The situation in which the parties agree that an appeal should be withdrawn as part of a settlement is dealt with by para 15.1 of the 2008 Practice Direction: **19.208**

> If a settlement is reached, the parties should inform the EAT as soon as possible. The appellant should submit to the EAT a letter signed by or on behalf of the appellant and signed also by or on behalf of the respondent, asking the EAT for permission to withdraw the appeal and to make a consent order in the form of an attached draft signed by or for both parties dismissing the appeal, together with any other agreed order.

Any withdrawal of an appeal should take place as soon as is practicable since if an appeal is withdrawn close to the hearing date the EAT may require the attendance of the appellant and/or a representative to explain the reasons for delaying in making the decision not to pursue the appeal (2008 Practice Direction, para 15.4). **19.209**

However, where the parties wish to consent to the appeal being allowed the position is a little more difficult. In *British Newspaper Publishing Ltd v Fraser* [1987] ICR 517, Popplewell J set out the practice by which settlement of an appeal could be reached by correspondence if the EAT **19.210** was satisfied that both parties were agreed. However, it was made clear that the EAT may, in its discretion, refuse to approve a settlement insofar as it overturns a decision of the employment tribunal. In that situation the EAT may well want full argument as to why the appeal should be allowed because the agreement not only affects the interests of the parties but also the role of the employment tribunal.

19.211 Paragraph 15.3 of the 2008 Practice Direction provides therefore:

> If the parties reach an agreement that the appeal should be allowed by consent, and that an order made by the Employment Tribunal should be reversed or varied or the matter remitted to the Employment Tribunal on the ground that the decision contains an error of law, it is usually necessary for the matter to be heard by the EAT to determine whether there is a good reason for making the proposed order. On notification by the parties, the EAT will decide whether the appeal can be dealt with on the papers or by a hearing at which one or more parties or their representatives should attend to argue the case for allowing the appeal and making the order that the parties wish the EAT to make.

19.212 In any case, in order for an appeal to be allowed by consent, the settlement must truly dispose of the matter. Mummery J stated in *Sainsbury's v Moger* [1994] ICR 800 that where the parties' agreement did not truly dispose of the matter it would have to be fully argued with reasons given by the EAT for a remission or allowing of the appeal. The EAT follows the practice of the Court of Appeal in this respect.

V. REVIEW OF THE EMPLOYMENT APPEAL TRIBUNAL'S JUDGMENT OR ORDER

19.213 Paragraph 20 of the 2008 Practice Direction sets out the procedure by which an application for review by the EAT is made:

> Where an application is made for a review of a judgment or order of the EAT, it can be considered on paper by a judge who may, if he or she heard the original appeal or made the original order alone, without lay members, make such order, granting, refusing, adjourning or otherwise dealing with such application, as he or she may think fit. If the original judgment or order was made by the judge together with lay members, then the judge may, pursuant to Rule 33, consider and refuse such application for review on the papers. If the judge does not refuse such application, he or she may make any relevant further order, but would not grant such application without notice to the opposing party and reference to the lay members, for consideration with them, either on paper or in open court.

19.214 By Rule 33 of the EAT Rules the EAT may of its own motion, or by application of one of the parties made within 14 days of the order, review its order where:

(a) the order was wrongly made as a result of an error on the part of the EAT or its staff;
(b) a party did not receive proper notice of the proceedings leading to the order; or
(c) the interests of justice require such a review.

19.215 The scope of the power to review is therefore limited and reviews have ordinarily only been successful where there have been issues of jurisdiction, where there have been fundamental process errors, where there has been a fraud which appears soon after the decision, or in simple cases of minor error or omission such as where the EAT had acted on the first occasion under a misapprehension of fact.

19.216 However, the EAT made use of its power to review in the unusual case of *O'Neill v Governors of St Thomas More Roman Catholic Voluntary Aided Upper School* [1997] ICR 33. The employment tribunal had dismissed Mrs O'Neill's complaint for sex discrimination in circumstances where she had been dismissed from a Roman Catholic school having had a baby by a Roman Catholic priest who had some connection with the school. On 10 February 1995, Mrs O'Neill's solicitors withdrew her appeal. However, subsequently, Mrs O'Neill sought advice from the European Commission who referred her to case law dealing with 'mixed motives' in discrimination claims and indicated that she might succeed in an appeal. On 4 April 1995, Mrs O'Neill sought to reinstate her appeal stating that before she had withdrawn her appeal, her solicitors had not advised her as to the availability of legal aid. The EAT treated the application as an application for a review of their original decision to allow withdrawal of the appeal. In the event the EAT allowed the appeal to be reinstated although stressed that the case was unusual and that no general rule should be seen to be promulgated by the decision. Future applications to review an order withdrawing a case would require 'an unusual and exceptional case' in order to be successful. Indeed the EAT was influenced in part by the fact that the case gave rise to an interesting and novel point of law and therefore it was in the public interest to permit the issue to be reopened. It is of some note that at the full hearing, the appeal was successful.

Similarly, in *Brain v Corby BC* EAT/376/04, the appellant's solicitors withdrew an appeal but then wrote to the EAT prior to the issuing of the sealed order by the EAT. They explained that their client had had a 'mini breakdown' when he instructed his solicitors that the appeal should be withdrawn. The EAT relied on *O'Neill v Governors of St Thomas More School* and permitted the withdrawal of a withdrawal of an appeal but the EAT once again emphasized that this would only be permitted in an exceptional case. **19.217**

As a superior court of record, the EAT has an inherent power to reconsider its judgment at any time before it is perfected. Therefore, in *Bass Leisure Ltd v Thomas* [1994] IRLR 104, the EAT was prepared to seek further argument from the parties in a case where there had been no appearance from the respondent. It was argued by the *amicus curiae* that in the light of r 26 of the EAT Rules, that the EAT should be slow to review a decision where a party had not appeared. However, the EAT considered that it was entitled as a superior court of record to reconsider its judgment at any time prior to an order being perfected and in the circumstances of that case, whilst finality and the question of costs were clearly relevant, there was a legitimate interest in not promulgating an avoidable error. The EAT stressed that although it was prepared to exercise its discretion in that case, its discretion should be exercised sparingly and with caution. **19.218**

The EAT, in *Asda Stores Ltd v Thompson, Pullan & Caller* [2004] IRLR 598, considered whether or not the EAT was entitled to reopen its own decisions in a similar manner to the Court of Appeal is able. It was decided by the Court of Appeal in *Taylor v Lawrence* [2003] QB 528 that the Court of Appeal could exercise such a power in limited situations such as in the case of apparent bias, discovery of any new matter, or of any fraud. The appeal in *Asda v Thompson* arose from a dismissal following an investigation into allegations that the claimants were using illegal drugs. Witness statements were obtained by a number of informants but the employers refused to disclose the witness statements on the basis that promises of confidentiality had been made to the informants that their identities would not be revealed. The employment tribunal made an order that the witness statements had to be disclosed to the claimants but the employers appealed to the EAT. The EAT (Wall J presiding) remitted the matter back to the tribunal in order that it could re-examine the documents and make such order as was appropriate for discovery and inspection with appropriate safeguards for the fair disposal of the case. The tribunal made such directions as it considered to be appropriate but the respondent was not happy with those directions on the basis that: **19.219**

(a) the respondent felt that it was important that it made submissions to the tribunal since only the respondent would understand why a particular redaction was sought; and
(b) the respondent opposed the idea that the parties could only make such applications to the tribunal following the tribunal's provision to the parties of its reasons and the statements redacted accordingly.

The respondent made an application to the EAT and attacked the previous decision of the EAT presided over by Wall J on the basis that it was ambiguous and alternatively that it was wrong. Either way, it was argued that the EAT should substitute the decision for a new decision. Counsel for the respondent sought to argue that the EAT had jurisdiction to overrule one of its earlier decisions, or to indicate that it should not be followed in the event that it was of the view **19.220** that the earlier decision of the EAT was wrong and sought to d aw an analogy with the jurisdiction of the Court of Appeal. However, the EAT found that if it did have such jurisdiction it was not prepared to exercise it in that case since:

(a) the EAT is not a final court of appeal;
(b) there was nothing to prevent the unsuccessful respondent in the case from appealing the judgment of Wall J to the Court of Appeal;
(c) if there were any ground of reconsideration of this question, it would not be based on apparent bias, or discovery of any new matter, or any fraud which has taken its time to be revealed but rather would be because a point had not been argued.

19.221 As such it is unclear whether or not, in an appropriate case, the EAT may overturn an earlier decision in the same case. It seems unlikely that the EAT will choose to exercise such jurisdiction in any case where the route of appeal to the Court of Appeal was open to the unsuccessful party. The decision in *Asda v Thompson* has recently been affirmed by the EAT (Burton P presiding) in *Vakante v Addey and Stanhope School (No 2)* [2004] ICR 279.

W. COSTS

Circumstances in which costs may be awarded

19.222 Rule 34 of the EAT Rules provides the EAT with a general discretion to award costs against a party. Costs are defined by r 34(2) as including 'fees charges disbursements expenses reimbursement allowed to a litigant in person or remuneration incurred by or on behalf of a party in relation to the proceedings'. The EAT's discretion to award costs against a party may be exercised in the circumstances set out in r 34A(1) of the EAT Rules:

> Where it appears to the Appeal Tribunal that any proceedings brought by the paying party were unnecessary, improper, vexatious or misconceived or that there has been unreasonable delay or other unreasonable conduct in the bringing or conducting of proceedings by the paying party, the Appeal Tribunal may make a costs order against the paying party.

19.223 Rule 34A(2) indicates three examples of cases where the EAT might exercise its discretion to award costs in particular. Those are where a party has not complied with a direction of the EAT, where a party has amended a pleading, or where a party has caused an adjournment of proceedings.

19.224 Case law provides further examples of when a party is at risk of having to pay the other side's costs:

(a) Where an appeal was abandoned shortly before the day of the hearing (*Maroof v JB Battye & Co Ltd* (1973) 8 ITR 489) or where there was unreasonable delay in communicating the decision to withdraw an appeal (*TVR Engineering Ltd v Johnson* [1978] IRLR 556) costs have been awarded. Thus in *Rocha v Commonwealth Holiday Inns of Canada Ltd* EAT/13/80, the EAT stated:

> Applicants to industrial tribunals and appellants to the EAT must take notice that if they withdraw their allegations at a late stage they will be at risk of an application being made for costs. If they desire to contest that application it is their duty to appear before the industrial tribunal or EAT in order to do so.

(b) Where there was no point of law involved in the appeal costs have been awarded against the appellant (*Redland Roof Tiles Ltd v Eveleigh* [1979] IRLR 11).
(c) Where the appellant was absent from the hearing and was unrepresented it has been held that the appellant had behaved unreasonably (*Croydon v Greenham (Plant Hire) Ltd* [1978] ICR 415).

19.225 In *Sodexho Ltd v Gibbons* [2005] IRLR 836 it was accepted by the EAT (Judge Peter Clark sitting alone) that the term 'misconceived' in r 34A includes the appeal having 'no reasonable prospect of success' since this was the definition as set out in reg 2 of ETR 2004. Therefore, the term 'misconceived' ought to be interpreted in the same manner in both the employment tribunals and the EAT.

However, no hard and fast rules can be enunciated as to when costs will be awarded against a party and when they will not. This is necessarily so since the EAT is bound to exercise its discretion before awarding such costs. Thus, while the EAT has been ready to award costs on many occasions where the appeal is abandoned shortly before the hearing, in *McPherson v BNP Paribas* [2004] IRLR 558, the Court of Appeal held that the question for employment tribunals and the EAT was whether in all the circumstances the claimant/appellant had conducted the proceedings reasonably and not whether or not the withdrawal of the claim/appeal was unreasonable. **19.226**

Appellants ought not to feel that they will avoid an award of costs simply because the appeal has progressed past a preliminary hearing or even in a case when the appeal is set down for a full hearing straight away. While it may appear that there is an arguable point of law at first sight, that might appear to be incorrect on a complete consideration of the case and therefore an award of costs might be appropriate (*Clifton Clinic Ltd v Monk* EAT/582/84; *Tesco Stores Ltd v Wilson* UKEAT/0749/98). **19.227**

Assessment of costs

The 2008 Practice Direction provides at para 19.2 that a party may make an application for costs at the end of a hearing or alternatively within 14 days of the seal date of the relevant order of the EAT. The party seeking the order must seek the legal ground on which the application is based and must show how the costs have been incurred. The production of a schedule of costs is the usual way of doing this. If an application for costs is made by paper, then the EAT may resolve the application on the papers provided that it has allowed all relevant parties to make representations in writing (2008 Practice Direction, para 19.4). **19.228**

Rule 34B of the EAT Rules provides for three methods of assessing costs: **19.229**

(1) summary assessment by the EAT;
(2) an order of the EAT ordering a sum agreed between the parties;
(3) detailed assessment in the High Court in accordance with the CPR.

If the assessment of costs takes place on a summary basis, then the EAT will look at the figures for fees charged and will compare them with the schedules in Appendices I and II of the Schedule to Part 48 of the CPR which contains notes on the applicable rates which might be charged by solicitors of various levels of experience and in various parts of the country. Barristers' fees are determined according to counsel's date of call. Summary assessments are a broad brush approach and therefore it is likely that the EAT will hear submissions and will then reduce any award of costs by either deducting some items claimed or alternatively by simply reducing by a percentage figure. On a summary assessment, the EAT may have regard to the ability of the paying party to pay costs when making an order (EAT Rules, r 34B(2)). **19.230**

Alternatively, if the EAT feels that a detailed assessment of costs is more appropriate the matter will be referred to the High Court and a costs judge will assess costs using the procedure set out in CPR Part 47. An appeal lies from the order of a costs judge to a High Court judge although permission to appeal is required. **19.231**

Rule 34D of the EAT Rules creates a special regime where costs are awarded in favour of a litigant in person. The litigant in person is able to make a claim for costs of work undertaken by him or her and disbursements made by a legal representative. However, those two items are treated differently. Costs of work which the litigant in person has undertaken are limited to two-thirds of the amount which would have been allowed if the litigant in person had been represented by a legal representative. Thus it is necessary to calculate the amount of loss by reference, for example, to the number of hours which the litigant in person has had to take off work in order to **19.232** prepare the appeal. It is then necessary to work out the rate which would have been charged by a legal representative. The litigant in person's loss is then capped at two-thirds of the amount that the legal representative would have charged. In a case where the litigant in person has incurred no financial loss in the preparation of the appeal he or she may make a claim for the time which the EAT considers was reasonably spent preparing the appeal at a rate of £25 per hour. That rate was increased to £26 per hour from 6 April 2006 and is increased by £1 each subsequent year from that date. Disbursements on the other hand can be claimed in full although they are subject to the usual cost rules and therefore must be reasonably incurred.

Wasted costs orders

19.233 The EAT can make a wasted costs order against a party's representative. Wasted costs are defined by r 34C of the EAT Rules:

> 'Wasted costs' means any costs incurred by a party (including the representative's own client and any party who does not have a legal representative):
>
> (a) as a result of any improper, unreasonable or negligent act or omission on the part of any representative; or
>
> (b) which, in the light of any such act or omission occurring after they were incurred, the Appeal Tribunal considers it reasonable to expect that party to pay.

19.234 Wasted costs may only be awarded against a party's representative as defined in r 34C(4). That definition only applies to representatives who are acting in pursuit of profit with regard to the proceedings. Therefore those individuals who are acting on a *pro bono* basis, be that as a voluntary sector representative while acting for a law centre or the Free Representation Unit, or a friend or relative of one of the parties, could not be ordered to pay wasted costs.

19.235 When an order is to be made against a representative, the representative will be given an opportunity to make oral or written submissions setting out why such an order should not be made by virtue of r 34C(5). Although there is no requirement on the EAT to provide oral reasons for the making of a wasted costs order, it is likely that the EAT will do so. If the EAT does not do so, then a request for written reasons can be made within 21 days of the date of the order. Written reasons will then be sent to all parties (EAT Rules, r 34C(8)).

19.236 The EAT may have regard to the representative's ability to pay a wasted costs order when determining the amount of such an order (EAT Rules, r 34C(5)).

Part B

Procedure in Other Jurisdictions

20

Employment Litigation in the Civil Courts

SUMMARY

(1) Certain types of employment law claims may be brought in the civil courts. Some disputes may only be brought in the civil courts; others may be brought either in the courts or in the tribunal.

(2) Where a claim may be brought in either venue, or where there are multiple claims in different venues, careful consideration is necessary as to which venue is the most appropriate. Careful consideration must be given the effects of the principles of *res judicata*, issue estoppel, and abuse of process.

(3) Claims in the High Court and county court are governed by the Civil Procedure Rules 1998. There are many similarities between practice in the courts and tribunals. Claims in the courts are characterized by a greater emphasis on pre-action work, greater formality, and a wider range of remedies, particularly interim remedies. *Inter partes* costs orders are the norm rather than the exception.

A. INTRODUCTION

Certain types of employment dispute may fall to be litigated in the civil courts, either in the High Court or in the county courts. This chapter will consider: **20.01**

(a) Tactical and procedural issues which arise from the potential overlap of claims in the tribunal and in the civil courts.
(b) The procedure for bringing claims in the civil courts pursuant to the CPR.

B. JURISDICTION OF THE COURTS AND THE EMPLOYMENT TRIBUNALS

Claims in the employment tribunal

20.02 The jurisdiction of the tribunal is statutory, and the tribunal may not hear claims in respect of which it is not specifically given jurisdiction. A full list of claims falling within the tribunal's jurisdiction is at the end of Chapter 1. The vast majority of claims in the tribunal concern statutory rights. Generally those rights can only be enforced in the tribunal and not in the civil courts. For example, a claim of unfair dismissal, or a claim of sex discrimination by an employee in relation to her employment, can only be brought in the tribunal. The rights upon which such claims are based are statutory and do not give rise to contractual rights which can be enforced in the civil courts: *Doherty v BMI* [2006] IRLR 90, EAT, paras 25–7 (although some statutory provisions do expressly and directly affect contractual terms, see, for example, the equality clause provided for by the Equal Pay Act 1970, and certain provisions of the National Minimum Wage Act 1998 and the Working Time Regulations 1998, SI 1998/1833).

Claims in the civil courts

20.03 A number of claims which are common in the context of employment fall outside the tribunal's general jurisdiction.

Breach of contract

20.04 The Employment Tribunals Extension of Jurisdiction (England and Wales) Order 1994, SI 1994/1623 gives to the tribunal limited jurisdiction over claims of breach of contract. Contract claims are considered in detail in Chapter 8. Claims of breach of contract which cannot be brought in the tribunal, and can only be brought in the civil courts include the following:

(a) claims which exceed the tribunal's jurisdictional limit of £25,000;
(b) claims in respect of restrictive covenants in restraint of trade or confidential information;
(c) claims in respect of personal injuries.

See *Fraser v HLMAD Ltd* [2006] EWCA Civ 738, [2006] IRLR 687.

Equitable claims

20.05 The tribunal has no equitable jurisdiction, and therefore cannot deal with claims of breach of fiduciary duty or restitutionary claims.

20.06 Whatever the nature of the claim, the tribunal has no jurisdiction to grant equitable remedies, so if an injunction is sought, or an account of profits, this must be pursued in the civil courts.

Tortious claims

20.07 The tribunal has no jurisdiction to deal with claims in tort other than the statutory torts which specifically fall within its jurisdiction. Common law claims, such as claims in negligence, can only be pursued in the civil courts. Many statutory torts also do not fall within the tribunal's jurisdiction, such as claims under the Protection from Harassment Act 1997.

Personal injuries

20.08 Claims in respect of personal injuries based upon negligence, breach of contract, or breach of statutory duty not falling within the tribunal's jurisdiction, cannot be pursued in the tribunal. Damages for personal injury can however be claimed as a head of loss in discrimination claims (see *Sheriff v Klyne Tugs (Lowestoft) Ltd* [1999] IRLR 481; *Essa v Laing Ltd* [2004] EWCA Civ 02, [2004] IRLR 31.

Discrimination outside the employment field

Discrimination claims outside the employment field fall within the exclusive jurisdiction of the county courts (and then only the county courts designated for this purpose). These include: **20.09**

(a) claims under Part III of the Sex Discrimination Act 1975 (education, good facilities, services, and premises);
(b) claims under Part III of the Race Relations Act 1975 (education, planning, public authorities, good facilities, services, and premises);
(c) claims under Part III and Part IV of Chapter 2 of the Disability Discrimination Act 1995 (goods facilities and services, disposal of premises, institutions of further and higher education);
(d) claims under reg 20 of the Employment Equality (Sexual Orientation) Regulations 2003, SI 2003/1661 and reg 20 of the Employment Equality (Religion or Belief) Regulations 2003, SI 2003/1660 (institutions of further or higher education).

C. OVERLAPPING CLAIMS

In a number of situations, a claimant may face the potential to bring a claim either in the tribunal or in the courts. **20.10**

There is one situation where a claimant may bring exactly the same claim, based on the same cause of action and claiming the same loss, in either the court or the tribunal, ie a breach of contract claim for less than £25,000. This may be brought in the tribunal (assuming the conditions of the Employment Tribunal (Extension of Jurisdiction) Orders 1994, SI 1994/1623 and SI 1994/1624 are met) or in the courts. **20.11**

Other circumstances arise where the claimant may have different causes of action arising out of the same facts, some of which may be brought in the courts, and some in the tribunal. **20.12**

The claimant may have suffered a number of different losses arising under different causes of action, but all arising out of the same broad set of facts. For example, a director of a company who is ousted in a boardroom coup may have claims in relation to unfair dismissal (tribunal), unlawful deduction from wages in relation to a previous year's bonus (tribunal), wrongful dismissal (court or tribunal depending on value), and in relation to his directorship and ownership of shares in the company (court). The right to a bonus may be the basis of a claim for the bonus in the High or county court or for loss of the ability to earn it in the employment tribunal. **20.13**

Alternatively the same loss could be attributed to different causes of action which fall to be litigated in different venues. For example, a claimant complaining about his summary dismissal and consequent loss of earnings may be able to frame his claim both as an unfair dismissal (within the exclusive jurisdiction of the tribunal) or as a wrongful dismissal. If the wrongful dismissal claim is worth more than £25,000 it can only be brought in the civil courts. In each claim he could recover in respect of loss of earnings, although sums recovered in one claim will have to be accounted for in the other claim in order to prevent double recovery. An employee must choose his jurisdiction carefully. An employee with a breach of contract claim worth more than £25,000 cannot bring a claim in the tribunal for the first £25,000 and then claim in the courts for the balance of the same claim: *Fraser v HLMAD Ltd* [2006] EWCA Civ 738, [2006] IRLR 687 and see Chapter 8 at para 8.33. **20.14**

A particularly difficult situation can arise where, for example, an employee has been subjected to a course of harassment by his fellow employees, as a result of which he sustains personal injury. The claimant may have a claim of discrimination, if the harassment was on grounds which constitute unlawful discrimination, or he may have claims which can only be brought in the courts: for instance for negligence, or under the Protection from Harassment Act 1997 (according to the House of Lords in *Majrowski v Guys and St Thomas's NHS Trust* [2006] UKHL 34, [2006] **20.15**

WLR 125, [2006] IRLR 695 the employer may be liable for harassment under the 1997 Act committed by an employee). One problem is that the employee will not necessarily know what the reason for the treatment is at the time he is deciding what claims to pursue.

20.16 Whichever proceedings are determined first, the decision in those proceedings will bind the court or the tribunal in the later proceedings. A decision of the civil courts may give rise to an issue estoppel, or *res judicata* in tribunal proceedings, and vice versa (*Green v Hampshire County Council* [1979] ICR 861, Ch D; *Munir v Jang Publications Ltd* [1989] IRLR 224, [1989] ICR 1, CA). There are three relevant doctrines which are considered in more detail at paras 11.90–11.139:

(1) *Res judicata*, or cause of action estoppel: a final adjudication against a party on a particular cause of action will be conclusive in later proceedings involving the same parties and the same cause of action as to all points decided in the previous judgment.
(2) Issue estoppel: a judgment which includes a decision on a particular issue forming a necessary ingredient in the cause of action will be binding as to that particular issue if it arises in subsequent proceedings between the same parties or related parties where that issue is relevant, subject to narrow exceptions.
(3) Abuse of process: it may be an abuse of process to make a claim which could and should have been brought forward as part of earlier proceedings: *Henderson v Henderson* (1843) 3 Hare 100.

20.17 The practical problems in this area do not ordinarily arise from cause of action estoppel: the fact that there are two sets of proceedings tends to be because there are two separate causes of action. The problems arise either from issue estoppel, where an issue decided in the first proceedings binds the court in the second proceedings, or from the abuse identified in *Henderson*, where it is argued that the claim in the second set of proceedings should have been brought in the first proceedings.

20.18 In *Sheriff v Klyne Tugs (Lowestoft) Ltd* [1999] IRLR 481, the claimant's personal injury claim against his former employers was struck out in the county court. The Court of Appeal held that damages claimed could and should have been claimed in earlier race discrimination proceedings in the tribunal. Those proceedings had been withdrawn on settlement. The county court claim was held to be a *Henderson* abuse. In *Enfield LBC v Sivanandan* [2005] EWCA Civ 10, the Court of Appeal appeared similarly alert to prevent the claimant from having a second bite at the cherry by recasting a failed claim under a different cause of action in a different forum. These cases are considered in more detail at paras 11.120–11.127 above.

20.19 Given the risk of the claimant being bound by or restricted to the outcome of the claims he brings in his first set of proceedings, it is important to set a clear strategy at an early stage wherever there is the potential for overlapping claims. The following questions should be considered:

(a) What losses has the claimant suffered?
(b) What causes of action can be relied on to recover those losses?
(c) In what forum can those claims be pursued? Can all of the causes of action be sued upon in a single forum, or are two sets of proceedings inevitable?
(d) What are the merits of the various causes of action? Where do the real strengths of the case lie?
(e) What remedies will be available for the various claims?
(f) Which claims have the higher monetary value?
(g) Consider the availability of remedies: is this a case where an injunction or an account of profits may be sought?
(h) Consider interim remedies: is this a case where use may be made of the wider range of interim remedies in the courts (for example summary judgment)?
(i) What is the best strategy for the sequence in which the claims should be resolved? Consider the risks of a decision in one forum prejudicing the claim in the other, on the basis of *res judicata*, issue estoppel, or abuse of process.

(j) Are there limitation issues which will potentially interfere with the best sequence for resolution of the claims?

The best tactical approach in any case will depend on the particular circumstances of the case, and upon the priorities of the particular claimant. 20.20

Where two sets of proceedings are inevitable (for example, where a claimant has a claim for unfair dismissal and a high value wrongful dismissal claim), and assuming both claims have potential merit, it may be thought desirable to leave the High Court judge as unfettered as possible by findings of the tribunal. 20.21

Where there are to be two sets of proceedings the tribunal claim is likely to be heard well before any civil claim. The limitation period for claims in the tribunal is much shorter; the civil court proceedings will have to be preceded by more extensive pre-action steps in order to avoid the risk of adverse costs orders; the procedural timetable in the courts is likely to be longer, although this depends on the claim (and the procedural steps to be taken). This problem can potentially be avoided by staying the tribunal claim pending resolution of the High Court claim. Stays of proceedings for this purpose are dealt with at paras 9.34–9.41 above. 20.22

D. PROCEEDINGS IN THE CIVIL COURTS

Introduction

The civil courts system

Civil claims may be brought in the High Court or the county court. The High Court of Justice is based at the Royal Courts of Justice, The Strand, London WC2. There are District Registries of the High Court in the major cities of England and Wales. The High Court forms part of the Supreme Court of England and Wales (along with the Crown Court and the Court of Appeal). The Supreme Court Act 1981 (SCA 1981) deals with the High Court's powers and jurisdiction. The county courts are established by the County Courts Act 1984 (CCA 1984). County courts are arranged into districts, and most cities and large towns have a county court. 20.23

Procedure in the High Court and county courts is governed by the Civil Procedure Rules 1998. Most of the rules are supplemented by detailed Practice Directions. Some rules from the old regime which existed prior to the introduction of the CPR (Rules of the Supreme Court and County Court Rules 1981) still apply, and are to be found in appendices to the CPR. 20.24

For a detailed exposition of the CPR, a specialist text on civil procedure should be consulted; see, for example, *Blackstone's Civil Practice*; the following is a brief outline. 20.25

Key distinctions between the civil courts and the tribunals

The following features of litigation in the civil courts mark it out from litigation in the tribunals: 20.26

(a) There is a greater emphasis in the courts on pre-action steps to avoid litigation. In the tribunals there are measures to avoid unnecessary litigation, for example, the rules governing statutory disciplinary and grievance procedures; and the overriding objective which seeks to encourage proportionate use of resources. However, the court system has a more formalized system of protocols governing steps to be taken to share information before proceedings are commenced.
(b) The normal position in civil proceedings is that the loser will pay the winner's legal costs.
(c) There are substantial court fees for the issue of proceedings and applications.
(d) Civil proceedings offer a greater opportunity to determine a claim before trial, for example by summary judgment or strike-out.
(e) Most interim remedies, such as injunctions or orders for delivery up, are available only in the courts.

(f) Court procedure is more complex and more formal, both in terms of case management and at trial, and legal representation may be considered more appropriate.
(g) The rules of evidence apply to proceedings in the courts.
(h) The majority of cases are dealt with by a judge sitting alone, rather than by the tribunal's 'industrial jury'.
(i) There is a wider range of final remedies in the civil courts, for example injunction, account of profits, restitutionary, and proprietary remedies. On the other hand, only the tribunal can make orders for reinstatement or re-engagement, or make protective awards.
(j) Lay representation is more rare in the courts.
(k) Costs are more frequently awarded in civil proceedings.

Pre-action steps

20.27 One of the cornerstones of Lord Woolf's reforms of civil justice which led to the CPR was an encouragement to parties to achieve settlement of their disputes, with litigation as a last resort. A number of features of the CPR are designed to assist and encourage settlement.

20.28 One key element is an encouragement to greater openness in communication between the parties at an earlier stage. Pre-action protocols set out procedures for the parties to identify their cases and share essential information before commencing proceedings, to promote the potential for settlement without litigation.

20.29 There are now several protocols dealing with disputes in a variety of common claims. Apart from the personal injury protocol, none are likely to impact directly on litigation in the employment field. However, the Protocol Practice Direction contains general guidance as to pre-action behaviour which covers both protocol and non-protocol cases (Protocol Practice Direction, para 4).

20.30 The court will expect the parties to act reasonably in exchanging information and documents relevant to the claim and generally in trying to avoid the necessity for the start of proceedings. A reasonable pre-action procedure should normally include:

(a) the claimant writing to give details of the claim;
(b) the defendant acknowledging the claim letter promptly;
(c) the defendant giving within a reasonable time a detailed written response; and
(d) the parties conducting genuine and reasonable negotiations with a view to settling the claim economically and without court proceedings.

20.31 Paragraph 4.3 of the Protocol Practice Direction sets out detailed guidance as to the contents of a claimant's letter before action. The letter should not only set out concisely the details of the proposed claim, but should enclose with it copies of the essential documents upon which the claimant relies. Similarly the defendant's response should give detailed reasons why the claim is not accepted, and should enclose documents: both those sought by the claimant and the essential documents relied on by the defendant. For the full guidance, see Protocol Practice Direction, para 4.

Commencement of proceedings

High Court or county court?

20.32 In addition to the SCA 1981 and the CCA 1984, the High Court and County Courts Jurisdiction Order 1991, SI 1991/724 deals with the jurisdiction of, and allocation of business between, the two courts.

20.33 Most employment-related claims fall within the jurisdiction of both the county court and the High Court. Section 15 of CCA 1984 gives the county court general jurisdiction in relation to claims in contract and tort. Section 23 gives the county court jurisdiction over certain equitable claims (including partnership matters) up to a limit of £30,000. Where both the High Court and the county court have jurisdiction to hear a claim, the claim may be commenced in either court. A money claim in respect of which both courts have jurisdiction may only be commenced in the High Court if its value exceeds £15,000 (1991 Order, art 4A). A claim for damages for personal injuries may only be brought in the High Court if the value of the claim is £50,000 or more (1991 Order, art 5).

Whilst the county court may grant injunctions, it should be noted that the county court does not have jurisdiction to grant freezing orders (other than in matrimonial proceedings) or search orders (CCA 1984, s 38 and the County Court Remedies Regulations 1991 (SI 1991/1222)). **20.34**

On the other hand, as noted at para 19.09 above, certain claims under the discrimination legislation may only be brought in the county court. **20.35**

In the High Court, most employment-related claims are suited for the Queen's Bench Division. If a claim raises issues concerning confidential information or intellectual property rights, company law issues, or pension issues, the Chancery Division may be more appropriate. **20.36**

Claim form and particulars of claim

There are two ways in which proceedings can be started in the civil courts: **20.37**

(a) by issuing a claim form (CPR Part 7);
(b) by issuing a claim under the alternative procedure in CPR Part 8.

The great majority of claims are commenced using the Part 7 claim form procedure. Part 8 claims are appropriate where a decision is sought on a dispute which is unlikely to involve a substantial dispute of fact, or for certain types of proceedings where a rule or a Practice Direction requires or permits a Part 8 claim (see CPR 8PD). **20.38**

It will be appropriate to use the normal Part 7 claim form procedure for the majority of employment disputes which are likely to be litigated in the civil courts. Part 8 claims are not considered further in this chapter. **20.39**

Tribunal awards may be enforced through the county court. The procedure for enforcement is in CPR Part 70, and is commenced by the issue of an application notice in form N322A. **20.40**

There is a prescribed claim form, form N1. A claim form must be issued by the court office of the court in which the proceedings are to be brought. A fee is payable on issue, the amount of which depends on the type and amount of the claim. **20.41**

Once issued a claim form must be served on the defendant within four months (CPR r 7.5), although the court may grant an extension of time (CPR r 7.6). An application for extension of time should be made before the time limit for service has expired. Although the court has the power to extend time after the expiry of the time limit, the grounds upon which it may do so are more limited (see CPR r 7.6(3)). The application may be without notice, and must be supported by evidence (CPR r 7.6(4)). The evidence should be in the form of a witness statement, and should explain all the circumstances relied on; the date of issue of the claim, the expiry date of any previous extension, and a full explanation of why the claim has not been served (CPR 7PD, para 8). It is prudent also to explain the reason for the particular duration of the extension sought. **20.42**

In a very simple case, the particulars of claim can be included in the space provided on the claim form. In most cases the claim form should contain brief particulars of the nature of the claim and the full detail of the claim should be set out in the particulars of claim. Particulars of claim may be served with the claim form or within 14 days of service of the claim form (but in any event no later than the last day for serving the claim form) (CPR r 7.4). **20.43**

Detailed provisions about service of the claim form are contained in CPR Part 6, in particular at rr 6.13–6.16. **20.44**

Acknowledgement of service and defence

20.45 This is dealt with at CPR Parts 9–11, 14 and 15. Once served with particulars of claim, a defendant may file an admission (CPR Part 14), an acknowledgement of service (CPR Part 10), or a defence (CPR Part 15). The time limit for doing so is 14 days from service of the particulars of claim.

20.46 An acknowledgement of service is a short standard form in which a defendant indicates that he has been served with the particulars of claim, and that he intends to dispute the claim in whole or in part. If the defendant intends to contest the jurisdiction of the court, he should indicate this in the acknowledgment of service. In filing an acknowledgment, the defendant does not lose the right to contest the jurisdiction of the court (CPR r 11.3). The defendant must, however, make an application to dispute the jurisdiction within 14 days of filing the acknowledgment.

20.47 The defence is the full response to the matters pleaded in the particulars of claim. A defence must be served within 14 days of service of the particulars of claim, or, if an acknowledgement of service is filed, within 28 days of the service of the particulars of claim (CPR r 15.4). The parties may agree to extend time for filing a defence by up to 28 days (CPR r 15.5).

20.48 A claimant may respond to a defence in a reply. A reply is optional, as failure to file a reply is not taken as an implied admission of the defence. A reply may be appropriate if the claimant wishes to allege matters in response to the defence which were not included in the particulars of claim. See CPR rr 15.8 and 16.7.

Default judgment

20.49 CPR Parts 12 and 13 set out a detailed regime for judgment in default of filing a defence or acknowledgement of service, and for applying to set aside such default judgments.

20.50 Judgment in default of acknowledgement of service can be obtained where the defendant has failed to file an acknowledgment of service, and the time for doing so has expired (CPR r 12.3(1)). Judgment in default of defence can be obtained where an acknowledgment of service has been filed, but the defendant fails to serve a defence within the time limit for doing so (CPR r 12.3(2)). It should be noted that judgment in default is also available where a claimant fails to file a defence to counterclaim in the time provided for doing so (CPR r 12.3(2)(b)). A default judgment may not be obtained if the defendant has made an application for a strike out or summary judgment; or has made an admission of a claim for money but has requested time to pay (CPR r 12.3(3)). There are some categories of case where judgment in default is not obtainable (CPR r 12.2) but none are likely to arise in employment litigation.

20.51 There are two types of process for obtaining judgment in default. In a money claim, either for a specific sum or an amount to be assessed, judgment can be obtained by filing a request (CPR r 12.4(1)). Judgment is then given as an administrative act. If the judgment is for a sum to be assessed the court will give directions for the assessment of damages (CPR r 12.7). Where any other remedy is sought, for example, an injunction, judgment can only be obtained by application (CPR r 12.4(2)). There are other categories of case where judgment can only be obtained on application which are set out at CPR r 12.9 and r 12.10; of note are judgments for costs only (other than fixed costs) (r 12.9) and judgments where the proceedings have been served out of the jurisdiction without leave (r 12.10(b)). Where an application is made for judgment, the court will make such judgment as it appears to the court the claimant is entitled to on his statement of case (CPR r 12.11(1)).

20.52 CPR Part 13 deals with applications to set aside default judgments. The court must set aside judgment in default if the judgment was wrongly entered, either because the conditions in CPR r 12.3(1),(2), or (3) were not satisfied, or if the whole claim was satisfied before the judgment was entered (CPR r 13.1). So if the claim was not served, or if the time limit for service of a defence had not expired at the point of judgment, the judgment must be set aside. In any other case, the court has a discretion to set aside the judgment if the defendant has a real prospect of success, or it appears to the court there is some other good reason why judgment should be set aside or varied, or the defendant should be allowed to defend the claim. The test is the same as that for summary judgment.

Counterclaims

A defendant may counterclaim against a claimant. The procedure for counterclaims is set out in CPR Part 20. In the employment tribunal, a respondent's entitlement to counterclaim is very limited. A counterclaim can only be brought where the claimant has brought a contract claim within the Employment Tribunals Extension of Jurisdiction (England and Wales) Order 1994 for certain defined types of contract claim. There are no such limits on counterclaims in the civil courts. A defendant may even, with permission of the court, bring a counterclaim against a person other than the claimant (CPR r 20.5) (what used to be referred to as 'third party proceedings'). The court has the power to determine that a Part 20 claim should be heard separately to the main claim, and will take into account the connection between the main claim and the counterclaim, and where a third party is introduced, the connection between the relief sought, and the connection between the issues in the various claims (see CPR r 20.9). **20.53**

Statements of case generally

The particulars of claim, defence, defence and counterclaim, reply and defence to counterclaim are all described as statements of case by the CPR. Prior to the CPR they were referred to as pleadings. General rules as to the form and content of statements of case are set out in CPR Part 16. A statement of case must be verified by a statement of truth (CPR r 22.1), in which the party states that he believes the facts stated in the statement of case are true. As an alternative, the party's solicitor may make a statement of truth, to the effect that the party believes the facts to be true. Rules as to the requirements for statements of truth are set out in CPR Part 22. See also CPR Parts 17 and 19 in relation to amendments to statement of case and addition of further parties. **20.54**

Case management

Allocation and tracks

There are three tracks to which a claim may be allocated. The court will allocate the claim to the appropriate track after taking into account a number of factors including the financial value of the claim, the complexity of the issues, the number of parties, the amount of oral and expert evidence, and the remedy sought. The general rule is as follows: **20.55**

(a) Small claims track: claims not more than £5,000, or, personal injury cases not more than £1,000.
(b) Fast track: claims more than £5,000 but not more than £15,000; normally appropriate for trials expected to last not more than one day.
(c) Multi-track: claims more than £15,000.

CPR 26 contains detailed rules as to allocation. To assist the court in allocating a case an allocation questionnaire is sent out to all parties once a defence is filed. A fee is payable by the claimant on filing of the allocation questionnaire, in all cases where the value of the claim is more than £1,000. **20.56**

Small claims track

The small claims track is a streamlined procedure appropriate for dealing with claims of limited financial value (CPR Part 27). Standard directions are given; there are very rarely preliminary hearings. Expert evidence is not allowed without permission of the court, and the court may limit the evidence of witnesses and their cross-examination at the hearing. Hearings are conducted more informally than in trials on the other tracks, and the rules of evidence do not apply. The court need not take evidence on oath. Lay representatives are allowed. The recovery of costs **20.57** is very limited: a party will normally recover only the fixed costs related to issuing the proceedings unless the other party has behaved unreasonably (CPR r 27.14).

Fast track

20.58 The fast-track procedure is contained in CPR Part 28. The procedure is designed to provide a proportionate way of dealing with claims which are more substantial than those on the small claims track, but are still of relatively limited value. Standard directions are normally given. Trial is limited to one day, and the management of the trial will be tightly timetabled. Whilst there is provision for disclosure and (if appropriate) expert evidence, these are kept within carefully controlled limits. Recovery of costs of trial is itself generally subject to limits (see CPR Part 46).

Multi-track

20.59 The multi-track is the normal track for all cases where the small claims or fast track are not appropriate, due either to their value or complexity.

20.60 Case management of multi-track cases is dealt with in CPR Part 29. Normally a case management conference (CMC) will be listed before a Master (or district judge in the county court) after the allocation questionnaires have been filed. At the CMC the Master will consider the issues in the case and fix an appropriate timetable of directions to take the claim through to trial. Each claim has a designated Master, appointed on issue, who will deal with all case management issues in the case (until close to trial when the trial judge may deal with certain case management issues). The parties may avoid the need for a CMC by submitting an appropriate set of agreed directions for approval by the Master. Any applications the parties wish to make should be made, if possible, at the same time as the CMC, or in any event as soon as possible. A useful checklist of matters which may need to be dealt with at a CMC is contained in the pro forma order for case management directions in the multi-track, Queens Bench Practice Form 52.

20.61 The court may order a pre-trial review, to be held close in time to the trial date, to ensure that the case is properly prepared and ready for trial.

Interim applications

20.62 A distinguishing feature of litigation in the courts from proceedings in the tribunal is the greater range of interim remedies that may be sought. In most employment-based civil litigation, one may encounter applications of two types:

(1) Applications which dispose of the proceedings, or of issues in proceedings, without trial: for example default judgment, strike-out, and summary judgment.
(2) Applications which give interim relief pending trial: for example injunctions, or delivery-up orders. Applications for interim injunctions are a primary area where the employment lawyer may become involved in High Court proceedings.

20.63 The general rules governing applications are found in CPR Part 23 and its Practice Direction. These are to be read in conjunction with: CPR Part 3.4 and 3.5 and 3PD (Striking Out), CPR Part 24 and 24PD (Summary Judgment), CPR Part 25 and 25PD (Interim Remedies and Security for Costs). See also the Queen's Bench Guide at 7.11 (Hearings), 7.12 (Applications), 7.13 (Interim Remedies), 8.5 (Interim Hearings List), and 8.7 (Listing before Interim Applications Judge); Chancery Guide, Chapter 5 (Applications).

Strike-out of statement of case

20.64 The court may strike out a statement of case on the following grounds: (CPR r 3.4(2)):

(a) the statement of case discloses no reasonable grounds for bringing or defending the claim;
(b) the statement of case is an abuse of process or is otherwise likely to obstruct the just disposal of the proceedings; or
(c) there has been a failure to comply with a rule, Practice Direction, or court order.

In addition, CPR r 3.4(2) does not limit the court's inherent jurisdiction to strike out a statement of case: CPR r 3.4(5). The court retains an inherent power to strike out for any abuse of process which does not fall within r 3.4(2), for example, where a party's conduct puts the fairness of the trial in jeopardy. **20.65**

There is therefore a distinction between grounds relating to the content of the claim or the defence (CPR r 3.4(2)(a) and, in part, (b)), and the manner in which the claim has been conducted (CPR r 3.4(2)(c) and, in part (b)) and the court's inherent jurisdiction. **20.66**

Applications based on the content of the claim or the defence

In determining whether the respondent to the application has reasonable grounds for bringing or defending the claim (CPR r 3.4(2)(a)), the court will examine the party's case as formulated on its statement of case. For the purposes of the application, the facts as pleaded will be treated as true: the question is whether the claim or defence, taken at face value, has a reasonable prospect of success. Thus strike-out is appropriate where the statement of case is defective on its face; this may be because even on the assumed facts the party's position is wrong in law; or it may be because there are no facts, or incoherent facts relied on to support an essential ingredient of a cause of action. Where the claim or defence is not on its face bound to fail, but turns on questions of fact, then a strike-out under this rule is not appropriate. However, if the party's case on the issue of fact is sufficiently weak, an application for summary judgment may still be appropriate. **20.67**

Even if a statement of case on its face has reasonable grounds to succeed, it may yet be an abuse of process. The categories of abuse of process are not fixed or defined (*Ashmore v British Coal Corporation* [1990] ICR 485). The court has a good degree of latitude in determining what amounts to an abuse of process. The abuse may lie in the nature of the claim, for example, attempts to re-litigate matters which have been raised or should have been raised in earlier proceedings (see further paras 11.90–11.139); or conduct of proceedings inconsistent with proceedings in another forum. Alternatively, the abuse may lie in the pursuit of proceedings with an improper ulterior motive, or use of repeated proceedings to vex or harass the other side (see, eg, *Grovit v Doctor* [1997] 1 WLR 640). **20.68**

A number of issues arising in employment litigation may come to be resolved on a strike-out application. For example, a strike-out application may be the suitable forum to resolve issues concerning the scope of a contractual duty, or a common law duty of care. A strike-out application will also be the appropriate stage to raise issues such as *res judicata* and estoppel arising out of earlier tribunal claims, or to raise arguments that the claim has been compromised by a compromise agreement or ACAS settlement. **20.69**

A statement of case should not be struck out if it raises serious issues of fact which can only be properly determined by oral evidence at trial or if it is in an area of developing jurisprudence, since decisions as to novel points of law should be based on actual findings of fact. **20.70**

There is an overlap between an application to strike out under CPR r 3.4 and an application for summary judgment under CPR Part 24; an application can be brought relying on both rules in the alternative. **20.71**

Applications based on the conduct of the parties

The conduct of the parties in the proceedings may result in a failure to comply with a rule, practice direction, or order, so as to fall within r 3.4(2)(c); or it may amount to an abuse of process under r 3.4(2)(b). An abuse of process in this case may entail conduct designed to prevent a fair trial, for example, forgery of documents (see, eg, *Arrow Nominees Inc v Blackledge* [2000] 2 BCLC 167). **20.72**

Where the strike-out application is based on the conduct of the other party in the course of the litigation, the court will have to consider whether strike-out is the appropriate sanction, or whether some lesser sanction is appropriate: for example, (indemnity) costs, payment into **20.73** court, penalty in interest on the sum found to be due. See *Biguzzi v Rank Leisure plc* [1999] 1 WLR 1926. Both in cases of non-compliance with a rule or order, and in cases of abuse of process, the court should regard a strike-out as a last resort, and consider whether a lesser sanction is consistent with the overriding objective, and whether a fair trial can still take place.

20.74 In the majority of cases of failure to comply with a rule, practice direction, or order, the party in default will apply for relief from sanction under CPR r 3.9. The principles relevant to the grant of relief are set out in CPR r 3.9(1): the court will consider all the circumstances, including:

- the interests of the administration of justice;
- whether the application for relief has been made promptly;
- whether there is a good explanation for the failure;
- the extent to which the party in default has complied with other rules, practice directions, court orders, and any relevant protocol;
- whether the failure to comply was caused by the party or his legal representative;
- whether the trial date or the likely date can still be met if relief is granted;
- the effect which the failure to comply had on each party; and
- the effect which the granting of relief would have on each party.

Procedure for application

20.75 An application to strike out is governed by the general principles in relation to interim applications, contained in CPR Part 23. The application should be made on an application notice N244, setting out the grounds for the application and the order sought, and should be supported by a witness statement, which should be served with the application notice.

20.76 There are no specific rules relating to the timing of the application in CPR r 3.4 (in contrast to the rules dealing with summary judgment in Part 24). Therefore the general rules in CPR Part 23 apply:

- The application should be made as soon as it becomes apparent that it is necessary or desirable to make it (23PD, para 2.7). Where the application is based on the statements of case, the application should be made soon after the service of the relevant statement of case.
- The application should be brought on at least three days' notice. However, for a contested application, the respondent will be likely to seek (and obtain) an extension of time in which to prepare and file evidence in response.

Summary judgment

20.77 CPR Part 24 deals with summary judgment. This procedure, which is not available in the employment tribunal, is a powerful tool by which a party may obtain judgment, or defeat a claim against him by a court considering the case on the papers only, without the expense of a full trial.

20.78 Summary judgment may be obtained either against the claimant or the defendant. Summary judgment may be given in respect of the whole of a claim, part of a claim, or a particular issue on which the claim in whole or part depends (see CPR r 24.1.2 and 24PD, para 1.2).

Grounds

20.79 The court may grant summary judgment if it considers (CPR r 24.2) that:

(a) the claimant has no real prospect of succeeding on the claim or issue; or that the defendant has no real prospect of successfully defending the claim or issue; and
(b) there is no other compelling reason why the case or issue should be disposed of at trial.

20.80 An application for summary judgment may be based on a point of law (including a question of construction of a document); the evidence which can reasonably be expected to be available at trial (or lack of it); or a combination of the two (CPR 24PD, para 1.3).

Timing of application

A claimant may not apply until the defendant against whom the application is made has filed an acknowledgement of service or defence unless the court gives permission, or a Practice Direction provides otherwise (CPR r 24.4(1)). If an application for summary judgment is made by a claimant before the defence is filed, the defendant need not file a defence before the hearing of the application (CPR r 24.4(2)). In most cases in practice there is little point in a claimant making an application for summary judgment before a defence is filed. It is difficult to assess whether there is a real prospect in a defence succeeding before one knows what that defence is. **20.81**

There is, however, no limitation on the time when a defendant can make an application for summary judgment. Whilst there is no express rule or Practice Direction governing how late in proceedings an application can be made, parties are encouraged to make applications before or upon filing allocation questionnaires. Certainly where the summary judgment application arises from matters known at the time this should be so, as a matter of efficient disposal of proceedings. However, where the applicant's view that summary judgment is appropriate is based on disclosure (or even the exchanged witness statements) the application could be made at a later stage. **20.82**

Procedure for application

The procedure for an application for summary judgment is dealt with in CPR rr 24.4 and 24.5, and in 24PD, para 2. The general rules for interim applications in CPR 23 are also relevant. **20.83**

(a) The application should be made by notice on Practice Form N244. CPR 24PD, para 2 sets out the following requirements for the application notice:
   (i) State that the application is brought under CPR 24 for summary judgment.
   (ii) Identify the order that is sought, and upon what grounds. Either the application notice, or the witness statement in support (see below) should state that the application must identify the point of law or provision in a document upon which the applicant relies; and/or state that the applicant believes that on the evidence the respondent has no real prospect of succeeding on the claim or issue (or of defending the claim or issue); and that the applicant knows of no other reason why the disposal of the claim should await trial.
   (iii) Identify the written evidence upon which the applicant relies.
   (iv) Draw the respondent's attention to the provisions of CPR r 24.5, which deals with filing of evidence by the respondent.
(b) The application should be supported by a witness statement. The witness statement should be served on the respondent with the application notice, and filed with the court (CPR 23PD, para 9).
(c) A summary judgment application is normally heard before a Master (or District Judge in a District Registry case). A Master can direct that the application be heard by a judge (CPR 24PD, para 3). If the applicant wishes to have the application heard before a judge, a direction to this effect should be sought in the application notice.
(d) The respondent must be given at least 14 days' notice of the date fixed for the hearing and the issues which it is proposed the court will decide at the hearing (CPR r 24.4(3)).
(e) A respondent must file and serve any evidence upon which he intends to rely at least seven days before the hearing. An applicant must file and serve any evidence in reply at least three days before the hearing (CPR r 24.5).

The court's powers

The court may (CPR 24PD, para 5) give judgment on the claim; strike out or dismiss the claim; dismiss the application, permitting the claim to proceed to trial; make a conditional order, permitting the claim to proceed to trial on condition that a party pay money into court or take a specified step. The court is likely to consider a conditional order where there is a real, but improbable prospect of success (CPR 24PD, para 4). **20.84**

20.85 Where the court dismisses the application, or makes an order which does not entirely dispose of the claim, it will give case management directions at the hearing of the application (CPR r 24.6).

The court's approach

20.86 The key question is whether there is sufficient in the impugned claim or defence to amount to a real prospect of success at trial. Often this will involve an assessment of whether factual evidence is of sufficient merit to give a real prospect of success, or whether factual assertions can be shown to be unmeritorious even on paper. A real prospect of success means better than merely an arguable prospect, but does not require the respondent to show he will probably succeed. The term is meant to exclude false, fanciful, or imaginary claims/defences: *ED & F Man Liquid Products Ltd v Patel* [2003] EWCA Civ 472; *Swain v Hillman* [2001] 1 All ER 91; *Three Rivers DC v Bank of England (No 3)* [2001] 2 All ER 513, HL. The court will not conduct a mini-trial of disputed evidence on a summary judgment application, but will not be bound to accept all evidence on its face, no matter how lacking in credibility.

20.87 The court must consider also whether there is any other 'compelling reason' for a trial.

20.88 What constitutes a 'compelling reason' for trial, other than the potential merits of the case, is unclear. Examples include cases where a defendant needs to interrogate or cross-examine the claimant (*Harrison v Bottenheim* (1878) 26 WR 362); cases where the defendant has been unable to contact key witnesses, or needs disclosure of documents within the claimant's possession, although the court is astute not to allow cases to continue to trial on the basis that 'something may turn up' (see *Miles v Bull* [1969] 1 QB 258 and *Lady Ann Tennant v Associated Newspapers* [1979] 5 FSR 298); or cases where the allegations are such that they demand resolution in a public trial. Although cases based on allegations of bad faith will normally need to be resolved at trial, there is no rule that this must be the case, and in some circumstances summary judgment based on allegations of bad faith may be appropriate: *Wrexham AFC Ltd v Crucialmove Ltd* [2006] EWCA Civ 237.

20.89 Where the application gives rise to a short point of law or construction, and if the court is satisfied that it has all the evidence necessary for a proper determination of the question and the parties have had an adequate opportunity to address it, the court should determine the point, rather than merely considering whether the point has a real prospect of success. Where a point of construction is said to turn on further documents or oral evidence, the court must consider whether the relevant facts, if established at trial, would have a bearing on the outcome: *ICI Chemicals & Polymers Ltd v TTE Training Ltd* [2007] EWCA Civ 725, paras 12–14.

20.90 The burden is on the claimant to show that the grounds for summary judgment are made out: see the *ED & F Man Liquid Products Ltd* case, cited above.

Tactical considerations

20.91 The tactical considerations under CPR Part 24 involve a careful weighing of any disputed evidence and the relevance of that evidence to the merits of the case.

(a) Does the claim turn on the law, or on disputed matters of fact?
(b) Can the evidence relied on by the respondent be shown to be demonstrably false on paper?
(c) Is the legal question upon which the case turns 'fact sensitive' or in a developing area of law?
(d) Is there a real cost-benefit in making an application? How complex are the issues? What extra preparation will be required for trial? Would it be as cheap and efficient to pursue the matter to trial? Are there discrete issues that can be disposed of, leading to a saving in trial preparation?
(e) Are there other advantages in making an application? For example, early sight of the other side's case; avoidance of exploration of issues orally at trial.

Interim injunctions

The employment tribunal does not have the power to grant injunctive relief. There are limited powers for a tribunal to order interim relief requiring an employer to continue to employ an employee where it is alleged that the dismissal has been for various prescribed reasons—notably trade union activities or public interest disclosure-related reasons (see ERA 1996, ss 128–132). Outside of these cases tribunals are not generally concerned with interim relief. 20.92

The civil courts have wide powers to grant interim relief pending trial: mandatory and prohibitory injunctions; orders for delivery up of property; search and seizure orders; orders for pre-action or early disclosure and inspection of documents. 20.93

Applications for injunctive relief will most commonly arise for employment practitioners in 'employee competition' disputes. Where an employee leaves, or threatens to leave, an employer to work in competition with the employer, there are a number of situations which may commonly give rise to the need for an injunction (either interim or final): 20.94

(a) The employee may have post termination restrictive covenants in his contract of employment (eg a restriction on working for a competitor, or dealing with or soliciting particular clients). Such covenants are in restraint of trade, and therefore unenforceable unless they are no wider than is reasonably necessary to protect a legitimate business interest of the employer (*Herbert Morris v Saxelby* [1916] AC 688, HL; *Office Angels Ltd v Rainer-Thomas* [1991] IRLR 214, CA);
(b) The employee may threaten to work for a competitor during his notice period, prompting the employer to apply for 'a garden leave' injunction, whereby the employee is not permitted to work either for the employer or for a competitor for the duration of his notice period. Such an injunction will also only be granted insofar as it is no more than necessary to protect the employer's legitimate interests (*Symbian Ltd v Christensen* [2001] IRLR 77, CA);
(c) The employee may threaten to misuse the employer's confidential information, prompting an application for an injunction to restrain misuse of confidential information, together with ancillary orders in support of such an order, eg delivery up of information, inspection of computers and electronic storage devices, destruction of electronic copies or hard copies of information;
(d) An employee may already have acted in breach of his obligations to the employer, and may be seeking to obtain further advantage, in a competing business, of an unlawful headstart obtained by his breaches of duty; such a situation may warrant a 'springboard' injunction to deprive the wrongdoer of taking further advantage of his unlawful actions (*Roger Bullivant v Ellis* [1987] ICR 464; *Midas IT Services v Opus Portfolio Ltd* (Ch D 21 December 1999).

Detailed consideration of interim injunctions generally, and in particular in the employment field are outside the scope of this work, and specialist practitioner works should always be consulted. The following is only a brief outline of the procedural principles applicable to such applications. 20.95

Section 37(1) of SCA 1981 gives the High Court power to grant injunctions (whether interim or final) in all cases in which it appears to the court to be 'just and convenient' to do so. The equivalent provision in the county court is s 38 of CCA 1984 (as amended by s 3 of the Courts and Legal Services Act 1990). County courts cannot grant freezing orders or search orders. CPR Part 25 and its Practice Direction deal with interim remedies and security for costs. The range of interim remedies that the court may grant are set out at CPR r 25.1(1). 20.96

The general rules governing applications are found in CPR Part 23 and its Practice Direction. See also the Queen's Bench Guide at 7.11 (Hearings), 7.12 (Applications), 7.13 (Interim Remedies), 8.5 (Interim Hearings List), and 8.7 (Listing before Interim Applications Judge); and the Chancery Guide, Chapter 5 (Applications). 20.97

The grant of an injunction is a matter of discretion. In interim applications evidence is almost always by way of written statement without the court having the benefit of seeing the evidence 20.98

tested by cross-examination. The court is required to 'hold the ring' as best it can. To obtain an interim injunction the claimant must give a cross-undertaking in damages so that in the event of the court at trial concluding that an injunction ought not to have been granted, the defendant can be compensated for any losses he has suffered by the grant of the injunction. The basic principles for grant of interim injunctions are set out in *American Cyanamid Co v Ethicon Ltd* [1975] AC 396, HL.

(a) The claimant must show a good arguable claim: a 'serious issue to be tried' (*American Cyanamid Co v Ethicon Ltd* [1975] AC 396, 407, *per* Lord Diplock) and that damages will not be an adequate remedy.
(b) Does the balance of convenience (the 'balance of the risk of doing an injustice'—see May LJ in *Cayne v Global Natural Resources* [1984] 1 All ER 225, 237) favour the grant or refusal of the injunction? Will more harm be done by the granting or refusal of an interim injunction? The court's aim at the interim stage is to take the course which runs the least risk of causing damage if it turns out to be wrong (in the sense that a different decision is reached at trial): *Films Rover International Ltd v Cannon Film Sales* [1987] 1 WLR 670, 680D–F, per Hoffman J.
(c) Where everything else is evenly balanced 'it is a counsel of prudence to take such measures as are calculated to preserve the status quo' said Lord Diplock in *Cyanamid*.

For cases involving issues of the right to free speech (for example, cases concerning use of confidential information) see also *Cream Holdings v Banerjee* [2004] UKHL 44, [2004] 1 AC 253.

20.99 In the employment field, a claimant is likely to need to apply for an injunction to enforce such provisions on an urgent interim basis: modern restrictive covenants are seldom more than 12 months long, and notice periods (such as may be enforced by a garden leave injunction) are often no longer or shorter. Further, the interim battle is frequently decisive of the dispute as a whole; few cases in fact reach a speedy trial, as most are settled between the interim injunction application and the trial.

20.100 So far as 'ordinary' restrictive covenant cases are concerned the following principles can be distilled from *Lawrence David Ltd v Ashton* [1989] IRLR 22; *Lansing Linde v Kerr* [1991] IRLR 80; and *Arbuthnot v Rawlings* [2003] EWCA Civ 518:

(a) If, without detailed examination of the factual background to the matter, it can be seen that the covenants relied upon plainly will not stand up or do not apply to restrict the employee from the activity in which he is engaged or proposes to be engaged, then that is an end of the matter and the court can, at an interim stage, dismiss the application for an injunction (*Arbuthnot*, at paras 20–30).
(b) If a speedy trial can be heard within the period of the restriction, then the court is unlikely to conduct a detailed examination of the strength of the respective cases of the parties; unless there is a compelling reason to do otherwise, then an interim injunction will ordinarily be granted and a speedy trial (with timetable) ordered.
(c) In such a case, a defendant should give serious consideration to giving appropriate undertakings until the determination of a speedy trial, to avoid the need for an unnecessary interlocutory battle: *Lawrence David*, para 54.
(d) If on the other hand a speedy trial cannot be heard within that period a more detailed examination of the strength of the respective cases may be required: *Lansing*, at paras 13–23; *Lawrence David*, at paras 50–1.

Application with or without notice

20.101 The general rule is that notice must be given of an application with a copy of the application notice being served on every defendant (CPR r 23.4). Three clear days' notice is normally required of any application, although the court can abridge time under CPR r 23.7(4) and/or r 3.1(2)(a). In an appropriate case, the court may hear an application and grant an interim injunction without notice (formerly known as '*ex parte*'). In cases of real urgency, applications can be made out of hours, and even by telephone. Applications without notice are only appropriate for cases of real urgency where there has been a true impossibility of giving notice; or cases where it is essential to maintain secrecy. Where possible (except in cases where secrecy is essential), short informal notice should be given: CPR 25PD, para 4.3(3).

It is the duty of the claimant and legal advisers on a without notice application to ensure that full and frank disclosure is made of all relevant matters. CPR 25PD, para 3.3 provides that the claimant's evidence must include 'all material facts of which the court should be aware'. This includes adverse evidence and extends to a duty to make reasonable investigation. 20.102

Where an application is made without notice, any order will normally be made for a short period of time only, over to a 'return date' on which the court considers with notice to all parties whether the relief granted without notice should be continued. 20.103

Documents in support of the application

When making an application for interim relief, the applicant will need an application notice; a draft order; one or more witness statements setting out the evidence supporting the application (an affidavit is necessary if a search order is being sought); a claim form and, if there is time, particulars of claim; and a skeleton argument. In urgent cases an order can be granted before issue of the claim form, provided an undertaking is given to issue and serve the claim form as soon as reasonably practicable after the injunction hearing. 20.104

Disclosure

CPR Part 31 distinguishes between two types of disclosure: standard disclosure (CPR r 31.6) and specific disclosure (CPR r 31.12). An order for disclosure will be an order for standard disclosure unless the court directs otherwise (CPR r 31.5). Standard disclosure will normally be ordered at the first case management conference in a case. Once standard disclosure has been given, the parties may need to consider whether any application for specific disclosure is required. 20.105

The rules also distinguish between disclosure and inspection. Disclosure requires a statement that a document exists, conventionally by reference to it on a disclosure list. In most cases, a party has a right to inspect a document disclosed to him, but there are circumstances in which inspection may be withheld: because the document is no longer in the disclosing party's possession; because there is a right to withhold disclosure (most commonly on grounds of privilege); or because inspection would be disproportionate (CPR r 31.2). Whilst in the employment tribunal disclosure and inspection are often elided, in court proceedings directions normally provide for inspection to follow a number of days after disclosure by list. 20.106

The principles applicable to disclosure, and in particular the right to withhold inspection, are relevant in the employment tribunal and are dealt with in Chapter 6 above, and are not repeated in detail here. 20.107

Standard disclosure

Standard disclosure (CPR r 31.6) is disclosure of: 20.108

- the documents on which the party relies; and
- the documents which adversely affect the party's, or another party's case or support another party's case; and
- the documents required to be disclosed under a relevant practice direction.

The duty of disclosure (standard or specific) relates to documents in the party's control; these are documents that: are or were in the party's physical possession; of which he has a right to possession; or of which he has or has had a right to inspect or take copies (CPR r 31.8). 20.109

The duty to search for documents when giving standard disclosure is limited by reasonableness (CPR r 31.7). The factors relevant in deciding the reasonableness of a search include: the 20.110

number of documents involved; the nature and complexity of the proceedings; the ease and expense of retrieval of any particular document; the significance of any document which is likely to be located in the search.

20.111 The manner in which standard disclosure is to be carried out is set out in CPR r 31.10. A party's disclosure list must be supported by a disclosure statement, unless the parties agree or the court directs otherwise. The appropriate form of disclosure statement is set out in CPR 31 PD.

Specific disclosure

20.112 Specific disclosure and inspection (CPR r 31.12) can be ordered in respect of documents or classes of document specified in the order. The court may require a party to carry out a search to the extent stipulated in an order and to disclose any documents located as a result of that search.

20.113 An application may be made by a party if the disclosure of documents is 'inadequate' (CPR r 31.12). In reaching its decision the court will take into account all of the circumstances of the case and the overriding objective. If the court concludes that the party from whom specific disclosure is sought has failed to comply with the obligations imposed by an order for disclosure, including by failing to make a sufficient search, the court will make such order as is necessary to ensure that the obligations are complied with.

Pre-action disclosure

20.114 The court has the power, under CPR r 31.16, to order disclosure prior to the commencement of proceedings in the following circumstances:

- the respondent is likely to become a party to proceedings;
- the applicant is also likely to be a party to those proceedings;
- if proceedings had started, the respondent's duty by way of standard disclosure, set out in CPR r 31.6, would extend to the documents or classes of document of which disclosure is sought; and
- disclosure before proceedings have started is desirable in order to:
    - dispose fairly of the anticipated proceedings;
    - assist the dispute to be resolved without proceedings; or
    - save costs.

20.115 It is not necessary to show a likelihood that proceedings will be commenced, only that if proceedings are commenced, the applicant and respondent may well be parties to them: *Black v Sumitomo Corp* [2001] EWCA Civ 1819, [2001] 1 WLR 1562. The court only has jurisdiction to make an order if there is a real prospect of an order being fair to the parties if proceedings are commenced, or assisting resolution of the dispute without proceedings, or saving costs. Once the jurisdictional threshold is satisfied, the court has a discretion whether to make an order (and if so what order to make) to be exercised in the light of all the circumstances: see *Black*, para 81. In determining the application, the court need only take a broad view of the merits of the case, and need not investigate legally complex issues: *Total v Edmonds* [2007] EWCA Civ 50.

Third party disclosure

20.116 The court may make an order for disclosure against a person who is not a party to the proceedings under CPR r 31.17 where:

- the documents of which disclosure is sought are likely to support the case of the applicant or adversely affect the case of one of the other parties to the proceedings; and
- disclosure is necessary in order to dispose fairly of the claim or to save costs.

20.117 An order under this rule must specify the documents or the classes of documents which the respondent must disclose, and require the respondent, when making disclosure, to specify any of those documents which are no longer in his control, or in respect of which he claims a right or duty to withhold inspection. Such an order may require the respondent to indicate what has happened to any documents which are no longer in his control; and specify the time and place for disclosure and inspection.

The court's power to order disclosure against a non-party is not limited to the power under CPR r 31.17: see CPR r 31.18. **20.118**

Disclosure may also be obtained against a non-party by obtaining a witness summons under CPR r 34.2 requiring the witness to attend court to produce documents to the court, either on the date fixed for a hearing or on such date as the court may direct. Under the provisions in CPR r 34.3(2) a party must obtain permission from the court where he wishes to have a summons issued for a witness to attend a hearing or produce documents on any date except the date fixed for the trial. **20.119**

Further, the court has the power to order disclosure against a non-party for the purposes of disclosing the identity of a wrongdoer: a 'Norwich Pharmacal order' see *Norwich Pharmacal v Customs & Excise Commissioners* [1974] AC 133. The *Norwich Pharmacal* jurisdiction is an exceptional one and one which is only exercised by the courts with caution, not least because the order may engage the respondent's right to privacy under Article 8 of ECHR. **20.120**

Evidence and witnesses

Rules concerning evidence and witnesses are in CPR Parts 32–4. Expert evidence is dealt with in CPR Part 34. The general principles, insofar as they are relevant to tribunal claims, have been touched on in Chapter 6 dealing with case management, and in relation to witnesses in Chapter 9, dealing with the hearing. Reference should be made to specialist works on civil procedure for the detailed principles as applied in the civil courts. **20.121**

A notable distinction between the tribunal and the civil courts is that the strict rules of evidence apply in the civil courts. The rules of evidence are a mixture of substantive and procedural law. CPR Parts 32–4 deal with procedural issues in relation to evidence. **20.122**

Trial

CPR Part 39 states the rules applicable to trials and other hearings. Hearings are normally held in public, unless the hearing falls within one of the categories in CPR r 39.2, which are similar to the cases in which private hearings may be held in the tribunal. **20.123**

A trial in the civil courts will normally be conducted by a judge sitting alone. There are categories of civil trial which may be heard by judge and jury (for example, defamation, false imprisonment) but these are unlikely to arise in the employment context. In race discrimination cases heard in the county court the judge may sit with expert assessors (RRA 1976, s 67(4)). As to the role of assessors, see *Ahmed v Governing Body of the University of Oxford* [2002] EWCA Civ 1907, [2003] 1 WLR 995. **20.124**

Generally, a trial will be listed in a trial window, that is a period of days or weeks during which the case may come on for trial, rather than having a fixed date. Parties can apply for a fixture in an appropriate case. **20.125**

Rights of audience in the High Court and county court are limited: see Access to Justice Act 1999, Part III and Courts and Legal Services Act 1990, Part II. Barristers and solicitors with appropriate rights of audience may appear in the courts. Fellows of the Institute of Legal Executives engaged in particular types of work may appear in certain hearings in the county court (County Courts (Right of Audience) Direction 1978). Lay representation is not widely permitted. The Lay Representatives (Rights of Audience) Order 1999, SI 1999/1225 enables lay representatives to appear in cases on the small claims track, but not in other cases. The court retains a power to permit to a lay representative rights of audience in exceptional cases: Courts and Legal Services Act 1990, s 27. A litigant may appear in person. In the case of a company which is party to proceedings, it may appear by a director or employee pursuant to CPR r 39.6. **20.126**

20.127 The conduct of trials is more formal in the civil courts than the conduct of hearings in the tribunal. Unless the judge directs otherwise, legal representatives are robed (although increasingly this formality is dispensed with in county courts). Strict court procedure as to the order of speeches and evidence is adopted. The strict rules of evidence apply, as indicated above. There is a requirement on the parties to have filed and exchanged bundles and skeleton arguments prior to trial. Whilst opening speeches may be made, in modern practice the judge will normally have read the skeletons, statements of case, and key documents prior to trial, and therefore in many cases the opening may be quite short. The witness statements stand as evidence in chief and are taken as read. Very limited additional cross-examination will be permitted.

Costs

20.128 The treatment of costs marks a great difference between proceedings in the employment tribunal and proceedings in the civil courts. Whereas in the tribunal costs orders remain the exception rather than the rule (see ETR 2004, rr 38–41 considered in Chapter 12), in the civil courts, the court has a wide discretion as to costs, and traditionally the normal rule has been that costs follow the event, that is, the loser pays the winner's costs.

20.129 The main provisions relating to costs are set out in CPR Parts 43–8, together with their associated Practice Directions. Parts 45 and 46 concern fixed costs and fast-track costs respectively. The following commentary concerns cases proceeding on the multi-track.

General principles

20.130 By CPR r 44.3 the court has a discretion as to whether costs are payable by one party to another; the amount of those costs; when they are to be paid; and whether costs are to be paid on a standard or indemnity basis.

20.131 The general rule is that the unsuccessful party will be ordered to pay the costs of the successful party, but the court is entitled to make a different order. When exercising that discretion, the court must have regard to all of the circumstances and in particular:

(a) The conduct of all of the parties. CPR r 44.3(5) sets out some detailed aspects of conduct to be taken into consideration.
(b) Whether a party has succeeded on part of his case.
(c) Any payment into court or other admissible offer to settle made by a party which is drawn to the court's attention (whether or not it is an offer in accordance with Part 36).

20.132 Under CPR r 44.3(6), the court has considerable margin of discretion to award a party part only of his costs, in order to do justice. The court may, for example, make an order that the winning party recovers a percentage of his total costs, or costs in respect of a particular period, or the costs of a distinct part of the proceedings.

Costs and ADR

20.133 One aspect of the parties' conduct which has become increasingly important in recent years is the attempt each party has made to resolve their dispute without recourse to the courts (CPR r 44.5(3)), and in particular the parties' approach to alternative dispute resolution (ADR; see further Chapter 5). A refusal on the part of one party to take part in ADR can affect an award of costs under CPR r 44.3(4)(a) since that party may be found to have conducted themselves unreasonably, see *Halsey v Milton Keynes NHS Trust* [2004] 1 WLR 3002. One of the key features of the CPR has been its encouragement of alternative dispute resolution methods, and the imposition of sanctions in costs has been one of the main tools by which the courts have given such encouragement.

Part 36 offers

20.134 An offer to settle made in accordance with the provisions of CPR Part 36 is referred to as a Part 36 offer.

Part 36 contains detailed provisions for the form and timing of Part 36 offers, and for the timing of acceptance. The rules repay detailed consideration. The acceptance or non-acceptance of a valid Part 36 offer can have important costs consequences. The following outlines the key provisions. **20.135**

A Part 36 offer must be in writing. It must (CPR r 36.2): **20.136**

- state that it is intended to have the consequences of Part 36;
- specify a period of not less than 21 days within which the offeror will be liable for the offeree's costs if the offer is accepted;
- state whether it relates to the whole of the claim or part of it;
- state whether it takes into account any counterclaim.

An offer by a defendant to pay a sum of money should be a single sum of money, and should be to pay the money within 14 days following the date of acceptance. If an offer is not in such terms, and the offer is not accepted the offer will not be treated as a Part 36 offer. However, if the offer is accepted, the normal costs consequences of acceptance of a Part 36 offer will apply (CPR r 36.4). **20.137**

A Part 36 offer may be made at any time, including prior to the commencement of proceedings. It may be made at any time up to the end of the trial itself, although the costs consequences of an offer made less than 21 days before trial differ from those applicable in the normal case. **20.138**

The Part 36 procedure relies on the concept of the 'relevant period' in the rules applicable to acceptance, withdrawal, and the costs consequences of any offer. This term is defined in CPR r 36.2(1)(c). Where an offer is made not less than 21 days before trial, the relevant period is the period stated in the offer, or such other period agreed between the parties. Where an offer is made less than 21 days before trial, the relevant period is the period up to the end of the trial, or such other period as the court has determined. **20.139**

Party accepts Part 36 offer

Pursuant to CPR r 36.10 where a claimant accepts a Part 36 offer within the relevant period he will be entitled to his costs of the proceedings up to the date of service of notice of acceptance of the offer (CPR r 36.9(3)). **20.140**

The court's permission is required to accept a Part 36 offer after commencement of the trial (CPR r 36.10(3)). **20.141**

Where a Part 36 offer is accepted after the expiry of the relevant period, or where an offer made less than 21 days before trial is accepted, the court will make an order for costs. Whilst the court has a discretion as to the appropriate order, the 'starting point' is that the offeree will be entitled to his costs up to the expiry of the relevant period, and the offeree will be liable for the offeror's costs between that date and the date of acceptance (CPR r 36.10(5)). **20.142**

On acceptance of a Part 36 offer, the proceedings are stayed, save for enforcement of the offer and costs (CPR r 36.11). Where the offer included an offer to pay a single sum of money, the sum must be paid within 14 days of acceptance (CPR r 36.11(6)). If the sum is not paid in time, the offeree may enter judgment (CPR r 36.11(7)). **20.143**

Claimant refuses defendant's offer, and fails to beat it at trial

Where a claimant fails to beat a Part 36 offer at trial then, unless it considers it unjust to do so, the court will order the claimant to pay the defendant's costs from the date on which the relevant period expired, together with interest on those costs (CPR r 36.14(2)). **20.144**

In considering whether it would be unjust to make such orders, the court shall consider all the circumstances, including: **20.145**

- the terms of any Part 36 offer;
- the stage in the proceedings when the Part 36 offer was made;

- the information available to the parties when the Part 36 offer was made;
- the conduct of the parties with regard to giving or refusing to give information for the purposes of evaluating the offer.

Defendant fails to beat claimant's Part 36 offer at trial

20.146 Where judgment against a defendant is at least as advantageous to the claimant as the proposals in the claimant's Part 36 offer, the court may 'punish' the defendant by (CPR r 36.14(3)):

(a) awarding interest on the whole or part of any sum of money awarded to the claimant at a rate not exceeding 10 per cent above the base rate for some or all of the period starting with the date when the relevant period expired; and
(b) the court may also order that the claimant is entitled to costs on an indemnity basis from the date on which the relevant period expired; and
(c) interest on those costs at a rate not exceeding 10 per cent above the base rate.

20.147 In determining whether it would be unjust to make any of the orders referred to in the previous paragraph, the same factors apply as referred to in para 20.145 above.

Costs against non-parties

20.148 Costs may be awarded in favour of, or against, a non-party to the proceedings as part of the general discretion to award costs under s 51 of SCA 1981. CPR r 48.2 states that if this discretion is to be exercised, then the individual must be added as a party to the proceedings and the individual must be given a reasonable opportunity to attend the hearing; see *Symphony Group plc v Hodgson* [1993] 4 All ER 143, CA.

Wasted costs orders

20.149 CPR r 48.7 permits the court to make a wasted costs order against a party's legal representative; see as to employment tribunals Chapter 12. The test was set out by the Court of Appeal in *Ridehalgh v Horsefield* [1994] Ch 205. An order may be made if:

(a) the representative, of whom the complaint has been made, has acted improperly, unreasonably, or negligently;
(b) such conduct has caused the applicant to incur unnecessary costs;
(c) in all the circumstances it is just to order the legal representative to compensate the applicant for the whole or part of the relevant costs.

Assessment of costs

Standard or indemnity basis

20.150 The court can assess the amount of costs under CPR r 44.4 on either a standard basis or an indemnity basis:

(a) Where costs are assessed on the standard basis, the court will allow costs which are proportionate to the matters in issue but any doubt as to whether the costs were reasonably incurred or are reasonable and proportionate in amount will be resolved in favour of the paying party.
(b) In contrast, where costs are assessed on the indemnity basis, the court will resolve any doubt as to whether costs were reasonably incurred or were reasonable in amount in favour of the receiving party.

Summary or detailed assessment

20.151 The court may assess costs either by summary assessment or detailed assessment (CPR r 44.7). The terms are defined in CPR rr 43.3–43.4.

(a) A summary assessment will be carried out by the judge who heard the trial or application and made the costs order, normally at the end of the trial or application. The assessment will be based on a summary statement of costs following form N260. The procedure for summary assessment is set out in CPR 44PD, paras 12–14.

(b) A detailed assessment will be carried out by a costs judge, on the basis of a detailed bill of costs. Detailed assessment is a whole contentious procedure in itself. The procedure to be followed on a detailed assessment is set out in CPR Part 47.

The factors relevant to the decision whether to order summary or detailed assessment are set out in paras 12–13 of CPR 44PD. As a general rule, the court should summarily assess costs at the end of a fast-track trial and at the end of any hearing (trial or application) which has lasted not more than one day. Where a detailed assessment is ordered, a payment on account of costs can be made prior to assessment pursuant to CPR r 44.3(8). **20.152**

Security for costs

A defendant may apply for security for costs pursuant to CPR r 25.12. An order for security for costs requires the party against whom it is made to pay an amount into court in respect of the other party's costs as a condition of proceeding with the claim. The court has a discretion to make such an order if it believes it to be just to do so in all the circumstances in certain specific situations set out in CPR r 25.12. The most common circumstances are cases where the claimant is outside the jurisdiction and not resident in a State covered by the EU Judgments Regulation, or the claimant is a company or other body and there is reason to believe that it will be unable to pay the defendant's costs if ordered to do so. **20.153**

CHECKLIST OF STEPS UP TO COMPLETION OF STATEMENTS OF CASE

- Claimant's pre-action letter: the letter should give a reasonable period for response, for many claims one month may be reasonable (Protocol Practice Direction para 4.3).
- Defendant's acknowledgment of claimant's pre-action letter: within 21 days of receipt (Protocol Practice Direction para 4.4). The acknowledgment should state when the defendant will give a full response. If the period is longer than that suggested by the claimant, the defendant should give reasons.
- Defendant's full response to pre-action letter: within the period stated by the claimant, or otherwise within a reasonable period.
- Issue of claim form: CPR r 7.2.
- Service of claim form: within four months of the date of issue (six months where the claim form is to be served out of the jurisdiction (CPR r 7.5), subject to extension by order of the court (CPR r 7.6).
- Particulars of claim: if not served with claim form, to be served within 14 days of service of claim form (CPR r 7.4(1)). Must be served no later than the latest date for serving the claim form (CPR r 7.4(2)).
- Defendant's Acknowledgment of Service: to be filed within 14 days after the service of the claim form, or 14 days after service of the Particulars of Claim (where the Particulars of Claim are served subsequently) (CPR r 10.3(1)). Special rules apply where the claim form is served out of the jurisdiction (CPR r 10.3(2)).
- Defendant's application to dispute jurisdiction: must be made within 14 days after filing an Acknowledgment of Service (CPR r 11(4)).
- Defence: to be filed and served by 14 days after service of the Particulars of Claim, or within 28 days, if the defendant has filed an acknowledgment of service (CPR r 15.4(1)). A defendant need not file a defence if he disputes the court's jurisdiction (CPR r 11).
- Counterclaim: to be filed and served with the defence, or at any other time with permission of the court (CPR r 20.4).

- Allocation questionnaire: to be served by the court on each party when a defence is filed (CPR r 26.3(1)).
- Completed allocation questionnaires: to be filed by each party on the date specified in the questionnaire, which must be at least 14 days after the deemed date of service (CPR r 26.3(6)).
- Reply: to be filed and served when the claimant files his allocation questionnaire (CPR r 15.8).
- Defence to counterclaim: to be filed and served by 14 days after service of the counterclaim (CPR r 15.4). However, the court will normally order that the defence to counterclaim must be filed by the same date as the reply (15PD, para 3.2A).

CHECKLIST OF MATTERS FOR CONSIDERATION AT CMC

- Allocation to a track (if this has not already been done).
- Transfer: is the case in the appropriate court or division?
- Alternative dispute resolution: one standard direction on the PF 52 form is a stay for alternative dispute resolution at an early stage of case management. The parties should consider whether this is appropriate, and if so, at what stage of the proceedings.
- Addition of parties.
- Consolidation with other cases: this involves consideration of Part 20 claims brought by the defendant, and unrelated claims, for example, claims brought by other claimants against the same defendant raising similar issues or evidence.
- Amendments to the statements of case, and/or provision of further information.
- Interim applications/trial of preliminary issues: are any such hearings appropriate? If so, they should be listed and a timetable of directions for those applications provided for.
- Disclosure.
- Witness statements.
- Expert evidence: the parties should be prepared to discuss the discipline(s) in which expert evidence is necessary, whether a joint expert is appropriate, the formulation of instructions, facilities for disclosure and examination, the date for service of reports, the mechanism for experts to attempt to agree or narrow the issues.
- Listing for trial: this will require consideration of the length of trial, the window in which it is to be listed, and its categorization as A, B, or C (in descending order of seriousness and complexity).
- Pre-trial review: this permits the court to ensure that the case will be ready for trial, but in many cases is now dispensed with.
- Preparation for trial: agreed lists of issues, bundles, skeleton arguments, agreed trial timetable.
- Settlement: the parties should notify the court immediately on settlement.
- Costs of the CMC: the usual order is costs in case.

21

Court of Appeal

SUMMARY

(1) An appeal to the Court of Appeal may only be made with the permission of the EAT or the Court of Appeal.

(2) In employment cases the Court of Appeal is a second tier appeal.

A. GENERAL PRINCIPLES

An application for permission to appeal to the Court of Appeal must be made unless the EAT orders otherwise at the hearing when a reserved judgment is handed down (EAT PD, para 21.1). If this is not done any later application must be made to the Court of Appeal which will want an explanation as to why it was not done earlier (*Balmoral Group v Borealis (UK) Ltd* [2006] EWHC 2228). **21.01**

Appeal to the Court of Appeal may only be made with the permission of the EAT or the Court of Appeal (ETA 1996, s 37(1), (2)). The rules are set out in CPR r 52 supplemented by CPR 52PD. The key points are as follows: **21.02**

(1) permission will be given only if the EAT or the Court of Appeal decides that the appeal:
  (a) would have a real prospect of success, or
  (b) there is some other compelling reason why the appeal should be heard (CPR r 52.3(6)).

  'Real prospect of success' means realistic and not fanciful (*Tanfern Ltd v Cameron MacDonald* [2000] 1 WLR 1311).
(2) An application is first made orally to the EAT and preferably on the day the appeal is heard or when judgment is given if later. It is not essential to do this before seeking permission to appeal from the Court of Appeal but it is advisable to do so.
(3) If the application is refused, an application may be made direct to the Court of Appeal (CPR r 52.3(2)). This should be made within 14 days of the date of the sealed order of the EAT.
(4) The Court of Appeal usually considers the application first without a hearing (CPR PD52, para 4.11).
(5) If permission is refused without a hearing, a request may be made for reconsideration of that refusal at an oral hearing (CPR r 52.3(4)); this must be requested within seven days after service of the notice that permission has been refused (CPR r 52.3(5)).

(6) Service of the notice of appeal must be made on the respondents as soon as practicable, and no later than seven days after it is filed.
(7) A notice of appeal must be accompanied by a skeleton argument or if this is not possible within this period, this has to be done within 14 days of filing the notice of appeal (CPR PD52, para 5.9(2)).
(8) The respondent's skeleton argument must be served no later than 21 days after the respondent receives the appellant's skeleton argument, although the court may make different directions in a particular case.
(9) The parties may not agree between themselves to any extension of the time stated, but the Court of Appeal itself may vary any part of this timetable (CPR PD52, para 5.2).
(10) The refusal by the Court of Appeal to give permission to appeal is not itself appealable.

B. SPECIAL FEATURES ABOUT EMPLOYMENT APPEALS

21.03 There are certain features of employment litigation in the Court of Appeal which are different from general cases in other areas. These are set out below.

Second tier appeal

21.04 One of the primary issues where practice in employment law is different from the norm is that in employment cases the Court of Appeal is a second tier appeal, the matter having already been heard by the employment tribunal and EAT. The Court of Appeal is 'primarily concerned to review the proceedings in and the decision of the ET in order to determine whether a question of law arises from them', according to Mummery LJ in *Yeboah v Crofton* [2002] IRLR 634, para 12; see also *Hennessy v Craigmyle & Co Ltd and ACAS* [1986] ICR 461, 470; *Campion v Hamworthy Engineering Ltd* [1987] ICR 966, 972; *Vento v Chief Constable of West Yorkshire Police* [2003] ICR 318 at para 25; and *Lambe v 186K Ltd* [2005] ICR 307 at para 80. This means that if the decision of the ET is correct in law the Court of Appeal will not allow the appeal because the EAT erred in its analysis in between.

21.05 This has always been applied with some flexibility since there may be fresh arguments or fresh evidence at the EAT.

21.06 In *Gover v Propertycare Limited* [2006] EWCA Civ 286, [2006] ICR 1073, para 9, however, Buxton LJ expressed 'some reserve' about the guidance in previous cases. He thought there was in no realistic sense an appeal from the employment appeal tribunal on a point of law, as the ETA 1996, s 37(1) expressly provided, if the Court of Appeal was only concerned with whether the tribunal was right. He said further: 'As to the business of this court, the assumption that we in effect repeat the exercise already performed by the expert appeal tribunal, of reviewing the decision of the employment tribunal, tends in practice to impose on this court an exercise that is inappropriate both in its nature and in its extent.' The argument in *Gover* was not full on this point which was not raised in argument.

21.07 Without reference to *Gover*, Sir Peter Gibson in *Balfour Beatty v Wilcox* [2007] IRLR 63 soon afterwards, reiterated the *Hennessy* approach and stressed that the fact that the EAT had 'erred in its reasoning will not necessarily be conclusive as to the outcome of the appeal'. This was not to suggest, however, that the judgment of the EAT must be ignored (para 71). Buxton LJ, however, expressed views similar to those he had expressed in *Gover*.

21.08 The Court of Appeal will only rarely remit a case to the EAT for further consideration (*Lambe v 186K Ltd* [2005] ICR 307) but examples have included a conclusion that the EAT lacked jurisdiction to hear the appeal (*Grady v Prison Service* [2003] ICR 1293) and where the Court of Appeal identified at permission stage grounds which had not been put before the EAT although the circumstances of the case were unusual (*Sukul Lennard v Croydon PCT* The Times, 22 July 2003).

Other procedural issues

This does not purport to be a complete guide to procedure in the Court of Appeal but we consider some aspects which are important for those who may appear there for the first time: **21.09**

(1) where a respondent wishes only to request that the court upholds the judgment or order of the lower court, whether for reasons given in the lower court or otherwise, no permission is required nor is a respondent's notice necessary (CPR 52PD, para 7.2), but if the respondent seeks to ask the court to uphold it for different or additional grounds a respondent's notice must be filed (CPR 52PD, para 7.3);
(2) the appeal bundle should be prepared in accordance with CPR 52PD, para 5.6 which sets down the general contents of bundles;
(3) in cases where the appeal bundle consists of more than 500 pages exclusive of transcripts, the appellant's solicitors must in consultation with the respondent's solicitors also prepare and file with the court a core bundle which must not exceed 150 pages (CPR 52PD,paras 15.2 and 15.3);
(4) if the appellant does not comply with the manifold requirements for bundles the appeal 'will be referred for consideration to be given as to why it should not be dismissed' (CPR 52PD, para 15.4(12));
(5) when the parties have been notified of the hearing date the appellant's advocate must after consulting his opposite number file a bundle containing photocopies of the authorities to be relied upon; this should be filed at least seven days before the hearing or where the period of notice of hearing is less than seven days immediately; relevant passages should be marked down the side so that the judges may carry out the relevant pre-reading (CPR 52PD, para 15.11(1));
(6) any supplementary skeleton argument for the appellant must be filed at least 14 days before the hearing (CPR 52PD, para 15.11A(1));
(7) there will be summary assessment of costs when appeals are listed for one day or less and parties must be prepared for this with schedules of costs swapped at least one day in advance of the hearing (CPR 52PD, para 14.1).

Costs

Normally if the Court of Appeal overturns the decision of the court below it will award costs of the appeal in the court below, but as the EAT is normally a costs-free jurisdiction it will not do so here, but the normal civil rules of costs apply to the Court of Appeal hearing itself. **21.10**

22

European Union Law and References to the European Court of Justice

A. EU LAW

The treatment of EU law in this book is necessarily summary but addresses the key principles which ultimately derive from Community law with which employment lawyers need to be familiar. In particular employment lawyers need to be familiar with: **22.01**

(a) sources of EU law and general principles;
(b) when and how EU law can be invoked in the Employment Tribunal;
(c) references to the ECJ under Article 234.

B. SOURCES OF EU LAW

The Treaties

The EC Treaty is the successor to the EEC Treaty ratified and incorporated by the UK in 1972. The EC Treaty is important because: **22.02**

- some of its provisions have direct effect (for example Art 141 on equal treatment has 'horizontal direct effect' (see below));
- it contains legislative competence for the Community institutions (Commission, Parliament, and Council) to enact European legislation which may directly confer rights on individuals (for example the Directive on Fixed Term Work).

Key provisions of the EC Treaty which employment lawyers should be aware of include: **22.03**

- Article 12 (any discrimination on grounds of nationality shall be prohibited)
- Article 13 (legislative competence to combat discrimination based on sex, racial or ethnic origin, religion or belief, disability, age, or sexual orientation)
- Article 141 (equal treatment of pay between men and women)
- Article 39 (free movement of workers)
- The other free movement provisions in relation to establishment and services (Articles 43 and 49)

- The legislative competences in the social chapter (Articles 136–145)
- Article 234 references to the ECJ
- Article 230 challenges to Community institutions.

EC legislation

22.04 The EC Treaty empowers the Community legislative organs to enact various different types of legislative instruments including:

- Regulations; and
- Directives.

22.05 These legislative instruments set out the exact mechanism by which the Member State must enact/give effect to a measure within the individual Member State. Regulations are automatically 'directly applicable' within each Member State. This means that individuals can rely on them regardless of whether they have actually been enacted domestically. The most important Regulation in the employment sphere is the Jurisdiction and Judgments Regulation (Regulation 44/2001 Council Regulation on Jurisdiction and the Recognition and Enforcement of Judgments in Civil and Commercial Matters) which supersedes the previous Brussels Convention on the conflicts of laws.

22.06 Directives are the more common instrument of choice in employment matters. Key examples include the Equal Treatment Framework Directive 2000/78/EC; the Race Directive 2000/43/EC; the Working Time Directive 93/104/EC; the Fixed Term Workers and Part Time Workers Directives 97/81/EC; the Posted Workers Directive 96/71/EC; and the Data Protection Directive 95/46/EC.

22.07 Directives set out the aim to be achieved by the Member State, but leave that Member State some degree of freedom to choose the method of implementation into the law of that State.

22.08 For employment lawyers it is important to remember the following features about Directives:

- They can confer rights directly on individuals which have 'direct effect' provided they are expressed to be sufficiently clear and precise (Cases C–397/01 to C–403/01 *Pfeiffer* [2005] ICR 1307). With Directives this is restricted generally to 'vertical' direct effect (unlike the Treaty)—ie rights which can be relied upon directly against organs of a Member State (defined by reference to the criteria in *Foster v British Gas* [1991] 2 AC 306).
- Not all provisions of a Directive will have direct effect.
- As Directives permit the Member State some degree of freedom in the manner in which they have been implemented, Directives have both a date of publication in the Official Journal of the European Communities, and a date by which they must be implemented. This principle is subject to the following conditions:
  - In the time prior to implementation the Member State must not do anything which is inconsistent with the Directive (the *Interenvironment Wallonie* principle [1998] Env LR 623 and Case C–427/06 *Bartsch v Bosch and Siemens Hausgeräte (BSH) Altersfürsorge GmbH* [2008] ECR I–0000);
  - The European Commission may bring proceedings under Article 226 EC against a Member State which has failed to implement a Directive in time;
  - An individual may rely on any directly effective rights conferred by the Directive in an action against a public body once the time for implementation has passed;
  - National legislation must be interpreted consistently with a Directive from the date of publication of that Directive, not just from the date for implementation (*Pfeiffer* Case C–106/89 *Marleasing* [1990] ECR I–4135; Case C–268/06 *Impact*; [2008] All ER (D) 194);
  - If a Member State completely fails to implement a Directive on time, this is generally speaking a sufficiently serious breach which would enable an individual to bring a damages action against the State for the State's breach of Community law in not

enacting legislation in time (under the principle in *Francovich v Italy* [1991] ECR 5357). This will only be a remotely desirable option in cases which involve either a:

- Directive which has been implemented late (and there is no national legislation to be interpreted consistently so as to protect those rights) for provisions which do not have direct effect. These were the facts of *Francovich*; or
- As for the first option, where the provision does have direct effect, but the individual lost the chance of a cause of action against a non-public entity.

It is important to consider the Treaty competence for legislation (ie the Article in the Treaty which gives the Community institutions the power to enact the legislation). This determines both: **22.09**

- the procedure (ie whether it is adopted by qualified majority voting and whether the 'Social Partners' are involved); and
- the principles behind the substantive rights (eg principles of non discrimination/free movement).

General principles of Community law

As in ordinary English common law, in EC law the sources of rights are not restricted to those under the EC Treaty directly or under legislation. There are also various 'general principles of Community law' which have been recognized/declared by the ECJ over the years. **22.10**

From an employment lawyer's perspective it is important to remember the following two key features about the doctrines of consistent interpretation and direct effect. **22.11**

- In all cases there is a duty on the national court to interpret national legislation consistently with Community law insofar as it is possible to do so. This is a powerful principle which permits the national court or tribunal to read out words in a national statute (or read words into one) where to do so would not go against a fundamental feature of the national legislation (for a recent summary of the principle see *Byrne v Motor Insurers Bureau* [2008] EWCA Civ 574;
- In a case involving a public body/emanation of the State, if it is not possible to interpret the national legislation compatibly with the relevant Directive/Treaty provision, it must be disapplied (eg *Marshall v Southampton and SW Hampshire HA (No 2)* [1994] 1 AC 530). Disapplication must also apply in cases where the article relied upon has horizontal direct effect (C 200/91 *Coloroll Pension Trustees Limited v James Russell and others* [1994] ECR I-04389).

Other international instruments

Sometimes there is confusion between the European Convention on Human Rights and the European Community. A full analysis is beyond the scope of this book, but the practical points to remember are: **22.12**

- The EU is not a party to the ECHR. Crucially, directly effective provisions of EC law have the capability of automatically disapplying legislation. Provisions which are incompatible with the ECHR are not disapplied. They can only be declared incompatible (but this has no legislative effect).
- The duty of consistent interpretation/indirect effect, however, is very similar under both the Human Rights Act and the European Communities Act. It is not unusual in HRA cases that EC cases are cited, and vice versa (see, eg, *Ghaidan v Godin Mendoza* [2004] 2 AC 557).
- The ECJ often makes reference to judgments of the ECHR when considering fundamental rights (eg *Viking v ITWF* [2008] ICR 741) and sometimes vice versa.
- Some legislation refers expressly to the ECHR (eg recitals 1 and 4 of the Framework Directive 2000/78 EC).

C. EU LAW IN THE EMPLOYMENT TRIBUNAL

Does the Tribunal have jurisdiction?

22.13 The starting point is that Employment Tribunals are creatures of statute. They have no inherent jurisdiction other than that provided by statute. The primary source of this is s 2 of ETA 1996 which provides:

> employment tribunals shall exercise the jurisdiction conferred on them by or by virtue of this Act or any other Act, whether passed before or after this Act.

22.14 Since 1996 there has been an increase in regulations conferring jurisdiction on the Employment Tribunal which wholly implement European legislation, for instance:

- Part-Time Workers (Prevention of Less Favourable Treatment) Regulations 2000
- Fixed-term Employees (Prevention of Less Favourable Treatment) Regulations 2002
- Employment Equality (Sexual Orientation) Regulation 2003
- Transfer of Undertakings (Protection of Employment) Regulations 2006
- Employment Equality (Age) Regulations 2006.

22.15 Pre-existing legislation has also more recently been amended to bring it into line with European legislation, for instance the Sex Discrimination Act 1975, the Race Relations Act 1976, and the Disability Discrimination Act 1995.

22.16 The employment tribunal does not have free-standing jurisdiction over employment matters derived from European law pursuant to s 2 of the European Communities Act 1972 (*Biggs v Somerset County Council* [1995] IRLR 811 at 829, approved by CA in [1996] IRLR 203). The question of whether the tribunal has jurisdiction is not as simple as looking at whether the wording of the governing statute provides for the particular right or remedy claimed in the tribunal. Although in EC law Member States have autonomy over matters of domestic civil procedure (*Preston v Wolverhampton Healthcare NHS Trust* [2000] IRLR 506, para 31) tribunals and courts must be able to comply with the general principles of Community law, including specifically:

- the principle of effectiveness of national remedies (that they not be impossible or excessively difficult);
- the principle of equivalence of national remedies for similar causes of action based in domestic and European law.

(eg *GMB v Mrs Brennan and Sunderland City Council* UKEAT/0580/07/MAA, paras 65–8 *per* Elias J; Case C–268/06 *Impact v Ministry of Agriculture and Food* [2008] All ER (D) 194 ('*Impact*') paras 37–55; Case C–432/05 *Unibet* [2007] ECR I–2271; Case 33/76 *Rewe-Zentralfinanz and Rewe-Zentral* [1976] ECR 1989, para 5; Case 45/76 *Comet* [1976] ECR 2043, para 13; Case C–312/93 *Peterbroeck* [1995] ECR I–4599 and Case C–326/96 *Levez* [1998] ECR I–7835).

22.17 In *Brennan*, Elias J applied AG Kokott's analysis from the *Impact v Ministry of Agriculture and Food* [2008] All ER (D) 194 case to the employment tribunal system (a couple of weeks before the ECJ followed her analysis in its judgment).

22.18 *Impact* was a case referred to the ECJ by the Irish Labour Court in a case brought under the Irish legislation implementing Directive 99/70 EC, the 'Fixed Term Work Directive'.

22.19 Ireland has a similar (although not identical) system to the English Employment Tribunal system. The similarities are more fully fleshed out in the Opinion of AG Kokott (herself a former Labour Court Judge from Germany) at paras 42, 60–3, 73, and 77.

(a) the Irish Labour Courts/Right Commissioners derive their jurisdiction wholly from statute;
(b) they are the forum of priority for disputes under various pieces of Employment Regulation/legislation;

(c) they have been generally presumed not to have jurisdiction to hear cases based purely on directly effective EC law rights; and
(d) they generally only award costs in exceptional circumstances.

There is an important distinction between: **22.20**

- the jurisdiction of tribunals under legislation which is derived solely from Parliament and domestic law(for example, the provisions on unfair dismissal in ERA 1996); and
- the jurisdiction of tribunals under legislation which implements provisions of Community law. This clearly applies to legislation such as the Fixed Term Employees (Prevention of Less Favourable Treatment) Regulations 2002 and may apply to legislation, for instance much of discrimination law, which began initially simply through national legislation, but subsequently has been covered by the Framework Directive on Equality and the Race Directive.

This newer line of case law fits in some ways rather uncomfortably with some of the older domestic case law, for example *Biggs v Somerset County Council* [1995] ICR 811, 830, EAT; *Secretary of State for Employment v Mann* [1996] ICR 197, 204; *Barber v Staffordshire County Council* [1996] ICR 376, 395; *Mensah v Northwick Park Hospital* UKEAT/711/99, para 10. These older cases stressed the first point, that the tribunal has no inherent jurisdiction other than under statute. **22.21**

Before *Impact* and *Brennan*, the strictness of this older approach had already begun to weaken in cases such as *R* (*on the application of Finian Manson*) *v Ministry of Defence* [2006] ICR 355 in which the Court of Appeal held that the employment tribunal had jurisdiction to determine whether a claimant came within the scope of the Directive 97/81/EC on Part Time Workers implemented by the Part Time Workers (Prevention of Less Favourable Treatment) Regulations 2000, even where this might mean the disapplication of some of the domestic regulations. This case is now best analysed as an example of the *Impact* principle in action. **22.22**

Under the older line of cases there was a strict demarcation between 'freestanding' rights in EC law, and those which had a statutory foundation under the relevant national legislation. The battle ground in many of the cases concerned Article 141 EC on equal treatment between men and women. The ECJ in *Impact* did not, however, draw any distinction between freestanding rights and those derived wholly from statute. **22.23**

One other point needs mentioning and that is the question of when time starts to run for an EU law claim where the Directive in question has not been properly transposed into domestic law. The ECJ in Case C–208/90 *Emmott v Minister for Social Welfare* [1991] ECR I–4269 held that time does not start to run until the Directive has been properly transposed and this is so even where the ECJ has delivered a judgment that the Member State is in default and that the obligations under the Directive are clear and precise. However, following the case of *R v Secretary of State for Employment, ex p EOC* [1994] IRLR 176 and *Rankin v British Coal Corporation* [1993] IRLR 69, most commentators and practitioners have taken a cautious line. The cases suggested that the time limit for claims not already pending, whether under the EC Treaty or a Directive, should be three months from the date of the legislation coming into force. This has been confirmed in *BP Supergas v Greece* [1995] All ER 684, where the ECJ held that domestic time limits will apply in a situation where the State has not properly transposed a Directive. **22.24**

To summarize the position, although domestic time limits will probably apply from the relevant date, there are two separate dates to consider depending on the EU source: **22.25**

(a) Where there is no direct effect, the date is that of the proper transposition of the Directive (*Cannon v Barnsley Metropolitan Borough Council* [1992] ICR 698, [1992] 2 CMLR 795; *Emmott v Minister for Social Welfare* [1993] ICR 8); if the application is held to be out of time because the employee has delayed bringing the claim until full implementation, there is a strong argument that it is just and equitable that the time limit be extended.

(b) Where there is direct effect or EC Treaty base, the date is when it becomes reasonably clear to any person affected that a claim could properly be made (*Rankin v British Coal*; *Emmott*).

22.26 As the time limits for bringing proceedings in the employment tribunal are often so short, it is particularly important to keep an eye on whether a timing point can be affected by Community law.

22.27 The general time limit for many European derived causes of action (such as sexual orientation discrimination) is three months (plus an additional three-month extension pursuant to the Employment Act 2002 if the grievance was made in time) and a discretionary extension when this is 'just and equitable'. The similarity to other domestic discrimination employment claims means that it is most unlikely, of itself, to be held to be contrary to the European principles of effectiveness and equivalence (see, eg, *Emmott and Livingstone v Hepworth Refractories plc* [1992] IRLR 63). In European claims it is important for employment lawyers to be sensitive to the following timing points:

- The Tribunal only has jurisdiction conferred on it by statute. However, the absence of a provision permitting retroactive application of the statute or regulations does not mean that claims cannot extend back to the date on which the Directive should have been implemented (*Impact*).
- In cases against public entities, the respondent cannot rely on the Member State's failure to implement a Directive on time to defeat a claimant's cause of action because to do so would permit the Member State to rely on its own wrong (*Emmott*, para 23).
- In similar cases against private entities, it is likely to be just and equitable to extend time to a claimant to when the Directive has been implemented into national law (conferring jurisdiction on the tribunal) (see *Cannon v Barnsley Metropolitan Council* [1992] ICR 698 at 704, where the principle was developed in relation to a public body).
- *Impact* also makes clear that this extension of time backwards applies both to directly effective and indirectly effective claims. However, a statute/regulation can only be disapplied if the right in the Directive has direct effect and the respondent is a public body.

Francovich claims

22.28 One type of claim under EC law which tribunals do not have jurisdiction over are claims for tortious State liability based on a Member State's failure properly to implement EC legislation/having committed a sufficiently serious breach of EC law (see *Secretary of State for Employment v Mann* [1997] ICR 209). Such claims are treated as being a species of the tort of breach of statutory duty, over which the tribunal has no jurisdiction (see *Spencer v Secretary of State for Work and Pensions* [2008] EWCA Civ 750, [2009] 2 WLR 593 [2008] IRLR 911 for an analysis of limitation issues).

D. REFERENCES TO THE EUROPEAN COURT OF JUSTICE

Discretion to refer

22.29 Article 234 of the EC Treaty declares that references to the ECJ may be made by 'any court or tribunal of a Member State'. This includes employment tribunals.

22.30 The criteria for seeking a reference are set out in the *CILFIT* case (Case 283/81 [1982] ECR 3415, paras 22.9–22.11):

> 9 In this regard, it must in the first place be pointed out that Article 177 (now 234) does not constitute a means of redress available to the parties to a case pending before a national court or tribunal. Therefore the mere fact that a party contends that the dispute gives rise to a question concerning the interpretation of community law does not mean that the court or tribunal concerned is compelled to consider that a question has been raised within the meaning of Article 177 (now 234). On the

> other hand, a national court or tribunal may, in an appropriate case, refer a matter to the Court of Justice of its own motion.
>
> 10 Secondly, it follows from the relationship between the second and third paragraphs of Article 177 (now 234) that the courts or tribunals referred to in the third paragraph have the same discretion as any other national court or tribunal to ascertain whether a decision on a question of community law is necessary to enable them to give judgment. Accordingly, those courts or tribunals are not obliged to refer to the Court of Justice a question concerning the interpretation of Community law raised before them if that question is not relevant, that is to say, if the answer to that question, regardless of what it may be, can in no way affect the outcome of the case.
>
> 11 If, however, those courts or tribunals consider that recourse to Community law is necessary to enable them to decide a case, Article 177 (now 234) imposes an obligation on them to refer to the Court of Justice any question of interpretation which may arise.

In *HP Bulmer v J Bollinger SA* [1974] Ch 40, Lord Denning MR set out a number of factors for a court to consider when making a reference. These guidelines have been criticized, as they considerably restrict the circumstances in which a court may make a reference, and in any event have been expressly overruled by Case C–106/89 *Marleasing SA v La Comercial Internacional de Alimentacion SA* [1990] ECR I–4135. The clearest statement by the United Kingdom courts of this principle is in *R v International Stock Exchange of the United Kingdom and the Republic of Ireland Ltd, ex p Else (1982) Ltd* [1993] 2 CMLR 677, (not an employment case) where it was said: **22.31**

> In relation to the determination of germane questions of Community law the correct approach in principle of a national court (other than a court of final appeal) is quite clear: if the facts have been found and the Community law issue is critical to the court's final decision, the appropriate course is ordinarily to refer the issue to the European Court unless the national court can with complete confidence resolve the issue itself. In considering whether it can resolve the issue itself the national court must be fully mindful of the difference between national and Community legislation, of the pitfalls which face a national court venturing into what may be an unfamiliar field, of the need for uniform interpretation throughout the Community and the great advantages enjoyed by the European Court in construing Community instruments. If the national court has any real doubt, it should refer.

Recently, in the ECJ Case C–303/06 *Coleman v Attridge Law* [2008] ICR 1128 the Netherlands Government sought to argue that the question was inadmissible on the basis that it did not determine the issues between the parties because the tribunal had not yet found that Ms Coleman had in fact suffered less favourable treatment or harassment because of her son's disability. The ECJ did not decline jurisdiction on this basis (paras 30–1), holding that the matter was primarily for the referring court. However, where the questions are 'manifestly unrelated to the reality or the subject matter' of the domestic proceedings the ECJ will be likely to decline jurisdiction. It is tactically important when considering whether a reference should be made to the ECJ (which takes between 18 months and two years to return to the tribunal) whether the tribunal should make key findings of fact first in order to determine whether it is necessary to make a reference. This point is reinforced in the Information Note on References from National Courts for a Preliminary Ruling in CPR 68 PD Annex, para 19. **22.32**

Form of reference

The reference takes the form of a question or questions for determination and is usually submitted in draft form by the parties' representatives for the tribunal to add to or amend as they see fit. If facts have been agreed or decided, they should be included in the reference, along with an outline of the opposing parties' contentions, a draft of the order sought, and a clear statement of the national law (so far as it can be agreed). **22.33**

There is useful and specific guidance which can be found in the CPR Part 68 PD 68 as to the form and content of a reference and the ECJ's information note on references from national courts for a preliminary ruling (published in the Official Journal 2005/C 143/01 and on the ECJ's website). The ECJ also provides notes for guidance to Council available from their website **22.34** which is essential reading for any party proposing a reference or dealing with European procedure once a reference is made.

22.35 It is the normal practice of the ECJ that costs incurred on a reference are to be treated as costs forming part of the proceedings before the national court, but the EAT has no power to award costs beyond those referred to in the rules so that no costs could in fact be awarded according to the EAT in *Burton v British Railways Board* [1983] ICR 544.

Stays

22.36 In order to avoid substantially identical references being made in cases which raise similar or the same issues, tribunals and courts generally order that those cases are stayed pending the outcome of the original reference (the principles are set out in *Johns v Solent* [2008] All ER (D) 18, CA, confirming the EAT [2008] IRLR 88, where it was stressed that it is not permissible for the domestic courts to speculate about the outcome of any referred case when deciding whether to stay or not).

23

Collective Labour Law Institutions—The Central Arbitration Committee and Certification Officer

SUMMARY

(1) The primary jurisdiction of the Central Arbitration Committee (CAC) is in respect of trade union recognition.

(2) The CAC may determine its own procedure.

(3) There is no direct appeal from the CAC in recognition cases but challenge may be made by way of an application for judicial review.

(4) The Certification Officer maintains a list of organizations which are trade unions or employers' associations and receives their annual returns and deals with matters in connection with political expenditure.

A. INTRODUCTION

The CAC is a permanent independent body of a judicial character established by statute (see TULR(C)A 1992, s 259(1) and (2)). Its main function now is to adjudicate on applications for statutory recognition and de-recognition of trade unions for collective bargaining purposes under Sch A1 to TULR(C)A 1992. It also has powers under the Information and Consultation of Employees Regulations 2004, SI 2004/3426, European Works Councils, the European Company Statute, and the disclosure of information for collective bargaining purposes. It can provide voluntary arbitration on a reference from ACAS. It has close ties to ACAS, who provide all its staff, equipment, and other facilities (TULR(C)A 1992, s 259(3)) and must be consulted on any appointment to its membership. **23.01**

The CAC is an unusual judicial body in that it does not have any formal rules of procedure because in the primary legislation, subject to specific provisions (of which there are few), it states that it 'shall determine its own procedure' (TULR(C)A 1992, s 263(5) and s 263A(7)). In all of its jurisdictions the CAC's approach is flexible and orientated towards practical problem solving. **23.02**

B. MEMBERSHIP

23.03 Appointment to membership of the CAC is by the Secretary of State (TULR(C)A 1992, s 260(1)). Members must be 'experienced in industrial relations' (TULR(C)A 1992, s 260(3)), and include persons who have experience as representatives of employers and persons who have experience as representatives of workers. Before making any appointment to the CAC the Secretary of State must consult ACAS and may also consult other persons (TULR(C)A 1992, s 260(3A)). Members normally have long experience in industry and are senior representatives of trade unions or employers' federations.

23.04 The Secretary of State also appoints from the members a chairman and deputy chairmen (TULR(C)A 1992, s 260(2)) of the CAC. The current Chairman is Sir Michael Burton, a High Court judge who was until 2006 also President of the EAT. The CAC consists of several deputy chairmen (who conduct most of the hearings, under powers contained in s 260(4) of TULR(C) A 1992 including well-known employment law academics such as Professors Paul Davies QC, Gillian Morris, and Roy Lewis) and lay members.

23.05 The only rules on the terms of appointment of members are set out in s 261 of TULR(C) A 1992. Amongst other rules, no term of appointment may exceed five years, but previous membership does not prevent reappointment beyond that five-year term (s 261(2)).

C. JURISDICTION

23.06 The CAC was first established by the Employment Protection Act 1975 as a permanent and independent industrial relations arbitration body. It succeeded what had been known as the Industrial Court. Its operation was at first quite narrowly focused and close to its precise name, that is it provided for voluntary and unilateral arbitrations. It then gained control of disclosure of information requests by trade unions (see TULR(C)A 1992, ss 183 and 184) but these are and always have been few and far between. The jurisdiction of the CAC was, however, much extended by the Employment Relations Act 1999 which introduced the compulsory trade union recognition provisions into Sch A1 to TULR(C)A 1992 and later by the Transnational Information and Consultation of Employee Regulations 1999, SI 1999/3323, and the European Company Statute (Council Regulation (EC) 2157/2001 [2001] OJ L294/1).

Information

23.07 Sections 181–5 of TULR(C)A 1992 gives the right of a recognized trade union to information from the employer for the purposes of collective bargaining, and the trade union may present a complaint to the CAC that an employer has failed to disclose the required information (s 183). If an employer then fails to disclose the necessary information the trade union may bring a further complaint under s 184 that the contracts of one or more descriptions of employees should include the terms and conditions specified in the complaint.

Union recognition

23.08 Under Sch A1 of TULR(C)A 1992 when a union(s) seeks recognition the CAC receives the applications under Part 1 and may make crucial decisions on the validity of the application for recognition, the bargaining unit, the method of balloting, and the method of collective bargaining. After recognition has been granted, it may need to decide whether a bargaining unit has in due course ceased to exist or to be appropriate in the particular circumstances, whether another bargaining unit is appropriate, and whether bargaining arrangements should cease to have effect.

European Works Councils

23.09 Under the Transnational Information and Consultation of Employees Regulations 1999 claims and complaints may be made to the CAC regarding the establishment and operation of European Works Councils. Employees may request information to assist them in determining whether their employer is part of a relevant EU-wide undertaking (reg 8) and the central management of that employer may apply to the CAC for a declaration that it is not such an undertaking (reg 10). Further applications may be made under regs 15 and 23. See also the Information and Consultation of Employees Regulations 2004, SI 2004/3426.

Trade disputes

Section 212 of TULR(C)A 1992 provides that where a trade dispute exists, the parties to that dispute may request ACAS to refer all or any of the matters in dispute to the CAC for settlement by way of arbitration. **23.10**

European public limited-liability company

The CAC now also has a role under the European Public Limited-Liability Company Regulations 2004, SI 2004/2326. Part 3 of the Regulations has requirements for the involvement of employees in such a company under the form of a Special Negotiating Body (SNB), and under reg 20 certain individuals may make a complaint to the CAC that a required SNB has not been or not been properly formed. **23.11**

D. PROCEEDINGS OTHER THAN UNDER SCH A1

When discharging its functions in any particular case (other than under Sch A1) the CAC consists of the chairman (or one of his deputies) and such other members as the chairman may direct (TULR(C)A 1992, s 263). **23.12**

The chairman also has the power to call in the aid of one or more assessors and rely on their assistance (TULR(C)A 1992, s 263(2)). **23.13**

The CAC has the power to sit in private if it appears expedient to do so, at the discretion of the chairman (TULR(C)A 1992, s 263(3)). Such situations are rare, and may involve the need to protect national security or commercial confidentiality. On occasions part of an application may be heard in private and the rest in public. **23.14**

The chairman has the powers of an umpire to decide on any award where the CAC cannot reach a unanimous decision (TULR(C)A 1992, s 263(4)). **23.15**

Subject to the above, the CAC determines its own procedures (TULR(C)A 1992, s 263(5)). **23.16**

E. RECOGNITION PROCEEDINGS

There are different provisions for trade union recognition cases. When discharging its functions in any matter under Sch A1 (its most usual fare), the CAC consists of a panel established under s 263A of TULR(C)A 1992. The chairman establishes particular panels to deal with particular cases (TULR(C)A 1992, s 263A(3)), to consist of the chairman (in fact this chairman has sat relatively infrequently) or a deputy chairman to chair the panel, a member whose experience is as a representative of employers, and a member whose experience is as a representative of workers (TULR(C)A 1992, s 263A(2)). **23.17**

Any panel has the power to sit in private if it appears expedient to do so (TULR(C)A 1992, s 263A(4)). Such situations are likely to be rare, and may only involve the need to protect national security or commercial confidentiality. **23.18**

Where a panel cannot reach a unanimous decision on a question arising before it the decision of the majority is held to be the decision of the panel (TULR(C)A 1992, s 263A(5)). However, if a panel cannot reach a unanimous decision on a question arising before it and there is no majority opinion, the chairman of the panel decides the question given the powers of an umpire, ie his decision is determinative of the issue. **23.19**

Subject to the above, the panel determines its own procedures (TULR(C)A 1992, s 263A(7)). **23.20**

23.21 Under Sch A1 panels have a general duty to 'have regard to the object of encouraging and promoting fair and efficient practices and arrangements in the workplace, so far as having regard to that object is consistent with applying other provisions of this Schedule is concerned' (para 171).

23.22 An application passes through various stages requiring input from the parties and the appropriate panel. Each application is assigned a case manager who takes an active role in procedural matters and seeks to ensure that deadlines are kept to and that there should be no adjournments because of lack of preparation of necessary documents. Especially tight deadlines are set down in the statutory recognition procedure with little scope for the CAC to waive a party's failure to meet a deadline. However, these deadlines may be extended with the consent of the parties or the CAC. Case managers usually sit in at the relevant hearing but have no decision-making role.

23.23 Generally, applications to start the recognition procedure and applications at various other stages (there are 17 possible applications) must be made 'in such form . . . and supported by such documentation as the CAC specifies'. Where such forms have been specified and an application is to be dealt with on paper, it will be important to comply with any requirements in relation to documentation. Both a Recognition Application Form and Employer's Questionnaire (to respond to an application) can be found on the CAC website.

23.24 Where the CAC is likely to decide a matter on paper and not by an oral hearing, it is important that a party asks for an oral hearing if the issue is sufficiently important that the parties wish for an oral hearing. Where it appears to the panel that a hearing will be necessary, the chairman of the panel may hold a preliminary meeting in order to set out procedures and identify the issues to be resolved.

23.25 Occasionally the CAC may appoint counsel specializing in employment law as an *amicus curiae* (friend of the court) to address a legal point which neither side has raised or wishes to raise, and which is thought to be of significance, or where neither party is legally represented nor wishes to be so and a legal point requires to be considered. By a statement in January 2004 (available at <http://www.cac.gov.uk/CHttpHandler.ashx?id=1166&p=0> (as accessed on 3 November 2009)), the Chairman of the CAC explained that the practice of appointing CAC panels is not affected by the decision of the House of Lords in *Lawal v Northern Spirit Ltd* [2003] IRLR 538. In that case it was decided that it was inappropriate for counsel to appear before panel members of the EAT with whom that counsel had previously sat as a (part-time) judge. Therefore counsel who has appeared as an *amicus curiae* before particular members will not be prevented from appearing as counsel for a party in a later case.

23.26 Decisions of the CAC on particular issues in one case do not bind later panels in other cases. However, such decisions may be referred to as guidance upon the manner in which issues have been resolved previously.

23.27 Two useful publications, 'Statutory Recognition—A guidance document for the Parties' and 'A guide for Employers and Employees to the role of the Central Arbitration Committee (CAC)' are available from the CAC website (see para 23.40 below).

F. HEARINGS

23.28 Cases are heard around the country, at places which are convenient to the parties in the particular matter, in hotels, country clubs, and other convenient venues. Most, however, are held in London, although currently not at the CAC's headquarters since there is no hearing room available there.

23.29 The approach of the CAC is generally quite informal (although the extent of this informality depends crucially on the personality of the deputy chairman involved) and normally all sit round a single table with name plates to indicate who everyone is and his or her role.

Some cases are dealt with in relative informality. Unusually sandwiches are served to the parties at lunch time.

There is often no formal divide between submissions and 'evidence', with each party being asked in turn to present their 'case'. Statements will have been exchanged between the parties at the discretion of the CAC and sent to the CAC itself in advance of the hearing. New evidence will be admitted at hearings only for good reasons and with the permission of the panel, and subject to any additional time being allowed for another party to consider it. Examination of the other side takes place with the consent of and through the deputy chair. The CAC may determine that in particular cases stricter, more conventional standards of evidence are required or that more formality in the proceedings is appropriate. **23.30**

The principles of natural justice (and Article 6 of ECHR) require that the CAC should consider any evidence put to it when deciding any particular questions, and that each side should have the opportunity to comment on the other side's evidence and submissions. Under the Transnational Information and Consultation of Employees Regulations 1999 (but not under the Sch 1A procedure) the CAC must make 'such enquiries as it sees fit' and seek out evidence (reg 38(2)). Under Sch 1A, the CAC has no power to order disclosure of documents other than those required for the initial application. **23.31**

G. ENFORCEMENT

The CAC does not have its own enforcement powers. However, the statutory procedures under which it has jurisdiction each provide directly or indirectly for various forms of enforcement in the civil courts and EAT. **23.32**

H. CHALLENGING DECISIONS

Under reg 38(8) of the Transnational Information and Consultation Regulations 1999, there exists a right of appeal to the EAT on any question of law arising from any declaration or order of, or arising from any proceedings of the CAC under the regulations. **23.33**

By para 165A of Sch 1A parties to the recognition procedure may appeal to the employment tribunal a demand for costs made under paras 19E(3), 28(4), or 120(4). **23.34**

Section 264 of TULR(C)A 1992 applies the 'slip rule' to awards, decisions, or declarations of the CAC, giving it the power to correct any clerical mistake or error arising from an accidental slip or omission. **23.35**

The only other way of challenging a CAC decision is by judicial review for which the procedure is set out in CPR r 52, and the only grounds on which an application for judicial review will succeed is if the CAC erred in law or reached a perverse conclusion which no reasonable CAC could reach. **23.36**

Where a decision to be challenged arises under Sch A1 the hearings may be very speedily arranged in order not to disrupt the strict time schedule imposed under the recognition procedure. Indeed, the CAC may not defer the ongoing timetable because an application for judicial review is made. Thus, in the case of *R v CAC, ex p Kwik Fit Ltd* [2002] EWCA Civ 512, [2002] IRLR 395, the hearing before the Administrative Court was held within three weeks of the CAC's decision and the Court of Appeal was convened three weeks thereafter. **23.37**

The claim for judicial review is brought against the CAC with the union potentially involved as an interested party. The interested party may gain costs of the proceedings if its arguments are successful. **23.38**

Parties considering a judicial review should note that the Administrative Court will be reluctant to interfere with decisions of the CAC given that it is a specialist body in an area which is **23.39** not suitable for detailed intervention by the courts (*ex p Kwik Fit Ltd*, above, see para 23.37; *R (on the application of the BBC) v CAC* [2003] EWHC 1375, [2003] ICR 1542, paras 14–16; *R (on the application of Ultraframe UK Ltd) v CAC* [2005] EWCA Civ 560, [2005] IRLR 1194, para 16; *R (NUJ) v CAC (Secretary of State for Trade and Industry intervening)* [2006] ICR 1). The CAC should not take a legalistic approach (*R (on the application of Cable & Wireless Services UK Ltd) v CAC and CWU* [2008] IRLR 425).

I. FURTHER INFORMATION

23.40 The CAC has a useful website at <http://www.cac.gov.uk> from which application forms to the CAC may be downloaded.

J. THE CERTIFICATION OFFICER

23.41 The certification officer is appointed by the Secretary of State for Business Enterprise and Regulatory Reform in consultation with ACAS under TULR(C)A 1992. He appoints his own assistants, including one for Scotland and his staff is provided by ACAS.

23.42 The certification officer carries on duties previously imposed on the Chief Registrar of Trade Unions and Employers' Associations under the Industrial Relations Act 1971. They are as follows:

(a) maintaining a list of organizations which are trade unions or employers' associations and receiving their annual returns under TULR(C)A 1992;
(b) dealing with matters in connection with political expenditure under TULR(C)A 1992;
(c) dealing with amalgamations of trade unions under the Trade Union (Amalgamations) Act 1964; and
(d) entertaining applications for breach of the requirement that a union elects its executive committee by secret ballot under TULR(C)A 1992.

23.43 In settling disputes between the union and one of its members, the certification officer often acts on the basis of written evidence and when hearings are necessary they are informal in procedure. There is an appeal from the certification officer's decision on both fact and law to the EAT.

23.44 In *Squibb UK Staff Association v Certification Officer* [1979] IRLR 76, the certification officer was put into the witness box and cross-examined on the validity of his decision on the granting of a certificate of independence to a trade union. The Court of Appeal considered that such practice was wrong. He was not to be treated as an opposing party, but rather as occupying a judicial position. He should not therefore be called upon to justify his adjudication under interrogation.

Part C

Remedies

24

Remedies for Unfair Dismissal

SUMMARY

(1) An award of unfair dismissal compensation is normally made up of a basic award and a compensatory award.

(2) An additional award of between 26 and 52 weeks' pay will be awarded where an employer fails to comply with an order for reinstatement or re-engagement unless it was not practicable to comply with such an order.

(3) An application for interim relief (interim re-employment) may be made in trade union dismissals (ie dismissals relating to union membership reasons), in dismissals for reasons relating to carrying out health and safety responsibilities and/or 'whistle-blowing' dismissals.

(4) The basic award is calculated in accordance with a statutory formula which is similar to a redundancy payment except that there is no minimum or maximum age requirement.

(5) The compensatory award is calculated in accordance with ERA 1996, s 123(1)–(3) and is based on the economic loss suffered by the claimant as a consequence of dismissal insofar as this is attributable to the actions of the employer.

(6) The assessment of future loss involves a consideration of both 'old job facts' involving a consideration of how long the old job was likely to continue and, where there is a continuing loss, 'new job facts', whether the claimant is likely to find a new job, if so when and how long the loss is likely to continue.

(7) Compensation for injured feelings may not be recovered as part of the compensatory award.

(8) There is statutory power to increase the compensatory award where an employer fails to comply with the statutory disputes resolution procedure set out in Sch 2 to the Employment Act 2002. Other than in exceptional circumstances, such a failure will result in the award being increased by a minimum of 10 per cent but may be increased by as much as 50 per cent. (There is an equivalent power to decrease the award where an employee fails to comply with the statutory disputes procedure—see Chapter 25.) These provisions were repealed by the Employment Act 2008 which introduced a new power to increase or reduce the award where there has been an unreasonable failure to comply with the ACAS Code of Practice.

A. INTRODUCTION

24.01 The remedies for unfair dismissal are set out in ERA 1996, ss 112–124.

24.02 An award of unfair dismissal compensation is usually made up of a basic award (ERA 1996, ss 119–120) and a compensatory award (ERA 1996, ss 123–4). However, where an employment tribunal makes an order for reinstatement or re-engagement pursuant to ERA 1996, s 113, and an employer fails to comply with such an order, the tribunal has the power to make an additional award (ERA 1996, s 117).

24.03 Each of the statutory awards is subject to prescribed statutory maxima. These are reviewed annually and increased or decreased by statutory instrument in line with changes in the RPI index. The new rates are normally announced and laid before Parliament in early December and come into force with effect from 1 February the following year (Employment Relations Act 1999, s 34).

B. RE-EMPLOYMENT ORDERS

24.04 Where a complaint of unfair dismissal is successful, the tribunal is required to explain to the claimant what orders may be made under ERA 1996, s 113, the circumstances in which they may be made, and to ask the claimant whether he or she wishes the tribunal to make such an order. If the claimant does wish the tribunal to make such an order, it may do so (ERA 1996, s 113(3)).

24.05 A failure to consider making such an order where it is requested by the claimant may amount to an error of law (*Cruickshank v London Borough of Richmond* EAT/483/97). The requirements of ERA 1996, s 113 are mandatory and a failure to explain the orders amounts to an error of law (*Pirelli General Cable Works Ltd v Murray* [1979] IRLR 190) but this may not apply in certain situations, ie *Richardson v Walker* EAT/312/79, where the claimant had found a new job, and *Pratt v Pickfords Removals Ltd* EAT/43/86, where the complainant contributed 100 per cent to the dismissal. A failure to comply with these provisions does not render the decision on compensation a nullity (*Cowley v Manson Timber Ltd* [1995] IRLR 153).

Types of order

24.06 An employment tribunal is empowered to make two types of orders: an order for reinstatement (ERA 1996, s 114) or an order for re-engagement (ERA 1996, s 115).

An order for reinstatement is an order that the employer shall treat the complaint in all respects as if he had not been dismissed (ERA 1996, s 114). An order for re-engagement is an order, on such terms as the employment tribunal may decide, that the complainant be engaged by the employer, or by a successor of the employer, or by an associated employer, in employment comparable to that from which he was dismissed or other suitable employment (ERA 1996, s 115). **24.07**

Choice of order

In exercising its discretion whether to make a re-employment order, the tribunal must first consider whether to make an order for reinstatement and in so doing the tribunal must take into account: **24.08**

(a) whether the complainant wishes to be reinstated;
(b) whether it is practicable for the employer to comply with an order for reinstatement; and
(c) where the complainant has caused or contributed to some extent to the dismissal, whether it would be just to order reinstatement.

(ERA 1996, s 116(1)(a))

If the tribunal decides not to make an order for reinstatement, it must then consider whether to make an order for re-engagement and, if so, on what terms (ERA 1996, s 116(2)). **24.09**

In so doing the tribunal must take into account: **24.10**

(a) any wish expressed by the complainant as to the nature of the order to be made;
(b) whether it is practicable for the employer (or a successor or an associated employer) to comply with an order for re-engagement; and
(c) where the complainant caused or contributed to some extent to the dismissal, whether it would be just to order his re-engagement and (if so) on what terms.

(ERA 1996, s 116(3))

These factors are looked at in greater detail below.

Wishes of complainant

No order can be made if the claimant does not want to be reinstated or re-engaged which accounts in part for the small number of orders that are made (ERA 1996, s 112(2) and (3)). **24.11**

Practicability of compliance

The practicability of compliance is an important factor in determining whether such an order should be made. It is also relevant to the issue of enforcement of such an order: a tribunal must consider this factor at both stages and cannot postpone its consideration until the enforcement stage (*Port of London Authority v Payne* [1994] IRLR 9). **24.12**

In deciding whether a re-employment order is practicable, the tribunal should consider whether, having regard to the employment relations realities of the situation, it is capable of being put into effect with success (*per* Stephenson LJ in *Coleman and Stephenson v Magnet Joinery Ltd* [1974] IRLR 343). What is 'practicable' should not be equated with what is 'possible' and in this context, the tribunal may take into account the impact the order has on other staff (*Meridian Ltd v Gomersall* [1977] IRLR 425). However, mere inexpediency is no bar to re-employment (*Qualcast (Wolverhampton) Ltd v Ross* [1979] IRLR 98). **24.13**

It should also be remembered that at this stage the tribunal is only required to 'consider' the issue of practicability and therefore the tribunal's assessment on the issue of practicability is provisional. It is not uncommon for tribunals to make an order to test whether or not employer claims of impracticability are justified (*Timex Corporation Ltd v Thomson* [1981] IRLR 522 and *Freemans plc v Flynn* [1984] IRLR 486). A tribunal may therefore make an order where an employer claims that there is no vacancy (*Electronic Data Processing Ltd v Wright* 1986 IRLR 8) **24.14** or where the reason for dismissal was redundancy (*Polkey v AE Dayton Services* [1988] AC 344, [1987] IRLR 503). But such orders are unlikely where the employer believes that the employee is incapable of doing the job or has a genuine fear that the employee will not be able to do the job without endangering those in his care (*ILEA v Gravett* [1988] IRLR 497). An order is also unlikely where there has been a fundamental loss of trust between the parties (*Nothman v London Borough of Barnet (No 2)* [1980] IRLR 65) particularly where the employer is small and the job involves a close working relationship (*Enessy Co SA (t/a The Tulcan Estate) v Minoprio* [1978] IRLR 489). It has been suggested that such a re-employment order will only be made in the rarest of cases where there has been a breakdown in trust and confidence (*Wood Group Heavy Industrial Turbines Ltd v Crossan* [1998] IRLR 680) but tribunals should not necessarily conclude that re-employment is impracticable because of the claimant's conduct of litigation (*Cruickshank v London Borough of Richmond* EAT/483/97).

Contributory fault

24.15 Tribunals are also required to consider whether re-employment is just in the light of the employee's contributory conduct. The test to be applied is the same as under ERA 1996, s 123(6) (*Boots Company Ltd v Lees-Collier* [1986] ICR 728), ie the conduct involved must be blameworthy (see para 25.40 *et seq*. below). However, a finding of contributory conduct does not rule out the possibility of a re-employment order being made although such an order is unlikely where the employee is substantially to blame for the dismissal (*Nairne v Highlands and Islands Fire Brigade* [1989] IRLR 366).

Other factors

24.16 In addition to these requirements, a tribunal may take into account other factors in deciding whether or not to make a re-employment order. For example, in *Port of London Authority v Payne*, the EAT thought that the tribunal should have taken into account the claimants' ability to repay the severance payments they had received from their employers. Similarly tribunals may take into account the impact the order would have on employment relations generally (*Coleman v Magnet Joinery Ltd* [1974] ICR 46) or the personal relationships with other employees (*Intercity East Coast Ltd v McGregor* EAT/473/96: reinstatement was not practicable because of the acrimonious relationship between employee and supervisor to which the employee had contributed).

Permanent replacements

24.17 Reinstatement or re-engagement is not necessarily considered impracticable simply because the employer has taken on a permanent replacement. ERA 1996, s 116(5) provides that where an employer has engaged a permanent replacement, this shall not be taken into account in deciding whether or not to make a re-employment order unless 'it was not practicable for [the employer] to arrange for the dismissed employee's work to be done without engaging a permanent replacement' or the employer engaged the replacement 'after the lapse of a reasonable period without having heard from the dismissed employee that he wished to be reinstated or re-engaged', and at the time the replacement was taken on, 'it was no longer reasonable for [the employer] to have the dismissed employee's work to be done except by a permanent replacement'(ERA 1996, s 116(6)).

24.18 The effect of ERA 1996, s 116 is that the employer will be required to dismiss a permanent replacement if an order is made unless the proviso referred to above applies. The effect of this provision appears to have been overlooked by the EAT in *Cold Drawn Tubes Ltd v Middleton* [1992] IRLR 160.

Duty to give reasons

24.19 The tribunal must give its reasons for making or refusing such an order and in particular the reasons why it considers the order to be practicable or otherwise (*Port of London Authority v Payne* [1992] IRLR 447, EAT and *Clancy v Cannock Chase Technical College & Parkers* [2001] IRLR 331).

Terms of the order

Reinstatement

ERA 1996, s 114(2) provides that on making an order for reinstatement, the tribunal must specify: **24.20**

(a) any amount payable by the employer in respect of any benefit which the complainant might reasonably be expected to have had but for the dismissal (including arrears of pay) for the period between the date of termination of employment and the date of reinstatement;
(b) any rights and privileges (including seniority and pension rights) which must be restored to the employee; and
(c) the date by which the order must be complied with.

(The amount under s 114(2)(a) is based on what the claimant would actually have earned during the period between dismissal and reinstatement.)

The tribunal can therefore require the employer to award full back pay, holiday pay, etc between the date of dismissal and reinstatement. This may include improvements in terms and conditions which have taken place in the interim (ERA 1996, s 114(3)). There is no statutory limit on the amount which the tribunal can award in this regard (ERA 1996, s 124(3)). **24.21**

However, in calculating the amount payable by the employer, tribunals must deduct the payments set out in ERA 1996, s 114(4), namely: **24.22**

(a) wages in lieu of notice or any *ex gratia* payment received by the employee from the employer in respect of the period between the date of termination and the date of reinstatement (see *Butlers v British Railways Board* EAT/510/89);
(b) any payments received by the employee in respect of employment with another employer in the same period; and
(c) such other benefits as the tribunal thinks fit in the circumstances.

No deduction should be made for contributory fault or a failure to mitigate (*City & Hackney Health Authority v Crisp* [1990] IRLR 47).

The Employment Protection (Recoupment of Jobseeker's Allowance and Income Support) Regulations 1996, SI 1996/2349 apply to the award. **24.23**

Re-engagement

ERA 1996, s 115(2) provides that on making an order for re-engagement, the tribunal must specify: **24.24**

(a) the identity of the employer;
(b) the nature of the employment;
(c) the remuneration for the employment;
(d) any amount payable by the employer in respect of any benefit which the complainant might reasonably be expected to have had but for the dismissal (including arrears of pay) for the period between the date of termination of employment and the date of re-engagement;
(e) any rights and privileges (including seniority and pension rights) which must be restored to the employee; and
(f) the date by which the order must be complied with.

Other than in cases where the claimant is found to have contributed to the dismissal, the tribunal is required to order re-engagement on such terms which are, so far as is reasonably practicable, as favourable as reinstatement (ERA 1996, s 116(4)) but the tribunal cannot order re-engagement on terms that are *more* favourable than if the employee had been reinstated (*Rank Xerox (UK) Ltd v Stryczek* [1995] IRLR 568). It is unclear whether the tribunal can require the employer to make reasonable adjustments to the employment where a dismissal is held to be both unfair and in breach of DDA 1995. **24.25**

24.26 The order should specify the place of employment and the nature of employment (*Rank Xerox (UK) Ltd v Stryczek* [1995] IRLR 568) and the date by which the order should be complied with (*Pirelli General Cable Works Ltd v Murray* [1979] IRLR 190).

24.27 The tribunal is entitled to award the full amount of back pay which has accrued between dismissal and the date when the order will take effect and the claimant may also recover compensation for any improvements in such terms and conditions between the date of dismissal and the date on which the order takes effect, though there is no authority on this point. There is no statutory limit on the amount the tribunal can award in this regard (ERA 1996, s 124(3)).

24.28 Credit must be given for payments that have been made to the claimant since dismissal such as wages in lieu, *ex gratia* payments, and any payments made by a new employer (ERA 1996, s 115(3)) but no deduction should be made for a failure to mitigate (*City & Hackney Health Authority v Crisp* [1990] IRLR 47).

24.29 The 1996 Recoupment Regulations (see Chapter 27 below) apply to the award.

Tribunal's duty to state terms

24.30 The tribunal is under a duty to state the terms of re-engagement. In effect, this means that it must write a new contract for the parties. It will not comply with the statutory requirements, if it leaves the parties to decide the terms of re-engagement (*Pirelli General Cable Works Ltd v Murray* [1979] IRLR 190) or leave the parties to agree the nature of the work and the rate of pay (*Stena Houlder Ltd v Keenan*, EATS/543/93).

Enforcing a re-employment order

24.31 The statutory provisions distinguish between partial compliance with the tribunal's order and non-compliance.

Partial compliance

24.32 The ERA 1996, s 117(1) provides that if an order for reinstatement or re-engagement is made and the complainant is reinstated or re-engaged but the terms of the order are not complied with, then the tribunal 'shall make an award of compensation'. In such circumstances, the amount of the award 'shall be such as the tribunal thinks fit having regard to the loss sustained by the complainant in consequence of the failure to comply fully with the terms of the order' (ERA 1996, s 117(2)). So where, for example, the employer fails to pay the arrears of pay due to the employee, the tribunal may order the employer to pay the arrears even if this exceeds the statutory maximum (ERA 1996, s 124(3)) but in relation to the other matters set out in ERA 1996, s 114(2) or 115(2), the tribunal can only award compensation up to the statutory maximum, £63,300 for the year beginning 1 February 2008, or where an award is made under either s 114(2)(a) or 115(2)(d), such residual amount as would take the award to the statutory maximum. There is no power to make an additional award in these circumstances.

Non-compliance

24.33 The ERA 1996, s 117(3) provides that if the claimant is not reinstated or re-engaged, the tribunal is required, subject to the defence of impracticability, to make an additional award as well as a standard award of compensation for unfair dismissal calculated in accordance with ERA 1996, ss 118–127. *Note*: reinstatement on different terms from that ordered by the tribunal amounts to non-compliance (*Artisan Press Ltd v Srawley and Parker* [1986] IRLR 126).

Additional award

24.34 The additional award is fixed by ERA 1996, s 117(3)(b) as an amount of not less than 26 weeks' pay and not more than 52 weeks' pay subject to the statutory maximum. The current statutory maximum is £19,760 with effect from 1 October 2009.(The rules on the calculation of a week's pay are summarized at para 24.56 below.)

The additional award is a penalty for non-compliance with the order and therefore the most important factor in deciding how much to award is the employer's conduct. The more serious the violation, the higher the award, but where it is found that even though it was practicable to comply, the employer faced genuine difficulties, the award may be lower (*Morganite Electrical Carbon Ltd v Donne* [1987] IRLR 363). Another relevant factor is the extent to which the employer has complied with the ancillary parts of the order, for example that he has paid any of the back-pay due to the employee. The tribunal may also take into account the extent to which the compensatory award compensates the employee for the financial loss suffered, whether the employee has taken steps to mitigate the loss (although no specific reduction should be made for this reason), the extent to which the employee contributed to the dismissal and, possibly, the injury to feelings suffered by the employee as a result of the dismissal, see *Morganite Electrical Carbon v Donne* and *Mabrizi v National Hospital for Nervous Diseases* [1990] IRLR 428. **24.35**

Defence of impracticability

No additional award is payable if the employer can show that 'it was not practicable to comply with the order' (ERA 1996, s 117(4)(a)). **24.36**

In determining whether the defence is made out, the tribunal is not restricted to considering the events which have taken place since the order was made. The tribunal may take account of all the relevant facts both before and after the date of the order (*Freemans plc v Flynn* [1984] IRLR 486). The employer therefore has a second opportunity to raise the objections raised in the first place to the order being made because, as stated at para 24.13, those objections do not necessarily prevent the order from being made. Employers are not under a duty to create a special job for the employee to do or to dismiss existing employees to enable them to re-employ the complainant (*Freemans plc v Flynn* [1984] IRLR 486). Subject to the rules on 'permanent replacements', it will not be practicable to comply with the order if this would result in over-manning or a redundancy situation (*Cold Drawn Tubes Ltd v Middleton* [1992] IRLR 160). Furthermore, whilst the tribunal will scrutinize the employer's reasons for failing to comply with the order, due weight should be given to the commercial judgment of management and the employer cannot be expected to explore every avenue which ingenuity might suggest (*Payne v Port of London Authority* [1994] IRLR 9). **24.37**

Non-compliance by employee

Where the tribunal finds that the claimant has unreasonably prevented an order under ERA 1996, s 114 or 115 from being complied with, it must treat the employee's conduct in this regard as a failure to mitigate under ERA 1996, s 123(4) (ERA 1996, s 117(8)). **24.38**

Relationship between additional and compensatory award

Where an employer fails to comply with an order for reinstatement and re-engagement, the tribunal is empowered to make an award in respect of arrears of pay and other matters specified in ERA 1996, s 114(2)(a) and s 115(2)(d) in excess of the statutory maximum, but in those circumstances it is not open to it to make an additional award or a compensatory award (*Selfridges Ltd v Malik* [1997] IRLR 577; *Parry v National Westminster Bank plc* [2005] IRLR 193). **24.39**

C. INTERIM RE-EMPLOYMENT

An application for interim relief (that is interim re-employment) may be made where an employee claims to have been dismissed for union-related reasons, for union membership reasons, for reasons relating to carrying out health and safety responsibilities, or for reasons relating to 'protected disclosures' under the Public Interest Disclosure Act 1998. **24.40**

24.41 The procedure in trade union cases is set out in TULR(C)A 1992, ss 161–3. The procedure in whistle-blowing and health and safety cases is set out in ERA 1996, ss 128–9.

24.42 An application for interim relief must be made within seven days of the effective date of dismissal (TULR(C)A 1992, s 161(2); ERA 1996, s 128(2)). In the case of dismissal for union membership, it must be supported by a certificate in writing signed by an authorized official of the independent trade union of which the employee was or had proposed to become a member stating that there are reasonable grounds for supposing that the reason or principal reason for dismissal was the one alleged in the complaint (TULR(C)A 1992, s 161(3)). There is no equivalent requirement in ERA 1996. On receipt of the application, the employment tribunal is under a statutory duty to determine the matter 'as soon as practicable', though the employer must be given at least seven days' notice of the hearing (TULR(C)A 1992, s 161(2); ERA 1996, s 128(4)). Furthermore, where it is proposed to join the trade union as a party to the proceedings, the union must be given at least three days' notice of the hearing (TULR(C)A 1992, s 162(3)). The tribunal may postpone the hearing in special circumstances (TULR(C)A 1992, s 162(4); ERA 1996, s 128(5)).

24.43 If at the hearing of the application for interim relief, the tribunal is satisfied that it is likely that on determining the complaint to which the application relates, the tribunal will find that the complaint was unfairly dismissed, it must announce its findings and explain to both parties its powers under TULR(C)A 1992, s 163; ERA 1996, s 129.

24.44 Broadly, these are:

(a) if the employer is willing to reinstate the employee, to order interim reinstatement until the case is heard or settled (TULR(C)A 1992, s 163(4); ERA 1996, s 129(3)(a));
(b) if the employer is willing to re-engage the employee, to order interim re-engagement until the case is heard or settled (TULR(C)A 1992, s 163(5); ERA 1996, s 129(3));
(c) if the employer is unwilling to reinstate or re-engage the employee, to order that the contract of employment shall continue in force, irrespective of whether it has been terminated until the case is heard or settled (TULR(C)A 1992, ss 163(6) and 164(2); ERA 1996, s 130(1)). The tribunal is required to specify in its order 'the amount which is to be paid by the employer to the employee' (TULR(C)A 1992, s 164(2); ERA 1996, s 130(2)), though in making the order it will take account of any payment made by the employer such as payment in lieu of notice (TULR(C)A 1992, s 164(5) and (6); ERA 1996, s 130(5) and (6)).

24.45 On the application of either party, the tribunal may 'at any time between the making of an order' under these provisions and 'the determination or settlement of the complaint, revoke or vary its order on the ground of a relevant change in circumstances' (TULR(C)A 1992, s 165; ERA 1996, s 131).

24.46 The penalty for a failure to comply with the terms of a continuation order is set out in TULR(C)A 1992, s 166 and ERA 1996, s 132. This provides that if, on the application of an employee, the tribunal is satisfied that the employer has failed to comply with an order of continuation of the contract, for example by not paying the employee the amount stated under the order, the tribunal is required to determine the amount of pay owed by the employer and order that the sum due is paid to the employee by way of additional compensation at the 'full' hearing. In cases where the employer has failed to comply with some other aspect of the tribunal's order, for example in relation to pension rights or similar matters, the tribunal may award such compensation as it considers just and equitable in the circumstances.

24.47 In effect these provisions enable the tribunal to ensure that the employee is either reinstated or re-engaged or suspended on full pay until the case is resolved. Any sums paid under these orders are not recoverable in the event that the employee loses the substantive complaint of unfair dismissal (*Initial Textile Services v Rendell* EAT/383/91).

D. COMPENSATION FOR UNFAIR DISMISSAL

ERA 1996, s 112 provides that if no order for reinstatement or re-engagement is made under s 113, the tribunal shall make an award of compensation for unfair dismissal calculated in accordance with ERA 1996, ss 118–127 to be paid by the employer to the employee. **24.48**

The unfair dismissal award consists of a basic award calculated in accordance with ERA 1996, ss 119–122 and a compensatory award calculated in accordance with ERA 1996, ss 124, 126, and 127. **24.49**

E. BASIC AWARD

Calculating the basic award

ERA 1996, s 119(1) provides that the basic award shall be calculated by: **24.50**

(a) determining the period, ending with the effective date of termination during which the employee has been continuously employed;
(b) reckoning backwards from the end of that period the number of years of employment falling within that period; and
(c) allowing the appropriate amount for each of those years of employment.

The statutory formula is subject to a maximum of 20 years of employment. Thus the maximum award is 30 weeks' pay (ERA 1996, s 119(3)) but this is not subject to any statutory age limit.

ERA 1996, s 119(2) defines the 'appropriate amount' as: **24.51**

(a) one and a half weeks' pay for a year of employment in which the employee was not below the age of forty-one,
(b) one week's pay for a year of employment (not within paragraph (a)) in which he was not below the age of twenty-two, and
(c) half a week's pay for a year of employment not within paragraph (a) or (b).

Note: This formula has not been changed as a result of the implementation of the EEAR 2006, SI 2006/1031.

Effective date of termination

The effective date of termination is defined in ERA 1996, s 97. Where an employer summarily dismisses an employee or gives him less than the period of notice guaranteed by the statutory provisions, the effective date of termination is the date on which the statutory period of notice would have expired had it been given (ERA 1996, s 97(2)(b)). Similarly if an employee is constructively dismissed, the effective date of termination is extended by the statutory period of notice (ERA 1996, s 97(4)). However, where the employer gives notice which is equivalent to or greater than the statutory minimum the effective date of termination is the date on which the notice expires (ERA 1996, s 97(2)). **24.52**

Age

The statutory provisions make it clear that years which span the 22nd or 41st year do count, but it is not entirely clear whether they count at the higher or lower rate. **24.53**

There is no minimum or lower age limit or upper age limit (Employment Equality (Age) Regulations, SI 2006/1031, Sch 8, Part 2, para 25). The previous provisions which provided for the scaling down of the award in the 64th year have been repealed by the EEAR 2006, SI 2006/1031 (Sch 8, Part 2, para 27). **24.54**

A week's pay

24.55 For the purpose of calculating the basic award, the calculation date, (ie the date on which a week's pay is calculated) is:

(a) the employee's last day of work, if the notice which is given is less than the statutory notice laid down in ERA 1996, s 86 or in the case of a woman who is not permitted to return from maternity leave, the last day she worked before the beginning of her maternity leave period;
(b) the date when notice is given if the employee gives or is given statutory notice (ERA 1996, s 226);
(c) the latest date when the employer would have needed to give statutory notice if more than the statutory minimum is given, ie this date is determined by ascertaining the statutory minimum period of notice and calculating the latest day when the employer would have needed to give notice in order for the employee's contract to have been terminated on the day that the employee actually left work (ERA 1996, s 226(6)).

24.56 The rules for calculating a week's pay are set out in ERA 1996, ss 220–9 and may be summarized as follows:

(a) The rules governing the calculation of a week's pay depend on whether or not the employment is one with normal working hours. There is no comprehensive definition of normal working hours but, in general, employments which follow a fixed pattern of work will be treated as employment with normal working hours. This will include time workers, piece workers, and most shift workers, but employees whose hours of work fluctuate with the demands of the business are likely to be treated as having no normal working hours.
(b) In most cases, the crucial issue is what hours count as *normal* working hours. This is based on the minimum number of hours of work the employer guarantees by the terms of the contract. Overtime hours do not normally count unless overtime is guaranteed and required to be worked (*Lotus Cars Ltd v Sutcliffe* [1982] IRLR 381).
(c) Not all payments received by employees count towards a week's pay. Most contractual payments do count such as wages, salaries, shift bonuses, and productivity bonuses, but overtime payments will not count unless these form part of an employee's normal working hours or the employment is one with no normal working hours.
(d) The calculation is based on an employee's gross earnings (ie earnings before the deduction of tax and national insurance).
(e) There are four different ways of calculating a week's pay. In the case of most workers (time workers) a week's pay is simply the amount which they earn during the normal working week but the rules are complicated in relation to piece workers, shift workers, and those who have no normal working hours.

24.57 The amount of a week's pay which counts towards a basic award is current capped at £380 per week with effect from 1 October 2009. The current maximum is therefore £11,400.

Example
An employee aged 30 earning £500 per week is dismissed after working for an employer for six years. The basic award is 6 x 1 x £380 = £2,280.

Minimum basic award

24.58 Generally, there is no minimum basic award. However, statute does provide for a minimum basic award in two specific situations:

Union-related and health and safety dismissals

24.59 Where employees are dismissed for reasons which are regarded as unfair under TULR(C)A 1992, ss 152 and 153 or ERA 1996, s 100(1)(a) and (b) and s 103, the statutory minimum remains at £4,700 for the year beginning 1 February 2010. This is reviewed annually as increased or decreased in line with the Employment Relations Act 1999, s 34.

Automatically unfair dismissals

A minimum basic award of four weeks' pay is awarded where a dismissal is regarded as automatically unfair pursuant to ERA 1996, s 98A(1) (ie where the employer has failed to comply with the statutory disputes procedure) if the compensatory award is less than this amount (ERA 1996, s 120(1A)). Such an award need not be made if it would result in injustice to the employer (ERA 1996, s 120(1B)). This provision was repealed with effect from 1 April 2009. **24.60**

Redundancy dismissals

An employee is not entitled to receive both a basic award and a redundancy payment. In cases of redundancy, therefore, the redundancy payment is deducted from the basic award (ERA 1996, s 122(4)). However, such a deduction will not be made if the tribunal finds that redundancy was not the real reason for dismissal (*Boorman v Allmakes Ltd* [1995] IRLR 553). For example, if an employer mistakenly makes a redundancy payment where the dismissal was unfair under TUPE 1981, the employee would be entitled to a basic award despite receiving a redundancy payment. **24.61**

This general exclusion does not apply in two situations: the first is where an employee is selected for redundancy in breach of TULR(C)A 1992, s 153, ie for a reason related to trade union membership or where a workers' representative is selected for redundancy for carrying out health and safety duties pursuant to ERA 1996, s 100(1)(a) and (b), and ss 101A(d), 102(1) and 103. In such circumstances, an employee is entitled to a minimum basic award as well as a redundancy payment (TULR(C)A 1992, s 159; ERA 1996, s 120(1)). The second is where the principal reason for dismissal is redundancy but the employee is ineligible for a redundancy payment because he has: (a) unreasonably refused an offer of suitable employment (ERA 1996, s 141(2)); or (b) unreasonably terminated or given notice to terminate a trial period (ERA 1996, s 141(4)(d)); or (c) had his contract renewed or is re-engaged under a new employment contract pursuant to ERA 1996, s 141(1), so that there is no dismissal. In such circumstances the employee is entitled to a maximum basic award of two weeks' pay (ERA 1996, s 121). **24.62**

Reducing the basic award

The basic award may be reduced or further reduced where any conduct of the employee (including any conduct which did not contribute to the dismissal) was such that it would be 'just and equitable' to reduce or further reduce the award (ERA 1996, s 122(2)). **24.63**

The power to reduce the basic award for contributory fault is therefore wider than the power to reduce the compensatory award for contributory fault (*Optikinetics Ltd v Whooley* EAT/1275/97) because any conduct may be taken into account and misconduct which was not known at the time of dismissal may be taken into account even though it did not contribute to the dismissal (*Parker Foundry Ltd v Slack* [1992] IRLR 11) but the case law relating to what amounts to contributory fault for this purpose is the same (see para 25.40 below). **24.64**

Unreasonable refusal of offer of reinstatement

The basic award may also be reduced by such extent as the tribunal considers just and equitable having regard to its finding that the employee 'has unreasonably refused an offer by the employer which (if accepted) would have the effect of reinstating the complainant in all respects as if he had not been dismissed' (ERA 1996, s 122(1)). This provision will apply only where the employer makes an offer which complies with the statutory provisions. An offer of a different job or the same job on less favourable terms would appear to be insufficient (*Artisan Press Ltd v Srawley and Parker* [1986] IRLR 126). Otherwise the factors in determining when it is unreasonable to turn down such an offer are similar to those referred to in mitigation cases (see para 25.31 below). Such a reduction will normally be made where the employee is found to have acted unreasonably, but a tribunal is not bound to make a reduction if it feels that this would not be just and equitable (see *Muirhead & Maxwell Ltd v Chambers* EAT/516/82, where the employee turned down the offer because he feared victimization). **24.65**

Restrictions in union membership dismissals

24.66 Special statutory rules apply to the reduction in the basic award in union membership cases. No reduction or further reduction in the basic award should be made where the employee's conduct amounts to a breach of a requirement to be a union member or non-member, or to take part in trade union activities. Tribunals should ignore a refusal to comply with a requirement to make a payment in lieu of union subscriptions or an objection to deduction from pay for that purpose. It is hard to imagine a case where the employee would be held to have contributed to a dismissal under TULR(C)A 1992, ss 152 and 153. Furthermore, as a general rule there can be no reduction in the basic award for contributory fault where the reason or principal reason for dismissal is redundancy. However, the restriction does not apply where an employee is entitled to receive a minimum basic award (see para 24.68 below). In such circumstances, the minimum basic award can be reduced for contributory fault but the reduction applies only to so much of the basic award as is payable under ERA 1996, s 120. For example, an employee with two years' service who earns £380 per week and is selected for redundancy for union-related reasons would normally be entitled to a redundancy payment of £760 but is entitled to a minimum basic award of £4,700 and therefore would be entitled to an award of £3,940.

Other deductions

24.67 The basic award is a statutory award and therefore may only be reduced where this is permitted by statute (*Cadbury Ltd v Doddington* [1977] IRLR 982); it cannot therefore be reduced where the employee failed to mitigate his loss (*Lock v Connell Estate Agents Ltd* [1994] IRLR 44) or where the tribunal considers it just and equitable (*Sahil v Kores Nordic (GB) Ltd* EAT/379/90). But it has been held that where an *ex gratia* payment is specifically referable to the employee's statutory right to unfair dismissal compensation (ie the payment is specifically referable to the basic and compensatory awards), the payment may be relied on as a defence to the employer's statutory liabilities (*Chelsea Football Club and Athletic Co Ltd v Heath* [1981] IRLR 73; cf *Pomphrey of Sittingbourne Ltd v Reed* EAT/457/94, where the payment was referred to as a payment in lieu of notice and therefore was not a defence to statutory liability).

F. THE COMPENSATORY AWARD

Introduction

24.68 The compensatory award will usually make up the largest part of the award of compensation for unfair dismissal. ERA 1996, s 123(1) provides that:

> Subject to the provisions of this section and sections 124 and 126, the amount of the compensatory award shall be such amount as the tribunal considers just and equitable in all the circumstances having regard to the loss sustained by the complainant in consequence of the dismissal in so far as that loss is attributable to action taken by the employer.

24.69 This provision gives employment tribunals a wide discretion over the assessment of the compensatory award. Where the claim is relatively small, tribunals are likely to approach the task with a minimum amount of technicality. In the past, this approach has been encouraged by the EAT and the Court of Appeal. In *Fougère v Phoenix Motor Co Ltd* [1976] IRLR 259, the EAT stressed that tribunals are 'bound by necessity to operate in a rough and ready manner and to paint the picture with a broad brush' rather than as skilled cost accountants or actuaries (although it should be noted that these decisions preceded the increase in the compensatory award). Nonetheless, in *Norton Tool Co Ltd v Tewson* [1973] 1 All ER 183, it was recognized that the discretion conferred by ERA 1996, s 123(1) must be exercised 'judiciously and upon the basis of principle' and a tribunal must set out its reasons in sufficient detail to show the principles it has applied in making its assessment and, if necessary, how it has quantified the loss.

Meaning of loss

'Loss' is limited to financial or economic loss. It does not extend to non-pecuniary loss such as injury to health or injury to feelings (*Dunnachie v Kingston Upon Hull City Council* [2004] IRLR 727). **24.70**

The principal heads of compensation were identified by the NIRC in *Norton Tool Co Ltd v Tewson* [1973] 1 All ER 183 as follows: **24.71**

(a) immediate loss of earnings, ie the loss of earnings between the date of dismissal and the date of the hearing;
(b) future loss of earnings, ie anticipated loss of earnings in the period following the hearing;
(c) loss arising from the manner of dismissal; and
(d) loss of statutory rights.

Although the *Norton Tool* case refers to loss of earnings (and in many cases loss of earnings will make up the most substantial part of the claim), compensation may also be claimed for loss of benefits including loss of pensions (see para 24.95 below). Furthermore, by ERA 1996, s 123(2) loss is also taken to include '(a) any expenses reasonably incurred by the complainant in consequence of the dismissal, and (b) loss of any benefit which he might reasonably be expected to have had but for the dismissal'. Special provision is made for the loss of any entitlement or potential entitlement to a redundancy payment (see para 24.109 below). **24.72**

Compensation, not punishment

Generally, the object of the compensatory award is to compensate the claimant but not to punish or express disapproval of the employer's policies (*Lifeguard Assurance Ltd v Zadrozny* [1977] IRLR 56). **24.73**

There are two possible exceptions to the general principle that the award should be based strictly on the financial loss suffered by the claimant. First it is well established that a claimant is entitled to be compensated for the loss of statutory rights (see para 24.156 below). Secondly, it has been established that, as a matter of justice and equity, claimants are normally entitled to receive a minimum award equivalent to their notice pay (*Norton Tool Co Ltd v Tewson* [1973] 1 All ER 183; *TBA Industrial Products Ltd v Locke* [1984] IRLR 48; *Babcock FATA Ltd v Addison* [1987] IRLR 173), although it would appear that this exception does not apply where the claimant is employed under a fixed term contract (*Isleworth Studios Ltd v Rickard* [1988] IRLR 137). These latter decisions are now open to doubt in the light of the EAT ruling in *Hardy v Polk Ltd* [2004] IRLR 420 and *Morgans v Alpha Plus Security Ltd* [2005] IRLR 234, both decisions of Burton P. In the latter case in particular, the EAT considered that the earlier interpretations were inconsistent with the approach taken by the House of Lords in the *Dunnachie* case that compensation should only be awarded to cover actual financial loss suffered by the claimant. But these recent EAT rulings were not followed by the EAT in *Voith Turbo Ltd v Stowe* [2005] IRLR 228 (presided over by Judge McMullen QC). The approach of Burton P was followed by the EAT majority in *Langley v Burlo* [2006] IRLR 460. The EAT's reasoning, based on the *Dunnachie* ruling, was rejected when the *Burlo* case went to the Court of Appeal ([2007] IRLR 145), even though the outcome, what the Court of Appeal calls the 'pay point' (the correct rate of pay), namely that the claimant's loss during her eight-week notice period should be calculated on the statutory sick pay rate rather than her normal rate of pay, was upheld. Mummery LJ (with whom Leveson LJ agreed) refused to resolve the conflict in case law on this issue, whereas Smith LJ cast doubt on the principle of whether it is good employment practice for an employer to pay an amount equivalent to a payment in lieu. Nonetheless, at the time of writing, it would appear that whilst it remains good employment practice to make a payment in lieu of notice, a failure to do so will not necessarily result in a minimum award of a sum equivalent to such a payment. The *Norton Tool* principle does not apply to constructive documents (*Stuart Peters Ltd v Bell* [2009] IRLR 941). **24.74**

Proof of loss

24.75 Whilst it is the duty of the tribunal to raise each of the heads of compensation referred to above (*Tidman v Aveling Marshall Ltd* [1977] IRLR 218), it is up to the claimant to particularize the sums claimed. This point was stressed by the EAT in *Adda International Ltd v Curcio* [1976] IRLR 425, where, in the context of a claim for future loss of earnings, Bristow J said (at 427):

> The industrial tribunal must have something to bite on, and if an applicant produces nothing for it to bite on he will only have himself to thank if he gets no compensation for loss of future earnings.

24.76 The claimant should come to the tribunal well prepared with evidence which shows what his or her loss is under each heading of compensation. Failure to make a claim under one of the heads or to quantify a particular type of loss cannot normally be remedied on appeal (*UBAF Bank Ltd v Davis* [1978] IRLR 442).

24.77 Any relevant information which is not in the possession of the claimant should be obtained by way of a request for further information or (if necessary) an order for disclosure. This will be particularly important in relation to a claim for loss of pension rights where much of the relevant information is likely to be in the employer's possession or control (see, for example, *Benson v Dairy Crest Ltd* EAT/192/89). Once the claimant has produced evidence of loss, the evidential burden will then switch to the employer if the employer wishes to challenge the sums claimed by the claimant.

Remoteness

24.78 The employer is liable for all financial loss which flows directly from the dismissal provided it is 'attributable to the employer's actions' (see *Royal Court Hotel v Cowans* EAT/48/84), but compensation cannot be recovered if the loss suffered by the employee is too remote, ie if it does not arise as a 'consequence of dismissal' and/or is not 'attributable to the employer's action' (ERA 1996, s 123(1)).

24.79 It has been argued that the employer's liability ceases once the claimant finds a new job or undergoes a period of training. In some cases the EAT has accepted this argument and adopted a relatively strict approach to the issue of causation (see *Courtaulds Northern Spinning Ltd v Moosa* [1984] IRLR 43 and *Simrad Ltd v Scott* [1997] IRLR 147) but in *Dench v Flynn & Partners* [1998] IRLR 63, the Court of Appeal adopted a more liberal interpretation of ERA 1996, s 123(1) and held that, as a matter of justice and equity, loss consequent upon dismissal does not necessarily cease when the claimant finds a new job at an equivalent or higher salary if that job turns out to be temporary. The effect of the *Dench* decision is to focus on whether it is just and equitable for the claimant to recover compensation for continuing loss if the claimant, having lost the new job, is out of work at the time of the remedies hearing. Relevant factors will include the nature of the new job, whether it was intended to be temporary or permanent, how long the new employment lasted, the reasons for the claimant leaving, and whether the claimant is able to bring an unfair dismissal claim against the new employer. The *Dench* principle applies to all elements of the award, so it is wrong in principle for an employment tribunal to conclude that a new job meant that the claimant had no claim in respect of continuing loss regarding loss of earnings but could claim for loss of pensions when she subsequently lost the new job since either the loss ceases in these circumstances or it does not (*Aegon UK Corp Serves Ltd v Roberts* [2009] IRLR 1042). The position would have been different if the employment tribunal had not found, as a matter of causation, that the loss came to an end when Ms Roberts found her new job.

24.80 A similar approach has been applied to cases where the employee elects to retrain rather than look for a new job. In such circumstances, a tribunal must also consider the question of mitigation (see para 25.27 below) as well as the issue of causation. In *Simrad Ltd v Scott* [1997] IRLR 147, it was successfully argued that the employer's liability ceases under ERA 1996, s 123(1) where an individual chooses to undergo a period of training prior to embarking on a new career since any subsequent loss can no longer be attributed to the employer's action. But in *Khanum v IBC Vehicles Ltd* EAT/785/98 and *Larkin v Korean Airlines Ltd* EAT/1241/98 the EAT ruled that the claimant's decision to embark on a training course for a new career did not preclude the claimant from recovering compensation from her old employers for the loss suffered thereafter and this approach would appear to be consistent with the Court of Appeal's ruling in *Dench v Flynn & Partners* above.

Loss under ERA 1996 A.123(1) can only be awarded if it is sustained by the claimant as a 'consequence of the dismissal'. In *GAB Robins (UK) Ltd v Triggs* [2008] IRLR 317 the Court of Appeal ruled that an employee's loss under s 123(1) of the ERA 1996 does not cover financial loss arising as a result of personal injury caused by the employer's actions prior to dismissal. In support of its analysis, the Court relies on the House of Lords' ruling in *Eastwood v Magnox Electric plc and McCabe v Cornwall County Council* [2004] IRLR 733, where it was held that where an employer's pre-dismissal conduct is in breach of the duty of trust and confidence, this could give rise to an action for damages in the ordinary courts, even if compensation could not be awarded for such loss in an employment tribunal as a result of the House of Lords' ruling in *Johnson v Unisys Ltd* [1999] IRLR 279 (see para 24.154 below). On the facts in *Triggs*, the Court of Appeal ruled that the employment tribunal was wrong to direct that compensation could be awarded for future loss of earnings arising after the claimant's constructive dismissal caused by the employer's repudiatory breaches of the implied duty of trust and confidence, as the dismissal arose as a result of the employee's acceptance of the breach and therefore the loss was not consequent upon dismissal. It is unclear how far the court's ruling extends beyond the particular circumstances of that case, but it would appear to substantially limit the compensation which can be claimed by an employee who suffers illness as a result of an employer's pre-dismissal conduct which leads to a complaint of constructive dismissal. It is also unclear whether the same principle would apply to a direct dismissal (see para 24.154 below). **24.81**

In the rather unusual circumstances of *Sheffield Forgemasters International Ltd v Fox* [2009] IRLR 192 the EAT ruled that the employment tribunal had not erred in holding that the receipt of incapacity benefit did not preclude the claimants from obtaining compensation for loss of earnings during the same period. This was because the wording of s 30A of the Social Security Contributions and Benefits Act 1992 (and the Social Security (Incapacity for Work) (General) Regulations 1995), which determined the eligibility for incapacity benefit, did not preclude the individual from obtaining paid employment during the relevant period when benefit was payable. However, credit would have to be given for the value of such benefits received during that period (see para 24.134 below). **24.82**

Industrial pressure disregarded

ERA 1996, s 123(5) provides that in assessing the compensatory award, an employment tribunal should take no account of 'any pressure which. . . by calling, organising, procuring, or financing a strike or other industrial action or . . . threatening to do so, was exercised on the employer to dismiss the employee'. The assessment of compensation must be determined 'as if no pressure had been exercised'. **24.83**

Types of loss

It is established that compensation may be awarded for the following types of loss: **24.84**

(a) salary;
(b) pay rises;
(c) notice pay;
(d) holiday pay;
(e) redundancy pay;
(f) bonus;
(g) commission;

(h) pension;
(i) travel concessions;
(j) clothing allowances or free goods;
(k) stock options;
(l) private medical insurance;
(m) permanent health insurance;
(n) life insurance;
(o) financial benefits;
(p) company cars and free petrol allowance;
(q) free or subsidized accommodation;
(r) free or subsidized meals;
(s) free telephone and other electronic equipment;
(t) childcare costs;
(u) free club membership.

This list is not exhaustive as compensation can be claimed for the loss of any benefit which can be valued in money terms and which forms part of an employee's remuneration package.

Quantifying the loss

24.85 The object of the compensatory award is 'to compensate and compensate fully, but not to award a bonus' (*per* Sir John Donaldson in *Norton Tool Co Ltd v Tewson* [1973] 1 All ER 183). As stated above, the burden is on the claimant to quantify the loss suffered as a result of the dismissal, and who will normally be required to prepare a 'schedule of loss' prior to the hearing.

24.86 Guidance on how to quantify some of the more typical types of claim is given below.

Pay

24.87 As the EAT points out in *Brownson v Hire Services Shops Ltd* [1978] IRLR 73, 'other things being equal, the first thing you lose in consequence of being dismissed is what you would have got in your pay packet'. Pay for this purpose means all payments which are included in the 'pay packet' whether payable under the contract of employment as of right or otherwise (ie overtime pay) excluding the payment of genuine tax-free reimbursement of expenses (*Tradewinds Airways Ltd v Fletcher* [1981] IRLR 272). Pay is assessed on actual earnings as a net figure, ie after deduction of tax and national insurance. It has been held, at employment tribunal level, that a claimant may be compensated for the loss of working tax credits received in the course of employment (*Mosse v Hastings and Rother Voluntary Association for the Blind* ET Case No 1103096/06/NW).

24.88 Normally the calculation is straightforward but difficulties can arise where the claimant's pay varies from week to week due to output or as a result of fluctuating payments such as tips, bonuses, and commission. In such circumstances, the normal practice is for tribunals to work out the average amount an employee was earning over the 12 weeks prior to dismissal, but it is open to the claimant or the respondent to put forward some different reference period or to award a lump sum.

24.89 The rate of pay is the contractual rate. It is for the tribunal to resolve any disputes relating to the correct rate based on what the claimant should have been receiving at that time (*Kinzley v Minories Finance Ltd* [1987] IRLR 490).

Pay rises

24.90 The claimant is entitled to be compensated for any pay rises which take place or are likely to take place over the period of the award (see para 24.140). In *Leyland Vehicles Ltd v Reston* [1981] IRLR 19 the EAT ruled that a pay increase awarded after the calculation date could not be included in the basic award even if it was backdated. The same principle applies to the additional award but in assessing the compensatory award a tribunal can take into account any pay increase awarded up to the date of the hearing, including a backdated increase and any increase which the employee might reasonably be expected to have had but for the dismissal. This may also include a future pay rise provided there is a high probability that, 'in conformity with company policy, the company would increase the salary of an employee' in the period of assessment (*York Trailer Co Ltd v Sparkes* [1973] IRLR 348).

Notice pay

Notice pay can be awarded as part of the claimant's lost earnings in the compensatory award (*TBA Industrial Products Ltd v Locke* [1984] IRLR 48). **24.91**

Holiday pay

Holiday pay can be recovered as part of the compensatory award (*Tradewinds Airways Ltd v Fletcher* [1981] IRLR 272), although a claimant cannot be compensated twice for the same loss and therefore such an award is unusual. **24.92**

Bonus and commission

An important difference between a claim for wrongful dismissal and unfair dismissal is that in an unfair dismissal compensation claim it is not necessary to show that the claimant has a contractual right to the sum claimed as a claim will lie for the loss of any benefit which the claimant 'might reasonably be expected to have had but for the dismissal' (ERA 1996, s 123(2)(b)). Claims can be made for lost bonuses and commission payments on this basis. **24.93**

However, it is still necessary to show, on a balance of probabilities, that the claimant had an 'expectation' of receiving such a payment and that that expectation was 'reasonable'. Such an expectation may be generated by the terms of the contract or by representations made to the claimant at an interview or in the employee handbook or at an appraisal. Furthermore, in relation to bonuses, even where a reasonable expectation is established, there may still be difficulties in quantifying the amount of the bonus, particularly where the scheme is completely discretionary. Tribunals may also base their awards on a 'percentage chance' approach if liability is established (*Allied Maples Group Ltd v Simmons & Simmons* [1995] 1 WLR 1602). The task may be easier where a bonus is a group bonus linked to targets where the evidence shows that the targets were achieved. Where the bonus is based on individual performance, evidence of bonuses paid to other people may set an appropriate benchmark. Quantification problems may also arise in relation to commission payments, although the rate of commission is likely to be stated in the scheme itself. **24.94**

Pension

The right to recover compensation for pension loss was established by the NIRC in *Copson v Eversure Accessories Ltd* [1974] IRLR 247. (It is also an established head of claim in discrimination cases (see *Ministry of Defence v Mutton* [1996] ICR 590).) However, as the EAT pointed out in *Benson v Dairy Crest Ltd* EAT/192/89 it can be one of the most difficult areas to quantify. **24.95**

The starting point is to identify the type of scheme under consideration. Employers commonly provide two types of pension: a defined contribution (or money purchase scheme); or a defined benefit (or final salary scheme). If the employee is not required to make a contribution, this is known as a 'non-contributory' scheme. A defined benefits scheme aims to provide a certain pension benefit on retirement and the level of contributions will be the amount necessary to fund that benefit. The level of benefit is expressed as a specified fraction of the employee's salary at or near retirement (normally one sixtieth in the private sector and one eightieth in the public sector) multiplied by the years of pensionable service. In a defined contribution scheme, the scheme defines the contributions made by the employer and (if appropriate) any made by the employee. On retirement the employee receives the pension which can be bought by the redemption of those contributions (usually by way of an annuity). **24.96**

In addition, in recent years personal pension plans have become popular as have 'stakeholder' pensions. These are varieties of defined contributions schemes. In a personal pension plan an employer and employee (or one or other) contributes to a private pension plan with an insurance company or other pension provider and the final pension on retirement will be an **24.97** annuity purchased from the accumulated contributions. A stakeholder pension is another form of personal pension whereby contributions are made to a policy with an insurance company or other pension provider. All employers (with some minor exceptions) must provide access to a stakeholder scheme unless they already offer a suitable pension scheme.

24.98 Quite apart from these provisions, there are pensions payable by the State. These can consist of a basic State pension, a graduated retirement benefit, and an additional State pension payable under the State Earnings Related Pension Scheme known as SERPS or a State Second Pension (S2P).

24.99 In *Copson v Eversure Accessories Ltd* [1974] IRLR 247, the NIRC held that compensation for pension loss falls to be considered under two heads: past loss and future loss. However, there may be cases where it may not be appropriate to make an award at all.

Tribunal guidelines

24.100 In 1990 a committee of judges of industrial tribunals was appointed by the President of the Industrial Tribunals (England and Wales) and in consultation with the Government Actuary's Department (GAD) produced a set of guidelines on compensation for pension loss. The guidelines were updated in 1991 and again in November 2003 when two employment judges (David Sneath and Colin Sara) together with Chris Daykin and Adrian Gallop from GAD produced a revised set of guidelines which are available in a booklet entitled *Compensation for loss of pension rights: Employment Tribunal*. Extracts from the booklet are set out in Appendix 4. In the absence of other evidence, tribunals are encouraged to apply the guidelines (*Orthet Ltd v Vince-Cain* [2004] IRLR 857). Nonetheless, the EAT has held that tribunals are not bound to apply the guidelines (*Bingham v Hobourn Engineering Ltd* [1992] IRLR 298) and it is open to the parties to call their own expert actuarial evidence if they wish to (*Port of Tilbury (London) Ltd v Birch* [2005] IRLR 92).

Pension loss in defined contributions schemes

24.101 In relation to defined contributions schemes and personal pension schemes, the calculation of past and future loss (see paras 24.103 and 24.104 below) is normally relatively straightforward as it is based on the loss of the employer's contributions to the scheme up to the date of the hearing and (if appropriate) beyond, subject to the guidance on the calculation on future loss set out below and the other rules on deductions. It is arguable that where the sums would have been paid into a fund, some allowance should be made for the increase in the value of the fund between the date of dismissal and the date of the hearing (although a tribunal may well ignore this if the change is minimal). If the claimant suffers any kind of penalty for leaving the scheme early, this will be recoverable as compensation.

Pension loss in defined benefit schemes (final salary schemes)

24.102 Unless the claimant is covered by a private scheme which confers greater benefits than the State scheme there will be no loss, although there may be a loss of S2P during any period of unemployment. (The guidelines on compensation for pension loss provide a formula and actuarial table (Table 3.2 in Appendix 4) to calculate this loss. The information required is gross annual earnings, state pension retirement date, age, and sex.) Furthermore, even where the claimant is covered by a pension scheme, there may be no loss if the claimant does not qualify for a pension under the rules of the scheme within the period covered by the award (*Manning v R & H Wale (Export) Ltd* [1979] ICR 433) or if the claimant's rights are valueless.

24.103 The first type of compensatable loss is *past loss*, that is the loss up to the date of dismissal. The reason why this loss arises is that the pension loss suffered by the individual is based on the salary the individual would have earned on the date of retirement rather than at the date of leaving. This type of loss is referred to as 'loss of enhancement of accrued pension rights'. However, in calculating this loss, allowance must be made for the fact that deferred pensions are now revalued in line with the statutory requirements of either the rise in the RPI or 5 per cent per annum compound interest (whichever is the lower) and this will reduce the amount of loss. There is no past loss if the claimant is offered the opportunity to transfer the full value of the accrued pension into a new fund provided that this takes into account any projected increases in salary (*Freemans plc v Flynn* [1984] IRLR 486 and *Yeats v Fairey Winches Ltd* [1974] IRLR 362). In this context, it should be borne in mind that employees leaving occupational pension schemes have the right to a 'transfer value' equivalent to the cash equivalent of the benefits to which the member leaving early would have been entitled had he or she remained in the scheme. However, there is no obligation to provide for projected increases in salary, so where there is a transfer value it will be necessary to check whether there is a residual loss. Most schemes make provision for the return of contributions if the employee leaves the scheme before completing two years of service. Allowance must be made for the return of contributions, although this does not compensate the claimant for the value of the lost contributions in pension terms (*Willment Bros v Oliver* [1979] IRLR 393). At the very least compound interest should be awarded on those contributions. The duty to mitigate may also be relevant to the assessment of past pension loss. For example, an employee may be found to have failed to mitigate his loss where the employee elects for a return of contributions instead of a deferred pension (as the latter is the more valuable benefit) but the question whether this amounts to a failure to mitigate will depend on the facts (see *Sturdy Finance v Bardsley* [1979] IRLR 65). Allowance must also be made for the possibility of *withdrawal*.

Compensation may also be awarded for *future loss* of pension rights. Future loss for this purpose **24.104** is divided between loss from the date of dismissal to the date of the hearing and future loss beyond the date of the hearing. Where, by the time of the hearing, the claimant has found a new job with equivalent pension benefits or is likely to do so in the near future and the period of 'future' loss is relatively short, a tribunal may well only award the loss of pension contributions over the period of loss (particularly if it uses the 'simplified method of assessment', see para 24.107 below). Indeed the tribunal may even conclude that there is no loss where the new and old schemes are equivalent (*Sturdy Finance v Bardsley* [1979] IRLR 65). Where the new scheme is less beneficial, the tribunal will have to assess the consequential loss to the employee bearing in mind the need to consider issues relating to 'new job facts' referred to at para 24.145 below and other relevant conditions of employment such as a higher salary. Credit must be given for future pension benefits from the new pension scheme, whether it is a final salary scheme or a money purchase scheme (*Network Rail Infrastructure Ltd v Booth* EAT/0071/06/ZT). Tribunals must also consider the possibility of *withdrawal* (see para 24.105 below) and make allowance for future pension contributions by the employee (if the scheme was non-contributory or contributions were at a lower rate) and the *accelerated receipt* of the payment (see para 25.63 below).

Risk of withdrawal The possibility of withdrawal, ie the chance that the claimant might have **24.105** left the scheme and therefore suffered some loss in any event, has to be discounted both in relation to the calculation of past loss and future loss. In addition, it may be argued in the current environment that the employer might have closed the scheme in any event (see *Glen Dimplex UK Ltd v Burrows* EAT/0265/03, where a tribunal decision was overturned by the EAT for not considering this issue). Under the guidelines on compensation for pension loss it is for the tribunal to consider the risk of withdrawal and reduce the award accordingly (previously the 1990 guidelines included a table based on the average risk of withdrawal but this is now a matter for evidence). Relevant factors will include the state of the business (ie the risk of future redundancy) and personal factors relating to the individual such as the chance of leaving on health grounds or for reasons relating to career development. The figure for future withdrawal may be the same or higher than the risk for past loss, although it is often the same. A failure to consider the possibility of withdrawal amounts to an error of law (*Manpower Services Ltd v Hearne* [1982] IRLR 281).

Methods of calculating the loss There are a number of different ways of putting a value on past and **24.106** future pension loss. The most straightforward is the *contributions method* which defines the loss in terms of the lost contributions made by the employer during the period of the award, but this (a) is not appropriate for the calculation of past loss in a final salary scheme, and (b) is unlikely to reflect the full value of future loss where the period of loss is substantial (see *Clancy v Cannock Chase Technical College* [2001] IRLR 331). Where this method is adopted consideration should be given to whether interest (simple or compound) should be added. The alternative method is the *benefits method* which involves an actuarial valuation of the loss either by valuing the capital cost of buying an annuity which would yield an equivalent pension which the employee would have had but for the dismissal and from this to deduct what the claimant has received (*John Millar & Sons v Quinn* [1974] IRLR 107) or to obtain an actuarial valuation of what the claimant has lost under the scheme taking account of the periods of both past loss and future loss.

24.107 *Tribunal guidelines* Two methods are put forward for calculating the loss: the 'simplified method' (which the guidelines on compensation for pension loss say should be applied in most cases (see 4.13 of the guidelines)) and the 'substantial method' (which should be used in the circumstances set out at 4.14 of the guidelines), ie where the tribunal is considering a career-long loss (although in *Orthet Ltd v Vince-Cain* [2004] IRLR 857 the EAT considered that the substantial loss approach may be more appropriate where the period of loss is likely to be more than two years). The simplified approach uses a combination of both actuarial tables and the contributions method. Under the simplified approach, the guidelines recognize three heads of loss: past loss, loss to the date of the hearing, and future loss. Compensation for past loss is deferred pension × multiplier taken from the relevant table less an appropriate percentage for withdrawal. Compensation per week between the date of dismissal and the date of the hearing is gross pensionable pay × employer's pension contribution × Appendix 6 adjustment. The same formula is used for future loss (although there must be an allowance for accelerated receipt). The substantial loss approach is the more complex. It is based on actuarial tables which are similar but not identical to the Ogden Tables for assessing future loss of earnings. The substantial approach does not differentiate between the three periods of loss. It is based on a formula that compensation = A minus B minus C less relevant withdrawal factors for A, B, and C where A = the value of prospective final salary pension rights up to the normal retirement age in the former employment; B = value of accrued final salary pension rights to the date of dismissal from the former employment; and C = the value of prospective final salary and pension rights to normal retirement age in any new employment. C will be zero if the tribunal concludes either that the claimant will not obtain future pensionable employment or if the claimant is likely to join a money purchase scheme, in which case the guidelines recommend that this is taken into account by adjusting the figure for loss of earnings (as distinct from pension loss). Loss of earnings is the difference between the net earnings in the old job (excluding the employer pension contributions) and the net earnings in the new job (including the employer's pension contributions). The calculation of A and B are based on the valuations set out in the relevant tables less the relevant withdrawal factor. In *Network Rail Infrastructure Ltd v Booth* EAT/0071/06/ZT, the EAT ruled that the employment tribunal had erred in law because, having found that the claimant was likely to find comparable employment with the benefit of a money purchase scheme, it failed to apply the 'C' factor at all. The result was an 'obvious injustice . . . conferring a windfall upon the employee'. The EAT observed that there may be 'some dispute about the best way in which credit can be given for future pension benefits, but what cannot be in doubt is that in a system which is designed to assess loss actually flowing from the unlawful act, credit must properly be given in one way or another'.

24.108 *Contributory fault* The normal rules on contributory fault (see para 25.39 below) apply to the sums awarded for loss of pension rights (*Port of Tilbury (London) Ltd v Birch* [2005] IRLR 92).

Redundancy pay

24.109 Where a redundancy payments scheme is more generous than the statutory scheme, compensation may be claimed for the loss of this benefit pursuant to ERA 1996, s 123(3) which provides that 'the loss referred to [in ERA 1996, s 123(1)] shall be taken to include in respect of any loss of (a) any entitlement or potential entitlement to a payment on account of dismissal by reason of redundancy (whether in pursuance of Part XI or otherwise), or (b) any expectation of such a payment'. This provision, on which there is a dearth of authority, means that a claim can be made where there is a contractual right to an enhanced redundancy payment (or otherwise) or where there is a reasonable expectation of such a payment, ie where such a payment formed part of a collective agreement. The right to claim compensation in such circumstances was recognized by the EAT in *Lee v IPC Business Press Ltd* [1984] ICR 306, where it was said:

> if it is shown that there was a term in the contract between Mr Lee and the company which was binding on the company and meant that, if Mr Lee was made redundant, he was entitled as a matter of contract to more than the statutory redundancy payment, that is something which he had lost as a result of being unfairly dismissed and it is one of the things which the industrial tribunal should be able to take into account in arriving at their award of compensation if any.

Such a claim can clearly be made where an employee is unfairly dismissed on grounds of redundancy but it is arguable that it can also be made where the employee would (or might) have been made redundant during the compensation period. **24.110**

Stock options

It has become common for senior staff to be granted stock options as part of an employee incentive package. There are a number of different schemes recognized by HM Revenue & Customs (HMRC) including Share Incentive Plans, approved SAYE Option Schemes, approved Company Share Option Schemes, and Enterprise Management Incentive Schemes. **24.111**

The value of these schemes will vary depending on their nature. In *Leonard v Strathclyde Buses Ltd* [1998] IRLR 693, the EAT accepted that compensation could be awarded for the loss in value caused by the premature sale of stock options. The claimants successfully recovered the difference between the share price on termination and the share price they would have received but for their unfair dismissal. **24.112**

Compensation may be awarded for the loss of the option itself provided the employment tribunal is satisfied that the claimant would have been granted such an option but for the dismissal (*O'Laoire v Jackel International Ltd* [1991] IRLR 170). But the loss may be difficult to quantify and prove where there is no more than a mere promise to grant such an option in the future. Nonetheless, where possible, tribunals should seek to place a value on these rights. In *Casey v Texas Homecare Ltd* EAT/632/87, an employment tribunal declined to estimate the value of an employee's share option because it was too 'speculative and indefinite'. The EAT held that this was wrong and, on the basis of the evidence presented to it, awarded £1,000 after making allowance for the chance that the share price might fall. This involves a separate assessment of any uncertainties connected with the future exercise of share options including an assessment of the likelihood of flotation, the likely value of the shares on flotation, and the likelihood that the claimant would have purchased some, or all, of the shares (*Selective Beauty (UK) Ltd v Hayes* UKEAT/0582/04/SM). **24.113**

Company cars

Compensation may be awarded for the loss of private use of a company car. The position is different if the car is used exclusively for business purposes or if private use is minimal (as, for example, where the employee has use of a 'pool' car for business purposes). In such circumstances, little or no compensation will be awarded. On the other hand, the award will be greater if, in addition to the use of the car, the employee also receives free maintenance, tax, insurance, and petrol. **24.114**

There is no single or universal method of valuing the loss of the use of a car. Indeed in many cases, tribunals do not always give any clear indication of their reasons for making an award or the method used in choosing a particular figure. In the past, some tribunals have awarded a conventional figure of between £40 and £120 per week for the loss of this benefit depending on the type of car but much will depend on the evidence presented to the employment tribunal. Three methods are commonly used: **24.115**

AA and RAC estimates One common method of establishing the value of being provided with a company car is to estimate the weekly costs of running a particular type of car based on the AA or RAC estimates which are published annually. The AA motoring tables are reproduced in Appendix 4. This method was used in *Shove v Downs Surgical plc* [1984] 1 All ER 7, where **24.116**

£10,000 was awarded for the loss of a company Daimler over a 30-month period and allowance was made for the ratio of business use to private use. Some employers have their own motor mileage allowances which may also form the basis of a valuation. Adjustments may need to be made if the employee contributes to the running costs of the car.

24.117 *HMRC scales* Another method of valuing the benefit of a company car is to rely on the scale charges drawn up by HMRC for tax purposes. The scale charges are based on the cylinder capacity and age of the car or in the case of a more expensive car, its original market value and its age. The problem with this approach is that the scales have been devised with a view to valuing the benefit for tax purposes and to some extent reflect changes in government policy on this issue. The use of the scales was rejected in *Shove v Downs Surgical plc* [1984] 1 All ER 7 for this reason.

24.118 *Cost of hire and other methods* Another possible way of valuing the loss of a company car is for the employee to buy or hire a car and claim a proportion of the cost from the employer. This approach was relied on by the claimant in *Nohar v Granitstone (Galloway) Ltd* [1974] ICR 273, where the tribunal awarded the difference between the cost of purchase and resale. However, it is open to employers to argue that this over-values the benefit and fails to make allowance for factors such as depreciation or the hirer's profit. A variant on this method, where the car is purchased on hire purchase, is to award the claimant a proportion of the outstanding hire purchase payments (see *S & U Stores v Wormleighton* EAT/477/77, where the EAT described this approach as 'unscientific' but not 'unreasonable').

24.119 Increasingly, employers are offering staff a car allowance or a travel allowance as an alternative to providing a company car. Compensation may be recovered for the loss of this allowance.

Accommodation

24.120 Compensation may be awarded for the loss of rent-free or subsidized accommodation. This has become a more valuable benefit in the light of the increases in the cost of accommodation (whether rented or bought). Clearly no compensation will be awarded if the claimant pays the market rent (*Nohar v Granitstone (Galloway) Ltd* [1974] ICR 273).

24.121 There is no single or universal method of valuing this benefit. The most favourable method from the claimant's point of view is the open market value of the accommodation (see, for example, *Butler v J Wendon & Son* [1972] IRLR 15, where the open market rental of a tied cottage was assessed at £3 a week). Evidence of open market values may be obtained from surveyors or local estate agents or even advertisements in the local newspapers for comparable property. The more favourable method for employers is the cost of providing suitable alternative accommodation. This method is commonly used where the claimant has found new accommodation at the time of the hearing and the award is based on the difference between the two (*Lloyd v Scottish Co-operative Wholesale Society* [1973] IRLR 93). Where the claimant buys a property rather than looking for suitable rented accommodation, it is arguable that the award should be based on a discounted proportion of the mortgage payment or alternatively the interest element in the mortgage over the period of the award but there are no reported cases where this approach has been adopted.

Company loans and mortgages

24.122 Some employers, particularly in the financial sector, offer their staff the benefit of interest-free (or reduced) loans or subsidized mortgages. The loss of such a perk may be recovered as part of the compensatory award. The problem is how to put a cash value on the benefit. In theory, the assessment should be fairly straightforward—the claimant's loss is the difference between the subsidy received and the market rate for the mortgage and the loan—but tribunals often opt for a broad brush approach rather than a mathematical quantification of the award. For example, in *UBAF Bank Ltd v Davis* [1978] IRLR 442, the tribunal awarded Mr Davis a lump sum of £2,000 for all the privileges he had lost as a result of his dismissal rather than the amount he said he would have to pay if he took out a mortgage from a high street building society.

Childcare costs

It is not uncommon for employers to offer either free childcare in the workplace or make a contribution to childcare costs. Where an employer does this, the loss may be claimed as part of the compensatory award. From an employer's point of view, the simplest way of calculating the loss will be the cost of providing the benefit to the employer, but from the employee's point of view, the loss will be based on the 'reasonable' cost of providing equivalent childcare. Where the employer makes a contribution to the childcare costs, the financial loss will be the loss of that contribution (*Visa International Ltd v Paul* [2004] IRLR 42). **24.123**

Medical and other health insurance

Private medical insurance is also a common benefit. Often the employer's 'group' scheme will also make provision for the employee's family and children. From an employer's point of view, the most favourable way of valuing this benefit is the cost of providing it to the employee. The problem from an employee's point of view, however, is that the cost to the employee of finding equivalent cover may be higher because the employer is able to gain the advantage of being a 'group' purchaser and therefore the value to the employee is the cost of alternative equivalent provision. The same principles apply to claims for loss of death in service benefits and other forms of life assurance. However, in *Knapton v ECC Card Clothing Ltd* [2006] IRLR 756 the EAT ruled that compensation is only recoverable for the loss of such benefits if the claimant has actually suffered the loss either through death or illness or has bought such cover. Where, as in *Knapton*, the claimant survived for the period covered by the award and did not take out life assurance cover during that period, there was no financial loss and therefore compensation could not be awarded for the loss of life assurance. **24.124**

Food

Some employers have their own staff catering facilities: sometimes the meals are provided free of charge but more often they are subsidized. The loss of this perk has been claimed in a number of cases where on the evidence the value of the benefit was substantial. **24.125**

Telephone and mobile

Sometimes employers pay for the rental and telephone/mobile charges. Compensation may be recovered for the value of this benefit (see *Dundee Plant Hire v Riddler* EAT/377/88 where £160 was awarded for the free use of a telephone covering both the rental and telephone charges). Claimants wishing to make such a claim would need to produce evidence of the rental fee and relevant bills showing the value of private use of the phone. **24.126**

Expenses

ERA 1996, s 123(2)(a) provides that the assessment of loss also includes any expenses reasonably incurred as a result of the dismissal. However, in relation to such claims, the tribunal must be satisfied: **24.127**

(a) the expenses were incurred as a result of dismissal;
(b) the expenses were reasonably incurred;
(c) the sums incurred were reasonable in themselves.

Costs associated with finding a new job are the most common kind of expenses awarded by tribunals. For example, the cost of attending interviews (*Leech v Berger, Jensen & Nicholson Ltd* [1972] IRLR 58) and, in appropriate cases, removal expenses and relocation costs (*Lloyd v Scottish Co-operative Wholesale Society* [1973] IRLR 93) and even estate agents' fees and legal costs (*Daykin v IHW Engineering Ltd* COIT 1440/117 and *United Freight Distribution Ltd v McDougall* EATS/218/94, where £500 was awarded to cover the legal fees necessary to sell the claimant's house). **24.128**

In addition, tribunals have allowed employees to recover some of the costs incurred in setting up a business where this was considered a reasonable way of mitigating the loss flowing from the **24.129** dismissal. For example, in *Gardiner-Hill v Roland Berger Technics Ltd* [1982] IRLR 498, the claimant successfully recovered £500 of expenses which he had incurred in setting up a business.

24.130 Legal costs associated with the tribunal hearing itself, however, are not recoverable as part of the compensatory award (*Raynor v Remploy* [1973] IRLR 3). (For the rules on legal and preparatory costs, see Chapter 12.)

Credit for payments received

24.131 In assessing the actual loss suffered by the claimant, it is necessary to give credit for any payment or benefits received since dismissal. The treatment of *ex gratia* payments is considered at para 25.59 below.

Payments in lieu

24.132 In the absence of an express or an implied agreement to the contrary, credit should be given for any payment in lieu of notice (*Babcock FATA Ltd v Addison* [1987] IRLR 173) but note that the position in Scotland may be different (*Finnie v Top Hat Frozen Foods Ltd* [1985] IRLR 365).

Payments received from the new employer

24.133 As a general rule, credit must also be given for any payment received from new employment since dismissal, including income from part-time employment (*Justfern Ltd v Skaife D'Ingerthorpe* [1994] IRLR 164). But this rule is subject to two provisos:

(1) It would appear that the claimant is not required to give credit for any payments or benefits received after the claimant has found permanent new employment (see para 24.140 below).
(2) Previously, there was a conflict of case law as to the extent that a claimant must account for payments received during the notice period (see para 24.74 above). In *Hardy v Polk Ltd* [2004] IRLR 420 and *Morgans v Alpha Plus Security Ltd* [2005] IRLR 234, the EAT ruled that credit should be given for such payments but in *Voith Turbo Ltd v Stowe* [2005] IRLR 228, the EAT decided that normally such payments should be ignored as a matter of good employment relations. The approach of Burton P was followed by the EAT in *Langley v Burlo* [2006] IRLR 460 but was doubted by the Court of Appeal in the same case ([2007] IRLR 145). The Court ruled that, on what it called a narrow interpretation of the NIRC's ruling in *Norton Tool Co Ltd v Tewson* [1973] 1 All ER 183, a claimant was not required to give credit for payments received from the new employer during the notice period.

Are State benefits deductible?

24.134 State benefits which are recoverable under the Recoupment Regulations (see Chapter 27) are not deducted from the compensatory award. This includes job seeker's allowance and income support (*Savage v Saxena* [1998] IRLR 182). Other State benefits such as invalidity or disability benefit and incapacity benefit are deductible in *full* (*Morgans v Alpha Plus Security Ltd* [2005] IRLR 234). It is unclear what impact the Court of Appeal's ruling in *Burlo v Langley* [2007] IRLR 145 (referred to in para 24.133 above) has on this decision. Furthermore, it is unclear whether the ruling in *Morgans* applies to all State benefits. For example, in the earlier case of *Savage v Saxena* [1998] IRLR 182, the Scottish EAT ruled that housing benefit should not be deducted because it would not be just and equitable for employers to benefit from such payments.

Remoteness

24.135 It is open to an employment tribunal to refuse to give credit for certain payments and benefits which an employee receives after dismissal on the basis that the sums are either too remote or arise independently of the employer's wrong. In *Justfern Ltd v Skaife D'Ingerthorpe* [1994] IRLR 164, the EAT upheld a tribunal's decision that the claimant need not give credit for an educational grant which the claimant had received to attend a training course. The same principle is likely to apply to payments received by an employee under a private insurance scheme (*Parry v Cleaver* [1970] AC 1). Similarly credit need not be given for payments received from the former employer's pension scheme as such payments are considered to be either analogous to payments from private insurance or are treated as collateral benefits (*Knapton v ECC Card Clothing Ltd* [2006] IRLR 756, EAT).

Tax rebates

Where, as a result of the dismissal, an employee is entitled to a tax rebate, the employer may argue that the amount of the award should be reduced to reflect this. Conversely, where the dismissal occurs towards the end of a tax year, the claimant may argue that account should be taken of the fact that had the correct process been followed, the dismissal might have occurred in the next tax year, leaving the claimant with a claim to a rebate. **24.136**

This issue has led to a number of conflicting decisions from the EAT ranging from the view that the tax implications should be completely ignored (*Adda International Ltd v Curcio* [1976] IRLR 425) to the view that compensation should be awarded for the loss of a rebate and by implication credit should be given for any rebate received (*Lucas v Laurence Scott Electromotors Ltd* [1983] IRLR 61). The current position would appear to be that the tax implications should be ignored unless the sums involved are substantial (*MBS Ltd v Calo* [1983] IRLR 189). **24.137**

Calculating the period of loss

As the NIRC pointed out in the *Norton Tool* case (see para 24.71 above), the compensation claim falls within two periods: the loss from the date of dismissal to the date of the hearing, and future loss. **24.138**

Date of assessment

The normal rule is that the claimant's loss is determined at the date of the remedies hearing, which may or may not be the same date as the liability hearing. This rule applies even where the assessment of compensation is delayed because of an appeal to the EAT against the ruling on liability (*Ging v Ellward Lancs Ltd* (1978) 12 ITR 265 and *Gilham v Kent County Council* [1986] IRLR 56), although it is now quite common for tribunals to assess compensation even if an appeal is pending. **24.139**

Loss between the date of dismissal and the date of the hearing

The tribunal will first assess the loss between the date of dismissal and the date of the hearing. Subject to mitigation, that loss will normally come to an end when the claimant has found a permanent new job on an equivalent remuneration package. It has been argued that where the claimant has found a permanent new job on a higher salary between the date of dismissal and the remedies hearing, the claimant should give credit for the payments received between the date when the claimant commenced the new job and the date of the hearing (ie these sums should be set off against any loss claimed during the period when the claimant was out of work), but this argument was rejected by the EAT in *Lytlarch Ltd (t/a The Viceroy Restaurant) v Reid* EAT/296/90, and *Fentimans v Fluid Engineering Products Ltd* [1991] IRLR 151. In the latter case, the EAT justified its decision on the basis that if this were not the case employees would be discouraged from mitigating their loss by finding new employment prior to the tribunal hearing and, as a matter of justice and equity, it would be unjust for the employer's liability to be reduced 'to a fraction of the loss sustained by the complainant during his period of unemployment'. On the other hand, it may be argued that 'justice and equity' work both ways and that on a strict application of the 'financial loss' principle, the claimant should give credit for all the payments received between dismissal and the date of the hearing. Furthermore, it could also be argued that the approach in these cases is inconsistent with the more flexible approach of the Court of Appeal in *Dench v Flynn and Partners* (para 24.79 above). It remains to be seen whether *Fentimans* is upheld in the future. **24.140**

24.141 A related issue is the extent to which a claimant has to account for payments received during the notice period. As noted at para 24.74 above, there is a conflict of authority on this point: in *Hardy v Polk Ltd* and *Morgans v Alpha Plus Security Ltd*, the EAT ruled that credit must be given for all payments received during the notice period, but in *Voith Turbo Ltd v Stowe*, the EAT relied on early authorities to conclude that the claimant should always, as a matter of good employment relations, receive compensation for loss of notice pay and should not be required to give credit for any payments received during that period. It was thought that this conflict of authority was resolved by the EAT's ruling in *Langley v Burlo* [2006] IRLR 460, but the issue has been left open by the Court of Appeal. It would seem that on the 'narrow' interpretation of the *Norton Tool* case adopted by the Court of Appeal in *Burlo* (referred to in para 24.74 above), the current position is that credit need not be given for payment received during the notice period.

Future loss

24.142 The more difficult task is to assess the award for future loss. This will often be a highly speculative exercise. Nonetheless, an employment tribunal is under a statutory duty to assess what is just and equitable and this may involve making a prediction based on the evidence it has heard. A tribunal cannot be allowed to 'opt out' of that task simply because the task is a difficult one and may involve speculation (*Scope v Thornett* [2007] IRLR 155). If the claimant has found a new job by the time of the hearing where the remuneration package is either equivalent to or better than the old job, then there will be no future loss. On the other hand, the task will be less straightforward where the new job is less well paid (or the overall package is less generous) or the claimant is still unemployed at the time of the hearing. This will involve having to assess how long the loss is likely to continue, what the EAT in *Kingston Upon Hull City Council v Dunnachie (No 3)* [2003] IRLR 843 called 'old job facts' and 'new job facts'.

Old job facts

24.143 'Old job facts' include whether the claimant would have remained in the job anyway and, if so, for how long? Overall, this will involve a reasonable assessment based on the evidence as to how long the employment would have lasted. So, for example, in *Scope v Thornett* [2007] IRLR 155 the employment tribunal was entitled to have considered how long the employment relationship would have lasted in the light of the relationship problems between the claimant and one of her colleagues but had not given adequate reasons for its conclusion that the employment would have come to an end after six months. Assuming that the claimant would have wished to have stayed in the old job, were there factors whether personal (such as health, family situations, or relocation) or economic factors (such as new technology, fall-off in orders, lay-offs, redundancies) which should on the available evidence (including the experience of the tribunal itself), be taken into account? Would the claimant have taken early retirement or have considered a second career? Would he or she have been promoted? Would his or her level of earnings have gone up or remained stable (other than by reference to the cost of living)?

24.144 In considering these questions tribunals should take into account the actual consequence (as well as the hypothetical issues referred to above). For example, if a business is closed, employees who are unfairly dismissed at an earlier date cannot recover compensation for any loss they suffer beyond the date of closure unless they are able to persuade the tribunal that the closure is not genuine (*Gilham v Kent County Council* [1986] IRLR 56; *James W Cook & Co (Wivenhoe) Ltd v Tipper* [1990] IRLR 386).

New job facts

24.145 'New job facts' include whether the claimant is likely to find a new job at all? If so, when and at what salary? (This will involve considering issues of mitigation.) How long is any pay differential likely to last? Is the claimant likely to change jobs to one which is better paid? Is the claimant likely to be promoted? Are the earnings in the new job likely to be stable, subject to cost of living increases, or will they improve?

In considering these factors, tribunals will take account of the personal characteristics of the claimant such as the claimant's age, skill, and qualifications. For example, in *Cartiers Superfoods Ltd v Laws* [1978] IRLR 315, the EAT held that the tribunal was entitled to take into account the claimant's age, the prospects of her having a child, and of being relocated to another part of the country in awarding future loss over a three-year period as these considerations were all relevant in considering the likely period of future loss (although tribunals must take care not to make discriminatory assumptions in making allowance for these contingencies). **24.146**

Age may be an important factor when a claimant is nearing retirement age (*Isle of Wight Tourist Board v Coombes* [1976] IRLR 413), particularly where this is combined with a poor state of health (*Fougère v Phoenix Motor Co Ltd* [1976] IRLR 259) or some other disadvantage in the labour market (*Brittains Aborfield Ltd v Van Uden* [1977] IRLR 211), though age of itself may become less relevant now that the new age discrimination law has come into force in October 2006. **24.147**

Tribunals will take into account the local and national state of the labour market in the light of any specific evidence which is presented to it. Where the tribunal relies on its own knowledge of the local labour market, the tribunal should give the parties an opportunity to comment on that knowledge (*Hammington v Berker Sportcraft Ltd* [1980] ICR 248). **24.148**

Subject to the guidance given by the EAT in *Dunnachie*, it is open to the tribunal to award compensation for the remainder of the claimant's working life if the tribunal is satisfied that the claimant will not work again, or will not work again in an equally remunerative employment, or has to undergo a change of career and thereby suffers a career-long loss as in *Chagger v Abbey National Plc* [2009] EWCA Civ 1202. Such awards are rare (see also *Kerley v New Forest Bakeries Ltd* ET Case No 7405/83, where a 59-year-old baker with no experience of any other trade was awarded compensation until retirement; *Barrel Plating and Phosphating Co Ltd v Danks* [1976] IRLR 262, where the evidence showed that the claimant would have worked beyond normal retirement age and the compensation was assessed accordingly). **24.149**

In broad terms, support for two different approaches may be found in the decided case law: first, the use of a 'multiplier' which takes account of contingencies referred to above and, secondly, the use of actuarial tables such as the Ogden Tables. **24.150**

Use of multiplier Some tribunals have used a basic multiplier, ie a figure in terms of weeks, months, or years, which reflects the employee's likely continuing loss of earnings and have then deducted or made allowance for the contingencies (referred to above) (see, for example, *Cartiers Superfoods Ltd v Laws* [1978] IRLR 315; *Tidman v Aveling Marshall Ltd* [1977] IRLR 218; and *Morgan Edwards Wholesale Ltd v Francis* EAT/205/78). Where such a multiplier is used, tribunals need not apply it with the same precision as a cost accountant or a skilled actuary (*Fougère v Phoenix Motor Co Ltd* [1977] IRLR 259). **24.151**

Use of actuarial tables More recently some claimants have relied on actuarial tables such as the Ogden Tables in support of their claims for future loss. The Ogden Tables, usually used in personal injury cases, provide a multiplier to be used for calculating future loss of earnings up to retirement age (and beyond, if pension loss is appropriate) where a severely injured claimant will never be able to work again in his or her chosen field and therefore will be in either less remunerative employment or unable to work for the rest of his or her working life. The Tables make allowance for accelerated payments and for mortality rates but not for other risks more directly associated with the employment relationship such as the possibility that the level of earnings may have been affected by periods of illness or unemployment or ceasing to work to care for children or other dependants. Nor do the Tables allow for specific risks associated with the particular employment such as redundancy. The circumstances in which the Ogden Tables (or other actuarial tables) may be used in the calculation of unfair dismissal compensation were considered by the EAT in *Kingston Upon Hull City Council v Dunnachie (No 3)* [2003] IRLR 843, where it was held that the Ogden Tables (or any other similar such table which may be **24.152** devised) should only be relied upon by an employment tribunal where it is satisfied that having considered the 'old job facts' and 'new job facts', the loss is likely to extend over the remainder of the claimant's life (ie a career-long loss) analogous to the circumstances where the table is used in personal injury claims. Such cases are likely to be rare. An example of such a case referred to by the EAT is *Kennard v Royal British Legion Industries* ET Case No 1100479/2001/R, where a disabled employee, aged 58, who was unfairly selected for redundancy, recovered compensation for the rest of his working life. Furthermore, for the reasons given above, the Ogden Tables do not take account of the many contingencies which fall to be discounted in the calculation of loss in an unfair dismissal claim and therefore even in those unusual cases where it is appropriate to use the Tables to calculate future loss, it will still be necessary to discount other contingencies such as specific risks associated with the particular individual or the particular employment. The EAT also warns of other 'dangers' of using actuarial tables such as: (a) difficulties in calculating loss of earnings over the relevant period as the differential may be variable, (b) the failure to address issues relating to tax and mitigation, and (c) the risk of double counting. Furthermore, it should be noted that the EAT's decision is not intended to apply to the calculation of pension loss where an actuarial method is used if the 'substantial loss' method is relevant to the calculation of pension loss. Similar points are made by the EAT in *Abbey National Plc v Chagger* [2009] IRLR 86 at page 104 where Underhill J makes it clear that even in a case where it is appropriate to use the Ogden Tables, it will never be right to use the multiplier taken from the main Tables without considering the contingencies (referred to above) which the Tables do not reflect.

No set amount

24.153 It should be stressed that a tribunal has considerable discretion to award what is appropriate in the particular circumstances of the case. Although many tribunals limit their award to a fixed period of around 12 months based on their perception of the labour market, they are not bound to do so and, subject to the statutory maximum, compensation may be awarded for such period as the tribunal considers appropriate in the circumstances (see *Morganite Electrical Carbon Ltd v Donne* [1987] IRLR 363, where an award of 30 weeks up to the date of the hearing and 52 weeks thereafter was not considered excessive).

Injury to feelings

24.154 As stated above, in *Dunnachie v Kingston Upon Hull City Council* [2004] IRLR 727, the House of Lords decided that the loss contemplated by ERA 1996, s 123(1) does not include compensation for injury to health or injury to feelings. Nonetheless, compensation for financial loss may be awarded where the manner of dismissal means that the claimant is likely to be at a disadvantage in the labour market or causes psychological injury which prevents the claimant from looking for a new job (*John Millar & Sons v Quinn* [1974] IRLR 107; *Devine v Designer Flowers Wholesale Florist Sundries Ltd* [1993] IRLR 517; *Vaughan v Weighpack Ltd* [1974] IRLR 105).

24.155 The correct approach to such situations was clarified by the Court of Session in *Dignity Funerals Ltd v Bruce* [2005] IRLR 189, where a tribunal declined to award the claimant compensation for reactive depression which was allegedly caused by the dismissal but did take this into account in its award for future loss. Confirming the correctness of the tribunal's approach, the Court of Session said that if it could be shown that the depressive illness was caused by the dismissal and it was this that prevented the claimant from working, then a full award of compensation for future loss of earnings should be made. On the other hand, where the dismissal is merely one of two or more concurrent causes of the claimant's loss or where the dismissal was a cause of the loss for only part of the period, a tribunal should consider what sum is 'just and equitable' to award and 'in all likelihood' this would be less than the full amount of the wages claimed by way of future loss. However, it is important to stress that such loss must be a consequence of the dismissal: losses arising from a series of events leading up to 'last straw' type constructive dismissal will not be recoverable. So, for example, in *GAB Robins (UK) Ltd v Triggs* [2008] IRLR 317 the Court of Appeal overturned the EAT's ruling that an employee was entitled to recover compensation for her loss of earnings for breaches of the duty of trust and confidence which preceded her constructive dismissal as such a loss was not a consequence of her dismissal. The claimant was therefore not entitled to recover compensation for 'wrongs already inflicted on her' as part of the tribunal's award of compensation for unfair dismissal. It may prove difficult to apply the Court's approach to cases where the loss of earning capacity is primarily, or substantially, a consequence of the final act which caused the constructive dismissal. In such circumstances, the approach in the *Dignity Funerals* case is still likely to be relevant.

Loss of statutory rights

A fixed award is normally made for the loss of statutory rights (ie the need to re-qualify for statutory protection against unfair dismissal and other statutory rights). In *SH Mufett v Head* [1986] IRLR 488, the EAT held that this should be in the region of £100 (although these days the conventional sum is closer to £250). A sum can also be claimed for the loss of other employment rights such as the loss of statutory notice. In *Daley v A E Dorset (Almar Dolls) Ltd* [1981] IRLR 385, the EAT suggested that this should be fixed at half the employee's statutory entitlement at the time of dismissal, though a tribunal which awards more than this conventional amount will not necessarily err in law (*Arthur Guinness Son & Co (GB) Ltd v Green* [1989] IRLR 288). 24.156

On the other hand, a tribunal will not necessarily err in law if it makes no award for loss of statutory rights (*Harvey v Institute of the Motor Industry (No 2)* [1995] IRLR 416), particularly where the loss is too remote (ie if it is found that the employee is unlikely to be on the labour market for some time due to illness (*Gourley v Kerr* EAT/692/81) or for some other reason like retraining (*Pagano v HGS* [1976] IRLR 9), or is going to become self-employed). 24.157

Power to increase the award

The compensatory award will be increased if an employer fails to comply with the statutory disputes resolution procedure set out in Sch 2 to the Employment Act 2002 (these provisions were repealed with effect from 6 April 2009 and are retained in this edition because there may be some cases in the pipeline which are covered by the transitional provisions in the Employment Act 2008). 24.158

The Employment Act 2002, s 31(3) provides that where the non-completion of the statutory procedure is 'wholly or mainly attributable to failure by the employer to comply with a requirement of the procedure', the tribunal must (other than in exceptional circumstances) increase the award to the employee by 10 per cent and may, if it considers it just and equitable, increase the award by a further amount up to a total increase of 50 per cent. There is no power to increase the award where the statutory procedure has been completed but the employer has failed to comply with the general requirements set out in Part 3 of Sch 2 of the Employment Act 2002 (*Selvarajan v Wilmot* [2008] IRLR 824). 24.159

This increase is made before the compensatory award is reduced for contributory fault or on account of a payment of an enhanced redundancy payment (ERA 1996, s 124A). It is also likely that any increase in the award will take place after account has been taken of the *Polkey* reduction (see para 25.05) as prior to this assessment, there is no 'award' to increase. 24.160

It should be noted that the duty to increase the compensatory award only arises where the breach of the statutory procedure is wholly or mainly attributable to the employer. So an award will not be increased where, for example, an employee fails to attend a dismissal meeting or an appeal meeting. 24.161

The provision is an exception to the normal principle that the purpose of the compensatory award is compensation not punishment and may give tribunals a limited power to take account 24.162

of non-economic factors in the increase of the award. There is no statutory guidance as to the amount by which the award should be increased above the 10 per cent minimum as this is left to the discretion of the tribunal. It is likely that any increase will reflect a number of factors including the seriousness of the procedural default, the degree of culpability on the part of the employer, and the size and resources of the employer. Arguably, a tribunal may also take account of the injury to the employee's feelings or health caused by the employer's default, for example, where the breach is one of unreasonable delay and this causes injury and upset to the employee. However, to rely on this factor alone may amount to an error of law. The EAT's ruling in *Aptuit (Edinburgh) Ltd v Kennedy* EATS/0057/06 is the first to address this issue. Hitherto, cases at an employment tribunal level have suggested that the degree of culpability on the part of the employer is the most significant factor in determining the level of uplift. However, in *Kennedy* the EAT said that the crucial consideration should be the circumstances surrounding the failure to complete the statutory procedure. The EAT therefore held that the employment tribunal in uplifting an award in a redundancy case by 40 per cent had taken irrelevant factors into account such as the size of the employer, the employer's failure to consult, and the 'shoddy' treatment of the employee. It should have concentrated on the reasons why the employer had failed to complete the statutory procedure. This has been confirmed by the EAT in *McKindless Group v McLaughlin* [2008] IRLR 678, where the tribunal had criticized the employer for conceding liability late in the day. It was also emphasized that if the tribunal increases the award by more than 10 per cent, it must give reasons for its decision.

24.163 The duty to increase the award by 10 per cent does not apply if there are 'exceptional circumstances' which would make an increase of that percentage unjust or inequitable, in which case the tribunal may make no increase or an increase of a lesser percentage (Employment Act 2002, s 31(4)). This is likely to apply in cases of proven dishonesty such as *W Devis & Sons v Atkins* [1977] IRLR 314 or other situations where it would be contrary to public policy and unfair to the employer to allow the claimant to benefit from his or her wrongdoing, although it should be noted that the statutory provisions do allow a lesser percentage to be awarded in these circumstances. It has also been held that an award need not be increased where the statutory process would amount to a charade (*Bainbridge v Redcar & Cleveland Borough Council (No 2)* [2007] IRLR 494, as confirmed by the Court of Appeal [2008] IRLR 776).

Employment Act 2008

24.164 With effect from 6 April 2009, Employment Act 2002, s 31(3) was replaced by Employment Act 2008, s 3 which inserts a new s 207A into the Trade Union and Labour Relations (Consolidation) Act 1992.

24.165 This empowers (but does not require) the employment tribunal to increase the compensatory award by such amount as it considers 'just and equitable' up to a maximum of 25 per cent where the employer 'unreasonably' fails to comply with the new ACAS Code of Practice (and it is a claim to which the Code of Practice applies).

Power to review

24.166 It is possible to review the tribunal's decision where new evidence comes to light which could not have been known or reasonably foreseen at the time of the hearing or where it is in the interests of justice to do so. In exceptional circumstances, awards for future loss have been set aside and varied where there has been a fundamental change of circumstances within a short time of the hearing. For example, in *Dicker v Seceurop Ltd* EAT/554/84 the employers successfully applied for a review when the claimant unexpectedly found a new job two days after the hearing. Similarly, in *Bateman v British Leyland* [1974] IRLR 101, the claimant successfully applied for a review when he lost his new job two weeks after the hearing. In both cases the tribunal considered that the fundamental basis of the decision had been falsified to a sufficiently substantial extent to invalidate the assessment (*Yorkshire Engineering Co Ltd v Burnham* [1974] ICR 77).

Interest

Interest is not automatically added to the assessment of loss (for interest on employment tribunal awards see Chapter 28, para 28.01). However, in *Melia v Magna Kansei Ltd* [2005] IRLR 449, the EAT held that it may be appropriate in some cases to compensate the claimant for the depreciation in the value of lost earnings between dismissal and judgment by applying the same premium as that used in making a deduction for an accelerated payment (ie 2.5 per cent). The EAT's ruling has been confirmed by the Court of Appeal ([2006] IRLR 117). It has been suggested that, alternatively, the 'loss' in such circumstances may be calculated, by analogy to personal injury awards, either at half the appropriate rate of interest (*Dexter v Courtaulds Ltd* [1984] 1 All ER 70) or full interest from the mid-date of the period of loss until judgment (*Prokop v Department of Health and Social Security* [1985] CLY 1037). It remains to be seen whether these alternatives are accepted by employment tribunals. **24.167**

25

Reducing Unfair Dismissal Compensation

SUMMARY

(1) The compensatory award may be limited where an employment tribunal considers this to be 'just and equitable', for example where the dismissal is held to be unfair for some technical procedural reason but would have been fair but for this procedural error.

(2) The options available to the tribunal are to make no award, limit the award to a period of time, make an assessment of the outcome on a percentage chance basis, or refuse to speculate on the outcome and make a full award. However, where there is a failure to comply with the statutory disputes resolution procedure, an employment tribunal should make a minimum award of four weeks' pay other than where this would cause injustice.

(3) The compensatory award may be reduced for contributory fault.

A. INTRODUCTION

The compensatory award may be reduced where: **25.01**

(a) the employment tribunal finds that the conduct of the employee caused or contributed to the dismissal (ERA 1996, s 123(6));

(b) the employee is shown to have failed to mitigate his or her loss (ERA 1996, s 123(4));
(c) the employment tribunal considers it just and equitable to limit the award for some other reason (ERA 1996, s 123(1));
(d) the employee has failed to comply with the requirements of the statutory disputes resolution procedure (Employment Act 2002, s 31(2)).

25.02 The compensatory award may also be reduced where a redundancy payment exceeds the statutory maximum (ERA 1996, s 123(7)), and where an *ex gratia* payment is received by the employee.

25.03 The grounds on which the compensatory award may be reduced or limited are considered in greater detail below.

B. 'JUST AND EQUITABLE' REDUCTION

25.04 ERA 1996, s 123(1) 'does not . . . provide that regard should be had only to the loss resulting from the dismissal being unfair. Regard must be had to that, but the award must be just and equitable in all the circumstances, and it cannot be just and equitable that a sum should be awarded in compensation when in fact the employee has suffered no injustice by being dismissed' (*per* Viscount Dilhourne in *W Devis & Sons v Atkins* [1977] IRLR 314). This principle has become particularly important since the House of Lords' ruling in *Polkey v AE Dayton Services* [1988] AC 344, [1987] IRLR 503, where the House of Lords held that the so-called 'any difference' rule did not apply to liability but that the degree of injustice suffered by the claimant was relevant to compensation. Although the House of Lords' ruling on liability must now be read in the context of ERA 1996, s 98(2), the ruling is still relevant to the assessment of compensation. As a consequence, there may be circumstances where a tribunal considers it just and equitable to make no award at all or to limit the award to a specific period of time.

General principles

25.05 In *Tele-Trading Ltd v Jenkins* [1990] IRLR 430 the Court of Appeal stated that it may be just and equitable to make no award where:

(a) at the time of the application to the employment tribunal, the employer can show that the employee is in fact guilty of the misconduct alleged against him or some other serious misconduct (see also *Polkey v AE Dayton Services Ltd* [1987] IRLR 503, 506–8, *per* Lord Mackay), or
(b) the employer would or might have fairly dismissed the employee if a thorough and just investigation had been conducted prior to the dismissal, whether or not the employee is guilty of the alleged misconduct (see also *Polkey v AE Dayton Services Ltd* [1987] IRLR 503, 508–9, *per* Lord Bridge).

25.06 Category (a) cases cover situations where the evidence clearly establishes dishonest behaviour on the part of the employee even if this was not known at the time of dismissal (as in *Devis*). It is not entirely clear whether category (a) cases also allow an employer to put forward an alternative reason for dismissal as a basis for limiting the award of compensation, ie to argue that even if dismissal for reason 'A' was unfair, it would have been fair to dismiss for reason 'B' on the facts as known at the time of dismissal and that therefore compensation should be limited accordingly. There is some support for this view in *McNee v Charles Tenant & Co Ltd* EAT/338/90, and *Melia v Magna Kansei Ltd* [2005] IRLR 449, where Burton P considered that it was consistent with the ruling in *Devis v Atkins*, but in *Trico-Folberth Ltd v Devonshire* [1989] IRLR 396 the Court of Appeal appears to have held that it is not just and equitable to limit the compensatory award where the employers could have dismissed for another reason. However, the Court of Appeal's ruling may also be justified on the alternative basis that the findings made by the employment tribunal did not establish that the employers would have dismissed the claimant on the alternative ground. The point therefore remains arguable.

Category (b) cases (which are the more common) are cases where the employer seeks to argue that dismissal would have been a reasonable response if a proper procedure had been followed, ie where there has been some relatively minor procedural irregularity. For example, where there is a failure to consult in a redundancy dismissal or there is some minor procedural irregularity in a misconduct dismissal. However, this argument will not succeed where the employer is unable to show that the dismissal would have been fair had a fair procedure been followed, for example there is insufficient evidence of the employee's guilt, as in *Tele-Trading Ltd v Jenkins* [1990] IRLR 430, or dismissal would not have been a reasonable response on the basis of the evidence (see *Panama v London Borough of Hackney* [2003] IRLR 278). **25.07**

Distinction between procedure and substance?

At one time, it was suggested that category (b) arguments would only apply where the error was one of procedure rather than one of substance (see *Steel Stockholders (Birmingham) Ltd v Kirkwood* [1993] IRLR 515), ie that it might be open to a tribunal to limit or make no award where there had been a failure to consult in a redundancy case but not where the defect related to the selection criteria used to select those to be made redundant. However, the position has since been clarified by the Court of Session's ruling in *King v Eaton Ltd (No 2)* [1998] IRLR 686, where the Court stated that the distinction between 'procedural' and 'substantive' errors may be of some practical use in deciding whether it is realistic or practicable or just and equitable to embark upon an attempt to reconstruct a hypothesis to assess what would have happened had the error not occurred. Where the lapse is procedural, 'it may be relatively straightforward to envisage what would have been if procedures had stayed on track', whereas if what went wrong was more fundamental (or substantive), 'it may be more difficult to envisage what track one would be on, in the hypothetical situation of the unfairness not having occurred'. If in a particular case such as *O'Dea v ISC Chemicals Ltd* [1995] IRLR 599, it is possible to say that the claimant would have been made redundant or dismissed for some other reason in any event, or the tribunal is able with a degree of certainty to reach such a conclusion on a percentage chance basis, then there is no reason why the *Polkey* principle should be limited to procedural errors alone. However, where (to follow the analogy in *King*) the process has been completely derailed, an employment tribunal will not necessarily be required to speculate on the outcome because, as the Court recognized in *King*, this would involve embarking 'upon a sea of speculation where the opinions of witnesses could have no reliable factual starting point'. The Court of Session's approach to this question was approved by the Court of Appeal in *Lambe v 186K Ltd* [2004] EWCA Civ 1045. The Court stressed that the distinction between procedural and substantive defects was not helpful as the real issue is whether or not it is possible for the tribunal to reach a reasoned conclusion on the issue. reduction will be upheld where adequate reasons are given. So in *Gover v Propertycare Ltd* an employment tribunal did not err in limiting its award to four months' loss of earnings as this represented the period which it would have taken for the employers to consult properly over a proposed variation in contractual commission. The EAT's decision dismissing the appeal (EAT/0458/05/2J) was subsequently confirmed by the Court of Appeal ([2006] EWCA Civ 286). **25.08**

Therefore the options open to tribunals in category (b) cases are as follows: **25.09**

(a) to make no award (but see para 25.16 below);
(b) to limit the award to a particular period of time;
(c) to make an assessment of the outcome on a percentage chance basis;
(d) to refuse to speculate on the outcome and make a full award. (See *Software 2000 Ltd v Andrews* [2007] IRLR 568, where the principles are usefully summarized by Elias P).

25.10 The tribunal is under a duty to consider whether or not it should limit its award for these reasons and a failure to do so may be grounds for appeal (*Wolesley Centres Ltd v Simmons* [1994] ICR 503). If the employer seeks to contend that the award should be limited for one or more of these reasons, the employer should call evidence in support of this contention. However, a tribunal must have regard to all the evidence when making the assessment, including any evidence given by the employee (*Software 2000 Ltd v Andrews* [2007] IRLR 568). The parties should then be given an opportunity to make representations on the nature and the extent of what is sometimes referred to as a *Polkey* reduction (*Market Force (UK) Ltd v Hunt* [2002] IRLR 863).

Some illustrations of category (b) cases

25.11 The application of these principles is particularly relevant to the assessment of compensation in redundancy dismissals where the dismissal is held unfair on procedural grounds such as a failure to consult or warn of impending redundancy, but it should be emphasized that the principles apply to any type of dismissal.

25.12 It is also important to bear in mind the nature and significance of the procedural defect. For example, in *Parker v D & J Tullis Ltd* EAT/306/91, the tribunal concluded that although the dismissal was unfair because the employers failed to show the witness statement of the employee who had witnessed the incident which led to the dismissal, the outcome would have been the same if the statement had been shown and therefore made no award (see also *Slaughter v C Brewer & Sons Ltd* [1990] IRLR 426, where a similar approach was taken to an ill-health case). In redundancy dismissals where there has been a failure to consult but the tribunal considers that the outcome would have been the same even if there had been proper consultation (ie where dismissal is inevitable), tribunals will often limit the award to the length of time it would have taken for such proper consultation to take place (*Mining Supplies (Longwall) Ltd v Baker* [1988] IRLR 417). The length of time will depend on the particular circumstances but a period of between 14 days and one month is common (*Abbotts v Wesson Glynwed Steels Ltd* [1982] IRLR 51). A period of six weeks was considered excessive in the *Baker* case referred to above. A similar period may be appropriate if the tribunal is satisfied that the employee would have rejected an offer of alternative employment had it been made (*Lambe v 186K Ltd* [2004] EWCA Civ 1045). However, there are no hard and fast rules: in *Elkouil v Coney Island* [2002] IRLR 174 the EAT held that the tribunal had erred in limiting the compensatory award to two weeks where the employers had been aware of the redundancy situation some 10 weeks earlier. The EAT held that had the claimant been made aware of the risk of redundancy at an earlier stage, he would have had a longer opportunity to find himself a new job and therefore substituted an award for a 10-week period.

25.13 On the other hand, a full award will be made if it is clear that the employee would have been retained if proper consultation had taken place. The position is more complicated if dismissal is a possible but not an inevitable outcome. In some cases, tribunals will adopt a percentage chance approach as in *Hough v Leyland DAF Ltd* [1991] IRLR 194, where the EAT upheld a tribunal's ruling that compensation should be reduced by 50 per cent to take account of the chance that the employee would have been retained. In *Rao v Civil Aviation Authority* [1992] IRLR 203, an illness case, it was held by both the EAT and the Court of Appeal that there was only a 20 per cent chance that the applicant would have kept his job if the employers would have postponed their decision on his future pending the outcome of further treatment for a back problem and accordingly reduced the award by 80 per cent, and in *O'Dea v ISC Chemicals Ltd* [1995] IRLR 599, the Court of Appeal held that the applicant had a 20 per cent chance of being retained and reduced the award by 80 per cent. A percentage chance approach may also be used in assessing the chances of the claimant obtaining alternative employment at the same or a lower salary. Where the alternative employment is based on a lower salary, then the percentage should be applied to that salary from the date when the employee would have started the new job (*Red Bank Manufacturing Ltd v Meadows* [1992] IRLR 209). In other cases, as stated above, particularly where different criteria would have been used, a tribunal may be unwilling to speculate on the outcome and will make a full award. *King v Eaton (No 2)* referred to at para 25.08 above is an example of such a case.

Other reasons for limiting the award

It is open to tribunals to limit the award to a specific period of time if it considers that it was inevitable that the claimant would have been fairly dismissed within that period. For example, in *Winterhalter Gastronom Ltd v Webb* [1973] IRLR 120, the tribunal limited the compensatory award to three months because even if the claimant had received a final warning, it felt that 'he would not have been able to hold down the job in the future'. Similarly, in *O'Donoghue v Redcar & Cleveland Borough Council* [2001] IRLR 615, the Court of Appeal upheld an employment tribunal's decision to award six months' salary to the claimant on the basis that she would have been fairly dismissed at that time because of her divisive and antagonistic approach to her colleagues. A tribunal may also limit its award if the evidence shows that the claimant would have been made redundant or there was a risk of redundancy (for example *Youngs of Gosport Ltd v Kendell* [1977] IRLR 433, where the award was limited to nine months for this reason). As indicated above, such a risk may be assessed on a percentage chance basis where appropriate (see *O'Donoghue*, where the court did not rule out the possibility that the risk of future dismissal could be assessed in percentage terms, although it rejected the argument that the tribunal should have done this in the case before it). Where an employee has resigned and is dismissed during the notice period, the award will be limited to the unexpired period of notice (see *Ford v Milthorn Toleman Ltd* [1980] IRLR 30). It is also possible that a tribunal retains a residual discretion to limit the award for other inequitable conduct, although the reductions in the reported cases may be justified for one or more of the reasons considered below. However, a tribunal may not take account of conduct which takes place after dismissal. For example, in *Soros and Soros v Davidson* [1994] IRLR 264, the EAT held that the tribunal was wrong to take account of the fact that the applicant had allegedly sold confidential information about their employment to national newspapers after they had left their employment. **25.14**

Statutory dismissal procedure

In *Alexander v Bridgen Enterprises Ltd* [2006] IRLR 422, the EAT ruled that the principles referred to in paras 25.05–25.09 apply where a dismissal is found to be automatically unfair as a result of an employer's failure to follow the statutory dismissal procedure set out in Sch 1 Part 1 of the Employment Act 2002. So, in *Alexander*, the tribunal was entitled to conclude that the claimants would have been made redundant even if the employers had complied with the statutory procedure and accordingly the decision to award no compensation (see para 25.08 above) was upheld (these provisions were repealed with effect from 6 April 2009 and are retained in this edition because there may be some cases in the pipeline which are covered by the transitional provisions in the Employment Act 2008). **25.15**

Impact of s 98A(2) of the Employment Rights Act 1996 on 'ordinary' dismissals?

It has been suggested in *Mason v Governing Body of Ward End Primary School* [2006] IRLR 432 and *Alexander v Bridgen Enterprises Ltd* [2006] IRLR 422 that as a result of s 98A(2) of the Employment Rights Act 1996 where an employment tribunal concludes that there is more than a 50 per cent chance that the employee would have been dismissed, it should hold that the dismissal is fair rather than make a so-called '*Polkey*' reduction. In *Mason*, the EAT suggested that a *Polkey* reduction should henceforth only be made where there is a less than 50 per cent chance of dismissal. At the time of writing these *obiter* comments have yet to be confirmed and are open to further argument in ordinary dismissals (ie dismissals which are not in breach of the statutory dismissal procedure) where the chance of dismissal is greater than 50 per cent but less than 100 per cent. These *obiter* comments have since been followed by the EAT in *Software 2000 Ltd v Andrews* [2007] IRLR 568 but is perhaps open to further argument in ordinary dismissals (ie dismissals which are not in breach of the statutory dismissal procedure) where the chance **25.16** of dismissal is greater than 50 per cent but less than 100 per cent. However, it is clear from the statutory provisions that where a tribunal is satisfied that a dismissal would have been reasonable if a fair procedure had been followed (ie 100 per cent reduction cases), then it should hold the dismissal to be fair in accordance with s 98A(2) of the Employment Rights Act 1996 rather than hold it unfair and make no award. Furthermore, in *Software 2000 Ltd v Andrews* [2007] IRLR 568, the EAT reminded tribunals that 'the s 98A(2) and *Polkey* exercises run in parallel and will often involve consideration of the same evidence, but they must not be conflated'. It follows that even if a tribunal considers that some of the evidence or potential evidence is too speculative to form any sensible view as to whether dismissal would have occurred on the balance of probabilities, it must nevertheless take into account any evidence on which it considers it can properly rely and from which it could in principle conclude that the employment may have come to an end when it did, or alternatively would not have continued indefinitely (this provision was repealed with effect from 6 April 2009 and is retained in this edition because there may be some cases in the pipeline which are covered by the transitional provisions in the Employment Act 2008).

Impact of age discrimination legislation

25.17 The Employment Equality (Age) Regulations 2006, SI 2006/1031 impose a statutory default retirement age of 65. Those who work beyond the statutory retirement age retain the right to complain of unfair dismissal and their compensation claims will be assessed in the ordinary way. However, in cases where the dismissal occurs before the statutory retirement age, it is unlikely that it will be 'just and equitable' to award compensation beyond the statutory retirement age unless the claimant can establish that he or she would have been retained or would be likely to have been retained beyond that date in response to a request under reg 49. This provision will be repealed when Employment Act 2008, s 2 comes into force.

C. POWER TO REDUCE THE AWARD UNDER THE EMPLOYMENT ACT 2002

25.18 The compensatory award will be reduced where an employee fails to comply with the statutory disputes resolution procedure set out in Sch 2 to the Employment Act 2002 (this provision was repealed with effect from 6 April 2009 and is retained in this edition because there may be some cases in the pipeline which are covered by the transitional provisions in the Employment Act 2008).

25.19 The EA 2002, s 31(2) provides that where the non-completion of the statutory procedure is 'wholly or mainly attributable to failure by the employee to comply with a requirement of the procedure' or 'to exercise a right of appeal under it', the tribunal must (other than in exceptional circumstances) reduce the award to the employee by 10 per cent and may, if it considers it just and equitable, reduce the award by a further amount up to a total decrease of 50 per cent. It is arguable that in the light of the Court of Appeal's ruling in *Selvarajan v Wilmot* [2008] IRLR 824, there is no power to reduce the award where the statutory procedure has been completed but the employee has failed to comply with the general requirements set out in Part 3 of Sch 2 of the Employment Act 2002, although the wording of s 31(2)(c) is slightly different from s 31(3). This reduction is made before the compensatory award is reduced for contributory fault or on account of a payment of an enhanced redundancy payment (ERA 1996, s 124A). It is also likely that any reduction in the award will be made after account has been taken of the *Polkey* reduction (referred to in para 25.05 above) as, prior to this assessment, there is no 'award' to reduce.

25.20 It should be noted that the duty to reduce the compensatory award only arises where the breach of the statutory procedure is wholly or mainly attributable to the employee. So an award will not be reduced where, for example, an employer fails to arrange a meeting in accordance with the statutory procedure or did not conduct the meeting in a manner which complies with the statutory requirements. There is no statutory guidance as to the amount by which the award should be reduced above the 10 per cent minimum as this is left to the discretion of the employment tribunal. The main factors in determining any reduction will relate to the reasons for the employee's failure to comply with the statutory procedure, seriousness of the default, the degree of culpability on the part of the employee (see para 24.162 above), and perhaps the impact the reduction will have on the overall size of the award since a tribunal may feel that it is inequitable for an employee to be deprived of a substantial part of the award where the dismissal is unfair. However, as stated above, an employee will still be entitled to a minimum basic award of four weeks' pay unless this causes injustice to the employer.

The duty to reduce the award by 10 per cent does not apply 'if there are exceptional circumstances' which would make an increase of that percentage unjust or inequitable, in which case the tribunal may make no increase or an increase of a lesser percentage (EA 2002, s 31(4)). **25.21**

There is no statutory guidance as to when such exceptional circumstances may arise as this is left to the employment tribunal to determine. Examples of such exceptional circumstances may arise where the employee's failure to comply with the statutory procedure was caused by illness or some other form of non-blameworthy conduct or possibly where the employer acted in such a high-handed manner that the employee was entitled to believe that compliance with the procedures would be futile or utterly useless. It has also been held that an award need not be reduced where the statutory process would amount to a charade (*Bainbridge v Redcar & Cleveland Borough Council (No 2)* [2007] IRLR 494, as confirmed by the Court of Appeal [2008] IRLR 776). **25.22**

Under the previous law, the award of compensation could be reduced by up to two weeks' pay where an employee failed to appeal against his or her dismissal (ERA 1996, s 127A). This provision has now been repealed and replaced by the power to make a reduction of 10–50 per cent in these circumstances (EA 2002, s 31). Such a reduction may well be substantial if the employee cannot give a good explanation for the failure to appeal as the policy behind the statutory provisions is that disputes should be resolved internally wherever possible. On the other hand, a reduction may not be made where there are serious doubts as to the transparency of the appeal process and in certain circumstances this may even lead to the award being increased. **25.23**

The legislation may be relied on in constructive dismissal cases. Under the statutory rules, subject to certain statutory exceptions, employees are normally required to raise their grievance in writing internally by following the statutory disputes resolution procedure before bringing a complaint to an employment tribunal. Where a written grievance is presented to the employer, the employee is debarred from presenting an employment tribunal complaint for a minimum period of 28 days. Thereafter a failure on the part of the employee to comply with the statutory procedure will result in the award of compensation being reduced in accordance with the terms of the statutory provisions (other than in exceptional circumstances). Again we would suggest that the extent of the reduction will depend on the culpability of the employee and that in certain exceptional circumstances, there may be no reduction. **25.24**

Employment Act 2008

With effect from 6 April 2009, Employment Act 2002, s 31(2) will be replaced by Employment Act 2008, s 3 which inserts a new s 207A into the Trade Union and Labour Relations (Consolidation) Act 1992. **25.25**

This empowers (but does not require) the employment tribunal to reduce the compensatory award by such amount as it considers 'just and equitable' up to a maximum of 25 per cent where the employee 'unreasonably' fails to comply with the new ACAS Code of Practice (and it is a claim to which the code of practice applies). **25.26**

D. MITIGATION

25.27 ERA 1996, s 123(4) provides that in ascertaining the loss to be awarded under ERA 1996, s 123(1), a tribunal 'shall apply the same rule concerning the duty of a person to mitigate his loss as applies to damages recoverable under the common law of England and Wales or (as the case may be) Scotland'. The common law duty to mitigate distinguishes between the duty to mitigate in law and in fact. Mitigation in law means that the claimant should not recover damages for any loss which could reasonably have been avoided. Mitigation in fact means that the claimant must give credit for any benefit received as a consequence of the respondent's breach (see para 24.131 above).

General principles

25.28 In the context of unfair dismissal law, the duty to mitigate in law means that the claimant must take reasonable steps to minimize the loss by finding another job or, as Donaldson J put it in *Archibold Freightage Ltd v Wilson* [1974] IRLR 10: 'It is the duty of an employee who has been dismissed to act as a reasonable man would do if he had no hope of receiving compensation from his previous employer.' Similarly, in *Wilding v British Telecommunications plc* [2002] IRLR 524, the Court of Appeal held that the steps taken by the employee must be reasonable as a claimant cannot recover compensation for any loss which he could have avoided by taking reasonable steps.

25.29 The burden of proving a failure to mitigate is on the employer: *Fyfe v Scientific Furnishing Ltd* [1989] IRLR 331 (as it is at common law: *Bessenden Properties Ltd v JK Corness* [1974] IRLR 338). There is some inconsistency in the case law as to whether the reasonableness of a claimant's attempts to mitigate loss are judged objectively, subjectively, or by the standard of a 'reasonable employee'. The Court of Appeal's ruling in *Wilding v British Telecommunications plc* (above) appears to support the latter, although Sedley LJ suggested that tribunals should consider whether the claimant's behaviour fell within a range of reasonable employee responses. The question of what is reasonable is essentially one of fact and pre-eminently one to be determined by the employment tribunal whose decision will only be overturned on appeal if it is shown to have misdirected itself in law or reached a decision to which no reasonable tribunal could have come. A failure to consider the issue of mitigation will, however, amount to an error of law (*Morganite Electrical Carbon Ltd v Donne* [1987] IRLR 363).

25.30 In *Savage v Saxena* [1998] IRLR 182, the EAT suggested that an employment tribunal should ask itself the following questions in relation to mitigation of loss: (1) what steps should the claimant have taken to mitigate his or her loss? and (2) on what date would such steps have produced an alternative income? Having answered those questions, the award should be reduced accordingly.

Re-employment as mitigation

25.31 In certain circumstances, the claimant may be required to accept an offer of re-employment by his or her old employer in mitigation of loss (see *Martin v Yeoman Aggregates Ltd* [1983] IRLR 49). In *Wilding v British Telecommunications plc* [2002] IRLR 524, a disability discrimination case, the Court of Appeal suggested that in applying the general principles referred to above to such an offer, it is necessary to consider the circumstances in which the offer was made and refused, the attitude of the former employer, the way in which the employee had been treated, and all the surrounding circumstances including the employee's state of mind. The Court advised tribunals not to be too stringent on the expectation of the employee. A relevant factor will include the timing of the offer. Normally it will not be unreasonable to turn down an offer made a long time after the dismissal, but as the *Wilding* case shows—where the offer was made after liability was established—there are no hard and fast rules. Another relevant fact is the clarity of the offer: the claimant may be reasonable in turning down an offer which is vague or unclear, but this will depend on the circumstances as it may be more 'reasonable' to ask the employer to clarify the terms. Other relevant factors include the reason for dismissal, the reasonableness of the dismissal, and in particular the impact it had on the relationship of trust which may be critical. It may be more reasonable to turn down an offer of reinstatement if the claimant has found a new job by the time it is made (*Yetton v Eastwoods Froy Ltd* [1966] 3 All ER 353; *How v Tesco Ltd* [1974] IRLR 194). Similar considerations apply to offers of re-engagement in alternative positions. Additional relevant factors will include the similarity of the positions and the length of time the claimant has been unemployed.

Offer of early retirement

It may be open to an employer to argue that employees who unreasonably turn down an offer of early retirement on generous terms in redundancy or ill-health dismissals have failed to mitigate their loss, but employees will not necessarily act unreasonably in turning down such an offer. For example, in *Fyfe v Scientific Furnishing Ltd* [1989] IRLR 331, the employment tribunal held that the applicant was unreasonable in turning down a generous offer of an early retirement package made after he was dismissed, but the decision was overturned by the EAT on the grounds that the employer had not explained its offer in clear terms and had not given the applicant sufficient time to think about it. Furthermore, it should be remembered that the duty to mitigate only arises after dismissal (see para 25.36 below), so any pre-dismissal offer is irrelevant for this purpose. **25.32**

Alternative employment

In most cases, the main issue will be whether the claimant has taken reasonable steps post-dismissal to find alternative employment with a new employer. As stated above, whether a claimant has acted reasonably in this regard is largely a question of fact and the citation of authority in this context is therefore mainly of illustrative value (*Bessenden Properties Ltd v JK Corness* [1974] IRLR 338). Much will depend on the state of the labour market and the personal characteristics of the employee. For example, an employee who is elderly or in poor health may experience particular difficulty in finding a new job and this is recognized by the tribunal (as are other discriminatory factors in the labour market). Claimants are expected not to turn down reasonable offers of alternative employment. However, this does not mean that they have to accept the first job offer that is made to them. As the NIRC said in *AG Bracey v Iles* [1973] IRLR 210: 'it may not be reasonable to take the first job that comes along. It may be much more reasonable, in the interests of the employee and of the employer who has to pay compensation, that he should wait a little time. He must, of course, use the time well and seek a better paid job which will reduce his overall loss and the amount of compensation which the previous employer ultimately will have to pay.' It should be observed that these comments were made at a time of high employment and the reasonableness of the claimant's behaviour needs to be considered in the context of the prevailing labour market. Claimants who have been out of work for some time may be required to be more flexible in their approach to job search both in relation to the level of pay (and terms and conditions) and the nature of the work they are looking for. Issues of relocation draw significant differences in response from tribunals: some tribunals expect the claimant to be willing to relocate whereas others less so (see *Ramsay v WB Anderson & Son Ltd* [1974] IRLR 164). The job search should extend to temporary or part-time work where the outlook for permanent employment is bleak (*Hardwick v Leeds Area Health Authority* [1975] IRLR 319). **25.33**

Setting up a business or becoming self-employed

If there is no suitable alternative employment available, it is possible to mitigate loss by setting up a business or becoming self-employed but it is for the tribunal to decide whether this was reasonable in the particular circumstances. The leading case on this point is **25.34**

Gardiner-Hill v Roland Berger Technics Ltd [1982] IRLR 498, where a former managing director aged 55 decided to set up his own business after being out of work for more than six and a half months. Furthermore, if the decision to set up the business was reasonable, the employee will not be penalized if the business subsequently fails (*Blick Vessels & Pipework Ltd v Sharpe* EAT/681/84).

Retraining

25.35 Similarly, tribunals will not necessarily penalize claimants who decide to improve their skills by retraining, thereby increasing their prospects of finding alternative employment. Again much will depend on the state of the labour market and the length of the particular course. Tribunals are more sympathetic to short-term or part-time courses (*Sealy v Avon Aluminium Co Ltd* EAT/516/78) than long-term academic courses (*Holroyd v Gravure Cylinders Ltd* [1984] IRLR 259). It is more difficult to show that it was reasonable to embark on a long-term course which involves a career change, but there are no hard and fast rules. For example, in *Khanum v IBC Vehicles* EAT/785/98, the tribunal found that it was reasonable for the complainant to take up a place at Luton University to study for a computer systems degree because she considered it would be difficult to find employment without it. The EAT dismissing the appeal agreed, noting that there were special factors supporting this decision. Similarly in *Orthet Ltd v Vince-Cain* [2004] IRLR 857, a sex discrimination case, the EAT held that the tribunal had not erred in law in awarding compensation covering the whole period of a four-year training course to become a dietician.

Limits to the duty to mitigate

25.36 The duty to mitigate only arises after dismissal. This may be relevant to offers of re-employment made prior to the termination of employment such as in *Gilham v Kent County Council* [1986] IRLR 56; *Trimble v Supertravel Ltd* [1982] IRLR 451; and *McAndrew v Prestwick Circuits Ltd* [1988] IRLR 514. There is nothing to prevent the employer from renewing such an offer after dismissal.

25.37 Similarly, employees will not be held to be in breach of their duty to mitigate by not pursuing an internal grievance prior to their dismissal or resignation (*Seligman & Latz Ltd v McHugh* [1979] IRLR 130). A failure to pursue an internal appeal may be in breach of the duty to mitigate where such an appeal stands a good prospect of success. In *Hoover Ltd v Forde* [1980] ICR 239 the award was reduced by 50 per cent for this reason, but contrast *William Muir (Bond 9) Ltd v Lamb* [1985] IRLR 95, where the award was not reduced because the appeal involved too many 'imponderable factors' and therefore the employee did not act unreasonably. These cases must now be seen in the light of the more general power to increase or reduce the award of compensation where an employee or employer fails to comply with the statutory disputes resolution procedure as the failure to comply with this procedure will, other than in exceptional circumstances, lead to an increase or decrease in the award of at least 10 per cent (see para 25.18). This provision was repealed when the Employment Act 2008 came into force (see para 25.25). A corollary of the procedure is that it may not be unreasonable for employees to delay their job search pending the outcome of such internal resolution and it will be interesting to see what impact, if any, the new rules have on mitigation.

Assessing the deduction

25.38 There is no specific statutory guidance on how the deduction for a failure to mitigate should be calculated. The normal approach is to decide when the employee would have found other work and limit the compensatory award accordingly (*Savage v Saxena* [1998] IRLR 182). If the tribunal concludes that the job will be less well paid, this will be reflected in the award for continuing loss (*Smith, Kline & French Laboratories Ltd v Coates* [1977] IRLR 276 and *Peara v Enderlin Ltd* [1979] ICR 804). Tribunals should not, however, reduce the award on a percentage basis as they do in assessing contributory fault.

E. CONTRIBUTORY FAULT

ERA 1996, s 123(6) provides that where a tribunal finds that the dismissal was to any extent caused or contributed to by an action of the claimant, it shall reduce the amount of the compensatory award by such proportion as it considers just and equitable having regard to that finding. **25.39**

In *Optikinetics Ltd v Whooley* EAT/1275/97, the EAT helpfully summarized the case law on reductions for contributory fault as follows: **25.40**

(a) The claimant must be found to have acted in a culpable, blameworthy, or wholly unreasonable manner.
(b) The tribunal's inquiry in this regard should be directed solely at the conduct of the claimant, not the employer.
(c) The conduct must be known to the employer prior to the dismissal and have been the cause of it.
(d) Once blameworthy conduct is established, a tribunal is bound to reduce the award by such amount as it considers just and equitable, although the tribunal retains a complete discretion over the amount of the reduction and may in some circumstances conclude that the behaviour was too trivial to justify any reduction.
(e) It is open to the tribunal to reduce the basic and compensatory awards by different amounts.
(f) Appellate courts will rarely interfere with a tribunal's assessment of a reduction for contributory fault.

Blameworthy conduct

A reduction for contributory fault should only take place if the claimant has acted in a culpable or blameworthy or wholly unreasonable manner. This was established by the Court of Appeal in *Nelson v BBC (No 2)* [1979] IRLR 346, 351, *per* Brandon LJ, who stated: **25.41**

> The concept does not, in my view, necessarily involve any conduct of the complainant amounting to a breach of contract or a tort. It includes, no doubt, conduct of that kind. But it also includes conduct which, while not amounting to a breach of contract or a tort, is nevertheless perverse or foolish, or, if I may use the colloquialism, bloody-minded. It may also include action which, though not meriting any of those more perjorative epithets, is nevertheless, unreasonable in all the circumstances. I should not, however, go so far as to say that all unreasonable conduct is necessarily culpable or blameworthy; it must depend on the degree of unreasonableness involved.

The issue whether or not the conduct in question amounts to blameworthy conduct is therefore largely a question of fact for a tribunal to determine and a tribunal's decision is unlikely to be overturned on appeal unless it misdirects itself in law or reaches a perverse decision on the facts (*Hollier v Plysu Ltd* [1983] IRLR 260). The conduct involved is judged objectively: it is irrelevant for this purpose whether the employee fully appreciates the extent of the blameworthy conduct (*Ladbroke Racing Ltd v Mason* [1978] IRLR 49), although this may be relevant in determining the extent of the reduction. The blameworthy conduct may be that of the claimant or his agents (see *Allen v Hammett* [1982] IRLR 89, where the applicant was held responsible for the negligent advice given to him by his solicitor). **25.42**

Most misconduct will be regarded as blameworthy. The following have all been so regarded: dishonesty, a breach of the company's rules, going on holiday or returning late without permission, soliciting customers for a rival business or working for a rival outside normal working hours, a poor attendance record, conduct setting back recovery from illness, failing to reply to a letter requiring an employee to attend a disciplinary hearing or a medical review. But such a reduction will only be made if there is sufficient evidence of such misconduct before the employment tribunal (*Tele-Trading Ltd v Jenkins* [1990] IRLR 430). **25.43**

Tribunals should not reduce compensation for contributory fault where employees are unfairly dismissed for taking part in industrial action as industrial action of itself is not blameworthy **25.44** conduct applying *Courtaulds Northern Spinning Ltd v Moosa* [1984] IRLR 43 (see *Crosville Wales Ltd v Tracey (No 2)* [1997] IRLR 691, HL, [1996] IRLR 91, CA). This reflects Parliament's intention that tribunals should not be involved in weighing up the merits of an employment dispute. However, the Court of Appeal and House of Lords in *Tracey* made clear that a reduction for contributory fault can be made if the conduct involved goes beyond mere participation in the industrial action, ie intimidatory conduct.

25.45 Tribunals are also reluctant to find blameworthy conduct where an employee is dismissed for capability-related reasons unless the employee was to blame for the performance which led to his dismissal. In *Kraft Foods Ltd v Fox* [1977] IRLR 43, the EAT drew a distinction between actions over which an employee has control and those outside his control. As regards the former, the claimant may be found to have contributed to his dismissal (see *Sutton & Gates (Luton) Ltd v Boxall* [1978] IRLR 486, where the EAT gave examples of laziness, idleness, or negligence where a reduction for contributory fault may be justified). But as regards the latter types of 'true capability dismissals', the claimant will not normally be to blame and therefore compensation should not normally be reduced for contributory fault. As the EAT put it, 'if an employee is incompetent or incapable and cannot, with the best will in the world measure up to the job, it seems to us to be wrong to say that that condition of incapacity is a contributory factor to his dismissal'.

25.46 Similarly, compensation will not normally be reduced for contributory fault in ill-health dismissals unless there is some aspect of the claimant's behaviour which justifies it, ie a failure to undergo a medical examination or refusal to provide a medical report (*Slaughter v C Brewer & Sons Ltd* [1990] IRLR 426) or acting in a manner which harms recovery (*A Links Ltd v Rose* [1991] IRLR 353).

25.47 The same principles apply to constructive dismissal cases. This was initially doubted in *Holroyd v Gravure Cylinders Ltd* [1984] IRLR 259, where the EAT said such a reduction should only be made in exceptional circumstances. However, in *Morrison v Amalgamated Transport and General Workers Union* [1989] IRLR 361 the Northern Ireland Court of Appeal disagreed and stated that insofar as *Holroyd* purported to lay down a general principle or rule of law, it was wrongly decided and the *Morrison* decision has since been followed and approved by the EAT in *Polentarutti v Autokraft Ltd* [1991] IRLR 457.

Conduct of the claimant

25.48 In deciding whether there should be a reduction for contributory fault, tribunals are concerned with the conduct of the claimant rather than the employer. In *Parker Foundry Ltd v Slack* [1992] IRLR 11 the court upheld the tribunal's decision to reduce the award by 50 per cent for contributory fault where the claimant had been dismissed for fighting and rejected the argument that the tribunal should have taken into account the conduct of another employee who had also been involved in the fight. This may be relevant to the issue of the extent of the reduction.

Contributory conduct

25.49 As far as the compensatory award is concerned, the statutory provisions make clear that the award may only be reduced where the conduct genuinely causes or contributes to the dismissal. For example, in *Hutchinson v Enfield Rolling Mills* [1981] IRLR 318, the EAT held that the tribunal was wrong to take into account the claimant's political views and the fact that the employers regarded him as a troublemaker. The EAT said that the only relevant factors are those which led to the dismissal. The principle was reiterated by the EAT in *Lindsay v General Contracting Ltd (t/a Pik a Pak Home Electrical)* EAT/1096/00 and 1126/00, where the claimant was found to have been unfairly dismissed for union membership-related reasons but the tribunal had reduced the award for unrelated conduct. However, tribunals may take into account subsidiary reasons which contributed to the decision to dismiss as in *Robert Whiting Designs Ltd v Lamb* [1978] ICR 89. Conduct which occurs post-dismissal such as conduct in the notice period or a failure to appeal (*Hoover Ltd v Forde* [1980] ICR 239) cannot be relied on as this does not cause or contribute to the dismissal. However, it should be noted that a failure to appeal may lead to a reduction in the award under EA 2002, s 31(2) (see para 25.18). This provision was repealed when the Employment Act 2008 came into force (see para 25.25).

Amount of reduction

Once the claimant's conduct has been found to be blameworthy, the tribunal will consider the extent to which it is just and equitable to reduce the award for this reason. **25.50**

In *Hollier v Plysu Ltd* [1983] IRLR 260, the Court of Appeal endorsed the EAT's guidance as to how tribunals should approach this task. The EAT suggested that there were four types of cases: **25.51**

(1) where the employee is wholly to blame for the dismissal, compensation could be reduced by 100 per cent;
(2) where the employee is largely to blame, the award should be reduced by 75 per cent;
(3) where both parties are equally to blame, the award should be reduced by 50 per cent;
(4) where the employee is slightly to blame, the award should be reduced by 25 per cent.

The EAT has also acknowledged that there may be cases where the degree of blameworthiness is so small that it may not be appropriate to make a reduction at all (see *Lindsay v General Contracting Ltd (t/a Pik a Pak Home Electrical)* EAT/1096/00 and 1126/00 and *York v Brown* EAT/262/84). **25.52**

Although the EAT's guidance in *Hollier* was endorsed by the Court of Appeal, the Court stressed that the question of apportionment should be approached by tribunals with a 'broad common sense view of the situation' and that appellate courts should not intervene unless a tribunal has misunderstood or misconstrued the statutory provisions or come to a decision to which no reasonable tribunal could have come. A failure to refer to the guidelines in itself will not justify an appeal. **25.53**

As stated above, it is open to a tribunal to reduce the award by 100 per cent for contributory fault but, as Chadwick LJ pointed out in *Friend v Civil Aviation Authority* [2001] IRLR 819, such a reduction is only appropriate in exceptional circumstances where the tribunal is satisfied that the employee was wholly to blame for the dismissal and it is just and equitable to make such a reduction (for example, *Maris v Rotherham Borough Council* [1974] IRLR 147, where the claimant made a fraudulent expenses claim and *Chaplin v Rawlinson* [1999] ICR 553, where the dismissal for urinating on a consignment of wheat was held to be procedurally unfair but a 100 per cent reduction was justified). Such a reduction will not normally be justified where any procedural irregularity which was the cause of the unfair dismissal judgment is significant (see *Gibson v British Transport Docks Board* [1982] IRLR 228). **25.54**

Tribunals must generally ignore industrial pressure in assessing compensation (ERA 1996, s 123(5)) but this does not prevent a tribunal from reducing the award for contributory fault where the employee was to blame for the actions which led to the industrial pressure. For example, in *Colwyn Borough Council v Dutton* [1980] IRLR 420, the tribunal found that the applicant's dismissal was the result of industrial pressure and was therefore unfair but the award was reduced for contributory fault because the cause of the industrial pressure was that his driving was so bad. **25.55**

Consistent reduction of awards

Normally a tribunal will reduce the basic and compensatory award for contributory fault by the same amount (*GM McFall & Co Ltd v Curran* [1981] IRLR 455; *RSPCA v Crudden* [1986] IRLR 83) but in exceptional circumstances it may be appropriate to reduce the awards by different amounts (*Les Ambassadeurs Club v Bainda* [1982] IRLR 5, where the EAT upheld a decision to reduce the compensatory award by 70 per cent but not to reduce the basic award at all). In **25.56** this context, it should be noted that the power to reduce the basic award is wider than the power to reduce the compensatory award (see para 24.63 above).

25.57 The reduction for contributory fault takes place before applying the statutory ceiling on the compensatory award (*Walter Braund (London) Ltd v Murray* [1991] IRLR 100).

Relationship with power to limit the award

25.58 It is open to the tribunal to both limit an award under ERA 1996, s 123(1) and to reduce it for contributory fault. The tribunal should first consider whether or not it wishes to limit its award and then consider a reduction for contributory fault if this is appropriate (*Rao v Civil Aviation Authority* [1994] IRLR 240).

F. EX GRATIA PAYMENTS

25.59 It is not uncommon for employers to make an *ex gratia* payment in addition to any payment which an employee is entitled to receive on dismissal. For this purpose an *ex gratia* payment is one which the employer pays without legal obligation to do so.

25.60 The case law on *ex gratia* payments is surprisingly confusing. The current position is that the claimant must normally give credit for all post-dismissal payments (*Digital Equipment Co Ltd v Clements (No 2)* [1998] IRLR 134). Where the payment is made under legal obligation such as a payment in lieu of notice, this will be taken into account in assessing the loss (*Heggie v Uniroyal Ltd* [1999] IRLR 802). The same will normally be true of an *ex gratia* payment (*Horizon Holiday Ltd v Grassi* [1987] IRLR 371; *Babcock FATA Ltd v Addison* [1987] IRLR 173) or payments made by mistake (*Boorman v Allmakes* [1995] IRLR 553), but in *Chelsea Football Club & Athletic Co Ltd v Heath* [1981] IRLR 73, the EAT ruled that where an *ex gratia* payment was expressly made with reference to the statutory liability for unfair dismissal compensation, the payment may be set off against the basic award and any excess may be set off against the final award of compensation. The case law therefore suggests that there is a distinction between *ex gratia* payments made as a goodwill gesture at the time of dismissal and payments made before a hearing on account of or without admission of liability. This issue is important because if the payment is not brought into account until the end of the process, the respondent will receive full credit for the total payment made to the claimant as in redundancy cases (see para 25.65 below).

25.61 Not all *ex gratia* payments fall to be deducted from the compensatory award. For example, in *Babcock FATA Ltd v Addison* [1987] IRLR 173, the applicant recovered compensation for the loss of an *ex gratia* payment which he would have received if he had been dismissed at the same time as his colleagues some 15 months later when the employer's business was closed. Similarly in *Roadchef Ltd v Hastings* [1988] IRLR 142, the EAT held that the tribunal was correct not to deduct an *ex gratia* payment which the employee would have received even if he had not been dismissed. The same reasoning was applied to the non-deduction of a bonus payment which an employee would have received had he remained in employment during the period covered by the award (*Quiring v Hill House International School* EAT/500/88, but contrast *DCM Optical plc v Stark* EAT/0124/04, where a retention payment was held to be deductible and *Rushton v Harcross Timber and Building Supplies Ltd* [1993] IRLR 254, where an *ex gratia* redundancy payment was held to be deductible).

G. OTHER REDUCTIONS

25.62 ERA 1996, s 123(7) provides that

> if the amount of any payment made by the employer to the employee on the ground that the dismissal was by reason of redundancy exceeds the amount of the basic award that would be payable . . . that excess goes to reduce the amount of the compensatory award.

So, for example, if the employer pays an enhanced redundancy payment to the claimant on dismissal, then the amount of the enhanced payment may be set off against the compensatory award.

H. ACCELERATED PAYMENT

Where an award is made for future loss of earnings and benefits, a deduction should be made for the accelerated receipt of the payment so as to ensure that the claimant is not put in a better position than would have been the case had the payment been received as and when it falls due (*York Trailer Co Ltd v Sparkes* [1973] IRLR 348). Such a reduction need not be made if the award for future loss is relatively small as it will be in many cases (*Les Ambassadeurs Club v Bainda* [1982] IRLR 5). **25.63**

There is no established method of calculating the reduction. Prior to the Court of Appeal's ruling in *Brentwood Bros (Manchester) Ltd v Shepherd* [2003] IRLR 364, it was not uncommon for tribunals simply to reduce the overall award for future loss by the prevailing discount rate in personal injury cases (currently 2.5 per cent). In *Shepherd*, a sex discrimination and unfair dismissal case, the tribunal awarded two and half years' loss of earnings and 10 years' loss of pension rights. It then reduced the award by 5 per cent to take account of the fact of accelerated receipt. The Court of Appeal held that the tribunal had erred in making a single reduction of 5 per cent pointing out that the conventional discount is based on an annual yield rather than a cumulative yield. **25.64**

I. ORDER OF REDUCTIONS

In *Digital Equipment Co Ltd v Clement (No 2)* [1998] IRLR 134 the Court of Appeal ruled that the order in which the reductions should be made depends on whether or not the dismissal is for redundancy. **25.65**

In ordinary cases, the correct approach is as follows: **25.66**

(a) to calculate the loss suffered by the claimant;
(b) to give credit for payments received on or since dismissal;
(c) to make a *Polkey* reduction (if appropriate);
(d) to reduce the award for contributory fault.

In redundancy cases, the correct approach is as follows: **25.67**

(a) to calculate the loss suffered by the claimant;
(b) to give full credit for any payments received by the claimant;
(c) to make a *Polkey* reduction (if appropriate);
(d) to reduce the award for contributory fault;
(e) to set off any enhanced redundancy payment made by the employer.

This means that the employer gets full credit for any enhanced redundancy payment made on the termination of employment. However, the position is slightly different where the award is increased or decreased under EA 2002, s 31. In such circumstances, ERA 1996, s 124A provides that the increase or decrease should take place before any reduction for contributory fault or credit is given for an enhanced redundancy payment. It is unclear whether such an increase or reduction should be made before or after a *Polkey* reduction. The better view is that it should be made *after* the *Polkey* reduction as the actual loss is only determined at that stage. **25.68**

J. STATUTORY MAXIMUM

The compensatory award is subject to a prescribed statutory maximum, £65,300 for the year beginning 1 February 2010. This is reviewed annually and increased (or decreased) in line with **25.69** changes in the RPI index. The new rate is normally announced in December and is varied by way of a statutory instrument laid before Parliament. The new rate comes into force with effect from 1 February of the following year, ie it applies to dismissals *after* that date.

25.70 ERA 1996, s 124(5) provides that the statutory maximum is applied *after* the quantification of the award under ERA 1996, s 123. This means that the statutory maximum is only applied after the total loss is assessed and reduced in accordance with the provisions of ERA 1996, ss 123 and 124A (*McCarthy v British Insulated Callenders Cables plc* [1985] IRLR 94 and *Walter Braund (London) Ltd v Murray* [1991] IRLR 100).

26

Remedies in Discrimination Cases

SUMMARY

(1) Where an employment tribunal finds a complaint of unlawful discrimination well founded it must, if it considers it just and equitable, make one of the following orders: a declaration, award of compensation, and/or a recommendation.

(2) The amount of compensation is assessed 'in like manner as any other claim in tort or (in Scotland) in reparation for breach of statutory duty'. The award may therefore include compensation for injury to feelings and, if appropriate, injury to health.

(3) An award for injury to feelings can be made where it is shown that the unlawful discrimination caused such an injury. Awards range from a minimum band of between £500 and £5,000, to a middle band of between £5,000 and £15,000, to a maximum band of between £15,000 and £30,000 depending on the gravity of the unlawful act and the employer's reaction to it (though these bands should be uprated to allow for inflation).

(4) Aggravated damages may be awarded where the discriminator has acted in a high-handed, malicious, insulting, or oppressive manner. The award must be compensatory, not punitive.

(5) The award of compensation may be increased or decreased where the respondent or claimant fails to comply with the statutory disputes resolution procedures set out in Schedule 2 to the Employment Act 2002. Other than in exceptional circumstances, such a failure will result in the award being increased or reduced by a minimum of 10 per cent but may be increased or reduced by as much as 50 per cent.

(6) Compensation may also be awarded for indirect discrimination where in race or sex discrimination cases, this is 'intentional' or in certain additional circumstances in 'provision, practice or criteria' cases.

(7) An employment tribunal has the power to make a recommendation that the respondent take action within a specified period which is practicable to remedy the adverse impact of the discrimination on the complainant. A failure to comply with such a recommendation may lead to an increase in the award of compensation.

A. INTRODUCTION

26.01 Compensation is the primary, though not the only, remedy open to an employee who is the victim of unlawful discrimination.

26.02 Compensation can be recovered under the following legislation:

(a) Sex Discrimination Act 1975 (SDA 1975);
(b) Race Relations Act 1976 (as amended) (RRA 1976);
(c) Disability Discrimination Act 1995 (as amended) (DDA 1995);
(d) Part-time Workers (Prevention of Less Favourable Treatment) Regulations 2000, SI 2000/1551 (PTWR 2000);
(e) Fixed Term Employees (Prevention of Less Favourable Treatment) Regulations 2002, SI 2002/2034 (FTER 2002);
(f) Employment Equality (Sexual Orientation) Regulations 2003, SI 2003/1661 (SOR 2003);
(g) Employment Equality (Religion or Belief) Regulations 2003, SI 2003/1660 (RBR 2003);
(h) Employment Equality (Age) Regulations 2006, SI 2006/1031 (EEAR 2006).

26.03 Recent discrimination cases have stressed the need for consistency in interpretation of the laws relating to sex and race discrimination and the other discrimination laws insofar as they incorporate the same concepts. The same policy considerations should apply to the interpretation of the statutory provisions which determine awards of compensation and other remedies available to the victims of unlawful discrimination. However, there are some significant differences in the powers to award compensation for indirect discrimination (para 26.61 below) and the power to make awards under EqPA 1970, PTWR 2000, and FTER 2002.

No statutory limit

26.04 There is no statutory limit to the amount of compensation which can be made in complaints of unlawful discrimination. There is also no statutory limit on awards made under EqPA 1970, PTWR 2000, or FTER 2002.

B. COMPENSATION FOR DIRECT DISCRIMINATION AND VICTIMIZATION

General principles

26.05 Where an employment tribunal finds a complaint of unlawful discrimination well founded, it must, if it considers it just and equitable to do so, make one or more of the following orders:

(a) an order declaring the rights of the claimant and respondent in relation to the act (or acts) to which the complaint relates;

(b) An order requiring the respondent to pay to the claimant compensation of an amount corresponding to any damages he could have been ordered to pay by a county court or by a sheriff court (in Scotland) if the complaint had fallen within the jurisdiction of one or other of those courts;
(c) a recommendation that the respondent take within a specified period action appearing to the tribunal to be practicable for the purpose of obviating or reducing the adverse effect on the claimant of any act of discrimination to which the complaint relates.

(SDA 1975, s 65(1); RRA 1976, s 56(1); DDA 1995, s 17A(2); SOR 2003, reg 30(1); RBR 2003, reg 30(1)); EEAR 2006, reg 38.)

Just and equitable discretion

These remedies, including compensation for discrimination, are not automatic. A tribunal must conclude that such an award is just and equitable. **26.06**

Whilst motive and intention are not relevant to liability in a complaint of direct discrimination, they may in certain circumstances be relevant to the issue of remedy (*per* Mummery J in *O'Neill v Governors of St Thomas More Roman Catholic Voluntary Aided Upper School* [1997] ICR 33 and *Chief Constable of Manchester v Hope* [1999] ICR 338, where a majority of the EAT allowed an appeal against an award of £750 for injury to feelings on the basis that the tribunal did not consider whether it was just and equitable to make such an award in the particular circumstances; alternatively the majority considered that the award was perverse). **26.07**

Claim to be assessed 'as any other claim in tort'

The amount of compensation is to be assessed 'in like manner as any other claim in tort or (in Scotland) in reparation for breach of statutory duty' (SDA 1975, s 66(1); RRA 1976, s 57(1); DDA 1995, s 17A(3); SOR 2003, reg 31(1); RBR 2003, reg 31(1); EEAR 2006, reg 39(1)). **26.08**

Unlike unfair dismissal cases, the amount of the award itself is not based on what the tribunal considers just and equitable in the particular circumstances (*Hurley v Mustoe (No 2)* [1983] ICR 422). Instead the general principle is that, as far as possible, claimants should be put in the same position they would have been but for the unlawful act (*Ministry of Defence v Wheeler* [1998] IRLR 23). **26.09**

In broad terms, the tort principles on causation and remoteness thus apply to the assessment of compensation in discrimination cases. The discriminator must therefore take his victim as he finds him (the 'eggshell skull' principle) as discriminatory behaviour affects people in different ways. This principle is of particular relevance in claims for injury to feelings as individuals will react differently to being the victims of discrimination but may also be relevant to the issue of mitigation. **26.10**

At common law, compensation will only be recoverable for injury which is reasonably foreseeable but in *Essa v Laing Ltd* [2004] ICR 746 the Court of Appeal, by a majority, ruled that this principle does not apply to all statutory torts and held that it did not apply to discrimination claims involving harassment. It was therefore open to a victim of harassment to claim compensation for any loss which flows directly from the discriminatory act. It is unclear whether the Court's ruling applies to all types of discrimination claims as, arguably, the majority's reasoning is based on the intentional nature of the particular behaviour in that case (racial abuse). Nonetheless, even if the reasoning does apply more generally, tribunals still have to consider difficult issues of causation particularly when it comes to assessing compensation for injury to feelings and injury to health as the complainant can only be compensated for the injury caused by the discriminatory act (see para 26.30 below). **26.11**

A tribunal award must be based on the loss caused by the substantive complaint (or complaints) it upholds (*Chapman v Simon* [1994] IRLR 124), although sometimes it may be appropriate to **26.12** take into account the findings made on the evidence in determining the extent of the injury to feelings (*British Telecommunications plc v Reid* [2004] IRLR 327).

Awards against individual respondents

26.13 Awards can be made against individual named respondents (*Gbaja-Biamila v DHL International (UK) Ltd* [2000] IRLR 730; *Armitage, Marsden and HM Prison Service v Johnson* [1997] ICR 275, where two prison officers were ordered to pay £500 respectively; and *HM Prison Service v Salmon* [2001] IRLR 425, where a named individual was ordered to pay £1,000). An employment tribunal also has jurisdiction to make an award on a joint and several basis rather than apportioning liability between the parties but should make clear its reason for doing so and in particular must have regard to the provisions of the Civil Liability (Contribution) Act 1978, s 2(1) in deciding how to apportion the liability of the parties. It is not relevant to take account of the relative financial resources of the respondent (*Way v Crouch* [2005] IRLR 603).

C. COMPENSATION FOR NON-FINANCIAL LOSS

26.14 An important difference between compensation claims for unlawful discrimination and unfair dismissal, is that compensation for unlawful discrimination under SDA 1975, s 66(4); RRA 1976, s 57(4); DDA 1995, s 17A(4); SOR 2003, reg 31(3); RBR 2003, reg 31(3); and EEAR 2006, reg 39(3) expressly provides for compensation for injury to feelings to be recoverable.

26.15 In addition, the tortious basis of awards for unlawful discrimination means that awards may be made for injury to health, aggravated damages, and, in exceptional circumstances, exemplary damages.

Injury to feelings

26.16 An award for injury to feelings includes compensation for loss of congenial employment (*Ministry of Defence v Cannock* [1994] ICR 918) but, in England and Wales, such an award does not include aggravated damages (*Scott v Commissioners of Inland Revenue* [2004] IRLR 713).

26.17 An award for injury to feelings will not be made automatically: it is for the claimant to show that such injury has been suffered as a result of the unlawful act (*Ministry of Defence v Cannock* [1994] ICR 918). However, the burden on the claimant is not a heavy one and the matter of hurt feelings may be simply stated. Tribunals should readily infer such injury in race discrimination cases (*Orthet Ltd v Vince-Cain* [2004] IRLR 857). It is then for the tribunal to consider the extent of the injury (*Murray v Powertech (Scotland) Ltd* [1992] IRLR 257).

26.18 It has been suggested in *Skyrail Oceanic v Coleman* [1981] ICR 864 and *Alexander v Home Office* [1988] ICR 685 that such an award can only be made where the claimant knows the act which led to the injury to be discriminatory, although there is nothing in the statutory provisions to support such a requirement but knowledge may be an aggravating factor.

Range of awards for injury to feelings

26.19 Translating hurt feelings, such as upset, anxiety, frustration, and humiliation, into an award is inevitably a somewhat artificial exercise but employment tribunals have to do the best they can on the evidence before them. The general policy considerations which tribunals should take into account were summarized by Smith J in *Armitage, Marsden and HM Prison Service v Johnson* [1997] ICR 275:

(a) Awards for compensation for injury to feelings are compensatory. They should be just to both parties. They should compensate fully without punishing the tortfeasor. Feelings of indignation should not be allowed to inflate the award.

(b) Awards should not be too low as that would diminish respect for the policy of anti-discrimination legislation. Society has condemned discrimination and awards must ensure that it is seen to be wrong. On the other hand, awards should be restrained as excessive awards may be seen as the way to untaxed riches.
(c) Awards should bear some broad general similarity to the range of awards in personal injury cases.
(d) In exercising their discretion, tribunals should remind themselves of the value in everyday life of the sum they have in mind. This can be done by reference to purchasing power or by reference to earnings.
(e) Tribunals should have regard to the need to retain public respect for the level of awards made.

More specific guidance on the categorization of awards was given by the Court of Appeal in *Vento v Chief Constable of West Yorkshire Police* [2003] ICR 318, where an award of £50,000 was reduced to £18,000. Three broad bands of award were identified which have now been received and uprated by the EAT in *Da'Bell v NSPCC* (UKEAT/0227/09). The current rates are: **26.20**

(a) a lower band of between £600 and £6,000 in 'less serious cases' where the unlawful act is isolated or one-off (see also *Sharifi v Strathclyde Regional Council* [1992] IRLR 259 and *Deane v London Borough of Ealing* [1993] IRLR 209);
(b) a middle band of between £6,000 and £18,000 for 'serious cases which do not merit an award in the highest band';
(c) an upper band of between £18,000 and £30,000 for the 'most serious' cases where there has been a 'lengthy campaign of harassment', although the court regarded awards of more than £25,000 as most exceptional.

The guidance given by the Court of Appeal in *Vento* 'was not intended to be applied like rules of law' (*per* Arden LJ in *Gilbank v Miles* [2006] IRLR 538). Furthermore, the issue of categorization and assessment is largely a matter for the tribunal's discretion and an appellate tribunal or court should not intervene unless the tribunal misdirects itself in law or reaches a perverse decision. An award may be challenged where it is manifestly excessive, as in *Vento*, or insufficient to represent the degree of harm suffered. In *Gilbank*, the Court of Appeal did not consider an award of £25,000 for injury to feelings to be 'manifestly excessive' as the tribunal was entitled to take the view that the circumstances of the case, which involved deliberate, intentional, and repeated harassment of a pregnant employee, justified an award at the top of the upper band. On the other hand, in *Doshoki v Draeger* [2002] IRLR 340 an award for taunts of a racial nature was increased from £750, which was described as 'very close to the bottom' of the range, to £4,000. **26.21**

Where there is more than one act of unlawful discrimination, a tribunal may use a global approach in assessing injury to feelings rather than make a separate award for each complaint as it may be unrealistic to make a separate award for each act of discrimination particularly where the acts form a pattern of conduct (*ICTS (UK) Ltd v Tchoula* [2000] ICR 1191). Such a 'global' approach will only be appropriate if either more than one type of unlawful discrimination arises out of the same facts or the act relied on is part of an overall pattern of behaviour. **26.22**

Where, as in *Al Jumard v Clywd Leisure Ltd* [2008] IRLR 345, complaints of different forms of discrimination (ie race, sex, disability) are made arising out of separate acts of discrimination, the employment tribunal should at least start by considering the appropriate award in relation to each act of discrimination. The EAT points out that the level of award should not necessarily be the same for different forms of discrimination as the offence, humiliation, or upset may vary if, for example, the act is one of deliberate racial discrimination as contrasted with a 'thoughtless' failure to comply with the duty to make reasonable adjustments under the Disability Discrimination Act. Furthermore, the EAT states that at the end of the exercise, a **26.23** tribunal should stand back to ensure that the overall award is 'proportionate' and that there has not been 'double counting'.

26.24 In some cases, it may be relevant to take into account the nature of the employment, ie whether the employment was full-time or part-time. In *Orlando v Didcot Power Stations Sports and Social Club* [1996] IRLR 262, the EAT observed that a 'person who unlawfully loses an evening job may be expected to be less hurt and humiliated. . . than a person who loses their entire professional career'.

26.25 In principle, it is open to a tribunal to make an award for both injury to feelings and injury to health (see para 26.30 below) provided compensation is not awarded twice for the same loss (*HM Prison Service v Salmon* [2001] IRLR 425).

26.26 In making its award a tribunal should ignore the fact that the claimant will receive interest on the award (*Ministry of Defence v Cannock* [1994] ICR 918) or that the claimant may be fairly dismissed at some future date (*O'Donoghue v Redcar and Cleveland Borough Council* [2001] IRLR 615).

26.27 Awards for injury to feelings are not taxable and therefore should not be grossed up (*Orthet Ltd v Vince-Cain* [2004] IRLR 857).

26.28 Awards for injury to feelings are fact specific but the EOR annual review of compensation in 2008, published in June and July 2009, reports that the median award for injury to feelings was £4,500, a slight decrease on the previous year.

Injury to health

26.29 The right of a complainant to bring a claim for injury to health (apart from or in addition to, a claim for injury to feelings) caused by an unlawful act of discrimination was recognized by the Court of Appeal in *Sheriff v Klyne Tugs (Lowestoft) Ltd* [1999] ICR 1170.

26.30 As stated above, compensation for injury to health may be claimed where the injury is a direct consequence of the discriminatory act and need not be reasonably foreseeable (*Essa v Laing Ltd* [2004] ICR 746). It is for the claimant to prove injury to health as a result of a discriminatory act. Where there is no specific medical evidence to support such a claim the award for injury to feelings should reflect general stress and emotional upset suffered by the claimant (*HM Prison Service v Salmon* [2001] IRLR 425) and tribunals may refuse to award additional compensation for injury to health in such circumstances.

26.31 The most common form of personal injury claim in discrimination cases involves psychiatric injury. Awards are often made with reference to the Judicial Studies Board *Guidelines for the Assessment of General Damages in Personal Injury Cases* (9th edn, 2008). According to these guidelines, relevant factors to be taken into account in valuing such damage include the injured person's ability to cope with life and work, the effect on the injured person's relationships, the extent of treatment and future vulnerability, prognosis, whether medical help is being sought, the nature of the abuse, and its duration.

26.32 There are four categories of award for psychiatric injury:

(1) Severe (£30,000–£63,000) where the claimant has serious problems and the prognosis is poor.
(2) Moderately severe (£10,500–£30,000) where there are significant problems in relation to the above factors but where the prognosis is more optimistic.
(3) Moderate (£3,250–£10,500) where there has been a significant improvement and the prognosis is good.
(4) Minor (£800–£3,250) where the illness is of limited duration such as temporary anxiety.

26.33 However, a discount should be made where the illness is not solely attributable to the discriminatory conduct, for example, where there is some pre-existing medical history or there are other contributory factors. In *HM Prison Service v Salmon* [2001] IRLR 425 compensation for psychiatric injury was reduced by 25 per cent on the basis that the depressive illness suffered by the claimant was not entirely caused by the unlawful discrimination suffered by the claimant.

Aggravated damages

Aggravated damages are recoverable in discrimination claims in England and Wales. The circumstances in which an award for aggravated damages may be made were summarized by Judge Burke in *Singh v University Hospital NHS Trust* EAT/1409/01, as follows: **26.34**

(a) Aggravated damages may only be awarded in a case in which it is established that the discriminator has acted in a high-handed, malicious, insulting, or oppressive manner in committing the discriminatory act or the way it was handled (*Alexander v Home Office* [1988] ICR 685). This does not apply in Scotland where aggravated damages are not known to the law of delict but aggravating factors are taken into account in determining the award for injury to feelings.
(b) While any discrimination is offensive and regrettable and may be potentially very distressing, the requirements set out in *Alexander* involve some special element in the conduct of the discriminator which takes the case beyond the ordinary run of discrimination cases. The fact that the victim is upset or distressed or even injured in his health as a result of the discrimination is not enough.
(c) It is a matter for the tribunal of fact in each case to decide whether, if the discriminator has acted in a high-handed, malicious, insulting, or oppressive manner, the case is one in which aggravated compensation should be awarded.
(d) Aggravated damages may be awarded even if the injury to feelings award is in the lower band.
(e) The award must be compensatory, not punitive.

The following are examples of circumstances where aggravated damages have been awarded: **26.35**

(a) where an employer failed to investigate a complaint of racial discrimination and failed to apologize (*Armitage, Marsden and HM Prison Service v Johnson* [1997] ICR 275);
(b) where the respondent attempted to cover up and trivialize the discriminatory acts (*HM Prison Service v Salmon* [2001] IRLR 425);
(c) where the respondent conducted the tribunal proceedings in an inappropriate and intimidatory manner (*Zaiwalla & Co v Walia* [2002] IRLR 697);
(d) where the respondent failed to give satisfactory answers in reply to a statutory discrimination questionnaire (*City of Bradford Metropolitan Council v Arora* [1989] IRLR 442);
(e) where the respondent promoted the perpetrator of an allegedly discriminatory act before completing its investigation (*British Telecommunications plc v Reid* [2004] IRLR 327). There is also some suggestion in this case that the conduct of the investigation itself and unreasonable delay may also be aggravating factors.

Exemplary damages

In *Deane v London Borough of Ealing* [1993] IRLR 209, the EAT ruled that exemplary or punitive damages could not be awarded under the RRA 1976. However, the EAT's ruling in *Deane* must now be seen in the light of the House of Lords' ruling in *Kuddus v Chief Constable of Leicestershire Constabulary* [2002] 2 AC 122, where it was held that exemplary damages are now recoverable if compensation is insufficient to punish the wrongdoer and if the conduct is either (a) oppressive, arbitrary, or unconstitutional action by agents of the Government, or (b) where the respondent's conduct has been calculated to make a profit which may exceed the compensation payable to the claimant. The *Kuddus* ruling is likely to have limited application in discrimination cases. **26.36**

26.37 Exemplary damages are also not available under the Equal Treatment Directive (*Ministry of Defence v Meredith* [1995] IRLR 539).

D. FINANCIAL LOSS

26.38 Compensation may be recovered for any financial loss flowing from the discriminatory act. As stated above, at least in cases of direct and intentional discrimination, claimants do not have to prove that the loss was reasonably foreseeable provided it can be shown to be a direct consequence of the discriminatory act.

Types of loss

26.39 Loss covers pecuniary loss as well as loss of benefits and expenses. In general, the types of recoverable loss are the same as in an unfair dismissal claim.

26.40 Earnings will include loss of pay, overtime, commission, and bonuses. The loss is assessed net rather than gross. Compensation may also be recovered for the loss of benefits such as private health care, private use of company car, pension, share schemes, travel concessions, loan facilities, clothing allowances and free goods, free accommodation, subsidized meals, and childcare costs. Compensation may also be awarded for the loss of the opportunity to be promoted to a higher position (*Ministry of Defence v Cannock* [1994] ICR 918).

26.41 Such losses are quantified in the same manner as in an unfair dismissal claim. For example, the tribunal's pension guidelines referred to at para 24.100 above also apply to the quantification of loss in discrimination claims.

26.42 Compensation claims can also be made for any expenses flowing from the discriminatory act. These can sometimes include medical expenses associated with treatment for recovery from the discriminatory act.

Calculating the loss

26.43 The process of calculating loss is also similar to that in an unfair dismissal claim. The loss will consist of the past loss up to the date of the hearing and future loss thereafter.

26.44 Although there is no equivalent power to ERA 1996, s 123(1) to limit the award for just and equitable reasons, it will still be necessary for the tribunal to consider the principles in *Kingston Upon Hull City Council v Dunnachie* (*No 3*) [2003] IRLR 843 in the calculation of future loss, ie 'old job facts' and 'new job facts'. Tribunals often have to consider whether the claimant would have remained in his or her employment but for the discrimination, ie whether the claimant would have left voluntarily or involuntarily at some future date or would have come back to work after the birth of a child or would have moved to another job or would have worked in the same job until retirement. At the time of writing, the issue of whether a '*Polkey*' type limitation can be applied in discrimination cases is being considered by the Court of Appeal, the EAT in *Abbey National plc v Chagger* [2009] IRLR 86 having ruled that such an argument is open to employers in discrimination cases. The EAT's ruling has been confirmed by the Court of Appeal in *Chagger v Abbey National plc* [2009] EWCA Civ 1202.

26.45 Statistical information may be admissible on the issue of job mobility. As Mummery LJ pointed out in *Vento v Chief Constable of West Yorkshire Police* [2003] ICR 318, 328: 'The question requires a forecast to be made about the course of future events. It has to be answered on the basis of the best assessment that can be made on the relevant material available to the court. That includes statistical material, such as that produced to the tribunal showing the percentage of women who have in the past continued to serve in the police force until the age of retirement.' The tribunal was therefore entitled to conclude that but for the discriminatory dismissal, there was a 75 per cent chance that the claimant, a probationary constable, would have stayed with the force until her retirement age of 55.

Given the inevitable uncertainty involved in making such an assessment on an all-or-nothing basis, tribunals will often quantify the loss in percentage terms or on a loss of a chance basis (*Ministry of Defence v Wheeler* [1998] IRLR 23). Where there are a number of contingent possibilities, the correct approach is to accumulate the percentage chance of each event occurring (*Ministry of Defence v Hunt* [1996] ICR 544, ie in that case there was a 75 per cent chance that she would have returned after her first child). This may need to be combined with making a percentage assessment of other contingencies such as a pay rise. **26.46**

The tribunal may also need to take into account the risk of future dismissal. For example, in *O'Donoghue v Redcar and Cleveland Borough Council* [2001] IRLR 615 the Court of Appeal held that the tribunal was entitled to find that although the claimant had been unfairly dismissed and victimized on the grounds of sex, it was inevitable that her divisive and antagonistic attitude towards her colleagues would have led to her dismissal within six months and to limit its award accordingly. There is a difference between the approach taken by a tribunal in a discrimination case in relation to this issue from that in an unfair dismissal case: in the former the tribunal is solely concerned with the behaviour of the actual employer whereas in the latter, a tribunal may take into account the actions of a reasonable employer (*Abbey National v Formoso* [1999] ICR 222). **26.47**

It is not entirely clear what bearing a future unfair dismissal has on an award of compensation for unlawful discrimination. In *HM Prison Service v Beart* (*No 2*) [2005] IRLR 171 the EAT, relying on the principle that a tortfeasor may not benefit from his wrong, concluded that a subsequent unfair dismissal does not break the chain of causation and that the claimant is entitled to recover full compensation for unlawful discrimination in these circumstances. The Court of Appeal upheld the EAT's ruling ([2005] IRLR 568) on the basis that, in the particular circumstances of that case, the 'second wrong' namely the unfair dismissal did not break the chain of causation. Rix LJ pointed out that all that happened was that the employer had committed two discrete wrongs in respect of which the statute provided a cap for one but not the other. Critically, in *Beart* the employment tribunal had found in relation to her discrimination claim that if the claimant had been redeployed (as recommended by an internal report), she would 'probably still have been employed' by the employer (ie there was a continuing loss) and that in relation to her unfair dismissal claim, the tribunal had found that the allegations of misconduct were unproven (ie there was no valid reason for dismissal). However, the Court of Appeal recognized that the position may be different if the employee 'commits a repudiatory breach of his own contract', ie if there is a 'new intervening act', either before or after the unlawful discriminatory act. In such circumstances, a subsequent dismissal for a valid and lawful reason may well break the chain of causation and it follows that in such a situation, the award should be limited to the current maximum for unfair dismissal even if it is held unfair for procedural reasons. **26.48**

Credit for payments received and ex gratia payments

The rules on giving credit for earnings and benefits received are the same as in unfair dismissal cases including the deduction of State benefits from the award paid to the claimant (*Chan v Hackney LBC* [1997] ICR 1014) but not benefits which are paid to the claimant's household or children (*Vento v Chief Constable of West Yorkshire Police* [2002] IRLR 177, EAT). Collateral benefits such as pension benefits should also normally be ignored but credit should be given for past or future payments received under a private health insurance scheme as these are not regarded as collateral benefits (*Atos Origin IT Services UK Ltd v Haddock* [2005] IRLR 20). **26.49**

Credit should be given for any *ex gratia* payment received in calculating the loss before applying the percentage chance reduction (see *Ministry of Defence v Hunt* [1996] ICR 544 and *Ministry of Defence v Wheeler* [1998] ICR 242). **26.50**

Mitigation

The normal common law principles on mitigation apply to the assessment of compensation. Claimants are under a duty to mitigate each and every head of loss and cannot expect to profit **26.51** from the unlawful discrimination. Whether the claimant has in fact mitigated his or her loss will be determined in accordance with the guidelines at paras 25.27–25.28 above and will depend on the facts of each case.

26.52 The loss will come to an end once (and if) the tribunal considers that the claimant has or should have found a new job at an equivalent rate of remuneration. This should be considered before the application of the multiplier or the percentage loss of a chance (*Ministry of Defence v Hunt* [1996] IRLR 139). For example, if the claimant earned £800 a week and finds a new job earning £500 a week, the net loss of £300 a week and the percentage chance will be applied to that figure (see also *Ministry of Defence v Wheeler* [1998] IRLR 23).

Future handicap in the labour market

26.53 Given that the award for unlawful discrimination is assessed in like manner as any other claim in tort, it is open to a claimant to recover compensation for any future handicap in the labour market. This is often referred to as a 'Smith and Manchester award' after the case *Smith v Manchester Corporation* (1974) 17 KIR 1. In making its assessment, the tribunal will have to quantify the risk that the claimant will suffer such damage in the labour market. In *Moeliker v Reyrolle & Co Ltd* [1976] ICR 253, the Court of Appeal suggested a two-stage approach in relation to such claims: where the claimant is in work at the time of the remedies hearing, the first question is whether there is a 'substantial' or real risk that the claimant will lose his job before the estimated end of his working life. If so, the second question is for the tribunal to assess and quantify that risk having regard to the degree of risk itself, the time in which it might materialize, and the factors which may influence the claimant's chances of finding another job at all or one which is equally well paid. The power to award 'stigma' compensation, based on the loss suffered by a claimant for a discriminatory reason, has been accepted by the Court of Appeal in *Chagger v Abbey National plc* [2009] EWCA Civ 1202 where it is suggested that a notional sum may be awarded for such loss. It remains to be seen how much employment tribunals award as a notional sum.

Dismissals which are both discriminatory and unfair

26.54 Compensation cannot be recovered twice for a dismissal which is discriminatory and unfair (ERA 1996, s 126). Where a dismissal is held to be both discriminatory and unfair, the tribunal should award compensation under the relevant discrimination legislation in order to give to the claimant full compensation, although it is still open to the tribunal to make a basic award (*D'Souza v London Borough of Lambeth* [1997] IRLR 677). On the other hand, if the dismissal is discriminatory but fair, no award will be made for financial loss, although an award can be made for non-pecuniary loss (*Lisk-Carew v Birmingham City Council* [2004] 2 All ER (D) 215).

Accelerated payment

26.55 The award of compensation for future loss falls to be discounted to make allowance for the accelerated receipt of the payment unless the sums involved are so small as to make this unnecessary. The case law in relation to discounts for accelerated payment is considered at para 25.63 above.

Power to adjust the award

26.56 The Employment Act 2002 (Dispute Resolution) Regulations 2004, SI 2004/752, which came into force on 1 October 2004, implement the statutory grievance and dismissal procedure provided for by the Employment Act 2002.

26.57 An award of compensation made for unlawful discrimination may be increased or reduced in accordance with the provisions of EA 2002, s 31(2) and (3) where either the employer or the employee has not complied with the statutory procedures. Other than in exceptional circumstances, the award must be increased or reduced by a minimum of 10 per cent. The award may be increased or reduced up to a maximum of 50 per cent where a tribunal considers this to be just and equitable.

These provisions are considered in greater detail at paras 24.158 and 25.18 above. However, these provisions will be repealed when the Employment Act 2008 comes into force (see para 25.25). It has also been suggested that it may be open to reduce an award for unlawful discrimination for contributory fault pursuant to the Law Reform (Contributory Negligence) Act 1945, although it may be questioned whether a claimant can contribute to unlawful discrimination by his or her conduct (*Way v Crouch* [2005] IRLR 603). **26.58**

These provisions were repealed with effect from 6 April 2009 and are retained in this edition because there may be some cases in the pipeline which are covered by the transitional provisions in the Employment Act 2008. Thereafter tribunals will have the power to increase or decrease the award for non-compliance with the ACAS Code of Practice pursuant to the Trade Union and Labour Relations (Consolidation) Act 1992, s 207A, the effect of which is summarized at paras 24.164, 24.165, 25.25 and 25.26 above. **26.59**

Overall size of awards

Compensation for a discriminatory dismissal must be adequate (*Marshall v Southampton and South-West Hampshire Area Health Authority (No 2)* [1993] ICR 893). In most cases, there is nothing wrong in principle with tribunals simply adding up the awards made under each head and awarding the total (including interest) (*Ministry of Defence v Hunt* [1996] IRLR 139) but in *Ministry of Defence v Cannock* [1994] ICR 918 the EAT stressed that awards should not be excessive and there is further support for this view in *Vento v Chief Constable of West Yorkshire Police* [2003] IRLR 102, CA. **26.60**

E. COMPENSATION FOR INDIRECT DISCRIMINATION

There is power to award compensation for indirect discrimination on a restricted basis. This is one of the few areas where there is some inconsistency in the statutory provisions. **26.61**

Indirect sex discrimination

For sex discrimination cases, insofar as a complaint of indirect discrimination is made under SDA 1975, s 1(1)(b) (ie condition or requirement cases), an award of compensation for indirect discrimination can be made either where the indirect discrimination is intentional (SDA 1975, s 66(3)) or where it would not be just and equitable merely to make a declaration and/or a recommendation (SDA 1975, s 65(1A)). **26.62**

There is a conflict of case law as to whether or not indirect discrimination can be intentional (see *Enderby v Frenchay Health Authority and Secretary of State for Health* [1991] IRLR 44, where this was rejected and *London Underground Ltd v Edwards* [1995] IRLR 355, where it was accepted). For the meaning of 'intention' for this purpose, see *JH Walker Ltd v Hussain* [1996] IRLR 11. **26.63**

Where a complaint is made under SDA 1975, s 1(2)(b), an order for compensation can be made where the provision, criterion, or practice in question was not applied with the intention of treating the claimant unfavourably on the ground of sex or marital status if the tribunal would have made the same declaration and/or recommendation if it had no power to order compensation and having made such a declaration and/or recommendation, it considers it just and equitable to order the respondent to pay the claimant damages (SDA 1975, s 65(1B)). There have been no reported cases on this provision. **26.64**

Indirect race discrimination

For race discrimination cases, RRA 1976, s 57(3) provides that compensation may not be awarded in cases of indirect discrimination unless it is shown that a discriminatory requirement or condition was applied with the intention of treating the complainant less favourably on the grounds of race. In *JH Walker Ltd v Hussain* [1996] IRLR 11, the EAT ruled that such intent may be inferred if at the time when the relevant discriminatory act took place, the employer **26.65** knew that certain consequences would flow from its actions and wanted those consequences to take place. So, for example, in *Hussain*, the EAT held that the tribunal was entitled to make an award of compensation for indirect discrimination where the company knew that the requirement to work on a holy day would indirectly discriminate against its Moslem workforce but nonetheless went ahead and enforced the requirement. The employer's motive (which was to promote business efficiency) did not mean that he did not intend to treat the claimants unfavourably on the prohibited grounds. The EAT also held that where such an intention is established, the award may include compensation for injury to feelings (see also *Orphanos v Queen Mary's College* [1985] AC 761).

26.66 No provision is made where the complaint is brought under RRA 1976, s 1(1A), ie where the complaint relates to a provision, practice, or criterion.

Indirect discrimination in sexual orientation, religious belief, or age cases

26.67 Where a complaint is brought under reg 30(1)(b) of SOR 2003 or RBR 2003, or reg 38(1)(b) of the EEAR 2006, an award of compensation for indirect discrimination can be made in similar circumstances to 'provision, criterion or practice' cases brought under the SDA 1975, ie where the employer proves that the provision, criterion, or practice was not applied with the intention of treating the claimant unfavourably on the ground of his sexual orientation or religion or belief, an order for compensation can only be made if the tribunal would have made the same declaration and/or recommendation if it had no power to order compensation and having made such a declaration and/or recommendation, it considers it just and equitable to order the respondent to pay to the claimant damages (SOR 2003, reg 30(2); RBR 2003, reg 30(2); EEAR 2006, reg 38 (2)).

F. RECOMMENDATIONS

Introduction

26.68 A tribunal is empowered to make a recommendation where it upholds the complaint and considers it just and equitable to do so. The power to make a recommendation is such that the respondent must take within a specified period action appearing to the tribunal to be practicable for the purpose of obviating or reducing the adverse effect on the complainant of any act of discrimination to which the complaint relates (SDA 1975, s 65(1)(c); RRA 1976, s 56(1)(c); DDA 1995, s 17A(2)(c); SOR 2003, reg 30(1)(c); RBR 2003, reg 30 (1)(c); EEAR 2006, reg 38 (1)).

Scope of the power to make recommendations

26.69 The discretion conferred by this provision is extremely wide (*Vento v Chief Constable of West Yorkshire Police* [2002] IRLR 177, EAT). For example, the tribunal may make a recommendation that the employer should make arrangements for racial awareness training if this is appropriate in the circumstances (*Southwark London Borough v Ayton* EAT/0515/03). Similarly a recommendation that the employer should consider its behaviour and discuss the tribunal's findings with certain named employees where the employer was in 'institutional denial' was upheld by the EAT in the *Vento* (*No 2*) case above, although the appeal was allowed against a further recommendation that the police officers should apologize to the claimant and the Deputy Chief Constable should report on whether or not the relevant officers were willing to apologize.

26.70 The discretion must be exercised in a judicial manner. The power does not permit tribunals to order the employer to increase the claimant's wages as this should be considered in determining the award of damages (*Irvine v Prestcold* [1981] IRLR 281). In *Atos Origin IT Services UK Ltd v Haddock* [2005] IRLR 20, however, the EAT considered that as an alternative to making an award for future loss, it could recommend that the employer should continue to employ the claimant to his normal retirement age to enable him to claim benefits under a private health insurance scheme. The power does not permit tribunals to order that the claimant is appointed to the next available vacancy as this would be unfair to other candidates (*Noone v North West

Regional Health Authority (*No 2*) [1988] IRLR 530) or, for the same reason, to order the claimant's promotion (*Sharma v British Gas* [1991] IRLR 101).

Regard must be had to the wording of the statutory provision. So, for example, a recommendation should not be made if it is 'completely impracticable' (*Leeds Rhinos Rugby Club v Sterling* EAT/267/01) or if it is too general to obviate or reduce the adverse effect of the discriminatory act (*Bayoomi v British Railways Board* [1981] IRLR 431, where the claimant had left the employment by the time of the tribunal hearing). **26.71**

Enforcement

There is no power to enforce a recommendation as such but where, without reasonable justification, the respondent fails to comply with a recommendation, the tribunal may, if it considers it just and equitable to do so, increase the amount of compensation previously awarded or (if no award was made) make an award of compensation (SDA 1975, s 65(3); RRA 1976, s 56(4); DDA 1995, s 17A(5); SOR 2003, reg 30(3); RBR 2003, reg 30(3); EEAR 2006, reg 38(3). **26.72**

G. EQUAL PAY CLAIMS

Equality clause

An employee's right to equal pay takes effect by way of operation of an equality clause, which is implied by EqPA 1970, s 1(1) in the contract of employment. An equality clause is a provision which relates to terms (whether concerned with pay or not) of a contract under which a woman is employed (EqPA 1970, s 1(2)) and may modify the terms of that contract. **26.73**

Remedies

The remedies available to the employee are therefore the same as those in any claim for breach of contract. Normally, this will involve a claim for damages for breach of contract but either side may apply for a declaration (EqPA 1970, s 2 (1A)) and possibly an injunction (although this remedy is not available in the employment tribunal). Where the equality clause has the effect of modifying any of the terms which relate to wages within the meaning of Part 2 of ERA 1996, s 27(1), a claim may be brought under those provisions for the recovery or non-payment of such wages. **26.74**

A claim under the EqPA 1970 is a financial claim only. Compensation cannot be recovered for non-economic loss such as injury to feelings, aggravated damages, and/or exemplary damages (*Council of City of Newcastle upon Tyne v Allen* [2005] IRLR 504). **26.75**

Arrears date

The normal period for a 'standard case' for which arrears of remuneration or damages may be claimed is six years (EqPA 1970, s 2ZB(1), (3)). However, in *Bainbridge v Redcar & Cleveland Borough Council* (*No 2*) [2007] IRLR 494, the EAT has ruled that employees whose jobs are rated equivalent under a job evaluation scheme do not have the right to seek compensation going back up to six years unless they have also established a right to equal pay in one or more of the other ways provided for under the statutory provisions (ie they can show that their jobs were of equal value during the relevant period). The ruling, which has been criticized as being inconsistent with the earlier decisions in *Dibro Ltd v Hore* [1990] IRLR 129; *Avon County Council v Foxall* [1989] IRLR 435; and *McAuley v Eastern Health and Social Services Board* [1991] IRLR 467, means that the outcome of a JES need not be backdated beyond the date on which it came into force. **26.76**

Special provision is also made for a 'concealment case' (EqPA 1970, s 2ZB(2)) or a 'disability case', ie where a woman is under a disability at the time of the contravention and the woman institutes proceedings within six years of the day on which she ceased to be under a disability **26.77**

(EqPA 1970, s 2ZB(2)). In such circumstances, the arrears date is the date of the contravention (EqPA 1970, s 2ZB (4)).

H. COMPENSATION FOR PART-TIME WORKERS AND FIXED TERM EMPLOYEES

26.78 Special provision is made for complaints under PTWR 2000 and FTER 2002.

26.79 Where a tribunal finds a complaint presented to it under PTWR 2000 or FTER 2002 well founded, it shall take such of the following steps as it considers just and equitable:

(a) make a declaration as to the rights of the complainant and the employer in relation to the matters to which the complaint relates;
(b) order the employer to pay compensation to the complainant;
(c) recommend that the employer takes, within a specified period, action appearing to the tribunal to be reasonable, in all the circumstances of the case, for the purpose of obviating or reducing the adverse effect on the complainant of any matter to which the complaint relates.

(PTWR 2000, reg 8(7); FTER 2002, reg 7(7))

26.80 Where a tribunal awards compensation, the amount of the compensation is such as the tribunal considers just and equitable in the circumstances having regard to (a) any infringement to which the complaint relates, and (b) any loss which is attributable to the infringement, having regard, in the case of an infringement conferred by PTWR 2000, reg 5, to the pro rata principle except where it is inappropriate to do so (PTWR 2000, reg 8(9); FTER 2002, reg 7 (8)).

26.81 Loss is taken to include any expenses reasonably incurred by the complainant in consequence of the infringement and loss of any benefit which he might reasonably be expected to have had but for the infringement (PTWR 2000, reg 8(1); FTER 2002, reg 7 (11)) but the loss does not include injury to feelings as a result of the less favourable treatment (PTWR 2000, reg 8(11); FTER 2002, reg 7(10)). The awards may be reduced for contributory conduct (PTWR 2000, reg 8(13); FTER 2002, reg 7 (13)).

26.82 The normal rules on mitigation apply to the assessment of loss under both regulations (PTWR 2000, reg 8(12); FTER 2002, reg 7(11)).

26.83 There is no statutory cap on the amount of compensation that can be awarded.

I. TAX

26.84 As stated above, there is no statutory limit to the amount of compensation which can be made in a complaint of unlawful discrimination but where the award (excluding any award for injury to feelings or injury to health) exceeds the tax threshold for lump sum payments (currently £30,000) (Income Tax (Earnings and Pensions) Act 2003, ss 401 and 403), the award is potentially taxable. This means that any such award falls to be 'grossed up' in accordance with the principles in *Shove v Downs Surgical plc* [1984] 1 All ER 7. The impact of taxation is considered in greater detail in Chapter 29.

27

Recoupment of Benefits

SUMMARY

(1) Some awards made by a tribunal may be subject to deductions in respect of two forms of social security payments received by the claimant: job seeker's allowance and income support. The deduction is of benefits paid to the claimant either to the date his loss ceased or to the date of the tribunal hearing or reserved decision, whichever is the earlier.

(2) If the claimant has been in receipt of job seeker's allowance or income support, any receipts are ignored for the purpose of deciding the compensation due to the claimant: the claimant retains the benefits, but the respondent deducts an equivalent amount from the compensation due to the claimant and sends it direct to Job Centre Plus.

(3) If the tribunal reduces an award for contributory fault or brings the award down to the statutory cap, the amount of recoupment will be reduced by the same proportion.

(4) A claimant can challenge the tribunal's decision on the recoupment certificate by notice to the Department for Work and Pensions.

(5) The Recoupment Regulations do not apply to out-of-court settlements.

A. INTRODUCTION

The Employment Protection (Recoupment of Job Seeker's Allowance and Income Support) Regulations 1996, SI 1996/2349 are intended to ensure that a dismissed employee is not compensated twice over for the same loss, by social security benefit and unfair dismissal compensation, and that the State can recover from the employer certain benefits previously paid to the successful claimant. **27.01**

B. WHEN APPLICABLE

The Recoupment Regulations only apply to job seeker's allowance and income support (reg 4(1)). They also apply where the claimant has claimed either allowance, whether or not he has received it (reg 4(8)). **27.02**

27.03 Any other forms of benefit (for example, incapacity benefit) must be deducted in their entirety from the amount of any compensatory award. This is because receipt of other benefits is regarded as a form of mitigation of loss (*Morgans v Alpha Plus Security Ltd* [2005] IRLR 234, EAT).

27.04 The Recoupment Regulations apply to any of 'the payments described in column 1 of the table contained in the Schedule to these Regulations' (reg 3(1)(a)). These include, but are not limited to, payments of unfair dismissal compensation, payments upon an order for re-engagement or reinstatement, payments where a reinstatement or re-engagement order is not complied with, protective awards, and guarantee payments. They do not apply to awards of compensation for any form of discrimination or to redundancy payments. The full description of payments to be made by a respondent to a claimant following an employment tribunal decision, to which the Recoupment Regulations apply, is set out at para 27.14 *et seq.* below.

C. THE WORKING OF THE SCHEME

27.05 When a tribunal makes an award of compensation to a claimant, it must not take into account, when deciding the appropriate level of compensation, any income support or job seeker's allowance which has been sought by or paid to the claimant. Instead, when the tribunal makes an award of compensation where the Regulations apply, it must set out (reg 4(3)):

(a) the monetary award;
(b) the amount of any 'prescribed element';
(c) the dates of the period to which the prescribed element relates;
(d) the amount, if any, by which the monetary award exceeds the prescribed element.

27.06 The 'prescribed element' of the compensation is defined in reg 3(1)(a) as being so much of the relevant monetary award as is attributable to loss of wages or arrears of pay or to the amounts found due to the claimant for a period before the conclusion of the tribunal proceedings. The conclusion of the tribunal proceedings is the date that the judgment making any compensatory award is given: if orally, on the date of the relevant hearing; and if judgment is reserved and the decision sent to the parties in writing, on the date when it is sent (reg 2(3)). Where benefits are to be deducted from a protective award (where a tribunal orders an employer to pay its employees remuneration for a protected period because it failed to consult a union or staff representatives in good time or at all on a redundancy or transfer of employment, pursuant to TULR(C) A 1992, s 189 or TUPE 1981, reg 11), the relevant period ends on the final day of the period covered by the protective award.

27.07 In essence, the prescribed element is:

(a) any arrears of pay in respect of a period before the conclusion of the tribunal proceedings;
(b) any compensation for loss of wages in respect of this period;
(c) any sum ordered to be paid by the employer under a protective award.

27.08 If a tribunal reduces an award on account of the claimant's contributory fault, or to take into account any statutory maximum limit (for example, to bring any substantial award of compensation for unfair dismissal down to the statutory maximum compensation limit, which is £330 for the year beginning 1 February 2008 and £350 for the yearperiod beginning 1 February 2009 and £380 for the period 1 October 2009–31 January 2011) the element of benefit which is to be recouped is correspondingly reduced (reg 4(2)). Therefore if, for example, there has been a 25 per cent reduction in an award of compensation for unfair dismissal because of contributory fault, only 75 per cent of the job seeker's allowance or income support which the employee has received during the relevant period will be subject to the recoupment provisions. The correct procedure is for the tribunal first to assess the compensatory award; secondly, to reduce it to the statutory maximum or for any element of contributory fault, and finally to reduce the prescribed element by the same proportion (*Tipton v West Midlands Co-operative Society* (*No 2*)

EAT/859/86; *Mason v (1) Wimpey Waste Management Ltd, (2) Secretary of State for Employment* [1982] IRLR 454).

Where the employer has made an *ex gratia* payment, this must be apportioned across all heads of compensation (save any basic award) which the claimant is awarded. The relevant amount should then be notionally added to any heads of compensation which are subject to the Regulations (*Digital Equipment Co Ltd v Clements (No 2)* [1998] IRLR 134, CA). For the purpose of calculating the prescribed element, it is only necessary to apportion the payment as to part against the earnings from dismissal to hearing, and the remaining part against any other losses lumped together. **27.09**

D. EXPLANATION OF RECOUPMENT

If the tribunal announces the remedy to be given to a claimant at a hearing, it must explain to the parties the consequences of any recoupment award. All written decisions—whether confirming an oral award or amounting to a reserved judgment—must also contain a similar explanation. **27.10**

E. NOTIFICATION TO THE DEPARTMENT FOR WORK AND PENSIONS

Where the tribunal is satisfied that the claimant has claimed or received job seeker's allowance or income support, and where he is to be awarded compensation to which the Recoupment Regulations apply (see para 27.04 above) it must send material information to the Department for Work and Pensions. The information must be sent as soon as reasonably practicable after the first announcement of the decision (whether orally or in writing) (regs 4(5) and (5)(1)). **27.11**

For all relevant payments save those which relate to a protective award, the Secretary of the tribunal sends the Department for Work and Pensions the information set out in reg 4(3) (see para 27.05). **27.12**

Where job seeker's allowance or income support is to be recouped against a protective award, the particulars to be supplied to the Department for Work and Pensions are: **27.13**

(a) the date when the decision was announced orally, or, if the decision was reserved, the date on which it was sent to the parties;
(b) the location of the tribunal;
(c) the name and address of the employer;
(d) the description of the employees to whom the protective award relates; and
(e) the dates of the protected period (reg 5(1)).

F. DUTIES ON THE EMPLOYER

The prescribed element of any award to an employee is initially ring-fenced. The employer should retain the prescribed element from the award to the employee until the Department for Work and Pensions has either served a notice on the employer, copied to the employee, requiring the employer to forward the money to it, or else has notified the employer that it does not intend to serve such a notice. **27.14**

If a recoupment notice is served on the employer, this operates as an instruction to the employer to pay, by way of deduction out of the sum due under the award, the recoupable amount to the Department for Work and Pensions. If the Department does not make an order for recoupment, the whole of the monetary sum awarded shall be paid to the employee. **27.15**

If the respondent fails to pay this recoupable amount to the Department for Work and Pensions, this can be recovered from the respondent as a debt (reg 8(11)). **27.16**

Worked example

A claimant is awarded compensation of £8,000. The prescribed element within this award is £5,000. The claimant has received income support of £2,000.

(a) The respondent should pay the claimant £3,000 immediately (ie the amount of the award less the prescribed element).
(b) The respondent should retain £5,000, pending receipt of information from the Department for Work and Pensions as to whether or not it intends to exercise its recoupment rights.
(c) If the Department for Work and Pensions notifies the employer it does wish to recoup against £2,000 income support, the employer must send £2,000 to the Department for Work and Pensions, and £3,000 (being the balance of the prescribed element) to the employee.
(d) If the Department for Work and Pensions notifies the employer it does not propose to exercise any recoupment rights, then the entire prescribed element of £5,000 should be sent to the employee.

G. APPEALS

27.17 A claimant may appeal against the calculation of the amount specified in the recoupment notice as the amount of job seeker's allowance or income support which he has been paid or is due for the period. Notice of the appeal must be given in writing to the Department for Work and Pensions within 21 days of the date upon which the Department's recoupment notice was served on him. This time limit can be extended by the Department for Work and Pensions for 'special reasons'. An appeal of this nature does not affect the respondent's duty to pay the recoupable amount specified in the Department for Work and Pensions' notice to the employer.

27.18 Where the claimant appeals, the Department for Work and Pensions will review its decision. The claimant then has a right of appeal to the Appeals Service tribunal against this decision.

27.19 If it is determined, either on review or on appeal, that the amount recovered by the Department for Work and Pensions from the respondent under the Recoupment Regulations exceeds the total amount paid by way of job seeker's allowance or income support, the Department shall pay the employee an amount equal to the excess (reg 10(4)).

H. CONSEQUENCES OF A SUCCESSFUL APPEAL AGAINST THE ORIGINAL JUDGMENT

27.20 If the original judgment, which gave rise to the recoupment exercise, is set aside in whole or in part on appeal, further adjustments occur. If the Department for Work and Pensions has by the time of any appeal or rehearing recovered any amount by way of recoupment of benefits, it shall repay the employer (or as appropriate the employee) all or part of the amount recovered as it is satisfied should properly be made having regard to the decision given on appeal or rehearing (reg 10(4)).

I. BENEFITS OF SETTLEMENT

27.21 The recoupment provisions do not apply where a sum is paid by way of settlement of a dispute. This may be before or after a finding of unfair dismissal is made. In this way there may be greater scope for settlement of unfair dismissal claims than other monetary claims, since what an employer may be prepared to pay by way of settlement may be less than the total of any potential monetary award, but greater than the amount the employee would receive after recoupment.

Worked example

In the situation described at para 27.16 above, if the claim were settled outside court on a payment of £7,000, this would advantage both employer and employee. The employer would pay out £7,000 instead of £8,000. The employee would receive £7,000 instead of £6,000.

28

Interest on Employment Tribunal Awards

SUMMARY

(1) Interest accrues on employment tribunal awards. The current rate of interest is 8 per cent.

(2) There are different rules for discrimination awards where interest can be ordered from the date of the act of discrimination (injury to feeling awards) or a mid-point date between the act of discrimination and the calculation date.

A. INTEREST ON AWARDS GENERALLY

The Employment Tribunals (Interest) Order 1990, SI 1990/479 (1990 Order) provides that where the whole or part of a sum of money has been awarded in a claim other than a discrimination claim and remains unpaid 42 days from the promulgation of the employment tribunal's decision, interest accrues at the rate specified in s 17 of the Judgments Act 1838. The relevant decisions are those requiring one party to pay a sum of money to the other. In relation to discrimination claims, the interest begins to accrue immediately that the award is made (Employment Tribunals (Interest on Awards in Discrimination Cases) Regulations 1996, SI 1996/2803). **28.01**

Interest accrues on the sum net of any recoupment, tax, or national insurance. **28.02**

Where there is a review or appeal, interest still accrues from the original decision but on such lesser or greater sum as is appropriate (1990 Order, arts 5, 6, 7, and 11). **28.03**

Where there is an appeal from a decision on liability and the appellate tribunal makes a monetary award the relevant decision is that of the appellate court (1990 Order, art 8). **28.04**

Finally, where a tribunal has made a declaration as to rights under a contract, interest is only payable if there was an obligation to pay the sum before the employment tribunal's decision. The Order came into force on 1 April 1990, but also applies to cases decided before that date, save that 1 April 1990 is deemed to be the date of the employment tribunal's decision. **28.05**

In terms of the interest rate, it is that specified under the Judgments Act 1838, s 17. Since 1 April 1993, this has been 8 per cent. **28.06**

B. INTEREST ON RACE AND SEX DISCRIMINATION AWARDS

28.07 The Employment Tribunals (Interest on Awards in Discrimination Cases) Regulations 1996, SI 1996/2803 give tribunals the power to award interest in EqPA 1970, SDA 1975, RRA 1976, and DDA 1995 cases and cases under SOR 2003, RBR 2003, and EEAR 2006. This is something that the tribunal is obliged to consider whether or not the applicant asks for interest (1996 Regulations, reg 2(1)(b)).

28.08 Regulation 3(1) of the 1996 Regulations provides that interest is to be calculated as simple interest, accruing from day to day at the interest rate specified in the Special Investment Account under r 27(1) of the Court Fund Rules 1987, SI 1987/821 (1996 Regulations, reg 3(2)). Where the rate of interest varies during the period for which interest is to be calculated, the median or average of the rates may be applied as the tribunal considers appropriate.

Injury to feelings

28.09 Regulation 6(1)(a) of the 1996 Regulations provides that the period of an award of interest under this heading begins at the date of the act of discrimination complained of and ends on the day on which the tribunal calculates compensation.

Other awards

28.10 In awards of interest under other headings, reg 6(1)(b) provides that interest is calculated from the period beginning on the 'mid-point date' and ends on the date of calculation of compensation—the 'mid-point date' is the date halfway through the period beginning on the date of the act of discrimination and ending on the date of calculation. The EAT has held, in *Ministry of Defence v Cannock* [1994] ICR 918, that no interest can be awarded for future loss, for example pension losses.

'Serious injustice' discretion

28.11 Regulation 6(3) of the 1996 Regulations permits tribunals to calculate interest using a different formula where 'serious injustice' would result from the normal calculation methods. An example can be found in *Cannock* where the losses had been incurred many years earlier.

28.12 The tribunal must state the total amount of interest awarded and, where the amount cannot be agreed by the parties, it must set out a table showing its methodology (reg 7(1)) and if no interest is awarded the tribunal must give its reasons.

Rates of interest

28.13 The rate of interest on discrimination awards up to judgment is the rate of interest prescribed for the Special Investment Account under r 27(1) of the Court Fund Rules 1987, SI 1987/821. These rates are as follows:

Date from which rate applies	Rate of interest
1 October 1991	0.25%
1 February 1993	8%
1 August 1999	7%
1 February 2002	**6%**

28.14 After the discrimination award has been made, the Judgments Act rate of 8 per cent will apply, unless payment of the full amount of the award (including any interest) is made within 14 days of the decision (1996 Regulations, reg 8(2)).

29

Tax Treatment of Tribunal Awards and Compromises

A. COMPENSATION PACKAGES

29.01 This chapter aims to deal with the issues which most frequently arise for employment practitioners. A payment by way of tribunal award or compromise agreement may constitute a package that includes a variety of different elements. This might include unpaid salary damages, a payment in lieu of notice, a payment for a restrictive covenant, compensation for loss of office, and the provision of a non-cash benefit after termination. The description of the payment may not be conclusive for tax purposes and the substance will be determinative. It will be necessary to identify each element within the package and treat it accordingly.

B. COMPROMISE AGREEMENTS

29.02 When an employment comes to an end, an employee may have various potential claims against the employer. The tax implications of compromise agreement will, like the other legal consequences, be dependant upon the normal rules for construction of contracts. Given the ability of parties to adjust the agreement to benefit from particular tax rules, the approach adopted by the courts in undertaking this exercise is to interpret the relevant tax rule purposively and construe the relevant transaction 'realistically' (*Barclays Mercantile Business Finance Ltd v Mawson* [2005] STC 1, HL, [2004] UKHL 51).

29.03 Any compromise of legal claims, whether a compromise agreement as statutorily defined or not, is a legal document separate and distinct from the employment contract. However, it will inevitably deal with rights which flow from the contract of employment and, consequently, will address both rights under the employment contract settling claims in respect of the employment and its termination. Thus in *Carter v Wadman* (1946) 28 TC 41 payment under such an agreement was held partly chargeable to tax because it satisfied a right to remuneration in the employee's contract, because the agreement was 'in full and final settlement of all claims'. Drafting or analysing compromise agreements requires classification of the bases of payment in accordance with the categories explained in paras 29.06–29.20 of this chapter.

29.04 PAYE Regulations apply to payments under compromise agreements in the same way as they do for any other payment. Where PAYE is properly due on the relevant sums the employer must deduct and account for it with the result that the employee may not receive, in cash, the full amount specified in the agreement. In certain circumstances where PAYE cannot be deducted (for example, where the payment is in the form of shares or other employment-related securities), the employer is treated as providing additional employment income equal to the PAYE unless the employee makes good the tax within 90 days of the notional payment (ITEPA 2003, s 222).

C. TRIBUNAL AWARDS

29.05 The broad jurisdiction of employment tribunals to order employers to pay compensation means that, in assessing the tax implications, it is important to establish the nature of the employee's claim and the type of award that the tribunal orders. The fact of payment pursuant to an award thus does not itself establish the tax character of the payment. The same care in drafting or analysing compromise agreements to make sure they reflect the relevant categories is explained in paras 29.06–29.20 of this chapter.

D. TAXATION OF EMPLOYMENT INCOME

29.06 Income tax is chargeable on employment income (Income Tax (Earnings and Pensions) Act 2003 (ITEPA 2003), s 1(1)(a)). 'Employment income earnings' includes all salaries, fees, wages, any incidental benefits of any kind if it is money's worth, and profits whatsoever (ITEPA 2003, s 62). Earnings may arise as a reward for services past, present, and future (*Hambleet v Godfrey* [1987] STC 60, CA). Thus, payment made pursuant to the terms of an employment contract will be liable to income tax. Where earnings from an office or employment would be for a year of assessment in which a person no longer holds the office or employment, the emoluments are treated as those for the last year of assessment in which the office or employment was held (ITEPA 2003, s 17(3)).

29.07 A number of items are deemed to be within the charge to income tax as employment income under ITEPA 2003. These include any pension paid other than by or on behalf of a person outside the United Kingdom (ITEPA 2003, ss 1(1)(b) and 569).

29.08 Sick pay, where sums are paid to or for the benefit of an employee or a member of his family or household in respect of any absence from work by reason of sickness or disability and are, by reason of his employment, paid as a result of any arrangements entered into by his employer (ITEPA 2003, s 221); maternity and paternity pay, and statutory sick pay (ITEPA 2003, s 600); income support and unemployment benefit (ITEPA 2003, s 661); job seeker's allowance (ITEPA 2003, s 670A); voluntary pensions (ITEPA, 2003, s 570).

29.09 Most benefits in kind provided by reason of employment are taxable and, in many cases, subject to complex rules (ITEPA 2003, Part 2, Chap 3). However certain benefits provided after employment has ceased are not taxable. Employment-related securities will also give rise to complex tax issues (ITEPA 2003, Part 7). In addition, employers are subject to detailed information reporting requirements in respect of the provision of benefits. In the case of shares or other employment-related securities this may be the case even where the reportable event does not trigger a tax liability (ITEPA 2003, s 424K).

E. PAYMENTS IN LIEU OF NOTICE

Payment in lieu of notice (PILON) is not a term of art but covers a variety of payments, the legal analysis of which differs (*Delaney v Staples* [1992] 1 AC 687). A PILON will be 'earnings' within ITEPA 2003, s 62 whether it is as a matter of entitlement or whether the employer reserves the right to make the payment under the terms of the employment contract (*EMI Group Electronics Ltd v Coldicott)(Inspector of Taxes)* [1997] STC 1372, Ch D). If a PILON is made without any entitlement to it under the employment contract on premature termination by the employer, then it may be damages for breach of contract and only taxable as a termination payment under ITEPA 2003, s 401 (see paras 29.13 and 29.14, below). In *SCA Packaging Limited v HMRC* [2007] EWHC 270, Ch, PILONs were made pursuant to a memorandum negotiated by the employees' union which specified that if employees wished to leave earlier than their contracts permitted, the PILON would be made. **29.10**

F. RESTRICTIVE COVENANTS

Payments in respect of restrictive covenants are taxed as income. This applies to any undertaking whether absolute or qualified, and whether legally valid or not, the tenure or effect of which is to restrict the individual as to conduct or activities (ITEPA 2003, s 225). **29.11**

G. DAMAGES FOR BREACH OF CONTRACT

This could include damages for wrongful repudiation of a contract, or a settlement of agreed damages, or a payment made in consideration of the employee giving up all contractual rights and ceasing to give services. These payments would not under ordinary principles be liable to income tax under ITEPA 2003. Payments of compensation for loss of employment are, however, chargeable under ITEPA 2003, s 401 (see below). **29.12**

H. TERMINATION PAYMENTS

Payments and other benefits not otherwise chargeable to tax which are received in connection with either the termination of a person's employment or any change in the duties of or emoluments from a person's employment are chargeable to tax (ITEPA 2003, s 401(1)). This rule only applies to the extent that the amount exceeds £30,000. Thus, termination payments are exempt from tax up to that amount. Several other categories of payment are excluded as detailed below. **29.13**

The distinction between contractual payments which give rise to earnings from employment and termination payments which arise in connection with the termination of the employment itself is often difficult to identify. Successive decisions of the Special Commissioners have emphasized the necessity for careful construction of the agreements and context in which payments are made (*Redundant Employee v McNally* [2005] UKSPC 440): employment terminated at the expiry of gardening leave although letter of termination was stated to be with immediate effect; *Porter v HMRC* [2005] UKSPC 501: entitlement under stock bonus plan extended to redundant employee by termination agreement was not from employment but in connection with termination; *SCA Packaging Ltd v HMRC* [2006] UKSPC 541: incorporation of entitlement to redundancy into employment contract by reference gives rise to earnings from employment but not for employees if the provisions were not so incorporated); compensation for loss of share option rights not found to be due and payable under service agreements but occasioned by termination in accordance with the compromise agreement; compensation for pension payments where the employer was not required by the service agreements to make them were likewise in connection with termination and only chargeable to tax under ITEPA 2003, s 401(1) **29.14**

(*Brander v HMRC* [2007] UKSPC 610. In *'A' v HMRC* [2009] UKSPC SPC734 the employee argued that the majority of the £250,000 compensation under a compromise agreement, which made no allocation, to settle an unfair dismissal dispute was for damage to reputation unconnected with the employment termination. The compensation was found to have been received in connection with the termination except £10,000 for injury to feelings and not in the most serious category within the Court of Appeal decision in *Vento v Chief Constable of West Yorkshire Police* [2002] EWCA Civ 1871. In *Resolute Management Services Ltd and Haderlein v HMRC* [2008] UKSPC SPC710, an employee, recognizing that the task for which she had been recruited was complete, resigned voluntarily notwithstanding loss of redundancy and other benefits. An ex-gratia payment was not a reward for work done but to compensate for benefits lost and to recognize that she was doing the right thing, and thus was not earnings but a termination payment. Compensation paid in *Crompton v HMRC* [2009] UKFTT 71 (TC) was held not causally connected with termination. It was paid because the employee had not been selected for posts for which he applied which he would have received whether he stayed or not. He left either of his own volition or by way of redundancy and not because of his failure to be selected.

I. TERMINATION BY DEATH, INJURY, OR DISABILITY

29.15 Tax is not charged on termination payments provided in connection with the termination of employment by the death of the employee or on account of injury to or disability of the employee. Thus, sums received by reason of disability are not taxed. This extends to where the disability results not from a sudden affliction, but from deterioration due to chronic illness (ITEPA 2003, s 405) (HM Revenue & Customs Statement of Practice 10/81). Again careful attention must be paid to the contractual arrangements. In *Minto v HMRC* [2007] STC (SCD) (SpC 625) payments were made to an employee under an employer-provided permanent health insurance policy. The employee was then made redundant and the benefit of the policy was assigned to him under a compromise agreement covering among other items a possible personal injury claim for work-related stress. Payments under the policy were found to be in the nature of pension payments, taxed as employment income rather than damages for personal injury.

J. REDUNDANCY PAYMENTS

29.16 Statutory redundancy payments are exempt from income tax as earnings (ITEPA 2003, s 309). Non-statutory lump sum redundancy payments are liable to income tax. They will only be liable to tax as termination payments under ITEPA 2003, s 401, provided they are genuinely made solely on account of redundancy as defined in ERA 1996 (HM Revenue & Customs Statement of Practice 1/94). Payments under non-statutory schemes which are not genuinely made to compensate for loss of employment through redundancy may be liable to tax in full. The practice of HM Revenue & Customs (HMRC) is to allow employers to submit proposed redundancy schemes to their tax inspectors for advance clearance, since redundancy arrangements can be complex and provide for a variety of payments.

K. TAX EXEMPT PENSION SCHEMES

29.17 Tax is also not charged on payments pursuant to certain approved retirement benefit schemes, either where the payment is by way of compensation for loss of employment, or for loss or diminution of earnings, and the loss or diminution is due to ill-health. Payments pursuant to retirement benefit schemes are also not taxed if the payment is properly regarded as earned by past service (ITEPA 2003, s 407(1)).

29.18 Where, as part of an arrangement relating to the termination of an employment, agreement is reached for the employer to make a special contribution into an approved retirement benefit scheme or approved personal pension scheme, in order to provide benefits for the employee, the payments are not charged as termination payments, provided that the retirement benefits are within the limits and in the form described by the rules of the scheme (ITEPA 2003, s 408).

L. QUALIFYING COUNSELLING SERVICES

No income tax charge arises in respect of the payment or reimbursement of fees for the provision to the employee of qualifying counselling services (ITEPA 2003, s 310). Qualifying counselling services include outplacement counselling, the purpose of which is to enable employees to adjust to termination of employment, or to find other gainful employment, as well as giving advice, guidance, and imparting or improving skills (ITEPA 2003, s 310(3)). Certain travelling expenses wholly, exclusively, and necessarily incurred in obtaining counselling services may be paid or reimbursed without income tax charge. **29.19**

M. LEGAL FEES AND INTEREST

Interest awarded by a tribunal is not liable to tax under ITEPA 2003 as employment income. It is, however, taxed under Schedule D Case III as interest income in the hands of the recipient (ITEPA 2003, s 18(3)). HMRC view payments made by way of recovery of costs by employees against former employers as liable to tax as termination payments. No deduction is allowable for legal costs incurred in pursuing the former employer for wrongful dismissal. However, HMRC will not seek to charge with tax payments of costs to former employees in the following circumstances: **29.20**

(a) Where the dispute is settled without recourse to the courts, no charge will be imposed on payments made by the former employer directly to the former employee's solicitor in full or partial discharge of the solicitor's costs incurred by the employee only in connection with termination of his or her employment. This must be included as a specific term in the settlement agreement.
(b) Where the dispute goes to court, no charge will be imposed on payment of costs made by the former employer, even where these are made direct to the employee in accordance with a court order (whether this is made following a judgment or compromise of the action).

The concession only applies to legal costs and not to other professional costs such as accountancy fees (Extra-Statutory Concession A81, and HMRC *Tax Bulletin*, November 1993, p 101). **29.21**

N. REPAYMENT OF EXPENSES TO EMPLOYERS

An employee whose employment contract requires repayment of certain expenses if the employment terminates will not normally be entitled to a deduction in calculating employment income for amounts paid to a former employer. Thus where an employer provides free training to an employee but is required to reimburse the cost of the training if the employee leaves, no deduction for the reimbursement is available (*Hinsley v HMRC* [2006] STC (SCD) 63 (SpC 569)). **29.22**

O. DAMAGES FOR DISCRIMINATION

Compensation for discrimination on grounds of race, sex, etc should not be liable to income tax under ITEPA on the basis that the compensation is in respect of a statutory tort (*Walker v Adams* [2003] STC (SCD) 239 (SpC 344)). If the discrimination takes place in connection with termination then HMRC take the view that it may be taxed as a termination payment under s 401 (see para 29.08). Although a person who receives a capital sum derived from an asset is treated for the purposes of capital gains tax as disposing of an asset (*Zim Properties Limited v Procter* [1985] STC 90, Ch D), compensation or damages for any wrong or injury suffered by an individual in his person are not chargeable to capital gains tax (Taxation of Chargeable Gains **29.23**

Act 1992; Taxes Act 1988, s 51(2)). The words 'wrong or injury' include breaches of contractual duties and torts (Extra-Statutory Concession D33).

P. PAYE AND NATIONAL INSURANCE CONTRIBUTIONS

29.24 PAYE is generally required to be operated on the making of any payment of or on account of any employment income assessable to income tax (ITEPA 2003, s 683(1)). Thus, employers will normally be required to deduct PAYE on payments in accordance with the PAYE Regulations, SI 2003/2682. Most payments that attract PAYE will also attract national insurance contributions (Social Security Contributions and Benefits Act 1992, ss 3 and 4). Special rules are applied for benefits in kind. Employers are required to make a report to HMRC at the latest by 6 July following the tax year in which the termination takes place if a package is provided, which includes non-cash benefits and is estimated over its lifetime to exceed £30,000. If the package consists of only, or includes, non-cash benefits but has an estimated value of £30,000 or less, no report is required.

29.25 Payments that may be made pursuant to a reinstatement order or a re-engagement order, an order for continuation of employment, or a protective award are treated as gross pay for both NIC and PAYE purposes.

29.26 The amount of PAYE depends on when and how the payment is made. If the payment is made before form P45 is issued, the employer must add taxable amounts to gross pay and apply normal PAYE procedures. If payment is made after employment has ceased and form P45 has been issued, then the employer must deduct tax from the taxable amount at the basic rate in force for the year in which payment is made (20 per cent in 2008–09) and employers are not required to operate PAYE on the non-cash element.

29.27 HMRC Practice, where a payment into court (or to a stakeholder or solicitor acting on behalf of an employer or employee) is made following arbitration, is to deal with amounts under self-assessment for the former employee when payment is made to them out of such amount. Employers may, if they wish, by agreement with HMRC (a PAYE Settlement Agreement (PSA)), settle the income tax liability on certain payments in a single payment under PAYE Regulations 105–117 (SI 2003/2682). Payment under a compromise agreement or order may qualify for PSA treatment on the basis that they are irregular or 'one-off'. This may help manage the effect of gross-up provisions where the employee becomes liable for additional tax that the employer must make good. An employer who enters into a PSA is liable for Class 1B NICs in place of any Class 1 or Class 1A NIC liability attached to the benefits and expenses that the PSA relates to.

Q. APPLICATION OF THE 'GOURLEY PRINCIPLE'

29.28 In *British Transport Commission v Gourley* [1956] AC 185, the House of Lords ruled that when assessing damages for wrongful dismissal for the actual or prospective loss of earnings, allowance must be made for any income tax on the earnings where the damages are not taxed in the hands of the recipient. The underlying principle is that a person should not be placed in a better or worse position than if the contract had actually been carried out. This approach is sometimes adopted by the courts in dealing with termination payments. The position of HMRC, however, is that any adjustment made in accordance with the *Gourley* principle is a matter for the parties and not HMRC. The *Gourley* principle, in their view, has to do with the calculation of damages under non-tax law and is not a matter that HMRC can become involved with. Their only interest is in the amount actually paid. Where a payment is reduced pursuant to this principle, it is not a reduction of tax. Only the actual payment made to the employee is considered under the normal taxation rules relating to that termination payment. If the taxation of that actual amount leaves the employee out of pocket, then in HMRC's view, this is a matter between the parties.

The damages are first calculated by reference to the pay and benefits that the employee would have received, for example, during the notice period if proper notice had been given, say, gross pay of £2,000. This is not pay but part of the calculation of the damages. But £2,000 would place the employee in a better position than if the contract had been carried out. If the employee had received pay during notice, it would have been taxed and liable to NICs, leaving (say) £1,500 in hand. As the damages payment itself is exempt from tax and not liable to NICs the employee would keep the whole £2,000. The damages calculation is therefore adjusted to £1,500. This payment made to the employee must be considered under the normal rules for termination payments. **29.29**

Tribunals have had difficulty in applying the principles in practice and reconciling the approach of HMRC with the *Gourley* decision particularly where the parties are uncertain about the tax treatment of the award and seek to protect their positions. In *Orthet v Vince-Cain* [2004] IRLR 857, the EAT ruled that a gross-up was inappropriate in the case of damages for injured feelings which was not liable to tax and noted that the risk of tax on the award could be addressed by way of indemnity or by seeking a review of the award as was the case there. **29.30**

R. INTERNATIONAL ASPECTS

The tax consequences of an employment relationship will vary according to the residence, ordinary residence, and domicile of the employee, where the employer is located, and where the duties of employment are performed. The position may be affected by double tax treaties. In addition, the amount taxable as a termination payment may be reduced or eliminated where foreign service is involved. There is no tax if three quarters or more of the whole period of service is foreign, or if the service is more than 10 years, the last 10 years is foreign, or, where the service is more than 20 years, one half of the service is foreign (ITEPA 2003, s 413); a proportionate reduction is permitted where the exclusion does not apply (ITEPA 2003, s 414). **29.31**

Part D

The Substantive Law

30

Dismissal

SUMMARY

(1) All employees have the right not to be wrongfully or unfairly dismissed.

(2) These rights are distinct but overlapping.

A. WRONGFUL DISMISSAL

Basic test

An employee is wrongfully dismissed if, without cause, he is dismissed without full notice or without money in lieu of notice. The notice period is either: that set out in the contract; the appropriate implied notice; or is determined in accordance with the statutory minimum period calculated in accordance with the employee's length of service. **30.01**

30.02 An employer may legitimately terminate an employee's employment without notice or money in lieu of notice if the employee has committed gross misconduct or some other serious breach of his contract of employment such as dishonesty, disobedience, or serious incompetence. The test whether an employee has committed a sufficiently serious breach of contract is similar to the test whether an employee's conduct or capability is such that he can be fairly dismissed (see paras 30.35–30.53 below).

Wrongful dismissal damages

30.03 If an employer, without legitimate reason, summarily terminates an employee's contract, the employee is entitled to compensation for his notice period. This is quantified by calculating the net amounts (salary and benefits) he should have received during the balance of his notice period. The first £30,000 of the total of all termination payments paid to employees (whether compensation for infringing a statutory right or damages for wrongful dismissal) is normally tax free (Income Tax (Earnings and Pensions) Act 2003, ss 403–6 (see Chapter 29 Section H), unless paid pursuant to a 'payment in lieu of notice' clause in an employment contract, and any balance above £30,000 is grossed up at the employee's marginal tax rate to arrive at the final figure. A claim can also be brought for any non-discretionary bonus or commission that would have fallen due during the notice period. Claims for discretionary bonuses will only succeed in exceptional circumstances where a court accepts that a decision to award no, or a low, bonus was irrational or perverse (*Commerzbank AG v Keen* [2007] IRLR 132, CA).

30.04 In addition, if procedural requirements such as disciplinary and warning procedures are incorporated into contracts of employment, but are ignored, this could give rise to a claim by the employee for damages representing the salary he would have received had proper warning procedures been undertaken, up to the date when the employer could lawfully have terminated the contract. In extreme cases, an employer who suspends an employee without any contractual right to do so, or who dismisses an employee without going through contractual disciplinary procedures, may be ordered to reverse the decision if the employee applies to the High Court for an injunction. If an employer dismisses an employee without notice, and by doing so deprives the employee of the benefit of statutory rights which would accrue if the notice period were worked out (eg by summarily dismissing someone whose notice period was three months after they had been employed for 50 weeks, thereby depriving them of the opportunity to claim unfair dismissal) no damages will be awarded for the loss of opportunity to bring any unfair dismissal claim (*Harper v Virgin Net Ltd* [2004] IRLR 390, CA).

Court jurisdiction in wrongful dismissal cases

30.05 Because the right to damages for wrongful dismissal is a common law right rather than a statutory right, the limitations and restrictions imposed by statute do not apply. For example, there is no minimum service requirement before one can claim damages for wrongful dismissal. In addition, an employee is not entitled to damages for wrongful dismissal merely because an employer has not followed fair procedural requirements, or because any serious breach by the employee of the contract of employment was only discovered subsequent to dismissal and was not cited as the reason for dismissal.

30.06 It used to be the case that a claim for wrongful dismissal could only be brought in the county court or High Court, but not in the employment tribunal. However, it is now possible to bring a claim in the employment tribunal instead, although the amount of any award is subject to a maximum of £25,000 (Employment Tribunals Extension of Jurisdiction (England and Wales) Order 1994 and Employment Tribunals Extension of Jurisdiction (Scotland) Order 1994 (1994 Orders)) and no interest can be awarded until 42 days after the judgment (see also Section B of Chapter 8). Although the compensation for wrongful dismissal and unfair dismissal overlaps to a certain extent, this will give the employee a useful additional weapon subject to two provisos: first, if a claim for wrongful dismissal is brought in the employment tribunal, the employer can counterclaim for losses it considers it has suffered as a result of the employee's breach of contract (other than where those losses have arisen as a result of a breach of the duty of confidence/fidelity by the employee) subject again to a maximum of £25,000 (1994 Orders, art 4); and second, an employee with a potentially large dismissal claim who succeeds in such a claim in the employment tribunal, where damages are limited to £25,000, or whose claim is dismissed, cannot seek to recover any excess in High Court proceedings as the issue will be *res judicata* (*Fraser v HLMAD Ltd* [2006] IRLR 687, CA), so high-earning employees would be ill-advised to bring such a claim in an employment tribunal. An employee does not have to bring a grievance before making any breach of contract claim against an employer in the employment tribunal. However, should he not have done so any award in relation to a claim lodged before 6 April 2009 will be reduced by 10–50 per cent (EA 2002, s 31) and may, if lodged after 1 April 2009, be reduced by 0–25 per cent (TULR(C)A 1992, s 207A.

WRONGFUL DISMISSAL/BREACH OF CONTRACT FLOWCHART

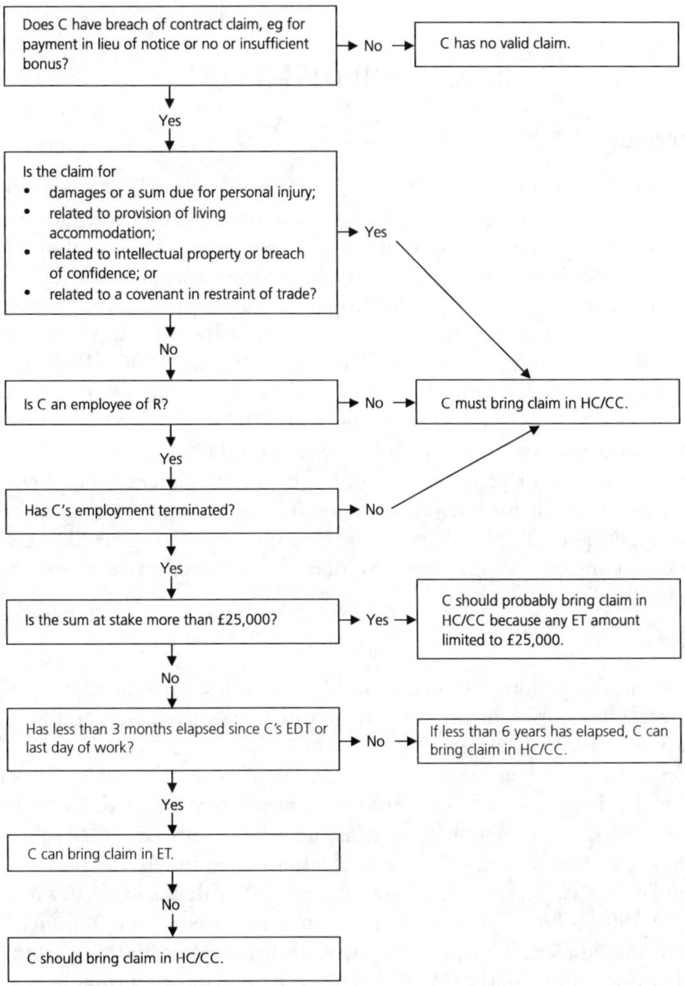

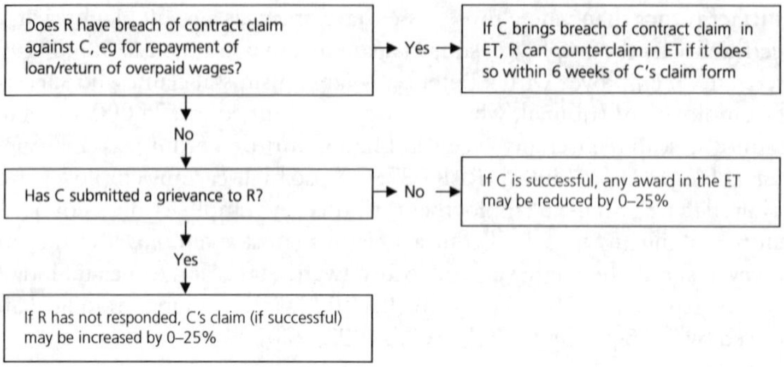

Key:
C = Claimant employee
R = Respondent employer
ET = Employment Tribunal
HC/CC = High Court or County Court
EDT = Effective date of termination of C's emp oyment

B. UNFAIR DISMISSAL

Qualifying periods

30.07 In addition to wrongful dismissal claims, most employees are entitled to claim compensation for unfair dismissal. Such a claim must generally be brought within three months of the EDT (see para 30.08 for definition of EDT), although this may be extended if a tribunal accepts it was not reasonably practicable to have done so. Only employees are able to bring unfair dismissal claims. An employee may include someone supplied to an employer by an agency—the court will examine whether it is necessary to imply an employment relationship between the end user or the agency and the individual (*Cable & Wireless plc v Muscat* [2006] IRLR 354, CA; *Dacas v Brook Street Bureau (UK) Ltd* [2004] IRLR 358, CA; *James v London Borough of Greenwich* [2008] IRLR 302, CA; *Cairns v Visteon UK Ltd* [2007] IRLR 175, EAT). To bring a claim for unfair dismissal, an employee has to overcome certain hurdles. The most important hurdle is that, in order to be entitled to complain of unfair dismissal, generally employees must have been employed continuously for one year or more. It does not matter how many hours a week they work during this period if they have one year's continuity. The general test is whether the employee has been continuously employed for one year by the effective date of termination of his employment (EDT).

30.08 The EDT may be:

(1) The date any notice period given expires or (if notice is less than the notice period to which the employee is statutorily entitled, the date statutory notice (see para 30.08(2)) would have expired (ERA 1996, s 97(1)(a)).

(2) If no notice is given, and employment is not legitimately terminated for gross misconduct, the EDT is the date on which statutory notice would have expired, had it been given on the date the employee was actually or constructively dismissed (ERA 1996, s 97(2) and (4)). Statutory notice is essentially one week after the employee has been employed for a month, and one week per completed year of service after that, subject to a maximum of 12 weeks (ERA 1996, s 86). This is so even if payment is given in lieu of notice but dismissal takes effect immediately. Thus, if someone is dismissed after 360 days' employment, the EDT will be on day 367, so the person will be deemed to have continuous employment for over a year and hence be able to bring an unfair dismissal claim even if the employee waives his right to notice (*Secretary of State for Employment v Staffordshire County Council* [1989] IRLR 117, CA).

GENERAL UNFAIR DISMISSAL FLOWCHART

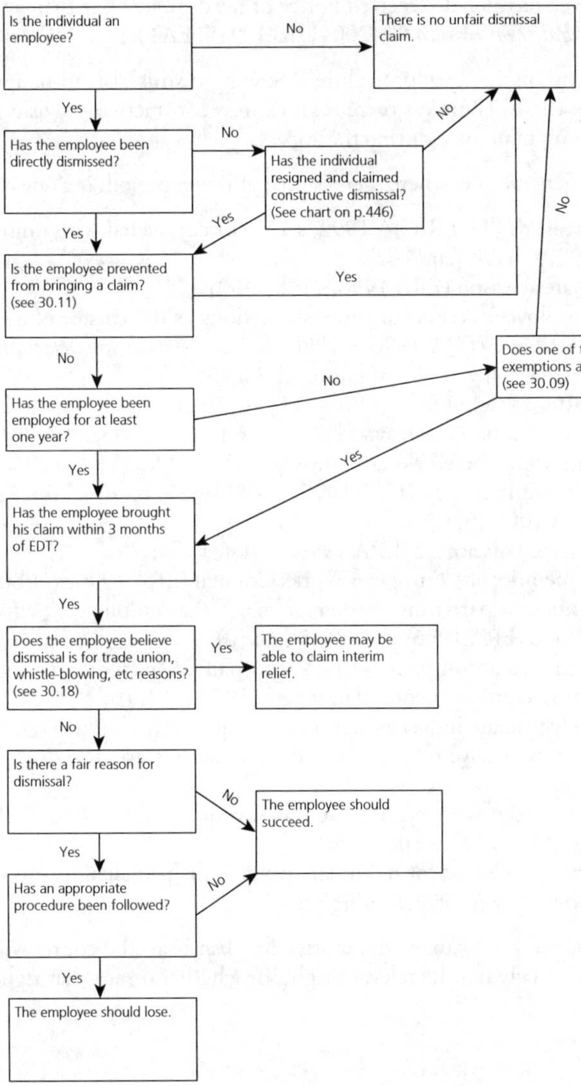

(3) The date the term of a fixed term contract expires (unless the parties agree that the contract should continue after that date) (ERA 1996, s 97(1)(c)).

(4) If the employee is dismissed with notice, but is not required to work during the notice period (gardening leave), the EDT is the date of expiry of the notice period (ie at the end of the gardening leave period), even if the employee is immediately given pay for the full notice period at the start of the gardening leave.

(5) The date an employee is summarily—and legitimately—dismissed for gross misconduct (ERA 1996, s 97(1)(b)); where a notice of summary dismissal was posted to an employee the EDT would be the date when the employee read the notice rather than the date it was posted (*Gisda Cyf v Barratt* [2009] EWCA Civ 648).

(6) If the employer serves notice on the employee to terminate a contract and the employee subsequently serves a counter notice terminating the contract on an earlier date, the EDT is nevertheless the date when the employer's notice would have expired.

(7) The date the employer and employee agree the employment will terminate. This is the case even if the employee has already received notice of his dismissal but then agrees an earlier termination date (*Palfrey v Transco plc* [2004] IRLR 916, EAT).

Note: Any appeal in any disciplinary procedure following dismissal is to be ignored for the purposes of estimating the EDT unless there is an express contractual provision which states that the contract will remain in force during the appeal.

30.09 The exceptions to this general rule, where there is no qualifying period, include dismissals:

(1) for trade union reasons (TULR(C)A 1992, s 154) or connected with union recognition (TULR(C)A 1992, Sch A1, para 162);
(2) for a health and safety reason (ERA 1996, s 108(3)(c));
(3) because of the employee's actions or proposed actions as the trustee of a relevant occupational pension scheme (ERA 1996, s 108(3)(e)) or as an employee representative for TUPE or redundancy collective consultation (ERA 1996, s 108(3)(f));
(4) for asserting a statutory right (ERA 1996, s 108(3)(g));
(5) for a pregnancy or other parental leave-related reason (ERA 1996, s 108(3)(b);
(6) for asserting rights under the Working Time Regulations 1998 (ERA, 1996, s 108(3)(dd)) or for a national minimum wage (ERA 1996, s 108(3)(gg)) or under the Tax Credits Act 1999 (ERA 1996, s 108(3)(gh));
(7) for making a protected disclosure (ERA 1996, s 108(3)(ff));
(8) for activities as a member of a European Works Council (ERA 1996, s 108(3)(hh));
(9) for asserting rights as a part-time worker or fixed term employee, or for supporting someone else to do so (ERA 1996, s 108(3)(i) and (j));
(10) for exercising rights to accompany, or be accompanied by, workers at grievance and disciplinary hearings (Employment Relations Act 1999, s 12(4));
(11) for taking part in legitimate industrial action after a properly conducted ballot, provided that at least eight weeks have elapsed since the employee started to do so (TULR(C)A 1992, s 238A);
(12) of protected shop workers who refuse to work on a Sunday (ERA 1996, s 108(3)(d));
(13) on grounds of age (ERA 1996, s 108(3)(n));
(14) where the employee is selected for redundancy where the principal reason was really one of those set out above (ERA 1996, s 108(3)(h)).

30.10 In all these exceptions, the key factor is the motive for dismissal: the courts will not look at whether the employee actually has the relevant right, or whether or not that right has actually been infringed.

Excluded employees

30.11 Certain categories of employees are excluded from bringing unfair dismissal claims. These include:

(1) those working under illegal contracts, though if an employer persuades an employee to accept an illegal contract (for example, one which enables the employer to defraud HMRC) it may still be enforceable by the employee. If the employee genuinely does not realize that the contract is illegal when he enters into it, or if he has wrongly but innocently been treated as self-employed by HMRC when on a correct legal analysis he is an employee, he will still be able to rely upon the contract (*Colen v Cebrian (UK) Ltd* [2004] ICR 568; *Enfield Technical Services Ltd v Payne* [2008] IRLR 500, CA). On the other hand, an employee who worked under a contract for the supply of services, under which she had not paid income tax or National Insurance contributions, who then claimed she was in fact an employee during the period failed in an unfair dismissal claim because the EAT held that her contract was tainted with illegality (*Daymond v Enterprise South Devon* EAT/0005/07/DA);
(2) those older than 65 (or the 'normal retiring age' for that category of employee employed by the particular employer, if lower) (ERA 1996, s 109(1)). *Note*: This only applies to

dismissals before 1 October 2006. The age limit is removed by the Employment Equality (Age) Regulations 2006;

(3) where the statutory grievance procedures still apply, those who are constructively dismissed but have failed to make proper use of the grievance procedure (Employment Act 2002, s 32);

(4) those in respect of whom an agreed settlement has been made either through the intervention of ACAS or in the form of a suitably comprehensive compromise agreement (ERA 1996, s 203(2); *University of East London v Hinton* [2005] IRLR 552, CA);

(5) those whose contracts of employment are frustrated by some circumstance unforeseen when the contract was entered into which renders performance of the contract very different from what was originally contemplated—for example, because the employee is severely incapacitated for a very long time as a result of sickness or because the employee is imprisoned (*Williams v Watsons Luxury Coaches Ltd* [1990] ICR 536, EAT);

(6) those employed in the police service; certain Crown employees, particularly those in the armed forces; and share fishermen and people employed on board ships registered outside Great Britain (ERA 1996, ss 191–200). *Note*: Those working on ships registered in Great Britain will be eligible to claim compensation for unfair dismissal unless they are wholly employed or resident outside Great Britain;

(7) those who are not employed in Great Britain (*Lawson v Serco Ltd* [2006] IRLR 289, HL) but peripatetic employees based in Great Britain or expatriate employees working for a business carried on in Great Britain, such as a foreign correspondent of a British newspaper, may be entitled to bring claims. Examples of the interpretation of these provisions are *ADT Fire & Security plc v Speyer* EAT/0125/06, where an employee recruited in the UK who worked in Asia (but not the UK) for the last 7½ years of his employment, reported only to Asian-based managers for the last 6 years of his employment, and whose pay was determined by his Asian managers (although payment was administered from the UK) was not regarded as having a sufficient connection with the UK to allow him to bring a claim in an employment tribunal here; and *Halliburton Manufacturing and Services Ltd v Ravat* [2008] 0012/08 EAT, where a claimant who had worked in the UK but was then employed by a German sister company to work in Libya, and who reported to a manager based in Cairo but employed by a different UK sister company, could not bring a claim before the EAT;

(8) those who are not employees, but are, say, casual workers (*Carmichael v National Power plc* [2000] IRLR 43, HL; *Ready Mixed Concrete (South East) Ltd v Minister of Pensions and National Insurance* [1968] 2 QB 497; *Redrow Homes (Yorkshire) Ltd v Wright* [2004] ICR 1126) or agency workers (*Dacas v Brook Street Bureau (UK) Limited* [2004] IRLR 358 CA; *Cable & Wireless v Muscat* [2006] IRLR 354 CA; *James v Greenwich Council* [2008] IRLR 302, CA; *Cairns v Visteon Ltd* [2007] IRLR 175, CA). Generally the court will look at the business reality considering two main issues: is the end user obliged to provide the individual with work and is the individual obliged to attend and do the work under the end user's direction and control (*Carmichael v National Power plc* [2000] IRLR 43 HL; *Ready Mixed Concrete (South East) Ltd v Minister of Pensions and National Insurance* [1968] 2 QB 487, HC)? The tribunal will generally assess the position by reference to the relevant contract, being reluctant to conclude that the contract is a sham unless both parties intended to create a false picture of their respective obligations (*Consistent Group Ltd v Kalwak* [2008] IRLR 505, CA, applied in *Autoclenz Ltd v Belcher* UK EAT/0160/08 in support of a decision that individuals who had answered advertisements calling for self-employed car valets were indeed workers, not employees; and in *Protectacoat Firthglow Ltd v Szilagyi* [2009] IRLR 365, CA where Smith LJ suggests that the appropriate question for the tribunal should be 'what are the parties' true intentions or expectations'. In *Redrow Homes (Yorkshire) Ltd v Buckborough* [2009] IRLR 34, EAT, the test was applied more generously to the employer, so that a sham may be found if in reality neither party intends the relevant provision of the contract to be effective). *Note*: secondees may be regarded as employed by the company to which they are seconded (*Fitton v City of Edinburgh*

Council EAT/0010/07. Company shareholders, even if they own a controlling stake in the company, may also be employees (*Secretary of State for BERR v Neufeld* [2009] IRLR 475 CA);

(9) employees who have resigned, without being pressured to do so. If the employee is told he faces a disciplinary process for misconduct but agrees to resign to avoid this, or if he is otherwise responding to a 'resign or be sacked' ultimatum, this will be regarded as a dismissal, not a resignation (*Sandhu v Jan de Rijk Transport Ltd* [2007] ICR 1137); and an employee who resigns in the heat of the moment, who is given a reasonable cooling-off period to reconsider and does not change his mind during that period, will be held to have resigned properly, even if, after the period, he asks to rescind the resignation but is refused (*Ali v Birmingham City Council* [2008] UK EAT/0313/08, EAT);

(10) employees who have not been dismissed. However, employees who are given formal notice to terminate their employment and are then re-engaged on new, less attractive terms are to be regarded as dismissed (*Darby v The Law Society of England and Wales* [2008] 0447/08 EAT). Removal from the payroll and ceasing to pay his salary while an employee is suspended and a compromise agreement is being negotiated also amounts to dismissal (*Radecki v Kirklees MBC* [2009] EWCA Civ 298, CA);

(11) employees who have been seconded to third parties may, depending on the circumstances, be employed by the third party during the secondment (*Fitton v City of Edinburgh BC* UKEATS/0010/07);

(12) employees who have resigned and are working out their notice but whose employment is subsequently terminated by their employer upon payment of the balance of the notice money due: this cannot be constructive dismissal—the cause of termination was the employee's resignation which cannot be unilaterally repudiated (*Tom Findlay & Co Ltd v Devlin* EATS/0071/06);

(13) partners in partnerships or members of limited liability partnerships, unless their role within the organization is not one of true partnership/membership (*Kovats v TFO Management LLP* [2009] All ER (D) 116 (May) EAT;

(14) employees who have entered into a valid compromise agreement with their employer, following advice from a solicitor, union official, or similar trained person, settling their unfair dismissal claims (ERA, s 203). To be binding, the agreement must be carefully worded and include a full description of the statutory claims to be settled and must follow exactly the provisions of ERA, s 203 (*Hinton v University of East London* [2005] IRLR 552, CA). In *Palihakkara v BT plc* EAT/0185/06, discrimination claims were not excluded because the compromise agreement did not conform to SDA 1975, s 77 or RRA 1976, s 72, and settlement of 'all claims past or future arising out of the termination of employment' only settled claims that arose from the termination itself—it did not settle earlier claims.

Constructive dismissal

The tests

30.12 If the employee believes that the employer has seriously breached the contract of employment, or has threatened to do so, he may resign and claim constructive dismissal. The tests are:

(1) The employer's breach of contract must be sufficiently important to justify the employee resigning, or must be the last in a series of less important incidents.

(2) The employer's conduct must amount to a fundamental breach of contract (*Western Excavating (ECC) Ltd v Sharp* [1978] QB 761). Unreasonable behaviour not amounting to a breach, for example, delaying the date on which salary payment is made, is not sufficient. The employer's actions will not amount to a constructive dismissal, however unreasonable, if there is an express contractual term allowing him to take that action. For example, a provision in a contract, or in a collective agreement or staff handbook, if its terms are incorporated into the contract of employment, that an employer is entitled to vary shift patterns,

will enable the employer to do so. However, the employer has a duty not to conduct himself in a manner, without reasonable or proper cause, likely to destroy or seriously damage the relationship of trust and confidence between the parties. Thus any change in shift pattern could not be wholly unreasonable, and would require reasonable prior notice (*United Bank Ltd v Akhtar* [1989] IRLR 507, EAT).

(3) An employee may rely on constructive dismissal citing a pattern of actions, the most recent of which is the 'last straw'. The last straw need not itself be a breach of contract so long as it is more than trivial and is capable of contributing to a breach of the implied term of mutual trust and confidence and has been preceded by blameworthy or unreasonable conduct in the past. This is an objective, not a subjective test (*Omilaju v Waltham Forest LBC* [2005] IRLR 35, CA). Examples of what might constitute the last straw could include a reduction in the number of hours worked, or a requirement to move to a workplace some way away, even if the contract allows such changes to be made, provided this has been preceded by previous unreasonable behaviour toward the employee. See also para 30.12(8).

(4) The employee must leave in response to the breach. In any resignation letter an employee would be wise to set out the employer's breach on which he relies in resigning and claiming constructive dismissal. If the employee has indeed breached the contract, it can still be a constructive dismissal even if the employee had an ulterior motive for resigning (*Shipperley v Nucleus Information Systems Ltd* UKEAT/0340/06).

(5) The employee must act promptly in resigning following the breach or he may be deemed to have waived the breach and agreed to vary the contract. What is 'prompt' will vary according to circumstances, but will normally be within at least one or two months. In *Quigley v University of St Andrews* UKEATS/0025/05, a two-month delay was sufficient to affirm the contract preventing the employee from arguing that he was constructively dismissed, even though he had claimed the gap was caused by the length of time it took him to consult his solicitor.

(6) The employee may rely upon the conduct of anyone employed by the employer in a supervisory capacity, and not only upon the conduct of the particular person who has the power to dismiss the employee.

(7) Deliberate misconduct or bad faith is not a necessary prerequisite for the obligation of mutual trust and confidence to be destroyed (*Post Office v Roberts* [1980] IRLR 347, EAT).

(8) A common argument in constructive dismissal cases is that the employee has acted in such a way that it has breached the implied term of trust and confidence that should exist in the employment relationship. To establish breach, the employee must show conduct by the employer 'which, objectively considered, is likely to seriously undermine the necessary trust and confidence in the employment relationship' (*Baldwin v Brighton & Hove City Council* [2007] IRLR 232, EAT; *Woods v WM Car Services (Peterborough) Ltd* [1981] 347, CA). Where breach of the implied term is raised in relation to a single act, the employment tribunal should ask itself the following questions:

- what was the conduct of the employer that is complained of;
- did the employer have reasonable and proper cause for that conduct including consideration of whether its action was within the range of reasonable responses; and if not
- was the conduct complained of calculated to destroy or seriously damage the employer/employee relationship of trust and confidence (*Fairbrother v Abbey National plc*) [2007] IRLR 320, EAT)?

However, where the employee is relying on the 'last straw' doctrine (see para 30.12(3)) the relevant principles are:

- the final straw act need not be of the same quality as the previous act relied on as cumulatively amounting to a breach of the implied term of trust and confidence, but it must, when taken in conjunction with the earlier acts, contribute something to that breach and be more than utterly trivial;

- where the employee, following a series of acts which amount to a breach of the term, does not accept the breach but continues in employment, thus affirming the contract, he cannot subsequently rely on the earlier acts if the final straw is entirely innocuous;
- the final straw, viewed alone, need not be unreasonable or blameworthy conduct on the part of the employer. It need not itself amount to a breach of contract, for example, it could be an invitation to attend a disciplinary meeting following acrimonious exchanges between employer and employee (*Thornton Print Ltd v Morton* [2008] 0090/08 EAT). However, it will be an unusual case where the 'final straw' consists of conduct which viewed objectively as reasonable and justifiable satisfies the final straw test. In 'last straw' cases, one does not need to review whether the action was within the range of reasonable responses (*GAB Robbins (UK) Ltd v Triggs* [2008] IRLR 317, CA);
- an entirely innocuous act on the part of the employer cannot be the final straw, even if the employee genuinely (and subjectively) but mistakenly interprets the employer's act as destructive of the necessary trust and confidence (*Waltham Forest v Omilaju* [2005] IRLR 35, CA).

Examples

30.13 Examples of constructive dismissal include the following actions if taken without the employee's consent or without an express contractual provision entitling the employer to do so (unless that provision is wholly unreasonable—for example, requiring an employee to change job location to a considerable distance from his home, or imposing material shift patterns, without reasonable notice):

(1) imposing a salary reduction (*Industrial Rubber Products v Gillon* [1977] IRLR 389, EAT);
(2) materially reducing benefits (*Gillies v Richard Daniels & Co Ltd* [1979] IRLR 45, EAT; *French v Barclays Bank plc* [1998] IRLR 646, CA);
(3) reduction in status (*Lewis v Motorworld Garages Ltd* [1985] IRLR 465, CA; *Coleman v S & W Baldwin* [1977] IRLR 342, EAT);
(4) change in hours or shift patterns;
(5) removing the most enjoyable or central aspect of a person's job if this reduces job satisfaction or prestige (*Hilton v Shiner Ltd* [2001] IRLR 727, EAT);
(6) moving someone from a hands-on role to a managerial one (*Land Securities Trillium Ltd v Thornley* [2005] IRLR 765, EAT);
(7) requiring someone to go on garden leave if there is no contractual provision entitling the employer to do so (*William Hill Organisation Ltd v Tucker* [1998] IRLR 313, CA) unless the employee has been guilty of serious misconduct or has otherwise demonstrated (here by planning to direct new business opportunities to his new employer) in a serious way that he is not able or willing to work (*SG&R Valuation Services Co v Boudrais* [2008] IRLR 770, EAT);
(8) suspending a person, when there is no contractual right to do so;
(9) imposing new restrictive covenants on an employee without going through proper procedure (*Willow Oak Developments Ltd (t/a Windsor Recruitment) v Silverwood* [2006] IRLR 607, CA);
(10) failing to bring an employee's attention to a right he holds which is about to expire, when the right has been negotiated collectively on behalf of employees, and the employee could not reasonably have been expected to be aware of the right (*Scally v Southern Health and Social Services Board* [1991] IRLR 522, HL);
(11) behaving without reasonable and proper cause in a manner likely to destroy or seriously damage the mutual relationship of trust and confidence which should exist between employer and employee, for example, by:
   (a) conducting a fraudulent business (*Malik v BCCI* [1997] IRLR 462, HL);
   (b) giving an employee no or a low salary rise or bonus out of all proportion to colleagues, without any justification (*Clarke v Nomura International plc* [2000] IRLR 766, HC);

CONSTRUCTIVE DISMISSAL FLOWCHART

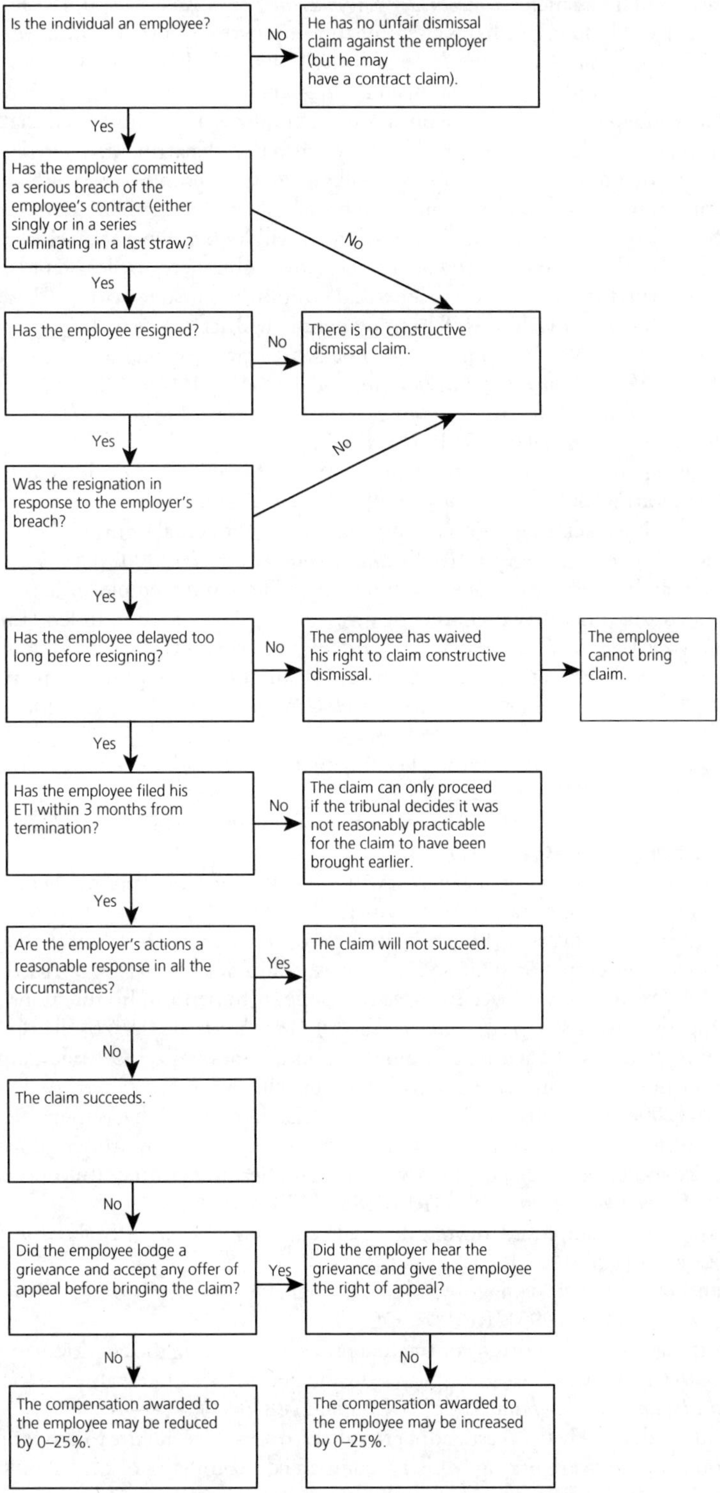

(c) allowing a bullying or harassing environment to persist, or failure to investigate allegations of harassment (*Bracebridge Engineering Ltd v Darby* [1990] IRLR 3, EAT);
(d) non-trivial bullying or harassment of the employee by another employee ((*1*) *Reed*, (*2*) *Bull Information Systems Ltd v Stedman* [1999] IRLR 299, EAT);
(e) offering an employee who has been on long-term absence from work through stress a new job in his old department, when the employee had maintained that his health problems would be exacerbated by a return to that department. There is an implied contractual term that the employer will safeguard its employee's health and safety at work. If it does not do so, it will be in breach of contract. When examining whether the employer's conduct is fair, the tribunal will look at whether, before requiring a return to the same department, the employer obtained medical reports and consulted with the employee on the medical position and on alternatives (*Thanet District Council v Webster* [2003] IDS Employment Law Brief 728, p 6);
(f) a senior executive acting in a high-handed and aggressive manner towards employees (*Horkulak v Cantor Fitzgerald International* [2004] ICR 697, QBD);
(g) rudely and unjustly criticizing an employee in front of others (*Isle of Wight Tourist Board v Coombes* [1976] IRLR 413, EAT);
(h) accusing an employee, without foundation, of inability to do his job (*Courtaulds Northern Textile Ltd v Andrew* [1979] IRLR 84, EAT);
(i) suspending an employee (even if pursuant to a contractual right) without reasonable and proper cause (*Gogay v Hertfordshire County Council* [2000] IRLR 703, CA);
(j) maintaining suspension of an employee even though the employer has already concluded that one of two charges against the employee is unfounded (*Camden and Islington Mental Health and Social Care Trust v Atkinson* EAT/0058/07);
(k) giving an unjust and unmerited warning or other disciplinary sanction out of all proportion to the offence (*Stanley Cole* (*Wainfleet*) *Ltd v Sheridan* [2003] IRLR 52, EAT);
(l) giving a bad reference without checking that it is fair and reasonable (*TSB Bank plc v Harris* [2000] IRLR 157, EAT);
(m) requiring an employee to relocate, without giving reasonable notice (*United Bank Ltd v Akhtar* [1989] IRLR 507, EAT);
(n) imposing a disciplinary suspension without pay, unless the employer has the power to do so under the contract of employment;
(o) laying off employees without pay, in the absence of an express contractual provision allowing the employer to do so (*D & J McKenzie Ltd v Smith* [1976] IRLR 345, CS);
(p) failing to give an employee the necessary support to perform his functions and duties properly (*Associated Tyre Specialists* (*Eastern*) *Ltd v Waterhouse* [1976] IRLR 386, EAT);
(q) failing to cooperate with an employee in his attempts to achieve sales targets which allow him to obtain benefits under a bonus scheme (*Takacs v Barclays Services Jersey Ltd*) [2006] IRLR 877, QBD—interim decision of the High Court);
(r) failing to provide a satisfactory working environment to enable the employee to work, for example, requiring people to work in an unpleasantly smoky atmosphere (*Waltons & Morse v Dorrington* [1997] IRLR 488, EAT);
(s) requiring the employee to work in unsafe conditions (*Marshall Specialist Vehicles Ltd v Osborne* [2003] IRLR 672, EAT);
(t) causing psychiatric damage by volume or character of work (*Walker v Northumberland County Council* [1995] IRLR 35, DC);
(u) in the absence of a written contractual provision entitling the employee to do so, failing to pay full wages to an employee during periods of sickness absence (*Secession Ltd* (*t/a Freud*) *v Bellingham* [2006] IRLB Issue 788, p 17);
(v) failing adequately to investigate a grievance, for example, failure to properly address a complaint of overworking (which accompanied a complaint of alleged bullying) was, when looked at cumulatively in the context of earlier unreasonable actions, constructive dismissal (*GAB Robbins* (*UK*) *Ltd v Triggs* [2008] IRLR 317, CA).

(w) refusing to provide work (in the absence of a reasonable contractual power to do so) for the employee if the employee's job is such (for example he is a scientist or doctor) that his skills constantly need exercising to avoid atrophy;

(x) refusing to provide work where a significant proportion of the employee's remuneration is based upon commission;

(y) not making reasonable adjustments to a disabled employee's job which would allow him to continue working (*Greenhof v Barnsley Metropolitan Council* [2006] IRLR 98, EAT);

(z) making public remarks about an employee which are highly damaging to his reputation (*Clements v RDF Medial Group Ltd* [2008] IRLR 207, HC);

(aa) discriminating against the employee (*Shaw v CCL Ltd* [2008] IRLR 284, EAT, where the employer unreasonably refused a woman's request to work flexibly following the birth of her child).

Employer's defence

Once an employee has shown there is a substantial breach going to the root of his contract of employment, the burden of proof is neutral as to whether the employee's dismissal was a reasonable response in all the circumstances, so that any 'dismissal' will be fair. The employer must show that: **30.14**

(1) it has not acted in substantial breach of contract. Conduct which will usually *not* amount to an event of constructive dismissal includes:

(a) minor alterations to the employee's contractual terms;

(b) changes allowed by the contract of employment (for example, pursuant to flexibility provisions—*White v Reflecting Roadstuds Ltd* [1991] IRLR 331, EAT);

(c) a delay in payment of wages, if not substantial;

(d) lack of consultation over the appointment of a subordinate;

(e) telling an employee he will be dismissed at some time in the future (this is not constructive dismissal because the employer may intend to give due notice, which would not be a breach of contract);

(f) introducing adverse changes to employees' contracts brought on in response to a necessary reorganization as the only perceived alternative to dismissing the employees (*St John of God (Care Services) Ltd v Brooks* [1992] IRLR 546, EAT);

(g) appointing someone to an internal interview panel whom the employee perceives to be prejudiced against transsexuals when the employer did not know the employee was a transsexual (*Baldwin v Brighton & Hove City Council* [2007] ICR 680, EAT);

(h) conducting a grievance raised by the employee in respect of co-workers in a way the tribunal concluded was a reasonable and proper manner (*Abbey National plc v Fairbrother* [2007] IRLR 320, EAT); or

(i) the actions of a third party, even one whom the employee considered her 'overall boss' over whom the employer had no control (*Yorke v Moonlight* EAT/0025/06);

(2) an employee's breach of a statutory duty (eg abuse of an employee's trade union rights) may not necessarily be a constructive dismissal (*Doherty v British Midland Airways Ltd* [2006] IRLR 90, EAT);

(3) there is a potentially fair reason for the constructive dismissals, and this reason falls within one of the potentially fair reasons set out in ERA 1998, s 98(2) or is some other substantial reason;

(4) the employee had, unbeknown to the employer at the time, already breached the implied term of trust and confidence before the employer subsequently breached the term (*RDF Media Group plc v Clements* [2008] IRLR 207, HC, where the employee had probably disclosed confidential information to a prospective employer and had assisted the prospective employer in press briefings to put pressure on the existing employer);

(5) it acted reasonably in acting in breach of contract (*Cape Industrial Services Ltd v Ambler* [2003] IDS Employment Law Brief 728, p 9); or

(6) it has remedied the breach (*Bournemouth University HEC v Buckland* [2009] UKEAT/0492/08 EAT) where upholding a grievance in relation to the behaviour which constituted the fundamental breach of contract, before the employee had resigned, meant that there was no 'live' fundamental breach to which the employee could respond.

Grievance procedure—pre 6 April 2009

30.15 If the employee claims to have been constructively dismissed, he must, if he brought tribunal proceedings before 6 April 2009 when the statutory grievance procedures were repealed (see paras 30.18 and 30.72), have lodged a grievance against his employer at least 28 days before bringing a claim (EA 2002, s 32). The grievance should be in relation to the whole claim; if it is only in relation to one aspect of it, yet in the claim form the employee relies upon a series of events to show constructive dismissal, the tribunal may not have jurisdiction to hear the claim (*Cyprus Airways Ltd v Lambrou* UKEAT/0526/06). If the employer is going to take the point that the claim is invalid because no grievance has been lodged in time, this must be specifically pleaded (*Plummer v DMC Business Machines* UKEAT/0381/06; *Hall v South Kent College* UKEAT/0087/07). *Note*: the requirement to follow the statutory grievance procedure was repealed on 1 April 2009.

30.16 The statutory grievance procedures are:

(1) *Step 1*: *Statement of grievance* The employee must set out the grievance in writing and send it to the employer. He must set out the basis for the grievance. This may be made without the use of the term 'grievance', for example by a solicitor's letter threatening to bring a claim or in a letter of resignation (*Mark Warner Ltd v Aspland* [2006] IRLR 87; *Shergold v Fieldway Medical Centre* [2006] IRLR 76; and *Galaxy Showers Ltd v Wilson* [2006] IRLR 83) or even by an informal letter indicating what the employee's complaints are, which is specifically expressed not to be a statutory grievance (*Procek v Oakford Farms Ltd* EAT/0049/08). The detail of the grievance need not be set out so long as the employer, on a fair reading of the statement, having regard to the context in which it was made, would have appreciated that the particular complaint was being raised (*Canary Wharf v Edebi* [2006] IRLR 416, EAT; *Ward v University of Essex* EAT/0391/07). The grievance must be made within a reasonable time, but the employer's timetable need not be strictly adhered to (*Martin v Class Security Installations Ltd* UKEAT/0188/06). In 'last straw' cases, the letter may be sent before the act relied on as the last straw has occurred (*Thornton Print v Morton* [2008] 0090/08, EAT).

(2) *Step 2*: *Meeting* The employer must invite the employee to attend a meeting to discuss the grievance, at a date which gives the employer reasonable opportunity to consider its response to the information. The employee must take all reasonable steps to attend the meeting.

After the meeting the employer must tell the employee its decision in response to the grievance and notify him of his right to appeal. Notification of the right to appeal can be oral, rather than in writing (*Aptuit* (*Edinburgh*) *Ltd v Kennedy* UKEATS/057/06).

(3) *Step 3*: *Appeal* If the employee appeals, the employer must invite him to a further meeting, normally with a more senior representative of the employer. The employee must attend the meeting and the employer must tell the employee, following the meeting, its final decision.

30.17 A modified procedure applies, amounting to Step 1 followed by an employer's written response, if the employee's employment has ended before the grievance starts *and* both the parties agree. In these circumstances, the employee must describe the grievance clearly, dealing with the essential questions 'who, what, where, when, why?' (*Clyde Valley Housing Association v MacAuley* [2008] IRLR 616, EAT).

Grievance procedure—post 6 April 2009

If there is no 'trigger event' before 6 April 2009, the statutory procedures do not apply. Trigger events, where the statutory grievance procedure will still apply are: 30.18

(1) where the actions of which the employee complains have all occurred before 6 April 2009;
(2) where the actions of which the employee complains began before 6 April 2009 and continue after that date, if the employee has submitted a grievance or brought tribunal proceedings before 4 July 2009;
(3) where the employee begins tribunal proceedings before 6 April 2009.

If an employee believes that he is being unfairly dismissed, and has not brought a grievance before 6 April 2009, the statutory procedures will not apply to the claim. Instead, the ACAS Code applies. The Code (see Appendix 3) sets out the five steps which should be followed without unreasonable delay. They are: 30.19

- the employee must let the employer know the nature of the grievance, in writing;
- the employer must hold a meeting with the employer to discuss the grievance;
- the employer must allow the employee to be accompanied at the meeting;
- the employer must decide on appropriate action;
- the employee should be offered the right of appeal.

If the employer fails to follow the grievance procedure, this does not make any dismissal automatically unfair. If an employee fails to follow the grievance procedure, the employee can still bring proceedings for unfair dismissal, and must do so within three months of the EDT (see para 30.08 for definition of EDT). If either party does not follow the grievance procedure (for example, if the employee does not lodge a grievance, or if the employer does not consider the grievance or does not allow the right of appeal), and if the employee wins the claim for unfair dismissal, the tribunal may adjust the compensation award up or down by up to 25 per cent either way, depending upon which party has failed to comply with the procedures. Tribunals should make such an award where there has been a failure to comply with the code which the tribunal finds is unreasonable. An award may then be granted if the Tribunal considers it just and equitable in all the circumstances to make the adjustment (TULR(C)A 1992, s 207A).

C. APPLICATION FOR INTERIM RELIEF

A person who believes he has been dismissed for: 30.20

(1) trade union reasons;
(2) most health and safety reasons;
(3) acting as trustee of his employer's occupational pension fund;
(4) acting as an employee representative in redundancy or TUPE consultations or a Working Time Regulations representative;
(5) making a protected disclosure;
(6) activities to do with union recognition; or
(7) asserting rights to accompany or be accompanied by someone facing disciplinary or grievance proceedings

may apply to an employment tribunal for interim relief (ERA 1996, s 128). The application must be presented to an employment tribunal within seven days of the EDT (see para 30.08 for definition of EDT). Interim relief may also be available if the claimant is likely to be able to establish that a dismissal made ostensibly on the ground of redundancy was in fact for one of the prohibited reasons (*McConnell v Bombardier Aerospace Short Bros plc* [2009] IRLR 201, CA).

Where dismissal is for trade union activities, an authorized official of the employee's trade union must within seven days of the EDT present a certificate to the tribunal stating that the employee is, or proposed to become, a member of the trade union, and that there appear to be reasonable 30.21

grounds for supposing that the principal reason for the dismissal was the one alleged in the employee's complaint.

30.22 An employment tribunal must decide, before making an order for interim relief, that the employee has a 'pretty good chance' of succeeding in his claim that he has been dismissed for one of the reasons set out (*Taplin v C Shippam Ltd* [1978] ICR 1068, EAT). The tribunal will normally call evidence on the issues, but will tend to shy away from giving a definitive account of the material facts. If an employee has ostensibly been dismissed for redundancy, the tribunal may still order interim relief if it believes the employee may well succeed in an argument that the redundancy was fabricated to obscure the fact that dismissal was really for one of the specified activities, such as his trade union activities (*Bombardier Aerospace v McConnell* [2008] IRLR 51, CA).

30.23 If the tribunal decides the employee's claim is likely to succeed, the employer will be asked to reinstate or re-engage the employee. If the employer refuses, or if it offers to re-engage but the employee reasonably refuses the offer, the employment tribunal will in effect order that the employee be suspended on full pay until the hearing.

D. GROUNDS FOR DISMISSAL

30.24 In respect of all qualifying employees, an employer must show that the reason for dismissal is one of the statutorily fair reasons set out in ERA 1996, s 98. These are incapability, lack of qualifications, misconduct, redundancy, retirement, or breach of statutory provisions. There is also a catch-all ground of 'some other substantial reason which would justify dismissal'. It is *automatically fair* to dismiss someone to safeguard national security, for retirement provided the statutory procedures are followed (ERA 1996, ss 98ZA–98ZG), or while they are taking part in an official strike or industrial action which has lasted for over 12 weeks when all those in a similar position are dismissed, or while taking part in unofficial action (TULR(C)A 1992, ss 237–238A) but even so the employer must show that appropriate steps were taken and dismissal was within the range of reasonable responses (for example, that there were no suitable redeployment options, *B v BAA plc* [2005] ICR 1530, EAT).

Time for assessing the reason for dismissal in unfair dismissal cases

30.25 A dismissal must be fair, based upon the facts known to the employer either at the date the employee was given notice of his dismissal or, if there is an appeal, at the date of the announcement of the appeal decision.

Subsequently discovered conduct

30.26 While conduct discovered after notice of dismissal or announcement of any appeal cannot be used to justify the dismissal in any unfair dismissal proceedings, it may be taken into account in the following circumstances:

(1) It may be relied upon to show the employer was reasonable in reaching any decision which it did, before dismissal, about the employee's performance or conduct.
(2) It may affect remedies. If subsequently discovered conduct is very serious, it could lead to a finding that it was not just and equitable for the tribunal to make any compensatory award at all because of the employee's conduct (see paras 25.05–25.07) (but see para 30.26(4)). If not in relation to the original reason for dismissal, the employer could allow an appeal but institute new disciplinary proceedings in relation to the newly discovered conduct.
(3) If new facts arise between the notice of dismissal and the termination date which show that the employer's conduct was unwarranted, this can be relied upon by the employee to show that the ultimate dismissal was unfair and vice versa. For example, if an employer gives an employee notice of termination of his employment as a result of misconduct but, before the termination date, discovers that it was another employee who committed the acts of

misconduct in question, if the employer still upholds the original employee's dismissal, this will be unfair.

(4) The employer can rely upon information relating to the original reason for dismissal received during the course of any appeal procedure even where the appeal takes place after the dismissal, though it may not use such information to introduce a fresh reason for dismissal. In these latter circumstances, if the employer wishes to rely upon the new information as a reason for dismissal, the original dismissal should be revoked upon appeal and further dismissal proceedings instituted.

Burden and standard of proof

The employer must show that the reason for dismissal is a potentially fair one. It is then for the tribunal to determine whether the employer has acted reasonably in all the circumstances in treating the reason for dismissal as a sufficiently serious one to dismiss the employee (ERA 1996, ss 98(1) and 98(4)). The tribunal will look at what the operative reason for dismissal was: even if the employee has committed an act of misconduct, if relying on the misconduct as the reason for dismissal was a sham device from an employer who had other reasons to wish to terminate the employment, dismissal may still be unfair (*ASLEF v Brady* [2006] IRLR 576, EAT). The process for establishing the reason for dismissal is as follows: **30.27**

(1) it is for the employer to prove a fair reason for his dismissal;
(2) there is no burden on the employee to disprove the reason put forward by the employer, or positively to prove a different reason;
(3) if the employee chooses to assert that there was a different and inadmissible reason for the dismissal (for example, making a protected disclosure) he must produce some evidence supporting his case and must challenge the employer's case;
(4) the employer can defeat a claim of inadmissible reason for dismissal either by proving a different reason or by successfully contesting the employee's proposed reason;
(5) if the tribunal does not accept the employer's case, it may, but is not obliged to, accept that the reason is one put forward by the employee (*Kuzel v Roche Products Ltd* [2008] IRLR 530, CA).

An employment tribunal cannot substitute its own reasoning and opinions for those of the employer (*Foley v Post Office*; *HSBC Bank plc v Madden* [2000] IRLR 827, CA). The matter must be judged by the objective standard of the way in which a reasonable employer in that line of business of that size in those circumstances would have behaved. The tribunal must ask the question: 'Was dismissal, as a sanction, one within the range of reasonable responses to the conduct which a reasonable employer might reasonably have imposed?' It is irrelevant whether other employers (or indeed the members of the employment tribunal hearing the case) might have behaved more leniently towards the individual. **30.28**

Automatically unfair grounds

Several types of dismissal are automatically unfair. These are where the principal reason for dismissal is: **30.29**

(1) *Spent convictions* Dismissal of the employee where the principal reason for the dismissal is a criminal conviction which is deemed to have been spent under the Rehabilitation of Offenders Act 1974 (Rehabilitation of Offenders Act 1974, s 4(3)(b)).
(2) *Trade union activities* Dismissal of the employee where the principal reason for the dismissal is a reason connected with membership or non-membership of, or participation in, the activities of an independent trade union (TULR(C)A 1992, s 152).
(3) *Health and safety reasons* Dismissal of the employee where the principal reason is the fact he is a health and safety representative or has taken reasonable action as a result of the inadequacy of health and safety procedures or refuses to work in what he reasonably believes are dangerous surroundings (ERA 1996, s 100). *Note*: there is no statutory maximum ceiling for compensation for dismissals on health and safety grounds (ERA 1996, s 124(1A)).

(4) *Pension trustee* Dismissal of the employee where the principal reason is that he is trustee of a relevant occupational pension scheme (ERA 1996, s 102).

(5) *Employee representative* Dismissal of the employee where the principal reason is that he is an employee representative performing consultation on redundancies or transfers of undertakings or that he takes part in an election for employee representatives (ERA 1996, s 103).

(6) *Assertion of statutory right* Dismissal of the employee where the principal reason is that he has asserted statutory rights (for example, the rights to written particulars of terms and conditions of employment; minimum statutory notice; time off, holiday and other rights under the Working Time Regulations 1998; to retain employment terms and rights following a TUPE transfer and similar rights) (ERA 1996, ss 101A and 104). This would include dismissal for the principal reason that the employee complained that her salary had not been paid on time, on the basis that she was asserting her statutory right not to have unlawful deductions made from her wages (*Elizabeth Claire Care Management Ltd v Francis* [2005] IRLR 858, EAT).

(7) *Family-related reasons* Dismissal of a woman where the principal reason for the dismissal is because she is pregnant or for a reason connected with pregnancy, maternity leave, adoption leave, ante-natal leave, paternity leave, parental leave, or compassionate leave (ERA 1996, s 99). This is so where the stated reason for dismissal is a reasonable one such as misconduct, but where the tribunal is satisfied that the real reason for dismissal relates to family matters (*Coulombeau v Enterprise Rent-a-Car (UK) Ltd* [2007] IDS Employment Law Brief 826, ET, where the tribunal found that the real reason for dismissal was the employer's view that the employee was likely to become entitled to additional leave because she was hoping to adopt a child). To succeed in arguing that the sole or principal reason for dismissal relates to paternity leave, the employee must probably show that the dismissal was caused by the paternity leave—this is a stronger test than just showing that the dismissal was associated with taking paternity leave (*Atkins v Coyle Personnel plc* EAT/0206/07).

(8) *Transfer of undertakings* Dismissal of the employee where the principal reason for the dismissal is a reason connected with a transfer of an undertaking (TUPE 2006, reg 7).

(9) *Industrial action* Dismissal of those taking part in official industrial action either during the first 12 weeks of the action, or (if the employee in question has stopped taking part in the industrial action) after this period (TULR(C)A 1992, s 238A(2), (3)).

(10) *Public interest disclosures* Dismissal of a person for being a 'whistle-blower' (ERA 1996, s 103A) and making a protected disclosure (see also ERA 1996, ss 43A–43K and, for example, *Street v Derbyshire Unemployed Workers' Centre* [2004] ICR 213, EAT). The disclosure must have been made, in good faith, to an appropriate person. These are:

    (a) his employer; or
    (b) a person who has legal responsibility for the behaviour in question (if not the employer's behaviour), in good faith (eg a building contractor, where the whistle-blower works for a sub-contractor); or
    (c) his legal adviser (see eg *Kirwan v First Corporate Shipping Ltd* EAT/0066/07); or
    (d) a Minister of the Crown (if the employee is a civil servant); or
    (e) to various listed regulatory bodies, such as the Charities Commission, the Financial Services Authority, or the Commissioners of the Inland Revenue concerning possible breaches of rules which are relevant to that body (Public Interest Disclosure (Prescribed Persons) Order 1999) provided that the employee reasonably believes the information to be substantially true;
    (f) to other people, such as the media, but only in the most stringent circumstances where:

        - the employee, in good faith, reasonably believes the allegations to be substantially true, and does not make the disclosure for purposes of financial gain; and

- when he makes the disclosure, the employee has: either made the disclosure to his employer (using relevant internal procedures, if any) or relevant regulator and nothing has been or is likely to be done; or has not made this disclosure only because he reasonably believes he will be subject to some detriment (eg dismissal or demotion) or evidence will be destroyed if he tells his employer; or
- it is nevertheless reasonable to make the disclosure to the individual, bearing in mind issues such as the identity of the recipient of the information, the seriousness of the allegations, whether they are continuing or likely to occur in future, and whether disclosure of the information puts the employer in breach of his obligations to another person;

(g) to someone else if the allegations are exceptionally serious, provided that the employee:

- acts reasonably and in good faith (including regarding his choice of person to whom he makes the disclosure);
- reasonably believes the allegation to be substantially true; and
- does not make the disclosure for personal gain.

The protection here only applies to any disclosure itself; it does not extend to misconduct designed to prove the employee's suspicions (*Bolton School v Evans* [2007] IRLR 140, CA, where hacking into a student's computer to point out weaknesses in the IT system merited dismissal). A disclosure is protected even if it reveals the wrongdoing of a third party (*Hibbins v Hesters Way Neighbourhood Project* [2009] IRLR 198, EAT). It is sufficient for the employee to believe that what he was disclosing fell within one of the whistle-blowing categories, eg the commission of a criminal offence, even if it does not do so; so long as their belief in the underlying facts is genuine, employees are not expected to have an encyclopaedic knowledge of the law (*Babula v Waltham Forest College* [2007] IRLR 346, CA). In deciding whether the reason for dismissal is that the employee has made a protected disclosure, the correct approach is:

- has the employee shown that there is a real issue as to whether the reason put forward by the employer for the dismissal was not the true reason: has he raised some doubt as to that reason by advancing a public interest disclosure reason under ERA 1996, s 103A?
- if so, has the employer proved its reason for dismissal?
- if not, has the employer disproved the s 103A reason advanced by the employee?
- if not, dismissal is for the s 103A reason.

In answering these questions, it follows:

- that failure by the employer to prove the potentially fair reason relied on does not automatically result in a finding of unfair dismissal under s 103A;
- but rejection of the employer's reason, coupled with the employee having raised a prima facie case that the reason is a s 103A reason, entitles the tribunal to infer that the s 103A reason is the true reason; but
- it remains open to the employer to satisfy the tribunal that the making of a protected disclosure was not the reason or the principal reason for dismissal, even if the real reason found by the tribunal is not the one advanced by the employer (*Kirwan v First Corporate Shipping Ltd* EAT/0066/07—where the EAT concluded that the employee had not suffered any detriment as a result of the disclosure because the reason for the dismissal was persistent lateness to work); and
- it is not at any stage for an employee with one year's qualifying service to prove the s 103A reason (though if the employee has less than one year's service, the onus will be on him to prove that the reason fell within s 103A: *Kuzel v Roche Products Ltd* [2007] IRLR 309, EAT, [2008] IRLR 530, CA).

(11) *Sunday working* Dismissal of a shop or betting worker, who has been continuously employed by the same employer since before 1995 and who has opted out of Sunday working, for refusing to work on a Sunday (ERA 1996, s 101).

(12) *Minimum wage* Dismissal of an employee for trying to enforce the rights of himself or others to a minimum wage (ERA 1996, s 104A).

(13) *Union recognition* Dismissal of an employee for getting involved or refusing to get involved in an application for union recognition (TULR(C)A 1992, Sch A1, para 161).

(14) *Tax credit rights* Dismissal of an employee for trying to enforce the rights of himself or others to working tax credits (formerly working families' tax credits) or disabled person's tax credits (ERA 1996, s 104B).

(15) *Accompanying colleagues at disciplinary or grievance hearings* Dismissal of an employee for accompanying or being accompanied by a colleague at a disciplinary or grievance hearing (Employment Relations Act 1999, s 12).

(16) *Part-time and fixed term workers* Dismissal of an employee for enforcing rights under the Part-time Workers (Prevention of Less Favourable Treatment) Regulations 2000, reg 7; or the Fixed-Term Employees (Prevention of Less Favourable Treatment) Regulations 2002, reg 6.

(17) *Works councils* Dismissal of an employee for activities in connection with European Works Councils (Transnational Information and Consultation of Employees Regulations 1999, reg 28) or information and consultation bodies (Information and Consultation of Employees Regulations 2004, reg 30).

(18) *Flexible working request* Dismissal for exercising rights to apply for flexible working (ERA 1996, s 104C).

(19) *No statutory disciplinary procedures* Dismissal where the employer has failed to comply with the minimum statutory disciplinary procedures before dismissal (ERA 1996, s 98A(1)). All the procedures must be complied with, including the obligation to do things in a timely fashion (*Patel v Leicester City Council* UKEAT/0368/2006). If (and only if) the employer concedes that the procedures were not followed, then the employment tribunal does not have to consider the question of ordinary unfair dismissal. If there is a dispute on the issue, the tribunal will consider both questions (*Metrobus v Cook* EAT/0490/06). This provision has been repealed with effect from 6 April 2009, and only applies where any of the following trigger events have occurred before that date:

- the employee has been dismissed; or
- the employer has sent the employee a Step 1 Statement (written notice setting out why dismissal is contemplated); or
- the employer has held a Step 2 meeting (disciplinary meeting) (see paras 30.72–30.76 for further details of Step 1 and Step 2); or
- the employer has taken relevant disciplinary action against the employee.

(20) *Unfair selection for redundancy* Selection for redundancy on one of the grounds set out above (save relating to flexible working arrangements and works councils) (ERA 1996, s 105).

(21) *Dismissal for retirement* without going through proper notification procedures (ERA 1996, s 98ZG).

Special provisions relating to retirement dismissal

30.30 Retirement dismissals after 1 October 2006 are not subject to the normal test of fairness of procedure set out in ERA 1996, s 98(4). Instead the provisions of ERA 1996, ss 98ZA–98ZG apply so that:

(1) Dismissal of an employee below the age of 65, in the absence of a normal retirement age below 65, is not for retirement.

(2) Dismissal of an employee 65 or older, in the absence of a normal retirement age or at the normal retirement age, is for retirement provided the employer has told the employee of his

right to request not to retire (Employment Equality (Age) Regulations 2006, Sch 6, para 2) and the dismissal takes effect on the intended date of retirement. If the normal retirement age is lower than 65 it must be objectively justified.

(3) Dismissal of an employee below the relevant normal retirement age is not for retirement.

(4) If an employee has not complied with the duty to notify the employee of his intended date of retirement at least 6–12 months in advance, and of his right to request not to retire, whether or not the decision is fairly for the reason of retirement will be decided taking into account:

(i) whether or not the employer notified the employee two weeks to six months in advance of his intended date of retirement and his right to request not to retire (Employment Equality (Age) Regulations 2006, Sch 6, para 4);
(ii) how long before dismissal the notification was given;
(iii) whether the employer followed or sought to follow the duty to consider procedure set out in the Employment Equality (Age) Regulations 2006, Sch 6, paras 5 to 9 if the employee has requested not to retire.

A dismissal for retirement will be fair if steps (i) to (iii) are followed and if the employer has properly considered any request to postpone retirement (see para 30.30(5)) provided that in reviewing these factors the tribunal determines that the real reason for dismissal was indeed retirement. (See also paras 32.71–32.82.)

(5) If the employee requests not to retire on the intended date of retirement, he must do so:

(a) within three months of any notification to retire, if the notification is given to him 6–12 months before the intended date of retirement;
(b) before the intended date of retirement, in any other circumstances.

The employer must meet the employee (who has the right to be accompanied by a colleague or trade union official) to consider the request (or, if not practicable to do so, must consider any written representations), and must then decide whether: (i) to extend employment indefinitely; (ii) to extend the employment to a specified date; or (iii) to reject the request. If (ii) or (iii) apply, the employee must be given the right of appeal.

(6) If the employer dismisses the employee before considering the employee's request not to retire on the proposed date then (except for the purposes of deciding on what date the employee was dismissed for the purposes of bringing employment tribunal proceedings) the employment will be deemed to continue until the day after the employer gives notice of his decision.

(7) If the tribunal reviews the three factors at para 30.30(4) (i) to (iii) and decides that the failures were sufficient to render the decision not for retirement, then the dismissal will be considered under normal unfair dismissal principles. However, the employee should have little difficulty then convincing a tribunal that such a dismissal was unfair because the employer will have to show the reason for the dismissal was for some other potentially fair reason and (at least until 1 April 2009) that the statutory dismissal procedures were followed.

Note: in December 2006 the High Court referred to the ECJ the issue of whether imposing a default retirement age of 65 properly implements the EC Equal Treatment Framework Directive (application for judicial review by National Council on Ageing). The ECJ has confirmed that in principle a country may lay down a mandatory retirement age. The case has now reverted to the High Court for a ruling on whether the current law, which permits retirement at 65, is justified and appropriate. All cases on the point brought before the Employment Tribunal are being stayed meanwhile. In similar but not identical circumstances, the ECJ decided that a retirement age of 65 in Spain was justified (*Palacios de la Villa v Cortefiel Servicios SA* [2007] IRLR 989, ECJ).

Written reasons for dismissal

An employee who has been continuously employed for one year or more has the right to request **30.31**
written reasons for his dismissal. No such continuity qualification applies if the employee is

pregnant at the time of the dismissal or if she is dismissed while pregnant or during her maternity or adoption leave, when reasons should be given whether or not requested. The employer must respond to such requests within 14 days (ERA 1996, ss 92 and 93). If the employer unreasonably fails to give reasons, he is liable to pay the employee two weeks' pay.

30.32 An employment tribunal is not bound to accept the employer's stated reason or reasons for dismissal if it finds that the reasons given conceal the true reason, but in any tribunal proceedings the employer is bound by the facts given in support of any dismissal, though not necessarily by the legal label given to those facts. When considering the reasons the tribunal will seek to ensure that they are genuinely held by the employer. If the employer relies on more than one reason, he may have to prove all of them to show a fair dismissal. If the tribunal decides that the stated reason for dismissal, even where misconduct has been committed which would potentially justify a dismissal, is not the true reason, the dismissal may be unfair (*ASLEF v Brady* [2006] IRLR 576, EAT).

Fair reasons

30.33 In any dismissal action, the burden is on the employer to show the reason for dismissal. In a case of wrongful dismissal, the employer must then show that the reason is sufficiently serious to have justified the employer terminating the contract, whether he knew of the reason at the date of termination or otherwise. For unfair dismissal, the tribunal will decide:

(1) what the reason for dismissal was;
(2) whether it was the actual reason why the decision to dismiss was taken; and
(3) whether it was a fair reason.

30.34 Potentially fair reasons are set out in ERA 1996, s 98, and are:

(1) that the employee was incapable (measured by reference to skills, aptitude, health, or any physical or mental quality) of performing the work of the kind he was currently employed by the employer to do (see paras 30.49–30.53 for incompetence and paras 30.54–30.64 for ill health);
(2) that the employee lacked the qualifications required to perform work of the kind that he was currently employed by the employer to do (see paras 30.65–30.66);
(3) misconduct (see paras 30.35–30.48);
(4) redundancy (see Chapter 31);
(5) that if the employee were to continue to be employed in the position he held, either he or the employer would be in breach of some statutory provision (see paras 30.67–30.68);
(6) retirement (see para 30.30); and
(7) some other substantial reason which will justify dismissal (see paras 30.69–30.71).

E. MISCONDUCT

30.35 Generally, misconduct amounts to behaviour which is unacceptable in the employment context. Most reasonably sized employers will have a code of conduct, either in a staff manual or in an employment contract, which gives examples of misconduct with differing degrees of seriousness.

Disciplinary code

30.36 A disciplinary code may be expressly incorporated into the employee's contract of employment. If it is, its provisions should be adhered to. In the absence of an express disciplinary code, any employment tribunal will decide whether the employer has followed the statutory disciplinary procedures (see paras 30.72–30.76) and will have regard to the ACAS disciplinary Code of Practice (see para 30.37). It will also expect any contractual disciplinary code to be along similar lines.

The new ACAS Code of Practice on Disciplinary and Grievance Procedures (set out in Appendix 3), which came into force on 6 April 2009, provides that facts should be established promptly following any disciplinary matter and an individual should be interviewed and given the opportunity to state his or her case and be advised of any rights under the procedure before a decision is made. They should have the right to be accompanied at any formal disciplinary meeting and a right of appeal (see para 30.80 for further details). **30.37**

Minor offences

The ACAS Code states that in the case of minor offences the individual should in general first be given a written warning setting out the nature of the offence and the likely consequence of further offences. Further misconduct might warrant a final written warning, which should contain a statement that any one occurrence could lead to suspension or dismissal. Minor offences include lateness, taking overly long meal breaks, minor acts of insubordination or rudeness, and so on. Appeals should be available at every stage. For dismissal following minor offences, normally, spent warnings cannot be relied on as part of the cumulative process (*Diosynth Ltd v Thomson* [2006] IRLR 284, CS), but this is not a hard and fast rule where the employee has committed gross misconduct (*Airbus UK Ltd v Webb* [2008] IRLR 309, CA—where five employees were watching television during working hours. One had a spent warning, the other four had clean disciplinary records. The fact that the employer viewed the clean records as a mitigating factor converting dismissal to a final warning for four of the employees did not make dismissal of the fifth employee unfair, where the employer viewed him differently because he had previously been subject to a final written warning, even though that warning was spent). **30.38**

Gross misconduct

Any single act of gross misconduct (ie serious breach of contract) will be sufficient to justify immediate dismissal without notice, money in lieu of notice, or compensation. Employers should be consistent (*Cain v Leeds Western Health Authority* [1990] ICR 585), and impose similar sanctions for similar offences; if not, the employee given the tougher sanction may be unfairly dismissed so long as the circumstances are truly comparable (*Levenes Solicitors v Dalley* EAT/0330/2006). They should also act reasonably speedily in taking disciplinary action—if they delay (even while an employee is taking time off for stress) without reserving their position, they may have waived the right to dismiss summarily (*Cook v MSHK Limited* [2009] EWCA Civ 624, CA). **30.39**

Misconduct involves some deliberate or reckless act or omission. Negligence or carelessness will generally be regarded as incapability (see paras 30.49–30.53). **30.40**

Examples of misconduct

Refusal to obey a lawful order

Refusal to obey a lawful instruction is misconduct. The nature of the refusal and the importance of the order will determine whether the misconduct is minor or gross (*UCATT v Brain* [1981] IRLR 224, CA). To determine what is lawful, one must look at the contract and any other incorporated documents such as a collective agreement or staff handbook, and at custom and practice. If the instruction is not lawful, that fact is not necessarily decisive when deciding whether any resulting dismissal was reasonable (*Farrant v Woodroffe School* [1998] ICR 184). **30.41**

Examples of refusals include: **30.42**

(1) refusal to comply with safety requirements;
(2) refusal to move location if the contract provides that the employee can be required to move to a proposed new site;
(3) refusal to perform a task which the employee is contractually obliged to perform;

(4) refusal to work reasonable overtime if the contract provides that the employees must work overtime so long as the employee is not being asked to work hours or at times that would involve a breach of the Working Time Regulations 1998;
(5) refusal to give new terms of employment a trial run, after having agreed (albeit reluctantly) to do so (*Robinson v Tescom Corporation* EAT 0567/07).

30.43 The following acts would not amount to misconduct under this head:

(1) refusal by employees to work in dangerous conditions (and indeed a dismissal on this basis may be automatically unfair);
(2) refusal to obey an unlawful order, for example, to falsify accounts;
(3) refusal to work overtime if the employee is not contractually obliged to do so;
(4) refusal to accept changes in terms and conditions of employment. However, if the employer can show that the changes are justifiable because of pressing business need, the dismissal may be for some other substantial reason and so the employer would be justified in dismissing the employee;
(5) frequent short-term self-certified absences should be dealt with under the procedure set out at para 30.55, and not as misconduct.

Breaches of discipline

30.44 If the employer's disciplinary code sets out an exhaustive list of disciplinary offences, no additional offences omitted from the list may be relied upon. If the disciplinary code sets out examples only of breaches of disciplinary procedure, then items which are not set out in the list may nevertheless, if sufficiently serious, be categorized by the employer as misconduct. To justify summary dismissal, the conduct must completely undermine the trust and confidence inherent in the employment relationship (*Neary v Dean of Westminster* [1999] IRLR 288).

30.45 Examples of breaches of discipline are:

(1) drunkenness at work (provided any alcohol policy which requires an employee to seek treatment for his alcoholism is drawn to his attention before the event in question—*Sinclair v Wandsworth Council* EAT/0145/07);
(2) being unfit to work as a result of drug abuse;
(3) theft of employer's, colleagues', clients', or suppliers' property (*Trusthouse Forte Hotels Ltd v Murphy* [1977] IRLR 186, EAT);
(4) physical violence or fighting;
(5) threatening behaviour;
(6) bad language;
(7) rudeness;
(8) fraud, for example, falsifying timesheets, or giving false information on a curriculum vitae (for example, not disclosing a past, unspent conviction);
(9) gross insubordination;
(10) failure to comply with legitimate management instructions, eg a director flouting his managing director's express instructions not to attend a particular meeting (*Annis v Eclipse Energy* [2007] All ER (D) 73, HC);
(11) working for or assisting a competitor whilst still employed, particularly where the employees are directors or have senior positions, so that they owe fiduciary duties or duties of fidelity to the employer (*Davidson and Maillou v Comparisons* [1980] IRLR 360, EAT; *Crowson Fabrics Ltd v Rider* [2008] IRLR 288, HC) (although merely seeking alternative employment even before the termination of the present contract is not unlawful: *Harris & Russell Ltd v Slingsby* [1973] IRLR 221, NIRC) and, in the absence of a contractual provision to the contrary, preparing to compete by developing a competitive product in one's spare time may not be a breach of fiduciary or other duties (*Helmet Integrated Systems v Tunnard* [2007] IRLR 126);
(12) misusing or unlawfully disclosing confidential information;
(13) unauthorized use of or tampering with a computer (*Denco Ltd v Joinson* [1991] IRLR 63, EAT);

(14) taking industrial action (but see para 30.29(9));
(15) taking bribes or secret commissions;
(16) serious breach of codes of relevant professional or governing bodies;
(17) failure to comply with important company policy, eg smoking on company premises (*Smith v Michelin Tyre plc* [2007] IDS Employment Law Brief 839, ET) or failure to disclose and seek formal approval for work performed for third parties, even though the employee had mentioned the work to her employers (*Guernina v Thames Valley University* [2008] EWCA Civ 34, CA);
(18) refusal to give consent to disclosure of medical records when there was a contractual obligation requiring the employee to do so, even though the employee had consented to undergo a medical examination (*Chaplin v Howard Kennedy* [2009] All ER (D) 16 (Jun) EAT).

Criminal offences

Criminal offences should only merit dismissal if they relate in some way to the employee's duties, for example, because they show that the employee is unsuitable for performing that type of work, or because the offence damages the employees' relationship with the employer, other employees and/or customers. This is a precept of the ACAS Code (see Appendix 3 at para 30). If the employer does not follow this principle a Tribunal may increase any award by 0–25 per cent (see paras 24.164–24.165 for details of the award increases). **30.46**

Examples of criminal offences which justify dismissal are: **30.47**

(1) dishonesty (fraud, theft, etc): this will normally justify dismissal unless, for example, the employee has been actively employed (ie not just on suspension) for a period;
(2) sexual offences: these will justify dismissal if the employee's duties often put him in contact with women or children, especially vulnerable ones, for example, where the job is in the education or health sectors (*X v Y* [2004] IRLR 665; *P v Nottinghamshire County Council* [1992] IRLR 362, CA);
(3) minor criminal offences which do not justify dismissal include minor drugs or traffic offences—these will not usually justify dismissal unless, for example, drug addiction affects the employee's capability or the employee's job requires a clean driving licence.

For appropriate procedure where misconduct is alleged, see paras 30.72–30.119. **30.48**

F. INCOMPETENCE

If the employer honestly believes, on reasonable grounds, that the employee is incompetent, he may dismiss him. It is, however, very rare that an employer may fairly dismiss an employee for incompetence if the employee has not had proper appraisals and warnings before a final decision is taken. **30.49**

Evidence of incompetence

The employment tribunal must rely to a large extent on the evidence of the employee's superiors in deciding whether or not an employee has been incompetent. An employer should have specific examples of incompetence, for example: **30.50**

(1) failure by the employee to perform part of his duties;
(2) complaints by colleagues or customers about the actions of the employee;
(3) inaccuracies committed by the employee;
(4) delays in finishing work by the employee;
(5) inflexibility and lack of adaptability on the part of the employee (*Abernethy v Mott Hay & Anderson* [1974] IRLR 213, CA);
(6) slovenliness or persistent carelessness on the part of the employee; or
(7) negligent acts or omissions on the part of the employee.

30.51 Separate and dissimilar acts of incompetence may cumulatively be relied upon by the employer. The employee is to be judged by the standards to be expected of someone in his present job, even if he has been over-promoted by the employer: the employee cannot demand to be returned to his former position, though in these circumstances a prudent employer would seek to establish whether there are any lower grade jobs to which the employee could be transferred.

Procedure

30.52 Before dismissing the employee for incompetence, the employer will normally need to adopt the following procedure (see also ACAS Disciplinary and Grievance Procedures. The guidance is available at <http://www.acas.org.uk/index.aspx?articleid=2179>):

(1) *Appraisal* The employer should discuss with the employee the criticisms he has of the employee's performance. The employer should maintain a system to monitor the employee's progress.
(2) *Warning* The employer should write to the employee telling him where his performance is deemed to be substandard, inviting him and a representative to come to a meeting to discuss his concerns and giving him an opportunity to express his point of view and explain why he might have been performing badly. If the explanation is not satisfactory, the employer should warn the employee of the consequences of a failure to improve. This should, preferably, be in writing. The warning should set out:

(a) where the employee has failed to meet the required standards;
(b) the time within which the employee must improve and a review date;
(c) the standard the employee must meet;
(d) any support/training the employer will provide to assist the employee;
(e) the fact that if the employee fails to improve, a further warning will be necessary (or, after the second warning that dismissal may be invoked); and
(f) the fact that the employee has a right to appeal.

(3) *Opportunity to improve* The employer must give the employee a reasonable period within which to improve. In establishing what is reasonable one must bear in mind the nature of the job, the employee's length of service, status, and past performance. The employer should give the employee the necessary support and assistance (which can include training) to enable the employee to improve. Normally, employees should receive at least two warnings before being dismissed for poor performance (but see para 30.53).
(4) The employee of previously good standing and long service will require special attention by the employer before any dismissal is made. He should be given reasonably substantial periods within which to improve unless there are very obvious reasons why an employee has suddenly become incapable, such as:

(a) the employee's capacity to do the job is altered, for example, because of ill health;
(b) the employee's job functions have altered, for example, as a result of new technology;
(c) the employee has failed to heed past warnings.

30.53 Warnings for incompetence may not be necessary in the following circumstances:

(1) gross incompetence or unsuitability;
(2) incompetence which has had serious physical consequences, for example, where a pilot has incompetently landed a plane causing actual or potential injury to passengers and/or expensive equipment (*Alidair Ltd v Taylor* [1976] IRLR 420, EAT);
(3) incompetence which has serious economic consequences, for example, deliberate or reckless incompetence leading to a loss of a whole production batch;
(4) incompetence where the employer reasonably believes that a warning would make no difference, for example, where an employee refuses to admit that there is any need for him to improve;

(5) the incompetence of a senior employee, who should appreciate what standards are required of him and whether he matches up to those standards. The employee must, however, be in a position to know (whether from his own experience or because he has been told his work is unsatisfactory) that he may be dismissed unless his work meets the required standard.

G. ILL HEALTH

Before dismissing the employee on the grounds of ill health, the employer should make proper inquiry into the actual state of the employee's health, its likely duration, and its effect upon the employee's ability to perform his tasks. **30.54**

Absenteeism

Where the employee takes frequent short-term, self-certificated absences, the employer should: **30.55**

(1) review the employee's attendance record and the reasons given for it;
(2) give the employee the opportunity to explain his attendance record (*International Sports Co Ltd v Thompson* [1980] IRLR 340, EAT);
(3) if the employee does not give a satisfactory explanation, but claims his absences are on grounds of ill health, or if there is any reason to suspect that the absences are caused by any disability, ask him to see a doctor to consider whether medical treatment is necessary. Any genuine illness must be treated with sympathy and under normal illness procedures (see paras 30.58–30.62). However, the fact that someone is disabled does not of itself prevent the employer from dismissing him for absenteeism (*Royal Liverpool Children's NHS Trust v Dunsby* [2006] IRLR 351), though an employer should consider whether it might be a 'reasonable adjustment' to disregard disability-related absences;
(4) if there is still no satisfactory explanation for the absences, give the employee a misconduct warning that further unwarranted absences are likely to result in dismissal;
(5) interview the employee after any subsequent absence to ascertain its cause.

If there is no improvement in the attendance record, and still no valid reason for the absences, the employer may dismiss the employee.

Disability

Where the employer knew, when it engaged the employee, of the existence and extent of a disability, it is most unlikely to be able to dismiss the employee fairly by reason only of the disability; if it does, this is likely to be discrimination under the terms of DDA 1995 (*Williams v J Walter Thompson Group Ltd* [2005] IRLR 376, CA), see para 32.43 *et seq*. In those circumstances the standard of work required of the employee will be that of a disabled person to do the particular job in hand. **30.56**

Where the employee becomes disabled during the course of his employment, he should be treated in the same manner as employees suffering from other illnesses but subject always to the provisions of DDA 1995, in particular in relation to the making of reasonable adjustments to the workplace (see paras 32.54–32.55). **30.57**

Illness

Before taking any action regarding the employee's illness, then, provided the employee is not disabled within the definition of DDA 1995 (see paras 32.44–32.50) the employer should take the following steps: **30.58**

(1) consult the employee about the situation and ask the employee for his own views on his health and abilities (*East Lindsey District Council v Daubney* [1977] IRLR 181, EAT);

(2) where appropriate, obtain a medical opinion. This medical opinion should be more detailed than a mere expression of opinion that the employee is unfit to work, and should deal with the likelihood of an improvement in health and attendance. The employee cannot be compelled (in the absence of an express contractual term) to undergo medical examinations;
(3) examine the sickness record;
(4) discuss the position again with the employee;
(5) review whether there is any alternative employment which might suit the employee;
(6) consider whether the employee can be 'medically retired' and granted an ill health pension—failure to do so could render a dismissal unfair (*First West Yorkshire Ltd v Haigh* [2008] IRLR 182, EAT).

If the employee is disabled within the definition of the DDA 1995, but the employer is contemplating dismissing the employee, for example because of incompetence or absenteeism, the employer must review whether any reasonable adjustments might improve the position, for example by giving training or adapting the working environment (in the case of incompetence) or changing the working hours (in the case of absenteeism), and if there are any he should make them. Failure to do so would render a dismissal a breach of DDA 1995, s 4(2)(d).

30.59 Where the absences are unconnected and intermittent, or where otherwise there will be no apparent benefit from a medical review of the position, there will be no obligation to obtain medical evidence (*Lynock v Cereal Packaging Ltd* [1988] IRLR 510, EAT).

30.60 Having formed a reasoned opinion of the employee's medical state, the employer should consider the following factors:

(1) the nature of the illness;
(2) the likelihood of it recurring;
(3) the length of absences likely and the intervening spaces of good health;
(4) the requirements of his business;
(5) whether the employee's tasks can smoothly be done by colleagues or temporary employees while the employee is absent;
(6) the impact on colleagues of the employee's absence;
(7) the employee's length of service;
(8) the need for the employer to have employees of this nature in rude health (for example, deep-sea divers, heavy manual workers);
(9) whether the ill health might cause potential problems at the workplace (for example, an epileptic may be thought unable to work with dangerous machinery or in a nightclub);
(10) whether continuing to employ the individual in his former job, or any suitable available employment, could give rise to injury for which the employer could be liable, if medical opinion is disregarded and the employee returns to work (*Liverpool Area Health Authority (Teaching) Central & Southern District v Edwards* [1977] IRLR 471, EAT);
(11) alternative employment (for example, a desk job) for the employee, even if at a reduced rate of pay. The employer is not, however, expected to create a special job for the employee but only to look to see whether he has any suitable vacancies (*Merseyside & North Wales Electricity Board v Taylor* [1975] IRLR 60, HC);
(12) whether it is possible to make adjustments to the workplace so that the employee could return to work;
(13) the employer's sick pay scheme. The employer should generally not dismiss an employee who is still entitled to benefits under the scheme, especially if by doing so, the employee is unable to benefit from the scheme in the future. Even if the employer has an express contractual right to dismiss, the courts are likely to strive to stop the employer blocking an employee's rights under, for example, a permanent health insurance scheme.

See, generally, *Spencer v Paragon Wallpapers Ltd* [1976] IRLR 373.

30.61 If it is clear, after consultation with the employee and his representative, that the employee will not within a reasonable time be able to resume his duties satisfactorily, and there are no alternative available jobs which the employee could be offered, and, for disabled employees, no reasonable adjustments that can be made to improve the position, it may be reasonable for the employer to dismiss the employee. This may be the case even where the employer's behaviour caused or contributed to the relevant incapacity, if there is no prospect of the employee being sufficiently well to return to work and the employer acted reasonably in all the circumstances (*McAldie v Royal Bank of Scotland* [2006] All ER (D) 393, EAT).

Very serious ill health, which will either mean the employee cannot in future carry out his old role or will be absent for long periods of time (at least more than the period when the employer's sick pay scheme operates) can in rare circumstances mean that the contract terminates by frustration, and there is, therefore, no dismissal. **30.62**

AIDS

An employer will generally not be able to dismiss an employee who is HIV positive unless AIDS has manifested itself and prevents the employee from working properly. The employer must consider the issues set out at paras 30.58–30.62 above and the provisions of DDA (see paras 32.43–32.63) in the normal way. The employer should seek to allay unreasoned fears of any of the employee's colleagues. A person who is HIV positive is now automatically regarded as disabled (DDA, Sch 1, para 6A). **30.63**

Responsibility for absences

When considering whether the employee was unfairly dismissed on grounds of ill health, the cause of the ill health is immaterial. An employer who caused the ill health may still dismiss an employee after going through the steps in paras 30.58–30.62, but may face High Court or county court proceedings for a personal injury claim. **30.64**

H. OTHER REASONS FOR DISMISSAL

Lack of qualifications

Generally, an employer has an opportunity to assess a prospective employee's qualifications before employing him. There are therefore only limited circumstances where this ground can be relied upon, for example: **30.65**

(1) where someone employed as a driver loses his driving licence; or
(2) where regulations, or new and profoundly sensible employer practice, require an employee carrying out work which the original employee had previously been doing to have particular qualifications, which the original employee does not possess.

Where an employer proposes to dismiss for lack of qualifications, he should still look to see whether there are any alternative jobs in which he can place the employee. **30.66**

Illegality

If an employer is to dismiss an employee under this head the employment must genuinely be in breach of the law. If the employer erroneously believes it is, then the dismissal may be fair for some other substantial reason but not under the heading of illegality (*Kelly v University of Southampton* [2008] IDS Employment Law Brief 846). Examples of illegality include: **30.67**

(1) the employee losing a work permit. If the employer mistakenly believes the employee does not have the appropriate work permit, this may be some other substantial reason justifying dismissal (see para 30.69) but an illegality defence can only be relied on when it would actually be illegal to continue the employment (*Klusova v London Borough of Hounslow* [2007] EWCA Civ 1127, CA);
(2) the employee being disqualified from driving if driving is an essential part of the job;
(3) the employee no longer having relevant professional qualifications (for example, an employed solicitor or doctor who is struck off his respective professional register).

30.68 Before dismissing on the ground of illegality the employer should consider whether it has any alternative vacancies which it could offer the employee that the employee would not legally be disqualified from performing. The employer does not have to create a suitable position if none is available.

Some other substantial reason

30.69 Examples include:

(1) An unreasonable refusal by the employee to accept changes in the terms and conditions of his employment whose imposition is necessary for sound business reasons (*Willow Oak Developments Ltd v Silverwood* [2006] IRLR 607, CA; *Catamaran Cruisers Ltd v Williams* [1994] IRLR 386, EAT).

(2) Where a genuine business reorganization dislodges an employee: the employer must show there is economic necessity for the reorganization and be prepared to produce supporting financial accounts (*Banerjee v City & Eastern London Health Authority* [1979] IRLR 147, EAT). If the reorganization is not genuine, but a pretext for getting rid of an old employee, it will be unfair (*Oakley v The Labour Party* [1988] IRLR 34, CA). When reviewing the employer's decision, the tribunal should conduct a balancing act, taking into account the advantages to the employer of its business reorganization and the disadvantages to employees—the employer does not have to go so far as to show that the changes are vital for the survival of the business (*Glasgow City Council v Deans* UKEATS/006/05).

(3) A personality clash if it disrupts the workplace. An employer should first try to establish whether the position is remediable, for example, by moving one of the employees to another department.

(4) The dismissal of the employee at the request of a third party (*Dobie v Burns International Security Services (UK) Ltd* [1984] IRLR 329, EAT). The employer must take into account, however, the potential injustice to the employee before acting on the third party's request. This will only be a fair dismissal in exceptional cases, for example, if a valued customer requires the employer to dismiss the employee (which the employer will have to prove—for example, by having a letter from the customer). This ground will not help any employer who, for example, gives in to union pressure to dismiss the employee. The employer should take into account issues such as the employee's length of service, work record, and potential difficulties in finding a new job (*Greenwood v Whiteghyll Plastics Ltd* EAT/0219/07).

(5) A breakdown of trust and confidence between employer and employee (*Perkin v St George's Healthcare NHS Trust* [2005] IRLR 93, CA, when behaviour at the disciplinary meeting was appropriately taken into account).

(6) Imprisonment of the employee.

(7) The wish of a small employer to appoint his child to do the relevant job.

(8) The protection of the employer's business, for example, where the employee refuses to sign a reasonable restrictive covenant (*Willow Oak Developments Ltd v Silverwood* [2006] IRLR 607, CA).

(9) The dismissal of an employee who refuses to agree a new shift pattern which would have resulted in him losing substantial overtime earnings (*Scott and Co v Richardson*, EAT/0074/04, IDS Employment Law Brief 786).

(10) A dismissal arising following a transfer of undertaking for an economic, technical, or organizational reason entailing changes in the workforce (*McGrath v Rank Leisure Ltd* [1985] IRLR 323, EAT).

(11) The non-renewal of a contract where the employee has been told in advance it is temporary and why (for example, because it replaces someone on maternity leave (ERA 1996, s 106(2)) or someone who is suspended on medical grounds). The employer should have told the employee at the outset that he is being employed to replace such a person and the employment will cease when the person returns to work.

(12) The mistaken belief that the employee did not have an appropriate work permit (*Klusova v London Borough of Hounslow* [2007] EWCA Civ 1127, CA).

The following have been held not to justify dismissal: **30.70**

(1) a rumour that the employee would leave to start up a rival business;
(2) the fact that a relative of the employee has been convicted of dishonesty;
(3) the fact that the employee is looking for alternative employment.

No employee should be dismissed for some other substantial reason unless appropriate warning and consultation procedures are first carried out. **30.71**

I. DISCIPLINARY PROCEDURE FOR ALL DISMISSALS

Statutory dismissal and disciplinary procedures

There are minimum procedures required for all dismissals where a 'trigger event' takes place before 6 April 2009 before an employer can dismiss an employee, irrespective of the reason (Employment Act 2002 (Dispute Resolution) Regulations 2004, regs 3 and 4(1)(b); EA 2002, s 30). If the procedures are not followed in those cases, a dismissal will be automatically unfair. A trigger event occurs when: **30.72**

- the employee has been dismissed; or
- the employer has sent the employee a Step 1 Statement (written notice setting out why dismissal is contemplated); or
- the employer has held a Step 2 meeting (disciplinary meeting) (see 30.72-30.76 for further details of Step 1 and Step 2); or
- the employer has taken relevant disciplinary action against the employee.

From 6 April 2009, employers are expected to follow the new ACAS Code on Disciplinary and Grievance Procedures (see Appendix 3). However, after 6 April 2009 it is no longer automatically unfair to dismiss someone without following the procedures. Instead, if the employee wins the claim, the award payable to him may be increased or decreased by 0–25 per cent where one of the parties has unreasonably failed to comply with a relevant element of the Code.

For dismissals where the trigger event is before 6 April 2009, the employer must follow the minimum procedure, set out in EA 2002, Sch 2, Part 2, which is: **30.73**

(1) *Step 1* The employer must write to the employee setting out the circumstances which lead it to contemplate dismissing the employee and inviting the employee to a meeting to discuss it. It is sensible for this information to include:

  (a) the reasons why dismissal is being contemplated (for example, for poor performance, one should detail specific lapses, or for misconduct, one should set out exactly what conduct is complained of though great detail may be unnecessary if, when viewed in context, the employee would clearly have understood what the misconduct was (*Draper v Mears Ltd* [2006] IRLR 869, EAT));
  (b) any evidence supporting the allegations, for example documents, witness statements, or notes of relevant conversations. The employee must be aware of this information (if not delivered with the Step 1 letter) in good time for him to consider it before the Step 2 hearing.

(2) *Step 2* The employer should invite the employee to a meeting to discuss the position before any decision to dismiss is taken. The timing and location of the meeting must be reasonable, and the meeting must be conducted in a manner that enables both employer and employee to explain their cases (EA 2002, Sch 3, Part 3). The employee may be accompanied by a colleague or a trade union official (ERA 1999, s 10; TUL(C)RA 1992, s 119) (see para 30.97). Following the meeting the employer must inform the employee of the decision and notify him that he has a right of appeal. This notification does not have to be in writing (*Aptuit (Edinburgh) Ltd v Kennedy* UKEATS/0057/06).

(3) *Step 3* If the employee exercises the right of appeal, the employer must invite the employee to an appeal meeting. Where possible, the appeal should be conducted by a more senior manager than the one who conducted the dismissal meeting. The employee may be accompanied at the meeting, as in Step 2 above. After the meeting, the employer must notify the employee of the decision.

Each step must be taken without unreasonable delay. An excessive delay, such as five months between disciplinary hearing and notification of the decision or six months between dismissal decision and appeal does not, however, make the dismissal automatically unfair (*Wilmot v Selvarajan* [2008] CA overturning *Yorkshire Housing Ltd v Swanson* [2008] IRLR 607, EAT) provided the core Steps 1–3 have been complied with.

30.74 In very rare cases, where an employee has reasonably been dismissed on the spot for gross misconduct, a *modified procedure* can be used consisting of, in place of Steps 1 and 2, a written document sent by the employer to the employee describing what misconduct the employee was dismissed for committing, why the employee was thought guilty of the misconduct, and his right of appeal. This process would not apply where the employee is not dismissed until the day after the misconduct in question (*O'Neil v Woolridge Ecotech Ltd* [2008] 0282/07, EAT).

30.75 These procedures do not have to be followed if either employer or employee would be in breach of any enactment if the employment continued; where the employee is legitimately dismissed for taking part in industrial action; where the employee is dismissed by reason of retirement (after 1 October 2006) where more than 20 people are to be made redundant (Employment Act (Dispute Resolution) Regulations 2004, reg 4). The procedures also need not be started or completed if either party has reasonable grounds to believe there may be a threat to any person or property; or that, having been harassed, he reasonably believes he will be harassed again; or that it was not reasonably practicable to begin to comply with the procedure within a reasonable period (Employment Act 2002 (Dispute Resolution) Regulations 2004, reg 11).

30.76 If the employer does not follow the procedure, and the employee wins the claim, the dismissal is automatically unfair (ERA 1996, s 98A). The amount of compensation (except in exceptional circumstances) must be increased by 10 per cent and may be increased by up to 50 per cent (in all cases subject to the statutory maximum award that may apply to the claim). If the employee fails to comply with the procedure (for example by unreasonably failing to attend a meeting) or does not appeal, but wins the claim, the award must (again, save in exceptional circumstances) be reduced by 10 per cent and may be reduced by up to 50 per cent (EA 2002, s 31). *Note*: these procedures were repealed on 6 April 2009.

Post 6 April 2009 dismissals: The ACAS Code

30.77 For dismissals where there is no trigger event before 6 April 2009, employees are expected to follow the ACAS Code of Practice on Disciplinary and Grievance Procedures (Appendix 3). Failure to do so may be taken into account by an employment tribunal and may entitle the tribunal to increase or decrease any award by up to 25 per cent (depending on whose fault it was that the Code was not complied with) (TULR(C)A 1992, s 207A).

30.78 The ACAS Code is short—11 pages. It is accompanied by lengthy guidance (see Appendix 3 for the Code). Tribunals are obliged to take into account any relevant element in the Code when adjudicating on cases. They are not, however, obliged to take into account all the guidance provisions. In an unfair dismissal context the Code applies to all employees (not workers) who are dismissed or constructively dismissed, except in two circumstances: the ACAS Code does not apply to those dismissed for redundancy, or on the expiry of a fixed term contract.

30.79 The core principles of the ACAS Code are:

- issues should be dealt with promptly;
- employers should act consistently;
- employers should carry out any necessary investigations to establish the facts of the case;

- employers should inform employees of the basis of the problem and give them an opportunity to put their case in response before any decisions are made;
- employers should allow employees to be accompanied at any formal disciplinary or grievance meeting; and
- employers should allow employees the right to appeal against any formal decision.

Key elements of the new ACAS Code are: **30.80**

(a) Employers should have a written disciplinary policy, though it does not have to be contractual. It should give examples of unacceptable behaviour including those which might be regarded as acts of gross misconduct.
(b) Employees and, if appropriate, their representatives, should be involved in the preparation of the disciplinary policy (though they do not have to agree to it), and should know where to find it.
(c) There should be an investigation before disciplinary action is taken (see para 30.82).
(d) The employee should be told in writing of the allegations which form the subject of any disciplinary action, preferably accompanied by any relevant documents and witness statements. The notification should invite the employee to a disciplinary meeting (see para 30.94).
(e) The disciplinary meeting should be held after the employee has had enough time to consider the position. The employee should make every effort to attend and be allowed to state his case and has the right to be accompanied at the meeting (see para 30.97).
(f) After the meeting, the employer must notify the employee in writing of its decision and give the employee the opportunity to appeal.
(g) If the employee appeals, this should be dealt with impartially, without unreasonable delay, and where possible by someone different from the person who took the original decision. Employees have the right to be accompanied at appeal meeting (see para 30.97). The employer must notify the result of the appeal to the employee in writing.
(h) Where the employee is a trade union representative, in addition to the normal steps it would be advisable to discuss the matter with a trade union official, after having obtained the employee's consent to do so.

If the employer does not follow the principles set out in para 30.80 and has no reasonable reason for not having done so, any award to an employee may be uplifted by 0–25 per cent. Similarly, if the employee does not follow the process without a reasonable reason, but wins an unfair dismissal case, an award may be reduced by 0–25 per cent (TULR(C)A 1992, s 207A and see para 24.164–24.165). **30.81**

Procedure for all dismissals

Investigation

Before taking disciplinary actions, and in particular before Step 1 in a statutory disciplinary procedure preparatory to possible dismissal, the employer should conduct a reasonable investigation into the issue (*British Home Stores Ltd v Burchell* [1978] IRLR 379, EAT—see paras 30.100–30.101). For pre6 April 2009 dismissals (see para 30.72 for transition provisions), if there is a minor failure to follow appropriate procedure in relation to the dismissal, then so long as the minimum statutory procedure is followed (see paras 30.72–30.76) this shall not be regarded, by itself, as making the decision to dismiss unreasonable if the employer can prove it would still have decided to dismiss the employee had it followed the proper procedure (ERA 1996, s 98A(2), overturning *Polkey v A E Dayton Services Ltd* [1988] AC 344, [1988] ICR 142, HL, on this point). For post 6 April 2009 disciplinary matters the ACAS Code also requires an investigation to be conducted. Where possible, the investigation, if for conduct issues, should be conducted by a different person from the one who takes the disciplinary decision. The employer should consider allowing the employee to be accompanied at the meeting (see para 30.97 for details) (ACAS Code paras 5–8). If, unreasonably, no investigation is undertaken, any award made to the employee may be increased by 0–25 per cent. **30.82**

30.83 The employer should always make proper investigation of all the circumstances. The tribunal will consider whether the employer's investigation was within the reasonable range of inquiries which should be made: it must not substitute its own view of exactly what it would have done (*Sainsbury's Supermarkets Ltd v Hitt* [2003] IRLR 23, CA). Nor should it come to conclusions on disputed facts about the employee's conduct and use its own conclusions to substitute its own view for that of the employer on the reasonableness of the dismissal—such a view facts can only be applied by tribunals when considering remedy (*London Ambulance Services NHS Trust v Small* [2009] EWCA Civ 220). However, there may be exceptional occasions where a proper investigation requires complainants to make their statements before the employees (*Dolan v Premier International Foods Ltd* [2005] All ER (D) 152, where the complainants, who were making allegations of harassment, included the employee's immediate supervisor).

30.84 The employer should take all necessary witness statements and examine all relevant documents. Even if the employee has been caught red-handed committing an act of gross misconduct, it is still not sensible to dismiss the employee on the spot if any anxiety about possible harm to the employer or its employees can be dealt with by suspending the employee and then pursuing the standard statutory procedures (Employment Act 2002 (Dispute Resolution) Regulations 2004, reg 3(2) for pre 6 April 2009 dismissals).

How rigorous should the investigation be?

30.85 The ACAS Guide (which is not statutorily enforceable) recommends that employers give employees advance notice of an investigatory meeting and time to prepare for it. There may, however, be circumstances where such a step is not reasonable. No decisions should taken at the meeting (ACAS Guidance p19).

30.86 Where charges which are criminal in nature have been made, and where the consequence of the dismissal may result in loss of reputation, loss of job, and possibly the prospect of securing future employment in the chosen field, a careful, conscientious, and full investigation is necessary (*A v B* [2003] IRLR 405, EAT). If the employee refuses to take part in the disciplinary process for fear of prejudicing his defence in the criminal proceedings, the employer should consider whether he has sufficient evidence to justify dismissal without hearing the employee. There should be an investigation, and where doubts remain it may be appropriate for the employer to postpone the decision until he can interview the employee (*Ali v Sovereign Buses (London) Ltd* EAT/0274/06).

30.87 If the employer has an established disciplinary policy, it is an implied term of the contract of employment that the employer will adhere to it unless it can establish a good reason not to do so. If it fails to do so, the court may grant an injunction preventing the dismissal, but only if it finds that a basis of mutual trust and confidence survives between employer and employee (*Lakshmi v Mid Cheshire Hospitals NHS Trust* [2008] IRLR 956, High Court, where the court declared that the NHS Trust was in breach of contract in refusing to postpone a disciplinary hearing against a doctor until the outcome of a police investigation, in contravention of the Trust's disciplinary policy, although no injunction was granted).

30.88 The employer should be responsible for the conduct of any investigation and should not rely on any parallel police investigation. It is also preferable not to have police present during any disciplinary meeting, particularly if the employee does not consent (*Read v Phoenix Preservation Ltd* [1985] IRLR 93, EAT).

30.89 The employer should consider whether to suspend the employee (with pay unless the contract provides otherwise) during the course of any investigation. Generally, there should be at least a preliminary enquiry before suspension (*Gogay v Hertfordshire County Council* [2000] IRLR 703, CA). If there is no contractual right to suspend, the employee may claim that suspension is an act of constructive dismissal or in rare circumstances, where suspension is likely to be a breach of contract and unduly harsh in its effect on the employee, may obtain an injunction requiring the suspension to be lifted (*Mezey v SW London and St George's Mental Health NHS Trust* [2007] IRLR 244, CA).

An employer can, however, make use of witness statements made to the police in an investigation into the same subject matter; it does not have to start from scratch again provided the witnesses confirm their original statements (*Rhondda Cynon Taf County Borough Council v Close* [2008] IRLR 868, EAT). **30.90**

Witnesses should ideally be asked to deal with the following points (*Linfood Cash & Carry Ltd v Thomson* [1989] IRLR 235, EAT): **30.91**

(1) the date, time, and place of any observation or incident;
(2) whether the individual had an opportunity to observe clearly what happened;
(3) the details of the event;
(4) any additional facts which have a bearing on the event;
(5) any circumstantial evidence giving credence to the key recollections;
(6) whether the individual has any reason to be biased against the employee.

Where witnesses do not wish to be identified, because they are frightened of reprisals from the employee under investigation, the employer should: **30.92**

(1) take statements, ignoring the fact the witness wishes to be anonymous;
(2) cover the items set out at para 30.91 above plus whether the witness has suffered at the hands of the accused, or has any other reason to fabricate;
(3) seek further evidence to corroborate/undermine the statement;
(4) make tactful inquiries as to the probity of the witness;
(5) if the witness is still not prepared to be named, decide whether the fear is justified and whether to proceed with the disciplinary action;
(6) where possible ask the people taking the decision to interview the witness;
(7) provide the statement, with any elements identifying the witness removed, along with any other relevant statements and documents, to the accused and his representatives. However, even this may not be required where it would be within the range of reasonable responses not to disclose the statements, even in anonymized form (*Surrey County Council v Henderson* UKEAT/0326/05, where the employee was alleged to have threatened serious violence against individuals, but they did not wish to be identified for fear of reprisals by the employee);
(8) if the accused raises any issues which need to be put to the witness, consider adjourning to allow the decision-maker to investigate them;
(9) make full and careful notes.

Note: there is still a risk that confidential witness statements may be disclosed to the employee if a court decides that doing so is necessary for the fair disposal of the case (*Arqiva Ltd v Sagoo* UKEAT/0135/06), but the employer may be able to provide copies of statements in redacted form, omitting confidential or sensitive information (*Defoe v HM Prison Service* UKEAT/0451/06).

Disciplinary meeting—general

Following internal investigation, the employer should hold a disciplinary meeting. If the employer has a written procedure about the conduct of the meeting, it should be followed. **30.93**

Notice of meeting

Once the employer has conducted its internal investigation it should ask the employee to attend a disciplinary meeting. In order to comply with the statutory procedure, the notification should be in writing (see para 30.72 and 30.80(d)). The employee should be told the following before the meeting: **30.94**

(1) The time and place of the meeting (which should give him reasonable time to consider his response to the allegations). (*Note*: If the employee's chosen companion is not available for the hearing at that time and the worker proposes a reasonable alternative time within

the next five wor! ing days, the employer must postpone the hearing to the suggested time (ERA 1999, s 10(4) and (5)), failing which the employer is liable to pay the employee up to two weeks' pay subject to the statutory maximum pay (ie up to £760 at the rates current from 1 October 2009) (ERA 1999, s 11(3)).)

(2) The fact that the meeting will be a disciplinary meeting.
(3) The topics which will be discussed at the meeting.
(4) The fact (if it be the case) that the employer is considering dismissal as an option.
(5) The right of the employee to be accompanied by a colleague or (if appropriate) trade union representative. *Note*: this is sensible but not obligatory. In exceptional circumstances, where a disciplinary decision could have far-reaching consequences affecting an employee's whole career (eg where criminal charges are threatened, or the prospective dismissal of a teaching assistant for abuse of an under-age pupil, where any dismissal would need to be reported to the Secretary of State for determination whether the assistant could work in schools again—*R v Governors of X School* [2009] EWHC 504 (Admin) High Court) the employee may be able to require to be represented by a lawyer.
(6) Preferably, and definitely in good time before any meeting which might lead to dismissal, provide the employee with the evidence and all key documents (for example any investigatory report or witness statements) which will be relied on against him.

Conduct of meeting

30.95 The meeting should preferably be chaired by the person who will be responsible for taking the decision to warn or dismiss. If possible, this should not be a witness or a complainant in the case. The decision-maker should plan the meeting in advance, and should where possible be accompanied by a note-taker (ACAS Guidance p 19—see Appendix 3). Ideally, the decision-maker should conduct the meeting in the following manner, though failure to adhere to this plan will not necessarily render a dismissal unfair (see para 30.81):

(1) identify those present;
(2) explain the role of any companion to the employee (see para 30.98);
(3) explain the purpose of the meeting;
(4) outline the structure at the meeting and inform the employee and any representative that they may ask questions or make observations at any stage, and that when the employer has set out the allegations, the employee will have the opportunity to respond to those allegations either by calling evidence or by argument, and to put forward any explanation or mitigating circumstances;
(5) if appropriate, arrange representation for the employee. The employee should have the opportunity to be accompanied by a colleague of his choice or, in some circumstances, a trade union representative. However, the employer is not obliged to allow the employee to be represented by a solicitor, particularly where the policy expressly disallows it (*Kulkarni v Milton Keynes Hospital NHS Trust* [2008] IRLR 949, High Court) unless the proceedings effectively amount to a criminal charge, or something similarly serious (eg if a dismissal could result in the employee suffering a ban from working in his chosen profession—*R v Governors of X School* [2009] IRLR 434, High Court);
(6) inform the employee of the allegations being made;
(7) make sure the employee has received all the evidence and has had a proper opportunity to consider it;
(8) the employee and/or his representative should then have an opportunity to put the employee's case, both relating to the allegations themselves and to any facts in mitigation. *Note*: If the employee is facing criminal prosecution, the employer must not prejudice a trial but should only give the employee the opportunity to make any statement he may volunteer: no pressure should be put upon the employee to admit guilt;
(9) if the employee asks to bring a witness to support his case, this should generally be allowed. The ACAS Guidance, in a change from what was earlier regarded as acceptable practice, suggests that all witnesses should be available at the hearing, unless it is clear that their oral

evidence will not affect the substance of the complaint. If this is not practicable, then the decision-maker should put any relevant supplementary questions to the witness after the disciplinary meeting, but before making the decision (see para 30.98);
(10) the employee should be asked whether there is any further evidence or inquiry which he considers could help his case and whether there are any mitigating circumstances;
(11) if an employee asks for additional questions to be put to witnesses an employer would be wise to adjourn the meeting to make further inquiries, or to ensure that those questions are put to the witnesses subsequently;
(12) the decision-maker should sum up the meeting;
(13) the meeting should be adjourned or concluded before the decision is taken.

A disciplinary procedure, though formal, is not a court of law. It used to be thought that an employee is not normally entitled to cross-examine witnesses. However, the ACAS Guidance (which is not statutorily enforceable) suggests that if the employee wishes to do so, and notifies the employer of this fact in good time, witnesses may be cross examined. Possible reasons for refusing this may be the following: **30.96**

(1) the decision-maker should consider whether it would be fair and reasonable to allow him to do so taking into account issues such as what cross-examination would achieve, and whether it might help the employee's case, and the likely effect on witnesses (especially in a harassment or bullying case);
(2) if there is a stark difference of evidence on fact, and this fact goes to the root of the disciplinary allegation, the decision-maker should very rarely refuse to allow cross-examination. A refusal would probably only be acceptable if, for example, the witnesses, having been asked if they will attend the disciplinary hearing, have refused to do so on the basis that it would be far too stressful—perhaps because they claim to have been bullied by the employee under investigation, or because the witnesses are not employees and cannot therefore be compelled to attend;
(3) the decision-maker would be wise to give reasons for any decision refusing to allow cross-examination;
(4) if cross-examination is refused, the employer should go back to the witnesses after the disciplinary hearing and put to them any allegations made by the employee which have not already been addressed (*Santamera v Express Cargo Forwarding* [2003] IRLR 273, EAT).

If the employee is accompanied, the companion: **30.97**

(1) may (unless the employee has indicated he does not wish the companion to do so) address the hearing by putting the employee's case, summing up that case, and responding on the employee's behalf to any view expressed at the hearing;
(2) may confer with the employee during the hearing;
(3) may not answer questions on the employee's behalf;
(4) may not act in such a way that either the employer is prevented from explaining his case or any other person is prevented from making any contribution to the hearing (ERA 1999, s 10(2)).

It may be necessary for the decision-maker to initiate further inquiries should the employee have raised fresh issues, for example where an employee is himself suspended and has been denied the opportunity of being able to contact potentially relevant witnesses, the employer needs to make sure that it focuses as much on any potential evidence that may exculpate or point towards the innocence of the employee as on the evidence directed towards proving the charges (*A v B* [2003] IRLR 405, EAT). **30.98**

If the employee raises a grievance about the way the disciplinary process has been handled, the employer shall consider whether the meeting should be adjourned until the grievance is dealt with. An adjournment might be appropriate if the employee alleges that the decision-maker has a conflict of interest or if biased management have been selective in producing **30.99** evidence for the meeting, or the process has been tainted by discrimination (ACAS Guidance p 22).

Standard of proof

30.100 The standard of proof is a reasonable suspicion, amounting to a belief in the guilt of the employee of that misconduct at that time.

30.101 The employer must establish:

(1) the fact of his belief in the guilt of the employee;
(2) that the employer had in his mind reasonable grounds on which to sustain that belief;
(3) that the employer had carried out an investigation which was reasonable in all the circumstances (*British Home Stores Ltd v Burchell* [1978] IRLR 379, EAT).

Where suspicion genuinely points to one or other of two employees, both may be dismissed (*Frames Snooker Centre v Boyce* [1992] IRLR 472).

30.102 If the employer has not acted consistently (for example, because employees had been led to believe that particular categories of conduct would be overlooked, or met with only a mild disciplinary sanction (*Hadjioannou v Coral Casinos Ltd* [1981] IRLR 352, EAT) or because in truly comparable cases one employee is dismissed while another has not been (*Securicor v Smith* [1989] IRLR 356, CA) then the dismissal is likely to be unfair. This is because it will not have passed the test in ERA 1996, s 98(4) that the tribunal must have regard to 'equity and the substantial merits of the case'.

Sanction

30.103 The tribunal must be satisfied that the sanction the employer has imposed is fair in all the circumstances. The ACAS Guidance recommends that the decision-maker considers the following:

(1) whether the employer's disciplinary policy indicates what the likely penalty will be as a result of the particular misconduct;
(2) the penalty imposed in similar cases in the past;
(3) whether the standards of other employees are acceptable, making sure that this employee is not being unfairly singled out;
(4) the employee's disciplinary record (including current warnings, general work record, work experience, position, and length of service) and any mitigating circumstances which might make it appropriate to reduce the severity of the penalty;
(5) whether the penalty is reasonable in all the circumstances;
(6) whether any training or additional support or adjustments to the work are necessary.

30.104 When reviewing the employer's decision to dismiss, an employment tribunal will look at whether the decision to dismiss is within the band of reasonable responses which a hypothetical reasonable employer might have adopted in the circumstances. The employment tribunal must not substitute its own decision for that of the employer (*Iceland Frozen Foods Ltd v Jones* [1982] IRLR 439, EAT and *Foley v Post Office*; *HSBC Bank plc v Madden* [2000] IRLR 827, CA).

Notification of decision

30.105 The employee, and any representative, should be notified of the employer's decision in writing. The employee should also be told of his right to appeal and to be accompanied to that appeal by a colleague or trade union representative, but not necessarily a solicitor. The employer should clearly specify any time limit within which the appeal should be lodged. It makes sense for notification of the right to appeal to be contained within the document recording the decision, but it is acceptable for the employee to be told of the right to appeal orally (*Aptuit (Edinburgh) Ltd v Kennedy* UKEATS/0057/06).

Appeals

If possible, the appeal body should be composed of different and more senior people from those who made the decision to dismiss (ACAS Code—see Appendix 3). **30.106**

Appeals may take into account additional facts learnt since the decision to dismiss. It used to be thought that an appeal cannot provide justification for unfairness at a lower level unless the appeal is a comprehensive rehearing. However, this is no longer the case, provided that the employee is given a proper opportunity in the appeal to understand the case against him and respond appropriately. **30.107**

Appeals should be heard promptly. An employer should not reject an appeal simply because the employee did not comply with the contractual time limit for bringing the appeal, so long as the employee appeals within a reasonable time—to do otherwise would be automatically unfair dismissal (*Masterfoods v Wilson*, [2007] ICR 370, EAT) for pre 6 April 2009 dismissals and contrary to the spirit of the ACAS Code for post 2009 dismissals. For pre 6 April 2009 dismissals, an appeal cannot remedy any failure to follow the statutory procedures (eg a failure to explain the reason for the dismissal before the Step 2 meeting between employer and employee—*Davies v Farnborough College of Technology* [2008] IRLR 14, EAT). **30.108**

Normally, a dismissal or resignation cannot be unilaterally withdrawn. However, by appealing, the employee impliedly consents to any subsequent withdrawal of the dismissal by the employer. Therefore, if the appeal is upheld, the employee cannot claim to have been dismissed (*Brock v Minerva Dental Ltd* EAT/0356/06). **30.109**

If an employee fails to exercise his right of appeal the employer may be able to argue that there should be a reduction in any compensation paid because the employee has failed to mitigate his loss. A dismissed employee who does not take up an invitation to appeal will, save in exceptional circumstances, have any compensatory award reduced by 10–50 per cent before 6 April 2009 and may face a 0–25 per cent after this date (see paras 30.76 and 30.77). **30.110**

For pre 6 April 2009 dismissals (see para 30.72 for the trigger events), where there is a failure to follow a proper procedure, the tribunal will consider whether the employer has shown that the employee would have been dismissed had a fair procedure been followed. There are six possible outcomes: **30.111**

(1) The employer may show that it is at least 51 per cent likely that if a fair procedure had been complied with, the dismissal should have occurred in any event. It will then be unfair under ERA, s 98A(2).
(2) The employer may persuade the tribunal that there was a chance of dismissal but it was less than 50 per cent, in which case the dismissal will be unfair but compensation should be reduced on *Polkey* principles. The court must attempt the task, however speculative, of evaluating the evidence on what might have happened had a proper procedure been followed (*Software 2000 Ltd v Andrews* [2007] ICR 825, EAT) unless evidence on this point is particularly sparse (*Clarke v Governing Body of Hastingbury School* EAT 0373/07 and 0374/07).
(3) The principles are set out in *Polkey v AE Dayton Services Ltd* [1987 IRLR 503, HL. In brief, in addition to the principle set out in para 30.111(2), they are that a dismissal will be unfair if inadequate procedures are followed, unless at the time the decision was taken and bearing in mind the facts the employer actually knew, a reasonable employer could have known that conducting a procedure (in this case, there was no consultation with individual employees before they were selected for redundancy) would be useless. The tribunal must consider the action of the employer in treating the reason as sufficient to dismiss as part of its review of

the manner of dismissal. It is not sufficient, to pass the *Polkey* test, for the employer to show that the result would have been the same had a proper procedure taken place.

(4) The tribunal may decide that the employment would have continued but only for a limited period, in which case compensation for loss of earnings should be restricted to the remuneration the employee would have received during this period; and

(5) The tribunal may decide the employment would continue indefinitely, in which case compensation will be assessed on normal principles. This decision should only be reached where the evidence is so scant or unreliable that it should be ignored because, even with a certain amount of legitimate speculation, it is impossible to reconstruct what might have happened (*Software 2000 Ltd v Andrews* [2007] IRLR 568, EAT).

30.112 For post 6 April 2009 dismissals (see para 30.72 for the trigger events), the tribunal will adopt the same processes as set out in para 30.111 (3)–(5). If the ACAS Code is not followed, a tribunal will have the discretion to increase or decrease any compensation award by 0–25 per cent.

J. WARNING PROCEDURE

Warnings

30.113 Except for gross misconduct, dismissal should not be the sanction for a first offence. The ACAS Guidance on Disciplinary and Grievance Procedures (see Schedule 3) lays down, for minor offences, a three-stage warning process before dismissal: oral warning, first written warning, and final written warning, and then dismissal. The number of warnings may, however, be reduced either because of practicalities or because an offence is of a more serious nature.

30.114 Dismissal will not normally be a valid response to a first act of misconduct, unless the misconduct is potentially serious. Generally, the employer should give the employee a first (perhaps oral) warning for minor offences, and a written warning for more serious offences or subsequent offences.

30.115 Successive warnings need not relate to similar subject matter.

30.116 *Lapsed warnings* In the absence of an express provision regarding the lapse of warnings, it is generally assumed that oral warnings should lapse after six months and written warnings after 6–12 months. It is unreasonable to take a lapsed warning into account when deciding whether to dismiss someone for gross misconduct: if it influences the decision, the dismissal will be unfair (*Diosynth Ltd v Thomson* [2006] IRLR 284). However, expired warnings may influence a decision not to reduce any appropriate sanction because of mitigating circumstances.

30.117 A warning subject to appeal can still be relied upon when taking action regarding a fresh offence, though the employer must, when deciding what weight to attach to the earlier warning, bear in mind that it is subject to appeal.

30.118 Warnings are especially important where rules have recently been disregarded in practice. For example, it would be unfair to dismiss a man for sleeping on a night shift where in practice his colleagues had been doing the same, to management's knowledge, for some time and management had not told employees that in future on-shift sleeping would be regarded as serious misconduct. If management had not known of the custom, dismissal would have been a reasonable sanction, provided it was applied consistently.

30.119 A warning will not be necessary in the following circumstances:

(1) where the employer's rules clearly and reasonably spell out that a particular action will result in instant dismissal;

(2) where the employee's conduct is likely to endanger safety;

(3) where a warning would make no difference, for example, because the employee refuses to accept he has done anything wrong;

(4) where the employee knew that he was putting his job in jeopardy.

K. STRESS ISSUES PRIOR TO INVESTIGATORY/ DISCIPLINARY MEETINGS

If an employee who is subject to a disciplinary or performance procedure goes off work and claims he cannot attend the procedure on the grounds of stress, the employer should postpone the procedure until the employee returns or do the following: 30.120

(1) Check his staff handbook to see if it contains procedures to follow in these circumstances. If it does, these should be followed. If not, proceed as below.
(2) Obtain the employee's consent to his GP giving the employer his opinion on:
  (a) whether the employee is fit to attend the disciplinary procedure;
  (b) if not, when he is likely to be;
  (c) whether there are any steps which could be taken to enable the meeting to take place.
(3) If concerned about the GP's response, seek the employee's consent to visiting a medical practitioner chosen by the employer, who should be asked similar questions.
(4) An employee is not obliged to give consent to sharing medical information, even if his contract of employment states that he must undergo any medical examinations that the employer reasonably requests. However, if this contractual term is in place and the employee refuses to see a doctor or to allow the employer to know the doctor's opinion, the employer can proceed carefully, making his own assumptions. If the employee allows his GP to give his opinion, but refuses to undergo a second opinion, the employer is effectively stuck with the first opinion.
(5) Make sure that all the allegations against the employee are set out clearly, and sent to him, together with copies or (where appropriate) summaries of witness statements and documents which will be relied on.
(6) Extend the time limit for any responses.
(7) Consider providing written questions to which answers will be sought in advance of the meeting, perhaps inviting written replies and/or representations.
(8) Consider permitting the employee to be accompanied by a relative or friend in addition to any colleague from work or union representative.
(9) Hold the hearing at a neutral venue, preferably close to the employee's home.
(10) Where possible, appoint someone with little or no prior involvement with the employee to chair the meeting and make the decision.
(11) Follow any recommendations from the medical practitioners on how the meeting should be held and conducted.
(12) Offer the employee breaks during the meeting.
(13) Send the employee and his representative a copy of written reasons for the decision.
(14) Allow an extended time for appeal.

CHECKLIST OF ISSUES FOR TRIBUNAL CLAIMS CONNECTED WITH DISMISSAL

Wrongful dismissal

1. Has the employer without cause terminated the employee's contract of employment without either:

   1.1 allowing the employee to work out all his notice; or

   1.2 paying the employee in lieu of his salary and benefits for all of his unworked notice period?

   If so, or if the employer has acted in such a way that he has constructively dismissed the employee (see paras 30.12–30.14) the employee has been wrongfully dismissed.

2. Is the maximum claim for £25,000 or less?

   The employment tribunal cannot award more than £25,000 damages for breach of contract. If the claim is for more, the employee might be better advised to bring proceedings in the High Court or county court (Employment Tribunals Extension of Jurisdiction (England and Wales) Order 1994, art 10; Employment Tribunals Extension of Jurisdiction (Scotland) Order 1994, art 10 (the 1994 Orders)). Any excess over any maximum £25,000 award cannot be recovered by a claim in the High Court see para 30.06).

3. Was the claim brought within three months of the EDT of the employee's contract? (See para 30.08 for the definition of EDT.)

   If not, it will be out of time (1994 Orders, art 7) and a claim should be brought in the High Court or county court).

4. Did the employer dismiss the employee for cause, but ignoring any contractual procedural requirements such as disciplinary and warning procedures which are expressly or impliedly incorporated into the employee's contract of employment (for example, because expressly referred to in the contract, staff handbook, or collective agreement)?

   If so, this will be wrongful dismissal (*Gunton v Richmond upon Thames LBC* [1980] ICR 755) but there are likely to be only two remedies:

   4.1 damages limited to the period between actual dismissal and the date dismissal should have taken place had proper procedures been followed; or

   4.2 (very rarely and only if sought promptly enough) an injunction obtained in the High Court preventing the employer from terminating the employment until proper procedures are undertaken (*Robb v London Borough of Hammersmith and Fulham* [1991] ICR 514, DC).

5. Did the employee commit a material breach of contract?

   If yes, the employer has a full defence to a wrongful dismissal claim.

   A breach of contract may be a breach of an express term of a contract or staff manual or it may be that the employee has shown himself to be so incompetent or to have conducted himself so badly as to entitle the employer to terminate the contract. In essence, the tests to be applied as to whether the employee's incompetence or misconduct are sufficiently serious to justify dismissal are the same as those which apply in unfair dismissal (see paras 30.35–30.47, 30.49–30.51). The court will examine all the employee's conduct before dismissal, whether or not the employer knew of the conduct before it terminated the contract (*Boston Deep Sea Fishing and Ice Company v Ansell* (1888) 39 Ch D 339).

UNFAIR DISMISSAL: GENERAL CHECKLIST

Issues

1. Was the individual an employee (see paras 30.07 and 30.11(8))?

   If not, he has no unfair dismissal rights.

2. Was the employee dismissed, either directly by the employer or as a result of constructive dismissal (see paras 30.12–30.14)?

   If not, for example because he has resigned (*Riordan v War Office* [1959] 3 All ER 774), without being forced to do so, he has no unfair dismissal claim.

3. Was the employee in one of the categories which prevents him from bringing a claim for unfair dismissal (see para 30.11).

   If he was, then the tribunal has no jurisdiction to hear the claim.

4. Has the employee brought his claim in time, within three months from the effective date of termination of his employment (ERA 1996, s 111(2)) (see paras 3.55–3.83 and 30.08)?

   If not he is unlikely to be allowed to pursue his claim unless the employment tribunal considers it was not reasonably practicable for the case to have been brought earlier

5. Did the employee have the necessary continuity of service—essentially one year from the effective date of termination of his employment (see para 30.08)—unless special situations apply (see para 30.09)?

   If not, in the absence of one of the special situations, he will not be able to maintain his claim.

6. If the employee believes he has been constructively dismissed:

   6.1 Has the employer committed a breach of contract which goes to the root of the employment relationship (see para 30.13 for examples) or a series of breaches culminating in a breach which is effectively the last straw (see para 30.12(3))?

   6.2 Did the employee resign as a result of this breach?

   6.3 Did the employee act promptly in resigning following the breach or last straw, so that he could not be said to have waived his rights in relation to the breach?

7. Does the employee believe he was dismissed for trade union, health and safety, or whistle-blowing reasons, or one of the other grounds set out in para 30.20?

   If so, he may apply for interim relief (for details, see paras 24.40–24.47, 30.20, and Chapter 7).

8. What is the principal reason for dismissal? Is it a potentially fair reason within ERA 1996, s 98(2) (see para 30.33)?

   If yes, the employer may have a defence to the claim.

9. Was the principal reason for dismissal one of the automatically unfair grounds listed at para 30.29?

   If yes, then the employee will win his unfair dismissal claim and the tribunal will determine the appropriate remedy.

10. Was the principal reason for dismissal one of the automatically fair grounds listed at para 30.24?

    If yes, then the employee will lose his unfair dismissal claim.

11. Did the employer make it clear why the employee is being dismissed? Was the employee continuously employed for one year or more (unless she is pregnant, when there is no qualifying period)? Has the employee requested written reasons for his dismissal?

    If the answer to all these questions is yes, and the employer has unreasonably not provided written reasons for dismissal, the tribunal will require the employer to pay the employee two weeks' pay, and may make a declaration as to what the reasons for dismissal were (ERA 1996, ss 92 and 93) (see para 30.31).

12. If the employer claims that the employee was dismissed for *misconduct*:

    12.1 Was the conduct sufficiently gross that dismissal was within the range of reasonable responses available to the employer (for examples, see paras 30.39–30.47).

If yes, the dismissal will potentially be fair. Go to 12.2.

If not, the dismissal will be unfair unless there have been previous warnings (see 13.3).

12.2 If the employer had an exhaustive list of matters which constituted gross misconduct, was the conduct of a type on the list?

If not, any summary dismissal will be unfair.

12.3 If the employee's misconduct is not so gross it justifies dismissal, has the employee previously been given warnings telling him that dismissal may be an option if there is further misconduct (see para 30.38 for examples of minor offences)?

If not, the employee will have been unfairly dismissed.

12.4 Is there another employee who has committed similar misconduct who was not dismissed, and did not have mitigating circumstances which would militate against dismissal?

If so, dismissal will probably be unfair (see para 30.39).

12.5 Was the misconduct known to the employer at the time of the dismissal? Did it form the real reason for the dismissal (see paras 30.25–30.27)?

If the answer to either question is no, the employee will have been unfairly dismissed, but his award may be reduced on the basis that it is not just and equitable to award compensation in these circumstances (see paras 30.25–30.26 and paras 25.05–25.07).

12.6 Was there a 'trigger event' (see para 30.72) before 6 April 2009?

If yes, did the employer follow a statutory procedure giving the employee written details of the relevant circumstances, inviting him to a meeting and offering an appeal (see paras 25.18 and 30.72–30.76)? If not, any financial award must (save in exceptional circumstances) be increased by 10–50 per cent (but still subject to any relevant statutory cap).

If no, did the employer comply with the key principles of the ACAS Code (see para 30.80). If not a tribunal may increase the award by 0–25 per cent (see 24.164).

12.7 Was there a 'trigger event' (see para 30.72) before 6 April 2009?

If yes, did the employee fail to participate in the statutory disciplinary procedure, for example by failing to appeal (see paras 25.18 and 30.72–30.76)? If yes, and if the employee is found to have been unfairly dismissed, his award must (save in exceptional circumstances) be reduced by 10–50 per cent.

If no, did the employee comply with the key principles of the ACAS Code, see para 30.80). If not, but the employee wins an unfair dismissal claim, the award may be reduced by 0–25 per cent (see para 24.164).

12.8 Did the employer conduct an appropriate investigation into the misconduct prior to the dismissal (see paras 30.82–30.92)? If not, was there an appeal and was the failure remedied prior to the appeal decision?

If the answer to both questions is no, the employee will have been unfairly dismissed. If it is yes to either question, go to 12.9.

12.9 Was the conduct of the disciplinary meeting fair (see paras 30.72(2) and 30.95–30.99)? If not, for pre 6 April 2009 dismissals (see para 30.72 for the trigger events) the dismissal will be unfair if the process outlined in para 30.72(2) is not followed, and may otherwise be unfair unless any lapses would not have affected the outcome of the decision (see para 30.82). If it was, go to 12.10.

12.10 Having conducted a reasonable investigation (see 12.8 and 12.9) did the decision-maker genuinely believe, on reasonable grounds, that the employee was guilty of the misconduct (see para 30.100)?

If no, the employee will have been unfairly dismissed. If yes, go to 12.11.

12.11 Was dismissal, given the conduct in question and the decision-maker's state of mind, within the range of reasonable responses available to the employer?
If yes, the dismissal will be fair (see paras 30.101–30.104). If no, it will be unfair.

12.12 If the procedure pre-appeal was insufficient, was the failure remedied by an appeal (see paras 30.106–30.110)?
If yes, the dismissal may be fair. If no, it will be unfair.

13. If the employer claims that the employee was dismissed for *incompetence*:

13.1 Had the employee had a prior warning of incompetence? If not, was the incompetence on one of those very rare occasions when it amounted to such gross negligence that the employer could not reasonably be expected to continue to employ the employee (see para 30.53)?
If yes, the employee may have been fairly dismissed. Go to 13.4.
If no, the employee will have been unfairly dismissed.

13.2 Has the employee been given a warning telling him that unless there is an improvement in his performance, he may be dismissed? Is that warning still current and unexpired (see paras 30.52 and 30.113–30.119)? Has sufficient time expired to allow the employee to demonstrate an improved performance?
If the answer to all questions is yes, the employee may have been fairly dismissed. Go to 13.3.
If the answer is no, unless 13.1 applies, the employee will have been unfairly dismissed.

13.3 Can the employer demonstrate that it is reasonable to conclude that the employee has been incompetent, for example does he have samples of poor quality work, or details of particular incidents (see paras 30.50–30.51)?
If yes, the employee may have been fairly dismissed—go to 13.4.
If no, the employee will have been unfairly dismissed.

13.4 Was there a 'trigger event (see para 30.72) before 6 April 2009?
If yes, did the employer follow a statutory procedure giving the employee written details of the relevant circumstances, inviting him to a meeting and offering an appeal (see paras 25.18 and 30.72–30.76)? If not, any financial award must (save in exceptional circumstances) be increased by 10–50 per cent (but still subject to any relevant statutory cap).
If no, did the employer comply with the key principles of the ACAS Code (see para 30.79). If not a tribunal may increase the award by 0–25 per cent (see para 24.164).

13.5 Was there a 'trigger event' (see para 30.72) before 6 April 2009?
If yes, did the employee fail to participate in the statutory disciplinary procedure, for example by failing to appeal (see paras 25.18 and 30.72–30.76)? If yes, and if the employee is found to have been unfairly dismissed, his award must (save in exceptional circumstances) be reduced by 10–50 per cent.
If no, did the employee comply with the key principles of the ACAS Code (see para 30.80). If not, but the employee wins an unfair dismissal claim, the award may be reduced by 0–25 per cent (see para 24.164).

13.6 Was the conduct of the pre-dismissal meeting fair (see paras 30.95–30.99)?
If not, the dismissal will probably be unfair unless any failures were minor. If it was, go to 13.7.

13.7 Are there any mitigating circumstances (for example, previous good record of long-standing employment) which would militate against dismissal in favour of a further warning?
If yes, dismissal may be unfair. Go to 13.8.

13.8 Was dismissal, given the incompetence in question, the conduct of the disciplinary meeting and any mitigating factors, within the band of reasonable responses open to the employer?
If yes, the dismissal will be fair (see paras 30.100–30.104).
If no, it will be unfair.

13.9 If the procedure pre-appeal was insufficient, was the failure remedied by an appeal (see paras 30.106–30.110)?
If yes, the dismissal may be fair. If not, it will be unfair.

14. If the employer claims the employee was dismissed by reason of ill health:

14.1 Has the employer made full inquiry (which would normally include meetings with the employee, obtaining a medical report, and examining the sickness record) about the employee's state of health (see para 30.55)?
If not, the dismissal is likely to be unfair.

14.2 Has the employer considered whether the employee is disabled and if so whether there are any reasonable adjustments he should make to allow the employee not to be at a disadvantage. If the employee is disabled and if the employer has not made reasonable adjustments (see para 32.54) the employee may have been both discriminated against and unfairly dismissed (see paras 30.56 and 30.57).

14.3 If the employee has been persistently absent, is there any medical excuse for this?
If yes, go to 14.4.
If not, treat the problem as misconduct. Go back to 12.

14.4 Has the employer considered all relevant factors before deciding whether or not he wishes to dismiss the employee (see para 30.58)?
If he has, and if there are no other steps (such as alternative employment) which he could take, the employee may fairly be dismissed. Go to 14.5.

14.5 Was there a 'trigger event' (see para 30.72) before 6 April 2009?
If yes, did the employee fail to participate in the statutory disciplinary procedure, for example by failing to appeal (see paras 25.18 and 30.72–30.76)? If yes, and if the employee is found to have been unfairly dismissed, his award must (save in exceptional circumstances) be reduced by 10–50 per cent.
If no, did the employee comply with the key principles of the ACAS Code (see para 30.80). If not, but the employee wins an unfair dismissal claim, the award may be reduced by 0–25 per cent (see para 24.164).

14.6 Was there a 'trigger event' (see para 30.72) before 6 April 2009?
If yes, did the employer follow a statutory procedure giving the employee written details of the relevant circumstances, inviting him to a meeting and offering an appeal (see paras 25.18 and 30.72–30.76)? If not, any financial award must (save in exceptional circumstances) be increased by 10–50 per cent (but still subject to any relevant statutory cap).
If no, did the employer comply with the key principles of the ACAS Code (see para 30.80). If not, a tribunal may increase the award by 0–25 per cent (see para 24.164).

14.7 Is the employee benefiting from permanent health insurance cover which will be withdrawn if dismissed (see para 30.60(13))?
If he is, then unless there is a clause in his contract of employment which nevertheless allows the employer to dismiss in those circumstances, any dismissal is likely to be unfair.

14.8 If the procedure pre-appeal was insufficient, was the failure remedied by an appeal (see paras 30.106–30.110)?
If yes, the dismissal, may be fair. If not, it will be unfair.

15. If the employer claims the employee has been dismissed by reason of lack of relevant qualifications, or illegality:

    15.1 Can the employer demonstrate why ownership of the qualifications has become necessary (see para 30.65)?
    If not, the dismissal will be unfair.
    If yes, go to 15.3.

    15.2 Can the employer demonstrate why the employment is now illegal (see para 30.67)?
    If no, the dismissal will be unfair. If yes, go to 15.3.

    15.3 Were there any alternative positions into which the employee could have been placed?
    If there were, and they were not offered to the employee, the dismissal is likely to be unfair.

    15.4 Was there a 'trigger event' (see para 30.72) before 6 April 2009?
    If yes, did the employer follow a statutory procedure giving the employee written details of the relevant circumstances, inviting him to a meeting and offering an appeal (see paras 25.18 and 30.72–30.76)? If not, any financial award must (save in exceptional circumstances) be increased by 10–50 per cent (but still subject to any relevant statutory cap).
    If no, did the employer comply with the key principles of the ACAS Code (see para 30.80). If not a tribunal may increase the award by 0–25 per cent (see para 24.164).

    15.5 Was there a 'trigger event' (see para 30.72) before 6 April 2009?
    If yes, did the employee fail to participate in the statutory disciplinary procedure, for example by failing to appeal (see paras 25.18 and 30.72–30.76)? If yes, and if the employee is found to have been unfairly dismissed, his award must (save in exceptional circumstances) be reduced by 10–50 per cent.
    If no, did the employee comply with the key principles of the ACAS Code (see para 30.80). If not, but the employee wins an unfair dismissal claim, the award may be reduced by 0–25 per cent (see para 24.164).

    15.6 If the procedure pre-appeal was insufficient, was the failure remedied by an appeal (see paras 30.106–30.110)?
    If yes, the dismissal, may be fair. If no, it will be unfair.

16. If the employer claims that the employee was dismissed for redundancy, please follow checklists at Chapter 31.

17. If the employer claims the employee was dismissed by reason of retirement (see para 30.30):

    17.1 Is the employee aged at or above the normal retirement age?
    If there is no normal retirement age, is the employee 65 or older?
    If not, the dismissal will not be fair for retirement reasons.

    17.2 Has the employer notified the employee 6–12 months in advance of his intended date of retirement and told him of his right to request not to retire?
    If not, the dismissal will be unfair except in the circumstances set out in 17.3.

    17.3 Has the employer notified the employee 2–26 weeks in advance of his intended date of retirement and his right to request not to retire?
    If yes, the dismissal may be fair, taking into account
    - the length of notice
    - whether the employer properly considered any right to request not to retire (see paras 32.71-32.82)
    - whether the retirement was the genuine reason for dismissal.

17.4 Following 17.3, if the tribunal considers dismissal was not for retirement, return to normal tribunal procedures (see, eg 13).

17.5 Has the employer properly considered any request not to retire?

If not, the dismissal is likely to be unfair, and the employment may continue for remedy purposes.

18. If the employer claims that the employee was dismissed for some other substantial reason:

18.1 If the reason is to do with a business reorganization the employer should follow a procedure similar to that described in Chapter 31.

18.2 For most other dismissals under this head, the employer should follow procedures similar to those described in 12, 13, or 14 above, whichever appears the most appropriate.

19. If the employee has been unfairly dismissed, consider remedies. Does the employee want to be reinstated or re-engaged? If he does, the tribunal must consider whether this is practicable and whether the employee has contributed to his dismissal so reinstatement or re-engagement would not be just or equitable. If it is practicable, the employment tribunal may well exercise its discretion to make the necessary order. For details of the consequences if the employer fails to reinstate or re-engage, see paras 24.32–24.39.

20. If compensation is the appropriate remedy, consider the following:

20.1 What is the actual loss the employee has suffered to date? Calculate the loss of salary and benefits.

20.2 For how long is this likely to last in future? Does the employee have another job?

If the salary is the same or more than with the employer, the employer's liability will cease from the moment the employee gains a new and ostensibly permanent job.

If less than the old salary, how long will this continue? If there is no new job, when is the employee likely to find one and at what salary? Further details are set out at paras 25.27–25.38.

20.3 Would the employee have been dismissed fairly by the employer in the near future in any event or if a fair procedure had been followed?

If yes, but the statutory procedures have not been followed, then the period for which the employee will be compensated will end when he would otherwise have been dismissed, although any basic award will still be payable (*Polkey v AE Dayton Services Ltd* [1988] AC 344, HL). For pre 6 April 2009 dismissals (see para 30.72 for 'trigger events'). If there is doubt whether, had a proper procedure been followed, dismissal would have resulted, but dismissal was at least 50 per cent likely then the dismissal will not be rendered unfair because of the procedural lapse (s 98A(2)). If dismissal was less than 50 per cent likely the dismissal will be unfair, but the award can be reduced to reflect this chance (see para 30.110). For post 6 April 2009 dismissals if a fair procedure has not been followed, dismissal will only be fair if the employer knew at the time that the process would be useless (see para 30.111(3). However, compensation may be reduced if the employee would have been dismissed anyway had a fair procedure been followed (see paras 30.111(2) and (3), and 25.08.

20.4 Has the employee mitigated his loss by finding another job? If the employee has failed to take appropriate steps to find another job, would he have found alternative employment had he taken those steps?

If the answer to either question is yes, there will be no further compensation to cover the period from which the alternative employment was or should have been obtained. The only caveat to this is that if the new job carries a lower salary and benefits package, the employee may recover damages representing the difference between the old and the new for such time as the tribunal decides this discrepancy will last. For further details, see paras 25.27–25.38.

20.5 Did the employee contribute to his own dismissal?
If there is an element of contributory fault, the compensation payments payable to the employee will be reduced by an appropriate percentage (see paras 25.39–25.58). *Note*: conduct arising after the dismissal or which did not cause or contribute to the dismissal, cannot be taken into account (*Mullinger v Department for Work and Pensions* UKEAT/0515/05).

20.6 Has the employer made any *ex gratia* payment to the employee? If so, it will be taken into account in reducing the award—see paras 25.59–25.61.

20.7 How much compensation should be awarded for the employee's loss of statutory rights (particularly because he will have to work for a year at his new employer before he is generally entitled to claim he has been unfairly dismissed and for two years before he is entitled to a redundancy payment)?
Generally an award in the region of £250 is made here.

20.8 In what order should any deductions from the compensation award be made?
See paras 25.65–25.68.

20.9 Should the employment tribunal add to the award on the basis that the employee has been deprived of the money due to him for a period?
The tribunal is entitled to make an allowance for loss caused by delayed payment and interest is a measure of the loss (*Melia v Magna Kansei Ltd* [2006] IRLR 117, CA).

21. *Evidence*

It is prudent for an employer and employee facing a dispute to obtain as much as possible of the following information:

(a) identity of employer, and any associated employer, its size and administrative resources;
(b) length of service of employee;
(c) contractual terms—value of salary/wages and benefits, plus general contractual obligations and entitlements, for example, duties, hours worked, etc. Documents should evidence contractual terms, for example, letter of appointment, contract, amendment letters, staff handbook, collective agreement, etc. Custom and practice may, too, be relevant in the absence of express written terms;
(d) any relevant disciplinary procedures;
(e) the reason for any termination of employment. Is the stated reason the true reason? Was a lesser sanction appropriate?
(f) what inquiries the employer made into the allegations against the employee—for cases involving poor performance, as many example of poor performance as possible should be produced;
(g) what warnings were given earlier to the employee;
(h) what warning, consultation, and disciplinary meetings were held relating to the dismissal;
(i) all correspondence and notes of meetings relating to the inquiries, disciplinary meetings, and dismissal;
(j) whether there was an appeal. If there was, all relevant documents and notes of meetings relating to the appeal;
(k) what effort has the employee made to find a new job? Has he retained details? He should, to show that he properly mitigated his loss;
(l) whether it is practicable to reappoint the employee in his old or any similar job;
(m) whether the employee received any settlement payment. If he did, was a legally enforceable settlement agreement completed?

31

Redundancy

SUMMARY

(1) An employer in financial difficulty often needs to reduce the number of its employees by making them redundant.

(2) Redundancy is potentially a fair reason for dismissal.

(3) An employee who has been employed for two years or more is entitled by statute to a redundancy payment on a sliding scale, calculated in accordance with his age and length of service.

(4) Most tribunal cases concerning redundancy revolve around: whether the people selected for redundancy are actually redundant; whether they have been selected for some unfair reason; whether proper individual consultation and/or collective consultation has been implemented; and the compensation to which any redundant person is entitled.

A. WHEN IS A PERSON REDUNDANT?

An employee is dismissed by reason of redundancy if the dismissal is attributable wholly or mainly to the fact that the employer has ceased or intends to cease to carry on the relevant business at all, or business in the particular place where the employee was employed; or because the requirement of the business for the employee to carry out work of a particular kind has ceased or diminished or is expected to do so (ERA 1996, s 139, *Murray v Foyle Meats Ltd* [1999] IRLR 562, HL). The commercial decision that the business needs fewer employees of a particular type rests with the employer, and the tribunal will generally not inquire into whether the employer was reasonable in taking that commercial decision. An employer selecting people for redundancy should be able to demonstrate to a tribunal that he has reviewed the number of staff he needs to maintain the business he proposes to carry on and the positions which will thereby become vacant: if he thinks in terms of which individuals he no longer requires, this may indicate that any selection process is unfair. **31.01**

When a tribunal looks at the issue of redundancy it takes into consideration not only the employing company but also, in reviewing the question whether the employee should be offered alternative employment elsewhere, any associated companies. **31.02**

31.03 When a whole business or office closes down there is rarely an issue whether the employee is redundant. If there is any question, it relates only (in a claim for unfair dismissal) to whether associated employers have appropriate alternative work for the employee. An employee will not be made redundant if he has a mobility clause in his contract of employment and is genuinely (and with advance notice as part of the redundancy consultation procedures) relocated pursuant to this clause (*Home Office v Evans* [2008] IRLR 59, which contrasted the position here from one where employers 'dodge' between implementing contractual redundancy procedures and invoking a mobility clause). However, it is at least arguable that the behaviour of employers who exercise mobility clauses solely in order to avoid the automatic TUPE transfer of certain employees is inconsistent with TUPE principles and unfair (*Royal Mail Group Ltd v Communication Workers Union* [2009] 0338/08 EAT).

31.04 When, however, the employer is merely reducing numbers rather than closing the business altogether, problems can arise if it cannot actually show that its cost-cutting measures are the direct cause of a particular person's departure. Company restructuring, which does not involve a reduction in numbers of employees, is unlikely to involve any redundancies, though anyone losing their job as a result may have been dismissed for 'some other substantial reason' (see para 30.69(2)). An employee may successfully claim unfair dismissal if he can show that no proper method of selecting people for redundancy was implemented or that there is some other motive for dismissal.

B. SELECTION OF THOSE EMPLOYEES TO BE MADE REDUNDANT

31.05 The employer must not use as his principal reason for selecting a person any facts relating to the individual's membership of or participation in the affairs of a trade union, or any other automatically unfair reason (see para 30.29 for automatically unfair reasons).

31.06 The employer must choose his own selection criteria, which must be reasonable (*Williams v Compair Maxam Ltd* [1982] IRLR 83, EAT) and followed in a consistent and unbiased way (*Dixon Stores Group v Sangster* [2004] 0205/04, EAT). Most fair criteria would include one or more of the following factors: the type of skills and capabilities for which there is a continuing employment need, and the suitability of the individuals to perform those tasks: competence, commitment and attitude, teamworking ability, health, absences, and conduct. In the past 'last in first out' has been applied as a criterion, although its use has been declining. Now, it may be unwise to adopt this as a criterion because it may disadvantage younger employees who will not have had the opportunity to build up substantial years of service, and may therefore be regarded as indirect age discrimination. However, in one of the first reported cases on the point, use of length of service as one of six criteria was upheld (*Rolls-Royce plc v Unite the Unions* [2009] EWCA Civ 387, CA, because its two aims, maintenance of a stable workforce during a redundancy exercise and rewarding loyalty, while potentially discriminatory, were objectively justifiable in the particular circumstances. (See also *MacCulloch v ICI plc* [2008] IRLR 846 which discussed, but reached no conclusion on, the use of age and service in the calculation of a contractual redundancy payment.) The criteria should be capable of being objectively checked, but can be weighted in favour of particular criteria (*Williams v Compair Maxam Ltd* [1982] ICR, 156, EAT, where the criterion to retain employees who 'would keep the company viable' was too subjective and unreasonable; and *Rees v Peninsula Business Services Ltd* [2006] 2401955, ET (where 'receipt of unsolicited commendations from clients' was unfair, depending entirely on luck). The employer should apply the criteria carefully: a glaring inconsistency may make the selection unfair (*Northgate HR Ltd v Mercy* [2008] IRLR 222, CA). Simply selecting on a cost-saving basis could also be unfair (*KGB Micros Ltd v Lewis*, EAT 573/90, where salesmen were unfairly selected for redundancy by comparing their overheads with their revenue generation (ie net profit per salesman) as this did not comprise an objective valuation of the salesmen's skills). If the employer cannot back up how the criteria were applied, for example by reference to previous appraisals or other records, but the marker has exercised his own judgment over a range of criteria, the process may be faulty and any selected employee may have been unfairly dismissed (*E-Zec Medical Transport Service Ltd v Gregory* [2008] 0192/08, EAT). Employees may have a discrimination claim against employers if selection criteria are chosen or applied in a discriminatory fashion. For example, a tribunal may detect a 'young' culture in the employer as a result of failure to consider other employees, all younger than the claimant, for redundancy, and conclude that there has been age discrimination (*Court v Dennis Publishing Ltd* 2200327/07, ET); and it is likely to be discriminatory to use absence as a criterion without taking into account that someone's absence may be as a result of their having a disability (*Harding v Eden Park Surgery* 1100367/05, ET).

In addition, the pool from which the employee is to be selected for redundancy needs to be ascertained. The pool which the employer chooses from which to select those to be made redundant must be within the band of reasonable choices for the employer; there may be more than one appropriate pool (*Hendy Banks City Print v Fairbrother* UKEAT/0691/04). Where there is a customary arrangement or agreed procedure about identifying the ambit of the pool, this should be followed unless the employer can show it was reasonable to depart from it (*Russell v LB Haringey* 12.6.00, CA). If, for example, the employer decides that he needs two fewer employees in one department, yet there are employees in another department who perform similar tasks and who, by their contract of employment, could be required to work in the first department, then those other employees could also be subject to the same criteria for selection. This 'bumping' rule is sound practice to follow, though it is not a hard and fast rule in every case (see *Lionel Leventhal Ltd v North* EAT/0265/04, IDS Employment Law Brief 778, where on the facts of the case the employer should have considered bumping a more junior employee, even though the potentially redundant employee had not requested it: factors to consider are how different the two jobs are, the difference in remuneration, and the qualifications of the potentially redundant employee). Further, an employer which is going to adopt this practice should have clear reasons for having done so, such as the need to maintain key skills: if it cannot show that it considered these issues at the time, the 'bumped' employee could be unfairly dismissed (see, eg, *O'Reilly v Welwyn and Hatfield DC* [1975] IRLR 334). **31.07**

C. CONSULTATION

Collective consultation

Consultation over the redundancies should take place on two levels, both the collective and the individual. **31.08**

Where 20 or more employees at any one establishment may be made redundant, the employer must consult with 'appropriate representatives'. The word 'establishment' is broadly defined. For example, a production unit can be an establishment if it, say, has a head of production and a substantial and specialized workforce, and is a stand-alone operation, even if it does not have any legal, economic, financial, administrative, or technological autonomy (*Athinaikim Chartopoiia AE v Panagiotidis* [2007] IRLR 284, ECJ). The representatives may be representatives of a recognized trade union, if there is one, or if not they must be employee representatives (see para 31.10). Those whom the employer plans to redeploy elsewhere in the business must be included in the headcount of those potentially redundant (*Hardy v Tourism South East* [2005] IRLR 242, EAT), as must those who voluntarily accept redundancy (*Optare Group Limited v Transport and General Workers Union* [2007] IRLR 931, EAT). **31.09**

If there is already a group of employees who have been appointed or elected to represent colleagues in general in circumstances such that they have authority to receive information about and be consulted about proposed redundancy dismissals, then, in the absence of a recognized **31.10** union, this group can be consulted with. If no such group exists, or if the employer does not wish to consult this group, he must consult with a group who has been specially elected by the affected employees in an election. The election must be held in the following way:

(a) The employer must make such arrangements as are reasonably practicable to ensure that the elections are fair;
(b) It is for the employer to decide:
    (i) how many representatives there should be, but they must be sufficient to represent all employee interests, having regard to the number and classes of affected employees;
    (ii) whether employees of different classes should be represented by all the representatives, or just be representatives of their class; and
    (iii) the length of the term of office—which must be sufficiently long to enable them to remain in place until the consultation concludes.
(c) The candidates for election must be affected employees as at the election date;
(d) No affected employee must be unreasonably excluded from standing for election;
(e) All affected employees as at the election date must have the opportunity to vote;
(f) The employees must be able to vote for as many candidates as are entitled to represent them;
(g) There should be a secret ballot; and
(h) Votes should be accurately counted (TULR(C)A 1992, s 188A).

31.11 Consultations must begin in good time and at least 30 days before any dismissal takes effect where the employer proposes to dismiss as redundant between 20 and 99 employees at one establishment within a 90-day period, and at least 90 days before any dismissal where the employer proposes to dismiss at least 100 employees within a 90-day period (TULR(C)A 1992, s 188(1) and (1A)). The dismissal 'takes effect' not on the day the employment terminates, but on the day that notice to terminate is given to the employees (*Junk v Kühnel* [2005] IRLR 310, ECJ). These time limits apply unless there are special circumstances which render it not reasonably practicable for them to be adhered to. 'In good time' does not mean 'at the earliest opportunity' and consultation may only take two weeks if that is sufficient time to produce a fair and meaningful consultation process (*Amicus v Nissan Motor Manufacturing (UK) Ltd* UKEAT/0184/05, IDS Employment Law Brief 793). Consultation must begin when there is a real proposal to dismiss, even if the proposal is a recommendation to management which has yet to be ratified (*Leicestershire County Council v Unison* [2005] IRLR 920, EAT), though if the proposals are still at a formative stage, the fact that there is a gap between their formulation and the start of consultations will not prevent the consultation being 'in good time' so long as there is sufficient consultation before proposals are finalized (*Amicus v Nissan Motor Manufacturing (UK) Ltd* UKEAT/0184/05, IDS Employment Law Brief 793, where constructive negotiations began several months after proposals had been announced and lasted two weeks).

31.12 Consultation must be about ways of avoiding dismissals, reducing the numbers of employees to be dismissed, and mitigating the consequences of the dismissals. The employer should undertake the consultation with a view to reaching agreement with the representatives/union (TULR(C)A 1992, s 188(2)). As part of the consultation, the employer must disclose the following information, in writing, to the representatives/union:

(a) its reasons for the proposals including the business reasons behind any proposed redundancies, eg the reasons for the closure of a business (*UK Mining Ltd v NUM* UKEAT/0397/06);
(b) the number and descriptions of employees whom it is proposed to dismiss as redundant;
(c) the total number of employees of any such description employed by it at the establishment in question;
(d) the proposed method of selecting the employees who may be dismissed;
(e) the proposed method of carrying out the dismissals—with due regard to any agreed procedure, including the period over which the dismissals are to take effect; and

(f) the proposed method of calculating the amount of any redundancy payments to be made (TULR(C)A 1992, s 188(4)).

The employer also has to give notice of the intention to effect redundancies to the Department for Business, Innovation and Skills if it proposes to make 20 or more people redundant over a 90-day period, and must use a form HR1. This must be done within similar time limits to those required for consultation with authorized representatives. **31.13**

If the employer has an agreement by which he has to inform and consult representatives under the Information and Consultation of Employees Regulations 2004, he need not discuss impending collective redundancies with those representatives if he tells them in writing that he will be consulting under TULR(C)A 1992, s 188 (Information and Consultation of Employees Regulations 2004, reg 20(1)(c)). **31.14**

Failure to consult with authorized representatives renders the employer liable to a protective award of up to 90 days' pay. This is a punitive, rather than compensatory award and tribunals are required to look at the seriousness of the employer's default. A proper approach where there is no consultation is to start with the maximum award and then reduce it only if there are mitigating circumstances which would justify a reduction (*Susie Radin Ltd v GMB* [2004] IRLR 400, CA; *Hutchins v Permacell Finesse Ltd* EAT/0350/07, IDS Employment Law Brief 848). Because the award is intended to be punitive, it applies even where employees remained employed throughout the protected period and were not dismissed or under notice until that period had ended (*Cranswick Country Foods Ltd v Beall* UKEAT/0222/06). If a protective award is obtained by a trade union, it can only be enforced by employees in respect of whom the union is recognized and not, for example, by employees from non-recognized unions, even where they were members of the union which obtained the award (*TGWU v Brauer Coley Ltd* [2007] ICR 226, EAT). *Note*: NIC contributions are payable on all of a protective award; they are also, in principle, treated by HMRC as taxable, but subject to the £30,000 limit set out in ITEPA, ss 401–403, see paras 29.13 and 29.25). **31.15**

Individual consultation

The employer must also consult with each individual employee whom it proposes to make redundant before any decision is finalized. **31.16**

The provisions regarding individual consultation have changed with effect from 6 April 2009. Where an employer proposes to make fewer redundancies than the 20 which trigger collective consultation obligations (see TULR(C)A 1992, s 188(1) and (1A)), it was obliged, in circumstances occurring before a 'trigger event' (see para 30.72), to go through a formal dismissal procedure with each employee (Employment Act 2002 (Dispute Resolution) Regulations 2004, regs 3 and 4(1)(b); EA 2002, s 30). The standard dismissal procedure set out in EA 2002, Sch 2, Part 2 is: **31.17**

- *Step 1*
  (1) The employer must write to the employee setting out the circumstances which lead him to contemplate dismissing the employee (ie that it is contemplating making the employee redundant) and invite the employee to a meeting to discuss it.
  (2) The information provided before the Step 2 meeting (ie either in writing or orally) must be sufficient to enable the employee to give a considered and informed response to the proposal. It must include:
  (a) reasons why there is a redundancy situation;
  (b) (if relevant) selection criteria, and the employee's performance against those selection criteria. It is not necessary for the purposes of the statutory procedure to produce the performance records of other employees, although it would be sensible to have the information to hand in an anonymized format (*Alexander v Bridgen Enterprises Ltd* [2006] IRLR 422).

Failure to consult an employee who has recently moved to a commercially risky and now potentially redundant role about the possibility of moving back to her old job does not necessarily make the dismissal unfair (*Hachette Filipacchi UK Ltd v Johnson* [2006] IDS Employment Law Brief 804).

- *Step 2*
  (1) The employer should invite the employee to a meeting to discuss the position, before any notice of redundancy is given.
  (2) The employee may be accompanied by a colleague or trade union official (Employment Relations Act 1999, s 10; TULR(C)A 1992, s 119).
  (3) Following the meeting the employer must inform the employee of the decision, and notify him that he has a right of appeal.

- *Step 3*
  (1) If the employee exercises the right of appeal, the employer must invite the employee to an appeal meeting.
  (2) The employee may be accompanied at the meeting, as in Step 2.
  (3) After the meeting, the employer must inform the employee of his decision.

31.18 For dismissals under the old rules (see para 31.17), if the employer does not follow the procedure, and the employee wins the claim, the dismissal is automatically unfair (ERA 1996, s 98A). This is the case even where dismissal would inevitably have resulted had the full procedure been followed (*Wareing v Stone Cladding International Limited* EAT/0498/06). The amount of the claim will (except in exceptional circumstances) be increased by 10–50 per cent (in all cases subject to any statutory maximum award that may apply to the claim). If the employee fails to comply with the procedure (for example, by unreasonably failing to attend a meeting) or does not appeal, but wins the action, the award will (again, save in exceptional circumstances) be reduced by 10–50 per cent (EA 2002, s 31). See also paras 24.156 and 25.15.

31.19 For dismissals where the old rules no longer apply (effectively where consultations with individuals did not start until 6 April 2009 or later—see para 30.72 for the 'trigger events') there are no formal rules to apply, and the ACAS Code (see Appendix 3) specifically exempts redundancy dismissals from its remit. Nevertheless, an employee will be expected to go through a fair consultation procedure, warning and consulting employees at risk of redundancy, using a fair selection basis, and taking steps to minimize the redundancies by exploring redeployment with employees (*Polkey v AE Dayton Services Ltd* [1987] IRLR 503, HL). This will involve explaining to them:

- why their role is at risk of redundancy;
- why they have been provisionally selected for redundancy, and what the selection criteria were;
- alternative roles available;
- financial proposals;

and giving the employee the opportunity to comment and respond before any final decision is taken. If this does not happen, an employee will be likely to have been unfairly dismissed. The only reason to avoid such a finding is if the employer convinces a tribunal that, on the basis of the facts it knew at the time, it would have been futile to have adopted the procedures (per Lord Bridge in *Polkey*). In all other circumstances, the employee will be unfairly dismissed, but compensation may be reduced by the '*Polkey* reduction' if the employer can demonstrate to the tribunal that a fair procedure would have resulted in dismissal anyway (see Chapter 25B). Also, if a tribunal finds that any redundancy label was a sham, masking a true (potentially unfair) reason for dismissal, it will expect the ACAS Code to be followed (see paras 30.77–30.81 for consequences of failure to follow the Code).

31.20 Even if the redundancies are subject to collective consultation, it is still advisable for the employer to conduct individual consultation with the employees, for example about available alternative employment. Failure to do so may well render any subsequent dismissal unfair.

D. ALTERNATIVE EMPLOYMENT

The employer also has a duty, if someone is provisionally selected for redundancy, to see whether there is any other role which might suit that particular employee, not only with the employer but also with any associated company of the employer. If this requirement is ignored, a dismissal is normally rendered unfair. If there are jobs, even if they are of lower status or carry lower wages than those which apply to the employee's present job, the prospect of moving to the alternative employment should nevertheless be raised. Where employees are potentially redundant but there are other vacant roles available, an employer should not invite applications for the vacant roles from the whole workforce before satisfying itself that the potentially redundant employees are not suitable to carry out the vacant role—and the selection process for deciding on their suitability must meet some criteria for fairness, though the test is not as stringent as those for the general selection procedure (*Ralph Martindale v Harris* EAT/0166/07). It is sensible for an employer to inform the employee of the proposed salary and benefits of any alternative position—failure to do so may make the dismissal unfair (*Fisher v Hoopoe Finance Ltd* [2005] IDS Employment Law Brief 784). Employees on *maternity leave* must be offered any suitable alternative jobs if their normal job is to be made redundant. Failure to consult an employee who had recently moved to a commercially risky and now potentially redundant role about the possibility of moving back to her old job does not necessarily make the dismissal unfair (*Hachette Filipacchi UK Ltd v Johnson* [2006] IDS Employment Law Brief 804). If there is no consideration given to alternative employment, but the employer can show it would not have appointed the employee to the vacant position in any event, the decision to make the employee redundant might still be regarded as fair if the breaches in procedure were not so serious as to make the decision to dismiss unreasonable (ERA 2006, s 98A and *Loosley v Social Action for Health* UKEAT/0378/06). **31.21**

If there is a mobility clause in the employee's contract, entitling the employer to transfer the employee to another work location, an employer can rely on this clause, upon giving the employee reasonable notice of the proposed relocation, to avoid a redundancy at one site if there are equivalent vacancies elsewhere. Any employee who refuses to transfer will not have been constructively dismissed if he refuses to transfer and resigns (*Home Office v Evans* [2008] IRLR 59, CA). This process must be adopted from the start—an employer cannot start a redundancy process and then evade the consequences by attempting to enforce a mobility clause (*Curling v Securicor Ltd* [1992] IRLR 549, EAT). If there is no mobility clause, an employer cannot go down this route, but must proceed as in paras 31.23–31.25. **31.22**

If the employer is able to identify suitable alternative work, either within its own company or with an associated company, which is substantially similar to the employee's previous position and commands a similar wage package, it is to the employer's advantage to offer such a job to the prospectively redundant employee. The job offer, which should be made before termination, to start within four weeks of the termination of the redundant job, is then generally subject to a four-week trial period (though the trial period may be extended if the employee has further training). If the employee accepts the job offer and continues to work after the trial period, there is no redundancy. If, however, he refuses a suitable job offer (either immediately or during the trial period) he will lose his right to a redundancy payment unless he can show that it was reasonable for him to reject the offer. If the job is not suitable, or if the employee acts reasonably in refusing it (respectively an objective and a subjective test) the employee will still be redundant unless he accepts the job offer and continues to work normally. If the employer invites potentially redundant employees to compete for other, vacant jobs, the selection process for the new post may not be so rigorous as it is for the original redundancy/selection itself, but the employer must simply act reasonably and fairly (*British Steel plc v Slater* EAT 644196; *Ralph Martindale and Co Ltd v Harris* EAT 0166/07). **31.23**

31.24 For the offer to be suitable, it must be made (orally or in writing) by the original employer or an associated employer before the employee's employment actually terminates. The new post should start within four weeks of the ending of the old one, and, if not on the same terms and conditions it is subject to an objective test of suitability. In determining this, the tribunal will review issues such as pay, status, location, and whether the new job is within the employee's skill set. If the terms and conditions differ at all from the original contract, the employee is allowed a trial period of four weeks to assess the new role, although this period may be extended by agreement.

31.25 If the terms of the new employment are suitable and the employee unreasonably refuses it, either immediately or during the trial period, he will not be entitled to a redundancy payment. Whether the employee is reasonable in refusing a job offer is a subjective test, viewed from the employee's perspective: the burden of proof is on the employer to show that the employee is behaving unreasonably (*Hudson v George Harrison Ltd* EAT/0571/02; *Executors of Everest v Cox* [1980] ICR 415). For example, an employee might reasonably refuse a job with apparently reasonable hours if it will prevent him or her from complying with childcare arrangements, or if he perceives it involves a loss of status (*Cambridge & District Co-operative Society v Ruse* [1993] IRLR 156, EAT). It is relevant to consider whether the new post is overwhelmingly suitable (as opposed, say, to only marginally suitable). If the post is only marginally suitable, it will be harder for the employer to persuade a tribunal that the employee was acting unreasonably in refusing it (*Commission for Health Care Audit & Inspection v Ward* EAT/0579/07).

E. CALCULATION OF REDUNDANCY PAYMENT

31.26 The redundancy payment is calculated according to a fixed formula. Provided that the employee has been employed for a minimum of two years (or would have been if given statutory notice (ERA 1996, ss 155 and 145(5) and see para 30.08) the employee will receive a redundancy payment calculated by multiplying his weekly gross remuneration (subject to a maximum payment, which, for dismissals after 1 February 2009 is set at £350 and for dismissals between 1 October 2009 and 31 January 2011 is £380) by a factor determined in accordance with age and length of service. Length of service means the period from commencement of employment to the Effective Date of Termination (see para 30.08 for the definition of Effective Date of Termination). (See Ready Reckoner in Appendix 4.) If an employee is not paid a redundancy payment, he can bring a claim in the employment tribunal (ERA 1996, s 163). Under the old rules relating to grievance procedures, no claim could be brought unless the employee had submitted a grievance. Under the new ACAS Code, employees who do not lodge a grievance run the risk that their award will be reduced by up to 25 per cent (see 24.164]).

31.27 If the employee is paid less than the national minimum wage, the award will be calculated as if the employee were receiving the national minimum wage (£5.80 per hour for those aged 22 or over; £4.83 per hour for those aged 18–21; and £3.57 per hour for 16- and 17-year-olds who are not apprentices with effect from 1 October 2009. (See Appendix 6 for earlier minimum wages.)

31.28 In addition to the redundancy payment, each employee is entitled either to work out his contractual notice period, or to be paid money in lieu of notice.

31.29 Some employers have contractually enhanced redundancy payment programmes. These may be included:

(a) in the employment contract itself;
(b) in a collective agreement incorporated into the employment contract, even if that collective agreement had expired before the redundancy took effect (*Framptons Ltd v Badger* [2006] All ER (D) 127 (Oct), EAT) and even if the policy expressly states that it is not part of the employee's contract if the policy has been followed without exception for a substantial period to such an extent that it has acquired contractual status by custom and practice (*Peries v Wirefast Ltd* EAT/0245/06); or

(c) a staff handbook (*Keeley v Fosroc International Ltd* [2006] IRLR 961, CA), including where it is one of a collection of contractual policies on the employer's intranet (*Christopher Harlow v Artemis International Corporation Limited* [2008] IRLR 629).

Employers may regularly pay enhanced redundancy payments, and if these have been consistently applied so that a custom and practice is established, future employees may have a contractual right to equivalent payments on redundancy. Questions designed to establish whether an enhanced redundancy payment scheme is included in an individual's contract of employment include: **31.30**

(1) whether the policy is 'reasonable, notorious and certain';
(2) whether the policy has been drawn to the attention of the employee, and if so was it in such a way that it indicated that the employer intended to be contractually bound by the policy;
(3) whether the policy has been followed consistently and without exception on every occasion where there have been redundancies for a substantial period;
(4) how many times the policy has been followed;
(5) whether payments have been made under the policy as a matter of course, or only as a result of specific negotiations (*Albion Automotive Ltd v Walker* [2002] EWCA Civ 946).

Enhancing the statutory minimum redundancy payments will not be regarded as age discrimination so long as the amount an employer offers to all the different employees is calculated in the same way, eg by applying the same multiplicand or substituting actual working wage for maximum weekly wage (Employment Equality (Age) Regulations 2006, reg 33). If the employer does not follow the pattern of the statutory scheme, for example if it increases payments according to age more sharply than the scheme, it faces the uphill task, if challenged by younger employees, of trying to justify why the greater differentials were a proportionate means of achieving a legitimate aim failing which the payments may be discriminatory on the ground of age (*MacCulloch v Imperial Chemical Industries Plc* [2008] IRLR 846, EAT; *Loxley v BAE Systems Land Systems (Munitions & Ordnance) Ltd* [2008] IRLR 853, EAT). **31.31**

An employee who is unfairly selected for redundancy will be entitled to compensation for unfair dismissal. **31.32**

REDUNDANCY FLOW CHART

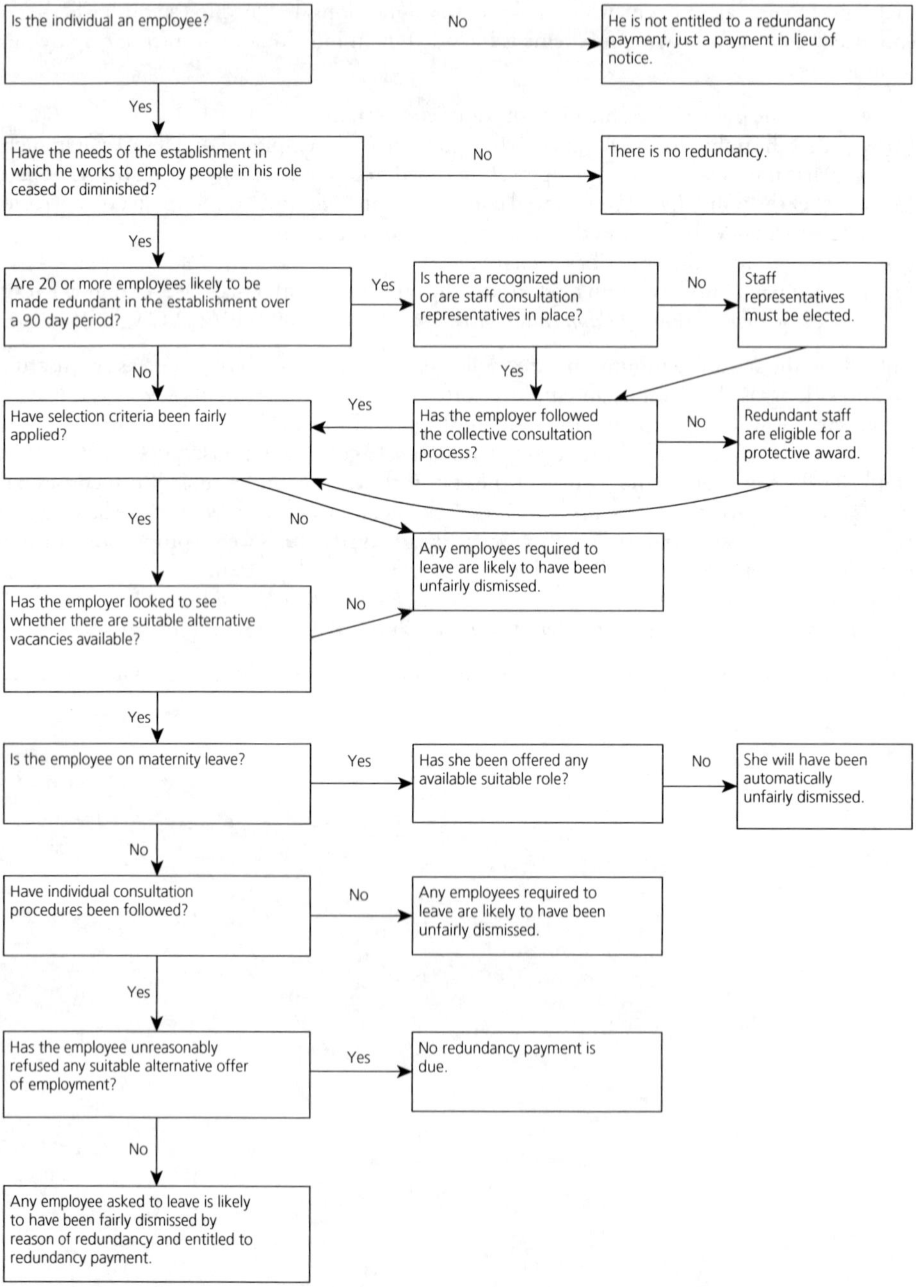

CHECKLIST OF ISSUES FOR TRIBUNAL CLAIMS CONNECTED WITH REDUNDANCY

1. Can the employer establish that it has or intends to close down the business where the employee works, or that the requirements of that business for employees to carry out work of a particular kind have ceased or diminished? (ERA 1996, s 139—see para 31.01.)

   If this cannot be established, then redundancy cannot be the reason for dismissal.

2. Were 20 or more employees potentially to be made redundant at the same establishment within 90 days or less? (TULR(C)A 1992, s 188—see para 31.09.)

   If 20 or more employees are potentially to be made redundant (or redeployed (*Hardy v Tourism South East* [2005] IRLR 242, EAT)) during this period, the employer will need to undertake collective consultation, either with a recognized trade union, or with special employee representatives. Any election for employee representatives must be fair (TULR(C)A 1992, s 188A) (see paras 31.10–31.12).

3. Was there a failure to consult or, where necessary, to hold a fair election of employee representatives—see para 31.15?

   If so, a claim may be brought against the employer for a protective award of up to 90 days' pay per affected employee (TULR(C)A 1992, s 189).

4. What is the reason for the employee's dismissal? Is it because his role is redundant, or is it for some other reason?

   If it is for some other reason but redundancy is given as the ostensible reason, the employee will probably have been unfairly dismissed.

5. Were fewer than 20 people to be made redundant by the establishment over a 90-day period? Did the employer begin to consult with individuals about the redundancy before 6 April 2009? If so, the employer should have followed the statutory disciplinary procedure (see paras 31.17–31.18).

   Failure to do so will render any dismissal automatically unfair (ERA 1996, s 98A). Any damages to be awarded will, except in exceptional circumstances, be increased by 10–50 per cent (EA 2002, s 31).

6. If 5 applies, did the employee unreasonably fail to participate in the statutory dismissal procedure, or has he not submitted an appeal (see paras 31.17–31.18)?

   If so, and if he wins an unfair dismissal claim, his damages will, save in exceptional circumstances, be reduced by 10–50 per cent (EA 2002, s 31).

7. If the employer proposed to make at least 20 employees redundant at one establishment within a 90-day period, did he notify the Department for Business, Innovation and Skills of his intention to do so using form HR1?

   If not, the employer could be convicted and fined up to level 5 on the standard scale in a magistrates' court (TULR(C)A 1992, s 194(1)).

8. Did the employer adopt a fair procedure leading up to the dismissal (see paras 31.05–31.07 and 31.19)? For example, have appropriate selection criteria been adopted/agreed and fairly applied? (*Williams v Compair Maxam Ltd* [1982] ICR 156, EAT and see generally for consultation obligations on an employer when dealing with union/employee representatives.)

If not, any consequent dismissal may well be (but is not bound to be—see *Grundy (Teddington) Ltd v Phimmer* [1983] ICR 367) unfair.

9. Was the consultation process reasonable or was it a sham?

   If the employee can demonstrate it was a sham, for example because the employer had reached a final but not inevitable decision before the process began, he is likely to have been unfairly dismissed (*Rowell v Hubbard Group Services Ltd* [1995] IRLR 195).

10. Was the employee on maternity leave at the time of her dismissal?

    If so, and she was not (before her old employment ends) offered alternative employment if any suitable vacancy exists, she will have been automatically unfairly dismissed (Maternity and Parental Leave etc Regulations 1999, SI 1999/3312, regs 10 and 20).

11. Did the employer review whether there are any suitable alternative jobs, within the employer company or any group companies, for the employee—see paras 31.21–31.25? Did it give the employee the available information about the proposed salary and benefits attaching to the alternatives?

    If not, the dismissal may be unfair (*Vokes Ltd v Bear* [1974] ICR 1; *Avonmouth Construction Co Ltd v Shipway* [1979] IRLR 14; *Fisher v Hoopoe Finance Ltd* [2005] IDS Employment Law Brief 784).

12. Did the employee unreasonably refuse any offers of suitable alternative employment (see para 31.25)?

    If so, he will not be entitled to a redundancy payment (ERA 1996, s 141).

13. Was it appropriate for the employer to consider 'bumping' so that an employee in a potentially redundant role would be given another's job (see para 31.07)?

    If not, there may be circumstances where this failure makes the dismissal unfair (*Thomas & Betts Manufacturing Ltd v Harding* [1980] IRLR 255).

14. Was the employee selected for redundancy for an automatically unfair reason? Automatically unfair reasons are set out at para 30.29.

    If so, the redundancy will be automatically unfair (ERA 1996, s 105).

15. Did the position regarding the potential redundancy, or any suitable alternative positions, change between the date on which notice was given and the date when the redundancy takes effect? If so, and if the employer does not take action which might allow the employee to remain employed, the dismissal may be regarded as unfair (*Dyke v Hereford and Worcester County Council* [1989] ICR 800).

16. Was an employee who is being made redundant asked to work out his notice period or paid salary in lieu?

    If neither, he may have a claim against his employer for breach of contract. If the amount is less than £25,000 the claim may be brought under art 3 of the Employment Tribunal (Employment Tribunals Extension of Jurisdiction) (England and Wales) Order 1994.

17. Was the employee employed for at least two years by the EDT (ie the termination date or, if no or inadequate statutory notice was given, the termination date plus this notice—see para 30.08 (ERA 1996, ss 145(5), 86, and 155))?

If so, he is entitled to a redundancy payment calculated in accordance with ERA 1996, s 162. See also Ready Reckoner for redundancy payments (Appendix 4) and current maximum week's pay (£380 per week with effect from 1 October 2009) (see Appendix 6) for calculating the sum due.

18. Did the employer have a contractually enhanced redundancy programme which is incorporated into the individuals' contracts of employment, or has he consistently applied an enhanced redundancy payment policy so that it has become custom and practice for it to be paid (see para 31.29)?

    If so, the employee may have a contractual claim against the employer, which can be brought in the employment tribunal up to a value of £25,000, or otherwise in the High Court or county court, for receipt of the enhanced redundancy payment (Employment Tribunals Extension of Jurisdiction (England and Wales) Order 1994, art 3).

19. Is the enhanced redundancy scheme modelled on the method for calculating statutory redundancy pay, but increased across the board by enhancing, consistently, any relevant multiplicands? If not, the scheme may be age discriminatory—see para 31.31.

32

Equal Pay and Discrimination

SUMMARY

(1) Employers may not discriminate on grounds of sex, race, disability, marital status, sexual orientation, religion, or age.

(2) Claims can be for direct or indirect discrimination, victimization, harassment, and, in the case of disability discrimination, a failure to make reasonable adjustments.

(3) Compensation for claims is uncapped and an award for injury to feelings may be made.

Employers who adopt discriminatory practices do so at their peril. The Equal Pay Act 1970 (EqPA 1970); the Sex Discrimination Act 1975 (SDA 1975); the Race Relations Act 1976 (RRA 1976); the Disability Discrimination Act 1995 (DDA 1995); the Employment Equality (Religion or Belief) Regulations 2003, SI 2003/1660 (RBR 2003); the Employment Equality (Sexual Orientation) Regulations 2003, SI 2003/1661 (SOR 2003); and the Employment Equality (Age) Regulations 2006, SI 2006/1031 (EEAR 2006) between them provide that employers cannot discriminate between people of different sexes and races, against those who intend to undergo, are undergoing, or who have undergone gender reassignment, against those who suffer from a disability, against employees because of their religion or belief or sexual orientation or age in their selection procedures, contractual terms, and treatment of employees. In addition, Article 141 (formerly Article 119) of the EC Treaty, and the Equal Treatment Directive (76/207/EEC [1976] OJ L39/40, as amended by Directive 2002/73/EC [2002] OJ L269/15) give additional protection to employees who are discriminated against on grounds of sex. There is also protection from discrimination of those who are or are not trade union members, take up other offices as part of their employment or who are whistle-blowers, those who work part-time, and those who work under fixed term contracts, but these types of discrimination will not be dealt with specifically here. **32.01**

A. EQUAL PAY

If an employee shows she does substantially similar work to a named member of the opposite sex, or performs work which has been rated as equivalent work under a job evaluation scheme, **32.02** or is of equal or greater value than work carried out by a named member of the opposite sex, and any element of the employee's contractual terms is worse than that of the chosen comparator, the EqPA 1970 operates (via a somewhat cumbersome route) to bring the worse contractual term up to the same level as the better one (EqPA 1970, s 1 and see *Sorbie v Trust Houses Forte Hotels Ltd* [1976] IRLR 371).

32.03 An employee for these purposes means one 'employed' under a contract of service or of apprenticeship or a contract personally to execute any work or labour at an establishment in Great Britain (EqPA 1970, s 1(6)(a)). It does, therefore, cover a wider category of individuals than employees, but probably does not extend to the full range of 'workers' (*Quinnen v Hovells* [1984] IRLR 227; *Allonby v Accrington and Rossendale College* [2004] IRLR 224). There can be no claim for equal pay where the complainant works wholly outside Great Britain. However, from October 2005, if the employer has a place of business at an establishment in Great Britain, the work the employee is doing is for the purposes of the business carried on at that establishment and the employee is ordinarily resident in Great Britain when she is recruited or at any time during the course of the employment, then she may have a claim (SDA 1975, s 10(1), (1A)).

32.04 The EqPA 1970 applies not only to wages but also to all contractual terms such as bonus, holiday entitlement, car policies, and sickness benefits. Each element that makes up a contract of employment is looked at individually, and employers cannot rely upon a general balancing out of benefits under the contract as a whole although terms relating to pay of the same kind can be aggregated (*Hayward v Cammell Laird Shipbuilders Ltd* [1988] ICR 464; *Degnan v Redcar and Cleveland Borough Council* [2005] IRLR 615).

32.05 Once an employee has shown that her job is substantially the same as or of equal value to the job of a member of the opposite sex, the employer's only excuse for any different contractual terms is that it is a material difference which is genuinely due to a material factor other than sex, such as length of service or degree of skill, which justifies the differential in pay or benefits (EqPA 1970, s 1(3)). If, however, this factor is found to be indirectly discriminatory, then the employee will be required to objectively justify the factor. The variation to be objectively justified must be both 'appropriate' and 'necessary' and a test of proportionality must be applied (*Rainey v Greater Glasgow Health Board* [1987] IRLR 26; *Strathclyde Regional Council v Wallace* [1998] IRLR 146; *Armstrong v Newcastle upon Tyne NHS Hospital Trust* [2006] IRLR 124). An employee may use a statistical approach to demonstrate indirect discrimination (*Enderby v Frenchay Health Authority* [1993] IRLR 591; *Bailey and ors v Home Office* [2005] IRLR 369). Note that an employer may have difficulties in relying on cost as a ground for objective justification (*Cross v British Airways plc* [2005] IRLR 423; *Grundy v British Airways plc* [2008] IRLR 74). (As to the genuine material factor defence and the need for justification see *Sharp v Caledonian Group Services Ltd* [2006] IRLR 4 and *Villalba v Merrill Lynch & Co Inc* [2006] IRLR 437. In the former, the EAT accepted the principle laid out in *Brunnhofer v Bank der Österreichischen Postsparkasse AG* [2001] IRLR 571 that all material factors must be objectively justified, not just those which are shown to be indirectly discriminatory. In the latter, the EAT stayed with the established position. Both cases were subject to appeal, but have now settled, so *Armstrong* (above) which states that only factors which are indirectly discriminatory need to be justified remains the leading authority. See, however, *Middlesbrough Borough Council v Surtees* [2007] IRLR 869 in the EAT and *Redcar and Cleveland BC v Bainbridge* [2008] IRLR 776, CA.)

32.06 The employee who is successful in her claim is entitled in future to remuneration and benefits on the higher level enjoyed by her comparator, and (generally) to have the difference refunded for the period starting six years before the court or tribunal application was made (EqPA 1970, s 2ZB(3)). There is no cap on the amount that may be recovered (EqPA 1970, s 2(5)). Interest can be ordered on these sums (see paras 28.07–28.14 above). There is no power for the tribunal to award compensation for injury to feelings and/or aggravated damages (*Newcastle upon Tyne City Council v Allan*; *Degnan v Redcar and Cleveland Borough Council* [2005] IRLR 504) (see also paras 25.71–25.73 above).

The EqPA 1970 applies Article 141 (formerly Article 119) of the EC Treaty and the Equal Pay Directive (75/117/EC and 2006/54/EC). Article 141 can be used by an employee to extend her rights under the EqPA 1970. The Equal Pay Directive works in a similar way, but only for employees of public authorities, for example local authorities or the health service. Further, as the ambit of Article 141 is in some ways wider than that of the EqPA 1970, many cases have been brought to highlight the incompatibility between the two. For example, under Article 141, the two-year time limit on claims has been held to be unenforceable leading to amendments to the EqPA 1970 (see also paras 15.05 above). The main exception to this principle is that Article 141 applies only to 'pay' and this has been construed more narrowly under Article 141 than the EqPA 1970. 32.07

The complainant may bring a claim in the employment tribunal, but must do so during employment or within six months of the termination of the contract in relation to which the claim arises (EqPA 1970, s 2(4)). This time limit has been considered to be compatible with European law (*Preston v Wolverhampton Healthcare NHS Trust* [2000] ICR 961) (see also Chapter 15, paras 15.05 above where more detail on time limits is set out). Where a TUPE transfer takes place, it appears that time may run on a claim for equal pay from the date of the TUPE transfer: see *Powerhouse Retail v Burroughs* [2006] IRLR 381; *Unison v Allen* [2007] IRLR 975; and *Sodexo Ltd v Gutridge* [2009] IRLR 721 (CA). Under the old regime, prior to bringing a claim the employee would have to raise a grievance under the statutory dispute procedures or she will be barred from bringing a claim (EA, 2002, s 32). In circumstances where the employee had brought a grievance, the six-month time limit would be extended (Employment Act (Dispute Resolution) Regulations 2004, reg 15 and see paras 3.93–3.99). From 6 April 2009 the requirement to raise a grievance will no longer apply. Regulation 15 has not been repealed, but presumably will have no legal effect. Note the transitional provisions set out in the Schedule to the Employment Act 2008 (Commencement No 1, Transitional Provisions and Savings) Order 2008 which suggest that the 'old grievance' rules will apply to claims brought before 4 October 2009 where the action complained of began before 5 April 2009 but continued beyond that date. 32.08

Equal pay questionnaires A person who considers he may have or has a complaint under the EqPA 1970 may ask questions via a statutory form of questionnaire to establish whether in fact there are grounds. The response to the questionnaire will stand as evidence in any subsequent proceedings. A failure to respond at all or to do so within an eight-week time limit will lead to an adverse inference by the tribunal (EqPA, 1970, s 7B and the Equal Pay (Questions and Replies) Order 2003) (see also Chapter 15, para 15.07 and *Barton v Investec Henderson Crosthwaite Securities Limited* [2003] ICR 1205, EAT). 32.09

Code of practice The Equal Opportunities Commission (EOC) (now amalgamated into the Equality and Human Rights Commission (EHRC)) first issued a code of practice in 1997 aimed at tackling disparity in pay in the workplace. It was updated, expanded, and re-issued with effect from 1 December 2003 (see Appendix 3). The application of this code or failure to apply it can be taken into account when an equal pay claim is being considered by the employment tribunal (SDA 1975, s 56A; Code of Practice on Equal Pay (2003)). 32.10

Equality of pay and contractual provisions for those undergoing or who have undergone gender reassignment, those who are discriminated against on grounds of marital status, those of different races, those who are disabled, those who are discriminated against on grounds of their religion or belief, sexual orientation, or age are dealt with under the SDA 1975, RRA 1976, DDA 1995, RBR 2003, SOR 2003, and EEAR 2006, respectively. 32.11

B. SEX DISCRIMINATION LEGISLATION

The EqPA 1970 and the SDA 1975 complement each other. While the EqPA 1970 deals with certain contractual terms, the SDA 1975 deals with all other aspects of employment, from 32.12

recruitment, through career structure to dismissal. (For a discussion as to the boundary lines between the two Acts see *Peake v Automotive Products* [1977] IRLR 105 and *Hoyland v Asda Stores* [2006] IRLR 468.) In order to bring a claim for sex discrimination, an employee must be employed under a contract of service or apprenticeship or any other contract to personally execute any work or labour (SDA 1975, s 82(1)). This is the same test as described at para 32.03 above, but see also *Mingley v Pennock & Ivory* [2004] IRLR 373. There can be no claim for sex discrimination (including by reason of marital status, civil partnership, and gender reassignment) where an employee works wholly outside Great Britain (SDA 1975, ss 6 and 10). However, from October 2005, if the employer has a place of business at an establishment in Great Britain, the work the employee is doing is for the purposes of the business carried on at that establishment and the employee is ordinarily resident in Great Britain when she is recruited or at any time during the course of the employment, then she may have a claim (SDA 1975, s 10(1), (1A)). As the provisions relating to race discrimination and discrimination on grounds of religion or belief or sexual orientation are substantially the same as those relating to sex discrimination, the substantive tests are not set out separately in the sections which deal with these claims and the statements of law made here will apply to those claims. The appropriate references to the RRA 1976 only are included below. Equally, cases relating to race discrimination are quoted as authority for the general propositions they support where appropriate.

32.13 There can be no claim for sex discrimination in the following cases:

(a) ministers of religion (SDA 1975, s 19);
(b) arrangements regarding the provision of certain accommodation facilities (SDA 1975, ss 46 and 47);
(c) prison officers (SDA 1975, s 18) (although the blanket exception only applies to requirements that people should be of a particular height);
(d) special treatment afforded to women in connection with pregnancy and childbirth (SDA 1975, s 2(2)).

32.14 The SDA applies not only to direct acts of discrimination, where an employee can show that a member of the opposite sex has been treated more favourably on any particular matter, but also to indirect discrimination, victimization, and harassment.

32.15 The basic test is whether the individual would have received the same treatment from the employer or potential employer but for his or her own sex, the fact he intends to undergo, is undergoing, or has undergone a gender reassignment, or his or her marital or civil partnership status (SDA 1975, ss 1(1), 2A, 3). For the remainder of this section, the term 'sex' shall also refer to discrimination on the basis of marital or civil partnership. Gender reassignment is dealt with at para 32.25 below.

32.16 Direct discrimination occurs when a person is receiving less favourable treatment on account of his or her sex (SDA 1975, ss 1(2)(a), 3; RRA 1976, s 1(1)(a)). Usually, this involves the identification of an actual comparator but it is also open to the claimant to base the claim on a 'hypothetical' comparator (*Shamoon v Chief Constable of the Royal Ulster Constabulary* [2003] ICR 337). The exception to this is where a pregnant woman is claiming. Case law has held that in this situation, no comparator is necessary as this is a gender-specific situation (*Dekker v Stichting VJV-Centrum Plus* [1992] ICR 325, ECJ; *Webb v EMO Air Cargo (UK) Ltd* [1994] ICR 770 but now enshrined in statute rather than simply being a product of case law (SDA 1975, s 3A and see *Equal Opportunities Commission v Secretary of State for Trade and Industry* [2007] IRLR 327). Note, however, the remarks by Mummery LJ in *Madarassy v Nomura International plc* [2007] IRLR 246 which suggest that comparators may be of use in pregnancy discrimination cases). In all other cases there are two key questions, as follows:

(1) Has the complainant been less favourably treated? Unreasonable treatment alone is not enough, if everyone else is being treated unreasonably; there has to be some differential

(*Glasgow City Council v Zafar* [1998] ICR 120, HL). Equally, different treatment is not enough; it has to be less favourable (*Smith v Safeway plc* [1996] ICR 868, CA). At this stage, the burden of proof is on the complainant (SDA 1975, s 63A; RRA 1976, s 54A). The claimant must prove the fact of less favourable treatment on a prescribed ground on the balance of probabilities. Inferences can be drawn from the primary facts and evasive or equivocal responses to a statutory questionnaire by the respondent employer can be taken into account (*Igen Ltd v Wong* [2005] IRLR 258; *Anya v University of Oxford* [2001] IRLR 377; *Barton v Investec Henderson Crosthwaite Securities Limited* [2003] ICR 1205, EAT; *Madarassy v Nomura International plc* [2007] IRLR 246).

(2) Was the less favourable treatment on the ground of the person's sex, marital status, civil partnership, or gender reassignment? Motive is generally irrelevant (in the sense that a good motive for discriminating will not absolve the discriminator of liability: *James v Eastleigh Borough Council* [1990] IRLR 288, HL). At this stage the burden of proof transfers to the respondent employer and the employer must prove that he did not commit and is not to be treated as committing that act. The test is on the balance of probabilities, but the tribunal will normally require cogent evidence. (SDA 1975, s 63A; RRA 1976, s 54A; *Igen Ltd v Wong* [2005] IRLR 258; *Anya v University of Oxford* [2001] IRLR 377; *Barton v Investec Henderson Crosthwaite Securities Limited* [2003] ICR 1205, EAT; *Madarassy v Nomura International plc* [2007] IRLR 246). There is no concept of transferred discrimination in the SDA 1975: see *MacDonald v Advocate General for Scotland* [2003] UKHL 34, although, arguably, such a concept exists in the Equal Treatment Directive.

Sexual harassment can take the form of unwelcome sexual attention, a suggestion that sexual activity or its refusal may help or hinder a career, sustained obscene or lewd language or behaviour, or sexually offensive material. There is also a self-standing claim of harassment in the SDA 1975, which is where a person engages in unwanted conduct that is related to the complainant's sex and which has the purpose or effect of violating another person's dignity or creating an intimidating, hostile, degrading, humiliating, or offensive environment for her (SDA 1975, s 4A(1)(a) and see the similar provision in RRA 1976, s 3A(1). As to the distinction between the words '*related to*' and '*on grounds of*' see *Equal Opportunities Commission v Secretary of State for Trade and Industry* [2007] IRLR 327). Additionally, for sex discrimination only, there will be sexual harassment if on the grounds of her sex, a person engages in any form of unwanted verbal, non-verbal, or physical conduct of a sexual nature that has the purpose of violating another person's dignity or creating an intimidating, hostile, degrading, or humiliating environment for her and/or on the ground of her rejection of or submission to unwanted conduct of this kind, a person treats her less favourably than the person would treat her had she not rejected, or submitted, to the conduct (SDA 1975, s 4A(1)(b) and (c)). Conduct will only be regarded as having this effect if, having regard to all the circumstances, including, in particular, the perception of the victim, it would be reasonably considered as having that effect (SDA 1975, s 4A(2) and see similar provision in RRA 1976, s 3(A)(2)). For a recent discussion of harassment (albeit in the context of the Race Relations Act 1976) see *Dhaliwal v Richmond Pharmacology* [2009] IRLR 336. **32.17**

The SDA 1975 also applies where a provision, criterion, or practice is applied to everyone, but which subtly discriminates against a class of people, the majority of whom are of one sex, and detriment is suffered by the complainant who is part of that group of people. Married people and those in civil partnerships can also complain of indirect discrimination, but those undergoing gender reassignment cannot. The test is that the treatment puts or would put a woman at a particular disadvantage when compared with a man and which puts her at that disadvantage (SDA 1975, s 1(2)(b); RRA 1976, s 1(1)(b) and 1(1)(c) but see also para 32.35 below). It also appears that where a group comprising mainly of men is treated more favourably than a group made up mainly of women, that a claim of indirect discrimination might be maintained even where a 'neutral' provision, criterion, or practice cannot be identified: see *GMB v Allen* [2008] EWCA Civ 810, [2008] IRLR 690. Treating groups less favourably can, therefore, amount to a provision, criterion, or practice. **32.18**

32.19 Although the test for indirect discrimination must be applied in each case, examples of indirect discrimination include:

(a) a requirement or policy that people should be a certain height;
(b) treatment that disadvantages workers with young children (which may also discriminate on the grounds of marital status) in particular, inflexibility in relation to flexible working, for example, part-time and home working, or job sharing (*Bilka-Kaufhaus GmbH v Weber von Hartz* [1987] ICR 110; *Clymo v Wandsworth Borough Council* [1989] ICR 250; *Robinson v Oddbins Ltd* [1996] 27 DCLD 1; *Lockworth v Crawley Warren Group Ltd* [2001] IDS Employment Law Brief 680, EAT);
(c) a requirement or practice that candidates should have a long period of previously uninterrupted working—which tends to exclude women who have taken time off work to look after children;
(d) a requirement or practice that applicants should be aged 25 to 35 (which excludes many women with young children) (*Price v Civil Service Commission and the Society of Civil and Public Servants* [1978] IRLR 3);
(e) a requirement that employees should work long and uncertain hours (*London Underground Ltd v Edwards (No 2)* [1998] IRLR 364).

32.20 Once an employee can show direct discrimination in that she is being treated less favourably than a named person, or even that she is being treated less favourably than a hypothetical member of the opposite sex and the employer has been unable to show that the reason for the treatment was something other than her sex, the employer has two possible defences: that it was an employee's actions, not the employer's, which were discriminatory and that the employer did everything reasonably practicable to prevent those actions (SDA 1975, s 41(3); RRA 1976, s 32(3)), or that gender was a genuine occupational qualification for the job (SDA 1975, s 7(2)).

32.21 Usually, it is very difficult for an employer to avoid a claim of discrimination on the grounds that it is not vicariously liable for it (SDA 1975, s 41(1)). In particular, an argument that the employee was not acting in the course of her employment when he did the discriminatory act will not succeed (*Jones v Tower Boot Co Ltd* [1997] IRLR 168) although this becomes more blurred at work-related social events (*Chief Constable of the Lincolnshire Police v Stubbs* [1991] IRLR 81; *Sidhu v Aerospace Composite Technology Ltd* [2000] IRLR 602). The exception to this is where the employer took such steps as were reasonably practicable to ensure that the act or type of act was proscribed (SDA 1975, s 41(3)). The employee himself or herself may, however, still be liable. It is to be noted that a principal cannot avail himself of the employers' defence in relation to the acts of an agent: SDA 1975, s 41(3).

32.22 The genuine occupational qualification defence applies to claims for sex discrimination (but not marital/civil partnership discrimination or discrimination against those undergoing gender reassignment) in relation to arrangements made for filling a job; refusal of a job; denial of opportunities for promotion, transfer, or training for the job in question or that there is a genuine need for a position to be filled by a person of a particular sex, for example:

(a) Physiology and authenticity in entertainment matters, for example, models and actors.
(b) Requirements of decency or privacy, for example, lavatory attendants.
(c) Jobs in a single-sex establishment such as a prison.
(d) Work abroad which can only be done by a man, for example, certain types of work in the Middle East.
(e) A job which is one of two to be done by a married couple.
(f) A job which requires personal services towards the welfare and education of others which can most effectively be done by a person of the same sex.
(g) A job which is likely to involve the holder living in or working in a private home with a degree of physical or social contact with other persons living there or involving intimate details of such person's life, such as a private nurse or companion.

(h) A job where the employee would have to live in, and there are no separate sleeping or toilet arrangements between the sexes.

(SDA 1975, s 7(2))

The defences to an allegation of indirect discrimination used to be that the conditions which have been imposed are justifiable on reasonable, non-sexual grounds, or grounds not related to marital status, for example, because of economic or administrative reasons, safety, hygiene, or management experience. In establishing these grounds, the employer must conduct a balancing exercise between the real business need dictating the imposition of the provision, criterion, or practice and the impact the imposition will have on the woman (*Rainey v Greater Glasgow Health Board* [1987] ICR 129; *Allonby v Accrington and Rossendale College* [2000] IRLR 364, CA; *GMB v Allen* [2008] EWCA Civ 810, [2008] IRLR 690). Now, the statutory test requires that the business reason for the imposition of the provision, criterion, or condition is a proportionate means of achieving a legitimate aim (SDA 1975, s 1(2)(b)(iii); RRA 1976, s 1(1A)(b)(iii) but see para 32.35 in relation to the differences in the tests in the SDA 1975 and RRA 1976). However, most commentators believe that the employer would be wise to consider both the old and the new tests. **32.23**

Victimization arises if an employer treats any person less favourably than others because that person threatens to bring proceedings, to give evidence or information, to take any action or to make any allegations concerning the employer with reference to SDA 1975 (or EqPA 1970) (SDA 1975, s 4(1); RRA 1976 s 2(1)). The allegation must be made in good faith to obtain the protection (SDA 1975, s 4(2); RRA 1976, s 2(2)). The test involves comparing the victimized person against someone who has not performed a protected act and looking at the subjective reasons for the employer's actions. There is no need for conscious motivation connected with the discrimination legislation (*Nagarajan v London Regional Transport* [1999] IRLR 572, HL; *Chief Constable of West Yorkshire Police v Khan* [2001] IRLR 830, HL). It is unlikely that honest and reasonable steps taken in the course of litigation could amount to victimization since they would be unlikely to amount to detriment for the purposes of the SDA 1975: see *St Helen's Metropolitan Borough Council v Derbyshire* [2007] IRLR 540 and *Bird v Sylvester* [2008] IRLR 232. **32.24**

SDA 1975 also protects against direct and indirect discrimination on grounds of marital status and gender reassignment: **32.25**

(a) *Gender reassignment* The test for discrimination on the grounds of gender reassignment is different. A person (A) will discriminate against a person (B) where A treats B less favourably and does so because B intends to undergo, is undergoing, or has undergone gender reassignment. 'Less favourably' has a specific meaning where it relates to absence from work for vocational training—it means either that the person is treated less favourably than he would be if the absence was due to sickness or injury or less favourably than he would be if the absence was due to some other cause and, having regard to the circumstances of the case, it is reasonable for him to be treated no less favourably (SDA 1975, s 2A).
(b) *Marital discrimination* Marital discrimination applies where there is direct or indirect discrimination by reason of a person's marital status or civil partnership (SDA 1975, s 3). The tests are identical to those relating to sex discrimination.

It will be a defence to a claim for discrimination on grounds of gender reassignment in relation to arrangements made for filling a job; refusal of a job; the terms on which employment is offered; denial of opportunities for promotion, transfer, or training for the job in question or where the employee is dismissed from it or subjected to detriment as a result of it, that being a man or woman is a genuine occupational qualification and the employer can show that the treatment was reasonable in view of the relevant circumstances (SDA 1975, s 7A). **32.26**

32.27 Relevant circumstances are all of those listed under para 32.22 above and additionally (but in relation to certain aspects of discrimination only) where:

(a) the job involves the holder of the job being liable to perform intimate searches under statutory powers;
(b) the job is in a private home and may result in objections due to the degree of physical or social contact with the person in the private home or the knowledge of the intimate details of such a person's life;
(c) the job involves living on the work premises and others may object to sharing premises with someone undergoing gender reassignment and no reasonable alternative arrangements can be made;
(d) the job involves the provision of personal services to vulnerable individuals and no cover can be provided while the gender reassignment is being done.

(SDA 1975, s 7B)

32.28 Remedies for sex discrimination include a declaration and unlimited compensation to put the employee in the position as if the discrimination had not taken place. The employee can also recover compensation for injury to feelings. See Chapter 26 in relation to this.

32.29 Again, there is a European aspect to sex discrimination which works in broadly the same way as in relation to equal pay, as both Article 141 and the Equal Treatment Directive provide for equal treatment of men and women. However, unlike Article 141, the Equal Treatment Directive is not directly effective albeit that employment tribunals are under a duty to read the SDA 1975 in a consistent manner with the Equal Treatment Directive: see Case C–106/89 *Marleasing SA v La Comercial Internacional de Alimentacion SA* [1990] ECR I–4135.

32.30 An employee may submit a questionnaire under the SDA 1975 (in prescribed form) asking the employer to confirm or deny certain facts. The employer must answer the questionnaire within eight weeks and any failure to answer, or an inaccurate or evasive answer, may be taken into account by any employment tribunal considering the issue of discrimination at a later date, and it may draw adverse inferences from such answers or failure to answer (SDA 1975, s 7 and see para 32.09 above). A failure to answer a statutory questionnaire (or an evasive or equivocal answer therein) does not automatically lead to the drawing of adverse inferences however, and employment tribunals must have regard to what inferences can properly be drawn in the light of such a failure: *D'Silva v NATFHE* [2008] IRLR 412.

32.31 Individuals who feel they may have been subject to discrimination may ask the Equality and Human Rights Commission (EHRC) either to conduct an official investigation on their behalf or to assist in the conduct of any claim.

32.32 If the EHRC gives notice that it intends to conduct a formal investigation, the employer must supply all information requested. Fines are imposed for failures to provide such evidence. In addition, the employer should comply with any unlawful act notice that may be sent following the investigation. An appeal against the notice must be made to an employment tribunal within six weeks of the notice being served (Equality Act 2006, ss 20 and 21, and Sch 2).

32.33 Prior to bringing a complaint, the employee might have to raise a grievance under the statutory dispute procedures or she will be barred from bringing a claim (EA 2002, s 32). Any complaint to the employment tribunal must be brought within three months of the act complained of (SDA 1975, s 76(1)) unless the tribunal thinks it just and equitable to extend the period (SDA 1975, s 76(5) and paras 3.84–3.88) or the employee does bring a grievance in which case the three-month time limit will be extended (Employment Act (Dispute Resolution) Regulations 2004, reg 15 and see paras 3.93–3.99). Continuing discrimination ends only when the practice ceases to be discriminatory. There is a distinction between a single act with continuing effect (where that single act will start the three-month time limit) and the constant repetition of discriminatory acts (where the last discriminatory act may start the time limit running, but all of the previous acts may also be in time too) (SDA 1975, s 76(6)(b), see Chapter 3, para 3.12 *et seq.*). The requirement to raise a grievance will no longer exist from 6 April 2009. However, it will continue to have effect for those cases where the acts complained of commenced before 6 April 2009 and in circumstances where a grievance was raised or a complaint was issued prior to 4 July 2009. Regulation 15 has not been repealed, but presumably will have no legal effect in circumstances where the statutory grievance procedures have no application.

The EOC (now amalgamated into the EHRC) issued a code of practice pursuant to its power to do so (SDA 1975, s 56A; Code of Practice on Sex Discrimination, Equal Opportunity Policies, Procedures and Practices in Employment (1985)). A failure to abide by the code will not render an employer liable to proceedings, but the code will be admissible in any employment tribunal proceedings. **32.34**

C. RACE RELATIONS ACT 1976

Employers must not discriminate on the grounds of colour, race, nationality, or ethnic or national origins against any person of either sex. This applies not only to recruitment policies, treatment during employment and career structures, and dismissal, but also to contractual terms. In order to bring a claim for race discrimination an employee must be employed under a contract of service or of apprenticeship or a contract to personally execute any work or labour (RRA 1976, s 78) (see para 32.12 above). There can be no claim for race discrimination where an employee works wholly outside Great Britain unless, if the employer has a place of business at an establishment in Great Britain, the work the employee is doing is for the purposes of the business carried on at the establishment and the employee is ordinarily resident in Great Britain when he is recruited or at any time during the course of the employment (RRA 1976, ss 4 and 8) when the employee may be able to claim. The provisions relating to race discrimination are substantially the same as those relating to sex discrimination in terms of the definitions of direct and indirect discrimination, victimization, and harassment, the defences available, and the burden of proof, and are therefore not dealt with separately in this book (although the relevant references to the RRA 1976 are included in the section on sex discrimination at paras 32.12 *et seq.* above). Note, however, that the burden of proof provisions in RRA 1976, s 54A do not apply to victimization claims: see *Oyarce v Cheshire County Council* [2008] IRLR 653. In addition the test for indirect discrimination under RRA 1976 is twofold: **32.35**

(a) where the discrimination relates to the employee's racial group, colour, or nationality the test is whether the application of a 'requirement or condition' (as opposed to the wider 'provision, criterion or practice') leads to the indirect discrimination, and justification is not subject to the 'legitimate aim/proportionate means' requirement (RRA 1976, s 1(1)(b)); and
(b) where the indirect discrimination is on grounds of race, ethnic, or national origins, the test is the same as indirect sex discrimination (see paras 32.19 and 32.23 above (RRA 1976, s 1(1A)).

Generally as the test under RRA 1976, s 1(1A) is regarded as easier to satisfy, most claims will now be brought under this section. The reason for the two separate tests is that the provisions of RRA 1976 are wider than the Race Directive. The RRA 1976 prohibits discrimination on grounds of colour and nationality whereas the Race Directive does not. As such, the test of indirect discrimination found in the Race Directive only applies to those grounds set out in the Race Directive (race, ethnic, or national origins) and not to those additional grounds which are not protected by the Race Directive. It follows that the burden of proof provisions in RRA 1976, s 54A (which also reflect the Race Directive) do not apply to claims of discrimination on grounds of colour or nationality. As such, the old rules set out in *King v Great Britain-China Centre* [1992] ICR 516 and *Anya v University of Oxford* [2004] ICR 847 will apply: see *Okonu v*

G4S Services UK Limited [2008] ICR 598, although in relation to 'colour', *Okonu* has not been followed in *Abbey National plc v Chagger* [2008] IRLR 86. In any event, the Equality Bill (in clause 130) will remove this anomaly in circumstances where it becomes law.

32.36 Examples of indirect race discrimination include:

(a) special treatment of workers from a particular area with a predominantly ethnic population;
(b) imposition of language tests which would exclude large numbers from ethnic minority groups.

32.37 There is a genuine occupational qualification defence to a race discrimination claim so that it will be a defence to a claim for race discrimination in relation to arrangements made for filling a job; refusal of a job; denial of opportunities for promotion, transfer, or training for the job in question, that there is a genuine need for a position to be filled by a person of a particular race. For example:

(a) To provide authenticity in entertainment (for example, acting).
(b) Jobs requiring personal services towards the welfare of others which can most effectively be done by a person of a particular race (for example, community officers).
(c) Jobs in establishments which require the maintenance of a particular ambience, for example, in an ethnic bar or restaurant.

(RRA 1976, s 5)

32.38 There can be no claim for race discrimination in the following cases:

(a) Employment in a private household (RRA 1976, s 4(3)).
(b) Selection for sports representation and competitions (RRA 1976, s 39).
(c) Acts safeguarding national security (RRA 1976, s 42).

32.39 An employee may submit a questionnaire in the same way as it is possible to do so in respect of sex discrimination claims (RRA 1976, s 69). The position in relation to grievances and the timing of claims is the same as described at para 32.33 above (see also RRA 1976, s 68). Note the change in the law from 6 April 2009.

32.40 The Commission for Racial Equality (CRE) fulfilled the same role in relation to race as the EOC did in relation to sex. It has now been replaced by the EHRC pursuant to the Equality Act 2006.

32.41 Note that segregation of individuals on racial grounds will always be discriminatory, even where it does not involve less favourable treatment. 'Racial grounds' for this and other purposes means colour, race, nationality, or ethnic or national origins (RRA 1976, s 3(1)). 'Ethnic origins' requires there to be a segment of the population distinguished from others by a sufficient combination of shared customs, beliefs, traditions, and characteristics derived from a common or presumed common past, even if not drawn from what, in biological terms, was a common racial stock (*Mandla v Dowell Lee* [1983] ICR 385). Sikhs, Jews, and those of the Romany race are all ethnic groups; Rastafarians are not. English and Scottish people are separate national groups. An employee will be discriminated against on 'racial grounds' if he is treated less favourably on the basis he refuses to implement a racially discriminatory policy or is affected by that policy irrespective of that person's race (*Showboat v Owens* [1984] 1 WLR 384; *Weathersfield v Sargent* [1999] IRLR 94; *Redfearn v Serco Ltd* [2006] IRLR 623, CA).

32.42 The CRE issued a Code of Practice in 1983 which has been recently updated (RRA 1976, s 47; Commission for Racial Equality: Code of Practice on Racial Equality in Employment (2005)). A failure to abide by the code will not render an employer liable to proceedings, but the code will be admissible in any employment tribunal proceedings.

D. DISABILITY DISCRIMINATION ACT 1995

Statute also provides that it is unlawful to discriminate against employees on grounds of their disability. An employee for these purposes means 'employed' under a contract of service or of apprenticeship or a contract personally to execute any work or labour (DDA 1995, s 68; see paras 32.03 and 32.12 above). There can be no claim for disability discrimination where the complainant works wholly outside Great Britain. However, if the employer has a place of business at an establishment in Great Britain, the work the employee is doing is for the purposes of the business carried on at that establishment and the employee is ordinarily resident in Great Britain when he is recruited or at any time during the course of the employment, then he may have a claim (DDA 1995, s 68(2) and (2A)). **32.43**

A person has a disability if he has a mental or physical impairment which has a substantial and long-term adverse effect (ie at least 12 months) on his ability to carry out normal day-to-day activities (DDA 1995, s 1(1), Sch 1). **32.44**

Physical or mental impairment includes any physical or mental illness, but does not include such conditions as alcoholism, drug or nicotine addiction, hay fever, pyromania, kleptomania, voyeurism (DDA 1995, Sch 1, para 1; Disability Discrimination (Employment) Regulations 1996, SI 1996/1455). With effect from December 2005, the requirement that a mental illness be clinically well recognized was removed. Further, a person who has cancer, HIV infection, or multiple sclerosis is to be deemed to have a disability and hence to be a disabled person (DDA 1995, Sch 1, para 6A). However, more recently the tribunals have been concentrating on effects of the disability rather than the precise cause of it (*Millar v The Board of the Inland Revenue* [2006] IRLR 112). **32.45**

The disability must actually affect the employee's ability to carry out normal day-to-day activities and must be long-term, that is, likely to last more than 12 months (even though its onset may only be in the future) (DDA 1995, Sch 1, paras 2 and 8). **32.46**

At present, an impairment may be taken to affect normal day-to-day activities only if it affects one of the following: **32.47**

(a) mobility;
(b) manual dexterity;
(c) physical coordination;
(d) continence;
(e) the ability to lift, carry, or otherwise move everyday objects;
(f) speech, hearing, or eyesight;
(g) memory or ability to concentrate, learn, or understand; or
(h) perception of the risk of physical danger.

(DDA 1995, Sch 1, para 4(1)).

However, the fact that the activities which are impaired are not ones which appear in the above list does not exclude a finding of disability: a broader approach should be taken (*Hewett v Motorola Ltd* [2004] IRLR 545, EAT). Indeed, the Government is, at present, proposing the removal of the above list in the forthcoming equality bill. Severe disfigurement is deemed to have a substantial effect on the ability of the person concerned to carry out normal day-to-day activities (DDA 1995, Sch 1, para 3).

The adverse effect must be substantial. Substantial means 'more than minor or trivial' rather than 'very large' (guidance on the Definition of Disability (2006), para B1—see para 32.50 below). The employment tribunal can take into account the fact that medication may reduce those affects. Furthermore, where an adverse effect ceases to be substantial but is likely to recur, it is deemed to recur: see DDA 1995, Sch 1, para 2(2); *Spence v Intype Libra Ltd* [2007] All ER (D) 261; and *Richmond Adult Community College v McDougall* [2008] IRLR 227. As to the **32.48** question of recurrence, see the decision of the House of Lords in *SCA Packaging v Boyle* [2009] UKHL 37 overturning *Swift v Chief Constable of Wiltshire Constabulary* [2004] IRLR 540. If an effect 'could well recur' it should be treated as being likely to recur for the purposes of the definition of disability.

32.49 Each case must be assessed on the facts and the available medical evidence. So, for example, stress or anxiety will not amount to a disability in every case and medical evidence will be important (although the employment tribunal has been known to take a more relaxed approach) (*Morgan v Staffordshire University* [2002] IRLR 190, EAT). Full guidance as to how to approach the issue of whether there is a disability on the basis of the questions set out above was given in *Goodwin v The Patent Office* [1999] IRLR 4.

32.50 The Government has also issued guidance as to the definition of disability ('Guidance on matters to be taken into account in determining questions relating to disability' (2006), issued pursuant to DDA 1995, s 3(9)). The Guidance came into force from 1 May 2006 replacing the 1996 Guidance. The Guidance must be taken into account by the employment tribunal (DDA 1995, s 3(3)). Case law has also stressed that this must be taken into account when considering claims under DDA 1995. Ultimately, an employer should look at all the circumstances but concentrate on those actions which the employee *cannot* do (*Goodwin v The Patent Office* [1999] IRLR 4; *Leonard v Southern Derbyshire Chamber of Commerce* [2001] IRLR 19).

32.51 Once the fact of disability has been established, there are a number of tests relating to disability discrimination: disability-related discrimination; direct discrimination; non-compliance with duty to make reasonable adjustments; justification; victimization; knowledge of the disability; and harassment.

32.52 *Disability-related discrimination* This is where, for a reason which relates to the disabled person's disability, the employer treats the complainant less favourably than he treats or would treat others to whom the reason does not or would not apply (DDA 1995, s 3A(1)). The correct comparator has historically been considered to be someone to whom the relevant reason did not apply rather than someone who did not have the relevant disability. For example, in *Clark v Novacold Ltd* [1999] ICR 951 the example of a restaurant which did not allow dogs on the premises, with the effect that a blind person with a guide dog could not eat there, was considered. It was held that for the purposes of disability-related discrimination the proper comparator was a person without a dog rather than a non-disabled person with a dog. However, in *Lewisham London Borough Council v Malcolm* [2008] 1 AC 1399 (a case unrelated to employment but interpreting the same provision in the DDA 1995) the House of Lords overruled *Clark v Novacold* and stated that the correct comparator in a disability-related discrimination case was a person who was not disabled. This would appear to have the effect that there is no difference as between direct discrimination (see below) and disability-related discrimination. However, the appellate courts have held in a series of decisions including *Child Suport Agency v Truman* [2009] IRLR 277 that *Malcolm* applies as much in the employment context as in other contexts.

32.53 *Direct discrimination* A person directly discriminates against a disabled person if, on the ground of the disabled person's disability, he treats the disabled person less favourably than he treats or would treat a person not having that particular disability whose relevant circumstances, including his abilities, are the same as or not materially different from, those of the disabled person (see DDA 1995, s 3A(5) and DRC Code of Practice: Employment and Occupation (2004), para 4.37 as well as the EAT's decision in *High Quality Lifestyles Limited v Watts* [2006] IRLR 850). The ECJ has recently held in *Coleman v Attridge Law* [2008] All ER (D) 245 that the Framework Directive includes a prohibition on transferred discrimination (otherwise known as associative discrimination). Further, in the same case, the London South Employment Tribunal has held that the DDA 1995, when read in line with the Framework Directive, includes transferred discrimination.

32.54 *Failure to implement adjustments* An employer also discriminates against a disabled person if he fails to comply with a duty to make reasonable adjustments (DDA 1995, s 3A(2)).

Where a provision, criterion, or practice applied by an employer, or any physical feature of premises occupied by an employer places the disabled person concerned at a substantial disadvantage which is personal to him, it is the duty of the employer to take such steps as it is reasonable for him to take, in all the circumstances of the case, in order to prevent the provision, criterion, or practice or feature, having that effect (DDA 1995, s 4A(1) and *O'Hanlon v Commissioners for HM Revenue & Customs* [2007] IRLR 404). Failure to take such steps will be a breach of DDA 1995. Examples of such adjustments would be the alteration of working hours, the provision of training, the modifying of instruction or reference manuals, and the modification of premises. What is reasonable will be determined by taking into account all the circumstances (DDA 1995, s 4(A)). The employment tribunal will judge this objectively (*Morse v Wiltshire County Council* [1998] ICR 1023). Examples of reasonable adjustments are:

(a) making adjustments to premises;
(b) allocating some of the disabled person's duties to another person;
(c) transferring him to fill an existing vacancy;
(d) altering his working hours;
(e) assigning him a different place of work;
(f) allowing him to be absent during working hours for rehabilitation, assessment, or treatment;
(g) giving him, or arranging for him to be given, training;
(h) acquiring or modifying equipment;
(i) modifying instructions or reference materials;
(j) modifying procedures for testing or assessment;
(k) providing a reader or interpreter;
(l) providing supervision.

(Disability Rights Commission (DRC) Code of Practice: Employment and Occupation (2004))

It is now clear that a failure to consider making reasonable adjustments does not amount to a failure to make reasonable adjustments in and of itself: see *Tarbuck v Sainsbury's* [2006] IRLR 664 and *Spence v Intype Libra Ltd* [2007] All ER (D) 261.

In looking at whether it is reasonable for an employer to take a particular step, a court will consider the effectiveness of the step in preventing the disadvantage, the practicability of the step, the financial and other costs of the adjustment, and the extent of any disruption involved, the extent of the employer's financial or other resources, the availability to the employer of financial or other assistance to help make the adjustment, the nature of the employer's activities, and the size of his undertaking and, in relation to private households, the extent to which taking the step would disrupt the household or disturb any person residing there (DRC Code of Practice: Employment and Occupation (2004). An employer may well be required to spend some money on the reasonable adjustments (*Ross v Ryanair Ltd and Stansted Airport Ltd* [2005] 1 WLR 2447). The House of Lords has also given a wide interpretation to the duty—'arrangements' appear to encompass almost anything which puts the disabled person at a disadvantage and steps include transferring the disabled person to a new role, not simply giving him an opportunity to apply for it (*Archibald v Fife Council* [2004] IRLR 197). However, it will rarely be a reasonable adjustment to pay an employee who is off sick full pay (*O'Hanlon v HMRC* [2007] IRLR 404) save for in circumstances where an employee could return to work with adjustments (*Meikle v Nottinghamshire County Council* [2004] IRLR 703). In a claim for adjustments, the burden of proof falls on the employee to show the application of a provision, criterion, or practice which puts disabled people at a particular disadvantage and puts the claimant at that disadvantage and to point to reasonable adjustments which could have prevented the same disadvantage. The burden will then shift to the employer to show that those adjustments were not reasonable: see *Project Institute Management v Latif* [2007] IRLR 579. **32.55**

32.56 *Justification* An employer can rely on a defence of justification in relation to disability-related discrimination but not direct discrimination. The defence will not apply in relation to disability-related discrimination where the employer had a duty to make reasonable adjustments and failed to do so, unless he can show the justification would have applied even if he had made the reasonable adjustments (DDA 1995, s 3A(6)). For discrimination to be justified, the reason for it must be both material to the circumstances of the particular case and substantial (DDA 1995, s 3A(3)). When looking at whether the grounds are material and substantial, an employment tribunal should not substitute its own view, but consider whether the employer has established that they are reasonable and substantial, and then whether the employer's response was within a range of reasonable responses (*Jones v Post Office* [2001] ICR 805; *Williams v J Walter Thompson Group Ltd* [2005] IRLR 376).

32.57 *Victimization* A person (A) discriminates against another person (B) if he treats B less favourably and does so because B has brought proceedings against A or any other person under DDA 1995, given evidence or information in relation to such a claim, otherwise done anything under DDA 1995 in relation to A, or alleged that A has breached DDA 1995 or where A believes B intends to do so (DDA 1995, s 55). Any allegation must be made in good faith and must not be false (DDA 1995, s 55(4)).

32.58 *Harassment* A person subjects a disabled person to harassment where for a reason which relates to the disabled person's disability he engages in unwanted conduct which has the purpose or effect of violating the disabled person's dignity or creating an intimidating, hostile, degrading, humiliating, or offensive environment for him (DDA 1995, s 3B(1)). Conduct shall only be regarded as having this effect if having regard to all the circumstances, including, in particular, the perception of the victim, it should be reasonably considered as having that effect (DDA 1995, s 3(B)(2)).

32.59 *Knowledge of disability* Lack of knowledge of the disability might well amount to a defence to claims of direct disability discrimination (since if an employer had no knowledge of a disability it would be difficult to show that the employer was treating the employee less favourably on grounds of the disability in question) and can possibly amount to a defence in relation to the obligation to make reasonable adjustments (DDA 1995, s 4A(3)). Until *Lewisham London Borough Council v Malcolm* [2008] 3 WLR 194 it was considered that lack of knowledge of a disability could not amount to a defence for the purposes of a claim of disability-related discrimination (*HJ Heinz Co Ltd v Kenrick* [2000] IRLR 144). However, that proposition has been thrown into question by *Malcolm*. In any event, lack of knowledge does not prevent the employer from putting forward a defence of justification (*Quinn v Schwarzkopf* [2002] IRLR 602).

32.60 There can be no claim for disability discrimination in the following cases:

(a) members of the armed forces (DDA 1995, s 64(7));
(b) employees who work wholly outside Great Britain (DDA 1995, s 68(2)) (unless they are resident in Great Britain and the employer is resident in Great Britain (s 68(2A));
(c) employees who work on board ships, aircraft, or hovercraft (DDA 1995, s 68(2C)).

32.61 An employer is responsible for a discriminatory act carried out by an employee or agent or in some circumstances other persons in the control of the employer. If the employer took such steps as were reasonably practicable to ensure that the act or type of act was not committed by his employees, the employer itself will not be found guilty of discrimination (DDA 1995, s 58) (see also para 32.21 in relation to the similar provisions which appear in the SDA 1975).

32.62 Individuals who feel they may have been subject to discrimination may ask the EHRC either to conduct an official investigation on their behalf or to assist in the conduct of any claim (see further paras 32.31 to 32.32 in relation to this). If the complainant wishes to bring a claim on an individual basis, he must apply to the employment tribunal. However, the complainant must, prior to bringing a claim, raise a grievance under the statutory dispute procedures or he will be barred from bringing a claim (EA 2002, s 31). The normal time limit for bringing a claim is three months from the act complained of (DDA 1995 Sch 3, Part 1, para 3(1)) unless the tribunal thinks it is just and equitable to extend the time limit (DDA 1995 Sch 3, Part 1 para 3(2) and see paras 3.84 to 3.88). However, if the employee does bring a grievance, the three-month period will be extended (Employment Act (Dispute Resolutions) Regulations 2004, reg 15 and see paras 3.93 to 3.99). The requirement to raise a grievance will no longer apply from 6 April 2009 (see para 32.33 above).

It is also possible to submit a DDA questionnaire in a similar way to the other discrimination legislation (DDA 1995, s 56(2), (4); Disability Discrimination (Questions and Replies) Order 2004). **32.63**

E. DISCRIMINATION ON THE GROUNDS OF RELIGION OR BELIEF OR SEXUAL ORIENTATION

Employers must not discriminate on grounds of religion or belief or sexual orientation. The provisions relating to this type of discrimination are substantially the same as those which apply to sex and race discrimination claims (although the test for indirect discrimination is the same as sex discrimination and RRA 1976, s 1(1A) (see para 32.35 above)). The provisions prohibiting direct discrimination on grounds of sexual orientation/religion or belief are broad and include transferred discrimination: see *English v Thomas Sanderson Blinds Ltd* [2008] EWCA Civ 1421, [2009] 2 All ER 468. **32.64**

Religion or belief means any religion, religious belief, or philosophical belief (RBR 2003, reg 2(1)). The definition of 'religion' is broad and includes all those religions widely recognized in this country (see also *Hussain v Bhullar Bros (t/a BB Supersave)* ET Case No 1806638/04). 'Religious belief' may include other beliefs founded on religion. A philosophical belief must be a profound belief affecting a person's way of life, or perception of the world, such as atheism and humanism. Both can include a lack of belief. In *McClintock v Department for Constitutional Affairs* [2008] IRLR 29 the EAT held that to fall within the RBR 2003, there must be a religious or philosophical belief in which the individual actually believes. **32.65**

Sexual orientation means orientation towards people of the same sex, the opposite sex, or both (SOR 2003, reg 2(1)). The definition of sexual orientation appears to exclude sexual behaviour although note the judgment of Richards J in *R v Secretary of State for Trade and Industry and Christian Action Research Education* [2004] IRLR 430. **32.66**

There can be no claim for this kind of discrimination unless the employee comes within the category of 'worker' described in paras 32.03, 32.12, and 32.35 above. Equally, where an employee works wholly outside Great Britain, he will not be able to bring a claim unless the employee is resident in Great Britain at some point during his recruitment or employment and the employer is based at an establishment in Great Britain (RBR 2003, reg 9(1) and (2)). There will also be a genuine occupational qualification defence to allegations in relation to religion or belief discrimination where having regard to the nature of the employment or the context in which it is carried out, being of a particular religion or belief is a genuine and determining occupational requirement and it is proportionate to apply that requirement and either the person to whom the requirement is applied does not meet it or the employer believes they do not meet it. This exception will also apply slightly less strictly where the employer has an ethos based on religion or belief, when the employer should apply the same test but religion or belief should be a genuine occupational requirement for the job (RBR 2003, reg 7). **32.67**

There is also a genuine occupational qualification defence for sexual orientation. Where the employment is *not* for the purposes of organized religion, it is that being of a particular sexual orientation is a genuine and determining occupational requirement, that it is proportionate to apply that requirement in this case, and that the person does not satisfy the requirement or the employer believes they do not. Where the employment is for the purposes of organized reli- **32.68** gion, it is that the requirement relating to sexual orientation is applied so as to comply with the doctrines of the religion or because of the nature of the employment and the context in which it is carried out, so as to avoid conflicting with the strongly held religious convictions of a significant number of the religious followers and the person to whom the requirement is applied does not satisfy it or the employer believes they will not satisfy it (SOR 2003, reg 7).

32.69 There are exceptions under both sets of Regulations where the acts relate to matters of national security (reg 24 in both) and under SOR 2003 for benefits dependent on marital status (reg 25), although the second of these exceptions may be incompatible with European law: see *Maruko v Versorgungsanstalt der Deutschen Bühnen* [2008] IRLR 450.

32.70 Employees may submit questionnaires in relation to their claim of discrimination in the same way they can for a sex or race discrimination claim (RBR 2003, reg 33; SOR 2003, reg 33). The position in relation to grievances and the timing of claims is the same as described at para 32.33 above. From 1 October 2007, the Equality and Human Rights Commission have also had responsibility for discrimination on the grounds of sexual orientation and religious belief in the same way as it has for sex (see paras 32.31–32.32 above).

F. DISCRIMINATION ON THE GROUNDS OF AGE

32.71 After an extensive period of consultation, the Employment Equality (Age) Regulations 2006 (EEAR 2006) come into force on 1 October 2006. The Regulations implement the last remaining strand of the Equal Treatment Framework Directive (2000/78/EC). The Regulations are supported by the ACAS Guide 'Age and the Workplace' (the 'ACAS Age Guidance'). This is currently the only official DTI guidance on EEAR 2006 and will, no doubt, be referred to in the Employment Tribunal (although note EEAR 2006 contains no specific provision for the issuance of Codes of Practice; cf the other discrimination legislation). EEAR 2006 introduces the concepts of direct and indirect discrimination, but also a new 'fair' means of dismissal on grounds of retirement. This chapter will deal only with the claim of age discrimination, defences to that claim, and exceptions.

32.72 In order to bring a claim for age discrimination, an employee must be employed under a contract of service or apprenticeship or a contract personally to do work (EEAR 2006, reg 2; see also paras 32.03 and 32.12 above). There can be no claim for age discrimination unless the employment of the employee is regarded as being at an establishment in Great Britain. This will be the case only where the employee does his work wholly or partly in Great Britain (EEAR 2006, reg 10(1)(a)). If he works outside Great Britain, he may still be covered if the employer has a place of business at an establishment in Great Britain, the work is for the purposes of the business carried on at that establishment, and the employee is ordinarily resident in Great Britain when he is recruited or at any time during the course of employment (EEAR 2006, reg 10(2)).

32.73 Employees in almost all professions will be able to bring a claim for age discrimination. There are no exemptions for the police, prison officers, etc, although see the general exemptions at para 10 of the checklist for claims of age discrimination below. However, those doing service in any of the naval, military, or air forces (EEAR 2006, reg 28), unpaid office holders (EEAR 2006, reg 10(8)), and unpaid volunteers (unless they are in an employment relationship or gaining vocational work experience) will not be protected.

32.74 EEAR 2006 outlaws both direct and indirect discrimination, discrimination by victimization, and harassment. However, unlike the other discrimination legislation it is possible to put forward a defence of objective justification for both direct *and* indirect discrimination. There is also a much more significant number of exceptions.

32.75 Direct discrimination occurs when on the grounds of a person's age, they receive less favourable treatment than other persons (EEAR 2006, reg 3(1)(a)). This test is the same as the test in the other discrimination legislation (see para 32.16 above). In relation to comparators, see EEAR 2006, reg 3(2) and para 32.16 above. It is arguable that reg 3(1)(a) does not properly implement the Framework Directive since it fails to include a prohibition on transferred discrimination: see *Coleman v Attridge Law* [2008] All ER (D) 245.

Indirect discrimination also mirrors the test in SDA 1975 (see para 32.18 above). Indirect discrimination will occur when an employer applies a provision, criterion, or practice to an employee which he would apply equally to persons not in the same age group as that employee, but which puts or would put people in the same age group as that employee at a disadvantage and does actually put that employee at a disadvantage (EEAR 2006, reg 3(1)(b)). **32.76**

For these purposes 'age' includes a person's apparent age, so a mistaken belief as to an individual's age which leads to discrimination will be no defence (EEAR 2006, reg 3(3)(b)). For the purposes of the definition of indirect discrimination, 'age group' is defined as being 'a group of persons defined by reference to age, whether by reference to a particular age or a range of ages' (EEAR 2006, reg 3(3)(b)). There is currently no further guidance as to what this will mean in practice. **32.77**

There will be a defence to a claim for direct and/or indirect discrimination where there is a genuine occupational requirement. This may apply where possessing a characteristic related to age is a genuine and determining occupational requirement and it is a proportionate requirement in the particular case (EEAR 2006, reg 8(2)). **32.78**

There will also be a defence to both direct and indirect discrimination where the employer's actions can be justified. Justification requires the employer to show that the otherwise discriminatory actions are a proportionate means of achieving a legitimate aim (EEAR 2006, reg 3(1)). The ACAS Age Guide suggests that a justification defence may be made out where it is necessary to fix a maximum age for the recruitment or promotion of employees in order to reflect the training requirements of the post or the need for a reasonable period of employment before retirement. It also points out that an employer will need clear evidence to support his defence; mere assertion will not be enough. The justification defence has recently been considered by the courts and tribunals at various levels: see *Hampton v Lord Chancellor* [2008] IRLR 258 for a decision of the Employment Tribunal; *MacCulloch v ICI* [2008] IRLR 846 and *Seldon v Clarkson, Wright & Jakes* [2009] IRLR 267 for decisions of the EAT; and *Rolls-Royce v Unite* [2009] IRLR 576 for a decision of the Court of Appeal. *Seldon's* case has been the subject of an appeal to the Court of Appeal. The appeal was heard in the Court of Appeal and, at the time of writing, judgment is awaited. **32.79**

The tests for harassment and victimization are the same as the tests in the rest of the discrimination legislation (EEAR 2006, regs 4 and 6 and see paras 32.17 and 32.24). Equally, the position in relation to vicarious liability for acts of employees is the same as that in the SDA 1975 (EEAR 2006, reg 25(3) and para 32.21). The justification defence referred to above will not apply to claims of victimization or harassment. **32.80**

EEAR 2006 also contains certain other exceptions relating to statutory authority, national security, positive action, retirement, national minimum wage, length of service, enhanced redundancy, and life insurance. See para 10 of the checklist for claims of age discrimination below in relation to this. **32.81**

The remedies for age discrimination are broadly the same as sex discrimination (EEAR 2006, reg 38 and see also Chapter 26). Equally there are similar provisions relating to burden of proof, questionnaires, grievances, and the time limits for claims (EEAR 2006, regs 37, 41, and 42 and paras 32.16, 32.30, and 32.33 above). From 1 October 2007, the Equality and Human Rights Commission has responsibility for age discrimination in the same way as it has for sex (see paras 32.31–32.32 above). **32.82**

G. EC TREATY, ARTICLE 141 (FORMERLY 119)

32.83 Article 141 provides that men and women should receive equal pay for equal work and is directly enforceable against employers (unlike the Equal Treatment Directive which is only enforceable against public authorities). There are some differences from the approach under Article 141 and the approach under the EqPA 1970, as follows.

32.84 Pay for these purposes includes claims relating to payments and benefits under occupational pension schemes, whether contributory or non-contributory (*Barber v Guardian Royal Exchange Assurance Group* [1990] ICR 616), contractual and *ex gratia* payments made following a compulsory redundancy, compensation for unfair dismissal (*R v Secretary of State for Employment, ex p Seymour Smith* [1999] IRLR 253), and non-contractual discretionary payments.

32.85 When looking at 'like work' ('same work' in Article 141) the case law will not simply look at the duties performed; it may take into account matters such as training qualifications.

32.86 Whilst Article 141 claims can be brought in the employment tribunal they can only be brought on the basis of modifying existing statutes (for example EqPA 1970) so as to make them compatible with EU law.

H. THE EQUALITY BILL

32.87 The Government and Parliament are currently considering a new Equality Bill. The provisions are wide ranging and since many do not relate, specifically, to employment law, they are beyond the scope of this work. However, the main proposed provisions affecting employment law are:

(a) a power on the part of the Government, to require reporting on the gender pay gap by public sector employers and private sector employers with more than 250 employees;
(b) the banning of 'gagging clauses' which prevent employees discussing pay with their colleagues;
(c) the permitting of more 'positive discrimination';
(d) the outlawing of 'multiple discrimination' where somebody is discriminated against on the basis of a combination of characteristics;
(e) extending the scope of 'transferred discrimination' so that it applies in respect of sex discrimination, disability discrimination, and age discrimination;
(f) the overturning of the decision of the House of Lords in *London Borough of Lewisham v Malcolm* [2008] UKHL 43.

It is expected that the bill will become law in spring 2010.

CHECKLIST FOR EQUAL PAY CLAIMS

1. Is the complainant employed under a contract of service or of apprenticeship or a contract personally to execute any work or labour? If not he may not have a claim under EqPA 1970 (EqPA 1970, s 1(6)(a) and see para 32.03 above).

2. Does the complainant work wholly outside Great Britain? If so, he will not be able to bring a claim under EqPA 1970, although there may be an exception for those who are posted abroad where the employee was resident in Great Britain when he was recruited or at some point during the employment and the employer has a place of business at an establishment in Great Britain and the work the employee was doing was for the business at that establishment (SDA 1975, s 10).

3. Does the claim relate to a contractual term relating to:

   (a) pay;
   (b) bonuses;
   (c) concessions and benefits in kind;
   (d) terms in collective agreements;
   (e) general contractual provisions such as those regarding holidays, sickness benefits, and hours?

   If so, it will come within the terms of the EqPA 1970 (EqPA 1970, s 1(1) and see para 32.04 above).

4. Does the claim relate to:

   (a) terms included in compliance with the law regarding women's employment (EqPA 1970, s 6(1)(a)—to a large degree, such provisions have been removed from the statute book and so this exception is now very limited);
   (b) terms relating to pregnancy and childbirth (EqPA 1970, s 6(1)(b));
   (c) terms relating to membership of or rights under occupational pension schemes, save that retirement ages must be the same and access to and benefits under occupational pension schemes must be equal (see EC Treaty, Article 141 (formerly Article 119), and the Pensions Act 1995) (EqPA 1970, s 6(1B)).

   If so, the complainant will not have a claim under the EqPA 1970 (see para 32.04 above).

5. Was there a difference in terms and conditions of employment, for example, is there a difference in:

   (a) pay;
   (b) hours of work;
   (c) method of allocation of bonuses or size of bonuses;
   (d) incentive payments;
   (e) concessions and benefits in kind such as advantageous loans, mortgage repayment allowances, participation in insurance schemes or share option schemes;
   (f) provisions in collective agreements, in respect of the above matters, incorporated into the contracts of employment;
   (g) terms relating to holidays, sickness benefits, and other contractual provisions?

   If so, the complainant may have a claim under the EqPA 1970 (see para 32.04 above).

6. Is there a comparator who is a genuine individual, and not a hypothetical comparator? There should be, other than in cases relating to pay during maternity leave (*Alabaster v Barclays Bank plc and Secretary of State for Social Security (No 2)* [2005] IRLR 576 and EqPA 1970, ss 1(2)(e) and (2)(f)). In non-maternity cases the complainant may, if she wishes, compare herself with her predecessor (*Kells v Pilkington plc* [2002] IRLR 693) but it would appear that she cannot compare herself with a successor (*Walton Centre for Neurology and Neurosurgery NHS Trust v Bewley* [2008] IRLR 588). Additionally, the comparator must work at the same establishment (EqPA 1970, s 1(6)). This is a question of fact, depending upon the following factors:

   (a) the degree of exclusive occupation of the premises;
   (b) the degree of permanence of the arrangements;
   (c) the organization of workers—whether they are organized as part of one group, or in separate and distinct entities;
   (d) how the administration is organized—if there is central administration and the head office runs several sites, such as building sites, those sites are likely to be part of the same

establishment. If each site is separately run, such as branches of a chain of shops, each site is likely to be a separate establishment.
(*Barley v Amey Roadstone Corp Ltd (No 2)* [1977] IRLR 299, in the context of a protective award under TULR(C)A 1992, but applicable here.)

7. If the comparator is not working at the same establishment, is he working at an establishment where broadly similar terms and conditions apply for the relevant class of employee? This must be the case, for example, where a collective agreement applies to both establishments (*Leverton v Clwyd County Council* [1989] ICR 33). If similar terms and conditions apply, the establishments may be owned by associated companies and not only by the employer.

   Where the differences identified in the pay of workers performing like work or work of equal value cannot be attributed to a single source (even where the employer is the same), the claim does not come within the legislation (or Article 141) since there is no body which is responsible for the inequality and which could restore equal treatment (*Lawrence v Regent Office Care Ltd* [2000] IRLR 822; *Robertson v Department for Environment, Food and Rural Affairs* [2005] IRLR 363; *Armstrong v Newcastle-upon-Tyne NHS Hospital Trust* [2006] IRLR 124).

8. Was the comparator engaged upon like work, work rated as equivalent, or work of equal value?

   Like work means work of the same or a broadly similar nature and where the differences (if any) are not of practical importance in relation to the terms and conditions of employment. Regard should be had to any such differences which occur in practice, as well as to the nature and extent of the differences (EqPA 1970, s 1(4)). This is a question of fact and the tribunal should not be too pedantic in its examination (*Capper Pass Ltd v Lawton* [1977] QB 852). The first issue is to examine the nature of the work done by the employee and what skill and knowledge are required to do it. Different training requirements may disqualify a job from being like work. The timing of the work will be irrelevant (*Dugdale v Kraft Foods* [1977] IRLR 368).

9. If there are differences, what are their nature and extent, and how frequently do they operate? If they operate infrequently (for example, if occasionally a man is asked to undertake heavy work) or are minor (for example, where canteen ladies sometimes wait at tables whereas their male comparator does not) work will still be regarded as like (*Capper Pass* (above); *Dorothy Perkins Ltd v Dance* [1977] IRLR 226).

10. Was the complainant engaged on work *rated as equivalent*, that is, her job and the comparator's job have been given equal value in terms of the demand made on the worker under various headings (for instance, effort, skill, decision) (EqPA 1970, s 1(5))? To establish this, the employer must have carried out a job evaluation scheme and the two jobs identified by the complainant must be rated by that scheme as equivalent (or the complainant's must have been ranked as having greater value: see *Redcar & Cleveland Borough Council v Bainbridge* [2007] IRLR 984). If they are, yet terms and conditions of employment between people of opposite sexes are different, the employee will succeed (subject to a justification defence). If they are not rated as equivalent, an employee will only succeed in a claim for equal pay if she can show that discriminatory criteria were used in setting up the job evaluation scheme (*Rummler v Dato-Druck GmbH* [1987] IRLR 32) or that the scheme has not been put into effect and complied with. Note, however, there is no legal obligation on an employer to conduct a job evaluation scheme (see also para 15.03 above).

11. Was the complainant engaged in work of *equal value* (or greater value: see *Murphy v An Bord Telecom Eireann* [1988] ECR 673), that is, work which would not fall within the tests for like work or work rated as equivalent, but which is, in terms of the demands made on her (for instance under such headings as effort, skill, and decision), of equal value to a man in the same

employment. If so, the complainant may apply to the employment tribunal which may proceed to determine the question or require a member of a panel or independent experts to prepare a report with respect to that question (EqPA 1970, s 1(2)(c) and see paras 15.08–15.25 in Chapter 15 above).

12. Can the employer show that, even where the two individuals are engaged in like work, or if their work is rated as equivalent under a job evaluation scheme, that where there is a variation between the woman's contract and that of the man, that the variation is genuinely due to a material factor which is not the difference of sex between the two cases, but is a material difference which causes the *whole* of the difference? If so, the employee's claim will fail. If the difference only explains part of the variation, then the employee's claim will succeed as to the unexplained part. Material factors include:
    (a) qualifications or level of experience (*McGregor v General Municipal Boilermakers and Allied Trades Union* [1987] ICR 505);
    (b) length of service (see *Cadman v Health and Safety Executive* [2006] All ER (D) 1, where the ECJ held that an employer does not need to specifically justify the use of length of service to determine pay, as long as there is no evidence which raises serious doubts that length of service is an appropriate means to attain the employer's objective with regard to that particular job);
    (c) degree of skills acquired (*Tyldesley v TML Plastics Ltd* [1996] IRLR 395);
    (d) place of employment (*Navy, Army and Air Force Institutes v Varley* [1976] IRLR 408);
    (e) regional pay variations or that market forces have dictated that a later applicant is paid more (or less) than someone who is already established in the job (*Ratcliffe v North Yorkshire CC* [1995] IRLR 439; *Rainey v Greater Glasgow Health Board* [1977] IRLR 26; *Enderby v Frenchay Health Authority and Secretary of State for Health* [1993] IRLR 591), but note that if the market or collective bargaining arrangements are tainted by sex, objective justification will be necessary (see para 14 below);
    (f) different economic circumstances affecting the business itself where the comparator was working at a different time from the complainant (*Waddington v Leicester Council for Voluntary Services* [1977] IRLR 32);
    (g) that the individuals are in differing levels in the grading structure (*Strathclyde Regional Council v Wallace* [1998] IRLR 146);
    (h) part-time working—but this can only be a justification if the differential between part-time and full-time rates is objectively justifiable and will satisfy the Part-time Workers (Prevention of Less Favourable Treatment) Regulations 2000;
    (i) the comparator is a 'red circled' worker (ie where the comparator has been demoted but his pay has not been reduced) although the differential in pay should be phased out over time, and there should be no outsiders within the 'red circle' (*Snoxell and Davies v Vauxhall Motors Ltd* [1977] 3 All ER 770; *United Biscuits Ltd v Young* [1978] IRLR 15; *Home Office v Bailey* [2005] IRLR 757; see also *SITA UK Ltd v Hope* EAT/0787/04/MAA, where a simple assertion of 'red circling' is insufficient to establish a material factor defence).

13. Where an independent report has concluded that the complainant's work is of equal value to that of a comparator, where there is a variation between the woman's contract and that of the man, is the variation genuinely due to a material factor which is not a difference of sex? If so, the employee's claim will fail. 'Factor' can encompass any issue, and not merely a material difference between the woman's case and the man's, and factors would include all those examples cited above. In particular, market forces will be construed widely so that, even where a lone individual demands, and receives, a higher wage this may be a defence.

14. Could the genuine material factor be indirectly discriminatory? If so, the employer will need to objectively justify the difference (see para 32.05 above).

15. Has the complainant brought a grievance in relation to her claim? If not, the complainant may not be able to bring a claim in the employment tribunal (EA 2002, s 32 and the Employment Act 2002 (Dispute Resolution) Regulations 2004, reg 15; also paras 3.98–3.103). Note that the requirement to raise a grievance will not apply after 6 April 2009 save for in circumstances where the facts giving rise to the claim began before that date and the claim has been commenced or a grievance raised before 4 October 2009.

16. Has the complainant brought the claim in the employment tribunal or county court during employment or within six months of the termination of the contract in relation to which the claim arises? If not, the complainant's claim will be time-barred unless the complainant has brought a grievance in relation to the inequality, in which case the time may be extended (see EA 2002, s 32 and the Employment Act 2002 (Dispute Resolution) Regulations 2004, reg 15; see also paras 3.93–3.99) (see also Chapter 15, paras 15.04–15.05). The requirement to raise a grievance will not apply from 6 April 2009. Note that the rules relating to TUPE transfers and time limits in the context of equal pay claims are complex: see para 32.08 above.

CHECKLIST FOR CLAIMS OF DISCRIMINATION BASED ON SEX (TO INCLUDE MARITAL/CIVIL PARTNERSHIP AND GENDER REASSIGNMENT), RACE, RELIGION OR BELIEF, AND SEXUAL ORIENTATION

1. Is the complainant employed under a contract of service or of apprenticeship or a contract personally to execute any work or labour? If not, he or she may not have the protection of the legislation (SDA 1975, s 82(1); RRA 1976, s 78; RBR 2003, reg 2(3); SOR 2003, reg 2 and see also paras 32.03 and 32.12 above as the same points will apply).

2. Do any of the genuine occupational qualification defences apply? If so, the complainant will not have a claim (see paras 32.22 (sex), 32.37 (race), and 32.68 (religion and sexual orientation) above).

3. Does the complainant work wholly outside Great Britain? If so, he will not have a claim, although there may be an exception for those who are posted abroad where the employee was resident in Great Britain when he was recruited or at some point during the employment and the employer has a place of business at an establishment in Great Britain and the work is for the purposes of the business carried out at that establishment (see paras 32.12 (sex), 32.37 (race), and 32.67 (religion and sexual orientation) above).

4. If claiming sex discrimination, is the complainant a minister of religion, claiming in relation to accommodation facilities, a prison officer, claiming about special treatment to women in connection with pregnancy and childbirth? If so, she may be excluded from claiming (see para 32.13 above).

5. If claiming race discrimination, is the complainant employed in a private household, claiming in relation to sports representation and competitions, claiming in relation to acts safeguarding national security? If so, the complainant may be prevented from claiming (see para 32.38 above).

6. If claiming discrimination based on religion or belief or sexual orientation, is the claim in relation to acts safeguarding national security, and (sexual orientation only) benefits dependent on marital status or status as a civil partner? If so, the complainant may be prevented from claiming (see para 32.69 above).

7. Is the complainant an employee, temporary worker, supplied by an employment agency, or a worker and claiming sex discrimination or race discrimination or discrimination based on religion or belief or sexual orientation in respect of the areas listed below?

   (a) Arrangements for recruitment (whether or not anyone is in fact recruited) (SDA 1975, s 6(1)(a); RRA 1976, s 4(1)(a); RBR 2003 and SOR 2003, reg 6(1)(a)).
   (b) Recruitment advertisements (SDA 1975, s 38; RRA 1976, s 29).
   (c) Contractual benefits, but only where discrimination is on grounds other than sex (see para 32.11 above).
   (d) Non-contractual benefits (see para 32.12 above).
   (e) Occupational pension schemes (race, marital status, gender reassignment, religion or belief, sexual orientation only) (see also para 32.02 *et seq*. in relation to sex).
   (f) Opportunities for promotion and transfer (SDA 1975, s 6(2)(b); RRA 1976 s 4(2)(b); RBR 2003 and SOR 2003, reg 6(2)(b)).
   (g) Training opportunities (save in a case where positive training of particular groups is allowed) (SDA 1975, s 6(2)(b); RRA 1976 s 4(2)(b); RBR 2003 and SOR 2003, reg 6(2)(b); see also SDA 1975, ss 47 and 48; RRA 1976, ss 37 and 38; RBR, reg 25; SOR 2003, reg 26).
   (h) Harassment (see para 32.17 above).
   (i) Grounds for dismissal.
   (j) Claims by employees in relation to their treatment after the termination of employment as long as the act complained of arose from the employment relationship or was closely connected with it (*Rhys-Harper v Relaxion Group plc* [2003] IRLR 484; SDA 1975, s 20A; RRA 1976, s 27A; RBR 2003 and SOR 2003, reg 21).

   If so, the complainant could have a claim under the relevant discrimination legislation.

8. In direct discrimination cases, would the employee have received the same treatment from the employer or potential employer but for his or her own sex, marital or civil partnership status, race, the fact he intends to undergo, is undergoing, or had undergone gender reassignment, religion or belief, or sexual orientation? If so, and the employee can convince the tribunal on the balance of probabilities that this is the case the employee concerned may have a claim for direct discrimination (see para 32.16).

9. Can the employer show on the balance of probabilities that sex, marital, or civil partnership status, race, the fact he intends to undergo, is undergoing, or had undergone gender reassignment, religion or belief, or sexual orientation are not the reason for less favourable treatment? If not, the employer may not be able to defend an allegation of direct discrimination (see paras 32.16 and 32.20).

10. In harassment cases, has the complainant been subject to unwanted conduct related to the person's sex, marital, civil partnership status, or the fact he intends to undergo gender reassignment, which has the purpose or effect of violating another person's dignity or creating an intimidating, hostile, degrading, humiliating, or offensive environment for them. Alternatively, was such conduct on the grounds of, race, religion or belief, or sexual orientation? If so, the complainant may have a claim of harassment (see para 32.17). As to the amendments to SDA 1975, s 4A see *Equal Opportunities Commission v Secretary of State for Trade and Industry* [2007] IRLR 327.

11. Is the complainant subject to a provision, criterion, or practice which is applied to everyone but which disadvantages a class of people, the majority of whom are one sex or race or married, or of the same religion or sexual orientation, and does the employee who is claiming suffer that disadvantage? If so, the employee concerned may have a claim for indirect discrimination (see paras 32.18 and 32.35).

12. To prove whether a provision, criterion, or practice amounts to indirect discrimination (which obligation is on the claimant SDA 1975, s 63A and *Nelson v Carillion Services Ltd* [2003] IRLR 428):

    (a) identify the criteria for selection;
    (b) identify the relevant pool of potential candidates;
    (c) divide the pool into those who satisfy the criteria and those who do not, and consider whether the members of the minority group are under-represented in the group which satisfies the criteria in comparison with the statistics and over-represented in the group which does not satisfy the criteria;
    (d) does the group which is over-represented suffer disadvantage as a result of the imposition of the provision, criteria, or practice, and does the employee complaining suffer that disadvantage? If so, it is potentially discriminatory.

13. Can the employer show that the conditions which have been imposed are a proportionate means of achieving a legitimate aim? If so, the employer may have a defence to a claim of indirect discrimination (see para 32.23).

14. Has the complainant been treated less favourably than others because that person threatens to bring proceedings, to give evidence or information, to take any action or to make any allegations concerning the employer under the discrimination legislation? If so, the complainant may have a claim of victimization as long as the allegation was made in good faith (see para 32.24).

15. If the complainant is an employee, did the employee bring a grievance in relation to her claim? If not, the claimant may not be able to bring a claim in the employment tribunal (EA 2002, s 32 and Employment Act 2002 (Dispute Resolution) Regulations 2003, reg 15; see also paras 3.93–3.99). The requirement to raise a grievance will no longer apply from 6 April 2009 unless the facts giving rise to the claim commenced before that date and the employee has brought a claim or raised a grievance before 4 July 2009.

16. Has the complainant brought the claim in the employment tribunal during employment or within three months of the act complained of? If not, the complainant's claim is likely to be out of time, unless the complainant is an employee and has brought a grievance in relation to the deduction, in which case the time may be extended (see EA 2002, s 32 and Employment Act 2002 (Dispute Resolution) Regulations 2004, reg 15; see also paras 3.93–3.99) or the tribunal decides it would be just and equitable to extend the time limit (see paras 3.84–3.88 above). The requirement to raise a grievance will no longer apply from 6 April 2009. Regulation 15 has not been repealed, but presumably will be of no legal effect where the grievance procedure does not apply.

CHECKLIST FOR DISABILITY DISCRIMINATION

1. Is the complainant employed under a contract of service or of apprenticeship or a contract personally to execute any work or labour? If not, he will not have the protection of the legislation (see para 32.43 above).

2. Is the complainant a member of the armed forces, an employee who works outside Great Britain (although there may be an exception for those who are posted abroad where the employee was resident in Great Britain when he or she was recruited or at some point during the employment and the employer has a place of business at an establishment in Great Britain and the work the employee is doing is for the business at that establishment) or an employee who works on a ship, aircraft, or hovercraft? If so, he will probably not have a claim (see para 32.60 above).

3. Does the complainant have a disability, ie a physical or mental impairment which has a substantial and long-term adverse effect on the employee's ability to carry out his normal day-to-day activities? (See para 32.44 *et seq.* above.) If so, he will be able to bring a claim under the DDA.

4. Does the employee suffer from alcoholism, drug, or nicotine addiction, hay fever, pyromania, kleptomania, exhibitionism, a tendency to physical or sexual abuse of other persons, or voyeurism? If so, these will not qualify as a disability and so the complainant will not have a claim (Disability Discrimination (Meaning of Disability) Regulations 1996, SI 1996/1455 and para 32.45 above).

5. Has the complainant been treated less favourably by someone than he treats or would treat a person not having that particular disability whose relevant circumstances, including his abilities, are the same as or not materially different from, those of the disabled person? If so, the complainant may have a claim of direct discrimination (DDA 1995, s 3A(5) and para 32.53 above).

6. Has the complainant received less favourable treatment for a reason relating to disability than a comparator would have received who did not have that disability (see *London Borough of Lewisham v Malcolm* [2008] 3 WLR 194 but also see para 32.52 above)? If so, the complainant may have a claim of disability-related discrimination (DDA 1995, s 3A(1) and para 32.52 above).

7. Has the employer complied with its duty to take steps as are reasonable to prevent substantial disadvantage to a disabled person? If not, the complainant will have a claim (DDA 1995, s 3A(2) and paras 32.54 and 32.55 above).

8. Can the employer justify its treatment of the complainant by showing a reason for it which is material to the particular circumstances of the case and substantial? If so, the employer may have a defence, but not if the claim is one of direct discrimination and it will have to show that it has complied with the duty to make reasonable adjustments as well (DDA 1995, s 3A(3), (5), and (6) and para 32.56 above).

9. Has the complainant been treated less favourably than others because that person has brought proceedings against another person under DDA 1995, given information or evidence in relation to such a claim, otherwise done anything under DDA 1995 in relation to the employer or alleged that the employer has breached DDA 1995 or believes the employer intends to do so? If so, the complainant may have a claim for victimization, as long as the allegation was made in good faith (DDA 1995, s 55 and para 32.57 above).

10. Has the complainant been subject to unwanted conduct which has the purpose or effect of violating another person's dignity or creating an intimidating, hostile, degrading, humiliating, or offensive environment for them? Can the conduct, having regard to all the circumstances, including, in particular, the perception of the victim, reasonably be considered as having that effect? If so, the complainant may have a claim of harassment on grounds of disability (DDA 1995, s 38 and para 32.58 above).

11. Is the employer unaware of the disability? This will potentially be a defence to claims of direct discrimination and disability related discrimination (see *London Borough of Lewisham v Malcolm* [2008] IRLR 700) and the duty to make reasonable adjustments (DDA 1995, s 4A(3) and para 32.59 above).

12. If the complainant is an employee, did the employee bring a grievance in relation to his claim? If not, the complainant may not be able to bring a claim in the employment tribunal (EA 2002, s 32 and the Employment Act 2002 (Dispute Resolution) Regulations 2004, reg 15; see also paras 3.93–3.99). The requirement to raise a grievance will no longer apply from 6 April 2009 unless the facts giving rise to the claim commenced before that date and the employee has brought a claim or raised a grievance before 4 July 2009.

13. Has the complainant brought the claim in the employment tribunal during employment or within three months of the act complained of? If not, the complainant's claim is likely to be out of time unless the complainant is an employee and has brought a grievance in relation to the deduction, in which case the time may be extended (see EA 2002, s 32 and the Employment Act 2002 (Dispute Resolution) Regulations 2004, reg 15; see also paras 3.93–3.99) or the tribunal decides it would be just and equitable to extend the time limit. The requirement to raise a grievance will no longer apply from 6 April 2009. Regulation 15 has not been repealed, but presumably will have no legal effect.

CHECKLIST FOR CLAIMS OF AGE DISCRIMINATION

1. Is the complainant employed under a contract of service or of apprenticeship or a contract personally to execute any work or labour? If not, he or she may not have the protection of the legislation (EEAR 2006, reg 2 and see paras 32.03 and 32.67 above for a similar test).

2. Does the employee work wholly outside Great Britain? If yes, he will not have a claim although there may be an exception for those who are posted abroad where the employee was resident in Great Britain when he was recruited or at some point during the employment and the employer has a place of business at an establishment in Great Britain and the work was for that establishment (EEAR 2006, reg 10).

3. Is the complainant doing service in any of the naval, military, or air forces, as an unpaid office holder or an unpaid volunteer? If so, they will not be covered by the legislation (see para 32.73 above).

4. Is the complainant claiming age discrimination about one of the areas below:

   (a) arrangements for recruitment (EEAR 2006, reg 7(1)(a));
   (b) contractual and non-contractual benefits (including occupational pension schemes);
   (c) opportunities for promotion and transfer and training (EEAR 2006, reg 7(2)(b) but see also reg 29 in relation to positive action);
   (d) harassment (see para 32.80);
   (e) grounds for dismissal (EEAR 2006, reg 7(2)(d) but see also paras 30.28 *et seq*. in relation to the specific rules governing dismissals);
   (f) claims by employees in relation to their treatment after the termination of employment as long as the act complained of arose from the employment relationship or was closely connected with it (EEAR 2006, reg 24);
   (g) vocational training (EEAR 2006, reg 20).

5. Would the employee have received the same treatment from the employer or potential employer but for his age (or apparent age)? If so, the employee concerned may have a claim for direct discrimination (see para 32.75 above).

6. Is the complainant subject to a provision, criterion, or practice which is applied to everyone but which disadvantages those in a specific age group and does the employee who is claiming suffer that disadvantage? If so, the employee concerned may have a claim for indirect discrimination (see para 32.76 above).

7. Can the employer show that the direct or indirect discrimination is a proportionate means of achieving a legitimate aim? In considering this, the employer will need to ask the following questions:

   (a) What is a legitimate aim?
      (i) economic factors such as business needs and efficiency;
      (ii) the health, welfare, and safety of the individual;
      (iii) the particular training requirements of the job.

   (b) Does the legitimate aim correspond with a real need of the business? It should do and not simply be cheaper.

   (c) What is proportionate?
      (i) it must actually contribute to the legitimate aim;
      (ii) the discriminatory effect should be significantly outweighed by the importance and benefits of the legitimate aim;
      (iii) the employer should have no reasonable alternative to the action it is taking.

   (ACAS Age Guide)

8. Has the complainant been subject to unwanted conduct which has the purpose or effect of violating another person's dignity or creating an intimidating, hostile, degrading, humiliating, or offensive environment on grounds of their age? If so, the employee may have a claim for harassment (EEAR 2006, reg 6).

9. Has the complainant been treated less favourably than others because that person threatens to bring proceedings, to give evidence or information, to take any action, or to make any allegations concerning the employer under EEAR 2006? If so, the complainant may have a claim for victimization as long as the allegation was made in good faith (EEAR 2006, reg 4).

10. Does one of the other exceptions to liability under EEAR 2006 apply? The exceptions are as follows:

   (a) The act was done in order to comply with a requirement of a statutory provision (EEAR 2006, reg 27);
   (b) A person (who is an employee as defined in ERA 1996, s 230(1)) is recruited whose age is greater than the employer's normal retirement age or, if the employer does not have a normal retirement age, 65, would be within a six-month period (EEAR 2006, reg 7(4)).
   (c) A person (who is an employee as defined in ERA 1996, s 230(1)) is dismissed at or over the age of 65 where the reason for the dismissal is retirement (EEAR 2006, reg 30(2) and see also para 29.28 *et seq*. above).
   (d) The act is done for the purposes of safeguarding national security (EEAR 2006, reg 28 and see also para 32.73).
   (e) The act prevents or compensates for disadvantages linked to age suffered by persons of that age or age group doing the work concerned (EEAR 2006, reg 29). Usually this will cover access to certain types of training or work. It will not, however, excuse positive discrimination, which will still need to be objectively justified.

(f) An exception to allow different rates of pay under NMWA 1998 for employees of different ages (EEAR, reg 31).

(g) An exception to allow certain benefits to be based on length of service (EEAR 2006, reg 32). An employee with a length of service of five years or less cannot bring a claim in relation to certain benefits. Where an employee has more than five years' service, he may be able to bring a claim in relation to benefits which place him at a disadvantage, unless the provider of the benefits can show that the provision of benefits in this way fulfils a business need of his undertaking (for example, by encouraging the loyalty or motivation or rewarding the experience, of some or all of his workers) (EEAR 2006, reg 32(2)). For this purpose, benefit does not include any benefit awarded to a worker by virtue of his ceasing to work for the employer (EEAR 2006, reg 32(7)). The ACAS Age Guide makes it clear that an employer must be able to produce evidence to support the justification described above.

(h) An exception which allows enhanced redundancy to be paid on the basis of age as long as the terms of the scheme mirror the terms of the statutory scheme, save that the cap on weekly pay need not apply and the multiplier may be more than one (EEAR 2006, reg 33). Also, those who take voluntary redundancy and have less than two years' service may take the benefit of enhanced redundancy as long as it mirrors the statutory scheme (EEAR 2006, reg 33(2)).

(i) An exception in relation to the provision of life assurance cover is to retired workers. It will not be age discrimination where an employer arranges for life assurance cover to cease on the early retirement of the employee or when they reach age 65 (EEAR 2006, reg 34). Note, however, this exception does not apply to other benefits and where these cease at a certain age, this will need to be objectively justified, which may be difficult as cost alone will usually be an insufficient justification.

(j) There are exceptions in relation to pension schemes. Generally, it will be unlawful to discriminate against a member or prospective member of a pension scheme (EEAR 2006, reg 11(1)). However, this will not apply to:
   (i) rights accrued or benefits payable in respect of periods of service prior to the coming into force of the EEAR 2006 (EEAR 2006, reg 11(1));
   (ii) certain parts of occupational pension schemes.

11. If the complainant is an employee, did the employee bring a grievance in relation to their claim? If not, the complainant may not be able to bring a claim in the employment tribunal (EA 2002, s 32 and Employment Act 2002 (Dispute Resolution) Regulations 2003, reg 15; see also paras 3.93–3.99). Note that the requirement to raise a grievance will no longer exist from 6 April 2009 unless the facts giving rise to the claim commenced before that date and the employee has brought a claim or raised a grievance before 4 July 2009.

12. Has the complainant brought the claim in the employment tribunal during employment or within three months of the act complained of? If not, the complainant's claim is likely to be out of time, unless the complainant is an employee and has brought a grievance in relation to the deduction, in which case the time may be extended (see EA 2002, s 32 and Employment Act 2002 (Dispute Resolution) Regulations 2004, reg 15; see also paras 3.93–3.99) or the tribunal decides it would be just and equitable to extend the time limit. The requirement to raise a grievance will no longer exist from 6 April 2009. Regulation 15 has not been repealed, but presumably will have no legal effect where the statutory grievance procedure does not apply.

33

Unlawful Deductions from Wages

SUMMARY

(1) Deductions by an employer from a worker's wages will be unlawful unless certain statutory requirements are fulfilled.

(2) Wages has a wide meaning and includes any fee, bonus, commission, holiday pay, or other emolument which is payable in connection with the worker's employment.

A. GENERAL PAY OBLIGATIONS

A worker's entitlement to be paid, when, and how much is generally governed by the contract of employment. Statute intervenes in the following ways: **33.01**

(a) an employer's right to make certain deductions from salary is circumscribed by statute, mainly ERA 1996, ss 13–27 (see the remainder of this chapter);
(b) by prescribing a minimum level of pay under the National Minimum Wage Act 1998 (not dealt with in this book);
(c) by not differentiating between men and women as to pay (see Chapters 15 and 32).

B. DEDUCTIONS FROM WAGES

The provisions contained in ss 13 to 27 of ERA 1996 apply to the wider category of individuals defined as 'workers' (see para 1 of the checklist below). **33.02**

During the course of employment the employer can only make the following deductions from the workers' wages: **33.03**

(a) Deductions required or authorized by statute such as PAYE and national insurance contributions or a relevant provision of the employee's contract (ERA 1996, s 13(1)(a)).
(b) Any deduction to which the worker has previously signified in writing his agreement or consent prior to it being made (ERA 1996, s 13(1)(b)).
(c) Any payment to a third party to which the employee has consented in writing (ERA 1996, s 14(4)).
(d) Any deductions made within a reasonable time for reimbursement of previous overpayments of wages or expenses (ERA 1996, s 14(1)).
(e) Any deductions made on account of a worker's participation in industrial action (including not only pay but also any damages suffered by the employer as a result of the industrial action) (ERA 1996, s 14(5)).

(f) Any payments the employer is required by statute to make to a public authority following an appropriate determination (ERA 1996, s 14(3)).
(g) Any sums the employer is required to pay pursuant to an attachment of earnings order made by the court (ERA 1996, s 14(6)).

33.04 The word 'wages' is very widely defined and includes fees, bonuses, commissions, and holiday pay (including statutory holiday pay pursuant to the Working Time Regulations 1998: see *Her Majesty's Revenue and Customs v Stringer* [2009] UKHL 31), statutory sick pay, statutory maternity, paternity, and adoption pay as well as some more esoteric statutory payments (ERA 1996, s 27(1)), but not (usually) pay in lieu of notice (*Delaney v Staples* [1992] ICR 483). Further, although bonuses fall within the definition of wages as set out in ERA 1996, s 27, a discretionary bonus which had yet to be determined and which, therefore, was not an identifiable sum, would not be recoverable under ERA 1996, Part II (*Farrell Matthews & Weir v Hansen* [2005] IRLR 160 and *Adcock v Coors Brewers Ltd* [2007] IRLR 440). Although there is no specific authority on the point, it is likely that the same is also true of share options. Claims in respect of these matters ought properly to be pursued as claims in contract for unliquidated damages either in the employment tribunal or in the civil courts.

33.05 Special provisions apply in the retail industry, where, even if the worker has consented in writing to deductions being made, deductions in any period to compensate for stock deficiencies or cash shortages (or any payments the employee is required to make as a result of deficiencies or shortages) cannot exceed 10 per cent of the worker's gross wages for the relevant period (ERA 1996, ss 17–22 (not included in this book)).

33.06 If the employer wrongfully makes deductions from pay or makes no payment whatsoever, the worker may complain to an employment tribunal within three months (subject to any extension of time in relation to which, see para 3.55 *et seq.*) of the relevant deduction, or of the last deduction in the series, seeking an order for payment of the sums due (ERA 1996, s 23). The worker may also, if he so wishes, bring proceedings in a county court or High Court for damages for breach of contract but cannot recover more than once in respect of any particular deduction.

CHECKLIST FOR UNLAWFUL DEDUCTION CLAIMS

1. Was or is the claimant a worker, ie someone who works under a contract of employment or any other contract, whether express or implied and (if it is express) whether oral or in writing whereby the individual undertakes to perform personally any work or services for another party to the contract whose status is not by virtue of the contract that of a client or customer of any profession or business undertaking carried on by the individual? If so, the individual can bring this claim (ERA 1996, s 230(3), s 13(1)).

2. Was or is the worker working in retail employment? If so, refer to the provisions of ERA 1996, ss 17–22 (not included in this book).

3. Was the deduction made from the wages of the worker, that is, a fee, bonus, commission, holiday pay, or other emolument referable to the employment, whether payable under the contract or not; statutory sick pay; statutory maternity pay; statutory paternity pay; statutory adoption pay; a guarantee payment; any payment for time off for carrying out trade union duties; any remuneration on suspension on medical or maternity grounds; any sums payable in pursuance of an order for reinstatement or re-engagement; any payment made under an order for interim relief leading to the continuation of the employment; any remuneration under a protective award (ERA 1996, s 27(1))? If it was, consider the question of deductions below.

4. Was the deduction made from payment in lieu of notice owed to the worker? Such a payment probably does not qualify as wages and therefore the claimant will not have a claim (*Delaney v Staples* [1992] ICR 483; *Farrell Matthews & Weir v Hanson* [2005] IRLR 160; and *Adcock v Coors Brewers Ltd* [2007] IRLR 440 for the position in relation to bonuses).

5. Was the payment an advance under an agreement for a loan or an advance of wages; payment in respect of expenses incurred by the employee in carrying out his employment; any payment by way of pension, allowance, or gratuity in connection with the worker's retirement or compensation for loss of office; any payment referable to the worker's redundancy or any payment to the worker otherwise than in his capacity as a worker? Such payments do not qualify as wages and therefore the claimant will not have a claim (ERA 1996, s 27(2)).

6. Was the deduction for tax or national insurance contributions made pursuant to relevant provision of the employee's contract, made with the employee's written consent, as a result of an overpayment of wages, as a result of industrial action, required by statute to be made to a public authority, or required to be made pursuant to an attachment of earnings order? If so, it is probably an allowed deduction and the claimant will not have a claim (ERA 1996, ss 13(1), (14)).

7. Was the claim brought within three months of the relevant deduction or the last in a series of deductions (ERA 1996, s 23(2) and (3))? If not, the claim is likely to be out of time.

8. Has the employer failed to make a payment which the employment tribunal then orders it to make? If so, the employer will be unable to recover the payment from the worker subsequently, even where the employer has the right to recover it (ERA 1996, s 25(4)).

34

Transfer of Undertakings

SUMMARY

(1) Employees working in an undertaking which is transferred are entitled to certain protections.

When an undertaking is transferred by one party to another, the Transfer of Undertakings (Protection of Employment) Regulations 2006, SI 2006/246 (TUPE 2006) operate so as to preserve, to a substantial extent, the employee's statutory and contractual employment rights which he had before the transfer. TUPE 2006 implements Council Directive 2001/23/EC which is commonly referred to as the 'Acquired Rights Directive'. They revoke the Transfer of Undertakings (Protection of Employment) Regulations 1981 (TUPE 1981). Although they are similar to TUPE 1981, they take advantage of certain policy options conferred by the Directive. TUPE 2006 applies to any relevant transfer that takes place on or after 6 April 2006. The Government has issued guidance to accompany TUPE 2006: 'Employment Rights on the Transfer of an Undertaking—A Guide to the 2006 TUPE Regulations for Employees, Employers and Representatives' (the 'Government Guidance'). Whilst this is not legally binding, it will no doubt be referred to by the courts and employment tribunals. **34.01**

A. DEFINITION OF 'TRANSFER' AND 'UNDERTAKING'

TUPE 2006 applies to a transfer of an 'undertaking' or business or to a part of an undertaking or business situated, prior to the transfer, in the United Kingdom where there is a transfer of an economic entity which retains its identity (TUPE 2006, reg 3(1)(a). As to transfers outside of the UK and outside of the European Union see *Holis Metal Industries v GMB* [2008] IRLR 187.) 'Economic' is defined as an organized grouping of resources which has the objective of pursuing an economic activity whether central or ancillary. Under TUPE 1981, an 'undertaking' was not expressly defined, and much case law has been devoted to determining its meaning *(Sanchez Hidalgo v Asociacion de Servicios Aser* [1999] IRLR 136; *Cheeseman v R Brewer Contracts Ltd* [2001] IRLR 144; *ECM (Vehicle Delivery Service) Ltd v Cox* [1999] IRLR 559). **34.02**

The test pursuant to TUPE 2006 is likely to be similar to that established by this case law and, indeed, this case law is referred to in the Government Guidance on TUPE 2006. The Government Guidance also states that business transfers covered by TUPE 2006 are those 'where there is an identifiable set of resources (which includes employees) assigned to the busi- **34.03** ness or part of the business which is transferred and that set of resources retains its identity after the transfer'. In relation to the transfer of part of a business:

> the resources do not need to be used exclusively in the transferring part of the business and by no other part. However, where resources are applied in a variable pattern over several parts of a business, then there is less likelihood that a transfer of any individual part of a business would qualify as a business transfer under [TUPE 2006].

A 'transfer' includes a sale, conditional sale, grant, transfer, or assignment of a lease or some other contract, or a transfer by way of gift. A sale of shares and a mere sale of bare assets is unlikely to amount to a transfer of undertaking (*Initial Supplies Ltd v McCall* 1992 SLT 67; *Brookes v Borough Care Services* [1998] IRLR 636, albeit these cases were under TUPE 1981 but confirmed in the Government Guidance. See also the decision of the EAT in *The Print Factory (London) 1991 v Millam* [2007] IRLR 526 which indicates that the mere fact of a share sale does not preclude a transfer taking place by other means.) The fact that employees are not taken on does not prevent TUPE applying in certain circumstances (see, for example, the decision of the Court of Appeal in *RCO Support Services v Unison* [2002] IRLR 401 and *ECM v Cox* [1999] IRLR 559).

34.04 Additionally, TUPE 2006 will apply to a 'service provision change'. This is now expressly set out in TUPE 2006 at reg 3(1)(b). A service provision change is, in effect, an initial outsourcing (TUPE 2006, reg 3(1)(b)(i)), a second round tender (TUPE 2006, reg 3(1)(b)(ii)), and a contracting back in (TUPE 2006, reg 3(1)(b)(iii)) which prior to that event is an organized grouping of employees situated in Great Britain which has the principal purpose of carrying out the activities on behalf of the client. It is not a contract for a specific event or of short-term duration and the activities must not consist wholly or mainly of the supply of goods for the customer's use (TUPE 2006, reg 3(3)). The Government Guidance makes it clear that there must be an identifiable group of employees providing the service, and gives the example of a courier service which uses different employees each day as an example of where this test would not be satisfied. It also makes it clear that 'service provision' can consist of just one employee. Difficulties can arise where, upon a transfer, there is fragmentation of a service: see *Kimberley Group Housing Limited v Hambley* [2008] IRLR 682 and *Clearsprings Management Limited v Ankers* [2009] All ER (D) 261. The multi-factoral test set out in *Cheesman* does not apply when considering whether or not a service provision change has occurred: *Metropolitan Resources v Churchill* [2009] IRLR 700.

34.05 TUPE 2006 will not apply to a transfer of an administrative function between public administrations or a reorganization of a public administration (TUPE 2006, reg 3(5)). However, the Cabinet Office's Statement of Practice 'Staff Transfers in the Public Sector' may apply separate regulations, and give employees similar rights to TUPE 2006.

34.06 A transfer under TUPE can be effected by a series of two or more transactions (TUPE 2006, reg 3(4)). The actual date of the transfer is determined by when, in fact, the responsibility as employer for carrying on the business or the unit transferred moves from the transferor to the transferee (*Celtec Ltd v Astley* [2005] IRLR 647).

34.07 Under TUPE 1981, there used to be an exception to the normal rule that when a transfer takes place is where a business is 'hived down' by a receiver or liquidator of a company, who may transfer a viable part of the business to a wholly owned subsidiary in the hope of making that part of the business more saleable to others. This exception no longer applies and this will be a transfer under TUPE 2006, provided the statutory definition is met.

B. WHICH EMPLOYEES?

34.08 TUPE 2006 only applies to people who are employed, under a contract of employment or apprenticeship (TUPE 2006, reg 2(1)), in the undertaking by the transferor *immediately before* the transfer or would have been so employed, if he had not been dismissed for an automatically unfair reason in accordance with reg 7(1) (TUPE 2006, reg 4(3)). Therefore, it is important to look carefully at whether the transferor and the employer are one and the same and to check which part of the business the employees are actually working in. If the employee was employed by another group company rather than the transferor, then the court may not look behind the formal legal position so TUPE 2006 may not apply to this employee (*Michael Peters Ltd v (1) Farnfield, (2) Michael Peters Group plc* [1995] IRLR 190; *Sunley Turriff Holdings Ltd v Stuart Lyle Thomson* [1995] IRLR 184; *Duncan Webb Offset (Maidstone) Ltd v Cooper* [1995] IRLR 633; *The Print Factory (London) 1991 v Millam* [2007] EWCA Civ 322, [2007] ICR 1331 (although these are all cases relating to TUPE 1981)).

It is necessary to consider whether the employee works in the undertaking or part of the business that is transferred. Factors under TUPE 1981 which would have shown that he is working in the relevant part of the undertaking are: that his contract of employment specifically assigns him to that part of the business (although this will not be decisive); that he is regarded as part of the human stock or permanent workforce of that business or part of the business, for example, he spends all his time working in that part of the business; that he values his work in that part of the business above his work in other areas; or that the cost of employing him is charged to that part of the business. If these factors are in favour of the employee being employed in the relevant part of the business it will not matter that there is a mobility clause in the contract which in theory allows the transferor to move the employee. Unless the transferor actually exercises his right to move the employee prior to the transfer he will be treated as if employed in the relevant part (Case 186/83 *Botzen v Rotterdamsche Droogdok Maatschappij BV* [1985] ECR 519; *CPL Distribution v Todd* [2003] IRLR 28). Under TUPE 2006, the Government Guidance makes it clear that those who are temporarily assigned to the business will not transfer—and whether someone is temporarily assigned will depend on a number of factors, such as the length of time the employee has been there and whether a date has been set for the employee's return or re-assignment. The EAT considered that the *Botzen* principles ought to apply in the context of a service provision change: see *Kimberley Group Housing Limited v Hambley* [2008] IRLR 682. **34.09**

Further, if the employee expressly informed either the transferor or transferee prior to the transfer that he objects to the transfer (which must mean a refusal to consent to it, at the least) the employee will not transfer; his employment will be deemed to terminate on the transfer of the undertaking, but that termination will usually not be regarded as a dismissal by the transferor (TUPE 2006, reg 4(7) and (8)). The exception to this is where the transfer would involve a substantial and detrimental change to his working conditions when the employee can still be treated as if they have been dismissed (TUPE 2006, reg 4(9)). See para 34.18 below in relation to the protection afforded to the employee in these circumstances. Although reg 4(7) only usually operates before the relevant transfer takes place (see, for example, *Capita Health Solutions v McLean* [2008] IRLR 595, where it was held that an agreement that an employee would work for the transferee for a short period did not amount to an objection), where the employees are not made aware of the identity of the transferee prior to the transfer, the employees will be permitted to object to the transfer, so as to prevent the operation of regs 4(1) and (2) even after the transfer has taken place: see *New ISG Limited v Vernon* [2008] IRLR 115. **34.10**

C. WHAT PROTECTION?

When an undertaking is transferred, TUPE 2006 provides that any contract of employment of any person employed by the transferor and assigned to the undertaking shall have effect as if originally made between the person so employed and the transferee (TUPE 2006, reg 4(1)). More particularly, the transferee takes over all the transferor's rights, powers, duties, and liabilities under the employment contracts so that after a transfer, any wrongful act committed by the transferor is deemed to have been done by the transferee, and similarly any breach of duty on the part of the employee before a transfer is deemed to have been a breach of duty to the transferee (TUPE 2006, reg 4(2)). The purpose of TUPE is therefore to preserve rights rather than to create new rights: see *Jackson v Computershare Investor Services plc* [2008] IRLR 80. **34.11**

34.12 The exception to the above is where the transfer to the transferor is subject to:

(a) relevant insolvency proceedings, where the obligation to pay certain amounts due to the employee will not transfer, for example, arrears in pay, statutory redundancy pay, payment in lieu of notice, holiday pay, or the basic award of compensation for unfair dismissal. These sums will instead be met by the Secretary of State through the National Insurance Fund (TUPE 2006, reg 8). A relevant insolvency procedure is defined at reg 8(6) as insolvency proceedings which have been opened in relation to the transferor, not with a view to the liquidation of the assets of the transferor and are under the supervision of an insolvency practitioner. According to the Government Guidance on TUPE 2006, this is intended to cover any collective insolvency procedures in which the whole or part of the business or undertaking is transferred to another entity as a going concern. It does not cover winding up by either creditors or members where there is no such transfer. The EAT gave guidance as to the definition of 'relevant insolvency proceedings' under TUPE 2006, reg 8 in *Secretary of State for Trade and Industry v Slater* [2007] IRLR 928;

(b) bankruptcy proceedings or analogous insolvency proceedings where regs 4 and 7 TUPE 2006 do not apply at all by virtue of reg 8(7). The scope of the these proceedings is not clear. Although liquidations are very likely to fall within the scope of reg 8(7) the status of 'pre-pack administrations' has been thrown into doubt as a result of the decisions of the EAT and Court of Appeal in *Oakland v Wellswood (Yorkshire) Limited* [2009] IRLR 250 (EAT).

34.13 All aspects of the employee's contract of employment and rights connected with that contract of employment are transferred save for criminal liability (TUPE 2006, reg 4(6)) and the rights concerning occupational pension schemes. Occupational pension schemes are specifically excluded from any transfer (TUPE 2006, reg 10). An occupational pension scheme is defined by reference to s 1 of the Pension Schemes Act 1993 as a pension scheme established by an employer for employees of a certain description for the purpose of providing benefits to, amongst others, persons of that description. It does not include a personal pension scheme, which is broadly a scheme registered and established in accordance with the Finance Act 2004. It is only those parts of the occupational pension scheme which relate to benefits for old age, invalidity, or survivors which shall be exempted from transfer; all other rights and obligations will transfer (TUPE 2006, reg 10(2)). TUPE 2006 now makes it clear that an employee will not have a claim as a result of a failure to transfer rights under an occupational pension scheme where that failure comes within reg 10 and took place after 6 April 2006 (TUPE 2006, reg 10(3)). However, where transferred employees were entitled to participate in an occupational pension scheme prior to the transfer, the transferee employer must establish a minimum level of pension provision for the transferred employees, which requires the transferee employer to match employee contributions, up to six per cent of salary, into a stakeholder pension or to offer an equivalent alternative (Pensions Act 2004).

34.14 Regulation 4(1) and (2) has the following effect:

(a) If the transferor fails to pay the employee's wages, the employee can sue the transferee to recover the underpayment save where the transfer is subject to relevant insolvency proceedings (see para 34.12 above).

(b) If the transferor dismissed the employee before the transfer, because of the transfer, or for a reason connected with the transfer which is not an economic, technical, or organizational reason entailing changes in the workplace, the employee can claim reinstatement or compensation for unfair dismissal and any other outstanding liabilities from the transferee (TUPE 2006, regs 4(3) and 7(1)) (see also para 34.15 below).

(c) If the transferor has discriminated against an employee on grounds of sex or race prior to the transfer (even where that discrimination took place when he was employed under a previous contract of employment) liability for that discrimination will transfer to the transferee.

(d) If the transferor was negligent towards the employee prior to the transfer, the employee can claim against the transferee in respect of that negligence and, potentially, under any connected insurance (*Martin v Lancashire County Council*; *Bernadone v Pall Mall Services Group* [2000] IRLR 487).

(e) If the employee has committed acts of misconduct for which he has or has not been given warnings, or if he has been given warnings for incapability, the transferee may rely upon such misconduct or warnings when considering subsequent stages in any disciplinary procedure affecting that employee.

(f) If the employee's contract of employment contains restrictive covenants, these will transfer, but their scope will be limited to protecting the undertaking transferred; they will not be construed as protecting the rest of the transferee's business as well (*Morris Angel & Son Ltd v Hollande* [1993] IRLR 169).

(g) The employee is generally deemed to have continuous employment so far as his statutory and contractual employment rights are concerned. These will include the right not to be unfairly dismissed, the right to redundancy or statutory maternity payments, and maternity rights.

(h) The rule applies to both express and implied contractual provisions. It also applies to collective agreements (TUPE 2006, reg 5). A customary arrangement or agreed procedure for selection of employees for redundancy would be deemed to be carried over (*Whent v T Cartledge Ltd* [1997] IRLR 153 as affirmed by the EAT in *Alemo-Herron v Parkwood Leisure Limited* [2009] IRLR 322).

(i) Share options, profit shares, bonus or equivalent schemes transfer, even if on a normal construction the provisions do not easily transfer. However, in that case the employee only has the right to participate in a scheme of 'substantial equivalencies, but one which is free from unjust, absurd or impossible features' (*Unicorn Consultancy Services v Westbrook* [2000] IRLR 80; MITIE *Management Ltd v French* [2002] IRLR 512).

(j) In relation to liability for a protective award in relation to a failure by the transferor to inform and consult, see para 34.28 below.

Any employee who has worked for one year for either the transferor or transferee, and whether or not in the undertaking or elsewhere, who is dismissed where the sole or principal reason for the dismissal is the transfer itself, or a reason connected with the transfer which was not an economic, technical, or organizational reason (ETO reason) entailing changes in the work force, is deemed to have been automatically unfairly dismissed (TUPE 2006, reg 7(1)(5)). If, however, the dismissal is not for a reason connected with the transfer, but for a justifiable reason, such as gross misconduct, it will not be automatically unfair. Under TUPE 1981, dismissals may also be for a reason connected with the transfer even where a potential transferee has not been identified (see *Morris v John Grose Group Ltd* [1998] IRLR 499 as discussed by the EAT in *CAB Automotive Limited v Blake* [2008] All ER (D) 155) and a dismissal which takes place some considerable time after the transfer (for example two years) can still be for a reason connected with the transfer (*Taylor v Connex South Eastern Ltd* [2000] IDS Employment Law Brief 670); there is no reason why this case law would not continue to apply in relation to TUPE 2006. **34.15**

There is a defence to this rule where the dismissal is as a result of an ETO reason entailing changes in the workforce of either the transferor or the transferee (TUPE 2006, reg 7(2)). The reason may apply to a dismissal which takes place either before or after the relevant transfer. Under TUPE 1981, the test applied has been a stringent one which, in effect, means that the reason must be connected with the conduct or running of the business. Thus dismissals carried out by the transferor at the insistence of the transferee, or dismissals whose main purpose is to raise the sale price of the business, would not have sufficient economic reason to justify fair termination of employment. Where the aim of the dismissal is to save the business this may qualify for the defence but only where, for example, the business was overstaffed, inefficient in terms of sales, and insolvent, and there was no collusion between seller and buyer (*Thomson v SCS Consulting Ltd* [2001] IRLR 801). In determining the reason for the dismissal in question, the reasoning of the person taking the decision must be analysed. As such, where an administrator took the decision to dismiss employees, it is his reasoning which must be considered: see *Dynamex Friction* **34.16**

Limited v Amicus [2008] IRLR 515. The reason must entail changes in the workforce; that is, a diminution of number of staff or a substantial reorganization (*Berriman v Delabole Slate Ltd* [1985] IRLR 305; *Green v Elan Care Ltd* EAT/018/01). It seems likely that this case law will continue to be good law under TUPE 2006. The Government Guidance states:

> the onus lies on the dismissing employer to show that the dismissal falls within the ETO exemption to the automatic unfairness rule. Neither the Regulations nor the Acquired Rights Directive define what an ETO reason may be. The courts and tribunals have not generally sought to distinguish between each of the three ETO categories, but rather have treated them as a single concept.

See also the Government Guidance relating to what is an ETO reason in the context of a variation of contract (Government Guidance, Part 3) which reflects the above case law. Even if a sufficient ETO reason does exist, the employer must still act fairly towards the employee and must follow all the appropriate procedures (TUPE 2006, reg 7(3)(b)). Previously, under TUPE 1981, case law had supported the fact that whilst liability for an automatically unfair dismissal would transfer to the transferee, where the dismissal by the transferor was for an ETO reason immediately before the transfer, that was then found to be substantively unfair, that liability may remain with the transferor. TUPE 2006 appears to continue this position—see regs 4(3) and 7(1); only liability for an automatically unfair dismissal under reg 7(1) transfers to the transferor. TUPE 2006 is silent as to what happens where there is an ETO reason but this dismissal is, nonetheless, unfair for procedural reasons.

34.17 Claims for TUPE-related unfair dismissals must be brought within the relevant time limits under the substantive legislation, that is usually within three months of the effective date of termination.

34.18 An employee who has resigned in response to a substantial change in working conditions to their material detriment and whose contract is or would otherwise be transferred in accordance with reg 4(1), will be treated as if he had been dismissed and could bring a claim for unfair dismissal (TUPE 2006, reg 4(9)). However, the dismissal will not necessarily be automatically unfair; it will be for the employee to prove that it is. Also, the employee will not be entitled to any damages in respect of a failure by the employer to pay the employee in respect of a notice period which he has failed to work (TUPE 2006, reg 4(10)). The Government Guidance states that a substantial change in working conditions could be a major relocation of the work place, or the withdrawal of a right to a tenured post. This protection is in addition to the employee's common law right to claim constructive dismissal (TUPE 2006, reg 4(11)).

34.19 An employee also has additional protection under TUPE 2006 where the transferor or, more usually, the transferee varies the terms and conditions of employment of the employee. Any variation of contract where the sole or principal reason is the transfer itself or a reason connected with the transfer that is not an ETO reason entailing changes in the workforce shall be void (TUPE 2006, reg 4(4)). Variations for an ETO reason entailing changes in the workforce or a reason unconnected with the transfer will, however, be valid (TUPE 2006, reg 4(5)). See para 34.15 above for a discussion of what constitutes an ETO reason entailing changes in the workforce. Note, however, that the Government Guidance states categorically that a desire to harmonize terms and conditions cannot constitute an ETO reason entailing changes in the workforce. Variations of contract will also be valid where those variations are purely beneficial to the employee(s) who are subject to the relevant transfer: see *Regent Security Services Limited v Power* [2008] IRLR 66.

34.20 Where the employee is employed in an undertaking which, at the time of the transfer, is subject to relevant insolvency proceedings, the protection in relation to variation of the contract of employment is different. Variations to the contract will be valid where they are agreed with appropriate representatives, who are either trade union representatives or, if there are none, elected representatives (TUPE 2006, reg 9(1) and (2)). Where the representatives are not trade union representatives, in addition to agreeing the variation with the appropriate representatives, the employer must obtain agreement in writing, signed by each of the representatives, and, before it is signed, provide all employees to whom it is intended to apply on the date on which it is intended to come into effect with copies of the text of the agreement and such guidance as those employees might reasonably require in order to understand it fully (TUPE 2006, reg 9(5)). For a variation to come within the scope of this additional flexibility, the sole or principal reason for it must be the transfer itself or a reason connected with the transfer which is not an ETO reason entailing changes in the workforce and it must be designed to safeguard employment opportunities by ensuring the survival of the undertakings or business (TUPE 2006, reg 9(7)).

D. TRADE UNIONS

TUPE 2006 also operates to transfer over any recognition agreement between the transferor and a recognized independent trade union but only where the transferred organized grouping of resources or employees maintains an identity distinct from the remainder of the transferee's undertaking (TUPE 2006, reg 6(1)). See also para 34.14(h) above in relation to collective agreements. **34.21**

E. DUTY TO INFORM AND CONSULT

Both the transferor and the transferee must notify representatives of employees who may be affected by the impending transfer of certain information and, if measures may be taken which could affect the employees, they also have consultation obligations (TUPE 2006, reg 13). **34.22**

Representatives for these purposes are, where a trade union is recognized in relation to the employees, representatives of the trade union, or, if not, representatives elected by the employees generally or specifically for the purposes of consultation under TUPE 2006 (TUPE 2006, reg 13(3)). **34.23**

If it is necessary to hold elections for the representatives, arrangements for elections must: **34.24**

(a) be fair;
(b) ensure that there are sufficient representatives to represent the interests of all the employees;
(c) identify the term for which the employee representatives shall be in office;
(d) ensure the candidates are affected employees and that no one is excluded from standing;
(e) equally, that all are able to vote;
(f) ensure that the election is conducted so as to secure that so far as reasonably practicable those voting do so in secret and the votes given are accurately counted.

(TUPE 2006, reg 14(1))

The transferor must inform the employee representatives of the following matters: **34.25**

(a) The fact that the transfer is to take place.
(b) The approximate date for the proposed transfer.
(c) The reason for the proposed transfer.
(d) The legal, economic, and social implications of the transfer for the affected employees.
(e) Any measure which it is envisaged the transferor or the transferee will take as a result of the transfer or, if no such measures will be taken, that fact. 'Measure' means an action which the transferor or transferee has a present plan to implement, and does not include a vague idea for the future.

(TUPE 2006, reg 13(2); *Institution of Professional Civil Servants v Secretary of State for Defence* [1987] IRLR 373)

If measures are to be taken by either the transferor or the transferee which may affect the employee, the party which is to take those measures must consult with the employee **34.26** representatives and consider the views expressed by the employee representatives with a view to seeking the representatives' agreement to them, before reaching a final decision to implement those measures (TUPE 2006, reg 13(6)). This means that the employer must discuss them with the representatives with an open mind and make every effort to secure the representatives' agreement to what is proposed and to accommodate their objections. The employer must consider any representations, reply to them, and, if they are to be rejected, state the reasons for doing so.

34.27 If the transferor fails to inform the representatives of the material facts, or if the representatives are not consulted about any measures which may be taken, the representatives may within three months of the transfer bring a complaint in an employment tribunal for a declaration and appropriate compensation for the failure to consult. The maximum award is 13 weeks' pay for each of the affected employees. The award is intended to be punitive rather than compensatory (*Sweetin v Coral Racing* [2006] IRLR 252). An award for failure to comply with the duty to inform and consult can be made against either the transferor, or the transferee. Where an award is made against the transferor, if, after being given notice, the transferee failed to provide information on time regarding any measures it proposed to take as a result of the transfer, or failed to consult about such measures, the transferee may also be liable (TUPE 2006, regs 15 and 16). However, there can be no obligation on the transferee to consult after the transfer: see *UCATT v Amicus* [2009] ICR 852.

34.28 In any case, the regulations expressly provide that the transferee and the transferor will be jointly liable for a failure to inform and consult. The transferee will be liable for its failure and will also be jointly and severally liable with the transferor for any failure by it (TUPE 2006, reg 15(7) to (9)).

F. DISCLOSURE OF 'EMPLOYEE LIABILITY INFORMATION'

34.29 TUPE 2006 introduces new obligations on the transferor to produce certain information to the transferee within certain specified timeframes (TUPE 2006, regs 11 and 12).

34.30 The obligation is in respect of any person employed by the transferor who is assigned to the organized grouping of resources or employees that is the subject of the transfer (TUPE 2006, reg 11(1)). The information must be notified in writing or some other readily accessible form. The information which must be provided is:

(a) the identity and age of the employee;
(b) the statutory particulars of employment;
(c) any information in relation to a disciplinary or grievance procedure which would come within the terms of the statutory dispute resolution procedures within the previous two years;
(d) information about any actual or pending court or tribunal case within the last two years;
(e) information about any collective agreement.

(TUPE 2006, reg 11(2))

34.31 The information must date from no more than 14 days before the date it is notified and must be notified no more than 14 days before the transfer (TUPE 2006, reg 11(3) and (6)).

34.32 If the transferor fails to provide the information in accordance with reg 11, the transferee may present a complaint to the employment tribunal within three months of the relevant transfer. The employment tribunal may make a declaration and award compensation (TUPE 2006, reg 12(1), (2), and (3)). The minimum award to be made by the employment tribunal shall be £500 per employee. Otherwise, the compensation should take into account the loss suffered by the transferee and the terms of any contract between the transferor and the transferee (TUPE 2006, reg 12(4) and (5)).

CHECKLIST FOR TUPE-RELATED CLAIMS

The checklist below is relevant to any claims (unfair dismissal, unlawful deduction, contractual claim, discrimination) where additional protection afforded by TUPE 2006 may be applicable.

Qualifying employee?

1. Is the relevant individual employed under a contract of service or of apprenticeship? If not, for example where the individual is a worker or otherwise employed under a contract for services or a partner in a partnership, TUPE 2006 will not apply (TUPE 2006, reg 2(1)).
2. Was the employee employed by the transferor or some other entity, for example, another company in the same group? If employed by another company in the group, TUPE 2006 may not apply (see para 34.08 above).
3. Was the employee temporarily assigned to the organized grouping of resources which was transferred? If yes, TUPE 2006 may not apply to him (see para 34.09).
4. Was the employee employed by the transferor in the undertaking immediately before the relevant transfer took place (ie before serious negotiations began between the parties leading to the transfer)? Subject to the next paragraph, unless they were, TUPE 2006 will not apply (TUPE 2006, reg 4(1)).
5. Was the employee dismissed prior to the transfer, because of the transfer or for a reason connected with the transfer which was not an economic, technical, or organizational reason? If so, TUPE 2006 will apply and liability for the individual's contract of employment will, nonetheless, be deemed to be transferred to the transferee of the business (TUPE 2006, reg 4(3)).
6. Was the employee dismissed prior to the transfer for some reason unconnected with the transfer, whether or not that reason is ultimately valid, such as misconduct? If so, TUPE 2006 will not apply and the employee's only remedy is against the transferor (TUPE 2006, reg 4(3)).
7. Did the employee carry on working for the transferor after the transfer? If so, even if the employee expressly agrees with the transferor that he would continue to work for the transferor, this will not necessarily preclude him from claiming that TUPE 2006 applies and that, in fact, their employment has or should have been transferred to the transferee (TUPE 2006, reg 18).

Qualifying undertaking?

1. Is the undertaking:
   - (a) in the United Kingdom prior to the transfer? If not, TUPE 2006 will not apply (TUPE 2006, reg 3(1));
   - (b) a transfer of shares in a company so that the only change is the identity of the shareholders and not the identity of the employing company? If so, TUPE 2006 will probably not apply, even where the share sale route is adopted to avoid the application of TUPE 2006;
   - (c) a transfer of assets only? For example, the sale of a building, where all the employees of the seller continue to work for the seller in a different building. If so, TUPE will not apply (TUPE 2006, reg 3(2));
   - (d) a non-commercial entity, for example, a non-profit-making body? Even if it is, TUPE 2006 will still apply;
   - (e) a transfer of administrative functions between public administrators or a reorganization of a public administration? If so, TUPE 2006 will not apply (TUPE 2006, reg 3(5)) but other similar provisions may apply.

APPENDICES

Appendix 1
Selected Legislation

Statutes

Rules

Statutory Instruments

STATUTES

Disability Discrimination Act 1995 (Extracts)

(1995 Chapter 50)

An Act to make it unlawful to discriminate against disabled persons in connection with employment, the provision of goods, facilities and services or the disposal or management of premises; to make provision about the employment of disabled persons; and to establish a National Disability Council.

[8th November 1995]

PART I
DISABILITY

Meaning of 'disability' and 'disabled person'

1.—(1) Subject to the provisions of Schedule 1, a person has a disability for the purposes of this Act if he has a physical or mental impairment which has a substantial and long-term adverse effect on his ability to carry out normal day-to-day activities.

(2) In this Act 'disabled person' means a person who has a disability.

Past disabilities

2.—(1) The provisions of this Part and Parts II [to 4] [and 5A] apply in relation to a person who has had a disability as they apply in relation to a person who has that disability.[1,2]

(2) Those provisions are subject to the modifications made by Schedule 2.

(3) Any regulations or order made under this Act [by the Secretary of State, the Scottish Ministers or the [Welsh Ministers]] may include provision with respect to persons who have had a disability.[3]

(4) In any proceedings under Part [2, 3, 4 or 5A] of this Act, the question whether a person had a disability at a particular time ('the relevant time') shall be determined, for the purposes of this section, as if the provisions of, or made under, this Act in force when the act complained of was done had been in force at the relevant time.[4]

(5) The relevant time may be a time before the passing of this Act.

PART II
[THE EMPLOYMENT FIELD] [AND MEMBERS OF LOCALLY ELECTABLE AUTHORITIES][5]

[Meaning of 'discrimination' and 'harassment'[6]

Meaning of 'discrimination'

3A.—(1) For the purposes of this Part, a person discriminates against a disabled person if—

(a) for a reason which relates to the disabled person's disability, he treats him less favourably than he treats or would treat others to whom that reason does not or would not apply, and

(b) he cannot show that the treatment in question is justified.

(2) For the purposes of this Part, a person also discriminates against a disabled person if he fails to comply with a duty to make reasonable adjustments imposed on him in relation to the disabled person.

(3) Treatment is justified for the purposes of subsection (1)(b) if, but only if, the reason for it is both material to the circumstances of the particular case and substantial.

---

1 As amended by the Special Educational Needs and Disability Act 2001 (c 10), s 38(1), (2).

2 As amended by the Disability Discrimination Act 2005 (c 13) Sch 1, para 2(2).

3 As amended by the Disability Discrimination Act 2005 (c 13) Sch 1, para 2(3) and by SI 2007/1388, Sch1, para 48.

4 As amended by the Special Educational Needs and Disability Act 2001 (c 10), s 38(1), (2) and by the Disability Discrimination Act 2005 (c 13) Sch 1, para 2(4).

5 As amended by SI 2003/1673, reg 4 and the Disability Discrimination Act 2005 (c 13) Sch 1, para 4.

6 Sections 3A and 3B and the heading immediately preceding them inserted by SI 2003/1673, reg 4.

(4) But treatment of a disabled person cannot be justified under subsection (3) if it amounts to direct discrimination falling within subsection (5).
(5) A person directly discriminates against a disabled person if, on the ground of the disabled person's disability, he treats the disabled person less favourably than he treats or would treat a person not having that particular disability whose relevant circumstances, including his abilities, are the same as, or not materially different from, those of the disabled person.
(6) If, in a case falling within subsection (1), a person is under a duty to make reasonable adjustments in relation to a disabled person but fails to comply with that duty, his treatment of that person cannot be justified under subsection (3) unless it would have been justified even if he had complied with that duty.

Meaning of 'harassment'

3B.—(1) For the purposes of this Part, a person subjects a disabled person to harassment where, for a reason which relates to the disabled person's disability, he engages in unwanted conduct which has the purpose or effect of—
(a) violating the disabled person's dignity, or
(b) creating an intimidating, hostile, degrading, humiliating or offensive environment for him.
(2) Conduct shall be regarded as having the effect referred to in paragraph (a) or (b) of subsection (1) only if, having regard to all the circumstances, including in particular the perception of the disabled person, it should reasonably be considered as having that effect.]

[Employment[7]

Employers: discrimination and harassment

4.—(1) It is unlawful for an employer to discriminate against a disabled person—
(a) in the arrangements which he makes for the purpose of determining to whom he should offer employment;
(b) in the terms on which he offers that person employment; or
(c) by refusing to offer, or deliberately not offering, him employment.
(2) It is unlawful for an employer to discriminate against a disabled person whom he employs—
(a) in the terms of employment which he affords him;
(b) in the opportunities which he affords him for promotion, a transfer, training or receiving any other benefit;
(c) by refusing to afford him, or deliberately not affording him, any such opportunity; or
(d) by dismissing him, or subjecting him to any other detriment.
(3) It is also unlawful for an employer, in relation to employment by him, to subject to harassment—
(a) a disabled person whom he employs; or
(b) a disabled person who has applied to him for employment.
(4) Subsection (2) des not apply to benefits of any description if the employer is concerned with the provision (whether or not for payment) of benefits of that description to the public, or to a section of the public which includes the employee in question, unless—
(a) that provision differs in a material respect from the provision of the benefits by the employer to his employees;
(b) the provision of the benefits to the employee in question is regulated by his contract of employment; or
(c) the benefits relate to training.
(5) The reference in subsection (2)(d) to the dismissal of a person includes a reference—
(a) to the termination of that person's employment by the expiration of any period (including a period expiring by reference to an event or circumstance), not being a termination immediately after which the employment is renewed on the same terms; and
(b) to the termination of that person's employment by any act of his (including the giving of notice) in circumstances such that he is entitled to terminate it without notice by reason of the conduct of the employer.
(6) This section applies only in relation to employment at an establishment in Great Britain.

[7] Section 4 and the heading immediately preceding it substituted and 4A inserted by SI 2003/1673, reg 5.

Employers: duty to make adjustments

4A.—(1) Where—

(a) a provision, criterion or practice applied by or on behalf of an employer, or

(b) any physical feature of premises occupied by the employer,

places the disabled person concerned at a substantial disadvantage in comparison with persons who are not disabled, it is the duty of the employer to take such steps as it is reasonable, in all the circumstances of the case, for him to have to take in order to prevent the provision, criterion or practice, or feature, having that effect.

(2) In subsection (1), 'the disabled person concerned' means—

(a) in the case of a provision, criterion or practice for determining to whom employment should be offered, any disabled person who is, or has notified the employer that he may be, an applicant for that employment;

(b) in any other case, a disabled person who is—

(i) an applicant for the employment concerned, or

(ii) an employee of the employer concerned.

(3) Nothing in this section imposes any duty on an employer in relation to a disabled person if the employer does not know, and could not reasonably be expected to know—

(a) in the case of an applicant or potential applicant, that the disabled person concerned is, or may be, an applicant for the employment; or

(b) in any case, that that person has a disability and is likely to be affected in the way mentioned in subsection (1).]

[Other unlawful acts[8]

Relationships which have come to an end

16A.—(1) This section applies where—

(a) there has been a relevant relationship between a disabled person and another person ('the relevant person'), and

(b) the relationship has come to an end.

(2) In this section a 'relevant relationship' is—

(a) a relationship during the course of which an act of discrimination against, or harassment of, one party to the relationship by the other party to it is unlawful under any preceding provision of this Part[, other than section 15B and 15C];[9] or

(b) a relationship between a person providing employment services [. . ..] and a person receiving such services.[10]

(3) It is unlawful for the relevant person—

(a) to discriminate against the disabled person by subjecting him to a detriment, or

(b) to subject the disabled person to harassment,

where the discrimination or harassment arises out of and is closely connected to the relevant relationship.

(4) This subsection applies where—

(a) a provision, criterion or practice applied by the relevant person to the disabled person in relation to any matter arising out of the relevant relationship, or

(b) a physical feature of premises which are occupied by the relevant person,

places the disabled person at a substantial disadvantage in comparison with persons who are not disabled, but are in the same position as the disabled person in relation to the relevant person.

(5) Where subsection (4) applies, it is the duty of the relevant person to take such steps as it is reasonable, in all the circumstances of the case, for him to have to take in order to prevent the provision, practice or criterion, or feature, having that effect.

(6) Nothing in subsection (5) imposes any duty on the relevant person if he does not know, and could not reasonably be expected to know, that the disabled person has a disability and is likely to be affected in the way mentioned in that subsection.

[8] Section 16A inserted by SI 2003/1673, reg 15.

[9] As amended by the Disability Discrimination Act 2005 (c 13) Sch 1, para 7(a).

[10] As amended by the Disability Discrimination Act 2005 (c 13) Sch 1, para 7(b) and Sch 2.

(7) In subsection (2), reference to an act of discrimination or harassment which is unlawful includes, in the case of a relationship which has come to an end before the commencement of this section, reference to such an act which would, after the commencement of this section, be unlawful.]

[Enforcement etc[11]

Enforcement, remedies and procedure

17A.—(1) A complaint by any person that another person—[12]

(a) has discriminated against him[, or subjected him to harassment,] in a way which is unlawful under this Part, or[13]

(b) is, by virtue of section 57 or 58, to be treated as having [done so],[14]

may be presented to an [employment tribunal].

[(1A) Subsection (1) does not apply to a complaint under section 14A(1) or (2) of an act in respect of which an appeal, or proceedings in the nature of an appeal, may be brought under any enactment.[15]

(1B) [. . .][16]

(1C) Where, on the hearing of a complaint under subsection (1), the complainant proves facts from which the tribunal could, apart from this subsection, conclude in the absence of an adequate explanation that the respondent has acted in a way which is unlawful under this Part, the tribunal shall uphold the complaint unless the respondent proves that he did not so act.]

(2) Where an [employment tribunal] finds that a complaint presented to it under this section is well-founded, it shall take such of the following steps as it considers just and equitable—[17]

(a) making a declaration as to the rights of the complainant and the respondent in relation to the matters to which the complaint relates;

(b) ordering the respondent to pay compensation to the complainant;

(c) recommending that the respondent take, within a specified period, action appearing to the tribunal to be reasonable, in all the circumstances of the case, for the purpose of obviating or reducing the adverse effect on the complainant of any matter to which the complaint relates.

(3) Where a tribunal orders compensation under subsection (2)(b), the amount of the compensation shall be calculated by applying the principles applicable to the calculation of damages in claims in tort or (in Scotland) in reparation for breach of statutory duty.

(4) For the avoidance of doubt it is hereby declared that compensation in respect of discrimination in a way which is unlawful under this Part may include compensation for injury to feelings whether or not it includes compensation under any other head.

(5) If the respondent to a complaint fails, without reasonable justification, to comply with a recommendation made by an [employment tribunal] under subsection (2)(c) the tribunal may, if it thinks it just and equitable to do so—[18]

(a) increase the amount of compensation required to be paid to the complainant in respect of the complaint, where an order was made under subsection (2)(b); or

(b) make an order under subsection (2)(b).

Section 1(1)

Schedule 1

Provisions Supplementing Section 1

Impairment

1.—(1) [. . .][19]

(2) Regulations may make provision, for the purposes of this Act—

(a) for conditions of a prescribed description to be treated as amounting to impairments;

(b) for conditions of a prescribed description to be treated as not amounting to impairments.

---

11 Section 17A (formerly s 8) substituted by SI 2003/1673, reg 9.

12 As amended by the Employment Rights (Dispute Resolution) Act 1998 (c 8),s 1(2)(c).

13 As amended by SI 2003/1673, reg 9.

14 As amended by SI 2003/1673, reg 9.

15 Inserted by SI 2003/1673, reg 9.

16 Repealed by the Disability Discrimination Act 2005 (c 13) Sch 1, para 9.

17 As amended by the Employment Rights (Dispute Resolution) Act 1998 (c 8),s 1(2)(c).

18 As amended by the Employment Rights (Dispute Resolution) Act 1998 (c 8),s 1(2)(c).

19 Repealed by the Disability Discrimination Act 2005 (c 13), s 18(2).

(3) Regulations made under sub-paragraph (2) may make provision as to the meaning of 'condition' for the purposes of those regulations.

Long-term effects

2.—(1) The effect of an impairment is a long-term effect if—
(a) it has lasted at least 12 months;
(b) the period for which it lasts is likely to be at least 12 months; or
(c) it is likely to last for the rest of the life of the person affected.
(2) Where an impairment ceases to have a substantial adverse effect on a person's ability to carry out normal day-to-day activities, it is to be treated as continuing to have that effect if that effect is likely to recur.
(3) For the purposes of sub-paragraph (2), the likelihood of an effect recurring shall be disregarded in prescribed circumstances.
(4) Regulations may prescribe circumstances in which, for the purposes of this Act—
(a) an effect which would not otherwise be a long-term effect is to be treated as such an effect; or
(b) an effect which would otherwise be a long-term effect is to be treated as not being such an effect.

Severe disfigurement

3.—(1) An impairment which consists of a severe disfigurement is to be treated as having a substantial adverse effect on the ability of the person concerned to carry out normal day-to-day activities.
(2) Regulations may provide that in prescribed circumstances a severe disfigurement is not to be treated as having that effect.
(3) Regulations under sub-paragraph (2) may, in particular, make provision with respect to deliberately acquired disfigurements.

Normal day-to-day activities

4.—(1) An impairment is to be taken to affect the ability of the person concerned to carry out normal day-to-day activities only if it affects one of the following—
(a) mobility;
(b) manual dexterity;
(c) physical co-ordination;
(d) continence;
(e) ability to lift, carry or otherwise move everyday objects;
(f) speech, hearing or eyesight;
(g) memory or ability to concentrate, learn or understand; or
(h) perception of the risk of physical danger.
(2) Regulations may prescribe—
(a) circumstances in which an impairment which does not have an effect falling within sub-paragraph (1) is to be taken to affect the ability of the person concerned to carry out normal day-to-day activities;
(b) circumstances in which an impairment which has an effect falling within sub-paragraph (1) is to be taken not to affect the ability of the person concerned to carry out normal day-to-day activities.

Substantial adverse effects

5. Regulations may make provision for the purposes of this Act—
(a) for an effect of a prescribed kind on the ability of a person to carry out normal day-to-day activities to be treated as a substantial adverse effect;
(b) for an effect of a prescribed kind on the ability of a person to carry out normal day-to-day activities to be treated as not being a substantial adverse effect.

Effect of medical treatment

6.—(1) An impairment which would be likely to have a substantial adverse effect on the ability of the person concerned to carry out normal day-to-day activities, but for the fact that measures are being taken to treat or correct it, is to be treated as having that effect.
(2) In sub-paragraph (1) 'measures' includes, in particular, medical treatment and the use of a prosthesis or other aid.
(3) Sub-paragraph (1) does not apply—
(a) in relation to the impairment of a person's sight, to the extent that the impairment is, in his case, correctable by spectacles or contact lenses or in such other ways as may be prescribed; or

(b) in relation to such other impairments as may be prescribed, in such circumstances as may be prescribed.

[**6A.**—(1) Subject to sub-paragraph (2), a person who has cancer, HIV infection or multiple sclerosis is deemed to have a disability, and hence to be a disabled person.

(2) Regulations may provide for sub-paragraph (1) not to apply in the case of a person who has cancer if he has cancer of a prescribed description.

(3) A description of cancer prescribed under sub-paragraph (2) may (in particular) be framed by reference to consequences for a person of his having it.][20]

Persons deemed to be disabled

7.—(1) Sub-paragraph (2) applies to any person whose name is, both on 12th January 1995 and on the date when this paragraph comes into force, in the register of disabled persons maintained under section 6 of the [1944 c 10.] Disabled Persons (Employment) Act 1944.

(2) That person is to be deemed—

(a) during the initial period, to have a disability, and hence to be a disabled person; and

(b) afterwards, to have had a disability and hence to have been a disabled person during that period.

(3) A certificate of registration shall be conclusive evidence, in relation to the person with respect to whom it was issued, of the matters certified.

(4) Unless the contrary is shown, any document purporting to be a certificate of registration shall be taken to be such a certificate and to have been validly issued.

(5) Regulations may provide for prescribed descriptions of person to be deemed to have disabilities, and hence to be disabled persons, for the purposes of this Act.

[(5A) The generality of sub-paragraph (5) shall not be taken to be prejudiced by the other provisions of this Schedule.][21]

(6) Regulations may prescribe circumstances in which a person who has been deemed to be a disabled person by the provisions of sub-paragraph (1) or regulations made under sub-paragraph (5) is to be treated as no longer being deemed to be such a person.

(7) In this paragraph—

'certificate of registration' means a certificate issued under regulations made under section 6 of the Act of 1944; and

'initial period' means the period of three years beginning with the date on which this paragraph comes into force.

Progressive conditions

8.—(1) Where—

(a) a person has a progressive condition (such as cancer, multiple sclerosis or muscular dystrophy or [HIV infection][22]),

(b) as a result of that condition, he has an impairment which has (or had) an effect on his ability to carry out normal day-to-day activities, but

(c) that effect is not (or was not) a substantial adverse effect,

he shall be taken to have an impairment which has such a substantial adverse effect if the condition is likely to result in his having such an impairment.

(2) Regulations may make provision, for the purposes of this paragraph—

(a) for conditions of a prescribed description to be treated as being progressive;

(b) for conditions of a prescribed description to be treated as not being progressive.

[Interpretation

9.—In this Schedule 'HIV infection' means infection by a virus capable of causing the Acquired Immune Deficiency Syndrome.][23]

---

[20] Inserted by the Disability Discrimination Act 2005 (c 13), s 18(3).

[21] Inserted by the Disability Discrimination Act 2005 (c 13), s 18(4).

[22] As amended by the Disability Discrimination Act 2005 (c 13) Sch 1, para 36.

[23] Inserted by the Disability Discrimination Act 2005 (c 13), s 18(5).

Employment Act 2002 (Extracts)

(2002 Chapter 22)

An Act to make provision for statutory rights to paternity and adoption leave and pay; to amend the law relating to statutory maternity leave and pay; to amend the Employment Tribunals Act 1996; to make provision for the use of statutory procedures in relation to employment disputes; to amend the law relating to particulars of employment; to make provision about compromise agreements; to make provision for questionnaires in relation to equal pay; to make provision in connection with trade union learning representatives; to amend section 110 of the Employment Rights Act 1996; to make provision about fixed-term work; to make provision about flexible working; to amend the law relating to maternity allowance; to make provision for work-focused interviews for partners of benefit claimants; to make provision about the use of information for, or relating to, employment and training; and for connected purposes.

[8th July 2002]

Part 3
Dispute Resolution etc

Statutory procedures[24]

Statutory dispute resolution procedures

29.—(1) Schedule 2 (which sets out the statutory dispute resolution procedures) shall have effect.

(2) The Secretary of State may by order—
  (a) amend Schedule 2;
  (b) make provision for the Schedule to apply, with or without modifications, as if—
    (i) any individual of a description specified in the order who would not otherwise be an employee for the purposes of the Schedule were an employee for those purposes; and
    (ii) a person of a description specified in the order were, in the case of any such individual, the individual's employer for those purposes.

(3) Before making an order under this section, the Secretary of State must consult the Advisory, Conciliation and Arbitration Service.

Non-completion of statutory procedure: adjustment of awards

31.—(1) This section applies to proceedings before an employment tribunal relating to a claim under any of the jurisdictions listed in Schedule 3 by an employee.

(2) If, in the case of proceedings to which this section applies, it appears to the employment tribunal that—
  (a) the claim to which the proceedings relate concerns a matter to which one of the statutory procedures applies,
  (b) the statutory procedure was not completed before the proceedings were begun, and
  (c) the non-completion of the statutory procedure was wholly or mainly attributable to failure by the employee—
    (i) to comply with a requirement of the procedure, or
    (ii) to exercise a right of appeal under it,

  it must, subject to subsection (4), reduce any award which it makes to the employee by 10 per cent, and may, if it considers it just and equitable in all the circumstances to do so, reduce it by a further amount, but not so as to make a total reduction of more than 50 per cent.

(3) If, in the case of proceedings to which this section applies, it appears to the employment tribunal that—
  (a) the claim to which the proceedings relate concerns a matter to which one of the statutory procedures applies,
  (b) the statutory procedure was not completed before the proceedings were begun, and
  (c) the non-completion of the statutory procedure was wholly or mainly attributable to failure by the employer to comply with a requirement of the procedure, it must, subject to subsection (4),

24 Sections 29 to 33 were repealed with effect from 6 April 2009 by the Employment Act 2008 (c.24), s 1 subject to transitional provisions and savings set out in SI 2008/3232, Sch 1 Pt 1 paras 1 to 3.

increase any award which it makes to the employee by 10 per cent and may, if it considers it just and equitable in all the circumstances to do

(4) The duty under subsection (2) or (3) to make a reduction or increase of 10 per cent does not apply if there are exceptional circumstances which would make a reduction or increase of that percentage unjust or inequitable, in which case the tribunal may make no reduction or increase or a reduction or increase of such lesser percentage as it considers just and equitable in all the circumstances.

(5) Where an award falls to be adjusted under this section and under section 38, the adjustment under this section shall be made before the adjustment under that section.

(6) The Secretary of State may for the purposes of this section by regulations—
- (a) make provision about the application of the statutory procedures;
- (b) make provision about when a statutory procedure is to be taken to be completed;
- (c) make provision about what constitutes compliance with a requirement of a statutory procedure;
- (d) make provision about circumstances in which a person is to be treated as not subject to, or as having complied with, such a requirement;
- (e) make provision for a statutory procedure to have effect in such circumstances as may be specified by the regulations with such modifications as may be so specified;
- (f) make provision about when an employee is required to exercise a right of appeal under a statutory procedure.

(7) The Secretary of State may by order—
- (a) amend Schedule 3 for the purpose of—
  - (i) adding a jurisdiction to the list in that Schedule, or
  - (ii) removing a jurisdiction from that list;
- (b) make provision, in relation to a jurisdiction listed in Schedule 3, for this section not to apply to proceedings relating to claims of a description specified in the order;
- (c) make provision for this section to apply, with or without modifications, as if—
  - (i) any individual of a description specified in the order who would not otherwise be an employee for the purposes of this section were an employee for those purposes, and
  - (ii) a person of a description specified in the order were, in the case of any such individual, the individual's employer for those purposes.

Complaints about grievances

32.—(1) This section applies to the jurisdictions listed in Schedule 4.

(2) An employee shall not present a complaint to an employment tribunal under a jurisdiction to which this section applies if—
- (a) it concerns a matter in relation to which the requirement in paragraph 6 or 9 of Schedule 2 applies, and
- (b) the requirement has not been complied with.

(3) An employee shall not present a complaint to an employment tribunal under a jurisdiction to which this section applies if—
- (a) it concerns a matter in relation to which the requirement in paragraph 6 or 9 of Schedule 2 has been complied with, and
- (b) less than 28 days have passed since the day on which the requirement was complied with.

(4) An employee shall not present a complaint to an employment tribunal under a jurisdiction to which this section applies if—
- (a) it concerns a matter in relation to which the requirement in paragraph 6 or 9 of Schedule 2 has been complied with, and
- (b) the day on which the requirement was complied with was more than one month after the end of the original time limit for making the complaint.

(5) In such circumstances as the Secretary of State may specify by regulations, an employment tribunal may direct that subsection (4) shall not apply in relation to a particular matter.

(6) An employment tribunal shall be prevented from considering a complaint presented in breach of subsections (2) to (4), but only if—
- (a) the breach is apparent to the tribunal from the information supplied to it by the employee in connection with the bringing of the proceedings, or
- (b) the tribunal is satisfied of the breach as a result of his employer raising the issue of compliance with those provisions in accordance with regulations under section 7 of the Employment Tribunals Act 1996 (c 17) (employment tribunal procedure regulations).

(7) The Secretary of State may for the purposes of this section by regulations—
 (a) make provision about the application of the procedures set out in Part 2 of Schedule 2;
 (b) make provision about what constitutes compliance with paragraph 6 or 9 of that Schedule;
 (c) make provision about circumstances in which a person is to be treated as having complied with paragraph 6 or 9 of that Schedule;
 (d) make provision for paragraph 6 or 9 of that Schedule to have effect in such circumstances as may be specified by the regulations with such modifications as may be so specified.
(8) The Secretary of State may by order—
 (a) amend, repeal or replace any of subsections (2) to (4);
 (b) amend Schedule 4;
 (c) make provision for this section to apply, with or without modifications, as if—
  (i) any individual of a description specified in the order who would not otherwise be an employee for the purposes of this section were an employee for those purposes, and
  (ii) a person of a description specified in the order were, in the case of any such individual, the individual's employer for those purposes.
(9) Before making an order under subsection (8)(a), the Secretary of State must consult the Advisory, Conciliation and Arbitration Service.
(10) In its application to orders under subsection (8)(a), section 51(1)(b) includes power to amend this section.

Consequential adjustment of time limits

33.—(1) The Secretary of State may, in relation to a jurisdiction listed in Schedule 3 or 4, by regulations make provision about the time limit for beginning proceedings in respect of a claim concerning a matter to which a statutory procedure applies.
(2) Regulations under this section may, in particular—
 (a) make provision extending, or authorising the extension of, the time for beginning proceedings,
 (b) make provision about the exercise of a discretion to extend the time for beginning proceedings, or
 (c) make provision treating proceedings begun out of time as begun within time.

Employment particulars

Failure to give statement of employment particulars etc

38.—(1) This section applies to proceedings before an employment tribunal relating to a claim by an employee under any of the jurisdictions listed in Schedule 5.
(2) If in the case of proceedings to which this section applies—
 (a) the employment tribunal finds in favour of the employee, but makes no award to him in respect of the claim to which the proceedings relate, and
 (b) when the proceedings were begun the employer was in breach of his duty to the employee under section 1(1) or 4(1) of the Employment Rights Act 1996 (c. 18) (duty to give a written statement of initial employment particulars or of particulars of change),

 the tribunal must, subject to subsection (5), make an award of the minimum amount to be paid by the employer to the employee and may, if it considers it just and equitable in all the circumstances, award the higher amount instead.
(3) If in the case of proceedings to which this section applies—
 (a) the employment tribunal makes an award to the employee in respect of the claim to which the proceedings relate, and
 (b) when the proceedings were begun the employer was in breach of his duty to the employee under section 1(1) or 4(1) of the Employment Rights Act 1996, the tribunal must, subject to subsection (5), increase the award by the minimum amount and may, if it considers it just and equitable in all the circumstances, increase the award by the higher amount instead.
(4) In subsections (2) and (3)—
 (a) references to the minimum amount are to an amount equal to two weeks' pay, and
 (b) references to the higher amount are to an amount equal to four weeks' pay.
(5) The duty under subsection (2) or (3) does not apply if there are exceptional circumstances which would make an award or increase under that subsection unjust or inequitable.
(6) The amount of a week's pay of an employee shall—
 (a) be calculated for the purposes of this section in accordance with Chapter 2 of Part 14 of the Employment Rights Act 1996 (c 18), and

(b) not exceed the amount for the time being specified in section 227 of that Act (maximum amount of week's pay).

(7) For the purposes of Chapter 2 of Part 14 of the Employment Rights Act 1996 as applied by subsection (6), the calculation date shall be taken to be—

(a) if the employee was employed by the employer on the date the proceedings were begun, that date, and

(b) if he was not, the effective date of termination as defined by section 97 of that Act.

(8) The Secretary of State may by order—

(a) amend Schedule 5 for the purpose of—

(i) adding a jurisdiction to the list in that Schedule, or

(ii) removing a jurisdiction from that list;

(b) make provision, in relation to a jurisdiction listed in Schedule 5, for this section not to apply to proceedings relating to claims of a description specified in the order;

(c) make provision for this section to apply, with or without modifications, as if—

(i) any individual of a description specified in the order who would not otherwise be an employee for the purposes of this section were an employee for those purposes, and

(ii) a person of a description specified in the order were, in the case of any such individual, the individual's employer for those purposes.

Schedule 2[25]

Statutory Dispute Resolution Procedures

Part I

Dismissal and Disciplinary Procedures

Chapter I

Standard Procedure

Step 1: statement of grounds for action and invitation to meeting

1.—(1) The employer must set out in writing the employee's alleged conduct or characteristics, or other circumstances, which lead him to contemplate dismissing or taking disciplinary action against the employee.

(2) The employer must send the statement or a copy of it to the employee and invite the employee to attend a meeting to discuss the matter.

Step 2: meeting

2.—(1) The meeting must take place before action is taken, except in the case where the disciplinary action consists of suspension.

(2) The meeting must not take place unless—

(a) the employer has informed the employee what the basis was for including in the statement under paragraph 1(1) the ground or grounds given in it, and

(b) the employee has had a reasonable opportunity to consider his response to that information.

(3) The employee must take all reasonable steps to attend the meeting.

(4) After the meeting, the employer must inform the employee of his decision and notify him of the right to appeal against the decision if he is not satisfied with it.

Step 3: appeal

3.—(1) f the employee does wish to appeal, he must inform the employer.

(2) If the employee informs the employer of his wish to appeal, the employer must invite him to attend a further meeting.

(3) The employee must take all reasonable steps to attend the meeting.

(4) The appeal meeting need not take place before the dismissal or disciplinary action takes effect.

(5) After the appeal meeting, the employer must inform the employee of his final decision.

[25] Repealed by the Employment Act 2008 (c.24), s 1 with effect from 6 April 2009, subject to transitional provisions and savings contained in SI 2008/3232, Sch 1 Pt 1 paras 1 to 3.

Chapter 2
Modified Procedure

Step 1: statement of grounds for action

4. The employer must—
   (a) set out in writing—
      (i) the employee's alleged misconduct which has led to the dismissal,
      (ii) what the basis was for thinking at the time of the dismissal that the employee was guilty of the alleged misconduct, and
      (iii) the employee's right to appeal against dismissal, and
   (b) send the statement or a copy of it to the employee.

Step 2: appeal

5.—(1) If the employee does wish to appeal, he must inform the employer.
(2) If the employee informs the employer of his wish to appeal, the employer must invite him to attend a meeting.
(3) The employee must take all reasonable steps to attend the meeting.
(4) After the appeal meeting, the employer must inform the employee of his final decision.

Part 2
Grievance Procedures

Chapter I
Standard Procedure

Step 1: statement of grievance

6. The employee must set out the grievance in writing and send the statement or a copy of it to the employer.

Step 2: meeting

7.—(1) The employer must invite the employee to attend a meeting to discuss the grievance.
(2) The meeting must not take place unless—
   (a) the employee has informed the employer what the basis for the grievance was when he made the statement under paragraph 6, and
   (b) the employer has had a reasonable opportunity to consider his response to that information.
(3) The employee must take all reasonable steps to attend the meeting.
(4) After the meeting, the employer must inform the employee of his decision as to his response to the grievance and notify him of the right to appeal against the decision if he is not satisfied with it.

Step 3: appeal

8.—(1) If the employee does wish to appeal, he must inform the employer.
(2) If the employee informs the employer of his wish to appeal, the employer must invite him to attend a further meeting.
(3) The employee must take all reasonable steps to attend the meeting.
(4) After the appeal meeting, the employer must inform the employee of his final decision.

Chapter 2
Modified Procedure

Step 1: statement of grievance

9. The employee must—
   (a) set out in writing—
      (i) the grievance, and
      (ii) the basis for it, and
   (b) send the statement or a copy of it to the employer.

Step 2: response

10. The employer must set out his response in writing and send the statement or a copy of it to the employee.

Part 3
General Requirements

Introductory

11. The following requirements apply to each of the procedures set out above (so far as applicable).

Timetable

12. Each step and action under the procedure must be taken without unreasonable delay.

Meetings

3.—(1) Timing and location of meetings must be reasonable.

(2) Meetings must be conducted in a manner that enables both employer and employee to explain their cases.

(3) In the case of appeal meetings which are not the first meeting, the employer should, as far as is reasonably practicable, be represented by a more senior manager than attended the first meeting (unless the most senior manager attended that meeting).

Part 4
Supplementary

Status of meetings

14. A meeting held for the purposes of this Schedule is a hearing for the purposes of section 13(4) and (5) of the Employment Relations Act 1999 (c 26) (definition of 'disciplinary hearing' and 'grievance hearing' in relation to the right to be accompanied under section 10 of that Act).

Scope of grievance procedures

15.—(1) The procedures set out in Part 2 are only applicable to matters raised by an employee with his employer as a grievance.

(2) Accordingly, those procedures are only applicable to the kind of disclosure dealt with in Part 4A of the Employment Rights Act 1996 (c 18) (protected disclosures of information) if information is disclosed by an employee to his employer in circumstances where—

(a) the information relates to a matter which the employee could raise as a grievance with his employer, and

(b) it is the intention of the employee that the disclosure should constitute the raising of the matter with his employer as a grievance.

Schedule 3[26]
Tribunal jurisdictions to which section 31 applies

Section 2 of the Equal Pay Act 1970 (c 41) (equality clauses)

Section 63 of the Sex Discrimination Act 1975 (c 65) (discrimination in the employment field)

Section 54 of the Race Relations Act 1976 (c 74) (discrimination in the employment field)

[Section 145A of the Trade Union and Labour Relations (Consolidation) Act 1992 (inducements relating to union membership or activities)

Section 145B of that Act (inducements relating to collective bargaining)

Section 146 of that Act (detriment in relation to union membership and activities)][27]

Paragraph 156 of Schedule A1 to that Act (detriment in relation to union recognition rights)

Section 17A of the Disability Discrimination Act 1995 (c 50) (discrimination in the employment field)

Section 23 of the Employment Rights Act 1996 (c 18) (unauthorised deductions and payments)

Section 48 of that Act (detriment in employment)

Section 111 of that Act (unfair dismissal)

Section 163 of that Act (redundancy payments)

---

[26] Repealed by the Employment Act 2008 (c.24), s 1 with effect from 6 April 2009, subject to transitional provisions and savings contained in SI 2008/3232, Sch 1 Pt 1 paras 1 to 3.

[27] Substituted by the Employment Relations Act 2004, Sch 1, para 43.

Section 24 of the National Minimum Wage Act 1998 (c 39) (detriment in relation to national minimum wage)

[. . .][28]

The Employment Tribunal Extension of Jurisdiction (England and Wales) Order 1994 (SI 1994/1623) (breach of employment contract and termination)

The Employment Tribunal Extension of Jurisdiction (Scotland) Order 1994 (SI 1994/1624) (corresponding provision for Scotland)

Regulation 30 of the Working Time Regulations 1998 (SI 1998/1833) (breach of regulations)

Regulation 32 of the Transnational Information and Consultation of Employees Regulations 1999 (SI 1999/3323) (detriment relating to European Works Councils)

[Regulation 28 of the Employment Equality (Religion or Belief) Regulations 2003 (discrimination in the employment field)][29]

[Regulation 45 of the European Public Limited-Liability Company Regulations 2004 (SI 2004/2326) (detriment in employment)

Regulation 33 of the Information and Consultation of Employees Regulations 2004 (SI 2004/3426) (detriment in employment)

Paragraph 8 of the Schedule to the Occupational and Personal Pension Schemes (Consultation by Employers and Miscellaneous Amendment) Regulations 2006 (SI 2006/349) (detriment in employment)][30]

[Regulation 28 of the Employment Equality (Sexual Orientation) Regulations 2003 (discrimination in the employment field)][31]

[Regulation 34 of the European Cooperative Society (Involvement of Employees) Regulations 2006 (detriment in relation to involvement in a European Cooperative Society)]

[Regulation 36 of the Employment Equality (Age) Regulations 2006 (dis crimination in the employment field)][32]

[Regulation 51 of the Companies (Cross-Border Mergers) Regulations 2007 (detriment in relation to special negotiating body or employee participation)][33]

[Regulation 17 of the Cross-border Railways Services (Working Time) Regulations 2008 (breach of regulations)][34]

Schedule 4[35]

Tribunal jurisdictions to which section 32 applies

Section 2 of the Equal Pay Act 1970 (c 41) (equality clauses)

Section 63 of the Sex Discrimination Act 1975 (c 65) (discrimination in the employment field)

Section 54 of the Race Relations Act 1976 (c 74) (discrimination in the employment field)

[Section 145A of the Trade Union and Labour Relations (Consolidation) Act 1992 (inducements relating to union membership or activities)

Section 145B of that Act (inducements relating to collective bargaining)

Section 146 of that Act (detriment in relation to union membership and activities)][36]

[28] Repealed by the Tax Credits Act 2002, s 60 Sch 6.

[29] Added by SI 2003/1660.

[30] Added by SI 2007/30 as from 6 April 2007.

[31] Added by SI 2003/1661.

[32] Added by SI 2006/1031 as from 1 October 2006.

[33] Added by SI 2007/2974 as from 15 December 2007.

[34] Added by SI 2008/1660 as from 27 July 2008.

[35] Repealed by the Employment Act 2008 (c.24), s 1 with effect from 6 April 2009, subject to transitional provisions and savings contained in SI 2008/3232, Sch 1 Pt 1 paras 1 to 3.

[36] Substituted by the Employment Relations Act 2004, Sch 1, para 43.

Paragraph 156 of Schedule A1 to that Act (detriment in relation to union recognition rights)

Section 17A of the Disability Discrimination Act 1995 (c 50) (discrimination in the employment field)

Section 23 of the Employment Rights Act 1996 (c 18) (unauthorised deductions and payments)

Section 48 of that Act (detriment in employment)

Section 111 of that Act (unfair dismissal)

Section 163 of that Act (redundancy payments)

Section 24 of the National Minimum Wage Act 1998 (c 39) (detriment in relation to national minimum wage)

[. . .][37]

Regulation 30 of the Working Time Regulations 1998 (SI 1998/1833) (breach of regulations)

Regulation 32 of the Transnational Information and Consultation of Employees Regulations 1999 (SI 1999/3323) (detriment relating to European Works Councils)

[Regulation 28 of the Employment Equality (Religion or Belief) Regulations 2003 (discrimination in the employment field)][38]

[Regulation 45 of the European Public Limited-Liability Company Regulations 2004 (SI 2004/2326) (detriment in employment)

Regulation 33 of the Information and Consultation of Employees Regulations 2004 (SI 2004/3426) (detriment in employment)

Paragraph 8 of the Schedule to the Occupational and Personal Pension Schemes (Consultation by Employers and Miscellaneous Amendment) Regulations 2006 (SI 2006/349) (detriment in employment)][39]

[Regulation 28 of the Employment Equality (Sexual Orientation) Regulations 2003 (discrimination in the employment field)][40]

[Regulation 34 of the European Cooperative Society (Involvement of Employees) Regulations 2006 (detriment in relation to involvement in a European Cooperative Society)]

[Regulation 36 of the Employment Equality (Age) Regulations 2006 (discrimination in the employment field)][41]

[Regulation 51 of the Companies (Cross-Border Mergers) Regulations 2007 (detriment in relation to special negotiating body or employee participation)][42]

[Regulation 17 of the Cross-border Railways Services (Working Time) Regulations 2008 (breach of regulations)][43]

Schedule 5

Tribunal jurisdictions to which section 38 applies

Section 2 of the Equal Pay Act 1970 (equality clauses)

Section 63 of the Sex Discrimination Act 1975 (c 65) (discrimination in the employment field)

Section 54 of the Race Relations Act 1976 (c 74) (discrimination in the employment field)

[Section 145A of the Trade Union and Labour Relations (Consolidation) Act 1992 (inducements relating to union membership or activities)

Section 145B of that Act (inducements relating to collective bargaining)

[37] Repealed by the Tax Credits Act 2002, s 60 Sch 6.
[38] Added by SI 2003/1660.
[39] Added by SI 2007/30 as from 6 April 2007.
[40] Added by SI 2003/1661.
[41] Added by SI 2006/1031 as from 1 October 2006.
[42] Added by SI 2007/2974 as from 15 December 2007.
[43] Added by SI 2008/1660 as from 27 July 2008.

Section 146 of that Act (detriment in relation to union membership and activities)][44]

Paragraph 156 of Schedule A1 to that Act (detriment in relation to union recognition rights)

Section 17A of the Disability Discrimination Act 1995 (c 50) (discrimination in the employment field)

Section 23 of the Employment Rights Act 1996 (c 18) (unauthorised deductions and payments)

Section 48 of that Act (detriment in employment)

Section 111 of that Act (unfair dismissal)

Section 163 of that Act (redundancy payments)

Section 24 of the National Minimum Wage Act 1998 (c 39) (detriment in relation to national minimum wage)

[. . .][45]

The Employment Tribunal Extension of Jurisdiction (England and Wales) Order 1994 (SI 1994/1623) (breach of employment contract and termination)

The Employment Tribunal Extension of Jurisdiction (Scotland) Order 1994 (SI 1994/1624) (corresponding provision for Scotland)

Regulation 30 of the Working Time Regulations 1998 (SI 1998/1833) (breach of regulations)

Regulation 32 of the Transnational Information and Consultation of Employees Regulations 1999 (SI 1999/3323) (detriment relating to European Works Councils)

[Regulation 28 of the Employment Equality (Religion or Belief) Regulations 2003 (discrimination in the employment field)] [46]

[Regulation 45 of the European Public Limited-Liability Company Regulations 2004 (SI 2004/2326) (detriment in employment)

Regulation 33 of the Information and Consultation of Employees Regulations 2004 (SI 2004/3426) (detriment in employment)

Paragraph 8 of the Schedule to the Occupational and Personal Pension Schemes (Consultation by Employers and Miscellaneous Amendment) Regulations 2006 (SI 2006/349) (detriment in employment)] [47]

[Regulation 28 of the Employment Equality (Sexual Orientation) Regulations 2003 (discrimination in the employment field)] [48]

[Regulation 34 of the European Cooperative Society (Involvement of Employees) Regulations 2006 (detriment in relation to involvement in a European Cooperative Society)]

[Regulation 36 of the Employment Equality (Age) Regulations 2006 (discrimination in the employment field)] [49]

[Regulation 51 of the Companies (Cross-Border Mergers) Regulations 2007 (detriment in relation to special negotiating body or employee participation)] [50]

[Regulation 17 of the Cross-border Railways Services (Working Time) Regulations 2008 (breach of regulations)][51]

44 Substituted by the Employment Relations Act 2004, Sch 1, para 43.
45 Repealed by the Tax Credits Act 2002, s 60 Sch 6.
46 Added by SI 2003/1660.
47 Added by SI 2007/30 as from 6 April 2007.
48 Added by SI 2003/1661.
49 Added by SI 2006/1031 as from 1 October 2006.
50 Added by SI 2007/2974 as from 15 December 2007.
51 Added by SI 2008/1660 as from 27 July 2008.

Employment Rights Act 1996 (Extracts)

(1996 Chapter 18)

An Act to consolidate enactments relating to employment rights.

[22nd May 1996]

Part I

Employment Particulars

Right to statements of employment particulars

Statement of initial employment particulars

1.—(1) Where an employee begins employment with an employer, the employer shall give to the employee a written statement of particulars of employment.

(2) The statement may (subject to section 2(4)) be given in instalments and (whether or not given in instalments) shall be given not later than two months after the beginning of the employment.

(3) The statement shall contain particulars of—

(a) the names of the employer and employee,

(b) the date when the employment began, and

(c) the date on which the employee's period of continuous employment began (taking into account any employment with a previous employer which counts towards that period).

(4) The statement shall also contain particulars, as at a specified date not more than seven days before the statement (or the instalment containing them) is given, of—

(a) the scale or rate of remuneration or the method of calculating remuneration,

(b) the intervals at which remuneration is paid (that is, weekly, monthly or other specified intervals),

(c) any terms and conditions relating to hours of work (including any terms and conditions relating to normal working hours),

(d) any terms and conditions relating to any of the following—

(i) entitlement to holidays, including public holidays, and holiday pay (the particulars given being sufficient to enable the employee's entitlement, including any entitlement to accrued holiday pay on the termination of employment, to be precisely calculated),

(ii) incapacity for work due to sickness or injury, including any provision for sick pay, and

(iii) pensions and pension schemes,

(e) the length of notice which the employee is obliged to give and entitled to receive to terminate his contract of employment,

(f) the title of the job which the employee is employed to do or a brief description of the work for which he is employed,

(g) where the employment is not intended to be permanent, the period for which it is expected to continue or, if it is for a fixed term, the date when it is to end,

(h) either the place of work or, where the employee is required or permitted to work at various places, an indication of that and of the address of the employer,

(j) any collective agreements which directly affect the terms and conditions of the employment including, where the employer is not a party, the persons by whom they were made, and

(k) where the employee is required to work outside the United Kingdom for a period of more than one month—

(i) the period for which he is to work outside the United Kingdom,

(ii) the currency in which remuneration is to be paid while he is working outside the United Kingdom,

(iii) any additional remuneration payable to him, and any benefits to be provided to or in respect of him, by reason of his being required to work outside the United Kingdom, and

(iv) any terms and conditions relating to his return to the United Kingdom.

(5) Subsection (4)(d)(iii) does not apply to an employee of a body or authority if—

(a) the employee's pension rights depend on the terms of a pension scheme established under any provision contained in or having effect under any Act, and

(b) any such provision requires the body or authority to give to a new employee information concerning the employee's pension rights or the determination of questions affecting those rights.

Statement of changes

4.—(1) If, after the material date, there is a change in any of the matters particulars of which are required by sections 1 to 3 to be included or referred to in a statement under section 1, the employer shall give to the employee a written statement containing particulars of the change.

(2) For the purposes of subsection (1)—

(a) in relation to a matter particulars of which are included or referred to in a statement given under section 1 otherwise than in instalments, the material date is the date to which the statement relates,

(b) in relation to a matter particulars of which—

(i) are included or referred to in an instalment of a statement given under section 1, or

(ii) are required by section 2(4) to be included in a single document but are not included in an instalment of a statement given under section 1 which does include other particulars to which that provision applies,

the material date is the date to which the instalment relates, and

(c) in relation to any other matter, the material date is the date by which a statement under section 1 is required to be given.

(3) A statement under subsection (1) shall be given at the earliest opportunity and, in any event, not later than—

(a) one month after the change in question, or

(b) where that change results from the employee being required to work outside the United Kingdom for a period of more than one month, the time when he leaves the United Kingdom in order to begin so to work, if that is earlier.

(4) A statement under subsection (1) may refer the employee to the provisions of some other document which is reasonably accessible to the employee for a change in any of the matters specified in sections 1(4)(d)(ii) and (iii) and 3(1)(a) and (c).

(5) A statement under subsection (1) may refer the employee for a change in either of the matters specified in section 1(4)(e) to the law or to the provisions of any collective agreement directly affecting the terms and conditions of the employment which is reasonably accessible to the employee.

(6) Where, after an employer has given to an employee a statement under section 1, either—

(a) the name of the employer (whether an individual or a body corporate or partnership) is changed without any change in the identity of the employer, or

(b) the identity of the employer is changed in circumstances in which the continuity of the employee's period of employment is not broken,

and subsection (7) applies in relation to the change, the person who is the employer immediately after the change is not required to give to the employee a statement under section 1; but the change shall be treated as a change falling within subsection (1) of this section.

(7) This subsection applies in relation to a change if it does not involve any change in any of the matters (other than the names of the parties) particulars of which are required by sections 1 to 3 to be included or referred to in the statement under section 1.

(8) A statement under subsection (1) which informs an employee of a change such as is referred to in subsection (6)(b) shall specify the date on which the employee's period of continuous employment began.

Enforcement

References to [employment tribunals][52]

11.—(1) Where an employer does not give an employee a statement as required by section 1, 4 or 8 (either because he gives him no statement or because the statement he gives does not comply with what is required), the employee may require a reference to be made to an [employment tribunal] to determine what particulars ought to have been included or referred to in a statement so as to comply with the requirements of the section concerned. [53]

(2) Where—

(a) a statement purporting to be a statement under section 1 or 4, or a pay statement or a standing statement of fixed deductions purporting to comply with section 8 or 9, has been given to an employee, and

[52] As amended by the Employment Rights (Dispute Resolution) Act 1998 (c 8), s 1(2).

[53] As amended by the Employment Rights (Dispute Resolution) Act 1998 (c 8), s 1(2).

Appendix 1 Selected Legislation

(b) a question arises as to the particulars which ought to have been included or referred to in the statement so as to comply with the requirements of this Part,[54] either the employer or the employee may require the question to be referred to and determined by an [employment tribunal].

(3) For the purposes of this section—

(a) a question as to the particulars which ought to have been included in the note required by section 3 to be included in the statement under section 1 does not include any question whether the employment is, has been or will be contracted-out employment (for the purposes of Part III of the Pension Schemes Act 1993), and

(b) a question as to the particulars which ought to have been included in a pay statement or standing statement of fixed deductions does not include a question solely as to the accuracy of an amount stated in any such particulars.

(4) An [employment tribunal] shall not consider a reference under this section in a case where the employment to which the reference relates has ceased unless an application requiring the reference to be made was made—[55]

(a) before the end of the period of three months beginning with the date on which the employment ceased, or

(b) within such further period as the tribunal considers reasonable in a case where it is satisfied that it was not reasonably practicable for the application to be made before the end of that period of three months.

Determination of references

12.—(1) Where, on a reference under section 11(1), an [employment tribunal] determines particulars as being those which ought to have been included or referred to in a statement given under section 1 or 4, the employer shall be deemed to have given to the employee a statement in which those particulars were included, or referred to, as specified in the decision of the tribunal.[56]

(2) On determining a reference under section 11(2) relating to a statement purporting to be a statement under section 1 or 4, an [employment tribunal] may—[57]

(a) confirm the particulars as included or referred to in the statement given by the employer,

(b) amend those particulars, or

(c) substitute other particulars for them,

as the tribunal may determine to be appropriate; and the statement shall be deemed to have been given by the employer to the employee in accordance with the decision of the tribunal.

(3) Where on a reference under section 11 an [employment tribunal] finds—[58]

(a) that an employer has failed to give an employee any pay statement in accordance with section 8, or

(b) that a pay statement or standing statement of fixed deductions does not, in relation to a deduction, contain the particulars required to be included in that statement by that section or section 9,

the tribunal shall make a declaration to that effect.

(4) Where on a reference in the case of which subsection (3) applies the tribunal further finds that any unnotified deductions have been made from the pay of the employee during the period of thirteen weeks immediately preceding the date of the application for the reference (whether or not the deductions were made in breach of the contract of employment), the tribunal may order the employer to pay the employee a sum not exceeding the aggregate of the unnotified deductions so made.

(5) For the purposes of subsection (4) a deduction is an unnotified deduction if it is made without the employer giving the employee, in any pay statement or standing statement of fixed deductions, the particulars of the deduction required by section 8 or 9.

[54] As amended by the Employment Rights (Dispute Resolution) Act 1998 (c 8), s 1(2).

[55] As amended by the Employment Rights (Dispute Resolution) Act 1998 (c 8), s 1(2).

[56] As amended by the Employment Rights (Dispute Resolution) Act 1998 (c 8), s 1(2).

[57] As amended by the Employment Rights (Dispute Resolution) Act 1998 (c 8), s 1(2).

[58] As amended by the Employment Rights (Dispute Resolution) Act 1998 (c 8), s 1(2).

Part II
Protection of Wages
Deductions by employer

Right not to suffer unauthorised deductions

13.—(1) An employer shall not make a deduction from wages of a worker employed by him unless—
(a) the deduction is required or authorised to be made by virtue of a statutory provision or a relevant provision of the worker's contract, or
(b) the worker has previously signified in writing his agreement or consent to the making of the deduction.

(2) In this section 'relevant provision', in relation to a worker's contract, means a provision of the contract comprised—
(a) in one or more written terms of the contract of which the employer has given the worker a copy on an occasion prior to the employer making the deduction in question, or
(b) in one or more terms of the contract (whether express or implied and, if express, whether oral or in writing) the existence and effect, or combined effect, of which in relation to the worker the employer has notified to the worker in writing on such an occasion.

(3) Where the total amount of wages paid on any occasion by an employer to a worker employed by him is less than the total amount of the wages properly payable by him to the worker on that occasion (after deductions), the amount of the deficiency shall be treated for the purposes of this Part as a deduction made by the employer from the worker's wages on that occasion.

(4) Subsection (3) does not apply in so far as the deficiency is attributable to an error of any description on the part of the employer affecting the computation by him of the gross amount of the wages properly payable by him to the worker on that occasion.

(5) For the purposes of this section a relevant provision of a worker's contract having effect by virtue of a variation of the contract does not operate to authorise the making of a deduction on account of any conduct of the worker, or any other event occurring, before the variation took effect.

(6) For the purposes of this section an agreement or consent signified by a worker does not operate to authorise the making of a deduction on account of any conduct of the worker, or any other event occurring, before the agreement or consent was signified.

(7) This section does not affect any other statutory provision by virtue of which a sum payable to a worker by his employer but not constituting 'wages' within the meaning of this Part is not to be subject to a deduction at the instance of the employer.

Excepted deductions

14.—(1) Section 13 does not apply to a deduction from a worker's wages made by his employer where the purpose of the deduction is the reimbursement of the employer in respect of—
(a) an overpayment of wages, or
(b) an overpayment in respect of expenses incurred by the worker in carrying out his employment,
made (for any reason) by the employer to the worker.

(2) Section 13 does not apply to a deduction from a worker's wages made by his employer in consequence of any disciplinary proceedings if those proceedings were held by virtue of a statutory provision.

(3) Section 13 does not apply to a deduction from a worker's wages made by his employer in pursuance of a requirement imposed on the employer by a statutory provision to deduct and pay over to a public authority amounts determined by that authority as being due to it from the worker if the deduction is made in accordance with the relevant determination of that authority.

(4) Section 13 does not apply to a deduction from a worker's wages made by his employer in pursuance of any arrangements which have been established—
(a) in accordance with a relevant provision of his contract to the inclusion of which in the contract the worker has signified his agreement or consent in writing, or
(b) otherwise with the prior agreement or consent of the worker signified in writing,
and under which the employer is to deduct and pay over to a third person amounts notified to the employer by that person as being due to him from the worker, if the deduction is made in accordance with the relevant notification by that person.

(5) Section 13 does not apply to a deduction from a worker's wages made by his employer where the worker has taken part in a strike or other industrial action and the deduction is made by the employer on account of the worker's having taken part in that strike or other action.

(6) Section 13 does not apply to a deduction from a worker's wages made by his employer with his prior agreement or consent signified in writing where the purpose of the deduction is the satisfaction (whether wholly or in part) of an order of a court or tribunal requiring the payment of an amount by the worker to the employer.

Payments to employer

Enforcement

Complaints to [employment tribunals]

23.—(1) A worker may present a complaint to an [employment tribunal]—[59]

(a) that his employer has made a deduction from his wages in contravention of section 13 (including a deduction made in contravention of that section as it applies by virtue of section 18(2)),

(b) that his employer has received from him a payment in contravention of section 15 (including a payment received in contravention of that section as it applies by virtue of section 20(1)),

(c) that his employer has recovered from his wages by means of one or more deductions falling within section 18(1) an amount or aggregate amount exceeding the limit applying to the deduction or deductions under that provision, or

(d) that his employer has received from him in pursuance of one or more demands for payment made (in accordance with section 20) on a particular pay day, a payment or payments of an amount or aggregate amount exceeding the limit applying to the demand or demands under section 21(1).

(2) Subject to subsection (4), an [employment tribunal] shall not consider a complaint under this section unless it is presented before the end of the period of three months beginning with—

(a) in the case of a complaint relating to a deduction by the employer, the date of payment of the wages from which the deduction was made, or

(b) in the case of a complaint relating to a payment received by the employer, the date when the payment was received.

(3) Where a complaint is brought under this section in respect of—

(a) a series of deductions or payments, or

(b) a number of payments falling within subsection (1)(d) and made in pursuance of demands for payment subject to the same limit under section 21(1) but received by the employer on different dates,

the references in subsection (2) to the deduction or payment are to the last deduction or payment in the series or to the last of the payments so received.

(4) Where the [employment tribunal] is satisfied that it was not reasonably practicable for a complaint under this section to be presented before the end of the relevant period of three months, the tribunal may consider the complaint if it is presented within such further period as the tribunal considers reasonable. [60]

[(5) No complaint shall be presented under this section in respect of any deduction made in contravention of section 86 of the Trade Union and Labour Relations (Consolidation) Act 1992 (deduction of political fund contribution where certificate of exemption or objection has been given).] [61]

Determination of complaints

24.—(1) Where a tribunal finds a complaint under section 23 well-founded, it shall make a declaration to that effect and shall order the employer—

(a) in the case of a complaint under section 23(1)(a), to pay to the worker the amount of any deduction made in contravention of section 13,

(b) in the case of a complaint under section 23(1)(b), to repay to the worker the amount of any payment received in contravention of section 15,

(c) in the case of a complaint under section 23(1)(c), to pay to the worker any amount recovered from him in excess of the limit mentioned in that provision, and

(d) in the case of a complaint under section 23(1)(d), to repay to the worker any amount received from him in excess of the limit mentioned in that provision.

---

[59] As amended by the Employment Rights (Dispute Resolution) Act 1998 (c 8), s 1(2).

[60] As amended by the Employment Rights (Dispute Resolution) Act 1998 (c 8), s 1(2).

[61] Inserted by the Employment Rights (Dispute Resolution) Act 1998 (c 8), s 15 and Sch 1, para 15.

[(2) Where a tribunal makes a declaration under subsection (1), it may order the employer to pay to the worker (in addition to any amount ordered to be paid under that subsection) such amount as the tribunal considers appropriate in all the circumstances to compensate the worker for any financial loss sustained by him which is attributable to the matter complained of.][62]

Supplementary

Meaning of 'wages' etc

27.—(1) In this Part 'wages', in relation to a worker, means any sums payable to the worker in connection with his employment, including—

(a) any fee, bonus, commission, holiday pay or other emolument referable to his employment, whether payable under his contract or otherwise,
(b) statutory sick pay under Part XI of the Social Security Contributions and Benefits Act 1992,
(c) statutory maternity pay under Part XII of that Act,
[(ca) statutory paternity pay under Part 12ZA of that Act,
(cb) statutory adoption pay under Part 12ZB of that Act,] [63]
(d) a guarantee payment (under section 28 of this Act),
(e) any payment for time off under Part VI of this Act or section 169 of the Trade Union and Labour Relations (Consolidation) Act 1992 (payment for time off for carrying out trade union duties etc),
(f) remuneration on suspension on medical grounds under section 64 of this Act and remuneration on suspension on maternity grounds under section 68 of this Act,
(g) any sum payable in pursuance of an order for reinstatement or re-engagement under section 113 of this Act,
(h) any sum payable in pursuance of an order for the continuation of a contract of employment under section 130 of this Act or section 164 of the Trade Union and Labour Relations (Consolidation) Act 1992, and
(j) remuneration under a protective award under section 189 of that Act,

but excluding any payments within subsection (2).

(2) Those payments are—

(a) any payment by way of an advance under an agreement for a loan or by way of an advance of wages (but without prejudice to the application of section 13 to any deduction made from the worker's wages in respect of any such advance),
(b) any payment in respect of expenses incurred by the worker in carrying out his employment,
(c) any payment by way of a pension, allowance or gratuity in connection with the worker's retirement or as compensation for loss of office,
(d) any payment referable to the worker's redundancy, and
(e) any payment to the worker otherwise than in his capacity as a worker.

(3) Where any payment in the nature of a non-contractual bonus is (for any reason) made to a worker by his employer, the amount of the payment shall for the purposes of this Part—

(a) be treated as wages of the worker, and
(b) be treated as payable to him as such on the day on which the payment is made.

(4) In this Part 'gross amount', in relation to any wages payable to a worker, means the total amount of those wages before deductions of whatever nature.

(5) For the purposes of this Part any monetary value attaching to any payment or benefit in kind furnished to a worker by his employer shall not be treated as wages of the worker except in the case of any voucher, stamp or similar document which is—

(a) of a fixed value expressed in monetary terms, and
(b) capable of being exchanged (whether on its own or together with other vouchers, stamps or documents, and whether immediately or only after a time) for money, goods or services (or for any combination of two or more of those things).

[62] Inserted by the Employment Act 2008 (c.24), s 7(1) with effect from 6 April 2009, subject to the transitional provisions and savings contained in SI 2008/3232, Sch 1 Pt 1 para 5.

[63] As amended by the Employment Act 2002 (c 22), Sch 7, para 25.

Part IVA
Protected Disclosures[64]

Meaning of 'protected disclosure'

43A. In this Act a 'protected disclosure' means a qualifying disclosure (as defined by section 43B) which is made by a worker in accordance with any of sections 43C to 43H.

Disclosures qualifying for protection

43B.—(1) In this Part a 'qualifying disclosure' means any disclosure of information which, in the reasonable belief of the worker making the disclosure, tends to show one or more of the following—

(a) that a criminal offence has been committed, is being committed or is likely to be committed,
(b) that a person has failed, is failing or is likely to fail to comply with any legal obligation to which he is subject,
(c) that a miscarriage of justice has occurred, is occurring or is likely to occur,
(d) that the health or safety of any individual has been, is being or is likely to be endangered,
(e) that the environment has been, is being or is likely to be damaged, or
(f) that information tending to show any matter falling within any one of the preceding paragraphs has been, is being or is likely to be deliberately concealed.

(2) For the purposes of subsection (1), it is immaterial whether the relevant failure occurred, occurs or would occur in the United Kingdom or elsewhere, and whether the law applying to it is that of the United Kingdom or of any other country or territory.

(3) A disclosure of information is not a qualifying disclosure if the person making the disclosure commits an offence by making it.

(4) A disclosure of information in respect of which a claim to legal professional privilege (or, in Scotland, to confidentiality as between client and professional legal adviser) could be maintained in legal proceedings is not a qualifying disclosure if it is made by a person to whom the information had been disclosed in the course of obtaining legal advice.

(5) In this Part 'the relevant failure', in relation to a qualifying disclosure, means the matter falling within paragraphs (a) to (f) of subsection (1).

Disclosure to employer or other responsible person

43C.—(1) A qualifying disclosure is made in accordance with this section if the worker makes the disclosure in good faith—

(a) to his employer, or
(b) where the worker reasonably believes that the relevant failure relates solely or mainly to—
  (i) the conduct of a person other than his employer, or
  (ii) any other matter for which a person other than his employer has legal responsibility,

to that other person.

(2) A worker who, in accordance with a procedure whose use by him is authorised by his employer, makes a qualifying disclosure to a person other than his employer, is to be treated for the purposes of this Part as making the qualifying disclosure to his employer.

Disclosure to legal adviser

43D. A qualifying disclosure is made in accordance with this section if it is made in the course of obtaining legal advice.

Disclosure to Minister of the Crown

43E. A qualifying disclosure is made in accordance with this section if—

(a) the worker's employer is—
  (i) an individual appointed under any enactment [(including any enactment comprised in, or in an instrument made under, an Act of the Scottish Parliament)] by a Minister of the Crown, or[65]
  (ii) a body any of whose members are so appointed, and
(b) the disclosure is made in good faith to a Minister of the Crown.

[64] As amended by SI 2000/2040, art 2 and Sch 1, para 19.
[65] As amended by SI 2000/2040, art 2 and Sch 1, para 19.

Disclosure to prescribed person

43F.—(1) A qualifying disclosure is made in accordance with this section if the worker—
- (a) makes the disclosure in good faith to a person prescribed by an order made by the Secretary of State for the purposes of this section, and
- (b) reasonably believes—
  - (i) that the relevant failure falls within any description of matters in respect of which that person is so prescribed, and
  - (ii) that the information disclosed, and any allegation contained in it, are substantially true.

(2) An order prescribing persons for the purposes of this section may specify persons or descriptions of persons, and shall specify the descriptions of matters in respect of which each person, or persons of each description, is or are prescribed.

Disclosure in other cases

43G.—(1) A qualifying disclosure is made in accordance with this section if—
- (a) the worker makes the disclosure in good faith,
- (b) he reasonably believes that the information disclosed, and any allegation contained in it, are substantially true,
- (c) he does not make the disclosure for purposes of personal gain,
- (d) any of the conditions in subsection (2) is met, and
- (e) in all the circumstances of the case, it is reasonable for him to make the disclosure.

(2) The conditions referred to in subsection (1)(d) are—
- (a) that, at the time he makes the disclosure, the worker reasonably believes that he will be subjected to a detriment by his employer if he makes a disclosure to his employer or in accordance with section 43F,
- (b) that, in a case where no person is prescribed for the purposes of section 43F in relation to the relevant failure, the worker reasonably believes that it is likely that evidence relating to the relevant failure will be concealed or destroyed if he makes a disclosure to his employer, or
- (c) that the worker has previously made a disclosure of substantially the same information—
  - (i) to his employer, or
  - (ii) in accordance with section 43F.

(3) In determining for the purposes of subsection (1)(e) whether it is reasonable for the worker to make the disclosure, regard shall be had, in particular, to—
- (a) the identity of the person to whom the disclosure is made,
- (b) the seriousness of the relevant failure,
- (c) whether the relevant failure is continuing or is likely to occur in the future,
- (d) whether the disclosure is made in breach of a duty of confidentiality owed by the employer to any other person,
- (e) in a case falling within subsection (2)(c)(i) or (ii), any action which the employer or the person to whom the previous disclosure in accordance with section 43F was made has taken or might reasonably be expected to have taken as a result of the previous disclosure, and
- (f) in a case falling within subsection (2)(c)(i), whether in making the disclosure to the employer the worker complied with any procedure whose use by him was authorised by the employer.

(4) For the purposes of this section a subsequent disclosure may be regarded as a disclosure of substantially the same information as that disclosed by a previous disclosure as mentioned in subsection (2)(c) even though the subsequent disclosure extends to information about action taken or not taken by any person as a result of the previous disclosure.

Disclosure of exceptionally serious failure

43H.—(1) A qualifying disclosure is made in accordance with this section if—
- (a) the worker makes the disclosure in good faith,
- (b) he reasonably believes that the information disclosed, and any allegation contained in it, are substantially true,
- (c) he does not make the disclosure for purposes of personal gain,
- (d) the relevant failure is of an exceptionally serious nature, and
- (e) in all the circumstances of the case, it is reasonable for him to make the disclosure.

(2) In determining for the purposes of subsection (1)(e) whether it is reasonable for the worker to make the disclosure, regard shall be had, in particular, to the identity of the person to whom the disclosure is made.

Contractual duties of confidentiality

43J.—(1) Any provision in an agreement to which this section applies is void in so far as it purports to preclude the worker from making a protected disclosure.

(2) This section applies to any agreement between a worker and his employer (whether a worker's contract or not), including an agreement to refrain from instituting or continuing any proceedings under this Act or any proceedings for breach of contract.

Extension of meaning of 'worker' etc for Part IVA[66,67]

43K.—(1) For the purposes of this Part 'worker' includes an individual who is not a worker as defined by section 230(3) but who—

(a) works or worked for a person in circumstances in which—

(i) he is or was introduced or supplied to do that work by a third person, and

(ii) the terms on which he is or was engaged to do the work are or were in practice substantially determined not by him but by the person for whom he works or worked, by the third person or by both of them,

(b) contracts or contracted with a person, for the purposes of that person's business, for the execution of work to be done in a place not under the control or management of that person and would fall within section 230(3)(b) if for 'personally' in that provision there were substituted '(whether personally or otherwise)',

[(ba) works or worked as a person performing services under a contract entered into by him with a Primary Care Trust [under section 84 or 100 of the National Health Service Act 2006 or with a Local Health Board under section 42 or 57 of the National Health Service (Wales) Act 2006],] [68]

[(bb) works or worked as a person performing services under a contract entered into by him with a Health Board under section 17J of the National Health Service (Scotland) Act 1978,] [69]

(c) works or worked as a person providing [. . .] general dental services, general ophthalmic services or pharmaceutical services in accordance with arrangements made—

(i) by a [Primary Care Trust [under section 126 of the National Health Service Act 2006,] or] [Local Health Board] under [section 71 or 80 of the National Health Service (Wales) Act 2006], or[70]

(ii) by a Health Board under section [. . .] 25, 26 or 27 of the National Health Service (Scotland) Act 1978, or

(d) is or was provided with work experience provided pursuant to a training course or programme or with training for employment (or with both) otherwise than—

(i) under a contract of employment, or

(ii) by an educational establishment on a course run by that establishment;

and any reference to a worker's contract, to employment or to a worker being 'employed' shall be construed accordingly.

(2) For the purposes of this Part 'employer' includes—

(a) in relation to a worker falling within paragraph (a) of subsection (1), the person who substantially determines or determined the terms on which he is or was engaged,

[(aa) in relation to a worker falling within paragraph (ba) of that subsection, the Primary Care Trust or Local Health Board referred to in that paragraph,] [71]

[(ab) in relation to a worker falling within paragraph (bb) of that subsection, the Health Board referred to in that paragraph,] [72]

---

66 Part IVA (ss 43A–43K) inserted by the Public Interest Disclosure Act 1998 (c 23), s 1.

67 Prospectively amended by SI 2006/1056, Sch 1, para 7.

68 Inserted by the Health and Social Care (Community Health and Standards) Act 2003 (c 43), Sch 11, para 65 and amended by the National Health Service (Consequential Provisions) Act 2006, Sch 1, para 178(a).

69 Inserted by SI 2004/957, Sch 1, para 8.

70 As amended by the National Health Service Reform and Health Care Professions Act 2002 (c 17), Sch 2, para 63; by the Health and Social Care (Community Health and Standards) Act 2003 (c 43), Sch 14, Part 4; by SI 2004/957, Sch 1, para 8; by the National Health Service (Consequential Provisions) Act 2006, Sch 1, para 178(b);and by SI2007/961, Sch, para 27.

71 Inserted by the Health and Social Care (Community Health and Standards) Act 2003 (c 43), Sch 11, para 65.

72 Inserted by the Health and Social Care (Community Health and Standards) Act 2003 (c 43), Sch 11, para 65.

(b) in relation to a worker falling within paragraph (c) of that subsection, the authority or board referred to in that paragraph, and
(c) in relation to a worker falling within paragraph (d) of that subsection, the person providing the work experience or training.
(3) In this section 'educational establishment' includes any university, college, school or other educational establishment.

PART V

PROTECTION FROM SUFFERING DETRIMENT IN EMPLOYMENT

[Protected disclosures]

[**47B.**—(1) A worker has the right not to be subjected to any detriment by any act, or any deliberate failure to act, by his employer done on the ground that the worker has made a protected disclosure.
(2) [. . .][73] This section does not apply where—
(a) the worker is an employee, and
(b) the detriment in question amounts to dismissal (within the meaning of [Part X][74]).
(3) For the purposes of this section, and of sections 48 and 49 so far as relating to this section, "worker", "worker's contract", "employment" and "employer" have the extended meaning given by section 43K.][75]

PART VIII

CHAPTER I MATERNITY LEAVE

71.—(1) An employee may, provided that she satisfies any conditions which may be prescribed, be absent from work at any time during an ordinary maternity leave period. [76]
(2) An ordinary maternity leave period is a period calculated in accordance with regulations made by the Secretary of State.
[(3) Regulations under subsection (2)—
(a) shall secure that, where an employee has a right to leave under this section, she is entitled to an ordinary maternity leave period of at least 26 weeks;
(b) may allow an employee to choose, subject to prescribed restrictions, the date on which an ordinary maternity leave period starts;
(c) may specify circumstances in which an employee may work for her employer during an ordinary maternity leave period without bringing the period to an end.] [77]
(4) Subject to section 74, an employee who exercises her right under subsection (1)— [78]
(a) is entitled[, for such purposes and to such extent as may be prescribed,] to the benefit of the terms and conditions of employment which would have applied if she had not been absent,
(b) is bound[, for such purposes and to such extent as may be prescribed] by any obligations arising under those terms and conditions (except in so far as they are inconsistent with subsection (1)), and
[(c) is entitled to return from leave to a job of a prescribed kind.]
(5) In subsection (4)(a) 'terms and conditions of employment'—
(a) includes matters connected with an employee's employment whether or not they arise under her contract of employment, but
(b) does not include terms and conditions about remuneration.
(6) The Secretary of State may make regulations specifying matters which are, or are not, to be treated as remuneration for the purposes of this section.
[(7) The Secretary of State may make regulations making provision, in relation to the right to return under subsection (4)(c) above, about—
(a) seniority, pension rights and similar rights;

---

73 Repealed by the Employment Relations Act 1999, ss 18(1), (2)(a), 44, Sch 9, Table 3.
74 Substituted by the Employment Relations Act 1999, s 18(1),(2)(b).
75 Inserted by the Public Interest Disclosure Act 1998, s 2.
76 Substituted by the Employment Relations Act 1999 (c 26), Sch 4, Part 1.
77 Substituted by the Work and Families Act 2006, Sch 1, para 31.
78 As amended by the Employment Act 2002 (c 22), s 17(2).

(b) terms and conditions of employment on return] [79]

Compulsory maternity leave[80]

72.—(1) An employer shall not permit an employee who satisfies prescribed conditions to work during a compulsory maternity leave period.

(2) A compulsory maternity leave period is a period calculated in accordance with regulations made by the Secretary of State.

(3) Regulations under subsection (2) shall secure—

(a) that no compulsory leave period is less than two weeks, and

(b) that every compulsory maternity leave period falls within an ordinary maternity leave period.

(4) Subject to subsection (5), any provision of or made under the Health and Safety at Work etc Act 1974 shall apply in relation to the prohibition under subsection (1) as if it were imposed by regulations under section 15 of that Act.

(5) Section 33(1)(c) of the 1974 Act shall not apply in relation to the prohibition under subsection (1); and an employer who contravenes that subsection shall be—

(a) guilty of an offence, and

(b) liable on summary conviction to a fine not exceeding level 2 on the standard scale.

Additional maternity leave[81]

73.—(1) An employee who satisfies prescribed conditions may be absent from work at any time during an additional maternity leave period.

(2) An additional maternity leave period is a period calculated in accordance with regulations made by the Secretary of State.

[(3) Regulations under subsection (2)—

(a) may allow an employee to choose, subject to prescribed restrictions, the date on which an additional maternity leave period ends;

(b) may specify circumstances in which an employee may work for her employer during an additional maternity leave period without bringing the period to an end.] [82]

(4) Subject to section 74, an employee who exercises her right under subsection (1)—

(a) is entitled, for such purposes and to such extent as may be prescribed, to the benefit of the terms and conditions of employment which would have applied if she had not been absent,

(b) is bound, for such purposes and to such extent as may be prescribed, by obligations arising under those terms and conditions (except in so far as they are inconsistent with subsection (1)), and

(c) is entitled to return from leave to a job of a prescribed kind.

(5) In subsection (4)(a) 'terms and conditions of employment'—

(a) includes matters connected with an employee's employment whether or not they arise under her contract of employment, but

(b) does not include terms and conditions about remuneration.

[(5A) In subsection (4)(c), the reference to return from leave includes, where appropriate, a reference to a continuous period of absence attributable partly to additional maternity leave and partly to ordinary maternity leave.] [83]

(6) The Secretary of State may make regulations specifying matters which are, or are not, to be treated as remuneration for the purposes of this section.

(7) The Secretary of State may make regulations making provision, in relation to the right to return under subsection (4)(c), about—

(a) seniority, pension rights and similar rights;

(b) terms and conditions of employment on return.

[79] Substituted by the Employment Act 2002 (c 22), s 17(3).

[80] Substituted by the Employment Relations Act 1999 (c 26), Sch 4, Part 1.

[81] Substituted by the Employment Relations Act 1999 (c 26), Sch 4, Part 1.

[82] Substituted by the Work and Families Act 2006, Sch 1, para32.

[83] Inserted by the Employment Act 2002 (c 22), s 17(4).

Part IX
Termination of Employment
Minimum period of notice

Rights of employer and employee to minimum notice

86.—(1) The notice required to be given by an employer to terminate the contract of employment of a person who has been continuously employed for one month or more—
(a) is not less than one week's notice if his period of continuous employment is less than two years,
(b) is not less than one week's notice for each year of continuous employment if his period of continuous employment is two years or more but less than twelve years, and
(c) is not less than twelve weeks' notice if his period of continuous employment is twelve years or more.
(2) The notice required to be given by an employee who has been continuously employed for one month or more to terminate his contract of employment is not less than one week.
(3) Any provision for shorter notice in any contract of employment with a person who has been continuously employed for one month or more has effect subject to subsections (1) and (2); but this section does not prevent either party from waiving his right to notice on any occasion or from accepting a payment in lieu of notice.
(4) Any contract of employment of a person who has been continuously employed for three months or more which is a contract for a term certain of one month or less shall have effect as if it were for an indefinite period; and, accordingly, subsections (1) and (2) apply to the contract.
(5) [. . .][84]
(6) This section does not affect any right of either party to a contract of employment to treat the contract as terminable without notice by reason of the conduct of the other party.

Rights of employee in period of notice

87.—(1) If an employer gives notice to terminate the contract of employment of a person who has been continuously employed for one month or more, the provisions of sections 88 to 91 have effect as respects the liability of the employer for the period of notice required by section 86(1).
(2) If an employee who has been continuously employed for one month or more gives notice to terminate his contract of employment, the provisions of sections 88 to 91 have effect as respects the liability of the employer for the period of notice required by section 86(2).
(3) In sections 88 to 91 'period of notice' means—
(a) where notice is given by an employer, the period of notice required by section 86(1), and
(b) where notice is given by an employee, the period of notice required by section 86(2).
(4) This section does not apply in relation to a notice given by the employer or the employee if the notice to be given by the employer to terminate the contract must be at least one week more than the notice required by section 86(1).

Employments with normal working hours

88.—(1) If an employee has normal working hours under the contract of employment in force during the period of notice and during any part of those normal working hours—
(a) the employee is ready and willing to work but no work is provided for him by his employer,
(b) the employee is incapable of work because of sickness or injury,
(c) the employee is absent from work wholly or partly because of pregnancy or childbirth [or on adoption leave, parental leave or paternity leave], or,[85,86]
(d) the employee is absent from work in accordance with the terms of his employment relating to holidays,

the employer is liable to pay the employee for the part of normal working hours covered by any of paragraphs (a), (b), (c) and (d) a sum not less than the amount of remuneration for that part of normal working hours calculated at the average hourly rate of remuneration produced by dividing a

[84] Omitted by SI 2002/2034, Sch 2, para 3.
[85] As amended by the Employment Relations Act 1999 (c 26), Sch 4, para 10.
[86] As amended by the Employment Act 2002 (c 22), Sch 7, para 29

week's pay by the number of normal working hours.

(2) Any payments made to the employee by his employer in respect of the relevant part of the period of notice (whether by way of sick pay, statutory sick pay, maternity pay, statutory maternity pay, [paternity pay, statutory paternity pay, adoption pay, statutory adoption pay,] holiday pay or otherwise) go towards meeting the employer's liability under this section. [87]

(3) Where notice was given by the employee, the employer's liability under this section does not arise unless and until the employee leaves the service of the employer in pursuance of the notice.

Employments without normal working hours

89.—(1) If an employee does not have normal working hours under the contract of employment in force in the period of notice, the employer is liable to pay the employee for each week of the period of notice a sum not less than a week's pay.

(2) The employer's liability under this section is conditional on the employee being ready and willing to do work of a reasonable nature and amount to earn a week's pay.

(3) Subsection (2) does not apply—

(a) in respect of any period during which the employee is incapable of work because of sickness or injury,

(b) in respect of any period during which the employee is absent from work wholly or partly because of pregnancy or childbirth [or on [adoption leave, parental leave or paternity leave]], or ,[88,89]

(c) in respect of any period during which the employee is absent from work in accordance with the terms of his employment relating to holidays.

(4) Any payment made to an employee by his employer in respect of a period within subsection (3) (whether by way of sick pay, statutory sick pay, maternity pay, statutory maternity pay, [paternity pay, statutory paternity pay, adoption pay, statutory adoption pay,] holiday pay or otherwise) shall be taken into account for the purposes of this section as if it were remuneration paid by the employer in respect of that period. [90]

(5) Where notice was given by the employee, the employer's liability under this section does not arise unless and until the employee leaves the service of the employer in pursuance of the notice.

Written statement of reasons for dismissal

Right to written statement of reasons for dismissal

92.—(1) An employee is entitled to be provided by his employer with a written statement giving particulars of the reasons for the employee's dismissal—

(a) if the employee is given by the employer notice of termination of his contract of employment,

(b) if the employee's contract of employment is terminated by the employer without notice, or

[(c) if the employee is employed under a limited-term contract and the contract terminates by virtue of the limiting event without being renewed under the same contract.] [91]

(2) Subject to [subsections (4) and (4A)], an employee is entitled to a written statement under this section only if he makes a request for one; and a statement shall be provided within fourteen days of such a request. [92]

(3) Subject to [subsections (4) and (4A)], an employee is not entitled to a written statement under this section unless on the effective date of termination he has been, or will have been, continuously employed for a period of not less than [one year] ending with that date. [93]

(4) An employee is entitled to a written statement under this section without having to request it and irrespective of whether she has been continuously employed for any period if she is dismissed—

(a) at any time while she is pregnant, or

(b) after childbirth in circumstances in which her [ordinary or additional maternity leave period] ends by reason of the dismissal. [94]

---

[87] As amended by the Employment Act 2002 (c 22), Sch 7, para 29.

[88] As amended by the Employment Relations Act 1999 (c 26), Sch 4, para 11.

[89] As amended by the Employment Act 2002 (c 22), Sch 7, para 30.

[90] As amended by the Employment Act 2002 (c 22), Sch 7, para 30.

[91] Substituted by SI 2002/2034, Sch 2, para 3.

[92] As amended by the Employment Act 2002 (c 22), Sch 7, para 31.

[93] As amended by SI 1999/1436, art 2.

[94] As amended by the Employment Relations Act 1999 (c 29), Sch 4, para 12.

[(4A) An employee who is dismissed while absent from work during an ordinary or additional adoption leave period is entitled to a written statement under this section without having to request it and irrespective of whether he has been continuously employed for any period if he is dismissed in circumstances in which that period ends by reason of the dismissal.] [95]

(5) A written statement under this section is admissible in evidence in any proceedings.

(6) Subject to subsection (7), in this section 'the effective date of termination'—
- (a) in relation to an employee whose contract of employment is terminated by notice, means the date on which the notice expires,
- (b) in relation to an employee whose contract of employment is terminated without notice, means the date on which the termination takes effect, and
- [(c) in relation to an employee who is employed under a limited-term contract which terminates by virtue of the limiting event without being renewed under the same contract, means the date on which the termination takes effect.] [96]

(7) Where—
- (a) the contract of employment is terminated by the employer, and
- (b) the notice required by section 86 to be given by an employer would, if duly given on the material date, expire on a date later than the effective date of termination (as defined by subsection (6)),

the later date is the effective date of termination.

(8) In subsection (7)(b) 'the material date' means—
- (a) the date when notice of termination was given by the employer, or
- (b) where no notice was given, the date when the contract of employment was terminated by the employer.

Part X
Unfair Dismissal

Chapter I Right not to be Unfairly Dismissed

The right

The right

94.—(1) An employee has the right not to be unfairly dismissed by his employer.

(2) Subsection (1) has effect subject to the following provisions of this Part (in particular sections 108 to 110) and to the provisions of the Trade Union and Labour Relations (Consolidation) Act 1992 (in particular sections 237 to 239).

Dismissal

Circumstances in which an employee is dismissed

95.—(1) For the purposes of this Part an employee is dismissed by his employer if (and, subject to subsection (2) [. . .], only if)— [97]
- (a) the contract under which he is employed is terminated by the employer (whether with or without notice),
- [(b) he is employed under a limited-term contract and that contract terminates by virtue of the limiting event without being renewed under the same contract, or] [98]
- (c) the employee terminates the contract under which he is employed (with or without notice) in circumstances in which he is entitled to terminate it without notice by reason of the employer's conduct.

(2) An employee shall be taken to be dismissed by his employer for the purposes of this Part if—
- (a) the employer gives notice to the employee to terminate his contract of employment, and
- (b) at a time within the period of that notice the employee gives notice to the employer to terminate the contract of employment on a date earlier than the date on which the employer's notice is due to expire;

---

95 Inserted by the Employment Act 2002 (c 22), Sch 7, para 31.
96 Substituted by the Employment Relations Act 2004 (c 24), Sch 1, para 28.
97 As amended by the Employment Relations Act 2004 (c 24), Sch 1, para 29.
98 Substituted by SI 2002/2034, Sch 2, para 3.

and the reason for the dismissal is to be taken to be the reason for which the employer's notice is given.

Effective date of termination

97.—(1) Subject to the following provisions of this section, in this Part 'the effective date of termination'—
(a) in relation to an employee whose contract of employment is terminated by notice, whether given by his employer or by the employee, means the date on which the notice expires,
(b) in relation to an employee whose contract of employment is terminated without notice, means the date on which the termination takes effect, and
[(c) in relation to an employee who is employed under a limited-term contract which terminates by virtue of the limiting event without being renewed under the same contract, means the date on which the termination takes effect.] [99]

(2) Where—
(a) the contract of employment is terminated by the employer, and
(b) the notice required by section 86 to be given by an employer would, if duly given on the material date, expire on a date later than the effective date of termination (as defined by subsection (1)),

for the purposes of sections 108(1), 119(1) and 227(3) the later date is the effective date of termination.

(3) In subsection (2)(b) 'the material date' means—
(a) the date when notice of termination was given by the employer, or
(b) where no notice was given, the date when the contract of employment was terminated by the employer.

(4) Where—
(a) the contract of employment is terminated by the employee,
(b) the material date does not fall during a period of notice given by the employer to terminate that contract, and
(c) had the contract been terminated not by the employee but by notice given on the material date by the employer, that notice would have been required by section 86 to expire on a date later than the effective date of termination (as defined by subsection (1)),

for the purposes of sections 108(1), 119(1) and 227(3) the later date is the effective date of termination.

(5) In subsection (4) 'the material date' means—
(a) the date when notice of termination was given by the employee, or
(b) where no notice was given, the date when the contract of employment was terminated by the employee.

(6) [. . .][100]

Fairness

General

98.—(1) In determining for the purposes of this Part whether the dismissal of an employee is fair or unfair, it is for the employer to show—
(a) the reason (or, if more than one, the principal reason) for the dismissal, and
(b) that it is either a reason falling within subsection (2) or some other substantial reason of a kind such as to justify the dismissal of an employee holding the position which the employee held.

(2) A reason falls within this subsection if it—
(a) relates to the capability or qualifications of the employee for performing work of the kind which he was employed by the employer to do,
(b) relates to the conduct of the employee,
[(ba) is retirement of the employee,] [101]
(c) is that the employee was redundant, or
(d) is that the employee could not continue to work in the position which he held without

[99] Substituted by SI 2002/2034, Sch 2, para 3.
[100] Repealed by the Employment Relations Act 1999 (c 26), Sch 4, para 14 and Sch 9, Part 2.
[101] Inserted by SI 2006/1031, Sch 8, para 22(2).

contravention (either on his part or on that of his employer) of a duty or restriction imposed by or under an enactment.

[(2A) Subsections (1) and (2) are subject to sections 98ZA to 98ZF.] [102]

(3) In subsection (2)(a)—

(a) 'capability', in relation to an employee, means his capability assessed by reference to skill, aptitude, health or any other physical or mental quality, and

(b) 'qualifications', in relation to an employee, means any degree, diploma or other academic, technical or professional qualification relevant to the position which he held.

[(3A) In any case where the employer has fulfilled the requirements of subsection (1) by showing that the reason (or the principal reason) for the dismissal is retirement of the employee, the question whether the dismissal is fair or unfair shall be determined in accordance with section 98ZG.] [103]

(4) [In any other case where] [104] the employer has fulfilled the requirements of subsection (1), the determination of the question whether the dismissal is fair or unfair (having regard to the reason shown by the employer)—

(a) depends on whether in the circumstances (including the size and administrative resources of the employer's undertaking) the employer acted reasonably or unreasonably in treating it as a sufficient reason for dismissing the employee, and

(b) shall be determined in accordance with equity and the substantial merits of the case.

(5) [. . .][105]

(6) [Subsection (4)] [is] subject to—[106]

(a) sections [98A] to 107 of this Act, and

(b) sections 152, 153[, 238 and 238A] of the Trade Union and Labour Relations (Consolidation) Act 1992 (dismissal on ground of trade union membership or activities or in connection with industrial action).

[Retirement[107]

No normal retirement age: dismissal before 65

98ZA.—(1) This section applies to the dismissal of an employee if—

(a) the employee has no normal retirement age, and

(b) the operative date of termination falls before the date when the employee reaches the age of 65.

(2) Retirement of the employee shall not be taken to be the reason (or a reason) for the dismissal.

No normal retirement age: dismissal at or after 65

98ZB.—(1) This section applies to the dismissal of an employee if—

(a) the employee has no normal retirement age, and

(b) the operative date of termination falls on or after the date when the employee reaches the age of 65.

(2) In a case where—

(a) the employer has notified the employee in accordance with paragraph 2 of Schedule 6 to the 2006 Regulations, and

(b) the contract of employment terminates on the intended date of retirement,

retirement of the employee shall be taken to be the only reason for the dismissal by the employer and any other reason shall be disregarded.

(3) In a case where—

(a) the employer has notified the employee in accordance with paragraph 2 of Schedule 6 to the 2006 Regulations, but

(b) the contract of employment terminates before the intended date of retirement,

retirement of the employee shall not be taken to be the reason (or a reason) for dismissal.

(4) In a case where—

---

[102] Inserted by SI 2006/1031, Sch 8, para 22(3).

[103] Inserted by SI 2006/1031, Sch 8, para 22(4).

[104] As amended by SI 2006/1031, Sch 8, para 22(5).

[105] Repealed by the Employment Relations Act 1999 (c 26), Sch 4, para 15 and Sch 9, Part 2.

[106] As amended by the Employment RelationsAct 1999 (c 26), Sch 4, para 15 and Sch 9, Part 2, the Employment Act 2002 (c 22), Sch 7, para 32 and the Employment RelationsAct 2004 (c 24), Sch 1, para 30.

[107] Sections 98ZA–98ZH inserted by SI 2006/1031, Sch 8, para 23.

(a) the employer has not notified the employee in accordance with paragraph 2 of Schedule 6 to the 2006 Regulations, and
(b) there is an intended date of retirement in relation to the dismissal, but
(c) the contract of employment terminates before the intended date of retirement,
retirement of the employee shall not be taken to be the reason (or a reason) for dismissal.

(5) In all other cases where the employer has not notified the employee in accordance with paragraph 2 of Schedule 6 to the 2006 Regulations, particular regard shall be had to the matters in section 98ZF when determining the reason (or principal reason) for dismissal.

Normal retirement age: dismissal before retirement age

98ZC.—(1) This section applies to the dismissal of an employee if—
(a) the employee has a normal retirement age, and
(b) the operative date of termination falls before the date when the employee reaches the normal retirement age.

(2) Retirement of the employee shall not be taken to be the reason (or a reason) for the dismissal.

Normal retirement age 65 or higher: dismissal at or after retirement age

98ZD.—(1) This section applies to the dismissal of an employee if—
(a) the employee has a normal retirement age,
(b) the normal retirement age is 65 or higher, and
(c) the operative date of termination falls on or after the date when the employee reaches the normal retirement age.

(2) In a case where—
(a) the employer has notified the employee in accordance with paragraph 2 of Schedule 6 to the 2006 Regulations, and
(b) the contract of employment terminates on the intended date of retirement,
retirement of the employee shall be taken to be the only reason for the dismissal by the employer and any other reason shall be disregarded.

(3) In a case where—
(a) the employer has notified the employee in accordance with paragraph 2 of Schedule 6 to the 2006 Regulations, but
(b) the contract of employment terminates before the intended date of retirement,
retirement of the employee shall not be taken to be the reason (or a reason) for dismissal.

(4) In a case where—
(a) the employer has not notified the employee in accordance with paragraph 2 of Schedule 6 to the 2006 Regulations, and
(b) there is an intended date of retirement in relation to the dismissal, but
(c) the contract of employment terminates before the intended date of retirement,
retirement of the employee shall not be taken to be the reason (or a reason) for dismissal.

(5) In all other cases where the employer has not notified the employee in accordance with paragraph 2 of Schedule 6 to the 2006 Regulations, particular regard shall be had to the matters in section 98ZF when determining the reason (or principal reason) for dismissal.

Normal retirement age below 65: dismissal at or after retirement age

98ZE.—(1) This section applies to the dismissal of an employee if—
(a) the employee has a normal retirement age,
(b) the normal retirement age is below 65, and
(c) the operative date of termination falls on or after the date when the employee reaches the normal retirement age.

(2) If it is unlawful discrimination under the 2006 Regulations for the employee to have that normal retirement age, retirement of the employee shall not be taken to be the reason (or a reason) for dismissal.

(3) Subsections (4) to (7) apply if it is not unlawful discrimination under the 2006 Regulations for the employee to have that normal retirement age.

(4) In a case where—
(a) the employer has notified the employee in accordance with paragraph 2 of Schedule 6 to the 2006 Regulations, and
(b) the contract of employment terminates on the intended date of retirement,

retirement of the employee shall be taken to be the only reason for dismissal by the employer and any other reason shall be disregarded.

(5) In a case where—
  (a) the employer has notified the employee in accordance with paragraph 2 of Schedule 6 to the 2006 Regulations, but
  (b) the contract of employment terminates before the intended date of retirement,

retirement of the employee shall not be taken to be the reason (or a reason) for dismissal.

(6) In a case where—
  (a) the employer has not notified the employee in accordance with paragraph 2 of Schedule 6 to the 2006 Regulations, and
  (b) there is an intended date of retirement in relation to the dismissal, but
  (c) the contract of employment terminates before the intended date of retirement,

retirement of the employee shall not be taken to be the reason (or a reason) for dismissal.

(7) In all other cases where the employer has not notified the employee in accordance with paragraph 2 of Schedule 6 to the 2006 Regulations, particular regard shall be had to the matters in section 98ZF when determining the reason (or principal reason) for dismissal.

Reason for dismissal: particular matters

98ZF.—(1) These are the matters to which particular regard is to be had in accordance with section 98ZB(5), 98ZD(5) or 98ZE(7)—
  (a) whether or not the employer has notified the employee in accordance with paragraph 4 of Schedule 6 to the 2006 Regulations;
  (b) if the employer has notified the employee in accordance with that paragraph, how long before the notified retirement date the notification was given;
  (c) whether or not the employer has followed, or sought to follow, the procedures in paragraph 7 of Schedule 6 to the 2006 Regulations.

(2) In subsection (1)(b) 'notified retirement date' means the date notified to the employee in accordance with paragraph 4 of Schedule 6 to the 2006 Regulations as the date on which the employer intends to retire the employee.

Retirement dismissals: fairness

98ZG.—(1) This section applies if the reason (or principal reason) for a dismissal is retirement of the employee.

(2) The employee shall be regarded as unfairly dismissed if, and only if, there has been a failure on the part of the employer to comply with an obligation imposed on him by any of the following provisions of Schedule 6 to the 2006 Regulations—
  (a) paragraph 4 (notification of retirement, if not already given under paragraph 2),
  (b) paragraphs 6 and 7 (duty to consider employee's request not to be retired),
  (c) paragraph 8 (duty to consider appeal against decision to refuse request not to be retired).

Interpretation

98ZH. In sections 98ZA to 98ZG—

'2006 Regulations' means the Employment Equality (Age) Regulations 2006;

'intended date of retirement' means the date which, by virtue of paragraph 1(2) of Schedule 6 to the 2006 Regulations, is the intended date of retirement in relation to a particular dismissal;

'normal retirement age', in relation to an employee, means the age at which employees in the employer's undertaking who hold, or have held, the same kind of position as the employee are normally required to retire;

'operative date of termination' means—
  (a) where the employer terminates the employee's contract of employment by notice, the date on which the notice expires, or
  (b) where the employer terminates the contract of employment without notice, the date on which the termination takes effect.

Other dismissals]

[Procedural fairness[108]

98A.—(1) An employee who is dismissed shall be regarded for the purposes of this Part as unfairly dismissed if—
(a) one of the procedures set out in Part 1 of Schedule 2 to the Employment Act 2002 (dismissal and disciplinary procedures) applies in relation to the dismissal,
(b) the procedure has not been completed, and
(c) the non-completion of the procedure is wholly or mainly attributable to failure by the employer to comply with its requirements.

(2) Subject to subsection (1), failure by an employer to follow a procedure in relation to the dismissal of an employee shall not be regarded for the purposes of section 98(4)(a) as by itself making the employer's action unreasonable if he shows that he would have decided to dismiss the employee if he had followed the procedure.

(3) For the purposes of this section, any question as to the application of a procedure set out in Part 1 of Schedule 2 to the Employment Act 2002, completion of such a procedure or failure to comply with the requirements of such a procedure shall be determined by reference to regulations under section 31 of that Act.]

[Protected disclosure]

[**103A.**—An employee who is dismissed shall be regarded for the purposes of this Part as unfairly dismissed if the reason (or, if more than one, the principal reason) for the dismissal is that the employee made a protected disclosure.][109]

Assertion of statutory right

104.—(1) An employee who is dismissed shall be regarded for the purposes of this Part as unfairly dismissed if the reason (or, if more than one, the principal reason) for the dismissal is that the employee—
(a) brought proceedings against the employer to enforce a right of his which is a relevant statutory right, or
(b) alleged that the employer had infringed a right of his which is a relevant statutory right.

(2) It is immaterial for the purposes of subsection (1)—
(a) whether or not the employee has the right, or
(b) whether or not the right has been infringed;
but, for that subsection to apply, the claim to the right and that it has been infringed must be made in good faith.

(3) It is sufficient for subsection (1) to apply that the employee, without specifying the right, made it reasonably clear to the employer what the right claimed to have been infringed was.

(4) The following are relevant statutory rights for the purposes of this section—[110]
(a) any right conferred by this Act for which the remedy for its infringement is by way of a complaint or reference to an [employment tribunal],
(b) the right conferred by section 86 of this Act, [. . .]
(c) the rights conferred by sections 68, 86, [145A, 145B,] 146, 168, [168A,] 169 and 170 of the Trade Union and Labour Relations (Consolidation) Act 1992 (deductions from pay, union activities and time off) [[. . .] [111]
[(d) the rights conferred by the Working Time Regulations 1998, the Merchant Shipping (Working Time: Inland Waterway) Regulations 2003[, the Fishing Vessels (Working Time: Sea-fisherman) Regulations 2004 or the Cross-border Railway Services (Working Time) Regulations 2008][112]]
[, and

[108] Inserted by the Employment Act 2002 (c 22), s 34. Repealed by the Employment Act 2008 (c.24), s 2 with effect from 6 April 2009, subject to the transitional provisions and savings contained in SI 2008/3232, Sch 1 Pt 1 paras 1 to 3.

[109] Inserted by the Public Interest Disclosure Act 1998, s 5.

[110] As amended by the Employment Rights (Dispute Resolution) Act 1998 (c 8), s 1 (2); the Employment Act 2002 (c 22), Sch 7, para 34; SI 2004/1713, Sch 2, para 2; and the Employment Relations Act 2004 (c 24), Sch 1, para31.

[111] Omitted by SI 2006/246, reg 19(a).

[112] Substituted by SI 2008/1660, Sch 3 para 2(4) as from 27 July 2008.

(e) the rights conferred by the Transfer of Undertakings (Protection of Employment) Regulations 2006.] [113]

[(5) In this section any reference to an employer includes, where the right in question is conferred by section 63A, the principal (within the meaning of section 63A(3)).] [114]

Exclusion of right

Qualifying period of employment

108.—(1) Section 94 does not apply to the dismissal of an employee unless he has been continuously employed for a period of not less than [one year] ending with the effective date of termination. [115]

(2) If an employee is dismissed by reason of any such requirement or recommendation as is referred to in section 64(2), subsection (1) has effect in relation to that dismissal as if for the words '[one year]' there were substituted the words 'one month'. [116]

(3) Subsection (1) does not apply if—

(a) [. . .][117]

[(aa) subsection (1) of section 98B (read with subsection (2) of that section) applies,] [118]

[(b) subsection (1) of section 99 (read with any regulations made under that section) applies,] [119]

(c) subsection (1) of section 100 (read with subsections (2) and (3) of that section) applies,

(d) subsection (1) of section 101 (read with subsection (2) of that section) or subsection (3) of that section applies,

[(dd) section 101A applies,] [120]

(e) section 102 applies,

(f) section 103 applies,

[(ff) section 103A applies,][121]

(g) subsection (1) of section 104 (read with subsections (2) and (3) of that section) applies,

[(gg) subsection (1) of section 104A (read with subsection (2) of that section) applies,] [122]

[(gh) subsection (1) of section 104B (read with subsection (2) of that section) applies,] [123]

[(gi) section 104C applies,] [124]

(h) section 105 applies.

[(hh) paragraph (3) or (6) of regulation 28 of the Transnational Information and Consultation of Employees Regulations 1999 (read with paragraphs (4) and (7) of that regulation) applies.] [125]

[(i) paragraph (1) of regulation 7 of the Part-time Workers (Prevention of Less Favourable Treatment) Regulations 2000 applies.] [126]

[(j) paragraph (1) of regulation 6 of the Fixed-term Employees (Prevention of Less Favourable Treatment) Regulations 2002 applies.] [127]

[(k) paragraph (3) or (6) of regulation 42 of the European Public Limited-Liability Company Regulations 2004 applies.] [128] [[. . .][129]

(l) paragraph (3) or (6) of regulation 30 of the Information and Consultation of Employees Regulations 2004 (read with paragraphs (4) and (7) of that regulation) applies.] [130] [, [. . .][131]

---

[113] Inserted by SI 2006/246, reg 19(b).
[114] Inserted by the Teaching and Higher Education Act 1998 (c 30), Sch 3, para 13.
[115] As amended by SI 1999/1436, art 2.
[116] As amended by SI 1999/1436, art 2.
[117] Repealed by the Employment Relations Act 1999 (c 26), Sch 4, para 19.
[118] Inserted by the Employment Relations Act 2004 (c 24), s 40.
[119] Substituted by the Employment Relations Act 2004 (c 24), Sch 1, para 32.
[120] Inserted by SI 1998/1833, reg32.
[121] Inserted by the Public Interest Disclosure Act 1998 (c 23), s 7.
[122] Inserted by the National Minimum Wage Act 1998 (c 39), s 25.
[123] Inserted by the Tax Credits Act 1999 (c 10), Sch 3, para 3 and by the Tax Credits Act 2002 (c 21), Sch 1, para 3.
[124] Inserted by the Employment Relations Act 2004 (c 24), s 40.
[125] Inserted by SI 1999/3323, reg 29.
[126] Inserted by SI 2000/1551, Sch, para 2.
[127] Inserted by SI 2002/2034, Sch 2, para 3.
[128] Inserted by SI 2004/2326, reg 43.
[129] Omitted by SI 2006/349, Sch, para 6(2)(a).
[130] Inserted by SI 2004/3426, reg31.
[131] Omitted by SI 2006/1031, Sch 8, para 24(a).

(m) paragraph 5(3) or (5) of the Schedule to the Occupational and Personal Pension Schemes (Consultation by Employers and Miscellaneous Amendment) Regulations 2006 (read with paragraph 5(6) of that Schedule) applies.] [132] [, [. . .]
(n) paragraph (a) or (b) of paragraph 13(5) of Schedule 6 to the Employment Equality (Age) Regulations 2006 applies.] [133] [, [. . .]
(o) paragraph (3) or (6) of regulation 31 of the European Cooperative Society (Involvement of Employees) Regulations 2006 (read with paragraphs (4) and (7) of that regulation) applies.] [134] [or
(p) regulation 46 or 47 of the Companies (Cross-Border Mergers) Regulations 2007 applies.] [135]

Chapter II Remedies for Unfair Dismissal

Introductory

Complaints to [employment tribunal] [136]

111.—(1) A complaint may be presented to an [employment tribunal] against an employer by any person that he was unfairly dismissed by the employer. [137]
(2) Subject to subsection (3), an [employment tribunal] shall not consider a complaint under this section unless it is presented to the tribunal—[138]
(a) before the end of the period of three months beginning with the effective date of termination, or
(b) within such further period as the tribunal considers reasonable in a case where it is satisfied that it was not reasonably practicable for the complaint to be presented before the end of that period of three months.
(3) Where a dismissal is with notice, an [employment tribunal] shall consider a complaint under this section if it is presented after the notice is given but before the effective date of termination. [139]
(4) In relation to a complaint which is presented as mentioned in subsection (3), the provisions of this Act, so far as they relate to unfair dismissal, have effect as if—
(a) references to a complaint by a person that he was unfairly dismissed by his employer included references to a complaint by a person that his employer has given him notice in such circumstances that he will be unfairly dismissed when the notice expires,
(b) references to reinstatement included references to the withdrawal of the notice by the employer,
(c) references to the effective date of termination included references to the date which would be the effective date of termination on the expiry of the notice, and
(d) references to an employee ceasing to be employed included references to an employee having been given notice of dismissal.

The remedies: orders and compensation

112.—(1) This section applies where, on a complaint under section 111, an [employment tribunal] finds that the grounds of the complaint are well-founded. [140]
(2) The tribunal shall—
(a) explain to the complainant what orders may be made under section 113 and in what circumstances they may be made, and
(b) ask him whether he wishes the tribunal to make such an order.
(3) If the complainant expresses such a wish, the tribunal may make an order under section 113.

[132] Inserted by SI 2006/349, Sch, para 6(2)(b).
[133] Inserted by SI 2006/1031, Sch 8, para 24(b).
[134] Inserted by SI 2006/2059, reg 32(2).
[135] Inserted by SI 2007/2974, reg 48(2).
[136] As amended by the Employment Rights (Dispute Resolution) Act 1998 (c 8), s 1(2).
[137] As amended by the Employment Rights (Dispute Resolution) Act 1998 (c 8), s 1(2).
[138] As amended by the Employment Rights (Dispute Resolution) Act 1998 (c 8), s 1(2).
[139] As amended by the Employment Rights (Dispute Resolution) Act 1998 (c 8), s 1(2).
[140] As amended by the Employment Rights (Dispute Resolution) Act 1998 (c 8), s 1(2).

(4) If no order is made under section 113, the tribunal shall make an award of compensation for unfair dismissal (calculated in accordance with sections 118 to [126]) to be paid by the employer to the employee. [141]

[(5) Where—[142]

(a) an employee is regarded as unfairly dismissed by virtue of section [98ZG *[or]* [143] *98A(1)]* [144] (whether or not his dismissal is unfair or regarded as unfair for any other reason), and

(b) an order is made in respect of the employee under section 113,

the employment tribunal shall, subject to subsection (6), also make an award of four weeks' pay to be paid by the employer to the employee.

(6) An employment tribunal shall not be required to make an award under subsection (5) if it considers that such an award would result in injustice to the employer.]

Orders for reinstatement or re-engagement

The orders

113. An order under this section may be—

(a) an order for reinstatement (in accordance with section 114), or

(b) an order for re-engagement (in accordance with section 115),

as the tribunal may decide.

Order for reinstatement

114.—(1) An order for reinstatement is an order that the employer shall treat the complainant in all respects as if he had not been dismissed.

(2) On making an order for reinstatement the tribunal shall specify—

(a) any amount payable by the employer in respect of any benefit which the complainant might reasonably be expected to have had but for the dismissal (including arrears of pay) for the period between the date of termination of employment and the date of reinstatement,

(b) any rights and privileges (including seniority and pension rights) which must be restored to the employee, and

(c) the date by which the order must be complied with.

(3) If the complainant would have benefited from an improvement in his terms and conditions of employment had he not been dismissed, an order for reinstatement shall require him to be treated as if he had benefited from that improvement from the date on which he would have done so but for being dismissed.

(4) In calculating for the purposes of subsection (2)(a) any amount payable by the employer, the tribunal shall take into account, so as to reduce the employer's liability, any sums received by the complainant in respect of the period between the date of termination of employment and the date of reinstatement by way of—

(a) wages in lieu of notice or ex gratia payments paid by the employer, or

(b) remuneration paid in respect of employment with another employer,

and such other benefits as the tribunal thinks appropriate in the circumstances.

(5) [. . .][145]

Order for re-engagement

115.—(1) An order for re-engagement is an order, on such terms as the tribunal may decide, that the complainant be engaged by the employer, or by a successor of the employer or by an associated employer, in employment comparable to that from which he was dismissed or other suitable employment.

---

[141] As amended by the Public Interest Disclosure Act 1998 (c 23), s 8 and by the Employment Relations Act 1999 (c 26), s 44 and Sch 9, Part 11 and the Employment Act 2002 (c 22), Sch 7, para 36.

[142] Inserted by the Employment Act 2002 (c 22), s 34.

[143] As amended by SI 2006/1031, Sch 8, para 26.

[144] Repealed by the Employment Act 2008 (c.24), Sch 1, Pt 1 with effect from 6 April 2009, subject to the transitional provisions and savings contained in SI 2008/3232, Sch 1 Pt 1 paras 1 to 3.

[145] Repealed by the Employment Relations Act 1999 (c 26), Sch 4, para 20 and Sch 9.

(2) On making an order for re-engagement the tribunal shall specify the terms on which re-engagement is to take place, including—
   (a) the identity of the employer,
   (b) the nature of the employment,
   (c) the remuneration for the employment,
   (d) any amount payable by the employer in respect of any benefit which the complainant might reasonably be expected to have had but for the dismissal (including arrears of pay) for the period between the date of termination of employment and the date of re-engagement,
   (e) any rights and privileges (including seniority and pension rights) which must be restored to the employee, and
   (f) the date by which the order must be complied with.

(3) In calculating for the purposes of subsection (2)(d) any amount payable by the employer, the tribunal shall take into account, so as to reduce the employer's liability, any sums received by the complainant in respect of the period between the date of termination of employment and the date of re-engagement by way of—
   (a) wages in lieu of notice or ex gratia payments paid by the employer, or
   (b) remuneration paid in respect of employment with another employer,

   and such other benefits as the tribunal thinks appropriate in the circumstances.

(4) [. . .][146]

Choice of order and its terms

116.—(1) An exercising its discretion under section 113 the tribunal shall first consider whether to make an order for reinstatement and in so doing shall take into account—
   (a) whether the complainant wishes to be reinstated,
   (b) whether it is practicable for the employer to comply with an order for reinstatement, and
   (c) where the complainant caused or contributed to some extent to the dismissal, whether it would be just to order his reinstatement.

(2) If the tribunal decides not to make an order for reinstatement it shall then consider whether to make an order for re-engagement and, if so, on what terms.

(3) In so doing the tribunal shall take into account—
   (a) any wish expressed by the complainant as to the nature of the order to be made,
   (b) whether it is practicable for the employer (or a successor or an associated employer) to comply with an order for re-engagement, and
   (c) where the complainant caused or contributed to some extent to the dismissal, whether it would be just to order his re-engagement and (if so) on what terms.

(4) Except in a case where the tribunal takes into account contributory fault under subsection (3)(c) it shall, if it orders re-engagement, do so on terms which are, so far as is reasonably practicable, as favourable as an order for reinstatement.

(5) Where in any case an employer has engaged a permanent replacement for a dismissed employee, the tribunal shall not take that fact into account in determining, for the purposes of subsection (1)(b) or (3)(b), whether it is practicable to comply with an order for reinstatement or re-engagement.

(6) Subsection (5) does not apply where the employer shows—
   (a) that it was not practicable for him to arrange for the dismissed employee's work to be done without engaging a permanent replacement, or
   (b) that—
      (i) he engaged the replacement after the lapse of a reasonable period, without having heard from the dismissed employee that he wished to be reinstated or re-engaged, and
      (ii) when the employer engaged the replacement it was no longer reasonable for him to arrange for the dismissed employee's work to be done except by a permanent replacement.

[146] Repealed by the Employment Relations Act 1999 (c 26), Sch 4, para 21 and Sch 9.

Enforcement of order and compensation[147]

117.—(1) An [employment tribunal] shall make an award of compensation, to be paid by the employer to the employee, if—[148]

(a) an order under section 113 is made and the complainant is reinstated or re-engaged, but

(b) the terms of the order are not fully complied with.

(2) Subject to section 124 [. . .], the amount of the compensation shall be such as the tribunal thinks fit having regard to the loss sustained by the complainant in consequence of the failure to comply fully with the terms of the order. [149]

[(2A) There shall be deducted from any award under subsection (1) the amount of any award made under section 112(5) at the time of the order under section 113.] [150]

(3) Subject to subsections (1) and (2) [. . .], if an order under section 113 is made but the complainant is not reinstated or re-engaged in accordance with the order, the tribunal shall make—[151]

(a) an award of compensation for unfair dismissal (calculated in accordance with sections 118 to [126]), and

(b) except where this paragraph does not apply, an additional award of compensation of [an amount not less than twenty-six nor more than fifty-two weeks' pay],

to be paid by the employer to the employee.

(4) Subsection (3)(b) does not apply where—[152]

(a) the employer satisfies the tribunal that it was not practicable to comply with the order, [. . .]

(b) [. . .]

(5) [. . .][153]

(6) [. . .][154]

(7) Where in any case an employer has engaged a permanent replacement for a dismissed employee, the tribunal shall not take that fact into account in determining for the purposes of subsection (4)(a) whether it was practicable to comply with the order for reinstatement or re-engagement unless the employer shows that it was not practicable for him to arrange for the dismissed employee's work to be done without engaging a permanent replacement.

(8) Where in any case an [employment tribunal] finds that the complainant has unreasonably prevented an order under section 113 from being complied with, in making an award of compensation for unfair dismissal [. . .] it shall take that conduct into account as a failure on the part of the complainant to mitigate his loss. [155]

Compensation

General

118.—(1) [. . .] Where a tribunal makes an award of compensation for unfair dismissal under section 112(4) or 117(3)(a) the award shall consist of—[156]

(a) a basic award (calculated in accordance with sections 119 to 122 and 126), and

(b) a compensatory award (calculated in accordance with sections 123, 124, 124A and 126]).

(2)–(3) [. . .][157]

(4) [. . .][158]

---

[147] For modifications of s 117 as regards the enforcement of re-employment orders in accordance with the ACAS Arbitration Scheme 2004, see the ACAS Arbitration Scheme (Great Britain) Order 2004, SI 2004/753, art 6 below.

[148] As amended by the Employment Rights (Dispute Resolution) Act 1998 (c 8), ss 1(2), 15 and Sch 2.

[149] As amended by the Employment Relations Act 1999, s 44 and Sch 9.

[150] Inserted by the Employment Act 2002, s 34(4).

[151] As amended by the Employment Relations Act 1999, ss 33, 44 and Sch 9 and the Employment Act 2002, Sch 7,paras 24 and 376.

[152] As amended by the Employment Relations Act 1999, ss 33, 44 and Sch 9.

[153] Repealed by the Employment Relations Act 1999, ss 33, 44 and Sch 9.

[154] Repealed by the Employment Relations Act 1999, ss 33, 44 and Sch 9.

[155] As amended by the Employment Rights (Dispute Resolution) Act 1998 (c 8), ss 1(2), 15 and Sch 2.

[156] As amended by the Employment Relations Act 1999, s 44 and Sch 9 and the Employment Act 2002, s 53 and Sch 7, paras 24 and 38.

[157] Repealed by the Employment Relations Act 1999, ss 33, 44 and Sch 9.

[158] Repealed by the Employment Act 2002, s 54 and Sch 8 (originally inserted by the Employment Rights (Dispute Resolution) Act 1998, Sch 1, para 21).

Basic award

119.—(1) Subject to the provisions of this section, sections 120 to 122 and section 126, the amount of the basic award shall be calculated by—

(a) determining the period, ending with the effective date of termination, during which the employee has been continuously employed,

(b) reckoning backwards from the end of that period the number of years of employment falling within that period, and

(c) allowing the appropriate amount for each of those years of employment.

(2) In subsection (1)(c) 'the appropriate amount' means—

(a) one and a half weeks' pay for a year of employment in which the employee was not below the age of forty-one,

(b) one week's pay for a year of employment (not within paragraph (a)) in which he was not below the age of twenty-two, and

(c) half a week's pay for a year of employment not within paragraph (a) or (b).

(3) Where twenty years of employment have been reckoned under subsection (1), no account shall be taken under that subsection of any year of employment earlier than those twenty years.

(4) [. . .][159]

(5) [. . .][160]

(6) [. . .][161]

Basic award: minimum in certain cases

120.—(1) The amount of the basic award (before any reduction under section 122) shall not be less than [£4,700] where the reason (or, if more than one, the principal reason)— [162]

(a) in a redundancy case, for selecting the employee for dismissal, or

(b) otherwise, for the dismissal,

is one of those specified in section 100(1)(a) and (b), [101A9d),] 102(1) or 103.

[(1A) Where—[163]

(a) an employee is regarded as unfairly dismissed by virtue of section [98ZG *[or]* [164] *98A(1)]*[165] (whether or not his dismissal is unfair or regarded as unfair for any other reason),

(b) an award of compensation falls to be made under section 112(4), and

(c) the amount of the award under section 118(1)(a), before any reduction under section 122(3A) or (4), is less than the amount of four weeks' pay,

the employment tribunal shall, subject to subsection (1B), increase the award under section 118(1)(a) to the amount of four weeks' pay.

(1B) An employment tribunal shall not be required by subsection (1A) to increase the amount of an award if it considers that the increase would result in injustice to the employer.]

(2) [. . .][166]

Basic award of two weeks' pay in certain cases

121. The amount of the basic award shall be two weeks' pay where the tribunal finds that the reason (or, where there is more than one, the principal reason) for the dismissal of the employee is that he was redundant and the employee—

(a) by virtue of section 138 is not regarded as dismissed for the purposes of Part XI, or

(b) by virtue of section 141 is not, or (if he were otherwise entitled) would not be, entitled to a redundancy payment.

---

159 Omitted by SI 2006/1031, Sch 8, para 27.

160 Omitted by SI 2006/1031, Sch 8, para 27.

161 Repealed by the Employment Relations Act 1999, ss 9, 14, Sch 4, para 23 and Sch 9.

162 As amended by SI 1998/1833, reg 32(5); SI 2004/2989, art 3 and Sch 9; SI 2005/3352, art 3 and Sch; SI 2006/3045, art 3 and Sch; and SI 2007/3570, art 3 and Sch.; and SI 2008/3055, art 3 and Sch.

163 Inserted by Employment Act 2002, s 34(6).

164 As amended by SI 2006/1031, Sch 8, para 28.

165 Repealed by the Employment Act 2008 (c.24), Sch 1, Pt 1 with effect from 6 April 2009, subject to the transitional provisions and savings contained in SI 2008/3232, Sch 1 Pt 1 paras 1 to 3.

166 Repealed by the Employment Relations Act 1999, ss36(1)(a), 44 and Sch 9.

Basic award: reductions

122.—(1) Where the tribunal finds that the complainant has unreasonably refused an offer by the employer which (if accepted) would have the effect of reinstating the complainant in his employment in all respects as if he had not been dismissed, the tribunal shall reduce or further reduce the amount of the basic award to such extent as it considers just and equitable having regard to that finding.

(2) Where the tribunal considers that any conduct of the complainant before the dismissal (or, where the dismissal was with notice, before the notice was given) was such that it would be just and equitable to reduce or further reduce the amount of the basic award to any extent, the tribunal shall reduce or further reduce that amount accordingly.

(3) Subsection (2) does not apply in a redundancy case unless the reason for selecting the employee for dismissal was one of those specified in section 100(1)(a) and (b), [101A(d),] 102(1) or 103; and in such a case subsection (2) applies only to so much of the basic award as is payable because of section 120.[167]

[(3A) Where the complainant has been awarded any amount in respect of the dismissal under a designated dismissal procedures agreement, the tribunal shall reduce or further reduce the amount of the basic award to such extent as it considers just and equitable having regard to that award.][168]

(4) The amount of the basic award shall be reduced or further reduced by the amount of—

(a) any redundancy payment awarded by the tribunal under Part XI in respect of the same dismissal, or

(b) any payment made by the employer to the employee on the ground that the dismissal was by reason of redundancy (whether in pursuance of Part XI or otherwise).

Compensatory award

123.—(1) Subject to the provisions of this section and sections 124[, 124A and 126], the amount of the compensatory award shall be such amount as the tribunal considers just and equitable in all the circumstances having regard to the loss sustained by the complainant in consequence of the dismissal in so far as that loss is attributable to action taken by the employer.[169]

(2) The loss referred to in subsection (1) shall be taken to include—

(a) any expenses reasonably incurred by the complainant in consequence of the dismissal, and

(b) subject to subsection (3), loss of any benefit which he might reasonably be expected to have had but for the dismissal.

(3) The loss referred to in subsection (1) shall be taken to include in respect of any loss of—

(a) any entitlement or potential entitlement to a payment on account of dismissal by reason of redundancy (whether in pursuance of Part XI or otherwise), or

(b) any expectation of such a payment,

only the loss referable to the amount (if any) by which the amount of that payment would have exceeded the amount of a basic award (apart from any reduction under section 122) in respect of the same dismissal.

(4) In ascertaining the loss referred to in subsection (1) the tribunal shall apply the same rule concerning the duty of a person to mitigate his loss as applies to damages recoverable under the common law of England and Wales or (as the case may be) Scotland.

(5) In determining, for the purposes of subsection (1), how far any loss sustained by the complainant was attributable to action taken by the employer, no account shall be taken of any pressure which by—

(a) calling, organising, procuring or financing a strike or other industrial action, or

(b) threatening to do so,

was exercised on the employer to dismiss the employee; and that question shall be determined as if no such pressure had been exercised.

(6) Where the tribunal finds that the dismissal was to any extent caused or contributed to by any action of the complainant, it shall reduce the amount of the compensatory award by such proportion as it considers just and equitable having regard to that finding.

167 As amended by SI 1998/1833, reg 32(5).

168 Inserted by the Employment Rights (Dispute Resolution) Act 1998, Sch 1, para 22.

169 As amended by the Employment Act 2002, Sch 7, paras 24 and 39.

(7) If the amount of any payment made by the employer to the employee on the ground that the dismissal was by reason of redundancy (whether in pursuance of Part XI or otherwise) exceeds the amount of the basic award which would be payable but for section 122(4), that excess goes to reduce the amount of the compensatory award.

[(8) Where the amount of the compensatory award falls to be calculated for the purposes of an award under section 117(3)(a), there shall be deducted from the compensatory award any award made under section 112(5) at the time of the order under section 113.] [170]

Limit of compensatory award etc

124.—(1) The amount of—[171]

(a) any compensation awarded to a person under section 117(1) and (2), or

(b) a compensatory award to a person calculated in accordance with section 123,

shall not exceed [£66,200].

[(1A) Subsection (1) shall not apply to compensation awarded, or a compensatory award made, to a person in a case where he is regarded as unfairly dismissed by virtue of section 100, 103A, 105(3) or 105(6A).] [172]

(2) [. . .][173]

(3) In the case of compensation awarded to a person under section 117(1) and (2), the limit imposed by this section may be exceeded to the extent necessary to enable the award fully to reflect the amount specified as payable under section 114(2)(a) or section 115(2)(d).

(4) Where—

(a) a compensatory award is an award under paragraph (a) of subsection (3) of section 117, and

(b) an additional award falls to be made under paragraph (b) of that subsection,

the limit imposed by this section on the compensatory award may be exceeded to the extent necessary to enable the aggregate of the compensatory and additional awards fully to reflect the amount specified as payable under section 114(2)(a) or section 115(2)(d).

(5) The limit imposed by this section applies to the amount which the [employment tribunal] would, apart from this section, award in respect of the subject matter of the complaint after taking into account—[174]

(a) any payment made by the respondent to the complainant in respect of that matter, and

(b) any reduction in the amount of the award required by any enactment or rule of law.

[Adjustments under the Employment Act 2002[175]

124A.—Where an award of compensation for unfair dismissal falls to be—

(a) reduced or increased under [section 207A of the Trade Union and Labour Relations (Consolidation) Act 1992 (effect of failure to comply with Code: adjustment of awards)][176], or

(b) increased under section 38 of that Act (failure to give statement of employment particulars),

the adjustment shall be in the amount awarded under section 118(1)(b) and shall be applied immediately before any reduction under section 123(6) or (7).]

---

[170] Inserted by the Employment Act 2002, s 34(5).

[171] As amended by the Employment Rights (Dispute Resolution) Act 1998 (c 8), s 1(2), SI 2004/2989, art 3 and Sch; SI 2006/3045, art 3 and Sch; and SI 2007/3570, art 3 and Sch.; and SI 2008/3055, art 3 and Sch.

[172] Inserted by the Employment Relations Act 1999, s 37(1).

[173] Repealed by the Employment Relations Act 1999, ss 36(1), 44 and Sch 9.

[174] As amended by the Employment Rights (Dispute Resolution) Act 1998 (c 8), s 1 (2) and SI 2004/2989, art 3 and Sch.

[175] Inserted by the Employment Act 2002, s 39.

[176] Substituted by the Employment Act 2008 (c.24), s 3(4) with effect from 6 April 2009, subject to the transitional provisions and savings contained in SI 2008/3232, Sch 1 Pt 1 paras 1 to 3.

PART XI
REDUNDANCY PAYMENTS ETC

CHAPTER I RIGHT TO REDUNDANCY PAYMENT

The right

135.—(1) An employer shall pay a redundancy payment to any employee of his if the employee—
 (a) is dismissed by the employer by reason of redundancy, or
 (b) is eligible for a redundancy payment by reason of being laid off or kept on short-time.
(2) Subsection (1) has effect subject to the following provisions of this Part (including, in particular, sections 140 to 144, 149 to 152, 155 to 161 and 164).

CHAPTER II RIGHT ON DISMISSAL BY REASON OF REDUNDANCY

Dismissal by reason of redundancy

Circumstances in which an employee is dismissed

136.—(1) Subject to the provisions of this section and sections 137 and 138, for the purposes of this Part an employee is dismissed by his employer if (and only if)—
 (a) the contract under which he is employed by the employer is terminated by the employer (whether with or without notice),
 [(b)) he is employed under a limited term contract and that contract terminates by virtue of the limiting event without being renewed under the same contract, or] [177]
 (c) the employee terminates the contract under which he is employed (with or without notice) in circumstances in which he is entitled to terminate it without notice by reason of the employer's conduct.
(2) Subsection (1)(c) does not apply if the employee terminates the contract without notice in circumstances in which he is entitled to do so by reason of a lock-out by the employer.
(3) An employee shall be taken to be dismissed by his employer for the purposes of this Part if—
 (a) the employer gives notice to the employee to terminate his contract of employment, and
 (b) at a time within the obligatory period of notice the employee gives notice in writing to the employer to terminate the contract of employment on a date earlier than the date on which the employer's notice is due to expire.
(4) In this Part the 'obligatory period of notice', in relation to notice given by an employer to terminate an employee's contract of employment, means—
 (a) the actual period of the notice in a case where the period beginning at the time when the notice is given and ending at the time when it expires is equal to the minimum period which (by virtue of any enactment or otherwise) is required to be given by the employer to terminate the contract of employment, and
 (b) the period which—
  (i) is equal to the minimum period referred to in paragraph (a), and
  (ii) ends at the time when the notice expires,
 in any other case.
(5) Where in accordance with any enactment or rule of law—
 (a) an act on the part of an employer, or
 (b) an event affecting an employer (including, in the case of an individual, his death),
 operates to terminate a contract under which an employee is employed by him, the act or event shall be taken for the purposes of this Part to be a termination of the contract by the employer.

Redundancy

139.—(1) For the purposes of this Act an employee who is dismissed shall be taken to be dismissed by reason of redundancy if the dismissal is wholly or mainly attributable to—
 (a) the fact that his employer has ceased or intends to cease—
  (i) to carry on the business for the purposes of which the employee was employed by him, or
  (ii) to carry on that business in the place where the employee was so employed, or

[177] Substituted by SI 2002/2034, reg 11 and Sch 2, para3(13).

(b) the fact that the requirements of that business—
   (i) for employees to carry out work of a particular kind, or
   (ii) for employees to carry out work of a particular kind in the place where the employee was employed by the employer,

have ceased or diminished or are expected to cease or diminish.

(2) For the purposes of subsection (1) the business of the employer together with the business or businesses of his associated employers shall be treated as one (unless either of the conditions specified in paragraphs (a) and (b) of that subsection would be satisfied without so treating them).

(3) For the purposes of subsection (1) the activities carried on by a local education authority with respect to the schools maintained by it, and the activities carried on by the [governing bodies] of those schools, shall be treated as one business (unless either of the conditions specified in paragraphs (a) and (b) of that subsection would be satisfied without so treating them). [178]

(4) Where—
   (a) the contract under which a person is employed is treated by section 136(5) as terminated by his employer by reason of an act or event, and
   (b) the employee's contract is not renewed and he is not re-engaged under a new contract of employment, he shall be taken for the purposes of this Act to be dismissed by reason of redundancy if the circumstances in which his contract is not renewed, and he is not re-engaged, are wholly or mainly attributable to either of the facts stated in paragraphs (a) and (b) of subsection (1).

(5) In its application to a case within subsection (4), paragraph (a)(i) of subsection (1) has effect as if the reference in that subsection to the employer included a reference to any person to whom, in consequence of the act or event, power to dispose of the business has passed.

(6) In subsection (1) 'cease' and 'diminish' mean cease and diminish either permanently or temporarily and for whatever reason.

Part XIII
Miscellaneous

Chapter II Other Miscellaneous Matters

Contracting out etc and remedies

Restrictions on contracting out

203.—(1) Any provision in an agreement (whether a contract of employment or not) is void in so far as it purports—[179]
   (a) to exclude or limit the operation of any provision of this Act, or
   (b) to preclude a person from bringing any proceedings under this Act before an [employment tribunal].

(2) Subsection (1)— [180]
   (a) does not apply to any provision in a collective agreement excluding rights under section 28 if an order under section 35 is for the time being in force in respect of it,
   (b) does not apply to any provision in a dismissal procedures agreement excluding the right under section 94 if that provision is not to have effect unless an order under section 110 is for the time being in force in respect of it,
   (c) does not apply to any provision in an agreement if an order under section 157 is for the time being in force in respect of it,
   (d) [. . .][181]
   (e) does not apply to any agreement to refrain from instituting or continuing proceedings where a conciliation officer has taken action under section 18 of the [Employment Tribunals Act 1996], and

---

[178] As amended by the Education Act 2002, s 215(1) and Sch 21, para 31.

[179] As amended by the Employment Rights (Dispute Resolution) Act 1998 (c 8),s 1(2).

[180] As amended by the Employment Rights (Dispute Resolution) Act 1998 (c 8),s 1(2).

[181] As amended by the Employment Rights (Dispute Resolution) Act 1998, ss 15,44, Sch 2 and Sch 9; SI 2001/1107, reg 3; and SI 2002/2034, reg 11 and Sch 2, para 3.

(f) does not apply to any agreement to refrain from instituting or continuing before an [employment tribunal] any proceedings within [the following provisions of section 18(1) of the Employment Tribunals Act 1996 (cases where conciliation available)—
 (i) paragraph (d) (proceedings under this Act),
 (ii) paragraph (h) (proceedings arising out of the Part-time Workers (Prevention of Less Favourable Treatment) Regulations 2000),]
 [(iii) paragraph (i) (proceedings arising out of the Fixed-term Employees (Prevention of Less Favourable Treatment) Regulations 2002),
 (iv) paragraph (j) (proceedings under those Regulations),]

if the conditions regulating compromise agreements under this Act are satisfied in relation to the agreement.

(3) For the purposes of subsection (2)(f) the conditions regulating compromise agreements under this Act are that—[182,183]
 (a) the agreement must be in writing,
 (b) the agreement must relate to the particular [proceedings],
 (c) the employee or worker must have received [advice from a relevant independent advisor] as to the terms and effect of the proposed agreement and, in particular, its effect on his ability to pursue his rights before an [employment tribunal],
 (d) there must be in force, when the adviser gives the advice, a [contract of insurance, or an indemnity provided for members of a professional body] covering the risk of a claim by the employee or worker in respect of loss arising in consequence of the advice,
 (e) the agreement must identify the adviser, and
 (f) the agreement must state that the conditions regulating compromise agreements under this Act are satisfied.

[(3A) A person is a relevant independent adviser for the purposes of subsection (3)(c)—[184]
 (a) if he is a qualified lawyer,
 (b) if he is an officer, official, employee or member of an independent trade union who has been certified in writing by the trade union as competent to give advice and as authorised to do so on behalf of the trade union,
 (c) if he works at an advice centre (whether as an employee or a volunteer) and has been certified in writing by the centre as competent to give advice and as authorised to do so on behalf of the centre, or
 (d) if he is a person of a description specified in an order made by the Secretary of State.

(3B) But a person is not a relevant independent adviser for the purposes of subsection (3)(c) in relation to the employee or worker—
 (a) if he is, is employed by or is acting in the matter for the employer or an associated employer,
 (b) in the case of a person within subsection (3A)(b) or (c), if the trade union or advice centre is the employer or an associated employer,
 (c) in the case of a person within subsection (3A)(c), if the employee or worker makes a payment for the advice received from him, or
 (d) in the case of a person of a description specified in an order under subsection (3A)(d), if any condition specified in the order in relation to the giving of advice by persons of that description is not satisfied.

(4) In subsection (3A)(a) 'qualified lawyer' means—
 (a) as respects England and Wales, a barrister (whether in practice as such or employed to give legal advice), a solicitor who holds a practising certificate, or a person other than a barrister or solicitor who is an authorised advocate or authorised litigator (within the meaning of the Courts and Legal Services Act 1990), and
 (b) as respects Scotland, an advocate (whether in practice as such or employed to give legal advice), or a solicitor who holds a practising certificate.]

182 As amended by the Employment Rights (Dispute Resolution) Act 1998 (c 8), s 1(2).

183 As amended by the Employment Rights (Dispute Resolution) Act 1998, ss 9, 10, 15 and Sch 1, para 24.

184 Substituted by the Employment Rights (Dispute Resolution) Act 1998, s 15 and Sch 1, para 24.

[(5) An agreement under which the parties agree to submit a dispute to arbitration—[185]
(a) shall be regarded for the purposes of subsection (2)(e) and (f) as being an agreement to refrain from instituting or continuing proceedings if—
(i) the dispute is covered by a scheme having effect by virtue of an order under section 212A of the Trade Union and Labour Relations (Consolidation) Act 1992, and
(ii) the agreement is to submit it to arbitration in accordance with the scheme, but
(b) shall be regarded as neither being nor including such an agreement in any other case.]

Part XIV
Interpretation

Chapter I Continuous Employment

Introductory

210.—(1) References in any provision of this Act to a period of continuous employment are (unless provision is expressly made to the contrary) to a period computed in accordance with this Chapter.
(2) In any provision of this Act which refers to a period of continuous employment expressed in months or years—
(a) a month means a calendar month, and
(b) a year means a year of twelve calendar months.
(3) In computing an employee's period of continuous employment for the purposes of any provision of this Act, any question—
(a) whether the employee's employment is of a kind counting towards a period of continuous employment, or
(b) whether periods (consecutive or otherwise) are to be treated as forming a single period of continuous employment,
shall be determined week by week; but where it is necessary to compute the length of an employee's period of employment it shall be computed in months and years of twelve months in accordance with section 211.
(4) Subject to sections 215 to 217, a week which does not count in computing the length of a period of continuous employment breaks continuity of employment.
(5) A person's employment during any period shall, unless the contrary is shown, be presumed to have been continuous.

Period of continuous employment

211.—(1) An employee's period of continuous employment for the purposes of any provision of this Act—
(a) (subject to [subsection] (3)) begins with the day on which the employee starts work, and[186]
(b) ends with the day by reference to which the length of the employee's period of continuous employment is to be ascertained for the purposes of the provision.
(2) [. . .][187]
(3) If an employee's period of continuous employment includes one or more periods which (by virtue of section 215, 216 or 217) while not counting in computing the length of the period do not break continuity of employment, the beginning of the period shall be treated as postponed by the number of days falling within that intervening period, or the aggregate number of days falling within those periods, calculated in accordance with the section in question.

Weeks counting in computing period

212.—(1) Any week during the whole or part of which an employee's relations with his employer are governed by a contract of employment counts in computing the employee's period of employment.
(2) [. . .][188]

---

[185] Inserted by the Employment Rights (Dispute Resolution) Act 1998, s 8(5).
[186] As amended by SI 2006/103 1,Sch 8, para35(2).
[187] Omitted by SI 2006/103 1, Sch 8, para35(3).
[188] Repealed by the Employment Relations Act 1999, ss 9, 44, Sch4,para38 andSch 9.

(3) Subject to subsection (4), any week (not within subsection (1)) during the whole or part of which an employee is—
(a) incapable of work in consequence of sickness or injury,
(b) absent from work on account of a temporary cessation of work, [or]
(c) absent from work in circumstances such that, by arrangement or custom, he is regarded as continuing in the employment of his employer for any purpose, [. . .]
(d) [. . .][189]
counts in computing the employee's period of employment.
(4) Not more than twenty-six weeks count under subsection (3)(a) or (subject to subsection (2)) subsection (3)(d) between any periods falling under subsection (1).

Intervals in employment

213.—(1) Where in the case of an employee a date later than the date which would be the effective date of termination by virtue of subsection (1) of section 97 is treated for certain purposes as the effective date of termination by virtue of subsection (2) or (4) of that section, the period of the interval between the two dates counts as a period of employment in ascertaining for the purposes of section 108(1) or 119(1) the period for which the employee has been continuously employed.
(2) Where an employee is by virtue of section 138(1) regarded for the purposes of Part XI as not having been dismissed by reason of a renewal or re-engagement taking effect after an interval, the period of the interval counts as a period of employment in ascertaining for the purposes of section 155 or 162(1) the period for which the employee has been continuously employed (except so far as it is to be disregarded under section 214 or 215).
(3) Where in the case of an employee a date later than the date which would be the relevant date by virtue of subsections (2) to (4) of section 145 is treated for certain purposes as the relevant date by virtue of subsection (5) of that section, the period of the interval between the two dates counts as a period of employment in ascertaining for the purposes of section 155 or 162(1) the period for which the employee has been continuously employed (except so far as it is to be disregarded under section 214 or 215).

Change of employer

218.—(1) Subject to the provisions of this section, this Chapter relates only to employment by the one employer.
(2) If a trade or business, or an undertaking (whether or not established by or under an Act), is transferred from one person to another—
(a) the period of employment of an employee in the trade or business or undertaking at the time of the transfer counts as a period of employment with the transferee, and
(b) the transfer does not break the continuity of the period of employment.
(3) If by or under an Act (whether public or local and whether passed before or after this Act) a contract of employment between any body corporate and an employee is modified and some other body corporate is substituted as the employer—
(a) the employee's period of employment at the time when the modification takes effect counts as a period of employment with the second body corporate, and
(b) the change of employer does not break the continuity of the period of employment.
(4) If on the death of an employer the employee is taken into the employment of the personal representatives or trustees of the deceased—
(a) the employee's period of employment at the time of the death counts as a period of employment with the employer's personal representatives or trustees, and
(b) the death does not break the continuity of the period of employment.
(5) If there is a change in the partners, personal representatives or trustees who employ any person—
(a) the employee's period of employment at the time of the change counts as a period of employment with the partners, personal representatives or trustees after the change, and
(b) the change does not break the continuity of the period of employment.

[189] Repealed by the Employment Relations Act 1999, ss 9, 44, Sch4,para38 andSch 9.

(6) If an employee of an employer is taken into the employment of another employer who, at the time when the employee enters the second employer's employment, is an associated employer of the first employer—

(a) the employee's period of employment at that time counts as a period of employment with the second employer, and

(b) the change of employer does not break the continuity of the period of employment.

(7) If an employee of the [governing body] of a school maintained by a local education authority is taken into the employment of the authority or an employee of a local education authority is taken into the employment of the [governing body] of a school maintained by the authority—[190]

(a) his period of employment at the time of the change of employer counts as a period of employment with the second employer, and

(b) the change does not break the continuity of the period of employment.

Reinstatement or re-engagement of dismissed employee

219.—(1) Regulations made by the Secretary of State may make provision—[191]

(a) for preserving the continuity of a person's period of employment for the purposes of this Chapter or for the purposes of this Chapter as applied by or under any other enactment specified in the regulations, or

(b) for modifying or excluding the operation of section 214 subject to the recovery of any such payment as is mentioned in that section,

in cases where [. . .] a dismissed employee is reinstated[, re-engaged or otherwise re-employed] by his employer or by a successor or associated employer of that employer [in any circumstances prescribed by the regulations].

(2)–(4) [. . .][192]

Chapter II A Week's Pay

Introductory

Introductory

220. The amount of a week's pay of an employee shall be calculated for the purposes of this Act in accordance with this Chapter.

Employments with normal working hours

General

221.—(1) This section and sections 222 and 223 apply where there are normal working hours for the employee when employed under the contract of employment in force on the calculation date.

(2) Subject to section 222, if the employee's remuneration for employment in normal working hours (whether by the hour or week or other period) does not vary with the amount of work done in the period, the amount of a week's pay is the amount which is payable by the employer under the contract of employment in force on the calculation date if the employee works throughout his normal working hours in a week.

(3) Subject to section 222, if the employee's remuneration for employment in normal working hours (whether by the hour or week or other period) does vary with the amount of work done in the period, the amount of a week's pay is the amount of remuneration for the number of normal working hours in a week calculated at the average hourly rate of remuneration payable by the employer to the employee in respect of the period of twelve weeks ending—

(a) where the calculation date is the last day of a week, with that week, and

(b) otherwise, with the last complete week before the calculation date.

(4) In this section references to remuneration varying with the amount of work done includes remuneration which may include any commission or similar payment which varies in amount.

(5) This section is subject to sections 227 and 228.

---

[190] As amended by the Education Act 2002, s 215 and Sch 21, para 32.

[191] As amended by the Employment Rights (Dispute Resolution) Act 1998 (c 8),s 1(2).

[192] Repealed by the Employment Rights (Dispute Resolution) Act 1998 (c 8), s 15 and Sch 1, para 25.

Remuneration varying according to time of work

222.—(1) This section applies if the employee is required under the contract of employment in force on the calculation date to work during normal working hours on days of the week, or at times of the day, which differ from week to week or over a longer period so that the remuneration payable for, or apportionable to, any week varies according to the incidence of those days or times.

(2) The amount of a week's pay is the amount of remuneration for the average number of weekly normal working hours at the average hourly rate of remuneration.

(3) For the purposes of subsection (2)—

(a) the average number of weekly hours is calculated by dividing by twelve the total number of the employee's normal working hours during the relevant period of twelve weeks, and

(b) the average hourly rate of remuneration is the average hourly rate of remuneration payable by the employer to the employee in respect of the relevant period of twelve weeks.

(4) In subsection (3) 'the relevant period of twelve weeks' means the period of twelve weeks ending—

(a) where the calculation date is the last day of a week, with that week, and

(b) otherwise, with the last complete week before the calculation date.

(5) This section is subject to sections 227 and 228.

Employments with no normal working hours

Employments with no normal working hours

224.—(1) This section applies where there are no normal working hours for the employee when employed under the contract of employment in force on the calculation date.

(2) The amount of a week's pay is the amount of the employee's average weekly remuneration in the period of twelve weeks ending—

(a) where the calculation date is the last day of a week, with that week, and

(b) otherwise, with the last complete week before the calculation date.

(3) In arriving at the average weekly remuneration no account shall be taken of a week in which no remuneration was payable by the employer to the employee and remuneration in earlier weeks shall be brought in so as to bring up to twelve the number of weeks of which account is taken.

(4) This section is subject to sections 227 and 228.

Maximum amount of week's pay

Maximum amount

227.—(1) For the purpose of calculating—[193]

[(za) an award of compensation under section 80I(1)(b),]

(a) a basic award of compensation for unfair dismissal,

(b) an additional award of compensation for unfair dismissal, or

[(ba) an award under section 112(5), or]

(c) a redundancy payment,

the amount of a week's pay shall not exceed [£350]. [194]

(2)–(4) [. . .][195]

Chapter III Other Interpretation Provisions

Employees, workers etc

230.—(1) In this Act 'employee' means an individual who has entered into or works under (or, where the employment has ceased, worked under) a contract of employment.

(2) In this Act 'contract of employment' means a contract of service or apprenticeship, whether express or implied, and (if it is express) whether oral or in writing.

(3) In this Act 'worker' (except in the phrases 'shop worker' and 'betting worker') means an individual who has entered into or works under (or, where the employment has ceased, worked under)—

(a) a contract of employment, or

[193] As amended by the Employment Act 2002, s 53 and Sch 7, paras 24 and 47; SI 2004/2989, art 3 and Sch; SI 2006/3045, art 3 and Sch; and SI 2007/3570, art 3 and Sch.

[194] As amended by SI 2006/3045, art 3 and Sch and SI 2008/3055, art 3 and Sch.

[195] Repealed by the Employment Relations Act 1999, ss 36, 44 and Sch 9.

(b) any other contract, whether express or implied and (if it is express) whether oral or in writing, whereby the individual undertakes to do or perform personally any work or services for another party to the contract whose status is not by virtue of the contract that of a client or customer of any profession or business undertaking carried on by the individual;

and any reference to a worker's contract shall be construed accordingly.

(4) In this Act 'employer', in relation to an employee or a worker, means the person by whom the employee or worker is (or, where the employment has ceased, was) employed.

(5) In this Act 'employment'—

(a) in relation to an employee, means (except for the purposes of section 171) employment under a contract of employment, and

(b) in relation to a worker, means employment under his contract;

and 'employed' shall be construed accordingly.

[(6) This section has effect subject to sections 43K and 47B(3); and for the purposes of Part XIII so far as relating to Part IVA or section 47B, 'worker', 'worker's contract' and, in relation to a worker, 'employer', 'employment' and 'employed' have the extended meaning given by section 43K.] [196]

Associated employers

231. For the purposes of this Act any two employers shall be treated as associated if—

(a) one is a company of which the other (directly or indirectly) has control, or

(b) both are companies of which a third person (directly or indirectly) has control;

and 'associated employer' shall be construed accordingly.

[196] Inserted by the Public Interest Disclosure Act 1998 (c 23), s 15.

Employment Tribunals Act 1996 (Extracts)[197]

(1996 Chapter 17)

An Act to consolidate enactments relating to [employment tribunals] and the Employment Appeal Tribunal.

[22nd May 1996]

Part I
[Employment Tribunals]

Membership etc

[Meaning of 'Employment Judge'

3A. A person who is a member of a panel of chairmen of employment tribunals which is appointed in accordance with regulations under section 1(1) may be referred to as an Employment Judge.] [198]

Composition of a tribunal

4.—(1) Subject to the following provisions of this section [and to section 7(3A)], proceedings before an [employment tribunal] shall be heard by—[199]

(a) the person who, [in accordance with regulation 11(a) of the Employment Tribunals (Constitution and Rules of Procedure) Regulations 2004,] is the [Employment Judge], and

[(b) two other members selected as the other members in accordance with regulation 11(b) of those Regulations or, with appropriate consent, one other member selected as the other member in accordance with regulations so made;

and in paragraph (b) 'appropriate consent' means either consent given at the beginning of the hearing by such of the parties as are then present in person or represented, or consent given by each of the parties.]

(2) Subject to subsection (5), the proceedings specified in subsection (3) shall be heard by the person mentioned in subsection (1)(a) alone [or alone by any Employment Judge who, in accordance with regulations made under section 1(1), is a member of the tribunal]. [200]

(3) The proceedings referred to in subsection (2) are—[201]

(a) proceedings on an application under [section 68A][, 87] or [192] of the Trade Union and Labour Relations (Consolidation) Act 1992 [or on an application under section 161, 165 or 166 of that Act],

(b) proceedings on a complaint under section 126 of the Pension Schemes Act 1993,

(c) proceedings [on a reference under section 11, 163 or 170 of the Employment Rights Act 1996,] on a complaint under section 23[, 34] or 188 of [that Act, on a complaint under section 70(1) of that Act relating to section 64 of that Act,] or on an application under section 128, 131 or 132 of that [Act or for an appointment under section 206(4) of that] Act,

[(ca) proceedings on a complaint under [regulation 15(10) of the Transfer of Undertakings (Protection of Employment) Regulations 2006],] [202]

[(cc) proceedings on a complaint under section 11 of the National Minimum Wage Act 1998;] [203]

[(cd) proceedings on an appeal under [section 19C] of the National Minimum Wage Act 1998;] [204]

[(ce) proceedings on a complaint under regulation 30 of the Working Time Regulations 1998

---

[197] All references in this Act to industrial tribunals were amended to references to employment tribunals by the Employment Rights (Dispute Resolution) Act 1998 (c 8), s 1(2).

[198] Inserted by the Tribunals, Courts and Enforcement Act 2007 (c 15), Sch 8, para 36.

[199] As amended by the Employment Rights (Dispute Resolution) Act 1998 (c 8), ss 3, 4, 5, 15 and Sch 1, para 12 and SI 2004/1861, reg 12.

[200] As amended by the Tribunals, Courts and Enforcement Act 2007 (c 15), Sch 8, para 37.

[201] As amended by the Employment Rights (Dispute Resolution) Act 1998 (c 8), ss 3,4, 5, 15 and Sch 1,para 12.

[202] As amended by SI 2006/246, Sch 2, para 8.

[203] Inserted by the National Minimum Wage Act 1998 (c 39), s 27.

[204] Inserted by the National Minimum Wage Act 1998 (c 39), s 27 and amended by the Employment Act 2008 (c 24), s 9(4).

relating to an amount due under regulation 14(2) or 16(1) of those Regulations,
(cf) proceedings on a complaint under regulation 18 of the Merchant Shipping (Working Time: Inland Waterways) Regulations 2003 relating to an amount due under regulation 11 of those Regulations,
(cg) proceedings on a complaint under regulation 18 of the Civil Aviation (Working Time) Regulations 2004 relating to an amount due under regulation 4 of those Regulations,
(ch) proceedings on a complaint under regulation 19 of the Fishing Vessels (Working Time: Sea-fishermen) Regulations 2004 relating to an amount due under regulation 11 of those Regulations,][205]
(d) proceedings in respect of which an [employment tribunal] has jurisdiction by virtue of section 3 of this Act,
(e) proceedings in which the parties have given their written consent to the proceedings being heard in accordance with subsection (2) (whether or not they have subsequently withdrawn it),
(f) [. . .]
(g) proceedings in which the person (or, where more than one, each of the persons) against whom the proceedings are brought does not, or has ceased to, contest the case.

(4) The Secretary of State [and the Lord Chancellor, acting jointly,] may by order amend the provisions of subsection (3).[206]

(5) Proceedings specified in subsection (3) shall be heard in accordance with subsection (1) if a person who, [in accordance with regulation 10(a) of the Employment Tribunals (Constitution and Rules of Procedure) Regulations 2004], may be the [Employment Judge] of an [employment tribunal], having regard to—[207]
(a) whether there is a likelihood of a dispute arising on the facts which makes it desirable for the proceedings to be heard in accordance with subsection (1),
(b) whether there is a likelihood of an issue of law arising which would make it desirable for the proceedings to be heard in accordance with subsection (2),
(c) any views of any of the parties as to whether or not the proceedings ought to be heard in accordance with either of those subsections, and
(d) whether there are other proceedings which might be heard concurrently but which are not proceedings specified in subsection (3),

decides at any stage of the proceedings that the proceedings are to be heard in accordance with subsection (1).

(6) Where (in accordance with the following provisions of this Part) the Secretary of State makes [employment tribunal] procedure regulations, the regulations may provide that [any act which is required or authorised by the regulations to be done by an employment tribunal and is of a description specified by the regulations for the purposes of this subsection may] be done by the person mentioned in subsection (1)(a) alone [or alone by any Employment Judge who, in accordance with regulations made under section 1(1), is a member of the tribunal].[208]

[(6A) Subsection (6) in particular enables employment tribunal procedure regulations to provide that—
(a) the determination of proceedings in accordance with regulations under section 7(3A), (3B) or (3C)(a),
(b) the carrying-out of pre-hearing reviews in accordance with regulations under subsection (1) of section 9 (including the exercise of powers in connection with such reviews in accordance with regulations under paragraph (b) of that subsection), or
(c) the hearing and determination of a preliminary issue in accordance with regulations under section 9(4) (where it involves hearing witnesses other than the parties or their representatives as well as where, in accordance with regulations under section 7(3C)(b), it does not),

may be done by the person mentioned in subsection (1)(a) alone [or alone by any Employment Judge who, in accordance with regulations made under section 1(1), is a member of the tribunal].][209]

[205] Inserted by SI 2009/789, art 2.
[206] As amended by the Tribunals, Courts and Enforcement Act 2007 (c 15), Sch 8, para 38.
[207] As amended by SI 2004/186 1, reg 12.
[208] As amended by the Tribunals, Courts and Enforcement Act 2007 (c 15), Sch 8, para 37.
[209] As amended by the Tribunals, Courts and Enforcement Act 2007 (c 15), Sch 8, para 37.

[(6B) Employment tribunal procedure regulations may (subject to subsection (6C)) also provide that any act which—
(a) by virtue of subsection (6) may be done by the person mentioned in subsection (1)(a) alone [or alone by any Employment Judge who, in accordance with regulations made under section 1(1), is a member of the tribunal], and[210]
(b) is of a description specified by the regulations for the purposes of this subsection,
may be done by a person appointed as a legal officer in accordance with regulations under section 1(1); and any act so done shall be treated as done by an employment tribunal.
(6C) But regulations under subsection (6B) may not specify—
(a) the determination of any proceedings, other than proceedings in which the parties have agreed the terms of the determination or in which the person bringing the proceedings has given notice of the withdrawal of the case, or
(b) the carrying-out of pre-hearing reviews in accordance with regulations under section 9(1).]
(7) Where a Minister of the Crown so directs in relation to any proceedings on grounds of national security—
(a) the proceedings shall be heard and determined, and
(b) any act required or authorised by [employment tribunal] procedure regulations to be done by an [employment tribunal] in relation to the proceedings shall be done,
by the President of the [employment tribunals] (England and Wales) appointed in accordance with regulations made under section 1(1), or by the President of the [employment tribunals] (Scotland) so appointed, alone.

Conciliation

Conciliation

18.—(1) This section applies in the case of [employment tribunal] proceedings and claims which could be the subject of [employment tribunal] proceedings—[211]
(a) under—
(i) section 2(1) of the Equal Pay Act 1970,
(ii) section 63 of the Sex Discrimination Act 1975, or
(iii) section 54 of the Race Relations Act 1976,
(b) arising out of a contravention, or alleged contravention, of section 64, 68, [86,] 137, 138, [145A, 145B,] 146, 168, [168A,] 169, 170, 174, 188 or 190 of the Trade Union and Labour Relations (Consolidation) Act 1992,
(c) under [section 17A or 25(8)] of the Disability Discrimination Act 1995,
(d) [under or] arising out of a contravention, or alleged contravention, of section 8, 13, 15, 18(1), 21(1), 28[, [80G(1), 80H(1)(b),] [80(1),] 92 or 135] of Part V, VI, VII or X, of the Employment Rights Act 1996,
[(dd) under or by virtue of section 11, 18, 20(1)(a) or 24 of the National Minimum Wage Act 1998;]
(e) which are proceedings in respect of which an [employment tribunal] has jurisdiction by virtue of section 3 of this Act, [. . .]
(f) arising out of a contravention, or alleged contravention, of a provision specified by an order under subsection (8)(b) as a provision to which this paragraph applies;
[(ff) under regulation 30 of the Working Time Regulations 1998,]
[(g) under regulation 27 or 32 of the Transnational Information and Consultation of Employees Regulations 1999,]
[(h) arising out of a contravention, or alleged contravention of regulation 5(1) or 7(2) of the Part-time Workers (Prevention of Less Favourable Treatment) Regulations 2000;]
[(i) arising out of a contravention, or alleged contravention of regulation 3 or 6(2) of the Fixed-term Employees (Prevention of Less Favourable Treatment) Regulations 2002;]

[210] As amended by the Tribunals, Courts and Enforcement Act 2007 (c 15), Sch 8, para 37.

[211] As amended by the Employment Rights (Dispute Resolution) Act 1998, ss 11, 15 and Sch 1, para 16; the National Minimum Wage Act 1998, s 30(1); the Employment Act 2002, Sch 7, para 23; the Employment Relations Act 2004, Sch 1, para 25; SI 1998/1833, reg 33; SI 1999/3323, reg 33(1); SI 2000/1299, art 2; SI 2000/1551, reg 10 and Sch, para 1; SI 2001/1107, reg 2; SI 2002/2034, reg 11 and Sch 2, para2; SI 2003/1660, reg 39, Sch 5, para 1; SI 2003/1661, reg 39, Sch 5, para 1; SI 2003/1673, reg 31(2); SI 2003/3049, reg 20 and Sch 2, para 2; SI 2004/1713, reg 21 and Sch 2, para 1; SI 2004/2326, reg 46; SI 2004/3426, reg 34.

[(j) under regulation 9 of those Regulations;]

[(k) under regulation 28 of the Employment Equality (Sexual Orientation) Regulations 2003;]

[(l) under regulation 28 of the Employment Equality (Religion or Belief) Regulations 2003;]

[(m) under regulation 18 of the Merchant Shipping (Working Time: Inland Waterways) Regulations 2003;]

[(o) under regulation 41 or 45 of the European Public Limited-Liability Company Regulations 2004][; [. . .][212]

[(p) under regulation 29 or 33 of the Information and Consultation of Employees Regulations 2004][,[. . .] [213]

(q) under paragraph 4 or 8 of the Schedule to the Occupational and Personal Pension Schemes (Consultation by Employers and Miscellaneous Amendment) Regulations 2006] [214] [, [. . .][215]

[(r) under regulation 36 of the Employment Equality (Age) Regulations 2006] [216] [, [. . .]

(s) under regulation 30 or 34 of the European Cooperative Society (Involvement of Employees) Regulations 2006,] [217] [[. . .]

(t) under regulation 45 or 51 of the Companies (Cross-Border Mergers) Regulations 2007] [218][, or

(u) under regulation 17 of the Cross-border Railway Services (Working Time) Regulations 2008.][219]

(2) Where an application has been presented to an [employment tribunal], and a copy of it has been sent to a conciliation officer, it is the duty of the conciliation officer—

(a) if he is requested to do so by the person by whom and the person against whom the proceedings are brought, or

(b) if, in the absence of any such request, the conciliation officer considers that he could act under this subsection with a reasonable prospect of success,

to endeavour to promote a settlement of the proceedings without their being determined by an [employment tribunal].

[(2A) Where employment tribunal procedure regulations include provision postponing the fixing of a time and place for a hearing for the purpose of giving an opportunity for the proceedings to be settled by way of conciliation and withdrawn, subsection (2) shall have effect from the end of the postponement to confer a power on the conciliation officer, instead of imposing a duty.] [220]

(3) Where at any time—

(a) a person claims that action has been taken in respect of which proceedings could be brought by him before an [employment tribunal], but

(b) before any application relating to that action has been presented by him a request is made to a conciliation officer (whether by that person or by the person against whom the proceedings could be instituted) to make his services available to them,

the conciliation officer [may endeavour to promote a settlement between the parties without proceedings being instituted].[221]

(4) Where a person who has presented a complaint to an [employment tribunal] under section 111 of the Employment Rights Act 1996 has ceased to be employed by the employer against whom the complaint was made, the conciliation officer shall (for the purpose of promoting a settlement of the complaint in accordance with subsection (2)) in particular—

(a) seek to promote the reinstatement or re-engagement of the complainant by the employer, or by a successor of the employer or by an associated employer, on terms appearing to the conciliation officer to be equitable, or

---

212 Omitted by SI 2006/349, Sch, para 9.

213 Omitted by SI 2006/103 1,Sch 8, para 19.

214 Inserted by SI 2006/349, Sch, para 9.

215 Omitted by SI 2006/2059, reg 35(a).

216 Inserted by SI 2006/1031, Sch 8, para 19.

217 Inserted by SI 2006/2059, reg35(b).

218 Inserted by SI 2007/2974, reg 52.

219 Inserted by SI 2008/1660, Sch 3 para 1.

220 Inserted by the Employment Act 2002, s 24(2). Repealed by the Employment Act 2008 (c.24), s 6(1) with effect from 6 April 2009, subject to the transitional provisions and savings contained in SI 2008/3232, Sch 1 Pt 1 paras 1 to 3.

221 Substituted by the Employment Act 2008 (c.24), s 5(2) with effect from 6 April 2009, subject to the transitional provisions and savings contained in SI 2008/3232, Sch 1 Pt 1 paras 1 to 3.

(b) where the complainant does not wish to be reinstated or re-engaged, or where reinstatement or re-engagement is not practicable, and the parties desire the conciliation officer to act, seek to promote agreement between them as to a sum by way of compensation to be paid by the employer to the complainant.

[(5) Where a conciliation officer acts pursuant to subsection (3) in a case where the person claiming as specified in paragraph (a) of that subsection has ceased to be employed by the employer and the proceedings which he claims could be brought by him are proceedings under section 111 of the Employment Rights Act 1996, the conciliation officer may in particular—

(a) seek to promote the reinstatement or re-engagement of that person by the employer, or by a successor of the employer or by an associated employer, on terms appearing to the conciliation officer to be equitable, or

(b) where the person does not wish to be reinstated or re-engaged, or where reinstatement or re-engagement is not practicable, seek to promote agreement between them as to a sum by way of compensation to be paid by the employer to that person.][222]

(6) In proceeding under this section a conciliation officer shall, where appropriate, have regard to the desirability of encouraging the use of other procedures available for the settlement of grievances.

(7) Anything communicated to a conciliation officer in connection with the performance of his functions under this section shall not be admissible in evidence in any proceedings before an [employment tribunal], except with the consent of the person who communicated it to that officer.

(8) The Secretary of State [and the Lord Chancellor, acting jointly,] may by order—[223]

(a) direct that further provisions of the Employment Rights Act 1996 be added to the list in subsection (1)(d), or

(b) specify a provision of any other Act as a provision to which subsection (1)(f) applies.

Conciliation procedure

19.—(1) [Employment tribunal] procedure regulations shall include in relation to [employment tribunal] proceedings in the case of which any enactment makes provision for conciliation—[224]

(a) provisions requiring a copy of the application by which the proceedings are instituted, and a copy of any notice relating to it which is lodged by or on behalf of the person against whom the proceedings are brought, to be sent to a conciliation officer,

(b) provisions securing that the applicant and the person against whom the proceedings are brought are notified that the services of a conciliation officer are available to them, [. . .]

(c) [. . .]

[(2) If employment tribunal procedure regulations include provision postponing the fixing of a time and place for a hearing for the purpose of giving an opportunity for the proceedings to be settled by way of conciliation and withdrawn, they shall also include provision for the parties to proceedings to which the provision for postponement applies to be notified that the services of a conciliation officer may no longer be available to them after the end of the postponement.] [225]

---

222 Repealed by the Employment Act 2008 (c.24), s 5(3) with effect from 6 April 2009, subject to the transitional provisions and savings contained in SI 2008/3232, Sch 1 Pt 1 paras 1 to 3.
S 18(5) formerly read:
[(5) Where at any time—
(a) a person claims that action has been taken in respect of which a complaint could be presented by him to an [employment tribunal] under section 111 of the Employment Rights Act 1996, but
(b) before any complaint relating to that action has been presented by him a request is made to a conciliation officer (whether by that person or by the employer) to make his services available to them,
the conciliation officer shall act in accordance with subsection (4) as if a complaint had been presented to an [employment tribunal] under section 111.]

223 As amended by the Tribunals, Courts and Enforcement Act 2007 (c 15), Sch 8, para 38.

224 As amended by the Employment Act 2002, ss 24(4), 53, 54, Sch 7, para 23 and Sch 8.

225 Inserted by the Employment Act 2002, s 24(4). Repealed by the Employment Act 2008 (c.24), s 6(2) with effect from 6 April 2009, subject to the transitional provisions and savings contained in SI 2008/3232, Sch 1 Pt 1 paras 1 to 3.

Part II
The Employment Appeal Tribunal
Jurisdiction

Jurisdiction of Appeal Tribunal

21.—(1) An appeal lies to the Appeal Tribunal on any question of law arising from any decision of, or arising in any proceedings before, an [employment tribunal] under or by virtue of—[226]

(a) the Equal Pay Act 1970,
(b) the Sex Discrimination Act 1975,
(c) the Race Relations Act 1976,
(d) the Trade Union and Labour Relations (Consolidation) Act 1992,
(e) the Disability Discrimination Act 1995, [. . .]
(f) the Employment Rights Act 1996, [. . .]
[(ff). . .]]
[(fg). . .]]
[(g) This Act,]
[(ga) The National Minimum Wage Act 1998,]
[(gb) The Employment Relations Act 1999,]
[(gc) The Equality Act 2006,] [227]
[(h) The Working Time Regulations 1998,]
[(i) the Transnational Information and Consultation of Employees Regulations 1999,]
[(j) the Part-time Workers (Prevention of Less Favourable Treatment) Regulations 2000,]
[(k) the Fixed-term Employees (Prevention of Less Favourable Treatment) Regulations 2002,]
[(l) the Employment Equality (Sexual Orientation) Regulations 2003]
[(m) the Employment Equality (Religion or Belief) Regulations 2003,]
[(n) the Merchant Shipping (Working Time: Inland Waterways) Regulations 2003;]
[(o) the Fishing Vessels (Working Time: Sea-fishermen) Regulations 2004.]
[(p) the European Public Limited-Liability Company Regulations 2004][; [. . .]
[(q) the Information and Consultation of Employees Regulations 2004][[;] [. . .]
(r) the Schedule to the Occupational and Personal Pension Schemes (Consultation by Employers and Miscellaneous Amendment) Regulations 2006][;] [. . .]
(s) the Employment Equality (Age) Regulations 2006] [, [. . .]
(t) the European Cooperative Society (Involvement of Employees) Regulations 2006.][228] [[. . .]
(u) the Companies (Cross-Border Mergers) Regulations 2007][229][, or
(v) the Cross-border Railway Services (Working Time) Regulations 2008].[230]

(2) No appeal shall lie except to the Appeal Tribunal from any decision of an [employment tribunal] under or by virtue of the Acts listed [or the Regulations referred to] in subsection (1).[231]

(3) Subsection (1) does not affect any provision contained in, or made under, any Act which provides for an appeal to lie to the Appeal Tribunal (whether from an [employment tribunal], the Certification Officer or any other person or body) otherwise than on a question to which that subsection applies.

---

226 As amended by the Employment Rights (Dispute Resolution) Act 1998, ss 15 and Sch 1, para 17 and Sch 2; the National Minimum Wage Act 1998, ss 29, 53 and Sch 3; the Tax Credits Act 2002, s 60 and Sch 6; the Employment Relations Act 2004, s 38; SI 1999/3323, reg 35(3); SI 2000/1551, reg 10 and Sch, para 1; SI 2002/2034, reg 11 and Sch 2, para 2; SI 2003/1660, reg 39, Sch 5, para 1; SI 2003/1661, reg 39, Sch 5, para 1; SI 2003/3049, reg 20 and Sch 2, para 2; SI 2004/1713, reg 21 and Sch 2, para 1; SI 2004/2326, reg 49; SI 2004/3426, reg 37; SI 2006/349, Sch 1, para 10; SI 2006/1031, Sch 8, para 20, and prospectively amended by the Equality Act 2006 (c 3), Sch 3, para 57.

227 Inserted by the Equality Act 2006, Sch 3, para 57.

228 Inserted by SI 2006/2059, reg 38(b).

229 Inserted by SI 2007/2974, reg 59.

230 Inserted by SI 2008/1661, Sch 3 para 1.

231 As amended by SI 1998/1833, reg 34(b).

[(4) The Appeal Tribunal also has any jurisdiction in respect of matters other than appeals which is conferred on it by or under—[232]

(a) the Trade Union and Labour Relations (Consolidation) Act 1992,

(b) this Act, or

(c) any other Act.]

Restriction of vexatious proceedings

33.—(1) If, on an application made by the Attorney General or the Lord Advocate under this section, the Appeal Tribunal is satisfied that a person has habitually and persistently and without any reasonable ground—

(a) instituted vexatious proceedings, whether [before the Certification Officer,] in an [employment tribunal] or before the Appeal Tribunal, and whether against the same person or against different persons, or

(b) made vexatious applications in any proceedings, whether [before the Certification Officer,] in an [employment tribunal] or before the Appeal Tribunal,

the Appeal Tribunal may, after hearing the person or giving him an opportunity of being heard, make a restriction of proceedings order.

(2) A 'restriction of proceedings order' is an order that—[233]

(a) no proceedings shall without the leave of the Appeal Tribunal be instituted [before the Certification Officer,] in any [employment tribunal] or before the Appeal Tribunal by the person against whom the order is made,

(b) any proceedings instituted by him [before the Certification Officer,] in any [employment tribunal] or before the Appeal Tribunal before the making of the order shall not be continued by him without the leave of the Appeal Tribunal, and

(c) no application (other than one for leave under this section) is to be made by him in any proceedings [before the Certification Officer,] in any [employment tribunal] or before the Appeal Tribunal without the leave of the Appeal Tribunal.

(3) A restriction of proceedings order may provide that it is to cease to have effect at the end of a specified period, but otherwise it remains in force indefinitely.

(4) Leave for the institution or continuance of, or for the making of an application in, any proceedings [before the Certification Officer,] in an [employment tribunal] or before the Appeal Tribunal by a person who is the subject of a restriction of proceedings order shall not be given unless the Appeal Tribunal is satisfied—[234]

(a) that the proceedings or application are not an abuse of [process], and

(b) that there are reasonable grounds for the proceedings or application.

(5) A copy of a restriction of proceedings order shall be published in the London Gazette and the Edinburgh Gazette.

[232] Inserted by the Employment Rights (Dispute Resolution) Act 1998, s 15 and Sch 1, para 17.

[233] As amended by the Employment Relations Act 2004, s 49.

[234] As amended by the Employment Relations Act 2004, s 49.

Equal Pay Act 1970 (Extracts)

(1970 Chapter 41)

An Act to prevent discrimination, as regards terms and conditions of employment, between men and women.

[29th May 1970]

Requirement of equal treatment for men and women in same employment

1.—[(1) If the terms of a contract under which a woman is employed at an establishment in Great Britain do not include (directly or by reference to a collective agreement or otherwise) an equality clause they shall be deemed to include one.][235]

[(2) An equality clause is a provision which relates to terms (whether concerned with pay or not) of a contract under which a woman is employed (the 'woman's contract'), and has the effect that—[236]

(a) where the woman is employed on like work with a man in the same employment—

(i) if (apart from the equality clause) any term of the woman's contract is or becomes less favourable to the woman than a term of a similar kind in the contract under which that man is employed, that term of the woman's contract shall be treated as so modified as not to be less favourable, and

(ii) if (apart from the equality clause) at any time the woman's contract does not include a term corresponding to a term benefiting that man included in the contract under which he is employed, the woman's contract shall be treated as including such a term;

(b) where the woman is employed on work rated as equivalent with that of a man in the same employment—

(i) if (apart from the equality clause) any term of the woman's contract determined by the rating of the work is or becomes less favourable to the woman than a term of a similar kind in the contract under which that man is employed, that term of the woman's contract shall be treated as so modified as not to be less favourable, and

(ii) if (apart from the equality clause) at any time the woman's contract does not include a term corresponding to a term benefiting that man included in the contract under which he is employed and determined by the rating of the work, the woman's contract shall be treated as including such a term.]

[(c) where a woman is employed on work which, not being work in relation to which paragraph (a) or (b) above applies, is, in terms of the demands made on her (for instance under such headings as effort, skill and decision), of equal value to that of a man in the same employment—[237]

(i) if (apart from the equality clause) any term of the woman's contract is or becomes less favourable to the woman than a term of a similar kind in the contract under which that man is employed, that term of the woman's contract shall be treated as so modified as not to be less favourable, and

(ii) if (apart from the equality clause) at any time the woman's contract does not include a term corresponding to a term benefiting that man included in the contract under which he is employed, the woman's contract shall be treated as including such a term.]

[(d) where—[238]

(i) any term of the woman's contract regulating maternity-related pay provides for any of her maternity-related pay to be calculated by reference to her pay at a particular time,

(ii) after that time (but before the end of the statutory maternity leave period) her pay is increased, or would have increased had she not been on statutory maternity leave, and

(iii) the maternity-related pay is neither what her pay would have been had she not been on statutory maternity leave nor the difference between what her pay would have been had she not been on statutory maternity leave and any statutory maternity pay to which she is entitled,

---

235 Substituted by the Sex Discrimination Act 1975 (c 65), s 8 and Sch 1, Part 1.

236 Substituted by the Sex Discrimination Act 1975 (c 65), s 8.

237 Inserted by SI 1983/1794, reg 2.

238 Inserted by SI 2005/2467, reg 36(2).

if (apart from the equality clause) the terms of the woman's contract do not provide for the increase to be taken into account for the purpose of calculating the maternity-related pay, the term mentioned in sub-paragraph (i) above shall be treated as so modified as to provide for the increase to be taken into account for that purpose;

(e) if (apart from the equality clause) the terms of the woman's contract as to—
   (i) pay (including pay by way of bonus) in respect of times before she begins to be on statutory maternity leave,
   (ii) pay by way of bonus in respect of times when she is absent from work in consequence of the prohibition in section 72(1) of the Employment Rights Act 1996 (compulsory maternity leave), or
   (iii) pay by way of bonus in respect of times after she returns to work following her having been on statutory maternity leave,

do not provide for such pay to be paid when it would be paid but for her having time off on statutory maternity leave, the woman's contract shall be treated as including a term providing for such pay to be paid when ordinarily it would be paid;

(f) if (apart from the equality clause) the terms of the woman's contract regulating her pay after returning to work following her having been on statutory maternity leave provide for any of that pay to be calculated without taking into account any amount by which her pay would have increased had she not been on statutory maternity leave, the woman's contract shall be treated as including a term providing for the increase to be taken into account in calculating that pay.]

[(3) An equality clause falling within subsection 2(a), (b) or (c) above shall not operate in relation to a variation between the woman's contract and the man's contract if the employer proves that the variation is genuinely due to a material factor which is not the difference of sex and that factor—[239]
   (a) in the case of an equality clause falling within subsection (2)(a) or (b) above, must be a material difference between the woman's case and the man's; and
   (b) in the case of an equality clause falling within subsection (2)(c) above, may be such a material difference.]

(4) A woman is to be regarded as employed on like work with men if, but only if, her work and theirs is of the same or a broadly similar nature, and the differences (if any) between the things she does and the things they do are not of practical importance in relation to terms and conditions of employment; and accordingly in comparing her work with theirs regard shall be had to the frequency or otherwise with which any such differences occur in practice as well as to the nature and extent of the differences.

(5) A woman is to be regarded as employed on work rated as equivalent with that of any men if, but only if, her job and their job have been given an equal value, in terms of the demand made on a worker under various headings (for instance effort, skill, decision), on a study undertaken with a view to evaluating in those terms the jobs to be done by all or any of the employees in an undertaking or group of undertakings, or would have been given an equal value but for the evaluation being made on a system setting different values for men and women on the same demand under any heading.

[(5A) For the purposes of subsection (2)(d) to (f) above—[240]
   (a) 'maternity-related pay', in relation to a woman, means pay (including pay by way of bonus) to which she is entitled as a result of being pregnant or in respect of times when she is on statutory maternity leave, except that it does not include any statutory maternity pay to which she is entitled;
   (b) 'statutory maternity leave period', in relation to a woman, means the period during which she is on statutory maternity leave;
   (c) an increase in an amount is taken into account in a calculation if in the calculation the amount as increased is substituted for the unincreased amount.

(5B) For the purposes of subsections (2)(d) to (f) and (5A) above, 'on statutory maternity leave' means absent from work—
   (a) in exercise of the right conferred by section 71(1) or 73(1) of the Employment Rights Act 1996 (ordinary or additional maternity leave), or
   (b) in consequence of the prohibition in section 72(1) of that Act (compulsory maternity leave).]

---

239 As amended by SI 2005/2467, reg 36(3).

240 Inserted by SI 2005/2467, reg 36(4).

(6) Subject to the following subsections, for purposes of this section—[241]
  (a) 'employed' means employed under a contract of service or of apprenticeship or a contract personally to execute any work or labour, and related expressions shall be construed accordingly;
  (b) [. . .]
  (c) Two employers are to be treated as associated if one is a company of which the other (directly or indirectly) has control or if both are companies of which a third person (directly or indirectly) has control,

[and men shall be treated as in the same employment with a woman if they are men employed by her employer or any associated employer at the same establishment or at establishments in Great Britain which include that one and at which common terms and conditions of employment are observed either generally or for employees of the relevant classes.]

Disputes as to, and enforcement of, requirement of equal treatment

2.—[(1) Any claim in respect of the contravention of a term modified or included by virtue of an equality clause, including a claim for arrears of remuneration or damages in respect of the contravention, may be presented by way of a complaint to an [employment tribunal]. [242]

(1A) Where a dispute arises in relation to the effect of an equality clause the employer may apply to an [employment tribunal] for an order declaring the rights of the employer and the employee in relation to the matter in question.][243]

(2) Where it appears to the [Minister] that there may be a question whether the employer of any women is or has been [contravening a term modified or included by virtue of their equality clauses], but that it is not reasonable to expect them to take steps to have the question determined, the question may be referred by him [as respects all or any of them] to an [employment tribunal] and shall be dealt with as if the reference were of a claim by the women or woman against the employer.[244]

(3) Where it appears to the court in which any proceedings are pending that a claim or counterclaim in respect of the operation of an [equality clause] could more conveniently be disposed of separately by an [employment tribunal], the court may direct that the claim or counterclaim shall be struck out; and (without prejudice to the foregoing) where in proceedings before any court a question arises as to the operation of an [equality clause], the court may on the application of any party to the proceedings or otherwise refer that question, or direct it to be referred by a party to the proceedings, to an [employment tribunal] for determination by the tribunal, and may stay or sist the proceedings in the meantime.[245]

[(4) No determination may be made by an employment tribunal in the following proceedings—[246]
  (a) on a complaint under subsection (1) above,
  (b) on an application under subsection (1A) above, or
  (c) on a reference under subsection (2) above,

unless the proceedings are instituted on or before the qualifying date (determined in accordance with section 2ZA below).]

[(5) A woman shall not be entitled, in proceedings brought in respect of a contravention of a term modified or included by virtue of an equality clause (including proceedings before an employment tribunal), to be awarded any payment by way of arrears of remuneration or damages—[247]
  (a) in proceedings in England and Wales, in respect of a time earlier than the arrears date (determined in accordance with section 2ZB below), and
  (b) in proceedings in Scotland, in respect of a time before the period determined in accordance with section 2ZC below.]

[(5A) In this section 'employer', in relation to the holder of an office or post to which section 1 above applies by virtue of subsection (6A) of that section, shall be construed in accordance with that subsection.][248]

---

[241] As amended by the Sex Discrimination Act 1975 (c 65), s 8 and Sch 1, Part 1.

[242] Substituted by the Sex Discrimination Act 1975, s 8(6) and Sch 1, Part I.

[243] Inserted by the Sex Discrimination Act 1975, s 8(6) and Sch 1, Part I.

[244] As amended by the Sex Discrimination Act 1975, s 8(6) and Sch 1, Part I and by SI 2007/2914, Sch, Para 3.

[245] As amended by the Sex Discrimination Act 1975, s 8(6) and Sch 1, Part I.

[246] Substituted by SI 2003/1656, reg 3.

[247] Substituted by SI 2003/1656, reg 3.

[248] Inserted by SI 2005/2467, reg 35(4).

(6) [. . .][249]
(7) [. . .][250]

'Qualifying date' under section 2(4)

[**2ZA.**—(1) This section applies for the purpose of determining the qualifying date, in relation to proceedings in respect of a woman's employment, for the purposes of section 2(4) above.[251]

(2) In this section—

'concealment case' means a case where—

(a) the employer deliberately concealed from the woman any fact (referred to in this section as a 'qualifying fact')—

(i) which is relevant to the contravention to which the proceedings relate, and

(ii) without knowledge of which the woman could not reasonably have been expected to institute the proceedings, and

(b) the woman did not discover the qualifying fact (or could not with reasonable diligence have discovered it) until after—

(i) the last day on which she was employed in the employment, or

(ii) the day on which the stable employment relationship between her and the employer ended,

(as the case may be);

'disability case' means a case where the woman was under a disability at any time during the six months after—

(a) the last day on which she was employed in the employment,

(b) the day on which the stable employment relationship between her and the employer ended, or

(c) the day on which she discovered (or could with reasonable diligence have discovered) the qualifying fact deliberately concealed from her by the employer (if that day falls after the day referred to in paragraph (a) or (b) above, as the case may be),

(as the case may be);

'stable employment case' means a case where the proceedings relate to a period during which a stable employment relationship subsists between the woman and the employer, notwithstanding that the period includes any time after the ending of a contract of employment when no further contract of employment is in force;

'standard case' means a case which is not—

(a) a stable employment case,

(b) a concealment case,

(c) a disability case, or

(d) both a concealment and a disability case.

(3) In a standard case, the qualifying date is the date falling six months after the last day on which the woman was employed in the employment.

(4) In a case which is a stable employment case (but not also a concealment or a disability case or both), the qualifying date is the date falling six months after the day on which the stable employment relationship ended.

(5) In a case which is a concealment case (but not also a disability case), the qualifying date is the date falling six months after the day on which the woman discovered the qualifying fact in question (or could with reasonable diligence have discovered it).

(6) In a case which is a disability case (but not also a concealment case), the qualifying date is the date falling six months after the day on which the woman ceased to be under a disability.

(7) In a case which is both a concealment and a disability case, the qualifying date is the later of the dates referred to in subsections (5) and (6) above.]

'Arrears date' in proceedings in England and Wales under section 2(5)

[**2ZB.**—(1)This section applies for the purpose of determining the arrears date, in relation to an award of any payment by way of arrears of remuneration or damages in proceedings in England and Wales in respect of a woman's employment, for the purposes of section 2(5)(a) above.[252]

249 Repealed by the Sex Discrimination Act 1975, s 8(6) and Sch 1, Part I.
250 Repealed by the Employment Protection (Consolidation) Act 1978, s 159 and Sch 17.
251 Inserted by SI 2003/1656, reg 4.
252 Inserted by SI 2003/1656, reg 5.

(2) In this section—
'concealment case' means a case where—
(a) the employer deliberately concealed from the woman any fact—
(i) which is relevant to the contravention to which the proceedings relate, and
(ii) without knowledge of which the woman could not reasonably have been expected to institute the proceedings, and
(b) the woman instituted the proceedings within six years of the day on which she discovered the fact (or could with reasonable diligence have discovered it);
'disability case' means a case where—
(a) the woman was under a disability at the time of the contravention to which the proceedings relate, and
(b) the woman instituted the proceedings within six years of the day on which she ceased to be under a disability;
'standard case' means a case which is not—
(a) a concealment case,
(b) a disability case, or
(c) both.
(3) In a standard case, the arrears date is the date falling six years before the day on which the proceedings were instituted.
(4) In a case which is a concealment or a disability case or both, the arrears date is the date of the contravention.]

Procedure before tribunal in certain cases

[**2A.**—(1) Where on a complaint or reference made to an [employment tribunal] under section 2 above, a dispute arises as to whether any work is of equal value as mentioned in section 1(2)(c) above the tribunal [may either—[253,254]
(a) proceed to determine that question; or
(b) require a member of the panel of independent experts to prepare a report with respect to that question;]
[(1A) Subsections (1B) and (1C) below apply in a case where the tribunal has required a member of the panel of independent experts to prepare a report under paragraph (b) of subsection (1) above.[255]
(1B) The tribunal may—
(a) withdraw the requirement, and
(b) request the member of the panel of independent experts to provide it with any documentation specified by it or make any other request to him connected with the withdrawal of the requirement.
(1C) If the requirement has not been withdrawn under paragraph (a) of subsection (1B) above, the tribunal shall not make any determination under paragraph (a) of subsection (1) above unless it has received the report.]
[(2) Subsection (2A) below applies in a case where—[256]
(a) a tribunal is required to determine whether any work is of equal value as mentioned in section 1(2)(c) above, and
(b) the work of the woman and that of the man in question have been given different values on a study such as is mentioned in section 1(5) above.]
[(2A) The tribunal shall determine that the work of the woman and that of the man are not of equal value unless the tribunal has reasonable grounds for suspecting that the evaluation contained in the study—[257]
(a) was (within the meaning of subsection (3) below) made on a system which discriminates on grounds of sex, or
(b) is otherwise unsuitable to be relied upon.]

---

253 Inserted by SI 1983/1794, reg 3.
254 As amended by the Employment Rights (Dispute Resolution) Act 1998 (c 8), s 1; SI 1996/438, reg 3; and SI 2004/2352, reg 2.
255 Inserted by SI 2004/2352, reg 2(3).
256 Substituted by SI 2004/2352, reg 2(4).
257 Inserted by SI 2004/2352, reg 2(5).

(3) An evaluation contained in a study such as is mentioned in section 1(5) above is made on a system which discriminates on grounds of sex where a difference, or coincidence, between values set by that system on different demands under the same or different headings is not justifiable irrespective of the sex of the person on whom those demands are made.

(4) [In this section a] reference to a member of the panel of independent experts is a reference to a person who is for the time being designated by the Advisory, Conciliation and Arbitration Service for the purposes of that paragraph as such a member, being neither a member of the Council of that Service nor one of its officers or servants.] [258]

Exclusion from sections 1 to 5 of pensions etc

6.—[(1) [An equality clause shall not] operate in relation to terms—[259]

(a) affected by compliance with the laws regulating the employment of women, or

(b) affording special treatment to women in connection with pregnancy or childbirth.]

[(1AA) Subsection (1)(b) does not affect the operation of an equality clause falling within section 1(2) (d), (e) or (f).] [260]

[(1B) An equality clause shall not operate in relation to terms relating to a person's membership of, or rights under, an occupational pension scheme, being terms in relation to which, by reason only of any provision made by or under sections 62 to 64 of the Pensions Act 1995 (equal treatment), an equal treatment rule would not operate if the terms were included in the scheme.[261]

(1C) In subsection (1B), 'occupational pension scheme' has the same meaning as in the Pension Schemes Act 1993 and 'equal treatment rule' has the meaning given by section 62 of the Pensions Act 1995.]

'Qualifying date' under section 7A(8)

[**7AA.**—(1) This section applies for the purpose of determining the qualifying date, in relation to proceedings on a complaint in respect of a woman's service in any of the armed forces, for the purposes of section 7A(8) above. [262]

(2) In this section—

'concealment case' means a case where—

(a) the employer deliberately concealed from the woman any fact (referred to in this section as a 'qualifying fact')—

(i) which is relevant to the contravention to which the complaint relates, and

(ii) without knowledge of which the woman could not reasonably have been expected to present the complaint, and

(b) the woman did not discover the qualifying fact (or could not with reasonable diligence have discovered it) until after the last day of the period of service during which the claim arose;

'disability case' means a case where the woman was under a disability at any time during the nine months after—

(a) the last day of the period of service during which the claim arose, or

(b) the day on which she discovered (or could with reasonable diligence have discovered) the qualifying fact deliberately concealed from her by the employer (if that day falls after the day referred to in paragraph (a) above),

(as the case may be);

'standard case' means a case which is not—

(a) a concealment case,

(b) a disability case, or

(c) both.

(3) In a standard case, the qualifying date is the date falling nine months after the last day of the period of service during which the claim arose.

---

258 As amended by SI 2004/2352, reg 2(6).

259 Substituted by the Sex Discrimination Act 1975 (c 65), s 8 and Sch 1, Part 1 and as amended by the Sex Discrimination Act 1986, s 9 and Sch, Part III.

260 Inserted by SI 2005/2467, reg 36(5).

261 Substituted for s 6(1A) and (2) by the Pensions Act 1995 (c 26), s 66(1).

262 Inserted by SI 2003/1656, reg 7.

(4) In a case which is a concealment case (but not also a disability case), the qualifying date is the date falling nine months after the day on which the woman discovered the qualifying fact in question (or could with reasonable diligence have discovered it).

(5) In a case which is a disability case (but not also a concealment case), the qualifying date is the date falling nine months after the day on which the woman ceased to be under a disability.

(6) In a case which is both a concealment and a disability case, the qualifying date is the later of the dates referred to in subsections (4) and (5) above.]

'Arrears date' in proceedings in England and Wales under section 7A(9)

[**7AB.**—(1) This section applies for the purpose of determining the arrears date, in relation to an award of any payment by way of arrears of pay or damages in proceedings in England and Wales on a complaint in respect of a woman's service in any of the armed forces, for the purposes of section 7A(9)(a) above.[263]

(2) In this section—[264]

'concealment case' means a case where—

(a) the employer deliberately concealed from the woman any fact—

(i) which is relevant to the contravention to which the proceedings relate, and

(ii) without knowledge of which the woman could not reasonably have been expected to institute the proceedings, and

(b) the woman made a [service complaint] within six years of the day on which she discovered the fact (or could with reasonable diligence have discovered it);

'disability case' means a case where—

(a) the woman was under a disability at the time of the contravention to which the proceedings relate, and

(b) the woman made a [service complaint] within six years of the day on which she ceased to be under a disability;

'standard case' means a case which is not—

(a) a concealment case,

(b) a disability case, or

(c) both.

(3) In a standard case, the arrears date is the date falling six years before the day on which the [service complaint] was made.

(4) In a case which is a concealment or a disability case or both, the arrears date is the date of the contravention.

(5) Subsection (6) below applies in a case where, in accordance with regulations made under section 7A(6) above, proceedings are instituted without a [service complaint having been made].

(6) In that case, references in this section to the making of a [service complaint] shall be read as references to the institution of proceedings.]

---

263 Inserted by SI 2003/1656, reg 8.

264 As amended by the Armed Forces Act 2006 (c 52), Sch 16, para 55.

Race Relations Act 1976 (Extracts)

(1976 Chapter 74)

An Act to make fresh provision with respect to discrimination on racial grounds and relations between people of different racial groups; and to make in the Sex Discrimination Act 1975 amendments for bringing provisions in that Act relating to its administration and enforcement into conformity with the corresponding provisions in this Act.

[22nd November 1976]

Racial discrimination

1.—(1) A person discriminates against another in any circumstances relevant for the purposes of any provision of this Act if—
- (a) on racial grounds he treats that other less favourably than he treats or would treat other persons; or
- (b) he applies to that other a requirement or condition which he applies or would apply equally to persons not of the same racial group as that other but—
  - (i) which is such that the proportion of persons of the same racial group as that other who can comply with it is considerably smaller than the proportion of persons not of that racial group who can comply with it; and
  - (ii) which he cannot show to be justifiable irrespective of the colour, race, nationality or ethnic or national origins of the person to whom it is applied; and
  - (iii) which is to the detriment of that other because he cannot comply with it.

[(1A) A person also discriminates against another if, in any circumstances relevant for the purposes of any provision referred to in subsection (1B), he applies to that other a provision, criterion or practice which he applies or would apply equally to persons not of the same race or ethnic or national origins as that other, but—[265]
- (a) which puts or would put persons of the same race or ethnic or national origins as that other at a particular disadvantage when compared with other persons,
- (b) which puts [or would put] that other at that disadvantage, and[266]
- (c) which he cannot show to be a proportionate means of achieving a legitimate aim.

(1B) The provisions mentioned in subsection (1A) are—
- (a) Part II;
- (b) sections 17 to 18D;
- (c) section 19B, so far as relating to—
  - (i) any form of social security;
  - (ii) health care;
  - (iii) any other form of social protection; and
  - (iv) any form of social advantage;

  which does not fall within section 20;
- (d) sections 20 to 24;
- (e) sections 26A and 26B;
- (f) sections 76 and 76ZA; and
- (g) Part IV, in its application to the provisions referred to in paragraphs (a) to (f).

(1C) Where, by virtue of subsection (1A), a person discriminates against another, subsection (1)(b) does not apply to him.]

(2) It is hereby declared that, for the purposes of this Act, segregating a person from other persons on racial grounds is treating him less favourably than they are treated.

Discrimination by way of victimisation

2.—(1) A person ('the discriminator') discriminates against another person ('the person victimised') in any circumstances relevant for the purposes of any provision of this Act if he treats the person

265 Inserted by SI 2003/1626, reg 3.

266 As amended by SI 2008/3008, reg 2 as from 22 December 2008.

victimised less favourably than in those circumstances he treats or would treat other persons, and does so by reason that the person victimised has—
(a) brought proceedings against the discriminator or any other person under this Act; or
(b) given evidence or information in connection with proceedings brought by any person against the discriminator or any other person under this Act; or
(c) otherwise done anything under or by reference to this Act in relation to the discriminator or any other person; or
(d) alleged that the discriminator or any other person has committed an act which (whether or not the allegation so states) would amount to a contravention of this Act,

or by reason that the discriminator knows that the person victimised intends to do any of those things, or suspects that the person victimised has done, or intends to do, any of them.

(2) Subsection (1) does not apply to treatment of a person by reason of any allegation made by him if the allegation was false and not made in good faith.

Applicants and employees

4.—(1) It is unlawful for a person, in relation to employment by him at an establishment in Great Britain, to discriminate against another—
(a) in the arrangements he makes for the purpose of determining who should be offered that employment; or
(b) in the terms on which he offers him that employment; or
(c) by refusing or deliberately omitting to offer him that employment.

(2) It is unlawful for a person, in the case of a person employed by him at an establishment in Great Britain, to discriminate against that employee—
(a) in the terms of employment which he affords him; or
(b) in the way he affords him access to opportunities for promotion, transfer or training, or to any other benefits, facilities or services, or by refusing or deliberately omitting to afford him access to them; or
(c) by dismissing him, or subjecting him to any other detriment.

[(2A) It is unlawful for an employer, in relation to employment by him at an establishment in Great Britain, to subject to harassment a person whom he employs or who has applied to him for employment.] [267]

(3) Except in relation to discrimination falling within section 2 [or discrimination on grounds of race or ethnic or national origins], subsections (1) and (2) do not apply to employment for the purposes of a private household. [268]

(4) Subsection (2) does not apply to benefits, facilities or services of any description if the employer is concerned with the provision (for payment or not) of benefits, facilities or services of that description to the public, or to a section of the public comprising the employee in question, unless—
(a) that provision differs in a material respect from the provision of the benefits, facilities or services by the employer to his employees; or
(b) the provision of the benefits, facilities or services to the employee in question is regulated by his contract of employment; or
(c) the benefits, facilities or services relate to training.

[(4A) In subsection (2)(c) reference to the dismissal of a person from employment includes, where the discrimination is on grounds of race or ethnic or national origins, reference—[269]
(a) to the termination of that person's employment by the expiration of any period (including a period expiring by reference to an event or circumstance), not being a termination immediately after which the employment is renewed on the same terms; and
(b) to the termination of that person's employment by any act of his (including the giving of notice) in circumstances such that he is entitled to terminate it without notice by reason of the conduct of the employer.]

[267] Inserted by SI 2003/1626, reg 6(2)(c).
[268] As amended by SI 2003/1626, reg 6(2)(b).
[269] Inserted by SI 2003/1626, reg 6(2)(c).

Exceptions for genuine occupational qualifications

5.—(1) In relation to racial discrimination [in cases where section 4A does not apply]—[270]

(a) section 4(1)(a) or (c) does not apply to any employment where being of a particular racial group is a genuine occupational qualification for the job; and

(b) section 4(2)(b) does not apply to opportunities for promotion or transfer to, or training for, such employment.

(2) Being of a particular racial group is a genuine occupational qualification for a job only where—

(a) the job involves participation in a dramatic performance or other entertainment in a capacity for which a person of that racial group is required for reasons of authenticity; or

(b) the job involves participation as an artist's or photographic model in the production of a work of art, visual image or sequence of visual images for which a person of that racial group is required for reasons of authenticity; or

(c) the job involves working in a place where food or drink is (for payment or not) provided to and consumed by members of the public or a section of the public in a particular setting for which, in that job, a person of that racial group is required for reasons of authenticity; or

(d) the holder of the job provides persons of that racial group with personal services promoting their welfare, and those services can most effectively be provided by a person of that racial group.

(3) Subsection (2) applies where some only of the duties of the job fall within paragraph (a), (b), (c) or (d) as well as where all of them do.

(4) Paragraph (a), (b), (c) or (d) of subsection (2) does not apply in relation to the filling of a vacancy at a time when the employer already has employees of the racial group in question—

(a) who are capable of carrying out the duties falling within that paragraph; and

(b) whom it would be reasonable to employ on those duties; and

(c) whose numbers are sufficient to meet the employer's likely requirements in respect of those duties without undue inconvenience.

[Relationships which have come to an end[271]

27A.—(1) In this section a 'relevant relationship' is a relationship during the course of which, by virtue of any provision referred to in section 1(1B), taken with section 1(1) or (1A), or (as the case may be) by virtue of section 3A—

(a) an act of discrimination by one party to the relationship ('the relevant party') against another party to the relationship, on grounds of race or ethnic or national origins, or

(b) harassment of another party to the relationship by the relevant party,

is unlawful.

(2) Where a relevant relationship has come to an end it is unlawful for the relevant party—

(a) to discriminate against another party, on grounds of race or ethnic or national origins, by subjecting him to a detriment, or

(b) to subject another party to harassment,

where the discrimination or harassment arises out of and is closely connected to that relationship.

(3) In subsection (1) reference to an act of discrimination or harassment which is unlawful includes, in the case of a relationship which has come to an end before 19th July 2003, reference to such an act which would, after that date, be unlawful.

(4) For the purposes of any proceedings in respect of an unlawful act under subsection (2), that act shall be treated as falling within circumstances relevant for the purposes of such of the provisions, or Parts, referred to in subsection (1) as determine most closely the nature of the relevant relationship.]

Liability of employers and principals

32.—(1) Anything done by a person in the course of his employment shall be treated for the purposes of this Act (except as regards offences thereunder) as done by his employer as well as by him, whether or not it was done with the employer's knowledge or approval.

(2) Anything done by a person as agent for another person with the authority (whether express or implied, and whether precedent or subsequent) of that other person shall be treated for the

[270] As amended by SI 2003/1626, reg 8.

[271] Inserted by SI 2003/1626, reg 29.

purposes of this Act (except as regards offences thereunder) as done by that other person as well as by him.

(3) In proceedings brought under this Act against any person in respect of an act alleged to have been done by an employee of his it shall be a defence for that person to prove that he took such steps as were reasonably practicable to prevent the employee from doing that act, or from doing in the course of his employment acts of that description.

Aiding unlawful acts

33.—(1) A person who knowingly aids another person to do an act made unlawful by this Act shall be treated for the purposes of this Act as himself doing an unlawful act of the like description.

(2) For the purposes of subsection (1) an employee or agent for whose act the employer or principal is liable under section 32 (or would be so liable but for section 32(3)) shall be deemed to aid the doing of the act by the employer or principal.

(3) A person does not under this section knowingly aid another to do an unlawful act if—

(a) he acts in reliance on a statement made to him by that other person that, by reason of any provision of this Act, the act which he aids would not be unlawful; and

(b) it is reasonable for him to rely on the statement.

(4) A person who knowingly or recklessly makes a statement such as is mentioned in subsection (3)(a) which in a material respect is false or misleading commits an offence, and shall be liable on summary conviction to a fine not exceeding [level 5 on the standard scale][272].

Jurisdiction of [employment tribunals] [273]

54.—(1) A complaint by any person ('the complainant') that another person ('the respondent')— [274]

(a) has committed an act [. . .] against the complainant which is unlawful by virtue of Part II[, section 76ZA or, in relation to discrimination on grounds of race or ethnic or national origins, or harassment, section 26A, 26B or 76]; or

(b) is by virtue of section 32 or 33 to be treated as having committed such an act [. . .] against the complainant,

may be presented to an [employment tribunal].

(2) Subsection (1) does not apply to a complaint under section 12(1) of an act in respect of which an appeal, or proceedings in the nature of an appeal, may be brought under any enactment [. . .].[275]

[Burden of proof: employment tribunals[276]

54A.—(1) This section applies where a complaint is presented under section 54 and the complaint is that the respondent—

(a) has committed an act of discrimination, on grounds of race or ethnic or national origins, which is unlawful by virtue of any provision referred to in section 1(1B)(a), (e) or (f), or Part IV in its application to those provisions, or

(b) has committed an act of harassment.

(2) Where, on the hearing of the complaint, the complainant proves facts from which the tribunal could, apart from this section, conclude in the absence of an adequate explanation that the respondent—

(a) has committed such an act of discrimination or harassment against the complainant, or

(b) is by virtue of section 32 or 33 to be treated as having committed such an act of discrimination or harassment against the complainant,

the tribunal shall uphold the complaint unless the respondent proves that he did not commit or, as the case may be, is not to be treated as having committed, that act.]

Remedies on complaint under section 54

56.—(1) Where an [employment tribunal] finds that a complaint presented to it under section 54 is well-founded, the tribunal shall make such of the following as it considers just and equitable—[277]

(a) an order declaring the rights of the complainant and the respondent in relation to the act to which the complaint relates;

---

272 Fine increased by the Criminal Justice Act 1982, ss 37, 38, 46

273 As amended by the Employment Rights (Dispute Resolution) Act 1998 (c 8), s 1(2).

274 As amended by SI 2003/1626, reg 40(b).

275 As amended by the Armed Forces Act 1996, s 35(2) and Sch 7, Pt III.

276 Inserted by SI 2003/1626, reg 41.

277 As amended by the Employment Rights (Dispute Resolution) Act 1998 (c 8), s 1(2).

(b) an order requiring the respondent to pay to the complainant compensation of an amount corresponding to any damages he could have been ordered by a county court or by a sheriff court to pay to the complainant if the complaint had fallen to be dealt with under section 57;

(c) a recommendation that the respondent take within a specified period action appearing to the tribunal to be practicable for the purpose of obviating or reducing the adverse effect on the complainant of any act of discrimination to which the complaint relates.

(2) [. . .][278]

(3) [. . .][279]

(4) If without reasonable justification the respondent to a complaint fails to comply with a recommendation made by an [employment tribunal] under subsection (1)(c), then, if it thinks it just and equitable to do so—[280]

(a) the tribunal may increase the amount of compensation required to be paid to the complainant in respect of the complaint by an order made under subsection (1)(b); or

(b) if an order under subsection (1)(b) could have been made but was not, the tribunal may make such an order.

[(5) The [Minister] may by regulations make provision—[281]

(a) for enabling a tribunal, where an amount of compensation falls to be awarded under subsection (1)(b), to include in the award interest on that amount; and

(b) specifying, for cases where a tribunal decides that an award is to include an amount in respect of interest, the manner in which and the periods and rate by reference to which the interest is to be determined; and the regulations may contain such incidental and supplementary provisions as the [Minister] considers appropriate.

(6) The [Minister] may by regulations modify the operation of any order made under [section 14 of the [Employment Tribunals Act 1996]] power to make provision as to interest on sums payable in pursuance of [employment tribunal] decisions) to the extent that it relates to an award of compensation under subsection (1)(b).] [282,283,284]

Claims under Part III etc

57.—(1) A claim by any person ('the claimant') that another person ('the respondent')—[285]

(a) has committed an act [. . .] against the claimant which is unlawful by virtue of Part III [other than, in relation to discrimination on grounds of race or ethnic or national origins, or harassment, section 26A or 26B]; or

(b) is by virtue of section 32 or 33 to be treated as having committed such an act [. . .] against the claimant,

may be made the subject of civil proceedings in like manner as any other claim in tort or (in Scotland) in reparation for breach of statutory duty.

(2) Proceedings under subsection (1)—

(a) shall, in England and Wales, be brought only in a designated county court; and

(b) shall, in Scotland, be brought only in a sheriff court;

but all such remedies shall be obtainable in such proceedings as, apart from this subsection and section 53(1), would be obtainable in the High Court or the Court of Session, as the case may be.

(3) As respects an unlawful act of discrimination falling within section 1(1)(b), no award of damages shall be made if the respondent proves that the requirement or condition in question was not applied with the intention of treating the claimant unfavourably on racial grounds.

(4) For the avoidance of doubt it is hereby declared that damages in respect of an unlawful act of discrimination may include compensation for injury to feelings whether or not they include compensation under any other head.

---

278 Repealed by the Race Relations (Remedies) Act 1994, ss 1, 3 and Sch.

279 Repealed by SI 1993/2798, reg 1(3) and Sch, para 1.

280 As amended by the Employment Rights (Dispute Resolution) Act 1998 (c 8), s 1(2).

281 Inserted by the Race Relations (Remedies) Act 1994, s 2 and as amended by SI 2007/2914, Sch, para 10(a).

282 As amended by the Employment Rights (Dispute Resolution) Act 1998 (c 8), s 1(2) and by SI 2007/2914, Sch, para 10(a).

283 Inserted by the Race Relations (Remedies) Act 1994, s 2.

284 As amended by the Employment Tribunals Act 1996, s 43 and Sch 1, para 4.

285 As amended by SI 2003/1626, reg 42(2)(b).

(4A) As respects an act which is done, or by virtue of section 32 or 33 is treated as done, by a person in carrying out public investigator functions or functions as a public prosecutor and which is unlawful by virtue of section 19B, no remedy other than—[286]

(a) damages; or

(b) a declaration or, in Scotland, a declarator;

shall be obtainable unless the court is satisfied that the remedy concerned would not prejudice a criminal investigation, a decision to institute criminal proceedings or any criminal proceedings.

Period within which proceedings to be brought[287]

58.—(1) An [employment tribunal] shall not consider a complaint under section 54 unless it is presented to the tribunal before the end of [—[288,289]

(a) the period of three months beginning when the act complained of was done; or

(b) in a case to which section 75(8) applies, the period of six months so beginning.]

(2) [Subject to subsection (2A)] a county court or a sheriff court shall not consider a claim under section 57 unless proceedings in respect of the claim are instituted before the end of—[290]

(a) the period of six months beginning when the act complained of was done;

(b) [. . .]

(2A)In relation to an immigration claim within the meaning of section 57A, the period of six months mentioned in subsection (2)(a) begins on the expiry of the period during which, by virtue of section 57A(1)(a), no proceedings may be brought under section 57(1) in respect of the claim.] [291]

(3) Where, in relation to proceedings or prospective proceedings by way of a claim under section 57, an application for assistance under section 66 is made to the Commission before the end of the period of six months mentioned in paragraph (a) [. . .] of subsection (2), the period allowed by that paragraph for instituting proceedings in respect of the claim shall be extended by two months. [292]

(3A) Where in England and Wales—[293]

(a) proceedings or prospective proceedings by way of a claim under section 57 relate to the act or omission of a qualifying institution,

(b) the dispute concerned is referred as a complaint under the student complaints scheme before the end of the period of six months mentioned in subsection (2), and

(c) subsection (3) does not apply,

the period allowed by subsection (2) for instituting proceedings in respect of the claim shall be extended by two months.

(3B) In subsection (3A)—

'qualifying institution' has the meaning given by section 11 of the Higher Education Act 2004;

'the student complaints scheme' means a scheme for the review of qualifying complaints, as defined by section 12 of that Act, that is provided by the designated operator, as defined by section 13(5)(b) of that Act.]

(4) An [employment tribunal], county court or sheriff court shall not consider an application under section 63(2)(a) unless it is made before the end of the period of six months beginning when the act to which it relates was done; and a county court or sheriff court shall not consider an application under section 63(4) unless it is made before the end of the period of five years so beginning. [294]

(5) An [employment tribunal] shall not consider a complaint under section 64(1) unless it is presented to the tribunal before the end of the period of six months beginning when the act complained of was done. [295]

(6) A court or tribunal may nevertheless consider any such complaint, claim or application which is out of time if, in all the circumstances of the case, it considers that it is just and equitable to do so.

---

[286] Inserted by the Race Relations (Amendment) Act 2000, ss 5, 9 and Sch 2, para 7.

[287] Prospectively amended by the Equality Act 2006, Sch 3, para 27 and Sch 4.

[288] As amended by the Employment Rights (Dispute Resolution) Act 1998, s 1(2).

[289] As amended by the Armed Forces Act 1996, s 23(4).

[290] As amended by the Race Relations (Amendment) Act 2000, s 9, Sch 2, para 13 and Sch 3.

[291] Inserted by the Race Relations (Amendment) Act 2000, s 9 and Sch 2, para 14.

[292] As amended by the Race Relations (Amendment) Act 2000, s 9 and Sch 3.

[293] Inserted by the Higher Education Act 2004 (c 8), s 19(2).

[294] As amended by the Employment Rights (Dispute Resolution) Act 1998, s 1(2).

[295] As amended by the Employment Rights (Dispute Resolution) Act 1998, s 1(2).

(7) For the purposes of this section—
  (a) when the inclusion of any term in a contract renders the making of the contract an unlawful act, that act shall be treated as extending throughout the duration of the contract; and
  (b) any act extending over a period shall be treated as done at the end of that period; and
  (c) a deliberate omission shall be treated as done when the person in question decided upon it;

and in the absence of evidence establishing the contrary a person shall be taken for the purposes of this section to decide upon an omission when he does an act inconsistent with doing the omitted act or, if he has done no such inconsistent act, when the period expires within which he might reasonably have been expected to do the omitted act if it was to be done.

Sex Discrimination Act 1975 (Extracts)

(1975 Chapter 65)

An Act to render unlawful certain kinds of sex discrimination and discrimination on the ground of marriage, and establish a Commission with the function of working towards the elimination of such discrimination and promoting equality of opportunity between men and women generally; and for related purposes.

[12th November, 1975]

Direct and indirect discrimination against women

[1.—(1) In any circumstances relevant for the purposes of any provision of this Act, other than a provision to which subsection (2) applies, a person discriminates against a woman if—[296]

(a) on the ground of her sex he treats her less favourably than he treats or would treat a man, or

(b) he applies to her a requirement or condition which he applies or would apply equally to a man but—

(i) which is such that the proportion of women who can comply with it is considerably smaller than the proportion of men who can comply with it, and

(ii) which he cannot show to be justifiable irrespective of the sex of the person to whom it is applied, and

(iii) which is to her detriment because she cannot comply with it.

(2) In any circumstances relevant for the purposes of a provision to which this subsection applies, a person discriminates against a woman if—

(a) on the ground of her sex, he treats her less favourably than he treats or would treat a man, or

[(b) he applies to her a provision, criterion or practice which he applies or would apply equally to a man, but—

(i) which puts or would put women at a particular disadvantage when compared with men,

(ii) which puts her at that disadvantage, and

(iii) which he cannot show to be a proportionate means of achieving a legitimate aim.] [297]

(3) Subsection (2) applies to—

(a) any provision of Part 2,

[(aa) sections 29 to 31, except in so far as they relate to an excluded matter,] [298]

(b) sections 35A and 35B, and

(c) any other provision of Part 3, so far as it applies to vocational training.

(4) [. . .][299]

Sex discrimination against men

2.—(1) Section 1, and the provisions of Parts II and III relating to sex discrimination against women, are to be read as applying equally to the treatment of men, and for that purpose shall have effect with such modifications as are requisite.

(2) In the application of subsection (1) no account shall be taken of special treatment afforded to women in connection with pregnancy or childbirth.

[Discrimination on the grounds of gender reassignment[300]

2A.—(1) A person ('A') discriminates against another person ('B') in any circumstances relevant for the purposes of—

(a) any provision of Part II,

[(aa) section 29, 30 or 31, except in so far as it relates to an excluded matter,] [301]

(b) section 35A or 35B, or

[296] Substituted by SI 2001/2660, reg 3.

[297] Substituted by SI 2005/2467, reg 3(1).

[298] Inserted by SI 2008/963, Sch 1, para 1.

[299] Repealed by the Civil Partnership Act 2004 (c 33) ss 251, 261 and Sch 30.

[300] Inserted by SI 1999/1102, reg 2(1).

[301] Inserted by SI 2008/963, Sch 1, para 2.

(c) any other provision of Part III, so far as it applies to vocational training, if he treats B less favourably than he treats or would treat other persons, and does so on the ground that B intends to undergo, is undergoing or has undergone gender reassignment.

(2) Subsection (3) applies to arrangements made by any person in relation to another's absence from work or from vocational training.

(3) For the purposes of subsection (1), B is treated less favourably than others under such arrangements if, in the application of the arrangements to any absence due to B undergoing gender reassignment—

(a) he is treated less favourably than he would be if the absence was due to sickness or injury, or

(b) he is treated less favourably than he would be if the absence was due to some other cause and, having regard to the circumstances of the case, it is reasonable for him to be treated no less favourably.

(4) In subsections (2) and (3) 'arrangements' includes terms, conditions or arrangements on which employment, a pupillage or tenancy or vocational training is offered.

(5) For the purposes of subsection (1), a provision mentioned in that subsection framed with reference to discrimination against women shall be treated as applying equally to the treatment of men with such modifications as are requisite.]

[Discrimination against married persons and civil partners in employment field

[3.—(1) In any circumstances relevant for the purposes of any provision of Part 2, a person discriminates against a person ('A') who fulfils the condition in subsection (2) if—

(a) on the ground of the fulfilment of the condition, he treats A less favourably than he treats or would treat a person who does not fulfil the condition, or

[(b) he applies to that person a provision, criterion or practice which he applies or would apply equally to an unmarried person, but—

(i) which puts or would put married persons at a particular disadvantage when compared with unmarried persons of the same sex,

(ii) which puts that person at that disadvantage, and

(iii) which he cannot show to be a proportionate means of achieving a legitimate aim.] [302]

(2) The condition is that the person is—

(a) married, or

(b) a civil partner.

(3) For the purposes of subsection (1), a provision of Part 2 framed with reference to discrimination against women is to be treated as applying equally to the treatment of men, and for that purpose has effect with such modifications as are requisite.] [303]

[Discrimination on the ground of pregnancy or maternity leave

[**3A.**—(1) In any circumstances relevant for the purposes of a provision to which this subsection applies, a person discriminates against a woman if—

(a) at a time in a protected period, and on the ground of the woman's pregnancy, the person treats her less favourably [. . .]; or

(b) on the ground that the woman is exercising or seeking to exercise, or has exercised or sought to exercise, a statutory right to maternity leave, the person treats her less favourably [. . .].[304]

(2) In any circumstances relevant for the purposes of a provision to which this subsection applies, a person discriminates against a woman if, on the ground that section 72(1) of the Employment Rights Act 1996 (compulsory maternity leave) has to be complied with in respect of the woman, he treats her less favourably [. . .].[305]

(3) For the purposes of subsection (1)—

(a) in relation to a woman, a protected period begins each time she becomes pregnant, and the protected period associated with any particular pregnancy of hers ends in accordance with the following rules—

(i) if she is entitled to ordinary but not additional maternity leave in connection with the pregnancy, the protected period ends at the end of her period of ordinary maternity leave

---

[302] Substituted by SI 2005/2467, reg 3(2).

[303] Substituted by the Civil Partnership Act 2004 (c 33), s 251(2).

[304] As amended by SI 2008/656, reg 2.

[305] As amended by SI 2008/656, reg 2.

connected with the pregnancy or, if earlier, when she returns to work after the end of her pregnancy;

(ii) if she is entitled to ordinary and additional maternity leave in connection with the pregnancy, the protected period ends at the end of her period of additional maternity leave connected with the pregnancy or, if earlier, when she returns to work after the end of her pregnancy;

(iii) if she is not entitled to ordinary maternity leave in respect of the pregnancy, the protected period ends at the end of the 2 weeks beginning with the end of the pregnancy;

(b) where a person's treatment of a woman is on grounds of illness suffered by the woman as a consequence of a pregnancy of hers, that treatment is to be taken to be on the ground of the pregnancy;

(c) a 'statutory right to maternity leave' means a right conferred by section 71(1) or 73(1) of the Employment Rights Act 1996 (ordinary and additional maternity leave).

(4) In subsection (3) 'ordinary maternity leave' and 'additional maternity leave' shall be construed in accordance with sections 71 and 73 of the Employment Rights Act 1996.

(5) Subsections (1) and (2) apply to—

(a) any provision of Part 2,

(b) sections 35A and 35B, and

(c) any other provision of Part 3, so far as it applies to vocational training.] [306]

[Discrimination on the ground of pregnancy or maternity: goods, facilities, services or premises

3B.— (1) In any circumstances relevant for the purposes of a provision to which this subsection applies, a person discriminates against a woman if he treats her less favourably—

(a) on the ground of her pregnancy, or

(b) within the period of 26 weeks beginning on the day on which she gives birth, on the ground that she has given birth.

(2) A person (P) is taken to discriminate against a woman on the ground of her pregnancy if—

(a) P refuses to provide her with goods, facilities or services because P thinks that providing them would, because of her pregnancy, create a risk to her health or safety, or

(b) P provides or offers to provide them on conditions intended to remove or reduce such a risk because P thinks that provision of them without the conditions would create such a risk.

(3) Subsection (2) does not apply if—

(a) it is reasonable for P to think as mentioned in paragraph (a) or (b), and

(b) P applies an equivalent policy.

(4) An equivalent policy is—

(a) for the purposes of subsection (2)(a), refusing to provide the goods, facilities or services to persons with other physical conditions because P thinks that to do so would, because of such physical conditions, create a risk to the health or safety of such persons;

(b) for the purposes of subsection (2)(b), imposing conditions on the provision of goods, facilities or services to such persons which are intended to remove or reduce the risk to their health or safety because P thinks that the provision without the conditions would create such a risk.

(5) Subsection (1) applies to sections 29 to 31, except in so far as they relate to an excluded matter.] [307]

Discrimination by way of victimisation

4.—(1) [308] A person ('the discriminator') discriminates against another person ('the person victimised') in any circumstances relevant for the purposes of any provision of this Act if he treats the person victimised less favourably than in those circumstances he treats or would treat other persons, and do so by reason that the person victimised has—

(a) brought proceedings against the discriminator or any other person under this Act or the Equal Pay Act 1970 [or Part I of Schedule 5 to the Social Security Act 1989] [or sections 62 to 65 of the Pensions Act 1995], or

306 Inserted by SI 2005/2467, reg 4.

307 Inserted by SI 2008/963, Sch 1, para 3(1).

308 As amended by the Social Security Act 1989 (c 24), s 23, Sch 5, para 14(1)(a) and by the Pensions Act 1995 (c26), s 66(2)(b).

(b) given evidence or information in connection with proceedings brought by any person against the discriminator or any other person under this Act or the Equal Pay Act 1970 [or Part I of Schedule 5 to the Social Security Act 1989] [or sections 62 to 65 of the Pensions Act 1995], or

(c) otherwise done anything under or by reference to this Act or the Equal Pay Act 1970 [or Part I of Schedule 5 to the Social Security Act 1989] [or sections 62 to 65 of the Pensions Act 1995] in relation to the discriminator or any other person, or

(d) alleged that the discriminator or any other person has committed an act which (whether or not the allegation so states) would amount to a contravention of this Act or give rise to a claim under the Equal Pay Act 1970 [or proceedings under Part I of Schedule 5 to the Social Security Act 1989] [or under sections 62 to 65 of the Pensions Act 1995], or by reason that the discriminator knows the person victimised intends to do any of those things, or suspects the person victimised has done, or intends to do, any of them.

(2) Subsection (1) does not apply to treatment of a person by reason of any allegation made by him if the allegation was false and not made in good faith.

(3) For the purposes of subsection (1), a provision of Part II or III framed with reference to discrimination against women shall be treated as applying equally to the treatment of men and for that purpose shall have effect with such modifications as are requisite.

[Harassment, including sexual harassment

4A.—(1) For the purposes of this Act, a person subjects a woman to harassment if—

(a) [he engages in unwanted conduct that is related to her sex or that of another person and] has the purpose or effect—[309]

(i) of violating her dignity, or

(ii) of creating an intimidating, hostile, degrading, humiliating or offensive environment for her,

(b) he engages in any form of unwanted verbal, non-verbal or physical conduct of a sexual nature that has the purpose or effect—

(i) of violating her dignity, or

(ii) of creating an intimidating, hostile, degrading, humiliating or offensive environment for her, or

(c) on the ground of her rejection of or submission to unwanted conduct of a kind mentioned in paragraph (a) or (b), he treats her less favourably than he would treat her had she not rejected, or submitted to, the conduct.

(2) Conduct shall be regarded as having the effect mentioned in sub-paragraph (i) or (ii) of subsection (1)(a) or (b) only if, having regard to all the circumstances, including in particular the perception of the woman, it should reasonably be considered as having that effect.

(3) For the purposes of this Act, a person ('A') subjects another person ('B') to harassment if—

(a) A, on the ground that B intends to undergo, is undergoing or has undergone gender reassignment, engages in unwanted conduct that has the purpose or effect—

(i) of violating B's dignity, or

(ii) of creating an intimidating, hostile, degrading, humiliating or offensive environment for B, or

(b) A, on the ground of B's rejection of or submission to unwanted conduct of a kind mentioned in paragraph (a), treats B less favourably than A would treat B had B not rejected, or submitted to, the conduct.

(4) Conduct shall be regarded as having the effect mentioned in sub-paragraph (i) or (ii) of subsection (3)(a) only if, having regard to all the circumstances, including in particular the perception of B, it should reasonably be considered as having that effect.

(5) Subsection (1) is to be read as applying equally to the harassment of men, and for that purpose shall have effect with such modifications as are requisite.

(6) For the purposes of subsections (1) and (3), a provision of Part 2 or 3 framed with reference to harassment of women shall be treated as applying equally to the harassment of men, and for that purpose will have effect with such modifications as are requisite.][310]

[309] As amended by SI 2008/656, reg 3.

[310] Inserted by SI 2005/2647, reg 5.

Applicants and employees[311]

6.—(1) It is unlawful for a person, in relation to employment by him at an establishment in Great Britain, to discriminate against a woman—

(a) in the arrangements he makes for the purpose of determining who should be offered that employment, or

(b) in the terms on which he offers her that employment, or

(c) by refusing or deliberately omitting to offer her that employment.

(2) It is unlawful for a person, in the case of a woman employed by him at an establishment in Great Britain, to discriminate against her—

(a) in the way he affords her access to opportunities for promotion, transfer or training, or to any other benefits, facilities or services, or by refusing or deliberately omitting to afford her access to them, or

(b) by dismissing her, or subjecting her to any other detriment.

[(2A) It is unlawful for an employer, in relation to employment by him at an establishment in Great Britain, to subject to harassment—

(a) a woman whom he employs, or

(b) a woman who has applied to him for employment.] [312]

[(2B) For the purposes of subsection (2A), the circumstances in which an employer is to be treated as subjecting a woman to harassment shall include those where—

(a) a third party subjects the woman to harassment in the course of her employment, and

(b) the employer has failed to take such steps as would have been reasonably practicable to prevent the third party from doing so.

(2C) Subsection (2B) does not apply unless the employer knows that the woman has been subject to harassment in the course of her employment on at least two other occasions by a third party.

(2D) In subsections (2B) and (2C), 'third party' means a person other than—

(a) the employer, or

(b) a person whom the employer employs,

and for the purposes of those subsections it is immaterial whether the third party is the same or a different person on each occasion.] [313]

(3) [. . .][314]

[(4) Subsections (1)(b) and (2) do not render it unlawful for a person to discriminate against a woman in relation to her membership of, or rights under, an occupational pension scheme in such a way that, were any term of the scheme to provide for discrimination in that way, then, by reason only of any provision made by or under sections 62 to 64 of the Pensions Act 1995 (equal treatment), an equal treatment rule would not operate in relation to that term. [315]

(4A) In subsection (4), 'occupational pension scheme' has the same meaning as in the Pension Schemes Act 1993 and 'equal treatment rule' has the meaning given by section 62 of the Pensions Act 1995.]

(5) Subject to section 8(3), subsection (1)(b) does not apply to any provision for the payment of money which, if the woman in question were given the employment, would be included (directly [. . .] or otherwise) in the contract under which she was employed. [316]

(6) Subsection (2) does not apply to benefits consisting of the payment of money when the provision of those benefits is regulated by the woman's contract of employment.

(7) Subsection (2) does not apply to benefits, facilities or services of any description if the employer is concerned with the provision (for payment or not) of benefits, facilities or services of that description to the public, or to a section of the public comprising the woman in question, unless—

(a) that provision differs in a material respect from the provision of the benefits, facilities or services by the employer to his employees, or

---

311 Amended by SI 2005/2467, reg 7(3).

312 Inserted by SI 2005/2467, reg 7(4).

313 Inserted by SI 2008/656, reg 4.

314 Repealed by the Sex Discrimination Act 1986, ss 1, 9 and Sch, Part II.

315 Substituted for the former subs (4) by the Pensions Act 1995, s 66(3).

316 As amended by the Sex Discrimination Act 1986, ss 1, 9 and Sch, Part II.

(b) the provision of the benefits, facilities or services to the woman in question is regulated by her contract of employment, or
(c) the benefits, facilities or services relate to training.

[(8) In its application to any discrimination falling within section 2A, this section shall have effect with the omission of subsections (4) to (6).] [317]

[Exception relating to terms and conditions during maternity leave

6A.—(1) Subject to subsection (2), section 6(1)(b) and (2) does not make it unlawful to deprive a woman who is on maternity leave of any benefit from the terms and conditions of her employment relating to remuneration.

(2) The reference in subsection (1) to benefit from the terms and conditions of a woman's employment relating to remuneration does not include a reference to—
(a) maternity-related remuneration (including maternity-related remuneration that is increase-related),
(b) remuneration (including increase-related remuneration) in respect of times when the woman is not on maternity leave, or
(c) remuneration by way of bonus in respect of times when a woman is on compulsory maternity leave.

(3) For the purposes of subsection (2), remuneration is increase-related so far as it falls to be calculated by reference to increases in remuneration that the woman would have received had she not been on maternity leave.

(4) In this section—
'maternity-related remuneration', in relation to a woman, means remuneration to which she is entitled as a result of being pregnant or being on maternity leave;
'on compulsory maternity leave' means absent from work in consequence of the prohibition in section 72(1) of the Employment Rights Act 1996; 'on maternity leave' means—
(a) on compulsory maternity leave,
(b) absent from work in exercise of the right conferred by section 71(1) of the Employment Rights Act 1996 (ordinary maternity leave), or
(c) absent from work in exercise of the right conferred by section 73(1) of that Act (additional maternity leave); and 'remuneration' means benefits—
(a) that consist of the payment of money to an employee by way of wages or salary, and
(b) that are not benefits whose provision is regulated by the employee's contract of employment.] [318]

Exception where sex is a genuine occupational qualification

7.—(1) In relation to sex discrimination—
(a) section 6(1)(a) or (c) does not apply to any employment where being a man is a genuine occupational qualification for the job, and
(b) section 6(2)(a) does not apply to opportunities for promotion or transfer to, or training for, such employment.

(2) Being a man is a genuine occupational qualification for a job only where—
(a) the essential nature of the job calls for a man for reasons of physiology (excluding physical strength or stamina) or, in dramatic performances or other entertainment, for reasons of authenticity, so that the essential nature of the job would be materially different if carried out by a woman; or
(b) the job needs to be held by a man to preserve decency or privacy because—
(i) it is likely to involve physical contact with men in circumstances where they might reasonably object to its being carried out by a woman, or
(ii) the holder of the job is likely to do his work in circumstances where men might reasonably object to the presence of a woman because they are in a state of undress or are using sanitary facilities; or

[317] Inserted by SI 1999/1102, reg 3(1).
[318] Inserted by SI 2005/2467, reg 8 and substituted by SI 2008/656, reg 5.

[(ba) the job is likely to involve the holder of the job doing his work, or living, in a private home and needs to be held by a man because objection might reasonably be taken to allowing to a woman—[319]
(i) the degree of physical or social contact with a person living in the home, or
(ii) the knowledge of intimate details of such a person's life, which is likely, because of the nature or circumstances of the job or of the home, to be allowed to, or available to, the holder of the job; or]
(c) the nature or location of the establishment makes it impracticable for the holder of the job to live elsewhere than in premises provided by the employer, and—
(i) the only such premises which are available for persons holding that kind of job are lived in, or normally lived in, by men and are not equipped with separate sleeping accommodation for women and sanitary facilities which could be used by women in privacy from men, and
(ii) it is not reasonable to expect the employer either to equip those premises with such accommodation and facilities or to provide other premises for women; or
(d) the nature of the establishment, or of the part of it within which the work is done, requires the job to be held by a man because—
(i) it is, or is part of, a hospital, prison or other establishment for persons requiring special care, supervision or attention, and
(ii) those persons are all men (disregarding any woman whose presence is exceptional), and
(iii) it is reasonable, having regard to the essential character of the establishment or that part, that the job should not be held by a woman; or
(e) the holder of the job provides individuals with personal services promoting their welfare or education, or similar personal services, and those services can most effectively be provided by a man, or
(f) [. . .][320]
(g) the job needs to be held by a man because it is likely to involve the performance of duties outside the United Kingdom in a country whose laws or customs are such that the duties could not, or could not effectively, be performed by a woman, or
(h) the job is one of two to be held—
(i) by a married couple,
[(ii) by a couple who are civil partners of each other, or
(iii) by a married couple who are civil partners of each other.] [321]
(3) Subsection (2) applies where some only of the duties of the job fall within paragraphs (a) to (g) as well as where all of them do.
(4) Paragraph (a), (b), (c), (d), (e) [. . .] or (g) of subsection (2) does not apply in relation to the filling of a vacancy at a time when the employer already has male employees—[322]
(a) who are capable of carrying out the duties falling within that paragraph, and
(b) whom it would be reasonable to employ on those duties, and
(c) whose numbers are sufficient to meet the employer's likely requirements in respect of those duties without undue inconvenience.

Relationships which have come to an end

[20A.—(1) This section applies where—[323]
(a) there has been a relevant relationship between a woman and another person ('the relevant person'), and
(b) the relationship has come to an end (whether before or after the commencement of this section).
(2) In this section, a 'relevant relationship' is a relationship during the course of which an act of discrimination by one party to the relationship against the other party to it is unlawful under any preceding provision of this Part.

[319] Inserted by the Sex Discrimination Act 1986 (c 59), s 1(2).
[320] Repealed by the Employment Act 1989 (c 38), ss 3(2), 29(4), Sch 7, Part II.
[321] As amended by the Civil Partnership Act (c 33), s 251(4).
[322] Words repealed by the Employment Act 1989 (c 38), s 29(4), Sch 7, Part II and Sch 9.
[323] Inserted by SI 2003/1657, reg 3.

(3) It is unlawful for the relevant person to discriminate against the woman by subjecting her to a detriment where the discrimination arises out of and is closely connected to the relevant relationship.]

[(4) It is unlawful for the relevant person to subject a woman to harassment where that treatment arises out of or is closely connected to the relevant relationship.] [324]

Liability of employers and principals[325]

41.—(1) Anything done by a person in the course of his employment shall be treated for the purposes of this Act as done by his employer as well as by him, whether or not it was done with the employer's knowledge or approval.

(2) Anything done by a person as agent for another person with the authority (whether express or implied, and whether precedent or subsequent) of that other person shall be treated for the purposes of this Act as done by that other person as well as by him.

(3) In proceedings brought under this Act against any person in respect of an act alleged to have been done by an employee of his it shall be a defence for that person to prove that he took such steps as were reasonably practicable to prevent the employee from doing that act, or from doing in the course of his employment acts of that description.

Aiding unlawful acts[326]

42.—(1) A person who knowingly aids another person to do an act made unlawful by this Act shall be treated for the purposes of this Act as himself doing an unlawful act of the like description.

(2) For the purposes of subsection (1) an employee or agent for whose act the employer or principal is liable under section 41 (or would be so liable but for section 41(3)) shall be deemed to aid the doing of the act by the employer or principal.

(3) A person does not under this section knowingly aid another to do an unlawful act if—

(a) he acts in reliance on a statement made to him by that other person that, by reason of any provision of this Act, the act which he aids would not be unlawful, and

(b) it is reasonable for him to rely on the statement.

(4) A person who knowingly or recklessly makes a statement such as is referred to in subsection (3)(a) which in a material respect is false or misleading commits an offence, and shall be liable on summary conviction to a fine not exceeding [level 5 on the standard scale].

Jurisdiction of [employment tribunals] [327]

63.—(1) A complaint by any person ('the complainant') that another person ('the respondent')—[328]

(a) has committed an act of discrimination [or harassment] against the complainant which is unlawful by virtue of Part II [or section 35A or 35B], or

(b) is by virtue of section 41 or 42 to be treated as having committed such an act of discrimination [or harassment] against the complainant, may be presented to an [employment tribunal].

(2) Subsection (1) does not apply to a complaint under section 13(1) of an act in respect of which an appeal, or proceedings in the nature of an appeal, may be brought under any enactment.

Burden of proof: employment tribunals[329]

[63A.—(1) This section applies to any complaint presented under section 63 to an employment tribunal.

(2) Where, on the hearing of the complaint, the complainant proves facts from which the tribunal could, apart from this section, conclude in the absence of an adequate explanation that the respondent—[330]

(a) has committed an act of discrimination [or harassment] against the complainant which is unlawful by virtue of Part 2 [or section 35A or 35B], or

(b) is by virtue of section 41 or 42 to be treated as having committed such an act of discrimination [or harassment] against the complainant,

---

324 Inserted by SI 2005/2467, reg 21.

325 Section 41 modified by SI 1989/901, art 3 and Sch.

326 As amended by the Criminal Justice Act 1982 (c 48), ss 38, 46 and by the Criminal Procedure (Scotland) Act 1975 (c 21), ss 289F and 289G.

327 As amended by the Employment Rights (Dispute Resolution) Act 1998 (c 8), s 1(2).

328 As amended by the Employment Rights (Dispute Resolution) Act 1998 (c 8), s 1(2) and SI 2005/2467, reg 28.

329 Inserted by SI 2001/2660, reg 5.

330 As amended by SI 2005/2467, reg 29.

the tribunal shall uphold the complaint unless the respondent proves that he did not commit, or, as the case may be, is not to be treated as having committed, that act.]

Remedies on complaint under section 63

65.—(1) Where an [employment tribunal] finds that a complaint presented to it under section 63 is well-founded the tribunal shall make such of the following as it considers just and equitable—[331]

(a) an order declaring the rights of the complainant and the respondent in relation to the act to which the complaint relates;

(b) an order requiring the respondent to pay to the complainant compensation of an amount corresponding to any damages he could have been ordered by a county court or by a sheriff court to pay to the complainant if the complaint had fallen to be dealt with under section 66;

(c) a recommendation that the respondent take within a specified period action appearing to the tribunal to be practicable for the purpose of obviating or reducing the adverse effect on the complainant of any act of discrimination to which the complaint relates.

[(1A) In applying section 66 for the purposes of subsection (1)(b), no account shall be taken of subsection (3) of that section.] [332]

(1B) As respects an unlawful act of discrimination falling within [section 1(2)(b) or section 3(1)(b)], if the respondent proves that the [provision, criterion or practice] in question was not applied with the intention of treating the complainant unfavourably on the ground of his sex [or (as the case may be) fulfilment of the condition in section 3(2)], an order may be made under subsection (1)(b) only if the [employment tribunal]— [333,334,335]

(a) makes such order under subsection (1)(a) and such recommendation under subsection (1)(c) (if any) as it would have made if it had no power to make an order under subsection (1)(b); and

(b) (where it makes an order under subsection (1)(a) or a recommendation under subsection (1)(c) or both) considers that it is just and equitable to make an order under subsection (1)(b) as well.]

(2) [. . .][336]

(3) If without reasonable justification the respondent to a complaint fails to comply with a recommendation made by an [employment tribunal] under subsection (1)(c), then, if they think it just and equitable to do so—[337,338]

(a) the tribunal may [. . .] increase the amount of compensation required to be paid to the complainant in respect of the complaint by an order made under subsection (1)(b), or

(b) if an order under subsection (1)(b) was not made, the tribunal may make such an order.

Period within which proceedings to be brought

76.[339]—(1) An [employment tribunal] shall not consider a complaint under section 63 unless it is presented to the tribunal before the end of [—[340,341]

(a) the period of three months beginning when the act complained of was done; or

(b) in a case to which section 85(9A) applies, the period of six months so beginning.]

(2) A county court or a sheriff court shall not consider a claim under section 66 unless proceedings in respect of the claim are instituted before the end of—

[(a) the period of six months beginning when the act complained of was done; or[342]

(b) in a case to which section 66(5) applies, the period of eight months so beginning.]

---

331 As amended by the Employment Rights (Dispute Resolution) Act 1998 (c 8), s 1(2).

332 Inserted by SI 1996/438, reg 2(2).

333 As amended by the Employment Rights (Dispute Resolution) Act 1998 (c 8), s 1(2).

334 Inserted by SI 1996/438, reg 2(2).

335 As amended by SI 2001/2660, reg 8(3) and the Civil Partnership Act 2004 (c 33), s 251(5).

336 Repealed by SI 1993/2798, regs 1(3) and 2.

337 As amended by the Employment Rights (Dispute Resolution) Act 1998 (c 8), s 1(2).

338 As amended by SI 1993/2798, reg 1(3) and Sch, para 1 and by SI 1996/438, reg 2(3).

339 Prospectively amended and repealed in part by the Equality Act 2006 (c 3), s 40, 91 and 93 and Sch 3, paras 14(1) and (4) and Sch 4.

340 As amended by the Employment Rights (Dispute Resolution) Act 1998 (c 8), s 1(2).

341 As amended by the Armed Forces Act 1996 (c 46), s 21(6).

342 As amended by the Race Relations Act 1976 (c 74), s 79(4) and Sch 4, para 8(a).

[(2A) Where in England and Wales—[343]
(a) proceedings or prospective proceedings under section 66 relate to the act or omission of a qualifying institution, and
(b) the dispute concerned is referred as a complaint under the student complaints scheme before the end of the period of six months mentioned in subsection (2)(a),
the period allowed by subsection (2)(a) shall be extended by two months.
(2B) In subsection (2A)—[344]
'qualifying institution' has the meaning given by section 11 of the Higher Education Act 2004;
'the student complaints scheme' means a scheme for the review of qualifying complaints, as defined by section 12 of that Act, that is provided by the designated operator, as defined by section 13(5)(b) of that Act.]
[(3) An [employment tribunal], county court or sheriff court shall not consider an application under section 72(2)(a) unless it is made before the end of the period of six months beginning when the act to which it relates was done; and a county court or sheriff court shall not consider an application under section 72(4) unless it is made before the end of the period of five years so beginning.][345,346]
(4) An [employment tribunal] shall not consider a complaint under section 73(1) unless it is presented to the tribunal before the end of the period of six months beginning when the act complained of was done.[347]
(5) A court or tribunal may nevertheless consider any such complaint, claim or application which is out of time if, in all the circumstances of the case, it considers that it is just and equitable to do so.
(6) For the purposes of this section—
(a) where the inclusion of any term in a contract renders the making of the contract an unlawful act that act shall be treated as extending throughout the duration of the contract, and
(b) any act extending over a period shall be treated as done at the end of that period, and
(c) a deliberate omission shall be treated as done when the person in question decided upon it,
and in the absence of evidence establishing the contrary a person shall be taken for the purposes of this section to decide upon an omission when he does an act inconsistent with doing the omitted act or, if he has done no such inconsistent act, when the period expires within which he might reasonably have been expected to do the omitted act if it was to be done.

343 Inserted by the Higher Education Act 2004 (c 8), s 19(1).
344 Inserted by the Higher Education Act 2004 (c 8), s 19(1).
345 As amended by the Employment Rights (Dispute Resolution) Act 1998 (c 8), s 1(2).
346 Substituted by the Race Relations Act 1976 (c 74), s 79(4) and Sch 4, para 8(b).
347 As amended by the Employment Rights (Dispute Resolution) Act 1998 (c 8), s 1(2).

Trade Union and Labour Relations (Consolidation) Act 1992 (Extracts)

(1992 Chapter 52)

An Act to consolidate the enactments relating to collective labour relations, that is to say, to trade unions, employers' associations, industrial relations and industrial action.

[16th July 1992]

Part III

Rights in Relation to Union Membership and Activities

[Detriment][348]

[Detriment] on grounds related to union membership or activities[349]

146.—(1) [A worker] has the right not to [be subjected to any detriment as an individual by any act, or any deliberate failure to act, by his employer if the act or failure takes place] for [the sole or main purpose] of—[350,351]

(a) preventing or deterring him from being or seeking to become a member of an independent trade union, or penalising him for doing so,

(b) preventing or deterring him from taking part in the activities of an independent trade union at an appropriate time, or penalising him for doing so,

[(ba) preventing or deterring him from making use of trade union services at an appropriate time, or penalising him for doing so, or] [352]

(c) compelling him to be or become a member of any trade union or of a particular trade union or of one of a number of particular trade unions.

(2) In subsection [(1)] 'an appropriate time' means—[353]

(a) a time outside the [worker's] working hours, or

(b) a time within his working hours at which, in accordance with arrangements agreed with or consent given by his employer, it is permissible for him to take part in the activities of a trade union [or (as the case may be) make use of trade union services];

and for this purpose 'working hours', in relation to [a worker], means any time when, in accordance with his contract of employment [(or other contract personally to do work or perform services)], he is required to be at work.

[(2A) In this section—[354]

(a) 'trade union services' means services made available to the worker by an independent trade union by virtue of his membership of the union, and

(b) references to a worker's 'making use' of trade union services include his consenting to the raising of a matter on his behalf by an independent trade union of which he is a member.

(2B) If an independent trade union of which a worker is a member raises a matter on his behalf (with or without his consent), penalising the worker for that is to be treated as penalising him as mentioned in subsection (1)(ba).

(2C) A worker also has the right not to be subjected to any detriment as an individual by any act, or any deliberate failure to act, by his employer if the act or failure takes place because of the worker's failure to accept an offer made in contravention of section 145A or 145B.

(2D) For the purposes of subsection (2C), not conferring a benefit that, if the offer had been accepted by the worker, would have been conferred on him under the resulting agreement shall be taken to be subjecting him to a detriment as an individual (and to be a deliberate failure to act).]

---

348 As amended by the Employment Relations Act 2004 (c 24), ss 30, 31, Sch 1, para 8 and Sch 2.
349 As amended by the Employment Relations Act 2004 (c 24), ss 30, 31, Sch 1, para 8 and Sch 2.
350 As amended by the Employment Relations Act 2004 (c 24), ss 30, 31, Sch 1, para 8 and Sch 2.
351 As amended by the Employment Relations Act 1999 (c 26), s 2 and Sch 2, para 2.
352 Inserted by the Employment Relations Act 2004 (c 24), s 31.
353 As amended by the Employment Relations Act 2004 (c 24), ss 30, 31, Sch 1, para 8 and Sch 2.
354 Inserted by the Employment Relations Act 2004 (c 24), s 31.

(3) [A worker] also has the right not to [be subjected to any detriment as an individual by any act, or any deliberate failure to act, by his employer if the act or failure takes place] for [the sole or main purpose] of enforcing a requirement (whether or not imposed by [a contract of employment] or in writing) that, in the event of his not being a member of any trade union or of a particular trade union or of one of a number of particular trade unions, he must make one or more payments.[355,356]

(4) For the purposes of subsection (3) any deduction made by an employer from the remuneration payable to [a worker] in respect of his employment shall, if it is attributable to his not being a member of any trade union or of a particular trade union or of one of a number of particular trade unions, be treated as [a detriment to which he has been subjected as an individual by an act of his employer taking place] for [the sole or main purpose] of enforcing a requirement of a kind mentioned in that subsection.[357,358]

(5) [A worker or former worker] may present a complaint to an industrial tribunal on the ground that [he has been subjected to a detriment] by his employer in contravention of this section.[359,360]

[(5A) This section does not apply where—[361]
  (a) the worker is an employee; and
  (b) the detriment in question amounts to dismissal.]

Time limit for proceedings

147.—(1) An [employment tribunal] shall not consider a complaint under section 146 unless it is presented—[362]
  (a) before the end of the period of three months beginning with the date of the [act or failure to which the complaint relates or, where that act or failure is part of a series of similar acts or failures (or both) the last of them], or
  (b) where the tribunal is satisfied that it was not reasonably practicable for the complaint to be presented before the end of that period, within such further period as it considers reasonable.

[(2) For the purposes of subsection (1)—[363]
  (a) where an act extends over a period, the reference to the date of the act is a reference to the last day of that period;
  (b) a failure to act shall be treated as done when it was decided on.

(3) For the purposes of subsection (2), in the absence of evidence establishing the contrary an employer shall be taken to decide on a failure to act—
  (a) when he does an act inconsistent with doing the failed act, or
  (b) if he has done no such inconsistent act, when the period expires within which he might reasonably have been expected to do the failed act if it was to be done.]

Duty of employer to consult [. . .][364] representatives

188.—[(1) Where an employer is proposing to dismiss as redundant 20 or more employees at one establishment within a period of 90 days or less, the employer shall consult about the dismissals all the persons who are appropriate representatives of any of the employees who may be [affected by the proposed dismissals or may be affected by measures taken in connection with those dismissals.][365]

(1A) The consultation shall begin in good time and in any event—
  (a) where the employer is proposing to dismiss 100 or more employees as mentioned in subsection (1), at least 90 days, and
  (b) otherwise, at least 30 days,

before the first of the dismissals takes effect.

---

355 As amended by the Employment Relations Act 2004 (c 24), ss 30, 31, Sch 1, para 8 and Sch 2.

356 As amended by the Employment Relations Act 1999 (c 26), s 2 and Sch 2, para 2.

357 As amended by the Employment Relations Act 2004 (c 24), ss 30, 31, Sch 1, para 8 and Sch 2.

358 As amended by the Employment Relations Act 1999 (c 26), s 2 and Sch 2, para 2.

359 As amended by the Employment Relations Act 2004 (c 24), ss 30, 31, Sch 1, para 8 and Sch 2.

360 As amended by the Employment Relations Act 1999 (c 26), s 2 and Sch 2, para 2.

361 Substituted by the Employment Relations Act 2004 (c 24), s 30.

362 Subsections (2) and (3) inserted and the original text renumbered as subs (1) and amended by the Employment Relations Act 1999 (c 26), s 2 and Sch 2, para 3.

363 As amended by the Employment Rights (Dispute Resolution) Act 1998 (c 8), s 1(2).

364 As omitted by SI 1995/2587, reg 3(10).

365 Substituted by SI 1999/1925, regs 2(2), 3(1)(2).

[(1B) For the purposes of this section the appropriate representatives of any affected employees are—

(a) if the employees are of a description in respect of which an independent trade union is recognised by their employer, representatives of the trade union, or

(b) in any other case, whichever of the following employee representatives the employer chooses:—

(i) employee representatives appointed or elected by the affected employees otherwise than for the purposes of this section, who (having regard to the purposes for and the method by which they were appointed or elected) have authority from those employees to receive information and to be consulted about the proposed dismissals on their behalf;

(ii) employee representatives elected by the affected employees, for the purposes of this section, in an election satisfying the requirements of section 188A(1).] [366]

(2) The consultation shall include consultation about ways of—

(a) avoiding the dismissals,

(b) reducing the numbers of employees to be dismissed, and

(c) mitigating the consequences of the dismissals,

and shall be undertaken by the employer with a view to reaching agreement with the appropriate representatives.] [367]

(3) In determining how many employees an employer is proposing to dismiss as redundant no account shall be taken of employees in respect of whose proposed dismissals consultation has already begun.

(4) For the purposes of the consultation the employer shall disclose in writing to the [appropriate] [368] representatives—

(a) the reasons for his proposals,

(b) the numbers and descriptions of employees whom it is proposed to dismiss as redundant,

(c) the total number of employees of any such description employed by the employer at the establishment in question,

(d) the proposed method of selecting the employees who may be dismissed, [. . .][369]

(e) the proposed method of carrying out the dismissals, with due regard to any agreed procedure, including the period over which the dismissals are to take effect. [and

(f) the proposed method of calculating the amount of any redundancy payments to be made (otherwise than in compliance with an obligation imposed by or by virtue of any enactment) to employees who may be dismissed.] [370]

(5) That information shall be [given to each of the appropriate representatives by being delivered to them], [371] or sent by post to an address notified by them to the employer, or [(in the case of representatives of a trade union)] [372] sent by post to the union at the address of its head or main office.

[(5A) The employer shall allow the appropriate representatives access to [the affected employees] [373] and shall afford to those representatives such accommodation and other facilities as may be appropriate.] [374]

(6) [. . .][375]

(7) If in any case there are special circumstances which render it not reasonably practicable for the employer to comply with a requirement of subsection [(1A), (2) or (4)], [376] the employer shall take all such steps towards compliance with that requirement as are reasonably practicable in

---

[366] Substituted by SI 1999/1925, regs 3(1)(3).

[367] Substituted for s 188(1)(2) by SI 1995/2587, reg 3(2).

[368] Substituted by SI 1995/2587, reg 3(3).

[369] Repealed by Trade Union Reform and Employment Rights Act 1993 (c 19), s 51, Sch 10; SI 1993/1908, art 2(1), Sch1.

[370] Inserted by Trade Union Reform and Employment Rights Act 1993 (c 19), s 34(2)(a); SI 1993/1908, art 2(1), Sch1.

[371] Substituted by SI 1995/2587, reg 3(4)(a).

[372] Inserted by SI 1995/2587, reg 3(4)(b).

[373] Substituted by SI 1999/1925, regs 2(2), 3(1)(4).

[374] Inserted by SI 1995/2587, reg 3(5).

[375] Omitted by SI 1995/2587, reg 3(6).

[376] Substituted by SI 1995/2587, reg 3(7).

those circumstances. [Where the decision leading to the proposed dismissals is that of a person controlling the employer (directly or indirectly), a failure on the part of that person to provide information to the employer shall not constitute special circumstances rendering it not reasonably practicable for the employer to comply with such a requirement.] [377]

[(7A) Where—

[(a) the employer has invited any of the affected employees to elect employee representatives, and] [378]

(b) the invitation was issued long enough before the time when the consultation is required by subsection (1A)(a) or (b) to begin to allow them to elect representatives by that time,

the employer shall be treated as complying with the requirements of this section in relation to those employees if he complies with those requirements as soon as is reasonably practicable after the election of the representatives.] [379]

[(7B) If, after the employer has invited affected employees to elect representatives, the affected employees fail to do so within a reasonable time, he shall give to each affected employee the information set out in subsection (4).] [380]

(8) This section does not confer any rights on a trade union [, a representative] [381] or an employee except as provided by sections 189 to 192 below.

Complaint by trade union and protective award

189.—(1) Where an employer has dismissed as redundant, or is proposing to dismiss as redundant, one or more employees of a description in respect of which an independent trade union is recognised by him, and has not complied with the requirements of section 188, the union may present a complaint to an industrial tribunal on that ground.

(2) If the tribunal finds the complaint well-founded it shall make a declaration to that effect and may also make a protective award.

(3) A protective award is an award in respect of one or more descriptions of employees—

(a) who have been dismissed as redundant, or whom it is proposed to dismiss as redundant, and

(b) in respect of whose dismissal or proposed dismissal the employer has failed to comply with a requirement of section 188,

ordering the employer to pay remuneration for the protected period.

(4) The protected period—

(a) begins with the date on which the first of the dismissals to which the complaint relates takes effect, or the date of the award, whichever is the earlier, and

(b) is of such length as the tribunal determines to be just and equitable in all the circumstances having regard to the seriousness of the employer's default in complying with any requirement of section 188;

but shall not exceed 90 days in a case falling within section 188(2)(a), 30 days in a case falling within section 188(2)(b), or 28 days in any other case.

(5) An industrial tribunal shall not consider a complaint under this section unless it is presented to the tribunal—

(a) before the proposed dismissal takes effect, or

(b) before the end of the period of three months beginning with the date on which the dismissal takes effect, or

(c) where the tribunal is satisfied that it was not reasonably practicable for the complaint to be presented within the period of three months, within such further period as it considers reasonable.

(6) If on a complaint under this section a question arises—

(a) whether there were special circumstances which rendered it not reasonably practicable for the employer to comply with any requirement of section 188, or

(b) whether he took all such steps towards compliance with that requirement as were reasonably practicable in those circumstances,

---

377 Inserted by Trade Union Reform and Employment Rights Act 1993 (c 19), s. 34(2) (c); SI 1993/1908, art 2(1), Sch 1.

378 Substituted by SI 1999/1925, regs 2(2), 3(1)(5).

379 Inserted by SI 1995/2587, reg 3(8).

380 Inserted by SI 1999/1925, regs 2(2), 3(1)(6).

381 Inserted by SI 1995/2587, reg 3(9).

it is for the employer to show that there were and that he did.

Entitlement under protective award

190.—(1) Where an industrial tribunal has made a protective award, every employee of a description to which the award relates is entitled, subject to the following provisions and to section 191, to be paid remuneration by his employer for the protected period.

(2) The rate of remuneration payable is a week's pay for each week of the period; and remuneration in respect of a period less than one week shall be calculated by reducing proportionately the amount of a week's pay.

(3) Any payment made to an employee by an employer in respect of a period falling within a protected period—

(a) under the employee's contract of employment, or

(b) by way of damages for breach of that contract,

shall go towards discharging the employer's liability to pay remuneration under the protective award in respect of that first mentioned period.

Conversely, any payment of remuneration under a protective award in respect of any period shall go towards discharging any liability of the employer under, or in respect of any breach of, the contract of employment in respect of that period.

(4) An employee is not entitled to remuneration under a protective award in respect of a period during which he is employed by the employer unless he would be entitled to be paid by the employer in respect of that period—

(a) by virtue of his contract of employment, or

(b) by virtue of Schedule 3 to the Employment Protection (Consolidation) Act 1978[382] (rights of employee in period of notice),

if that period fell within the period of notice required to be given by section 49(1) of that Act.

(5) Schedule 14 to the Employment Protection (Consolidation) Act 1978 applies with respect to the calculation of a week's pay for the purposes of this section.

The calculation date for the purposes of Part II of that Schedule is the date on which the protective award was made or, in the case of an employee who was dismissed before the date on which the protective award was made, the date which by virtue of paragraph 7(1)(k) or (l) of that Schedule is the calculation date for the purpose of computing the amount of a redundancy payment in relation to that dismissal (whether or not the employee concerned is entitled to any such payment).

(6) If an employee of a description to which a protective award relates dies during the protected period, the award has effect in his case as if the protected period ended on his death.

Supplementary provisions

Meaning of 'redundancy'

195.—(1) In this Chapter, references to redundancy or to being redundant, in relation to an employee, are references to—

(a) the fact that the employer has ceased, or intends to cease, to carry on the business for the purposes of which the employee is or was employed by him, or has ceased, or intends to cease, to carry on that business in the place where the employee is or was so employed, or

(b) the fact that the requirements of that business for employees to carry out work of a particular kind, or for employees to carry out work of a particular kind in the place where he is or was so employed, have ceased or diminished or are expected to cease or diminish.

(2) In subsection (1)—

'business' includes a trade or profession and includes any activity carried on by a body of persons, whether corporate or unincorporate; and

'cease' means cease either permanently or temporarily and from whatever cause, and 'diminish' has a corresponding meaning.

(3) For the purposes of any proceedings under this Chapter, the dismissal or proposed dismissal of an employee shall be presumed, unless the contrary is proved, to be by reason of redundancy.

[382] 1978 c 44

Consolidated Version of the Treaty Establishing the European Community[383]

(Official Journal C325 of 24.12.2002)

Article 141

1. Each Member State shall ensure that the principle of equal pay for male and female workers for equal work or work of equal value is applied.
2. For the purpose of this article, 'pay' means the ordinary basic or minimum wage or salary and any other consideration, whether in cash or in kind, which the worker receives directly or indirectly, in respect of his employment, from his employer.
   Equal pay without discrimination based on sex means:
   (a) that pay for the same work at piece rates shall be calculated on the basis of the same unit of measurement;
   (b) that pay for work at time rates shall be the same for the same job.
3. The Council, acting in accordance with the procedure referred to in Article 251, and after consulting the Economic and Social Committee, shall adopt measures to ensure the application of the principle of equal opportunities and equal treatment of men and women in matters of employment and occupation, including the principle of equal pay for equal work or work of equal value.
4. With a view to ensuring full equality in practice between men and women in working life, the principle of equal treatment shall not prevent any Member State from maintaining or adopting measures providing for specific advantages in order to make it easier for the underrepresented sex to pursue a vocational activity or to prevent or compensate for disadvantages in professional careers.

[383] Reproduced with thanks to EUR-Lex and the European Communities. However, only European Community legislation printed in the paper edition of the Official Journal of the European Union is deemed authentic.

RULES

The Employment Appeal Tribunal Rules 1993[384]

(SI 1993/2854)

Citation and commencement

1.—(1) These Rules may be cited as the Employment Appeal Tribunal Rules 1993 and shall come into force on 16th December 1993.

(2) As from that date the Employment Appeal Tribunal Rules 1980, the Employment Appeal Tribunal (Amendment) Rules 1985 and the Employment Appeal Tribunal (Amendment) Rules 1988 shall be revoked.

Interpretation

[2.—(1) In these rules—[385]

'the 1992 Act' means the Trade Union and Labour Relations (Consolidation) Act 1992;

'the 1996 Act' means the Employment Tribunals Act 1996;

'the 1999 Regulations' means the Transnational Information and Consultation of Employees Regulations 1999;

['the 2004 Regulations' means the European and Public Limited-Liability Company Regulations 2004;] [386]

['the Information and Consultation Regulations' means the Information and Consultation of Employees Regulations 2004;] [387]

['the 2007 Regulations' means the Companies (Cross-Border Mergers) Regulations 2007;] [388]

'the Appeal Tribunal' means the Employment Appeal Tribunal established under section 87 of the Employment Protection Act 1975 and continued in existence under section 20(1) of the 1996 Act and includes the President, a judge, a member or the Registrar acting on behalf of the Tribunal;

'the CAC' means the Central Arbitration Committee;

'the Certification Officer' means the person appointed to be the Certification Officer under section 254(2) of the 1992 Act;

'costs officer' means any officer of the Appeal Tribunal authorised by the President to assess costs or expenses;

'Crown employment proceedings' has the meaning given by section 10(8) of the 1996 Act;

['document' includes a document delivered by way of electronic communication; [389]

'electronic communication' shall have the meaning given to it by section 15(1) of the Electronic Communications Act 2000;]

'excluded person' means, in relation to any proceedings, a person who has been excluded from all or part of the proceedings by virtue of—

(a) a direction of a Minister of the Crown under rule 30A(1)(b) or (c); or

(b) an order of the Appeal Tribunal under rule 30A(2)(a) read with rule 30A(1)(b) or (c);

'judge' means a judge of the Appeal Tribunal nominated under section 22(1)(a) or (b) of the 1996 Act and includes a judge nominated under section 23(2) of, or a judge appointed under section 24(1) of, the 1996 Act to be a temporary additional judge of the Appeal Tribunal;

['legal representative' shall mean a person, including a person who is a party's employee, who—[390]

(a) has a general qualification within the meaning of the Courts and Legal Services Act 1990;

---

[384] References within these rules to industrial tribunals were amended to read employment tribunals by the Employment Rights (Dispute Resolution) Act 1998 (c 8), s 1.

[385] Substituted by SI 2001/1128, r 2.

[386] Inserted by SI 2004/2526, r 2(1).

[387] Inserted by SI 2004/3426, reg 41.

[388] Inserted by SI 2007/2974, reg 64(1).

[389] Inserted by SI 2004/2526, r 2(1).

[390] Inserted by SI 2004/2526, r 2(1).

(b) is an advocate or solicitor in Scotland; or
(c) is a member of the Bar of Northern Ireland or a Solicitor of the Supreme Court of Northern Ireland.]

'member' means a member of the Appeal Tribunal appointed under section 22(1)(c) of the 1996 Act and includes a member appointed under section 23(3) of the 1996 Act to act temporarily in the place of a member appointed under that section;

['national security proceedings' shall have the meaning given to it in regulation 2 of the Employment Tribunals (Constitution and Rules of Procedure) Regulations 2004] [391]

'the President' means the judge appointed under section 22(3) of the 1996 Act to be President of the Appeal Tribunal and includes a judge nominated under section 23(1) of the 1996 Act to act temporarily in his place;

'the Registrar' means the person appointed to be Registrar of the Appeal Tribunal and includes any officer of the Tribunal authorised by the President to act on behalf of the Registrar;

'the Secretary of Employment Tribunals' means the person acting for the time being as the Secretary of the Central Office of the Employment Tribunals (England and Wales) or, as may be appropriate, of the Central Office of the Employment Tribunals (Scotland);

'special advocate' means a person appointed pursuant to rule 30A(4).

['writing' includes writing delivered by means of electronic communication;] [392]

(2) [. . .][393]

(3) Any reference in these Rules to a person who was the [claimant] or, as the case may be, the respondent in the proceedings before an employment tribunal includes, where those proceedings are still continuing, a reference to a person who is the [claimant] or, as the case may be, is the respondent in those proceedings.] [394]

[Overriding objective[395]

2A.—(1) The overriding objective of these Rules is to enable the Appeal Tribunal to deal with cases justly.

(2) Dealing with a case justly includes, so far as practicable—
(a) ensuring that the parties are on an equal footing;
(b) dealing with the case in ways which are proportionate to the importance and complexity of the issues;
(c) ensuring that it is dealt with expeditiously and fairly; and
(d) saving expense.

(3) The parties shall assist the Appeal Tribunal to further the overriding objective.]

[Institution of appeal[396]

3.—(1) Every appeal to the Appeal Tribunal shall, subject to paragraphs (2) and (4), be instituted by serving on the Tribunal the following documents—
(a) a notice of appeal in, or substantially in, accordance with Form 1, 1A or 2 in the Schedule to these rules;
[(b) in the case of an appeal from a judgment of an employment tribunal a copy of any claim and response in the proceedings before the employment tribunal or an explanation as to why either is not included; and] [397]
[(c) in the case of an appeal from a judgment of an employment tribunal a copy of the written record of the judgment of the employment tribunal which is subject to appeal and the written reasons for the judgment, or an explanation as to why written reasons are not included;] [398]
(d) in the case of an appeal made pursuant to regulation 38(8) of the 1999 Regulations [or regulation 47(6) of the 2004 Regulations] [or regulation 35(6) of the Information and Consultation

[391] Inserted by SI 2004/2526, r 2(1).
[392] Inserted by SI 2004/2526, r 2(1).
[393] As amended by SI 2004/2526, r 2.
[394] As amended by SI 2004/2526, r 2.
[395] Inserted by SI 2004/2526, r 3.
[396] Substituted by SI 2001/1128, r 3.
[397] Substituted by SI 2004/2526, r 4.
[398] Substituted by SI 2004/2526, r 4.

Regulations] [or regulation 57(6) of the 2007 Regulations] from a declaration or order of the CAC, a copy of that declaration or order[; and] [399]

[(e) in the case of an appeal from an order of an employment tribunal a copy of the written record of the order of the employment tribunal which is subject to appeal and (if available) the written reasons for the order; [400]

(f) in the case of an appeal from a decision or order of the Certification Officer a copy of the decision or order of the Certification Officer which is subject to appeal and the written reasons for that decision or order.]

[(2) In an appeal from a judgment or order of the employment tribunal in relation to national security proceedings where the appellant was the claimant—[401]

(i) the appellant shall not be required by virtue of paragraph (1)(b) to serve on the Appeal Tribunal a copy of the response if the response was not disclosed to the appellant; and

(ii) the appellant shall not be required by virtue of paragraph (1)(c) or (e) to serve on the Appeal Tribunal a copy of the written reasons for the judgment or order if the written reasons were not sent to the appellant but if a document containing edited reasons was sent to the appellant, he shall serve a copy of that document on the Appeal Tribunal.]

(3) The period within which an appeal to the Appeal Tribunal may be instituted is—

[(a) in the case of an appeal from a judgment of the employment tribunal—[402]

(i) where the written reasons for the judgment subject to appeal—

(aa) were requested orally at the hearing before the employment tribunal or in writing within 14 days of the date on which the written record of the judgment was sent to the parties; or

(bb) were reserved and given in writing by the employment tribunal 42 days from the date on which the written reasons were sent to the parties;

(ii) in an appeal from a judgment given in relation to national security proceedings, where there is a document containing edited reasons for the judgment subject to appeal, 42 days from the date on which that document was sent to the parties; or

(iii) where the written reasons for the judgment subject to appeal—

(aa) were not requested orally at the hearing before the employment tribunal or in writing within 14 days of the date on which the written record of the judgment was sent to the parties; and

(bb) were not reserved and given in writing by the employment tribunal 42 days from the date on which the written record of the judgment was sent to the parties;]

[(b) in the case of an appeal from an order of an employment tribunal, 42 days from the date of the order;] [403]

(c) in the case of an appeal from a decision of the Certification Officer, 42 days from the date on which the written record of that decision was sent to the appellant;

(d) in the case of an appeal from a declaration or order of the CAC under regulation 38(8) of the 1999 Regulations [or regulation 47(6) of the 2004 Regulations] [or regulation 35(6) of the Information and Consultation Regulations] [or regulation 57(6) of the 2007 Regulations], 42 days from the date on which the written notification of that declaration or order was sent to the appellant. [404]

(4) In the case of [an appeal from a judgment or order of the employment tribunal in relation to national security proceedings], the appellant shall not set out the grounds of appeal in his notice of appeal and shall not append to his notice of appeal the [written reasons for the judgment] of the tribunal. [405]

(5) In [an appeal from the employment tribunal in relation to national security proceedings] in relation to which the appellant was the respondent in the proceedings before the employment tribunal, the appellant shall, within the period described in paragraph (3)(a), provide to the Appeal Tribunal a document setting out the grounds on which the appeal is brought. [406]

---

[399] As amended by SI 2004/2526, r 4; SI 2004/3426, reg 41; and SI 2007/2974, reg 64(2).

[400] Inserted by SI 2004/2526, r 4.

[401] Substituted by SI 2004/2526, r 4.

[402] Substituted by SI 2004/2526, r 4.

[403] Substituted by SI 2004/2526, r 4.

[404] As amended by SI 2004/2526, r 4; SI 2004/3426, reg 41; and SI 2007/2974, reg 64(2).

[405] As amended by SI 2004/2526, r 4.

[406] As amended by SI 2004/2526, r 4.

(6) In [an appeal from the employment tribunal in relation to national security proceedings] in relation to which the appellant was the [claimant] in the proceedings before the employment tribunal—[407]
(a) the appellant may, within the period described in [paragraph 3(a)(ii) or (iii) or paragraph 3(b), whichever is applicable,] provide to the Appeal Tribunal a document setting out the grounds on which the appeal is brought; and
(b) a special advocate appointed in respect of the appellant may, within the period described in [paragraph 3(a)(ii) or (iii) or paragraph 3(b), whichever is applicable,] or within 21 days of his appointment, whichever is later, provide to the Appeal Tribunal a document setting out the grounds on which the appeal is brought or providing supplementary grounds of appeal.

[(7) Where it appears to a judge or the Registrar that a notice of appeal or a document provided under paragraph (5) or (6)—[408]
(a) discloses no reasonable grounds for bringing the appeal; or
(b) is an abuse of the Appeal Tribunal's process or is otherwise likely to obstruct the just disposal of proceedings,

he shall notify the Appellant or special advocate accordingly informing him of the reasons for his opinion and, subject to paragraphs (8) and (10), no further action shall be taken on the notice of appeal or document provided under paragraph (5) or (6).]

[(7A) In paragraphs (7) and (10) reference to a notice of appeal or a document provided under paragraph (5) or (6) includes reference to part of a notice of appeal or document provided under paragraph (5) or (6).][409]

(8) Where notification has been given under paragraph (7), the appellant or the special advocate, as the case may be, may serve a fresh notice of appeal, or a fresh document under paragraph (5) or (6), within the time remaining under paragraph (3) or (6) or within 28 days from the date on which [the notification given under paragraph (7)] was sent to him, whichever is the longer period.[410]

(9) Where the appellant or the special advocate serves a fresh notice of appeal or a fresh document under paragraph (8), [the judge or the Registrar] shall consider such fresh notice of appeal or document with regard to jurisdiction as though it were an original notice of appeal lodged pursuant to paragraphs (1) and (3), or as though it were an original document provided pursuant to paragraph (5) or (6), as the case may be.[411]

[(10) Where notification has been given under paragraph (7) and within 28 days of the date the notification was sent, an appellant or special advocate expresses dissatisfaction in writing with the reasons given by the judge or Registrar for his opinion, he is entitled to have the matter heard before a judge who shall make a direction as to whether any further action should be taken on the notice of appeal or document under paragraph (5) or (6).]][412]

Service of notice of appeal

4.—[(1) On receipt of notice under rule 3, the Registrar shall seal the notice with the Appeal Tribunal's seal and shall serve a sealed copy on the appellant and on—[413]
(a) every person who, in accordance with rule 5, is a respondent to the appeal; and
(b) The Secretary of [Employment Tribunals] in the case of an appeal from an [employment tribunal]; or
(c) the Certification Officer in the case of an appeal from any of his decisions; or
(d) the Secretary of State in the case of an appeal under [. . .] Chapter II of Part IV of the 1992 Act [or Part XI of the Employment Rights Act 1996] to which he is not a respondent[; or
(e) the Chairman of the CAC in the case of an appeal from the CAC under regulation 38(8) of the 1999 Regulations [or regulation 47(6) of the 2004 Regulations] [or regulation 35(6) of the Information and Consultation Regulations] [or regulation 57(6) of the 2007 Regulations].[414]

[407] As amended by SI 2004/2526, r 4.
[408] Substituted by SI 2004/2526, r 4.
[409] Inserted by SI 2004/2526, r 4.
[410] As amended by SI 2004/2526, r 4.
[411] As amended by SI 2004/2526, r 4.
[412] Substituted by SI 2004/2526, r 4.
[413] As amended by SI 2001/1128, r 4.
[414] As amended by SI 2004/2526, r 5; SI 2004/3426, reg 41; and SI 2007/2974, reg 64(2).

(2) On receipt of a document provided under rule 3(5)—
  (a) the Registrar shall not send the document to a person in respect of whom a Minister of the Crown has informed the Registrar that he wishes to address the Appeal Tribunal in accordance with rule 30A(3) with a view to the Appeal Tribunal making an order applicable to this stage of the proceedings under rule 30A(2)(a) read with 30A(1)(b) or (c) (exclusion of a party or his representative), at any time before the Appeal Tribunal decides whether or not to make such an order; but if it decides not to make such an order, the Registrar shall, subject to sub-paragraph (b), send the document to such a person 14 days after the Appeal Tribunal's decision not to make the order; and
  (b) the Registrar shall not send a copy of the document to an excluded person, but if a special advocate is appointed in respect of such a person, the Registrar shall send a copy of the document to the special advocate.

(3) On receipt of a document provided under rule 3(6)(a) or (b), the Registrar shall not send a copy of the document to an excluded person, but shall send a copy of the document to the respondent.]

Respondents to appeals

5. The respondents to an appeal shall be—[415]
  (a) in the case of an appeal from an [employment tribunal] or of an appeal made pursuant to [section 45D, 56A, 95, 104 or 108C] of the 1992 Act from a decision of the Certification Officer, the parties (other than the appellant) to the proceedings before the [employment tribunal] or the Certification Officer;
  (b) in the case of an appeal made pursuant to [section 9 or 126] of the 1992 Act from a decision of the Certification Officer, that Officer;
  [(c) in the case of an appeal made pursuant to regulation 38(8) of the 1999 Regulations [or regulation 47(6) of the 2004 Regulations] [or regulation 35(6) of the Information and Consultation Regulations] [or regulation 57(6) of the 2007 Regulations] from a declaration or order of the CAC, the parties (other than the appellant) to the proceedings before the CAC.][416]

Respondent's answer and notice of cross-appeal

6.—(1) The Registrar shall, as soon as practicable, notify every respondent of the date appointed by the Appeal Tribunal by which any answer under this rule must be delivered.

(2) A respondent who wishes to resist an appeal shall, [subject to paragraph (6), and] within the time appointed under paragraph (1) of this rule, deliver to the Appeal Tribunal an answer in writing in, or substantially in, accordance with Form 3 in the Schedule to these Rules, setting out the grounds on which he relies, so, however, that it shall be sufficient for a respondent to an appeal referred to in rule 5(a) [or 5(c)] who wishes to rely on any ground which is the same as a ground relied on by the [employment tribunal][, the Certification Officer or the CAC] for making the [judgment,] decision[, declaration] or order appealed from to state that fact in his answer.[417]

(3) A respondent who wishes to cross-appeal may[, subject to paragraph (6),] do so by including in his answer a statement of the grounds of his cross-appeal, and in that event an appellant who wishes to resist the cross-appeal shall, within a time to be appointed by the Appeal Tribunal, deliver to the Tribunal a reply in writing setting out the grounds on which he relies.[418]

(4) The Registrar shall serve a copy of every answer and reply to a cross-appeal on every party other than the party by whom it was delivered.

(5) Where the respondent does not wish to resist an appeal, the parties may deliver to the Appeal Tribunal an agreed draft of an order allowing the appeal and the Tribunal may, if it thinks it right to do so, make an order allowing the appeal in the terms agreed.

[(6) In [an appeal from the employment tribunal in relation to national security proceedings], the respondent shall not set out the grounds on which he relies in his answer to an appeal, nor include in his answer a statement of the grounds of any cross-appeal.[419]

---

415 As amended by SI 2001/1128, r 5.

416 As amended by SI 2004/2526, r 6; SI 2004/3426, reg 41; and SI 2007/2974, reg 64(2).

417 As amended by SI 2001/1128, r 6 and SI 2004/2526, r 7.

418 As amended by SI 2001/1128, r 6.

419 As amended by SI 2004/2526, r 7.

[(7) In [an appeal from the employment tribunal in relation to national security proceedings] in relation to which the respondent was not the [claimant] in the proceedings before the employment tribunal, the respondent shall, within the time appointed under paragraph (1), provide to the Registrar a document, setting out the grounds on which he intends to resist the appeal, and may include in that document a statement of the grounds of any cross-appeal.[420]

(8) In [an appeal from the employment tribunal in relation to national security proceedings] in relation to which the respondent was the [claimant] in the proceedings before the employment tribunal—[421]

(a) the respondent may, within the time appointed under paragraph (1) provide to the Registrar a document, setting out the grounds on which he intends to resist the appeal, and may include in that document a statement of the grounds of any cross-appeal; and

(b) a special advocate appointed in respect of the respondent may, within the time appointed under paragraph (1), or within 21 days of his appointment, whichever is the later, provide to the Registrar a document, setting out the grounds, or the supplementary grounds, on which the respondent intends to resist the appeal, and may include in that document a statement of the grounds, or the supplementary grounds, of any cross-appeal.

(9) In [an appeal from the employment tribunal in relation to national security proceedings], if the respondent, or any special advocate appointed in respect of a respondent, provides in the document containing grounds for resisting an appeal a statement of grounds of cross-appeal and the appellant wishes to resist the cross-appeal—[422]

(a) where the appellant was not the [claimant] in the proceedings before the employment tribunal, the appellant shall within a time to be appointed by the Appeal Tribunal deliver to the Tribunal a reply in writing setting out the grounds on which he relies; and

(b) where the appellant was the [claimant] in the proceedings before the employment tribunal, the appellant, or any special advocate appointed in respect of him, may within a time to be appointed by the Appeal Tribunal deliver to the Tribunal a reply in writing setting out the grounds on which the appellant relies.

(10) Any document provided under paragraph (7) or (9)(a) shall be treated by the Registrar in accordance with rule 4(2), as though it were a document received under rule 3(5).

(11) Any document provided under paragraph (8) or (9)(b) shall be treated by the Registrar in accordance with rule 4(3), as though it were a document received under rule 3(6)(a) or (b).]

[(12) Where it appears to a judge or the Registrar that a statement of grounds of cross-appeal contained in respondent's answer or document provided under paragraph (7) or (8)—[423]

(a) discloses no reasonable grounds for bringing the cross-appeal; or

(b) is an abuse of the Appeal Tribunal's process or is otherwise likely to obstruct the just disposal of proceedings,

he shall notify the appellant or special advocate accordingly informing him of the reasons for his opinion and, subject to paragraphs (14) and (16), no further action shall be taken on the statement of grounds of cross-appeal.

(13) In paragraphs (12) and (16) reference to a statement of grounds of cross-appeal includes reference to part of a statement of grounds of cross-appeal.

(14) Where notification has been given under paragraph (12), the respondent or special advocate, as the case may be, may serve a fresh statement of grounds of cross-appeal before the time appointed under paragraph (1) or within 28 days from the date on which the notification given under paragraph (12) was sent to him, whichever is the longer.

(15) Where the respondent or special advocate serves a fresh statement of grounds of cross-appeal, a judge or the Registrar shall consider such statement with regard to jurisdiction as though it was contained in the original Respondent's answer or document provided under (7) or (8).

(16) Where notification has been given under paragraph (12) and within 28 days of the date the notification was sent, a respondent or special advocate expresses dissatisfaction in writing with the reasons given by the judge or Registrar for his opinion, he is entitled to have the matter heard

[420] Inserted by SI 2001/1128, r 6 and amended by SI 2004/2526, r 7.

[421] As amended by SI 2004/2526, r 7.

[422] As amended by SI 2004/2526, r 7.

[423] Inserted by SI 2004/2526, r 7.

before a judge who shall make a direction as to whether any further action should be taken on the statement of grounds of cross-appeal.]

Disposal of appeal

7.—(1) The Registrar shall, as soon as practicable, give notice of the arrangements made by the Appeal Tribunal for hearing the appeal to—

(a) every party to the proceedings; and
(b) the Secretary of [Employment Tribunals] in the case of an appeal from an [employment tribunal]; or
(c) the Certification Officer in the case of an appeal from one of his decisions; or
(d) the Secretary of State in the case of an appeal under [Part XI of the Employment Rights Act 1996] or Chapter II of Part IV of the 1992 Act to which he is not a respondent[; or[424]
(e) the Chairman of the CAC in the case of an appeal from a declaration or order of, or arising in any proceedings before, the CAC under regulation 38(8) of the 1999 Regulations] [or regulation 47(6) of the 2004 Regulations] [or regulation 35(6) of the Information and Consultation Regulations] [or regulation 57(6) of the 2007 Regulations].[425]

(2) Any such notice shall state the date appointed by the Appeal Tribunal by which any [interim] application must be made.[426]

Application for restriction of proceedings order

13. Every application to the Appeal Tribunal by the Attorney General or the Lord Advocate under [section 33 of the 1996 Act] for a restriction of proceedings order shall be made in writing in, or substantially in, accordance with Form 6 in the Schedule to these Rules, accompanied by an affidavit in support, and shall be served on the Tribunal.[427]

[Disposal of interim applications[428]

20.—(1) Every interim application made to the Appeal Tribunal shall be considered in the first place by the Registrar who shall have regard to rule 2A (the overriding objective) and, where applicable, to rule 23(5).

(2) Subject to sub-paragraphs (3) and (4), every interim application shall be disposed of by the Registrar except that any matter which he thinks should properly be decided by the President or a judge shall be referred by him to the President or judge who may dispose of it himself or refer it in whole or part to the Appeal Tribunal as required to be constituted by section 28 of the 1996 Act or refer it back to the Registrar with such directions as he thinks fit.

(3) Every interim application for a restricted reporting order shall be disposed of by the President or a judge or, if he so directs, the application shall be referred to the Appeal Tribunal as required to be constituted by section 28 of the 1996 Act who shall dispose of it.

(4) Every interim application for permission to institute or continue or to make a claim or application in any proceedings before an employment tribunal or the Appeal Tribunal, pursuant to section 33(4) of the 1996 Act, shall be disposed of by the President or a judge, or, if he so directs, the application shall be referred to the Appeal Tribunal as required to be constituted by section 28 of the 1996 Act who shall dispose of it.]

Appeals from Registrar

21.—(1) Where an application is disposed of by the Registrar in pursuance of rule 20(2) any party aggrieved by his decision may appeal to a judge and in that case [. . .] the judge may determine the appeal himself or refer it in whole or in part to the Appeal Tribunal as required to be constituted by [section 28 of the 1996 Act].[429]

(2) Notice of appeal under paragraph (1) of this rule may be given to the Appeal Tribunal, either orally or in writing, within five days of the decision appealed from and the Registrar shall notify every

[424] As amended by SI 2001/1128, r7.
[425] As amended by SI 2004/2526, r 8; SI 2004/3426, reg 41; and SI 2007/2974, reg 64(2).
[426] As amended by SI 2004/2526, r 8.
[427] AsamendedbySI2001/1128, r 8.
[428] Substituted by SI 2004/2526, r 13.
[429] As amended by SI 2001/1128, r 12.

other party who appears to him to be concerned in the appeal and shall inform every such party and the appellant of the arrangements made by the Tribunal for disposing of the appeal.

Hearing of interim applications

22.—(1) The Appeal Tribunal may, subject to [any direction of a Minister of the Crown under rule 30A(1) or order of the Appeal Tribunal under rule 30A(2)(a) read with rule 30A(1),] and, where applicable, to rule 23(6), sit either in private or in public for the hearing of any [interim] application. [430]

(2) [. . .][431]

Cases involving allegations of sexual misconduct or the commission of sexual offences

23.—(1) This rule applies to any proceedings to which [section 31 of the 1996 Act] applies. [432]

(2) In any such proceedings where the appeal appears to involve allegations of the commission of a sexual offence, the Registrar shall omit from any register kept by the Appeal Tribunal, which is available to the public, or delete from any order, judgment or other document, which is available to the public, any identifying matter which is likely to lead members of the public to identify any person affected by or making such an allegation.

(3) In any proceedings to which this rule applies where the appeal involves allegations of sexual misconduct the Appeal Tribunal may at any time before promulgation of its decision either on the application of a party or of its own motion make a restricted reporting order having effect, if not revoked earlier by the Appeal Tribunal, until the promulgation of its decision.

(4) A restricted reporting order shall specify the persons who may not be identified.

[(5) Subject to paragraph (5A) the Appeal Tribunal shall not make a full restricted reporting order unless it has given each party to the proceedings an opportunity to advance oral argument at a hearing, if they so wish.] [433]

[(5A) The Appeal Tribunal may make a temporary restricted reporting order without a hearing. [434]

(5B) Where a temporary restricted reporting order has been made the Registrar shall inform the parties to the proceedings in writing as soon as possible of:

(a) the fact that the order has been made; and

(b) their right to apply to have the temporary restricted reporting order revoked or converted into a full restricted reporting order within 14 days of the temporary order being made.

(5C) If no such application is made under subparagraph (5B)(b) within the 14 days, the temporary restricted reporting order shall lapse and cease to have any effect on the fifteenth day after it was made. When such an application is made the temporary restricted reporting order shall continue to have effect until the Hearing at which the application is considered.]

(6) Any [. . .] hearing shall, subject to [any direction of a Minister of the Crown under rule 30A(1) or order of the Appeal Tribunal under rule 30A(2)(a) read with rule 30A(1),] or unless the Appeal Tribunal decides for any of the reasons mentioned in rule 29(2) to sit in private to hear evidence, be held in public. [435]

(7) The Appeal Tribunal may revoke a restricted reporting order at any time where it thinks fit.

(8) Where the Appeal Tribunal makes a restricted reporting order, the Registrar shall ensure that a notice of that fact is displayed on the notice board of the Appeal Tribunal at the office in which the proceedings in question are being dealt with, on the door of the room in which those proceedings are taking place and with any list of the proceedings taking place before the Appeal Tribunal.

(9) In this rule, 'promulgation of its decision' means the date recorded as being the date on which the Appeal Tribunal's order finally disposing of the appeal is sent to the parties.

[Restricted reporting orders in disability cases[436]

23A.—(1) This rule applies to proceedings to which section 32(1) of [the] [1996 Act] applies. [437]

430 As amended by SI 2001/1128, r 13 and SI 2004/2526, r 14.
431 Repealed by SI 2001/1128, r 13.
432 As amended by SI 2001/1128, r 14.
433 Substituted by SI 2004/2526, r 15.
434 Inserted by SI 2004/2526, r 15.
435 As amended by SI 2001/1128, r 14 and SI 2004/2526, r 15.
436 Inserted by SI 1996/3216, r 2.
437 As amended by SI 2001/1128, r 15.

(2) In proceedings to which this rule applies the Appeal Tribunal may, on the application of the complainant or of its own motion, make a restricted reporting order having effect, if not revoked earlier by the Appeal Tribunal, until the promulgation of its decision.

(3) Where the Appeal Tribunal makes a restricted reporting order under paragraph (2) of this rule in relation to an appeal which is being dealt with by the Appeal Tribunal together with any other proceedings, the Appeal Tribunal may direct that the order is to apply also in relation to those other proceedings or such part of them as it may direct.

(4) Paragraphs (5) to (9) of rule 23 apply in relation to the making of a restricted reporting order under this rule as they apply in relation to the making of a restricted reporting order under that rule.]

Appointment for direction

24.—(1) Where it appears to the Appeal Tribunal that the future conduct of any proceedings would thereby be facilitated, the Tribunal may (either of its own motion or on application) at any stage in the proceedings appoint a date for a meeting for directions as to their future conduct and thereupon the following provisions of this rule shall apply.

(2) The Registrar shall give to every party in the proceedings notice of the date appointed under paragraph (1) of this rule and any party applying for directions shall, if practicable, before that date give to the Appeal Tribunal particulars of any direction for which he asks.

(3) The Registrar shall take such steps as may be practicable to inform every party of any directions applied for by any other party.

(4) On the date appointed under paragraph (1) of this rule, the Appeal Tribunal shall consider every application for directions made by any party and any written representations relating to the application submitted to the Tribunal and shall give such directions as it thinks fit for the purpose of securing the just, expeditious and economical disposal of the proceedings, including, where appropriate, directions in pursuance of rule 36, for the purpose of ensuring that the parties are enabled to avail themselves of opportunities for conciliation.

(5) Without prejudice to the generality of paragraph (4) of this rule, the Appeal Tribunal may give such directions as it thinks fit as to—
  (a) the amendment of any notice, answer or other document;
  (b) the admission of any facts or documents;
  (c) the admission in evidence of any documents;
  (d) the mode in which evidence is to be given at the hearing;
  (e) the consolidation of the proceedings with any other proceedings pending before the Tribunal;
  (f) the place and date of the hearing.

(6) An application for further directions or for the variation of any directions already given may be made in accordance with rule 19.

Appeal Tribunal's power to give directions

25. The Appeal Tribunal may either of its own motion or on application, at any stage of the proceedings, give any party directions as to any steps to be taken by him in relation to the proceedings.

Review of decisions and correction of errors

33.—(1) The Appeal Tribunal may, either of its own motion or on application, review any order made by it and may, on such review, revoke or vary that order on the grounds that—
  (a) the order was wrongly made as the result of an error on the part of the Tribunal or its staff;
  (b) a party did not receive proper notice of the proceedings leading to the order; or
  (c) the interests of justice require such review.

(2) An application under paragraph (1) above shall be made within 14 days of the date of the order.

(3) A clerical mistake in any order arising from an accidental slip or omission may at any time be corrected by, or on the authority of, a judge or member.

[(4) The decision to grant or refuse an application for review may be made by a judge.] [438]

[438] Inserted by SI 2004/2526, r 19.

[General power to make costs or expenses orders[439]

34.—(1) In the circumstances listed in rule 34A the Appeal Tribunal may make an order ('a costs order') that a party or a special advocate, ('the paying party') make a payment in respect of the costs incurred by another party or a special advocate ('the receiving party').

(2) For the purposes of these Rules 'costs' includes fees, charges, disbursements and expenses incurred by or on behalf of a party or special advocate in relation to the proceedings, including the reimbursement allowed to a litigant in person under rule 34D. In Scotland, all references to costs or costs orders (except in the expression 'wasted costs') shall be read as references to expenses or orders for expenses.

(3) A costs order may be made against or in favour of a respondent who has not had an answer accepted in the proceedings in relation to the conduct of any part which he has taken in the proceedings.

(4) A party or special advocate may apply to the Appeal Tribunal for a costs order to be made at any time during the proceedings. An application may also be made at the end of a hearing, or in writing to the Registrar within 14 days of the date on which the order of the Appeal Tribunal finally disposing of the proceedings was sent to the parties.

(5) No costs order shall be made unless the Registrar has sent notice to the party or special advocate against whom the order may be made giving him the opportunity to give reasons why the order should not be made. This paragraph shall not be taken to require the Registrar to send notice to the party or special advocate if the party or special advocate has been given an opportunity to give reasons orally to the Appeal Tribunal as to why the order should not be made.

(6) Where the Appeal Tribunal makes a costs order it shall provide written reasons for doing so if a request for written reasons is made within 21 days of the date of the costs order. The Registrar shall send a copy of the written reasons to all the parties to the proceedings.]

[When a costs or expenses order may be made[440]

34A.—(1) Where it appears to the Appeal Tribunal that any proceedings brought by the paying party were unnecessary, improper, vexatious or misconceived or that there has been unreasonable delay or other unreasonable conduct in the bringing or conducting of proceedings by the paying party, the Appeal Tribunal may make a costs order against the paying party.

(2) The Appeal Tribunal may in particular make a costs order against the paying party when—

(a) he has not complied with a direction of the Appeal Tribunal;

(b) he has amended its notice of appeal, document provided under rule 3 sub-paragraphs (5) or (6), Respondent's answer or statement of grounds of cross-appeal, or document provided under rule 6 sub-paragraphs (7) or (8); or

(c) he has caused an adjournment of proceedings.

(3) Nothing in paragraph (2) shall restrict the Appeal Tribunal's discretion to award costs under paragraph (1).]

[The amount of a costs or expenses order[441]

34B.—(1) Subject to sub-paragraphs (2) and (3) the amount of a costs order against the paying party can be determined in the following ways:

(a) the Appeal Tribunal may specify the sum which the paying party must pay to the receiving party;

(b) the parties may agree on a sum to be paid by the paying party to the receiving party and if they do so the costs order shall be for the sum agreed; or

(c) the Appeal Tribunal may order the paying party to pay the receiving party the whole or a specified part of the costs of the receiving party with the amount to be paid being determined by way of detailed assessment in the High Court in accordance with the Civil Procedure Rules 1998 or in Scotland the Appeal Tribunal may direct that it be taxed by the Auditor of the Court of Session, from whose decision an appeal shall lie to a judge.

(2) The Appeal Tribunal may have regard to the paying party's ability to pay when considering the amount of a costs order.

---

[439] Substituted by SI 2004/2526, r 20.

[440] Inserted by SI 2004/2526, r 21.

[441] Inserted by SI 2004/2526, r 21.

(3) The costs of an assisted person in England and Wales shall be determined by detailed assessment in accordance with the Civil Procedure Rules.]

[Personal liability of representatives for costs[442]

34C.—(1) The Appeal Tribunal may make a wasted costs order against a party's representative.

(2) In a wasted costs order the Appeal Tribunal may disallow or order the representative of a party to meet the whole or part of any wasted costs of any party, including an order that the representative repay to his client any costs which have already been paid.

(3) 'Wasted costs' means any costs incurred by a party (including the representative's own client and any party who does not have a legal representative):
- (a) as a result of any improper, unreasonable or negligent act or omission on the part of any representative; or
- (b) which, in the light of any such act or omission occurring after they were incurred, the Appeal Tribunal considers it reasonable to expect that party to pay.

(4) In this rule 'representative' means a party's legal or other representative or any employee of such representative, but it does not include a representative who is not acting in pursuit of profit with regard to the proceedings. A person is considered to be acting in pursuit of profit if he is acting on a conditional fee arrangement.

(5) Before making a wasted costs order, the Appeal Tribunal shall give the representative a reasonable opportunity to make oral or written representations as to reasons why such an order should not be made. The Appeal Tribunal may also have regard to the representative's ability to pay when considering whether it shall make a wasted costs order or how much that order should be.

(6) When the Appeal Tribunal makes a wasted costs order, it must specify in the order the amount to be disallowed or paid.

(7) The Registrar shall inform the representative's client in writing—
- (a) of any proceedings under this rule; or
- (b) of any order made under this rule against the party's representative.

(8) Where the Appeal Tribunal makes a wasted costs order it shall provide written reasons for doing so if a request is made for written reasons within 21 days of the date of the wasted costs order. The Registrar shall send a copy of the written reasons to all parties to the proceedings.]

[Litigants in person and party litigants[443]

34D.—(1) This rule applies where the Appeal Tribunal makes a costs order in favour of a party who is a litigant in person.

(2) The costs allowed under this rule must not exceed, except in the case of a disbursement, two-thirds of the amount which would have been allowed if the litigant in person had been represented by a legal representative.

(3) The litigant in person shall be allowed—
- (a) costs for the same categories of—
  - (i) work; and
  - (ii) disbursements,

  which would have been allowed if the work had been done or the disbursements had been made by a legal representative on the litigant in person's behalf;
- (b) the payments reasonably made by him for legal services relating to the conduct of the proceedings;
- (c) the costs of obtaining expert assistance in assessing the costs claim; and
- (d) other expenses incurred by him in relation to the proceedings.

(4) The amount of costs to be allowed to the litigant in person for any item of work claimed shall be—
- (a) where the litigant in person can prove financial loss, the amount that he can prove he had lost for the time reasonably spent on doing the work; or
- (b) where the litigant in person cannot prove financial loss, an amount for the time which the Tribunal considers reasonably spent on doing the work at the rate of £25.00 per hour;

[442] Inserted by SI 2004/2526, r 21.
[443] Inserted by SI 2004/2526, r 21.

(5) For the year commencing 6th April 2006 the hourly rate of £25.00 shall be increased by the sum of £1.00 and for each subsequent year commencing on 6 April, the hourly rate for the previous year shall also be increased by the sum of £1.00.
(6) A litigant in person who is allowed costs for attending at court to conduct his case is not entitled to a witness allowance in respect of such attendance in addition to those costs.
(7) For the purpose of this rule, a litigant in person includes—
 (a) a company or other corporation which is acting without a legal representative; and
 (b) in England and Wales a barrister, solicitor, solicitor's employee or other authorised litigator (as defined in the Courts and Legal Services Act), who is acting for himself; and
 (c) in Scotland, an advocate or solicitor (within the meaning of the Solicitors (Scotland) Act 1980) who is acting for himself.
(8) In the application of this rule to Scotland, references to a litigant in person shall be read as references to a party litigant.]

Schedule

Rule 3 Form[444]

Notice of Appeal from Decision of Employment Tribunal

1. The appellant is (*name and address of appellant*).
2. Any communication relating to this appeal may be sent to the appellant at (*appellant's address for service, including telephone number if any*).
3. The appellant appeals from (*here give particulars of the judgment, decision or order of the employment tribunal from which the appeal is brought including the location of the employment tribunal and the date*).
4. The parties to the proceedings before the employment tribunal, other than the appellant, were (*name and addresses of other parties to the proceedings resulting in judgment, decision or order appealed from*).
5. Copies of—
 (a) the written record of the employment tribunal's judgment, decision or order and the written reasons of the employment tribunal;
 (b) the claim (ET1);
 (c) the response (ET3); and/or (*where relevant*);
 (d) an explanation as to why any of these documents are not included;
 are attached to this notice.
6. If the appellant has made an application to the employment tribunal for a review of its judgment or decision, copies of—
 (a) the review application;
 (b) the judgment;
 (c) the written reasons of the employment tribunal in respect of that review application; and/or;
 (d) a statement by or on behalf of the appellant, if such be the case, that a judgment is awaited
 are attached to this Notice. If any of these documents exist but cannot be included, then a written explanation must be given.
7. The grounds upon which this appeal is brought are that the employment tribunal erred in law in that (*here set out in paragraphs the various grounds of appeal*).

Signed: Date:

NB.—The details entered on your Notice of Appeal must be legible and suitable for photocopying or electronic scanning. The use of black ink or typescript is recommended.]

444 Substituted by SI 2005/1871, r 3.

The Employment Tribunals (Constitution and Rules of Procedure) Regulations 2004

(SI 2004/1861)

Overriding objective

3.—[(1) The overriding objective of these Regulations and the rules in Schedules 1, 2, 3, 4, 5 and 6 is to enable tribunals and [Employment Judges][445] to deal with cases justly.] [446]

(2) Dealing with a case justly includes, so far as practicable:—

(a) ensuring that the parties are on an equal footing;

(b) dealing with the case in ways which are proportionate to the complexity or importance of the issues;

(c) ensuring that it is dealt with expeditiously and fairly; and

(d) saving expense.

[(3) A tribunal or [Employment Judge][447] shall seek to give effect to the overriding objective when it or he: [448]

(a) exercises any power given to it or him by these Regulations or the rules in Schedules 1, 2, 3, 4, 5 and 6; or

(b) interprets these Regulations or any rule in Schedules 1, 2, 3, 4, 5 and 6.]

(4) The parties shall assist the tribunal or the [Employment Judge][449] to further the overriding objective.

Composition of tribunals—general

9.—(1) For each hearing, the President, Vice President or the Regional [Employment Judge] shall select [an Employment Judge], who shall, subject to regulation 11, be a member of the panel of [Employment Judges], and the President, Vice President or the Regional [Employment Judge] may select himself.[450]

(2) In any proceedings which are to be determined by a tribunal comprising [an Employment Judge] and two other members, the President, Regional [Employment Judge] or Vice President shall, subject to regulation 11, select one of those other members from the panel of persons appointed by the [Lord Chancellor] under regulation 8(3)(b) and the other from the panel of persons appointed under regulation 8(3)(c).[451]

Calculation of time limits

15.—[(1) Any period of time for doing any act required or permitted to be done under any of the rules in Schedules 1, 2, 3, 4, 5 and 6, or under any decision, order or judgment of a tribunal or [an Employment Judge][452], shall be calculated in accordance with paragraphs (2) to (6).]

(2) Where any act must or may be done within a certain number of days of or from an event, the date of that event shall not be included in the calculation. For example, a respondent is sent a copy of a claim on 1st October. He must present a response to the Employment Tribunal Office within 28 days of the date on which he was sent the copy. The last day for presentation of the response is 29th October.

(3) Where any act must or may be done not less than a certain number of days before or after an event, the date of that event shall not be included in the calculation. For example, if a party wishes to submit representations in writing for consideration by a tribunal at a hearing, he must submit them not less than 7 days before the hearing. If the hearing is fixed for 8th October, the representations must be submitted no later than 1st October.

[445] Substituted by SI 2008/2683, Sch 1 para 242.
[446] As amended by SI 2004/2351, reg 2.
[447] Substituted by SI 2008/2683, Sch 1 para 242.
[448] As amended by SI 2004/2351, reg 2.
[449] Substituted by SI 2008/2683, Sch 1 para 242.
[450] As amended by SI 2008/2683, Sch 1 para 248.
[451] As amended by SI 2008/2683, Sch 1 para 248 and by SI 2008/3240, reg 3(2).
[452] Substituted by SI 2008/2683, Sch 1 para 252.

(4) Where the tribunal or [an Employment Judge][453] gives any decision, order or judgment which imposes a time limit for doing any act, the last date for compliance shall, wherever practicable, be expressed as a calendar date.

(5) In rule 14(4) of Schedule 1 the requirement to send the notice of hearing to the parties not less than 14 days before the date fixed for the hearing shall not be construed as a requirement for service of the notice to have been effected not less than 14 days before the hearing date, but as a requirement for the notice to have been placed in the post not less than 14 days before that date. For example, a hearing is fixed for 15th October. The last day on which the notice may be placed in the post is 1st October.

(6) Where any act must or may have been done within a certain number of days of a document being sent to a person by the Secretary, the date when the document was sent shall, unless the contrary is proved, be regarded as the date on the letter from the Secretary which accompanied the document. For example, a respondent must present his response to a claim to the Employment Tribunal Office [within 28 days of the date on which] he was sent a copy of the claim. If the letter from the Secretary sending him a copy of the claim is dated 1st October, the last day for presentation of the response is 29th October.[454]

Regulation 16

Schedule 1

The Employment Tribunals Rules of Procedure

How to Bring a Claim

Starting a claim

1.—(1) A claim shall be brought before an employment tribunal by the claimant presenting to an Employment Tribunal Office the details of the claim in writing. Those details must include all the relevant required information (subject to [. . .][455] rule 53 (Employment Agencies Act 1973)).

(2) The claim may only be presented to an Employment Tribunal Office in England and Wales if it relates to English and Welsh proceedings (defined in regulation 19(1)). The claim may only be presented to an Employment Tribunal Office in Scotland if it relates to Scottish proceedings (defined in regulation 19(2)).

(3) Unless it is a claim in proceedings described in regulation 14(3), a claim which is presented on or after [1st October 2005] must be presented on a claim form which has been prescribed by the Secretary of State in accordance with regulation[456,457]

(4) Subject to [. . .][458] rule 53, the required information in relation to the claim is—
- (a) each claimant's name;
- (b) each claimant's address;
- (c) the name of each person against whom the claim is made ('the respondent');
- (d) each respondent's address;
- (e) details of the claim.
- (f)–(i) [. . .][459]

(5) [. . .][460]

(6) [. . .][461]

[453] Substituted by SI 2008/2683, Sch 1 para 252.

[454] As amended by SI 2004/2351, reg 2.

[455] Omitted by SI 2008/3240, reg 4(2)(a) subject to transitional provisions contained in reg 8 of those Regulations.

[456] Inserted by SI 2004/2351, reg 2.

[457] As amended by SI 2005/435, reg 2.

[458] Omitted by SI 2008/3240, reg 4(2)(b) subject to transitional provisions contained in reg 8 of those Regulations.

[459] Omitted by SI 2008/3240, reg 4(2)(c) subject to transitional provisions contained in reg 8 of those Regulations.

[460] Omitted by SI 2008/3240, reg 4(2)(d) subject to transitional provisions contained in reg 8 of those Regulations.

[461] Omitted by SI 2008/3240, reg 4(2)(d) subject to transitional provisions contained in reg 8 of those Regulations.

(7) Two or more claimants may present their claims in the same document if their claims arise out of the same set of facts.

(8) [. . .][462]

Acceptance of Claim Procedure

What the tribunal does after receiving the claim

2.—(1) On receiving the claim the Secretary shall consider whether the claim or part of it should be accepted in accordance with rule 3. If a claim or part of one is not accepted the tribunal shall not proceed to deal with any part which has not been accepted (unless it is accepted at a later date). If no part of a claim is accepted the claim shall not be copied to the respondent.

(2) If the Secretary accepts the claim or part of it, he shall—

(a) send a copy of the claim to each respondent and record in writing the date on which it was sent;

(b) inform the parties in writing of the case number of the claim (which must from then on be referred to in all correspondence relating to the claim) and the address to which notices and other communications to the Employment Tribunal Office must be sent;

(c) inform the respondent in writing about how to present a response to the claim, the time limit for doing so, what may happen if a response is not entered within the time limit and that the respondent has a right to receive a copy of any judgment disposing of the claim;

(d) when any enactment relevant to the claim provides for conciliation, notify the parties that the services of a conciliation officer [may be] available to them; [and][463]

(e) [. . .][464]

(f) if only part of the claim has been accepted, inform the claimant and any respondent which parts of the claim have not been accepted and that the tribunal shall not proceed to deal with those parts unless they are accepted at a later date.

When the claim will not be accepted by the Secretary

3.—(1) When a claim is required by rule 1(3) to be presented using a prescribed form, but the prescribed form has not been used, the Secretary shall not accept the claim and shall return it to the claimant with an explanation of why the claim has been rejected and provide a prescribed claim form.

(2) The Secretary shall not accept the claim (or a relevant part of one) if it is clear to him that one or more of the following circumstances applies—

(a) the claim does not include all the relevant required information; [or]

(b) the tribunal does not have power to consider the claim (or that relevant part of it).

(c) [. . .][465]

(3) If the Secretary decides not to accept a claim or part of one for any of the reasons in paragraph (2), he shall refer the claim together with a statement of his reasons for not accepting it to [an Employment Judge]. The [Employment Judge] shall decide in accordance with the criteria in paragraph (2) whether the claim or part of it should be accepted and allowed to proceed.[466]

(4) If the [Employment Judge] decides that the claim or part of one should be accepted he shall inform the Secretary in writing and the Secretary shall accept the relevant part of the claim and then proceed to deal with it in accordance with rule 2(2).[467]

(5) If the [Employment Judge] decides that the claim or part of it should not be accepted he shall record his decision together with the reasons for it in writing in a document signed by him. The Secretary shall as soon as is reasonably practicable inform the claimant of that decision and the reasons for it in writing together with information on how that decision may be reviewed or appealed.[468]

---

462 Omitted by SI 2008/3240, reg 4(2)(d) subject to transitional provisions contained in reg 8 of those Regulations.

463 As amended by SI 2008/3240, reg 4(3)(a).

464 Omitted by SI 2008/3240, reg 4(3)(b).

465 As amended by SI 2008/3240, reg 4(4)(a) and (b) subject to transitional provisions contained in reg 8 of those Regulations.

466 As amended by SI 2008/2683, Sch 1 para 255.

467 As amended by SI 2008/2683, Sch 1 para 255.

468 As amended by SI 2008/2683, Sch 1 para 255.

(6) [. . .][469]
(7) Except for the purposes of paragraph [. . .] (8) or any appeal to the Employment Appeal Tribunal, where [an Employment Judge] has decided that a claim or part of one should not be accepted such a claim (or the relevant part of it) is to be treated as if it had not been received by the Secretary on that occasion.[470]
(8) Any decision by [an Employment Judge] not to accept a claim or part of one may be reviewed in accordance with rules 34 to 36. If the result of such review is that any parts of the claim should have been accepted, then paragraph (7) shall not apply to the relevant parts of that claim and the Secretary shall then accept such parts and proceed to deal with it as described in rule 2(2).[471]
(9) A decision to accept or not to accept a claim or part of one shall not bind any future tribunal or [Employment Judge] where any of the issues listed in paragraph (2) fall to be determined later in the proceedings.[472]
(10) Except in rule 34 (review of other judgments and decisions), all references to a claim in the remainder of these rules are to be read as references to only the part of the claim which has been accepted.

Response

Responding to the claim

4.—(1) If the respondent wishes to respond to the claim made against him he must present his response to the Employment Tribunal Office within 28 days of the date on which he was sent a copy of the claim. The response must include all the relevant required information. The time limit for the respondent to present his response may be extended in accordance with paragraph (4).
(2) Unless it is a response in proceedings described in regulation 14(3), any response presented on or after [1st October 2005] must be on a response form prescribed by the Secretary of State pursuant to regulation 14.[473]
(3) The required information in relation to the response is—
(a) the respondent's full name;
(b) the respondent's address;
(c) whether or not the respondent wishes to resist the claim in whole or in part; and
(d) if the respondent wishes to so resist, on what grounds.
(4) The respondent may apply [. . .] for an extension of the time limit within which he is to present his response. The application must be presented to the Employment Tribunal Office within 28 days of the date on which the respondent was sent a copy of the claim (unless the application is made under rule 33(1)) and must explain why the respondent cannot comply with the time limit. Subject to rule 33, the [Employment Judge] shall only extend the time within which a response may be presented if he is satisfied that it is just and equitable to do so.[474]
[(4A) When a respondent is legally represented in relation to the application the respondent or the respondent's representative must, at the same time as the application is sent to the Employment Tribunal Office, provide all other parties with the following information in writing—
(a) details of the application and the reasons why it is made;
(b) notification that any objection to the application must be sent to the Employment Tribunal office within 7 days of receiving the application or, if a hearing of any type is due to take place before the expiry of that 7 days period, before the date of that hearing; and
(c) that any objection to the application must be copied to both the Employment Tribunal office and all other parties,
and the respondent or that representative must confirm in writing to the Employment Tribunal office that this rule has been complied with.

[469] Omitted by SI 2008/3240, reg 4(4)(c) subject to transitional provisions contained in reg 8 of those Regulations.
[470] As amended by SI 2008/2683, Sch 1 para 255. Also amended by SI 2008/3240, reg 4(4)(d) subject to transitional provisions contained in reg 8 of those Regulations.
[471] As amended by SI 2008/2683, Sch 1 para 255.
[472] As amended by SI 2008/2683, Sch 1 para 255.
[473] As amended by SI 2005/435, reg 2.
[474] As amended by SI 2008/2683, Sch 1 para 255 and by SI 2008/3240, reg 4(5)(a).

(4B) The time limit described in sub-paragraph (4A)(b) may be amended where the Employment Judge or tribunal considers it in the interests of justice to do so.

(4C) Where a respondent is not legally represented in relation to the application, the Secretary shall send a copy of the application to all other parties and inform them of the matters listed in sub-paragraphs (4A) (b) and (c).

(4D) Where a respondent's application under paragraph (4) is refused the Secretary shall inform the parties in writing of such refusal unless the application is refused at a hearing.

(4E) This rule is subject to section 12 of the State Immunity Act 1978 (a).][475]

(5) A single document may include the response to more than one claim if the relief claimed arises out of the same set of facts, provided that in respect of each of the claims to which the single response relates—

(a) the respondent intends to resist all the claims and the grounds for doing so are the same in relation to each claim; or

(b) the respondent does not intend to resist any of the claims.

(6) A single document may include the response of more than one respondent to a single claim provided that—

(a) each respondent intends to resist the claim and the grounds for doing so are the same for each respondent; or

(b) none of the respondents intends to resist the claim.

Acceptance of Response Procedure

What the tribunal does after receiving the response

5.—(1) On receiving the response the Secretary shall consider whether the response should be accepted in accordance with rule 6. If the response is not accepted it shall be returned to the respondent and (subject to paragraphs (5) and (6) of rule 6) the claim shall be dealt with as if no response to the claim had been presented.

(2) If the Secretary accepts the response he shall send a copy of it to all other parties and record in writing the date on which he does so.

When the response will not be accepted by the Secretary

6.—(1) Where a response is required to be presented using a prescribed form by rule 4(2), but the prescribed form has not been used, the Secretary shall not accept the response and shall return it to the respondent with an explanation of why the response has been rejected and provide a prescribed response form.

(2) The Secretary shall not accept the response if it is clear to him that any of the following circumstances apply—

(a) the response does not include all the required information (defined in rule 4(3));

(b) the response has not been presented within the relevant time limit.

(3) If the Secretary decides not to accept a response for either of the reasons in paragraph (2), he shall refer the response together with a statement of his reasons for not accepting the response to [an Employment Judge]. The [Employment Judge] shall decide in accordance with the criteria in paragraph (2) whether the response should be accepted.[476]

(4) If the [Employment Judge] decides that the response should be accepted he shall inform the Secretary in writing and the Secretary shall accept the response and then deal with it in accordance with rule 5(2).[477]

(5) If the [Employment Judge] decides that the response should not be accepted he shall record his decision together with the reasons for it in writing in a document signed by him. The Secretary shall inform both the claimant and the respondent of that decision and the reasons for it. The Secretary shall also inform the respondent of the consequences for the respondent of that decision and how it may be reviewed or appealed.[478]

(6) Any decision by [an Employment Judge] not to accept a response may be reviewed in accordance with rules 34 to 36. If the result of such a review is that the response [is to be] accepted, then

[475] Inserted by SI 2008/3240, reg 4(5)(b).

[476] As amended by SI 2008/2683, Sch 1 para 255.

[477] As amended by SI 2008/2683, Sch 1 para 255.

[478] As amended by SI 2008/2683, Sch 1 para 255.

the Secretary shall accept the response and proceed to deal with the response as described in rule 5(2).[479]

Counterclaims

7.—(1) When a respondent wishes to present a claim against the claimant ('a counterclaim') in accordance with article 4 of the Employment Tribunals Extension of Jurisdiction (England and Wales) Order 1994, or as the case may be, article 4 of the Employment Tribunals Extension of Jurisdiction (Scotland) Order 1994, he must present the details of his counterclaim to the Employment Tribunal Office in writing. Those details must include—

(a) the respondent's name;

(b) the respondent's address;

(c) the name of each claimant whom the counterclaim is made against;

(d) the claimant's address;

(e) details of the counterclaim.

(2) [An Employment Judge] may in relation to particular proceedings by order made under rule 10(1) establish the procedure which shall be followed by the respondent making the counterclaim and any claimant responding to the counterclaim.[480]

(3) The President may by a practice direction made under regulation 13 make provision for the procedure which is to apply to counterclaims generally.

Consequences of a Response Not Being Presented or Accepted

Default judgments

8.—[(1) Subject to paragraphs (2A) and (6), in any proceedings if the relevant time limit for presenting a response has passed, an Employment Judge shall, in the circumstances listed in paragraph (2), issue a default judgment to determine the claim without a hearing.][481]

[(1A) If the Employment Judge is not satisfied that he has sufficient information to issue a default judgment, he shall make an order (as described in rule 10 (2) (b)) requiring such additional information as he considers appropriate to enable him, subject to paragraphs (2A) and (6), to issue a default judgment.

(1B) Where an order is made as described in paragraph (1A), and the additional information requested has not been received within the specified time limit, a default judgment shall be issued in accordance with paragraph (1).][482]

[(2) [Subject to paragraphs (2A) and (6), those circumstances] are when either—

(a) no response in those proceedings has been presented to the Employment Tribunal Office within the relevant time limit;

(b) a response has been so presented, but a decision has been made not to accept the response either by the Secretary under rule 6(1) or by [an Employment Judge] under rule 6(3), and the Employment Tribunal Office has not received an application under rule 34 to have that decision reviewed; or

(c) a response has been accepted in those proceedings, but the respondent has stated in the response that he does not intend to resist the claim.][483]

[(2A) No default judgment need be issued where the Employment Judge—

(a) is not satisfied that the tribunal has jurisdiction to consider the claim, or part of it; or

(b) has sufficient evidence to conclude that the claim form has not been received by the respondent.][484]

(3) A default judgment may determine liability only or it may determine liability and remedy. If a default judgment determines remedy it shall be such remedy as it appears to the [Employment Judge] that the claimant is entitled to on the basis of the information before him.[485]

---

[479] As amended by SI 2008/2683, Sch 1 para 255 and by SI 2008/3240, reg 4(6).

[480] As amended by SI 2008/2683, Sch 1 para 255.

[481] Substituted by SI 2008/3240, reg 4(7)(a) subject to transitional provisions contained in reg 8 of those Regulations.

[482] Added by SI 2008/3240, reg 4(7)(b) subject to transitional provisions contained in reg 8 of those Regulations.

[483] Substituted by SI 2004/2351, reg 2 and as amended by SI 2008/2683, Sch 1 para 255 and SI 2008/3240, reg 4(7)(c) subject to transitional provisions contained in reg 8 of SI 2008/3240.

[484] Added by SI 2008/3240, reg 4(7)(d) subject to transitional provisions contained in reg 8 of those Regulations.

[485] As amended by SI 2008/2683, Sch 1 para 255.

(4) Any default judgment issued by [an Employment Judge] under this rule shall be recorded in writing and shall be signed by him. The Secretary shall send a copy of that judgment to the parties, to ACAS, and, if the proceedings were referred to the tribunal by a court, to that court. The Secretary shall also inform the parties of their right to [apply to] have the default judgment reviewed under rule 33. The Secretary shall put a copy of the default judgment on the Register (subject to rule 49 (sexual offences and the Register)).[486]

(5) The claimant or respondent may apply to have the default judgment reviewed in accordance with rule 33.

[(6) A default judgment shall not be issued where the parties have settled the proceedings (either by means of a compromise agreement or through ACAS). If a default judgment is issued in these circumstances it shall have no effect.][487]

(7) When paragraph (6) applies, either party may apply under rule 33 to have the default judgment revoked.

Taking no further part in the proceedings

9. A respondent who has not presented a response to a claim or whose response has not been accepted shall not be entitled to take any part in the proceedings except to—
 [(aa) make a request under rule 30 (written reasons);][488]
 (a) make an application under rule 33 (review of default judgments);
 (b) make an application under rule 35 (preliminary consideration of application for review) in respect of [rule 34(3)(a), (b) or (e)]; [489]
 (c) be called as a witness by another person; or
 (d) be sent a copy of a document or corrected entry in accordance with rule 8(4), 29(2) or 37;

and in these rules the word 'party' or 'respondent' includes a respondent only in relation to his entitlement to take such a part in the proceedings, and in relation to any such part which he takes.

Case Management

General power to manage proceedings

10.—(1) Subject to the following rules, the [Employment Judge] may at any time either on the application of a party or on his own initiative make an order in relation to any matter which appears to him to be appropriate. Such orders may be any of those listed in paragraph (2) or such other orders as he thinks fit. Subject to the following rules, orders may be issued as a result of [an Employment Judge] considering the papers before him in the absence of the parties, or at a hearing (see regulation 2 for the definition of 'hearing').

(2) Examples of orders which may be made under paragraph (1) are orders—
 (a) as to the manner in which the proceedings are to be conducted, including any time limit to be observed;
 (b) that a party provide additional information;
 (c) requiring the attendance of any person in Great Britain either to give evidence or to produce documents or information;
 (d) requiring any person in Great Britain to disclose documents or information to a party [or] to allow a party to inspect such material as might be ordered by a County Court (or in Scotland, by a sheriff);[490]
 (e) extending any time limit, whether or not expired (subject to rules 4(4), 11(2), 25(5), 30(5), 33(1), 35(1), 38(7) and 42(5) of this Schedule, and to rule 3(4) of Schedule 2);
 (f) requiring the provision of written answers to questions put by the tribunal or [Employment Judge];
 (g) [. . .][491]
 (h) staying (in Scotland, sisting) the whole or part of any proceedings;

[486] As amended by SI 2008/2683, Sch 1 para 255 and SI 2008/3240, reg 4(7)(e) subject to transitional provisions contained in reg 8 of SI 2008/3240.

[487] Substituted by SI 2008/3240, reg 4(7)(f) subject to transitional provisions contained in reg 8 of SI 2008/3240.

[488] Added by SI 2008/3240, reg 4(8).

[489] As amended by SI 2005/1865, reg 2.

[490] As amended by SI 2008/3240, reg 4(9)(a).

[491] Omitted by SI 2008/3240, reg 4(9)(b).

(i) that part of the proceedings be dealt with separately;
(j) that different claims be considered together;
(k) that any person who the [Employment Judge] or tribunal considers may be liable for the remedy claimed should be made a respondent in the proceedings;
(l) dismissing the claim against a respondent who is no longer directly interested in the claim;
(m) postponing or adjourning any hearing;
(n) varying or revoking other orders;
(o) giving notice to the parties of a pre-hearing review or the Hearing;
(p) giving notice under rule 19;
(q) giving leave to amend a claim or response;
(r) that any person who the [Employment Judge] or tribunal considers has an interest in the outcome of the proceedings may be joined as a party to the proceedings;
(s) that a witness statement be prepared or exchanged; or
(t) as to the use of experts or interpreters in the proceedings.

(3) An order may specify the time at or within which and the place at which any act is required to be done. An order may also impose conditions and it shall inform the parties of the potential consequences of non-compliance set out in rule 13.

(4) When a requirement has been imposed under paragraph (1) the person subject to the requirement may make an application under rule 11 (applications in proceedings) for the order to be varied or revoked.

(5) An order described in [. . .] [sub-]paragraph (2)(d) which requires a person other than a party to grant disclosure or inspection of material may be made only when the disclosure sought is necessary in order to dispose fairly of the claim or to save expense.[492]

(6) Any order containing a requirement described in either sub-paragraph (2)(c) or (d) shall state that under section 7(4) of the Employment Tribunals Act, any person who without reasonable excuse fails to comply with the requirement shall be liable on summary conviction to a fine, and the document shall also state the amount of the maximum fine.

(7) An order as described in [sub-]paragraph (2)(j) may be made only if all relevant parties have been given notice that such an order may be made and they have been given the opportunity to make oral or written representations as to why such an order should or should not be made.[493]

(8) Any order made under this rule shall be recorded in writing and signed by the [Employment Judge] and the Secretary shall [(except where the order is for a witness order described in rule 10(2)(c) only)] inform all parties to the proceedings of any order made as soon as is reasonably practicable.[494]

Applications in proceedings

11.—(1) At any stage of the proceedings a party may apply for an order to be issued, varied or revoked or for a case management discussion or pre-hearing review to be held.

(2) An application for an order must be made not less than 10 days before the date of the hearing at which it is to be considered (if any) unless it is not reasonably practicable to do so, or the [Employment Judge] or tribunal considers it in the interests of justice that shorter notice be allowed. The application must (unless [an Employment Judge] orders otherwise) be in writing to the Employment Tribunal Office and include the case number for the proceedings and the reasons for the request. If the application is for a case management discussion or a pre-hearing review to be held, it must identify any orders sought.[495]

(3) An application for an order must include an explanation of how the order would assist the tribunal or [Employment Judge] in dealing with the proceedings efficiently and fairly.[496]

(4) When a party is legally represented in relation to the application (except where the application is for a witness order described in rule 10(2)(c) only), that party or his representative must, at the same time as the application is sent to the Employment Tribunal Office, provide all other parties with the following information in writing—
(a) details of the application and the reasons why it is [made];

---

492 As amended by SI 2005/1865, reg 2 and by SI 2008/3240, reg 4(9)(c).
493 As amended by SI 2008/3240, reg 4(9)(d).
494 As amended by SI 2008/2683, Sch 1 para 255 and by SI 2008/3240, reg 4(9)(e).
495 As amended by SI 2008/2683, Sch 1 para 255.
496 As amended by SI 2008/2683, Sch 1 para 255.

(b) [notification that any objection to the application must be sent to the Employment Tribunal Office within 7 days of receiving the application or, if a hearing of any type is due to take place before the expiry of that 7 day period, before the date of that hearing;]
(c) that any objection to the application must be copied to both the Employment Tribunal Office and all other parties;

and the party or his representative must confirm in writing to the Employment Tribunal Office that this rule has been complied with.[497]

[(4A) The time limit described in sub-paragraph (4)(b) may be amended where the Employment Judge or tribunal considers it in the interests of justice to do so.][498]

[(5) Where a party is not legally represented in relation to the application, the Secretary shall (except where the application is for a witness order described in rule 10(2)(c) only) send a copy of the application to all other parties and inform them of the matters listed in sub-paragraphs (4)(b) and (c).][499]

(6) [An Employment Judge] may refuse a party's application and if he does so the Secretary shall inform the parties in writing of such refusal unless the application is refused at a hearing.[500]

[Employment Judge] acting on his own initiative[501]

12.—(1) Subject to paragraph (2) and to rules 10(7) and 18(7), [an Employment Judge] may make an order on his own initiative with or without hearing the parties or giving them an opportunity to make written or oral representations. He may also decide to hold a case management discussion or pre-hearing review on his own initiative.[502]

(2) Where [an Employment Judge] makes an order without giving the parties the opportunity to make representations—
(a) the Secretary must send to the party affected by such order a copy of the order and a statement explaining the right to make an application under [sub-]paragraph (2)(b); and
(b) a party affected by the order may apply to have it varied or revoked.[503]

(3) An application under [sub-]paragraph (2)(b) must (subject to rule 10(2)(e)) be made before the time at which, or the expiry of the period within which, the order was to be complied with. Such an application must (unless [an Employment Judge] orders otherwise) be made in writing to an Employment Tribunal Office and it must include the reasons for the application. Paragraphs (4) and (5) of rule 11 apply in relation to informing the other parties of the application.[504]

Compliance with orders and practice directions

13.—(1) If a party does not comply with an order made under these rules, under rule 8 of Schedule 3, rule 7 of Schedule 4 or a practice direction, [an Employment Judge] or tribunal—[505]
(a) may make, an order in respect of costs or preparation time under rules 38 to 46; or
(b) may (subject to paragraph (2) and rule 19) at a pre-hearing review or a Hearing make an order to strike out the whole or part of the claim or, as the case may be, the response and, where appropriate, order that a respondent be debarred from responding to the claim altogether.

(2) An order may also provide that unless the order is complied with, the claim or, as the case may be, the response shall be struck out on the date of non-compliance without further consideration of the proceedings or the need to give notice under rule 19 or hold a pre-hearing review or Hearing.

(3) [Employment Judges] and tribunals shall comply with any practice directions issued under regulation 13.[506]

---

497 As amended by SI 2008/3240, reg 4(10)(a) and (b).
498 Added by SI 2008/3240, reg 4(10)(c).
499 Substituted by SI 2008/3240, reg 4(10)(d).
500 As amended by SI 2008/2683, Sch 1 para 255.
501 As amended by SI 2008/2683, Sch 1 para 255.
502 As amended by SI 2008/2683, Sch 1 para 255.
503 As amended by SI 2008/2683, Sch 1 para 255 and by SI 2008/3240, reg 4(11)(a).
504 As amended by SI 2008/2683, Sch 1 para 255 and by SI 2008/3240, reg 4(11)(b).
505 As amended by SI 2008/2683, Sch 1 para 255.
506 As amended by SI 2008/2683, Sch 1 para 255.

Different Types of Hearing

Hearings—general

14.—(1) [An Employment Judge] or a tribunal (depending on the relevant rule) may hold the following types of hearing—[507]

(a) a case management discussion under rule 17;

(b) a pre-hearing review under rule 18;

[(bb) a hearing dealing with interim relief as described in rule 18A;][508]

(c) a Hearing under rule 26; or

(d) a review hearing under rule 33 or 36.

(2) So far as it appears appropriate to do so, the [Employment Judge] or tribunal shall seek to avoid formality in his or its proceedings and shall not be bound by any enactment or rule of law relating to the admissibility of evidence in proceedings before the courts.[509]

(3) The [Employment Judge] or tribunal (as the case may be) shall make such enquiries of persons appearing before him or it and of witnesses as he or it considers appropriate and shall otherwise conduct the hearing in such manner as he or it considers most appropriate for the clarification of the issues and generally for the just handling of the proceedings.[510]

(4) Unless the parties agree to shorter notice, the Secretary shall send notice of any hearing (other than a case management discussion) to every party not less than 14 days before the date fixed for the hearing and shall inform them that they have the opportunity to submit written representations and to advance oral argument. The Secretary shall give the parties reasonable notice before a case management discussion is held.

(5) If a party wishes to submit written representations for consideration at a hearing (other than a case management discussion) he shall present them to the Employment Tribunal Office not less than 7 days before the hearing and shall at the same time send a copy to all other parties.

(6) The tribunal or [Employment Judge] may, if it or he considers it appropriate, consider representations in writing which have been submitted otherwise than in accordance with paragraph (5).[511]

Use of electronic communications

[**15.**—(1) A hearing may be conducted (in whole or in part) by use of electronic communications provided that the Employment Judge or tribunal conducting the hearing considers it just and equitable to do so.

(2) Where a hearing is required by these rules to be held in public and electronic communications are to be used in accordance with this rule then, subject to rule 16, it must be held in a place to which the public has access and using equipment so that, when oral evidence is given the public is able to see and hear all parties to the communication.

(3) Where a hearing is to be held in private, and electronic communications are to be used in accordance with this rule, when oral evidence is given the tribunal or Employment Judge must be able to see and hear all parties to the communication.][512]

Hearings which may be held in private

16.—(1) A hearing or part of one may be conducted in private for the purpose of hearing from any person evidence or representations which in the opinion of the tribunal or [Employment Judge] is likely to consist of information—[513]

(a) which he could not disclose without contravening a prohibition imposed by or by virtue of any enactment;

(b) which has been communicated to him in confidence, or which he has otherwise obtained in consequence of the confidence placed in him by another person; or

[507] As amended by SI 2008/2683, Sch 1 para 255.
[508] Added by SI 2008/3240, reg 4(12).
[509] As amended by SI 2008/2683, Sch 1 para 255.
[510] As amended by SI 2008/2683, Sch 1 para 255.
[511] As amended by SI 2008/2683, Sch 1 para 255.
[512] Substituted by SI 2008/3240, reg 4(13).
[513] As amended by SI 2008/2683, Sch 1 para 255.

(c) the disclosure of which would, for reasons other than its effect on negotiations with respect to any of the matters mentioned in section 178(2) of TULR(C)A, cause substantial injury to any undertaking of his or any undertaking in which he works.

(2) Where a tribunal or [Employment Judge] decides to hold a hearing or part of one in private, it or he shall give reasons for doing so. [. . .][514]

Case Management Discussions

Conduct of case management discussions

17.—(1) Case management discussions are interim hearings and may deal with matters of procedure and management of the proceedings and they [shall be held in private]. Case management discussions shall be conducted by [an Employment Judge]. [515]

(2) Any determination of a person's civil rights or obligations shall not be dealt with in a case management discussion. The matters listed in rule 10(2) are examples of matters which may be dealt with at case management discussions. Orders and judgments listed in rule 18(7) may not be made at a case management discussion.

Pre-hearing Reviews

Conduct of pre-hearing reviews

18.—(1) Pre-hearing reviews are interim hearings and shall be conducted by [an Employment Judge] unless the circumstances in paragraph (3) are applicable. Subject to rule 16, they shall take place in public.[516]

(2) At a pre-hearing review the [Employment Judge] may carry out a preliminary consideration of the proceedings and he may—[517]

(a) determine any interim or preliminary matter relating to the proceedings;

(b) issue any order in accordance with rule 10 or do anything else which may be done at a case management discussion;

(c) order that a deposit be paid in accordance with rule 20 without hearing evidence;

(d) consider any oral or written representations or evidence;

(e) [. . .][518]

(3) Pre-hearing reviews shall be conducted by a tribunal composed in accordance with section 4(1)[. . .] of the Employment Tribunals Act if—

(a) a party has made a request in writing not less than 10 days before the date on which the pre-hearing review is due to take place that the pre-hearing review be conducted by a tribunal instead of [an Employment Judge]; and

(b) [an Employment Judge] considers that one or more substantive issues of fact are likely to be determined at the pre-hearing review, that it would be desirable for the pre-hearing review to be conducted by a tribunal and he has issued an order that the pre-hearing review be conducted by a tribunal.[519]

(4) If an order is made under paragraph (3), any reference to [an Employment Judge] in relation to a pre-hearing review shall be read as a reference to a tribunal.[520]

(5) Notwithstanding the preliminary or interim nature of a pre-hearing review, at a pre-hearing review the [Employment Judge] may give judgment on any preliminary issue of substance relating to the proceedings. Judgments or orders made at a pre-hearing review may result in the proceedings being struck out or dismissed or otherwise determined with the result that a Hearing is no longer necessary in those proceedings.[521]

(6) Before a judgment or order listed in paragraph (7) is made, notice must be given in accordance with rule 19. The judgments or [orders] listed in paragraph (7) must be made at a pre-hearing review or a

514 As amended by SI 2008/2683, Sch 1 para 255.

515 As amended by SI 2005/1865, reg 2 and by SI 2008/2683, Sch 1 para 255.

516 As amended by SI 2008/2683, Sch 1 para 255.

517 As amended by SI 2008/2683, Sch 1 para 255.

518 Omitted by SI 2008/3240, reg 4(14)(a).

519 As amended by SI 2008/2683, Sch 1 para 255 and by SI 2008/3240, reg 4(14)(b).

520 As amended by SI 2008/2683, Sch 1 para 255.

521 As amended by SI 2008/2683, Sch 1 para 255.

Hearing if one of the parties has so requested. If no such request has been made such judgments or [orders] may be made in the absence of the parties. [522]

(7) Subject to paragraph (6), [an Employment Judge] or tribunal may make a judgment or order:—
- (a) as to the entitlement of any party to bring or contest particular proceedings;
- (b) striking out or amending all or part of any claim or response on the grounds that it is scandalous, or vexatious or has no reasonable prospect of success;
- (c) striking out any claim or response (or part of one) on the grounds that the manner in which the proceedings have been conducted by or on behalf of the claimant or the respondent (as the case may be) has been scandalous, unreasonable or vexatious;
- (d) striking out a claim which has not been actively pursued;
- (e) striking out a claim or response (or part of one) for non-compliance with an order or practice direction;
- (f) striking out a claim where the [Employment Judge] or tribunal considers that it is no longer possible to have a fair Hearing in those proceedings;
- (g) making a restricted reporting order (subject to rule 50).[523]

(8) A claim or response or any part of one may be struck out under these rules only on the grounds stated in sub-paragraphs (7)(b) to (f).

(9) If at a pre-hearing review a requirement to pay a deposit under rule 20 has been considered, the [Employment Judge] who conducted that pre-hearing review shall not be a member of the tribunal at the Hearing in relation to those proceedings.[524]

[Interim relief

18A. —(1) Hearings dealing with interim relief are interim hearings

(2) Subject to the provisions applying to interim relief of TULR(C) A, the Employment Rights Act, and the Employment tribunals Act, these rules shall apply when dealing with the following applications as they apply to pre-hearing reviews—
- (a) an application made under section 161 of TULR(C)A or section 128 of the Employment Rights Act for interim relief;
- (b) an application made under section 165 of TULR(C)A or section 131 of the Employment Rights Act to vary or revote an order.][525]

Notice requirements

19.—(1) Before [an Employment Judge] or a tribunal makes a judgment or order described in rule 18(7), except where the order is one described in rule 13(2) or it is a temporary restricted reporting order made in accordance with rule 50, the Secretary shall send notice to the party against whom it is proposed that the order or judgment should be made. The notice shall inform him of the order or judgment to be considered and give him the opportunity to give reasons why the order or judgment should not be made. This paragraph shall not be taken to require the Secretary to send such notice to that party if that party has been given an opportunity to give reasons orally to the [Employment Judge] or the tribunal as to why the order should not be made.[526]

(2) Where a notice required by paragraph (1) is sent in relation to an order to strike out a claim which has not been actively pursued, unless the contrary is proved, the notice shall be treated as if it were received by the addressee if it has been sent to the address specified in the claim as the address to which notices are to be sent (or to any subsequent replacement for that address which has been notified to the Employment Tribunal Office).

Payment of a Deposit

Requirement to pay a deposit in order to continue with proceedings

20.—(1) At a pre-hearing review if [an Employment Judge] considers that the contentions put forward by any party in relation to a matter required to be determined by a tribunal have little reasonable prospect of success, the [Employment Judge] may make an order against that party requiring the

---

522 As amended by SI 2005/1865, reg 2.
523 As amended by SI 2008/2683, Sch 1 para 255.
524 As amended by SI 2008/2683, Sch 1 para 255.
525 Added by SI 2008/3240, reg 4(15).
526 As amended by SI 2008/2683, Sch 1 para 255.

party to pay a deposit of an amount not exceeding £500 as a condition of being permitted to continue to take part in the proceedings relating to that matter.[527]

(2) No order shall be made under this rule unless the [Employment Judge] has taken reasonable steps to ascertain the ability of the party against whom it is proposed to make the order to comply with such an order, and has taken account of any information so ascertained in determining the amount of the deposit.[528]

(3) An order made under this rule, and the [Employment Judge]'s grounds for making such an order, shall be recorded in a document signed by the [Employment Judge]. A copy of that document shall be sent to each of the parties and shall be accompanied by a note explaining that if the party against whom the order is made persists in making those contentions relating to the matter to which the order relates, he may have an award of costs or preparation time made against him and could lose his deposit.[529]

(4) If a party against whom an order has been made does not pay the amount specified in the order to the Secretary either:—

(a) within the period of 21 days of the day on which the document recording the making of the order is sent to him; or

(b) within such further period, not exceeding 14 days, as the [Employment Judge] may allow in the light of representations made by that party within the period of 21 days;

[an Employment Judge] shall strike out the claim or response of that party or, as the case may be, the part of it to which the order relates.[530]

(5) The deposit paid by a party under an order made under this rule shall be refunded to him in full except where rule 47 applies.

Conciliation

Documents to be sent to conciliators

21. In proceedings brought under the provisions of any enactment providing for conciliation, the Secretary shall send copies of all documents, orders, judgments, written reasons and notices to an ACAS conciliation officer except where the Secretary and ACAS have agreed otherwise.

22—24. [. . .][531]

Withdrawal of Proceedings

Right to withdraw proceedings

25.—(1) A claimant may withdraw all or part of his claim at any time—this may be done either orally at a hearing or in writing in accordance with paragraph (2).

(2) To withdraw a claim or part of one in writing the claimant must inform the Employment Tribunal Office of the claim or the parts of it which are to be withdrawn. Where there is more than one respondent the notification must specify against which respondents the claim is being withdrawn.

(3) The Secretary shall inform all other parties of the withdrawal. Withdrawal takes effect on the date on which the Employment Tribunal Office (in the case of written notifications) or the tribunal (in the case of oral notification) receives notice of it and where the whole claim is withdrawn, subject to paragraph (4), proceedings are brought to an end against the relevant respondent on that date. Withdrawal does not affect proceedings as to costs, preparation time or wasted costs.

(4) Where a claim has been withdrawn, a respondent may make an application to have the proceedings against him dismissed. Such an application must be made by the respondent in writing to the Employment Tribunal Office within 28 days of the notice of the withdrawal being sent to the respondent. If the respondent's application is granted and the proceedings are dismissed[, the claimant may not commence a further claim against the respondent for the same, or substantially the same, cause of action (unless the decision to dismiss is successfully reviewed or appealed).][532]

[527] As amended by SI 2008/2683, Sch 1 para 255.
[528] As amended by SI 2008/2683, Sch 1 para 255.
[529] As amended by SI 2008/2683, Sch 1 para 255.
[530] As amended by SI 2008/2683, Sch 1 para 255.
[531] Omitted by SI 2008/3240, reg 4(16).
[532] As amended by SI 2008/3240, reg 4(17)(a)

(5) The time limit in paragraph (4) may be extended by [an Employment Judge] if he considers it just and equitable to do so.[533]

[Automatic dismissal of proceedings following withdrawal of a claim (or part of a claim) where an ACAS settlement has been reached

25A.—(1) where—

(a) the parties settle the whole or part of the proceedings through ACAS;

(b) the settlement is agreed in writing;

(c) the parties to the settlement have confirmed in the settlement agreement, or otherwise in writing, their understanding that the proceedings covered by the settlement will, following the withdrawal of the claim (or relevant part of the claim) by the claimant, be dismissed; and

(d) the claimant withdraws the whole of, or the part of, the claim that is covered by the settlement by informing the Employment Tribunal Office of the withdrawal in accordance with rule 25(2),

the Employment Judge shall dismiss the proceedings covered by the settlement.

(2) The dismissal shall take place no later than 28 days after the date on which the Employment Tribunal Office receives—

(a) written evidence that the requirement described in sub-paragraph (1)(c) has been satisfied; and

(b) the written notification of withdrawal described in sub-paragraph (1)(d).

(3) If proceedings are dismissed under paragraph (1), the claimant may not commence a further claim against the respondent for the same, or substantially the same, cause of action (unless the decision to dismiss is successfully reviewed or appealed).][534]

The Hearing

Hearings

26.—(1) A Hearing is held for the purpose of determining outstanding procedural or substantive issues or disposing of the proceedings. In any proceedings there may be more than one Hearing and there may be different categories of Hearing, such as a Hearing on liability, remedies, costs (in Scotland, expenses) or preparation time.

(2) Any Hearing of a claim shall be heard by a tribunal composed in accordance with section 4(1) and (2) of the Employment Tribunals Act.

(3) Any Hearing of a claim shall take place in public, subject to rule 16.

[(4) The President, Vice President, or Regional Employment Judge shall fix the date, time and place of the Hearing and the Secretary shall send to each party a notice of the Hearing together with information and guidance as to procedure at the Hearing.][535]

What happens at the Hearing

27.—(1) [. . .][536]

(2) Subject to rule 14(3), at the Hearing a party shall be entitled to give evidence, to call witnesses, to question witnesses and to address the tribunal.

(3) The tribunal shall require parties and witnesses who attend the Hearing to give their evidence on oath or affirmation.

(4) The tribunal may exclude from the Hearing any person who is to appear as a witness in the proceedings until such time as they give evidence if it considers it in the interests of justice to do so.

(5) If a party fails to attend or to be represented (for the purpose of conducting the party's case at the Hearing) at the time and place fixed for the Hearing, the tribunal may dismiss or dispose of the proceedings in the absence of that party or may adjourn the Hearing to a later date.

(6) If the tribunal wishes to dismiss or dispose of proceedings in the circumstances described in paragraph (5), it shall first consider any information in its possession which has been made available to it by the parties.

(7) At a Hearing a tribunal may exercise any powers which may be exercised by [an Employment Judge] under these rules.[537]

---

533 As amended by SI 2008/2683, Sch 1 para 255.

534 Added by SI 2008/3240, reg 4(17)(b) subject to transitional provisions contained in reg 8 of those Regulations.

535 Added by SI 2008/3240, reg 4(18).

536 Omitted by SI 2008/3240, reg 4(19)

537 As amended by SI 2008/2683, Sch 1 para 255.

Orders, Judgments and Reasons

Orders and judgments

28.—(1) [Employment Judges] or tribunals may issue the following—[538]

(a) a 'judgment', which is a final determination of the proceedings or of a particular issue in those proceedings; it may include an award of compensation, a declaration or recommendation and it may also include orders for costs, preparation time or wasted costs;

(b) an 'order', which may be issued in relation to interim matters and it will require a person to do or not to do something.

(2) If the parties agree in writing upon the terms of any order or judgment [an Employment Judge] or tribunal may, if he or it thinks fit, make such order or judgment.[539]

(3) At the end of a hearing the [Employment Judge] (or, as the case may be, the tribunal) shall either issue any order or judgment orally or shall reserve the judgment or order to be given in writing at a later date.[540]

(4) Where a tribunal is composed of three persons any order or judgment may be made or issued by a majority; and if a tribunal is composed of two persons only, the [Employment Judge] has a second or casting vote.[541]

Form and content of judgments

29.—(1) When judgment is reserved a written judgment shall be sent to the parties as soon as practicable. All judgments (whether issued orally or in writing) shall be recorded in writing and signed by the [Employment Judge].[542]

(2) The Secretary shall provide a copy of the judgment to each of the parties and, where the proceedings were referred to the tribunal by a court, to that court. The Secretary shall include guidance to the parties on how the judgment may be reviewed or appealed.

(3) Where the judgment includes an award of compensation or a determination that one party is required to pay a sum to another (excluding an order for costs, expenses, allowances, preparation time or wasted costs), the document shall also contain a statement of the amount of compensation awarded, or of the sum required to be paid.

Reasons

30.—(1) A tribunal or [Employment Judge] must give reasons (either oral or written) for any—[543]

(a) judgment; or

(b) order, if a request for reasons is made before or at the hearing at which the order is made.

(2) Reasons may be given orally at the time of issuing the judgment or order or they may be reserved to be given in writing at a later date. If reasons are reserved, they shall be signed by the [Employment Judge] and sent to the parties by the Secretary.[544]

(3) [[Where oral reasons have been provided], written reasons shall only be provided]:—[545]

(a) in relation to judgments if requested by one of the parties within the time limit set out in paragraph (5); or

(b) in relation to any judgment or order if requested by the Employment Appeal Tribunal at any time.

(4) When written reasons are provided, the Secretary shall send a copy of the reasons to all parties to the proceedings and record the date on which the reasons were sent. Written reasons shall be signed by the [Employment Judge].[546]

(5) A request for written reasons for a judgment must be made by a party either orally at the hearing (if the judgment is issued at a hearing), or in writing within 14 days of the date on which the judgment

[538] As amended by SI 2008/2683, Sch 1 para 255.
[539] As amended by SI 2008/2683, Sch 1 para 255.
[540] As amended by SI 2008/2683, Sch 1 para 255.
[541] As amended by SI 2008/2683, Sch 1 para 255.
[542] As amended by SI 2008/2683, Sch 1 para 255.
[543] As amended by SI 2008/2683, Sch 1 para 255.
[544] As amended by SI 2008/2683, Sch 1 para 255.
[545] As amended by SI 2005/1865, reg 2.
[546] As amended by SI 2008/2683, Sch 1 para 255.

was sent to the parties. This time limit may be extended by [an Employment Judge] where he considers it just and equitable to do so.[547]

(6) Written reasons for a judgment shall include the following information—
  (a) the issues which the tribunal or [Employment Judge] has identified as being relevant to the claim;
  (b) if some identified issues were not determined, what those issues were and why they were not determined;
  (c) findings of fact relevant to the issues which have been determined;
  (d) a concise statement of the applicable law;
  (e) how the relevant findings of fact and applicable law have been applied in order to determine the issues; and
  (f) where the judgment includes an award of compensation or a determination that one party make a payment to the other, a table showing how the amount or sum has been calculated or a description of the manner in which it has been calculated.[548]

Absence of [Employment Judge][549]

31. Where it is not possible for a judgment, order or reasons to be signed by the [Employment Judge] due to death, incapacity or absence—
  (a) if the [Employment Judge] has dealt with the proceedings alone the document shall be signed by the Regional [Employment Judge], Vice President or President when it is practicable for him to do so; and
  (b) if the proceedings have been dealt with by a tribunal composed of two or three persons, the document shall be signed by the other person or persons;

and any person who signs the document shall certify that the [Employment Judge] is unable to sign.[550]

The Register

32.—(1) Subject to rule 49, the Secretary shall enter a copy of the following documents in the Register—
  (a) any judgment (including any costs, expenses, preparation time or wasted costs order); and
  (b) any written reasons provided in accordance with rule 30 in relation to any judgment.

(2) Written reasons for judgments shall be omitted from the Register in any case in which evidence has been heard in private and the tribunal or [Employment Judge] so orders. In such a case the Secretary shall send the reasons to each of the parties and where there are proceedings before a superior court relating to the judgment in question, he shall send the reasons to that court, together with a copy of the entry in the Register of the judgment to which the reasons relate.[551]

Power to Review Judgments and Decisions

Review of default judgments

33.—(1) A party may apply to have a default judgment against or in favour of him reviewed. An application must be made in writing and presented to the Employment Tribunal Office within 14 days of the date on which the default judgment was sent to the parties. The 14 day time limit may be extended by [an Employment Judge] if he considers that it is just and equitable to do so.[552]

(2) The application must state the reasons why the default judgment should be varied or revoked. When it is the respondent applying to have the default judgment reviewed, the application must include with it the respondent's proposed response to the claim, [(where that has not been received by the Employment Tribunal Office)] an application for an extension of the time limit for presenting the response and an explanation (where that has not been received by the Employment Tribunal Office) of why rules 4(1) and (4) were not complied with.[553]

---

547 As amended by SI 2008/2683, Sch 1 para 255.
548 As amended by SI 2008/2683, Sch 1 para 255.
549 As amended by SI 2008/2683, Sch 1 para 255.
550 As amended by SI 2008/2683, Sch 1 para 255.
551 As amended by SI 2008/2683, Sch 1 para 255.
552 As amended by SI 2008/2683, Sch 1 para 255.
553 As amended by SI 2008/3240, reg 4(20(a).

[(2A) An application under paragraph (1) may be given preliminary consideration (without the need to hold a hearing) by an Employment Judge, who may refuse the application if the requirements of paragraph (2) have not been met.][554]

(3) A review of a default judgment shall be conducted by an Employment Judge in public [unless all the parties to the proceedings consent in writing to the review without a hearing]. Notice of the hearing and a copy of the application shall be sent by the Secretary to all other parties.[555]

(4) The [Employment Judge] may—
 (a) refuse the application for a review;
 (b) vary the default judgment;
 (c) revoke all or part of the default judgment;
 (d) confirm the default judgment;

and all parties to the proceedings shall be informed by the Secretary in writing of the [Employment Judge]'s judgment on the application.[556]

(5) A default judgment must be revoked if the whole of the claim was satisfied before the judgment was issued or if rule 8(6) applies. [an Employment Judge] may revoke or vary all or part of a default judgment if the respondent has a reasonable prospect of successfully responding to the claim or part of it.[557]

(6) In considering the application for a review of a default judgment the [Employment Judge] must have regard to whether there was good reason for the response not having been presented within the applicable time limit.[558]

(7) If the [Employment Judge] decides that the default judgment should be varied or revoked and that the respondent should be allowed to respond to the claim the Secretary shall accept the response and proceed in accordance with rule 5(2).[559]

[(8) An Employment Judge may on his own initiative review a default judgment on the grounds listed at rule 34(3)(a), (b) and (e).][560]

Review of other judgments and decisions

34.—(1) Parties may apply to have certain judgments and decisions made by a tribunal or [an Employment Judge] reviewed under rules 34 to 36. Those judgments and decisions are—[561]
 (a) a decision not to accept a claim, response or counterclaim;
 (b) a judgment (other than a default judgment but including an order for costs, expenses, preparation time or wasted costs); and
 (c) a decision made under rule 6(3) of Schedule 4;

and references to 'decision' in rules 34 to 37 are references to the above judgments and decisions only. Other decisions or orders may not be reviewed under these rules.

(2) In relation to a decision not to accept a claim or response, only the party against whom the decision is made may apply to have the decision reviewed.

(3) Subject to paragraph (4), decisions may be reviewed on the following grounds only—
 (a) the decision was wrongly made as a result of an administrative error;
 (b) a party did not receive notice of the proceedings leading to the decision;
 (c) the decision was made in the absence of a party;
 (d) new evidence has become available since the conclusion of the hearing to which the decision relates, provided that its existence could not have been reasonably known of or foreseen at that time; or
 (e) the interests of justice require such a review.

(4) A decision not to accept a claim or response may only be reviewed on the grounds listed in [sub-] paragraphs (3)(a) and (e).[562]

---

554 Added by SI 2008/3240, reg 4(20)(b).
555 As amended by SI 2008/3240, reg 4(20)(c).
556 As amended by SI 2008/2683, Sch 1 para 255.
557 As amended by SI 2008/2683, Sch 1 para 255.
558 As amended by SI 2008/2683, Sch 1 para 255.
559 As amended by SI 2008/2683, Sch 1 para 255.
560 Added by SI 2008/3240, reg 4(20)(d) subject to transitional provisions contained in reg 8 of those Regulations.
561 As amended by SI 2008/2683, Sch 1 para 255.
562 As amended by SI 2008/3240, reg 4(21).

(5) A tribunal or [Employment Judge] may on its or his own initiative review a decision made by it or him on the grounds listed in paragraphs (3) or (4).[563]

Preliminary consideration of application for review

35.—(1) An application under rule 34 to have a decision reviewed must be made to the Employment Tribunal Office within 14 days of the date on which the decision was sent to the parties. The 14 day time limit may be extended by [an Employment Judge] if he considers that it is just and equitable to do so.[564]

(2) The application must be in writing and must identify the grounds of the application in accordance with rule 34(3), but if the decision to be reviewed was made at a hearing, an application may be made orally at that hearing.

(3) The application to have a decision reviewed shall be considered (without the need to hold a hearing) by the [Employment Judge] of the tribunal which made the decision or, if that is not practicable, by—

(a) a Regional [Employment Judge] or the Vice President;

(b) any [Employment Judge] nominated by a Regional [Employment Judge] or the Vice President; or

(c) the President;

and that person shall refuse the application if he considers that there are no grounds for the decision to be reviewed under rule 34(3) or there is no reasonable prospect of the decision being varied or revoked.[565]

(4) If an application for a review is refused after such preliminary consideration the Secretary shall inform the party making the application in writing of the [Employment Judge]'s decision and his reasons for it. If the application for a review is not refused the decision shall be reviewed under rule 36.[566]

The review

36.—(1) When a party has applied for a review and the application has not been refused after the preliminary consideration above, the decision shall be reviewed by the [Employment Judge] or tribunal who made the original decision. If that is not practicable a different [Employment Judge] or tribunal (as the case may be) shall be appointed by a Regional [Employment Judge], the Vice President or the President.[567]

(2) Where no application has been made by a party and the decision is being reviewed on the initiative of the tribunal or [Employment Judge], the review must be carried out by the same tribunal or [Employment Judge] who made the original decision and—

(a) a notice must be sent to each of the parties explaining in summary the grounds upon which it is proposed to review the decision and giving them an opportunity to give reasons why there should be no review; and

(b) such notice must be sent before the expiry of 14 days from the date on which the original decision was sent to the parties.[568]

(3) A tribunal or [Employment Judge] who reviews a decision under paragraph (1) or (2) may confirm, vary or revoke the decision. If the decision is revoked, the tribunal or [Employment Judge] must order the decision to be taken again. When an order is made that the original decision be taken again, if the original decision was taken by [an Employment Judge] without a hearing, the new decision may be taken without hearing the parties and if the original decision was taken at a hearing, a new hearing must be held.[569]

[563] As amended by SI 2008/2683, Sch 1 para 255.
[564] As amended by SI 2008/2683, Sch 1 para 255.
[565] As amended by SI 2008/2683, Sch 1 para 255.
[566] As amended by SI 2008/2683, Sch 1 para 255.
[567] As amended by SI 2008/2683, Sch 1 para 255.
[568] As amended by SI 2008/2683, Sch 1 para 255.
[569] As amended by SI 2008/2683, Sch 1 para 255.

Correction of judgments, decisions or reasons

37.—(1) Clerical mistakes in any order, judgment, decision or reasons, or errors arising in those documents from an accidental slip or omission, may at any time be corrected by certificate by the [Employment Judge], Regional [Employment Judge], Vice President or President.[570]

(2) If a document is corrected by certificate under paragraph (1), or if a decision is revoked or varied under rules 33 or 36 or altered in any way by order of a superior court, the Secretary shall alter any entry in the Register which is so affected to conform with the certificate or order and send a copy of any entry so altered to each of the parties and, if the proceedings have been referred to the tribunal by a court, to that court.

(3) Where a document omitted from the Register under rules 32 or 49 is corrected by certificate under this rule, the Secretary shall send a copy of the corrected document to the parties; and where there are proceedings before any superior court relating to the decision or reasons in question, he shall send a copy to that court together with a copy of the entry in the Register of the decision, if it has been altered under this rule.

(4) In Scotland, the references in paragraphs (2) and (3) to superior courts shall be read as referring to appellate courts.

Costs Orders and Orders for Expenses

General power to make costs and expenses orders

38.—(1) Subject to paragraph (2) and in the circumstances listed in rules 39, 40 and 47 a tribunal or [Employment Judge] may make an order ('a costs order') that—[571]

(a) a party ('the paying party') make a payment in respect of the costs incurred by another party ('the receiving party');

(b) the paying party pay to the Secretary of State, in whole or in part, any allowances (other than allowances paid to members of tribunals) paid by the Secretary of State under section 5(2) or (3) of the Employment Tribunals Act to any person for the purposes of, or in connection with, that person's attendance at the tribunal.

(2) A costs order may be made under rules 39, 40 and 47 only where the receiving party has been legally represented at the Hearing or, in proceedings which are determined without a Hearing, if the receiving party is legally represented when the proceedings are determined. If the receiving party has not been so legally represented a tribunal [or [Employment Judge]] may make a preparation time order (subject to rules 42 to 45). (See rule 46 on the restriction on making a costs order and a preparation time order in the same proceedings.)[572]

(3) For the purposes of these rules 'costs' shall mean fees, charges, disbursements or expenses incurred by or on behalf of a party, in relation to the proceedings. In Scotland all references to costs (except when used in the expression 'wasted costs') or costs orders shall be read as references to expenses or orders for expenses.

(4) A costs order may be made against or in favour of a respondent who has not had a response accepted in the proceedings in relation to the conduct of any part which he has taken in the proceedings.

(5) In these rules legally represented means having the assistance of a person (including where that person is the receiving party's employee) who—

(a) has a general qualification within the meaning of section 71 of the Courts and Legal Services Act 1990;

(b) is an advocate or solicitor in Scotland; or

(c) is a member of the Bar of Northern Ireland or a solicitor of the Supreme Court of Northern Ireland.

(6) Any costs order made under rules 39, 40 or 47 shall be payable by the paying party and not his representative.

(7) A party may apply for a costs order to be made at any time during the proceedings. An application may be made at the end of a hearing, or in writing to the Employment Tribunal Office. An application for costs which is received by the Employment Tribunal Office later than 28 days from

[570] As amended by SI 2008/2683, Sch 1 para 255.

[571] As amended by SI 2008/2683, Sch 1 para 255.

[572] As amended by SI 2005/1865, reg 2 and by SI 2008/2683, Sch 1 para 255.

the issuing of the judgment determining the claim shall not be accepted or considered by a tribunal or [Employment Judge] unless it or he considers that it is in the interests of justice to do so.[573]

(8) In paragraph (7), the date of issuing of the judgment determining the claim shall be either—
   (a) the date of the Hearing if the judgment was issued orally; or
   (b) if the judgment was reserved, the date on which the written judgment was sent to the parties.

(9) No costs order shall be made unless the Secretary has sent notice to the party against whom the order may be made giving him the opportunity to give reasons why the order should not be made. This paragraph shall not be taken to require the Secretary to send notice to that party if the party has been given an opportunity to give reasons orally to the [Employment Judge] or tribunal as to why the order should not be made.[574]

(10) Where a tribunal or [Employment Judge] makes a costs order it or he shall provide written reasons for doing so if a request for written reasons is made within 14 days of the date of the costs order. The Secretary shall send a copy of the written reasons to all parties to the proceedings.[575]

When a costs or expenses order must be made

39.—(1) Subject to rule 38(2), a tribunal [or [Employment Judge]] must make a costs order against a respondent where in proceedings for unfair dismissal a Hearing has been postponed or adjourned and—[576]
   (a) the claimant has expressed a wish to be reinstated or re-engaged which has been communicated to the respondent not less than 7 days before the Hearing; and
   (b) the postponement or adjournment of that Hearing has been caused by the respondent's failure, without a special reason, to adduce reasonable evidence as to the availability of the job from which the claimant was dismissed, or of comparable or suitable employment.

(2) A costs order made under paragraph (1) shall relate to any costs incurred as a result of the postponement or adjournment of the Hearing.

When a costs or expenses order may be made

40.—(1) A tribunal or [Employment Judge] may make a costs order when on the application of a party it has postponed the day or time fixed for or adjourned a Hearing or pre-hearing review. The costs order may be against or, as the case may require, in favour of that party as respects any costs incurred or any allowances paid as a result of the postponement or adjournment.[577]

(2) A tribunal or [Employment Judge] shall consider making a costs order against a paying party where, in the opinion of the tribunal or [Employment Judge] (as the case may be), any of the circumstances in paragraph (3) apply. Having so considered, the tribunal or [Employment Judge] may make a costs order against the paying party if it or he considers it appropriate to do so.[578]

(3) The circumstances referred to in paragraph (2) are where the paying party has in bringing the proceedings, or he or his representative has in conducting the proceedings, acted vexatiously, abusively, disruptively or otherwise unreasonably, or the bringing or conducting of the proceedings by the paying party has been misconceived.

(4) A tribunal or [Employment Judge] may make a costs order against a party who has not complied with an order or practice direction.[579]

The amount of a costs or expenses order

41.—(1) The amount of a costs order against the paying party shall be determined in any of the following ways—
   (a) the tribunal may specify the sum which the paying party must pay to the receiving party, provided that sum does not exceed £10,000;
   (b) the parties may agree on a sum to be paid by the paying party to the receiving party and if they do so the costs order shall be for the sum so agreed;

[573] As amended by SI 2008/2683, Sch 1 para 255.
[574] As amended by SI 2008/2683, Sch 1 para 255.
[575] As amended by SI 2008/2683, Sch 1 para 255.
[576] As amended by SI 2005/1865, reg 2 and by SI 2008/2683, Sch 1 para 255.
[577] As amended by SI 2008/2683, Sch 1 para 255.
[578] As amended by SI 2008/2683, Sch 1 para 255.
[579] As amended by SI 2008/2683, Sch 1 para 255.

(c) the tribunal may order the paying party to pay the receiving party the whole or a specified part of the costs of the receiving party with the amount to be paid being determined by way of detailed assessment in a County Court in accordance with the Civil Procedure Rules 1998 or, in Scotland, as taxed according to such part of the table of fees prescribed for proceedings in the sheriff court as shall be directed by the order.

(2) The tribunal or [Employment Judge] may have regard to the paying party's ability to pay when considering whether it or he shall make a costs order or how much that order should be.[580]

(3) For the avoidance of doubt, the amount of a costs order made under paragraphs (1)(b) or (c) may exceed £10,000.

Preparation Time Orders

General power to make preparation time orders

42.—(1) Subject to paragraph (2) and in the circumstances described in rules 43, 44 and 47 a tribunal or [Employment Judge] may make an order ('a preparation time order') that a party ('the paying party') make a payment in respect of the preparation time of another party ('the receiving party').[581]

(2) A preparation time order may be made under rules 43, 44 or 47 only where the receiving party has not been legally represented at a Hearing or, in proceedings which are determined without a Hearing, if the receiving party has not been legally represented when the proceedings are determined. (See: rules 38 to 41 on when a costs order may be made; rule 38(5) for the definition of legally represented; and rule 46 on the restriction on making a costs order and a preparation time order in the same proceedings.)

(3) For the purposes of these rules preparation time shall mean time spent by—

(a) the receiving party or his employees carrying out preparatory work directly relating to the proceedings; and

(b) the receiving party's legal or other advisers relating to the conduct of the proceedings;

up to but not including time spent at any Hearing.

(4) A preparation time order may be made against a respondent who has not had a response accepted in the proceedings in relation to the conduct of any part which he has taken in the proceedings.

(5) A party may apply to the tribunal for a preparation time order to be made at any time during the proceedings. An application may be made at the end of a hearing or in writing to the Secretary. An application for preparation time which is received by the Employment Tribunal Office later than 28 days from the issuing of the judgment determining the claim shall not be accepted or considered by a tribunal or [Employment Judge] unless they consider that it is in the interests of justice to do so.[582]

(6) In paragraph (5) the date of issuing of the judgment determining the claim shall be either—

(a) the date of the Hearing if the judgment was issued orally; or,

(b) if the judgment was reserved, the date on which the written judgment was sent to the parties.

(7) No preparation time order shall be made unless the Secretary has sent notice to the party against whom the order may be made giving him the opportunity to give reasons why the order should not be made. This paragraph shall not be taken to require the Secretary to send notice to that party if the party has been given an opportunity to give reasons orally to the [Employment Judge] or tribunal as to why the order should not be made.[583]

(8) Where a tribunal or [Employment Judge] makes a preparation time order it or he shall provide written reasons for doing so if a request for written reasons is made within 14 days of the date of the preparation time order. The Secretary shall send a copy of the written reasons to all parties to the proceedings.[584]

---

[580] As amended by SI 2008/2683, Sch 1 para 255.

[581] As amended by SI 2008/2683, Sch 1 para 255.

[582] As amended by SI 2008/2683, Sch 1 para 255.

[583] As amended by SI 2008/2683, Sch 1 para 255.

[584] As amended by SI 2008/2683, Sch 1 para 255.

When a preparation time order must be made

43.—(1) Subject to rule 42(2), a tribunal [or [Employment Judge]] must make a preparation time order against a respondent where in proceedings for unfair dismissal a Hearing has been postponed or adjourned and—[585]

(a) the claimant has expressed a wish to be reinstated or re-engaged which has been communicated to the respondent not less than 7 days before the Hearing; and

(b) the postponement or adjournment of that Hearing has been caused by the respondent's failure, without a special reason, to adduce reasonable evidence as to the availability of the job from which the claimant was dismissed, or of comparable or suitable employment.

(2) A preparation time order made under paragraph (1) shall relate to any preparation time spent as a result of the postponement or adjournment of the Hearing.

When a preparation time order may be made

44.—(1) A tribunal or [Employment Judge] may make a preparation time order when on the application of a party it has postponed the day or time fixed for or adjourned a Hearing or a pre-hearing review. The preparation time order may be against or, as the case may require, in favour of that party as respects any preparation time spent as a result of the postponement or adjournment.[586]

(2) A tribunal or [Employment Judge] shall consider making a preparation time order against a party (the paying party) where, in the opinion of the tribunal or the [Employment Judge] (as the case may be), any of the circumstances in paragraph (3) apply. Having so considered the tribunal or [Employment Judge] may make a preparation time order against that party if it considers it appropriate to do so.[587]

(3) The circumstances described in paragraph (2) are where the paying party has in bringing the proceedings, or he or his representative has in conducting the proceedings, acted vexatiously, abusively, disruptively or otherwise unreasonably, or the bringing or conducting of the proceedings by the paying party has been misconceived.

(4) A tribunal or [Employment Judge] may make a preparation time order against a party who has not complied with an order or practice direction.[588]

Calculation of a preparation time order

45.—(1) In order to calculate the amount of preparation time the tribunal or [Employment Judge] shall make an assessment of the number of hours spent on preparation time on the basis of—

(a) information on time spent provided by the receiving party; and

(b) the tribunal or [Employment Judge]'s own assessment of what it or he considers to be a reasonable and proportionate amount of time to spend on such preparatory work and with reference to, for example, matters such as the complexity of the proceedings, the number of witnesses and documentation required.[589]

(2) Once the tribunal or [Employment Judge] has assessed the number of hours spent on preparation time in accordance with paragraph (1), it or he shall calculate the amount of the award to be paid to the receiving party by applying an hourly rate of £25.00 to that figure (or such other figure calculated in accordance with paragraph (4)). No preparation time order made under these rules may exceed the sum of £10,000.[590]

(3) The tribunal or [Employment Judge] may have regard to the paying party's ability to pay when considering whether it or he shall make a preparation time order or how much that order should be.[591]

(4) For the year commencing on 6th April 2006, the hourly rate of £25 shall be increased by the sum of £1.00 and for each subsequent year commencing on 6 April, the hourly rate for the previous year shall also be increased by the sum of £1.00.

585 As amended by SI 2005/1865, reg 2 and by SI 2008/2683, Sch 1 para 255.
586 As amended by SI 2008/2683, Sch 1 para 255.
587 As amended by SI 2008/2683, Sch 1 para 255.
588 As amended by SI 2008/2683, Sch 1 para 255.
589 As amended by SI 2008/2683, Sch 1 para 255.
590 As amended by SI 2008/2683, Sch 1 para 255.
591 As amended by SI 2008/2683, Sch 1 para 255.

Restriction on making costs or expenses orders and preparation time orders

46.—(1) A tribunal or [Employment Judge] may not make a preparation time order and a costs order in favour of the same party in the same proceedings. However where a preparation time order is made in favour of a party in proceedings, the tribunal or [Employment Judge] may make a costs order in favour of another party or in favour of the Secretary of State under rule 38(1)(b) in the same proceedings.[592]

(2) If a tribunal or [an Employment Judge] wishes to make either a costs order or a preparation time order in proceedings, before the claim has been determined, it or he may make an order that either costs or preparation time be awarded to the receiving party. In such circumstances a tribunal or [Employment Judge] may decide whether the award should be for costs or preparation time after the proceedings have been determined.[593]

Costs, expenses or preparation time orders when a deposit has been taken

47.—(1) When:—

(a) a party has been ordered under rule 20 to pay a deposit as a condition of being permitted to continue to participate in proceedings relating to a matter;

(b) in respect of that matter, the tribunal or [Employment Judge] has found against that party in its or his judgment; and

(c) no award of costs or preparation time has been made against that party arising out of the proceedings on the matter;

the tribunal or [Employment Judge] shall consider whether to make a costs or preparation time order against that party on the ground that he conducted the proceedings relating to the matter unreasonably in persisting in having the matter determined; but the tribunal or [Employment Judge] shall not make a costs or preparation time order on that ground unless it has considered the document recording the order under rule 20 and is of the opinion that the grounds which caused the tribunal or [Employment Judge] to find against the party in its judgment were substantially the same as the grounds recorded in that document for considering that the contentions of the party had little reasonable prospect of success.[594]

(2) When a costs or preparation time order is made against a party who has had an order under rule 20 made against him (whether the award arises out of the proceedings relating to the matter in respect of which the order was made or out of proceedings relating to any other matter considered with that matter), his deposit shall be paid in part or full settlement of the costs or preparation time order—

(a) when an order is made in favour of one party, to that party; and

(b) when orders are made in favour of more than one party, to all of them or any one or more of them as the tribunal or [Employment Judge] thinks fit, and if to all or more than one, in such proportions as the tribunal or [Employment Judge] considers appropriate;

and if the amount of the deposit exceeds the amount of the costs or preparation time order, the balance shall be refunded to the party who paid it.[595]

Wasted Costs Orders Against Representatives

Personal liability of representatives for costs

48.—(1) A tribunal or [Employment Judge] may make a wasted costs order against a party's representative.[596]

(2) In a wasted costs order the tribunal or [Employment Judge] may:—

(a) disallow, or order the representative of a party to meet the whole or part of any wasted costs of any party, including an order that the representative repay to his client any costs which have already been paid; and

(b) order the representative to pay to the Secretary of State, in whole or in part, any allowances (other than allowances paid to members of tribunals) paid by the Secretary of State under section 5(2)

592 As amended by SI 2008/2683, Sch 1 para 255.

593 As amended by SI 2008/2683, Sch 1 para 255.

594 As amended by SI 2008/2683, Sch 1 para 255.

595 As amended by SI 2008/2683, Sch 1 para 255.

596 As amended by SI 2008/2683, Sch 1 para 255.

or (3) of the Employment Tribunals Act to any person for the purposes of, or in connection with, that person's attendance at the tribunal by reason of the representative's conduct of the proceedings.[597]

(3) 'Wasted costs' means any costs incurred by a party:—
(a) as a result of any improper, unreasonable or negligent act or omission on the part of any representative; or
(b) which, in the light of any such act or omission occurring after they were incurred, the tribunal considers it unreasonable to expect that party to pay.

(4) In this rule 'representative' means a party's legal or other representative or any employee of such representative, but it does not include a representative who is not acting in pursuit of profit with regard to those proceedings. A person is considered to be acting in pursuit of profit if he is acting on a conditional fee arrangement.

(5) A wasted costs order may be made in favour of a party whether or not that party is legally represented and such an order may also be made in favour of a representative's own client. A wasted costs order may not be made against a representative where that representative is an employee of a party.

(6) Before making a wasted costs order, the tribunal or [Employment Judge] shall give the representative a reasonable opportunity to make oral or written representations as to reasons why such an order should not be made. [The tribunal or [Employment Judge] may also have regard to the representative's ability to pay] when considering whether it shall make a wasted costs order or how much that order should be.[598]

(7) When a tribunal or [Employment Judge] makes a wasted costs order, it must specify in the order the amount to be disallowed or paid.

(8) The Secretary shall inform the representative's client in writing:—
(a) of any proceedings under this rule; or
(b) of any order made under this rule against the party's representative.[599]

(9) Where a tribunal or [Employment Judge] makes a wasted costs order it or he shall provide written reasons for doing so if a request is made for written reasons within 14 days of the date of the wasted costs order. This 14 day time limit may not be extended under rule 10. The Secretary shall send a copy of the written reasons to all parties to the proceedings.[600]

Powers in Relation to Specific Types of Proceedings

Sexual offences and the Register

49. In any proceedings appearing to involve allegations of the commission of a sexual offence the tribunal, the [Employment Judge] or the Secretary shall omit from the Register, or delete from the Register or any judgment, document or record of the proceedings, which is available to the public, any identifying matter which is likely to lead members of the public to identify any person affected by or making such an allegation.[601]

Restricted reporting orders

50.—(1) A restricted reporting order may be made in the following types of proceedings:—
(a) any case which involves allegations of sexual misconduct;
(b) a complaint under section 17A or 25(8) of the Disability Discrimination Act in which evidence of a personal nature is likely to be heard by the tribunal or [an Employment Judge].[602]

(2) A party (or where a complaint is made under the Disability Discrimination Act, the complainant) may apply for a restricted reporting order (either temporary or full) in writing to the Employment Tribunal Office, or orally at a hearing, or the tribunal or [Employment Judge] may make the order on its or his own initiative without any application having been made.[603]

(3) [An Employment Judge] or tribunal may make a temporary restricted reporting order without holding a hearing or sending a copy of the application to other parties.[604]

---

[597] As amended by SI 2008/2683, Sch 1 para 255.
[598] As amended by SI 2005/1865, reg 2 and by SI 2008/2683, Sch 1 para 255.
[599] As amended by SI 2008/2683, Sch 1 para 255.
[600] As amended by SI 2008/2683, Sch 1 para 255.
[601] As amended by SI 2008/2683, Sch 1 para 255.
[602] As amended by SI 2008/2683, Sch 1 para 255.
[603] As amended by SI 2008/2683, Sch 1 para 255.
[604] As amended by SI 2008/2683, Sch 1 para 255.

(4) Where a temporary restricted reporting order has been made the Secretary shall inform all parties to the proceedings in writing as soon as possible of—
(a) the fact that the order has been made; and
(b) their right to apply to have the temporary restricted reporting order revoked or converted into a full restricted reporting order within 14 days of the temporary order having been made.

(5) If no application under [sub-]paragraph (4)(b) is made within the 14 days, the temporary restricted reporting order shall lapse and cease to have any effect on the fifteenth day after the order was made. If such an application is made the temporary restricted reporting order shall continue to have effect until the pre-hearing review or Hearing at which the application is considered.[605]

(6) All parties must be given an opportunity to advance oral argument at a pre-hearing review or a Hearing before a tribunal or [Employment Judge] decides whether or not to make a full restricted reporting order (whether or not there was previously a temporary restricted reporting order in the proceedings).[606]

(7) Any person may make an application to the [Employment Judge] or tribunal to have a right to make representations before a full restricted reporting order is made. The [Employment Judge] or tribunal shall allow such representations to be made where he or it considers that the applicant has a legitimate interest in whether or not the order is made.[607]

(8) Where a tribunal or [Employment Judge] makes a restricted reporting order—
(a) it shall specify in the order the persons who may not be identified;
(b) a full order shall remain in force until both liability and remedy have been determined in the proceedings unless it is revoked earlier; and
(c) the Secretary shall ensure that a notice of the fact that a restricted reporting order has been made in relation to those proceedings is displayed on the notice board of the employment tribunal with any list of the proceedings taking place before the employment tribunal, and on the door of the room in which the proceedings affected by the order are taking place.[608]

(9) Where a restricted reporting order has been made under this rule and that complaint is being dealt with together with any other proceedings, the tribunal or [Employment Judge] may order that the restricted reporting order applies also in relation to those other proceedings or a part of them.[609]

(10) A tribunal or [Employment Judge] may revoke a restricted reporting order at any time.[610]

(11) For the purposes of this rule liability and remedy are determined in the proceedings on the date recorded as being the date on which the judgment disposing of the claim was sent to the parties, and references to a restricted reporting order include references to both a temporary and a full restricted reporting order.

Proceedings involving the National Insurance Fund

51. The Secretary of State shall be entitled to appear as if she were a party and be heard at any hearing in relation to proceedings which may involve a payment out of the National Insurance Fund, and in that event she shall be treated for the purposes of these rules as if she were a party.

General Provisions

Powers

60.—(1) Subject to the provisions of these rules and any practice directions, a tribunal or [Employment Judge] may regulate its or his own procedure.[611]

(2) At a Hearing, or a pre-hearing review held in accordance with rule 18(3), a tribunal may make any order which [an Employment Judge] has power to make under these rules, subject to compliance with any relevant notice or other procedural requirements.[612]

(3) Any function of the Secretary may be performed by a person acting with the authority of the Secretary.

[605] As amended by SI 2008/3240, reg 4(22).
[606] As amended by SI 2008/2683, Sch 1 para 255.
[607] As amended by SI 2008/2683, Sch 1 para 255.
[608] As amended by SI 2008/2683, Sch 1 para 255.
[609] As amended by SI 2008/2683, Sch 1 para 255.
[610] As amended by SI 2008/2683, Sch 1 para 255.
[611] As amended by SI 2008/2683, Sch 1 para 255.
[612] As amended by SI 2008/2683, Sch 1 para 255.

[(4) Where the Attorney-General, or Lord Advocate, makes a request to search for, inspect and take a copy of any relevant documents within a case file (including documents held electronically) for the purposes of preparing or considering whether to make an application under section 42 of the Supreme Court Act 1981, (or where the request is made by the Lord Advocate, section 1 of the Vexatious Actions (Scotland) Act 1898) or section 33 of the Employment Tribunals Act 1996 (restriction of vexatious proceedings), the Secretary shall send notice of or a copy of any relevant document which relates to any proceedings before the tribunal, or any decision, order or award of the tribunal.][613]

SCHEDULE 6 [614]

Regulation 16(4)

THE EMPLOYMENT TRIBUNALS (EQUAL VALUE) RULES OF PROCEDURE

General

1. The rules in this Schedule shall only apply in proceedings involving an equal value claim and they modify and supplement the rules in Schedule 1. If there is conflict between Schedule 1 and this Schedule, the provisions of this Schedule shall prevail.

Interpretation

2.—(1) In this Schedule and in relation to proceedings to which this Schedule applies:

'comparator' means the person of the opposite sex to the claimant in relation to whom the claimant claims that his work is of equal value as described in section 1(2)(c) of the Equal Pay Act;

'Equal Pay Act' means the Equal Pay Act 1970;

'equal value claim' means a claim by a claimant which rests upon entitlement to the benefit of an equality clause by virtue of the operation of section 1(2)(c) of the Equal Pay Act;

'the facts relating to the question' has the meaning in rule 7(3);

'independent expert' means a member of the panel of independent experts mentioned in section 2A(4) of the Equal Pay Act;

'indicative timetable' means the indicative timetable set out in the Annex to this Schedule;

'the question' means whether the claimant's work is of equal value to that of the comparator as described in section 1(2)(c) of the Equal Pay Act; and

'report' means a report required by a tribunal to be prepared by an independent expert, in accordance with section 2A(1)(b) of the Equal Pay Act.

(2) A reference in this Schedule to a rule, is a reference to a rule in this Schedule unless otherwise provided.

(3) A reference in this Schedule to 'these rules' is a reference to the rules in Schedules 1 and 6 unless otherwise provided.

General power to manage proceedings

3.—(1) In addition to the power to make orders described in rule 10 of Schedule 1, the tribunal or [Employment Judge] shall have power (subject to rules 4(3) and 7(4)) to make the following orders:

(a) the standard orders set out in rules 5 or 8, with such addition to, omission or variation of those orders (including specifically variations as to the periods within which actions are to be taken by the parties) as the [Employment Judge] or tribunal considers is appropriate;

(b) that no new facts shall be admitted in evidence by the tribunal unless they have been disclosed to all other parties in writing before a date specified by the tribunal (unless it was not reasonably practicable for a party to have done so);

(c) that the parties may be required to send copies of documents or provide information to the other parties and to the independent expert;

(d) that the respondent is required to grant the independent expert access to his premises during a period specified by the tribunal or [Employment Judge] in order for the independent expert to conduct interviews with persons identified as relevant by the independent expert;

[613] Added by SI 2008/3240, reg 4(24).

[614] Inserted by SI 2004/2351, reg 2(11).

(e) when more than one expert is to give evidence in the proceedings, that those experts present to the tribunal a joint statement of matters which are agreed between them and those matters on which they disagree;

(f) where proceedings have been joined, that lead claimants be identified.[615]

(2) Any reference in Schedule 1 or 2 to an order made under rule 10 of Schedule 1 shall include reference to an order made in accordance with this Schedule.

Conduct of stage 1 equal value hearing

4.—(1) When in an equal value claim there is a dispute as to whether any work is of equal value as mentioned in section 1(2)(c) of the Equal Pay Act, the tribunal shall conduct a 'stage 1 equal value hearing' in accordance with both this rule and the rules applicable to pre-hearing reviews in Schedule 1.

(2) [. . .][616]

(3) At the stage 1 equal value hearing the [Employment Judge or] tribunal shall: [617]

(a) where section 2A(2) of the Equal Pay Act applies, strike out the claim (or the relevant part of it) if, in accordance with section 2A(2A) of that Act, the tribunal must determine that the work of the claimant and the comparator are not of equal value;

(b) decide, in accordance with section 2A(1) of the Equal Pay Act, either that:

(i) the tribunal shall determine the question; or

(ii) it shall require a member of the panel of independent experts to prepare a report with respect to the question;

(c) subject to rule 5 and with regard to the indicative timetable, make the standard orders for the stage 1 equal value hearing as set out in rule 5;

(d) if the tribunal has decided to require an independent expert to prepare a report on the question, require the parties to copy to the independent expert all information which they are required by an order to disclose or agree between each other;

(e) if the tribunal has decided to require an independent expert to prepare a report on the question, fix a date for the stage 2 equal value hearing, having regard to the indicative timetable;

(f) if the tribunal has not decided to require an independent expert to prepare a report on the question, fix a date for the Hearing, having regard to the indicative timetable;

(g) consider whether any further orders are appropriate.

(4) Before a claim or part of one is struck out under [sub-]paragraph (3)(a), the Secretary shall send notice to the claimant giving him the opportunity to make representations to the tribunal as to whether the evaluation contained in the study in question falls within paragraph (a) or (b) of section 2A(2A) of the Equal Pay Act. The Secretary shall not be required to send a notice under this paragraph if the claimant has been given an opportunity to make such representations orally to the tribunal as to why such a judgment should not be issued.[618]

(5) The tribunal may, on the application of a party, hear evidence upon and permit the parties to address it upon the issue contained in section 1(3) of the Equal Pay Act (defence of a genuine material factor) before determining whether to require an independent expert to prepare a report under paragraph (3)(b)(ii).

(6) When the Secretary gives notice to the parties of the stage 1 equal value hearing under rule 14(4) of Schedule 1, he shall also give the parties notice of the matters which the tribunal may and shall consider at that hearing which are described in paragraphs (3) and (5) of this rule and he shall give the parties notice of the standard orders in rule 5.

(7) The tribunal's power to strike out the claim or part of it under [sub-]paragraph (3)(a) is in addition to powers to strike out a claim under rule 18(7) of Schedule 1.[619]

---

[615] As amended by SI 2008/2683, Sch 1 para 259.

[616] Omitted by SI 2008/3240, reg 7(2) subject to a transitional provision contained in reg 12 of those Regulations.

[617] As amended by SI 2008/3240, reg 7(3) subject to a transitional provision contained in reg 12 of those Regulations.

[618] As amended by SI 2008/3240, reg 7(4).

[619] As amended by SI 2008/3240, reg 7(4).

Standard orders for stage 1 equal value hearing

5.—(1) At a stage 1 equal value hearing a tribunal shall, unless it considers it inappropriate to do so and subject to paragraph (2), order that:

(a) before the end of the period of 14 days after the date of the stage 1 equal value hearing the claimant shall:

(i) disclose in writing to the respondent the name of any comparator, or, if the claimant is not able to name the comparator he shall instead disclose such information as enables the comparator to be identified by the respondent; and

(ii) identify to the respondent in writing the period in relation to which he considers that the claimant's work and that of the comparator are to be compared;

(b) before the end of the period of 28 days after the date of the stage 1 equal value hearing:

(i) where the claimant has not disclosed the name of the comparator to the respondent under sub-paragraph (a), if the respondent has been provided with sufficient detail to be able to identify the comparator, he shall disclose in writing the name of the comparator to the claimant;

(ii) the parties shall provide each other with written job descriptions for the claimant and any comparator;

(iii) the parties shall identify to each other in writing the facts which they consider to be relevant to the question;

(c) the respondent is required to grant access to the claimant and his representative (if any) to his premises during a period specified by the tribunal or [Employment Judge] in order for him or them to interview any comparator;[620]

(d) the parties shall before the end of the period of 56 days after the date of the stage 1 equal value hearing present to the tribunal a joint agreed statement in writing of the following matters:

(i) job descriptions for the claimant and any comparator;

(ii) facts which both parties consider are relevant to the question;

(iii) facts on which the parties disagree (as to the fact or as to the relevance to the question) and a summary of their reasons for disagreeing;

(e) the parties shall, at least 56 days prior to the Hearing, disclose to each other, to any independent or other expert and to the tribunal written statements of any facts on which they intend to rely in evidence at the Hearing; and

(f) the parties shall, at least 28 days prior to the Hearing, present to the tribunal a statement of facts and issues on which the parties are in agreement, a statement of facts and issues on which the parties disagree and a summary of their reasons for disagreeing.

(2) Any of the standard orders for the stage 1 equal value hearing may be added to, varied or omitted as the tribunal considers appropriate.

Involvement of independent expert in fact finding

6.—(1) This rule applies only to proceedings in relation to which the tribunal has decided to require an independent expert to prepare a report on the question.

(2) In proceedings to which this rule applies a tribunal or [Employment Judge] may if it or he considers it appropriate at any stage of the proceedings order an independent expert to assist the tribunal in establishing the facts on which the independent expert may rely in preparing his report.[621]

(3) Examples of the circumstances in which the tribunal or [Employment Judge] may make an order described in paragraph (2) may include:

(a) a party not being legally represented;

(b) the parties are unable to reach agreement as required by an order of the tribunal or [Employment Judge];

(c) the tribunal or [Employment Judge] considers that insufficient information may have been disclosed by a party and this may impair the ability of the independent expert to prepare a report on the question;

(d) the tribunal or [Employment Judge] considers that the involvement of the independent expert may promote fuller compliance with orders made by the tribunal or [an Employment Judge].[622]

---

[620] As amended by SI 2008/2683, Sch 1 para 259.

[621] As amended by SI 2008/2683, Sch 1 para 259.

[622] As amended by SI 2008/2683, Sch 1 para 259.

(4) A party to proceedings to which this rule applies may make an application under rule 11 of Schedule 1 for an order under paragraph (2).

Conduct of stage 2 equal value hearing

7.—(1) This rule applies only to proceedings in relation to which the tribunal has decided to require an independent expert to prepare a report on the question. In such proceedings the tribunal shall conduct a 'stage 2 equal value hearing' in accordance with both this rule and the rules applicable to pre-hearing reviews in Schedule 1.

(2) Notwithstanding rule 18(1) and (3) of Schedule 1, a stage 2 equal value hearing shall be [conducted by a tribunal] composed in accordance with section 4(1) of the Employment Tribunals Act.[623]

(3) At the stage 2 equal value hearing the tribunal shall make a determination of facts on which the parties cannot agree which relate to the question and shall require the independent expert to prepare his report on the basis of facts which have (at any stage of the proceedings) either been agreed between the parties or determined by the tribunal (referred to as 'the facts relating to the question').

(4) At the stage 2 equal value hearing the tribunal shall:
- (a) [subject] to rule 8 and having regard to the indicative timetable, make the standard orders for the stage 2 equal value hearing as set out in rule 8;[624]
- (b) make any orders which it considers appropriate;
- (c) fix a date for the Hearing, having regard to the indicative timetable.

(5) Subject to paragraph (6), the facts relating to the question shall, in relation to the question, be the only facts on which the tribunal shall rely at the Hearing.

(6) At any stage of the proceedings the independent expert may make an application to the tribunal for [. . .] some or all of the facts relating to the question to be amended, supplemented or omitted.[625]

(7) When the Secretary gives notice to the parties and to the independent expert of the stage 2 equal value hearing under rule 14(4) of Schedule 1, he shall also give the parties notice of the standard orders in rule 8 and draw the attention of the parties to paragraphs (4) and (5) of this rule.

Standard orders for stage 2 equal value hearing

8.—(1) At a stage 2 equal value hearing a tribunal shall, unless it considers it inappropriate to do so and subject to paragraph (2), order that:
- (a) by a date specified by the tribunal (with regard to the indicative timetable) the independent expert shall prepare his report on the question and shall (subject to rule 14) have sent copies of it to the parties and to the tribunal; and
- (b) the independent expert shall prepare his report on the question on the basis of the facts relating to the question and no other facts which may or may not relate to the question.

(2) Any of the standard orders for the stage 2 equal value hearing may be added to, varied or omitted as the tribunal considers appropriate.

The Hearing

9.—(1)In proceedings in relation to which an independent expert has prepared a report, unless the tribunal determines that the report is not based on the facts relating to the question, the report of the independent expert shall be admitted in evidence in those proceedings.

(2) If the tribunal does not admit the report of an independent expert in accordance with paragraph (1), it may determine the question itself or require another independent expert to prepare a report on the question.

(3) The tribunal may refuse to admit evidence of facts or hear argument as to issues which have not been disclosed to the other party as required by these rules or any order made under them, unless it was not reasonably practicable for the party to have so complied.

Duties and powers of the independent expert

10.—(1) When a tribunal requires an independent expert to prepare a report with respect to the question or an order is made under rule 6(2), the Secretary shall inform that independent expert of the duties and powers he has under this rule.

---

623 As amended by SI 2005/1865, reg 2(6)(a).

624 As amended by SI 2005/1865, reg 2(6)(b).

625 As amended by SI 2005/1865, reg 2(6)(c).

(2) The independent expert shall have a duty to the tribunal to:
(a) assist it in furthering the overriding objective in regulation 3;
(b) comply with the requirements of these rules and any orders made by the tribunal or [an Employment Judge] in relation to the proceedings;
(c) keep the tribunal informed of any delay in complying with any order in the proceedings with the exception of minor or insignificant delays in compliance;
(d) comply with any timetable imposed by the tribunal or [Employment Judge] in so far as this is reasonably practicable;
(e) inform the tribunal or [an Employment Judge] on request by it or him of progress in the preparation of the independent expert's report;
(f) prepare a report on the question based on the facts relating to the question and (subject to rule 14) send it to the tribunal and the parties;
(g) make himself available to attend hearings in the proceedings.[626]

(3) The independent expert may make an application for any order or for a hearing to be held as if he were a party to the proceedings.
(4) At any stage of the proceedings the tribunal may, after giving the independent expert the opportunity to make representations, withdraw the requirement on the independent expert to prepare a report. If it does so, the tribunal may itself determine the question, or it may determine that a different independent expert should be required to prepare the report.
(5) When paragraph (4) applies the independent expert who is no longer required to prepare the report shall provide the tribunal with all documentation and work in progress relating to the proceedings by a date specified by the tribunal. Such documentation and work in progress must be in a form which the tribunal is able to use. Such documentation and work in progress may be used in relation to those proceedings by the tribunal or by another independent expert.
(6) When an independent expert has been required to prepare a report in proceedings the Secretary shall give the independent expert notice of all hearings, orders or judgments in those proceedings as if the independent expert were a party to those proceedings and when these rules require a party to provide information to another party, such information shall also be provided to the independent expert.

Use of expert evidence

11.—(1) Expert evidence shall be restricted to that which, in the opinion of the tribunal, is reasonably required to resolve the proceedings.
(2) An expert shall have a duty to assist the tribunal on matters within his expertise. This duty overrides any obligation to the person from whom he has received instructions or by whom he is paid.
(3) No party may call an expert or put in evidence an expert's report without the permission of the tribunal. No expert report shall be put in evidence unless it has been disclosed to all other parties and any independent expert at least 28 days prior to the Hearing.
(4) In proceedings in which an independent expert has been required to prepare a report on the question, the tribunal shall not admit evidence of another expert on the question unless such evidence is based on the facts relating to the question. Unless the tribunal considers it inappropriate to do so, any such expert report shall be disclosed to all parties and to the tribunal on the same date on which the independent expert is required to send his report to the parties and to the tribunal.
(5) If an expert (other than an independent expert) does not comply with these rules or an order made by the tribunal or [an Employment Judge], the tribunal may order that the evidence of that expert shall not be admitted.[627]
(6) Where two or more parties wish to submit expert evidence on a particular issue, the tribunal may order that the evidence on that issue is to be given by one joint expert only. When such an order has been made, if the parties wishing to instruct the joint expert cannot agree who should be the expert, the tribunal may select the expert.

Written questions to experts

12.—(1) When any expert (including an independent expert) has prepared a report, a party or any other expert (including an independent expert) involved in the proceedings may put written questions about the report to the expert who has prepared the report.

[626] As amended by SI 2008/2683, Sch 1 para 259.
[627] As amended by SI 2008/2683, Sch 1 para 259.

(2) Unless the tribunal or [Employment Judge] agrees otherwise, written questions under paragraph (1):
   (a) may be put once only;
   (b) must be put within 28 days of the date on which the parties were sent the report;
   (c) must be for the purpose only of clarifying the factual basis of the report;
   (d) must be copied to all other parties and experts involved in the proceedings at the same time as they are sent to the expert who prepared the report.[628]

(3) When written questions have been put to an expert in accordance with paragraph (2) he shall answer those questions within 28 days of receiving them.

(4) An expert's answers to questions put in accordance with paragraph (2) shall be treated as part of the expert's report.

(5) Where a party has put a written question in accordance with this rule to an expert instructed by another party and the expert does not answer that question, or does not do so within 28 days, the tribunal may order that the party instructing the expert may not rely on the evidence of that expert.

Procedural matters

13.—(1) In proceedings in which an independent expert has been required to prepare a report, the Secretary shall send him notices and inform him of any hearing, application, order or judgment in those proceedings as if he were a party to those proceedings.

(2) For the avoidance of doubt, any requirement in this Schedule to hold a stage 1 or a stage 2 equal value hearing does not preclude holding more than one of each of those types of hearing or other hearings from being held in accordance with Schedule 1.

(3) Any power conferred on [an Employment Judge] in Schedule 1 may (subject to the provisions of this Schedule) be carried out by a tribunal or [an Employment Judge] in relation to proceedings to which this Schedule applies.[629]

National security proceedings

14.—(1) In equal value cases which are also national security proceedings, if a tribunal has required an independent expert to prepare a report on the question, the independent expert shall send a copy of the report to the tribunal and shall not send it to the parties. In such proceedings if written questions have been put to the independent expert under rule 12, the independent expert shall send any answers to those questions to the tribunal and not to the parties.

(2) Before the Secretary sends to the parties a copy of a report or answers which have been sent to him by the independent expert under paragraph (1), he shall follow the procedure set out in rule 10 of Schedule 2 as if that rule referred to the independent expert's report or answers (as the case may be) instead of written reasons, except that the independent expert's report or answers shall not be entered on the Register.

(3) If the Minister does not give a direction under rule 10(3) of Schedule 2 within the period of 28 days from the date on which the Minister was sent the report or answers to written questions the Secretary shall send a copy of the independent expert's report or answers to written questions (as the case may be) to the parties.

---

628 As amended by SI 2008/2683, Sch 1 para 259.

629 As amended by SI 2008/2683, Sch 1 para 259.

STATUTORY INSTRUMENTS

The Employment Act 2002 (Dispute Resolution) Regulations 2004*

(SI 2004/752)

Citation and commencement

1. These Regulations may be cited as the Employment Act 2002 (Dispute Resolution) Regulations 2004 and shall come into force on 1st October 2004.

Interpretation

2.—(1) In these Regulations—

'the 1992 Act' means the Trade Union and Labour Relations (Consolidation) Act 1992;

'the 1996 Act' means the Employment Rights Act 1996;

'the 1999 Act' means the Employment Relations Act 1999;

'the 2002 Act' means the Employment Act 2002;

'action' means any act or omission;

'applicable statutory procedure' means the statutory procedure that applies in relation to a particular case by virtue of these Regulations;

'collective agreement' has the meaning given to it by section 178(1) of the 1992 Act;

'dismissal and disciplinary procedures' means the statutory procedures set out in Part 1 of Schedule 2;

'dismissed' has the meaning given to it in section 95(1)(a) and (b) of the 1996 Act;

'employers' association' has the meaning given to it by section 122 of the 1992 Act;

'grievance' means a complaint by an employee about action which his employer has taken or is contemplating taking in relation to him;

'grievance procedures' means the statutory procedures set out in Part 2 of Schedule 2;

'independent trade union' has the meaning given to it by section 5 of the 1992 Act;

'modified dismissal procedure' means the procedure set out in Chapter 2 of Part 1 of Schedule 2;

'modified grievance procedure' means the procedure set out in Chapter 2 of Part 2 of Schedule 2;

'non-completion' of a statutory procedure includes non-commencement of such a procedure except where the term is used in relation to the non-completion of an identified requirement of a procedure or to circumstances where a procedure has already been commenced;

'party' means the employer or the employee;

'relevant disciplinary action' means action, short of dismissal, which the employer asserts to be based wholly or mainly on the employee's conduct or capability, other than suspension on full pay or the issuing of warnings (whether oral or written);

'standard dismissal and disciplinary procedure' means the procedure set out in Chapter 1 of Part 1 of Schedule 2;

'standard grievance procedure' means the procedure set out in Chapter 1 of Part 2 of Schedule 2;

and a reference to a Schedule is a reference to a Schedule to the 2002 Act.

(2) In determining whether a meeting or written communication fulfils a requirement of Schedule 2, it is irrelevant whether the meeting or communication deals with any other matter (including a different matter required to be dealt with in a meeting or communication intended to fulfil a requirement of Schedule 2).

Application of dismissal and disciplinary procedures

3.—(1) Subject to paragraph (2) and regulation 4, the standard dismissal and disciplinary procedure applies when an employer contemplates dismissing or taking relevant disciplinary action against an employee.

(2) Subject to regulation 4, the modified dismissal procedure applies in relation to a dismissal where—

(a) the employer dismissed the employee by reason of his conduct without notice,

(b) the dismissal occurred at the time the employer became aware of the conduct or immediately thereafter,

(c) the employer was entitled, in the circumstances, to dismiss the employee by reason of his conduct without notice or any payment in lieu of notice, and

* Repealed from 6/4/09, see p551 at note 24.

(d) it was reasonable for the employer, in the circumstances, to dismiss the employee before enquiring into the circumstances in which the conduct took place,

but neither of the dismissal and disciplinary procedures applies in relation to such a dismissal where the employee presents a complaint relating to the dismissal to an employment tribunal at a time when the employer has not complied with paragraph 4 of Schedule 2.

Dismissals to which the dismissal and disciplinary procedures do not apply

4.—(1) Neither of the dismissal and disciplinary procedures applies in relation to the dismissal of an employee where—

(a) all the employees of a description or in a category to which the employee belongs are dismissed, provided that the employer offers to re-engage all the employees so dismissed either before or upon the termination of their contracts;

(b) the dismissal is one of a number of dismissals in respect of which the duty in section 188 of the 1992 Act (duty of employer to consult representatives when proposing to dismiss as redundant a certain number of employees) applies;

(c) at the time of the employee's dismissal he is taking part in—

(i) an unofficial strike or other unofficial industrial action, or

(ii) a strike or other industrial action (being neither unofficial industrial action nor protected industrial action), unless the circumstances of the dismissal are such that, by virtue of section 238(2) of the 1992 Act, an employment tribunal is entitled to determine whether the dismissal was fair or unfair;

(d) the reason (or, if more than one, the principal reason) for the dismissal is that the employee took protected industrial action and the dismissal would be regarded, by virtue of section 238A(2) of the 1992 Act, as unfair for the purposes of Part 10 of the 1996 Act;

(e) the employer's business suddenly ceases to function, because of an event unforeseen by the employer, with the result that it is impractical for him to employ any employees;

(f) the reason (or, if more than one principal reason) for the dismissal is that the employee could not continue to work in the position which he held without contravention (either on his part or on that of his employer) of a duty or restriction imposed by or under any enactment; [. . .][630]

(g) the employee is one to whom a dismissal procedures agreement designated by an order under section 110 of the 1996 Act applies at the date of dismissal[, or

(h) the reason (or, if more than one, the principal reason) for the dismissal is retirement of the employee (to be determined in accordance with section 98ZA to 98ZF of the 1996 Act.][631]

(2) For the purposes of paragraph (1)—

'unofficial' shall be construed in accordance with subsections (2) to (4) of section 237 of the 1992 Act;

'strike' has the meaning given to it by section 246 of the 1992 Act;

'protected industrial action' shall be construed in accordance with section 238A(1) of the 1992 Act;

and an employer shall be regarded as offering to re-engage an employee if that employer, a successor of that employer or an associated employer of that employer offers to re-engage the employee, either in the job which he held immediately before the date of dismissal or in a different job which would be suitable in his case.

Circumstances in which parties are treated as complying with the dismissal and disciplinary procedures

5.—(1)Where—

(a) either of the dismissal and disciplinary procedures is the applicable statutory procedure in relation to a dismissal,

(b) the employee presents an application for interim relief to an employment tribunal pursuant to section 128 of the 1996 Act (interim relief pending determination of complaint) in relation to his dismissal, and

(c) at the time the application is presented, the requirements of paragraphs 1 and 2 or, as the case may be, paragraph 4 of Schedule 2 have been complied with but the requirements of paragraph 3 or 5 of Schedule 2 have not,

the parties shall be treated as having complied with the requirements of paragraph 3 or 5 of Schedule 2.

[630] Omitted by SI 2006/1031, Sch 8, para 64(a)

[631] Inserted by SI 2006/1031, Sch 8, para 64(b)

(2) Where either of the dismissal and disciplinary procedures is the applicable statutory procedure in relation to the dismissal of an employee or to relevant disciplinary action taken against an employee but—
  (a) at the time of the dismissal or the taking of the action an appropriate procedure exists,
  (b) the employee is entitled to appeal under that procedure against his dismissal or the relevant disciplinary action taken against him instead of appealing to his employer, and
  (c) the employee has appealed under that procedure,

the parties shall be treated as having complied with the requirements of paragraph 3 or 5 of Schedule 2.

(3) For the purposes of paragraph (2) a procedure is appropriate if it—
  (a) gives the employee an effective right of appeal against dismissal or disciplinary action taken against him, and
  (b) operates by virtue of a collective agreement made between two or more employers or an employers' association and one or more independent trade unions.

Application of the grievance procedures

6.—(1)The grievance procedures apply, in accordance with the paragraphs (2) to (7) of this regulation, in relation to any grievance about action by the employer that could form the basis of a complaint by an employee to an employment tribunal under a jurisdiction listed in Schedule 3 or 4, or could do so if the action took place.

(2) Subject to paragraphs (3) to (7), the standard grievance procedure applies in relation to any such grievance.

(3) Subject to paragraphs (4) to (7), the modified grievance procedure applies in relation to a grievance where—
  (a) the employee has ceased to be employed by the employer;
  (b) the employer—
    (i) was unaware of the grievance before the employment ceased, or
    (ii) was so aware but the standard grievance procedure was not commenced or was not completed before the last day of the employee's employment; and
  (c) the parties have agreed in writing in relation to the grievance, whether before, on or after that day, but after the employer became aware of the grievance, that the modified procedure should apply.

(4) Neither of the grievance procedures applies where—
  (a) the employee has ceased to be employed by the employer;
  (b) neither procedure has been commenced; and
  (c) since the employee ceased to be employed it has ceased to be reasonably practicable for him to comply with paragraph 6 or 9 of Schedule 2.

(5) Neither of the grievance procedures applies where the grievance is that the employer has dismissed or is contemplating dismissing the employee.

(6) Neither of the grievance procedures applies where the grievance is that the employer has taken or is contemplating taking relevant disciplinary action against the employee unless one of the reasons for the grievance is a reason mentioned in regulation 7(1).

(7) Neither of the grievance procedures applies where regulation 11(1) applies.

Circumstances in which parties are treated as complying with the grievance procedures

7.—(1)Where the grievance is that the employer has taken or is contemplating taking relevant disciplinary action against the employee and one of the reasons for the grievance is—
  (a) that the relevant disciplinary action amounted to or, if it took place, would amount to unlawful discrimination, or
  (b) that the grounds on which the employer took the action or is contemplating taking it were or are unrelated to the grounds on which he asserted that he took the action or is asserting that he is contemplating taking it,

the standard grievance procedure or, as the case may be, modified grievance procedure shall apply but the parties shall be treated as having complied with the applicable procedure if the employee complies with the requirement in paragraph (2).

(2) The requirement is that the employee must set out the grievance in a written statement and send the statement or a copy of it to the employer—
(a) where either of the dismissal and disciplinary procedures is being followed, before the meeting referred to in paragraph 3 or 5 (appeals under the dismissal and disciplinary procedures) of Schedule 2, or
(b) where neither of those procedures is being followed, before presenting any complaint arising out of the grievance to an employment tribunal.

(3) In paragraph (1)(a) 'unlawful discrimination' means an act or omission in respect of which a right of complaint lies to an employment tribunal under any of the following tribunal jurisdictions (specified in Schedules 3 and 4)—
section 2 of the Equal Pay Act 1970;
section 63 of the Sex Discrimination Act 1975;
section 54 of the Race Relations Act 1976;
section 17A of the Disability Discrimination Act 1995;
regulation 28 of the Employment Equality (Religion or Belief) Regulations 2003;
regulation 28 of the Employment Equality (Sexual Orientation) Regulations 2003;
[regulation 36 of the Employment Equality (Age) Regulations 2006].[632]

8.—(1) Where—
(a) the standard grievance procedure is the applicable statutory procedure,
(b) the employee has ceased to be employed by the employer,
(c) paragraph 6 of Schedule 2 has been complied with (whether before or after the end of his employment); and
(d) since the end of his employment it has ceased to be reasonably practicable for the employee, or his employer, to comply with the requirements of paragraph 7 or 8 of Schedule 2,
the parties shall be treated, subject to paragraph (2), as having complied with such of those paragraphs of Schedule 2 as have not been complied with.

(2) In a case where paragraph (1) applies and the requirements of paragraphs 7(1) to (3) of Schedule 2 have been complied with but the requirement in paragraph 7(4) of Schedule 2 has not, the employer shall be treated as having failed to comply with paragraph 7(4) unless he informs the employee in writing of his decision as to his response to the grievance.

9.—(1) Where either of the grievance procedures is the applicable statutory procedure, the parties shall be treated as having complied with the requirements of the procedure if a person who is an appropriate representative of the employee having the grievance has—
(a) written to the employer setting out the grievance; and
(b) specified in writing to the employer (whether in setting out the grievance or otherwise) the names of at least two employees, of whom one is the employee having the grievance, as being the employees on behalf of whom he is raising the grievance.

(2) For the purposes of paragraph (1), a person is an appropriate representative if, at the time he writes to the employer setting out the grievance, he is—
(a) an official of an independent trade union recognised by the employer for the purposes of collective bargaining in respect of a description of employees that includes the employee having the grievance, or
(b) an employee of the employer who is an employee representative elected or appointed by employees consisting of or including employees of the same description as the employee having the grievance and who, having regard to the purposes for which and method by which he was elected or appointed, has the authority to represent employees of that description under an established procedure for resolving grievances agreed between employee representatives and the employer.

(3) For the purposes of paragraph (2)(a) the terms 'official', 'recognised' and 'collective bargaining' have the meanings given to them by, respectively, sections 119, 178(3) and 178(1) of the 1992 Act.

10. Where either of the grievance procedures is the applicable statutory procedure but—
(a) at the time the employee raises his grievance there is a procedure in operation, under a collective agreement made between two or more employers or an employers' association and one or more

[632] Inserted by SI 2007/825, reg 8(2).

independent trade unions, that provides for employees of the employer to raise grievances about the behaviour of the employer and have them considered, and

(b) the employee is entitled to raise his grievance under that procedure and does so, the parties shall be treated as having complied with the applicable statutory procedure.

General circumstances in which the statutory procedures do not apply or are treated as being complied with

11.—(1)Where the circumstances specified in paragraph (3) apply and in consequence the employer or employee does not commence the procedure that would otherwise be the applicable statutory procedure (by complying with paragraph 1, 4, 6 or 9 of Schedule 2), the procedure does not apply.

(2) Where the applicable statutory procedure has been commenced, but the circumstances specified in paragraph (3) apply and in consequence a party does not comply with a subsequent requirement of the procedure, the parties shall be treated as having complied with the procedure.

(3) The circumstances referred to in paragraphs (1) and (2) are that—

(a) the party has reasonable grounds to believe that commencing the procedure or complying with the subsequent requirement would result in a significant threat to himself, his property, any other person or the property of any other person;

(b) the party has been subjected to harassment and has reasonable grounds to believe that commencing the procedure or complying with the subsequent requirement would result in his being subjected to further harassment; or

(c) it is not practicable for the party to commence the procedure or comply with the subsequent requirement within a reasonable period.

(4) In paragraph (3)(b), 'harassment' means conduct which has the purpose or effect of—

(a) violating the person's dignity, or

(b) creating an intimidating, hostile, degrading, humiliating or offensive environment for him,

but conduct shall only be regarded as having that purpose or effect if, having regard to all the circumstances, including in particular the perception of the person who was the subject of the conduct, it should reasonably be considered as having that purpose or effect.

Failure to comply with the statutory procedures

12.—(1)If either party fails to comply with a requirement of an applicable statutory procedure, including a general requirement contained in Part 3 of Schedule 2, then, subject to paragraph (2), the non-completion of the procedure shall be attributable to that party and neither party shall be under any obligation to comply with any further requirement of the procedure.

(2) Except as mentioned in paragraph (4), where the parties are to be treated as complying with the applicable statutory procedure, or any requirement of it, there is no failure to comply with the procedure or requirement.

(3) Notwithstanding that if regulation 11(1) applies the procedure that would otherwise be the applicable statutory procedure does not apply, where that regulation applies because the circumstances in sub-paragraph (a) or (b) of regulation 11(3) apply and it was the behaviour of one of the parties that resulted in those circumstances applying, that party shall be treated as if—

(a) the procedure had applied, and

(b) there had been a failure to comply with a requirement of the procedure that was attributable to him.

(4) In a case where regulation 11(2) applies in relation to a requirement of the applicable statutory procedure because the circumstances in sub-paragraph (a) or (b) of regulation 11(3) apply, and it was the behaviour of one of the parties that resulted in those circumstances applying, the fact that the requirement was not complied with shall be treated as being a failure, attributable to that party, to comply with a requirement of the procedure.

Failure to attend a meeting

13.—(1) Without prejudice to regulation 11(2) and (3)(c), if it is not reasonably practicable for—

(a) the employee, or, if he is exercising his right under section 10 of the 1999 Act (right to be accompanied), his companion; or

(b) the employer,

to attend a meeting organised in accordance with the applicable statutory procedure for a reason which was not foreseeable when the meeting was arranged, the employee or, as the case may be, employer shall not be treated as having failed to comply with that requirement of the procedure.

(2) In the circumstances set out in paragraph (1), the employer shall continue to be under the duty in the applicable statutory procedure to invite the employee to attend a meeting and, where the employee is exercising his rights under section 10 of the 1999 Act and the employee proposes an alternative time under subsection (4) of that section, the employer shall be under a duty to invite the employee to attend a meeting at that time.
(3) The duty to invite the employee to attend a meeting referred to in paragraph (2) shall cease if the employer has invited the employee to attend two meetings and paragraph (1) applied in relation to each of them.
(4) Where the duty in paragraph (2) has ceased as a result of paragraph (3), the parties shall be treated as having complied with the applicable statutory procedure.

Questions to obtain information not to constitute statement of grievance

14.—(1) Where a person aggrieved questions a respondent under any of the provisions set out in paragraph (2), those questions shall not constitute a statement of grievance under paragraph 6 or 9 of Schedule 2.
(2) The provisions referred to in paragraph (1) are—
section 7B of the Equal Pay Act 1970;
section 74 of the Sex Discrimination Act 1975;
section 65 of the Race Relations Act 1976;
section 56 of the Disability Discrimination Act 1995;
regulation 33 of the Employment Equality (Religion or Belief) Regulations 2003;
regulation 33 of the Employment Equality (Sexual Orientation) Regulations 2003;
[regulation 41 of the Employment Equality (Age) Regulations 2006].[633]

Extension of time limits

15.—(1) Where a complaint is presented to an employment tribunal under a jurisdiction listed in Schedule 3 or 4 and—
(a) either of the dismissal and disciplinary procedures is the applicable statutory procedure and the circumstances specified in paragraph (2) apply; or
(b) either of the grievance procedures is the applicable statutory procedure and the circumstances specified in paragraph (3) apply;
the normal time limit for presenting the complaint is extended for a period of three months beginning with the day after the day on which it would otherwise have expired.
(2) The circumstances referred to in paragraph (1)(a) are that the employee presents a complaint to the tribunal after the expiry of the normal time limit for presenting the complaint but had reasonable grounds for believing, when that time limit expired, that a dismissal or disciplinary procedure, whether statutory or otherwise (including an appropriate procedure for the purposes of regulation 5(2)), was being followed in respect of matters that consisted of or included the substance of the tribunal complaint.
(3) The circumstances referred to in paragraph (1)(b) are that the employee presents a complaint to the tribunal—
(a) within the normal time limit for presenting the complaint but in circumstances in which section 32(2) or (3) of the 2002 Act does not permit him to do so; or
(b) after the expiry of the normal time limit for presenting the complaint, having complied with paragraph 6 or 9 of Schedule 2 in relation to his grievance within that normal time limit.
(4) For the purposes of paragraph (3) and section 32 of the 2002 Act the following acts shall be treated, in a case to which the specified regulation applies, as constituting compliance with paragraph 6 or 9 of Schedule 2—
(a) in a case to which regulation 7(1) applies, compliance by the employee with the requirement in regulation 7(2);
(b) in a case to which regulation 9(1) applies, compliance by the appropriate representative with the requirement in sub-paragraph (a) or (b) of that regulation, whichever is the later; and
(c) in a case to which regulation 10 applies, the raising of his grievance by the employee in accordance with the procedure referred to in that regulation.

[633] Inserted by SI 2007/825, reg 8(3).

(5) In this regulation 'the normal time limit' means—
   (a) subject to sub-paragraph (b), the period within which a complaint under the relevant jurisdiction must be presented if there is to be no need for the tribunal, in order to be entitled to consider it to—
      (i) exercise any discretion, or
      (ii) make any determination as to whether it is required to consider the complaint, that the tribunal would have to exercise or make in order to consider a complaint presented outside that period; and
   (b) in relation to claims brought under the Equal Pay Act 1970, the period ending on the date on or before which proceedings must be instituted in accordance with section 2(4) of that Act.

The Employment Equality (Age) Regulations 2006

(SI 2006/1031)

Part I
General

Interpretation

2.—(1) In these Regulations, references to discrimination are to any discrimination falling within regulation 3 (discrimination on grounds of age), regulation 4 (discrimination by way of victimisation) or regulation 5 (instructions to discriminate) and related expressions shall be construed accordingly, and references to harassment shall be construed in accordance with regulation 6 (harassment on grounds of age).

(2) In these Regulations—

'1996 Act' means the Employment Rights Act 1996;[634]

'act' includes a deliberate omission;

'benefit', except in regulation 11 and Schedule 2 (pension schemes), includes facilities and services;

'commencement date' means 1st October 2006;

'Crown employment' means—

(a) service for purposes of a Minister of the Crown or government department, other than service of a person holding a statutory office; or

(b) service on behalf of the Crown for purposes of a person holding a statutory office or purposes of a statutory body;

'detriment' does not include harassment within the meaning of regulation 6;

'employment' means employment under a contract of service or of apprenticeship or a contract personally to do any work, and related expressions (such as 'employee' and 'employer') shall be construed accordingly, but this definition does not apply in relation to regulation 30 (exception for retirement) or to Schedules 2, 6, 7 and 8;

'Great Britain' includes such of the territorial waters of the United Kingdom as are adjacent to Great Britain;

'Minister of the Crown' includes the Treasury and the Defence Council;

'proprietor', in relation to a school, has the meaning given by section 579 of the Education Act 1996;[635]

'relevant member of the House of Commons staff' means any person who was appointed by the House of Commons Commission or who is a member of the Speaker's personal staff;

'relevant member of the House of Lords staff' means any person who is employed under a contract of employment with the Corporate Officer of the House of Lords;

'school', in England and Wales, has the meaning given by section 4 of the Education Act 1996,[636] and, in Scotland, has the meaning given by section 135(1) of the Education (Scotland) Act 1980,[637] and references to a school are to an institution in so far as it is engaged in the provision of education under those sections;

'service for purposes of a Minister of the Crown or government department' does not include service in any office mentioned in Schedule 2 (Ministerial offices) to the House of Commons Disqualification Act 1975;[638]

'statutory body' means a body set up by or in pursuance of an enactment, and 'statutory office' means an office so set up; and

---

[634] 1996 c 18.

[635] 1996 c 56; s 579 has been amended on a number of occasions. The relevant amendments for the purposes of these Regulations were those made by s 140(1) of, and para 183(a)(iii) of Sch 30 to, the School Standards and Framework Act 1998 and reg 3 of SI 2003/2045.

[636] Section 4 was amended by s 51 of the Education Act 1997 and Part 3 of Sch 22 to the Education Act 2002.

[637] 1980 c 44.

[638] 1975 c 24; Sch 2 was amended by the Scotland Act 1998, ss 48(6) and 87(1) and Sch 9, and by SI 2002/794.

'worker' in relation to regulations 32 and 34 and to Schedule 2, means, as the case may be—
(a) an employee;
(b) a person holding an office or post to which regulation 12 (office-holders etc) applies;
(c) a person holding the office of constable;
(d) a partner within the meaning of regulation 17 (partnerships);
(e) a member of a limited liability partnership within the meaning of that regulation;
(f) a person in Crown employment;
(g) a relevant member of the House of Commons staff;
(h) a relevant member of the House of Lords staff.

(3) In these Regulations references to 'employer', in their application to a person at any time seeking to employ another, include a person who has no employees at that time.

Discrimination on grounds of age

3.—(1) For the purposes of these Regulations, a person ('A') discriminates against another person ('B') if—
(a) on grounds of B's age, A treats B less favourably than he treats or would treat other persons, or
(b) A applies to B a provision, criterion or practice which he applies or would apply equally to persons not of the same age group as B, but—
(i) which puts or would put persons of the same age group as B at a particular disadvantage when compared with other persons, and
(ii) which puts B at that disadvantage,

and A cannot show the treatment or, as the case may be, provision, criterion or practice to be a proportionate means of achieving a legitimate aim.

(2) A comparison of B's case with that of another person under paragraph (1) must be such that the relevant circumstances in the one case are the same, or not materially different, in the other.

(3) In this regulation—
(a) 'age group' means a group of persons defined by reference to age, whether by reference to a particular age or a range of ages; and
(b) the reference in paragraph (1)(a) to B's age includes B's apparent age.

Discrimination by way of victimisation

4.—(1) For the purposes of these Regulations, a person ('A') discriminates against another person ('B') if he treats B less favourably than he treats or would treat other persons in the same circumstances, and does so by reason that B has—
(a) brought proceedings against A or any other person under or by virtue of these Regulations;
(b) given evidence or information in connection with proceedings brought by any person against A or any other person under or by virtue of these Regulations;
(c) otherwise done anything under or by reference to these Regulations in relation to A or any other person; or
(d) alleged that A or any other person has committed an act which (whether or not the allegation so states) would amount to a contravention of these Regulations,

or by reason that A knows that B intends to do any of those things, or suspects that B has done or intends to do any of them.

(2) Paragraph (1) does not apply to treatment of B by reason of any allegation made by him, or evidence or information given by him, if the allegation, evidence or information was false and not made (or, as the case may be, given) in good faith.

Instructions to discriminate

5. For the purposes of these Regulations, a person ('A') discriminates against another person ('B') if he treats B less favourably than he treats or would treat other persons in the same circumstances, and does so by reason that—
(a) B has not carried out (in whole or in part) an instruction to do an act which is unlawful by virtue of these Regulations, or
(b) B, having been given an instruction to do such an act, complains to A or to any other person about that instruction.

Harassment on grounds of age

6.—(1)For the purposes of these Regulations, a person ('A') subjects another person ('B') to harassment where, on grounds of age, A engages in unwanted conduct which has the purpose or effect of—

(a) violating B's dignity; or
(b) creating an intimidating, hostile, degrading, humiliating or offensive environment for B.

(2) Conduct shall be regarded as having the effect specified in paragraph (1)(a) or (b) only if, having regard to all the circumstances, including in particular the perception of B, it should reasonably be considered as having that effect.

PART 2

DISCRIMINATION IN EMPLOYMENT AND VOCATIONAL TRAINING

Applicants and employees

7.—(1) It is unlawful for an employer, in relation to employment by him at an establishment in Great Britain, to discriminate against a person—
(a) in the arrangements he makes for the purpose of determining to whom he should offer employment;
(b) in the terms on which he offers that person employment; or
(c) by refusing to offer, or deliberately not offering, him employment.

(2) It is unlawful for an employer, in relation to a person whom he employs at an establishment in Great Britain, to discriminate against that person—
(a) in the terms of employment which he affords him;
(b) in the opportunities which he affords him for promotion, a transfer, training, or receiving any other benefit;
(c) by refusing to afford him, or deliberately not affording him, any such opportunity; or
(d) by dismissing him, or subjecting him to any other detriment.

(3) It is unlawful for an employer, in relation to employment by him at an establishment in Great Britain, to subject to harassment a person whom he employs or who has applied to him for employment.

(4) Subject to paragraph (5), paragraph (1)(a) and (c) does not apply in relation to a person—
(a) whose age is greater than the employer's normal retirement age or, if the employer does not have a normal retirement age, the age of 65; or
(b) who would, within a period of six months from the date of his application to the employer, reach the employer's normal retirement age or, if the employer does not have a normal retirement age, the age of 65.

(5) Paragraph (4) only applies to a person to whom, if he was recruited by the employer, regulation 30 (exception for retirement) could apply.

(6) Paragraph (2) does not apply to benefits of any description if the employer is concerned with the provision (for payment or not) of benefits of that description to the public, or to a section of the public which includes the employee in question, unless—
(a) that provision differs in a material respect from the provision of the benefits by the employer to his employees; or
(b) the provision of the benefits to the employee in question is regulated by his contract of employment; or
(c) the benefits relate to training.

(7) In paragraph (2)(d) reference to the dismissal of a person from employment includes reference—
(a) to the termination of that person's employment by the expiration of any period (including a period expiring by reference to an event or circumstance), not being a termination immediately after which the employment is renewed on the same terms; and
(b) to the termination of that person's employment by any act of his (including the giving of notice) in circumstances such that he is entitled to terminate it without notice by reason of the conduct of the employer.

(8) In paragraph (4) 'normal retirement age' is an age of 65 or more which meets the requirements of section 98ZH of the 1996 Act.[639]

Exception for genuine occupational requirement etc

8.—(1) In relation to discrimination falling within regulation 3 (discrimination on grounds of age)—
(a) regulation 7(1)(a) or (c) does not apply to any employment;

---

639 Section 98ZH of the 1996 Act is inserted into that Act by reg 49 of, and para 23 of Sch 8 to, these Regulations

(b) regulation 7(2)(b) or (c) does not apply to promotion or transfer to, or training for, any employment; and
(c) regulation 7(2)(d) does not apply to dismissal from any employment,
where paragraph (2) applies.
(2) This paragraph applies where, having regard to the nature of the employment or the context in which it is carried out—
(a) possessing a characteristic related to age is a genuine and determining occupational requirement;
(b) it is proportionate to apply that requirement in the particular case; and
(c) either—
(i) the person to whom that requirement is applied does not meet it, or
(ii) the employer is not satisfied, and in all the circumstances it is reasonable for him not to be satisfied, that that person meets it.

Part 3
Other Unlawful Acts

Liability of employers and principals

25.—(1) Anything done by a person in the course of his employment shall be treated for the purposes of these Regulations as done by his employer as well as by him, whether or not it was done with the employer's knowledge or approval.
(2) Anything done by a person as agent for another person with the authority (whether express or implied, and whether precedent or subsequent) of that other person shall be treated for the purposes of these Regulations as done by that other person as well as by him.
(3) In proceedings brought under these Regulations against any person in respect of an act alleged to have been done by an employee of his it shall be a defence for that person to prove that he took such steps as were reasonably practicable to prevent the employee from doing that act, or from doing in the course of his employment acts of that description.

Aiding unlawful acts

26.—(1) A person who knowingly aids another person to do an act made unlawful by these Regulations shall be treated for the purpose of these Regulations as himself doing an unlawful act of the like description.
(2) For the purposes of paragraph (1) an employee or agent for whose act the employer or principal is liable under regulation 25 (or would be so liable but for regulation 25(3)) shall be deemed to aid the doing of the act by the employer or principal.
(3) A person does not under this regulation knowingly aid another to do an unlawful act if—
(a) he acts in reliance on a statement made to him by that other person that, by reason of any provision of these Regulations, the act which he aids would not be unlawful; and
(b) it is reasonable for him to rely on the statement.
(4) A person who knowingly or recklessly makes a statement such as is referred to in paragraph (3)(a) which in a material respect is false or misleading commits an offence, and shall be liable on summary conviction to a fine not exceeding level 5 on the standard scale.

Part 4
General Exceptions from Parts 2 and 3

Exception for provision of certain benefits based on length of service

32.—(1) Subject to paragraph (2), nothing in Part 2 or 3 shall render it unlawful for a person ('A'), in relation to the award of any benefit by him, to put a worker ('B') at a disadvantage when compared with another worker ('C'), if and to the extent that the disadvantage suffered by B is because B's length of service is less than that of C.
(2) Where B's length of service exceeds 5 years, it must reasonably appear to A that the way in which he uses the criterion of length of service, in relation to the award in respect of which B is put at a disadvantage, fulfils a business need of his undertaking (for example, by encouraging the loyalty or motivation, or rewarding the experience, of some or all of his workers).

(3) In calculating a worker's length of service for these purposes, A shall calculate—
   (a) the length of time the worker has been working for him doing work which he reasonably considers to be at or above a particular level (assessed by reference to the demands made on the worker, for example, in terms of effort, skills and decision making); or
   (b) the length of time the worker has been working for him in total;

   and on each occasion on which he decides to use the criterion of length of service in relation to the award of a benefit to workers, it is for him to decide which of these definitions to use to calculate their lengths of service.

(4) For the purposes of paragraph (3), in calculating the length of time a worker has been working for him—
   (a) A shall calculate the length of time in terms of the number of weeks during the whole or part of which the worker was working for him;
   (b) A may discount any period during which the worker was absent from work (including any period of absence which at the time it occurred was thought by A or the worker to be permanent) unless in all the circumstances (including the way in which other workers' absences occurring in similar circumstances are treated by A in calculating their lengths of service) it would not be reasonable for him to do so;
   (c) A may discount any period of time during which the worker was present at work ('the relevant period') where—
      (i) the relevant period preceded a period during which the worker was absent from work, and
      (ii) in all the circumstances (including the length of the worker's absence, the reason for his absence, the effect his absence has had on his ability to discharge the duties of his work, and the way in which other workers are treated by A in similar circumstances) it is reasonable for A to discount the relevant period.

(5) For the purposes of paragraph (3)(b), a worker shall be treated as having worked for A during any period during which he worked for another if—
   (a) that period is treated as a period of employment with A for the purposes of the 1996 Act by virtue of the operation of section 218 of that Act; [. . .]
   (b) were the worker to be made redundant by A, that period and the period he has worked for A would amount to 'relevant service' within the meaning of section 155 of that Act [or,
   (c) in any case to which sub-paragraph (a) or (b) does not apply, that period is treated as a period of employment with A by or under an enactment pursuant to which his employment was transferred to A.][640]

(6) In paragraph (5)—
   (a) the reference to being made redundant is a reference to being dismissed by reason of redundancy for the purposes of the 1996 Act;
   (b) the reference to section 155 of that Act is a reference to that section as modified by the Redundancy Payments (Continuity of Employment in Local Government, etc.) (Modification) Order 1999.[641]

(7) In this regulation—

   'benefit' does not include any benefit awarded to a worker by virtue of his ceasing to work for A;

   ['enactment' includes an enactment comprised in, or in an instrument made under, an Act of the Scottish Parliament;] and

   'year' means a year of 12 calendar months.[642]

Exception for provision of enhanced redundancy payments to employees

33.—(1) Nothing in Part 2 or 3 shall render it unlawful for an employer—
   (a) to give a qualifying employee an enhanced redundancy payment which is less in amount than the enhanced redundancy payment which he gives to another such employee if both amounts are calculated in the same way;
   (b) to give enhanced redundancy payments only to those who are qualifying employees by virtue of sub-paragraph (a) or (c)(i) of the definition of qualifying employee below.

[640] As amended by SI 2008/573, reg3(a) and (b).

[641] SI 1999/2277. See Sch 2, Part 1, para 2.

[642] As amended by SI 2008/573, reg 3(c)

(2) In this regulation—

'the appropriate amount', 'a redundancy payment' and 'a week's pay' have the same meaning as they have in section 162 of the 1996 Act;[643]

'enhanced redundancy payment' means a payment of an amount calculated in accordance with paragraph (3) or (4);

'qualifying employee' means—

(a) an employee who is entitled to a redundancy payment by virtue of section 135 of the 1996 Act;

(b) an employee who would have been so entitled but for the operation of section 155 of that Act;

(c) an employee who agrees to the termination of his employment in circumstances where, had he been dismissed—

(i) he would have been a qualifying employee by virtue of sub-paragraph (a) of this definition; or

(ii) he would have been a qualifying employee by virtue of sub-paragraph (b).

(3) For an amount to be calculated in accordance with this paragraph it must be calculated in accordance with section 162(1) to (3) of the 1996 Act.

(4) For an amount to be calculated in accordance with this paragraph—

(a) it must be calculated as in paragraph (3);

(b) however, in making that calculation, the employer may do one or both of the following things—

(i) he may treat a week's pay as not being subject to a maximum amount or as being subject to a maximum amount above the amount laid down in section 227 of the 1996 Act;[644]

(ii) he may multiply the appropriate amount allowed for each year of employment by a figure of more than one;

(c) having made the calculation as in paragraph (3) (whether or not in making that calculation he has done anything mentioned in sub-paragraph (b)) the employer may increase the amount thus calculated by multiplying it by a figure of more than one.

(5) For the purposes of paragraphs (3) and (4), the reference to 'the relevant date' in section 162(1)(a) of the 1996 Act is to be read, in the case of a qualifying employee who agrees to the termination of his employment, as a reference to the date on which that termination takes effect.

Part 5
Enforcement

Jurisdiction of employment tribunals

36.—(1) A complaint by any person ('the complainant') that another person ('the respondent')—

(a) has committed against the complainant an act to which this regulation applies; or

(b) is by virtue of regulation 25 (liability of employers and principals) or 26 (aiding unlawful acts) to be treated as having committed against the complainant such an act;

may be presented to an employment tribunal.

(2) This regulation applies to any act of discrimination or harassment which is unlawful by virtue of any provision of Part 2 other than—

(a) where the act is one in respect of which an appeal or proceedings in the nature of an appeal may be brought under any enactment, regulation 19 (qualifications bodies);

(b) regulation 23 (institutions of further and higher education); or

(c) where the act arises out of and is closely connected to a relationship between the complainant and the respondent which has come to an end but during the course of which an act of discrimination against, or harassment of, the complainant by the respondent would have been unlawful by virtue of regulation 23, regulation 24 (relationships which have come to an end).

---

643 Subsections (4), (5), and (8) of s 162 of the 1996 Act have been repealed by reg 49 of, and para 32 of Sch 8 to, these Regulations. Subsection (6) was amended by the Employment Rights (Dispute Resolution) Act 1998, s 1(2)(a). Subsection (7) was repealed by the Employment Relations Act 1999, ss 9 and 44 and Sch 4, Part 3, paras 5 and 30.

644 The amount laid down in s 227 may be increased or decreased by Order made by the Secretary of State unders 34 of the Employment Relations Act 1999. The amount laid down in s 227 is currently £290: see SI 2005/3352.

(3) In paragraph (2)(c), reference to an act of discrimination or harassment which would have been unlawful includes, in the case of a relationship which has come to an end before [the date on which the act of discrimination or harassment became unlawful by virtue of these Regulations], reference to an act of discrimination or harassment which would, after [that date], have been unlawful.[645]

(4) In this regulation, 'enactment' includes an enactment comprised in, or in an instrument made under, an Act of the Scottish Parliament.

Burden of proof: employment tribunals

37.—(1) This regulation applies to any complaint presented under regulation 36 to an employment tribunal.

(2) Where, on the hearing of the complaint, the complainant proves facts from which the tribunal could, apart from this regulation, conclude in the absence of an adequate explanation that the respondent—

(a) has committed against the complainant an act to which regulation 36 applies; or

(b) is by virtue of regulation 25 (liability of employers and principals) or 26 (aiding unlawful acts) to be treated as having committed against the complainant such an act,

the tribunal shall uphold the complaint unless the respondent proves that he did not commit, or as the case may be, is not to be treated as having committed, that act.

Remedies on complaints in employment tribunals

38.—(1) Where an employment tribunal finds that a complaint presented to it under regulation 36 is well-founded, the tribunal shall make such of the following as it considers just and equitable—

(a) an order declaring the rights of the complainant and the respondent in relation to the act to which the complaint relates;

(b) an order requiring the respondent to pay to the complainant compensation of an amount corresponding to any damages he could have been ordered by a county court or by a sheriff court to pay to the complainant if the complaint had fallen to be dealt with under regulation 39 (jurisdiction of county and sheriff courts);

(c) a recommendation that the respondent take within a specified period action appearing to the tribunal to be practicable for the purpose of obviating or reducing the adverse effect on the complainant of any act of discrimination or harassment to which the complaint relates.

(2) As respects an unlawful act of discrimination falling within regulation 3(1)(b) (discrimination on the grounds of age), if the respondent proves that the provision, criterion or practice was not applied with the intention of treating the complainant unfavourably on grounds of age, an order may be made under paragraph (1)(b) only if the employment tribunal—

(a) makes such order under paragraph (1)(a) (if any) and such recommendation under paragraph (1)(c) (if any) as it would have made if it had no power to make an order under paragraph (1)(b); and

(b) (where it makes an order under paragraph (1)(a) or a recommendation under paragraph (1)(c) or both) considers that it is just and equitable to make an order under paragraph (1)(b) as well.

(3) If without reasonable justification the respondent to a complaint fails to comply with a recommendation made by an employment tribunal under paragraph (1)(c), then, if it thinks it just and equitable to do so—

(a) the tribunal may increase the amount of compensation required to be paid to the complainant in respect of the complaint by an order made under paragraph (1)(b); or

(b) if an order under paragraph (1)(b) was not made, the tribunal may make such an order.

(4) Where an amount of compensation falls to be awarded under paragraph (1)(b), the tribunal may include in the award interest on that amount subject to, and in accordance with, the provisions of the Employment Tribunals (Interest on Awards in Discrimination Cases) Regulations 1996.[646]

(5) This regulation has effect subject to paragraph 6 of Schedule 2 (pension schemes).

Period within which proceedings to be brought

42.—(1) In employment tribunal shall not consider a complaint under regulation 36 unless it is presented to the tribunal before the end of the period of three months beginning when the act

[645] As amended by SI 2006/2408, reg 2(1), (4).

[646] SI 1996/2803. Regulation 1(2) of those Regulations is amended by para 56 of, and Sch 8 to, these Regulations.

complained of was done.

[(1A) Where the period within which a complaint must be presented in accordance with paragraph (1) is extended by regulation 15 of the Employment Act 2002 (Dispute Resolution) Regulations 2004, the period within which the complaint must be presented shall be the extended period rather than the period in paragraph (1).][647]

(2) A county court or a sheriff court shall not consider a claim brought under regulation 39 unless proceedings in respect of the claim are instituted before the end of the period of six months beginning when the act complained of was done.

(3) A court or tribunal may nevertheless consider any such complaint or claim which is out of time if, in all the circumstances of the case, it considers that it is just and equitable to do so.

(4) For the purposes of this regulation and regulation 41 (help for persons in obtaining information etc)—

(a) when the making of a contract is, by reason of the inclusion of any term, an unlawful act, that act shall be treated as extending throughout the duration of the contract; and

(b) any act extending over a period shall be treated as done at the end of that period; and

(c) a deliberate omission shall be treated as done when the person in question decided upon it,

and in the absence of evidence establishing the contrary a person shall be taken for the purposes of this regulation to decide upon an omission when he does an act inconsistent with doing the omitted act or, if he has done no such inconsistent act, when the period expires within which he might reasonably have been expected to do the omitted act if it was to be done.

[647] Inserted by SI 2008/573, reg 5.

The Employment Equality (Religion or Belief) Regulations 2003

(SI 2003/1660)

1.—(1) These Regulations may be cited as the Employment Equality (Religion or Belief) Regulations 2003, and shall come into force on 2nd December 2003.
(2) These Regulations do not extend to Northern Ireland.

Interpretation

2.—[(1) In these Regulations—
(a) 'religion' means any religion,
(b) 'belief' means any religious or philosophical belief,
(c) a reference to religion includes a reference to lack of religion, and
(d) a reference to belief includes a reference to lack of belief.][648]
(2) In these Regulations, references to discrimination are to any discrimination falling within regulation 3 (discrimination on grounds of religion or belief) or 4 (discrimination by way of victimisation) and related expressions shall be construed accordingly, and references to harassment shall be construed in accordance with regulation 5 (harassment on grounds of religion or belief).
(3) In these Regulations—
'act' includes a deliberate omission;
['benefits', except in regulation 9A (trustees and managers of occupational pension schemes), includes facilities and services;] [649]
'detriment' does not include harassment within the meaning of regulation 5;
references to 'employer', in their application to a person at any time seeking to employ another, include a person who has no employees at that time;
'employment' means employment under a contract of service or of apprenticeship or a contract personally to do any work, and related expressions shall be construed accordingly;
'Great Britain', except where the context otherwise requires in regulation 26 (protection of Sikhs from discrimination in connection with requirements as to wearing of safety helmets), includes such of the territorial waters of the United Kingdom as are adjacent to Great Britain;
'Minister of the Crown' includes the Treasury and the Defence Council; [. . .]
['proprietor', in relation to a school in England and Wales, has the meaning given by section 579 of the Education Act 1996, and, in relation to a school in Scotland, means the governing body, trustees, or other person or body of persons responsible for the management of the school; and][650]
'school', in England and Wales, has the meaning given by section 4 of the Education Act 1996, and, in Scotland, has the meaning given by section 135(1) of the Education (Scotland) Act 1980, and references to a school are to an institution in so far as it is engaged in the provision of education under those sections.

Discrimination on grounds of religion or belief

3.—(1) For the purposes of these Regulations, a person ('A') discriminates against another person ('B') if—
(a) on grounds of religion or belief, A treats B less favourably than he treats or would treat other persons; or[651]
(b) A applies to B a provision, criterion or practice which he applies or would apply equally to persons not of the same religion or belief as B, but—
(i) which puts or would put persons of the same religion or belief as B at a particular disadvantage when compared with other persons,
(ii) which puts B at that disadvantage, and
(iii) which A cannot show to be a proportionate means of achieving a legitimate aim.
(2) [. . .] [652]

---

648 Substituted by the Equality Act 2006 (c 3), s 77.
649 Substituted by SI 2003/2828, reg 3.
650 Inserted by SI 2007/2269, reg 4(2).
651 Prospectively amended by the Equality Act 2006 (c 3), s 77.
652 Omitted by the Equality Act 2006 (c 3), s 77.

(3) A comparison of B's case with that of another person under paragraph (1) must be such that the relevant circumstances in the one case are the same, or not materially different, in the other.

Discrimination by way of victimisation

4.—(1) For the purposes of these Regulations, a person ('A') discriminates against another person ('B') if he treats B less favourably than he treats or would treat other persons in the same circumstances, and does so by reason that B has—

(a) brought proceedings against A or any other person under these Regulations;
(b) given evidence or information in connection with proceedings brought by any person against A or any other person under these Regulations;
(c) otherwise done anything under or by reference to these Regulations in relation to A or any other person; or
(d) alleged that A or any other person has committed an act which (whether or not the allegation so states) would amount to a contravention of these Regulations,

or by reason that A knows that B intends to do any of those things, or suspects that B has done or intends to do any of them.

(2) Paragraph (1) does not apply to treatment of B by reason of any allegation made by him, or evidence or information given by him, if the allegation, evidence or information was false and not made (or, as the case may be, given) in good faith.

Harassment on grounds of religion or belief

5.—(1) For the purposes of these Regulations, a person ('A') subjects another person ('B') to harassment where, on grounds of religion or belief, A engages in unwanted conduct which has the purpose or effect of—

(a) violating B's dignity; or
(b) creating an intimidating, hostile, degrading, humiliating or offensive environment for B.

(2) Conduct shall be regarded as having the effect specified in paragraph (1)(a) or (b) only if, having regard to all the circumstances, including in particular the perception of B, it should reasonably be considered as having that effect.

Part II

Discrimination in Employment and Vocational Training

Applicants and employees

6.—(1) It is unlawful for an employer, in relation to employment by him at an establishment in Great Britain, to discriminate against a person—

(a) in the arrangements he makes for the purpose of determining to whom he should offer employment;
(b) in the terms on which he offers that person employment; or
(c) by refusing to offer, or deliberately not offering, him employment.

(2) It is unlawful for an employer, in relation to a person whom he employs at an establishment in Great Britain, to discriminate against that person—

(a) in the terms of employment which he affords him;
(b) in the opportunities which he affords him for promotion, a transfer, training, or receiving any other benefit;
(c) by refusing to afford him, or deliberately not affording him, any such opportunity; or
(d) by dismissing him, or subjecting him to any other detriment.

(3) It is unlawful for an employer, in relation to employment by him at an establishment in Great Britain, to subject to harassment a person whom he employs or who has applied to him for employment.

(4) Paragraph (2) does not apply to benefits of any description if the employer is concerned with the provision (for payment or not) of benefits of that description to the public, or to a section of the public which includes the employee in question, unless—

(a) that provision differs in a material respect from the provision of the benefits by the employer to his employees; or
(b) the provision of the benefits to the employee in question is regulated by his contract of employment; or
(c) the benefits relate to training.

(5) In paragraph (2)(d) reference to the dismissal of a person from employment includes reference—
   (a) to the termination of that person's employment by the expiration of any period (including a period expiring by reference to an event or circumstance), not being a termination immediately after which the employment is renewed on the same terms; and
   (b) to the termination of that person's employment by any act of his (including the giving of notice) in circumstances such that he is entitled to terminate it without notice by reason of the conduct of the employer.

Exception for genuine occupational requirement

7.—(1) In relation to discrimination falling within regulation 3 (discrimination on grounds of religion or belief)—
   (a) regulation 6(1)(a) or (c) does not apply to any employment;
   (b) regulation 6(2)(b) or (c) does not apply to promotion or transfer to, or training for, any employment; and
   (c) regulation 6(2)(d) does not apply to dismissal from any employment,

   where paragraph (2) or (3) applies.

(2) This paragraph applies where, having regard to the nature of the employment or the context in which it is carried out—
   (a) being of a particular religion or belief is a genuine and determining occupational requirement;
   (b) it is proportionate to apply that requirement in the particular case; and
   (c) either—
      (i) the person to whom that requirement is applied does not meet it, or
      (ii) the employer is not satisfied, and in all the circumstances it is reasonable for him not to be satisfied, that that person meets it,

   and this paragraph applies whether or not the employer has an ethos based on religion or belief.

(3) This paragraph applies where an employer has an ethos based on religion or belief and, having regard to that ethos and to the nature of the employment or the context in which it is carried out—
   (a) being of a particular religion or belief is a genuine occupational requirement for the job;
   (b) it is proportionate to apply that requirement in the particular case; and
   (c) either—
      (i) the person to whom that requirement is applied does not meet it, or
      (ii) the employer is not satisfied, and in all the circumstances it is reasonable for him not to be satisfied, that that person meets it.

Relationships which have come to an end

21.—(1)In this regulation a 'relevant relationship' is a relationship during the course of which an act of discrimination against, or harassment of, one party to the relationship ('B') by the other party to it ('A') is unlawful by virtue of any preceding provision of this Part.

(2) Where a relevant relationship has come to an end, it is unlawful for A—
   (a) to discriminate against B by subjecting him to a detriment; or
   (b) to subject B to harassment,

   where the discrimination or harassment arises out of and is closely connected to that relationship.

(3) In paragraph (1), reference to an act of discrimination or harassment which is unlawful includes, in the case of a relationship which has come to an end before the coming into force of these Regulations, reference to an act of discrimination or harassment which would, after the coming into force of these Regulations, be unlawful.

Part III

Other Unlawful Acts

Liability of employers and principals

22.—(1) Anything done by a person in the course of his employment shall be treated for the purposes of these Regulations as done by his employer as well as by him, whether or not it was done with the employer's knowledge or approval.

(2) Anything done by a person as agent for another person with the authority (whether express or implied, and whether precedent or subsequent) of that other person shall be treated for the purposes of these Regulations as done by that other person as well as by him.

(3) In proceedings brought under these Regulations against any person in respect of an act alleged to have been done by an employee of his it shall be a defence for that person to prove that he took such steps as were reasonably practicable to prevent the employee from doing that act, or from doing in the course of his employment acts of that description.

Aiding unlawful acts

23.—(1) A person who knowingly aids another person to do an act made unlawful by these Regulations shall be treated for the purpose of these Regulations as himself doing an unlawful act of the like description.

(2) For the purposes of paragraph (1) an employee or agent for whose act the employer or principal is liable under regulation 22 (or would be so liable but for regulation 22(3)) shall be deemed to aid the doing of the act by the employer or principal.

(3) A person does not under this regulation knowingly aid another to do an unlawful act if—

(a) he acts in reliance on a statement made to him by that other person that, by reason of any provision of these Regulations, the act which he aids would not be unlawful; and

(b) it is reasonable for him to rely on the statement.

(4) A person who knowingly or recklessly makes a statement such as is referred to in paragraph (3)(a) which in a material respect is false or misleading commits an offence, and shall be liable on summary conviction to a fine not exceeding level 5 on the standard scale.

Part V
Enforcement

Restriction of proceedings for breach of Regulations

27.—(1) Except as provided by these Regulations no proceedings, whether civil or criminal, shall lie against any person in respect of an act by reason that the act is unlawful by virtue of a provision of these Regulations.

(2) Paragraph (1) does not prevent the making of an application for judicial review [or the investigation or determination of any matter in accordance with Part X (investigations: the Pensions Ombudsman) of the Pension Schemes Act 1993 by the Pensions Ombudsman].[653]

Jurisdiction of employment tribunals

28.—(1) A complaint by any person ('the complainant') that another person ('the respondent')—

(a) has committed against the complainant an act to which this regulation applies; or

(b) is by virtue of regulation 22 (liability of employers and principals) or 23 (aiding unlawful acts) to be treated as having committed against the complainant such an act,

may be presented to an employment tribunal.

(2) This regulation applies to any act of discrimination or harassment which is unlawful by virtue of any provision of Part II other than—

(a) where the act is one in respect of which an appeal or proceedings in the nature of an appeal may be brought under any enactment, regulation 16 (qualifications bodies);

(b) regulation 20 (institutions of further and higher education); or

(c) where the act arises out of and is closely connected to a relationship between the complainant and the respondent which has come to an end but during the course of which an act of discrimination against, or harassment of, the complainant by the respondent would have been unlawful by virtue of regulation 20, regulation 21 (relationships which have come to an end).

(3) In paragraph (2)(c), reference to an act of discrimination or harassment which would have been unlawful includes, in the case of a relationship which has come to an end before the coming into force of these Regulations, reference to an act of discrimination or harassment which would, after the coming into force of these Regulations, have been unlawful.

(4) In this regulation, 'enactment' includes an enactment comprised in, or in an instrument made under, an Act of the Scottish Parliament.

Burden of proof: employment tribunals

29.—(1) This regulation applies to any complaint presented under regulation 28 to an employment tribunal.

---

653 As amended by SI 2003/2828, reg 3.

(2) Where, on the hearing of the complaint, the complainant proves facts from which the tribunal could, apart from this regulation, conclude in the absence of an adequate explanation that the respondent—
(a) has committed against the complainant an act to which regulation 28 applies; or
(b) is by virtue of regulation 22 (liability of employers and principals) or 23 (aiding unlawful acts) to be treated as having committed against the complainant such an act,
the tribunal shall uphold the complaint unless the respondent proves that he did not commit, or as the case may be, is not to be treated as having committed, that act.

Remedies on complaints in employment tribunals

30.—(1) Where an employment tribunal finds that a complaint presented to it under regulation 28 is well-founded, the tribunal shall make such of the following as it considers just and equitable—
(a) an order declaring the rights of the complainant and the respondent in relation to the act to which the complaint relates;
(b) an order requiring the respondent to pay to the complainant compensation of an amount corresponding to any damages he could have been ordered by a county court or by a sheriff court to pay to the complainant if the complaint had fallen to be dealt with under regulation 31 (jurisdiction of county and sheriff courts);
(c) a recommendation that the respondent take within a specified period action appearing to the tribunal to be practicable for the purpose of obviating or reducing the adverse effect on the complainant of any act of discrimination or harassment to which the complaint relates.

(2) As respects an unlawful act of discrimination falling within regulation 3(1)(b), if the respondent proves that the provision, criterion or practice was not applied with the intention of treating the complainant unfavourably on grounds of religion or belief, an order may be made under paragraph (1)(b) only if the employment tribunal—
(a) makes such order under paragraph (1)(a) (if any) and such recommendation under paragraph (1)(c) (if any) as it would have made if it had no power to make an order under paragraph (1)(b); and
(b) (where it makes an order under paragraph (1)(a) or a recommendation under paragraph (1)(c) or both) considers that it is just and equitable to make an order under paragraph (1)(b) as well.

(3) If without reasonable justification the respondent to a complaint fails to comply with a recommendation made by an employment tribunal under paragraph (1)(c), then, if it thinks it just and equitable to do so—
(a) the tribunal may increase the amount of compensation required to be paid to the complainant in respect of the complaint by an order made under paragraph (1)(b); or
(b) if an order under paragraph (1)(b) was not made, the tribunal may make such an order.

(4) Where an amount of compensation falls to be awarded under paragraph (1)(b), the tribunal may include in the award interest on that amount subject to, and in accordance with, the provisions of the Employment Tribunals (Interest on Awards in Discrimination Cases) Regulations 1996.

[(5) This regulation has effect subject to paragraph 7 of Schedule 1A (occupational pension schemes).][654]

Period within which proceedings to be brought

34.—(1) In employment tribunal shall not consider a complaint under regulation 28 unless it is presented to the tribunal before the end of—
(a) the period of three months beginning when the act complained of was done; or
(b) in a case to which regulation 36(7) (armed forces) applies, the period of six months so beginning.

[(1A) Where the period within which a complaint must be presented in accordance with paragraph (1) is extended by regulation 15 of the Employment Act 2002 (Dispute Resolution) Regulations 2004, the period within which the complaint must be presented shall be the extended period rather than the period in paragraph (1).][655]

[654] Inserted by SI 2003/2828, reg 3.
[655] Inserted by SI 2004/752, reg 17.

(2) A county court or a sheriff court shall not consider a claim brought under regulation 31 unless proceedings in respect of the claim are instituted before the end of the period of six months beginning when the act complained of was done.

(3) A court or tribunal may nevertheless consider any such complaint or claim which is out of time if, in all the circumstances of the case, it considers that it is just and equitable to do so.

(4) For the purposes of this regulation and regulation 33 (help for persons in obtaining information etc)—

(a) when the making of a contract is, by reason of the inclusion of any term, an unlawful act, that act shall be treated as extending throughout the duration of the contract; and

(b) any act extending over a period shall be treated as done at the end of that period; and

(c) a deliberate omission shall be treated as done when the person in question decided upon it,

and in the absence of evidence establishing the contrary a person shall be taken for the purposes of this regulation to decide upon an omission when he does an act inconsistent with doing the omitted act or, if he has done no such inconsistent act, when the period expires within which he might reasonably have been expected to do the omitted act if it was to be done.

The Employment Equality (Sexual Orientation) Regulations 2003

(SI 2003/1661)

1.—(1) These Regulations may be cited as the Employment Equality (Sexual Orientation) Regulations 2003, and shall come into force on 1st December 2003.

(2) These Regulations do not extend to Northern Ireland.

Interpretation

2.—(1) In these Regulations, 'sexual orientation' means a sexual orientation towards—

(a) persons of the same sex;

(b) persons of the opposite sex; or

(c) persons of the same sex and of the opposite sex.

(2) In these Regulations, references to discrimination are to any discrimination falling within regulation 3 (discrimination on grounds of sexual orientation) or 4 (discrimination by way of victimisation) and related expressions shall be construed accordingly, and references to harassment shall be construed in accordance with regulation 5 (harassment on grounds of sexual orientation).

(3) In these Regulations—

'act' includes a deliberate omission;

['benefits', except in regulation 9A (trustees and managers of occupational pension schemes), includes facilities and services;] [656]

'detriment' does not include harassment within the meaning of regulation 5;

references to 'employer', in their application to a person at any time seeking to employ another, include a person who has no employees at that time;

'employment' means employment under a contract of service or of apprenticeship or a contract personally to do any work, and related expressions shall be construed accordingly;

'Great Britain' includes such of the territorial waters of the United Kingdom as are adjacent to Great Britain;

'Minister of the Crown' includes the Treasury and the Defence Council; [. . .]

['proprietor', in relation to a school in England and Wales, has the meaning given by section 579 of the Education Act 1996, and, in relation to a school in Scotland, means the governing body, trustees, or other person or body of persons responsible for the management of the school; and] [657]

'school', in England and Wales, has the meaning given by section 4 of the Education Act 1996, and, in Scotland, has the meaning given by section 135(1) of the Education (Scotland) Act 1980, and references to a school are to an institution in so far as it is engaged in the provision of education under those sections.

Discrimination on grounds of sexual orientation

3.—(1) For the purposes of these Regulations, a person ('A') discriminates against another person ('B') if—

(a) on grounds of sexual orientation, A treats B less favourably than he treats or would treat other persons; or

(b) A applies to B a provision, criterion or practice which he applies or would apply equally to persons not of the same sexual orientation as B, but—

(i) which puts or would put persons of the same sexual orientation as B at a particular disadvantage when compared with other persons,

(ii) which puts B at that disadvantage, and

(iii) which A cannot show to be a proportionate means of achieving a legitimate aim.

(2) A comparison of B's case with that of another person under paragraph (1) must be such that the relevant circumstances in the one case are the same, or not materially different, in the other.

[(3) For the purposes of paragraph (2), in a comparison of B's case with that of another person the fact that one of the persons (whether or not B) is a civil partner while the other is married shall not be treated as a material difference between their respective circumstances.][658]

[656] As amended by SI 2003/2827, reg 3.

[657] Inserted by SI 2007/573, reg 3(2).

[658] Inserted by SI 2005/2114, Sch 17, para 7.

Discrimination by way of victimisation

4.—(1) For the purposes of these Regulations, a person ('A') discriminates against another person ('B') if he treats B less favourably than he treats or would treat other persons in the same circumstances, and does so by reason that B has—

(a) brought proceedings against A or any other person under these Regulations;

(b) given evidence or information in connection with proceedings brought by any person against A or any other person under these Regulations;

(c) otherwise done anything under or by reference to these Regulations in relation to A or any other person; or

(d) alleged that A or any other person has committed an act which (whether or not the allegation so states) would amount to a contravention of these Regulations, or by reason that A knows that B intends to do any of those things, or suspects that B has done or intends to do any of them.

(2) Paragraph (1) does not apply to treatment of B by reason of any allegation made by him, or evidence or information given by him, if the allegation, evidence or information was false and not made (or, as the case may be, given) in good faith.

Harassment on grounds of sexual orientation

5.—(1) For the purposes of these Regulations, a person ('A') subjects another person ('B') to harassment where, on grounds of sexual orientation, A engages in unwanted conduct which has the purpose or effect of—

(a) violating B's dignity; or

(b) creating an intimidating, hostile, degrading, humiliating or offensive environment for B.

(2) Conduct shall be regarded as having the effect specified in paragraph (1)(a) or (b) only if, having regard to all the circumstances, including in particular the perception of B, it should reasonably be considered as having that effect.

Part II

Discrimination in Employment and Vocational Training

Applicants and employees

6.—(1) It is unlawful for an employer, in relation to employment by him at an establishment in Great Britain, to discriminate against a person—

(a) in the arrangements he makes for the purpose of determining to whom he should offer employment;

(b) in the terms on which he offers that person employment; or

(c) by refusing to offer, or deliberately not offering, him employment.

(2) It is unlawful for an employer, in relation to a person whom he employs at an establishment in Great Britain, to discriminate against that person—

(a) in the terms of employment which he affords him;

(b) in the opportunities which he affords him for promotion, a transfer, training, or receiving any other benefit;

(c) by refusing to afford him, or deliberately not affording him, any such opportunity; or

(d) by dismissing him, or subjecting him to any other detriment.

(3) It is unlawful for an employer, in relation to employment by him at an establishment in Great Britain, to subject to harassment a person whom he employs or who has applied to him for employment.

(4) Paragraph (2) does not apply to benefits of any description if the employer is concerned with the provision (for payment or not) of benefits of that description to the public, or to a section of the public which includes the employee in question, unless—

(a) that provision differs in a material respect from the provision of the benefits by the employer to his employees; or

(b) the provision of the benefits to the employee in question is regulated by his contract of employment; or

(c) the benefits relate to training.

(5) In paragraph (2)(d) reference to the dismissal of a person from employment includes reference—

(a) to the termination of that person's employment by the expiration of any period (including a period expiring by reference to an event or circumstance), not being a termination immediately after which the employment is renewed on the same terms; and

(b) to the termination of that person's employment by any act of his (including the giving of notice) in circumstances such that he is entitled to terminate it without notice by reason of the conduct of the employer.

Exception for genuine occupational requirement etc

7.—(1) In relation to discrimination falling within regulation 3 (discrimination on grounds of sexual orientation)—

(a) regulation 6(1)(a) or (c) does not apply to any employment;

(b) regulation 6(2)(b) or (c) does not apply to promotion or transfer to, or training for, any employment; and

(c) regulation 6(2)(d) does not apply to dismissal from any employment,

where paragraph (2) or (3) applies.

(2) This paragraph applies where, having regard to the nature of the employment or the context in which it is carried out—

(a) being of a particular sexual orientation is a genuine and determining occupational requirement;

(b) it is proportionate to apply that requirement in the particular case; and

(c) either—

(i) the person to whom that requirement is applied does not meet it, or

(ii) the employer is not satisfied, and in all the circumstances it is reasonable for him not to be satisfied, that that person meets it,

and this paragraph applies whether or not the employment is for purposes of an organised religion.

(3) This paragraph applies where—

(a) the employment is for purposes of an organised religion;

(b) the employer applies a requirement related to sexual orientation—

(i) so as to comply with the doctrines of the religion, or

(ii) because of the nature of the employment and the context in which it is carried out, so as to avoid conflicting with the strongly held religious convictions of a significant number of the religion's followers; and

(c) either—

(i) the person to whom that requirement is applied does not meet it, or

(ii) the employer is not satisfied, and in all the circumstances it is reasonable for him not to be satisfied, that that person meets it.

Contract workers

8.—(1) It is unlawful for a principal, in relation to contract work at an establishment in Great Britain, to discriminate against a contract worker—

(a) in the terms on which he allows him to do that work;

(b) by not allowing him to do it or continue to do it;

(c) in the way he affords him access to any benefits or by refusing or deliberately not affording him access to them; or

(d) by subjecting him to any other detriment.

(2) It is unlawful for a principal, in relation to contract work at an establishment in Great Britain, to subject a contract worker to harassment.

(3) A principal does not contravene paragraph (1)(b) by doing any act in relation to a contract worker where, if the work were to be done by a person taken into the principal's employment, that act would be lawful by virtue of regulation 7 (exception for genuine occupational requirement etc).

(4) Paragraph (1) does not apply to benefits of any description if the principal is concerned with the provision (for payment or not) of benefits of that description to the public, or to a section of the public to which the contract worker in question belongs, unless that provision differs in a material respect from the provision of the benefits by the principal to his contract workers.

(5) In this regulation—

'principal' means a person ('A') who makes work available for doing by individuals who are employed by another person who supplies them under a contract made with A;

'contract work' means work so made available; and

'contract worker' means any individual who is supplied to the principal under such a contract.

Relationships which have come to an end

21.—(1) In this regulation a 'relevant relationship' is a relationship during the course of which an act of discrimination against, or harassment of, one party to the relationship ('B') by the other party to it ('A') is unlawful by virtue of any preceding provision of this Part.

(2) Where a relevant relationship has come to an end, it is unlawful for A—

(a) to discriminate against B by subjecting him to a detriment; or

(b) to subject B to harassment,

where the discrimination or harassment arises out of and is closely connected to that relationship.

(3) In paragraph (1), reference to an act of discrimination or harassment which is unlawful includes, in the case of a relationship which has come to an end before the coming into force of these Regulations, reference to an act of discrimination or harassment which would, after the coming into force of these Regulations, be unlawful.

PART III
OTHER UNLAWFUL ACTS

Liability of employers and principals

22.—(1) Anything done by a person in the course of his employment shall be treated for the purposes of these Regulations as done by his employer as well as by him, whether or not it was done with the employer's knowledge or approval.

(2) Anything done by a person as agent for another person with the authority (whether express or implied, and whether precedent or subsequent) of that other person shall be treated for the purposes of these Regulations as done by that other person as well as by him.

(3) In proceedings brought under these Regulations against any person in respect of an act alleged to have been done by an employee of his it shall be a defence for that person to prove that he took such steps as were reasonably practicable to prevent the employee from doing that act, or from doing in the course of his employment acts of that description.

Aiding unlawful acts

23.—(1) A person who knowingly aids another person to do an act made unlawful by these Regulations shall be treated for the purpose of these Regulations as himself doing an unlawful act of the like description.

(2) For the purposes of paragraph (1) an employee or agent for whose act the employer or principal is liable under regulation 22 (or would be so liable but for regulation 22(3)) shall be deemed to aid the doing of the act by the employer or principal.

(3) A person does not under this regulation knowingly aid another to do an unlawful act if—

(a) he acts in reliance on a statement made to him by that other person that, by reason of any provision of these Regulations, the act which he aids would not be unlawful; and

(b) it is reasonable for him to rely on the statement.

(4) A person who knowingly or recklessly makes a statement such as is referred to in paragraph (3)(a) which in a material respect is false or misleading commits an offence, and shall be liable on summary conviction to a fine not exceeding level 5 on the standard scale.

PART V
ENFORCEMENT

Restriction of proceedings for breach of Regulations

27.—(1) Except as provided by these Regulations no proceedings, whether civil or criminal, shall lie against any person in respect of an act by reason that the act is unlawful by virtue of a provision of these Regulations.

(2) Paragraph (1) does not prevent the making of an application for judicial review [or the investigation or determination of any matter in accordance with Part X (investigations: the Pensions Ombudsman) of the Pension Schemes Act 1993 by the Pensions Ombudsman].[659]

[659] As amended by SI 2003/2827, reg 3.

Jurisdiction of employment tribunals

28.—(1) A complaint by any person ('the complainant') that another person ('the respondent')—

(a) has committed against the complainant an act to which this regulation applies; or

(b) is by virtue of regulation 22 (liability of employers and principals) or 23 (aiding unlawful acts) to be treated as having committed against the complainant such an act,

may be presented to an employment tribunal.

(2) This regulation applies to any act of discrimination or harassment which is unlawful by virtue of any provision of Part II other than—

(a) where the act is one in respect of which an appeal or proceedings in the nature of an appeal may be brought under any enactment, regulation 16 (qualifications bodies);

(b) regulation 20 (institutions of further and higher education); or

(c) where the act arises out of and is closely connected to a relationship between the complainant and the respondent which has come to an end but during the course of which an act of discrimination against, or harassment of, the complainant by the respondent would have been unlawful by virtue of regulation 20, regulation 21 (relationships which have come to an end).

(3) In paragraph (2)(c), reference to an act of discrimination or harassment which would have been unlawful includes, in the case of a relationship which has come to an end before the coming into force of these Regulations, reference to an act of discrimination or harassment which would, after the coming into force of these Regulations, have been unlawful.

(4) In this regulation, 'enactment' includes an enactment comprised in, or in an instrument made under, an Act of the Scottish Parliament.

Burden of proof: employment tribunals

29.—(1) This regulation applies to any complaint presented under regulation 28 to an employment tribunal.

(2) Where, on the hearing of the complaint, the complainant proves facts from which the tribunal could, apart from this regulation, conclude in the absence of an adequate explanation that the respondent—

(a) has committed against the complainant an act to which regulation 28 applies; or

(b) is by virtue of regulation 22 (liability of employers and principals) or 23 (aiding unlawful acts) to be treated as having committed against the complainant such an act,

the tribunal shall uphold the complaint unless the respondent proves that he did not commit, or as the case may be, is not to be treated as having committed, that act.

Remedies on complaints in employment tribunals

30.—(1) Where an employment tribunal finds that a complaint presented to it under regulation 28 is well-founded, the tribunal shall make such of the following as it considers just and equitable—

(a) an order declaring the rights of the complainant and the respondent in relation to the act to which the complaint relates;

(b) an order requiring the respondent to pay to the complainant compensation of an amount corresponding to any damages he could have been ordered by a county court or by a sheriff court to pay to the complainant if the complaint had fallen to be dealt with under regulation 31 (jurisdiction of county and sheriff courts);

(c) a recommendation that the respondent take within a specified period action appearing to the tribunal to be practicable for the purpose of obviating or reducing the adverse effect on the complainant of any act of discrimination or harassment to which the complaint relates.

(2) As respects an unlawful act of discrimination falling within regulation 3(1)(b), if the respondent proves that the provision, criterion or practice was not applied with the intention of treating the complainant unfavourably on grounds of sexual orientation, an order may be made under paragraph (1)(b) only if the employment tribunal—

(a) makes such order under paragraph (1)(a) (if any) and such recommendation under paragraph (1)(c) (if any) as it would have made if it had no power to make an order under paragraph (1)(b); and

(b) (where it makes an order under paragraph (1)(a) or a recommendation under paragraph (1)(c) or both) considers that it is just and equitable to make an order under paragraph (1)(b) as well.

(3) If without reasonable justification the respondent to a complaint fails to comply with a recommendation made by an employment tribunal under paragraph (1)(c), then, if it thinks it just and equitable to do so—

(a) the tribunal may increase the amount of compensation required to be paid to the complainant in respect of the complaint by an order made under paragraph (1)(b); or
(b) if an order under paragraph (1)(b) was not made, the tribunal may make such an order.

(4) Where an amount of compensation falls to be awarded under paragraph (1)(b), the tribunal may include in the award interest on that amount subject to, and in accordance with, the provisions of the Employment Tribunals (Interest on Awards in Discrimination Cases) Regulations 1996.

[(5) This regulation has effect subject to paragraph 7 of Schedule 1A (occupational pension schemes).][660]

Period within which proceedings to be brought

34.—(1) In employment tribunal shall not consider a complaint under regulation 28 unless it is presented to the tribunal before the end of—
(a) the period of three months beginning when the act complained of was done; or
(b) in a case to which regulation 36(7) (armed forces) applies, the period of six months so beginning.

[(1A) Where the period within which a complaint must be presented in accordance with paragraph (1) is extended by regulation 15 of the Employment Act 2002 (Dispute Resolution) Regulations 2004, the period within which the complaint must be presented shall be the extended period rather than the period in paragraph (1).] [661]

(2) A county court or a sheriff court shall not consider a claim brought under regulation 31 unless proceedings in respect of the claim are instituted before the end of the period of six months beginning when the act complained of was done.

(3) A court or tribunal may nevertheless consider any such complaint or claim which is out of time if, in all the circumstances of the case, it considers that it is just and equitable to do so.

(4) For the purposes of this regulation and regulation 33 (help for persons in obtaining information etc)—
(a) when the making of a contract is, by reason of the inclusion of any term, an unlawful act, that act shall be treated as extending throughout the duration of the contract; and
(b) any act extending over a period shall be treated as done at the end of that period; and
(c) a deliberate omission shall be treated as done when the person in question decided upon it,

and in the absence of evidence establishing the contrary a person shall be taken for the purposes of this regulation to decide upon an omission when he does an act inconsistent with doing the omitted act or, if he has done no such inconsistent act, when the period expires within which he might reasonably have been expected to do the omitted act if it was to be done.

660 Inserted by SI 2003/2827, reg 3.
661 As amended by SI 2004/752, reg 17.

The [Employment Tribunals] Extension of Jurisdiction (England and Wales) Order 1994[662]

(SI 1994/1623)

Citation, commencement and interpretation

1.—(1) This Order may be cited as the [Employment Tribunals] Extension of Jurisdiction (England and Wales) Order 1994 and comes into force on the first day after it is made.

(2) In this Order—

'contract claim' means a claim in respect of which proceedings may be brought before an [employment tribunal] by virtue of article 3 or 4; and

'the 1978 Act' means the Employment Protection (Consolidation) Act 1978.

Transitional provision

2. This Order does not enable proceedings in respect of a contract claim to be brought before an [employment tribunal] unless—

(a) the effective date of termination (as defined in section 55(4) of the 1978 Act) in respect of the contract giving rise to the claim, or

(b) where there is no effective date of termination, the last day upon which the employee works in the employment which has terminated,

occurs on or after the day on which the Order comes into force.

Extension of jurisdiction

3. Proceedings may be brought before an [employment tribunal] in respect of a claim of an employee for the recovery of damages or any other sum (other than a claim for damages, or for a sum due, in respect of personal injuries) if—

(a) the claim is one to which section 131(2) of the 1978 Act applies and which a court in England and Wales would under the law for the time being in force have jurisdiction to hear and determine;

(b) the claim is not one to which article 5 applies; and

(c) the claim arises or is outstanding on the termination of the employee's employment.

4. Proceedings may be brought before an [employment tribunal] in respect of a claim of an employer for the recovery of damages or any other sum (other than a claim for damages, or for a sum due, in respect of personal injuries) if—

(a) the claim is one to which section 131(2) of the 1978 Act applies and which a court in England and Wales would under the law for the time being in force have jurisdiction to hear and determine;

(b) the claim is not one to which article 5 applies;

(c) the claim arises or is outstanding on the termination of the employment of the employee against whom it is made; and

(d) proceedings in respect of a claim of that employee have been brought before an [employment tribunal] by virtue of this Order.

5. This article applies to a claim for breach of a contractual term of any of the following descriptions—

(a) a term requiring the employer to provide living accommodation for the employee;

(b) a term imposing an obligation on the employer or the employee in connection with the provision of living accommodation;

(c) a term relating to intellectual property;

(d) a term imposing an obligation of confidence;

(e) a term which is a covenant in restraint of trade.

In this article 'intellectual property' includes copyright, rights in performances, moral rights, design right, registered designs, patents and trade marks.

---

[662] References in this Order to industrial tribunals were amended to read as references to employment tribunals by the Employment Rights (Dispute Resolution) Act 1998 (c 8), s 1.

Manner in which proceedings may be brought

6. Proceedings on a contract claim may be brought before an [employment tribunal] by presenting a complaint to an [employment tribunal].

Time within which proceedings may be brought

7. An [employment tribunal] shall not entertain a complaint in respect of an employee's contract claim unless it is presented—
   (a) within the period of three months beginning with the effective date of termination of the contract giving rise to the claim, or
   (b) where there is no effective date of termination, within the period of three months beginning with the last day upon which the employee worked in the employment which has terminated,
   [(ba) where the period within which a complaint must be presented in accordance with paragraph (a) or (b) is extended by regulation 15 of the Employment Act 2002 (Dispute Resolution) Regulations 2004, the period within which the complaint must be presented shall be the extended period rather than the period in paragraph (a) or (b); or][663]
   (c) where the tribunal is satisfied that it was not reasonably practicable for the complaint to be presented within whichever of those periods is applicable, within such further period as the tribunal considers reasonable.

8. An [employment tribunal] shall not entertain a complaint in respect of an employer's contract claim unless—
   (a) it is presented at a time when there is before the tribunal a complaint in respect of a contract claim of a particular employee which has not been settled or withdrawn;
   (b) it arises out of a contract with that employee; and
   (c) it is presented—
      (i) within the period of six weeks beginning with the day, or if more than one the last of the days, on which the employer (or other person who is the respondent party to the employee's contract claim) received from the tribunal a copy of an originating application in respect of a contract claim of that employee; or
      (ii) where the tribunal is satisfied that it was not reasonably practicable for the complaint to be presented within that period, within such further period as the tribunal considers reasonable.

Limit on payment to be ordered

10. An [employment tribunal] shall not in proceedings in respect of a contract claim, or in respect of a number of contract claims relating to the same contract, order the payment of an amount exceeding £25,000.

[663] As amended by SI 2004/752, reg 17.

The [Employment Tribunals] (Interest) Order 1990[664]

(SI 1990/479)

Citation, commencement and transitional provisions

1.—(1) This Order may be cited as the [Employment Tribunals] (Interest) Order 1990 and shall come into force on 1st April 1990.

(2) Where a relevant decision day or a day to be treated as if it were a relevant decision day would, but for this paragraph of this Article, fall on a day before 1st April 1990, the relevant decision day or day to be treated as if it were that day shall be 1st April 1990.

Interpretation

2.—(1) In this Order, except in so far as the context otherwise requires—

'appellate court' means the Employment Appeal Tribunal, the High Court, the Court of Appeal, the Court of Session or the House of Lords as the case may be;

'the calculation day' in relation to a relevant decision means the day immediately following the expiry of the period of 42 days beginning with the relevant decision day;

'interest' means simple interest which accrues from day to day;

'relevant decision' in relation to a tribunal means any award or other determination of the tribunal by virtue of which one party to proceedings before the tribunal is required to pay a sum of money, excluding a sum representing costs or expenses, to another party to those proceedings;

'Rules of Procedure' means rules having effect in relation to proceedings before a tribunal by virtue of any regulations or order made pursuant to an enactment;

'the stipulated rate of interest' has the meaning assigned to it in Article 4 below;

'tribunal' means in England and Wales an [employment tribunal] (England and Wales) established in pursuance of the [Employment Tribunals] (England and Wales) Regulations 1965 and in Scotland an [employment tribunal] (Scotland) established in pursuance of the [Employment Tribunals] (Scotland) Regulations 1965.

(2) For the purposes of this Order a sum of money is required to be paid by one party to proceedings to another such party if, and only if, an amount of money required to be so paid is:—

(a) specified in an award or other determination of a tribunal or, as the case may be, in an order or decision of an appellate court; or

(b) otherwise ascertainable solely by reference to the terms of such an award or determination or, as the case may be, solely by reference to the terms of such an order or decision,

but where a tribunal or, as the case may be, appellate court has made a declaration as to entitlement under a contract nothing in this Order shall be taken to provide for interest to be payable on any payment under that contract in respect of which no obligation to make the payment has arisen under that contract before the declaration was made.

(3) In this Order, except in so far as the context otherwise requires, 'decision day' means the day signified by the date recording the sending of the document which is sent to the parties recording an award or other determination of a tribunal and 'relevant decision day', subject to Article 5, 6 and 7 below, means the day so signified in relation to a relevant decision.

(4) In this Order 'party' includes the Secretary of State where he has elected to appear as if he were a party in accordance with a Rule of Procedure entitling him so to elect.

Computation of interest

3.—(1) Subject to paragraphs (2) and (3) of this Article and to Article 11 below, where the whole or any part of a sum of money payable by virtue of a relevant decision of a tribunal remains unpaid on the calculation day the sum of money remaining unpaid on the calculation day shall carry interest at the stipulated rate of interest from the calculation day (including that day).

(2) Where, after the calculation day, a party pays to another party some but not all of such a sum of money remaining unpaid on the calculation day, then beginning with the day on which the payment is made interest shall continue to accrue only on that part of the sum of money which then remains unpaid.

[664] References in this Order to industrial tribunals were amended to read as references to employment tribunals by the Employment Rights (Dispute Resolution) Act 1998 (c 8),

(3) For the purposes of the computation of interest under this Order, there shall be disregarded—
(a) any part of a sum of money which pursuant to the Employment Protection (Recoupment of Unemployment Benefit and Supplementary Benefit) Regulations 1977 has been claimed by the Secretary of State in a recoupment notice; and
(b) any part of a sum of money which the party required to pay the sum of money is required, by virtue of any provision contained in or having effect under any enactment, to deduct and pay over to a public authority in respect of income tax or contributions under Part I of the Social Security Act 1975.

Rate of interest

4. The stipulated rate of interest shall be the rate of interest specified in section 17 of the Judgments Act 1838 on the relevant decision day.

Reviews

5. Where a tribunal reviews its decision pursuant to the Rules of Procedure and the effect of the review, or of any re-hearing which takes place as a result of the review, is that a sum of money payable by one party to another party is confirmed or varied the relevant decision day shall be the decision day of the decision which is the subject of the review.

Decisions on remission to a tribunal

6. Where an appellate court remits a matter to a tribunal for re-assessment of the sum of money which would have been payable by virtue of a previous relevant decision or by virtue of an order of another appellate court, the relevant decision day shall be the decision day of that previous relevant decision or the day on which the other appellate court promulgated its order, as the case may be.

Appeals from relevant decisions

7. Where, on an appeal from a relevant decision, or on a further appeal arising from a relevant decision an appellate court makes an order which confirms or varies the sum of money which would have been payable by virtue of that relevant decision if there had been no appeal, the relevant decision day shall be the decision day of that relevant decision.

Other appeals

8.—(1) This Article applies in relation to any order made by an appellate court on an appeal from a determination of any issue by a tribunal which is not a relevant decision, or on any further appeal arising from such a determination, where the effect of the order is that for the first time in relation to that issue one party to the proceedings is required to pay a sum of money, other than a sum representing costs or expenses, to another party to the proceedings.

(2) Where this Article applies in relation to an order, Articles 3 and 4 above shall apply to the sum of money payable by virtue of the order as if it was a sum of money payable by virtue of a relevant decision and as if the day on which the appellate court promulgated the order was the relevant decision day.

9. Where, on an appeal from an order in relation to which Article 8 applies or on a further appeal arising from such an order, an appellate court makes an order which confirms or varies the sum of money which would have been payable by virtue of the order in relation to which Article 8 applies if there had been no appeal, the day to be treated as the relevant decision day shall be the day on which the order in relation to which Article 8 applies was promulgated.

Reviews by the Employment Appeal Tribunal

10. Where the Employment Appeal Tribunal reviews an order to which Article 8 above applies, the day to be treated as the relevant decision day shall be the day on which the order reviewed was promulgated.

Variations of the sum of money on appeal etc

11. Where a sum of money payable by virtue of a relevant decision is varied under one of the procedures referred to in Articles 5, 6 and 7 above, or a sum of money treated as being so payable by virtue of Article 8 above is varied under one of the procedures referred to in Articles 6, 9 and 10 above, the reference in paragraph (1) of Article 3 above, to a sum of money payable by virtue of a relevant decision shall be treated as if it were a reference to that sum as so varied.

Notices

12.—(1) Where a decision of a tribunal is a relevant decision and a copy of a document recording that decision is sent to all parties entitled to receive that decision, it shall be the duty of the Secretary of the Central Office of the [Employment Tribunals] (England and Wales) or the Secretary of the Central Office of the [Employment Tribunals] (Scotland), as the case may be, to cause a notice containing the matters detailed in paragraph (2) below to accompany that document.

(2) The notice referred to in paragraph (1) above shall specify the decision day, the stipulated rate of interest and the calculation day in respect of the decision concerned.

(3) The failure to discharge the duty under paragraph (1) above correctly or at all shall have no effect on the liability of one party to pay to another party any sum of money which is payable by virtue of this Order.

The [Employment Tribunals] (Interest on Awards in Discrimination Cases) Regulations 1996[665]

(SI 1996/2803)

Citation, commencement, interpretation and revocation

1.—(1) These Regulations may be cited as the [Employment Tribunals] (Interest on Awards in Discrimination Cases) Regulations 1996 and shall come into force on 2nd December 1996.

(2) In these Regulations—

'the 1970 Act' means the Equal Pay Act 1970;

'the 1975 Act' means the Sex Discrimination Act 1975;

'the 1976 Act' means the Race Relations Act 1976;

'the 1995 Act' means the Disability Discrimination Act 1995 and;

'an award under the relevant legislation' means—

(a) an award under the 1970 Act of arrears of remuneration or damages, or

(b) an order under section 65(1)(b) of the 1975 Act, section 56(1)(b) of the 1976 Act [. . .] section 8(2)(b) of the 1995 Act [. . .regulation 30(1)(b) of the Employment Equality (Sexual Orientation) Regulations 2003,] [. . .regulation 30(1)(b) of the Employment Equality (Religion or Belief) Regulations 2003] [or regulation 38(1)(b) of the Employment Equality (Age) Regulations 2006] for payment of compensation,

but does not include an award of costs under rule 12 in Schedule 1 to the [Employment Tribunals] (Constitution and Rules of Procedure) Regulations 1993, or of expenses under rule 12 in Schedule 1 to the [Employment Tribunals] (Constitution and Rules of Procedure) (Scotland) Regulations 1993, even if the award of costs or expenses is made in the same proceedings as an award under the 1970 Act or such an order [666]

(3) The Sex Discrimination and Equal Pay (Remedies) Regulations 1993 and the Race Relations (Interest on Awards) Regulations 1994 are revoked.

Interest on awards

2.—(1) Where, at any time after the commencement of these Regulations, an [employment tribunal] makes an award under the relevant legislation—

(a) it may, subject to the following provisions of these Regulations, include interest on the sums awarded; and

(b) it shall consider whether to do so, without the need for any application by a party in the proceedings.

(2) Nothing in paragraph (1) shall prevent the tribunal from making an award or decision, with regard to interest, in terms which have been agreed between the parties.

Rate of interest

3.—(1) Interest shall be calculated as simple interest which accrues from day to day.

(2) Subject to paragraph (3), the rate of interest to be applied shall be, in England and Wales, the rate from time to time prescribed for the Special Investment Account under rule 27(1) of the Court Funds Rules 1987 and, in Scotland, the rate fixed, for the time being, by the Act of Sederunt (Interest in Sheriff Court Decrees or Extracts) 1975.

(3) Where the rate of interest in paragraph (2) has varied during a period for which interest is to be calculated, the tribunal may, if it so desires in the interests of simplicity, apply such median or average of those rates as seems to it appropriate.

Calculation of interest

4.—(1) In this regulation and regulations 5 and 6, 'day of calculation' means the day on which the amount of interest is calculated by the tribunal.

(2) In regulation 6, 'mid-point date' means the day which falls half-way through the period mentioned

665 References in these Regulations to industrial tribunals were amended to read as references to employment tribunals by the Employment Rights (Dispute Resolution) Act 1998 (c 8), s 1.

666 As amended by SI 2003/1660, Sch 5, para3; SI 2003/1661, Sch 5, para3; and SI 2006/103 1, Sch 8, para 56.

in paragraph (3) or, where the number of days in that period is even, the first day of the second half of the period.

(3) The period referred to in paragraph (2) is the period beginning on the date, in the case of an award under the 1970 Act, of the contravention and, in other cases, of the act of discrimination complained of, and ending on the day of calculation.

5. No interest shall be included in respect of any sum awarded for a loss or matter which will occur after the day of calculation or in respect of any time before the contravention or act of discrimination complained of.

6.—(1) subject to the following paragraphs of this regulation—

(a) in the case of any sum for injury to feelings, interest shall be for the period beginning on the date of the contravention or act of discrimination complained of and ending on the day of calculation;

(b) in the case of all other sums of damages or compensation (other than any sum referred to in regulation 5) and all arrears of remuneration, interest shall be for the period beginning on the mid-point date and ending on the day of calculation.

(2) Where any payment has been made before the day of calculation to the complainant by or on behalf of the respondent in respect of the subject matter of the award, interest in respect of that part of the award covered by the payment shall be calculated as if the references in paragraph (1), and in the definition of 'mid-point date' in regulation 4, to the day of calculation were to the date on which the payment was made.

(3) Where the tribunal considers that in the circumstances, whether relating to the case as a whole or to a particular sum in an award, serious injustice would be caused if interest were to be awarded in respect of the period or periods in paragraphs (1) or (2), it may—

(a) calculate interest, or as the case may be interest on the particular sum, for such different period, or

(b) calculate interest for such different periods in respect of various sums in the award,

as it considers appropriate in the circumstances, having regard to the provisions of these Regulations.

Decision in writing

7.—(1) The tribunal's written statement of reasons for its decision shall contain a statement of the total amount of any interest awarded under regulation 2 and, unless this amount has been agreed between the parties, either a table showing how it has been calculated or a description of the manner in which it has been calculated.

(2) The tribunal's written statement of reasons shall include reasons for any decision not to award interest under regulation 2.

Interest for period after award

8.—(1) The [Employment Tribunals] (Interest) Order 1990 shall apply in relation to an award under the relevant legislation (whether or not including interest under regulation 2) as if references in that Order to the calculation day were references to the day immediately following the relevant decision day (as defined in Article 2(3) of the Order) and accordingly interest shall accrue under the Order from that day onwards (including that day).

(2) Notwithstanding paragraph (1), no interest shall be payable by virtue of that Order if payment of the full amount of the award (including any interest under regulation 2) is made within 14 days after the relevant decision day.

The Fixed-term Employees (Prevention of Less Favourable Treatment) Regulations 2002

(SI 2002/2034)

Part 1
General and Interpretation

Citation, commencement and interpretation

1.—(2) In these Regulations—

'the 1996 Act' means the Employment Rights Act 1996;

'collective agreement' means a collective agreement within the meaning of section 178 of the Trade Union and Labour Relations (Consolidation) Act 1992; the trade union parties to which are independent trade unions within the meaning of section 5 of that Act;

'employer', in relation to any employee, means the person by whom the employee is (or, where the employment has ceased, was) employed;

'fixed-term contract' means a contract of employment that, under its provisions determining how it will terminate in the normal course, will terminate—

(a) on the expiry of a specific term,

(b) on the completion of a particular task, or

(c) on the occurrence or non-occurrence of any other specific event other than the attainment by the employee of any normal and bona fide retiring age in the establishment for an employee holding the position held by him,

and any reference to 'fixed-term' shall be construed accordingly;

'fixed-term employee' means an employee who is employed under a fixed-term contract;

'permanent employee' means an employee who is not employed under a fixed-term contract, and any reference to 'permanent employment' shall be construed accordingly;

'pro rata principle' means that where a comparable permanent employee receives or is entitled to pay or any other benefit, a fixed-term employee is to receive or be entitled to such proportion of that pay or other benefit as is reasonable in the circumstances having regard to the length of his contract of employment and to the terms on which the pay or other benefit is offered;

'renewal' includes extension and references to renewing a contract shall be construed accordingly;

'workforce agreement' means an agreement between an employer and his employees or their representatives in respect of which the conditions set out in Schedule 1 to these Regulations are satisfied.

Comparable employees

2.—(1) For the purposes of these Regulations, an employee is a comparable permanent employee in relation to a fixed-term employee if, at the time when the treatment that is alleged to be less favourable to the fixed-term employee takes place,

(a) both employees are—

(i) employed by the same employer, and

(ii) engaged in the same or broadly similar work having regard, where relevant, to whether they have a similar level of qualification and skills; and

(b) the permanent employee works or is based at the same establishment as the fixed-term employee or, where there is no comparable permanent employee working or based at that establishment who satisfies the requirements of sub-paragraph (a), works or is based at a different establishment and satisfies those requirements.

(2) For the purposes of paragraph (1), an employee is not a comparable permanent employee if his employment has ceased.

Part 2
Rights and Remedies

Less favourable treatment of fixed-term employees

3.—(1) A fixed-term employee has the right not to be treated by his employer less favourably than the employer treats a comparable permanent employee—

(a) as regards the terms of his contract; or
(b) by being subjected to any other detriment by any act, or deliberate failure to act, of his employer.

(2) Subject to paragraphs (3) and (4), the right conferred by paragraph (1) includes in particular the right of the fixed-term employee in question not to be treated less favourably than the employer treats a comparable permanent employee in relation to—
(a) any period of service qualification relating to any particular condition of service,
(b) the opportunity to receive training, or
(c) the opportunity to secure any permanent position in the establishment.

(3) The right conferred by paragraph (1) applies only if—
(a) the treatment is on the ground that the employee is a fixed-term employee, and
(b) the treatment is not justified on objective grounds.

(4) Paragraph (3)(b) is subject to regulation 4.

(5) In determining whether a fixed-term employee has been treated less favourably than a comparable permanent employee, the pro rata principle shall be applied unless it is inappropriate.

(6) In order to ensure that an employee is able to exercise the right conferred by paragraph (1) as described in paragraph (2)(c) the employee has the right to be informed by his employer of available vacancies in the establishment.

(7) For the purposes of paragraph (6) an employee is 'informed by his employer' only if the vacancy is contained in an advertisement which the employee has a reasonable opportunity of reading in the course of his employment or the employee is given reasonable notification of the vacancy in some other way.

Objective justification

4.—(1) Where a fixed-term employee is treated by his employer less favourably than the employer treats a comparable permanent employee as regards any term of his contract, the treatment in question shall be regarded for the purposes of regulation 3(3)(b) as justified on objective grounds if the terms of the fixed-term employee's contract of employment, taken as a whole, are at least as favourable as the terms of the comparable permanent employee's contract of employment.

(2) Paragraph (1) is without prejudice to the generality of regulation 3(3)(b).

Unfair dismissal and the right not to be subjected to detriment

6.—(1) An employee who is dismissed shall be regarded as unfairly dismissed for the purposes of Part 10 of the 1996 Act if the reason (or, if more than one, the principal reason) for the dismissal is a reason specified in paragraph (3).

(2) An employee has the right not to be subjected to any detriment by any act, or any deliberate failure to act, of his employer done on a ground specified in paragraph (3).

(3) The reasons or, as the case may be, grounds are—
(a) that the employee—
(i) brought proceedings against the employer under these Regulations;
(ii) requested from his employer a written statement under regulation 5 or regulation 9;
(iii) gave evidence or information in connection with such proceedings brought by any employee;
(iv) otherwise did anything under these Regulations in relation to the employer or any other person;
(v) alleged that the employer had infringed these Regulations;
(vi) refused (or proposed to refuse) to forgo a right conferred on him by these Regulations;
(vii) declined to sign a workforce agreement for the purposes of these Regulations, or
(viii) being—
(aa) a representative of members of the workforce for the purposes of Schedule 1, or
(bb) a candidate in an election in which any person elected will, on being elected, become such a representative,

performed (or proposed to perform) any functions or activities as such a representative or candidate, or

(b) that the employer believes or suspects that the employee has done or intends to do any of the things mentioned in sub-paragraph (a).

(4) Where the reason or principal reason for dismissal or, as the case may be, ground for subjection to any act or deliberate failure to act, is that mentioned in paragraph (3)(a)(v), or (b) so far as it relates

thereto, neither paragraph (1) nor paragraph (2) applies if the allegation made by the employee is false and not made in good faith.

(5) Paragraph (2) does not apply where the detriment in question amounts to dismissal within the meaning of Part 10 of the 1996 Act.

Complaints to employment tribunals etc

7.—(1) An employee may present a complaint to an employment tribunal that his employer has infringed a right conferred on him by regulation 3, or (subject to regulation 6(5)), regulation 6(2).

(2) Subject to paragraph (3), an employment tribunal shall not consider a complaint under this regulation unless it is presented before the end of the period of three months beginning—

(a) in the case of an alleged infringement of a right conferred by regulation 3(1) or 6(2), with the date of the less favourable treatment or detriment to which the complaint relates or, where an act or failure to act is part of a series of similar acts or failures comprising the less favourable treatment or detriment, the last of them;

(b) in the case of an alleged infringement of the right conferred by regulation 3(6), with the date, or if more than one the last date, on which other individuals, whether or not employees of the employer, were informed of the vacancy.

(3) A tribunal may consider any such complaint which is out of time if, in all the circumstances of the case, it considers that it is just and equitable to do so.

(4) For the purposes of calculating the date of the less favourable treatment or detriment under paragraph (2)(a)—

(a) where a term in a contract is less favourable, that treatment shall be treated, subject to paragraph (b), as taking place on each day of the period during which the term is less favourable;

(b) a deliberate failure to act contrary to regulation 3 or 6(2) shall be treated as done when it was decided on.

(5) In the absence of evidence establishing the contrary, a person shall be taken for the purposes of paragraph (4)(b) to decide not to act—

(a) when he does an act inconsistent with doing the failed act; or

(b) if he has done no such inconsistent act, when the period expires within which he might reasonably have been expected to have done the failed act if it was to be done.

(6) Where an employee presents a complaint under this regulation in relation to a right conferred on him by regulation 3 or 6(2) it is for the employer to identify the ground for the less favourable treatment or detriment.

(7) Where an employment tribunal finds that a complaint presented to it under this regulation is well founded, it shall take such of the following steps as it considers just and equitable—

(a) making a declaration as to the rights of the complainant and the employer in relation to the matters to which the complaint relates;

(b) ordering the employer to pay compensation to the complainant;

(c) recommending that the employer take, within a specified period, action appearing to the tribunal to be reasonable, in all the circumstances of the case, for the purpose of obviating or reducing the adverse effect on the complainant of any matter to which the complaint relates.

(8) Where a tribunal orders compensation under paragraph (7)(b), the amount of the compensation awarded shall be such as the tribunal considers just and equitable in all the circumstances having regard to—

(a) the infringement to which the complaint relates, and

(b) any loss which is attributable to the infringement.

(9) The loss shall be taken to include—

(a) any expenses reasonably incurred by the complainant in consequence of the infringement, and

(b) loss of any benefit which he might reasonably be expected to have had but for the infringement.

(10) Compensation in respect of treating an employee in a manner which infringes the right conferred on him by regulation 3 shall not include compensation for injury to feelings.

(11) In ascertaining the loss the tribunal shall apply the same rule concerning the duty of a person to mitigate his loss as applies to damages recoverable under the common law of England and Wales or (as the case may be) the law of Scotland.

(12) Where the tribunal finds that the act, or failure to act, to which the complaint relates was to any extent caused or contributed to by action of the complainant, it shall reduce the amount

of the compensation by such proportion as it considers just and equitable having regard to that finding.

(13) If the employer fails, without reasonable justification, to comply with a recommendation made by an employment tribunal under paragraph (7)(c) the tribunal may, if it thinks it just and equitable to do so—

(a) increase the amount of compensation required to be paid to the complainant in respect of the complaint, where an order was made under paragraph (7)(b); or

(b) make an order under paragraph (7)(b).

The Part-time Workers (Prevention of Less Favourable Treatment) Regulations 2000

(SI 2000/1551)

Unfair dismissal and the right not to be subjected to detriment

7.—(1) An employee who is dismissed shall be regarded as unfairly dismissed for the purposes of Part X of the 1996 Act if the reason (or, if more than one, the principal reason) for the dismissal is a reason specified in paragraph (3).

(2) A worker has the right not to be subjected to any detriment by any act, or any deliberate failure to act, by his employer done on a ground specified in paragraph (3).

(3) The reasons or, as the case may be, grounds are—

(a) that the worker has—

(i) brought proceedings against the employer under these Regulations;

(ii) requested from his employer a written statement of reasons under regulation 6;

(iii) given evidence or information in connection with such proceedings brought by any worker;

(iv) otherwise done anything under these Regulations in relation to the employer or any other person;

(v) alleged that the employer had infringed these Regulations; or

(vi) refused (or proposed to refuse) to forgo a right conferred on him by these Regulations, or

(b) that the employer believes or suspects that the worker has done or intends to do any of the things mentioned in sub-paragraph (a).

(4) Where the reason or principal reason for dismissal or, as the case may be, ground for subjection to any act or deliberate failure to act, is that mentioned in paragraph (3)(a)(v), or (b) so far as it relates thereto, neither paragraph (1) nor paragraph (2) applies if the allegation made by the worker is false and not made in good faith.

(5) Paragraph (2) does not apply where the detriment in question amounts to the dismissal of an employee within the meaning of Part X of the 1996 Act.

Complaints to employment tribunals etc

8.—(1) Subject to regulation 7(5), a worker may present a complaint to an employment tribunal that his employer has infringed a right conferred on him by regulation 5 or 7(2).

(2) Subject to paragraph (3), an employment tribunal shall not consider a complaint under this regulation unless it is presented before the end of the period of three months (or, in a case to which regulation 13 applies, six months) beginning with the date of the less favourable treatment or detriment to which the complaint relates or, where an act or failure to act is part of a series of similar acts or failures comprising the less favourable treatment or detriment, the last of them.

(3) A tribunal may consider any such complaint which is out of time if, in all the circumstances of the case, it considers that it is just and equitable to do so.

(4) For the purposes of calculating the date of the less favourable treatment or detriment under paragraph (2)—

(a) where a term in a contract is less favourable, that treatment shall be treated, subject to paragraph (b), as taking place on each day of the period during which the term is less favourable;

(b) where an application relies on regulation 3 or 4 the less favourable treatment shall be treated as occurring on, and only on, in the case of regulation 3, the first day on which the applicant worked under the new or varied contract and, in the case of regulation 4, the day on which the applicant returned; and

(c) a deliberate failure to act contrary to regulation 5 or 7(2) shall be treated as done when it was decided on.

(5) In the absence of evidence establishing the contrary, a person shall be taken for the purposes of paragraph (4)(c) to decide not to act—

(a) when he does an act inconsistent with doing the failed act; or

(b) if he has done no such inconsistent act, when the period expires within which he might reasonably have been expected to have done the failed act if it was to be done.

(6) Where a worker presents a complaint under this regulation it is for the employer to identify the ground for the less favourable treatment or detriment.

(7) Where an employment tribunal finds that a complaint presented to it under this regulation is well founded, it shall take such of the following steps as it considers just and equitable—

(a) making a declaration as to the rights of the complainant and the employer in relation to the matters to which the complaint relates;

(b) ordering the employer to pay compensation to the complainant;

(c) recommending that the employer take, within a specified period, action appearing to the tribunal to be reasonable, in all the circumstances of the case, for the purpose of obviating or reducing the adverse effect on the complainant of any matter to which the complaint relates.

(8) [. . .][667]

(9) Where a tribunal orders compensation under paragraph (7)(b), the amount of the compensation awarded shall be such as the tribunal considers just and equitable in all the circumstances [. . .] having regard to—[668]

(a) the infringement to which the complaint relates, and

(b) any loss which is attributable to the infringement having regard, in the case of an infringement of the right conferred by regulation 5, to the pro rata principle except where it is inappropriate to do so.

(10) The loss shall be taken to include—

(a) any expenses reasonably incurred by the complainant in consequence of the infringement, and

(b) loss of any benefit which he might reasonably be expected to have had but for the infringement.

(11) Compensation in respect of treating a worker in a manner which infringes the right conferred on him by regulation 5 shall not include compensation for injury to feelings.

(12) In ascertaining the loss the tribunal shall apply the same rule concerning the duty of a person to mitigate his loss as applies to damages recoverable under the common law of England and Wales or (as the case may be) Scotland.

(13) Where the tribunal finds that the act, or failure to act, to which the complaint relates was to any extent caused or contributed to by action of the complainant, it shall reduce the amount of the compensation by such proportion as it considers just and equitable having regard to that finding.

(14) If the employer fails, without reasonable justification, to comply with a recommendation made by an employment tribunal under paragraph (7)(c) the tribunal may, if it thinks it just and equitable to do so—

(a) increase the amount of compensation required to be paid to the complainant in respect of the complaint, where an order was made under paragraph (7)(b); or

(b) make an order under paragraph (7)(b).

Restrictions on contracting out

9. Section 203 of the 1996 Act (restrictions on contracting out) shall apply in relation to these Regulations as if they were contained in that Act.

Armed forces

13.—(1) These Regulations, shall have effect in relation—

(a) subject to paragraphs (2) and (3) and apart from regulation 7(1), to service as a member of the armed forces, and

(b) to employment by an association established for the purposes of Part XI of the Reserve Forces Act 1996.

(2) These Regulations shall not have effect in relation to service as a member of the reserve forces in so far as that service consists in undertaking training obligations—

(a) under section 38, 40 or 41 of the Reserve Forces Act 1980,

(b) under section 22 of the Reserve Forces Act 1996,

(c) pursuant to regulations made under section 4 of the Reserve Forces Act 1996,

or consists in undertaking voluntary training or duties under section 27 of the Reserve Forces Act 1996.

[667] As amended by SI 2002/2035, reg 2.

[668] As amended by SI 2002/2035, reg 2.

(3) No complaint concerning the service of any person as a member of the armed forces may be presented to an employment tribunal under regulation 8 unless—
  (a) that person has made a complaint in respect of the same matter to an officer under the service redress procedures, and
  (b) that complaint has not been withdrawn.

[(4) For the purpose of paragraph (3)(b), a person shall be treated as having withdrawn his complaint if, having made a complaint to an officer under the service redress procedures—
  (a) where the service redress procedures are those referred to in section 334 of the Armed Forces Act 2006, neither that officer nor a superior officer has decided to refer the complaint to the Defence Council, and the person who made the complaint fails to apply for such a reference to be made;
  (b) in any other case, the person who made the complaint fails to submit the complaint to the Defence Council under the service redress procedures.][669]

(5) Where a complaint of the kind referred to in paragraph (3) is presented to an employment tribunal, the service redress procedures may continue after the complaint is presented.

(6) In this regulation, 'the service redress procedures' means the procedures, excluding those which relate to the making of a report to Her Majesty, referred to in section 180 of the Army Act 1955, section 180 of the Air Force Act 1955[, section 130 of the Naval Discipline Act 1957 or section 334 of the Armed Forces Act 2006].[670]

669 Substituted by SI 2008/1696, art 3(2).
670 Substituted by SI 2008/1696, art 3(3).

The Transfer of Employment (Pension Protection) Regulations 2005

(SI 2005/649)

Citation, commencement, application and interpretation

1.—(1) These Regulations may be cited as the Transfer of Employment (Pension Protection) Regulations 2005 and shall come into force on 6th April 2005.

(2) These Regulations apply in the case of a person ('the employee') in relation to whom section 257 of the Act (conditions for pension protection) applies, that is to say a person who, in the circumstances described in subsection (1) of that section, ceases to be employed by the transferor of an undertaking or part of an undertaking and becomes employed by the transferee.

(3) In these Regulations 'the Act' means the Pensions Act 2004.

Requirements concerning a transferee's pension scheme

2.—(1) In a case where these Regulations apply, and the transferee is the employer in relation to a pension scheme which is not a money purchase scheme, that scheme complies with section 258(2)(c)(ii) of the Act (alternative standard for a scheme which is not a money purchase scheme) if it provides either—

(a) for members to be entitled to benefits the value of which equals or exceeds 6 per cent. of pensionable pay for each year of employment together with the total amount of any contributions made by them, and, where members are required to make contributions to the scheme, for them to contribute at a rate which does not exceed 6 per cent. of their pensionable pay; or

(b) for the transferee to make relevant contributions to the scheme on behalf of each employee of his who is an active member of it.

(2) In this regulation—

'pensionable pay' means that part of the remuneration payable to a member of a scheme by reference to which the amount of contributions and benefits are determined under the rules of the scheme.

Requirements concerning a transferee's pension contributions

3.—(1) In a case where these Regulations apply, the transferee's pension contributions are relevant contributions for the purposes of section 258(2)(b) of the Act in the case of a money purchase scheme, section 258(3) to (5) of the Act in the case of a stakeholder pension scheme, and regulation 2(1)(b) above in the case of a scheme which is not a money purchase scheme, if—

(a) the contributions are made in respect of each period for which the employee is paid remuneration, provided that the employee also contributes to the scheme in respect of that period, and

(b) the amount contributed in respect of each such period is—

(i) in a case where the employee's contribution in respect of that period is less than 6 per cent. of the remuneration paid to him, an amount at least equal to the amount of the employee's contribution;

(ii) in a case where the employee's contribution in respect of that period equals or exceeds 6 per cent. of the remuneration paid to him, an amount at least equal to 6 per cent. of that remuneration.

(2) In calculating the amount of an employee's remuneration for the purposes of paragraph (1)—

(a) only payments made in respect of basic pay shall be taken into account, and bonus, commission, overtime and similar payments shall be disregarded, and

(b) no account shall be taken of any deductions which are made in respect of tax, national insurance or pension contributions.

(3) In calculating the amount of a transferee's pension contributions for the purposes of paragraph (1) in the case of a scheme which is contracted-out by virtue of section 9 of the Pension Schemes Act 1993, minimum payments within the meaning of that Act shall be disregarded.

The Transfer of Undertakings (Protection of Employment) Regulations 2006

(SI 2006/246)

Interpretation

2.—(1) In these Regulations—

'assigned' means assigned other than on a temporary basis;

'collective agreement', 'collective bargaining' and 'trade union' have the same meanings respectively as in the 1992 Act;

'contract of employment' means any agreement between an employee and his employer determining the terms and conditions of his employment;

references to 'contractor' in regulation 3 shall include a sub-contractor;

'employee' means any individual who works for another person whether under a contract of service or apprenticeship or otherwise but does not include anyone who provides services under a contract for services and references to a person's employer shall be construed accordingly;

'insolvency practitioner' has the meaning given to the expression by Part XIII of the Insolvency Act 1986;[671]

references to 'organised grouping of employees' shall include a single employee;

'recognised' has the meaning given to the expression by section 178(3) of the 1992 Act;

'relevant transfer' means a transfer or a service provision change to which these Regulations apply in accordance with regulation 3 and 'transferor' and 'transferee' shall be construed accordingly and in the case of a service provision change falling within regulation 3(1)(b), 'the transferor' means the person who carried out the activities prior to the service provision change and 'the transferee' means the person who carries out the activities as a result of the service provision change;

'the 1992 Act' means the Trade Union and Labour Relations (Consolidation) Act 1992;[672]

'the 1996 Act' means the Employment Rights Act 1996;[673]

'the 1996 Tribunals Act' means the Employment Tribunals Act 1996;[674]

'the 1981 Regulations' means the Transfer of Undertakings (Protection of Employment) Regulations 1981.[675]

(2) For the purposes of these Regulations the representative of a trade union recognised by an employer is an official or other person authorised to carry on collective bargaining with that employer by that trade union.

(3) In the application of these Regulations to Northern Ireland the Regulations shall have effect as set out in Schedule 1.

A relevant transfer

3.—(1) These Regulations apply to—

(a) a transfer of an undertaking, business or part of an undertaking or business situated immediately before the transfer in the United Kingdom to another person where there is a transfer of an economic entity which retains its identity;

---

671 1986 c 45; s 388, which explains the meaning of acting as insolvency practitioner, was amended by the Insolvency Act 2000 (c 39) ss 4(1), 4(2)(a), 4(2)(b), 4(2)(c); the Bankruptcy (Scotland) Act 1993 s 11(1); SI 1994/2421; SI 2002/1240; and SI 2002/2708.

672 1992 c 52.

673 1996 c 18.

674 1996 c 17; s 18, which defines conciliation, was amended by the Employment Rights (Dispute Resolution) Act 1998 (c 8) ss 1(2)(a), 11(1), 15 and Sch 1; the National Minimum Wage Act 1998 (c 39) ss 24 and 30(1); the Employment Act 2002 (c 22) ss 24(2), 53 and Sch 7; the Employment Relations Act 2004 (c 24) s 57(1) and Sch 1; SI 1998/1833; SI 1999/3323; SI 2000/1299; SI 2000/1551; SI 2001/1107; SI 2002/2034; SI 2003/1660; SI 2003/1661; SI 2003/1673; SI 2003/3049; SI 2004/2326; SI 2004/1713; and SI 2004/3426.

675 SI 1981/1794, amended by the Dock Work Act 1989 (c 13), s 7(2); the Trade Union Reform and Employment Rights Act 1993 (c 19), ss 33, 51 and Sch 10, the Employment Rights (Dispute Resolution) Act 1998 (c 8), s 1(2)(a); SI 1987/442; SI 1995/2587; SI 1998/1658; SI 1999/1925; and SI 1999/2402.

(b) a service provision change, that is a situation in which—
   (i) activities cease to be carried out by a person ('a client') on his own behalf and are carried out instead by another person on the client's behalf ('a contractor');
   (ii) activities cease to be carried out by a contractor on a client's behalf (whether or not those activities had previously been carried out by the client on his own behalf) and are carried out instead by another person ('a subsequent contractor') on the client's behalf; or
   (iii) activities cease to be carried out by a contractor or a subsequent contractor on a client's behalf (whether or not those activities had previously been carried out by the client on his own behalf) and are carried out instead by the client on his own behalf,

and in which the conditions set out in paragraph (3) are satisfied.

(2) In this regulation 'economic entity' means an organised grouping of resources which has the objective of pursuing an economic activity, whether or not that activity is central or ancillary.

(3) The conditions referred to in paragraph (1)(b) are that—
(a) immediately before the service provision change—
   (i) there is an organised grouping of employees situated in Great Britain which has as its principal purpose the carrying out of the activities concerned on behalf of the client;
   (ii) the client intends that the activities will, following the service provision change, be carried out by the transferee other than in connection with a single specific event or task of short-term duration; and
(b) the activities concerned do not consist wholly or mainly of the supply of goods for the client's use.

(4) Subject to paragraph (1), these Regulations apply to—
(a) public and private undertakings engaged in economic activities whether or not they are operating for gain;
(b) a transfer or service provision change howsoever effected notwithstanding—
   (i) that the transfer of an undertaking, business or part of an undertaking or business is governed or effected by the law of a country or territory outside the United Kingdom or that the service provision change is governed or effected by the law of a country or territory outside Great Britain;
   (ii) that the employment of persons employed in the undertaking, business or part transferred or, in the case of a service provision change, persons employed in the organised grouping of employees, is governed by any such law;
(c) a transfer of an undertaking, business or part of an undertaking or business (which may also be a service provision change) where persons employed in the undertaking, business or part transferred ordinarily work outside the United Kingdom.

(5) An administrative reorganisation of public administrative authorities or the transfer of administrative functions between public administrative authorities is not a relevant transfer.

(6) A relevant transfer—
(a) may be effected by a series of two or more transactions; and
(b) may take place whether or not any property is transferred to the transferee by the transferor.

(7) Where, in consequence (whether directly or indirectly) of the transfer of an undertaking, business or part of an undertaking or business which was situated immediately before the transfer in the United Kingdom, a ship within the meaning of the Merchant Shipping Act 1995[676] registered in the United Kingdom ceases to be so registered, these Regulations shall not affect the right conferred by section 29 of that Act (right of seamen to be discharged when ship ceases to be registered in the United Kingdom) on a seaman employed in the ship.

Effect of relevant transfer on contracts of employment

4.—(1) Except where objection is made under paragraph (7), a relevant transfer shall not operate so as to terminate the contract of employment of any person employed by the transferor and assigned to the organised grouping of resources or employees that is subject to the relevant transfer, which would otherwise be terminated by the transfer, but any such contract shall have effect after the transfer as if originally made between the person so employed and the transferee.

---

[676] 1995 c 21.

(2) Without prejudice to paragraph (1), but subject to paragraph (6), and regulations 8 and 15(9), on the completion of a relevant transfer—
   (a) all the transferor's rights, powers, duties and liabilities under or in connection with any such contract shall be transferred by virtue of this regulation to the transferee; and
   (b) any act or omission before the transfer is completed, of or in relation to the transferor in respect of that contract or a person assigned to that organised grouping of resources or employees, shall be deemed to have been an act or omission of or in relation to the transferee.

(3) Any reference in paragraph (1) to a person employed by the transferor and assigned to the organised grouping of resources or employees that is subject to a relevant transfer, is a reference to a person so employed immediately before the transfer, or who would have been so employed if he had not been dismissed in the circumstances described in regulation 7(1), including, where the transfer is effected by a series of two or more transactions, a person so employed and assigned or who would have been so employed and assigned immediately before any of those transactions.

(4) Subject to regulation 9, in respect of a contract of employment that is, or will be, transferred by paragraph (1), any purported variation of the contract shall be void if the sole or principal reason for the variation is—
   (a) the transfer itself; or
   (b) a reason connected with the transfer that is not an economic, technical or organisational reason entailing changes in the workforce.

(5) Paragraph (4) shall not prevent the employer and his employee, whose contract of employment is, or will be, transferred by paragraph (1), from agreeing a variation of that contract if the sole or principal reason for the variation is—
   (a) a reason connected with the transfer that is an economic, technical or organisational reason entailing changes in the workforce; or
   (b) a reason unconnected with the transfer.

(6) Paragraph (2) shall not transfer or otherwise affect the liability of any person to be prosecuted for, convicted of and sentenced for any offence.

(7) Paragraphs (1) and (2) shall not operate to transfer the contract of employment and the rights, powers, duties and liabilities under or in connection with it of an employee who informs the transferor or the transferee that he objects to becoming employed by the transferee.

(8) Subject to paragraphs (9) and (11), where an employee so objects, the relevant transfer shall operate so as to terminate his contract of employment with the transferor but he shall not be treated, for any purpose, as having been dismissed by the transferor.

(9) Subject to regulation 9, where a relevant transfer involves or would involve a substantial change in working conditions to the material detriment of a person whose contract of employment is or would be transferred under paragraph (1), such an employee may treat the contract of employment as having been terminated, and the employee shall be treated for any purpose as having been dismissed by the employer.

(10) No damages shall be payable by an employer as a result of a dismissal falling within paragraph (9) in respect of any failure by the employer to pay wages to an employee in respect of a notice period which the employee has failed to work.

(11) Paragraphs (1), (7), (8) and (9) are without prejudice to any right of an employee arising apart from these Regulations to terminate his contract of employment without notice in acceptance of a repudiatory breach of contract by his employer.

Dismissal of employee because of relevant transfer

7.—(1) Where either before or after a relevant transfer, any employee of the transferor or transferee is dismissed, that employee shall be treated for the purposes of Part X of the 1996 Act (unfair dismissal) as unfairly dismissed if the sole or principal reason for his dismissal is—
   (a) the transfer itself; or
   (b) a reason connected with the transfer that is not an economic, technical or organisational reason entailing changes in the workforce.

(2) This paragraph applies where the sole or principal reason for the dismissal is a reason connected with the transfer that is an economic, technical or organisational reason entailing changes in the workforce of either the transferor or the transferee before or after a relevant transfer.

(3) Where paragraph (2) applies—
   (a) paragraph (1) shall not apply;

(b) without prejudice to the application of section 98(4) of the 1996 Act (test of fair dismissal), the dismissal shall, for the purposes of sections 98(1) and 135 of that Act (reason for dismissal), be regarded as having been for redundancy where section 98(2)(c) of that Act applies, or otherwise for a substantial reason of a kind such as to justify the dismissal of an employee holding the position which that employee held.

(4) The provisions of this regulation apply irrespective of whether the employee in question is assigned to the organised grouping of resources or employees that is, or will be, transferred.

(5) Paragraph (1) shall not apply in relation to the dismissal of any employee which was required by reason of the application of section 5 of the Aliens Restriction (Amendment) Act 1919[677] to his employment.

(6) Paragraph (1) shall not apply in relation to a dismissal of an employee if the application of section 94 of the 1996 Act to the dismissal of the employee is excluded by or under any provision of the 1996 Act, the 1996 Tribunals Act or the 1992 Act.

Insolvency

8.—(1) If at the time of a relevant transfer the transferor is subject to relevant insolvency proceedings paragraphs (2) to (6) apply.

(2) In this regulation 'relevant employee' means an employee of the transferor—

(a) whose contract of employment transfers to the transferee by virtue of the operation of these Regulations; or

(b) whose employment with the transferor is terminated before the time of the relevant transfer in the circumstances described in regulation 7(1).

(3) The relevant statutory scheme specified in paragraph (4)(b) (including that sub-paragraph as applied by paragraph 5 of Schedule 1) shall apply in the case of a relevant employee irrespective of the fact that the qualifying requirement that the employee's employment has been terminated is not met and for those purposes the date of the transfer shall be treated as the date of the termination and the transferor shall be treated as the employer.

(4) In this regulation the 'relevant statutory schemes' are—

(a) Chapter VI of Part XI of the 1996 Act;

(b) Part XII of the 1996 Act.

(5) Regulation 4 shall not operate to transfer liability for the sums payable to the relevant employee under the relevant statutory schemes.

(6) In this regulation 'relevant insolvency proceedings' means insolvency proceedings which have been opened in relation to the transferor not with a view to the liquidation of the assets of the transferor and which are under the supervision of an insolvency practitioner.

(7) Regulations 4 and 7 do not apply to any relevant transfer where the transferor is the subject of bankruptcy proceedings or any analogous insolvency proceedings which have been instituted with a view to the liquidation of the assets of the transferor and are under the supervision of an insolvency practitioner.

Variations of contract where transferors are subject to relevant insolvency proceedings

9.—(1) If at the time of a relevant transfer the transferor is subject to relevant insolvency proceedings these Regulations shall not prevent the transferor or transferee (or an insolvency practitioner) and appropriate representatives of assigned employees agreeing to permitted variations.

(2) For the purposes of this regulation 'appropriate representatives' are—

(a) if the employees are of a description in respect of which an independent trade union is recognised by their employer, representatives of the trade union; or

(b) in any other case, whichever of the following employee representatives the employer chooses—

(i) employee representatives appointed or elected by the assigned employees (whether they make the appointment or election alone or with others) otherwise than for the purposes of this regulation, who (having regard to the purposes for, and the method by which they were appointed or elected) have authority from those employees to agree permitted variations to contracts of employment on their behalf;

(ii) employee representatives elected by assigned employees (whether they make the appointment or election alone or with others) for these particular purposes, in an election satisfying requirements identical to those contained in regulation 14 except those in regulation 14(1)(d).

---

677 1919 c 92; s 5 was amended by the Former Enemy Aliens (Disabilities Removal) Act 1925, s 1 and Sch 2; the Merchant Shipping Act 1970, s 100(3) and Sch 5; and the Merchant Shipping Act 1995, s 314 and Sch 12.

(3) An individual may be an appropriate representative for the purposes of both this regulation and regulation 13 provided that where the representative is not a trade union representative he is either elected by or has authority from assigned employees (within the meaning of this regulation) and affected employees (as described in regulation 13(1)).

(4) In section 168 of the 1992 Act (time off for carrying out trade union duties) in subsection (1), after paragraph (c) there is inserted—

', or

(d) negotiations with a view to entering into an agreement under regulation 9 of the Transfer of Undertakings (Protection of Employment) Regulations 2006 that applies to employees of the employer, or

(e) the performance on behalf of employees of the employer of functions related to or connected with the making of an agreement under that regulation.'

(5) Where assigned employees are represented by non-trade union representatives—

(a) the agreement recording a permitted variation must be in writing and signed by each of the representatives who have made it or, where that is not reasonably practicable, by a duly authorised agent of that representative; and

(b) the employer must, before the agreement is made available for signature, provide all employees to whom it is intended to apply on the date on which it is to come into effect with copies of the text of the agreement and such guidance as those employees might reasonably require in order to understand it fully.

(6) A permitted variation shall take effect as a term or condition of the assigned employee's contract of employment in place, where relevant, of any term or condition which it varies.

(7) In this regulation—

'assigned employees' means those employees assigned to the organised grouping of resources or employees that is the subject of a relevant transfer;

'permitted variation' is a variation to the contract of employment of an assigned employee where—

(a) the sole or principal reason for it is the transfer itself or a reason connected with the transfer that is not an economic, technical or organisational reason entailing changes in the workforce; and

(b) it is designed to safeguard employment opportunities by ensuring the survival of the undertaking, business or part of the undertaking or business that is the subject of the relevant transfer;

'relevant insolvency proceedings' has the meaning given to the expression by regulation 8(6).

Pensions

10.—(1) Regulations 4 and 5 shall not apply—

(a) to so much of a contract of employment or collective agreement as relates to an occupational pension scheme within the meaning of the Pension Schemes Act 1993;[678] or

(b) to any rights, powers, duties or liabilities under or in connection with any such contract or subsisting by virtue of any such agreement and relating to such a scheme or otherwise arising in connection with that person's employment and relating to such a scheme.

(2) For the purposes of paragraphs (1) and (3), any provisions of an occupational pension scheme which do not relate to benefits for old age, invalidity or survivors shall not be treated as being part of the scheme.

(3) An employee whose contract of employment is transferred in the circumstances described in regulation 4(1) shall not be entitled to bring a claim against the transferor for—

(a) breach of contract; or

(b) constructive unfair dismissal under section 95(1)(c) of the 1996 Act,

arising out of a loss or reduction in his rights under an occupational pension scheme in consequence of the transfer, save insofar as the alleged breach of contract or dismissal (as the case may be) occurred prior to the date on which these Regulations took effect.

Duty to inform and consult representatives

13.—(1) In this regulation and regulations 14 and 15 references to affected employees, in relation to a relevant transfer, are to any employees of the transferor or the transferee (whether or not assigned to the organised grouping of resources or employees that is the subject of a relevant transfer) who may

[678] 1993 c 48; s 1, which defines occupational pension scheme, was amended by the Welfare Reform & Pensions Act 1999 (c 30), s 18 and Sch 2; the Pensions Act 2004 (c 35), s 239; and SI 1999/1820.

be affected by the transfer or may be affected by measures taken in connection with it; and references to the employer shall be construed accordingly.

(2) Long enough before a relevant transfer to enable the employer of any affected employees to consult the appropriate representatives of any affected employees, the employer shall inform those representatives of—
  (a) the fact that the transfer is to take place, the date or proposed date of the transfer and the reasons for it;
  (b) the legal, economic and social implications of the transfer for any affected employees;
  (c) the measures which he envisages he will, in connection with the transfer, take in relation to any affected employees or, if he envisages that no measures will be so taken, that fact; and
  (d) if the employer is the transferor, the measures, in connection with the transfer, which he envisages the transferee will take in relation to any affected employees who will become employees of the transferee after the transfer by virtue of regulation 4 or, if he envisages that no measures will be so taken, that fact.

(3) For the purposes of this regulation the appropriate representatives of any affected employees are—
  (a) if the employees are of a description in respect of which an independent trade union is recognised by their employer, representatives of the trade union; or
  (b) in any other case, whichever of the following employee representatives the employer chooses—
    (i) employee representatives appointed or elected by the affected employees otherwise than for the purposes of this regulation, who (having regard to the purposes for, and the method by which they were appointed or elected) have authority from those employees to receive information and to be consulted about the transfer on their behalf;
    (ii) employee representatives elected by any affected employees, for the purposes of this regulation, in an election satisfying the requirements of regulation 14(1).

(4) The transferee shall give the transferor such information at such a time as will enable the transferor to perform the duty imposed on him by virtue of paragraph (2)(d).

(5) The information which is to be given to the appropriate representatives shall be given to each of them by being delivered to them, or sent by post to an address notified by them to the employer, or (in the case of representatives of a trade union) sent by post to the trade union at the address of its head or main office.

(6) An employer of an affected employee who envisages that he will take measures in relation to an affected employee, in connection with the relevant transfer, shall consult the appropriate representatives of that employee with a view to seeking their agreement to the intended measures.

(7) In the course of those consultations the employer shall—
  (a) consider any representations made by the appropriate representatives; and
  (b) reply to those representations and, if he rejects any of those representations, state his reasons.

(8) The employer shall allow the appropriate representatives access to any affected employees and shall afford to those representatives such accommodation and other facilities as may be appropriate.

(9) If in any case there are special circumstances which render it not reasonably practicable for an employer to perform a duty imposed on him by any of paragraphs (2) to (7), he shall take all such steps towards performing that duty as are reasonably practicable in the circumstances.

(10) Where—
  (a) the employer has invited any of the affected employee to elect employee representatives; and
  (b) the invitation was issued long enough before the time when the employer is required to give information under paragraph (2) to allow them to elect representatives by that time,

the employer shall be treated as complying with the requirements of this regulation in relation to those employees if he complies with those requirements as soon as is reasonably practicable after the election of the representatives.

(11) If, after the employer has invited any affected employees to elect representatives, they fail to do so within a reasonable time, he shall give to any affected employees the information set out in paragraph (2).

(12) The duties imposed on an employer by this regulation shall apply irrespective of whether the decision resulting in the relevant transfer is taken by the employer or a person controlling the employer.

Failure to inform or consult

15.—(1) Where an employer has failed to comply with a requirement of regulation 13 or regulation 14, a complaint may be presented to an employment tribunal on that ground—

(a) in the case of a failure relating to the election of employee representatives, by any of his employees who are affected employees;

(b) in the case of any other failure relating to employee representatives, by any of the employee representatives to whom the failure related;

(c) in the case of failure relating to representatives of a trade union, by the trade union; and

(d) in any other case, by any of his employees who are affected employees.

(2) If on a complaint under paragraph (1) a question arises whether or not it was reasonably practicable for an employer to perform a particular duty or as to what steps he took towards performing it, it shall be for him to show—

(a) that there were special circumstances which rendered it not reasonably practicable for him to perform the duty; and

(b) that he took all such steps towards its performance as were reasonably practicable in those circumstances.

(3) If on a omplaint under paragraph (1) a question arises as to whether or not an employee representative was an appropriate representative for the purposes of regulation 13, it shall be for the employer to show that the employee representative had the necessary authority to represent the affected employees.

(4) On a complaint under paragraph (1)(a) it shall be for the employer to show that the requirements in regulation 14 have been satisfied.

(5) On a complaint against a transferor that he had failed to perform the duty imposed upon him by virtue of regulation 13(2)(d) or, so far as relating thereto, regulation 13(9), he may not show that it was not reasonably practicable for him to perform the duty in question for the reason that the transferee had failed to give him the requisite information at the requisite time in accordance with regulation 13(4) unless he gives the transferee notice of his intention to show that fact; and the giving of the notice shall make the transferee a party to the proceedings.

(6) In relation to any complaint under paragraph (1), a failure on the part of a person controlling (directly or indirectly) the employer to provide information to the employer shall not constitute special circumstances rendering it not reasonably practicable for the employer to comply with such a requirement.

(7) Where the tribunal finds a complaint against a transferee under paragraph (1) well-founded it shall make a declaration to that effect and may order the transferee to pay appropriate compensation to such descriptions of affected employees as may be specified in the award.

(8) Where the tribunal finds a complaint against a transferor under paragraph (1) well-founded it shall make a declaration to that effect and may—

(a) order the transferor, subject to paragraph (9), to pay appropriate compensation to such descriptions of affected employees as may be specified in the award; or

(b) if the complaint is that the transferor did not perform the duty mentioned in paragraph (5) and the transferor (after giving due notice) shows the facts so mentioned, order the transferee to pay appropriate compensation to such descriptions of affected employees as may be specified in the award.

(9) The transferee shall be jointly and severally liable with the transferor in respect of compensation payable under sub-paragraph (8)(a) or paragraph (11).

(10) An employee may present a complaint to an employment tribunal on the ground that he is an employee of a description to which an order under paragraph (7) or (8) relates and that—

(a) in respect of an order under paragraph (7), the transferee has failed, wholly or in part, to pay him compensation in pursuance of the order;

(b) in respect of an order under paragraph (8), the transferor or transferee, as applicable, has failed, wholly or in part, to pay him compensation in pursuance of the order.

(11) Where the tribunal finds a complaint under paragraph (10) well-founded it shall order the transferor or transferee as applicable to pay the complainant the amount of compensation which it finds is due to him.

(12) An employment tribunal shall not consider a complaint under paragraph (1) or (10) unless it is presented to the tribunal before the end of the period of three months beginning with—

(a) in respect of a complaint under paragraph (1), the date on which the relevant transfer is completed; or

(b) in respect of a complaint under paragraph (10), the date of the tribunal's order under paragraph (7) or (8),

or within such further period as the tribunal considers reasonable in a case where it is satisfied that it was not reasonably practicable for the complaint to be presented before the end of the period of three months.

Restriction on contracting out

18. Section 203 of the 1996 Act (restrictions on contracting out) shall apply in relation to these Regulations as if they were contained in that Act, save for that section shall not apply in so far as these Regulations provide for an agreement (whether a contract of employment or not) to exclude or limit the operation of these Regulations.

(2) Section 33 of, and paragraph 4 of Schedule 9 to, the Trade Union Reform and Employment Rights Act 1993[679] are repealed.

(3) Schedule 2 (consequential amendments) shall have effect.

Transitional provisions and savings

21.—(1) These Regulations shall apply in relation to—

(a) a relevant transfer that takes place on or after 6 April 2006;

(b) a transfer or service provision change, not falling within sub-paragraph (a), that takes place on or after 6 April 2006 and is regarded by virtue of any enactment as a relevant transfer.

(2) The 1981 Regulations shall continue to apply in relation to—

(a) a relevant transfer (within the meaning of the 1981 Regulations) that took place before 6 April 2006;

(b) a transfer, not falling within sub-paragraph (a), that took place before 6 April 2006 and is regarded by virtue of any enactment as a relevant transfer (within the meaning of the 1981 Regulations).

(3) In respect of a relevant transfer that takes place on or after 6 April 2006, any action taken by a transferor or transferee to discharge a duty that applied to them under regulation 10 or 10A of the 1981 Regulations shall be deemed to satisfy the corresponding obligation imposed by regulations 13 and 14 of these Regulations, insofar as that action would have discharged those obligations had the action taken place on or after 6 April 2006.

(4) The duty on a transferor to provide a transferee with employee liability information shall not apply in the case of a relevant transfer that takes place on or before 19 April 2006.

(5) Regulations 13, 14, 15 and 16 shall not apply in the case of a service provision change that is not also a transfer of an undertaking, business or part of an undertaking or business that takes place on or before 4 May 2006.

(6) The repeal of paragraph 4 of Schedule 9 to the Trade Union Reform and Employment Rights Act 1993 does not affect the continued operation of that paragraph so far as it remains capable of having effect.

[679] 1993 c 19.

The Working Time Regulations 1998

(SI 1998/1833)

Part II

Rights and Obligations Concerning Working Time

Maximum weekly working time

4.—(1) [Unless his employer has first obtained the worker's agreement in writing to perform such work], a worker's working time, including overtime, in any reference period which is applicable in his case shall not exceed an average of 48 hours for each seven days.[680]

(2) An employer shall take all reasonable steps, in keeping with the need to protect the health and safety of workers, to ensure that the limit specified in paragraph (1) is complied with in the case of each worker employed by him in relation to whom it applies [and shall keep up-to-date records of all workers who carry out work to which it does not apply by reason of the fact that the employer has obtained the worker's agreement as mentioned in paragraph (1)].[681]

(3) Subject to paragraphs (4) and (5) and any agreement under regulation 23(b), the reference periods which apply in the case of a worker are—

(a) where a relevant agreement provides for the application of this regulation in relation to successive periods of 17 weeks, each such period, or

(b) in any other case, any period of 17 weeks in the course of his employment.

(4) Where a worker has worked for his employer for less than 17 weeks, the reference period applicable in his case is the period that has elapsed since he started work for his employer.

(5) Paragraphs (3) and (4) shall apply to a worker who is excluded from the scope of certain provisions of these Regulations by regulation 21 as if for each reference to 17 weeks there were substituted a reference to 26 weeks.

(6) For the purposes of this regulation, a worker's average working time for each seven days during a reference period shall be determined according to the formula—

$$\frac{A+B}{C}$$

where—

A is the aggregate number of hours comprised in the worker's working time during the course of the reference period;

B is the aggregate number of hours comprised in his working time during the course of the period beginning immediately after the end of the reference period and ending when the number of days in that subsequent period on which he has worked equals the number of excluded days during the reference period; and

C is the number of weeks in the reference period.

(7) In paragraph (6), 'excluded days' means days comprised in—[682]

(a) any period of annual leave taken by the worker in exercise of his entitlement under regulation 13;

(b) any period of sick leave taken by the worker;

(c) any period of maternity[, paternity, adoption or parental] leave taken by the worker; and[683]

(d) any period in respect of which the limit specified in paragraph (1) did not apply in relation to the worker [by reason of the fact that the employer has obtained the worker's agreement as mentioned in paragraph (1)].

Entitlement to annual leave

13.—[(1) Subject to paragraph (5), a worker is entitled to four weeks' annual leave in each leave year.][684]

680 As amended by SI 1999/3372, reg 3.

681 As amended by SI 1999/3372, reg 3.

682 As amended by SI 1999/3372, reg 3.

683 As amended by SI 2002/3128, reg 5.

684 As amended by SI 2001/3256, reg 2.

(2) [. . .] [685]

(3) A worker's leave year, for the purposes of this regulation, begins—
  (a) on such date during the calendar year as may be provided for in a relevant agreement; or
  (b) where there are no provisions of a relevant agreement which apply—
    (i) if the worker's employment began on or before 1st October 1998, on that date and each subsequent anniversary of that date; or
    (ii) if the worker's employment begins after 1st October 1998, on the date on which that employment begins and each subsequent anniversary of that date.

(4) Paragraph (3) does not apply to a worker to whom Schedule 2 applies (workers employed in agriculture) except where, in the case of a worker partly employed in agriculture, a relevant agreement so provides.

(5) Where the date on which a worker's employment begins is later than the date on which (by virtue of a relevant agreement) his first leave year begins, the leave to which he is entitled in that leave year is a proportion of the period applicable under [paragraph (1)] equal to the proportion of that leave year remaining on the date on which his employment begins.[686]

(6) Where by virtue of paragraph [. . .] (5) the period of leave to which a worker is entitled is or includes a proportion of a week, the proportion shall be determined in days and any fraction of a day shall be treated as a whole day.[687]

(7) [. . .] [688]

(8) [. . .] [689]

(9) Leave to which a worker is entitled under this regulation may be taken in instalments, but—
  (a) it may only be taken in the leave year in respect of which it is due, and
  (b) it may not be replaced by a payment in lieu except where the worker's employment is terminated.

Compensation related to entitlement to leave

14.—(1) This regulation applies where—[690]
  (a) a worker's employment is terminated during the course of his leave year, and
  (b) on the date on which the termination takes effect ('the termination date'), the proportion he has taken of the leave to which he is entitled in the leave year under [regulation 13] differs from the proportion of the leave year which has expired.

(2) Where the proportion of leave taken by the worker is less than the proportion of the leave year which has expired, his employer shall make him a payment in lieu of leave in accordance with paragraph (3).

(3) The payment due under paragraph (2) shall be—[691]
  (a) such sum as may be provided for for the purposes of this regulation in a relevant agreement, or
  (b) where there are no provisions of a relevant agreement which apply, a sum equal to the amount that would be due to the worker under regulation 16 in respect of a period of leave determined according to the formula—

$$(A \times B) - C$$

where—

A is the period of leave to which the worker is entitled under [regulation 13];
B is the proportion of the worker's leave year which expired before the termination date, and
C is the period of leave taken by the worker between the start of the leave year and the termination date.

(4) A relevant agreement may provide that, where the proportion of leave taken by the worker exceeds the proportion of the leave year which has expired, he shall compensate his employer, whether by a payment, by undertaking additional work or otherwise.

685 As amended by SI 2001/3256, reg 2.
686 As amended by SI 2001/3256, reg 2.
687 As amended by SI 2001/3256, reg 2.
688 As amended by SI 2001/3256, reg 2.
689 As amended by SI 2001/3256, reg 2.
690 As amended by SI 2001/3256, reg 3.
691 As amended by SI 2001/3256, reg 3.

Dates on which leave is taken

15.—(1) A worker may take leave to which he is entitled under [regulation 13] on such days as he may elect by giving notice to his employer in accordance with paragraph (3), subject to any requirement imposed on him by his employer under paragraph (2).

(2) A worker's employer may require the worker—[692]

(a) to take leave to which the worker is entitled under [regulation 13]; or

(b) not to take such leave,

on particular days, by giving notice to the worker in accordance with paragraph (3).

(3) A notice under paragraph (1) or (2)—

(a) may relate to all or part of the leave to which a worker is entitled in a leave year;

(b) shall specify the days on which leave is or (as the case may be) is not to be taken and, where the leave on a particular day is to be in respect of only part of the day, its duration; and

(c) shall be given to the employer or, as the case may be, the worker before the relevant date.

(4) The relevant date, for the purposes of paragraph (3), is the date—

(a) in the case of a notice under paragraph (1) or (2)(a), twice as many days in advance of the earliest day specified in the notice as the number of days or part-days to which the notice relates, and

(b) in the case of a notice under paragraph (2)(b), as many days in advance of the earliest day so specified as the number of days or part-days to which the notice relates.

(5) Any right or obligation under paragraphs (1) to (4) may be varied or excluded by a relevant agreement.

(6) This regulation does not apply to a worker to whom Schedule 2 applies (workers employed in agriculture) except where, in the case of a worker partly employed in agriculture, a relevant agreement so provides.

[Leave during the first year of employment[693]

15A.—(1) During the first year of his employment, the amount of leave a worker may take at any time in exercise of his entitlement under regulation 13 is limited to the amount which is deemed to have accrued in his case at that time under paragraph (2), as modified under paragraph (3) in a case where that paragraph applies, less the amount of leave (if any) that he has already taken during that year.

(2) For the purposes of paragraph (1), leave is deemed to accrue over the course of the worker's first year of employment, at the rate of one-twelfth of the amount specified in regulation 13(1) on the first day of each month of that year.

(3) Where the amount of leave that has accrued in a particular case includes a fraction of a day other than a half-day, the fraction shall be treated as a half-day if it is less than a half-day and as a whole day if it is more than a half-day.

(4) This regulation does not apply to a worker whose employment began on or before 25th October 2001.]

Payment in respect of periods of leave

16.—(1) A worker is entitled to be paid in respect of any period of annual leave to which he is entitled under regulation 13, at the rate of a week's pay in respect of each week of leave.

(2) Sections 221 to 224 of the 1996 Act shall apply for the purpose of determining the amount of a week's pay for the purposes of this regulation, subject to the modifications set out in paragraph (3).

(3) The provisions referred to in paragraph (2) shall apply—

(a) as if references to the employee were references to the worker;

(b) as if references to the employee's contract of employment were references to the worker's contract;

(c) as if the calculation date were the first day of the period of leave in question; and

(d) as if the references to sections 227 and 228 did not apply.

(4) A right to payment under paragraph (1) does not affect any right of a worker to remuneration under his contract ('contractual remuneration').

692 As amended by SI 2001/3256, reg 3.

693 Inserted by SI 2001/3256, reg 4.

(5) Any contractual remuneration paid to a worker in respect of a period of leave goes towards discharging any liability of the employer to make payments under this regulation in respect of that period; and, conversely, any payment of remuneration under this regulation in respect of a period goes towards discharging any liability of the employer to pay contractual remuneration in respect of that period.

Entitlements under other provisions

17. Where during any period a worker is entitled to a rest period, rest break or annual leave both under a provision of these Regulations and under a separate provision (including a provision of his contract), he may not exercise the two rights separately, but may, in taking a rest period, break or leave during that period, take advantage of whichever right is, in any particular respect, the more favourable.

Appendix 2
Practice Directions

Practice Direction (Employment Appeal Tribunal—Procedure) 2008

1 Introduction and Objective

1.1 This Practice Direction ('PD') supersedes all previous Practice Directions. It comes into force on 22 May 2008.

1.2 The Employment Appeal Tribunal Rules 1993 (SI 1993/2854) as amended by the Employment Appeal Tribunal (Amendment) Rules 2001 (SI 2001/1128 and 2001/1476) and the Employment Appeal Tribunal (Amendment) Rules 2004 (SI 2004/2526) ('the Rules') apply to all proceedings irrespective of when those proceedings were commenced.

1.3 By s 30(3) of the Employment Tribunals Act 1996 ('ETA 1996') the Employment Appeal Tribunal ('the EAT') has power, subject to the Rules, to regulate its own procedure. In so doing, the EAT regards itself as subject in all its actions to the duties imposed by Rule 2A. It will seek to apply the overriding objective when it exercises any power given to it by the Rules or interprets any Rule.

1.4 The overriding objective of this PD is to enable the EAT to deal with cases justly. Dealing with a case justly includes, so far as is practicable:

1.4.1 ensuring that the parties are on an equal footing;

1.4.2 dealing with the case in ways which are proportionate to the importance and complexity of the issues;

1.4.3 ensuring that it is dealt with expeditiously and fairly;

1.4.4 saving expense.

1.5 The parties are required to help the EAT to further the overriding objective.

1.6 Where the Rules do not otherwise provide, the following procedure will apply to all appeals to the EAT.

1.7 The provisions of this PD are subject to any specific directions which the EAT may make in any particular case. Otherwise, the directions set out below must be complied with in all appeals from Employment Tribunals. In national security appeals, and appeals from the Certification Officer and the Central Arbitration Committee, the Rules set out the separate procedures to be followed and the EAT will normally give specific directions.

1.8 Where it is appropriate to the EAT's jurisdiction, procedure, unrestricted rights of representation and restricted costs regime, the EAT is guided by the Civil Procedure Rules. So, for example:

1.8.1 For the purpose of serving a valid Notice of Appeal under Rule 3 and para 3 below, when an Employment Tribunal decision is sent to parties on a Wednesday, that day does not count and the Notice of Appeal must arrive at the EAT by 4.00pm on or before the Wednesday 6 weeks (i.e. 42 days) later.

1.8.2 When a date is given for serving of a document or for doing some other act, the complete document must be received by the EAT or the relevant party by 4.00pm on that date. Any document received after 4.00pm will be deemed to be lodged on the next working day.

1.8.3 Except as provided in 1.8.4 below, all days count, but if a time limit expires on a day when the central office of the EAT, or the EAT office in Edinburgh (as appropriate), is closed, it is extended to the next working day.

1.8.4 Where the time limit is five days (e.g. an appeal against a Registrar's order or direction), Saturdays, Sundays, Christmas Day, Good Friday and Bank Holidays do not count. For example an appeal against an order made on a Wednesday must arrive at the EAT on or before the following Wednesday.

1.9 In this PD any reference to the date of an order shall mean the date stamped upon the relevant order by the EAT ('the seal date').

1.10 The parties can expect the EAT normally to have read the documents (or the documents indicated in any essential reading list if permission is granted under para 6.3 below for an enlarged appeal bundle) in advance of any hearing.

2 Institution of Appeal

2.1 The Notice of Appeal must be, or be substantially, in accordance with Form 1 (in the amended form annexed to this Practice Direction) or Forms 1A or 2 of the Schedule to the Rules and must identify the date of the judgment, decision or order being appealed. Copies of the judgment, decision or order appealed against and of the Employment Tribunal's written reasons, together with a copy of the claim (ET1) and the response (ET3) must be attached, or if not, a written explanation must be given. A Notice of Appeal without such documentation will not be validly lodged.

2.2 If the appellant has made an application to the Employment Tribunal for a review of its judgment or decision, a copy of such application should accompany the Notice of Appeal together with the judgment and written reasons of the Employment Tribunal in respect of that review application, or a statement, if such be the case, that a judgment is awaited. If any of these documents cannot be included, a written explanation must be given. The appellant should also attach (where they are relevant to the appeal) copies of any orders including case management orders made by the Employment Tribunal.

2.3 Where written reasons of the Employment Tribunal are not attached to the Notice of Appeal, either (as set out in the written explanation) because a request for written reasons has been refused by the Employment Tribunal or for some other reason, an appellant must, when lodging the Notice of Appeal, apply in writing to the EAT to exercise its discretion to hear the appeal without written reasons or to exercise its power to request written reasons from the Employment Tribunal, setting out the full grounds of that application.

2.4 The Notice of Appeal must clearly identify the point(s) of law which form(s) the ground(s) of appeal from the judgment, decision or order of the Employment Tribunal to the EAT. It should also state the order which the appellant will ask the EAT to make at the hearing.

2.5 Rules 3(7)–(10) give a judge or the Registrar power to decide that no further action shall be taken in certain cases where it appears that the Notice of Appeal or any part of it (a) discloses no reasonable grounds for bringing the appeal, or (b) is an abuse of the Employment Appeal Tribunal's process or is otherwise likely to obstruct the just disposal of proceedings. The Rules specify the rights of the appellant and the procedure to be followed. The appellant can request an oral hearing before a judge to challenge the decision. If it appears to the judge or Registrar that a Notice of Appeal or an application gives insufficient grounds of, or lacks clarity in identifying, a point of law, the judge or Registrar may postpone any decision under Rule 3(7) pending the appellant's amplification or clarification of the Notice of Appeal or further information from the Employment Tribunal.

2.6 **Perversity Appeals:** an appellant may not state as a ground of appeal simply words to the effect that 'the judgment or order was contrary to the evidence', or that 'there was no evidence to support the judgment or order', or that 'the judgment or order was one which no reasonable Tribunal could have reached and was perverse' unless the Notice of Appeal also sets out full particulars of the matters relied on in support of those general grounds.

2.7 A party cannot reserve a right to amend, alter or add, to a Notice of Appeal or a respondent's Answer. Any application for permission to amend must be made as soon as practicable and must be accompanied by a draft of the amended Notice of Appeal or amended Answer which makes clear the precise amendments for which permission is sought.

2.8 A respondent to the appeal who wishes to resist the appeal and/or to cross-appeal, but who has not delivered a respondent's Answer as directed by the Registrar, or otherwise ordered, may be precluded from taking part in the appeal unless permission is granted to serve an Answer out of time.

2.9 Where an application is made for permission to institute or continue relevant proceedings by a person who has been made the subject of a Restriction of Proceedings Order pursuant to s 33 of ETA 1996, that application will be considered on paper by a judge, who may make an order granting, refusing or otherwise dealing with such application on paper.

3 Time for Instituting Appeals

3.1 The time within which an appeal must be instituted depends on whether the appeal is against a judgment or against an order or decision of the Employment Tribunal.

3.2 If the appeal is against an order or decision, the appeal must be instituted within 42 days of the date of the order or decision. The EAT will treat a Tribunal's refusal to make an order or decision as itself constituting an order or decision. The date of an order or decision is the date when the order or decision was sent to the parties, which is normally recorded on or in the order or decision.

3.3 If the appeal is against a judgment, the appeal must be instituted within 42 days from the date on which the written record of the judgment was sent to the parties. However in three situations the time for appealing against a judgment will be 42 days from the date when written reasons were sent to the parties. This will be the case only if (1) written reasons were requested orally at the hearing before the Tribunal or (2) written reasons were requested in writing within 14 days of the date on which the written record of the judgment was sent to the parties or (3) the Tribunal itself reserved its reasons and gave them subsequently in writing: such exception will not apply if the request to the Tribunal for written reasons is made out of time (whether or not such request is granted). The date of the written record and of the written reasons is the date when they are sent to the parties, which is normally recorded on or in the written record and the written reasons.

3.4 The time limit referred to in paras 3.1 to 3.3 above apply even though the question of remedy and assessment of compensation by the Employment Tribunal has been adjourned or has not been dealt with and even though an application has been made to the Employment Tribunal for a review.

3.5 An application for an extension of time for appealing cannot be considered until a Notice of Appeal in accordance with para 2(1) above has been lodged with the EAT.

3.6 Any application for an extension of time for appealing must be made as an interim application to the Registrar, who will normally determine the application after inviting and considering written representations from each side. An interim appeal lies from the Registrar's decision to a judge. Such an appeal must be notified to the EAT within 5 days of the date when the Registrar's decision was sent to the parties. [See para 4.3 below.]

3.7 In determining whether to extend the time for appealing, particular attention will be paid to whether any good excuse for the delay has been shown and to the guidance contained in the decisions of the EAT and the Court of Appeal, as summarised in *United Arab Emirates v Abdelghafar* [1995] ICR 65, *Aziz v Bethnal Green City Challenge Co Ltd* [2000] IRLR 111 and *Jurkowska v HLMAD Ltd* [2008] EWCA Civ 231.

3.8 It is not usually a good reason for late lodgement of a Notice of Appeal that an application for litigation support from public funds has been made, but not yet determined; or that support is being sought from, but has not yet been provided by, some other body, such as a trade union, employers' association or the Equality and Human Rights Commission.

3.9 In any case of doubt or difficulty, a Notice of Appeal should be lodged in time and an application made to the Registrar for directions.

4 Interim Applications

4.1 Interim applications should be made in writing (no particular form is required) and will be initially referred to the Registrar who after considering the papers may deal with the case or refer it to a judge. The judge may dispose of it himself or refer it to a full EAT hearing. Parties are encouraged to make any such applications at a Preliminary Hearing ('PH') or an Appointment for Directions if one is ordered (see paras 9.7–9.18 and 11.2 below).

4.2 Unless otherwise ordered, any application for extension of time will be considered and determined as though it were an interim application to the Registrar, who will normally determine the application after inviting and considering written representations from each side.

4.3 An interim appeal lies from the Registrar's decision to a judge. Such an appeal must be notified to the EAT within five days of the date when the Registrar's decision was sent to the parties.

5 The Right to Inspect the Register and Certain Documents and to Take Copies

5.1 Any document lodged in the Central Office of the EAT in London or in the EAT office in Edinburgh in any proceedings before the EAT shall be sealed with the seal of the EAT showing the date (and time, if received after 4.00pm) on which the document was lodged.

5.2 Particulars of the date of delivery at the Central Office of the EAT or in the EAT office in Edinburgh of any document for filing or lodgement together with the time, if received after 4.00pm, the date of the document and the title of the appeal of which the document forms part of the record shall be entered in the Register of Cases kept in the Central Office and in Edinburgh or in the file which forms part of the Register of Cases.

5.3 Any person shall be entitled during office hours by appointment to inspect and request a copy of any of the following documents filed or lodged in the Central Office or the EAT office in Edinburgh, namely:

5.3.1 any Notice of Appeal or respondent's Answer or any copy thereof;

5.3.2 any judgment or order given or made in court or any copy of such judgment or order; and

5.3.3 with the permission of the EAT, which may be granted on an application, any other document.

5.4 A copying charge per page will be payable for those documents mentioned in para 5.3 above.

5.5 Nothing in this Direction shall be taken as preventing any party to an appeal from inspecting and requesting a copy of any document filed or lodged in the Central Office or the EAT office in Edinburgh before the commencement of the appeal, but made with a view to its commencement.

6 Papers for Use at the Hearing

6.1 It is the responsibility of the parties or their advisers (see paras 6.5 and 6.6 below) to prepare a core bundle of papers for use at any hearing. Ultimate responsibility lies with the appellant, following consultation with other parties. The bundle must include only those exhibits (productions in Scotland) and documents used before the Employment Tribunal which are considered to be necessary for the appeal. It is the duty of the parties or their advisers to ensure that only those documents are included which are (a) relevant to the point(s) of law raised in the appeal and (b) likely to be referred to at the hearing. It is also the responsibility of parties to retain copies of all documents and correspondence, including hearing bundles, sent to EAT. Bundles (see para 6.2 below) used at one EAT hearing will not be retained by the EAT for a subsequent hearing.

6.2 The documents in the core bundle should be numbered by item, then paginated continuously and indexed, in the following order:

6.2.1 Judgment, decision or order appealed from and written reasons
6.2.2 Sealed Notice of Appeal
6.2.3 Respondent's Answer if a Full Hearing ('FH'), respondent's Submissions if a PH
6.2.4 ET1 claim (and any Additional Information or Written Answers)
6.2.5 ET3 response (and any Additional Information or Written Answers)
6.2.6 Questionnaire and Replies (discrimination and equal pay cases)
6.2.7 Relevant orders, judgments and written reasons of the Employment Tribunal
6.2.8 Relevant orders and judgments of the EAT
6.2.9 Affidavits and Employment Tribunal comments (where ordered)
6.2.10 Any documents agreed or ordered pursuant to para 7 below.

6.3 Other documents relevant to the particular hearing (for example the particulars or contract of employment and any procedures) referred to at the Employment Tribunal may follow in the core bundle, if the total pages do not exceed 100. No bundle containing more than 100 pages should be agreed or lodged without the permission of the Registrar or order of a judge which will not be granted without the provision of an essential reading list as soon as practicable thereafter. If permitted or ordered, further pages should follow, with consecutive pagination, in an additional bundle or bundles if appropriate.

6.4 All documents must be legible and unmarked.

6.5 **PH cases** (see para 9.5.2 below), **Appeals from Registrar's Order, Rule 3(10) hearings, Appointments for Directions**: the appellant must prepare and lodge four copies (two copies if judge sitting alone) of the bundle as soon as possible after service of the Notice of Appeal and no later than 28 days from the seal date of the relevant order unless otherwise directed.

6.6 **FH cases** (see para 9.5.3 below): the parties must co-operate in agreeing a bundle of papers for the hearing. By no later than 28 days from the seal date of the relevant order, unless otherwise directed, the appellant is responsible for ensuring that four copies (two copies if judge sitting alone) of a bundle agreed by the parties is lodged at the EAT.

6.7 **Warned List and Fast Track FH cases:** the bundles should be lodged as soon as possible and (unless the hearing date is within seven days) in any event within seven days after the parties have been notified that the case is expedited or in the Warned List.

6.8 In the event of disagreement between the parties or difficulty in preparing the bundles, the Registrar may give appropriate directions, whether on application in writing (on notice) by one or more of the parties or of his/her own initiative.

7 Evidence Before the Employment Tribunal

7.1 An appellant who considers that a point of law raised in the Notice of Appeal cannot be argued without reference to evidence given (or not given) at the Employment Tribunal, the nature or substance of which does not, or does not sufficiently, appear from the written reasons, must ordinarily submit an application with the Notice of Appeal. The application is for the nature of such evidence (or lack of it) to be admitted, or if necessary for the relevant parts of the employment judge's notes of evidence to be produced. If such application is not so made, then it should be made:

7.1.1 if a PH is ordered, in the skeleton or written submissions lodged prior to such PH; or
7.1.2 if the case is listed for FH without a PH, then within 14 days of the seal date of the order so providing.

Any such application by a respondent to an appeal, must, if not made earlier, accompany the respondent's Answer.

7.2 The application must explain why such a matter is considered necessary in order to argue the point of law raised in the Notice of Appeal or respondent's Answer. The application must identify:

7.2.1 the issue(s) in the Notice of Appeal or respondent's Answer to which the matter is relevant;

7.2.2 the names of the witnesses whose evidence is considered relevant, alternatively the nature of the evidence the absence of which is considered relevant;

7.2.3 (if applicable) the part of the hearing when the evidence was given;

7.2.4 the gist of the evidence (or absence of evidence) alleged to be relevant; and

7.2.5 (if the party has a record), saying so and by whom and when it was made, or producing an extract from a witness statement given in writing at the hearing.

7.3 The application will be considered on the papers, or if appropriate at a PH, by the Registrar or a judge. The Registrar or a judge may give directions for written representations (if they have not already been lodged), or may determine the application, but will ordinarily make an order requiring the party who seeks to raise such a matter to give notice to the other party(ies) to the appeal/cross-appeal. The notice will require the other party(ies) to co-operate in agreeing, within 21 days (unless a shorter period is ordered), a statement or note of the relevant evidence, alternatively a statement that there was no such evidence. All parties are required to use their best endeavours to agree such a statement or note.

7.4 In the absence of such agreement within 21 days (or such shorter period as may be ordered) of the requirement, any party may make an application within seven days thereafter to the EAT, for directions. The party must enclose all relevant correspondence and give notice to the other parties. The directions may include: the resolution of the disagreement on the papers or at a hearing; the administration by one party to the others of, or a request to the employment judge to respond to, a questionnaire; or, if the EAT is satisfied that such notes are necessary, a request that the employment judge produce his/her notes of evidence either in whole or in part.

7.5 If the EAT requests any documents from the employment judge, it will supply copies to the parties upon receipt.

7.6 In an appeal from an Employment Tribunal which ordered its proceedings to be tape recorded, the EAT will apply the principles above to any application for a transcript.

7.7 A note of evidence is not to be produced and supplied to the parties to enable the parties to embark on a 'fishing expedition' to establish grounds or additional grounds of appeal or because they have not kept their own notes of the evidence. If an application for such a note is found by the EAT to have been unreasonably made or if there is unreasonable lack of co-operation in agreeing a relevant note or statement, the party behaving unreasonably is at risk of being ordered to pay costs.

8 Fresh Evidence and New Points of Law

8.1 Where an application is made by a party to an appeal to put in, at the hearing of the appeal, any document which was not before the Employment Tribunal, and which has not been agreed in writing by the other parties, the application and a copy of the documents sought to be admitted should be lodged at the EAT with the Notice of Appeal or the respondent's Answer, as appropriate. The application and copy should be served on the other parties. The same principle applies to any oral evidence not given at the Employment Tribunal which is sought to be adduced on the appeal. The nature and substance of such evidence together with the date when the party first became aware of its existence must be disclosed in a document, where appropriate a witness statement from the relevant witness with signed statement of truth, which must be similarly lodged and served.

8.2 In exercising its discretion to admit any fresh evidence or new document, the EAT will apply the principles set out in *Ladd v Marshall* [1954] 1WLR 1489, having regard to the overriding objective, i.e.:

8.2.1 the evidence could not have been obtained with reasonable diligence for use at the Employment Tribunal hearing;

8.2.2 it is relevant and would probably have had an important influence on the hearing;

8.2.3 it is apparently credible.

Accordingly the evidence and representations in support of the application must address these principles.

8.3 A party wishing to resist the application must, within 14 days of its being sent, submit any representations in response to the EAT and other parties.

8.4 The application will be considered by the Registrar or a judge on the papers (or, if appropriate, at a PH) who may determine the issue or give directions for a hearing or may seek comments from the employment judge. A copy of any comments received from the employment judge will be sent to all parties.

8.5 If a respondent intends to contend at the FH that the appellant has raised a point which was not argued below, the respondent shall so state:

8.5.1 if a PH has been ordered, in writing to the EAT and all parties, within 14 days of receiving the Notice of Appeal;

8.5.2 if the case is listed for a FH without a PH, in a respondent's Answer.

In the event of dispute the employment judge should be asked for his/her comments as to whether a particular legal argument was deployed.

9 Case Tracks and Directions: the Sift of Appeals

9.1 Consistent with the overriding objective, the EAT will seek to give directions for case management so that the case can be dealt with quickly, or better considered, and in the most effective and just way.

9.2 Applications and directions for case management will usually be dealt with on the papers ('the sift') by a judge, or by the Registrar with an appeal to a judge. Any party seeking directions must serve a copy on all parties. Directions may be given at any stage, before or after the registration of a Notice of Appeal. An order made will contain a time for compliance, which must be observed or be the subject of an application by any party to vary or discharge it, or to seek an extension of time. Otherwise, failure to comply with an order in time or at all may result in the EAT exercising its power under Rule 26 to strike out the appeal, cross-appeal or respondent's Answer or debar the party from taking any further part in the proceedings or to make any other order it thinks fit, including an award of costs.

9.3 Any application to vary or discharge an order, or to seek an extension of time, must be lodged at the EAT and served on the other parties within the time fixed for compliance. Such other parties must, if opposing the application and within 14 days (or such shorter period as may be ordered) of receiving it, submit their representations to the EAT and the other parties.

9.4 An application to amend a Notice of Appeal or respondent's Answer must include the text of the original document with any changes clearly marked and identifiable, for example with deletions struck through in red and the text of the amendment either written or underlined in red. Any subsequent amendments will have to be in a different identifiable colour.

9.5 Notices of Appeal are sifted by a judge or the Registrar so as to determine the most effective case management of the appeal. The sift will result in a decision as to which track the appeal will occupy, and directions will be given. There are four tracks:

9.5.1 Rule 3(7) cases [see para 9.6 below].

9.5.2 Preliminary Hearing (PH) cases [see paras 9.7–9.18 below].

9.5.3 Full Hearing (FH) cases [see para 9.19 below].

9.5.4 Fast Track Full Hearing ('FTFH') cases [see paras 9.20–9.21 below].

The judge or Registrar may also stay (or sist in Scotland) the appeal for a period, normally 21 days, pending the making or the conclusion of an application by the appellant to the Employment Tribunal (if necessary out of time) for a review or pending the response by the Employment Tribunal to an invitation from the judge or Registrar to clarify, supplement or give its written reasons.

Rule 3(7) Cases (9.5.1)

9.6 The judge or Registrar, having considered the Notice of Appeal and, if appropriate, having obtained any additional information, may decide that it or any of the grounds contained in it discloses no reasonable grounds for bringing the appeal or is an abuse of the process or otherwise likely to obstruct the just disposal of the proceedings. Reasons will be sent and within 28 days the appellant may submit a fresh Notice of Appeal for further consideration or request an oral hearing before a judge. At that hearing the judge may confirm the earlier decision or order that the appeal proceeds to a Preliminary or Full Hearing. A hearing under Rule 3(10), including judgment and any directions, will normally last not more than one and a half hours. A judge or Registrar may also follow the Rule 3(7) procedure, of his or her own initiative, or on application, at any later stage of the proceedings, if appropriate.

Preliminary Hearing Cases (9.5.2)

9.7 The purpose of a PH is to determine whether:

9.7.1 the grounds in the Notice of Appeal raise a point of law which gives the appeal a reasonable prospect of success at a FH; or

9.7.2 for some other compelling reason the appeal should be heard e.g. that the appellant seeks a declaration of incompatibility under the Human Rights Act 1998; or to argue that a decision binding on the EAT should be considered by a higher court.

9.8 Prior to the PH there will be automatic directions. These include sending the Notice of Appeal to the respondent(s) to the appeal. The direction may order or in any event will enable the respondent(s) to lodge and serve, within 14 days of the seal date of the order (unless otherwise directed), concise written submissions in response to the Notice of Appeal, dedicated to showing that there is no reasonable prospect of success for all or any grounds of any appeal. Such submissions will be considered at the PH.

9.9 If the respondent to the appeal intends to serve a cross-appeal this must be accompanied by written submissions and must be lodged and served within 14 days of service of the Notice of Appeal. The respondent to the appeal must make clear whether it is intended to advance the cross-appeal:

9.9.1 in any event (an unconditional cross-appeal); or

9.9.2 only if the appellant succeeds (a conditional cross-appeal).

In either case the respondent is entitled to attend the PH, which will also amount to a PH of the cross-appeal, and make submissions.

9.10 All parties will be notified of the date fixed for the PH. In the normal case, unless ordered otherwise, only the appellant and/or a representative should attend to make submissions to the EAT on the issue whether the Notice of Appeal raises a point of law with a reasonable prospect of success:

9.10.1 Except where the respondent to the appeal makes a cross-appeal, or the EAT orders a hearing with all parties present, the respondent to the appeal is not required to attend the hearing and is not usually permitted to take part in it. But any written submissions as referred to in (8) above will be considered at the PH.

9.10.2 If the appellant does not attend, the appeal may nevertheless be dealt with as above on written submissions, and be wholly or in part dismissed or allowed to proceed.

9.11 The PH, including judgment and directions, will normally last no more than one hour.

9.12 The sift procedure will be applied to cross-appeals as well as appeals. If an appeal has been assigned to the FH track, without a PH, and the respondent includes a cross-appeal in the respondent's Answer, the respondent must immediately apply to the EAT in writing on notice to the appellant for directions on the papers as to whether the EAT considers that there should be a PH of the cross-appeal.

9.13 If satisfied that the appeal (and/or the cross-appeal) should be heard at a FH on all or some of the grounds of appeal, the EAT will give directions relating to, for example, a time estimate, any application for fresh evidence, a procedure in respect of matters of evidence before the Employment Tribunal not sufficiently appearing from the written reasons, the exchange and lodging of skeleton arguments and an appellant's Chronology, and bundles of documents and authorities.

9.14 Permission to amend a Notice of Appeal (or cross-appeal) may be granted:

9.14.1 **If the proposed amendment is produced at the hearing**, then, if such amendment has not previously been notified to the other parties, and the appeal (or cross-appeal) might not have been permitted to proceed but for the amendment, the opposing party(ies) will have the opportunity to apply on notice to vary or discharge the permission to proceed, and for consequential directions as to the hearing or disposal of the appeal or cross-appeal.

9.14.2 **If a draft amendment is not available at the PH**, an application for permission to amend, in writing on notice to the other party(ies) in accordance with para 9.4 above, will be permitted to be made within 14 days. Where, but for such proposed amendment, the appeal (or cross-appeal) may not have been permitted to proceed to a FH, provision may be made in the order on the PH for the appeal (or cross-appeal) to be dismissed if the application for permission to amend is not made. Where such an application is made and refused, provision will be made for any party to have liberty to apply, in writing on notice to the other party(ies), as to the hearing or disposal of the appeal.

9.15 If not satisfied that the appeal, or any particular ground of it, should go forward to a FH, the EAT at the PH will dismiss the appeal, wholly or in part, and give a judgment setting out the reasons for doing so.

9.16 If an appeal is permitted to go forward to an FH on all grounds, a reasoned judgment will not normally be given.

9.17 Parties who become aware that a similar point is raised in other proceedings at an Employment Tribunal or the EAT are encouraged to co-operate in bringing this to the attention of the Registrar so that consideration can be given to the most expedient way of dealing with the cases, in particular to the possibility of having two or more appeals heard together.

9.18 If an appeal is permitted to go forward to an FH, a listing category will be assigned i.e.:
P (recommended to be heard in the President's list);
A (complex, and raising point(s) of law of public importance);
B (any other cases).The President reserves the discretion to alter any relevant category as circumstances require.

Full Hearing Cases (9.5.3)

9.19 If a judge or the Registrar decides to list the case for an FH without a PH s/he will consider appropriate directions, relating for example to amendment, further information, any application for fresh evidence, a procedure in respect of matters of evidence at the Employment Tribunal not sufficiently appearing from the written reasons, allegations of bias, apparent bias or improper conduct, provisions for skeleton arguments, appellant's Chronology and bundles of documents and of authorities, time estimates and listing category (as set out in para 9.18 above).

Fast Track Full Hearing Cases (9.5.4)

9.20 FH cases are normally heard in the order in which they are received. However, there are times when it is expedient to hear an appeal as soon as it can be fitted into the list. Appeals placed in this Fast Track, at the discretion of a judge or the Registrar, will normally fall into the following cases:

9.20.1 appeals where the parties have made a reasoned case on the merits for an expedited hearing;

9.20.2 appeals against interim orders or decisions of an Employment Tribunal, particularly those which involve the taking of a step in the proceedings within a specified period, for example adjournments, further information, amendments, disclosure, witness orders;

9.20.3 appeals on the outcome of which other applications to the Employment Tribunal or the EAT or the civil courts depend;

9.20.4 appeals in which a reference to the European Court of Justice (ECJ), or a declaration of incompatibility under the Human Rights Act 1998, is sought;

9.20.5 appeals involving reinstatement, re-engagement, interim relief or a recommendation for action (discrimination cases).

9.21 Category B cases estimated to take two hours or less may also be allocated to the Fast Track.

10 Respondent's Answer and Directions

10.1 After the sift stage or a PH, at which a decision is made to permit the appeal to go forward to an FH, the EAT will send the Notice of Appeal, with any amendments which have been permitted, and any submissions or skeleton argument lodged by the appellant, to all parties who are respondents to the appeal. Within 14 days of the seal date of the order (unless otherwise directed), respondents must lodge at the EAT and serve on the other parties a respondent's Answer. If it contains a cross-appeal, the appellant must within 14 days of service (unless otherwise directed), lodge and serve a Reply.

10.2 After lodgement and service of the respondent's Answer and of any Reply to a cross-appeal, the Registrar may, where necessary, invite applications from the parties in writing, on notice to all other parties, for directions, and may give any appropriate directions on the papers or may fix a day when the parties should attend on an Appointment for Directions.

10.3 A judge may at any time, upon consideration of the papers or at a hearing, make an order requiring or recommending consideration by the parties or any of them of compromise, conciliation, mediation or, in particular, reference to ACAS.

11 Complaints about the Conduct of the Employment Tribunal Hearing

11.1 An appellant who intends to complain about the conduct of the Employment Tribunal (for example bias, apparent bias or improper conduct by the employment judge or lay members or any procedural irregularity at the hearing) must include in the Notice of Appeal full particulars of each complaint made.

11.2 An appeal which is wholly or in part based on such a complaint will be sifted by a judge or the Registrar as set out in para 9.5 above and this may result in a decision as to the appropriate track which the appeal will occupy. At the sift stage or before, the judge or Registrar may postpone a decision as to track, and direct that the appellant or a representative provide an affidavit setting out full particulars of all allegations of bias or misconduct relied upon. At the sift stage the Registrar may enquire of the party making the complaint whether it is intended to proceed with it and may draw attention to para 11.6 below.

11.3 If the appeal is allocated to the PH or FH track, the EAT may take the following steps prior to such hearing within a time-limit set out in the relevant order:

11.3.1 require the appellant or a representative to provide, if not already provided, an affidavit as set out in para 11.2 above;

11.3.2 require any party to give an affidavit or to obtain a witness statement from any person who has represented any of the parties at the Tribunal hearing, and any other person present at the Tribunal hearing or a relevant part of it, giving their account of the events set out in the affidavit of the appellant or the appellant's representative. For the above purpose, the EAT will provide copies of any affidavits received from or on behalf of the appellant to any other person from whom an account is sought;

11.3.3 seek comments, upon all affidavits or witness statements received, from the employment judge of the Employment Tribunal from which the appeal is brought and may seek such comments from the lay members of the Tribunal. For the above purpose, copies of all relevant documents will be provided by the EAT to the employment judge and, if appropriate, the lay members; such documents will include any affidavits and witness statements received, the Notice of Appeal and other relevant documents.

11.3.4 the EAT will on receipt supply to the parties copies of all affidavits, statements and comments received.

11.4 A respondent who intends to make such a complaint must include such particulars as set out in paras 11.1 and 11.2 above:

11.4.1 (in the event of a PH being ordered in respect of the appellant's appeal, in accordance with para 9.5.2 above) in the cross-appeal referred to in para 9.9 above, or, in the absence of a cross-appeal, in written submissions, as referred to in para 9.8 above;

11.4.2 (in the event of no PH being ordered, in accordance with para 9.5.3 above) in his respondent's Answer. A similar procedure will then be followed as in para 11.3 above.

11.5 In every case which is permitted to go forward to an FH the EAT will give appropriate directions, ordinarily on the papers after notice to the appellant and respondent, as to the procedure to be adopted at, and material to be provided to, the FH; but such directions may be given at the sift stage or at a PH.

11.6 Parties should note the following:

11.6.1 The EAT will not permit complaints of the kind mentioned above to be raised or developed at the hearing of the appeal unless this procedure has been followed.

11.6.2 The EAT recognises that employment judges and Employment Tribunals are themselves obliged to observe the overriding objective and are given wide powers and duties of case management (see Employment Tribunal (Constitution and Rules of Procedure) Regulations 2004 (SI No 1861)), so appeals in respect of the conduct of Employment Tribunals, which is in exercise of those powers and duties, are the less likely to succeed.

11.6.3 Unsuccessful pursuit of an allegation of bias or improper conduct, particularly in respect of case management decisions, may put the party raising it at risk of an order for costs.

12 Listing of Appeals

12.1 **Estimate of Length of Hearing**: the lay members of the EAT are part-time members. They attend when available on pre-arranged dates. They do not sit for continuous periods. Consequently appeals which run beyond their estimated length have to be adjourned part-heard (often with substantial delay) until a day on which the judge and members are all available. To avoid inconvenience to the parties and to the EAT, and to avoid additional delay and costs suffered as a result of adjournment of part-heard appeals, all parties are required to ensure that the estimates of length of hearing (allowing for the fact that the parties can expect the EAT to have pre-read the papers and for deliberation and the giving of a judgment) are accurate when first given. Any change in such estimate, or disagreement with an estimate made by the EAT on a sift or at a PH, is to be notified immediately to the Listing Officer.

12.2 If the EAT concludes that the hearing is likely to exceed the estimate, or if for other reasons the hearing may not be concluded within the time available, it may seek to avoid such adjournment by placing the parties under appropriate time limits in order to complete the presentation of the submissions within the estimated or available time.

12.3 Subject to para 12.6 below a date will be fixed for a PH as soon as practicable after the sift (referred to in para 9.5 above) and for an FH as soon as practicable after the sift if no PH is ordered, or otherwise after the PH.

12.4 The Listing Officer will normally consult the parties on dates, and will accommodate reasonable requests if practicable, but is not bound to do so. Once the date is fixed, the appeal will be set down in the list. A party finding that the date which has been fixed causes serious difficulties may apply to the Listing Officer for it to be changed, having first notified all other parties entitled to appear on the date, of their application and the reasons for it.

12.5 Parties receiving such an application must, as soon as possible and within seven days, notify the Listing Officer of their views.

12.6 In addition to this fixed date procedure, a list ('the warned list') may be drawn up. Cases will be placed in such warned list at the discretion of the Listing Officer or may be so placed by the direction of a judge or the Registrar. These will ordinarily be short cases, or cases where expedition has been ordered. Parties or their representatives will be notified that their case has been included in this list, and as much notice as possible will be given of the intention to list a case for hearing, when representations by way of objection from the parties will be considered by the Listing Officer and if necessary on appeal to the Registrar or a judge. The parties may apply on notice to all other parties for a fixed date for hearing.

12.7 Other cases may be put in the list by the Listing Officer with the consent of the parties at shorter notice: for example, where other cases have been settled or withdrawn or where it appears that they will take less time than originally estimated. Parties who wish their cases to be taken as soon as possible and at short notice should notify the Listing Officer. Representations by way of objection may be made by the parties to the Listing Officer and if necessary by appeal to a judge or the Registrar.

12.8 Each week an up-to-date list for the following week will be prepared, including any changes which have been made, in particular specifying cases which by then have been given fixed dates. The list appears on the EAT website.

13 Skeleton Arguments

(This part of the Practice Direction does not apply to an appeal heard in Scotland, unless otherwise directed in relation to that appeal by the EAT)

13.1 Skeleton arguments must be provided by all parties in all hearings, unless the EAT is notified by a party or representative in writing that the Notice of Appeal or respondent's Answer or relevant application contains the full argument, or the EAT otherwise directs in a particular case. It is the practice of the EAT for all the members to read the papers in advance. A well-structured skeleton argument helps the members and the parties to focus on the point(s) of law required to be decided and so makes the oral hearing more effective.

13.2 The skeleton argument should be concise and should identify and summarise the point(s) of law, the steps in the legal argument and the statutory provisions and authorities to be relied upon, identifying them by name, page and paragraph and stating the legal proposition sought to be derived from them. It is not, however, the purpose of the skeleton argument to argue the case on paper in detail. The parties should be referred to by name or as they appeared at the Employment Tribunal i.e. Claimant (C) and Respondent (R).

13.3 The skeleton argument should state the form of order which the party will ask the EAT to make at the hearing: for example, in the case of an appellant, whether the EAT will be asked to remit the whole or part of the case to the same or to a different Employment Tribunal, or whether the EAT will be asked to substitute a different decision for that of the Employment Tribunal.

13.4 The appellant's skeleton argument must be accompanied by a Chronology of events relevant to the appeal which, if possible, should be agreed by the parties. That will normally be taken as an uncontroversial document, unless corrected by another party or the EAT.

13.5 Unless impracticable, the skeleton argument should be prepared using the pagination in the index to the appeal bundle. In a case where a note of the evidence at the Employment Tribunal has been produced, the skeleton argument should identify the parts of the record to which that party wishes to refer.

13.6 Represented parties should give the instructions necessary for their representative to comply with this procedure within the time limits.

13.7 The fact that conciliation or settlement negotiations are in progress in relation to the appeal does not excuse delay in lodging and exchanging skeleton arguments.

13.8 A skeleton argument may be lodged by the appellant with the Notice of Appeal or by the respondent with the respondent's Answer.

13.9 Skeleton arguments must (if not already so lodged):

13.9.1 be lodged at the EAT not less than 10 days (unless otherwise ordered) before the date fixed for the PH, appeal against Registrar's Order, Rule 3 (10) hearing or Appointment for Directions; or, if the hearing is fixed at less than seven days' notice, as soon as possible after the hearing date has been notified. In the event that the hearing has been ordered to be heard with all parties present, the skeleton arguments must also then be exchanged between the parties;

13.9.2 be lodged at the EAT, and exchanged between the parties, not less than 14 days before the FH;

13.9.3 in the case of warned list and fast track FH cases be lodged at the EAT and exchanged between the parties as soon as possible and (unless the hearing date is less than seven days later) in any event within seven days after the parties have been notified that the case is expedited or in the warned list.

13.10 Failure to follow this procedure may lead to an adjournment of an appeal or to dismissal for non-compliance with the PD pursuant to Rule 26, and to an award of costs. The party in default may also be required to attend before the EAT to explain their failure. It will always mean that the defaulting party must immediately despatch any delayed skeleton argument to the EAT by hand or by fax or by email to londoneat@tribunals.gsi.gov.uk or, as appropriate, edinburgheat@tribunals.gsi.gov.uk and (unless notified by the EAT to the contrary) bring to the hearing sufficient copies (a minimum of 6) of the skeleton argument and any authorities referred to. The EAT staff will not be responsible for supplying or copying these on the morning of the hearing.

14 Citation of Authorities

General

14.1 It is undesirable for parties to cite the same case from different sets of reports. The parties should, if practicable, agree which report will be used at the hearing. Where the Employment Tribunal has cited from a report it may be convenient to cite from the same report.

14.2 It is the responsibility of a party wishing to cite any authority to provide photocopies for the use of each member of the Tribunal and photocopies or at least a list for the other parties. All authorities should be indexed and incorporated in an agreed bundle.

14.3 Parties are advised not to cite an unnecessary number of authorities either in skeleton arguments or in oral argument at the hearing. It is of assistance to the EAT if parties could highlight or sideline passages relied on within the bundle of authorities.

14.4 It is unnecessary for a party citing a case in oral argument to read it in full to the EAT. Whenever a case is cited in a skeleton argument or in an oral argument it is helpful if the legal proposition for which it is cited is stated. References need only be made to the relevant passages in the report. If the formulation of the legal proposition based on the authority cited is not in dispute, further examination of the authority will often be unnecessary.

14.5 For decisions of the ECJ, the official report should be used where possible.

PH Cases

14.6 If it is thought necessary to cite any authority at a PH, appeal against Registrar's Order, Rule 3(10) hearing or Appointment for Directions, three copies should be provided for the EAT (one copy if a judge is sitting alone) no less than 10 days before the hearing, unless otherwise ordered: and additional copies for any other parties notified. All authorities should be bundled, indexed and incorporated in one agreed bundle.

FH Cases

14.7 The parties must co-operate in agreeing a list of authorities and must jointly or severally lodge a list and three bundles of copies (one copy if judge sitting alone) of such authorities at the EAT not less than seven days before the FH, unless otherwise ordered.

15 Disposal of Appeals by Consent

15.1 An appellant who wishes to abandon or withdraw an appeal should notify the other parties and the EAT immediately. If a settlement is reached, the parties should inform the EAT as soon as possible. The appellant should submit to the EAT a letter signed by or on behalf of the appellant and signed also by or on behalf of the respondent, asking the EAT for permission to withdraw the appeal and to make a consent order in the form of an attached draft signed by or for both parties dismissing the appeal, together with any other agreed order.

15.2 If the other parties do not agree to the proposed order the EAT should be informed. Written submissions should be lodged at the EAT and served on the parties. Any outstanding issue may be determined on the papers by the EAT, particularly if it relates to costs, but the EAT may fix an oral hearing to determine the outstanding matters in dispute between the parties.

15.3 If the parties reach an agreement that the appeal should be allowed by consent, and that an order made by the Employment Tribunal should be reversed or varied or the matter remitted to the Employment Tribunal on the ground that the decision contains an error of law, it is usually necessary for the matter to be heard by the EAT to determine whether there is a good reason for making the proposed order. On notification by the parties, the EAT will decide whether the appeal can be dealt with on the papers or by a hearing at which one or more parties or their representatives should attend to argue the case for allowing the appeal and making the order that the parties wish the EAT to make.

15.4 If the application for permission to withdraw an appeal is made close to the hearing date the EAT may require the attendance of the appellant and/or a representative to explain the reasons for delay in making a decision not to pursue the appeal.

16 Appellant's Failure to Present a Response

16.1 If the appellant in a case did not present a response (ET3) to the Employment Tribunal and did not apply to the Employment Tribunal for an extension of time for doing so, or applied for such an extension and was refused, the Notice of Appeal must include particulars directed to the following issues, namely whether:

16.1.1 there is a good excuse for failing to present a response (ET3) and (if that be the case) for failing to apply for such an extension of time; and

16.1.2 there is a reasonably arguable defence to the claim (ET1).

16.2 In order to satisfy the EAT on these issues, the appellant must lodge at the EAT, together with the Notice of Appeal, a witness statement explaining in detail the circumstances in which there has been a failure to serve a response (ET3) in time or apply for such an extension of time, the reason for that failure and the facts and matters relied upon for contesting the claim (ET1) on the merits. There should be exhibited to the witness statement all relevant documents and a completed draft response (ET3).

17 Hearings

17.1 Where consent is to be obtained from the parties pursuant to s 28(3) of the ETA 1996 to an appeal commencing or continuing to be heard by a judge together with only one lay member, the parties must, prior to the commencement or continuation of such hearing in front of a two-member court, themselves or by their representatives each sign a form containing the name of the one member remaining, and stating whether the member is a person falling within s 28(1)(a) or (b) of the ETA 1996.

17.2 **Video and Telephone Hearings:** facilities can be arranged for the purpose of holding short PHs or short Appointments for Directions by video or telephone link, upon the application (in writing) of an appellant or respondent who, or whose representative, has a relevant disability (supported by appropriate medical evidence). Such facilities will only be made available for a hearing at which the party or, if more than one party will take part, both or all parties is or are legally represented. An application that a hearing should be so held will be determined by a judge or the Registrar, and must be made well in advance of the date intended for the hearing, so that arrangements may be made. So far as concerns video conferencing facilities, they may not always be available, dependent on the location of the parties; as for telephone hearings or, especially, telephone conferencing facilities, consideration may need to be given as to payment by a party or parties of any additional expenditure resulting.

18 Handing Down of Judgments

(England and Wales)

18.1 When the EAT reserves judgment to a later date, the parties will be notified of the date when it is ready to be handed down. It is not necessary for a party or representative to attend.

18.2 Copies of the judgment will be available to the parties or their representatives on the morning on which it is handed down or, if so directed by a judge, earlier to the parties' representatives in draft subject to terms as to confidentiality.

18.3 The judgment will be pronounced without being read aloud, by the judge who presided or by another judge, on behalf of the EAT. The judge may deal with any application or may refer it to the judge and/or the Tribunal who heard the appeal, whether to deal with on the papers or at a further oral hearing on notice. Applications for permission to appeal should be made pursuant to para 21 below. Applications for costs should be made pursuant to para 19 below.

18.4 Transcripts of unreserved judgments at a PH, appeal against Registrar's Order, Appointment for Directions and Rule 3(10) hearing will not (save as below) be produced and provided to the parties:

18.4.1 Where an appeal, or any ground of appeal, is dismissed in the presence of the appellant, no transcript of the judgment is produced unless, within 14 days of the seal date of the order, either party applies to the EAT for a transcript, or the EAT of its own initiative directs that a judgment be transcribed (in circumstances such as those set out in para 18.5.2 below).

18.4.2 Where an appeal or any ground of appeal is dismissed in the absence of the appellant, a transcript will be supplied to the appellant.

18.4.3 Where an appeal is allowed to go forward to a PH or an FH, a judgment will not normally be delivered, but, if it is, the judge may order it to be transcribed, in which case a transcript is provided to the parties.

18.5 Transcripts of unreserved judgments at an FH: where judgment is delivered at the hearing, no transcript will be produced and provided to the parties unless:

18.5.1 either party applies for it to the EAT within 14 days of that hearing; or

18.5.2 the EAT of its own initiative directs that the judgment be transcribed, e.g. where it is considered that a point of general importance arises or that the matter is to be remitted to, or otherwise continued before, the Employment Tribunal.

18.6 Where judgment at either a PH or an FH is reserved, and later handed down in writing, a copy is provided to all parties, and to recognised law reporters.

(Scotland)

18.7 Judgments are normally reserved in Scotland and will be handed down as soon as practicable thereafter on a provisional basis to both parties who will thereafter have a period of 14 days to make any representations with regard to expenses, leave to appeal or any other relevant matter. At the expiry of that period or after such representations have been dealt with, whichever shall be the later, an order will be issued to conform to the original judgment.

EAT Website

18.8 All FH judgments which are transcribed or handed down will be posted on the EAT website. Any other judgment may be posted on the EAT website if so directed by the Registrar or a Judge.

19 Costs (referred to as Expenses in Scotland)

19.1 In this PD 'costs' includes legal costs, expenses, allowances paid by the Secretary of State and payment in respect of time spent in preparing a case. Such costs may relate to interim applications or hearings or to a PH or FH.

19.2 An application for costs must be made either during or at the end of a relevant hearing, or in writing to the Registrar within 14 days of the seal date of the relevant order of the EAT or, in the case of a reserved judgment, as provided for in paragraph 18.3 above, copied to all parties.

19.3 The party seeking the order must state the legal ground on which the application is based and the facts on which it is based and, by a schedule or otherwise, show how the costs have been incurred. If the application is made in respect of only part of the proceedings, particulars must be given showing how the costs have been incurred on that specific part. If the party against whom the order is sought wishes the EAT to have regard to means and/or an alleged inability to pay, a witness statement giving particulars and exhibiting any documents must be served on the other party(ies) and lodged with the EAT. Further directions may be required to be given by the EAT in such cases.

19.4 Such application may be resolved by the EAT on the papers, provided that the opportunity has been given for representations in writing by all relevant parties, or the EAT may refer the matter for an oral hearing, and may assess the costs either on the papers or at an oral hearing, or refer the matter for detailed assessment.

19.5 **Wasted Costs:** An application for a wasted costs order must be made in writing, setting out the nature of the case upon which the application is based and the best particulars of the costs sought to be recovered. Such application must be lodged with the EAT and served upon the party(ies) sought to be charged. Further directions may be required to be given by the EAT in such cases.

19.6 Where the EAT makes any costs order it shall provide written reasons for so doing if such order is made by decision on the papers. If such order is made at a hearing, then written reasons will be provided if a request is made at the hearing or within 21 days of the seal date of the costs order. The Registrar shall send a copy of the written reasons to all the parties to the proceedings.

20 Review

20.1 Where an application is made for a review of a judgment or order of the EAT, it can be considered on paper by a judge who may, if he or she heard the original appeal or made the original order alone, without lay members, make such order, granting, refusing, adjourning or otherwise dealing with such application, as he or she may think fit. If the original judgment or order was made by the judge together with lay members, then the judge may, pursuant to Rule 33, consider and refuse such application for review on the papers. If the judge does not refuse such application, he or she may make any relevant further order, but would not grant such application without notice to the opposing party and reference to the lay members, for consideration with them, either on paper or in open court. A request to review a judgment or order of the EAT must be made within 14 days of the seal date of the order, or must include an application, with reasons for an extension of time copied to all parties.

21 Appeals from the EAT

Appeals Heard in England and Wales

21.1 An application to the EAT for permission to appeal to the Court of Appeal must be made (unless the EAT otherwise orders) at the hearing or when a reserved judgment is handed down or in writing within seven days thereafter as provided in para 18.3 above. If not made then, or if refused, or unless the EAT otherwise orders, any such applications must be made to the Court of Appeal within 21 days of the sealed order. An application for an extension of time for permission to appeal may be entertained by the EAT where a case is made out to the satisfaction of a judge or Registrar that there is a need to delay until after a transcript is received (expedited if appropriate). Applications for an extension of time for permission to appeal should however normally be made to the Court of Appeal.

21.2 The party seeking permission must state the point of law to be advanced and the grounds.

Appeals Heard in Scotland

21.3 An application to the EAT for permission to appeal to the Court of Session must be made within 42 days of the date of the hearing where judgment is delivered at that hearing: if judgment is reserved, within 42 days of the date the transcript was sent to parties.

21.4 The party seeking permission must state the point of law to be advanced and the grounds.

22 Conciliation

22.1 Pursuant to Rule 36 and the overriding objective, the EAT encourages alternative dispute resolution. To this end it has agreed a pilot scheme with ACAS for ACAS to provide conciliation in certain cases. See 2007 Protocol.

22.2 In all cases the parties should, and when so directed must, consider conciliation of their appeals. The Registrar or a judge may at any stage make such a direction and require the parties to report on steps taken, but not the substance, to effect a conciliated settlement with the assistance of an ACAS officer notified by ACAS to the EAT.

THE HONOURABLE MR JUSTICE ELIAS, PRESIDENT

Dated: 22 May 2008

Form 1

Notice of Appeal from Decision of Employment Tribunal

1. The Appellant is (*name and address of the Appellant*):—
2. Any communication relating to this appeal may be sent to the Appellant at (*Appellant's address for service, including telephone number if any*):—
3. The Appellant appeals from (*here give particulars of the judgment, decision or order of the Employment Tribunal from which the appeal is brought including the location of the Employment Tribunal and the date*):—
4. The parties to the proceedings before the Employment Tribunal, other than the Appellant, were (*names and addresses of other parties to the proceedings resulting in judgment, decision or order appealed from*):—
5. Copies of:
   - the written record of the Employment Tribunal's judgment, decision or order and the Written Reasons of the Employment Tribunal
   - the Claim (ET1) and Response (ET3)

   or
   - an explanation as to why any of these documents are not included are attached to this notice.

   [If relevant.]

   [If the Appellant has made an application to the Employment Tribunal for a review of its judgment or decision, a copy of such application, together with the judgment and Written Reasons of the Employment Tribunal in respect of that review application, or a statement by or on behalf of the Appellant, if such be the case, that a judgment is awaited, is attached to this Notice. If any of these documents exist but cannot be included, then a written explanation must be given.]
6. The grounds upon which this appeal is brought are that the Employment Tribunal erred in law in that (*here set out in paragraphs the various grounds of appeal*):—

Signed: . . . .   Date: . . . .

N.B. The details entered on your Notice of Appeal must be legible and suitable for photocopying. The use of black ink or typescript is recommended.

EAT Practice Statement (2005)

This is a Practice Statement handed down by the President of the Employment Appeal Tribunal on 3 February 2005.

1. The attention of litigants and practitioners in the Employment Appeal Tribunal is expressly drawn to the wording and effect of Rules 3(1)(b) and 3(3) of the Employment Appeal Tribunal Rules (1993) (as amended). As is quite clear from the terms of paragraph 2.1 of the Employment Appeal Tribunal Practice Direction 2004 handed down on 9 December 2004, a Notice of Appeal without the specified documentation will not be validly lodged. The documentation required to accompany the Notice of Appeal in order for it to be valid now includes a copy of the Claim (ET1) and the Response (ET3) in the Employment Tribunal proceedings appealed from, if such be available to the appellant, and in any event if such not be available for whatever reason then a written explanation as to why they are not provided. Paragraph 2.1 of the Practice Direction makes this entirely clear:

   '*2.1. . . Copies of the judgment, decision or order appealed against and of the Employment Tribunal's written reasons, together with a copy of the Claim (ET1) and the Response (ET3) must be attached, or if not, a written explanation must be given. A Notice of Appeal without such documentation will not be validly lodged.*'
2. The reported decision of the Employment Appeal Tribunal in *Kanapathiar* v *London Borough of Harrow* [2003] IRLR 571 made quite clear that the effect of failure to lodge documents required by the Rules with the Notice of Appeal within the time limit specified for lodging of a Notice of Appeal would mean that the Notice of Appeal had not been validly lodged in time. The same now applies to the additional documents required by the amended Rule, namely the Claim and the Response.
3. It is apparent that both practitioners and litigants in person are not complying with the new Rules and Practice Direction, and not appreciating the consequences of their non-compliance. Between 2 and 26 January 2005, 20 Notices of Appeal were received by the Employment Appeal Tribunal and returned as invalid (compared with 4 during the similar period in 2004). Of those 20 Notices of Appeal, 7 would have been invalid in any event under the old Rules. 13 however were only invalid because they were neither accompanied by the Claim nor the Response nor by any explanation as to their absence or unavailability. If the Notices of Appeal are relodged well within the very generous 42-day time limit, there may still be time for the missing documents to be supplied and the time limit to be complied with. If however, as is very often the case, such Notices of Appeal are delivered either at, or only immediately before, the expiry of the time limit, the absence of the relevant documents is, even if speedily pointed out by the Employment Appeal Tribunal, likely to lead to the Notice of Appeal being out of time.
4. Of the 20 Notices of Appeal which were invalidly lodged during the period above referred to, only 10 were lodged by litigants in person and 10 by solicitors or other representatives: and it is plain that the latter ought certainly to have known of the requirements, although, given the wide publication both of the Rules and the Practice Direction, together with the guidance given by the Employment Tribunals, both at the Tribunal and sent with their judgments, there can be no excuse for litigants in person either.
5. The reason for this Statement in open court is to re-emphasise these requirements and the consequence of failure to comply with them, namely that an appeal not lodged within the 42 days validly constituted, i.e. accompanied by the required documents, will be out of time, and extensions of time are only exceptionally granted (see paragraph 3.7 of the Practice Direction).
6. From the date of this Practice Statement, ignorance or misunderstanding of the requirements as to service of the documents required to make a Notice of Appeal within the 42 days valid will not be accepted by the Registrar as an excuse.

THE HONOURABLE MR JUSTICE BURTON

President of the Employment Appeal Tribunal

3 February 2005

Appendix 3
Codes of Practice

Equal Opportunities Commission Code of Practice on Sex Discrimination, Equal Opportunity Policies, Procedures and Practices in Employment (1985, as amended)

Code of Practice—Sex Discrimination

The EOC issues this Code of Practice for the following purposes:

- for the elimination of discrimination in employment;
- to give guidance as to what steps it is reasonably practicable for employers to take to ensure that their employees do not in the course of their employment act unlawfully contrary to the Sex Discrimination Act (SDA);
- for the promotion of equality of opportunity between men and women in employment.

The SDA prohibits discrimination against men, as well as against women. It also requires that married people should not be treated less favourably than single people of the same sex. It should be noted that the provisions of the SDA—and therefore this Code—apply to the UK-based subsidiaries of foreign companies.

Scope of the Code

The Equal Opportunities Commission (the EOC) was set up under the Sex Discrimination Act 1975 (as amended) and is empowered to issue Codes of Practice under section 58(A)(1) of that Act. A failure on the part of any person to observe any provision of a code of practice shall not of itself render him [or her] liable to any proceedings; but in any proceedings under this Act before an employment tribunal any code of practice issued under this section shall be admissible in evidence, and if any provision of such a code appears to the tribunal to be relevant to any question arising in the proceedings it shall be taken into account in determining that question. [Sex Discrimination Act 1975 (as amended), section 56A(10)]

Purpose of the Code

The Code gives guidance to employers, trade unions and employment agencies on measures that can he taken to achieve equality. The chances of success of any organisation will clearly be improved if it seeks to develop the abilities of all employees, and the Code shows the close link that exists between equal opportunity and good employment practice. In some cases, an initial cost may be involved, but this should be more than compensated for by better relationships and better use of human resources.

Small Businesses

The Code has to deal in general terms and it will be necessary for employers to adapt it in a way appropriate to the size and structure of their organisations. Small businesses, for example, will require much simpler procedures than organisations with complex structures and it may not always be reasonable for them to carry out all the Code's detailed recommendations. In adapting the Code's recommendations, small firms should, however, ensure that their practices comply with the Sex Discrimination Act.

Employers' Responsibility

The primary responsibility at law rests with each employer to ensure that there is no unlawful discrimination. It is important, however, that measures to eliminate discrimination or promote equality of opportunity should be understood and supported by all employees. Employers ate therefore recommended to involve their employees in equal opportunity policies.

Individual Employees' Responsibility

While the main responsibility for eliminating discrimination and providing equal opportunity is that of the employer, individual employees at all levels have responsibilities too. They must not discriminate or knowingly aid their employer to do so.

Trade Union Responsibility

The full commitment of trade unions is essential for the elimination of discrimination and for the successful operation of an equal opportunities policy. Much can be achieved by collective bargaining and throughout the Code it is assumed that all the normal procedures will be followed.

It is recommended that unions should co-operate in the introduction and implementation of equal opportunities policies where employers have decided to introduce them, and should urge that such policies be adopted where they have not yet been introduced.

Trade unions have a responsibility to ensure that their representatives and members do not unlawfully discriminate on grounds of sex or marriage in the admission or treatment of members. The guidance in this Code also applies to trade unions in their role as employers.

Employment Agencies

Employment agencies have a responsibility as suppliers of job applicants to avoid unlawful discrimination on the grounds of sex or marriage in providing services to clients. The guidance in this Code also applies to employment agencies in their role as employers.

Definitions

For case of reference, the main employment provisions of the Sex Discrimination Act, including definitions of direct and indirect sex and marriage discrimination, are provided in a Legal Annex to this Code. [. . .].

The Role Of Good Employment Practices In Eliminating Sex And Marriage Discrimination

This section of the Code describes those good employment practices, which will help to eliminate unlawful discrimination. It recommends the establishment and use of consistent criteria for selection, training, promotion, redundancy and dismissal that are made known to all employees. Without this consistency, decisions can be subjective and leave the way open for unlawful discrimination to occur.

Recruitment

It is unlawful: unless the job is covered by an exception: to discriminate directly or indirectly on the grounds of sex or marriage—in the arrangements made for deciding who should be offered a job—in any terms of employment—by refusing or omitting to offer a person employment.

It is therefore recommended that:

- each individual should be assessed according to his or her personal capability to carry out a given job. It should not be assumed that men only or women only will be able to perform certain kinds of work;
- any qualifications or requirements applied to a job which effectively inhibit applications from one sex or from married people should be retained only if they are justifiable in terms of the job to be done;
- any age limits should be retained only if they are necessary for the job. An unjustifiable age limit could constitute unlawful indirect discrimination, for example, against women who have taken time out of employment for child-rearing;
- where trade unions uphold such qualifications or requirements as union policy, they should amend that policy in the light of any potentially unlawful effect.

Genuine Occupational Qualifications (GOQs)

It is unlawful: except for certain jobs when a person's sex is a genuine occupational qualification (GOQ) for that job to select candidates on the ground of sex.

There are very few instances in which a job will qualify for a GOQ on the ground of sex. However, exceptions may arise, for example, where considerations of privacy and decency or authenticity are involved. The SDA expressly states that the need of the job for strength and stamina does not justify restricting it to men. When a GOQ exists for a job, it applies also to promotion, transfer, on training for that job, but cannot be used to justify a dismissal.

In some instances, the GOQ will apply to some of the duties only. A GOQ will not be valid, however, where members of the appropriate sex are already employed in sufficient numbers to meet the employer's likely requirements without undue inconvenience. For example, in a job where sales assistants may be required to undertake changing room duties, it might not be lawful to claim a GOQ in respect of ***all*** the assistants on the grounds that any of them might be required to undertake changing room duties from time to time.

It is therefore recommended that:—A job for which a GOQ was used in the past should be re-examined if the post falls vacant to see whether the GOQ still applies. Circumstances may well have changed, rendering the GOQ inapplicable.

Sources of Recruitment

It is unlawful: unless the job is covered by an exception:—to discriminate on grounds of sex or marriage in the arrangements made for determining who should be offered employment whether recruiting by advertisements, through employment agencies, job centres, or career offices to imply that applications from one sex or from married people will not be considered to instruct or put pressure on others to omit to refer for employment people of one sex or married people unless the job is covered by an exception.

It is also unlawful when advertising job vacancies,—to publish or cause to be published an advertisement that indicates or might reasonably be understood as indicating an intention to discriminate unlawfully on grounds of sex or marriage.

Advertising

It is therefore recommended that job advertising should be carried out in such a way as to encourage applications from suitable candidates of both sexes. This can be achieved both by wording of the advertisements and, for example by placing advertisements in publications likely to reach both sexes. All advertising material and accompanying literature relating to employment or training issues should be reviewed to ensure that it avoids presenting men and women in stereotyped roles. Such stereotyping tends to perpetuate sex segregation in jobs and can also lead people of the opposite sex to believe that they would be unsuccessful in applying for particular jobs:

- where vacancies are filled by promotion or transfer, they should be published to all eligible employees in such a way that they do not restrict applications from either sex
- recruitment solely or primarily by word of mouth may unnecessarily restrict the choice of applicants available. The method should be avoided in a workforce predominantly of one sex, if in practice it prevents members of the opposite sex from applying
- where applicants are supplied through trade unions and members of one sex only come forward, this should be discussed with the unions and an alternative approach adopted.

Careers Service/Schools

When notifying vacancies to the Careers Service, employers should specify that these are open to both boys and girls. This is especially important when a job has traditionally been done exclusively or mainly by one sex. If dealing with single sex schools, they should ensure, where possible, that both boys' and girls' schools are approached: it is also a good idea to remind mixed schools that jobs are open to boys and girls.

Selection Methods

Tests

If selection tests are used, they should be specifically related to job and/or career requirements and should measure an individual's actual or inherent ability to do or train for the work or career.

Tests should be reviewed regularly to ensure that they remain relevant and free from any unjustifiable bias, either in content or in scoring mechanism

Applications and interviewing

It is unlawful: unless the job is covered by an exception: to discriminate on grounds of sex or marriage by refusing or deliberately omitting to offer employment.
It is therefore recommended that:

- employers should ensure that personnel staff, line managers and all other employees who may come into contact with job applicants, should be trained in the provisions of the SDA, including the fact that it is unlawful to instruct or put pressure on others to discriminate;
- applications from men and women should he processed in exactly the same way. For example, there should not be separate lists of male and female or married and single applicants. All those handling applications and conducting interviews should be trained in the avoidance of unlawful discrimination and records of interviews kept, where practicable, showing why applicants were or were not appointed;
- questions should relate to the requirements of the job. Where it is necessary to assess whether personal circumstances will affect performance of the job (for example, where it involves unsocial hours or extensive travel) this should be discussed objectively without detailed questions based on assumptions about marital status, children and domestic obligations. Questions about marriage plans or family intentions should not be asked, as they could be construed as showing bias against women. Information necessary for personnel records can be collected after a job offer has been made.

Promotion, Transfer and Training

It is unlawful: unless the job is covered by an exception, for employers to discriminate directly or indirectly on the grounds of sex or marriage in the way they afford access to opportunities for promotion, transfer or training.

It is therefore recommended that:

- where an appraisal system is in operation, the assessment criteria should be examined to ensure that they are not unlawfully discriminatory and the scheme monitored to assess how it is working in practice;
- when a group of workers predominantly of one sex is excluded from an appraisal scheme, access to promotion, transfer and training and to other benefits should be reviewed, to ensure that there is no unlawful indirect discrimination;
- promotion and career development patterns are reviewed to ensure that the traditional qualifications are justifiable requirements for the job to be done. In some circumstances, for example, promotion on the basis of length of service could amount to unlawful indirect discrimination, as it may unjustifiably affect more women than men;
- when general ability and personal qualifies are the main requirements for promotion to a post, care should be taken to consider favourably candidates of both sexes with differing career patterns and general experience;
- rules which restrict or preclude transfer between certain jobs should be questioned and charged if they are found to unlawfully discriminatory. Employees of one sex may be concentrated in sections from which transfers are traditionally restricted without real justification;
- policies and practices regarding selection for training, day release and personal development should be examined for unlawful direct and indirect discrimination. Where there is found to be an imbalance in training as between sexes, the cause should be identified to ensure that it is not discriminatory;
- age limits for access to training and promotion should be questioned.

Health and Safety Legislation

Equal treatment of men and women may be limited by statutory provisions, which require men and women to be treated differently. For example, the Factories Act 1961 places restrictions on the hours of work of female manual employees, although the Health and Safety Executive can exempt employers from these restrictions, subject to certain conditions. The Mines and Quarries Act 1954 imposes limitations on women's work and there are restrictions where there is special concern for the unborn child (e.g. lead and ionising radiation). However the broad duties placed on employers by the Health and Safety at Work Act, 1974 makes no distinctions between men and women Section 2(1) requires employers to ensure, so far as is reasonably practicable, the health and safety and welfare at work of all employees.

Specific health and safety requirements under earlier legislation are unaffected by the act.

It is therefore recommended that: company policy should be reviewed and serious consideration given to any significant differences in treatment between men and women, and there should be well-founded reasons if such differences are maintained or introduced.

Note. Some statutory restrictions placed on adult women's hours of work were repealed in February 1987 and others in February 1988. They now no longer apply. Paragraph 26 of the code is still relevant, however, to other health and safety legislation that requires men and women to be treated differently, and which has not been repealed.

Terms of Employment, Benefits, Facilities and Services

It is unlawful: unless the job is covered by an exception: to discriminate on the grounds of sex or marriage, directly or indirectly, in the terms on which employment is offered or in affording access to any benefits, facilities or services.

It is therefore recommended that: all terms of employment, benefits, facilities and services are reviewed to ensure that there is no unlawful discrimination on grounds of sex or marriage. For example, part-time work, domestic leave, company cars and benefits for dependants should be available to both male and female employees in the same or not materially different circumstances.

In an establishment where part-timers are solely or mainly women, unlawful indirect discrimination may arise if, as a group, they are treated less favourably than other employees without justification.

It is therefore recommended that: where part-time workers do not enjoy pro-rata pay or benefits with full-time workers, the arrangements should be reviewed to ensure that they are justified without regard to sex.

Grievances, Disciplinary Procedures and Victimisation

It is unlawful: to victimise an individual for a complaint made in good faith about sex or marriage discrimination or for giving evidence about such a complaint.
It is therefore recommended that:

- particular care is taken to ensure that an employee who has in good faith taken action under the Sex Discrimination Act or the Equal Pay Act does not receive less favourable treatment than other employees, for example by being disciplined or dismissed
- employees should be advised to use the internal procedures, where appropriate, but this is without prejudice to the individual's right to apply to an employment tribunal within the statutory time limit, i.e. before the end of the period of three months beginning when the act complained of was done. (There is no time limit if the victimisation is continuing.)
- particular care is taken to deal effectively with all complaints of discrimination, victimisation or harassment. It should not be assumed that they are made by those who are over-sensitive.

Dismissals, Redundancies and Other Unfavourable Treatment of Employees

It is unlawful: to discriminate directly or indirectly on grounds of sex or marriage in dismissals or by treating an employee unfavourably in any other way.
It is therefore recommended that:

- care is taken that members of one sex are not disciplined or dismissed for performance or behaviour which would be overlooked or condoned in the other sex;
- redundancy procedures affecting a group of employees predominantly of one sex should be reviewed, so as to remove any effects which could be disproportionate and unjustifiable;
- conditions of access to voluntary redundancy benefit should be made available on equal terms to male and female employees in the same or not materially different circumstances;
- where there is down-grading or short-time working (for example, owing to a change in the nature or volume of an employer's business) the arrangements should not unlawfully discriminate on the ground of sex;
- all reasonably practical steps should be taken to ensure that a standard of conduct or behaviour is observed which prevents members of either sex from being intimidated, harassed or otherwise subjected to unfavourable treatment on the ground of their sex.

The Role Of Good Employment Practices In Promoting Equality Of Opportunity

This section of the Code describes those employment practices that help to promote equality of opportunity. It gives information about the formulation and implementation of equal opportunities policies. While such policies are not required by law, their value has been recognised by a number of employers who have voluntarily adopted them. Others may wish to follow this example.

Formulating An Equal Opportunities Policy

An equal opportunities policy will ensure the effective use of human resources in the best interests of both the organisation and its employees, It is a commitment by an employer to the development and use of employment procedures and practices which do not discriminate on grounds of sex or marriage and which provide genuine equality of opportunity for all employees. The detail of the policy will vary according to size of the organisation.

Implementing the Policy

An equal opportunities policy must be seen to have the active support of management at the highest level. To ensure that the policy is fully effective, the following procedure is recommended:

- the policy should be clearly stated and where appropriate, included in a collective agreement;
- overall responsibility for implementing the policy should rest with senior management;
- the policy should be made known to all employees and, where reasonably practicable, to all job applicants.

Trade unions have a very important part to play in implementing genuine equality of opportunity and they will obviously be involved in the review of established procedures to ensure that these are consistent with the law.

Monitoring

It is recommended that the policy be monitored regularly to ensure that it is working in practice. Consideration could he given to setting up a joint Management/Trade Union Review Committee.

In a small firm with a simple structure it may be quite adequate to assess the distribution and payment of employees from personal knowledge.

In a large and complex organisation a more formal analysis will be necessary, for example, by sex, grade and payment in each unit. This may need to be introduced by stages as resources permit. Any formal analysis should be regularly updated and available to Management and Trade Unions to enable any necessary action to be taken.

Sensible monitoring will show, for example, whether members of one sex:

- do not apply for employment or promotion, or that fewer apply than might be expected;
- are not recruited, promoted or selected for training and development or are appointed/selected in a significantly lower proportion than their rate of application;
- are concentrated in certain jobs, sections or departments.

Positive Action

Recruitment, Training and Promotion

Selection for recruitment or promotion must be on merit, irrespective of sex. However, the Sex Discrimination Act does allow certain steps to redress the effects of previous unequal opportunities. Where there have been few or no members of one sex in particular work in their employment for the previous 12 months, the Act allows employers to give special encouragement to, and provide specific training for, the minority sex. Such measures are usually described as Positive Action.

Employers may wish to consider positive measures such as:

- training their own employees (male or female) for work which is traditionally the preserve of the other sex, for example, training women for skilled manual or technical work
- positive encouragement to women to apply for management posts—special courses may be needed.
- advertisements which encourage applications from the minority sex, but make it clear that selection will be on merit without reference to sex
- notifying job agencies, as part of a Positive Action Programme that they wish to encourage members of one sex to apply for vacancies, where few or no members of that sex are doing the work in question. In these circumstances, job agencies should tell both men and women about the posts and, in addition, let the under-represented sex know that applications from them are particularly welcome. Withholding information from one sex in an attempt to encourage applications from the opposite sex would be unlawful.

Other Working Arrangements

There are other forms of action that could assist both employer and employee by helping to provide continuity of employment to working parents, many of whom will have valuable experience or skills. Employers may wish to consider with their employees whether:

(a) certain jobs can be carried out on a part-time or flexi-time basis

(b) personal leave arrangements are adequate and available to both sexes. It should not be assumed that men may not need to undertake domestic responsibilities on occasion, especially at the time of childbirth

(c) childcare facilities are available locally or whether it would be feasible to establish nursery facilities on the premises or combine with other employers to provide them

(d) residential training could be facilitated for employees with young children. For example, where this type of training is necessary, by informing staff who are selected well in advance to enable them to make childcare and other personal arrangements; employers with their own residential training centres could also consider whether childcare facilities might he provided

(e) the statutory maternity leave provisions could he enhanced, for example, by reducing the qualifying service period, extending the leave period, or giving access to part-time arrangements on return.

These arrangements, and others, are helpful to both sexes but are of particular benefit to women in helping them to remain in gainful employment during the years of child-rearing.

Annex: Legal Background

This section gives general guidance only and should not be regarded as a complete or definitive statement of law.

The Relationship Between the Equal Pay Act and the Sex Discrimination Act

The Sex Discrimination Act 1975 (as amended) (the SDA) covers a wide range of non-contractual benefits, in addition to covering practices and procedures relating to recruitment, training, promotion and dismissal. A claim relating to a contractual benefit may also be brought under the SDA provided the benefit does not consist of the payment of money.

The Equal Pay Act 1970 (as amended) (the EPA) provides for an individual to be treated not less favourably than a person of the opposite sex who works for the same employer, as regards pay and other terms of the contract of employment where they are employed on like work (i.e. the same work or work which is broadly similar) or on work which has been rated as equivalent under a job evaluation scheme or on work which is of equal value. There is no overlap between an individual's rights under the Equal Pay Act and those under the Sex Discrimination Act. All complaints of discrimination in the circumstances covered by the EPA are dealt with under that Act. All complaints of discrimination about access to jobs and matters not included in a contract of employment and about contractual matters (other than those relating to the payment of money) in situations not covered by the EPA are dealt with under the SDA.

Who is covered by the SDA?

The provisions of the SDA apply to both men and women. It is unlawful to discriminate, directly or indirectly, against a person on the grounds of sex or marriage, unless the situation is covered by one of the Exceptions. It is also unlawful to instruct or bring pressure to bear on others to discriminate.

Exceptions from the Act

Geographical scope—section 10(1)
The SDA does not relate to employment that is wholly or mainly outside Great Britain.

Private household or small employer—section 6(3)(a); section 6(3)(b)
These exceptions made it lawful under the Sex Discrimination Act to discriminate in relation to existing or potential employment in a private household, or an organisation that employed five people or fewer. These exceptions did not apply to matters covered by the Equal Pay Act. These exceptions were, however, repealed in February 1987.

Small employer
Note: Small employers, as all other employers, are now covered by the SDA. This means that there is now no distinction between small employers and any other employer. There are, however, still certain exclusions which apply to all employers relating to, for example (i) death or retirement, and (ii) Genuine Occupational Qualifications, in accordance with sections 6(4) and 7 of the SDA. Paragraph 3 of the Code, which states that it will be necessary for employers to adapt the Code in a way appropriate to the size and structure of their organisations, has not been superseded.

Private household
Note: There is no longer any distinction between employment in a private household and any other employment for the purposes of the SDA. There can no longer be any sex or marriage discrimination in choosing someone to work in your home except that, in order to respect personal privacy, discrimination on the basis of a person's sex may still be allowed if the job involves physical or social contact with someone in the family, or having knowledge of intimate details of someone's life.

Death or retirement—section 6(4)
Certain provisions relating to death or retirement are exempt from the SDA. However, retirement ages for male and female employees should be equal.

Pregnancy or childbirth—section 2(2)
Special treatment (i.e. more favourable treatment) may lawfully be afforded to women in connection with pregnancy or childbirth.

Genuine Occupational Qualifications—section 7
A person's sex may be a Genuine Occupational Qualification (GOQ) for a job, in which case discrimination in recruitment, opportunities for promotion or transfer to, or training for such employment would not

be unlawful. A GOQ cannot, however, apply to the treatment of employees once they are in post, not too discrimination on grounds of marriage, nor to victimisation. The GOQ is not an automatic exception for general categories of jobs. In every case it will be necessary for an employer to show that the criteria detailed in the SDA apply to the job or part of the job in question. A GOQ may be claimed only because of:

- physiology (excluding physical strength and stamina) or authenticity—for example, a model or an actor;
- decency or privacy—for example, some changing room attendants;

Note: The job being likely to involve the holder of the job doing work, or living, in a private home and needs to be held by a member of one sex because objection might reasonably be taken to allowing a member of the other sex—

> the degree of physical or social contact with a person living within the home, the knowledge of intimate details of such a person's life, which is likely because of the nature or circumstances of the job or of the home, to be allowed to, or available to, the holder of the job; the nature or location of the establishment which makes it impracticable for the jobholder to live in premises other than those provided by the employer (e.g. if the job is in a ship or on a remote site) and the only available premises for persons doing that kind of job do not provide both separate sleeping accommodation for each sex, and sanitary facilities which can he used in privacy from the other. In such a case, the employer may discriminate by choosing for the job only persons of the same sex as those who are already living, or normally live, in these premises. However, the exception does not apply if the employer could reasonably be expected either to equip the premises with the necessary separate sleeping accommodation and private sanitary facilities, or to provide other premises, for a jobholder of the opposite sex;

- the fact that the establishment, or part of it, provides special care, supervision or attention to people of one sex only—for example, some jobs in a single-sex hospital;
- the fact that the job involves the provision of personal services, promoting welfare or education, that are most effectively provided by men (or by women)—for example, some probation officers or wardens of residential hostels;
- laws regulating the employment of women;
- the laws and customs of the country in which part of the job is to be carried out—for example, a job involving driving in a country where women are forbidden to drive;
- the fact that the job is one of two to be held by a married couple.

Definition of 'employment'—section 82

'Employment' is defined in the SDA as meaning employment under a contract of service or of an apprenticeship or a contract personally to carry out any work or labour.

Direct sex discrimination—section 1(1)(a)

This occurs where a person of one sex is treated less favourably, on the ground of sex, than a person of the other sex would be in the same or not material different circumstances.

Indirect sex discrimination—section 1(1)(b)

Indirect sex discrimination occurs when an unjustifiable requirement or condition is applied equally to both sexes, but has a proportionately adverse effect on one sex, because the proportion of one sex which can comply with it is much smaller than the proportion of the other sex which can comply with it. For example, a requirement to be mobile might bar more women than men. A complainant would have to show that fewer women than men could comply with such a requirement and that it is to her detriment that she cannot comply. Where she cannot comply. Where the employer can justify such a requirement without regard to sex there will be no unlawful act. A finding of unlawful discrimination may be made even though the employer has no intention to discriminate.

Marriage discrimination—section 3(1)(a); section 3(1)(b)

Direct discrimination against a married person occurs where a married person is treated less favourably on the grounds of marital status, than an unmarried person of the same sex would be in the same or not materially different circumstances. Indirect discrimination against a married person is similar in concept to indirect sex discrimination and may arise when a condition or requirement is applied equally to married and unmarried persons of the same sex but which is in fact discriminatory in its effect on married persons. For example, a requirement to be mobile might bar more married than single women.

Discrimination by way of victimisation—section 4

This occurs where a person is treated less favourably than other persons would be treated because he/she has done something by reference to the EPA or the SDA, for example, brought proceedings or given evidence or information in a case under either of those Acts or alleged (expressly or otherwise) that anyone has committed an act which could constitute a breach of those Acts. Victimisation is not unlawful if the allegation was false and not made in good faith.

Discrimination in recruitment—section 6(1)

This section makes it unlawful for an employer to discriminate when recruiting employees in the following ways:

- Section 6(1)(a)—in the arrangements made for deciding who should be offered a job. (One example might be the instructions given to a Personnel Officer or to an Employment Agency. Another example might be advertising a job in a place where only one sex would have the opportunity of seeing the advertisement.)
- Section 6(1)(b)—in relation to any terms offered (for instance, in respect of pay or holidays). It is, for instance, unlawful to offer a job (whether or not the candidate accepts), where the terms would be a breach of the EPA should an employment contract be entered into;
- Section 6(1)(c)—by refusing or deliberately omitting to offer a person employment (for example, by rejecting an application or deliberately refusing consideration of an application).

Discrimination in the treatment of present employees—section 6(2)

This section makes it unlawful for an employer to discriminate in the following ways:

- Section 6(2)(a)—in the way access is afforded to opportunities for promotion, transfer or training, or to any other benefits, facilities or services, or by refusing or deliberately omitting to afford access to them; or
- Section 6(2)(b)—by dismissal or the subjection to any other unfavourable treatment.

Discrimination against contract workers—section 9(1)

This section covers contract workers, i.e. workers who are sent to work for an organisation by another organisation that employs them.

Section 9(2)
It is unlawful for the principal firm to discriminate on grounds of sex or marriage:

- in the terms on which it allows the contract worker to do the work or
- by not allowing the contract worker to do it or continue to do it or
- in the way the contract worker is afforded access to any benefits, facilities or services or by refusing or deliberately omitting to afford access to any of them or
- by subjecting the contract worker to any other unfavourable treatment.

Section 9(3)
A principal may rely upon the GOQ exception, where it is applicable, to refuse to allow a contract worker to do, or to continue to do the contract work.

Section 9(4)
Where a principal provides his contract workers with benefits, facilities or services not materially different from those he provides to the public, a complaint relating to the discriminatory provision of such benefits, etc. would not fall under section 9, but under section 29 of the SDA.

Discrimination by trade unions and employers' organisations, etc—section 12(1) and 12(2)

It is unlawful, for an organisation of workers or of employers or any other organisation whose members carry on a particular profession or trade for the purposes of which the organisation exists, to discriminate on grounds of sex or marriage against anyone applying for membership:

- in the terms on which it is prepared to admit the person to membership; or
- by refusing or deliberately omitting to accept an application for membership.

Section 12(3)
It is unlawful for such an organisation to discriminate on grounds of sex or marriage against a member:

- in the way it affords access to any benefits, facilities or services or by refusing or deliberately omitting to afford access to them; or

- by depriving a person of membership or varying the terms of membership; or
- subjecting to any other unfavourable treatment.

Discrimination by employment agencies—section 15(1)

It is unlawful for an employment agency to discriminate on grounds of sex or marriage:

- in the terms on which they offer to provide any of their services; or
- by refusing or deliberately omitting to provide them; or
- in the way in which they provide any of them.

Section 15(4)
Section 15(1) will not apply if the discrimination only concerns employment that an employer could lawfully refuse to offer to a woman (or a man).

Section 15(5) and 15(6)
Where an employment agency has the employer's assurance that a vacancy is covered by one of the exceptions and this turns out not to be the case, the agency has a defence if it can prove both that it acted in reliance on a statement by the employer that its action would not be unlawful and that it was reasonable for it to rely on the statement. It is a summary offence punishable by a fine not exceeding £5,000, knowingly or recklessly to make such a statement that in a material respect is false or misleading.

Discriminatory advertisements—section 38(1) and 38(2)

The SDA makes it unlawful to publish or cause to be published an advertisement that indicates, or might reasonably be taken to indicate, an intention to discriminate unlawfully. An advertisement would not he unlawful if it dealt with a job that was covered by an exception.

Section 38(3)
An advertisement that uses a job description with a sexual connotation (for example, 'waiter' 'salesgirl' or 'stewardess') is taken as an intention to commit an unlawful discriminatory act, unless the advertisement states that the job is open to men and women or uses descriptions applying to both sexes (e.g. 'waiter' or 'waitress').

Section 38(4)
There will be cases where a publisher may not know whether a particular advertisement is lawful. A publisher will not be held liable if:

- he or she relied on a statement by the person placing the advertisement that the publication would not be unlawful, for example because the vacancy was covered by an exception and
- it was reasonable for the publisher to rely on the statement.

Section 38(5)
It is an offence punishable on summary conviction with a fine not exceeding £5,000, for anyone placing an advertisement knowingly or recklessly to make a materially false or misleading statement to the publisher as to its lawfulness.

Instructions to discriminate—section 39

It is unlawful for a person who has authority over another person or whose wishes are normally carried out by that other person to instruct or attempt to procure another person (e.g. a member of staff) to carry out an act of unlawful discrimination, e.g. an instruction to an employment agency to discriminate.

Pressure to discriminate—section 40

It is unlawful for a person to bring pressure to hear on another person to carry out an act of unlawful discrimination, by providing or offering any benefit or threatening any detriment; for example, by a threat of industrial action to persuade an employer to discriminate.

Liability of employers and principals—section 41

An employer is liable for any act done by an employee in the course of the employment with or without the employer's knowledge or approval, unless the employer can show that such steps were taken as were reasonably practicable to prevent the employee doing the act in question. Similarly, a principal is liable for any act done by an agent with the principal's authority.

Section 42
A person (for example, an employee or agent) who knowingly aids another to do an unlawful act is also to be treated as having done that act, unless it can be shown that he or she acted in reliance on a statement that the act would not be unlawful and that it was reasonable to rely on such a statement.

Positive action by training bodies—section 47

Training bodies may apply to the Secretary of State for Employment to become designated for the purpose of providing:

- training or encouragement for particular work where in the previous 12 months one sex has been substantially under-represented or;
- special training for persons following absence from employment because of domestic or family responsibilities.

Note. Until February 1987, training bodies that wished to run single sex courses needed special designation by the Secretary of State. This is no longer required.
Positive Action is, however, confined to training and is still not allowed in recruitment. Section 47 of the Act now applies to any person, not just to training bodies.

Positive action by employers—section 48

This section of the SDA allows for positive action by employers to overcome the effects of past discrimination, it allows for training and encouragement where few or no members of one sex have been doing particular work in the preceding 12 months. It does not cover recruitment or promotion. Advice on the promotion of equality of opportunity in employment is available from the EOC. All EOC publications referred to are available from the EOC Offices in Manchester.

Other publications

Many Policy Statements will cover race as well as sex discrimination. For advice on racial discrimination refer to the Code of Practice issued by the Commission for Racial Equality. Examples of equal opportunities policy statements are the Trade Union Congress Model Clause and the Confederation of British Industry's Statement Guide.

Equal Opportunities Commission Code of Practice on Equal Pay (2003)

Introduction

1. The Equal Pay Act gives women (or men) a right to equal pay for equal work. An employer can only pay a man more than a woman for doing equal work if there is a genuine and material reason for doing so which is not related to sex. The Equal Opportunities Commission (EOC) has issued this revised Code of Practice on Equal Pay in order to provide practical guidance on how to ensure pay is determined without sex discrimination. The revised Code (the Code) is aimed at employers, but employees and their representatives or advisers—for example, from a trade union, or Citizens Advice Bureau, may also find it useful.[1]
2. The Act applies to both men and women but to avoid repetition the Code is written as though the claimant is a woman comparing her work and pay with those of a man. The Equal Pay Act specifically deals with the pay of women compared to men, (or vice versa), and not to comparisons between people of the same sex.
3. The Code is admissible in evidence in any proceedings under the Sex Discrimination Act 1975 or the Equal Pay Act 1970 (each as amended), before the Employment Tribunal. This means that, while the Code is not binding, the Employment Tribunal may take into account an employer's failure to act on its provisions.
4. Despite the fact that it is over 30 years since the Equal Pay Act became law, women working full-time earn on average 81 per cent of the hourly earnings of male full-time employees.[2] Part-time working further accentuates the gender pay gap with women working part-time earning on average only 41% of the hourly earnings of male full-time employees. Both the Government and the EOC regard this as unacceptable. By helping employers to check the pay gap in their organisation and by encouraging good equal pay practice, this Code reinforces the Government's commitment to closing the gap between men's and women's pay.
5. Depending on the particular circumstances a number of other pieces of legislation can give rise to claims related to pay discrimination. They include the Race Relations Act, the Disability Discrimination Act, the Pensions Act 1995, the Part-Time (Prevention of Less Favourable Treatment) Regulations 2000 and the Fixed-Term Employees (Prevention of Less Favourable Treatment) Regulations 2002. A female part-time cleaner, for example, could claim equal pay under the Equal Pay Act with a male part-time cleaner, but she could also claim under the Part-Time Workers Regulations, that she was being treated less favourably than a female full-time cleaner. These other pieces of legislation are dealt with in Annex A, but employers should be aware of the need to pay particular attention to the situation in respect of part-time, black and minority ethnic employees and employees with a disability.
6. It is in everyone's interest to avoid litigation, and the Code recommends equal pay reviews as the best means of ensuring that a pay system delivers equal pay. Employers can avoid equal pay claims by regularly reviewing and monitoring their pay practices, in consultation with their workforce. Consultation is likely to increase understanding and acceptance of any changes required. Involving recognised trade unions or other employee representatives also helps to ensure that pay systems meet the legal requirement for transparency.
7. The Code includes, as good equal pay practice, a summary of EOC guidance on how to carry out an equal pay review. The full guidance is in the EOC's Equal Pay Review Kit.[3] The EOC has also produced a separate kit for smaller organisations without specialist personnel expertise.[4] Both are available on the EOC website at www.eoc.org.uk or from the EOC Helpline 0845 601 5901.
8. Whilst every effort has been made to ensure that the explanations given in the Code are accurate, only the Courts or Tribunals can give authoritative interpretations of the law.

[1] For ease of communication the word 'employee' is used throughout this document, but it is not used as a legal term. 'Employee' should be read as referring to all people who work in your organisation.

[2] *New Earnings Survey 2002*, Office for National Statistics.

[3] The EOC Equal Pay Review Kit.

[4] EOC Equal Pay, Fair Pay: a guide to effective pay practices in small businesses.

Section One: Equal Pay Legislation

The Treaty of Rome and the Equal Pay Directive

9. The principle that a woman is entitled to equal pay for equal work is set out in European Union and British legislation.[5] The British Courts take into account the decisions of the European Court of Justice in interpreting the Equal Pay Act and the Sex Discrimination Act. A woman bringing an equal pay claim will usually do so under the domestic British legislation, but in some circumstances she can claim under European law.

10. **Article 141 of the Treaty of Amsterdam** (previously Article 119 of the Treaty of Rome) requires Member States to ensure that the principle of equal pay for male and female workers for equal work or work of equal value is applied. The **Equal Pay Directive**[6] explains the practical application of the principle of equal pay, namely the elimination of sex discrimination in pay systems. European law defines pay as:

   'The ordinary basic or minimum wage or salary and any other consideration, whether in cash or kind, which the worker receives directly or indirectly, in respect of his employer or employment.'

   Pensions are treated as pay.

The Equal Pay Act 1970

11. The Equal Pay Act 1970, as amended, entitles a woman doing equal work with a man in the same employment to equality in pay and terms and conditions. The meaning of 'same employment' is considered in paragraph 21. The Act does so by giving her the right to equality in the terms of her contract of employment. The man with whom she is claiming equal pay is known as her comparator. Equal work is work that is the same or broadly similar, work that has been rated as equivalent, or work that is of equal value (see paragraphs 27–32).

12. Claims for equal pay are taken through the Employment Tribunal. If a woman succeeds in a claim:
    - Her pay, including any occupational pension rights, must be raised to that of her male comparator
    - Any beneficial term in the man's contract but not in hers must be inserted into her contract
    - Any term in her contract that is less favourable than the same term in the man's contract must be made as good as it is in his
    - Compensation consisting of arrears of pay (if the claim is about pay) and/or damages (if the complaint is about some other contractual term).

13. The woman can compare any term in her contract with the equivalent term in her comparator's contract. This means that each element of the pay package has to be considered separately and it is not sufficient to compare total pay. For example, a woman can claim equal pay with a male comparator who earns a higher rate of basic pay than she does, even if other elements of her pay package are more favourable than his.

14. Once a woman establishes that she and her comparator are doing equal work it is up to her employer to show that the explanation for the pay difference is genuinely due to a 'material factor' that is not tainted by sex discrimination. This defence is known as the 'genuine material factor' defence. In practice, an employer may identify more than one factor. For example, an employer may argue that the man is paid more because he is better qualified than the woman *and* because it is difficult to recruit people with his particular skills.

The Sex Discrimination Act 1975

15. The Equal Pay Act applies to pay or benefits provided under the contract of employment. The Sex Discrimination Act 1975, as amended, complements the Equal Pay Act. It covers noncontractual issues such as recruitment, training, promotion, dismissal and the allocation of benefits, for example, flexible working arrangements or access to a workplace nursery.

16. The Sex Discrimination Act also covers non-contractual pay matters, such as promotion and discretionary bonuses. Decisions about performance markings in a performance-related pay scheme are aspects of treatment which could be challenged under the Sex Discrimination Act if discriminatory. By contrast, where those decisions result in different levels of pay, that difference and the terms of the scheme could be challenged under the Equal Pay Act. This means that if a woman

---

[5] This Code applies to Great Britain. Northern Ireland has its own equivalent equal pay and sex discrimination legislation and Equality Commission.

[6] European Council Directive 75/117/EEC.

wishes to make a claim in respect of non-contractual or discretionary payments her claim will be made under the Sex Discrimination Act.[7] If there is any doubt as to which Act a payment falls under, legal advice should be sought.

Protection Against Victimisation

17. The Sex Discrimination Act also protects employees from being victimised for making a complaint (unless this is both untrue and made in bad faith) about equal pay or sex discrimination, or for giving evidence about such a complaint. Victimisation because a woman intends to bring a claim is also unlawful. The 'complaint' does not have to be by way of filing a claim with the Employment Tribunal, but includes any discussion or correspondence about the matter between the woman and her employer. The protection against victimisation also includes not only the woman bringing the claim, but also anyone who assists her, for example, her comparator and any trade union or employee representatives.

The Scope of the Equal Pay Act

Employers

18. The Equal Pay Act applies to all employers irrespective of their size and whether they are in the public or the private sector.

Employees

19. The Equal Pay Act applies to:
    - All employees (including apprentices and those working from home), whether on full-time, part-time, casual or temporary contracts, regardless of length of service
    - Other workers (e.g. self employed) whose contracts require personal performance of the work
    - Employment carried out for a British employer unless the employee works wholly outside Great Britain[8]
    - Employment carried out on British registered ships or UK registered aircraft operated by someone based in Great Britain unless the employee works wholly outside Great Britain.

20. The Equal Pay Act also applies to Armed Services personnel, but there is a requirement to first make a complaint to an officer under the relevant service redress procedures and submit a complaint to the Defence Council under those procedures before presenting a claim to the Employment Tribunal.[9]

Same employment

21. A woman can claim equal pay with a man working:
    - For the same employer at the same workplace
    - For the same employer but at a different workplace where common terms and conditions apply, for example at another branch of a store
    - For an associated employer; for example, at her employer's parent company
    - European law also allows a comparison to be made between employees who do not work for the same employer, but who are '*in the same establishment or service*'. As there is no clear definition of '*in the same establishment or service*' this is an area of law on which specific legal advice should be sought. However, European law as it currently stands suggests a comparison can only be made where the differences in pay are attributable to a 'common source' and there is a single body, responsible for and capable of remedying the pay inequality, for example where pay differences arise from a sector-wide collective agreement or from legislation.

The pay package

22. The Equal Pay Act covers all aspects of the pay and benefits package, including:
    - Basic pay
    - Non-discretionary bonuses

---

[7] Also, if a woman considers that a term in a collective agreement, or an employer's rule, provides for the doing of an unlawful discriminatory act, and that the term or rule may at some time have effect in relation to her, she can challenge that term or rule under the Sex Discrimination Act 1986 as amended by section 32 of the Trade Union Reform and Employment Rights Act 1993.

[8] Great Britain includes such of the territorial waters of the UK as are adjacent to Great Britain and certain areas designated in relation to employment in the offshore oil and gas industry.

[9] Section S7A (5) of the Equal Pay Act read with the Service Redress Procedures.

- Overtime rates and allowances
- Performance related benefits
- Severance and redundancy pay
- Access to pension schemes
- Benefits under pension schemes
- Hours of work
- Company cars
- Sick pay
- Fringe benefits such as travel allowances.

Comparators

23. A woman can claim equal pay for equal work with a man, or men, in the same employment. It is for the woman to select the man or men with whom she wishes to be compared, and her employer cannot interfere with her choice of comparator(s). She can claim equal pay with more than one comparator, but to avoid repetition the Code (and the law) is written as though there is only one comparator.
24. The comparator can be:
    - Someone with whom she is working at the present time, subject to the usual time limits (see paragraphs 47–48)
    - Her predecessor, however long ago he did the job, or her successor.
25. The comparator does not have to give his consent to being named. If the woman's equal pay claim is successful, the result will be that her pay is raised to the same level as his. There will not be any reduction in the comparator's pay and benefits.
26. There are a number of ways in which a woman may be able to select a comparator. These include:
    - Her own knowledge and experience
    - The internal grievance procedure (see paragraph 36)
    - The Equal Pay Questionnaire (see paragraph 37)
    - Discovery (asking for documents through the Employment Tribunal). Once a woman has filed her claim with the Employment Tribunal, provided that she has shown that her contractual terms are less favourable than those of male colleagues, she can apply for discovery to enable her to name appropriate comparators.

Equal pay for equal work

27. The comparator may be doing the *same* job as the woman, or he may be doing a *different* job. She can claim equal pay for equal work with a comparator doing work that is:
    - The *same*, or broadly similar (known as **like work**)
    - *Different*, but which is rated under the same job evaluation scheme as equivalent to hers (known as **work rated as equivalent**)
    - *Different*, but of equal value in terms of demands such as effort, skill and decision-making (known as **work of equal value**).

Like work

28. Like work means the woman and her comparator are doing the same or broadly similar work. Job titles could be different, yet the work being done could be broadly similar—the nature of the work actually being done needs to be considered. Where differences exist the Employment Tribunal will look at the nature and extent of the differences, how frequently they occur, and whether they are of practical importance in relation to the terms and conditions of the job.

Like work comparisons that have succeeded, in the particular circumstances of the case, include:

- Male and female cleaners doing 'wet' and 'dry' cleaning in different locations on the same site
- A woman cook preparing lunches for directors and a male chef cooking breakfast, lunch and tea for employees.

Work rated as equivalent

29. Work rated as equivalent means that the jobs being done by the woman and her comparator have been assessed under the same job evaluation scheme as being equivalent, that is, they have been assessed as having the same number of points, or as falling within the same job evaluation grade.

Work rated as equivalent comparisons that have succeeded in the particular circumstances of the case, include:
- Where a woman and a man had been placed in the same job evaluation grade, but the employer had refused to pay the woman (who had been evaluated as having fewer points) the rate for the grade.

Work of equal value

30. Work of equal value means that the jobs done by the woman and her comparator are different, but can be regarded as being of equal value or worth. This can be measured by comparing the jobs under headings such as effort, skill and decision-making.

31. Comparing jobs on the basis of equal value means jobs that are entirely different in their nature can be used as the basis for equal pay claims. Job comparisons can be made both within a particular pay/grading structure and between different structures or departments, for example, in a printing firm, between a bindery and a press room. Equal value is likely to be relevant where men and women are in the same employment but do different types of work.

Equal value comparisons that have succeeded in the particular circumstances of the case, include:
- Cooks and carpenters
- Speech therapists and clinical psychologists
- Kitchen assistants and refuse workers.

32. A woman can claim equal pay under more than one heading. For example, a woman working as an administrator in a garage could claim 'like work' with a male administrator working alongside her and 'equal value' with a mechanic.

Pregnant women and women on maternity leave

33. During the period of Ordinary Maternity Leave a woman's contract remains in place and all of her contractual terms and conditions must continue, with the exception of her normal pay (i.e. wages or salary).[10] The position with regard to bonuses, occupational pension rights, and the provision of maternity benefits over and above those required by the statutory scheme is unclear, and specific legal advice will be needed.

34. When a woman is on Additional Maternity Leave,[11] even though her contract remains in place, her contractual terms cease to apply, except for some limited exceptions not relevant to pay. However, her entitlement to paid leave under the Working Time Regulations continues to accrue, and in some circumstances it may be unlawful under either the Equal Pay Act or the Sex Discrimination Act to treat a woman on maternity leave differently from other workers, e.g. by failing to pay her a bonus. The situation will vary according to the facts and again, this is an area where detailed legal advice should be sought.

35. Pay increases continue to accrue while a woman is on maternity leave and she is entitled to the benefit of any pay increases that she would have received had she been at work.[12]

Raising the Matter with the Employer

Using the grievance procedure

36. Before making a complaint to the Employment Tribunal, a woman should try to resolve the issue of equal pay by mutual agreement with her employer, perhaps through the employer's own grievance procedure. Employers and employees can also seek advice from an Acas conciliator. Acas can be contacted at www.acas.org.uk. However, the time limit for making a complaint to the Employment

[10] Under the Employment Rights Act 1996, and the Maternity and Parental Leave Regulations 1999, as amended by the Maternity and Parental Leave (Amendment) Regulations 2002, Ordinary Maternity Leave is 26 weeks for all mothers whose expected week of childbirth is after 6 April 2003.

[11] Under the Employment Rights Act 1996, as amended by the Employment Relations Act 1999, women who have at least 26 weeks service at the beginning of the 14th week before the expected week of childbirth are entitled to 26 weeks Additional Maternity Leave starting after their Ordinary Maternity Leave.

[12] *Gillespie & others v Northern Health and Social Services Board (1996 ECJ).*

Tribunal will still apply and will not be extended to take account of the time taken to complete the grievance procedure.[13] Although there is no legal requirement to do so it is good practice for the employer, the employee, and/or her union representative, to keep records of any meetings.

The equal pay questionnaire

37. A woman is entitled to write to her employer asking for information that will help her establish whether she has received equal pay and if not, what the reasons for the pay difference are. There is a standard questionnaire form which can be used to do this. The focus of the questionnaire is on establishing whether she is receiving less favourable pay and contractual terms and conditions than a colleague or colleagues of the opposite sex, and whether the employer agrees that she and her comparator are doing 'equal work'. The woman can send the questionnaire to her employer either before she files her claim with the Employment Tribunal or within 21 days of doing so. Copies of the questionnaire can be obtained from the Women and Equality Unit website at www.womenandequalityunit.gov.uk.
38. If the woman takes a case to the Employment Tribunal, the information provided by her employer should enable her to present her claim in the most effective way and the proceedings should be simpler because the key facts will have been identified in advance. If her employer fails, without reasonable excuse, to reply within 8 weeks, or responds with an evasive or equivocal reply, the Employment Tribunal may take this into account at the hearing. The Employment Tribunal may then draw an inference unfavourable to the employer, for example, that the employer has no genuine reason for the difference in pay.

Responding to Requests from an Employee for Information

Transparency

39. The European Court of Justice has held that pay systems must be transparent. Transparency means that pay and benefit systems should be capable of being understood by everyone (employers, employees and their trade unions). Employees should be able to understand how each element of their pay packet contributes to total earnings in a pay period. Where the pay structure is not transparent, and a woman is able to show some indication of sex discrimination, the burden of proof switches to the employer who then has to demonstrate that the pay system does not discriminate.
40. It is advisable for an employer to keep records that will allow him or her to explain why he or she did something, showing clearly what factors he or she relied on at the time that the decision on pay was made. Employers should be aware that employees may bring complaints or make enquiries about pay decisions which were taken many years previously, since when the person who took the decision may have left the organisation. For this reason it is advisable for employers to keep records that may, in the future, help them to explain why pay decisions were made.
41. Bearing in mind the guidance given in the preceding paragraphs, when responding either to a grievance or to the questionnaire employers need to:
    - Decide whether or not they agree that the woman is doing equal work
    - Consider the reasons for any difference in pay
    - If they do not agree that the woman's work is equal to that of her comparator, they should explain in what way the work is not equal
    - Explain the reasons for any difference in pay.

    Further guidance is given in the notes accompanying the questionnaire.

Confidentiality

42. The principle of transparency set out above does not mean that an individual has the automatic right to know what another individual earns. The principle of transparency means that a woman has the right to know how the calculations are made, not the content of the calculation. It is necessary to balance the ideal of transparency with the rights of individual privacy. The equal pay questionnaire cannot be used to require an employer to disclose confidential information, unless the Employment Tribunal orders the employer to do so. A woman can use the questionnaire to request key information and it is likely that in many cases an employer will be able to answer detailed questions in general terms, while still preserving the anonymity and confidentiality of employees.

[13] A woman will be obliged to use the grievance procedure once the relevant provisions of the Employment Act 2002 have come into effect in October 2004. Time limits will be amended to allow the grievance procedure to be used.

The Data Protection Act

43. Much of the information requested will not be confidential but some information, such as the exact details of a comparator's pay package, may be confidential to that person. Personal data is protected by the Data Protection Act 1998 and can only be disclosed in accordance with data protection principles. Pay records will usually be personal data covered by the Data Protection Act. Moreover, other issues such as ethnic origin and medical details are sensitive personal data to which particular safeguards apply. The disclosure of confidential information in the employment context is also protected by the implied duty of trust and confidence owed by an employer to an employee.
44. The EOC has produced a guidance note that explains an employer's legal obligations when responding to an equal pay questionnaire or to a request for information during the course of tribunal proceedings.[14] However, this is a developing area of law and, if in doubt, an employer should seek specific advice from the Information Commissioner www.informationcommissioner.gov.uk and/or take legal advice.

Disclosure of information to trade unions or employee representatives

45. Under the Trade Union and Labour Relations (Consolidation) Act 1992 an employer is under a duty, on request, to disclose to a recognised trade union, information to enable constructive collective bargaining. Information about pay and terms and conditions of employment usually comes within the duty to disclose, but it is important to note that the duty applies only to information for collective bargaining.
46. It also represents good practice for employers who do not recognise trade unions to communicate regularly with their workforce and, where appropriate, their representatives.

Bringing an Equal Pay Claim

The time limits for applying to an Employment Tribunal

47. If a woman wishes to lodge a claim with the Employment Tribunal she must do so within the prescribed time limits. **It is her responsibility to ensure that she does so.** The woman bringing the claim and her representatives should be alert to the importance of lodging the equal pay claim with the Employment Tribunal within the time limits. Using the internal grievance procedure does not extend the time limits set for lodging a claim, nor does serving the questionnaire.[15]
48. The Equal Pay Act and the Sex Discrimination Act have different time limits.
    - Claims under the Equal Pay Act can be taken at any time up to six months after leaving the employment with the employer (as opposed to leaving the particular post about which the equal pay claim is made, but remaining in the same employment). This time limit also applies to equal pay claims taken where a stable relationship with an employer has come to an end. The time limit can be extended only where the employer deliberately conceals the existence of pay inequality from the complainant, or the complainant is a minor or of unsound mind[16]
    - In contracting out situations the time limit runs from the date of the contracting out in respect of periods of service up to that date
    - Claims under the Sex Discrimination Act can be taken within three months of the alleged act of discrimination, subject to the tribunal's discretion to extend the time limit where it is just and equitable to do so
    - Because of the requirement on Armed Services personnel to use the relevant Service Redress Procedure referred to in paragraph 20 different rules apply. In the case of the Equal Pay Act, the time limit is nine months from the end of the period of service, and in the case of the Sex Discrimination Act, the time limit is six months from the date of the act complained of. The time limits can be extended only as described above.

The burden of proof

49. The woman bringing an equal pay claim has to show the Employment Tribunal that on the face of it she is receiving less pay than a man in the same employment who is doing equal work. Her employer must then either accept her claim or prove to the Employment Tribunal that the difference in pay was for a genuine and material reason, which was not the difference of sex.

[14] EOC practical tips: responding to an equal pay questionnaire and requests for information during tribunal proceedings in accordance with Data Protection Act principles.

[15] See footnote 13.

[16] The Equal Pay Act 1970 (Amendment) Regulations 2003 (SI 2003/1656).

The Employment Tribunal procedure

50. The fact that a woman is paid less than a man doing equal work does not necessarily mean that she is suffering sex discrimination in pay. In making a decision about a case the Employment Tribunal has to assess the evidence about:
    - The work done by the woman and her comparator
    - The value placed on the work (sometimes with the advice of an Independent Expert), in terms of the demands of the jobs
    - The pay of the woman and her comparator and how it is arrived at
    - The reasons for the difference in pay.
51. In *like work* and *work rated as equivalent* claims the procedure is the same as in any other employment case. There are special tribunal procedures for *work of equal value* claims.[17]

Assessing equal value

52. The concept of equal pay for work of equal value means that a woman can claim equal pay with a man doing a completely different job. In comparing such jobs the Employment Tribunal will apply techniques akin to analytical job evaluation, whereby the demands on the jobholders and the skills required of them are assessed using objective criteria. The Employment Tribunal may also appoint an Independent Expert to assess the value of the jobs. The Employment Tribunal-appointed Independent Expert may make a detailed study of an employer's pay system and the employer would be expected to co-operate with any such exercise.
53. Employers should be aware that they, and the woman bringing the claim, might also appoint someone with equal pay expertise to act as an expert on their behalf. It is important when dealing with experts to be clear who is the Independent Expert appointed by the Employment Tribunal and who is acting for the parties to the claim.

The employer's defence

54. The possible defences against an equal pay claim are as follows:
    - The woman and the man are not doing equal work
    - For equal value claims only—the jobs being done by the woman and the man have been evaluated and rated differently under an analytical job evaluation scheme that is free of sex bias. An analytical job evaluation scheme evaluates jobs according to the demands made on the jobholders. **A non-analytical job evaluation scheme does not provide a defence to a claim**
    - The difference in pay is genuinely due to a material factor, which is not the difference of sex.

The job evaluation defence

55. Where employers use analytical job evaluation schemes they need to check that the scheme has been designed and implemented in such a way that it does not discriminate on grounds of sex. An analytical evaluation discriminates on the grounds of sex where values have been attributed to the different demands against which it has measured the jobs, and these values cannot be justified irrespective of the sex of the person on whom these demands are made.
56. A job evaluation scheme will be discriminatory if it fails to include, or properly take into account, a factor, or job demand, that is an important element in the woman's job (e.g. caring demands in a job involving looking after elderly people), or if it gives an unjustifiably heavy weighting to factors that are more typical of the man's job (e.g. the physical demands of being employed as a gardener).
57. A woman may also challenge a job evaluation scheme on the basis that instead of a factor, say, 'mental concentration' (in her job) being awarded fewer points than 'physical effort' (in her comparator's job), it should have received the same or more points. Similarly, she may argue that 'physical effort' (in his job) has been overrated compared with the skill her job requires for 'manual dexterity'. Even where she has received the same or more points than a man for a particular factor, she may still argue that the demands of her job under this factor have been underrated, that is, that the difference in points under the factor should have been bigger.

[17] These are to be found in the Employment Tribunals (Constitution and Rules of Procedure) Regulations 2001 (SI 2001/1171) and the Employment Tribunals (Constitution and Rules of Procedure) (Scotland) Regulations 2001 (SI 2001/1170) and s 2A of the Equal Pay Act itself.

58. Employers also need to check the outcomes of the job evaluation for sex bias. This means checking what impact the scheme has had on women and men, that is, how many women and how many men have moved up or down the grades? Any ensuing pay protection (red-circling) should also be free of sex bias and should be phased out as soon as is practicable.[18]
59. The EOC has produced a guidance note recommending that matters, such as the following, should be considered as a matter of good practice.[19] In order to check that a scheme is non-discriminatory, an employer needs to look at matters such as:
    - Whether statistics recorded on pay are broken down by gender
    - Whether the scheme is appropriate to the jobs it will cover
    - If a proprietary scheme is used does the supplier have equal opportunities guidelines?
    - If any groups of workers are excluded from the scheme, are there clear and justifiable reasons for their exclusion?
    - Is the composition of the job evaluation panel/steering committee representative of the jobs covered by the scheme and are the members trained in job evaluation and avoiding sex bias?
    - Are the job descriptions written to an agreed format and assessed to a common standard? Are trained job analysts used and have the jobholders been involved in writing their own job descriptions?
    - Where the scheme uses generic/bench mark jobs are these free from sex bias?
    - Are the factor definitions and levels exact and are detailed descriptions provided for each factor? Do the factors cover **all** the important job demands?

    If a job evaluation scheme is to remain free of sex bias it should be monitored. The employer (and not the job evaluation supplier or consultant) will need to show that the scheme is non-discriminatory.

The 'genuine material factor defence'—testing for sex discrimination

60. The Employment Tribunal tests for sex discrimination by first establishing a difference in pay or terms between the woman bringing the claim and a man doing equal work, and then asking whether the difference is due to discrimination or some other factor that does not amount to sex discrimination. This means that an employer can pay a man more than a woman for doing equal work, but only if the reason for doing so—the factor which the employer regards as the reason for the difference in pay—is not related to the sex of the jobholders.
61. The employer will have to show that the factor, or factors, on which he or she relies is free from both direct and indirect sex discrimination:
    - Direct sex discrimination occurs when the difference in pay or terms is directly related to the difference of sex
    - Indirect sex discrimination arises when the pay difference is due to a provision, criterion or practice which:
      — Applies to both men and women, but
      — Adversely affects a considerably larger proportion of women than men, and
      — Is not objectively justified irrespective of the sex of the jobholders.
62. Whether a defence succeeds or fails will always depend on the circumstances of the case and there is no such thing as an automatic or blanket defence. The defences that are likely to succeed include allowances such as London weighting and night-shift payments. Factors such as different market rates of pay for different specialisms or different levels of skills and experience have been successful in some cases but not in others.
63. The factor put forward to explain the difference in pay has to be significant; it has to be the real reason for the difference and it must not be connected with the sex of the people doing the job. For example, if the employer considers that the reason for paying the comparator more than the woman bringing the claim is that people will not do the work for the lower rate of pay, then the employer would have to bring evidence of actual difficulties in recruiting and retaining people to do the job being done by the male comparator.
64. Where a woman is claiming equal pay on the basis that the two jobs are work of equal value, indirect discrimination may arise where one of the jobs is done by a much higher proportion of women than

[18] The EOC Equal Pay Review Kit Guidance Note 4: Job Evaluation Schemes Free of Sex Bias.
[19] The EOC Equal Pay Review Kit Guidance Note 4: Job Evaluation Schemes Free of Sex Bias.

the other job. The onus lies on the employee to provide evidence of significant disparate impact.[20]

65. In such a case, if the Employment Tribunal accepts that the jobs are of equal value, the employer will need to provide objective justification for the pay difference between the two kinds of job. This is a higher standard of justification than that of the material factor defence.

66. The employer must show that:
    - The purpose of the provision or practice is to meet a real business need
    - The provision or practice is appropriate and necessary as a means of meeting that need.

An example of objective justification is:

- A pay system that makes an additional payment to employees working unsocial hours, in which most of the employees getting the bonus are men. Here the employer would have to show that:
  — There is a real business need to create a system to encourage a particular group of employees to
  work unsociable hours, and
  — The additional payments meet that need, and
  — The payments are an effective way of meeting that need, and do not go beyond what is necessary to achieve it (i.e. without the payment, the extra work would not be done, and the payment is only made when the workers actually do the work).

Awards of equal pay

67. If the woman succeeds in her claim she is entitled to:
    - An order from the Employment Tribunal declaring her rights
    - Equalisation of contractual terms for the future (if she is still in employment)
    - Compensation consisting of arrears of pay (if the claim is about pay) and/or damages (if the complaint is about some other contractual term).

    Back pay can be awarded up to a maximum of six years (five years in Scotland) from the date that proceedings were filed with the Employment Tribunal.[21] In addition, the Employment Tribunal may award interest on the award of compensation. With up to six year's worth of back pay being awarded, the interest element of any award is likely to be considerable.

[20] The advice given here is based on *Nelson v Carillion Services Ltd*, Court of Appeal decision 15 April 2003. Specific legal advice should be sought.

[21] Special rules apply where the woman is under a disability or the employer has concealed a breach of the Equal Pay Act.

ACAS Code of Practice 1: Disciplinary and Grievance Procedures (2009)

Foreword

The Acas statutory Code of Practice on discipline and grievance is set out at paras 1 to 45 on the following pages. It provides basic practical guidance to employers, employees and their representatives and sets out principles for handling disciplinary and grievance situations in the workplace. The Code does not apply to dismissals due to redundancy or the non-renewal of fixed term contracts on their expiry. Guidance on handling redundancies is contained in Acas' advisory booklet on Redundancy handling.

The Code is issued under section 199 of the Trade Union and Labour Relations (Consolidation) Act 1992 and was laid before both Houses of Parliament on 9 December 2008. It comes into effect by order of the Secretary of State on 6 April 2009 and replaces the Code issued in 2004.

A failure to follow the Code does not, in itself, make a person or organisation liable to proceedings. However, employment tribunals will take the Code into account when considering relevant cases. Tribunals will also be able to adjust any awards made in relevant cases by up to 25 per cent for unreasonable failure to comply with any provision of the Code. This means that if the tribunal feels that an employer has unreasonably failed to follow the guidance set out in the Code they can increase any award they have made by up to 25 per cent. Conversely, if they feel an employee has unreasonably failed to follow the guidance set out in the code they can reduce any award they have made by up to 25 per cent.

Employers and employees should always seek to resolve disciplinary and grievance issues in the workplace. Where this is not possible employers and employees should consider using an independent third party to help resolve the problem. The third party need not come from outside the organisation but could be an internal mediator, so long as they are not involved in the disciplinary or grievance issue. In some cases, an external mediator might be appropriate.

Many potential disciplinary or grievance issues can be resolved informally. A quiet word is often all that is required to resolve an issue. However, where an issue cannot be resolved informally then it may be pursued formally. This Code sets out the basic requirements of fairness that will be applicable in most cases; it is intended to provide the standard of reasonable behaviour in most instances.

Employers would be well advised to keep a written record of any disciplinary or grievances cases they deal with.

Organisations may wish to consider dealing with issues involving bullying, harassment or whistleblowing under a separate procedure.

More comprehensive advice and guidance on dealing with disciplinary and grievance situations is contained in the Acas booklet, 'Discipline and grievances at work: the Acas guide'. The booklet also contains sample disciplinary and grievance procedures. Copies of the guidance can be obtained from Acas.

Unlike the Code employment tribunals are not required to have regard to the Acas guidance booklet. However, it provides more detailed advice and guidance that employers and employees will o ten find helpful both in general terms and in individual cases.

Introduction

1. This Code is designed to help employers, employees and their representatives deal with disciplinary and grievance situations in the workplace.
   - Disciplinary situations include misconduct and/or poor performance. If employers have a separate capability procedure they may prefer to address performance issues under this procedure. If so, ho ever, the basic principles of fairness set out in this Code should still be followed, albeit that they may need to be adapted.
   - Grievances are concerns, problems or complaints that employees raise with their employers. The Code does not apply to redundancy dismissals or the non renewal of fixed term contracts on their expiry.
2. Fairness and transparency are promoted by developing and using rules and procedures for ha dling disciplinary and grievance situations. These should be set down in writing, be specific and clear. Employees and, where appropriate, their representatives should be involved in the development of

rules and procedures. It is also important to help employees and managers understand what the rules and procedures are, where they can be found and how they are to be used.

3. Where some form of formal action is needed, what action is reasonable or justified will depend on all the circumstances of the particular case. Employment tribunals will take the size and resources of an employer into account when deciding on relevant cases and it may sometimes not be practicable for all employers to take all of the steps set out in this Code.
4. That said, whenever a disciplinary or grievance process is being followed it is important to deal with issues fairly. There are a number of elements to this:
   - Employers and employees should raise and deal with issues promptly and should not unreasonably delay meetings, decisions or confirmation of those decisions.
   - Employers and employees should act consistently.
   - Employers should carry out any necessary investigations, to establish the facts of the case.
   - Employers should inform employees of the basis of the problem and give them an opportunity to put their case in response before any decisions are made.
   - Employers should allow employees to be accompanied at any formal disciplinary or grievance meeting.
   - Employers should allow an employee to appeal against any formal decision made.

Discipline

Keys to handling disciplinary issues in the workplace

Establish the facts of each case

5. It is important to carry out necessary investigations of potential disciplinary matters without unreasonable delay to establish the facts of the case. In some cases this will require the holding of an investigatory meeting with the employee before proceeding to any disciplinary hearing. In others, the investigatory stage will be the collation of evidence by the employer for use at any disciplinary hearing.
6. In misconduct cases, where practicable, different people should carry out the investigation and disciplinary hearing.
7. If there is an investigatory meeting this should not by itself result in any disciplinary action. Although there is no statutory right for an employee to be accompanied at a formal investigatory meeting, such a right may be allowed under an employer's own procedure.
8. In cases where a period of suspension with pay is considered necessary, this period should be as brief as possible, should be kept under review and it should be made clear that this suspension is not considered a disciplinary action.

Inform the employee of the problem

9. If it is decided that there is a disciplinary case to answer, the employee should be notified of this in writing. This notification should contain sufficient information about the alleged misconduct or poor performance and its possible consequences to enable the employee to prepare to answer the case at a disciplinary meeting. It would normally be appropriate to provide copies of any written evidence, which may include any witness statements, with the notification.
10. The notification should also give details of the time and venue for the disciplinary meeting and advise the employee of their right to be accompanied at the meeting.

Hold a meeting with the employee to discuss the problem

11. The meeting should be held without unreasonable delay whilst allowing the employee reasonable time to prepare their case.
12. Employers and employees (and their companions) should make every effort to attend the meeting. At the meeting the employer should explain the complaint against the employee and go through the evidence that has been gathered. The employee should be allowed to set out their case and answer any allegations that have been made. The employee should also be given a reasonable opportunity to ask questions, present evidence and call relevant witnesses. They should also be given an opportunity to raise points about any information provided by witnesses. Where an employer or employee intends to call relevant witnesses they should give advance notice that they intend to do this.

Allow the employee to be accompanied at the meeting

13. Workers have a statutory right to be accompanied by a companion where the disciplinary meeting could result in:
    - a formal warning being issued; or

- the taking of some other disciplinary action; or
- the confirmation of a warning or some other disciplinary action (appeal hearings).

14. The chosen companion may be a fellow worker, a trade union representative, or an official employed by a trade union. A trade union representative who is not an employed official must have been certified by their union as being competent to accompany a worker.
15. To exercise the statutory right to be accompanied workers must make a reasonable request. What is reasonable will depend on the circumstances of each individual case. However, it would not normally be reasonable for workers to insist on being accompanied by a companion whose presence would prejudice the hearing nor would it be reasonable for a worker to ask to be accompanied by a companion from a remote geographical location if someone suitable and willing was available on site.
16. The companion should be allowed to address the hearing to put and sum up the worker's case, respond on behalf of the worker to any views expressed at the meeting and confer with the worker during the hearing. The companion does not, however, have the right to answer questions on the worker's behalf, address the hearing if the worker does not wish it or prevent the employer from explaining their case.

Decide on appropriate action

17. After the meeting decide whether or not disciplinary or any other action is justified and inform the employee accordingly in writing.
18. Where misconduct is confirmed or the employee is found to be performing unsatisfactorily it is usual to give the employee a written warning. A further act of misconduct or failure to improve performance within a set period would normally result in a final written warning.
19. If an employee's first misconduct or unsatisfactory performance is sufficiently serious, it may be appropriate to move directly to a final written warning. This might occur where the employee's actions have had, or are liable to have, a serious or harmful impact on the organisation.
20. A first or final written warning should set out the nature of the misconduct or poor performance and the change in behaviour or improvement in performance required (with timescale). The employee should be told how long the warning will remain current. The employee should be informed of the consequences of further misconduct, or failure to improve performance, within the set period following a final warning. For instance that it may result in dismissal or some other contractual penalty such as demotion or loss of seniority.
21. A decision to dismiss should only be taken by a manager who has the authority to do so. The employee should be informed as soon as possible of the reasons for the dismissal, the date on which the employment contract will end, the appropriate period of notice and their right of appeal.
22. Some acts, termed gross misconduct, are so serious in themselves or have such serious consequences that they may call for dismissal without notice for a first offence. But a fair disciplinary process should always be followed, before dismissing for gross misconduct.
23. Disciplinary rules should give examples of acts which the employer regards as acts of gross misconduct. These may vary according to the nature of the organisation and what it does, but might include things such as theft or fraud, physical violence, gross negligence or serious insubordination.
24. Where an employee is persistently unable or unwilling to attend a disciplinary meeting without good cause the employer should make a decision on the evidence available.

Provide employees with an opportunity to appeal

25. Where an employee feels that disciplinary action taken against them is wrong or unjust they should appeal against the decision. Appeals should be heard without unreasonable delay and ideally at an agreed time and place. Employees should let employers know the grounds for their appeal in writing.
26. The appeal should be dealt with impartially and wherever possible, by a manager who has not previously been involved in the case.
27. Workers have a statutory right to be accompanied at appeal hearings.
28. Employees should be informed in writing of the results of the appeal hearing as soon as possible.

Special cases

29. Where disciplinary action is being considered against an employee who is a trade union representative the normal disciplinary procedure should be followed. Depending on the circumstances, however, it is advisable to discuss the matter at an early stage with an official employed by the union, after obtaining the employee's agreement.

30. If an employee is charged with, or convicted of a criminal offence this is not normally in itself reason for disciplinary action. Consideration needs to be given to what effect the charge or conviction has on the employee's suitability to do the job and their relationship with their employer, work colleagues and customers.

Grievance

Keys to handling grievances in the workplace

Let the employer know the nature of the grievance

31. If it is not possible to resolve a grievance informally employees should raise the matter formally and without unreasonable delay with a manager who is not the subject of the grievance. This should be done in writing and should set out the nature of the grievance.

Hold a meeting with the employee to discuss the grievance

32. Employers should arrange for a formal meeting to be held without unreasonable delay after a grievance is received.
33. Employers, employees and their companions should make every effort to attend the meeting. Employees should be allowed to explain their grievance and how they think it should be resolved. Consideration should be given to adjourning the meeting for any investigation that may be necessary.

Allow the employee to be accompanied at the meeting

34. Workers have a statutory right to be accompanied by a companion at a grievance meeting which deals with a complaint about a duty owed by the employer to the worker. So this would apply where the complaint is, for example, that the employer is not honouring the worker's contract, or is in breach of legislation.
35. The chosen companion may be a fellow worker, a trade union representative or an official employed by a trade union. A trade union representative who is not an employed official must have been certified by their union as being competent to accompany a worker.
36. To exercise the right to be accompanied a worker must first make a reasonable request. What is reasonable will depend on the circumstances of each individual case. However it would not normally be reasonable for workers to insist on being accompanied by a companion whose presence would prejudice the hearing nor would it be reasonable for a worker to ask to be accompanied by a companion from a remote geographical location if someone suitable and willing was available on site.
37. The companion should be allowed to address the hearing to put and sum up the worker's case, respond on behalf of the worker to any views expressed at the meeting and confer with the worker during the hearing. The companion does not however, have the right to answer questions on the worker's behalf, address the hearing if the worker does not wish it or prevent the employer from explaining their case.

Decide on appropriate action

38. Following the meeting decide on what action, if any, to take. Decisions should be communicated to the employee, in writing, without unreasonable delay and, where appropriate, should set out what action the employer intends to take to resolve the grievance. The employee should be informed that they can appeal if they are not content with the action taken.

Allow the employee to take the grievance further if not resolved

39. Where an employee feels that their grievance has not been satisfactorily resolved they should appeal. They should let their employer know the grounds for their appeal without unreasonable delay and in writing.
40. Appeals should be heard without unreasonable delay and at a time and place which should be notified to the employee in advance.
41. The appeal should be dealt with impartially and wherever possible by a manager who has not previously been involved in the case.
42. Workers have a statutory right to be accompanied at any such appeal hearing.
43. The outcome of the appeal should be communicated to the employee in writing without unreasonable delay.

Overlapping grievance and disciplinary cases

44. Where an employee raises a grievance during a disciplinary process the disciplinary process may be temporarily suspended in order to deal with the grievance. Where the grievance and disciplinary cases are related it may be appropriate to deal with both issues concurrently.

Collective grievances

45. The provisions of this code do not apply to grievances raised on behalf of two or more employees by a representative of a recognised trade union or other appropriate workplace representative. These grievances should be handled in accordance with the organisation's collective grievance process. Discipline and Grievances at work: The ACAS Guide, 2009 can be found at <http://www.acas.org.uk/index.aspx?articleid=2179>.

Disability Discrimination Act

Guidance On Matters To Be Taken Into Account In Determining Questions Relating To The Definition Of Disability

Status And Purpose Of The Guidance

This guidance is issued by the Secretary of State under section 3 of the Disability Discrimination Act 1995, as amended.[1] In this document, any reference to 'the Act' means the Disability Discrimination Act 1995 (as amended).

This guidance concerns the definition of disability in the Act. Section 3 of the Act enables the Secretary of State to issue guidance about matters to be taken into account in determining whether a person is a disabled person. The guidance gives examples.

This guidance does not impose any legal obligations in itself, nor is it an authoritative statement of the law. However, section 3(3) of the Act requires that an adjudicating body[2] which is determining for any purpose of the Act whether a person is a disabled person, must take into account any aspect of this guidance which appears to it to be relevant.

This guidance applies to England, Wales and Scotland. Similar, but separate, guidance applies to Northern Ireland.

Part I

Introduction

The Disability Discrimination Act 1995

1. The Act prohibits discrimination against disabled people in a range of circumstances, covering employment and occupation, education, transport, and the provision of goods, facilities, services, premises and the exercise of public functions. Only those people who are defined as disabled in accordance with section 1 of the Act, and the associated schedules and Regulations made thereunder, will be entitled to the protection that the Act provides.

Using the guidance

2. This guidance is primarily designed for adjudicating bodies which determine cases brought under the Act. The definition of who is a disabled person for the purposes of the Act is a legal definition and it is only adjudicating bodies which can determine whether a person meets that definition. However, the guidance is also likely to be of value to a range of people and organisations as an explanation of how the definition operates.
3. **In the vast majority of cases there is unlikely to be any doubt whether or not a person has or has had a disability, but this guidance should prove helpful in cases where the matter is not entirely clear.**
4. The definition of disability has a number of elements. The guidance covers each of these elements in turn. Each section contains an explanation of the relevant provisions of the Act which supplement the basic definition. Guidance and examples are provided where relevant. Those using this guidance for the first time should read it all, as each part of the guidance builds upon the part(s) preceding it.
5. Throughout the guidance, descriptions of statutory provisions in the legislation are immediately preceded by bold text and followed by a reference to the relevant provision of the Act or to Regulations made under the Act. References to sections of the Act are marked '**S**'; references to schedules are marked '**Sch**'; and references to paragraphs in schedules are marked '**Para**'.

Other references to 'disability'

6. The definition of disability set out in the Act and described in this guidance is the only definition relevant to determining whether someone is a disabled person for the purposes of the Act. References to 'disability' or to mental or physical impairments in the context of other legislation are not relevant to determining whether someone is a disabled person under this Act and should be disregarded.
7. There is a range of services, concessions, schemes and financial benefits for which disabled people may qualify. These include, for example: local authority services for disabled people; the Blue Badge parking scheme; tax concessions for people who are blind; and disability-related social security benefits. However, each of these has its own individual eligibility criteria and qualification for any one of them does not automatically confer entitlement to protection under the Act, nor does

entitlement to the protection of the Act confer eligibility for benefits, or concessions. Similarly, a child who has been identified as having special educational needs is not necessarily disabled for the purposes of the Act.

8. **In order to be protected by the Act, a person must meet the Act's definition of disability as explained below.**

PART 2
GUIDANCE ON MATTERS TO BE TAKEN INTO ACCOUNT IN DETERMINING QUESTIONS RELATING TO THE DEFINITION OF DISABILITY
Section A: General

Main elements of the definition of disability

A1. **The Act defines** a disabled person as a person with 'a physical or mental impairment which has a substantial and long-term adverse effect on his ability to carry out normal day-to-day activities' (**S1**).

A2. This means that, in general:
- the person must have an impairment that is either physical or mental (**see paragraphs A3 to A8 below**);
- the impairment must have adverse effects which are substantial (**see Section B**);
- the substantial adverse effects must be long-term (**see Section C**); and
- the long-term substantial adverse effects must be effects on normal day-to-day activities (**see Section D**).

This definition is subject to the provisions in **Schedule 1 (Sch1)** and **Schedule 2 (Sch2)**.

Meaning of 'impairment'

A3. The definition requires that the effects which a person may experience must arise from a physical or mental impairment. The term mental or physical impairment should be given its ordinary meaning. In many cases, there will be no dispute whether a person has an impairment. Any disagreement is more likely to be about whether the effects of the impairment are sufficient to fall within the definition. Even so, it may sometimes be necessary to decide whether a person has an impairment so as to be able to deal with the issues about its effects.

A4. Whether a person is disabled for the purposes of the Act is generally determined by reference to the **effect** that an impairment has on that person's ability to carry out normal day-to-day activities. It is not possible to provide an exhaustive list of conditions that qualify as impairments for the purposes of the Act. Any attempt to do so would inevitably become out of date as medical knowledge advanced.

A5. It is important to remember that not all impairments are readily identifiable. While some impairments, particularly visible ones, are easy to identify, there are many which are not so immediately obvious.

A6. A disability can arise from a wide range of impairments which can be:
- sensory impairments, such as those affecting sight or hearing;
- impairments with fluctuating or recurring effects such as rheumatoid arthritis, myalgic encephalitis (ME)/chronic fatigue syndrome (CFS), fibromyalgia, depression and epilepsy;
- progressive, such as motor neurone disease, muscular dystrophy, forms of dementia and lupus (SLE);
- organ specific, including respiratory conditions, such as asthma, and cardiovascular diseases, including thrombosis, stroke and heart disease;
- developmental, such as autistic spectrum disorders (ASD), dyslexia and dyspraxia;
- learning difficulties;
- mental health conditions and mental illnesses, such as depression, schizophrenia, eating disorders, bipolar affective disorders, obsessive compulsive disorders, as well as personality disorders and some self-harming behaviour;
- produced by injury to the body or brain.

A7. It may not always be possible, nor is it necessary, to categorise a condition as either a physical or a mental impairment. The underlying cause of the impairment may be hard to establish. There may be adverse effects which are both physical and mental in nature. Furthermore, effects of a mainly physical nature may stem from an underlying mental impairment, and vice versa.

A8. It is not necessary to consider how an impairment is caused, even if the cause is a consequence of a condition which is excluded. For example, liver disease as a result of alcohol dependency would count as an impairment, although alcoholism itself is expressly excluded from the scope of the definition of disability in the Act. What it is important to consider is the effect of an impairment not its cause—provided that it is not an excluded condition. **See also paragraph A12 below (exclusions from the definition)**.

A woman has obesity which gives rise to impairments such as mobility restrictions and breathing difficulties. She is unable to walk more than 50 yards without having to rest.

A man has borderline moderate learning difficulties which have an adverse impact on his short-term memory and his levels of literacy and numeracy. For example, he cannot write any original material, as opposed to slowly copying existing text, and he cannot write his address from memory.

It is the effects of these impairments that need to be considered, rather than the underlying conditions themselves.

Mental illness

A9. The Act previously required that where an impairment arose from, or consisted of, a mental illness, that illness had to be clinically well-recognised in order for it to be regarded as a mental impairment for the purposes of the Act. The Disability Discrimination Act 2005 amended the original Act to remove this requirement with effect from 5 December 2005. However, anyone who has an impairment **including one resulting from a mental illness** will still need to meet the requirements of the definition as set out in paragraph A1, in order to demonstrate that they have a disability under the Act.

Persons deemed to be disabled

A10. The following people are deemed to meet the definition of disability without having to show that they have an impairment that has (or is likely to have) a substantial, adverse, long-term effect on the ability to carry out normal day-to-day activities:

- A person who has cancer, HIV infection or multiple sclerosis (MS) (**Sch1, Para 6A**). **See also paragraphs B16 to B19 below (progressive conditions)**.
- A person who is certified as blind or partially sighted by a consultant ophthalmologist, or is registered as such with a local authority.[3]

A11. Anyone who has an impairment which is not listed in A10 above will need to meet the requirements of the definition as set out in paragraph A1 in order to demonstrate that they have a disability under the Act.

Exclusions from the definition

A12. Certain conditions are not to be regarded as impairments for the purposes of the Act. These are:

- addiction to, or dependency on, alcohol, nicotine, or any other substance (other than in consequence of the substance being medically prescribed);
- the condition known as seasonal allergic rhinitis (e.g. hayfever), except where it aggravates the effect of another condition;
- tendency to set fires;
- tendency to steal;
- tendency to physical or sexual abuse of other persons;
- exhibitionism;
- voyeurism.

A13. Also, disfigurements which consist of a tattoo (which has not been removed), non-medical body piercing, or something attached through such piercing, are to be treated as not having a substantial adverse effect on the person's ability to carry out normal day-to-day activities.[4]

A14. A person with an excluded condition may nevertheless be protected as a disabled person if he or she has an accompanying impairment which meets the requirements of the definition. For example, a person who is addicted to a substance such as alcohol may also have depression, or a physical impairment such as liver damage, arising from the alcohol addiction. While this person would not meet the definition simply on the basis of having an addiction, he or she may still meet the definition as a result of the effects of the depression or the liver damage.

People who have had a disability in the past

A15. **The Act says** that Part 1 of the Act (disability), Part 2 (the employment field and members of locally-electable authorities), Part 3 (discrimination in other areas[5]), Part 4 (education), and Part 5A (public authorities[6]) also apply in relation to a person who previously has had a disability as defined in paragraphs A1 and A2 above. For this purpose, those Parts of the Act are subject to the provisions in Schedule 2 to the Act (**S2, Sch2**). This means that someone who is no longer disabled, but who met the requirements of the definition in the past, will still be covered by those Parts of the Act listed above. For example, a woman who, four years ago, experienced a mental illness that had a substantial and long-term adverse effect on her ability to carry out normal day-to-day activities, but who has experienced no recurrence of the condition, is still entitled to the protection afforded by the Act, as a person with a past disability.

A16. A particular instance of someone who is treated under the Act as having had a disability in the past is someone whose name was on the register of disabled persons under provisions in the Disabled Persons (Employment) Act 1944.

A17. The introduction of the employment provisions in the Disability Discrimination Act 1995 coincided with the abolition of the Quota scheme which had operated under the Disabled Persons (Employment) Act 1944. Special provisions still apply, however, to any person who was registered under the Disabled Persons (Employment) Act 1944. **The Disability Discrimination Act 1995 says** that anyone who was registered as a disabled person under the Disabled Persons (Employment) Act 1944 and whose name appeared on the register both on 12 January 1995 and on 2 December 1996 (the date on which the employment provisions came into force) was to be treated as having a disability for the purposes of the Disability Discrimination Act 1995 during the period of three years starting on 2 December 1996. This applied regardless of whether the person otherwise met the definition of a 'disabled person' during that period. As the three-year transitional period has ended, those people who were treated by this provision as being disabled are now treated as having had a disability in the past (**Sch1, Para 7**).

Section B: Substantial

Meaning of 'substantial adverse effect'

B1. The requirement that an adverse effect on normal day-to-day activities should be a substantial one reflects the general understanding of disability as a limitation going beyond the normal differences in ability which may exist among people. A substantial effect is one that is greater than the effect which would be produced by the sort of physical or mental conditions experienced by many people which have only 'minor' or 'trivial' effects. This section looks in more detail at what 'substantial' means. It should be read in conjunction with Section D which considers what is meant by 'normal day-to-day activities'.

The time taken to carry out an activity

B2. The time taken by a person with an impairment to carry out a normal day-to-day activity should be considered when assessing whether the effect of that impairment is substantial. It should be compared with the time it might take a person who did not have the impairment to complete an activity.

A ten-year-old child has cerebral palsy. The effects include muscle stiffness, poor balance and uncoordinated movements. The child is still able to do most things for himself, but he gets tired very easily and it is harder for him to accomplish tasks like eating and drinking, washing, and getting dressed. Although he has the ability to carry out everyday activities such as these, everything takes longer compared to a child of a similar age who does not have cerebral palsy. This amounts to a substantial adverse effect.

The way in which an activity is carried out

B3. Another factor to be considered when assessing whether the effect of an impairment is substantial is the way in which a person with that impairment carries out a normal day-to-day activity. The comparison should be with the way that the person might be expected to carry out the activity if he or she did not have the impairment.

A person who has obsessive compulsive disorder follows a complicated ritual of hand washing. When preparing a simple meal, he washes his hands carefully after handling each ingredient and each utensil. A person without the disorder might wash his or her hands at appropriate points in preparing the meal, for example after handling raw meat, but would not normally do this after every stage in the process of preparation.

Cumulative effects of an impairment

B4. An impairment might not have a substantial adverse effect on a person's ability to undertake a particular day-to-day activity in isolation, but its effects on more than one activity, taken together, could result in an overall substantial adverse effect.

B5. For example, a person whose impairment causes breathing difficulties may, as a result, experience minor effects on the ability to carry out a number of activities such as getting washed and dressed, preparing a meal, or travelling on public transport. But taken together, the cumulative result would amount to a substantial adverse effect on his or her ability to carry out these normal day-to-day activities.

A man with depression experiences a range of symptoms that include a loss of energy and motivation that makes even the simplest of tasks or decisions seem quite difficult. For example, he finds it difficult to get up in the morning, get washed and dressed, and prepare breakfast. He is forgetful and cannot plan ahead. As a result he has often run out of food before he thinks of going shopping again. Household tasks are frequently left undone, or take much longer to complete than normal. Together, the effects amount to a substantial adverse effect.

B6. A person may have more than one impairment, any one of which alone would not have a substantial effect. In such a case, account should be taken of whether the impairments together have a substantial effect overall on the person's ability to carry out normal day-to-day activities. For example, a minor impairment which affects physical co-ordination and an irreversible but minor injury to a leg which affects mobility, when taken together, might have a substantial effect on the person's ability to carry out certain normal day-to-day activities.

Effects of behaviour

B7. Account should be taken of how far a person can **reasonably** be expected to modify his or her behaviour to prevent or reduce the effects of an impairment on normal day-to-day activities. If a person can reasonably be expected to behave in such a way that the impairment ceases to have a substantial adverse effect on his or her ability to carry out normal day-to-day activities the person would no longer meet the definition of disability. For example, when considering modification of behaviour, it would be reasonable to expect a person who has back pain to avoid extreme activities such as parachuting. It would not be reasonable to expect him or her to give up, or modify, more normal activities that might exacerbate the symptoms; such as moderate gardening, shopping, or using public transport.

B8. Account should also be taken of where a person avoids doing things which, for example, cause pain, fatigue or substantial social embarrassment; because of a loss of energy and motivation. It would **not** be reasonable to conclude that a person who employed an avoidance strategy was not a disabled person. In determining a question as to whether a person meets the definition of disability it is important to consider the things that a person cannot do, or can only do with difficulty, rather than focussing on those things that a person can do.

In order to manage her condition, a woman with a persistent stammer uses coping strategies, such as avoiding using the telephone, not giving verbal instructions at work, limiting social contact outside her immediate family, and avoiding challenging situations with service providers. As a consequence, it may not be readily obvious that she has an impairment which adversely affects her ability to carry out normal day-to-day activities. In determining whether she meets the definition of disability, consideration should be given to the extent to which it is reasonable to expect her to place such restrictions on her working and domestic life.

B9. In some cases, people have coping strategies which cease to work in certain circumstances (for example, where someone who has dyslexia is placed under stress). If it is possible that a person's ability to manage the effects of an impairment will break down so that effects will sometimes still occur, this possibility must be taken into account when assessing the effects of the impairment.

See also paragraphs B11 to B15 below (effects of treatment), paragraph C8 (likelihood of recurrence) and D11 (indirect effects).

Effects of environment

B10. Environmental conditions may exacerbate the effect of an impairment. Factors such as temperature, humidity, lighting, the time of day or night, how tired the person is, or how much stress he or she is under, may have an impact on the effects. When assessing whether adverse effects are substantial, the extent to which such environmental factors are likely to exacerbate the effects should, therefore, also be considered. **See also paragraphs C4 to C7 below, meaning of 'long-term' (recurring or fluctuating effects).**

> A woman has had rheumatoid arthritis for the last three years and has difficulty carrying out day-to-day activities such as walking, undertaking household tasks, and getting washed and dressed. The effects are particularly bad during autumn and winter months when the weather is cold and damp. Symptoms are mild during the summer months. The effect on ability to carry out normal day-to-day activities fluctuates according to the weather conditions, but because the effect of the impairment is likely to recur, this person meets the definition of disability requirement on the meaning of 'long-term' (Sch1, Para 2(2)).

Effects of treatment

B11. **The Act provides** that, where an impairment is subject to treatment or correction, the impairment is to be treated as having the effect that it would have without the measures in question (**Sch1, Para 6(1)**). **The Act states** that the treatment or correction measures which are to be disregarded for these purposes include, in particular, medical treatment and the use of a prosthesis or other aid (**Sch1, Para 6(2)**).

B12. This provision applies even if the measures result in the effects being completely under control or not at all apparent. Where treatment is continuing it may be having the effect of masking or ameliorating a disability so that it does not have a substantial adverse effect. If the final outcome of such treatment cannot be determined or if it is known that removal of the medical treatment would result in either a relapse or a worsened condition, it would be reasonable to disregard the medical treatment in accordance with paragraph 6 of Schedule 1.

B13. For example, if a person with a hearing impairment wears a hearing aid the question as to whether his or her impairment has a substantial adverse effect is to be decided by reference to what the hearing level would be without the hearing aid. Similarly, in the case of someone with diabetes which is being controlled by medication or diet, or the case of a person with depression which is being treated by counselling, whether or not the effect is substantial should be decided by reference to what the effects of the condition would be if he or she were not taking that medication or following the required diet, or were not receiving counselling (the so-called 'deduced effects').

B14. **The Act states** that this provision does not apply to sight impairments to the extent that they are capable of correction by spectacles or contact lenses. In other words, the only effects on the ability to carry out normal day-to-day activities which are to be considered are those which remain when spectacles or contact lenses are used (or would remain if they were used). This does not include the use of devices to correct sight which are not spectacles or contact lenses (**Sch1, Para 6(3)**).

B15. Account should be taken of where the effect of the continuing medical treatment is to create a permanent improvement rather than a temporary improvement. For example, a person who develops pneumonia may be admitted to hospital for treatment including a course of antibiotics. This cures the impairment and no effects remain. **See also paragraph C9 below, regarding medical or other treatment that permanently reduces or removes the effects of an impairment.**

Progressive conditions

B16. A progressive condition is one which is likely to change and develop over time. **The Act gives** examples of progressive conditions, including cancer, multiple sclerosis, and HIV infection. It should be noted that, following the amendments made by the Disability Discrimination Act 2005 (**see paragraph A10**), persons with cancer, multiple sclerosis or HIV infection are all now deemed to be disabled persons, for the purposes of the Act, from the point at which they have that condition: thus effectively from diagnosis.

B17. Progressive conditions are subject to the special provisions set out in **Sch1, Para 8**. These provisions provide that a person with a progressive condition is to be regarded as having an impairment which has a substantial adverse effect on his or her ability to carry out normal day-to-day activities **before** it does so. A person who has a progressive condition, will be treated as having an impairment which has a **substantial** adverse effect from the moment any impairment resulting from that condition first has **some** adverse effect on his or her ability to carry out normal day-to-day activities, provided that in the future the adverse effect is **more likely than not** to become substantial. Medical prognosis of the likely impact of the condition will be the normal route to establishing protection under this provision. The effect need not be continuous and need not be substantial. **(See also paragraphs C4 to C7 on recurring or fluctuating effects)**. The person will still need to show that the impairment meets the requirements of **Sch1**, **Para 2** (meaning of long-term).

B18. Further examples of progressive conditions to which the special provisions apply include systemic lupus erythematosis (SLE), various types of dementia, rheumatoid arthritis, and motor neurone disease. This list, however, is not exhaustive.

A young boy aged 8 has been experiencing muscle cramps and some weakness. The effects are quite minor at present, but he has been diagnosed as having muscular dystrophy. Eventually it is expected that the resulting muscle weakness will cause substantial adverse effects on his ability to walk, run and climb stairs. Although there is no substantial adverse effect at present, muscular dystrophy is a progressive condition, and this child will still be entitled to the protection of the Act under the special provisions in Sch1, Para 8 of the Act if it can be shown that the effects are likely to become substantial.

A woman has been diagnosed with lupus (SLE) following complaints to her GP that she is experiencing mild aches and pains in her joints. She has also been feeling generally unwell, with some flu-like symptoms. The initial symptoms do not have a substantial adverse effect on her ability to carry out normal day-to-day activities. However, SLE is a progressive condition, with fluctuating effects. She has been advised that the condition may come and go over many years, and in the future the effects may become substantial, including severe joint pain, inflammation, stiffness, and skin rashes. Providing it can be shown that the effects are likely to become substantial, she will be covered by the special provisions in Sch1, Para 8. She will, however, still need to meet the 'long-term' condition of the definition in order to be protected by the Act.

B19. A person with a progressive condition which has no effect on day-to-day activities because it is successfully treated (for example by surgery) may still be covered by **Sch1**, **Para 8** where the effects of that treatment give rise to a further impairment which does have an effect on normal day-to-day activities. For example, treatment for the condition may result in an impairment which has some effect on normal day-to-day activities and the effects of that impairment are likely to become substantial in the future.

A man has an operation to remove the colon because of progressing and uncontrollable ulcerative colitis. This is a treatment that is fairly routine for severe colitis. The operation results in his no longer experiencing adverse effects from the colitis. He requires a colostomy, however, which means that his bowel actions can only be controlled by a sanitary appliance. The effect of the incontinence should be taken into account as an effect arising from the original impairment.

Whether the effects of any treatment can qualify for the purposes of **Sch1**, **Para 8** will depend on the circumstances of the individual case.

Severe disfigurements

B20. **The Act provides** that where an impairment consists of a severe disfigurement, it is to be treated as having a substantial adverse effect on the person's ability to carry out normal day-to-day activities. There is no need to demonstrate such an effect (**Sch1**, **Para 3**). Regulations provide that a disfigurement which consists of a tattoo (which has not been removed) is not to be considered as a severe disfigurement. Also excluded is a piercing of the body for decorative purposes including anything attached through the piercing.[7]

B21. Examples of disfigurements include scars, birthmarks, limb or postural deformation (including restricted bodily development), or diseases of the skin. Assessing severity will be mainly a matter of the degree of the disfigurement. However, it may be necessary to take account of where the disfigurement in question is (e.g. on the back as opposed to the face).

Section C: Long term

Meaning of 'long-term effects'

C1. **The Act states** that, for the purpose of deciding whether a person is disabled, a long-term effect of an impairment is one:

- which has lasted at least 12 months; or
- where the total period for which it lasts, from the time of the first onset, is likely to be at least 12 months; or
- which is likely to last for the rest of the life of the person affected (**Sch1, Para 2**).

For the purpose of deciding whether a person has had a disability in the past, a long-term effect of an impairment is one which has lasted at least 12 months (**Sch2, Para 5**).

Meaning of 'likely'

C2. It is likely that an event will happen if it is more probable than not that it will happen.

C3. In assessing the likelihood of an effect lasting for 12 months, account should be taken of the total period for which the effect exists. This includes any time before the point at which the alleged incident of discriminatory behaviour which is being considered by the adjudicating body occurred. Account should also be taken of both the typical length of such an effect on an individual, and any relevant factors specific to this individual (for example, general state of health or age).

Recurring or fluctuating effects

C4. **The Act states** that, if an impairment has had a substantial adverse effect on a person's ability to carry out normal day-to-day activities but that effect ceases, the substantial effect is treated as continuing if it is likely to recur. In other words, it is more likely than not that the effect will recur. (In deciding whether a person has had a disability in the past, the question is whether a substantial adverse effect has in fact recurred.) Conditions with effects which recur only sporadically or for short periods can still qualify as impairments for the purposes of the Act, in respect of the meaning of 'long-term' (**Sch1, Para 2(2); Sch2, Para 5**).

C5. For example, a person with rheumatoid arthritis may experience substantial adverse effects for a few weeks after the first occurrence and then have a period of remission. **See also example at B10 above.** If the substantial adverse effects are likely to recur, they are to be treated as if they were continuing. If the effects are likely to recur beyond 12 months after the first occurrence, they are to be treated as long-term. Other impairments with effects which can recur, or where effects can be sporadic, include Menières disease and epilepsy as well as mental health conditions such as schizophrenia, bipolar affective disorder, and certain types of depression, though this is not an exhaustive list. It should be noted that some impairments with recurring or fluctuating effects may be less obvious in their impact on the individual concerned than is the case with other impairments where the effects are more constant.

> A young man has bipolar affective disorder, a recurring form of depression. The first episode occurred in months one and two of a 13-month period. The second episode took place in month 13. This man will satisfy the requirements of the definition in respect of the meaning of long-term, because the adverse effects have recurred beyond 12 months after the first occurrence and are therefore treated as having continued for the whole period (in this case, a period of 13 months).

> A woman has two discrete episodes of depression within a ten-month period. In month one she loses her job and has a period of depression lasting six weeks. In month nine she suffers a bereavement and has a further episode of depression lasting eight weeks. Even though she has experienced two episodes of depression she will not be covered by the Act. This is because, as at this stage, the effects of her impairment have not yet lasted more than 12 months after the first occurrence, and there is no evidence that these episodes are part of an underlying condition of depression which is likely to recur beyond the 12-month period.

C6. It is not necessary for the effect to be the same throughout the period which is being considered in relation to determining whether the 'long-term' element of the definition is met. A person may still satisfy the long-term element of the definition even if the effect is not the same throughout the period. It may change: for example activities which are initially very difficult may become possible to a much greater extent. The effect might even disappear temporarily. Or other effects on the ability to carry out normal day-to-day activities may develop and the initial effect may disappear altogether.

C7. Regulations specifically exclude seasonal allergic rhinitis (e.g. hayfever) except where it aggravates the effects of an existing condition.[8] For example, this may occur in some cases of asthma. **See also paragraph A12 (exclusions).**

Likelihood of recurrence

C8. Likelihood of recurrence should be considered taking all the circumstances of the case into account. This should include what the person could reasonably be expected to do to prevent the recurrence. For example, the person might reasonably be expected to take action which prevents the impairment from having such effects (e.g. avoiding substances to which he or she is allergic). This may be unreasonably difficult with some substances. In addition, it is possible that the way in which a person can control or cope with the effects of an impairment may not always be successful: for example, because a routine is not followed or the person is in an unfamiliar environment. If there is an increased likelihood that the control will break down, it will be more likely that there will be a recurrence. That possibility should be taken into account when assessing the likelihood of a recurrence. **See also paragraphs B7 to B9 above (effects of behaviour, including coping strategies and medical advice), paragraph B10 (environmental effects); and paragraphs B11 to B15 (effect of treatment).**

A woman experiences stress-related anxiety. She is able to manage her workload and meet normal deadlines provided that she avoids too much responsibility. She achieves this through careful monitoring of her workload and regular supervision by her manager. She can cope with the symptoms of her condition most of the time, provided that she is not exposed to stressful situations.

The possibility that she might be exposed to stressful situations should be taken into account when deciding whether there is a likelihood of recurrence.

C9. If medical or other treatment is likely to permanently cure a condition and therefore remove the impairment, so that recurrence of its effects would then be unlikely even if there were no further treatment, this should be taken into consideration when looking at the likelihood of recurrence of those effects. However, if the treatment simply delays or prevents a recurrence, and a recurrence would be likely if the treatment stopped, as is the case with most medication, then the treatment is to be ignored and the effect is to be regarded as likely to recur.

Assessing whether a past disability was long-term

C10. **The Act provides** that a person who has had a disability within the definition is protected from some forms of discrimination even if he or she has since recovered or the effects have become less than substantial. In deciding whether a past condition was a disability, its effects count as long-term if they lasted 12 months or more after the first occurrence, or if a recurrence happened or continued until more than 12 months after the first occurrence (**S2, Sch2, Para 5**). **For the forms of discrimination covered by this provision see paragraph A15 above. For examples of how this provision works, see above at C5.**

Section D: Normal day-to-day activities

List of 'capacities'

D1. **The Act states** that an impairment is to be taken to affect the ability of a person to carry out normal day-to-day activities **only** if it affects that person in respect of one or more of the following (**Sch1, Para 4**):

- mobility;
- manual dexterity;
- physical co-ordination;
- continence;
- ability to lift, carry or otherwise move everyday objects;
- speech, hearing or eyesight;
- memory or ability to concentrate, learn or understand; or
- perception of the risk of physical danger.

For the purposes of this guidance, the above list will be referred to as a list of 'capacities'.

D2. The list of capacities should be looked at in a broad sense, and applied equally to both physical and mental impairments. For example, it is often assumed that for people with a mental impairment the relevant capacity will be 'memory or ability to concentrate, learn or understand'. The capacities of mobility and physical co-ordination, for example, are often seen as relevant only where there is a physical impairment. However, in many instances this will not be the case. A person with a mental impairment may also have difficulties carrying out activities that involve mobility or other 'physical' skills, and people with a physical impairment may also have effects that involve mental processes such as the ability to concentrate (for example, as a result of pain or fatigue).

D3. **An impairment will only be treated as affecting a normal day-to-day activity if it involves at least one of the capacities set out at D1 above.** The substantial effect is determined by looking at the effect on the particular day-to-day activity, not the relevant capacity. So, for example, an inability to go shopping because of restricted mobility is in itself a substantial effect on a normal day-to-day activity: it is not necessary to show that all or any other aspects of the capacity of mobility are substantially affected.

Meaning of 'normal day-to-day activities'

D4. **It should be noted that the list of capacities set out in D1 above is not a list of day-to-day activities.** It is not possible to provide an exhaustive list of day-to-day activities, although guidance on this matter is given here. In general, day-to-day activities are things people do on a regular or daily basis, and examples include shopping, reading and writing, having a conversation or using the telephone, watching television, getting washed and dressed, preparing and eating food, carrying out household tasks, walking and travelling by various forms of transport, and taking part in social activities.

D5. The term 'normal day-to-day activities' is not intended to include activities which are normal only for a particular person, or a small group of people. In deciding whether an activity is a normal day-to-day activity, account should be taken of how far it is normal for a large number of people, and carried out by people on a daily or frequent and fairly regular basis. In this context, 'normal' should be given its ordinary, everyday meaning.

D6. A normal day-to-day activity is not necessarily one that is carried out by a majority of people. For example, it is possible that some activities might be carried out only, or more predominantly, by people of a particular gender, such as applying make-up or using hair curling equipment, and cannot therefore be said to be normal for **most** people. They would nevertheless be considered to be normal day-to-day activities.

Work-related and other specialised activities

D7. Normal day-to-day activities do not include work of any particular form because no particular form of work is 'normal' for most people. In any individual case, the activities carried out might be highly specialised. For example, carrying out delicate work with specialised tools may be a normal working activity for a watch repairer, whereas it would not be normal for a person who is employed as a semi-skilled worker. The Act only covers effects which go beyond the normal differences in skill or ability.

D8. The same is true of other specialised activities such as playing a musical instrument to a high standard of achievement; taking part in a particular game or hobby where very specific skills or level of ability are required; or playing a particular sport to a high level of ability, such as would be required for a professional footballer or athlete.

D9. However, many types of work or specialised hobby, sport or pastime may still involve normal day-to-day activities. For example; sitting down, standing up, walking, running, verbal interaction, writing, making a cup of tea, using everyday objects such as a keyboard, and lifting, moving or carrying everyday objects such as chairs.

> A woman plays the piano to a high standard, and often takes part in public performances. She has developed carpal tunnel syndrome in her wrists, an impairment that adversely affects manual dexterity. She can continue to play the piano, but not to such a high standard, and she has to take frequent breaks to rest her arms. This would not of itself be an adverse effect on a normal day-to-day activity. However, as a result of her impairment she also finds it difficult to operate a computer keyboard and cannot use her PC to send emails or write letters. This is an adverse effect on a normal day-to-day activity.
>
> A man works in a warehouse, loading and unloading heavy stock. He develops heart problems and no longer has the ability to lift or move heavy items of stock at work. Lifting and moving such unusually heavy types of item is not a normal day-to-day activity. However, he is also unable to lift, carry or move moderately heavy everyday objects such as chairs, either at work or around the home. This is an adverse effect on a normal day-to-day activity.

D10. The effects experienced by a person as a result of environmental conditions, either in the workplace or in another location where a specialised activity is being carried out, should not be discounted simply because there may be a work-related or other specialised activity involved. It is important to consider whether there may also be an adverse effect on the ability to carry out a normal day-to-day activity.

A middle-aged man works in a factory where chemical fumes cause him to have breathing difficulties, and this has made it impossible for him to continue to do his job. He has been diagnosed with occupational asthma, which has a substantial adverse effect while he is at work. As a result he is no longer able to work where he would continue to be exposed to the fumes. Even in a non-work situation he finds any general exertion difficult and this adversely affects activities which involve the capacities of mobility and ability to lift and carry everyday objects. The effects fluctuate, and when he is not at work his asthma attacks are very infrequent. Although the substantial effect is only apparent while at work, the man is able to demonstrate that his impairment has an adverse effect on normal day-to-day activities and at least one capacity in the list in D1.

Indirect effects

D11. An impairment may not directly **prevent** someone from carrying out one or more normal day-to-day activities, but it may still have a substantial adverse long-term effect on how he or she carries out those activities. For example:

- pain or fatigue: where an impairment causes pain or fatigue in performing normal day-to-day activities the person may have the capacity to do something but suffer pain in doing so; or the impairment might make the activity more than usually fatiguing so that the person might not be able to repeat the task over a sustained period of time. **See also paragraphs B7 and B9 above (effects of behaviour)**;

  A man has had chronic fatigue syndrome for several years and although he has the physical capability to walk and to stand, he finds these very difficult to sustain for any length of time because of the overwhelming fatigue he experiences. As a consequence, he is restricted in his ability to take part in normal day-to-day activities such as travelling, so he avoids going out socially, and works from home several days a week. Therefore there is a substantial adverse effect on normal day-to-day activities.

- medical advice: where a person has been advised by a medical practitioner or other health professional, as part of a treatment plan, to change, limit or refrain from a normal day-to-day activity on account of an impairment or only do it in a certain way or under certain conditions. **See also paragraphs B11 to B15 above (effects of treatment)**.

  A woman who works as a teacher develops sciatic pain which is attributed to a prolapsed inter-vertebral disc. Despite physiotherapy and traction her pain became worse. As part of her treatment plan her doctor prescribes daily pain relief medication and advises her to avoid repetitive bending or lifting, and to avoid carrying heavy items. This prevents her from carrying out a range of normal day-to-day activities such as shopping.

Children with a disability

D12. The effects of impairments may not be apparent in babies and young children because they are too young to have developed the ability to act in a way which falls within the capacities listed in D1. Regulations provide that where an impairment to a child under six years old does not have an effect in respect of any of the capacities, it is to be treated as having a substantial and longterm adverse effect on the ability of that child to carry out normal day-to-day activities where it would normally have a substantial and long-term adverse effect on the ability of a person aged six years or over to carry out normal day-to-day activities.[9]

D13. Children aged six and older are subject to the normal requirements of the definition.

A six-year-old child has been diagnosed as having autism. He has difficulty communicating through speech and in recognising when someone is happy or sad. Without a parent or carer with him he will often try to run out of the front door and on to the road to look at the wheels of parked or sometimes passing cars, and he has no sense of danger at all. When going somewhere new or taking a different route he can become very anxious. This amounts to a substantial adverse effect on his ability to carry out normal day-to-day activities, even for such a young child. The capacities of mobility, speech, and perception of risk are all affected.

D14. Since September 2002, provisions in the Special Educational Needs and Disability Act 2001 have extended Part 4 of the Disability Discrimination Act 1995 to cover every aspect of education.[10] These provisions provide protection for disabled pupils and students by preventing discrimination against them at school or in post–16 education for a reason related to their disability. A pupil or student must satisfy the definition of disability as described in this guidance in order to be protected by Part 4 of the Act. The duties for schools in the Act are designed to dovetail with duties under the Special Educational Needs (SEN) framework which are based on a separate definition of special educational needs. Further information on these duties can be found in the SEN Code of Practice[11] and the Code of Practice for Schools.12

Examples of children in an educational setting where their impairment has a substantial and long-term adverse effect on ability to carry out normal day-to-day activities:

A 10-year-old girl has learning difficulties. She has a short attention span and has difficulties remembering facts from one day to the next. She can read only a few familiar words and has some early mathematical skills. To record her work in class she needs to use a tape recorder, pictures and symbols.

A 14-year-old boy has been diagnosed as having attention deficit hyperactivity disorder (ADHD). He often forgets his books, worksheets or homework. In class he finds it difficult to concentrate and skips from task to task forgetting instructions. He often fidgets and makes inappropriate remarks in class or in the playground. Sometimes there can be outbursts of temper.

In both of these examples reading, writing and participating in activities in class and/or in the playground, which are all normal day-to-day activities, are adversely affected to a substantial degree. The capacity affected is 'memory, or ability to concentrate, learn or understand'.

List of capacities, with examples of normal day-to-day activities

D15. The following section looks at the **list of capacities**, and provides examples of normal day-to-day activities which might affect those capacities. The examples given are purely illustrative and should not in any way be considered as a prescriptive list of activities related to a specific capacity.

D16. Examples are given of circumstances where it **would be reasonable** to regard the effect as substantial. In addition, examples are given of circumstances where it would **not be reasonable** to regard the effect as substantial. In these examples, the effect described should be thought of as if it were the **only** effect of the impairment.

D17. The examples of what it would, and what it would not, be reasonable to regard as substantial adverse effects on normal day-to-day activities are indicators and not tests. They do not mean that if a person can do an activity listed then he or she does not experience any substantial adverse effects: the person may be affected in relation to other activities, and this instead may indicate a substantial effect. Or the person may be affected in a minor way in a number of different activities, and the cumulative effect could amount to a substantial adverse effect. **See also paragraphs B4 to B6 (cumulative effects).**

D18. The examples describe the effect which would occur when the various factors described in Sections A, B and C above have been allowed for, including for example the effects of a person making such modifications of behaviour as might reasonably be expected, or of disregarding the impact of medical or other treatment.

D19. Some of the examples show how an adverse effect may arise from either a physical or a mental impairment. Where illustrations of both types of impairment have not been given, this does not mean that only one type of impairment could result in that particular effect. **Regard should be given to the fact that physical impairments can result in mental effects, and mental impairments can have physical manifestations.**

Mobility

D20. This covers moving or changing position in a wide sense. Account should be taken of the extent to which, because of either a physical or a mental impairment, a person finds difficult such day-to-day activities as: getting around unaided or using a normal means of transport; leaving home with or without assistance; walking a short distance; climbing stairs; travelling in a car or completing a journey on public transport; sitting, standing, bending, or reaching; or getting around in an unfamiliar place.

Examples

It would be reasonable to regard as having a substantial adverse effect:

- difficulty in travelling a short journey as a passenger in a vehicle, because, for example, it would be painful getting in and out of a car, or sitting in a car for even a short time; the person has a frequent need for a lavatory; or perhaps, as a result of a mental impairment, the person would become distressed while in the car;
- total inability to walk, or difficulty walking other than at a slow pace or with unsteady or jerky movements;
- difficulty in going up or down steps, stairs or gradients; for example, because movements are painful, uncomfortable or restricted in some way;
- difficulty using one or more forms of public transport; for example, as a result of physical restrictions, pain or fatigue, or as a result of a mental impairment;
- difficulty going out of doors unaccompanied; for example, because the person has a phobia.

A young man with severe anxiety and symptoms of agoraphobia is unable to go out because he fears being outside in open spaces and gets panic attacks in stressful situations such as shopping or travelling on a route that is less than familiar.

A woman with Downs Syndrome has learning difficulties, and finds difficulty in travelling unaccompanied because she often gets lost in areas that are slightly unfamiliar.

A man with Menière's disease experiences dizziness and nausea. This restricts his ability to move around within his home without some form of support.

In these cases, the restricted ability to travel and move around affects the capacity of mobility and has a substantial adverse effect on the ability to carry out normal day-to-day activities.

It would not be reasonable to regard as having a substantial adverse effect:

- experiencing some discomfort as a result of travelling in a car for a journey lasting more than two hours;
- experiencing some tiredness or minor discomfort as a result of walking unaided for a distance of about 1.5 kilometres or one mile.

Manual dexterity

D21. This covers the ability to use hands and fingers with precision. Account should be taken of the extent to which a person can manipulate the fingers on each hand or co-ordinate the use of both hands together to do a task. This includes the ability to carry out normal day-to-day activities that involve things like picking up or manipulating small objects, operating a range of equipment manually, or communicating through writing or typing on standard machinery. Loss of function in the dominant hand would be expected to have a greater effect than equivalent loss in the non-dominant hand.

Examples

It would be reasonable to regard as having a substantial adverse effect:

- difficulty co-ordinating the use of a knife and fork at the same time;
- difficulty preparing a meal because of problems doing things like opening cans or other packages; peeling vegetables; lifting saucepans; and opening the oven door;
- difficulty opening doors which have door knobs rather than lever handles, or gripping handrails on steps or gradients;
- difficulty pressing the buttons on keyboards or keypads at the same speed as someone who does not have an impairment;
- difficulty in dealing with buttons and fasteners when dressing and activities associated with toileting.

A man with tenosynovitis experiences significant pain in his hands and lower arms when undertaking repetitive tasks such as using a keyboard at home or work, peeling vegetables, and writing. The impairment substantially adversely affects these normal day-to-day activities and it has an impact on the capacity of manual dexterity.

It would not be reasonable to regard as having a substantial adverse effect:

- inability to undertake activities requiring delicate hand movements, such as threading a small needle;
- inability to reach typing speeds standardised for secretarial work;
- inability to pick up a single small item, such as a pin.

Physical co-ordination

D22. This covers balanced and effective interaction of body movement, including hand and eye co-ordination. In the case of a child, it is necessary to take account of the level of achievement which would be normal for a person of a similar age. In any case, account should be taken of the ability to carry out 'composite' activities such as walking and using hands at the same time.

Examples

It would be reasonable to regard as having a substantial adverse effect:

- ability to pour hot water into a cup to make a cup of tea only with unusual slowness or concentration;
- difficulty placing food into one's own mouth with a fork or spoon, without unusual concentration or assistance;
- inability to place a key in a lock without unusual concentration or requiring assistance.

A young man who has dyspraxia experiences a range of effects which include difficulty co-ordinating physical movements. He is frequently knocking over cups and bottles of drink and cannot combine two activities at the same time, such as walking while holding a plate of food upright, without spilling the food. It would be reasonable to regard this as a substantial adverse effect on normal day-to-day activities affecting manual dexterity.

It would not be reasonable to regard as having a substantial adverse effect:

- simple clumsiness;
- inability to catch a tennis ball.

Continence

D23. This covers the ability to control urination and/or defecation. Account should be taken of the frequency and extent of the loss of control.

Examples

It would be reasonable to regard as having a substantial adverse effect:

- infrequent loss of control of the bowels, if it is entirely unpredictable and leads to immediate major soiling;
- loss of control of the bladder while asleep at least once a month;
- frequent minor faecal incontinence or frequent minor leakage from the bladder, particularly if it is unpredictable.

A young woman has developed colitis, an inflammatory bowel disease. The condition is a chronic one which is subject to periods of remission and flare-ups. During a flare-up she experiences severe abdominal pain and bouts of diarrhoea. This makes it very difficult for her to travel or go to work as she must ensure she is always close to a lavatory. This has a substantial adverse effect on her ability to carry out normal day-to-day activities.

It would not be reasonable to regard as having a substantial adverse effect:

- infrequent (less than once a month) loss of control of the bladder while asleep;
- infrequent and minor leakage from the bladder;
- incontinence in a very young child who would not be expected to be able to control urination and/or defecation.

Ability to lift, carry or otherwise move everyday objects

D24. Account should be taken of a person's ability to repeat such functions or, for example, to bear weights over a reasonable period of time. Everyday objects might include such items as books, a kettle of water, bags of shopping, a briefcase, an overnight bag, a chair or other piece of light furniture.

Examples

It would be reasonable to regard as having a substantial adverse effect:

- difficulty picking up objects of moderate weight with one hand;
- difficulty opening a moderately heavy door;
- difficulty carrying a moderately loaded tray steadily.

A man with achondroplasia has unusually short stature, and arms which are disproportionate in size to the rest of his body. He has difficulty lifting or manipulating everyday items like a vacuum cleaner, or bulky items of household furniture, and has difficulty opening moderately heavy doors, and operating revolving barriers at the entrance to some stations and buildings. It would be reasonable to regard this as a substantial adverse effect on normal day-today activities.

It would not be reasonable to regard as having a substantial adverse effect:
- inability to carry heavy luggage without assistance;
- inability to move heavy objects without a mechanical aid, such as moving a heavy piece of furniture without a trolley.

Speech, hearing or eyesight

D25. This covers the ability to speak, hear or see and includes face-to-face, telephone and written communication. Account should be taken of the extent to which, as a result of either a physical or mental impairment, a person may have the capacity to speak, hear or see, but may nevertheless be substantially adversely affected in a range of activities involving one of these capacities as a result of the effects of his or her impairment.

(i) Speech

Account should be taken of how far a person is able to speak clearly at a normal pace and rhythm and to understand someone else speaking normally in the person's native language. It is necessary to consider any effects on speech patterns or which impede the acquisition or processing of a person's native language, for example by someone who has had a stroke.

Examples

It would be reasonable to regard as having a substantial adverse effect:
- difficulty giving clear basic instructions orally to colleagues or providers of a service;
- difficulty asking specific questions to clarify instructions;
- taking longer than someone who does not have an impairment to say things.

A man has had a stammer since childhood. He does not stammer all the time, but his stammer can appear, particularly in telephone calls, to go beyond the occasional lapses in fluency found in the speech of people who do not have the impairment. However, this effect can often be hidden by his coping strategy. He may try to avoid telephone calls where he believes he will stammer, or he may not speak as much during telephone calls. He may sometimes try to avoid stammering by substituting words, or by inserting extra words or phrases.

A six-year-old boy has verbal dyspraxia which adversely affects his ability to speak. He is unable to make himself clear to other people, including his friends and teachers at school.

A woman has bipolar disorder. Her speech may sometimes become over-excited and irrational, making it difficult for others to understand what she is saying.

In these cases it would be reasonable to regard these effects as substantial adverse effects.

It would not be reasonable to regard as having a substantial adverse effect:
- inability to articulate fluently due to a lisp or other minor speech impediment;
- inability to speak in front of an audience simply as a result of nervousness;
- inability to be understood because of having a strong accent;
- inability to converse in a language which is not the speaker's native language.

(ii) Hearing

Account should be taken of effects where the level of background noise is within such a range and of such a type that most people would be able to hear adequately. If a person uses a hearing aid or similar device, what needs to be considered is the effect that would be experienced if the person were not using the hearing aid or device.

Examples

It would be reasonable to regard as having a substantial adverse effect:
- difficulty hearing someone talking at a sound level which is normal for everyday conversations, and in a moderately noisy environment;
- difficulty hearing and understanding another person speaking clearly over the voice telephone (where the telephone is not affected by bad reception);
- difficulty hearing or understanding normal conversations because of interference caused by auditory hallucinations as a result of a mental impairment.

A woman has tinnitus which interferes with, and makes difficult, the ability to hear or understand normal conversation, to the extent that she cannot hear and respond to what a supermarket checkout assistant is saying if the two people behind her in the queue are holding a conversation at the same time. This has a substantial adverse effect on her ability to carry out the normal day-to-day activity of shopping.

It would not be reasonable to regard as having a substantial adverse effect:
- inability to hold a conversation in a very noisy place, such as a factory floor, a pop concert or alongside a busy main road;
- inability to sing in tune.

(iii) Eyesight

If a person's sight is corrected by spectacles or contact lenses, or could be corrected by them, what needs to be considered is the effect remaining while he or she is wearing such spectacles or lenses.

If a person's eyesight is impaired sufficiently to lead to registration or certification as a blind or partially sighted person he or she is deemed to be a disabled person,[13] and does not need to prove that he or she has an impairment which has a substantial and long-term adverse effect on his or her ability to carry out normal day-to-day activities.

Account should be taken of the possible effects on a person who has monocular vision, particularly if the sight in the remaining eye is compromised in any way.

Examples

It would be reasonable to regard as having a substantial adverse effect:
- inability to see to pass the eyesight test for a standard driving test (however where this is corrected by glasses, this is not a substantial adverse effect);
- difficulty recognising by sight a known person across a moderately-sized room (unless this can be corrected by glasses);
- inability to distinguish any colours at all;
- difficulty reading ordinary newsprint (unless this can be corrected by reading glasses);
- difficulty walking safely without bumping into things (unless this can be corrected by glasses).

A man has retinitis pigmentosa (RP), a heredity eye disorder which affects the retina. In RP sight loss is gradual but progressive. It is unusual for people with RP to become totally blind – most retain some useful vision well into old age. In this case the man has difficulty seeing in poor light and a marked reduction in his field of vision (referred to as tunnel vision). As a result he often bumps into furniture and doors when he is in an unfamiliar environment, and can only read when he is in a very well-lit area. It would be reasonable to conclude that the adverse effects of this impairment on normal day-to-day activities are substantial.

It would not be reasonable to regard as having a substantial adverse effect:
- inability to read very small or indistinct print without the aid of a magnifying glass;
- inability to distinguish a known person across a substantial distance (e.g. across the width of a football pitch);
- simple inability to distinguish between red and green, which is not accompanied by any other effect such as blurring of vision.

Memory or ability to concentrate, learn or understand

D26. Account should be taken of the person's ability to remember, organise his or her thoughts, plan a course of action and carry it out, take in new knowledge, and to understand spoken or written information. This includes considering whether the person has cognitive difficulties or learns to do things significantly more slowly than a person who does not have an impairment. Account should be taken of whether the person has persistent and significant difficulty in reading and understanding text in his or her native language despite adequate educational opportunities or in reading and understanding straightforward numbers. The ability to learn or understand covers human non-factual information and non-verbal communication such as body language and facial expressions. Account should be taken of whether the inability to understand communication leads to difficulties in understanding and following verbal instructions.

Examples

It would be reasonable to regard as having a substantial adverse effect:

- intermittent loss of consciousness and associated confused behaviour;
- persistent difficulty in remembering the names of familiar people such as family or friends;
- difficulty in adapting after a reasonable period to minor changes in work routine;
- persistent and significant difficulty with reading;
- persistent difficulty in remembering the spelling and meaning of words in common usage;
- considerable difficulty in following a short sequence such as a simple recipe or a brief list of domestic tasks;
- significant difficulty taking part in normal social interaction or forming social relationships;
- disordered perception of reality.

A man has Asperger's syndrome, a form of autism, and this causes him to have difficulty communicating with people. He finds it hard to understand non-verbal communications such as facial expressions, and non-factual communication such as jokes. He takes everything that is said very literally, and therefore has difficulty in making or keeping friends or developing close relationships. He is given verbal instructions during office banter with his manager, but his ability to understand the instruction is impaired because he is unable to isolate the instruction from the social conversation.

A woman with bipolar affective disorder is easily distracted. This results in her frequently not being able to concentrate on performing an activity like making a sandwich without being distracted from the task. Consequently, it takes her significantly longer than a person without the disorder to complete the task.

It would be reasonable to regard these impairments as having a substantial adverse effect on normal day-to-day activities, which involve the capacity of 'memory or ability to concentrate, learn or understand'.

It would not be reasonable to regard as having a substantial adverse effect:

- occasionally forgetting the name of a familiar person, such as a colleague;
- inability to concentrate on a task requiring application over several hours;
- inability to fill in a long, detailed, technical document without assistance;
- inability to read at faster than normal speed;
- some shyness or timidity;
- minor problems with writing or spelling.

Perception of the risk of physical danger

D27. This includes both the underestimation and overestimation of physical danger, including danger to well-being. Account should be taken, for example, of whether the person is inclined to neglect basic functions such as eating, drinking, sleeping, keeping warm or personal hygiene; reckless behaviour which puts the person or others at risk; or excessive avoidance behaviour without a good cause.

Examples

It would be reasonable to regard as having a substantial adverse effect:

- difficulty in safely operating properly-maintained equipment;
- persistent difficulty crossing a road safely;
- persistent failure to nourish oneself (where nourishment is available);
- inability to recognise the physical dangers of touching an object which is very hot or cold.

A man has had paranoid schizophrenia for five years, and one of the effects of this impairment is an inability to make proper judgements about activities that may result in a risk to his personal safety. For example, he will walk into roads without checking if cars are coming. This makes normal day-to-day activities such as shopping very difficult.

A woman has had anorexia, an eating disorder, for two years. She fails to eat properly, and this results in a risk to her well-being. She has no regard for self-preservation, so her perception of physical danger is compromised.

In both cases, these people have an impaired appreciation of danger which results in a substantial adverse effect on their ability to carry out normal day-to-day activities.

It would not be reasonable to regard as having a substantial adverse effect:

- fear of significant heights;
- underestimating the risk associated with dangerous hobbies, such as mountain climbing;
- a person consciously taking a higher than normal risk on their own initiative, such as persistently crossing a road when the signals are adverse, or driving fast on highways for own pleasure;
- underestimating risks – other than obvious ones—in unfamiliar workplaces.

Notes

1 Including by the Special Educational Needs and Disability Act 2001, the Disability Discrimination Act 1995 (Amendment) Regulations 2003, and the Disability Discrimination Act 2005.

2 Section 3(3A) defines an 'adjudicating body' as a court, tribunal, or any other person who, or body which, may decide a claim under Part 4 of the Act.

3 The Disability Discrimination (Blind and Partially Sighted Persons) Regulations 2003. Note: these may be subject to amendment in 2006.

4 The Disability Discrimination (Meaning of Disability) Regulations 1996.

5 Part 3 covers goods, facilities, and services; public authorities; private clubs; and premises.

6 Part 5A covers the duties of a public authority, as opposed to the functions of a public authority, which are dealt with in Part 3.

7 The Disability Discrimination (Meaning of Disability) Regulations 1996.

8 The Disability Discrimination (Meaning of Disability) Regulations 1996.

9 The Disability Discrimination (Meaning of Disability) Regulations 1996.

10 The Special Educational Needs and Disability Act 2001 amends Part 4 of the Disability Discrimination Act 1995 to prevent discrimination against disabled people in their access to education.

11 The Special Educational Needs Code of Practice (November 2001), Department for Education and Skills.

12 Code of Practice for Schools: Disability Discrimination Act 1995: Part 4 (July 2002), Disability Rights Commission.

13 The Disability Discrimination (Blind and Partially Sighted Persons) Regulations 2003. Note: these may be subject to amendment in 2006.

Commission for Racial Equality: Code of Practice on Racial Equality in Employment (2005) (Extracts)

Introduction

1.1 This code replaces the statutory *Code of Practice for the Elimination of Racial Discrimination and the Promotion of Equality of Opportunity in Employment*, issued by the Commission for Racial Equality (CRE) in 1984 under the Race Relations Act 1976 (RRA).

Status of the code

1.6 This code is a statutory code. This means it has been approved by the secretary of state and laid before parliament. The code does not impose any legal obligations. Nor is it an authoritative statement of the law; only the courts and employment tribunals can provide this. However, the code can be used in evidence in legal proceedings brought under the RRA. Courts and tribunals must take account of any part of the code that might be relevant to a question arising during those proceedings.

The Legal Context

Types of Discrimination

2.4 The RRA defines four main types of unlawful discrimination:

a. direct discrimination;
b. indirect discrimination;
c. victimisation; and
d. harassment.

Direct discrimination [Section 1 (1) (a) of the RRA]

2.5 Direct discrimination occurs when a person is treated less favourably, on racial grounds, than another person is or would be treated in the same or similar circumstances (see Example 2, p 17). Apart from limited exceptions (see paras 2.33–2.36) to the general prohibition of discrimination in the RRA, direct discrimination is automatically unlawful, whatever the reason for it. There can be no justification for the difference in treatment.

Example 2:: Direct discrimination

Hussain v Alfred Brown (Worsted Mills) Ltd, Case No. 1805479/98

An Asian with 15 years' experience in textile work applied, for the fourth time, for a job as a warper at a textile mill, close to where he lived in Bradford. As before, he did not receive a reply to his application. However, his son, who had applied at the same time, in the name of J A Taylor, and as someone with ten years' experience, was called in for a trial. The employment tribunal upheld his father's claim that he had been discriminated against on racial grounds. The tribunal took account of the fact that, in four years, not one of the company's 70 workers had been from an ethnic minority group, even though the mill was very near Bradford, with its large ethnic minority population, many of whom had considerable skills in the textile trade. The complainant was awarded a total of around £7,000 in compensation, including £2,500 for injury to feelings.

2.6 In considering whether there has been less favourable treatment, the employment tribunal will examine evidence of any disadvantage the complainant has suffered as a result of the alleged act of discrimination. This may include evidence that the person has been disciplined or dismissed, or any other evidence that shows that the circumstances in which the complainant has to continue to work are to her or his disadvantage (see Example 3, p 17).

Example 3: Proving less favourable treatment

Shamoon v Chief Constable of the Royal Ulster Constabulary (RUC)[2003] IRLR 285

When complaints were made about the appraisal reports written by a chief inspector at the RUC, her appraisal duties were withdrawn. Meanwhile, the other two chief inspectors at her grade continued to carry out appraisals. The RUC argued that carrying out appraisals was not a right, but, at most, a practice; that it was a small part of the complainant's duties; and that she did not suffer loss of rank or any financial disadvantage when the function was removed from her. The chief inspector brought legal proceedings under the Sex Discrimination Act 1975. In an important case for all discrimination law, the House of Lords held that a reasonable employee might well feel demeaned, both in the eyes of those whom she managed and in the eyes of her colleagues, once it was known that a part of her normal duties had been taken away from her following a complaint. The House of Lords concluded that, if an employee reasonably believes that the circumstances in which they would have to continue to work would put them at a disadvantage, this would be sufficient to prove they had suffered a detriment.

2.7 In cases alleging direct racial discrimination, the way a person has been treated will be compared with the way a person from a different racial group has been, or would be, treated in the same or similar circumstances. The courts have recognised that it may not always be possible to compare the alleged treatment with the treatment of an actual other person, and that a hypothetical comparison might have to be made with a person from a different racial group in a similar situation. The question to be asked is: 'how would a person from a different racial group be treated, in circumstances that are not identical, but not too dissimilar?' (see Example 4, p 18).

Example 4: A hypothetical comparator

Balamoody v UK Central Council for Nursing, Midwifery and Health Visiting [*2002*] *IRLR 288*

The complainant, a Mauritian, was the owner of a nursing home. He was convicted in a magistrates' court of failures in relation to the administration of drugs and staffing at the home. As a result, the UK Central Council for Nursing, Midwifery and Health Visiting found him guilty of professional misconduct and struck him off its register. The complainant blamed his matron, a white woman, for the offences he had been convicted for. He complained that the disparity in their treatment – she had not faced disciplinary proceedings – was due to his race.

In a case of direct discrimination, one has to compare like with like (section 3(4) of the RRA). If the complainant can point to an actual person whose circumstances are sufficiently similar to his or her own, so much the better. In this case, the employment tribunal found that the matron was not an appropriate comparator, and dismissed the claim. The Employment Appeals Tribunal went on to uphold the tribunal's decision. However, the Court of Appeal held that both tribunals had made an error of principle: in those circumstances where it was not possible to find an actual comparator who had been treated less favourably, the tribunal would have to construct a hypothetical comparator, as a benchmark, to show how a person from other racial groups would have been treated. In this case, the court felt there was evidence to allow an inference that the council's refusal to reinstate the applicant on the register was racially discriminatory.

Segregation [Section 1(2) of the RRA]

2.8 Segregating a person from others, on racial grounds, automatically means treating her or him less favourably, and constitutes unlawful direct discrimination. The segregation of workers, by racial group, will be unlawful even if they have the same access to promotion, training or pay and conditions as other workers.

Indirect discrimination [Sections 1(1)(b) and 1(1A) of the RRA]

2.9 The RRA contains two definitions of indirect discrimination, depending on the grounds of discrimination. The definition of indirect discrimination introduced under section 1(1A) to comply with the EC Race Directive applies when the discrimination is on grounds of race or ethnic or national origins, but not colour or nationality. When the discrimination is on grounds of colour or nationality, the original definition under section 1(1)(b) applies (see Example 5).

Example 5: Indirect discrimination

Aina v Employment Service [*2002*] *DCLD 103D*

A Black African employee applied for the post of equal opportunities manager in his organisation. He was assessed as having the skills and ability for the job. However, his application was rejected because, unknown to him, the post was open only to permanent staff at higher grades than his. Monitoring data showed that the organisation had no permanent Black African employees at the grades in question. The employment tribunal held that there was no justification for the requirement, and that it amounted to discrimination on racial grounds.

a. Grounds of race or ethnic or national origins [section 1(1A) of the RRA]

This occurs when a provision, criterion or practice which, on the face of it has nothing to do with race or ethnic or national origin, and is applied equally to everyone –

i. puts or would put people of a certain race or ethnic or national origins at a particular disadvantage when compared with others; *and*
ii. puts a person of that race or ethnic or national origins at that disadvantage; *and*
iii. cannot be shown to be a 'proportionate means of achieving a legitimate aim'.

b. Grounds of colour or nationality [section 1(1)(b) of the RRA]

This occurs when an apparently non-discriminatory requirement or condition which applies equally to everyone –
i. can only be met by a considerably smaller proportion of people from a particular racial group than the proportion not from that group who can meet it; *and*
ii. cannot be justified on non-racial grounds; *and*
iii. puts a person from that group at a disadvantage because he or she cannot meet it.

2.10 Although the definition of indirect discrimination introduced to meet the EC Race Directive does not apply to grounds of colour or nationality, in practice, a criterion that disadvantaged someone because of his or her colour would also be likely to disadvantage that person because of his or her race or ethnic or national origins.
- **Example A**. A prohibition on workers wearing their hair in locks would disproportionately disadvantage black people, compared with white people, but this prohibition could also be challenged on grounds of ethnic or national origins, for example, Jamaican.

2.11 'Proportionate means' may be defined as means that are appropriate and necessary to achieve a legitimate business or other objective, such as meeting health and safety requirements (see also para 2.12).
- **Example B**. A blanket ban on beards in a food packaging factory might not be a proportionate means of meeting health and safety requirements, if face masks could be used satisfactorily instead.
- **Example C**. Y, a white English woman, applies for a job as a receptionist with a hospital trust in Wales. Under the Welsh Language Act 1993, the trust has drawn up a Welsh Language Scheme, which permits the trust to require applicants for posts involving the provision of services to the public to be able to speak Welsh, or to be prepared to learn it to an acceptable degree within six months. Y does not speak Welsh and is not prepared to learn it. She does not get the job and her complaint that she has been discriminated against on grounds of national origins fails, because the requirement is considered to be a reasonable means of achieving a legitimate aim. It should be noted that Y might have had a stronger case if the post she had applied for had been one of many receptionist posts at the hospital trust, or, if the trust had had enough Welsh-speaking receptionists to do the work. Meanwhile, W, a man of Pakistani origin, who also does not speak Welsh, successfully applies for a post in the trust's finance department; as the post does not involve contact with the public, it carries no Welsh language requirement.

2.12 The test of indirect discrimination is the same under both definitions; it involves drawing an objective balance between the discriminatory effects of the provision, criterion, practice, requirement or condition and the employer's reasonable need to apply it. When assessing the justification for policies and practices that could have a disproportionate effect on some racial groups, it would be useful to consider the following questions:
a. Does the provision, criterion, practice, requirement or condition correspond to a real need?
b. Does the need pursue a legitimate aim, for example health and safety?
c. Are the means used to achieve the aim appropriate and necessary?
d. Is there any other way of achieving the aim in question?
e. Is there a way of reducing any potentially unlawful discriminatory effect?

Example 6: Victimisation

Mann v Gloucester County Council Fire and Rescue Services (1) and Gibb (2) [1997]
Case No. 1400859/96

A complaint by an Asian fire fighter that the sub-officer in charge of the station had made racially derogatory remarks was initially upheld during the informal stage of an investigation, but later dismissed. The fire station's divisional officer made recommendations, to make sure there were no recriminations. However, almost immediately, the Asian fire fighter was 'sent to Coventry' and his colleagues refused to speak to him. The tribunal upheld his claim of unlawful victimisation, rejecting the fire authority's claim that it had taken all reasonably practicable steps to prevent this. The tribunal thought it was unrealistic of the authority to expect either of the parties, and everybody else concerned, to rise above the situation before a good deal of skilled counselling had been given to them all.

2.13 The concept of 'provision, criterion or practice', which was introduced to comply with the EC Race Directive, is broader and less restrictive than the concept of 'requirement or condition' in the original definition of indirect discrimination in the RRA. The concept of 'provision, criterion or practice' covers the full breadth of formal and informal practices in employment.

- **Example D.** M, who is of Nigerian origin, is informed of a vacancy for a managing director. M phones and is told that the company's normal practice is to use head-hunters for recruitment to senior management posts. If M can show that this practice makes it more difficult for people of Nigerian origin than others to get senior management jobs in this company, and that this puts her at a disadvantage, the practice could amount to unlawful indirect discrimination.

Victimisation [Section 2 of the RRA]

2.14 It is unlawful to treat a person less favourably on racial grounds because he or she has:

a. brought proceedings under the RRA; or
b. given evidence or information in connection with any proceedings under the RRA; or
c. alleged that an act of unlawful discrimination has been committed; or
d. done anything under the RRA in relation to someone, or intends to do so, or is suspected of having done or intending to do so.

2.15 For a claim of victimisation under the RRA to succeed, a complainant would also have to show that:

a. he or she has been or would have been treated less favourably, on racial grounds, than others in those circumstances; and
b. the treatment was a result of his or her action in relation to allegations or proceedings under the RRA.

Harassment [Section 3A(1) of the RRA]

2.16 The definition of harassment introduced by the 2003 Race Regulations applies when the conduct in question is on grounds of race or ethnic or national origins, but not colour or nationality. Harassment on grounds of colour or nationality involves less favourable treatment and may constitute unlawful direct discrimination (see Example 7, and Examples 19 and 20, p 64).

2.17 A person harasses another on grounds of race or ethnic or national origins when he or she engages in unwanted conduct that has the purpose or effect of:

a. violating the other person's dignity; or
b. creating an intimidating, hostile, degrading, humiliating or offensive environment for that person.

Harassment on grounds of colour or nationality may be recognisable by the same type of behaviour.

Example 7: Harassment

Anisetti v Tokyo-Mitsubishi International plc Case No. 6002429/98

The Indian-born head of credit derivatives at an international Japanese bank in London resigned, claiming he had been made to feel like a 'second-class citizen' by his Japanese employers. He said he had been humiliated, excluded by workers speaking Japanese and underpaid, simply because he was not Japanese. The bank argued that it was 'natural' for Japanese staff to use their own language among themselves. An employment tribunal upheld the complainant's claim that he had been discriminated against unlawfully, not because of his Indian national origins, but because he was not Japanese. The tribunal noted that the bank had maintained a practice which had effectively excluded the complainant from various activities, and treated him less favourably than others. The complainant was awarded around £1 million in compensation.

2.18 The definition of what is intimidating, hostile, degrading, humiliating or offensive is mainly a subjective one. In considering a claim of harassment, unless the conduct was intentionally hostile, it would only be considered to have the effects described above (see para 2.17) if, after considering all the circumstances, including, especially, the perceptions of the person affected, it was reasonable to do so. This means a court could decide that a complainant was oversensitive and had unreasonably taken offence.

2.19 While the statutory definition of harassment in the RRA applies only to grounds of race or ethnic or national origins, and not to those of colour and nationality, in cases where abuse is overtly directed at a person's skin colour, employment tribunals and courts may interpret 'race' widely, to include colour.

2.20 Similarly, offensive behaviour in relation to a person's nationality may also be regarded as offensive on the grounds of that person's actual or perceived national origins (see Example 1, p 16), and would therefore be covered by the statutory definition of harassment in the RRA.

2.21 Employers should note that a single incident, for example a racist joke, on any racial grounds, could be sufficient to cause a person to feel harassed.

Discriminatory advertisements [Section 29 of the RRA]

2.22 It is unlawful to publish, or to be responsible for publishing, any advertisement (see the glossary at Appendix 7) that indicates, or may reasonably be understood to indicate, an intention to discriminate, even if the act of discrimination were lawful.

- **Example E.** An advertisement in a local newspaper for a Turkish machinist for a dress manufacturing company would be unlawful.

2.23 The test for deciding whether an advertisement indicates an intention to discriminate is whether a reasonable person would consider it to be discriminatory. The definition of advertisement is very wide and includes any form of advertisement or notice, whether public or not; for example, internal circulars or newsletters announcing staff vacancies, emails, displays on notice boards or shop windows, and job advertisements, banners and pop-up windows on websites.

2.24 The RRA allows a small number of limited exceptions, where the advertisement refers to a situation where discrimination is not unlawful; for example, a lawful positive action training measure (see paras 2.33 and 3.43–3.45 and Appendix 1) or a genuine occupational qualification (see para 2.36 and Appendix 1). The advertisement should make it clear that the employer is making use of the exception.

Example 8: Instructions to discriminate

Weatherfield Ltd t/a Van and Truck Rentals v Sargent* [*1999*] *IRLR 94

A white woman was told as part of an induction course for her new job as a receptionist that the company, a van and truck rental firm, had a special policy on ethnic minority customers. She was instructed to identify 'coloured or Asian callers' by the sound of their voice and to tell them there were no vehicles available. The woman was so upset by this that she resigned, giving her reasons in a letter. The Court of Appeal ruled that she had been discriminated against on racial grounds when she resigned in response to being given an instruction to discriminate against black and Asian customers.

Pressure to discriminate [Section 31 of the RRA]

2.25 It is unlawful to induce, or attempt to induce, a person to discriminate against, or harass, someone on racial grounds. The pressure may amount to no more than persuasion, and need not necessarily involve a benefit or loss. Nor does the pressure have to be applied directly; it is unlawful if it is applied in such a way that the other person is likely to hear of it. And it is unlawful in itself, even if the person who was put under pressure does not go on to commit an unlawful act of discrimination.

Instructions to discriminate [Section 30 of the RRA]

2.26 It is unlawful for a person who has authority over another person, or whose wishes that person normally follows, to instruct him or her to discriminate against, or harass, someone on racial grounds (see Example 8).

Aiding unlawful acts [Section 33 of the RRA]

2.27 A person who knowingly helps another person to discriminate against, or harass, someone unlawfully, on racial grounds, will be treated as having discriminated similarly themselves. Their only defence would be that they had been told the act would not be unlawful, and it was reasonable for them to believe that statement – it is an offence to make a reckless statement on such matters. In an employment situation, anything a worker does in the course of his or her employment is treated as having been done by his or her employer as well, whether or not the employer knew about it or approved of it. A person who knowingly takes part in an act of unlawful discrimination or harassment will therefore be deemed to have helped his or her employer in acting unlawfully.

The responsibilities of employers: A framework for action

Train workers on the equal opportunities policy

3.20 Employers should make sure all their workers understand the organisation's equal opportunities policy, and how it affects them, and that they are aware of any plans for putting it into practice.

This could be done by providing basic training and providing written information and guidance on the policy and plan. Some workers may need more advanced training, depending on their jobs. Equal opportunities should also be a standard component of other training courses, at all levels.

Example 10: Interview

Umerji v Blackburn Borough Council, Case No. 29273/94 [*1995*] *DCLD 47*

An Asian part-time worker on a short-term contract with a local council was one of six candidates interviewed by a panel for the full-time post of welfare officer with the council. He performed better than any of the other candidates, scoring higher than a white council worker. The panel agreed to offer the Asian applicant the job. The panel subsequently reversed its decision and decided to offer the post to the white worker. According to the council, the Asian applicant was not selected because he had failed to meet the criterion of 'written communication' skills, which only became apparent when the application forms were considered after the interview process.

The tribunal upheld the Asian worker's claim of unlawful racial discrimination. It found that he had not only achieved the highest score in both the test of his technical ability and in the interview as a whole, but had also overcome the 'hurdle' of the application form, by being put on the shortlist in the first place. Further, as a council worker, 'his written communication skills were well known to his employer'. The tribunal found the council's replies to the race relations questionnaire (see the glossary at Appendix 7) to be 'evasive and/or equivocal', and rejected its explanations as 'a cover-up'.

The tribunal criticised the council for failing to follow its own equal opportunities and selection procedures: 'It is quite pointless for the respondent to go to the trouble and expense of creating an elaborate selection procedure and an elaborate equal opportunities policy, if it then breaches that procedure and the policy by following an entirely separate procedure, directed apparently by events, and by the personal whim of individual officers.' The tribunal awarded compensation of around £14,000.

3.21 The training will benefit from consulting workers and their representatives about their needs, and incorporating feedback from any training into future courses.

3.22 Employers should make sure in-house trainers are themselves trained before running courses for other staff. External trainers also need to be fully informed about the organisation's policies, including its equal opportunities policy.

3.23 Employers will find it helpful to give a named manager responsibility for equal opportunities training in the organisation.

3.24 In the event of legal proceedings being brought against them under the RRA, employers may find it easier to defend themselves if they are able to show that the basic equal opportunities training all workers receive includes the following:

a. the law against racial discrimination and harassment;
b. the organisation's equal opportunities policy, why it has been introduced and how it will be put into practice;
c. what is acceptable and unacceptable conduct in the workplace;
d. workers' responsibilities under the equal opportunities policy to maintain and promote a workplace free of unlawful racial discrimination and harassment; and
e. how prejudice can affect the way an organisation functions, and the effects that generalisations about racial groups, and bias in day-to-day operations, can have on people's chances of obtaining work, promotion, recognition and respect.

Example 11: Monitoring

Richards v Brighton Borough Council [*1992*] *Case No. 14213/91 and EAT 431/92* [*1993*] *DCLD 19*

A black woman, who had been turned down for the post of information officer in a council's housing department, in favour of a white woman with much less relevant work experience, won her claim of racial discrimination against the council. The tribunal noted the council's failure to monitor its equal opportunities policy

Monitor workers and applicants by racial group, and review all employment policies, procedures and practices

3.25 Monitoring, by racial group, gives employers the information they need to understand how their policies, practices and procedures in the field of employment affect people from different racial groups.

3.26 Monitoring is a process that involves collecting, analysing and evaluating information, to measure performance, progress and change. It can be done in several ways, including questionnaires, surveys, consultation and feedback. Monitoring, by racial group, will allow employers to:

a. determine the composition of their workforce, by racial group, and compare this information with benchmarks, such as census data;
b. know how their workforce is distributed across the organisation, by location, type of job and grade;
c. uncover any disparities between racial groups, in the workforce as a whole and at different levels of the organisation, and investigate the underlying causes;
d. find out whether people from certain racial groups are typically taking longer to obtain promotion;
e. examine whether the practices, provisions, criteria, requirements or conditions used to select candidates for employment, training and promotion might be indirectly discriminatory, and why, and consider how they might be changed to avoid any negative effects on candidates from a particular racial group (or groups);
f. set realistic targets and timetables for reducing any significant racial disparities, both within the workforce as a whole, and at different levels of the organisation;
g. send a clear message to its workers, and to job seekers, that the organisation is serious about achieving fair and equitable participation, and encourage them to cooperate fully; and
h. judge whether the equal opportunities policy is achieving its aims.

3.27 Monitoring, by racial group, should cover the following:

a. applications for jobs, temporary and permanent, advertised and non-advertised, and success rates at each stage of the process;
b. distribution of workers in the organisation, by type of job, location, and grade;
c. applications for promotion, transfer and training, and success rates for each;
d. results of performance appraisals;
e. grievances and disciplinary action, including the results, and tribunal decisions involving claims of racial discrimination or harassment; and
f. terminations of contract (for whatever reason).

3.28 Section 8 of the RRA gives the meaning of employment at an establishment in Great Britain (see 'employment' in the glossary at Appendix 7). Employers who have operations or subsidiaries in other countries, or who have outsourced functions to other countries, need to make arrangements to keep their monitoring data for workers at establishments in Great Britain separate (or in a form that is readily identifiable).

- **Example F.** A bank outsources its payroll function to a company in Manila. It transfers a senior manager to Manila from its office in London, to oversee the work. The bank would include the senior manager, but not the payroll workers in Manila, in the monitoring data it keeps to meet the recommendations of this code.

3.29 The information needed for effective monitoring may be obtained in a number of ways. The best course is to ask workers and applicants for jobs, training and promotion to select the racial group they want to be associated with from a list of categories. The 2001 census provides the most comprehensive and reliable data about the population in England, Scotland and Wales, increasingly supplemented by the Labour Force Survey and other survey statistics (see the Office for National Statistics in Appendix 5). Employers should therefore use categories that are compatible with those used in the 2001 census. Employers who wish to include a group that is not separately listed in the census classification should add the group as a sub-group of the appropriate main group in the census classification system. For example, Somali would be a sub-group of Other in the broad Black or Black British category, Sikh a sub-group of Indian in the Asian or Asian British category, and Roma/Gypsy a sub-group of Other in the White category. In response to increasing national consciousness in England, Scotland and Wales, employers may also want to consider offering workers and applicants the opportunity to classify themselves in terms of a national identity. It is important to remember that any aggregation of data, especially when the numbers are small, risks masking significant disparities between sub-groups, for example between Indian and Bangladeshi, if they are considered only as part of the broad Asian group.

3.30 Smaller organisations may only need a simple method of collecting information about workers' and job applicants' racial groups, such as a questionnaire. Larger organisations are likely to need more sophisticated procedures and computerised systems as well, to capture the full picture across their subsidiaries and branches in Britain.

3.31 To ensure the integrity of their monitoring systems, employers should consider the following steps:

a. consult workers, trade unions and other representatives in the workplace, and make sure they understand the reasons for introducing monitoring, before asking workers for information about their racial group;
b. assure everyone concerned that information about ethnic or racial background will be treated in the strictest confidence;
c. analyse the information regularly, preferably together with other available information, for example, on sex, sexual orientation, disability, religion or belief, or age;
d. review the information periodically, and make sure it is current; and
e. make sure managers responsible for monitoring, and anyone else involved in the process, are properly trained in data protection and sensitive data processing.

Public authorities and monitoring

3.32 Most of the public authorities bound by the statutory general duty to promote race equality (see paras 2.28–2.29) also have a specific duty to monitor, by racial group, all their workers, and all applicants for jobs, promotion and training. Public authorities with 150 or more full-time-equivalent workers must also monitor the number of workers from each racial group who:

a. receive training;
b. benefit or suffer detriment from performance assessment;
c. are involved in grievances;
d. are subject to disciplinary action; and
e. end employment with the organisation (for whatever reason).

3.33 Public authorities must publish the results of this monitoring each year.

3.34 Educational institutions are not bound by the specific duty for public authorities as employers. However, schools do have to give their local education authorities (education authorities in Scotland) information about staff, so that the authorities can meet their duty to monitor, by racial group, employment in the schools they manage, and publish a report on it each year. Further and higher education institutions have a specific duty to monitor, by racial group, the recruitment of staff and their career progress. They are also expected to take reasonable and practicable steps to publish the results of their monitoring each year.

3.35 A statutory Code of Practice on the Duty to Promote Race Equality was laid before parliament and came into effect in May 2002. The CRE has also produced non-statutory guidance for public authorities on different aspects of the duty (see Appendix 6).

Take steps to prevent unlawful discrimination, and reduce any significant disparities between racial groups

3.36 If the monitoring data show significant disparities between racial groups, employers should investigate the possible causes, and examine all the arrangements, procedures and practices that give effect to their policies in the field of employment, including recruitment, training, promotion, grievance and discipline, performance assessment and dismissal. The absence of disparities for ethnic minorities as a whole, or for one racial group in particular (see para 3.29), should not be taken as evidence that 'discrimination is not a problem'. The aim should be to make sure none of the rules, requirements, procedures or practices used, formally or informally, put any racial groups at a significant disadvantage; for example, indirectly discriminatory eligibility rules for promotion, or restrictive advertising techniques. It is recommended that employers approach this as systematically as possible, taking the following steps:

a. review the selection criteria used, to make sure they are strictly related to the job or training opportunity, and do not have an unjustifiable adverse effect on any racial groups;
b. examine all decision-making processes, to make sure they are fair, and are followed consistently across the full range of recruitment and assessment exercises;
c. review the policy on advertising jobs, and training and promotion opportunities, to make sure the information is reaching any under-represented groups, and that people from these groups feel encouraged to apply;
d. reassess the labour markets from which they traditionally recruit;

e. set targets (see paras 3.38–3.42) for employment, training and promotion, as part of a programme of action to reduce any significant disparities between racial groups, and regularly review progress; and
f. consider whether lawful positive action (see Appendix 1) might be appropriate.

3.37 Larger employers may find it useful to:
a. nominate a person with specialist knowledge of discrimination and equality to monitor the effectiveness of the organisation's equal opportunities policy, conduct independent investigations of complaints of discrimination and harassment, and advise on, and coordinate, action; and
b. encourage their branches or subsidiaries to draw up and implement their own equal opportunities action plan, against standards set and controlled centrally.

Racial equality targets

3.38 Employers could consider setting racial equality targets as a means of planning the reduction of any significant disparities between racial groups. A racial equality target could represent improvements in representation for particular racial groups or progress towards equality of treatment. For example, it could show the percentage of workers from a particular racial group (or groups) that an organisation is aiming to have in particular areas or types of work within a certain period of time; or a reduction or elimination of any unfavourable disparity in assessment ratings between racial groups over a certain period of time.

3.39 Racial equality targets are not quotas. Restricting recruitment to people from particular racial groups, in order to improve their representation in the workforce, would be positive discrimination. This is unlawful in Britain. All selection for employment must be, and be seen to be, fair, and based solely on merit.

3.40 Racial equality targets for recruitment, promotion and training should be based on the ethnic and racial composition of the area from which an organisation decides to recruit for particular jobs, and on the ethnic and racial composition of its own workforce. Progress towards racial equality targets can then be monitored against the steps being taken, including positive action training and encouragement (see paras 3.43–3.45 and Appendix 1), to make recruitment and other employment policies and practices fairer and more equal.

3.41 Employers should consider publishing their racial equality targets, for example, in their annual reports, to show how their organisation is working towards fair participation.

3.42 Employers should base their corporate priorities, objectives, approaches and any racial equality targets on the outcomes listed below.
a. The ethnic and racial composition of the workforce, at each location and level, reflects the composition of the labour markets used for different types of work.
b. Vacancies attract applications from the full range of qualified candidates in the relevant labour markets, including candidates from ethnic minorities.
c. The ratio of appointments to applications is proportionate across all racial groups.
d. The organisation's board and senior management team (where applicable) reflect the ethnic and racial backgrounds of all potential candidates, both internally and externally.
e. Workers from all racial groups are equally likely to apply for, and be offered, training.
f. Applications for promotion and deputising are received from across the full spectrum of workers, irrespective of racial group.
g. Workers spend the same length of time at a particular grade, on average, irrespective of racial group.
h. Progress from one grade to another is unaffected by workers' racial groups.
i. Workers are not disproportionately subject to disciplinary proceedings, because of their racial group.
j. Workers from all racial groups benefit equally from bonuses or performance pay.
k. Grievances are not more likely to be brought by workers from particular racial groups.
l. The number of complaints alleging racial discrimination or harassment is negligible.
m. There are no significant disparities between racial groups among staff leaving the organisation, for whatever reason.

Positive action [Sections 35, 37 and 38 of the RRA]

3.43 The RRA recognises that, due to past discrimination or other disadvantages, people from particular racial groups may not have fully realised their potential, and may not have the qualifications or experience to make them eligible for particular jobs. The aim of positive action, as permitted under the RRA, is to give people from a particular racial group (or groups) the opportunity to compete for work in which they have been under-represented or absent. The RRA also allows action to be taken to make facilities or services, such as language classes or training or education in basic work skills, available for people from a particular racial group (or groups) who would otherwise be excluded from opportunities.

3.44 If the results of monitoring show under-representation, or the complete absence of a racial group (or groups) in particular work (see Appendix 1), for example among senior managers or shop floor supervisors, it is recommended that employers take the following steps:

a. consider positive action training or encouragement;

b. make sure the positive action scheme offers only training or encouragement, and not employment – employers making use of the positive action provisions of the RRA should be especially careful that the training or encouragement provided as a form of positive action does not constitute employment, or lead automatically to employment; for example, 'on-the-job' training or apprenticeships, which are defined as employment, and not training, cannot form part of a positive action programme (see Example 12 below); and

c. inform workers, trade unions and other workplace representatives about their plans, explaining that the aim of positive action training or encouragement is to help create a level playing field, not to favour any particular racial group.

Example 12: Positive action

Hughes and others v London Borough of Hackney (unreported) [1986]

A local authority included a statement in an advertisement for gardening apprentices encouraging young people from 'black and ethnic minorities' to apply, and referring to section 38 of the RRA. Three white people applied for the jobs and were told they were open only to people from ethnic minorities. The employment tribunal upheld their claims that they had been unlawfully discriminated against on racial grounds, pointing out that 'encouragement' under the positive action provisions of the RRA did not extend to providing job opportunities for any section of the community.

- **Example G.** A national broadcaster used section 37 of the RRA to set up a mentoring scheme for would-be sports journalists. The scheme gave 12 young people from ethnic minorities a year's training and work placements in the sports broadcasting department, leading to a postgraduate certificate in broadcast journalism from a leading institution. Twelve specially selected and trained senior managers from the sports department were matched with the trainees.

3.45 Positive action may, and should, be used to encourage or train workers to compete for jobs where they are under-represented (section 38 of the RRA).

Equal opportunities conditions in contracts

3.46 Employers should encourage companies and other organisations, with whom they have, or propose to enter into, contracts for goods, facilities or services, to take practical steps to promote equality of opportunity in their employment practices. Employers should therefore:

a. make acceptance on tender lists, and the award or renewal of a contract, conditional on the organisation's providing information about any findings of racial discrimination or harassment, and adopting the recommendations of this code;

b. include terms and conditions in contracts that require contractors to follow the recommendations of this code; and

c. encourage individuals and organisations from under-represented racial groups to tender or compete for contracts.

3.47 Most public authorities have a legal duty to promote race equality when carrying out their functions (see also paras 2.28–2.31). The duty applies whether they carry out these functions themselves or contract them out to private businesses or voluntary organisations. While bound by the RRA's general prohibition of unlawful racial discrimination, private businesses and voluntary organisations are not bound by the duty. Public authorities therefore need to make arrangements during the tendering process, and through the contract itself, to make sure contractors are able to meet the duty on their behalf, if it applies to the goods, works, facilities or services being contracted out. The CRE has produced guides to procurement for local authorities and other public authorities (see Appendix 6).

The responsibilities of employers: Equality of opportunity and good employment practice

What the law says [Sections 4 and 4A of the RRA]

4.1 The Race Relations Act 1976 (RRA) makes it unlawful for employers to discriminate against a person on racial grounds, or subject them to harassment, in the arrangements they make for recruitment and selection, and in the terms and conditions on which they offer employment, training or promotion.

4.2 Employers must therefore make sure their policies, procedures and practices in the field of employment are not potentially discriminatory, and that they promote equality of opportunity, not obstruct it.

4.3 The framework for action (see Chapter 3) emphasises the importance of applying the organisation's equal opportunities policy to all aspects of employment, from recruitment to termination of the employment contract. This chapter of the code makes recommendations on good equal opportunities procedures and practice in key areas of employment.

RECRUITMENT

Principles of good practice

4.4 The following principles apply to all aspects of recruitment for employment, including promotion, and training.

a. Recruitment policies, procedures and practices should meet all the terms and objectives of the organisation's equal opportunities policy and action plan.
b. All staff responsible for recruitment should receive training in the equal opportunities policy.
c. Opportunities for employment, including promotion, and training should be equally open to all eligible candidates, and selection should be based solely on merit (except where the positive action exception applies to training; see Appendix 1).
d. No applicant or worker should be placed at a disadvantage by rules, requirements, conditions or practices that have a disproportionately adverse effect on his or her racial group.

Planning

Job descriptions

4.5 It is recommended that employers prepare a job description for any vacant post they decide to fill.

4.6 To avoid claims that a job description includes a requirement that might be indirectly discriminatory on racial grounds, employers need to make sure that:

a. they are able to justify each duty or task as being necessary;
b. the job description does not overstate a duty, or the responsibilities attached to it; and
c. the job description is written in plain English (or Welsh in Wales), and is free of jargon.

4.7 A helpful way of drawing up a job description might be to describe the duties and the tasks a person would be expected to carry out over a certain period of time, for example an average working day or week, in order to get a clear picture of what the job actually entails.

Person specifications

4.8 A person specification describes the skills, knowledge, abilities, qualifications, experience and qualities that are considered necessary or desirable in a candidate, in order to perform all the duties in the job description satisfactorily. It is recommended that employers prepare a written person specification to accompany the job description.

4.9 To avoid claims that a person specification includes potentially discriminatory requirements, criteria or conditions, employers need to make sure of the following.

a. The person specification includes only the criteria needed to perform the duties in the job description satisfactorily.
b. The person specification does not overstate the requirements; for example, by calling for 'excellent knowledge of English' (or Welsh in Wales) when 'good understanding' is more appropriate, or by asking for higher qualifications than are actually needed to do the job satisfactorily.
c. The person specification makes clear the relative importance placed on each criterion, and whether it is necessary or desirable.
d. As far as possible, all the criteria are capable of being tested objectively. This means avoiding vague or subjective qualities. Attributes such as 'leadership', which are widely used in the selection process, need to be precisely and objectively defined in terms of the measurable skills and qualities that contribute to it; for example, fairness, knowledge, diplomacy, imagination and decisiveness.
e. The person specification makes clear that degrees or diplomas obtained abroad are acceptable, if they are of an equivalent standard to UK qualifications (see Appendix 5 for details of UK National Academic Recognition Information Centre).

f. To reduce the risk of including criteria that reflect personal preferences rather than justifiable requirements, as far as possible, the manager responsible for the post obtains approval of the person specification from the person responsible for equal opportunities in the organisation (in smaller organisations, this might be the director or proprietor).

4.10 Employers should consider reviewing the person specifications they have used over a period of time, or a representative sample of them, as part of their equal opportunities review of the recruitment process, to make sure the requirements and criteria applied do not contribute to any significant disparities between the success rates for different racial groups.

Job advertisements

4.11 It is recommended that employers take the following steps, to make sure all opportunities for employment or training are advertised widely, fairly and openly.

a. Employers should avoid recruitment, solely or in the first instance, on the basis of recommendations by existing staff, particularly when the workforce is wholly or predominantly from one racial group.

b. The advertisement, in all its forms (including signs in shop windows, and on notice boards and recruitment websites), must not indicate an intention to discriminate unlawfully (see paras 2.22–2.24). Nor should it be possible for an ordinary member of the public to understand the advertisement as discriminating against people from a particular racial group (or groups), unless a statutory exception to discriminate applies (see paras 2.33–2.36), and this is clearly stated in the advertisement.

c. Employers should consider including a reference to the organisation's equal opportunities policy in the advertisement. However, statements encouraging applicants from particular racial groups to apply should not be used, unless the job in question meets the conditions for taking positive action (see paras 3.43–3.45 and Appendix 1). Advertisements for a job relying on a genuine occupational requirement or qualification should make clear how the exception applies to the duties of the job (see Appendix 1).

d. Every effort should be made to ensure that the advertisement accurately reflects the job description and the requirements listed in the person specification.

e. Employers should remember, when recruiting through recruitment agencies, job centres, careers offices, schools or online agencies, that it is unlawful to:

i. instruct them to discriminate, for example by suggesting that certain groups would (or would not) be preferred; or

ii. put pressure on them to discriminate against people from a particular racial group (or groups).

f. Recruitment and other agencies should be made aware of the employer's equal opportunities policy, as well as other relevant policies. They should also be given copies of the job descriptions and person specifications for posts they are helping the employer to fill.

g. To avoid indirect discrimination, employers should not unjustifiably restrict job advertisements or information about vacant posts to areas, publications, recruitment agencies, job centres, careers offices and schools that would result in excluding or disproportionately reducing the number of applicants from a particular racial group (or groups). All staff should be informed of any opportunities for promotion or career development (see Example 13 above).

h. Employers should consider reviewing the job advertisements they have placed over a period of time, or a representative sample of advertisements, as part of their equal opportunities review of the recruitment process, to make sure the advertisements, and where they were placed, did not contribute to any significant disparities between the success rates for different racial groups.

Application forms

4.12 It is recommended that, where practicable, all employers should use a standard application form (see Appendix 4). This has the following advantages.

a. It reduces the time spent in sifting through a great deal of information that is not relevant to the job, which is usually the case with CVs and application letters.

b. It helps employers obtain the information they need, and in the form in which they need it, to make an objective assessment of the applicant's ability to do the job.

c. It makes it easier to obtain information about applicants' racial groups; this is mandatory for public authorities under their legal duty to monitor various aspects of employment, by racial group (see paras 3.32–3.34).

d. It provides employers with evidence that they have tried to meet their legal obligations, should they face legal proceedings under the RRA.
e. It gives all applicants the opportunity to compete on equal terms.

4.13 To reduce the risk of unlawful racial discrimination, employers should follow the guidelines below; smaller organisations may adapt these to their particular circumstances.

a. The section of the application form requesting personal information (including information about racial group) should be detachable from the rest of the form, and not made known to members of the selection panel before the interview.
b. The question about an applicant's racial group should include a clear explanation as to why this information is needed, and an assurance that the information will be treated in strictest confidence, and will not be used to assess suitability for the job, or in the selection decision.
c. Information about eligibility to work in the UK, which employers are required to obtain under the Asylum and Immigration Act 1996, should preferably be verified in the final stages of the selection process, to make sure the appointment is based on merit alone, and is not influenced by other factors. Employers can apply for work permits and should not exclude potentially suitable candidates from the selection process. Depending on the employer's recruitment process, and the type of job being filled, candidates might be asked for the relevant documents when they are invited to an interview, or when an offer of employment is made. It is important to carry out these checks before the person's employment begins. The Home Office (see Appendix 5) has published a code of practice for employers on how to avoid unlawful racial discrimination when complying with this requirement.
d. Only information that is relevant to the job, and to the skills and qualifications listed in the person specification, should be requested in the application form (apart from the questions in the personal details section of the form).
e. Applicants should not be asked to provide photographs, unless a genuine occupational requirement or qualification applies (see Appendix 1).
f. Applicants should be assured that their referees will not be approached unless they are offered the job.
g. Recruitment and employment agencies acting on behalf of an organisation should have copies of its equal opportunities policy, and understand its recruitment policies, and the role of the application form in the selection process.

Example 13: Job advertisements

Gulsher v Gateway Foodmarkets Ltd, Case No. 17036/92 [1994] DCLD 19

An employer promoted a worker to a new post without advertising the vacancy internally. As a result, no one in the organisation was given the opportunity to apply. The tribunal ruled that the employer had unlawfully discriminated against a black worker who was qualified for the post, and would have applied for it if he had known about it. The complainant was awarded £500 for injury to feelings.

4.14 Employers who accept CVs might consider publishing guidance on their websites, to help applicants organise their CVs as closely as possible to the organisation's job application form (if they use one), or the form in which employers would prefer to receive the information.

4.15 Employers should review their job application form periodically, as part of their equal opportunities review of the recruitment process, to make sure it does not contribute to any significant disparities between the success rates for different racial groups.

The selection process

4.16 Employers are responsible for making sure their selection procedures are fair, and operate consistently, to ensure the appointment of the best person for the job, irrespective of race, colour, nationality (including citizenship) or ethnic or national origins.

4.17 Every selection decision, from short-listing to appointment, is equally important and it is recommended that employers keep records that will allow them to justify each decision, and the process by which it was reached. Employers need to be able to show that:

a. each selection decision was based on objective evidence of the candidate's ability to do the job satisfactorily, and not on assumptions or prejudices about the capabilities of people from certain racial groups; and
b. all staff involved in the selection process had received training on the equal opportunities policy, and its application to recruitment.

4.18 Actual selection procedures will vary from one organisation to another, depending on size and administrative resources – for example, some organisations may be able to ensure that a member of staff with expertise in personnel matters is involved in the selection process – but the principles of fair selection apply to all.

4.19 As far as possible, to ensure consistency, it would be best if the same staff were responsible for selection decisions at all stages of the recruitment process for each vacancy.

4.20 Employers should make sure the arrangements they make for holding tests or interviews, or using assessment centres, do not put any candidates at a disadvantage, on racial grounds; for example, because the dates or times coincide with religious festivals or observance, or because they fail to take account of dietary needs or cultural norms.

Shortlisting

4.21 It is recommended that employers build the following guidelines for good practice into their selection procedures and practice.

a. Wherever possible, more than one person should be involved in shortlisting candidates, to reduce the chance of one individual's bias prejudicing an applicant's chances of being selected.
b. The marking system, including the cut-off score for selection, should be agreed before the applications are assessed, and applied consistently to all applications.
c. Each person involved in the selection should mark the applications separately, before meeting to agree a final mark.
d. Assumptions about candidates as members of particular racial groups, and the type of work they would be able or willing to do, should play no part in the process. Selection should be based only on information provided in the application form (where one is used), or in any formal performance assessment reports, in the case of internal applicants.
e. The weight given to each item in the person specification should not be changed during shortlisting; for example, in order to include someone who would otherwise not be shortlisted.

4.22 As part of their equal opportunities review of the recruitment process, employers should use the information they have collected about applicants' racial groups to see whether decisions at the shortlisting stage might have contributed to any significant disparities between the success rates for different racial groups. If so, they should investigate further, and take steps to remove any barriers.

Selection tests and assessment centres

4.23 It is recommended that ability tests and personality questionnaires should only be used as one of several assessment methods.

Example 14: Selection tests

Mallidi v The Post Office, Case No. 2403719/98 [2001] DCLD 47

An Asian woman who had worked for the Post Office on a casual basis for a number of years was asked to take a written aptitude test in order to remain in employment on a contractual basis. She failed the test, and her employment was terminated. Her complaint, when she found that white workers in the same situation had been given temporary or permanent contracts without having to take a test, was not investigated, and she brought legal proceedings claiming racial discrimination.

The tribunal found that whole batches of casual workers were given contracts without passing a test. Nor was the Post Office able to explain why workers had to sit the test at certain times, and in certain cases but not in others. The tribunal inferred that the only explanation for the Asian woman's dismissal was her race (the tribunal also found that the aptitude test was indirectly discriminatory). It also found no evidence that the Post Office's 'intention to operate an equal opportunities policy . . . was actually implemented on a day-to-day basis'. The tribunal awarded compensation of nearly £20,000, including £10,000 for injury to feelings.

4.24 Well-designed, properly administered and professionally validated ability tests can be a useful method of predicting candidates' performance in a particular job. However, this depends critically on the design of the test; its validation (see the glossary at Appendix 7) as a reliable predictor of performance, irrespective of racial group; and its fair administration by professionals trained in assessment and in the organisation's equal opportunities policy. (See Appendix 5 for details of the British Psychological Centre, the representative body for psychologists and psychology in the UK, and its online Psychological Testing Centre.)

4.25 If tests and assessment centres are used as part of the selection process, it is recommended that employers take account of the following guidelines.

a. Tests should correspond to the job in question, and measure as closely as possible the appropriate levels of the skills and abilities included in the person specification.
b. Special care should be taken to make sure candidates whose first language is not English (or Welsh in Wales) understand the instructions. Tests that are fair for speakers of English (or Welsh) as a first language may present problems for people who are less proficient in the language. The Welsh Language Act 1993 puts Welsh and English on an equal basis in the delivery of public services in Wales and bilingual tests may need to be used for recruitment to some public sector jobs, where the ability to speak Welsh is deemed to be essential or desirable.4
c. All the candidates, without exception, should take the same test (see Example 14 above).
d. Test papers, assessment notes and records of decisions should be kept on file for at least 12 months.

4.26 As part of their equal opportunities review of the recruitment process, employers should use the information they have received about applicants' racial groups to see whether the tests and assessment methods used might have contributed to any significant disparities between the success rates for different racial groups. If so, they should investigate further and take steps to remove any barriers.

Interviews

4.27 For many employers, the interview is the decisive stage of the selection process.
It is also the stage when it is easiest to make judgements about a candidate based on instant, subjective and, sometimes, wholly irrelevant impressions. If assumptions about the capabilities or characteristics of people from a particular racial group contribute to an unfavourable impression, this could lead to an unlawful, racially discriminatory selection decision.

4.28 To strengthen their legal defence in any proceedings alleging unlawful racial discrimination, it is recommended that employers take steps to make sure all job interviews are conducted strictly on the basis of the application form, the job description, the person specification, the agreed weight given to each criterion, and the results of any selection tests, so that all applicants are assessed objectively, and solely on their ability to do the job satisfactorily.

4.29 Staff involved in selection panels would benefit especially from equal opportunities training in interviewing techniques, to help them:

a. recognise when they are making stereotyped assumptions about people;
b. apply a scoring method objectively;
c. prepare questions based on the person specification, and the information in the application form; and
d. avoid questions about hobbies, social activities or religious or cultural beliefs or practices, unless these are demonstrably relevant to the job.

4.30 Employers need to make arrangements to keep application forms, and documents relating to each stage of the recruitment process, for 12 months, in case of any complaints about decisions or procedures, or requests for the information under the Data Protection Act 1998, or, where appropriate, the Freedom of Information Act 2000. The documentation should include:

a. records of discussions and decisions by members of the selection panel; for example, on marking standards or interview questions;
b. notes taken by each member of the panel during the interviews; and
c. each panel member's marks at each stage of the process; for example, on the application form, any selection tests and each interview question.

4.31 Employers should remind gate, reception and personnel staff that it would be unlawful to treat people from a particular racial group (or groups) less favourably than others, and should consider issuing written guidance to this effect.

4.32 Evidence of good practice throughout the recruitment process will help avoid litigation, or end it at an early stage. Employers will be in a better position to show that they took reasonably practicable steps to prevent unlawful racial discrimination or harassment, should the matter reach an employment tribunal.

4.33 As part of their equal opportunities review of the recruitment process, employers should use the information they have received about applicants' racial groups to see whether selection decisions at the interview stage might have contributed to any significant disparities between the success rates for different racial groups. If so, they should investigate further and take steps to remove any barriers.

References

4.34 To make sure the selection decision is based strictly on the application form, the job description, the person specification, any selection tests and interviews, and is not influenced by other factors, such as potentially subjective judgements about a candidate by referees, employers should avoid making references part of the selection process. It is recommended that references should only be obtained, and circulated to members of the selection panel, after a selection decision has been reached.

4.35 Employers will find it more useful to avoid asking for general character references, and to send referees copies of the job description and person specification instead, requesting evidence of the candidate's ability to meet the specific requirements of the job. This is more likely to ensure that the reference focuses on information that is relevant to the job.

Eligibility to work in the UK

4.36 Under the Asylum and Immigration Act 1996, employers have to carry out checks of a job applicant's eligibility to work in the UK. Employers should preferably do this in the final stages of the selection process, to ensure appointment on the basis of merit alone (see para 4.13c).

Terms and conditions

4.37 It is unlawful for employers to discriminate, on racial grounds, in the terms and conditions of work they offer, including pay, hours of work, overtime, bonuses, holiday entitlement, sickness leave, and maternity and paternity leave.

4.38 It is recommended that employers make sure their rules and requirements on access to any benefits, facilities or services, such as luncheon vouchers, discount travel services or membership of a gym, do not unlawfully discriminate against a particular racial group (or groups) (see paras 2.9–2.13).

4.39 When employees' cultural or religious practices, such as those expressed in dress codes, conflict with an employer's policies or workplace requirements, it is recommended that the employer consider whether it is practicable to vary or adapt these requirements. Employers should consult staff, trades unions and other workplace representatives on practical ways in which they can accommodate workers' needs. Discrimination in the field of employment on grounds of religion or belief is unlawful under the Employment Equality (Religion or Belief) Regulations 2003. If the policy or requirement affects people from a particular racial group (or groups), it might also amount to unlawful indirect racial discrimination (see paras 2.9–2.13).

Induction

4.40 Induction is an opportunity for employers to make sure all new staff understand the organisation's commitment to equality of opportunity. Employers might consider providing translations or interpreters, if necessary.

4.41 As a minimum, good employment practice would see employers using the induction process to make new recruits familiar with:

a. equal opportunities principles and workers' legal rights and responsibilities under the RRA;
b. what is acceptable and unacceptable conduct in the workplace, in the light of the organisation's policies on harassment, discipline and grievances; and
c. the organisation's procedures for bringing complaints of racial discrimination or harassment against colleagues or managers.

4.42 For permanent or long-term workers, it is recommended that employers include training on the organisation's equal opportunities policy and action plan (see para 3.20). Employers might consider asking new recruits to sign a statement, affirming that they have read and understood all the policies covered during the induction. This may serve as evidence that they have taken reasonably practicable steps to prevent unlawful racial discrimination or harassment, should they face legal proceedings under the RRA.

4.43 Staff responsible for induction will need to be trained on the organisation's equal opportunities policy, and on how assumptions about new recruits, based on their racial group, can affect the degree to which they are informed, for example, about their rights at work, access to staff facilities and benefits, and the complaints procedure.

Probation

4.44 The RRA protects all workers from unlawful discrimination or harassment on racial grounds during any probationary period.

4.45 To strengthen their legal defence in any proceedings alleging unlawful racial discrimination or harassment, employers are advised to make sure that:

a. any job plan agreed with the probationer includes:
   i. what the probationer is expected to achieve during the probation period; and
   ii. the standards by which performance will be assessed – as far as possible, these should be objectively measurable;
b. managers carry out regular supervision and keep written records of all supervision meetings held during the probation period;
c. any concerns about performance are put in writing, following discussions with the probationer, and a copy sent to the probationer and the personnel office (if the organisation has one); and
d. training on the equal opportunities policy includes guidance for managers on how to avoid judgements about a new worker based on fixed ideas of what it means to 'get on' with other members of staff, or 'fit in'.

IN THE COURSE OF EMPLOYMENT

Language in the workplace

4.46 There is a clear business interest in having a common language in the workplace, to avoid misunderstandings, with all the risks these can entail, whether legal, financial or in relation to health and safety. It is also a matter of courtesy, conducive to good working relations, not to exclude people from conversations that might concern them, when they are present. In the main, English is the language of business in Britain and is likely to be the preferred language of communication in most workplaces (see Example 15 on p 57), unless other languages are specifically required.

4.47 The situation is different in Wales, where Welsh, as an indigenous language, is protected by the Welsh Language Act 1993, and promoted by *Iaith Pawb* (*Everyone's Language*), the Welsh Assembly Government's *Action Plan for a Bilingual Wales.*

Many organisations in the public, private and voluntary sectors in Wales operate through the medium of Welsh, or bilingually in Welsh and English. It is therefore recommended that employers in Wales seek advice from the Welsh Language Board in relation to the use of Welsh in the workplace, as well as following the recommendations of this code.

4.48 However, employers should make sure that any rules, requirements, conditions, policies or practices involving the use of a particular language during or outside working hours, for example during work breaks, do not amount to unlawful racial discrimination or harassment against a worker or job applicant (see Example 7, p 22). Employers should be able to justify these as being a reasonable means of achieving a legitimate business end. Blanket rules, requirements or practices involving the use of a particular language are often unlikely to be justifiable. Even during working hours, most types of work permit casual conversation at the same time, for example while picking fruit, or filing papers. An employer who prohibits workers from talking casually to each other in a language they do not share with all colleagues, or uses occasions when this happens to trigger disciplinary or capability procedures or impede progress, may be considered to be acting unreasonably.

4.49 Employers should always consult workers, trade unions and other workplace representatives before drawing up any proposals on the use of language in the workplace.

4.50 Where the workforce includes people who are not proficient in the language of the workplace, employers should consider taking reasonable steps to improve communication (see Example I at para 4.58). These might include providing:

a. interpreting and translation facilities; for example, multilingual safety signs and notices, to make sure workers understand health and safety requirements;
b. training in language and communication skills; and
c. training for managers and supervisors on the various populations and cultures that make up Britain today.

Example 15: Language

Shah v George Grassic t/a The Suite Factory [*1995*] *DCLD 24*

An Asian worker in a furniture factory (where there were eight Asians in a workforce of 40) came out of a disciplinary meeting onto the shop floor and, in the owner's presence, began to speak to other Asian workers in their own language. The owner instructed him to speak English, so that he knew what was being said. The worker refused and was warned that if he did not do as he had been instructed he would be dismissed immediately. The worker said he could speak in any language he wished and continued to ignore the instruction. He was then summarily dismissed.

The tribunal dismissed the worker's complaint that he had been discriminated against on racial grounds, and ruled that, whether or not it is discriminatory to forbid people to speak in their native language depends on the circumstances: 'If the worker had been told not to speak in his native tongue at all on any occasion at work, in any circumstances, then that, in our view, would clearly be a discriminatory instruction. . . . [but in these circumstances] It was not unreasonable for [the owner] to expect the common courtesy of being spoken to, or about, in a way in which he could understand.'

Language requirements for a job

4.51 A language requirement for a job may be indirectly discriminatory and unlawful unless it is necessary for the satisfactory performance of the job.

4.52 Under the Welsh Language Act 1993, public bodies providing services to the public in Wales must make their services available in Welsh as well as English. This means a wide range of posts in public bodies in Wales, and some in public bodies outside Wales, will need workers who can speak, write and read Welsh sufficiently well for the post in question. In some cases, this may make Welsh language skills an essential requirement for appointment, in others it may require the applicant to agree to learn the language to the required level within a reasonable period of time after appointment (see Example C, para 2.11).

Performance assessment

4.53 It is unlawful to discriminate against, or harass, a worker, on racial grounds in assessing his or her performance.

4.54 To strengthen their legal defence in any proceedings alleging unlawful racial discrimination, employers need to make sure that performance assessments are not used to pass judgements about the person, based on assumptions about their capabilities as members of certain racial groups. Employers will find it helpful to base all assessments on actual performance of specific tasks, measured by impartial and objective standards. This is particularly important when performance is linked to promotion or a benefit, such as pay or bonuses (see Example 16, p 59).

4.55 It is recommended that training courses for managers on the equal opportunities policy (see para 3.20) should include guidance on objective performance assessment. Equally, any training on assessment methods should take the organisation's equal opportunities policy fully into account.

4.56 To be sure workers are being assessed fairly, and consistently, employers will find it helpful to monitor the results of performance assessments, by racial group (see paras 3.25–3.31), and use the data to inform their review of the organisation's policies, procedures and practices in this area. any significant disparities in assessment marks between racial groups should be investigated, and steps taken to deal with possible causes.

Example 16: Performance assessment

Nasr v Salisbury Health Care NHS Trust, Case No. 3102492/99

A consultant of Egyptian origin was not awarded a discretionary point to take his salary above the standard, whereas his 12 colleagues, who were white and of British origin, had each been awarded at least one point. The tribunal upheld his claim of unlawful direct discrimination. It found that the members of the discretionary points committee did not independently record their assessment of each of the candidates against the appropriate criteria and guidelines. Nor were any notes kept of the discussions or the assessment process. The tribunal concluded that 'such a high level of subjectivity is anathema to the successful application of equal opportunity guidelines, since it works to the disadvantage of ethnic minorities, both in operation and perception'. The complainant was awarded £18,000 in exemplary damages.

- **Example** H. A large-scale study of appraisal in 13 civil service departments in 2000 found that staff from white racial groups were consistently awarded higher marks than staff from other racial groups. This was true across grades, age groups, and length-of-service bands. The researchers found no evidence of significant differences in education or training between the groups that were likely to affect performance. Interviews with staff from all racial groups revealed common concerns about the appraisal system itself. Staff from 'non-white' groups were concerned that their performance reviews and appraisal markings reflected stereotyped attitudes about their racial groups. The researchers produced reports and made recommendations for each department. Departments are now acting on these and are themselves monitoring appraisal results and carrying out further investigations and analyses, for example of the language used in appraisal reports, depending on the racial groups concerned.

Training and development

4.57 It is unlawful for employers to discriminate against, or harass, a person, on racial grounds, in the arrangements they make for training, transfer and other development opportunities, or by deliberately refusing to make these available to all workers (see Example 17, p 60). The RRA permits some exceptions, including an exception for training provided as part of a positive action initiative (see paras 3.43–3.45 and Appendix 1).

4.58 Employers should consider adopting a policy on training, transfer and development, linked to the organisation's business plan (if it has one), and based on regularly updated audits of workers' skills and training needs. The policy should describe the range of development opportunities open to all staff, such as mentoring and shadowing schemes, and to any support its staff will receive.

Example 17: Training and development

Bath v Bedfordshire County Council, Case No. 36632/91** [**1993**] **DCLD 17

An Asian careers officer found that, although he had been employed to spend one-third of his time counselling pupils about careers, the council refused to let him do this, because he did not have a diploma in careers guidance. No qualifications had been specified in either the job advertisement or the job description. Three years later, five candidates – two white, and three Asian or African Caribbean – were interviewed for one place on a diploma course. The Asian officer was the best qualified academically and the successful white candidate the least qualified. The tribunal ruled that the interviews had been conducted 'for the sake of form' and that the result was a foregone conclusion that amounted to unlawful racial discrimination.

- **Example I.** Employers might consider providing language training for workers whose language skills are weak. Even when their skills are adequate for the job they are doing, a better command of the language will open the door to better career prospects. Good communication in the workplace also improves overall efficiency, and health and safety, and contributes to better understanding between workers from all racial groups as well as between managers and workers and their representatives.

4.59 To help avoid claims of unlawful discrimination or harassment on racial grounds, it is recommended that employers ensure that managers and supervisors responsible for selecting workers for training and other development opportunities are themselves trained to:

a. understand their legal responsibilities under the RRA, and how the organisation's equal opportunities policy applies to matters of training and career development;
b. recognise workers' training needs, regardless of racial group;
c. encourage all workers to apply for training and other development opportunities, so that no one is overlooked as a result of subjective judgements about their abilities as members of particular racial groups;
d. monitor the take-up of training and other development opportunities, by racial group, and take steps to deal with any significant disparities in take-up between racial groups;
e. regularly review the selection criteria for training and other development opportunities, to make sure they are not potentially discriminatory on racial grounds; and
f. advertise all training and other development opportunities as widely as possible throughout the organisation, for example, through notice boards, and internal websites and bulletins.

Promotion

4.60 It is unlawful for employers to discriminate against, or harass, workers on racial grounds in the way they make opportunities for promotion available, or by refusing or deliberately failing to make them available (see Example 18 below).

4.61 It is recommended that all promotion opportunities, including development opportunities that could lead to permanent promotion, should be advertised widely throughout the organisation, and filled in line with the organisation's equal opportunities and recruitment policies and procedures. This would mean using the organisation's standard job application form (if it has one) to fill all promotion and development opportunities, and making sure that selection is based strictly on demonstrable merit.

Example 18: Promotion

Dr Halim v Moray College, Case No. S/200267/02

The complainant, who was a lecturer at a college in Scotland, was twice overlooked for promotion, even though he was better qualified than those who were promoted. He believed this was because he had complained to the college principal that his line manager was racist and that he had given him unfair appraisals. The principal had advised the complainant to raise the matter directly with his line manager.

There were nine applicants for the first post, including the complainant and his line manager, and the panel included the principal. The principal's sole comment on the complainant was 'This man's not for shortlisting'. At the tribunal hearing, he said he did not consider the application to be 'a serious one' and thought it was all 'part of a sad ruse'. The complainant's line manager was appointed to the post. The panel for the second promotion included the complainant's line manager and the principal and deputy principal. This time he was rejected because the panel said he did not meet some of the essential criteria. The principal also told the tribunal that the complainant 'did not understand what the job was about'.

The tribunal found the college's explanations unconvincing. In upholding the complainant's claim, it took into account the following: unlike the shortlisted candidates, the complainant had met some of the essential criteria; the panel members had been aware of the complainant's grievance; and the person who was the subject of the grievance had been a member of the panel. The tribunal awarded £14,000 in damages.

4.62 Employers should avoid by-passing their recruitment procedures, unless a temporary promotion is absolutely necessary. In this case, the promotion should last no longer than the time needed to fill the post permanently, and openly, through the organisation's recruitment procedures.

4.63 Employers will find it helpful to build the following guidelines into their policies and procedures for promotion and career development.

a. Where posts are advertised internally and externally, the same selection procedures and criteria should apply to both internal and external candidates. Discussions about candidates, particularly internal candidates, should not be based on rumours or unsubstantiated opinions.

b. As far as possible, selection decisions based on performance assessments should be endorsed by the organisation's personnel department (if it has one).

c. No assumptions should be made about the eligibility of staff, based on their grade, current post or racial group, and information about all promotion and other development opportunities that could lead to permanent promotion, such as deputising and secondments, should be communicated to all staff; restricting applications for promotion and other development opportunities to staff at a particular grade or level could indirectly discriminate against some racial groups.

d. Records should be kept, by racial group, of who is taking up different types of opportunities, and who is not (see paras 3.25–3.31); who is successful, and who is not.

4.64 As part of their equal opportunities review of the recruitment process, employers should use the monitoring data on promotions to see if there are significant disparities between racial groups in the take-up of promotion and other development opportunities, success rates and length of time spent at a particular grade. If disparities are found, employers should investigate the possible causes in each case and take steps to remove any barriers.

Discipline and grievance

4.65 Employers must not discriminate on racial grounds in the way they respond to grievances, or invoke disciplinary measures. Disciplinary action is an extreme measure and should be taken fairly and consistently, regardless of the worker's racial group. Equally, allegations of racial discrimination or harassment must always be taken seriously and investigated promptly, not dismissed as 'oversensitivity' on a worker's part.

4.66 All employers (irrespective of their size) must now have minimum statutory procedures in place for dealing with dismissal, disciplinary action and grievances in the workplace (section 3 of the Employment Rights Act 1996, as amended by the Employment Act 2002) (see 'disciplinary procedure' and 'grievance procedure' in the glossary at Appendix 7, and ACAS in Appendix 5). These provisions apply only to employees (see the glossary at Appendix 7).

4.67 It is in the interests of employers to attempt, wherever possible, to resolve grievances as they arise, and before they become major problems, through mediation. Grievance procedures can provide an open and fair way for complainants to make their concerns known, and for their grievances to be resolved quickly, without having to bring legal proceedings.

4.68 It is recommended that employers monitor, by racial group, the number of workers who have brought grievances or been subjected to disciplinary action (public authorities with at least 150 full-time-equivalent workers have a legal duty to do this; see paras 3.32–3.34), and the outcomes of each case. It will also be useful to be able to match the data with information about the workers' grades, their managers and the areas of the organisation where they work.

4.69 If an investigation into a grievance or disciplinary matter finds evidence that the grievance was brought in bad faith, for example, to get another worker into trouble, the employer should take steps to make sure this does not happen again, either by recommending training or taking disciplinary action against the worker in question, as appropriate. However, employers must be careful not to punish someone for having made a complaint that proves to have been unfounded, but that was made in good faith, as that could amount to unlawful victimisation (see paras 2.14–2.15).

4.70 It is recommended that, before taking disciplinary action, employers should consider the possible effect on a worker's behaviour of the following:

a. racist abuse or other provocation on racial grounds;
b. difficulty in communicating with, or understanding, colleagues; and
c. different cultural norms.

4.71 As part of their equal opportunities review, employers should use the monitoring data on grievances and disciplinary action to see if there are significant disparities between racial groups, investigate the possible causes in each case, and take steps to deal with them.

Harassment

4.72 It is unlawful for employers to engage in, or condone, unwanted conduct that will violate the dignity of workers or job applicants, or create an intimidating, hostile, degrading, offensive or humiliating atmosphere for that person (see Example 7, p 22, and Examples 19 and 20 above).

Example 19: Harassment

Milovanovic v Hebden Dyeing and Finishing Co Ltd, Case No. 29691/94 **[*1995*] *DCLD No. 24***

A Serbian worker, who had lived in Britain for over 40 years, was one of 25 workers in a dyeing company. He complained in vain of persistent harassment based on his ethnic background, especially after the war in Bosnia began. He faced comments such as 'Go back to Bosnia or wherever you belong, and fight and die like a dog instead of our lads'; and 'If all foreigners and blacks go back to their own country, we will have a better environment in this country'. He handed in his notice and brought a successful claim of direct racial discrimination against the company (see para 2.16). The complainant was awarded around £4,000 in damages.

Example 20: Harassment

Mohammed Wahid Zia v Killermont Polo Club **(*Scotland*)** ***Ltd, Case No. S/105430/2001***

A Muslim of Pakistani origin, who was employed as a part-time waiter in Glasgow, claimed that his employers, who were Indian Sikhs, harassed, humiliated and demeaned him on racial grounds, and that they also made derogatory remarks about his religion. The tribunal upheld his claims of direct racial discrimination (see para 2.16), victimisation and unfair dismissal. The application was made before 19 July 2003, when it became unlawful to treat a worker or a job applicant less favourably on grounds of religion or belief. Since then, in similar circumstances, the case could have been brought on religious as well as racial grounds. The complainant was awarded a total of around £33,000 in compensation, including £22,000 for injury to feelings.

4.73 It is recommended that employers introduce a policy for dealing with racial harassment. The policy could be part of a wider anti-harassment policy or the organisation's policies on discipline and grievance, or a policy covering dignity in the workplace. Whatever form the policy takes, it should make clear what is and what is not acceptable behaviour in the organisation (see the sample policy at Appendix 3).

4.74 To make sure the policy is effective, it is recommended that employers:

a. publicise the policy through the organisation's websites, notice boards and other forms of communication, so that all staff know about it and understand why it has been adopted, how it will work and how it affects them;

b. make both the policy for dealing with racial harassment and the equal opportunities policy standard components of all training, including induction and specialist courses; and

c. offer an informal route to resolving a grievance as well as the formal one of an investigation.

4.75 If an allegation of racial harassment or discrimination is upheld, it is in the interest of good workplace relations for the employer to make sure that:

a. the harassment has actually stopped, particularly if the parties continue to work together, and

b. the complainant is not victimised for having brought the grievance.

Dismissal and termination of employment

4.76 It is unlawful for employers to discriminate against, or harass, workers on racial grounds, by dismissing them or subjecting them to any other detriment (see Example 21 below and Example 22, p 66). Dismissal includes termination of a contract by the employer (with or without notice), and non-renewal or expiry of a fixed-term contract, unless a genuine occupational requirement applies (see para 2.36 and Appendix 1).

4.77 It is recommended that employers make sure the criteria they use for dismissal (including redundancies) are not indirectly discriminatory, and that their procedures are fair and objective, and are followed consistently.

4.78 Dismissal, or any other detriment – such as demotion or compulsory transfer – must always be fair and reasonable. Employers should make sure such decisions are based on a worker's actual performance or conduct during his or her employment, as reflected in any performance assessments. Any aptitude tests designed to select people for redundancy should be objective, and fairly and consistently administered (see paras 4.23–4.26). Wherever possible, employers should consult their workers, and trade unions and other workplace representatives, about proposed redundancies, and the criteria for selection.

Example 21: Dismissal

Birdi v Waites (1) and Waites Architecture (2), Case No. 37708/95 [1996] DCLD 30

A tribunal found that a firm of architects had a record of dismissing black and Asian professional staff after short service, and that this amounted to unlawful racial discrimination. It found that an Asian architect had been criticised without reason during his employment with the firm, marginalised and then dismissed after nine months, for poor performance. He was the third consecutive ethnic minority worker to be dismissed in under 12 months.

Example 22: Redundancy

Sahota and ORS v Shareporter Ltd, [1983] COIT 1414/148

Three sewing machinists, each with less than a year's service, claimed compensation for their selection for redundancy. Two were of Indian origin and the third was an Italian. The machine room supervisor, whose views of black and Asian workers were known to be both strong and derogatory, had made the selection.

The tribunal did not accept the company's claim that the machinists had been selected objectively, on the grounds of skill, as one of the machinists was a high bonus earner of some speed and reliability. The tribunal ruled that all three complainants had been dismissed in a redundancy situation because of their race.

4.79 Staff responsible for selecting workers for dismissal should be instructed not to discriminate on racial grounds, and trained in the organisation's equal opportunities policy, and how it might apply to dismissal and redundancy.

4.80 Workers who are eligible for redeployment should be given the chance to show they have the skills or abilities required in alternative jobs. Employers should use their normal recruitment policy to fill these jobs.

4.81 It is recommended that employers monitor all dismissals, by racial group (see also paras 3.25 and 3.31). They will find it useful to be able to match this data with information about the workers' grades, the areas of the organisation where they work, and their managers.

4.82 As well as the guidelir ~s proposed in relation to disciplinary action (see paras 4.65–4.71), employers will find it helpful to:

a. make sure the decision to dismiss is not made by one individual, but, as far as possible, in discussion with a senior member of staff in the personnel department (if the organisation has one);
b. keep written records of all decisions to dismiss; and
c. encourage leavers to give feedback about their employment.

4.83 Employers should use the monitoring data to see if policies, procedures or practices that might have been criticised in the feedback could be contributing to any significant disparities between racial groups, for example in performance ratings or promotion.

RESPONSIBILITIES TO FORMER EMPLOYEES [Section 27A of the RRA]

4.84 It is unlawful for employers to discriminate against, or harass, former workers, on racial grounds.

- **Example J**. Employers will find themselves in a stronger position, should they face legal proceedings under the RRA, if they can show that they gave their staff clear guidance on supplying references to former workers. References need to be true and accurate, and give a fair representation of the worker's performance, based on evidence of the work they actually did, and not on rumours or assumptions based on their racial group. Best practice would consist of giving the worker a copy of the reference.

Core Principles of Reasonable Behaviour

- Use procedures primarily to help and encourage employees to improve rather than just as a way of imposing a punishment.
- Inform the employee of the complaint against them, and provide them with an opportunity to state their case before decisions are reached.
- Allow employees to be accompanied at disciplinary meetings.
- Make sure that disciplinary action is not taken until the facts of the case have been established and that the action is reasonable in the circumstances.
- Never dismiss an employee for a first disciplinary offence, unless it is a case of gross misconduct.
- Give the employee a written explanation for any disciplinary action taken and make sure they know what improvement is expected.
- Give the employee an opportunity to appeal.
- Deal with issues as thoroughly and promptly as possible.
- Act consistently.

Work rated as equivalent comparisons that have succeeded in the particular circumstances of the case, include:

- Where a woman and a man had been placed in the same job evaluation grade, but the employer had refused to pay the woman (who had been evaluated as having fewer points) the rate for the grade.

An example of objective justification is:

- A pay system that makes an additional payment to employees working unsocial hours, in which most of the employees getting the bonus are men. Here the employer would have to show that:
  - — There is a real business need to create a system to encourage a particular group of employees to work unsociable hours, and
  - — The additional payments meet that need, and
  - — The payments are an effective way of meeting that need, and do not go beyond what is necessary to achieve it (i.e. without the payment, the extra work would not be done, and the payment is only made when the workers actually do the work).

Equal value comparisons that have succeeded in the particular circumstances of the case, include:

- Cooks and carpenters
- Speech therapists and clinical psychologists
- Kitchen assistants and refuse workers.

Like work comparisons that have succeeded, in the particular circumstances of the case, include:

- Male and female cleaners doing 'wet' and 'dry' cleaning in different locations on the same site
- A woman cook preparing lunches for directors and a male chef cooking breakfast, lunch and tea for employees.

Appendix 4
Financial Information

Income Tax Rates

Current only shown	2003/04 £	2004/05 £	2005/06 £	2006/07 £	2007/08 £
Lower rate (10%)	0–1,960	0–2,020	0–2,090	0–2,150	0-2,230
Basic rate (22%)	1,961–30,500	2,021–31,400	2,091–32,400	2,151–33,300	2,231–34,600
Higher rate (40%)	30,500+	31,400+	32,400+	33,300 +	34, 600+

Current only shown	2008/09£	2009/10£
Basic rate (20%)*	0–34,800	0–37,400
Higher rate (40%)*	34,800+	0–37,400+

* From 2008–09, there is a 10 per cent starting rate for savings income only, with a limit of £2,320. If an individual's taxable non-savings income is above this limit then the 10 per cent starting rate for savings will not apply. There are no changes to the 10 per cent dividend ordinary rate or the 32.5 per cent dividend upper rate. For 2009–10 the 10 per cent limit for savings income will be increased to £2,440.

Personal Allowances and Reliefs

	2003/04 £	2004/05 £	2005/06 £	2006/07 £
Single person	4,615	4,745	4,895	5,035
Married couple's allowance	2,150	2,210	2,280	2,350
Additional personal allowance for children (TA 1988, s 259, as amended)	—	—	—	—
Children's tax credit	—	—	—	—

	2007/08 £	2008/09 £	2009/10 £
Personal allowance	5,225	6,035	6,475
Personal allowance for people aged 65–74 (1)	7,550	9,030	9,490
Personal allowance for people aged 75 and over (1)	7,690	9,180	9,640
Married couple's allowance (born before 6th April 1935 but aged under 75) (1) (2)	6,285	6,535	n/a
Married couple's allowance – aged 75 and over (1) (2)	6,365	6,625	6,965
Income limit for age-related allowances	20,900	21,800	22,900
Minimum amount of married couple's allowance	2,440	2,540	2,670
Blind person's allowance	1,730	1,800	1,890

NI Contributions

Employers' Rates

2003/2004		2004/2005		2005/2006		2006/2007		2007/2008	
Below £77	Nil	Below £79	Nil	Below £82	Nil	Below £84	Nil	Below £87	Nil
£77–£89	0%	£79–£91	0%	£82–£94	0%	£84–97	0%	£87–100	0%
£91.01–£610	12.8%	£94.01–£630	12.8%			£97.01–645	12.8%	£100–670	12.8%
£610+	12.8%	£630+	12.8%			£645+	12.8%	£670+	12.8%

2008-2009		**2009-2010**	
Below £90	Nil	Below £95	Nil
£90–£105	0%	£95–110	0%
£105–770	12.8%	£110–844	12.8%
£770+	12.8%	£844+	12.8%

Employees' Standard Rates

2003/2004		2004/2005		2005/2006		2006/2007		2007/2008	
First £89	Nil	First £91	Nil	First £94	Nil	First £97	Nil	First £100	Nil
£89–£595	11%	£91–£610	11%	£94–£630	11%	£97–645	11%	£100–670	11%
								£670+	1%

2008/2009		2009/2010	
First £105	Nil	First £110	Nil
£105–770	11%	£770+	1%
£110–844	11%	£844+	1%

Note: For years prior to 2003/04, 2004/05, 2005/06, 2007/08, 2008/09 and 2009/10 the contracted-out rebate was 1.0%.

Employees' Class 2 Contributions

2003/04	2004/05	2005/06	2006/07	2007/08	2008/09	2009/10
£2.00	£2.05	£2.10	£2.10	£2.20	£2.30	£2.40

Appendix 4 Financial Information

Main Social Security Benefits

Jobseeker's Allowance (updated in April)

Rate for adult dependants in brackets

2003/04	2004/05	2005/06	2006/07	2007/08	2008/09	2009/10
£54.65 (25+yr-olds)	£55.65 (25+yr-olds)	£56.20 (25+yr-olds)	£57.45 (25+yr-olds)	£59.15 (25+yr-olds)	£60.50 (25+yr-olds)	£64.30 (25+yr-olds)
£43.25 (18–24 yr-olds)	£44.05 (18–24 yr-olds)	£44.50 (18–24 yr-olds)	£45.50 (18–24 yr-olds)	£46.85 (18–24 yr-olds)	£47.95 (18–24 yr-olds)	£50.95 (18–24 yr-olds)
			£34.60 (16–17 yr-olds)	£35.65/ £46.85 (16–17 yr-olds)	£47.95 (16–17 yr-olds)	£50.95 (16–17 yr-olds)

The jobseeker's allowance came into force on 7 October 1996 and replaces both income support and unemployment benefit.

Incapacity Benefit (before 1995 known as Sickness Benefit) (updated in April)

Weeks	2003/04	2004/05	2005/06	2006/07	2007/08	2008/09	2009/10
1–28	£54.40	£55.90	£57.65	£59.20	£61.35	£63.75	£67.75
29–52	£64.35	£66.15	£68.20	£70.05	£72.55	£75.40	£80.15
52+	£72.15	£74.15	£76.45	£78.50	£81.35	£84.50	£89.80

Statutory Sick Pay (updated in April)

The amount of SSP depends upon the level of gross earnings.

2003/04	2004/05	2005/06	2006/07	2007/08	2008/09	2009/10
£64.35	£66.15	£68.20	£70.05	£72.55	£75.40	£79.15

Statutory Maternity Pay

2003/04	2004/05	2005/06	2006/07	2007/08	2008/09	2009/10
90% of average weekly earnings for 6 weeks and then £100.00 for 20 weeks	90% of average weekly earnings for 6 weeks and then £102.80 for 20 weeks	90% of average weekly earnings for 6 weeks and then £106.00 (if lower) for 20 weeks	90% of average weekly earnings for 6 weeks and then £108.85 (if lower) for 20 weeks. For babies due on or after 1 April 2007, 90% of average weekly earnings for 6 weeks and then £108.85 (if lower) for 33 weeks	90% of average weekly earnings for 6 weeks and then £112.75 (if lower) for 33 weeks	90% of average weekly earnings for 6 weeks and then £117.18 (if lower) for 33 weeks	90% of average weekly earnings for 6 weeks and then £123.06 (if lower) for 33 weeks

AA Motoring Costs Tables 2007–2009

Motoring Costs 2007

Petrol Cars Running Costs, Basic Guide for 2007

	New car purchase price (£)				
	Up to 10,000	10,000 to 13,000	13,000 to 20,000	20,000 to 30,000	Over 30,000
Standing charges per annum (£s)					
A. Road tax	115	140	165	205	205
B. Insurance	396	445	572	764	907
C. Cost of capital	328	426	545	897	1,515
D. Depreciation at 10,000 miles/annum	1,132	1,557	2,349	3,441	5,670
E. Breakdown cover	40	40	40	40	40
TOTAL (£)	2,011	2,608	3,671	5,347	8,337
Standing charges per mile (in pence)					
at 5,000 per year	39.78	51.54	72.48	105.56	164.48
10,000	20.11	26.08	36.71	53.47	83.37
15,000	13.71	17.80	25.10	36.56	87.09
20,000	10.62	13.82	19.53	28.46	44.52
25,000	8.59	11.18	15.81	23.04	36.07
30,000	7.19	9.37	13.25	19.31	30.25
Running costs per mile (in pence)					
F. Petrol*	9.33	10.50	11.98	15.68	18.79
G. Tyres	0.5	0.65	0.99	1.62	1.88
H. Service labour costs	2.89	3.08	3.31	3.82	4.69
I. Replacement parts	1.61	1.68	1.81	2.03	2.11
J. Parking and tolls	1.8	1.8	1.8	1.8	1.8
TOTAL (PENCE)	16.13	17.71	19.89	24.95	29.27
* Unleaded petrol at 95.9 pence per litre. For each penny more or less, add or subtract	0.1	0.11	0.12	0.16	0.2
Total of Standing and Running Costs (in pence)					
Based on annual mileage of:					
5,000 miles	55.91	69.25	92.37	130.51	193.75
10,000 miles	36.24	43.79	56.60	78.42	112.64
15,000 miles	29.85	35.51	44.99	61.51	86.36
20,000 miles	26.75	31.53	39.42	53.41	73.79
25,000 miles	24.720	28.89	35.70	47.99	65.34
30,000 miles	23.33	27.08	33.14	44.26	

	New car purchase price (£)				
	Up to 10,000	10,000 to 13,000	13,000 to 20,000	20,000 to 30,000	Over 30,000
Standing charges per annum (£)					
A. Road tax	115	115	140	205	205
B. Insurance	396	445	572	764	907
C. Cost of capital	343	440	611	930	1,489
D. Depreciation at 10,000 miles/annum	1,204	1,585	2,425	3,191	4,384
E. Breakdown cover	40	40	40	40	40
TOTAL (£)	2,098	2,625	3,788	5,130	7,025
Standing charges per mile (in pence)					
5,000	41.48	51.86	74.78	101.34	138.74
10,000	20.98	26.25	37.88	51.30	7.25
15,000	14.31	17.92	25.90	35.05	48.00
20,000	11.10	13.92	20.15	27.25	37.32
25,000	8.97	11.26	16.32	22.05	30.20
30,000	7.52	9.44	13.68	18.48	25.31
Running costs per mile (in pence)					
F. Diesel*	7.38	7.61	9.00	11.40	14.38
G. Tyres	0.5	0.65	0.99	1.62	1.88
H. Service labour costs	2.61	2.96	3.27	3.82	5.11
I. Replacement parts	1.9	11.76	1.98	2.23	2.3
J. Parking and tolls	1.8	1.8	1.8	1.8	1.8
TOTAL (PENCE)	14.19	14.78	17.04	20.87	25.47
* Diesel fuel at 96.8 pence per litre. For each penny more or less, add or subtract:					
	0.08	0.08	0.09	0.12	0.15
Total of Standing and Running Costs (in pence)					
Based on annual mileage of:					
5,000 miles	55.67	66.64	91.82	122.21	164.21
10,000 miles	35.17	41.03	54.92	72.17	95.72
15,000 miles	28.50	32.70	42.94	55.92	73.47
20,000 miles	25.29	28.70	37.19	48.12	62.78
25,000 miles	23.16	26.04	33.35	42.92	55.67
30,000 miles	21.71	24.22	30.71	39.35	50.78

Quick Reference Guide

How our costs are calculated

We base our standing and running costs on various sources of information. The following are the sort of things that we bear in mind.

Breakdown cover

The initial figure provided in all the guides is based on the cost of Option 100 for an individual not paying by continuous payment.

Claiming mileage

How much your employer will give you for mileage depends on the employer. The Inland Revenue operates an Approved Mileage Allowance Payment (AMAP) system. Prices in our tables include VAT.

More information

Contact your tax office
Websites: http://www.inlandrevenue.gov.uk/cars/fuel_company_cars.htm
http://www.inlandrevenue.gov.uk/cars/using_own.htm

Cost of capital

This sum represents the loss of income from the owner having money tied up in a vehicle, which otherwise could be earning interest in a deposit account. It is calculated at 4.75% of the average value for the car-size group. Any further charges for a loan or hire purchase will be on top of this.

Depreciation

Cars lose their values at different rates depending on make, age, mileage, and condition, etc. The tables assume that depreciation costs are averaged over five years from purchase, and include typical adjustments for the different annual mileage in that period. Older cars generally depreciate at a slower rate than when they were brand new.

Fuel

- The price of fuel used is the UK average value from our fuel price report.
- The fuel consumption figures used are typical for each of the car groups listed.

Insurance

For cars, the value displayed is an average cost for a fully comprehensive policy with 60% no-claims discount.

Parking and tolls

Car parking and toll payments are based on a national average. But you may pay more or less depending on how much you use your car.

Road tax

- The value displayed on the basic guides assumes that the car was first registered after March 2001 and is the average in each price group.
- See our Road Tax Calculator for more information on Variable Vehicle Excise Duty (VED) which links new car road tax to CO_2 emissions and applies to cars first registered on or after 1 March 2001.

Replacement parts

The replacement parts included cover those likely to be needed under normal driving conditions, such as brake materials, timing belts, batteries, filters, oils, bulbs, and hoses.

Service labour costs

The labour costs cover normal servicing and parts replacement at a dealer, taking average UK labour rates for each of the car-cost groups concerned.

Tyres

The figure used is based on an estimated tyre life of 20,000 miles. Different values are used depending on the engine size or price band.

[Please note that the Automobile Association stopped producing Motoring Cost figures for Mopeds, Motorcycles, and Scooters from 2004 onwards.]

Motoring Costs 2008

Petrol Cars Running Costs, Basic Guide for 2008

	Cost new (£s)				
	Up to 10,000	10,000 to 13,000	13,000 to 20,000	20,000 to 30,000	Over 30,000
Standing charges per annum (£s)					
Road tax	120.0	145.0	170.0	210.0	400.0
Insurance	420.0	472.0	606.0	810.0	961.0
Cost of capital	401.0	578.0	806.0	1245.0	1835.0
Depreciation (at 10,000 miles/ annum)	1097.0	1636.0	2486.0	3247.0	7099.0
Breakdown cover	44.0	44.0	44.0	44.0	44.0
Total (£s)	2082.00	2875.00	4112.00	5556.00	10339.00
Standing charges per mile (pence)					
5,000	41.20	56.84	81.24	109.82	203.94
10,000	20.82	28.75	41.12	55.56	103.39
15,000	14.17	19.60	28.07	37.91	70.82
20,000	10.96	15.20	21.80	29.40	55.24
25,000	8.86	12.28	17.64	23.78	44.76
30,000	7.42	10.29	14.78	19.93	37.54
Running costs per mile (pence)					
Petrol*	12.04	12.86	15.13	17.97	21.62
Tyres	0.52	0.68	1.03	1.68	1.96
Service labour costs	3.2	2.94	2.79	2.91	3.22
Replacement parts	1.67	1.75	1.88	3.03	3.35
Parking and tolls	1.8	1.8	1.8	1.8	1.8
Total (pence)	19.23	20.03	22.63	27.39	31.95
* Unleaded petrol @ 118.2p/litre. For every penny more or less, add or subtract	0.1	0.11	0.13	0.15	0.18
Total of standing charges and running costs (in pence) based on annual mileage of					
5,000 miles	60.43	76.87	103.87	137.21	235.89
10,000 miles	40.05	48.78	63.75	82.95	135.34
15,000 miles	33.40	39.63	50.70	65.30	102.77
20,000 miles	30.19	35.22	44.43	56.79	87.20
25,000 miles	28.09	32.31	40.27	51.17	66.71
30,000 miles	26.65	30.32	37.41	47.32	69.49

Diesel Car Running Costs, Basic Guide for 2008

	Cost new (£s)				
	Up to 10,000	10,000 to 13,000	13,000 to 20,000	20,000 to 30,000	Over 30,000
Standing charges per annum (£s)					
Road tax	35.0	120.0	170.0	210.0	400.0
Insurance	420.0	472.0	606.0	210.0	961.0
Cost of capital	468.0	582.0	829.0	1170.0	2061.0
Depreciation (at 10,000 miles/ annum)	1,202.0	1,858.0	2,410.0	3,156.0	5,461.0
Breakdown cover	44.0	44.0	44.0	44.0	44.0
Total (£s)	2,169.00	3,076.00	4,059.00	5,390.00	8,927.00
Standing charges per mile (pence)					
5,000	42.90	60.78	80.22	106.54	176.36
10,000	21.69	30.76	40.59	53.90	89.27
15,000	14.78	21.00	27.70	36.77	60.97
20,000	11.44	16.31	21.50	28.53	47.36
25,000	9.25	13.20	17.39	23.08	38.33
30,000	7.75	11.06	14.57	19.33	32.12
Running costs per mile (pence)					
Diesel*	9.43	10.09	13.01	14.13	18.98
Tyres	0.52	0.68	1.03	1.68	1.96
Service labour costs	2.75	2.71	2.79	2.79	4.33
Replacement parts	1.98	1.83	2.06	2.32	2.39
Parking and tolls	1.8	1.8	1.8	1.8	1.8
Total (pence)	16.48	17.11	20.69	22.72	29.46
* Diesel @ 131.6p/litre. For every penny more or less, add or subtract	0.07	0.08	0.1	0.11	0.14
Total of standing charges and running costs (in pence)					
Based on annual mileage of					
5,000 miles	59.38	77.89	100.91	129.26	205.82
10,000 miles	38.17	47.87	61.28	76.62	118.73
15,000 miles	31.26	38.11	48.39	59.50	90.42
20,000 miles	27.93	33.42	42.19	51.25	76.82
25,000 miles	25.73	30.31	38.08	45.80	67.79
30,000 miles	24.23	28.17	35.27	42.06	61.58

Quick Reference Guide

How our costs are calculated

We base our standing and running costs on various sources of information. The following are the sort of things that we bear in mind.

Breakdown cover

The figure shown is based on the cost of Roadside annual vehicle based cover.

Claiming mileage

How much your employer will give you for using your own car for company business depends on the employer and is a matter for negotiation as circumstances vary. The Inland Revenue operates an Approved Mileage Allowance Payment (AMAP) system. Prices in our tables include VAT.

More information

Contact your tax office
websites: http://www.inlandrevenue.gov.uk/cars/fuel_company_cars.htm
http://www.hmrc.gov.uk/mileage/index.htm

Cost of capital

This sum represents the loss of income from the owner having money tied up in a vehicle, which otherwise could be earning interest in a deposit account. This year we used the AA's online saving rate of 5.99 per cent in conjunction with the average value for the cars chosen for each cost group.
Any further charges for a loan or hire purchase will be on top of this.

Depreciation

Cars lose value at different rates depending on make, age, mileage and condition etc. The tables assume that depreciation costs are averaged over four years from purchase, and include typical adjustments for the different annual mileage in that period. Older cars generally depreciate at a slower rate than when brand new.
We use various depreciation rates for mileages which differ from the average 10 000 miles per annum.

Fuel

- The price of fuel used is the UK average value from our fuel price report.
- The fuel consumption figures used are typical for each of the car groups listed.

Insurance

The value displayed is a UK average cost for a fully comprehensive policy with 60% no-claims discount.

Parking and tolls

Car parking and toll payments are based on a national average for an urban driver. But you may pay more or less depending on how much you use your car.

Road tax

The value displayed on the basic guides assumes that the car was first registered after March 2001 and is the average in each price group.
See our Road Tax Calculator for more information on Variable Vehicle Excise Duty (VVED) which links new car road tax to CO_2 emissions and applies to cars first registered on or after 1 March 2001.
This year we have used the band G tax rate of £400 for the most expensive cars.

Replacement parts

The replacement parts included cover those likely to be needed under normal driving conditions, such as brake materials, oils, filters, bulbs, wipers, and hoses.

Service and labour costs

The labour costs cover normal servicing and parts replacement at a dealer, taking average UK labour rates..

Tyres

The figure used is based on an estimated tyre life of 27,000 miles. Different values are used depending on the vehicle size or price band.

Prices are based on online tyre dealer prices. They are not main dealer prices - which will inevitably be higher.

Motoring Costs 2009

Petrol Cars Running Costs, Basic Guide for 2009

	Cost new (£s)				
	Up to 12,000	12,000 to 14,000	14,000 to 22,000	22,000 to 30,000	Over 30,000
Standing charges per annum (£s)					
Road tax	120.0	120.0	150.0	215.0	405.0
Insurance	379.0	397.0	485.0	619.0	892.0
Cost of capital	341.0	436.0	546.0	805.0	1512.0
Depreciation (at 10,000 miles/annum)	1284.0	1937.0	2942.0	3845.0	7794.0
Breakdown cover	42.0	42.0	42.0	42.0	42.0
Total (£s)	2166.0	2932.0	4165.0	5526.0	10645.0
Standing charges per mile (pence)					
5,000	42.81	57.87	82.12	108.98	209.78
10,000	21.66	29.32	41.65	55.26	106.45
15,000	14.78	20.06	28.55	37.87	73.05
20,000	11.47	15.63	22.30	29.55	57.12
25,000	9.28	12.66	18.07	23.95	46.32
30,000	7.78	10.61	15.16	20.09	38.86
Running costs per mile (pence)					
Petrol*	10.56	11.42	13.70	15.11	18.65
Tyres	0.95	0.79	0.78	1.14	1.68
Service labour costs	3.48	3.54	3.33	3.70	3.59
Replacement parts	1.85	2.03	2.00	2.13	2.52
Parking and tolls	1.80	1.80	1.80	1.80	1.80
Total (pence)	18.64	19.58	21.61	23.88	28.24
* Unleaded petrol @ 104.4p/litre. For every penny more or less, add or subtract	0.10	0.11	0.13	0.14	0.17
Total of standing charges and running costs (in pence) based on annual mileage of					
5,000 miles	61.45	77.44	103.74	132.86	238.02
10,000 miles	40.30	48.90	63.26	79.14	134.69
15,000 miles	33.42	39.64	50.17	61.74	101.28
20,000 miles	30.11	35.21	43.91	53.43	85.36
25,000 miles	27.92	32.24	39.69	47.82	74.56
30,000 miles	26.42	30.19	36.77	43.96	67.10

Diesel Car Running Costs, Basic Guide for 2009

	Cost new (£s)				
	Up to 12,000	12,000 to 16,000	16,000 to 24,000	24,000 to 32,000	Over 32,000
Standing charges per annum (£s)					
Road tax	120.0	120.0	150.0	215.0	405.0
Insurance	379.0	397.0	485.0	619.0	892.0
Cost of capital	371.0	477.0	629.0	922.0	1622.0
Depreciation (at 10,000 miles/annum)	1441.0	2284.0	3152.0	4114.0	8313.0
Breakdown cover	42.0	42.0	42.0	42.0	42.0
Total (£s)	2353.0	3320.0	4458.0	5912.0	11274.0
Standing charges per mile (pence)					
5,000	46.48	65.49	87.90	116.59	222.15
10,000	23.53	33.20	44.58	59.12	112.74
15,000	16.07	22.74	30.56	40.51	77.38
20,000	12.49	17.74	23.87	31.62	60.53
25,000	10.10	14.38	19.34	25.62	49.09
30,000	8.47	12.06	16.23	21.49	41.18
Running costs per mile (pence)					
Diesel*	7.92	8.68	10.34	12.08	15.31
Tyres	0.78	0.80	0.86	1.19	2.03
Service labour costs	2.79	2.82	2.69	2.99	3.12
Replacement parts	2.29	2.30	2.37	2.46	3.01
Parking and tolls	1.80	1.80	1.80	1.80	1.80
Total (pence)	15.58	16.40	18.06	20.52	25.27
* Diesel @ 105.0p/litre. For every penny more or less, add or subtract	0.07	0.08	0.10	0.11	0.14
Total of standing charges and running costs (in pence)					
Based on annual mileage of					
5,000 miles	62.06	81.89	105.96	137.12	247.43
10,000 miles	39.11	49.60	62.64	79.64	138.01
15,000 miles	31.65	39.14	48.62	61.03	102.65
20,000 miles	28.06	34.14	41.93	52.14	85.80
25,000 miles	25.68	30.78	37.40	46.15	74.36
30,000 miles	24.05	28.46	34.28	42.01	66.46

Quick Reference Guide

How our costs are calculated

We base our standing and running costs on various sources of information. The following are the sort of things that we bear in mind.

Breakdown cover

The figure shown is based on the cost of Roadside annual vehicle based cover.

Claiming mileage

How much your employer will give you for using your own car for company business depends on the employer and is a matter for negotiation as circumstances vary. The Inland Revenue operates an Approved Mileage Allowance Payment (AMAP) system.Prices in our tables include VAT.

More information

Contact your tax office
Websites: http://www.inlandrevenue.gov.uk/cars/fuel_company_cars.htm
http://www.hmrc.gov.uk/mileage/index.htm

Cost of capital

This sum represents the loss of income from the owner having money tied up in a vehicle, which otherwise could be earning interest in a deposit account. This year we used the AA's online saving rate of 1.85 per cent in conjunction with the average value for the cars chosen for each cost group. Any further charges for a loan or hire purchase will be on top of this.

Depreciation

Cars lose value at different rates depending on make, age, mileage and condition etc. The tables assume that depreciation costs are averaged over four years from purchase, and include typical adjustments for the different annual mileage in that period. Older cars generally depreciate at a slower rate than when brand new.
We use various depreciation rates for mileages which differ from the average 10 000 miles per annum.

Fuel

- The price of fuel used is the UK average value from our fuel price report.
- The fuel consumption figures used are typical for each of the car groups listed.

Insurance

The value displayed is a UK average cost for a fully comprehensive policy with 60% no-claims discount.

Parking and tolls

Car parking and toll payments are based on a national average for an urban driver. But you may pay more or less depending on how much you use your car.

Road tax

- The value displayed on the basic guides assumes that the car was first registered after March 2001 and is the average in each price group.
- See our Road Tax Calculator for more information on Variable Vehicle Excise Duty (VED) which links new car road tax to CO_2 emissions and applies to cars first registered on or after 1 March 2001.

Replacement parts

The replacement parts included cover those likely to be needed under normal driving conditions, such as brake materials, oils, filters, bulbs, wipers, and hoses.

Service and labour costs

The labour costs cover normal servicing and parts replacement at a dealer, taking average UK labour rates.

Tyres

The figure used is based on an estimated tyre life of 27,000 miles. Different values are used depending on the vehicle size or price band.
Prices are based on online tyre dealer prices. They are not main dealer prices - which will inevitably be higher.

Extract from Judicial Studies Board, *Guidelines for the Assessment of General Damages in Personal Injury Cases* (9th edn, 2008)

3 Psychiatric Damage

In part (A) of this chapter some of the brackets contain an element of compensation for post-traumatic stress disorder. This is of course not a universal feature of cases of psychiatric injury and hence a number of the awards upon which the brackets are based did not reflect it. Where it does figure any award will tend towards the upper end of the bracket.

[. . .][1]

(A) Psychiatric Damage Generally

The factors to be taken into account in valuing claims of this nature are as follows:

(i) the injured person's ability to cope with life and work;
(ii) the effect on the injured person's relationships with family, friends and those with whom he or she comes into contact;
(iii) the extent to which treatment would be successful;
(iv) future vulnerability;
(v) prognosis;
(vi) whether medical help has been sought;
(vii) (a) whether the injury results from sexual and/or physical abuse and/or breach of trust;
(b) if so, the nature of the relationship between victim and abuser, the nature of the abuse, its duration and the symptoms caused by it.

(a) Severe **£35,000 to £74,000**

In these cases the injured person will have marked problems with respect to factors (i) to (iv) above and the prognosis will be very poor.

(b) Moderately Severe **£12,250 to £35,000**

In these cases there will be significant problems associated with factors (i) to (iv) above but the prognosis will be much more optimistic than in (a) above. While there are awards which support both extremes of this bracket, the majority are somewhere near the middle of the bracket. Cases of work-related stress resulting in a permanent or long-standing disability preventing a return to comparable employment would appear to come within this category.

(c) Moderate **£3,750 to £12,250**

While there may have been the sort of problems associated with factors (i) to (iv) above there will have been marked improvement by trial and the prognosis will be good.

(d) Minor **£1,000 to £3,750**

[1] Text has been deleted to limit the material to that which is relevant to employment law claims.

Ready Reckoner for Redundancy Payments

Redundancies after 1 October 2006

Following the Employment Equality (Age) Discrimination Regulations 2006 the upper and lower limits of redundancy payments have been removed. This means that people may potentially qualify for a redundancy payment at any age, and the 'taper' payments which used to apply to employees aged 64 have been removed.

There is a limit on the amount of a week's pay that can be taken into account in working out the entitlement. The limit changes annually in line with the Retail Price Index. The limit was raised from £330 to £350 on 1 February 2009 and to £380 from 1 October 2009. This rate will continue until 1 February 2011. Calculation of entitlement where the lower reckonable period of service ended between 1 October 2009 and 1 February 2010 should therefore be subject to the £380 maximum.

To calculate the payment refer to the table at pp 916–17 to determine the number of weeks' pay the employee is entitled to. Then multiply this by the week's pay subject to the relevant statutory limit. The definition of a week's pay is set out at para 24.55.

The redundancy payment is:

- half a week's pay for every year of employment under the age of 22;
- a week's pay for every year of employment aged 22 and 40;
- one and a half week's pay for every year of employment aged 41 or over;

subject to an overall maximum of 20 years.

Further information, including an online calculator, can be found at <http://www.berr.gov.uk/whatwed/employment/employment-legislation/employment-guidance/page33157.html> (although DTI tends to change this reference from time to time, and the page can often be accessed by searching for 'BERR ready reckoner redundancy payment'.

Please note: the information contained above and on the web page is intended only as a guide and shows how statutory redundancy pay is calculated for people who are entitled to receive it. Whether or not you are entitled to redundancy pay will depend on your individual circumstances.

Table of statutory redundancy entitlement—Redundancies on or after 1.10.06

Age (years)	Service (years) 2	3	4	5	6	7	8	9	10	11	12	13	14	15	16	17	18	19	20
18	1	1½	2																
19	1	1½	2	2½															
20	1	1½	2	2½	3														
21	1	1½	2	2½	3	3½													
22	1	1½	2	2½	3	3½	4												
23	1½	2	2½	3	3½	4	4½	5											
24	2	2½	3	3½	4	4½	5	5½	6										
25	2	3	3½	4	4½	5	5½	6	6½	7									
26	2	3	4	4½	5	5½	6	6½	7	7½	8								
27	2	3	4	5	5½	6	6½	7	7½	8	8½	9							
28	2	3	4	5	6	6½	7	7½	8	8½	9	9½	10						
29	2	3	4	5	6	7	7½	8	8½	9	9½	10	10½	11					
30	2	3	4	5	6	7	8	8½	9	9½	10	10½	11	11½	12				
31	2	3	4	5	6	7	8	9	9½	10	10½	11	11½	12	12½	13			
32	2	3	4	5	6	7	8	9	10	10½	11	11½	12	12½	13	13½	14		
33	2	3	4	5	6	7	8	9	10	11	11½	12	12½	13	13½	14	14½	15	
34	2	3	4	5	6	7	8	9	10	11	12	12½	13	13½	14	14½	15	15½	16
35	2	3	4	5	6	7	8	9	10	11	12	13	13½	14	14½	15	15½	16	16½
36	2	3	4	5	6	7	8	9	10	11	12	13	14	14½	15	15½	16	16½	17
37	2	3	4	5	6	7	8	9	10	11	12	13	14	15	15½	16	16½	17	17½
38	2	3	4	5	6	7	8	9	10	11	12	13	14	15	16	16½	17	17½	18

Age (years)	Service (years) 2	3	4	5	6	7	8	9	10	11	12	13	14	15	16	17	18	19	20
39	2	3	4	5	6	7	8	9	10	11	12	13	14	15	16	17	17½	18	18½
40	2	3	4	5	6	7	8	9	10	11	12	13	14	15	16	17	18	18½	19
41	2	3	4	5	6	7	8	9	10	11	12	13	14	15	16	17	18	19	19½
42	2½	3½	4½	5½	6½	7½	8½	9½	10½	11½	12½	13½	14½	15½	16½	17½	18½	19½	20½
43	3	4	5	6	7	8	9	10	11	12	13	14	15	16	17	18	19	20	21
44	3	4½	5½	6½	7½	8½	9½	10½	11½	12½	13½	14½	15½	16½	17½	18½	19½	20½	21½
45	3	4½	6	7	8	9	10	11	12	13	14	15	16	17	18	19	20	21	22
46	3	4½	6	7½	8½	9½	10½	11½	12½	13½	14½	15½	16½	17½	18½	19½	20½	21½	22½
47	3	4½	6	7½	9	10	11	12	13	14	15	16	17	18	19	20	21	22	23
48	3	4½	6	7½	9	10½	11½	12½	13½	14½	15½	16½	17½	18½	19½	20½	21½	22½	23½
49	3	4½	6	7½	9	10½	12	13	14	15	16	17	18	19	20	21	22	23	24
50	3	4½	6	7½	9	10½	12	13½	14½	15½	16½	17½	18½	19½	20½	21½	22½	23½	24½
51	3	4½	6	7½	9	10½	12	13½	15	16	17	18	19	20	21	22	23	24	25
52	3	4½	6	7½	9	10½	12	13½	15	16½	17½	18½	19½	20½	21½	22½	23½	24½	25½
53	3	4½	6	7½	9	10½	12	13½	15	16½	18	19	20	21	22	23	24	25	26
54	3	4½	6	7½	9	10½	12	13½	15	16½	18	19½	20½	21½	22½	23½	24½	25½	26½
55	3	4½	6	7½	9	10½	12	13½	15	16½	18	19½	21	22	23	24	25	26	27
56	3	4½	6	7½	9	10½	12	13½	15	16½	18	19½	21	22½	23½	24½	25½	26½	27½
57	3	4½	6	7½	9	10½	12	13½	15	16½	18	19½	21	22½	24	25	26	27	28
58	3	4½	6	7½	9	10½	12	13½	15	16½	18	19½	21	22½	24	25½	26½	27½	28½
59	3	4½	6	7½	9	10½	12	13½	15	16½	18	19½	21	22½	24	25½	27	28	29
60	3	4½	6	7½	9	10½	12	13½	15	16½	18	19½	21	22½	24	25½	27	28½	29½
61*	3	4½	6	7½	9	10½	12	13½	15	16½	18	19½	21	22½	24	25½	27	28½	30

* The same figures should be used when calculating the redundancy payment for a person aged 61 and above.

Employment Tribunals' Guidelines on Compensation for Loss of Pension Rights (3rd edn, 2003)

I. Introduction

1.1 This is the Third Edition of this Booklet which was last edited in 1991. The original Booklet received judicial approval in *Benson v Dairy Crest Ltd* (EAT/192/89) but the Second Edition was criticised in *Clancy v Cannock Chase Technical College & Parkers* [2001] IRLR 331 where Lindsay J. President of the Employment Appeals Tribunal said:—

> The rest of Mr Clancy's appeal is dismissed for the reasons we have given but we would not wish to leave the case without adding a plea. It arises especially now that the cap is £50,000 and because full pension compensation is therefore more likely to require to be accurately computed than it was in the past. Our plea is that careful consideration needs to be given to whether the 1991 guidelines can still be relied on to give the valuable help they have done in the past or whether a fresh edition ought not to be prepared if the tribunals up and down the country are to be given the assistance they deserve in this 'most difficult element' of the calculation of loss in unfair dismissal cases.

This criticism and the removal since 1991 of any statutory limits on compensation in discrimination cases led to the formation of the present working party.

1.2 In re-drafting the previous Edition we have tried to steer a middle course between over-simplification and over-elaboration. We have come to the conclusion that a distinction has to be drawn between the normal run of tribunal cases, where the amount of compensation is limited and the pension element is, therefore, comparatively small and those few cases, many of them discrimination cases, where the sums involved are considerable.

1.3 We have, therefore, developed alternative approaches. On the one hand we have retained the method set out in the previous editions, which has received considerable support from Chairmen and, indeed, from the bodies consulted about this Booklet. We call this *the simplified approach.* Meanwhile we have added a new approach, which we call *the substantial loss approach* which will be appropriate to those cases where the tribunal is considering 'career loss' of a particular employment. This approach makes more use of actuarial tables than *the simplified approach.*

1.4 The structure of this booklet is that at Chapters 2 and 3 we make some general remarks about pensions provision. Then in Chapter 4 we set out the decisions which have to be made by tribunals in deciding which approach to take. Chapters 5 to 7 explain how assessment should be made under *the simplified approach* while Chapter 8 sets out how to make the assessment under *the substantial loss approach.*

2. State Pension Provision

2.1 The State Pension payable by the State may comprise the Basic State Pension, a Graduated Retirement Benefit and an Additional State Pension payable pursuant to the State Earnings-Related Pension Scheme (SERPS) and, from April 2002, the State Second Pension (S2P). State Pension benefits are normally payable from the State Pension age (currently 65 for males and 60 for females, although the female State Pension age will be 65 from 2020 and will be increased gradually from 60 to 65 between 2010 and 2020 for those born between 1950 and 1955—see Appendix 3 Table 3.1).

The Basic State Pension

2.2 This pension is flat-rate and therefore independent of earnings levels. Provided that certain contribution requirements are met, the Basic State Pension is payable to everyone over State Pension age, with the amount depending on the number of contributions paid or credited.

Graduated Retirement Benefit

2.3 Graduated Retirement Benefit (GRB) is based on the amount of graduated National Insurance contributions paid by the employer and employee in the period between April 1961 and April 1975. The amount of an individual's GRB varies according to the number of units of graduated contributions paid by them. GRB payments are usually very modest and will soon cease to be of any significance for people in the active labour force.

The State Earnings-Related Pension Scheme ('SERPS')

2.4 This pension is earnings-related and varies according to an individual's earnings in respect of which he has paid full National Insurance contributions as an employee between April 1978 and March 2002. This is also called 'Additional State Pension'. It was based on earnings between the Lower Earnings Limit and the Upper Earnings Limit (£72 per week and £575 per week respectively in 2001–02, the last year in which SERPS benefits accrued).

State Second Pension ('S2P')

2.5 Following the enactment of the Child Support, Pensions and Social Security Act 2000, SERPS benefits ceased to accrue from April 2002 and were replaced from that date by the State Second Pension (S2P). Initially, the benefits accruing to employees earning less than £25,600 (in 2003–04, and increasing thereafter) will be higher under S2P than they would under SERPS. However, for those reaching State Pension age after a date yet to be specified, it is expected that the benefit payable will effectively become a flat-rate benefit.

Minimum Income Guarantee and Pension Credits

2.6 Currently, people aged 60 or over on low incomes and with savings of less than £12,000 have their income increased to the minimum income guarantee. From October 2003 the Minimum Income Guarantee will be replaced by the Pension Credit. This will guarantee the same minimum income of £102 per week for single pensioners and £156 per week for a couple (in 2003–04 terms). However, in addition, where pensioners have income from other sources, the 'clawback' will be at a rate of 40%, rather than the 100% used with the Minimum Income Guarantee. Thus, pensioners with modest savings will not lose one pound of benefit for every pound of pensions or other savings they have built up. From age 65 people with incomes up to around £139 a week (£204 for couples) will receive some benefit through the operation of Pension Credit. These limits will be increased annually.

Contracting Out

2.7 Since its introduction in 1978 it has been possible for employers to contract out of SERPS those employees who are members of a final salary occupational pension scheme which satisfies certain criteria. National Insurance contributions payable in respect of employees who are members of such a scheme which is contracted-out are paid at a lower rate than that payable for employees not in such a scheme (employers also pay National Insurance contributions at a reduced rate).

2.8 Before April 1997, a final salary scheme which was contracted-out had to provide a Guaranteed Minimum Pension ('GMP') as a substitute for the Additional State Pension. The GMP was broadly equivalent to the Additional State Pension paid under SERPS and was the minimum amount of occupational pension that must be paid from a contracted-out final salary scheme. Often such a scheme would provide benefits that were higher than and additional to the GMP. For service prior to 6 April 1997 it is possible for someone who had been contracted-out to build up rights to a partial Additional State Pension as well as their Basic State Pension and the pension from the contracted-out scheme.

2.9 GMPs no longer accrue for service after 6 April 1997. From that date, final salary schemes wishing to contract out have to pass a Reference Scheme Test (RST). This requires that the pensions provided by the scheme are broadly equivalent to, or better than, those required by the RST.

2.10 Employees who have served all their pensionable service as members of a contracted-out scheme will receive the Basic State Pension paid by the State as well as a pension from the contracted-out scheme. When the State Pension is paid, the Basic State Pension and Additional State Pension have an inflation protection element built into them. While an employee is still employed, any accrued GMP element increases broadly in line with wage inflation. For pension relating to the tax years 1988–89 and later, the GMP element of the retired employee's pension after retirement will be increased in line with price inflation, subject to an upper limit of 3% per annum. Where inflation exceeds that amount any excess will be paid by the State through increasing the Additional Pension.

2.11 From 6 April 1988 it has been possible for occupational money purchase schemes to be contracted-out of SERPS. Since July 1988 individual employees have been able to make their own arrangements to purchase an Appropriate Personal Pension and use this to opt out of SERPS and/or their employer's pension scheme. In this case both the employer and the employee pay the full rate National Insurance contributions and at the end of the tax year to which the contributions relate, the Inland Revenue pays an age-related rebate (which increases with age) direct to the pension scheme for investment on behalf of the employee. Since April 2001 employees have also been able to use a stakeholder pension to contract out of SERPS.

2.12 As with SERPS, it is possible to contract out of the new S2P either by means of an occupational or personal pension scheme or with a stakeholder pension.

Potential Loss

2.13 Accrual of State Pension benefits may be interrupted if an employee is out of work, although credits are available for the Basic State Pension whilst in receipt of Jobseekers Allowance or Income Support and some credits are available for S2P. Assuming that an employee is re-employed without too long a delay, the loss of Basic State Pension arising from dismissal is likely to be nil or relatively small. Thus we recommend the assumption that there is no loss of Basic State Pension in respect of a dismissed employee. The onus will then be on him or her to show otherwise.

2.14 The Working Party have, however, identified a new area of potential loss which arises when an employee who is not in a contracted out occupational or personal pension scheme is dismissed. Where a dismissed employee is not in a pension scheme or is in a scheme which is not contracted out, he is liable to lose the Second State Pension element for the period that he is out of work. The full method of calculating this is set out in section 7.5 and Appendix 3.

3. Occupational Pension Schemes

3.1 Occupational pension schemes fall into two main categories: final salary (otherwise known as defined benefit) and money purchase (otherwise known as defined contribution). An increasing number of schemes are a mixture of the two but it will usually be possible to calculate the two elements separately.

Final Salary Schemes

3.2 These are schemes where the amount of pension paid is based not on the contributions made by the employer or the employee, but on a proportion of the earnings of the employee for each year of service (e.g. 10/60ths of final salary after 10 years in the company pension scheme).

Example:
A joined the company scheme in 1980. He retires in 2000 and his salary in the year before his retirement is £30,000 p.a. The pension from the scheme is based on 1/60th of his final year's salary for each year. Therefore his annual pension will be 20/60ths of his final year's salary, i.e. £10,000 p.a.

3.3 In most cases the employee makes a contribution of a fixed percentage of his income into the fund throughout his employment. The employer usually agrees to make contributions to the fund at least matching those made by the employees but such as to ensure that the benefit costs are met. There is usually little difficulty in establishing the contributions currently made by the employer as a percentage of the total pay-roll but this may vary from year to year depending on how well the pension fund is keeping up with the demands that are likely to be made on it. Sometimes the employer may be enjoying a contribution 'holiday', with reduced, or even zero, contributions for a period. Such a temporary reduction should not be taken into account for the purposes of compensating an employee for loss of pension rights. Where there is a lack of accurate evidence, or where the current contribution position is anomalous, the Government Actuary advises that on average the overall standard contribution for a good scheme is 20% of the pay-roll, made up, in a contributory scheme, as to 15% from the employer and 5% from the employee. It is important to note that the employer's contribution is not earmarked for the pension of any individual employee and the pension that an employee actually receives will not necessarily be proportional to his and the company's contributions.

3.4 On the face of it non-funded schemes (particularly publicly financed schemes like the Principal Civil Service Pension Scheme) might seem to be different from normal final salary schemes because, as there is no fund, there is no need for contributions to be paid in advance to meet the accruing benefits and benefits could just be paid as they arise. However, an appropriate level of employer contributions is usually fixed by the scheme's actuary as though they were funded and should be easily obtainable. These non-funded schemes, therefore, can be treated in the same way as any other final salary scheme. It should be noted, however, that they tend to be more generous in the way in which they increase as a deferred pension before retirement and as a pension in payment during retirement. Typically public service schemes increase by the full percentage increase in the cost of living index whereas private schemes are only obliged to increase up to 5%. In a period of low inflation this may be seen as a minor issue.

3.5 Not all final salary schemes use the same pension fraction. However, by far the most common fraction in the private sector is 1/60th of final salary per year of service and most public sector schemes have a fraction of 1/80th but also provide a tax-free lump sum benefit equivalent to three years' pension payments. Members of private sector schemes usually have the right to give up part of their pension in return for a tax-free lump sum of a similar amount to that provided by public sector schemes. Taking this into account, a private sector scheme with 1/60th benefits can be roughly equivalent to a public sector scheme with 1/80th benefits. Some schemes use the best of the employee's last few years for the calculation of final salary; others may use the average of the last few years or even a career average, which may be substantially less favourable to the employee. However, the essence of a final salary scheme is that the employee's pension is based on his earnings and length of service and not directly on what the employee or the employer have contributed to the fund.

3.6 'Additional Voluntary Contributions' (AVCs) have existed for many years and employers offering occupational final salary schemes must allow them to be made, if the employee wants to top up the company pension. AVCs usually operate on a money purchase basis, even where the main scheme is a final salary scheme. As such they should be treated in the same way as company money purchase schemes (see 3.9 below). However, some schemes (mainly public sector) allow employees to buy extra years. If this has been done the additional years already bought will be put into the equation of loss of final salary pension rights as if the employee had actually worked those extra years.

3.7 AVCs are usually made by the employee alone. They, therefore, have no significant bearing when future loss of pension rights comes to be considered, unless the employer was making some contribution towards their cost. They are not 'portable', however, and the loss of the facility to make AVCs could in some circumstances be regarded as a financial loss to the individual, where they were relying on being able to top up their pension in this way. Any loss is likely to be in the form of additional charges paid out to the pension provider in setting up a replacement scheme.

3.8 'Free-Standing Additional Voluntary Contributions' (FSAVCs), introduced in October 1987, are in effect separate and, therefore, 'portable' money purchase plans and should be dealt with as Appropriate Personal Pension plans. There will be no loss to be taken into account unless the employer was contributing towards the cost.

Money Purchase Schemes

Company Money Purchase Schemes:

3.9 These are quite different from final salary schemes. The pension payable is directly related to the contributions made by the employer and the employee to the fund over the years. In the past they gave inadequate compensation for the effect of inflation and became unpopular, but there is a move back to them, because they enable the employer to know exactly how much the scheme will cost each year and to budget accordingly, whereas a final salary scheme may be an open-ended commitment.

Example:
A joined the company in 1982. He retires in 2002. Over the 20 years he and his employers have contributed £20,000 to the scheme, but let us say that the accumulated contributions are now worth £50,000. For this, on annuity rates current at the time of writing, a pension of about £3,600 per annum can be provided. The amount of the pension, of course, varies not only according to the success of the investment policy but also with the age and the sex of the annuitant, whether dependants' benefits are also purchased and the interest rates current at the date of retirement.

Personal pension plans including individual life insurance backed schemes:

3.10 The idea of these plans, very simply, is that the employee and the employer or either of them makes contributions to a private pension policy with an insurance company or other pensions provider of the employee's choice. On retirement the employee then receives an annuity based on the value of his personalised fund. The main difference between these plans and company money purchase schemes is that it is usually the employee and not the employer who decides where the money is to be invested. Whilst employers are required to contribute to occupational plans, this is not the case in respect of personal pensions. Appropriate Personal Pension plans can also be used to contract out of SERPS and S2P.

3.11 FSAVCs are a form of personalised plan designed as a private top up for employees in company pension schemes (see paragraph 3.8).

Stakeholder pensions:

3.12 Stakeholder pensions were introduced under the Welfare Reform and Pensions Act 1999 with the aim of encouraging private pension provision. Stakeholder pension schemes provide money purchase benefits only, but the employer is not required to contribute to the arrangement. All employers must provide access to a stakeholder scheme for their employees unless there are fewer than 5 employees or the employer already offers a suitable pension scheme. Although this means that it is likely that an increasing proportion of employees will have access to a pension scheme of some sort, there may not be any increase in the number of cases of loss of pension rights on dismissal, since it is unlikely that all employers will contribute to stakeholder pension plans.

Life Assurance Cover

3.13 Many pension schemes provide, or have separate schemes associated with them to provide, life assurance benefits for their members. In appropriate cases it may be just and equitable or otherwise appropriate to compensate former employees for the loss of the benefit of belonging to such schemes by awarding as compensation the average market rate for providing equivalent cover.

4. Pension Loss—Introduction

4.1 Anyone who leaves pensionable employment before retirement is known as an 'early leaver'. Persons who are unfairly dismissed or are the victims of discrimination and lose their jobs are examples. The effect of leaving early will depend on whether the scheme is a final salary or a money purchase scheme.

4.2 With a money purchase scheme, whether company or personal, the fund built up to the date of leaving by the contributions of the employer and the employee remains invested for the employee's benefit. Accordingly, what the employee loses on dismissal is the prospective value of the further contributions that his employer would have made. As far as his own future contributions are concerned, there is no loss, since he can use the compensation awarded for lost earnings and/or any earnings in a new job to pay into a pension scheme associated with his new employment. If he is not re-employed, he should still be able to make contributions to a stakeholder pension or enjoy similar advantages from investing in an ISA.

4.3 A person dismissed who is a member of a money purchase scheme may be required to pay a penalty for leaving the scheme early. This is also a loss directly attributable to the dismissal, but it is easily quantifiable. Apart from this he does not lose any part of the current value of contributions already made by his employer and himself.

4.4 In a final salary scheme the position is much more complicated. On being dismissed the employee loses the prospective right to a pension based on his final salary. In most cases that come before the Tribunal, however, he will be entitled to a deferred pension. It is the difference between this deferred pension (including any cost of living increases and other benefits) and the pension and other benefits that he would have received had he not been unlawfully dismissed that constitutes his loss.

4.5 The applicant's loss of pension rights on dismissal is the difference between the pension he will receive in due course and the pension he would have received if he had not been dismissed. The value of the former can only be truly assessed when he dies and the value of the latter includes a number of imponderables. Although the benefit does not come into payment until the applicant retires, it is still a fringe benefit derived from the employment like a company car or private health insurance, albeit considerably more valuable once accrued.

4.6 Often the applicant has not found other employment by the date of the hearing. In this situation the tribunal is engaged in the highly speculative process of deciding when he is likely to find other employment and how much he is likely to earn if and when he does. Forecasting the likely pension, if any, in such employment is just one part of this highly speculative process, which includes deciding whether the applicant would have left his previous job anyway and whether he would have been promoted if he had not been dismissed.

4.7 The key choice to be made by the tribunal is whether to look at the whole career loss to retirement which can then be discounted to allow for the eventuality that the applicant would not have remained in the employment throughout, or to look only to the next few years and assume that by that time he will have obtained comparable employment either with a similar pension scheme or a higher salary to compensate. Tribunals have tended to find in many cases that the applicant would obtain comparable employment within a fairly short period, ranging from 3 months to 2 years. Where the likely period of unemployment was longer the tribunal would quickly find that compensation had reached the previous statutory limit of £12,000, so that assessing future loss over a period of years was largely an academic exercise. However, the increase in the limit in respect of compensatory award for unfair dismissal to £50,000 (now £53,500) and the removal of any limit in discrimination cases and some unfair dismissal cases require, where appropriate, an approach akin to that adopted in personal injury cases.

4.8 The Ogden Tables were prepared by the Government Actuary's Department for use in typical personal injury cases. They enable the courts to convert a total loss of employment continuing to retirement into a lump sum based on the annualised loss of earnings, age at trial and likely retirement age of the individual. They also include tables which assess loss where the loss of earnings is for a fixed number of years. Whilst these Tables are just a guide, they are used routinely by the courts unless there are circumstances calling for a different approach. These Tables have occasionally been used by tribunals to assess future loss of earnings whether whole or partial. The EAT in *Kingston upon Hull City Council v Dunnachie (No. 3) EAT/0848/02* have laid down guidelines for their use in that context, but have specifically excluded compensation for loss of pension rights. However, the guidelines in that case may be helpful in deciding which of the two approaches in 4.10 below to use.

4.9 In a case where the Ogden Tables are being used to assess future loss of earnings, there is a clear need for a comparable approach to pensions using similar assumptions. There may also be cases where the loss of earnings is slight and the loss of the pension is the most significant aspect of the compensation.

4.10 We consider that, in assessing future pension loss, the tribunal has to select one of two approaches, which we will call *the simplified approach* and *the substantial loss approach*. As we have indicated, the decision by the tribunal as to which approach to use will be a crucial one. It has led to considerable debate in the consultation process and the final conclusion will be a matter for the tribunal. It can, however, make a substantial difference to the amount of compensation under this heading.

4.11 *The simplified approach* is set out in Chapters 5, 6 and 7. It involves three stages—(a) in the case of a final salary scheme, the loss of the enhancement to the pension already accrued because of the increase of salary which would have occurred had the applicant not been dismissed, (b) in all cases, the loss of rights accruing up to the hearing and (c) the loss of future pension rights. These last two elements are calculated on the assumption that the contribution made by the employer to the fund during the period will equate to the value of the pension (attributable to the employer) that would have accrued. In the case of a final salary scheme, it may be necessary to make an adjustment to the employer's contribution as discussed in section 6.5. No such adjustment is necessary in the case of a money purchase scheme because the scheme is personal to the employee.

4.12 *The substantial loss approach*, by contrast, uses actuarial tables comparable to the Ogden Tables to assess the current capitalised value of the pension rights which would have accrued up to retirement. There may be cases where the tribunal decides that a person will return to a job at a comparable salary, but will never get a comparable pension see *Bentwood Bros. (Manchester) Ltd. v Shepherd* [2003] IRLR 364. In such cases *the substantial loss approach* may be needed even where the future loss of earnings is for a short period. But it must be remembered that loss of pension rights is the loss of a fringe benefit and may be compensated by an increase in salary in new employment.

4.13 Experience suggests that *the simplified approach* will be appropriate in most cases. Tribunals have been reluctant to embark on assessment of whole career loss because of the uncertainties of employment in modern economic conditions. In general terms *the substantial loss approach* may be chosen in cases where the person dismissed has been in the respondent's employment for a considerable time, where the employment was of a stable nature and unlikely to be affected by the economic cycle and where the person dismissed has reached an age where he is less likely to be looking for new pastures. The decision will, however, always depend on the particular facts of the case.

4.14 More particularly, we suggest that *the substantial loss approach* is appropriate in the following circumstances:

(a) when the applicant has found permanent new employment by the time of the hearing and assuming no specific uncertainties about the continuation of the lost job such as a supervening redundancy a few months after dismissal; further, the tribunal has found that the applicant is not likely to move on to better paid employment in due course;

(b) when the applicant has not found permanent new employment and the tribunal is satisfied on the balance of probabilities that he or she will not find new employment before State Pension age (usually confined to cases of significant disability where the applicant will find considerable difficulty in the job market);

(c) when the applicant has not found new employment but the tribunal is satisfied that the applicant will find alternative employment (which it values, for example, with the help of employment consultants) and is required then to value all losses to retirement and beyond before reducing the total loss by the percentage chance that the applicant would not have continued to retirement in the lost career. See *Ministry of Defence v Cannock* [1994] ICR 918 et al. subject to our comment below.

The simplified approach becomes inappropriate in these cases because there is a quantifiable continuing loss which can be assessed using the pensions data and Tables 1 to 4 of Appendices 5 and 6. These tables use factors similar to those in the Ogden Tables for personal injury and fatal accident cases. Although tables for pension loss are included in those tables, the tables in this booklet use some different assumptions to those underlying the Ogden Tables (see Appendix 2).

5. *The Simplified Approach* (i)—Loss of Enhancement of Pension Rights Accrued Prior to Dismissal in Final Salary Schemes

5.1 When a person who is a member of a final salary scheme is dismissed or leaves for any other reason, he is entitled to a pension payable at what would have been his retirement date as an annuity for the rest of his life. This is referred to in this booklet as a 'deferred pension'.

5.2 In the most common form of private sector final salary scheme, an employee when he retires receives 1/60th of his final salary for each year he has worked for the employer. For the employee retiring at the scheme's normal retirement age there is a maximum of 40/60ths. Frequently part of this pension is commuted to provide a lump sum.

5.3 The early leaver receives a deferred pension representing 1/60th of his final salary (at the time he leaves) for each year he has worked for the employer (providing he has 2 years' service—if not, he usually receives repayment of his own contributions). The Pensions Schemes Act 1993 requires this deferred pension to be revalued in line with increases in the cost of living index up to the retirement age, when the pension comes into payment, subject to a cap of 5% a year over the accumulation period. (There are separate revaluation requirements for that portion of any deferred pension representing a guaranteed minimum pension.) Even with this revaluation, the deferred pension is likely to be much less than if it had been based on the final salary which the member could have expected to have had if he had remained with the company until retirement.

Example:
A worked for his employers for 15 years; he left, aged 50, on 1 December 1985 with a final salary of £10,000. His basic deferred pension was 15/60ths of £10,000 = £2,500 p.a., payable from his retirement age 15 years later at the age of 65. By the time he reached retirement age, the cost of living index had increased by 56% (about 3% a year), so the pension which came into payment was £3,900 p.a.

Alternative example:
Instead of leaving he stayed with the company for another 15 years when he retired at 65 with a final salary of £21,000 (an increase of about 5% a year). His pension was £10,500 a year, of which £5,250 is referable to his first 15 years service.

5.4 By leaving early he has lost £1,350 a year from retirement to his death in respect of his first 15 years of service. This is the case whether or not he obtains fresh employment with identical salary and identical increases and with an identical pension scheme. There will be a corresponding reduction in any lump sum on retirement and any widow or widower's benefit.

5.5 What he has lost, however, is not necessarily the £1,350 a year pension difference between the two examples in 5.3. For example, he might well not have stayed with the company until retirement, even if he had not left at 50 years of age. He might have left or been sacked or the company might have gone into liquidation. On the other hand, he might have ended up as managing director with a salary of £100,000 a year and a pension of £50,000 a year. Alternatively he might have moved to a new job where his pension could be transferred in such a way as to preserve the full value of his past years of service. Who knows? Nevertheless his real loss on leaving could be substantial and there will usually be a loss arising from the difference between earnings revaluation of the accrued pension rights if he remained in service up to retirement age and the cost of living revaluation (capped at 5% a year) of the deferred pension.

5.6 Part IV of the Pension Schemes Act 1993 entitles a person to require his ex-employer to transfer the value of his accrued pension either to a similar scheme run by a new employer or personally to make other arrangements meeting the prescribed requirements (Para 13(2) of Schedule 1A to the Social Security Pensions Act 1975 as subsequently amended).

5.7 The transfer value is calculated in accordance with Regulations which refer in turn to the guidance note 'Retirement Benefit Schemes—Transfer Values (GN11)' This gives the actuary a certain amount of discretion which has been enlarged to the employee's disadvantage by recent amendments or, exceptionally, the pension fund trustees may, if they wish, be more generous to early leavers than the law requires. However, our understanding is that the transfer value is an actuarial figure which is intended to represent the present value of the deferred pension he can anticipate.

5.8 In theory, he should be no better or worse off by taking the transfer value and re-investing it than if he chooses to leave the deferred pension in the fund. However, it does create the additional possibility that the employee will find a better private pension fund to put his money into or that the transfer values will be assessed on a generous basis, or, on the other hand, that the new scheme may credit the transfer value on a less generous basis.

5.9 A common fallacy is the belief that an employee does not lose financially if his pension is transferred from his old employer's pension fund to his new employer's pension fund. In fact the transfer value will usually be assessed on the basis of the value of the deferred pension, as in the first example, and will not take account of the additional benefits that he might have received based on salary increases if he had stayed on to retirement age, or, usually, the value of any discretionary post-award pensions increases. Meanwhile, the scheme receiving the transfer value will allow for the fact that salary is likely to increase up to retirement age and may charge for the cost of discretionary post-award increases, so there may be no advantage to be gained from taking a transfer value. It follows that, where an applicant from the private sector has taken a transfer value to a new pension scheme, he will still need to be compensated for loss of enhancement of accrued pension rights as described in part (b) below. Transfer values operate more favourably than this between the public sector pension schemes.

(a) No Compensation at All

5.10 We consider that in respect of certain categories of cases it would be just and equitable not to make any award of compensation in respect of loss of enhancement of accrued pension rights. In particular, we recommend there should be no compensation for loss of enhancement of pension rights in cases where the applicant is fairly near to his anticipated retirement date i.e. within 5 years of retirement, because the difference between cost of living increases and anticipated increases in earnings has less cumulative effect over this shorter period.

5.11 Where the Tribunal finds as a fact that the employment would have terminated in any event within a period of up to a year it would not be appropriate to order any compensation for loss of accrued pension rights.

(b) The Government Actuary's New Tables

5.12 Where the Applicant had 5 years or more to retirement we recommend a different approach. The Government Actuary has put forward a revised and simplified actuarial method which is described in Appendix 2 and which uses the four Tables of multipliers in Appendix 4. Public and private sector schemes attract different tables because the former usually provide a pension of 1/80th final salary plus a lump sum, whereas the latter usually provide 1/60th final salary with the option of partial commutation. There are also often differences between public and private sector schemes in the increases awarded to pensions in payment and the treatment of revaluation of pensions in deferment.

5.13 The approach is similar to that in the 1980 and 1991 Editions. It takes as the starting point the deferred pension to which the applicant is entitled (without any allowance for anticipated cost of living increases or other benefits) and then applies a multiplier based on the applicant's age. The figure resulting from this calculation is the starting point for working out the award for loss of enhancement of accrued benefit rights.

5.14 To calculate this figure, therefore, all that is needed is the deferred annual pension (which is usually to be found in the pension information document sent by employers to early leavers), the applicant's age and either the scheme retirement age or any earlier retirement age found by the tribunal. It is entirely an arithmetical calculation. The table assumes that the Applicant would not have left his or her employment before retirement for reasons other than death or disability.

5.15 The figure obtained by applying the multiplier should be reduced if appropriate by a percentage representing the likelihood that the applicant would have lost his job before retirement for reasons other than unfair dismissal or discrimination, such as a fair dismissal, redundancy, leaving voluntarily etc. The 1980 paper set out a table of such deductions called the 'withdrawal factor', but, as stated in the previous guidelines, we remain of the view that any such figures are inappropriate and that it is best to leave this percentage to the discretion of the Tribunal.

5.16 The rationale of this scheme is that the amount a person will lose over the years can be seen as a proportion of the value of his pension and can be related to his age. Generally the younger he is the greater the loss.

5.17 Because of the simplification on which we have insisted, Tables 1 to 4 of Appendix 4 make various assumptions. They are that:

(1) private sector pensions are based on a defined amount of pension (usually 1/60th of final salary) of which part can be commuted to a lump sum. Public sector pensions have a lump sum payable in addition to the pension—at an amount equal to three years of pension payments at the initial rate.
(2) there is a widow or widower's pension at 50% of the member's rate.
(3) the maximum possible amount of pension is commuted for a lump sum.
(4) pensions after retirement are increased annually in line with the Retail Price Index (subject to an annual limit of 5% pa for private sector scheme pensions).
(5) no allowance has been made for the effects of contracting out.

5.18 The effects of inflation and taxation have been taken into account in the assumptions used in those tables, with particular regard to the assumed net rates of return and the allowance for a tax free lump sum, either as of right in public sector schemes or through commutation of part of the pension in private sector schemes. The actuarial basis is set out in Appendix 2 principally for the benefit of any expert who may be instructed in an individual case.

5.19 Assumptions of this nature are the only way in which the kind of simple tables set out in Appendix 4 can be put into effect. However, the assumptions are liable to change over time and we feel that the tables and the assumptions on which they are based should be reviewed periodically.

5.20 We have come to the conclusion that despite these crude assumptions it is the best system that can be devised in the circumstances. We therefore recommend it for use. If either party considers that it is inapplicable in any particular case he can put forward his arguments. The point is that it provides a starting point which can be used in the absence of more detailed evidence and modified as necessary.

5.21 Readers must note that the calculation in this section is not needed if *the substantial loss approach* described in section 8 is used to calculate future pension loss. The methodology and factors which apply to that section already allow for loss of enhancement (cf 8.3).

6. *The Simplified Approach* (2)—Loss of Pension Rights from the Date of Dismissal to the Date of Hearing

6.1 Had the applicant remained in employment between the date of his dismissal and the hearing he would have gained the right to additional pension benefits. Equally he would have made additional contributions to the pension fund and his employer might well have also made contributions to the pension fund because of his continued employment.

6.2 In the case of a money purchase scheme it is usually easy to calculate the money value of the additional benefits he would have received in respect of the employer's contributions. In a final salary scheme this is not possible. Had he remained in the scheme until the date of the hearing and then left he would have qualified for a slightly higher deferred pension, but had he still been in employment at the date of the hearing then he would simply have gained additional service to put into the calculation of his final pension.

6.3 We consider that the simplest method, though not technically correct, is to look not at the additional contingent benefits he would have gained, but at the contributions which his employer would have made to the pension fund. If this is done it is not necessary to consider refinements such as widows' benefits or inflation-proofing after retirement, since the better the scheme the more money will have to go into it.

6.4 When calculating loss of earnings during this period it is necessary to work out the weekly loss and multiply it by the number of weeks between the applicant's dismissal and the hearing (allowing for any sums paid in lieu of notice). Our recommendation for calculating the loss of pension rights during this period, where there is no Recoupment, is simply to include with the weekly loss a sum to represent what the employer would have contributed notionally towards the applicant's pension had he still been employed. Of course, in the case of a final salary scheme this is not strictly a correct method of assessing the applicant's loss, since the benefit that would have accrued to the applicant by remaining in employment does not necessarily correspond to this figure, but it would, we believe, be regarded as just and equitable by both applicants and respondents.

6.5 In a typical final salary pension scheme the employer does not make a specific contribution to each person's pension, but makes a contribution to the general pension fund which is a percentage of the total wages bill or of some part of the wages bill, such as basic wages excluding commission and/or overtime. The proportion of such overall payments which is attributable to an individual employee increases with age. While in a simple case it may be felt that it is unnecessary to try to allow for this, not to do so can make a difference of as much as 25% to the multiplicand. Accordingly, tribunals should apply the factors in Tables 1 and 2 of Appendix 7 (see the example at section 6.7).

6.6 If the percentage contributed by the employer is currently anomalous (e.g. because of a 'contributions holiday'), care should be taken to use the true 'standard rate of contribution'. This should be available in the report and accounts of the pension scheme or in the statement of pension costs for inclusion in the accounts of the employer.

6.7 If the percentage contributed by the employer cannot easily be ascertained, assume that the figure is 15% (or 20% for a non-contributory scheme) of pensionable pay. Whether a scheme is contributory or not can usually be determined by inspection of a wages slip. In each case the percentage for the employer's contribution should be multiplied by the factor from the Tables in Appendix 7 relating to the age of the employee at the date of dismissal. Applying the resulting percentage to the applicant's gross pensionable pay is, in our view, the fairest and simplest way of calculating his continuing loss of pension rights.

Example:
A is a man aged 35 and earns £300 a week gross, which is his pensionable pay. He contributes £15.00 a week (5%) to the pension fund. His employers contribute 15% of the gross wage bill to the pension fund. His normal retirement age is 65. The factor from Table 1 of Appendix 7 is 0.88, so that A's continuing loss of pension rights is £300 × 0.15 × 0.88 = £39.60 a week.

6.8 Although to this extent pension provision is being treated as part of the applicant's weekly loss, it is not part of his wages and the Recoupment Regulations do not apply to the pension element. Thus where there is Recoupment, the pension loss element should be calculated separately.

6.9 Where there is a company money purchase scheme or where the employer is contributing to a personalised plan or a money purchase top up then assessing the contribution that the employer would have made is both the simplest and the most accurate way of assessing the employee's loss. The same system, therefore, can be applied using the percentage contributed by the employer towards the pension on a weekly basis, but without the need to apply any adjustment using the Tables in Appendix 7.

6.10 Again, readers must note that the calculation in this section is not necessary if *the substantial loss approach* described in section 8 is used to calculate future pension loss.

7. *THE SIMPLIFIED APPROACH* (3)—LOSS OF FUTURE PENSION RIGHTS FROM THE DATE OF HEARING

7.1 This is essentially the same as the approach to assessing loss for the period between dismissal and hearing. It may be used where the period of loss of future earnings is not likely to be more than two years. In such cases, the tribunal is making a finding which subsequent events may prove entirely incorrect, particularly where the applicant is in white-collar employment. For the applicant may find himself in a new job at a lower level with none of the prospects he had with his former employment. He may also find himself in a job which, though otherwise comparable, has no pension scheme other than a stakeholder scheme to which the employer does not contribute. Nevertheless if the tribunal decides that, when the applicant finds employment, it will be either with a comparable pension scheme or at a higher salary to offset the absence of such a scheme, the loss of future pension rights can be assessed by *the simplified approach*.

7.2 Where the pension is a money purchase scheme, the value of the loss during the fixed period is essentially the aggregate of the contributions which the employer would have made to the scheme during this period, bearing in mind that they are not taxable. Care must be taken, however, following the judgment of the Court of Appeal in *Bentwood Bros (Manchester) Ltd v Shepherd* 2003 IRLR 364 to make allowance for accelerated payment by using, for example, Ogden Table 38. Where the pension is a final salary scheme, the loss is represented by the aggregate of contributions which the employer would have made to the pension fund during this period but subject to the same caveat.

7.3 The two qualifications to a final salary scheme calculation are:

- The employer may be taking a contributions holiday. In this case there will usually be a standard rate of contribution disclosed by the scheme and this should form the basis of the calculation.
- As discussed in section 6.5, the contributions made in respect of younger employees are used to balance out the contributions for older employees. Table 1 or 2 of Appendix 7 should be used to make any necessary adjustment. Thus the value of the lost pension rights is the contributions which would have been paid by the employer, adjusted to allow for age.

7.4 Again this calculation does not apply where *the substantial loss approach* is used.

7.5 All the above relates to occupational pension schemes but, as explained at section 2.14, if the applicant was not in a pension scheme in the lost job or is in a scheme which is not contracted out, he may still suffer a loss owing to his future S2P not accruing. Then it may be appropriate to make an award for loss of S2P accrual by using Table 3.2 in Appendix 3. This is done by taking the applicant's age at dismissal, his or her sex and gross annual earnings and reading off the percentage at those coordinates. Small adjustments to the percentage can be made to reflect actual ages and earnings. That percentage applied to annual gross earnings reflects one year's accrual of S2P which should then be multiplied by the estimated numbers of years of loss.

8. The Substantial Loss Approach

8.1 We have set out in Chapter 4 the factors which the tribunal should take into account in deciding whether to use *the simplified approach* or *the substantial loss approach*. Once a decision is made to take *the substantial loss approach* the calculation is not as complex as it might at first appear.

8.2 In such cases the value of the loss of pension rights can be calculated using factors similar to those available in the Ogden Tables for personal injury and fatal accident cases. Those tables are used to calculate future loss of earnings whereas the tables in this booklet use some different assumptions (see Appendix 2). This method will be reasonably accurate either if the employee is thought unlikely to find alternative employment or when the dismissed employee has already obtained pensionable employment in a final salary or defined benefit scheme when it is possible to value the difference in benefits between the former pension scheme and the new pension scheme.

8.3 The calculation required is:

> Loss of future pension rights = A minus B minus C where:
> A = value of prospective final salary pension rights up to normal retirement age in former employment (if he or she had not been dismissed)
> B = value of accrued final salary pension rights to date of dismissal from former employment
> C = value of prospective final salary pension rights to normal retirement age in new employment C will of course be zero if it is found that the applicant will probably not obtain further pensionable employment or if he or she has joined a money purchase scheme in the new employment. In that case, see 8.11 below.

8.4 Once these figures have been calculated, the tribunal has a further decision to make as to the amounts of any withdrawal factors. The Tables work on the basis that the applicant would have remained in his previous employment until retirement, subject to the usual risks of mortality and disability. However, it is recognised that people leave even the most stable employment for a variety of reasons. As with the Ogden Tables, no Tables are available to assist the tribunal in making this deduction. It will vary with the age, status, work record and health of the applicant and with the perceived future viability of the respondent's business.

8.5 In the case of A and B the annual amount of pension (and separate retirement lump sum where applicable, principally from public service pension schemes) is calculated on the basis of the pensionable earnings in the year up to the date of dismissal (or according to the rules of the scheme). The period of service in B is up to the date of dismissal, whereas for A the period of service is from the beginning of the employment to the individual's normal retirement age in that employment. In the case of C the annual amount of pension (and separate lump sum where applicable) is calculated on the basis of the current pensionable pay in the new employment (or the deemed pensionable pay in any assumed future employment). The period of service in C is from the date of taking up the new post to the normal retirement age in the new employment.

8.6 In each case the annual amount of pension is calculated according to the rules of the scheme, so that the annual amount of pension = pension fraction (1/60th or 1/80th for example) × relevant period of service × pensionable salary. As explained above, in private sector defined benefit schemes the scheme pension fraction will often be 1/60th, with no separately identified lump sum but with the option of partial commutation. In most of the large public sector schemes the scheme pension fraction is 1/80th and there is a separately identified lump sum equivalent to 3 times the annual amount of pension. The tables in Appendices 5 and 6 are based on these distinctions and, in the case of the private sector tables, assume commutation of pension at retirement to the maximum extent permitted. In order to simplify the calculations, guaranteed minimum pension rights are ignored. As described in Appendix 3, in certain circumstances members of contracted-out pension arrangements will be entitled to receive a 'top up pension' paid by the State from state pension age. These amounts are generally small and in the interests of simplifying the calculations this top-up pension is ignored in the calculations.

8.7 The lump sum value of A and C is found by multiplying the respective annual amounts by the factors from Tables 1 to 4 of Appendix 5 corresponding to the age of the individual. The lump sum value of B is found in the same way by using the factors from Tables 1 to 4 of Appendix 6. In the case of A and B the relevant age is at the date of dismissal. In the case of C the relevant age is at the date of commencing the new job.

8.8 Example:

A female employee is dismissed in 2002–03 at age 40 from private sector employment, which had a contracted-out pension scheme offering a pension of 1/60th of final year's salary per year of service. Her pensionable pay in the year before she was dismissed was £20,000. She had completed 15 years of service before being dismissed and had a pensionable age of 65.

She is employed again one year later, at age 41, in a public sector job, with a salary of £15,000 and a contracted-out pension scheme offering a pension of 1/80th of final year's salary per year of service and a lump sum of 3 years' pension, payable at normal retirement age of 60.

For the calculation of A:
Pension expected at normal retirement age in former employment
= 1/60th × 40 (i.e. 15 years' service + 25 years to retirement) × 20,000
= £13,333.33 a year

For the calculation of B:
Pension expected at normal retirement age in former employment with service cut short at date of dismissal
= £ 1/60th × 15 × 20,000
= £ 5,000.00 a year

For the calculation of C:
Pension expected at normal retirement age in new employment = 1/80th × 19 × 15,000 = £ 3,562.50 a year

In addition, as a matter of fact there is an expected lump sum at normal retirement age of three years' pension, namely £10,687.50, but no separate calculation is required for the lump sum in C as this is incorporated within the factors for public sector schemes. The pension schemes in both employments are contracted-out. All amounts are calculated in current terms, that is to say there is no specific allowance made for inflation, future career progression and so on, since these factors are taken into account in the multiplier factors to be applied.

Factor for the calculation of the value of A = 11.45 from Table 5.3
Factor for the calculation of the value of B = 7.56 from Table 6.3
Factor for the calculation of the value of C = 17.54 from Table 5.4
Loss of pension rights
Pension amount × factor for A (£13,333.33 × 11.45) = £152,667
Pension amount × factor for B (£5,000.00 × 7.56) = £37,800
Pension amount × factor for C (£3,562.50 × 17.54) = £62,486
Loss = £52,381

8.9 The blanket percentage chance or withdrawal factor, derived from *Clancy v Cannock Chase Technical College & Parkers* [2001] IRLR 331, applies to future loss of earnings. The Government Actuary, however, has argued that a blanket withdrawal factor is wrong in principle because the tribunal might have material upon which to decide, for example, that the chance of the applicant losing his new job before retirement was not as great as that of losing the old job before retirement. If the tribunal is persuaded to adopt that approach, then care must be taken to apply separate withdrawal factors to A and B on the one hand and C on the other. Accordingly, taking the example in 8.8 above and assuming the tribunal determines a 40% withdrawal factor for the lost job and a 25% withdrawal factor for the new job, the calculation will look like this:

A = £13,333.33 × 11.45 × 60% = £91,600
B = £5,000.00 × 7.56 × 60% = £22,680
C = £3,562.50 × 17.54 × 75% = £46,865
Loss = £22,055

8.10 Where the pension scheme in the previous job is a contributory scheme, allowance must be made for the fact that the applicant no longer has to pay his own contributions to the scheme. The most accurate method is to devise another table relating to such contributions. However, to simplify the calculations we suggest that this be allowed for by treating his earnings in his old employment as reduced accordingly. Thus, in calculating compensation for loss of earnings (as opposed to pension loss), any employee contributions need to be taken off the net earnings before applying the appropriate multiplier. Payslips normally show net earnings after all deductions including employee pension contributions. Similarly, if the pension scheme with the new employment is a contributory final salary scheme, the value assessed at C includes the value of the employee's contributions and hence the value of the net earnings in the new job should also be reduced accordingly.

8.11 If the applicant loses a job with a final salary pension scheme and obtains one with a money purchase scheme or signs up to a stakeholder pension, the loss is calculated as in 8.3 but only A minus B. There is no need to worry about any loss of employer pension contributions in the new job because those contributions have already been factored into the A minus B calculation. When assessing loss of earnings, however, it will be appropriate to take account of any employer contributions in the new job in order to ascertain whether there is a continuing loss of earnings or not. Thus the comparison will be the difference between net earnings in the old job (ignoring employer payroll contributions) and net earnings plus any employer pension contributions in the new.

8.12 If the applicant obtains a new job in which S2P accrues, then its value should be deducted from the value of A minus B. The value of the future accrual of S2P can be assessed using Table 3.2 in Appendix 3 based on earnings in the new employment.

Example:
As in 8.8 but instead of obtaining a public sector job, she finds work in the private sector with no pension scheme and no prospect of one. She has made no personal pension arrangements but pays her National Insurance contribution at the full rate so as to entitle her to S2P. Age at date of re-employment is 41 and her state retirement age is 65—as she was born after 1955 (see Table 3.2). Thus: A minus B as before but also minus C calculated in accordance with Appendix 3 £15,000 × 5.0% (extrapolated from 4.8% rising to 5.6% between 40 and 45) × 24 = £18,000.
Loss = £152,667 minus £37,800 minus £18,000 = £96,867
The result will be a smaller award if withdrawal factors are applied.

8.13 Although not strictly within *the substantial loss approach* but for the sake of completeness, if the applicant loses a job with a money purchase scheme to which the employer contributed and finds a lower paid job with no such pension scheme, the employer's contributions should be added to the continuing loss of earnings before applying the appropriate multiplier in the Ogden Tables. Any accrued S2P will have to be deducted from the result as in the above example. The use of Ogden Tables will only be appropriate where the Tribunal has decided that the loss is long term. If it is not, then *the simplified approach* in sections 6 and 7 will be used.

8.14 It should be emphasized that *the substantial loss approach* automatically includes compensation for loss of enhancement of accrued pension rights at the date of dismissal (section 5) and for loss of pension rights from the date of dismissal to the date of hearing (section 6) as well as the loss of future pension rights from the date of the hearing (section 7). Thus no further compensation needs to be added to the value derived from this approach.

9. General Conclusions

9.1 It is important to note that where the compensation exceeds the statutory limit even without consideration of loss of pension rights, the need to calculate the sum involved may remain. For it must be remembered that the Recoupment Regulations (r. 4(2)) provide for a proportionate reduction of the sum repayable to the Benefits Agency where the statutory limit applies.

9.2 Appendix 1 sets out a simple checklist for parties and tribunals to use. Appendix 2 is the Government Actuary's paper on which our conclusions as to loss of enhancement of accrued pension rights are based and also sets out the assumptions underlying the other tables. It is there primarily for the benefit of any actuarial expert who may wish to challenge the assumptions on the facts of a particular case. Appendix 3 contains a description of the State Earnings-related Pension Scheme and State Second Pension and the table for assessing the loss or future accrual of State Second Pension rights. Appendix 4 contains the tables of multipliers for assessing the loss of enhancement on accrued pension rights. Appendix 5 contains the tables of multipliers for assessing the loss of future pension rights in the lost job and Appendix 6 in the new job, using *the substantial loss approach*. Appendix 7 gives tables of factors to be applied to the contribution rates in respect of defined benefit schemes in assessing the loss of pension rights between the date of dismissal and the date of hearing and the loss of future pension rights using *the simplified approach*.

. . .

Appendix 1: Check list for assessing pension loss

1. Was the applicant a member of any personal or occupational pension scheme at the date of dismissal?
2. If not, is it necessary to award compensation for loss of S2P rights? See section 7.5 and Appendix 3.
3. If the applicant was a member of a personal pension scheme, did the respondent contribute to it? If so, see sections 6, 7 and 8.13.
4. If the applicant was a member of an occupational scheme, do the circumstances call for use of *the simplified approach*? See section 4. If so, see sections 5, 6 and 7.
5. If not, do the circumstances call for use of *the substantial loss approach*? If so, see section 8.
6. If the scheme was not contracted out, is it necessary to award compensation for loss of both occupational pension and S2P? See sections 7.5 and 8 and Appendix 3.

Appendix 2: Memorandum by the Government Actuary Assessing loss of occupational pension scheme rights following a finding of unfair dismissal or discrimination by an employment tribunal

Background

The 1980 paper under the above title produced by the Government Actuary's Department provided chairmen of Industrial Tribunals with a simple system of assessing the loss in respect of service before dismissal by calculating the difference between the value of the deferred pension to which the applicant remained entitled and what he would have received had he not been dismissed. The formula became less satisfactory over time because of legislative changes aimed at preserving at least some of the pension entitlement of early leavers; very approximate adjustments for this were proposed in notes issued in 1980 and 1987.

A revised system was put forward in 1989, at the time of the compilation of the first edition of the Industrial Tribunals Booklet on compensation for loss of pension rights, to take account of the legislation, together with an approximate simple formula which might be useful to chairmen in the absence of expert evidence. The formula related to a pension derived from final salary at exit, continuing (at one-half rate) to a dependant.

If a member of a final-salary pension scheme withdraws, he loses potential benefits in respect of his past service to the extent that the accrued benefits are not fully indexed in line with salaries (including an allowance for possible future promotion) until normal retirement age.

The value of each pension unit depends on many factors, in particular:

- sex, attained age, normal retirement age
- estimates of future rates of salary progression and promotion, of inflation (prices and/or pensions) and of interest on investments

- estimates of rates of withdrawal (dismissal, redundancy, resignation, transfer), death (in service and after retirement), retirement (age and ill-health) and (for dependants' benefits) age and death rates of dependants and the proportion of staff leaving an eligible dependant on their own death.

Tables were constructed for the 1989 edition and were subsequently revised for the second edition, issued in 1991. For the second edition, the tables were constructed on simplified assumptions. The method used required each pension to be divided into three parts, namely the continuing benefit value, pre- and post-1988 guaranteed minimum pension (GMP) and any balance above the GMP; a different factor was applied to each part. Tables were provided in the booklet.

To simplify procedures, a single factor was found (varying with age) to apply to the accrued pension to estimate the loss of pension rights assuming:

(i) the accrued pension for past service equalled that preserved on dismissal;
(ii) the GMP represented two-thirds of the total pension and would be revalued at least to the same extent as any balance.

It was noted these fractions would change with time.

All estimates of loss needed to be reduced by an individual assessment of the likelihood of withdrawal from the pension fund other than on account of unfair dismissal.

Loss of enhancement of accrued pension rights

One possible method to value benefit loss is to deduct the transfer value from a standard table of continuing benefit values. This methodology was considered for use in the 1991 edition of the Booklet. However, transfer values of pension rights are calculated on different assumptions from those used in valuing benefits to continuing staff. A transfer value passes between pension schemes in cash form, so the transferring scheme has to realize assets at current market rates, not the long-term average assessment. Further, there is a change in benefit expectations: the salary linkage is broken, and there are often differences in death and ill-health benefits between schemes (especially enhancement on early exit). Consequently it can be inequitable to value benefit loss by this method and it was felt to be fairer to use a table representing the loss of benefit on dismissal allowing for standard deferred benefits valued on a specified basis. This approach is still valid and it is used in this edition of the tables.

Tables 1 to 4 of Appendix 4 give factors to be applied to the amount of accrued pension at the date of dismissal to value the loss of enhancement. The approach is to value the accrued pension had it continued to increase in line with earnings until retirement age and deduct the value assuming the accrued pension increases in line with statutory revaluations (or in line with price inflation in the case of public sector schemes) until retirement age. The bases used for valuing these are set out below.

As described in Chapter 2, GMPs no longer accrue in respect of service since April 1997: thus this element will become a decreasing proportion of the pension in future. The presence of GMPs complicates the calculations and can only be allowed for in a very approximate way which will not be correct for the majority of cases. Also, GMPs did not accrue in respect of schemes which were not contracted out of SERPS. Given the preceding considerations and the Working Party's desire that any methodology adopted should be comprehensible and relatively simple to apply, it is proposed that the calculations for this edition should make no direct allowance for the effects of GMPs.

Financial assumptions

The assumptions underlying the calculations have also been reviewed in the light of changes in the demographic and economic outlook. The new calculations assume that money could be invested to earn an average of 6½% per annum. For continuing benefits, based on final salary with a half-rate pension continuing to a dependent spouse, salary is assumed to increase at 5% per annum. However, in valuing pension benefits, it is the assumptions as to the rate of return net of increases in earnings, net of increases in pensions in deferment and net of increases in pensions in payment which are important, rather than the absolute values of the assumed rates of increase.

The assumptions made for increases in pensions both in deferment and in payment are slightly different for private sector and public sector schemes to allow for the different practices in granting such increases. The level of guaranteed increases in pensions in payment varies between schemes within the private sector but must be at least equivalent to a statutory minimum for pensions accrued in respect of service since 5 April 1997 of increasing annually in line with the increase in the Retail Price Index, subject to an upper limit of 5% per annum. This statutory minimum is assumed for the increase in pensions in payment from private sector schemes. Pensions in payment from most public sector schemes increase in line with the increase in the Retail Price Index, with no upper limit. This assumption has been adopted for public sector schemes.

Frozen (deferred) benefits provided by private sector schemes are assumed to increase from the time of deferment to the time the benefit comes into payment at the lower of the increase in the Retail Price Index over that period and 5% per annum over the same period. This is equivalent to the statutory minimum increase of pensions in deferment. Frozen (deferred) benefits provided by public sector schemes are assumed to increase from the time of deferment to the time the benefit comes into payment by the increase in the Retail Price Index over that period, with no upper limit, in line with the revaluation provided by most public sector schemes.

Awards made by Employment Tribunals for loss of pension rights are tax free; however, tax is payable on the income and gains arising through any investment of the award, although it may be possible to defray the extent of this by investing in suitable tax efficient vehicles. After discussion with the ET chairmen on the working party, it was agreed that some allowance for the possible effects of tax being payable on the proceeds arising from investment of the compensation award should be made in determining the financial assumptions to be used for the rates of return net of earnings and net of revaluation of deferred pension.

It was the intention of the working party that the methodology for assessing loss of pension rights should be brought more into line with the approach used for assessing damage awards in court cases involving personal injury where heads of claim are multiplied by an appropriate multiplier, based on those given in the Ogden Tables. However, some differences remain. For instance, certain awards for loss of pension rights made by Employment Tribunals often incorporate an allowance for future increases in earnings. In general, earnings have risen on average at a faster rate than prices; it is this difference that mainly gives rise to a loss of enhancement on accrued pension rights at the date of dismissal. Awards made using the Ogden Tables approach make no allowance for any difference in the future rates of increase in earnings and prices; a rate of return net of prices rather than net of earnings is used to value earnings loss. In June 2001 the Lord Chancellor, having regard to the then recent experience of yields available on UK index-linked gilts and other considerations, specified a rate of discount of 2½% per annum to be used in court cases involving damages for personal injury and fatal accidents. This yield was net of tax at the standard rate and is used for discounting future earnings, costs of care and other monetary amounts.

Having regard to the discount rate of 2½%, net of standard rate tax, prescribed by the Lord Chancellor for use in court cases involving personal injury, discount rates used for various purposes in the public sector, the yields available on index-linked gilts in recent years and likely future movements in these yields and the effects of tax during the roll-up period, the following financial assumptions have been made in the calculations as summarised in the following table:

Assumption	Private sector	Public sector
Gross yield	6.5%	6.5%
Yield net of earnings	1.0%	1.0%
Yield net of revaluation of deferred pensions	2.75%	2.5%
Yield net of increases in pensions in payment	3.5%	3.0%

These assumptions are not fully market-related, as they are only expected to be changed relatively infrequently.

A higher rate of statutory revaluation for pensions in deferment than for pensions in payment is assumed for private sector schemes because the revaluation in deferment is cumulative, rather than being lost if RPI exceeds 5% in a given revaluation year. Hence, the yield net of increases in deferment is lower than the yield net of increases of pensions in payment. Also a larger part of the past service benefit is statutorily subject to this revaluation than is subject to LPI in payment.

Demographic and other assumptions

The Continuous Mortality Investigation Bureau (CMIB) set up by the actuarial profession in the United Kingdom publishes tables of mortality rates derived from data relating to people who are members of insured pension schemes. The mortality rates used in the calculations have been taken as those assumed by age and gender for the calendar year 2010 in the PMA/PFA92 tables (the latest tables on insured pensioner mortality issued by the CMIB). Ill-health retirement benefits are assumed to be worth as much as those on normal retirement. No allowance is made for exits except by death; chairmen are expected to assess for themselves the reduction for the possibility of withdrawal (by resignation etc. but not unfair dismissal) before normal pension age. In valuing the pension benefits, it is assumed that the member would be married at death and that the spouse would be entitled to a pension of half that payable to the member in the case of death after retirement or death in deferment or which would have been payable to the member based on potential service to normal retirement age at the date of death in the case of death in service.

No allowance has been made for expenses of any kind which might be incurred by the individual were he or she to purchase pension benefits equivalent to those lost.

The factors in the tables in Appendices 4, 5 and 6 also make allowance for the availability of a tax free lump sum; either, for private sector schemes, by commutation to the maximum extent permitted or, in the case of public sector schemes, by inclusion of the benefit of a lump sum of three times the annual pension paid at the date of retirement. The lump sum amounts have been grossed up within the total figures, so that the whole amount can be regarded as the equivalent taxable payment.

Loss of future pension rights

Simplified approach

The 1991 edition of the booklet assessed the loss of future pension rights by assuming that the loss was equivalent in value to the contributions that the employer would have made to the pension scheme in respect of the employee's employment. *The simplified approach* discussed in Chapters 4 to 7 of the booklet follows this approach. However, as discussed in paragraph 6.5 of the booklet, in a typical final salary pension scheme the employer does not make a specific contribution to each person's pension, but makes a contribution to the general pension fund which is a proportion of the total wages bill or of some part of the wages bill. To make some allowance for the fact that the accrual of pension in respect of a year's pensionable service usually increases with age, whereas the employer is paying an aggregate contribution in respect of all members of the scheme and which does not usually vary by age, the overall percentage contribution payable by the employer should be multiplied by a factor related to the employee's age at the date of dismissal. These factors are set out in Tables 1 and 2 of Appendix 7. These have been obtained by calculating the value of the pension earned through one year of pensionable service at each year of age from age 20 onwards until the assumed retirement age, allowing for increases in salary before retirement but with no allowance made for exit from the scheme before the scheme retirement age is reached other than death. The average of the resulting contribution rates is then taken. The figure given for a particular age in the tables is the ratio of the assessed contribution rate for that age divided by the average contribution rate.

Substantial loss approach

This approach does not use future contributions that would have been made to the pension scheme to assess the value of future pension rights. Instead, the value of the pension benefits up to normal retirement age which would have been earned had the employee not been dismissed is determined. From this is deducted the value of the accrued pension rights at the date of dismissal and the value of any prospective pension rights arising from any new employment since dismissal. The various values required are assessed by multiplying the accrued or estimated total pension by appropriate multipliers.

This approach is akin to that used for assessing damages awards in personal injury cases and uses factors similar to those given in the Ogden Tables. These factors are given in tables in Appendices 5 and 6. The methodology, termed *the substantial loss approach*, is discussed in more detail in Chapter 8. The factors have been calculated using the same financial and demographic assumptions as those used in the simplified loss approach for calculating loss of enhancement of accrued pension rights.

Loss of accrual of future state second pension rights

The various types of pension benefit provided by the State are discussed in Chapter 2. It is proposed there that it be assumed there is no loss of accrual of Basic State Pension but that the loss of any State Second Pension (S2P) should be compensated.

S2P is essentially an earnings-related benefit under which tranches of earnings between various lower and upper limits in any tax year are revalued in line with the general increase in earnings until the year preceding that in which state pension age is attained. These revalued earnings are then averaged over the period from age 16, or April 1978, if later, to the end of the year preceding state pension age.

The resulting pension is payable from state pension age and is indexed in line with the general level of prices.

Under the State Earnings-Related Pension Scheme (SERPS), the accrual rate depended on the year in which state pension age was attained; for those retiring up to April 2009 there was a phased reduction in the accrual rate from 25/N to 20/N where N is the number of tax years in the earner's working life from April 1978 to the end of the year preceding state pension age. Under the changes initiated by the Child Support, Pensions and Social Security Act 2000, SERPS was reformed into S2P. These reforms introduced the different accrual rates on different bands of earnings that are double, half and equal to the previous SERPS accrual rates.

Given assumptions about future increases in the general levels of earnings, the amount of the S2P benefits which would arise from state pension age in respect of earnings in a particular tax year can be estimated. This accrued S2P would not then alter regardless of whether the person remained in employment in the future or not. Given assumptions about the rate of state pension increases, the discount yield and future mortality rates, a value can be assigned to £1 of earnings accrued in each of the three various bands in a given year.

Table 3.2 in Appendix 3 show the values of the S2P pension arising from £1 of gross earnings, calculated using the financial and demographic assumptions used to value the loss of pension rights from occupational and other pension arrangements, described earlier in this Appendix, together with other demographic assumptions used in the calculations of contracting-out rebates in the report *Review of certain contracting-out terms* (Cm 5076).

If it is assumed that the claimant's earnings in his old employment would have increased in line with the earnings revaluations applied to the accrual of S2P then an estimate of the S2P accrued over a given number of years can be found by multiplying the gross earnings by the appropriate factors given in Table 3.2 in Appendix 3 and then by the number of years over which S2P is assumed to accrue. The value of any S2P accrued in any new employment can be assessed in the same way.

General

It should be noted that the basis used for assessing the loss of pension rights is intended to provide a just and equitable level of compensation to individuals found to have been wrongly dismissed for whatever reason, taking into account the interests of all the parties involved. It does not necessarily correspond to actuarial funding bases used by pension schemes in general.

The tables of factors in Appendix 4 are for use in calculating the loss of enhancement on accrued pension rights, as discussed in Chapter 5. The tables in Appendices 5 and 6 are for use in cases assessing the loss of future pension rights using *the substantial loss approach*, described in Section 8. The factors in Appendix 7 are those to be applied to the overall contribution rate to the scheme to estimate the appropriate age specific contribution rates.

Where the value of scheme benefits is not known, it is suggested that an average (sixtieths) scheme should be assumed with a standard contribution rate taken as 20% of pensionable salary, then multiplied by a factor from Appendix 7, as appropriate. It must be emphasized that pensionable salary may not be the same as total salary.

. . .

Appendix 3: State Earnings-Related Pension Scheme (SERPS) and State Second Pension (S2P)

SERPS

Since April 1978, employees who have paid national insurance contributions on earnings over the lower earnings limit have been entitled to an earnings-related additional pension payable by the State and generally referred to as the State Earnings-Related Pension Scheme (SERPS). Since April 2000 employees earning between the lower earnings limit and the primary threshold for National Insurance contributions are treated as having paid the necessary NI contributions and hence qualified for SERPS accrual. Earnings between the lower earnings and upper earnings limits in any tax year ('relevant earnings') are revalued in line with the general level of increase in earnings up to the year before that in which state pension age is attained. These revalued earnings are then averaged over the period from age 16, or April 1978 if later, to the end of the year preceding state pension age. The retirement pension is payable from state pension age and is indexed after that age in line with the general level of prices.

State pension age for men is 65. State pension age is age 60 for women retiring up to 5 April 2010. For women retiring from 6 April 2020 onwards state pension age will be 65, as it is for men. Between these dates, state pension age for women will increase by one month in every two month interval as set out in Table 3.1.

Table 3.1 State pension age for women—adjustments

Date of birth	State pension age (year. month)	Pension date	Date of birth	State pension age (year. month)	Pension date
06.03.50	60.0	06.03.2010	06.10.52	62.7	06.05.2015
06.04.50	60.1	06.05.2010	06.11.52	62.8	06.07.2015
06.05.50	60.2	06.07.2010	06.12.52	62.9	06.09.2015
06.06.50	60.3	06.09.2010	06.01.53	62.10	06.11.2015
06.07.50	60.4	06.11.2010	06.02.53	62.11	06.01.2016
06.08.50	60.5	06.01.2011	06.03.53	63.0	06.03.2016
06.09.50	60.6	06.03.2011	06.04.53	63.1	06.05.2016
06.10.50	60.7	06.05.2011	06.05.53	63.2	06.07.2016
06.11.50	60.8	06.07.2011	06.06.53	63.3	06.09.2016
06.12.50	60.9	06.09.2011	06.07.53	63.4	06.11.2016
06.01.51	60.10	06.11.2011	06.08.53	63.5	06.01.2017
06.02.51	60.11	06.01.2012	06.09.53	63.6	06.03.2017
06.03.51	61.0	06.03.2012	06.10.53	63.7	06.05.2017
06.04.51	61.1	06.05.2012	06.11.53	63.8	06.07.2017
06.05.51	61.2	06.07.2012	06.12.53	63.9	06.09.2017
06.06.51	61.3	06.09.2012	06.01.54	63.10	06.11.2017
06.07.51	61.4	06.11.2012	06.02.54	63.11	06.01.2018
06.08.51	61.5	06.01.2013	06.03.54	64.0	06.03.2018
06.09.51	61.6	06.03.2013	06.04.54	64.1	06.05.2018
06.10.51	61.7	06.05.2013	06.05.54	64.2	06.07.2018
06.11.51	61.8	06.07.2013	06.06.54	64.3	06.09.2018
06.12.51	61.9	06.09.2013	06.07.54	64.4	06.11.2018
06.01.52	61.10	06.11.2013	06.08.54	64.5	06.01.2019
06.02.52	61.11	06.01.2014	06.09.54	64.6	06.03.2019
06.03.52	62.0	06.03.2014	06.10.54	64.7	06.05.2019
06.04.52	62.1	06.05.2014	06.11.54	64.8	06.07.2019
06.05.52	62.2	06.07.2014	06.12.54	64.9	06.09.2019
06.07.52	62.4	06.11.2014	06.02.55	64.11	06.01.2020
06.08.52	62.5	06.01.2015	06.03.55	65.0	06.03.2020
06.09.52	62.6	06.03.2015	06.04.55	65.0	06.04.2020

Following the Social Security Contributions and Benefits Act 1992 the additional pension was eventually to be 20 per cent of revalued earnings as defined above and could be regarded as accruing uniformly over the working life between age 16 and the end of the tax year preceding state pension age. For those over 16 in April 1978 when the accrual of additional pension commenced, the working life was taken to be between April 1978 and the end of the tax year preceding state pension age.

For people reaching state pension age after April 1999, the accrual rate will be 25/N per cent in respect of earnings up to April 1988, where N is the number of tax years in the earner's working life from April 1978 or age 16, if later, to the end of the one preceding state pension age. However, the accrual rate in respect of earnings after April 1988 depends on the year in which state pension age is attained as follows:

Year of retirement	Percentage accrual rate for period 1988–89 onwards
2003–04	23/25
2004–05	22.5/26
2005–06	22/27
2006–07	21.5/28
2007–08	21/29
2008–09	20.5/30
2009–10	20/31
2010–11	20/32
....	....
2027–28 and later	20/49

The State Second Pension

The Child Support, Pensions and Social Security Act 2000 introduced a number of changes to additional pension, which is now known as The State Second Pension (S2P). The main changes, which took effect from the tax year 2002–03, were:

- The introduction of three different accrual rates on different bands of earnings
- Treating those earning between the annualized lower earnings limit (the qualifying earnings factor or QEF set to be £4,004 in 2003–04) up to the 'low earnings threshold'—£11,200 in terms of 2003–04 earnings—as though they earned the low earnings threshold
- Treating qualified carers and people with long-term disabilities who have no earnings or earnings below the annual lower earnings limit, as if they had earnings at the level of the low earnings threshold.

S2P will accrue on earnings (actual or treated as earned) between the lower earnings limit and the upper earnings limit. These earnings ('relevant earnings') will initially be divided into three bands. Band 1 will be from the annual lower earnings limit to the low earnings threshold (LET). Band 2 will be from the low earnings threshold plus £1 to an amount equal to 3 × LET–2 × QEF. This would be £25,600 in terms of 2003–04 earnings. Band 3 will be from the top of the second band plus £1 to the upper earnings limit. The lower and upper earnings limits and the low earnings threshold will be revalued from year to year.

The S2P accrual rates will be double, half and equal to the SERPS accrual rates on bands 1, 2 and 3 of earnings respectively. Thus, for example, for retirements in 2009–10 and later the S2P will be based on 40%, 10% and 20% of earnings in bands 1, 2 and 3 respectively.

Potential loss of S2P

S2P will be accrued by all employees earning over the lower earnings limit who are in pension arrangements which are not contracted-out of the S2P. Thus, for any employee who is not a member of an occupational scheme or is a member of an occupational pension scheme which was not contracted out of S2P (circumstances which currently apply to about three-quarters of the private sector working population, but to only a small proportion of public sector workers) there is a potential loss of rights in relation to S2P.

The value of the loss of future accrual of S2P can be obtained by using the relevant factor from Table 3.2 of this appendix which reflects the value of one year's accrual of S2P by age and sex. To obtain the value of the loss of S2P rights, the appropriate factor is taken from Table 3.2 according to the applicant's age at the date of dismissal and sex. The gross earnings of the applicant at the date of dismissal are then multiplied by this factor to give the value of one year's accrual of S2P. The resulting amount should then be multiplied by the length of the period, in years, for which the loss is being valued. The basis used for calculating the factors is described in Appendix 2.

> Example
> A male employee is dismissed in 2003–04 at age 50 from private sector employment with gross earnings of £35,000 a year and no prospect of reemployment before state pension age of 65. The claimant was not a member of any pension arrangements run by the employer and hence was accruing S2P since his earnings are above the lower earnings limit. The loss for future accrual of S2P is assessed as
> £35,000 × 0.043 × 15 = £22,575
> where the factor of 0.043 is taken from Table 3.2 at age 50 for males with gross earnings of £35,000.

If the employee was a member of a pension arrangement which was contracted out of the Additional Pension under SERPS and/or S2P, there will be a potential loss of state pension benefits under S2P for members of employer contracted-out final salary schemes and contracted-out money purchase schemes with earnings below 3 × LET – 2 × QEF (= £25,600 in 2003–04 terms) and for employee members of Appropriate Personal Pensions with earnings below the Lower Earnings Threshold (= £11,200 in 2003–04 terms). Had the member not been dismissed, a top-up pension would have been paid by the State from the state pension age equal to the amount of S2P the member would have accrued less the amount of SERPS the member would notionally have accrued. The loss of the SERPS accrual is effectively allowed for in the assessment of the loss of occupational pension rights, as discussed in section 5 et seq. Hence, the loss of state pension benefits in respect of future service which are not allowed for elsewhere can be assessed as the value of the S2P which would have been paid in respect of future service less the value of the amount of SERPS the member would notionally have accrued. However, the value of this top-up is complex to calculate and is usually small relative to the value of the loss of pension from the pension scheme. In keeping with the aim of simplifying the calculations as far as possible, it is recommended that no award of compensation be made in respect of the potential loss of any top-up pension payable to members of contracted out pension arrangements.

There may be cases where the employee was a member of a company occupational pension scheme which was not contracted out. This means that there are two potential losses which have to be assessed separately; one under S2P and the second under the occupational pension scheme. The methods for assessing this second loss are discussed in Chapters 5, 6, 7 and 8. An employee who was not previously a member of an occupational pension scheme will not suffer a loss of future pension rights (other than those payable by the State) unless the employer was contributing to a personal pension or stakeholder pension on behalf of the employee, in which case the loss can be measured as the loss of that contribution (see Chapter 7).

In general, the lower and upper earnings limits and the lower earnings threshold will be uprated at the beginning of each tax year. Thus the figures in Table 3.2 will need to be revised on an annual basis; in calculating the value of the S2P loss on dismissal, factors relevant to the tax year in which dismissal took place should be applied to the gross earnings as at the date of dismissal.

Where the factors are used to value the S2P accruing from some future employment, the table of factors for the latest available tax year should be used and applied to the assessed gross earnings in the new employment.

Table 3.2 Factor to be applied to gross earnings for valuing loss of future accruals of S2P for one year

QEF = 4004 LET = 11200 UEL = 30940 (2003-2004)

Salary	5,000	6,000	7,000	8,000	9,000	10,000	11,000	12,000	13,000	14,000	15,000	20,000	25,000	30,000	35,000	40,000	45,000	50,000
Men (age)																		
20	9.2%	7.7%	6.6%	5.8%	5.1%	4.6%	4.2%	3.9%	3.8%	3.6%	3.5%	3.0%	2.7%	2.8%	2.5%	2.2%	1.9%	1.7%
25	9.7%	8.1%	6.9%	6.0%	5.4%	4.8%	4.4%	4.1%	4.0%	3.8%	3.6%	3.2%	2.9%	2.9%	2.6%	2.3%	2.0%	1.8%
30	10.2%	8.5%	7.3%	6.4%	5.7%	5.1%	4.7%	4.4%	4.2%	4.0%	3.9%	3.3%	3.0%	3.1%	2.7%	2.4%	2.1%	1.9%
35	10.9%	9.1%	7.8%	6.8%	6.0%	5.4%	4.9%	4.7%	4.4%	4.3%	4.1%	3.6%	3.2%	3.3%	2.9%	2.5%	2.3%	2.0%
40	11.5%	9.6%	8.2%	7.2%	6.4%	5.8%	5.2%	4.9%	4.7%	4.5%	4.3%	3.8%	3.4%	3.5%	3.1%	2.7%	2.4%	2.2%
45	13.5%	11.3%	9.7%	8.5%	7.5%	6.8%	6.1%	5.8%	5.5%	5.3%	5.1%	4.4%	4.0%	4.1%	3.6%	3.2%	2.8%	2.5%
50	16.2%	13.5%	11.6%	10.1%	9.0%	8.1%	7.4%	7.0%	6.6%	6.4%	6.1%	5.3%	4.8%	4.9%	4.3%	3.8%	3.4%	3.0%
55	19.9%	16.6%	14.2%	12.4%	11.1%	10.0%	9.1%	8.5%	8.1%	7.8%	7.5%	6.5%	5.9%	6.0%	5.3%	4.7%	4.1%	3.7%
60	26.0%	21.6%	18.5%	16.2%	14.4%	13.0%	11.8%	11.1%	10.6%	10.2%	9.8%	8.5%	7.7%	7.8%	6.9%	6.1%	5.4%	4.9%
63	32.5%	27.1%	23.2%	20.3%	18.1%	16.3%	14.8%	13.9%	13.3%	12.7%	12.3%	10.6%	9.6%	9.8%	8.7%	7.6%	6.8%	6.1%
Women (age)																		
20	10.2%	8.5%	7.3%	6.4%	5.7%	5.1%	4.7%	4.4%	4.2%	4.0%	3.9%	3.3%	3.0%	3.1%	2.7%	2.4%	2.1%	1.9%
25	10.8%	9.0%	7.7%	6.7%	6.0%	5.4%	4.9%	4.6%	4.4%	4.2%	4.1%	3.5%	3.2%	3.2%	2.9%	2.5%	2.2%	2.0%
30	11.3%	9.5%	8.1%	7.1%	6.3%	5.7%	5.2%	4.9%	4.6%	4.4%	4.3%	3.7%	3.4%	3.4%	3.0%	2.7%	2.4%	2.1%
35	12.0%	10.0%	8.6%	7.5%	6.7%	6.0%	5.5%	5.2%	4.9%	4.7%	4.5%	3.9%	3.6%	3.6%	3.2%	2.8%	2.5%	2.3%
40	12.7%	10.6%	9.0%	7.9%	7.0%	6.3%	5.8%	5.4%	5.2%	5.0%	4.8%	4.1%	3.7%	3.8%	3.4%	3.0%	2.6%	2.4%
45	14.7%	12.3%	10.5%	9.2%	8.2%	7.4%	6.7%	6.3%	6.0%	5.8%	5.6%	4.8%	4.4%	4.4%	3.9%	3.4%	3.1%	2.8%
50	20.7%	17.2%	14.8%	12.9%	11.5%	10.3%	9.4%	8.9%	8.4%	8.1%	7.8%	6.7%	6.1%	6.2%	5.5%	4.8%	4.3%	3.9%
55	31.8%	26.5%	22.7%	19.9%	17.7%	15.9%	14.4%	13.6%	13.0%	12.5%	12.0%	10.4%	9.4%	9.6%	8.5%	7.4%	6.6%	5.9%
58	39.4%	32.8%	28.1%	24.6%	21.9%	19.7%	17.9%	16.9%	16.1%	15.4%	14.9%	12.9%	11.7%	11.9%	10.5%	9.2%	8.2%	7.4%

Appendix 4 Financial Information

Appendix 4: Tables of multipliers to be applied to the deferred annual pension to assess compensation for loss of enhancement of accrued pension rights (Chapter 5)

Table 4.1 Men in private sector schemes

Age last birthday at dismissal	Normal retirement age—men			Age last birthday at dismissal	Normal retirement age—men		
	55	60	65		55	60	65
20 and under	5.62	5.22	4.63	43	2.85	3.31	3.37
21	5.55	5.18	4.60	44	2.65	3.16	3.28
22	5.49	5.13	4.57	45	2.45	3.02	3.17
23	5.41	5.09	4.55	46	2.23	2.86	3.07
24	5.34	5.03	4.51	47	2.01	2.70	2.96
25	5.25	4.98	4.48	48	1.77	2.53	2.84
26	5.17	4.92	4.44	49	1.53	2.36	2.72
27	5.08	4.86	4.41	50	1.28	2.18	2.59
28	4.98	4.80	4.37	51	1.01	1.99	2.46
29	4.88	4.73	4.32	52	0.74	1.79	2.32
30	4.78	4.66	4.28	53	0.45	1.58	2.18
31	4.67	4.58	4.23	54	0.15	1.37	2.03
32	4.55	4.50	4.18	55		1.14	1.87
33	4.43	4.42	4.12	56		0.91	1.71
34	4.30	4.33	4.06	57		0.66	1.54
35	4.17	4.24	4.00	58		0.40	1.37
36	4.03	4.14	3.94	59		0.14	1.18
37	3.88	4.03	3.87	60			0.99
38	3.73	3.93	3.79	61			0.79
39	3.57	3.81	3.72	62			0.57
40	3.40	3.70	3.64	63			0.35
41	3.22	3.57	3.55	64			0.12
42	3.04	3.44	3.47				

Table 4.2 Men in public sector schemes

Age last birthday at dismissal	Normal retirement age—men			Age last birthday at dismissal	Normal retirement age—men		
	55	60	65		55	60	65
20 and under	6.26	5.91	5.33	43	3.10	3.65	3.80
21	6.19	5.85	5.30	44	2.88	3.49	3.69
22	6.10	5.80	5.26	45	2.66	3.33	3.57
24	5.92	5.68	5.18	47	2.17	2.97	3.32
25	5.83	5.61	5.14	48	1.92	2.78	3.18

Table 4.2 Men in public sector schemes (continued)

Age last birthday at dismissal	Normal retirement age—men			Age last birthday at dismissal	Normal retirement age—men		
	55	60	65		55	60	65
27	5.62	5.47	5.05	50	1.38	2.39	2.90
28	5.51	5.39	4.99	51	1.09	2.18	2.75
29	5.39	5.31	4.94	52	0.79	1.96	2.59
30	5.27	5.22	4.88	53	0.49	1.73	2.43
31	5.14	5.13	4.82	54	0.16	1.49	2.26
32	5.01	5.04	4.76	55		1.24	2.09
33	4.87	4.94	4.69	56		0.99	1.90
34	4.72	4.83	4.62	57		0.72	1.71
35	4.57	4.72	4.54	58		0.44	1.52
36	4.41	4.61	4.47	59		0.15	1.31
37	4.25	4.49	4.38	60			1.10
38	4.08	4.36	4.30	61			0.87
39	3.90	4.23	4.21	62			0.64
40	3.71	4.10	4.11	63			0.39
41	3.51	3.96	4.01	64			0.13
42	3.31	3.81	3.91				

Table 4.3 Women in private sector schemes

Age last birthday at dismissal	Normal retirement age—women			Age last birthday at dismissal	Normal retirement age—women		
	55	60	65		55	60	65
20 and under	5.89	5.54	4.96	43	2.98	3.50	3.61
21	5.83	5.49	4.94	44	2.77	3.35	3.50
22	5.75	5.44	4.91	45	2.56	3.19	3.39
23	5.68	5.39	4.88	46	2.33	3.02	3.28
24	5.59	5.34	4.84	47	2.10	2.85	3.16
25	5.51	5.28	4.81	48	1.85	2.68	3.04
26	5.42	5.22	4.77	49	1.60	2.49	2.91
27	5.32	5.15	4.73	50	1.33	2.30	2.77
28	5.22	5.09	4.68	51	1.06	2.09	2.63
29	5.12	5.01	4.63	52	0.77	1.88	2.48
30	5.00	4.94	4.58	53	0.47	1.67	2.33
31	4.89	4.85	4.53	54	0.16	1.44	2.17
32	4.77	4.77	4.47	55		1.20	2.00
33	4.64	4.68	4.42	56		0.95	1.83
34	4.50	4.58	4.35	57		0.69	1.64
35	4.36	4.48	4.28	58		0.42	1.46

Table 4.3 Women in private sector schemes (continued)

Age last birthday at dismissal	Normal retirement age—women			Age last birthday at dismissal	Normal retirement age—women		
	55	60	65		55	60	65
37	4.06	4.27	4.14	60			1.05
38	3.90	4.16	4.06	61			0.84
39	3.73	4.03	3.98	62			0.61
40	3.55	3.91	3.89	63			0.37
41	3.37	3.78	3.80	64			0.13
42	3.18	3.64	3.71				

Table 4.4 Women in public sector schemes

Age last birthday at dismissal	Normal retirement age—women			Age last birthday at dismissal	Normal retirement age—women		
	55	60	65		55	60	65
20 and under	6.53	6.22	5.68	43	3.23	3.84	4.04
21	6.45	6.17	5.65	44	3.00	3.67	3.92
22	6.36	6.11	5.61	45	2.76	3.49	3.79
23	6.27	6.04	5.57	46	2.51	3.31	3.66
24	6.18	5.98	5.52	47	2.26	3.12	3.53
25	6.08	5.91	5.48	48	1.99	2.92	3.38
26	5.97	5.83	5.43	49	1.72	2.72	3.24
27	5.86	5.75	5.38	50	1.43	2.50	3.08
28	5.74	5.67	5.32	51	1.13	2.28	2.92
29	5.62	5.59	5.26	52	0.82	2.05	2.75
30	5.49	5.49	5.20	53	0.50	1.81	2.58
31	5.36	5.40	5.14	54	0.17	1.56	2.40
32	5.22	5.30	5.07	55		1.30	2.21
33	5.07	5.19	4.99	56		1.03	2.02
34	4.92	5.08	4.92	57		0.75	1.81
35	4.76	4.97	4.84	58		0.46	1.60
36	4.59	4.85	4.75	59		0.15	1.38
37	4.42	4.72	4.66	60			1.16
38	4.24	4.59	4.57	61			0.92
39	4.05	4.45	4.48	62			0.67
40	3.86	4.31	4.37	63			0.41
41	3.66	4.16	4.27	64			0.14
42	3.44	4.00	4.16				

Appendix 5: Tables of multipliers to be applied to the estimated final annual pension to assess value of pension arising from service to Normal Retirement Age (Chapter 8)

Table 5.1 Men in private sector schemes

Age last birthday at dismissal	Normal retirement age—men			Age last birthday at dismissal	Normal retirement age—men		
	55	60	65		55	60	65
20 and under	12.79	10.83	8.91	43	16.24	13.75	11.29
21	12.92	10.94	9.00	44	16.42	13.89	11.41
22	13.05	11.05	9.09	45	16.60	14.04	11.53
23	13.19	11.16	9.18	46	16.78	14.20	11.66
24	13.32	11.28	9.27	47	16.97	14.35	11.78
25	13.46	11.39	9.36	48	17.16	14.51	11.91
26	13.60	11.51	9.46	49	17.35	14.67	12.04
27	13.74	11.63	9.56	50	17.55	14.84	12.17
28	13.88	11.75	9.66	51	17.76	15.01	12.30
29	14.02	11.87	9.76	52	17.97	15.18	12.44
30	14.17	11.99	9.86	53	18.19	15.36	12.58
31	14.32	12.12	9.96	54	18.42	15.55	12.72
32	14.47	12.25	10.07	55		15.74	12.87
33	14.62	12.37	10.17	56		15.95	13.03
34	14.77	12.50	10.28	57		16.16	13.19
35	14.93	12.64	10.39	58		16.38	13.36
36	15.08	12.77	10.50	59		16.61	13.54
37	15.24	12.90	10.61	60			13.73
38	15.40	13.04	10.72	61			13.93
39	15.57	13.18	10.83	62			14.14
40	15.73	13.32	10.95	63			14.37
41	15.90	13.46	11.06	64			14.62
42	16.07	13.60	11.18				

Table 5.2 Men in public sector schemes

Age last birthday at dismissal	Normal retirement age—men			Age last birthday at dismissal	Normal retirement age—men		
	55	60	65		55	60	65
20 and under	15.97	13.65	11.36	43	20.26	17.31	14.40
21	16.13	13.79	11.47	44	20.48	17.50	14.55
22	16.30	13.93	11.59	45	20.70	17.68	14.70
23	16.46	14.07	11.71	46	20.93	17.88	14.86
24	16.63	14.21	11.82	47	21.16	18.07	15.02
25	16.80	14.36	11.95	48	21.40	18.27	15.18

Table 5.2 Men in public sector schemes (continued)

Age last birthday at dismissal	Normal retirement age—men			Age last birthday at dismissal	Normal retirement age—men		
	55	60	65		55	60	65
27	17.15	14.66	12.19	50	21.89	18.69	15.52
28	17.33	14.81	12.32	51	22.15	18.90	15.69
29	17.51	14.96	12.44	52	22.41	19.12	15.87
30	17.69	15.12	12.57	53	22.69	19.35	16.05
31	17.87	15.27	12.70	54	22.97	19.59	16.24
32	18.06	15.43	12.84	55		19.83	16.44
33	18.25	15.59	12.97	56		20.09	16.64
34	18.44	15.75	13.11	57		20.35	16.85
35	18.63	15.92	13.24	58		20.63	17.07
36	18.82	16.08	13.38	59		20.92	17.30
37	19.02	16.25	13.52	60			17.55
38	19.22	16.42	13.66	61			17.81
39	19.42	16.60	13.80	62			18.08
40	19.63	16.77	13.95	63			18.38
41	19.83	16.95	14.10	64			18.70
42	20.05	17.13	14.24				

Table 5.3 omen in private sector schemes

Age last birthday at dismissal	Normal retirement age—women			Age last birthday at dismissal	Normal retirement age—women		
	55	60	65		55	60	65
20 and under	13.26	11.32	9.37	43	16.74	14.28	11.81
21	13.39	11.43	9.47	44	16.92	14.43	11.93
22	13.53	11.55	9.56	45	17.10	14.58	12.05
23	13.67	11.67	9.66	46	17.28	14.73	12.18
24	13.80	11.78	9.75	47	17.47	14.89	12.30
25	13.94	11.90	9.85	48	17.66	15.05	12.43
26	14.08	12.02	9.95	49	17.85	15.21	12.56
27	14.23	12.14	10.05	50	18.05	15.38	12.70
28	14.37	12.27	10.15	51	18.25	15.55	12.84
29	14.52	12.39	10.26	52	18.46	15.72	12.98
30	14.66	12.51	10.36	53	18.67	15.90	13.12
31	14.81	12.64	10.46	54	18.89	16.08	13.27
32	14.96	12.77	10.57	55		16.27	13.42
33	15.11	12.90	10.67	56		16.47	13.58
34	15.27	13.03	10.78	57		16.67	13.74
35	15.42	13.16	10.89	58	16.88		13.91

Table 5.3 omen in private sector schemes (continued)

Age last birthday at dismissal	Normal retirement age—women			Age last birthday at dismissal	Normal retirement age—women		
	55	60	65		55	60	65
37	15.74	13.43	11.11	60			14.27
38	15.90	13.57	11.22	61			14.46
39	16.07	13.71	11.34	62			14.66
40	16.23	13.85	11.45	63			14.88
41	16.40	13.99	11.57	64			15.10
42	16.57	14.13	11.69				

Table 5.4 omen in public sector schemes

Age last birthday at dismissal	Normal retirement age—women			Age last birthday at dismissal	Normal retirement age—women		
	55	60	65		55	60	65
21	16.64	14.33	12.02	44	21.02	18.09	15.16
22	16.81	14.48	12.15	45	21.25	18.28	15.32
23	16.98	14.62	12.27	46	21.47	18.48	15.48
24	17.15	14.77	12.39	47	21.70	18.67	15.64
25	17.32	14.92	12.51	48	21.94	18.87	15.81
26	17.50	15.07	12.64	49	22.18	19.08	15.98
27	17.68	15.22	12.77	50	22.42	19.28	16.15
28	17.86	15.37	12.90	51	22.67	19.50	16.33
29	18.04	15.53	13.03	52	22.93	19.72	16.51
30	18.22	15.69	13.16	53	23.19	19.94	16.69
31	18.40	15.85	13.29	54	23.46	20.17	16.88
32	18.59	16.01	13.43	55		20.41	17.08
33	18.78	16.17	13.56	56		20.65	17.28
34	18.97	16.33	13.70	57		20.90	17.48
35	19.16	16.50	13.84	58		21.16	17.70
36	19.36	16.67	13.98	59		21.43	17.92
37	19.56	16.84	14.12	60			18.15
38	19.76	17.01	14.26	61			18.40
39	19.96	17.18	14.41	62			18.65
40	20.17	17.36	14.56	63			18.92
41	20.38	17.54	14.70	64			19.21
42	20.59	17.72	14.86				

Appendix 6: Tables of multipliers to be applied to the deferred annual pension to assess value of deferred pension (Chapter 8)

Table 6.1 Men in private sector schemes

Age last birthday at dismissal	Normal retirement age—men			Age last birthday at dismissal	Normal retirement age—men		
	55	60	65		55	60	65
20 and under	7.17	5.61	4.28	43	13.39	10.44	7.92
21	7.37	5.76	4.40	44	13.76	10.73	8.14
22	7.57	5.92	4.51	45	14.15	11.03	8.36
23	7.77	6.08	4.63	46	14.55	11.33	8.59
24	7.98	6.24	4.76	47	14.96	11.65	8.83
25	8.20	6.41	4.88	48	15.38	11.98	9.07
26	8.43	6.59	5.02	49	15.82	12.31	9.32
27	8.66	6.77	5.15	50	16.28	12.66	9.57
28	8.90	6.95	5.29	51	16.75	13.02	9.84
29	9.14	7.14	5.43	52	17.24	13.40	10.12
30	9.39	7.34	5.58	53	17.74	13.78	10.40
31	9.65	7.54	5.73	54	18.27	14.19	10.69
32	9.92	7.74	5.89	55		14.60	11.00
33	10.19	7.96	6.05	56		15.04	11.32
34	10.47	8.18	6.22	57		15.50	11.65
35	10.76	8.40	6.39	58		15.97	12.00
36	11.06	8.63	6.56	59		16.47	12.36
37	11.36	8.87	6.74	60			12.74
38	11.68	9.11	6.92	61			13.14
39	12.00	9.36	7.11	62			13.56
40	12.33	9.62	7.31	63			14.02
41	12.67	9.89	7.51	64			14.50
42	13.03	10.16	7.71				

Table 6.2 Men in public sector schemes

Age last birthday at dismissal	Normal retirement age—men			Age last birthday at dismissal	Normal retirement age—men		
	55	60	65		55	60	65
20 and under	9.71	7.74	6.03	43	17.16	13.66	10.59
21	9.95	7.93	6.18	44	17.60	14.00	10.86
22	10.19	8.13	6.33	45	18.05	14.36	11.13
23	10.45	8.33	6.48	46	18.51	14.72	11.41
24	10.71	8.54	6.64	47	18.99	15.10	11.70
25	10.97	8.75	6.81	48	19.48	15.49	12.00

Table 6.2 Men in public sector schemes (continued)

Age last birthday at dismissal	Normal retirement age—men			Age last birthday at dismissal	Normal retirement age—men		
	55	60	65		55	60	65
27	11.53	9.19	7.15	50	20.51	16.30	12.62
28	11.82	9.42	7.32	51	21.06	16.73	12.94
29	12.11	9.65	7.50	52	21.62	17.17	13.27
30	12.42	9.89	7.69	53	22.20	17.62	13.62
31	12.73	10.14	7.88	54	22.81	18.10	13.98
32	13.05	10.40	8.08	55		18.59	14.35
33	13.37	10.66	8.28	56		19.10	14.74
34	13.71	10.92	8.49	57		19.63	15.14
35	14.05	11.20	8.70	58		20.19	15.56
36	14.41	11.48	8.91	59		20.78	15.99
37	14.77	11.76	9.14	60			16.45
38	15.14	12.06	9.36	61			16.94
39	15.53	12.36	9.60	62			17.45
40	15.92	12.67	9.84	63			17.99
41	16.32	12.99	10.08	64			18.57
42	16.73	13.32	10.34				

Table 6.3 Women in private sector schemes

Age last birthday at dismissal	Normal retirement age—women			Age last birthday at dismissal	Normal retirement age—women		
	55	60	65		55	60	65
20 and under	7.37	5.79	4.41	43	13.76	10.79	8.20
21	7.57	5.94	4.53	44	14.15	11.08	8.42
22	7.78	6.11	4.66	45	14.54	11.39	8.66
23	7.99	6.27	4.78	46	14.95	11.71	8.90
24	8.21	6.44	4.91	47	15.37	12.04	9.14
25	8.43	6.62	5.05	48	15.80	12.37	9.40
26	8.67	6.80	5.18	49	16.25	12.72	9.66
27	8.90	6.99	5.33	50	16.71	13.08	9.93
28	9.15	7.18	5.47	51	17.19	13.45	10.21
29	9.40	7.38	5.62	52	17.69	13.84	10.49
30	9.66	7.58	5.77	53	18.20	14.23	10.79
31	9.92	7.79	5.93	54	18.73	14.65	11.10
32	10.20	8.00	6.09	55		15.07	11.42
33	10.48	8.22	6.26	56		15.52	11.75
34	10.77	8.45	6.43	57		15.98	12.10
35	11.06	8.68	6.61	58		16.46	12.45

Table 6.3 Women in private sector schemes (continued)

Age last birthday at dismissal	Normal retirement age—women			Age last birthday at dismissal	Normal retirement age—women		
	55	60	65		55	60	65
37	11.68	9.16	6.97	60			13.22
38	12.00	9.41	7.16	61			13.63
39	12.34	9.67	7.36	62			14.05
40	12.68	9.94	7.56	63			14.50
41	13.03	10.21	7.77	64			14.98
42	13.39	10.49	7.98				

Table 6.4 Women in public sector schemes

Age last birthday at dismissal	Normal retirement age—women			Age last birthday at dismissal	Normal retirement age—women		
	55	60	65		55	60	65
20 and under	9.94	7.97	6.22	43	17.58	14.07	10.97
21	10.19	8.17	6.38	44	18.03	14.42	11.24
22	10.45	8.37	6.54	45	18.49	14.79	11.53
23	10.71	8.58	6.70	46	18.96	15.16	11.82
24	10.97	8.79	6.87	47	19.45	15.55	12.12
25	11.25	9.01	7.04	48	19.95	15.95	12.43
26	11.53	9.24	7.21	49	20.46	16.36	12.74
27	11.82	9.47	7.39	50	20.99	16.78	13.07
28	12.11	9.70	7.58	51	21.54	17.22	13.41
29	12.42	9.94	7.76	52	22.11	17.67	13.75
30	12.73	10.19	7.96	53	22.69	18.13	14.11
31	13.05	10.45	8.16	54	23.29	18.61	14.48
32	13.37	10.71	8.36	55		19.11	14.86
33	13.71	10.98	8.57	56		19.62	15.26
34	14.05	11.25	8.78	57		20.15	15.67
35	14.40	11.53	9.00	58		20.70	16.10
36	14.77	11.82	9.22	59		21.28	16.54
37	15.14	12.12	9.45	60			17.00
38	15.52	12.42	9.69	61			17.48
39	15.91	12.73	9.93	62			17.98
40	16.31	13.05	10.18	63			18.51
41	16.72	13.38	10.44	64			19.07
42	17.15	13.72	10.70				

Appendix 7: Tables of factors to be applied to the standard contribution rate to assess the age specific contribution rate

Table 7.1 Men

Age last birthday at dismissal	Normal retirement age—men			Age last birthday at dismissal	Normal retirement age—men		
	55	60	65		55	60	65
20 and under	0.77	0.74	0.71	43	1.09	1.04	1.00
21	0.78	0.75	0.72	44	1.11	1.06	1.01
22	0.79	0.76	0.73	45	1.12	1.08	1.03
23	0.80	0.77	0.74	46	1.14	1.09	1.05
24	0.82	0.78	0.75	47	1.16	1.11	1.06
25	0.83	0.79	0.76	48	1.18	1.13	1.08
26	0.84	0.81	0.77	49	1.20	1.15	1.09
27	0.85	0.82	0.78	50	1.22	1.16	1.11
28	0.87	0.83	0.80	51	1.24	1.18	1.13
29	0.88	0.84	0.81	52	1.26	1.20	1.15
30	0.89	0.86	0.82	53	1.28	1.22	1.17
31	0.91	0.87	0.83	54	1.30	1.24	1.18
32	0.92	0.88	0.84	55		1.27	1.20
33	0.93	0.90	0.86	56		1.29	1.22
34	0.95	0.91	0.87	57		1.31	1.24
35	0.96	0.92	0.88	58		1.33	1.27
36	0.98	0.94	0.90	59		1.36	1.29
37	0.99	0.95	0.91	60			1.31
38	1.01	0.97	0.93	61			1.34
39	1.02	0.98	0.94	62			1.37
40	1.04	1.00	0.95	63			1.39
41	1.06	1.01	0.97	64			1.42
42	1.07	1.03	0.98				

Table 7.2 Women

Age last birthday at dismissal	Normal retirement age—women			Age last birthday at dismissal	Normal retirement age—women		
	55	60	65		55	60	65
20 and under	0.77	0.74	0.70	43	1.09	1.04	0.99
21	0.78	0.75	0.71	44	1.11	1.06	1.00
22	0.79	0.76	0.72	45	1.12	1.08	1.02
23	0.81	0.77	0.73	46	1.14	1.09	1.03
24	0.82	0.78	0.75	47	1.16	1.11	1.05

Table 7.2 Women (continued)

Age last birthday at dismissal	Normal retirement age—women			Age last birthday at dismissal	Normal retirement age—women		
	55	60	65		55	60	65
26	0.84	0.81	0.77	49	1.20	1.14	1.08
27	0.86	0.82	0.78	50	1.21	1.16	1.10
28	0.87	0.83	0.79	51	1.23	1.18	1.12
29	0.88	0.85	0.80	52	1.25	1.20	1.14
30	0.90	0.86	0.81	53	1.28	1.22	1.15
31	0.91	0.87	0.83	54	1.30	1.24	1.17
32	0.92	0.88	0.84	55		1.26	1.19
33	0.94	0.90	0.85	56		1.28	1.21
34	0.95	0.91	0.86	57		1.30	1.23
35	0.96	0.92	0.88	58		1.33	1.25
36	0.98	0.94	0.89	59		1.35	1.27
37	0.99	0.95	0.90	60			1.30
38	1.01	0.97	0.92	61			1.32
39	1.02	0.98	0.93	62			1.35
40	1.04	1.00	0.95	63			1.37
41	1.06	1.01	0.96	64			1.40
42	1.07	1.03	0.97				

Appendix 5
Forms and Precedents

For a specimen Compromise Agreement see Chapter 5, page 74

Employment Tribunal

THE CLAIM

The Claim Form ET1

The form can be found on the ETS website at <http://www.employmenttribunals.gov.uk/Documents/FormsGuidance>.

New forms were introduced with effect from 6 April 2009. At the time of writing the ETS website carried both the new forms and the old forms, which continue to apply in some transitional cases after 6 April 2009. Care must be taken to ensure that the correct form is used.

Specimen Grounds of Complaint

Claim alleging constructive unfair dismissal

IN THE [ ] EMPLOYMENT TRIBUNAL Claim No
BETWEEN:

MISS A

Claimant

-and-

XYZ IT SYSTEMS LIMITED

Respondent

RIDER TO ET1

1. The Respondent carries on business as a provider of bespoke IT solutions to commercial clients. The Claimant was employed as a sales representative between 6 January 2006 and 22 March 2007.
2. It was an implied term of the Claimant's contract of employment that the Respondent would not, without reasonable cause, act in a manner calculated or likely to destroy or seriously damage the relationship of trust and confidence between the employer and employee.
3. The Claimant's role involved two distinct functions. First, generating 'sales leads' through cold calling companies with whom the Respondent had no previous contact, such contact was deemed to be successful if the potential client agreed to a meeting with the Respondent's representatives. Secondly, the Claimant would form part of a two person team, along with a technical expert, who attended such meetings and attempted to persuade the client to agree to buy a system from the Respondent. It was the Respondent's policy that where a sales lead was generated by a particular representative, they would normally attend the meeting. However, if the meeting could not be arranged to fit in with that individual's availability, another representative would be designated by the sales manager to attend.
4. The Claimant was paid two monthly bonuses based on the number of successful cold calls she made and the value of the contracts signed as a result of her sales meetings. The Claimant and other sales representatives were given individual targets for each of these bonuses.
5. When the Claimant commenced employment the sales manager she reported to was Mr B. During the first six months of her employment the Claimant met all her targets. At her six month appraisal Mr B complimented her performance and indicated that she had a bright future within the Respondent's organization.
6. Shortly after the appraisal, Mr B left the company and was replaced by Mr C. Mr C had a very different style of management to Mr C and he sought to achieve results by intimidating the sales staff. During the period July 2006 to February 2007 Mr C increasingly singled out the Claimant. In particular:
   (a) Mr C frequently swore in the office, and would direct this at the Claimant.
   (b) Mr C told the Claimant that she was 'crap' at sales and didn't understand the Respondent's products. He repeated this in front of other employees.
   (c) Mr C never gave the Claimant the opportunity to go to sales meetings that other representatives could not attend. Whenever possible he removed her sales meetings and gave them to other employees. This resulted in a decrease in the value of contracts agreed by the Claimant and she began to fail to meet her targets.
   (d) Mr C unreasonably increased the Claimant's targets, thereby 'setting her up to fail'. Other employees targets remained the same.

7. On 23 February 2007 the Claimant discovered that Mr C had asked another employee to attend a scheduled sales meeting with a company called 123 Ltd the following week. 123 Ltd is a large educational publisher with offices all over the country, if they were to agree to allow the Respondent to replace their IT system it would be an extremely valuable contract. The Claimant had made contact with 123 Ltd and developed the relationship over several weeks, she believed that she would be attending the sales meeting.
8. The Claimant went to Mr C's office to challenge him in relation to the 123 Ltd meeting. Mr C confirmed that he had asked another employee, Ms D, to attend the sales meeting. He said that the reason for this was that he was not confident that the Claimant had the skills or experience to manage such a potentially large order. The Claimant said that she disagreed that Ms D was any more able than her to successfully conduct the meeting. The Claimant said she believed that Mr C unfairly favoured Ms D.
9. At this point Mr C began to shout at the Claimant. He told her that she was 'always whinging' and that she was 'useless' and should be glad that she still had a job. He said that he would be 'a fool' to send her to such an important meeting as the 123 Ltd meeting and continued to shout at her for about five minutes. The Claimant was reduced to tears by Mr C's outburst. She ran out of his office and immediately left the building.
10. Mr C's actions, on behalf of the Respondent, both separately and cumulatively, amounted to repudiatory breaches of the implied term of trust and confidence in the Claimant's contract of employment.
11. The following day, in response to the Respondent's repudiatory breach, the Claimant resigned in writing giving one months' notice as required by her contract. The Claimant made it clear in the letter that she considered that she had been left with no option to resign due to Mr C's unacceptable treatment of her. The Respondent and Claimant agreed that she would take the notice as garden leave.
12. The Claimant also raised a grievance in her letter of resignation. The grievance was heard on 5 March 2007 and subsequently rejected. The appeal was heard on 29 March 2007 and was also rejected.
13. In all the circumstances the Claimant claims that she was constructively dismissed by the Respondent, and that such dismissal was unfair. The Claimant claims compensation for unfair dismissal.

[*Name*]

[*Date*]

Claim alleging discrimination on grounds of sex and maternity

IN THE [ ] EMPLOYMENT TRIBUNAL Claim No
BETWEEN:

MRS A

Claimant

-and-

R & R
A FIRM

Respondent

RIDER TO ET1

1. The Claimant was employed by the Respondent as a marketing executive from 1 December 2004 until her dismissal on 16 May 2007. The Respondent employed eight marketing executives in its marketing department.
2. In December 2005 the Claimant told her manager, Mr B, that she was pregnant. Mr B said 'congratulations' but then added that this was not the best timing as three other members of the department were either on maternity leave or shortly to commence maternity leave.
3. Prior to the Claimant commencing maternity leave two new, male, marketing executives joined the team. In the months preceding the start of her maternity leave the Claimant noticed that many of her clients were handed over to the new marketing executives and that she was left with very little to do.
4. The Claimant commenced maternity leave on 13 March 2006. The Claimant took full ordinary and additional maternity leave, as she was entitled to do, and returned to work on 12 March 2007.
5. When the Claimant returned to work none of the marketing executives remained on maternity leave. The total number of marketing executives now numbered ten, of which four were female. The Claimant was not given her previous client accounts to look after and found she had relatively little work to do. The other marketing executives, particularly the male ones, were very busy and were working long hours.
6. On or around 30 March 2007 Mr B called a meeting of all the marketing executives. Mr B said that the department needed to make cost savings and that it would perhaps be necessary to make a redundancy. Mr B asked if anyone would be prepared to reduce their hours but none of the executives volunteered to do this. Mr B did not ask whether anyone would be prepared to take voluntary redundancy.
7. The Claimant was invited to a meeting with Mr B on 4 April 2007 and informed her that she could be accompanied at that meeting. The Claimant attended the meeting with Miss C, a colleague. At the meeting, the Claimant was told that she had been provisionally selected for redundancy.
8. The Claimant was presented with a 'score sheet' which showed only her scores and appeared to show marks out of ten for length of service, qualifications, appraisal outcomes, attendance/timekeeping and performance. The Claimant was unable properly to argue against the scores she had been given without being able to compare herself to other employees. The Claimant had scored only 5 out of 10 for performance and argued that she would have scored higher if proper account had been taken of the fact that she had been absent on maternity leave and had not been given the same level of work as others before and afterwards.
9. The meeting was adjourned for approximately 10 minutes. Mr B returned and said that, in light of the Claimant's comments, he would increase her 'qualifications' mark from 4 to 5 out of 10. Mr B then said that the Claimant's score remained the lowest and said that he was terminating her contract by reason of redundancy on six weeks' notice.
10. The Claimant received a letter dated 4 April 2007 confirming Mr B's decision and informing her of her right to appeal. The Claimant appealed and argued that the redundancy process was a sham and merely designed to allow the Respondent to terminate her employment, or alternatively, that she had been unfairly selected for redundancy because of her maternity leave. The appeal was unsuccessful.

11. In the circumstances, the Claimant claims that the Respondent unlawfully discriminated against her on grounds of pregnancy and/or on grounds that she was seeking to exercise, or had exercised, her statutory right to maternity leave. The following acts of discrimination are relied upon:
    (a) Mr B requiring the Claimant to 'hand over' her accounts to new marketing executives prior to commencing her maternity leave.
    (b) Mr B failing to give the Claimant her accounts or equivalent accounts on her return to work following maternity leave.
    (c) The Claimant's dismissal.
12. Further, or in the alternative, the Claimant claims that the acts set out at paragraph 11(a) to (c) above are acts of direct sex discrimination.
13. Further, or in the alternative, the Claimant claims that her dismissal was automatically unfair under s 99 of the Employment Rights Act 1996 ('ERA') and regulation 20 of the Maternity and Parental Leave etc Regulations 1999, that is, that the dismissal was for a reason connected with:
    (a) the fact that she took, sought to take, or availed herself of the benefits of, ordinary maternity leave; further or alternatively,
    (b) the fact that she took or sought to take additional maternity leave.
14. The Claimant's primary case is that her position was not redundant as defined by s 139 ERA, and redundancy was not the reason for dismissal. The Respondent decided, as a result of her pregnancy and maternity leave, that it wished to dismiss the Claimant, and that the alleged redundancy was contrived to achieve this end.
15. In the alternative, should the ET find that there was a genuine redundancy, the Claimant was unfairly selected for redundancy by reason of her pregnancy and maternity leave and her dismissal was automatically unfair.
16. Further or in the alternative, should the ET find that dismissal was by reason of redundancy, and was not connected with the Claimant's pregnancy and maternity leave, the dismissal was nevertheless unfair as the Claimant was not adequately consulted, was not subject to objective selection criteria and was not offered any alternative employment.
17. The Claimant seeks a declaration that she has been discriminated against and unfairly dismissed and appropriate compensation.

[*Name*]

[*Date*]

Claim alleging discrimination on grounds of age and disability and whistle-blowing

IN THE [ ] EMPLOYMENT TRIBUNAL Claim No
BETWEEN:

MR A

Claimant

-and-

R ESTATE AGENTS LIMITED

Respondent

RIDER TO ET1

The Parties

1. The Claimant is employed by the Respondent as a sales assistant.
2. The Claimant's date of birth is 10 December 1949.
3. The Respondent is an estate agency and property management company operating within the residential sales and letting market in the Manchester area.

The Claimant's disability

4. In 1995 the Claimant was involved in a road traffic accident which resulted in serious injuries being sustained to both of his legs. The Claimant's injuries continue to constitute a physical impairment which has a substantial effect on his ability to carry out day-to-day activities and, in particular, upon his mobility. The Claimant walks with a pronounced limp and requires rest breaks when walking distances beyond around 200 metres. The Claimant can negotiate stairs only with extreme difficulty and pain and takes much longer to do so than an able-bodied person. As a result of his injuries, the Claimant can no longer drive.
5. In the premises, at all material times the Claimant was a disabled person within the meaning of the Disability Discrimination Act 1995 ('DDA').
6. The Respondent was at all times aware of the Claimant's disability.
   (a) The Claimant informed Mr B of the Respondent of his disability during his interview on 4 March 2006;
   (b) The Claimant's impairment is in any event obvious and apparent.

The Claimant's role

7. The Claimant was appointed to the role of sales assistant by letter dated 6 March 2002. His appointment commenced on 4 April 2002. From the commencement of his employment the Claimant's place of work was the Respondent's offices at 14 Hillside Road, Manchester ('Hillside Road'). The role was a part-time role working 9am to 1.30pm Monday to Friday.

The move to Riverside House

8. In or around May 2006 the Claimant and other employees were informed that they would be relocated to the Respondent's offices at Riverside Road, Salford ('Riverside House'). No consultation took place as to this relocation. The relocation took effect on 5 July 2006.
9. The offices at Riverside House were only accessible via a flight of 35 stairs. The Claimant experienced great difficulty accessing Riverside House via the flight of stairs.
10. On 5 July 2006 Mr B told the Claimant that he recognised the stairs would cause problems for the Claimant. Mr B indicated that he envisaged installing a stairlift, subject to obtaining quotes in relation to that work. Mr B informed the Claimant that he felt it appropriate that the Claimant change his hours to work from 9am to 6pm on two days and then from 9am to 1.30pm on a third day in order to reduce the number of times that the Claimant had to come into the office (and therefore use the stairs) in any given week. The Claimant reluctantly agreed to this on the basis that it would be for a short time only.
11. From 6 July 2006 the Claimant worked at Riverside House attending for full days on Mondays and Thursdays and half days on Wednesdays. The Respondent has failed to take any steps to install a stairlift.

The employment of Miss C

12. In or around October 2006 the Respondent employed another office assistant, Miss C.
13. On numerous occasions from October 2006 onwards, Miss C made age-specific disparaging comments, both to the Claimant's face and to other employees. These included 'old git', 'granddaddy' and 'slaphead'. Various junior members of the sales negotiation team particularly Mr D, Mr E and Miss F, also began to use these terms.
14. Mr B was at all material times aware of the disparaging comments, and sent an email to all members of staff on 18 January 2007 reminding them that conduct should be professional and appropriate at all times. However, the Respondent took no further steps to stop the comments, which continued, a fact of which Mr B of the Respondent was aware.

Breach of Estate Agency Act 1979

15. On or about 15 December 2006 it came to the Claimant's attention that one of the sales negotiators, Mr D, had failed to pass on an offer from a potential property purchaser to the vendor. The Claimant raised this with Mr D. Mr D said 'Be cool, grandad, sometimes you've got to let them sweat a bit to get the best deal'.
16. As a result of the information referred to in the previous paragraph, the Claimant believed (on reasonable grounds) that:
    (a) Mr D was deliberately failing to pass on an offer from a purchaser to a vendor;
    (b) The failure to do so constitutes an undesirable practice within the Estate Agency Act 1979 and the Estate Agency (Undesirable Practices) (No 2) Order 1991 and thus Mr D was failing to comply with his legal obligations towards his clients.

Meeting 24 January 2006

17. At the Claimant's request, the Claimant had a meeting with Mr B on 23 January 2006. In the meeting the Claimant raised the following matters:
    (a) He complained about the age-related harassment that he had suffered at the hands of the above-mentioned employees and asked that action be taken in this respect.
    (b) He asked what progress had been made in respect of a stairlift.
    (c) He requested to return to his previous hours, and/or to be permitted to work from Hillside Road.
    (d) He informed Mr B about Mr D's actions in respect of failing to inform vendors of offers made by prospective purchasers.
18. The Claimant's disclosure at paragraph 17(d) above was a protected disclosure within s 43A Employment Rights Act 1996 ('ERA').
    (a) The Claimant disclosed information which, in his reasonable belief, tended to show that a person had failed to comply with a legal obligation, within the meaning of s 43B(1)(b) ERA;
    (b) The disclosure was made in good faith to the Claimant's employer, within s 43C(1) ERA.
19. Further, or in the alternative, in raising the matters referred to in paragraph 17(a)–(c) the Claimant alleged that the Respondent and its employees had committed acts which would be in contravention of the DDA and the Employment Equality (Age) Regulations 2006 ('the Age Regulations'). The Claimant's actions in raising the said matters were protected acts for the purposes of s 55 DDA and regulation 4 of the Age Regulations.
20. The Respondent has failed to take any or any adequate steps to remedy the matters complained of by the Claimant.

Meeting 31 January 2007

21. The Claimant was asked by Mr B to attend a further meeting on 31 January 2007. The Claimant was not told what this meeting was about, nor was he offered the opportunity to be accompanied.
22. At the meeting on 31 January 2007 Mr B informed the Claimant that he was concerned that the Claimant's performance had been deteriorating in recent weeks and cited two allegations that the Claimant had failed to diarise appointments with the result that appointments were missed. Mr B informed the Claimant that he was to be given a formal written warning and that this would be kept on file. At the end of the meeting Mr B gave the Claimant a pre-prepared warning letter.
23. The allegations which formed the subject matter of the warning were false and without foundation.
24. The Respondent conducts an annual pay review on 28 February each year. As a result of having a written warning on his record, under the Respondent's remuneration policy, the Claimant was eligible for a pay increase of only 1.5%. The Claimant's pay increase would otherwise have been 3.5%.

Grievance procedure

25. The Claimant wrote a letter to Mr B dated 2 February 2007 which was stated to be both an appeal against the written warning and a grievance letter in respect of disability discrimination, age discrimination and detriment on the grounds of making a protected disclosure.
26. Mr B met with the Claimant to hear his grievance on 16 February 2007, the grievance was rejected. Mr B appealed the rejection and this was heard by Mr G, the Managing Director of the Respondent on 21 March 2007. The appeal was rejected.

Claims

Disability discrimination

27. The stairs in Riverside House placed the Claimant at a substantial disadvantage compared to people without his disability. The Respondent failed to make reasonable adjustments to alleviate this disadvantage by:
    (a) failing to install a stairlift or similar device.
    (b) failing to permit the Claimant to work from Hillside Road.
28. The Respondent has failed in its duty to the Claimant under s 4A DDA and has therefore discriminated against the Claimant under s 3A(2) of the DDA.
29. The implementation of these reasonable adjustments would have allowed him to revert to his original contractual hours.
30. Further or in the alternative, the Respondent has discriminated against the Claimant on grounds of his disability under s 3A(1) DDA by:
    (a) changing the Claimant's hours from five mornings per week to two days and one morning per week; and/or
    (b) requiring the Claimant to relocate to Riverside House.
31. Further or in the alternative, the Respondent's actions in issuing him with an unjustified written warning on 31 January 2007 was by reason, or in part by reason, of the allegations of disability discrimination made by the Claimant to Mr B at the 24 January 2007 meeting and therefore constitutes unlawful discrimination by way of victimisation contrary to s 55 DDA.

Age discrimination

32. The actions of Miss C, Mr D, Mr E and Miss F, as outlined above constituted unlawful harassment on the grounds of age under regulation 6 of the Age Regulations. The Respondent is liable for such harassment by virtue of regulation 25(1) of the Age Regulations.
33. The Claimant further contends that the Respondent's actions in issuing him with an unjustified written warning on 31 January 2006 was by reason, or in part by reason, of the allegations of age discrimination made by the Claimant to Mr B at the 24 January 2007 meeting and therefore constitutes unlawful discrimination by way of victimisation contrary to regulation 4(1) of the Age Regulations.

Protected disclosure

34. The Claimant further contends that the Respondent's actions in issuing him with an unjustified written warning on 31 January 2006 was by reason, or in part by reason, of the allegations made by the Claimant to Mr B at the 24 January 2007 meeting in respect of Mr D's professional conduct. In the premises, the Claimant has suffered a detriment on the ground that he had made a protected disclosure contrary to s 47B ERA.

Remedy

35. The Claimant seeks declarations that he has been subject to discrimination and/or victimisation and/or detriment on grounds of making a protected disclosure as set out above.
36. The Claimant seeks a recommendation that the Respondent shall, within such time as the Tribunal determines to be appropriate, relocate the Claimant to the Hillside Road office and/or install a stairlift or similar apparatus in the Riverside House office.
37. By reason of the matters aforesaid the Claimant has suffered loss and damage. The Claimant seeks compensation in respect of each of his claims. In particular, the Claimant claims:
    (a) Compensation for injury to feelings.
    (b) Compensation in respect of financial loss resulting from his failure to obtain a 3.5% pay increase.
    (c) Compensation in respect of anticipated financial loss resulting from his failure to obtain a 3.5% pay increase.

[*Name*]
[*Date*]

THE RESPONSE

The Response Form ET3

The form can be found on the ETS website at <http://www.employmenttribunals.gov.uk/Documents/FormsGuidance>.

New forms were introduced with effect from 6 April 2009. At the time of writing the ETS website carried both the new forms and the old forms, which continue to apply in some transitional cases after 6 April 2009. Care must be taken to ensure that the correct form is used.

Specimen Grounds of Response

Response to claim of constructive unfair dismissal

IN THE [ ] EMPLOYMENT TRIBUNAL Claim No
BETWEEN:

MISS A

Claimant

-and-

XYZ IT SYSTEMS LIMITED

Respondent

RIDER TO ET3

14. References to paragraph numbers are references to the Claimant's Rider to ET1.
15. Paragraph 1, 2, 3 and 4 of the ET1 are admitted.
16. Paragraph 5 of the ET1 is admitted. However, the Respondent's policy is to set easily obtainable targets in the first six months of employment to encourage new sales representatives and recognise the fact that it takes some time to build up a list of contacts which will ultimately result in a stream of potential business.
17. As to the appraisal conducted by Mr B in June 2006, Mr B did compliment the Claimant in relation to her cold-calling ability, but noted a concern that she appeared to have some difficulty in turning the opportunities she created into sales. The appraisal records that this is an area for further monitoring and development.
18. As to paragraph 6:
    (a) It is admitted that Mr B left the company and was replaced by Mr C in July 2006.
    (b) It is denied that Mr C 'sought to achieve results by intimidating the sales staff'.
    (c) It is admitted that Mr C occasionally swore in the office. It is denied that this was specifically directed at the Claimant or was such that a reasonable person would find it offensive. The Claimant made no complaint about this language until her resignation and has herself been known to use similar language on occasion.
    (d) Mr C quickly identified problems with the Claimant's performance. She had not met her targets for July and August in respect of contracts agreed and was still performing at the level expected of new starters. Mr C had several discussions with the Claimant where she accepted these problems and resolved to try to improve.
    (e) It is denied that Mr C ever told the Claimant she was 'crap'.
    (f) As the Claimant continued to perform well in cold-calling, Mr C was concerned that perhaps her lack of in-depth knowledge of the products was causing problems at the meeting stage. This was confirmed by technical staff who had accompanied the Claimant to meetings. Mr C addressed this by increasing the Claimant's cold-calling targets for November and December and reducing her contracts target. He also arranged for her to spend two afternoons with technical staff to develop a further understanding of the business. The Claimant did not indicate any objection to these proposals.
    (g) If is denied that the objective in increasing the Claimant's cold-calling target was to set her up to fail, rather it was to protect her ability to earn whilst recognising that neither she nor the company were benefiting from her poor performance in sales meetings.
    (h) As a result of this policy, Mr C did arrange for certain opportunities generated by the claimant through cold-calling to be handled at the meeting stage by other employees. Mr C also allowed the Claimant to continue to attend meetings so as to develop her skills in this area.
19. As to paragraph 7, on or around 22 February 2007 it came to Mr C's attention that the Claimant had diarised to attend a sales meeting with 123 Ltd. It is admitted that this was a contact established by the Claimant and admitted and averred that this was potentially an extremely important and valuable contract for the Respondent. Mr C therefore asked another sales representative to take on this meeting.

20. Paragraphs 8 and 9 are denied, save that it is admitted that the Claimant came to Mr C's office to challenge him in relation to the 123 Ltd meeting. The Claimant appeared very angry. The Claimant asked Mr C if it was correct that she was no longer going to the 123 Ltd meeting. He confirmed that it was and began to provide an explanation. The Claimant refused to listen to Mr C's explanation and instead told him that she hated working for the Respondent and that she had only taken the job because she believed she would earn huge bonuses. The Claimant told Mr C that she intended to resign. Mr C asked the Claimant to think about her decision overnight and explained that he felt that she could still develop into a successful sales representative. The Claimant agreed to do this. The Claimant had become tearful as she told Mr C that she wished to resign.
21. It is denied that Mr C shouted at the Claimant or said that she was 'whinging', 'useless' or a 'fool'. There was no discussion as to the identity of another person who would conduct the meeting in place of the Claimant.
22. For the reasons set out above, paragraph 10 is denied.
23. Mr C had told the Claimant that she could take the rest of the afternoon off, and understood that she returned to her desk to collect her handbag and then left the office.
24. As to paragraph 11, it is admitted that the Claimant tendered her resignation the following day and that she claimed that Mr C's conduct had left her with no option but to resign. Mr C called the Claimant and asked her if she would like any more time to reconsider her decision and she said that she already had another job and that she would not wish to return to the Respondent. It is admitted that both parties agreed the Claimant would serve her notice as garden leave.
25. Paragraph 12 is admitted, the Respondent conducted a full investigation and concluded that there was no evidence that Mr C had acted in anything other than an appropriate manner towards the Claimant.
26. Paragraph 13 is denied.
    (a) There was no breach of the implied term of trust and confidence as alleged by the Claimant or at all.
    (b) Further or in the alternative, the Claimant did not resign in response to any breach of contract on the part of the Respondent, but resigned to pursue other employment opportunities.
    (c) Further or in the alternative, if the ET find that the Claimant was constructively dismissed, such dismissal was due to the Claimant's capability and was a fair dismissal.
    (d) Further or in the alternative, if the ET find that the Claimant was unfairly dismissed, the Claimant contributed to her dismissal and that her compensation should be reduced accordingly.
    (e) Further or in the alternative, if the ET find that the Claimant was unfairly dismissed, it is likely that the Claimant would have been fairly dismissed and/or would have resigned in any event within a short period and that her compensation should be assessed accordingly.

[*Name*]

[*Date*]

Response to claim alleging discrimination on grounds of sex and maternity

IN THE [ ] EMPLOYMENT TRIBUNAL Claim No
BETWEEN:

MRS A

Claimant

-and-

R & R

A FIRM

Respondent

RIDER TO ET3

18. References to paragraph numbers are references to the Claimant's Rider to ET1.
19. The first sentence of paragraph 1 is admitted. It is admitted that from the commencement of the Claimant's employment until November 2005 the headcount of the marketing department was eight. In September 2005, in response to significant new business, the Respondent decided to increase the headcount to 10. The new marketing executives, Mr D and Mr E, began work in October and November 2005 respectively.
20. As to paragraph 2, it is admitted that the Claimant informed the Respondent, through Mr B, of her pregnancy in December 2005 and that Mr B congratulated her. The remainder of paragraph 2 is denied. In fact, the Respondent's position with regard to employees on maternity leave was as follows:
    (a) Ms F had commenced maternity leave in February 2005. She had informed the Respondent that she did not intend to return to work and a permanent replacement had been recruited in June 2005.
    (b) Ms G was on maternity leave and due to return in June 2006. An employee had been hired to cover this maternity leave on a temporary contract. Ms G returned as planned and this employee left.
    (c) Ms H was due to commence maternity leave on 6 January 2006. Temporary cover was arranged for both Ms H and Mrs A. Ms H ultimately informed the company that she did not wish to return and the employee covering her role, Ms I, was offered a permanent role.
21. Save that it is admitted that Mr D and Mr E joined the team in late 2005, as set out above, paragraph 3 is denied. Some clients from each member of the team were transferred to Mr D and Mr E, as they had been recruited to reduce the workload of other team members, the Claimant was not treated any differently in this respect from other team members. A temporary employee, Ms J, was engaged from 27 February 2006 to cover the Claimant's maternity leave, there was therefore a two-week handover period during which the Claimant introduced Ms J to her clients.
22. Paragraph 4 is admitted.
23. Save that it is admitted that the headcount of the marketing department was 10, as it had been since autumn 2005, paragraph 5 is denied. Five of the marketing executives at this time were female. The Claimant was given her three most important previous clients—X Ltd, Y Ltd and Z Ltd. All the executives were relatively quiet at this time as two very large contracts had been lost in February 2007.
24. It was apparent to the Respondent in February 2007 that the loss of the two large contracts meant that it would be uneconomic to sustain a marketing department of ten people. Mr B worked for around six weeks attempting to secure other business before concluding that the Respondent would need to reduce personnel costs.
25. Paragraph 6 is admitted. The Respondent does not make enhanced redundancy payments, its experience is that in these circumstances voluntary redundancy is not attractive to employees. The employees were asked about reducing their hours and about any other suggestions.

26. Following the meeting Mr B decided that there was no alternative but to make one member of the team redundant. He constructed an assessment matrix and obtained advice from a human resources consultancy as to the appropriateness of the criteria used. The categories were as set out in the Claimant's paragraph 8. In relation to performance, this was based on feedback on file from clients.
27. Mr B was aware that the Claimant had been on maternity leave and this did not result in her having a reduced score in any category. In relation to performance, the Respondent considered feedback received prior to the Claimant's maternity leave and assumed that she would have continued to receive this level of feedback had she been undertaking the role in the period of her maternity leave.
28. The Claimant received an overall score of 22 out of 50. The next lowest score was 28.
29. Paragraph 7 is admitted.
30. As to paragraph 8, the Claimant and Mr B had an extensive discussion around her scores and the Claimant accepted most of them. It is admitted that the Claimant was not shown the scores of other employees but the Respondent contends that such an approach was neither necessary nor appropriate. Mr B explained that the Claimant had been assessed on her previous performance as if this was replicated throughout the period of her maternity leave. The Claimant received 5 out of 10 because she had significant neutral feedback and a small amount of negative feedback from the period prior to her maternity leave.
31. As to paragraph 9, in discussing her qualifications the Claimant noted that she had recently passed a further module in a professional marketing distance learning course. This had not appeared on her personnel file and Mr B accordingly increased her score in this area by one mark. The Claimant's total score following the meeting was therefore 23 out of 50 and she remained the lowest scoring employee by some margin. Mr B therefore verbally dismissed the Claimant on notice.
32. Paragraph 10 is admitted. It is denied that there was any foundation in the Claimant's allegations relating to the reasons for dismissal. The letter dated 4 April 2007 also set out the Claimant's entitlement to a statutory redundancy payment which was paid with her final wage.
33. For the reasons set out above, the reason for the Claimant's dismissal was redundancy and that the dismissal was fair in all the circumstances.
34. For the reasons set out above, it is denied that Mr B's instructions to the Claimant regarding the management of her clients either before or after her maternity constituted less favourable treatment, whether on the grounds of sex or pregnancy/maternity status.
35. Further, the Claimant failed to raise a statutory grievance in relation to the alleged management of clients and therefore is precluded from pursuing such a claim by operation of s 32 Employment Act 2002.
36. Further, insofar as the Claimant's claim relates to actions undertaken by Mr B prior to her maternity leave, the claim is out of time and it would not be just and equitable for the ET to extend time. The ET therefore has no jurisdiction to hear this claim.
37. For the reasons set out above, paragraphs 11–16 are denied.
38. The Respondent carried out reasonable consultation with the Claimant. Objective criteria were used to select for redundancy, and were fairly applied. There were no vacancies at the time of the Claimant's dismissal.
39. The Respondent denies that the Claimant is entitled to any remedy as claimed or at all.

[*Name*]

[*Date*]

Response to claim alleging discrimination on grounds of age and disability and whistle-blowing

IN THE [ ] EMPLOYMENT TRIBUNAL Claim No
BETWEEN:

MR A

Claimant

-and-

R ESTATE AGENTS LIMITED

Respondent

RIDER TO ET3

Introduction

1. References to paragraph numbers are references to paragraphs contained within the Claimant's Rider to ET1.
2. Paragraphs 1–3 are admitted.
3. The Respondent is a small company currently employing 16 employees, 14 of which are based at Riverside House and two at Hillside Road.
4. Paragraph 4 is not admitted, as the Respondent does not have detailed knowledge of the Claimant's medical history and medical condition. It is, however, admitted, that the Claimant is, and was at all material times, a disabled person within the meaning of the Disability Discrimination Act 1995 ('DDA') and that the Respondent had knowledge of such.
5. For the reasons set out above, paragraphs 5 and 6 are admitted.
6. Paragraph 7 is admitted. The Claimant's role was specifically to provide administrative support to the Respondent's sales and lettings negotiations.

The move to Riverside House

7. As to paragraph 8, it is admitted that the Claimant and other employees were relocated to Riverside House on 5 July 2006. It is denied that there was no consultation in relation to this move. There were regular meetings and discussions between the employees and management in the period between May and July 2006. These meetings addressed *inter alia* the issue of accessibility at Riverside House. Mr B offered to visit Riverside House with the Claimant in advance of the relocation in order to properly assess the difficulties the new location would present, but the Claimant refused to undertake such a visit.
8. Paragraph 9 is admitted.
9. As to paragraph 10, it is admitted that the Claimant and Mr B had a private discussion on 5 July 2006 regarding accessibility. It is further admitted that Mr B agreed to investigate the cost and practicality of installing a stairlift. It is denied that Mr B suggested to the Claimant that he should change his hours as described. The Claimant suggested this change. Mr B agreed to this change in hours solely in order to assist the Claimant.
10. Save that the start date and hours of work are admitted, paragraph 11 is denied. Mr B took steps to obtain quotes from three suppliers as to fitting a stairlift. Each supplier expressed concerns about the age of the building and the physical structure of the staircase. One supplier said that he could not undertake the work, the other two quotes were £15,000 and £18,000 respectively. The two companies which did provide quotes each estimated that it would take at least four months before they would be able to carry out the work.
11. The Respondent envisages continued expansion necessitating a further office move in around 18 months to 2 years. Taking into account the high price of the work, the fact that the Respondent is a small business with a modest turnover, and the relatively short time for which the Respondent is likely to remain in occupation of Riverside House, it is the Respondent's case that the installation of a stairlift is not a reasonable adjustment in all the circumstances.

The employment of Miss C

12. Paragraph 12 is admitted.
13. Paragraph 13 is denied. The Respondent conducted extensive interviews with the employees in question as part of the grievance process and could find no evidence of disparaging comments having been made.
14. Paragraph 14 is denied. Mr B was never aware of any disparaging comments made by the named members of staff, or any other member of staff, towards the Claimant. Mr B was aware that the Claimant on several occasions made inappropriate personal comments regarding Miss C's dress and appearance. Miss C has several body piercings and the Claimant was in the habit of telling her that she looked 'like the nails section in B&Q'.
15. During early January 2007 Mr B became aware of a culture among the sales assistants and some sales negotiators of making inappropriate comments about customers and deliberately keeping people waiting on the telephone. It was this which caused Mr B to send the email dated 18 January 2007.

Breach of Estate Agents Act 1979

16. Paragraphs 15 and 16 are denied, save that it is admitted that had Mr D acted in the manner alleged by the Claimant, this would constitute a breach of his legal obligations under the Estate Agents Act 1979 and subordinate legislation.

Meeting 24 January 2006

17. As to paragraph 17, it is admitted that a meeting took place between the Claimant and Mr B on the 23 January 2007.
    (a) It is admitted that the Claimant made a general complaint that he had been 'called names' related to his age by Miss C. It is denied that the Claimant made this allegation against any employee other than Miss C.
    (b) It is admitted that the Claimant asked what progress had been made in respect of the stairlift.
    (c) It is denied that the Claimant requested to return to his previous hours but admitted that he asked if it would be possible to work from Hillside Road.
    (d) It is denied that the Claimant raised any issue at all in respect of Mr D's alleged actions or in respect of the professional conduct of any sales negotiator.
18. Paragraph 18 is denied.
19. To the extent that the allegations made were restricted to those set out above, paragraph 19 is admitted.
20. Paragraph 20 is denied:
    (a) Mr B had an informal meeting with Miss C where she admitted that she did not get on with the Claimant but denied using age-specific disparaging terms. Mr B took the view that this was a simple clash of personalities and asked both employees to act respectfully towards one another.
    (b) Mr B informed the Claimant that he was waiting for quotes in respect of the stairlift, which was correct at that time.
    (c) Mr B explained to the Claimant that it would not be possible for him to work from Hillside Road. That office had been reduced to only two sales negotiators and all the administration systems had been relocated. There was not a sufficient requirement for administrative support to provide the Claimant with work at Hillside Road.
    (d) As set out above, the Claimant raised no issue in respect of regulatory breach and so this point was not addressed.

Meeting 31 January 2007

21. Paragraphs 21 and 22 are admitted.
22. Paragraph 23 is denied. The Claimant had recorded appointments in the diary for two clients, X and Y, on 25 and 27 January 2007. The appointments are recorded in the Claimant's handwriting, which is distinctive. The appointments should both have been recorded on the 26 January. As a result, the client attended the appointments and nobody from the Respondent attended. Both clients called to complain. Mr and Mrs X were looking to place their property on the market and subsequently did so with another agent, without agreeing to another appointment with the Respondent. The Respondent therefore lost a potentially valuable client as a result of the Claimant's mistake..

23. Save that it is admitted that the Respondent conducts a pay review on 28 February each year, paragraph 24 is denied. In the 2007 pay review the majority of employees received a 1.5% pay increase. Only two employees, who had performed particularly well, received a 3.5% increase. The Claimant would have received a pay increase of 1.5% regardless of the written warning.
24. At the conclusion of this meeting the Claimant informed Mr B of the matters set out at paragraph 15 of the Rider to ET1. This disclosure was therefore made, for the first time, after the Claimant had received the written warning.
25. It is denied that the disclosure was a qualifying disclosure within s 43B Employment Rights Act 1996 ('ERA'). It is denied that the Claimant believed, or had reasonable grounds to believe that the information he disclosed tended to show a breach of a legal obligation. The Claimant was aware at the time of his disclosure that the content of his disclosure was not true.
26. Further or in the alternative, it is denied that the allegation was made in accordance with s 43C ERA because it is denied that the allegation was made in good faith. The allegation was made in response to the Claimant having received a written warning. For these reasons it is denied that the disclosure is a protected disclosure within s 43A ERA.

Grievance procedure

27. Paragraphs 25 and 26 are admitted.

Claims

Disability discrimination

28. As to paragraph 27, it is admitted that the stairs at Riverside house placed the Claimant at a substantial disadvantage compared to people without his disability. For the reasons set out above, it is denied that either of the adjustments proposed by the Claimant were, or are, reasonable.
29. Paragraph 28 is denied for the reasons set out above.
30. Paragraph 29 is admitted, save that it is denied the adjustments were, or are, reasonable.
31. Paragraph 30 is denied. As to 30(a), this change was proposed by the Claimant who has never asked to revert to his original hours. In any event, it is the Respondent's case that this change in hours was an appropriate adjustment to accommodate the Claimant's disability following the relocation to Riverside House. As to 30(b), it is denied that this relocation constitutes discrimination against the claimant. Further or in the alternative, to the extent that it would otherwise constitute such discrimination the requirement to relocate was justified in all the circumstances.
32. Paragraph 31 is denied. The Respondent's actions in issuing the Claimant with a written warning were for the alleged reasons.

Age discrimination

33. Paragraph 32 is denied for the reasons set out above. In the event that the Tribunal find that the Claimant has been subjected to harassment the Respondent admits that it is vicariously liable for the actions of the employees and does not rely on the statutory defence set out at Regulation 25(3) of the Age Regulations.
34. For the reasons set out in paragraph 31 above, paragraph 33 is denied.

Protected disclosure

35. Paragraph 34 is denied. The Respondent's case is that:
    (a) The Claimant made the disclosure relied upon subsequent to the treatment complained of, further or in the alternative;
    (b) The disclosure is not a protected disclosure, for the reasons set out above, further or in the alternative;
    (c) In any event, the written warning was issued solely for the reasons set out above.

Remedy

36. For the reasons set out above it is denied that the Claimant is entitled to any remedy as claimed in paragraphs 35–37 or at all.

[Name]

[Date]

Employment Appeal Tribunal (EAT)

NOTICE OF APPEAL

[See Form 1, Schedule 1 to the Employment Appeal Tribunal Rules 1993, SI 1993/2854 as substituted by SI 2005/1871.]

Notice of Appeal from Decision of Employment Tribunal

1. The appellant is [name and address of the appellant].
2. Any communication relating to this appeal may be sent to the appellant at [appellant's address for service, including telephone number if any].
3. The appellant appeals from [here give particulars of the judgment, decision or order of the employment tribunal from which the appeal is brought including the location of the employment tribunal and the date].
4. The parties to the proceedings before the employment tribunal, other than the appellant, were [names and addresses of other parties to the proceedings resulting in judgment, decision or order appealed from].
5. Copies of—
   (a) the written record of the employment tribunal's judgment, decision or order and the written reasons of the employment tribunal;
   (b) the claim (ET1);
   (c) the response (ET3); and/or (*where relevant*)
   (d) an explanation as to why any of these documents are not included;
   are attached to this notice.
6. If the appellant has made an application to the employment tribunal for a review of its judgment or decision, copies of—
   (a) the review application;
   (b) the judgment;
   (c) the written reasons of the employment tribunal in respect of that review application; and/or
   (d) a statement by or on behalf of the appellant, if such be the case, that a judgment is awaited
   are attached to this Notice. If any of these documents exist but cannot be included, then a written explanation must be given.
7. The grounds upon which this appeal is brought are that the employment tribunal erred in law in that [*here set out in paragraphs the various grounds of appeal*].

Signed ....

Date ....

N.B. The details entered on your Notice of Appeal must be legible and suitable for photocopying. The use of black ink or typescript is recommended.

RESPONDENT'S ANSWER

[See Form 3, Schedule 1 to the Employment Appeal Tribunal Rules 1993, SI 1993/2854 as amended by SI 2005/1871.]

Respondent's Answer
Appeal from Decision of Employment Tribunal

1. The respondent is [name and address of respondent].
2. Any communication relating to this appeal may be sent to the respondent at [*respondent's address for service, including telephone number if any*].
3. The respondent intends to resist the appeal of [*here give the name of appellant*]. The grounds on which the respondent will rely are [the grounds relied upon by the employment tribunal/Certification Officer for making the judgment, decision or order appealed from] [and] [the following grounds]: *[here set out any grounds which differ from those relied upon by the employment tribunal or Certification Officer, as the case may be].*

4. The respondent cross-appeals from
   [*here give particulars of the decision appealed from*].
5. The respondent's grounds of appeal are:
   [*here state the grounds of appeal*].

Date
Signed

High Court and County Court

THE CLAIM

Claim Form N1

The N1 claim form, reproduced below, can be found at <http://www.hmcourts-service.gov.uk/HMCSCourtFinder/FormFinder.do>

Specimen Claim Form Endorsement: Wrongful Dismissal

Where Particulars of Claim are to be served with the Claim Form, it is sufficient to say in the Claim Form 'Particulars of Claim attached'. Where Particulars of Claim are to be served at a later date, brief particulars should be inserted in the space provided on the second page of the Claim Form.

For example:

'The Claimant's claim is for wrongful dismissal, in breach of a contract of employment made between the Claimant and the Defendant dated [*date*].

The Claimant claims damages and interest pursuant to section 35A Supreme Court Act 1981

The Claimant expects to recover more than £15,000.'

[*Note 1*: CPR, r 16.3 requires a statement of value to assist the court in allocation. The valuation brackets are: not more than £5,000; more than £5,000 but not more than £15,000; more than £15,000. For claims involving damages for personal injury, see CPR, r 16.3(4).

Note 2: in a county court claim, interest should be claimed under s 69 of the County Courts Act 1984.]

Specimen Particulars of Claim: Wrongful Dismissal

IN THE HIGH COURT OF JUSTICE CLAIM No.

QUEEN'S BENCH DIVISION

BETWEEN

A Claimant

—and—

B Defendant

PARTICULARS OF CLAIM

1. The Defendant is a limited company carrying on business in the manufacture, sale and distribution of electronic components.
2. The Claimant was employed by the Defendant from [*date*] as a Sales Manager.
3. The terms of the Claimant's employment are set out in a written contract of employment made between the Claimant and the Defendant and dated [*date*] ('the Contract'). A copy of the Contract is attached to these Particulars of Claim.
   There were (amongst others) the following express terms of the Contract:
   3.1 The Claimant's salary was £[] per annum.
   3.2 The Claimant was entitled to benefits as follows:
   [*insert details of other benefits provided for by the contract insofar as relevant to losses during the notice period, for example bonus, share options, car, insurance, private health care, etc*]
   3.3 By clause [ ], the period of notice to be given by either the Claimant or the Defendant to terminate the Claimant's employment was three months.
4. On [*date*], in breach of contract, the Defendant summarily dismissed the Claimant. At about 16.00 on [*date*] the Claimant was called to a meeting with [ ]. The Claimant was told that he was dismissed with immediate effect and was given a letter dated the same date confirming the same. The Claimant was not given three months', or any, notice as required by clause [ ] of the contract.
5. By reason of the Defendant's breach of contract the Claimant has suffered loss and damage.

PARTICULARS

5.1 The Defendant was not entitled to terminate the Claimant's employment summarily. The Defendant could only have terminated the Claimant's employment lawfully by giving three months' notice under clause [ ]. The Claimant has lost the benefit of the remuneration and other benefits he was entitled to and would have received from the Defendant during a three months' notice period.

5.2 A schedule of loss is attached to this statement of case.

6. Further, at the date of termination of his employment the Claimant was owed arrears of salary in respect of the months [insert details], in the sum of £[ ]. The Defendant has not paid the Claimant the said arrears or any part thereof.

7. The Claimant is entitled to and claims interest pursuant to section 35A of the Supreme Court Act 1981, at the Judgments Act rate of 8 per cent (or alternatively at such rates as the court shall find fit):

7.1 On the arrears of salary from [*date salary due*] to the date hereof, in the sum of £[ ], and thereafter continuing at a daily rate of £[ ]; or, alternatively for such periods as the court finds fit. A calculation of interest due until the date hereof is attached to these Particulars of Claim.

7.2 On such damages as are awarded to her for breach of contract at the Judgment Act rate of 8% from 31st December 2001; or, alternatively, at such rate and for such period as the court finds fit.

AND the Claimant claims:

1. The sum of £[ ] arrears of salary.
2. Damages for wrongful dismissal.
3. Interest pursuant to section 35A of the Supreme Court Act 1981 as set out at paragraph 7 above.

[Signature of Draftsman]

STATEMENT OF TRUTH

The Claimant believes that the facts stated in these Particulars of Claim are true.

I am duly authorized by the Claimant to sign this statement.

[Full Name]

[Date]

Signed

Solicitor,

of [ ]

Solicitors for the Claimant

[In a county court claim, interest should be claimed under s 69 of the County Courts Act 1984.]

THE DEFENCE

Specimen Defence: Wrongful Dismissal

IN THE HIGH COURT OF JUSTICE CLAIM No.

QUEEN'S BENCH DIVISION

BETWEEN

A Claimant

—and—

B Defendant

DEFENCE

1. Paragraphs 1 and 2 of the Particulars of Claim are admitted.
2. The Contract referred to in paragraph 3 is admitted. The Defendant will refer to the Contract at trial for its full meaning and effect.

3. It is admitted that the Claimant was summarily dismissed on [*date*]. It is admitted that the dismissal was without notice.
4. Prior to the termination of the Claimant's employment, on dates between [*date*] and [*date*], the Claimant had submitted false expenses claims, in the total sum of £500, to the Defendant in respect of expenses which had not been incurred by the Claimant and/or in respect of items which were not legitimate business expenditure incurred in the course of the Defendant's business. A schedule of the said expenses claims is attached to these Particulars of Claim. The submission of the said claims was gross misconduct on the part of the Claimant.
5. In the premises the Defendant was entitled to dismiss the Claimant summarily, and it is denied that the dismissal was in breach of contract as alleged or at all.
6. The Defendant disputes the Claimant's assessment of the value of the claim. A counter schedule is attached to these Particulars of Claim.
7. It is denied that the Claimant is entitled to the alleged or any relief.

[Signature of Draftsman]

STATEMENT OF TRUTH

The Defendant believes that the facts stated in this Defence are true.

I am duly authorized by the Defendant to sign this statement.

[Full Name]

[Date]

Signed

Solicitor,

of [ ]

Solicitors for the Defendant

Appendix 6
Tables

Current and Recent Maximum Awards

Complaint	Detail	Limit 1 February 2009 to 31 January 2010	Limit 1 February 2010 to 31 January 2011
Unfair dismissal			
Basic award (ERA 1996, s 119)	Based on week's pay and length of service	£10,500 (£11,400 wef 1.10.09)	£11,400
Maximum week's pay (ERA 1996, ss 220–229)		£350 (£380 from 1.10.09)	£380
Minimum basic award (TULR(C)A 1992 ss 152–167; ERA 1996, ss 100, 101A, 102, 103)	Applies on dismissals for health and safety, union or pension trustee reasons		
Compensation award (ERA 1996, ss 123–124)	Most dismissals	£66,200	£65,300
	Dismissals for health and safety/protected disclosure reasons	Unlimited	Unlimited
Additional award (ERA 1996, s 117)	26–52 weeks' pay	£18,200 (£19,760 wef 1.10.09)	£19,760
Redundancy payment (ERA 1996, s 162)	Based on week's pay and length of service	£10,500 (£11,400 wef 1.10.09)	£11,400
Guarantee pay per day (ERA 1996, ss 30–31)		£21.50	£21.20
Contract claims in employment tribunal			
Employment Tribunals (Extension of Jurisdiction) Order 1994		£25,000	£25,000
Insolvency payments (ERA 1996, s 18H)			
Arrears of pay	Up to 8 weeks' pay	£2,800 (£3,040 wef 1.10.09)	£3,040
Notice pay	Up to 12 weeks' pay	£4,260 (£4,560 wef 1.10.09)	£4,560
Holiday pay	Up to 6 weeks' pay	£1,980	£2,100
Redundancy payment	See above up to	£10,500 (£11,400 wef 1.10.09)	£11,400
Consultation/Notification rights			
Protective award (TULR(C)A 1992, s 192; TUPE 1981, reg 11)	Up to 90 days' pay	Unlimited	Unlimited
Failure to comply with information and consultation provisions (ICER 2004)		£75,000	£75,000
Failure to comply with notification of retirement rights (EE(A)R 2006, Sch 6, paras 2 and 11)	Up to 8 weeks' pay	£2,800 (£3,040 wef 1.10.09)	£3,040
Failure to allow right to be accompanied (ERA 1999, s 11)	Up to 2 week's pay	£700 (£760 wef 1.10.09)	£760
Discrimination		Unlimited	Unlimited
Flexible working			
Failure to follow procedure (FWR reg 7)	Up to 8 weeks' pay	£2,800 (£3,040 wef 1.10.09)	£3,040

Past Awards Limits

Complaint	Limit	Limit	Limit	Limit	Limit	Limit
	1 February 2003 to 31 January 2004 (SI 2002/2927)	1 February 2004 to 31 January 2005 (SI 2003/3038)	1 February 2005 to 31 January 2006 (SI 2004/2989)	1 February 2006 to 31 January 2007 (SI 2005/3352)	1 February 2007 to 31 January 2008 (SI 2006/3045)	1 February 2008 to 31 January 2009
Unfair dismissal						
Basic award (ERA 1996, s 119)	£7,800	£8,100	£8,400	£8,700	£9,300	£9,900
Maximum week's pay (ERA 1996, ss 220–229)	£260	£270	£280	£290	£310	£330
Minimum basic award (TULR(C) A 1992 ss 152–167; ERA 1996, ss 100, 101A, 102, 103)	£3,500 min.	£3,600 min.	£3,800 min.	£4,000 min.	£4,200 min.	£4,700 min
Compensation award (ERA 1996, ss 123–124)	£53,500	£55,000	£56,800	£58,400	£60,600	£63,000
Additional award (ERA 1996, s 117)	£13,520	£14,040	£14,560	£15,080	£16,120	£17,160
Redundancy payment (ERA 1996, s 162)	£7,800	£8,100	£8,400	£8,700	£9,300	£9,900
Guarantee pay per day (ERA 1996, ss 30–31)	£17.30	£17.80	£18.40	£18.90	£19.60	£20.40
Insolvency payments						
Week's pay for insolvency debts (ERA 1996, s 18H)	£260	£270	£280	£290	£310	£330

National Minimum Hourly Wage

Age	From October 2001	From October 2002	From October 2003	From October 2004	From October 2005	From October 2006	From October 2007	From October 2008	From October 2009
16–17	—	—	—	£3.00	£3.00	£3.30	£3.40	£3.53	3.57
18–21	£3.50	£3.60	£3.80	£4.10	£4.25	£4.45	£4.60	£4.77	4.83
22 and above	£4.10	£4.20	£4.50	£4.85	£5.05	£5.35	£5.52	£5.73	5.80

Time Limits

Qualifying Periods and Time Limits

Employment right and statutory provision	When application must be made	Qualifying period	Discretionary power to extend time limit
Equal pay/value claim under the EC Treaty, Art 141, and/or Directive 75/117/EEC, Art 1	3–6 months from termination of employment, but in the case of a Directive time does not run until it has been properly implemented (see *Emmott v Minister for Social Welfare and anor* [1991] IRLR 387)	None	None
Equal pay: EPA 1970, s 2(1)	Whilst working or within 6 months of leaving employment: ss 2(4), s 2ZA(3)	None	
Sex discrimination in employment: SDA 1975, s 63	(i) 3 months from the date when the discriminatory act was done: s 76(1)(a)	None	Just and equitable: s 76(5)
	(ii)In the case of discriminatory advertisements (s 38), instructions to discriminate (s 39), persistent discrimination (s 71) and pressure to discriminate (s 40), all of which can only be enforced by the EHRC: Equality Act 2006, s 21(5).	None	
Appeal from EHRC unlawful act notice:	6 weeks from service of notice	None	None
Application by EHRC in respect of discriminatory advertising, instructions and/or pressure to discriminate: EA 2006, s 25	6 months from the date of the act complained of or with the permission of the court or tribunal: EA 2006, s 26(1)	None	
Race discrimination in employment: RRA 1976, s 54	3 months from the date of the act complained of: RRA 1976, s 68(1) and (6). An act that extends over a period, as opposed to a one-off act, is treated as done at the end of the period (s 68(7)(b) and *Barclays Bank plc v Kapur* [1991] ICR 208)	None	Just and equitable: s 68(1) and (6)
Appeal from EHRC unlawful notice:	6 weeks from service of notice: EA 2006, s 21(5)	None	None
Application by EHRC in connection with discriminatory advertising, instructions and/or pressure to discriminate: RRA 1976, s 63(2)(a)	6 months from the date of the act complained of or with the permission of the court or tribunal: EA 2006, s 26(1)	None	Just and equitable: RRA 1976, s 68(6)

Employment right and statutory provision	When application must be made	Qualifying period	Discretionary power to extend time limit
Sex discrimination claim: under Directive 76/207/EEC, Art 5	3 months starting with termination of employment (time limit analogous to time limit in national law)	None	None
Sexual orientation discrimination: EE (SO) Regs 2003, reg 28	3 months from act complained of (6 months for complaints within armed forces): reg 34	None	Just and equitable: reg 34(3).
Religion or belief discrimination: EE (RB) Regs 2003, reg 28	3 months from act complained of (6 months for complaints within armed forces): reg 34	None	Just and equitable: reg 34(3).
Age discrimination EE (A) Regs 2006, reg 36	3 months from act complained of: reg 42(1).	None	Just and equitable: reg 42(3).
Claim for failure to be notified of intended retirement age: EE (A) Regs 2006, Sch 6, para 2	3 months from last day permitted to employers to notify or (if the employee did not then know the date that would be the intended retirement date) 3 months from the first day on which he knew or should have known that date: EE (A) Regs 2006, Sch 6, para 11		Reasonably practicable: Sch 6, para 11(2)(b)
Written particulars of employment: ERA 1996, ss 1–4	While working or within 3 months of employee leaving: ERA 1996, s 11(4)(a)	Employee should be provided with statement no later than 2 months after employment begins: s 1(2); employees with less than 1 month's service do not qualify: s 198	Reasonably practicable: s 11(4)(b)
Itemized pay statement: ERA 1996, s 8	While working or within 3 months of employee leaving: ERA 1996, s 11(4)(a)	None	Reasonably practicable: s 11(4)(b)
Unlawful deduction from wages: ERA 1996, s 23	3 months from date of deduction (or last in a series of deductions) made: s 23(2)	None	Reasonably practicable: s 23(4).
Guarantee payments: ERA 1996, ss 28–35	3 months from the day the guarantee payment should have been made: ERA 1996, s 34(2)(a)	1 month: s 29	Reasonably practicable: s 34(2)(b)
Detriment in health and safety cases: ERA 1996, ss 44, 48, 49	3 months from act complained of: s 48(3)(a)	None	Reasonably practicable: s 48(3)(b).
Detriment or dismissal in connection with time off work for study or training: ERA 1996, s 47A	3 months from act complained of: s 48(3)(a)	None	Reasonably practicable: s 48(3)(b)
Time off for public duties: ERA 1996, ss 50–51	3 months from the date when failure to permit time off occurred: s 50(2)(a)	None	Reasonably practicable: s 50(2)(b)

Employment right and statutory provision	When application must be made	Qualifying period	Discretionary power to extend time limit
Time off to look for work or training on redundancy: ERA 1996, s 52	3 months from the date of refusal: s 54(2)(a)	2 years: s 52(2)	Reasonably practicable: s 54(2)(b)
Time off for ante-natal care: ERA 1996, s 55	3 months beginning with the day of the relevant appointment for ante-natal care: s 57(2)(a)	None	Reasonably practicable: s 57(2)(b)
Right to remuneration on suspension on medical grounds: ERA 1996, ss 64–65	3 months from the date payment during suspension was due: s 70(2)(a)	1 month: s 65(1)	Reasonably practicable: s 70(2)(b)
Paid time off for employee representative (or candidate in an election as such an employee representative) for the purpose of consultation in relation to collective redundancies or the transfer of an undertaking or to undergo training in relation to their functions: ERA 1996, ss 61(1) and 62	3 months from the date when the failure to permit time off occurred: s 63(2)(a)	None	Reasonably practicable: s 63(2)(b)
Claim for remuneration on suspension from work on maternity grounds: ERA 1996, ss 68 and 70(1)	3 months beginning with date of failure to pay: s 70(2)(a)	None	Reasonably practicable: s 70(2)(b)
Right to additional maternity leave: ERA 1996, s 73	3 months from notified day of return when employer refuses right	6 months employment at beginning of 14th week before expected week of childbirth: MPLR 1999, reg 5	Reasonably practicable
Written reasons for dismissal: ERA 1996, s 92	3 months from the effective date of termination: s 93(3) when read with s 111(2)(a)	1 year	Reasonably practicable: s 93(3) when read with s 111(2)(b)
Unfair dismissal in connection with health and safety functions: ERA 1996, s 100	3 months from effective date of termination: s 111(2)(a)	None: s 108(3)(c)	Reasonably practicable: s 111(2)(b).
Unfair dismissal of a shop or betting worker for refusing to work on a Sunday: ERA 1996, s 101	3 months from effective date of termination: s 111(2)(a)	None: s 108(3)(d)	Reasonably practicable: s 111(2)(b).
Unfair dismissal in connection with leave for family reasons: ERA 1996, s 99	3 months from effective date of termination: s 111(2)(a)	None: s 108(3)(b)	Reasonably practicable: s 111(2)(b).

Employment right and statutory provision	When application must be made	Qualifying period	Discretionary power to extend time limit
Unfair dismissal for a reason connected with WTR 1998: ERA 1996, s 101A	3 months from effective date of termination: s 111(2)(a)	None: s 108(3)(dd)	Reasonably practicable: s 111(2)(b).
Unfair dismissal for performing occupational pension trustee functions or those as an employee representative: ERA 1996, ss 102–103	3 months from effective date of termination: s 111(2)(a)	None: s 108(3)(e) and (f)	Reasonably practicable: s 111(2)(b).
Unfair dismissal related to making a protected disclosure: ERA 1996, s 103A	3 months from effective date of termination: s 111(2)(a)	None: s 108(3)(ff)	Reasonably practicable: s 111(2)(b).
Unfair dismissal in connection with asserting a statutory right: ERA 1996, s 104	3 months from effective date of termination: s 111(2)(a)	None: s 108(3)(g)	Reasonably practicable: s 111(2)(b).
Detriment to shop or betting worker for refusing Sunday work: ERA 1996, s 45	3 months from effective date of termination or act complained of: s 48(3)(a)	None	Reasonably practicable: s 48(3)(b).
Unfair dismissal related to national minimum wage: ERA 1996, s 104A	3 months from effective date of termination: s 111(2)(a)	None: s 108(3)(gg)	Reasonably practicable: s 111(2)(b).
Unfair dismissal in connection with suspension on medical grounds: ERA 1996, s 64(2) when read with s 108(2)	3 months from effective date of termination	1 month: s 108(2)	Reasonably practicable: s 111(2)(b).
Interim relief on a complaint under ERA 1996, ss 100, 101A, 102, 103, 103A or under TULR(C)A 1992, Sch A1, para 161(2): ERA 1996, s 128	7 days immediately following EDT, s 128(2)	None	None
Unfair dismissal: ERA 1996, s 98	(i) Before effective date of termination if employee is dismissed with notice: ERA 1996, s 111(4), or (ii) within 3 months from effective date of termination but (iii) in the case of unfair selection of strikers for re-engagement, 6 months from applicant's day of dismissal: TULR(C)A 1992, s 239(2)	1 year: s 108(1)	Reasonably practicable: s 111(2)(b).
Constructive Unfair Dismissal: ERA 1996, s 95(1)(c)	After 28 days has elapsed from lodging a grievance with the employer, provided this is lodged within 3 months of the date of termination, but within 6 months of the date of termination	1 year: s 108(1)	Reasonably practicable ERA 1996, s 111(2)(b).

Employment right and statutory provision	When application must be made	Qualifying period	Discretionary power to extend time limit
Interim relief in health and safety cases: ERA 1996, s 128(1)	7 days after effective date of termination: s 128(2)	None	None except where employer has committed fraud
Redundancy payment: ERA 1996, ss 135–170	Within 6 months of the relevant date defined in ERA 1996, s 164. This is similar to the effective date of termination.	2 years: s 115, subject to *Seymour-Smith* comments ([1999] ICR 447). Any service before the age of 18 does not count: ERA 1996, s 211(2) when read with s 155	Just and equitable: ERA 1996, s 164(2). If the employee dies during the 6-month period it is extended to 1 year: ERA 1996, s 176(7). If the employee dies after the 6-month period before end of the following 6 months the tribunal can extend the period for 1 year: s 176(7)
Payments on insolvency of employer: ERA 1996, ss 182–190	3 months from date of communication of Secretary of State's decision: s 188(2)(a)	Each of the payments claimed are dependent upon qualifying periods	Reasonably practicable: s 188(2)(b)
Unfair dismissal in connection with transfer of an undertaking: TUPE 2006, reg 7	3 months from the effective date of termination: ERA 1996, s 111(2)(a)	1 year	Reasonably practicable: ERA 1996, s 111(2)(b).
Failure to notify transferee of employee liability information: TUPE 2006, reg 11	3 months from date of transfer: reg 12(2)a	None	Reasonably practicable: reg 12(2)(b)
Consultation and provision of information on transfer of undertaking: TUPE 2006, regs 13 and 14	3 months from the date of the relevant transfer: reg 15(12)(a)	None	Reasonably practicable: reg 15(12)
Failure to pay compensation ordered by employment tribunal in respect of failure to consult on a transfer of undertakings: TUPE 2006, reg 15(7)	3 months from the employment tribunal's decision: reg 15(12)(b)	None	Reasonably practicable: reg 15(12)
Unlawful deduction from wages: ERA 1996, ss 13–27	3 months from date of last deduction (ie date payment was contractually due): s 23(2) and (3)	None	Reasonably practicable: s 23(4)

Employment right and statutory provision	When application must be made	Qualifying period	Discretionary power to extend time limit
Unjustifiable discipline by a union: TULR(C)A 1992, ss 64–66	3 months starting with date of decision: s 66(2)(a)	None	Reasonably practicable or if delay is wholly or party attributable to reasonable attempts to appeal a decision: s 66(2)(b)
Application for compensation after successful s 66 complaint: TULR(C)A 1992, s 67	Not before 4 weeks and not later than 6 months starting with the date of the employment tribunal's decision: s 67(1).	None	None
Unauthorized deduction of union member's subscriptions: TULR(C) A 1992, ss 68, 68A	3 months from date of deduction: s 68A(1)(a)	None	Reasonably practicable: s 68A(1)(b)
Refusal of employment because of union membership: TULR(C) A 1992, s 137	3 months from date of refusal: s 139(1)(a)	None	Reasonably practicable: s 139(1)(b)
Refusal of services of employment agency because of union membership: TULR(C) A 1992, s 138	3 months from date of refusal: s 139(1)(a)	None	Reasonably practicable: s 139(1)(b)
Right not to receive inducements relating to union membership and activities or collective bargaining: TULR(C)A 1992, ss 145A and 145B	3 months from inducement (or last in a series of inducements): s 145C	None	Reasonably practicable: s 145C(b)
Detriment on grounds related to union membership or activities: TULR(C)A 1992, ss 146–151	3 months from the date on which there occurred the action complained of or, where that action is part of a series of similar actions, from the last of those actions: s 147(1)(a)	None	Reasonably practicable: s 147(1)(b). Dispute resolution extension*
Unfair dismissal in connection with trade union membership and activities: TULR(C)A 1992, ss 152 and 153	3 months from effective date of termination: ERA 1996, s 111(2)(a)	None	Reasonably practicable: ERA 1996, s 111(2)(b). Dispute resolution extension*
Right of employee representative (or candidate or participant in election of employee representative) in respect of consultation over transfer of undertaking or collective redundancies not to suffer detriment: ERA 1996, s 47(1) and (1A)	3 months from the date on which there occurred the action complained of. If the act is one of a series of similar acts, then the date of the last such act: s 48(3)(a)	None	Reasonably practicable: s 48(3)(b)

Employment right and statutory provision	When application must be made	Qualifying period	Discretionary power to extend time limit
Unfair dismissal on account of employee being an employee representative (or candidate or participant in election of employee representative) in respect of consultation over transfer of undertaking or collective redundancies: ERA 1996, s 103	3 months from effective date of termination: s 111(2)(a)	None: s 108(2)(f)	Reasonably practicable: s 111(2)(b).
Interim relief in dismissal for trade union membership and activities: TULR(C)A 1992, s 161	7 days from the effective date of termination: s 161(2)	None	None unless fraud involved
Time off for trade union activities and duties and for union learning representatives: TULR(C)A 1992, ss 168, 168A, 169 and 170	3 months from the date when failure to permit time off for union activities or to pay remuneration, occurred: TULR(C)A 1992, s 171(a)	None	Reasonably practicable: s 171(b)
Unlawful exclusion or expulsion from trade union: TULR(C)A 1992, s 174	6 months from the date of expulsion for initial application: s 175(a); following which an application may be made for compensation between 4 weeks and 6 months after the date of a declaration by employment tribunal: s 176(3)	None	Reasonably practicable: s 175(b)
Consultation with recognized union over redundancy: TULR(C)A 1992, s 188	Before the proposed dismissal or 3 months from the date on which the last dismissal takes effect: s 189(5)(a) and (b)	None	Reasonably practicable: s 189(5)(c)
Protective award claim by trade union for failing to consult over redundancies: TULR(C) A 1992, s 192	3 months from the date when the application of failure to pay was made: s 192(2) (a)	None	Reasonably practicable: s 192(2)(b)
Unfair dismissal in connection with official industrial action: TULR(C)A 1992, ss 238 and 238A	6 months from date of dismissal—where contract terminated by notice, date on which employer's notice given and in any other case, the EDT: s 238(5) when read with s 239(2)(a)	None: s 239(1)	Reasonably practicable: s 239(2)(b)
Levy appeal: Employment Tribunals (Constitution and Rules of Procedure) Regulations 2004, Sch 3	None—except that Board must forward notice of appeal to the employment tribunal within 21 days of receipt: Sch 3, r 4	None	None

Employment right and statutory provision	When application must be made	Qualifying period	Discretionary power to extend time limit
Appeal against health & safety improvement notice: Employment Tribunals (Constitution and Rules of Procedure) Regulations 2004, Sch 4	21 days from date of service of notice: Sch 4, r 4(1)	None	Reasonably practicable: Sch 4, r 4(2)
Right of safety representatives to take time off to perform functions/for training: SRCR 1977, r 4(2)	3 months from failure: r 11(2)	None	Reasonable period: r 11(2)
Paid time off for pension scheme trustees to undergo training: ERA 1996, ss 58–60	3 months from the date when the failure to permit time off occurred: s 60(2)(a)	None	Reasonably practicable: s 60(2)(b)
Discrimination on grounds of disability DDA 1995: s 17A	3 months beginning with date of act complained of: Part 1, Sch 3, para 3(1)	None	Just and equitable: Part 1, Sch 3, para 3(2).
Employee's contract claim: ETEJ (E&W) O 1994; ETEJ O 1994, para 3	In employment tribunal, 3 months beginning with EDT or if no EDT, last working day. In county court/ High Court, 6 years from breach of contract: para 7	None	Reasonably practicable: para 7(c).
Employer's contract claim: ETEJ (E&W) O 1994; ETEJ (S) O 1994	In employment tribunal, 6 weeks beginning with date of receipt of employee's claim. In county court/ High Court, 6 years from breach of contract: para 8	None	Reasonably practicable
Right to daily rest: WTR 1998, reg 10	3 months from the date when the right should have been permitted	None	Reasonably practicable: reg 30.
Right to weekly rest: WTR 1998, reg 11	3 months from the date when the right should have been permitted	None	Reasonably practicable: reg 30.
Right to rest breaks: WTR 1998, reg 12	3 months from the date when the right should have been permitted	None	Reasonably practicable: reg 30.
Right to compensatory rest in cases where regulations modified or excluded: WTR 1998, reg 24	3 months from the date when the right should have been permitted	None	Reasonably practicable: reg 30.
Right to annual leave: WTR 1998, reg 13	3 months from the date when the right should have been permitted	None	Reasonably practicable: reg 30.
Right to payment in lieu of holiday on termination of employment: WTR 1998, reg 14(2)	3 months from the date when the payment should have been made	None	Reasonably practicable: reg 30.

Employment right and statutory provision	When application must be made	Qualifying period	Discretionary power to extend time limit
Right to pay during annual leave: WTR 1998, reg 16(1)	3 months from the date when the payment should have been made	None	Reasonably practicable: reg 30.
Failure to allow access to records: NMWA 1998, s 11	3 months from end of 14 days from receipt of production notice or 3 months from agreed later date: s 11(3)(a) and (b)	None	Reasonably practicable: s 11(4)
Detriment arising from enforcement of rights: NMWA 1998, s 24	3 months beginning with date of act or failure	None	Reasonably practicable.
Appeal against enforcement notice: NMWA 1998, s 19(4)	4 weeks following date of service of notice	Not applicable	None
Appeal against penalty notice: NMWA 1998, s 22(1)	4 weeks following date of service of notice	Not applicable	None
Failure or threat to fail to comply with right to be accompanied at a disciplinary or grievance hearing: ERelA 1999	3 months beginning with date of failure or threat: s 11(2)(a)	None	Reasonably practicable: s 11(2)(b)
Time off for members of European Works Council, etc: TICER 1999, reg 25	3 months beginning with date when time off should have been allowed or day taken off: reg 27(2)(a)	None	Reasonably practicable: reg 27(2)(b)
Detriment relating to membership of EWC, etc: TICER 1999, reg 31	3 months beginning with last date of less favourable treatment or detriment	None	Just and equitable.
Right not to be treated less favourably as a part-time worker: PTWR 2000, reg 5	3 months starting from date of less favourable treatment: reg 8(2)	None	Just and equitable: reg 8(3)
Right of part-time worker to receive written statement of reasons for less favourable treatment: PTWR 2000, reg 6	3 months starting from date of less favourable treatment (6 months if complaint relates to armed forces): reg 8(2)	None	Just and equitable: reg 8(3)
Unfair dismissal or right not to suffer detriment related to a part-time worker status: PTWR 2000, reg 7	3 months starting from date of last act or failure to act: reg 8(2)	None	Just and equitable: reg 8(3)

Appeal Time Limits

Employment right and statutory provision	When application must be made	Discretionary power to extend time limit
Review of employment tribunal decision: Employment Tribunals (Constitution and Rules of Procedure) Regulations 2004, Sch 1, rr 34 and 35	14 days from date decision sent to parties: r 35(1)	General discretion to extend time if chairman considers it just and equitable to do so: r 35(1)
Appeal from employment tribunal decision or order	42 days from date full written reasons for decision or order were sent: EAT Rules 1993, r 3(3), as amended by SI 2004/2526, reg 4(3)	May be extended or abridged under broad power in r 37, but no specific power
Review of EAT decision or order: EAT Rules, r 33	Within 14 days of the order: r 33(2)	General discretion to extend time under EAT Rules, r 37
Appeal from EAT to Court of Appeal: ETA 1996, s 37	14 days from date on which order or judgment of EAT drawn up unless EAT gives longer period: CPR, r 52.4	General discretion to extend time limits: r 3.1(2)(a) when read with CPR, r 52.6

Tribunal Statistics

Most 2008/09 figures have not been published by the Employment Tribunals Service at the time of going to press.

Total Number of Applications

Tribunal	2003/04	2004/05	2005/06	2006/07	2007/08	2008/09
Employment Tribunal	115,042	86,181	115,039	132,577	189,303	151,028
Employment Appeal Tribunal	1,062	881	836	781	1,841	1,794
Central Arbitration Committee	106	83	58	64	64	42

Total Number of Employment Tribunal Claims in Key Categories

Claim	2003/04	2004/05	2005/06	2006/07	2007/08	2008/09
Unfair dismissal	46,370	39,727	41,832	44,491	40,941	52,711
Working time	16,869	3,223	35,474	21,127	55,712	23,976
Redundancy/TUPE—failure to inform and consult	6,951	4,695	4,955	5,910	5,860	12,633
Discrimination						
Sex	17,722	11,726	14,250	28,153	26,907	18,637
Equal pay	4,412	8,229	17,268	44,013	62,706	45,748
Race	3,492	3,317	4,103	3,780	4,130	4,983
Disability	5,655	4,942	4,585	5,533	5,833	6,578
Part-time workers	833	561	402	776	595	664
Religion/belief	70	307	486	648	709	832
Sexual orientation	61	349	395	470	582	600
Age	n/a	n/a	n/a	972	2,949	3,801

Outcomes 2008/09

Court/Claim	Withdrawn/Settled/ Struck out before trial	Successful at trial	Not successful at trial*
Employment Tribunal	72%	13%	15%
Unfair dismissal	75%	10%**	15%
Working time	62%	20%	18%
Discrimination			
Sex	89%	3%	8%
Equal pay	99%	0.5%	0.5%
Race	73%	3%	24%
Disability	83%	3%	14%
Age	82%	2%	16%

*Including judgments in default.

**Reinstatement/re-engagement was ordered as a remedy in only 7 of the 3,935 unfair dismissal cases which were upheld.

Outcomes 2007/08

Court/Claim	Withdrawn/Settled/ Struck out before trial	Successful at trial	Not successful at trial*
Employment Tribunal	73%	17%	9%
Unfair dismissal	76%	10%**	14%
Working time	66%	19%	15%
Discrimination	91%	3%	6%
Sex	91%	7%	2%
Equal pay	76%	3%	21%
Race	84%	3%	13%
Disability	84%	3%	13%
Age			

*Including judgments in default.

**Reinstatement/re-engagement was ordered as a remedy in only 8 of the 3,791 unfair dismissal cases which were upheld.

Outcomes 2006/07

Court/Claim	Withdrawn/Settled before trial	Successful at trial	Not successful at trial*
Employment Tribunal	77%	12%	11%
Employment Appeal Tribunal	27%	34%	39%
Unfair dismissal	76%	10%**	14%
Working time	85%	9%	6%
Discrimination			
Sex	94%	2%	4%
Equal pay	96%	2%	2%
Race	76%	3%	21%
Disability	85%	3%	12%

*Including judgments in default.

**Reinstatement/re-engagement was ordered as a remedy in only 23 of the 3,870 unfair dismissal cases which were upheld.

Outcomes 2005/06

Court/Claim	Withdrawn/Settled before trial	Successful at trial	Not successful at trial*
Employment Tribunal	71%	18%	11%
Employment Appeal Tribunal	18%	45%	37%
Unfair dismissal	77%	10%**	13%
Working time	71%	15%	14%
Discrimination	80%	17%	3%
Sex	66%	33%	1%
Equal pay	79%	3%	18%
Race	83%	4%	13%
Disability			

*Including judgments in default.

**Reinstatement/re-engagement was ordered as a remedy in only 14 of the 3,425 unfair dismissal cases which were upheld.

Outcomes 2004/05

Court/Claim	Withdrawn/Settled before trial	Successful at trial	Not successful at trial
Employment Tribunal	74%	18%	8%
Employment Appeal Tribunal	N/A	40%	60%
Unfair dismissal	79%	10%*	11%
Working time	23%	75%	2%
Discrimination	93%	2%	5%
Sex	97%	1%	2%
Equal pay	77%	3%	20%
Race	83%	5%	12%
Disability			

*Reinstatement/re-engagement was ordered as a remedy in only 14 of the 3,493 unfair dismissal cases which were upheld.

Size of Awards 2008/09

Claim	Maximum award	Award above £50,000		Median award	Average award
		No.	%		
Unfair dismissal	£84,005	49	2%	£4,269	£7,959
Sex discrimination	£113,106	3	1.7%	£7,000	£11,025
Race discrimination	£1,353,432	4	5.9%	£5,172	£32,115
Disability discrimination	£388,612	7	8.6%	£7,226	£27,235
Age discrimination	£90,031	1	4.8%	£3,000	£8,869

Size of Awards 2007/08

Claim	Maximum award	Award above £50,000		Median award	Average award
		No.	%		
Unfair dismissal	£76,536	60	2.4%	£4,000	£8,058
Sex discrimination	£131,466	4	2.7%	£5,200	£11,263
Race discrimination	£68,991	4	6.2%	£8,120	£14,566
Disability discrimination	£227,208	7	7.6%	£8,363	£19,523
Age discrimination	£12,124	0	0	£1,526	£3,334

Size of Awards 2006/07

Claim	Maximum award	Award above £50,000		Median award	Average award
		No.	%		
Unfair dismissal	£250,470	84	2.54	£3,800	£7,974
Sex discrimination	£64,862	2	1.03	£6,724	£10,652
Race discrimination	£123,898	6	6.32	£7,000	£14,049
Disability discrimination	£138,684	7	6.03	£8,232	£15,059

Size of Awards 2005/06

Claim	Maximum award	Award above £50,000		Median award	Average award
		No.	%		
Unfair dismissal	£477,603	62	2.6	£4,228	£8,679
Sex discrimination	£217,961	4	2.4	£5,546	£10,807
Race discrimination	£984,465	5	6.8	£6,640	£30,361
Disability discrimination	£138,650	9	11.8	£9,021	£19,360

Size of Awards 2004/05

Claim	Maximum award	Award above £50,000		Median award	Average award
		No.	%		
Unfair dismissal	£75,250*	48	2	£3,476	£7,303
Sex discrimination	£179,026	11	6.6	£6,235	£14,158
Race discrimination	£170,953	6	10.2	£6,699	£19,114
Disability discrimination	£148,681	7	8	£7,500	£17,736

*Includes an additional award for failure to reinstate.

Size of Awards 2003/04

Claim	Maximum award	Award above £50,000		Median award	Average award
		No.	%		
Unfair dismissal	£113,117*	46	1.6	£3,375	£7,275
Sex discrimination	£504,433	5	2.3	£5,425	£12,971
Race discrimination	£635,150	6	7.5	£8,410	£26,660
Disability discrimination	£173,139	5	6.5	£5,652	£16,214

*Includes additional award for failure to reinstate.

Employment Tribunal Costs Awards 2008/09

Number of claims in which costs awarded:	367
Costs awarded to claimant	102
Costs awarded to respondent	265
Maximum cost award	£25,000
Median cost award	£1,100
Average cost award	£2,470

Employment Tribunal Costs Awards 2007/08

Number of claims in which costs awarded:	461
Costs awarded to claimant	134
Costs awarded to respondent	327
Maximum cost award	£17,775
Median cost award	£1,000
Average cost award	£2,095

Employment Tribunal Costs Awards 2006/07

Number of claims in which costs awarded:	469
Costs awarded to claimant	152
Costs awarded to respondent	317
Maximum cost award	£65,000
Median cost award	£1,000
Average cost award	£2,079

Employment Tribunal Costs Awards 2005/06

Number of claims in which costs awarded:	580
Costs awarded to claimant	148
Costs awarded to respondent	432
Maximum cost award	£20,000
Median cost award	£1,000
Average cost award	£2,256

Employment Tribunal Costs Awards 2004/05

Number of claims in which costs awarded:	1,036
Costs awarded to claimant	281
Costs awarded to respondent	755
Maximum cost award	£15,000*
Median cost award	£1,000
Average cost award	£1,828

*Costs in excess of £10,000 by agreement between parties.

Appendix 7
Note on Tribunal Procedure and Appeals in Scotland

The ETR 2004 apply equally to England and Wales, and to Scotland. Provision is made in the Regulations (Rule 19) for the different bases on which the separate geographical jurisdictions operate, and where the ground of jurisdiction relied on is 'a contract of employment, the place of . . . performance of which is in Scotland' it has been held by the Court of Session (*Prescription Pricing Authority v Ferguson* [2005] CSIH 5) that properly interpreted these words require performance that is wholly or at least substantially in Scotland.

There is no reason why a party who has knowledge of the conduct of tribunal proceedings in England and Wales should have particular concerns about bringing a claim before a Scottish tribunal, though it should be noted there are three Practice Directions which are specific to proceedings in the Scottish tribunals (see below). The same comment applies to the taking of appeals from decisions of tribunals to the Employment Appeal Tribunal, which sits separately in Scotland and is chaired by a Scottish judge of the Court of Session (equivalent to an English High Court judge). The EAT's Practice Direction of May 2008 and its Practice Statement of 2005 apply to the EAT wherever it is sitting, although there are certain modifications in the former relevant to appeals held in Scotland. There are, however, differences of importance in how hearings before employment tribunals proceed, and additionally there are certain differences in the legal terminology governing tribunal procedure, and in substantive law. A full discussion of the nature and extent of differences between England and Wales and Scotland in the substantive law of employment lies outside the scope of this Appendix, but the following general comments may be of assistance. Insofar as tribunal claims turn upon questions of common law, it should be remembered that the common law of Scotland in matters of contract, tort (delict), and in public law is not identical to that of England and Wales. There is, for example, no doctrine of consideration known to Scots contract law, and there are also, inter alia, differences in the rules of estoppel (personal bar) and *res judicata*. While in the interpretation and application of statutory rights these differences are usually not important, there will be occasions, especially when considering contractual and other common law entitlements, when an understanding of the technical rules of Scots law is a necessary prerequisite of properly presenting or defending. The more one is required to consider technical issues of the law of procedure or evidence in their application to proceedings in employment tribunals, the less likely it is that the detailed rules of English law will apply, although often the end result is very similar. (See, eg, *Renfrewshire Council v Adamson* UKEATS/0013/07/MT, a case dealing with the circumstances in which there is a right to withdraw a concession made in the course of proceedings.) The point is illustrated by the existence of situations where the powers of the tribunal are assimilated to those of a Sheriff (in Scotland) or County Court (in England). (See, eg, the ETR 2004, Sch 1, r 41(1)(c), which deals with the amount of a costs or expenses order.) Similarly, under ETR 2004 (r 10(2)(d)) the power which a tribunal has in Scotland to require the disclosure of documents or information is the same as the power enjoyed by a Sheriff under the general rules of civil procedure. The Scottish regime for the recovery of expenses (costs) in the employment tribunal is quite different from that found in England and Wales, and it should be noted, in particular, that there is no provision for the recovery of expenses on an indemnity basis under Scots law.

The view has been expressed by the EAT (*McGuire v Centrewest London Buses Ltd* UKEAT/0576/06) that in exercising discretion under ETR, Sch 1, r 34(3)(e) (power to order strike-out when the interests of justice so require) it is appropriate to follow the approach taken by the civil courts under CPR Rule 3.9. That sets out a number of specific considerations, including the interests of the administration of justice, which are to be taken into account when applying for relief from any sanction imposed for failure to comply with any rule, practice direction, or court order. The Civil Procedure Rules are not, of course, applicable to civil proceedings in Scotland, and it is less than obvious why they should provide an authoritative guidance to employment tribunals in that jurisdiction.

As a matter of formal hierarchy, while decisions of the Employment Appeal Tribunal (being a court which has jurisdiction throughout Great Britain) have equal status within Great Britain, decisions of the Court of Appeal are not formally binding within Scotland. Similarly, decisions of the Court of Session in appeals from the EAT are not binding on English tribunals. Nevertheless, as a matter of practice it would be rare for decisions of the Court of Appeal on a matter where there is no difference in the substantive law between the two jurisdictions not to be followed. In practice, decisions of the Court of Appeal are regularly cited and followed within the Scottish tribunal system and in the EAT. And the same applies in the reverse. The point was well put by Laws LJ in *Clarke v Frank Staddon Ltd*; *Caulfield v Marshalls Clay Products Ltd* [2004] ICR 1502, when he said (at para 31): 'As a matter of pragmatic good sense the ET and the EAT in either jurisdiction will ordinarily expect to follow decisions of the higher appeal court in the other jurisdiction (whether the Court of Session or the Court of Appeal) where the point confronting them is indistinguishable from what was there decided.' That approach was foreshadowed by remarks made in 1992 by Lord Mayfield, a Scottish EAT judge, in the following terms: this Court, being part of a United Kingdom body in the field of employment law, would only depart from an opinion of the Court of Appeal on a matter which was purely related to a particular aspect of Scots Law (*Brown v Rentokil Ltd* [1992] IRLR 302, EAT, at para 17).

One recent decision of the Inner House of the Court of Session relates to a procedural matter of some importance that can often arise in connection with the reporting of tribunal proceedings. In *Fiona Davidson v Dallas McMillan* [2009] CSIH 70 (4 August 2009) it was decided that, contrary to the view expressed by the EAT below, an employment tribunal did have power to allow a journalist to be heard in connection with the variation or revocation of a Restricted Reporting Order. Even although the power under Rule 50(7) of the ETR 2004 envisages a right to be heard only in connection with the making of the Order, Rules 10(1) and 60(1) give a tribunal power to allow a journalist to be heard. On the other hand, in the same case, the Inner House held that once a claimant had communicated her withdrawal of her claim, the tribunal had no jurisdiction to entertain any application that a RRO be revoked. So, on the facts, the tribunal had erred in ordering the lifting of an RRO following representations made by a journalist to that effect.

What, however, would be the position in the event of there being a difference between a decision of the EAT (sitting in England) and a decision of the Court of Session (sitting in Scotland, on an appeal from the EAT)? While it is unlikely that such direct conflict will arise, it is not impossible that it could, especially in the event of one court being unaware of the decision of the other. The scope for conflict is apparent in the differences between the reasoning of the EAT in *Sharma v Manchester CC* [2008] IRLR 336 and that of the Court of Session (Inner House) in *McMenemy v Capital Systems Ltd* [2007] IRLR 400. While the point has never had to be decided, it is thought that in such a situation an employment tribunal in Scotland would be bound to follow the decision of the Court of Session in preference to that of the EAT.

Appeals from the EAT sitting in Scotland go to the Court of Session (Inner House) and thence to the Supreme Court. In the event of considering an appeal to the Court of Session, it would always be appropriate to take advice from advisers qualified in Scots law. The Rules of the Court of Session (applicable to all proceedings before the Court of Session) are significantly different from the Civil Procedure Rules. Only party-litigants and those with rights of audience in the higher courts (ie advocates and solicitor-advocates) may appear in the Court of Session, unlike the EAT (where English-qualified barristers and solicitors regularly appear).

In the past, employment tribunals in Scotland have generally tended to adopt a less formalistic approach to proceedings than their counterparts in England and Wales. There are signs that this relative informality may be changing, particularly as there is now, since 2004, a common set of regulations for both jurisdictions. As already mentioned, there are three Scottish practice directions, all of which date from December 2006. Practice Direction No 1 requires the intimation of lists of documents 14 days in advance of hearing where a party is legally represented. Practice Direction No 2 makes provision for the sist (stay) of proceedings where parties are agreed to do so in order to allow mediation to go ahead. Practice Direction No 3 applies in proceedings involving the jurisdiction of tribunals to hear claims of breach of contract, where a party seeks to present a counter claim. A respondent who wishes so to proceed must (if reasonably practicable) specify the amount which is claimed, along with other information, and the claimant who receives notice of a counter claim must tell the tribunal office if it is intended to resist the counter claim and the reasons for so doing. But notwithstanding these recent regulatory interventions, practitioners may still expect a less regulated regime, with more control left to the parties in the organization and presentation of their cases.

Presentation of Claims

All claims are presented to the Central Office of Tribunals in Glasgow.

Witness Statements

While the rules for Scotland provide for witness statements they are still very much the exception. In general, unless a tribunal has previously ruled to the contrary, it should be assumed that witness statements will neither be expected nor acceptable, and that witnesses will give their evidence in chief by answering questions from the party's representative. If a party wishes to make use of a witness statement then it is important to ascertain in advance whether this would be acceptable to the tribunal. The absence of witness statements means of course there is a risk that the full case being argued by a party will not be known to his or her opponent until the hearing itself. For this reason the use of the powers under ETR 2004, r 10 to obtain further information of the claimant's case in advance of the hearing is particularly important within the Scottish system. Should a party be taken by surprise by unexpected and important evidence given at the hearing, of which notice has not been given, then application to the tribunal should of course be made for adjournment or other appropriate procedure to allow for investigation and answer.

Witnesses

During the course of the hearing witnesses are, in the terminology of Scots law, 'sequestrated'—that is to say they remain outside the tribunal until they have given their evidence. That is the general rule. In special circumstances (for example, where the party giving instructions to the legal representative is also a witness in the case or the witness is a director of the company) leave may be sought from the tribunal to permit the attendance of the individual before he or she gives evidence.

Hearing

Separate hearings dealing with the issue of liability and remedy are not as common in Scotland as they are in England. Care should therefore be taken to ascertain the position at the start, and parties should generally assume that they will be required to deal with both aspects at the scheduled hearing.

Closing Speeches

In contrast to the position in England in which the party who starts the case presents their closing speech last, in Scotland the closing speeches will usually follow the order in which the evidence was led. But practice varies and confirmation of the wishes of the particular tribunal should be sought.

Opening Speeches

It is very unusual for there to be any opening speech in tribunal proceedings, though where a matter is especially complex or technical some explanatory remarks may be appropriate. Where the differences between the parties are largely dependent on questions of law or on narrowly focused issues of fact, it is increasingly common, with the approval of the tribunal, to submit agreed summaries of facts, sometimes referred to as 'joint minutes', which may eliminate or substantially reduce the need for witness evidence.

Disclosure of Documents

The process of disclosure—finding and obtaining documents in the hands of another party—is known as recovery in Scotland.

Use of Documents at Hearing

The documents are known as productions and each document is numbered, rather than the pages of the bundle. It is not uncommon for each party to produce its own productions as opposed to a bundle, but this of course is subject to any particular directions to the contrary that may be given in a particular case by a tribunal.

Costs

A costs order in Scotland is known as an expenses order.

Enforcement of Awards

In Scotland the tribunal issues a certificate and any award can be enforced directly without having to go to the Sheriff Court (ETA 1996, s 15(1), (2)).

Appeals

Appeals from the employment tribunal to the EAT are governed, as in England and Wales, by the provisions of the Employment Tribunals Act 1996. It should be noted, however, that aspects of the EAT practice in Scotland are different to those in England and Wales, and attention should be paid to the EAT Practice Direction which explains where differences lie. It is, for example, not general practice for skeleton arguments to be submitted to the EAT in advance of the hearing, although in complex cases it is quite common for oral submissions to be supplemented by written submissions. (Part 13 of the EAT Practice Direction 2008, which governs skeleton arguments, states that it does not apply to an appeal heard in Scotland unless there is a contrary direction by the EAT in Edinburgh.) Appeals from the EAT are made to the Inner House of the Court of Session. Leave to appeal is required, as in England, and this may be obtained either from the EAT or from the Court of Session itself. In addition to raising a point of law, it is a requirement that *probabilis causa* be shown. See *Campbell v Dunoon & Cowal Housing Association* [1992] IRLR 528, para 3, *per* Lord Murray. It has also been emphasized by the Court of Session that no appeal should be allowed to proceed on grounds other than those in respect of which leave has been granted. See *Hynd v (1) Armstrong; and (2) Messrs Bishops* [2005] CSIH 12.

Staying or Sisting Proceedings

Under ETR 2004, r 10(2)(h) proceedings in the tribunal may be sisted which is the equivalent of a stay.

Index